FOREWORD

The International Computing Symposium 1977 is the fifth of its kind to be organized by the European Chapters of ACM.

The present Symposium, whose moto is "Computing's many Facets", intends to cover the whole range of current developments in the fields of computing systems theory and usage, with an emphasis on new trends and applications. Therefore, interesting contributions from a variety of fields of specialization were included in the Symposium programme. This volume was published and distributed in advance of the presentations, for the benefit of the participants. The same material will be published in book-form by North-Holland Publishing Company, after the Conference.

The collection of papers is organized in three groups :

- Invited papers.
- Contributed papers (49 papers were selected by the Programme Committee and the referees from over 100 submitted).
- As an innovation in ICS Conferences, three parallel tutorial sessions were organized on the first day in order to give the participants an opportunity to prepare themselves for the more specialized presentations. The volume contains most of the texts supporting these tutorials.

The ICS 77 Programme Committee was composed of :

- G.A. Blaauw, Technische Hogeschool Twente, Netherlands.
- J.L. Bonnet, Brown-Boveri, Baden, Switzerland.
- G. Bracchi, Politecnico di Milano, Italy.
- D.W. Davies, NPL, Teddington, England.
- J.D. Ichbiah, CII, Louveciennes, France.
- E. Morlet, IBM ESRI, La Hulpe, Belgium (Co-Chairman).
- G. Nijssen, Control Data Europe, Brussels, Belgium.
- D. Ribbens, Université de Liège, Belgium (Co-Chairman).
- J. Witt, Siemens, Munich, Germany.
- P. Wodon, MBLE Research, Brussels, Belgium.

In presenting this volume, we would like to express our sincere thanks to the invited authors, to the contributors and to those who prepared and delivered the tutorials.

Also, we are indebted to our colleagues on the Programme Committee and to their referees, as well as to the publisher and the Symposium secretary Mrs. Marie-Rose Heynen for their efficient and competent cooperation.

E. Morlet

D. Ribbens

Liège, April 1977

International Computing Symposium 1977

Proceedings of the International Computing Symposium 1977,
Liège, Belgium, 4–7 April 1977

Organized by
The European Chapters of the Association for Computing Machinery (ACM)

With the support of
the European Cooperation in Informatics (E.C.I)

Edited by
E. Morlet, IBM ESRI, la Hulpe, Belgium
and
D. Ribbens, Université de Liège, Belgium

1977

NORTH-HOLLAND PUBLISHING COMPANY
AMSTERDAM-NEW YORK-OXFORD

North-Holland ISBN: 0 7204 0741 9

PUBLISHERS:
NORTH-HOLLAND PUBLISHING COMPANY - AMSTERDAM · NEW YORK · OXFORD

SOLE DISTRIBUTORS FOR THE U.S.A. AND CANADA:
AMERICAN ELSEVIER PUBLISHING COMPANY, INC.
52 VANDERBILT AVENUE
NEW YORK, N.Y. 10017

Library of Congress Cataloging in Publication Data

International Computing Symposium, 5th, Liège, Belgium, 1977.
International Computing Symposium, 1977.

Bibliography: p.
1. Electronic data processing--Congresses.
2. Computers--Congresses. 3. Programming (Electronic computers)--Congresses. I. Morlet, E. II. Ribbens, Daniel. III. Association for Computing Machinery. IV. European Cooperation in Informatics (Organization).
QA75.5.I57 1977 001.6'4 77-10016
ISBN 0-7204-0741-9

PRINTED IN THE NETHERLANDS

CONTENTS

1. INVITED PAPERS

papers preceded by * have an entry in the ERRATA Section.

2. CONTRIBUTED PAPERS

PROGRAMMING

PROPERTIES OF PROGRAMS

COMPILERS

COMPUTER APPLICATIONS

MODELLING OF PROGRAMS BEHAVIOR

MODELLING

COMPUTER NETWORKS/DISTRIBUTED PROCESSING

SORTING

THEORETICAL DP

GRAPHICS

INTERACTIVE LANGUAGES

SYSTEMS PROGRAMMING

DATA BASE SYSTEMS

3. TUTORIALS

4. LATE PAPERS

E. Morlet and D. Ribbens, (Eds.), International Computing Symposium 1977.

PROGRAMMING LANGUAGES: FORMAL DEVELOPMENT of INTERPRETERS & COMPILERS

An Invited Paper

Dines Bjørner,
Department of Computer Science, Bldg. 343,
Technical University of Denmark,
DK-2800 Lyngby, DENMARK.

Abstract: Starting with a denotational semantics definition of a simple applicative language, SAL, we systematically develop the specifications of a compiler for SAL. We do so by presenting, in a unifying framework and steps of increasing concretization, the commonly known semantics definition styles of the 1960's: first-order functional, abstract and concrete state machine, macro-substitution and attribute semantics. By way of illustration we exemplify refinements of abstract-, functional- into concrete first-order objects, and decompositions of functional-, applicatively expressed transformations into state variable-, imperatively stated processes. Examples of proofs of correctness in terms of commuting diagrams and applying so-called retrieve functions are briefly stated. The first four semantics styles are employed in the definition of an interpetive semantics, whilst the fifth style is engaged in the final description of a compiling algorithm. The target machine for which the compiler is to generate code is likewise interpretively defined.

1. INTRODUCTION

The quadruple aims of this paper are: to show that generally complex software, which is the result of a non-automatable development process, can indeed be simply derived and (simply) proven correct; to advocate a different approach to the teaching of software-, and in particular compiler-, design; to expound certain, basic programming techniques; and to illustrate that the spectrum of semantics definition methods of the 1960's fit into a development hierarchy. The main contribution of the paper is seen as the exemplification of a disciplined software development methodology, especially as applicable to programming language design [1] and compiler development, and the demonstration of its feasability. The implied, derived and constituent contributions are then these: the design of a hierarchy of meta-languages for expressing levels of concretization & abstraction; the actual proofs of correctness of chosen representations; and the proper context placement, blending and exploitation of a number of seemingly diverse software techniques. These latter include the conscious choice &/or mixture of levels of representational- & operational abstraction, configurational (bottom-up) & hierarchical (top-down) abstractions, and functional vs. state programming [2-3].

We believe, seemingly contrary to all textbooks on compiler design, that the very initial stages of any compiler development must concentrate first on a precise description of the source language ('to be compiled') and the target language ('into which compiling is to take place'), to be followed by a precise description of the compiling algorithm. That is: the complete specification, irrespective of the eventually evolving, internal compiler structure, of the compiler's input/output relation: source program texts into target code sequences. We secondly believe that an activity such as the one whose initial steps have been outlined above, can be meaningfully embedded within a more generally applicable software development methodology. This software engineering discipline views programming within the following, briefly sketched, framework, and as proceeding by means of the application of the corresponding techniques and tools: A first stage in which the requirements of the software are identified and analyzed, and which evolves into an informal formation of believed underlying concepts and facilities. A second stage in which an abstract specification is given for the intended software [2-3]. A description which 'as abstractly as possible & reasonable' models, or abstracts only the relevant domains and functions. This stage to result in a formal document whose consistency and completeness can be verified. That is: a specification which can be formally proved to contain no contradictions and to define a meaning to any applicable input. A third stage in which one derives, from the abstract model, a concrete, efficient realization such that this implementation can be proven correct with respect to the abstract model.

We now relate the methodology stages above to the compiler development so far only partially sketched. The inital stage of gathering requirements for a (new) programming language, their analysis, and the foundational formation of basic concepts and facilities reflected by this source language will not be dealt with here. As soon, however, as intrinsic notions have been isolated we start expressing these as parts of a formal model. [1] of these proceedings illustrate techniques used in this activity. The borderline between modelling the source language abstractly for purposes of language design and compiler- and program development are these: the language designer experiments with different models in attempts to understand, discover, purify, generalize and simplify language constructs. The compiler development uses the final abstraction document as a basis for implementation of the compiler. And the source language programmer refers to the mathematical semantics definition when proving correctness of source programs. In this paper we shall exemplify only the compiler developers' view. We choose abstraction in order to expose most succintly intrinsic source language ideas. We choose formalism so as to be able to carry out proofs. And we choose mathematical semantics because it permits us to guarantee existence of (denoted) objects, and to prove correctness of source program functions. We finally choose a meta-language which in successive refinement steps allow first a mathematical reading, then an interpretive (program-like) reading, and finally a macro-expansion like reading. This greatly simplifies the entire development process. Our models, whether abstract or concrete, essentially consists of three parts. A part describing the input/output object domains, a part describing the internally manipulated object domains, and a part describing the manipulations. These parts will be referred to as the definition of the syntactic- & semantic domains, respectively the elaboration (or evaluation & interpretation) functions. Concise abstractions can be achieved by the judicious use of representational- & operational abstractions. Representational abstraction emphasizes the implementation-independent expression of intrinsic and relevant object (domain) properties, avoiding as far as is possible implying properties irrelevant to the concepts modelled. Operational abstraction means the implicit definition of functions by what they do, i.e. their input/output relationships, rather than by how they (e.g. algorithmically) achieve their results. We shall use abstract syntax [4-6] to define both the syntactic & semantic domains since that allows us to express such domains at an arbitrary level of representational abstraction. We shall in this paper almost exclusively use constructively expressed elaboration function definitions. Well-structured (abstract) models can be obtained by a proper balance between configurational & hierarchic abstractions. In a pure configurationally abstracted model the definition successively bottom-up builds increasing layers of abstraction from a basic set of simple, mechanical or concrete, machine-near components. In a pure hierarchic abstraction the definition iteratively decomposes the model in a top-down fashion into decreasing layers of abstraction. Configurational abstraction in a sense represents a synthesized realization, whereas a hierarchical abstraction represents an analytic model, still to be implemented. In our first, the denotational semantics definition of SAL only hierarchical abstraction is used. As we move towards more concrete implementation definitions we shall configure from simpler, in particular storage cell like notions the more abstract ideas of dynamic- & static chaining of stacks of activations, etc.. Finally abstract models can be expressed transparently by a suitable conscious mixture of functional-, referentially transparent specifications and the abstract 'programming' of local & global state (abstract & concrete) machines. In functional semantics the meaning of a syntactic object is defined explicitly in terms of application of elaboration functions to argument values being (themselves) the result of application(s) of (other) elaboration functions to components of the syntactic objects, etc.. Such programming entails referential transparency. An expression is referentially transparent iff the value denoted is a function of the values of the subexpressions, and any subexpression can be replaced by any other expression having the same value. Denotational semantics is functional with the denoted objects usually being of higher order, i.e. themselves functions (maps). Functional programs usually result in long argument lists and often results in function definitions for which it is difficult to see what the function values depend on, and of what they 'change' with respect to their input. This is especially true of functional, first-order programs, not so much of denotationally expressed semantics due to its use of higher order objects. In pure 'state' (or: variable) programming, all referenced objects (whether constants or not) are potentially assignable, global variables. Now most elaboration functions achieve their results almost exclusively by so-called side-effects. Usually, but not very directly expressed in this paper, we find that pleasing abstractions models as (global or local) states only such semantic domain objects which are both referenced and updated by elaboration functions. That is: for which a pure functional definition would require such objects explicitly as arguments and produce as explicit part of their result-values, such objects. Section 5 of [1] of these proceedings exemplify varieties of functional and state machine definitions of identical (semantical) notions.

In the denotational (or: mathematical) semantics definition, the semantic domains usually consists of higher-order objects, viz.: maps whose range elements are either maps or more arbitrary functions. The purpose of object refinement is to decompose such object domains into first-order, non-functional domains. In order to prove correctness we must show that the more concrete objects properly 'simulates' their more abstract ancestors from which they were systematically derived. The notion of simulation will be defined in sect. 5. It requires here that each refinement be followed/paired by the definition of a so-called retrieve function. These apply to refined objects and yield the corresponding abstract object. Since object refinement usually is a transformation which adds properties, retrieval is normally a filtering function which removes, to the abstraction, irrelevant properties. Since the abstract model's semantic objects usually are abstract, and perhaps even higher-order, the operations performed on them are themselves very simple. In refining the objects we therefore find a related need to decompose the corresponding, constructively defined functions into compositions of more concrete operations. Operation decomposition is also, independently of any object refinement, needed wherever functions, or parts thereof, have been implicitly defined. By implicit definitions we shall include, besides function specification by pre- and post-conditions, such which build objects (sets, maps, tuples) by stating predicates which constituent objects must satisfy. Finally we include among implicit constructs those of the meta-language's own block structure and recursion capability. In our examples we shall mostly find a need for the former kind of function decompositon.

1.1 Informal Description of SAL

Syntax: SAL is a simple, purely applicative language. Its programs are expressions. There are eight expression categories:

*Cons*tants	*k*
*Var*iables	*id*
Infix expressions	*e1 + e2*
*Con*ditional expressions	*if et then ec else ea*
Simple *Let* Blocks	*(let id = ed; eb)*
*Rec*ursive Functions	*(letrec g(id) = ed; eb)*

Lambda Functions $\lambda id.ed$
Applications $ef(ea)$

(Most of our elaboration functions will be expres=sed in a simple language like SAL.) Blocks with multiple definitions can be 'mimiced' by multiply nested simple (Let) blocks.Multiply,mutually recur=sive functions,however,cannot be explicitly defined other than through the use of formal function argu=ments.

Data Types: Constants stand for either NUMbers, BOOLeans,etc..The infix operators are then the u=sual ones: ADDition, SUBtraction, AND etc.. In our models we shall additionally use meta-language da=ta types such as sets, maps, tuples and trees,with corresponding objects and operators.

Comment: SAL may seem awfully trivial to those of you who are used to programming with an ample supply and type variety of assignable variables -- but its realization illustrates most of the more tricky aspects of interpreter,i.e. run-time code,and com=piler design.The main reason for this should be seen in SALs ability to yield FUNction VALues out of their defining scope (i.e. the FUNARG property). In addition,our development concentrates on imple=menting the block-structure and function invoca=tion aspects,complicated technicalities regrettably ignored by all,so far published accounts on varie=ties of semantics definition styles [7-9].

Semantics: SAL programs speak of only three kinds of VALues: NUMbers,truth VALued BOOLeans,and FUNc=tion VALues,i.e. objects which are functions from VALues to VALues,these again including FUNctions, etc..The DENotation,i.e.VALue,of a variable iden=tifier,*id*,is that of the possibly recursively de=fining expression: *ed* (respectively: $Y\lambda g.\lambda id.ed$) of the lexicographically youngest incarnation,i.e. the 'outward-going' statically closest containing block. Y is the fixed point finding function which when applied to $\lambda g.\lambda id.ed$ yields the 'smallest' solution to the equation: $g(id) = ed$,in which g occurs free in *ed*.Infix and conditional expression VALues are as you expect them to be.The VALue of a block is that of the expression body,*eb*,in which all free occurrences of the *id* of a *let*,respective=ly the *g* of a *letrec*,block header definition have been replaced (or: substituted) by their VALues. That is: *ed* is evaluated in an environment,*env'*, which is exactly that extension of the block em=bracing environment,*env*,which binds *id* (respecti=vely *g*) to its VALue,and otherwise binds as *env*. The VALue of a lambda-expression,$\lambda id.ed$,is the FUNction of *id* that *ed* denotes in the environment in which it is first encountered,i.e.defined.Final=ly: the VALue of an application,$ef(ea)$,is the re=sult of (mathematically) applying the FUNction VAL=ue that *ef* (hopefully) denotes (i.e.has as DENota=tion) to the VALue denoted by *ea*.For a more com=plete linguistic treatment of the above notions we refer to [1] of these proceedings.

2. INTERPETIVE SEMANTICS DEFINITIONS

Four styles will be given.In the first definition we express the semantics of SAL in terms of mathe=matical functions.Thus the semantics of a compound syntactic object is expressed as the (homomorphic) function (i.e.as functional composition) of the semantics of the individual,proper components.The denoted functions are themselves expressed in terms of so-called semantic domains,and these are again functional.The remaining definitions are increas=ingly more 'computational',i.e.can best be under=stood as specifying sequences of computations given an input,i.e.an initial binding af variables to their meaning.For a more detailed description of the distinction between denotational- & computa=tional semantics we refer again to [1].The last, fourth,interpretive definition unzips user-defined functions by permitting a compile-time macro-ex=pansion of the definition,pre-processing SAL pro=gram-defined functions into label/goto encapsula=ted meta-language texts,and calls of these funct=ions into (branch & link-like) gotos to such texts. The principles of properly saving-,updating- (i.e. 'setting-up') and restoring- (i.e.'taking-down' & 'reinstalling') calling and defining environments form a more detailed version of those of any of the preceding definitions,and of otherwise pub=lished accounts of this so-called dynamic- & static (environmentally preceding) and dynamic (call) ac=tivation chain mechanisms.This amounts therefore to a complete,comprehensive and concise descrip=tion of what is otherwise known as a variant of the DISPLAY method for variable & formal parameter referencing in a block-structured,recursive,proce=dure-oriented language [10-14].

2.1 Denotational Semantics

Without much further ado we now present the first in a series of seven specifications of SAL.

I.1 Syntactic Domains

```
(1)  Prog  = Expr
(2)  Expr  = Const|Var|Infix|Cond|Let|Rec|Lamb|Appl
(3)  Const :: INTG
(4)  Var   :: Id
(5)  Infix :: Expr Op Expr
(6)  Cond  :: Expr Expr Expr
(7)  Let   :: Id Expr Expr
(8)  Rec   :: Id Lamb Expr
(9)  Lamb  :: Id Expr
(10) Appl  :: Expr Expr
(11) Id    ⊂ TOKEN
(12) Op    = ADD|SUB|AND|...
```

I.2 Semantic Domains

```
(13) ENV  = Id →m VAL        (maps)
(14) VAL  = NUM|BOOL|FUN
(15) FUN  = VAL ⥲ VAL        (partial functions)
```

I.3 Elaboration Functions

```
(16) type: eval-prog:  Prog → VAL
(17) type: eval-expr:  Expr → (ENV → VAL)
(18) type: eval-fun:   Lamb → (ENV → FUN)

eval-prog(e)=                                  (16)
  eval-expr(e)([])

eval-fun(mk-Lamb(id,e))env=                    (18)
  (let f(a) = (let env' = env + [id→a];
                   eval-expr(e)env');
   result is f)
```

```
eval-expr(e)env=                                        (17)
 cases e:                                                .1
  mk-Const(k)       →k,                                  .2
  mk-Var(id)        →env(id),                            .3
  mk-Infix(e1,o,e2)→(let v1=eval-expr(e1)env,            .4
                          v2=eval-expr(e2)env;           .5
                     cases o:                            .6
                      (ADD→ v1+v2,SUB→ v1-v2,...)),      .7
  mk-Cond(t,c,a)    →if eval-expr(t)env                  .8
                     then eval-expr(c)env                .9
                     else eval-expr(a)env,               .10
  mk-Let(id,d,b)    →(let env'=                          .11
                          env+[id→eval-expr(d)env];      .12
                     eval-expr(b)env'),                  .13
  mk-Rec(g,d,b)     →(let env'=                          .14
                          env+[g→eval-fun(d)env'];       .15
                     eval-expr(b)env'),                  .16
  mk-Lamb(id,d)     →eval-fun(e)env,                     .17
  mk-Appl(f,a)      →(let fun=eval-expr(f)env,           .18
                          val=eval-expr(a)env;           .19
                     if is-FUN(fun)                      .20
                      then fun(val) else error           .21
```

Denotational semantics can be traced back to Landin [15],real activity in the area seems to start with Strachey [16],and complete proposals set up by Strachey & Scott [17-18].Foundational work on the mathematics of the applied domains is due to Scott,see [19] and its wealth of references.Examples of denotational semantics applications and explications can be found in [20-23].The present meta-language style is that of the IBM Vienna [24] Lab. and was developed with compiler development in view [25-26].McCarthy & Painter and Landin & Burstall seem to first propose basing compiler correctness on denotational/functional semantics [27-28].Lockwood-Morris develops this viewpoint applying concepts from Universal Algebra [29] and experiments in an earlier unpublished paper [30] with variants of definition styles.Compiler correctness proofs based on similar notions are those of Milner & Weyhrauch [31],and Lucas [32].Our example is taken from Reynolds [33],as is the next step of development.[34] explains/develops the foundations for derived semantics in terms of homomorphisms of initial algebras.[35] finally attempts to place the whole thing in a categorical setting.

2.2 First-Order Functional Semantics

By a first-order functional semantics definition we mean one all of whose objects,and then notably those of the semantics domains,are non-functional, but which is still referentially transparently expressed.Hence,if we were given,as a basis,a denotational semantics we would have to object refine its functional components into such which by means of suitable simulations can mimic the essential aspects of the denotational definition.In the case of SAL two kinds of objects are to be refined: *ENV= Id ⇀ VAL* and,among *VAL*ues: *FUN = VAL ⇝ VAL*.The former objects were constructed by means of expressions:

I.18.1: *env' = env + [id→a]*
I.17.12: *env' = env + [id→eval-expr(d)env]*
I.17.15: *env' = env + [g→eval-fun(d)env']*

The latter objects by an expression basically of the lambda form:

I.18.1-3: *λa.(eval-expr(e)(env+[id→a]))*

We shall not in this paper motivate the refinement choices further (see: [33,2-3]),nor state general derivation principles,but rather present the refined objects as 'faits-accomplis': *ENV* objects, which are *MAPs* (⇀) as *ENV1* objects of the *TUPLE* (*) type,with extensions (+) accomplished in terms of concatenations (⌢),and functional application (()) as directed,linear searches (*look up*).The mathematical functions,*fun*, (⇝) denoted by lambda-expressions are then realized as so-called *closures* -- these are 'passive' structures,which physically pairs the expression, *d* ,to be evaluated,with the defining environment,*env'*,so that when *fun* is to be applied,*fun(val)*,then a simulation of *clos* with the refined counterpart,*arg*,of *val*,is performed: *apply1(clos,arg)*.Instead of now presenting the more concrete,first-order functional elaboration functions we first present arguments for why we believe that our choice(s) will do the job.Those arguments are stated as *retrieve functions*,*retr-ENV*& *retr-VAL*, which applies to the refined objects and yield the more abstract 'ancestors' from which they were (supposedly) derived.In sect.5 we then express in which way the denotational and this,the first-order functional,definition can be considered equivalent.The theorems stated there are subsequently proved.We next observe that the definition is still functional, as was the denotational (of course).All arguments are explicit,there is no reference to,nor any,assignable/declared variables.And we finally note that we cannot,given a specific expression,*e*,'stick' it into the *m1-eval-expr* (together with an initial, say null,environment) and by macro-substitution eliminate all references to *m1-eval-expr*.The reason for this 'failure' will be seen in our 'stacking' closures whose subsequent application requires *m1-eval-expr*.

II.1 Syntactic Domains -- as in I.1

II.2 Semantic Domains

```
(1)  ENV1  =  IdVal*
(2)  IdVal =  SIMP|REC
(3)  SIMP  :: Id VAL1
(4)  REC   :: Id Lamb
(5)  VAL1  =  NUM|BOOL|CLOS
(6)  CLOS  :: Lamb ENV1
```

II.2.1 Retrieve Functions

```
(7)  type: retr-ENV:  ENV1 → ENV
(8)  type: retr-VAL:  VAL1 → VAL

retr-ENV(env1)=                                          (7)
 (env1=<> → [],
  T→(let env=retr-ENV(tenv1);
      cases henv1:
       mk-SIMP(id,val1)
        →  env + [id→retr-VAL(val1)],
       mk-REC(g,d)
        →  (let env' = env+[g→eval-fun(d)env'];
            result is env' )))

retr-VAL(val1)=                                          (8)
 cases val1: mk-CLOS(l,env1)
              →eval-fun(l)retr-ENV(env1),
          T→val1
```

II.2.2 Auxiliary Function

```
(9) type: look-up1: Id ENV1 → VAL1

look-up1(id,env1)=                                          (9)
 if env1=<>
  then error
  else cases h env1:
        mk-SIMP(id,val1) → val1,
        mk-REC(id,lamb)  → mk-CLOS(lamb,env1),
        T                → look-up1(id,t env1)
```

II.3 Elaboration Functions

```
(10)type: m1-eval-prog: Prog        → VAL1
(11)type: m1-eval-expr: Expr ENV1  → VAL1
(12)type: apply1:       CLOS VAL1  → VAL1

m1-eval-prog(e)=                                            (10)
 m1-eval-expr(1,<>)

m1-eval-expr(e,env1)=                                       (11)
 cases e:
  mk-Const(k)
   → k,
  mk-Var(id)
   → look-up1(id,env1),                                     .5
  mk-Infix(e1,o,e2)
   → (let v1=m1-eval-expr(e1,env1),                         .7
          v2=m1-eval-expr(e2,env1);                         .8
      cases o:
       (ADD → v1+v2,SUB → v1-v2,...)),
  mk-Cond(t,c,a)
   → if m1-eval-expr(t,env1)                                .12
      then m1-eval-expr(c,env1)                             .13
      else m1-eval-expr(a,env1),                            .14
  mk-Let(id,d,b)
   → (let v=m1-eval-expr(d,env1);                           .16
      let env1'=<mk-SIMP(id,v)>⌢env1;
      m1-eval-expr(b,env1')),                               .18
  mk-Rec(g,d,b)
   → (let env1'=<mk-REC(g,d)>⌢env1;
      m1-eval-expr(b,env1')),                               .19
  mk-Lamb(,)
   → mk-CLOS(e,env1),                                       .21
  mk-Appl(f,a)
   → (let clos=m1-eval-expr(f,env1),                        .23
          arg = m1-eval-expr(a,env1);                       .24
      apply1(clos,arg))

apply1(clos,arg)=                                           (12)
 cases clos:
  mk-CLOS(mk-Lamb(id,d),env1)
   → (let env1'=<mk-SIMP(id,arg)>⌢env1;
      m1-eval-expr(d,env1')),
  T → error
```

end-of-definition.

The first first-order functional semantics was that of LISP 1.5 [36] (a denotational semantics study of LISP 1.5 was recently carried out by Gordon [37]). The 1960's saw further exercises in first-order functional semantics,notably among which we find the IBM Vienna Lab. series of PL/I definitions: ULD III versions 1,2,3 [38-40],Reynolds' GEDANKEN [41],and,as mentioned before,the sketches of Lock=wood Morris [31].Common to all,however,is the fact that none were derived from other semantic defini=tions (except perhaps in an intuitive sense those of [31]),but marked the only available 'abstract=ion'.The present derivation of SAL.I into SAL.II is essentially that of [33],the statement of the retrieve functions and the (proof of the) theorem (sect.5) is however new.

2.3 Abstract Machine Operational Semantics

By an abstract machine semantics we understand a definition which primarily employs (globally) de=clared variables of abstract,possibly higher-level, type,and expresses the semantics (not in terms of applicatively defined,'grand' transformations on this state,but) in terms of statement sequences denoting a computational process of individually, smaller state transformations.In the SAL case we choose to map the semantic *ENV1* arguments onto a globally declared variable,*env2*,thereby removing these arguments from the elaboration function re=ferences.By doing so we must additionally mimic the meta-language's own recursion capability which is exploited e.g.in lines II.11.7-8,12-14,...Thus the type of *env2* is to become a stack of stacks,i.e.a *TUPLE* of *TUPLE*s: $ENV2 = ENV1^*$,where $ENV1 = IdVal^*$. Each *cenv2* element is that stack of *Id*'s and their values,which when *look*ed-*up* properly (cf.*retr-ENV*) reflects the bindings of the so-called 'lexico=graphically youngest incarnations' of each iden=tifier in the static scope (going outwards from the identifier use through embracing blocks towards the outermost program expression level).As long as no *let* or *rec* defined function is being *Appl*ied,the *env2* will contain exactly one *ENV1* element.As soon as a defined function is *Appl*ied,the calling envi=ronment is dumped on the *env2* stack onto whose top is pushed the *ENV1* environment current when the function was defined.In addition we choose also to mechanize the recursive stacking of temporaries (e. g.II.11.7-8,16,23-24) by means of a global stack, *STK*.We could have merged *STK* into *ENV2*,but decide presently not to.Hence this abstract machine defi=nition also requires further decomposition of the *look-up* operation.As before,we state our beliefs why we think the present development is on a right track,by presenting *retr*ieve functions.The abstract state machine semantics definition is said to be o=perational,or to be an operational semantics defi=nition,since it specifies the meaning of SAL by de=scribing the operation of a machine effecting the computation of the desired value.Such definitions rather directly suggests,or are,realizations,since they do not possess,or involve,implicit,implemen=tation language processor controlled-,but explicit (albeit in this case,abstract) state machine seman=tics definee determined allocation and freeing (⌢, respectively *t* (III.16.2,17,20,25,34 respectively III.16.9,13,23,27,37 etc.)) of otherwise recursive=ly nested (i.e.stacked pushing/popping) objects. The definition,however,still requires the presence, at run-time,of *m2-eval-expr* (III.16.36),it still cannot be completely factored out of the definition for any given,non-trivial expression.Thus there still cannot be an exhaustive,macro-substitution process which completely eliminates the interpre=tive nature of the definition.The reason is as be=fore: *CLOS*ures are triplets of a function defini=tion bound variable,*id*,a function 'body',*d*,and the recursive,defining environment,*env2'*.Together they represent,but are not,the function, *fun* (I.18.3), which must be mimiced,hence the required presence.

III.1 Syntactic Domains -- as in I.1

III.2 Semantic Domains

```
(1) ENV2   =   ENV1*
(2) ENV1   =   IdVal*
(3) IdVal  =   SIMP|REC
(4) SIMP   ::  Id VAL1
(5) REC    ::  Id Lamb
(6) VAL1   =   NUM|BOOL|CLOS
(7) CLOS   ::  Lamb ENV1
(8) STK    =   VAL1*
(9) Σ      =   REF → (ENV2|STK)
```

III.2.1 State Initialization

```
(10) dcl env2 := <<>>  type ENV2,
(11)     stk  := <>    type STK;
```

III.2.2 Retrieve Functions

```
(12) type: retr-ENV1:  Σ → ENV1
(13) type: retr-VAL1:  Σ → VAL1

retr-ENV1() = h c env2                                (12)

retr-VAL1() = h c stk                                 (13)
```

III.2.3 Auxiliary Function

```
(14) type: look-up2:  Id → (Σ → Σ)

look-up2(id)=                                         (14)
 (trap exit() with I;
  for j = 1 to l h c env2 do
   cases (h c env2)[j]:
    mk-SIMP(id,val2)
      →(stk := <val2>⌢c stk;
        exit),
    mk-REC(id,e)
      →(let env2' : <(h c env2)[k]|j ≤ k ≤ l h c env2 >;
        stk := <mk-CLOS(e,env2')>⌢c stk;
        exit)
    T→I)
```

III.3 Elaboration Functions

```
(15) type: m2-eval-prog: Prog → (Σ → Σ  VAL1)
(16) type: m2-eval-expr: Expr → (Σ → Σ)

m2-eval-prog(e)=                                      (15)
 (env2 := <<>>;                                        .1
  m2-eval-expr(e);                                     .2
  env2 := t c env2;                                    .3
  return(h c stk))                                     .4

m2-eval-expr(e)=                                      (16)
 cases e:                                              .1
  mk-Const(k)      → stk := <k>⌢c stk,                 .2
  mk-Var(id)       → look-up2(id),                     .3
  mk-Infix(e1,o,e2)                                    .4
  → (m2-eval-expr(e1);                                 .5
     m2-eval-expr(e2);                                 .6
     stk := <h t c stk                                 .7
             cases o: ADD→+,SUB→-,...                  .8
             h c stk>⌢t t c stk),                      .9
  mk-Cond(t,c,a)                                      .10
  → (m2-eval-expr(t);                                 .11
     let b : h c stk;                                 .12
     stk := t c stk;                                  .13
     if b then m2-eval-expr(c)                        .14
          else m2-eval-expr(a)),                      .15
  mk-Lamb(,)                                          .16
  → stk := <mk-CLOS(e,h c env2)>⌢c stk,               .17
  mk-Let(id,d,b)                                      .18
  → (m2-eval-expr(d);                                 .19
     env2 := <<mk-SIMP(id,h c stk)>⌢h c env2>⌢t c env2;
     stk := t c stk;                                  .21
     m2-eval-expr(b);                                 .22
     env2 := <t h c env2>⌢t c env2),                  .23
  mk-Rec(g,d,b)                                       .24
  → (env2 :=<<mk-REC(id,d)>⌢h c env2>⌢t c env2;       .25
     m2-eval-expr(b);                                 .26
     env2 := <t h c env2>⌢t c env2),                  .27
  mk-Appl(f,a)                                        .28
  → (m2-eval-expr(f);                                 .29
     m2-eval-expr(a);                                 .30
     if is-CLOS(h c stk)                              .31
      then                                            .32
       (let mk-CLOS(mk-Lamb(id,e'),env2') : h c stk;
        env2 :=<<mk-SIMP(id,h t c stk)>⌢env2'>⌢c env2;
        stk := t t c stk ;                            .35
        m2-eval-expr(e');                             .36
        env2 := t c env2)                             .37
      else                                            .38
       error)                                         .39
```

end-of-definition.

Abstract state machine,interpretive,operational se= mantics definitions were first reported by Landin [15],and received their full development with the IBM Vienna Lab. series of PL/I definitions, ULD III versions 1-2-3 (Universal Language Descriptions,as expressed in the so-called VDL,Vienna Definition Language [42-47]).Whereas Landin's definition of an even simpler applicative expression language,AE, than SAL was also paired with a denotational de= finition,no attempt was then reported on proving their 'equivalence',let alone deriving the former systematically from the latter.Landin's mechanical version was since referred to as the SECD,Stack/ Environment/Control/Dump,machine specification sty= le,since the structure was amenable to a variety of language definitions.The VDL based definitions [42,48-49],too,were free-standing,in that no more abstract model was used as a departure point.The recent PL/I ANS/ECMA standards proposal [50] is ba= sically a derivative of the ULD/VDL style of seman= tics,as also explained in [51].[8-9] presents ex= amples of abstract state machine semantics,with[8] proving equivalence among several variants of these and also axiomatically stated versions.

2.4 Concrete Machine,Meta-Language (Pre-Processor) Compiled,Interpretive Semantics

By a concrete machine,interpretive semantics we un= derstand a definition which again exploits global= ly declared variables,but now of more concrete,ef= ficiently realizable type.We shall in particular mean such forms which model,or rather closely ex= hibits,the actual run-time structure(s) of e.g. such objects as activation stacks,but such that the definition is still interpretable within (,at this time,possibly extended) meta-language.It is obser= ved that the borderline between the definition sty= les is smooth,and thus that too rigid delineations serve no purpose.In the abstract state machine se= mantics of SAL we observe a number of storage-wise inefficient object representations;these are caused (almost) exclusively by our choice to stay with the CLOSure representation of FUNctions as first derived in sect.2.2.Closures 'drag' along with them,not on=

ly the function body text,but also the entire de= fining environment.This generally results in ex= tensive redundancy (duplication) of (dynamic) scope information (elsewhere) being kept 'stored) in *ENV2*. The basic object refinement objective therefore of this development step is now to keep only non-re= dundant (but not necessarily only elsewhere refe= renced) environment information in the refined ac= tivation stack.We shall achieve this by 'folding' the *ENV2* stack of *ENV1* stacks 'back into' a tree structured activation stack (*STG*).Each 'path' from a leaf to the root signifies a chain of dynamically preceding activations,with one of these chains sig= nifying the current-,all others those of defining environment chains of FUNARG functions.Each chain is statically and dynamically linked,corresponding to the subchain of environmentally preceding,lexi= cographically youngest,i.e.most recent,incarnations of statically embracing blocks;respectively the complete chain of dynamically (call/invocation) preceding activations.Our definition thus entails a complete,self-contained description of a common= ly used variant of the so-called DISPLAY variable referencing scheme first attributed to Dijkstra [10-11].We believe ours to be a first such compre= hensive specification published,and also systemati= cally derived from non-implementation oriented for= mulations.We can,however,only succeed in achieving this realization of activations if,at the same time we refine *CLOS*ures into pairs (*mk-CLOS* III.16.17) of (not *Lamb*da expressions and *1*st level *ENV*iron= ments,but,e.g.pairs (*mk-FCT* IV.30.8) of) resulting program *lab*el points,*lfct*,and defining environment (activation stack) pointers (*cp*);where from *lfct* we are able to *retr*ieve the *Lamb*da expression,and from *cp* we are able to *retr*ieve the defining *env*ironment.

Compiler-Compilers: To realize this goal we also, in this step,refine *CLOS*ures by a macro-expansion compilation of SAL texts (*e*) into (extended) meta-language (*META-IV*) texts.It is thus we have chosen here to introduce,somewhat belatedly,but - we think - in an appropriate context,the issue of viewing a meta-language expressed definition of some source language construct as specifying a compilation of source language texts into meta-language texts,see also [52].By a meta-language,macro-substitution, compiled (interpretive) semantics we basically un= derstand a definition in the meta-language not con= taining any references to specifier defined elabo= ration functions.We shall,however,widen the above term definition to admit forms,which contain such references,but where these now are to be thought of as references to elaboration macros,hence specify= ing a pre-processing stage,called compiling,prior to interpretation of 'pure',elaboration function reference free meta-text.To achieve a(n extended) meta-language definition which can be so macro-ex= panded (given an input source text in the form of an argument to an elaboration function) recursive definitions of objects (like e.g. *env'* I.17.14-15) & functions must be eliminated either by taking the (their) fixed points,or by unzipping them into me= chanical constructions.Taking fixed points,e.g. re= sults in:

$$\underline{let}\ env' = Y\lambda\rho.(env + [id \rightarrow eval\text{-}expr(d)\rho])$$

but that does'nt help us very much when we come to actual,effective realizations on computers - it is, or may be,beautiful in theory,but 'costly' in prac= tice.Even though machines,or their languages,may be claimed to possess fixed point finding,Y,instruct= ions,they would have to be general enough to cater for the most complex case.Instead we unravel each individual use of recursion separately,and so-far by hand.In the case of *env'* by providing suitable stacks,pointer initializations & manipulations.The guiding principle being: to derive,from the more abstract definition,which for 'brevity' and trans= parency may use recursion 'excessively',to each oc= currence of an otherwise recursive definition,its, or a,most fitting,efficient and economical realiza= tion. In the next five subsections we now go into a characterization of the resulting definition at this stage.Again we present it as a fait-accompli, leaving to other treatments [53] the formulation of (and partial,theoretical support for) the general derivation techniques applied.

The Definition: Thus the definition represents two, intertwined efforts: the further concretization of run-time objects,here the *ENV2* stack into the Σ complex,and the further decomposition of elabora= tion function definitions so that we may achieve that e.g. references to *m3-int-expr* can be succes= sively eliminated.

A: The Environmentally Preceding Activation Vari= able Referencing Scheme, The Run-Time State.

The *ENV2* and *STK* of III is merged into the separa= tely allocated *DSA*s of *STG*.And these are chained together:dynamic chains by *CP*,for: Calling Poin= ter;lexicographic chains to (defining) youngest in= carnations by *EP*,for: Environment Pointer.The ex= act functioning,reason for and behavior of this EPA scheme,its set-up,sue and only for the case of lan= guages not possessing the FUNARG property,the eli= mination of environment chain objects is precisely described by the formulae.Hence it will not be in= formally described here.Our objective in presenting the formulae is twofold: to indicate a stepwise re= finement process which leads to their derivation and the possibility now of a correctness proof with respect to a far shorter definition,and to show that,even when starting with the concrete,which most textbooks unfortunately still do,and then in= variably only very incompletely,one can indeed a= chieve a complete yet terse formulation.

B: Macro-Expansion.

A conditional (*if-then-else*) expression results in all of the text corresponding to IV.26.1,4,5 being generated first,in a pre-processing 'compile' sta= ge. A simple *Let* defining block expression results in all of the text corresponding to IV.27.1,3 being so expanded before any elaboration. Etcetera.Thus lines IV.21.1, -28.1, -31.4 etc.,do not denote themselves,i.e. run-time references to *m3-int-expr*, but the text resulting from similar expansions.One may choose to do likewise for the auxiliary funct= ions *pop* & *push*,or one may wish to keep these as standard run-time routines.

C: Realization of *CLOS*ures.

Note the *Rec* or *Lamb* cases: ($\underline{letrec}\ g(id) = d;\ b$) respectively: $\lambda id.d$ .Upon evaluation of a *Rec* or a *Lamb* their defined function bodies,*d*,are not elaborated (till actually *Appl*ied).Since,however,in order to eliminate *CLOS*ures,or at least as much as possible of what before,in III,could be said to be *CLOS*ure,we have decided to macro-expand these texts 'in-line' with the text in which they were defined. And since we are not to execute this text when otherwise elaborating the two definition cases,we shall *lab*el their expansions,*lab*el the text immediately following these expansions,precede the expansion with a (meta-language) *GOTO* around the thus expanded text,and terminate the expanded text itself with a *GOTO* intended to *return* to the caller, who, it is expected, 'dropped' a suitable return address in a global *ra* branch label register before GOing TO the *lab*el of the expanded function text. All this is 'performed' in functions 30,respectively 29.So what is left in the EPA of the former *CLOS*ures? The answer is: just the 'barebones'.Enough to reconstruct (i.e.*retr*ieve) the *id*,the *d*, and their defining *env*ironment: the former two from *lab(lfct)*,the *env*ironment from *cp* (IV.30.4, IV.30.8).Thus,in this definition,a function *CLOS*ure has been realized as a *FCT* pair: '*fct*,*ptr*'.This solution closely mirrors the way in which formal procedures and BY-NAME thunks are realized in actual programming language systems.

D: The Compiler State.

We observe that *Labels* had to be generated for each *Lamb*,*Appl* and *Rec* (actually its *Lamb* part),and since we describe only once (in IV.30 & IV.29) what meta-language text to be generated,i.e. how to schematically elaborate these,we shall have to view the formulae (IV.21-31) as subject to (as already mentioned) a two stage process: the 'compiler' stage which macro-expands the SAL program into 'pure' meta-text,and the 'interpreter' which executes the expanded text.Thus all lines of the formulae with lower case let are 'executed' at compile-time,all *dict* (in *DICT*) objects are likewise compile-time computed,and all references to *m3*- functions are eliminated by the compile-time macro-substitution process already mentioned.All upper-case *LET*s,e.g., are then to be executed at 'run-time',i.e.in the interpreter stage.Thus the abstract compiler,whose 'working behavior' will not be formalized in this paper,performs three actions: generate labels;compute,distribute and use dictionaries;and generate *META-IV* code. Whereas in *ENV1* and *ENV2* *VAL*ues of *ids* were explicitly paired with these,in the *DSA*s (for: Dynamic Storage/Save Area's) only the *VAL*ues are left,but in fixed positions (*VR*).Consider any variable,*id*.It is defined at block depth *n*,and uniquely so.And it is used e.g. at block depth *ln*, where: $0 \leq n \leq ln$.The *DICT* components serve exactly this singular purpose (at least in this sample definition): for all *ids* in some context,to map them into the static block depth,*n*,at which they were defined.Since the static chain also touches exactly the embracing blocks,*ln-n* denotes the number of levels one has to chain back to get to the *VAL*ue corresponding to *id*! (IV.24.3-4).In fact,that is the whole,singular purpose of the static (*EP*) chain. Since it is furthermore observed (IV.24.1) that the only place *dict* is used,is in the compile stage,any reference to *dict* is seen also to be eliminatable

Finally observe that the unique label objects denoted by *lfct*,*lbyp* and *lret* shall be substituted into respective (meta-language scope-determined) cases of use (IV.30.4,8; IV30.3,7; IV.29.9,11).

E: Execution:

The result of executing a SAL program is (to be) found on top of the temporaty list (IV.19.2), about which we can assert a length of exactly one in line (IV.21.2)! So *m3-int-expr* places (*m3-push*es) the result of any expression elaboration on top of the current *DSA*'s *TL* -- with the working register,*u*,invariably holding this result too at the instance of *push*ing. A simple *Let Expr* is executed by first finding the *VAL*ue of the locally defined variable,*id*,in the environment in which the *Let* is encountered.Then a new activation is set up to elaborate the body,*b*,of the *Let*.Working register *u* is used to store the result temporarily while the activation is terminated,but not necessarily disposed off.The the result is *push*ed on the *TL* of the invoking activations' *DSA*.Since the *VAL*ue so yielded might be a function which was concocted by the activation just left,and since that *FunCT*ion may depend on its locally defined *Var*iable *VAL*ues,we cannot,in general,dispose of the activation.This 'story' then shall account for our use of the (--) dashed line around the reclamation of *Storage* shown in (IV.31.9).The yielded *FunCT*ion *VAL*ue would be (realized as) a 'pair': *mk-FCT(lfct,ptr)* where *ptr* is a *pointer* to that,or a contained,activation.This is (again) the FUNARG situation previously mentioned.By not disposing (IV.31.9) of the *DSA* we are later able to 'reactivate' the *FunCT*ion defining activation.We leave it to the reader to 'exercise' remaining aspects of the definition.

Discussion: The illustrated solution is much too cumbersome.As is also done in actual run-time situations and commercially available ALGOL & PL/I systems,we could merge all (statically nested) *Lets* and *Recs* into one body,avoiding stacking and unstacking activations.Now such would only be created and suspended (or destroyed) when functions (of an embracing block) were actually invoked,respectively left.And now we would need a *ParaMeter* component, as well as a *VaRiable List* (of statically knowable) length) in the *DSA*s:

DSA :: CP EP RA PM VR TL*

The length to be set aside in each *dsa* of the *VR** component is the maximal *depth* of nested *Let* and *Rec* expressions in the program-,respectively any *Lamb*da-,expression.

IV.1 Syntactic Domains -- as in I.1

IV.2 Semantic Domains

IV.2.1 Dynamic State Components

(1)	Σt	=	$REF \underset{m}{\rightarrow} ([Ptr] \mid [Lbl] \mid [VAL2] \mid STG)$
(2,3,4)	P, EP, CP	=	$[Ptr]$
(5,6)	BR, RA	=	$[Lbl]$
(7)	U, W	=	$[VAL2]$
(8)	STG	=	$Ptr \underset{m}{\rightarrow} DSA$
(9)	Ptr	$\subset$	$TOKEN$
(10)	Lbl	$\subset$	$TOKEN$
(11)	DSA	::	$CP\ EP\ RA\ VR\ TL$
(12)	VR	=	$[VAL2]$

```
(13)  TL    =  VAL2*
(14)  VAL2  =  NUM|BOOL|FCT
(15)  FCT   ::  BR EP
```

IV.2.1.1 Initial State

```
(16)  LET ptr ∈ Ptr;
(17)  DCL Stg := [ptr→mk-DSA(nil,nil,nil,nil,<>)],
          p   := ptr,
          ep  := ptr,
          br  := nil  type BR,
          ra  := nil  type RA,
          u,w := nil  type [VAL2];
```

IV.2.2 Compiler State

IV.2.2.1 Global:

```
(32)  Σc  = Lbl-set
```

Initialization:

```
(33)  dcl ls := {} type Lbl-set;
```

IV.2.2.2 Local:

```
(34)  LN    = N0
(35)  DICT = Id ↔m N1
```

IV.3 Elaboration Functions

Function Types:

```
(21) Prog              → (Σc→Σc) → (Σt→Σt)
(22) Expr  DICT LN → (Σc→Σc) → (Σt→Σt)
(23) Const DICT LN             → (Σt→Σt)
(24) Var   DICT LN → (Σc→Σc) → (Σt→Σt)
(25) Infix DICT LN → (Σc→Σc) → (Σt→Σt)
(26) Cond  DICT LN → (Σc→Σc) → (Σt→Σt)
(27) Let   DICT LN → (Σc→Σc) → (Σt→Σt)
(28) Rec   DICT LN → (Σc→Σc) → (Σt→Σt)
(29) Appl  DICT LN → (Σc→Σc) → (Σt→Σt)
(30) Lamb  DICT LN → (Σc→Σc) → (Σt→Σt)
(31) Expr  DICT LN → (Σc→Σc) → (Σt→Σt)

(18) REF                       → (Σt→Σt)
(19) REF                       → (Σt→Σt)

(20)               → (Σc→Σc)
```

IV.3.1 Auxiliary Functions

Run-Time Functions:

```
m3-pop(r)=                                              (18)
   (LET mk-DSA(c,e,a,v,tl) : (cStg)(cp);                .1
    Stg := cStg + [cp→mk-DSA(c,e,a,v,t tl)] ;           .2
    r := h tl)                                          .3

m3-push(r)=                                             (19)
   (LET mk-DSA(c,e,a,v,tl) : (cStg)(cp);                .1
    Stg := cStg + [cp→mk-DSA(c,e,a,v,<cr>⌢tl)])         .2
```

Compile-Time Functions:

```
make-lbl()=                                             (20)
   (let l ∈ Lbl be s.t. l ∉ cls;                        .1
    ls := cls ∪ {l};                                    .2
    return l )                                          .3
```

IV.3.2 Compile/Execute Functions

```
m3-int-prog(e)=                                         (21)
 (m3-int-expr(e,[],0);
  u := h(s-TL((cStg)(cp)));
  return(cu))

m3-int-expr(e,dict,ln)=                                 (22)
 is-Const(e)  → m3-int-const(e),
 is-Var(e)    → m3-int-var(e,dict,ln),
 is-Infix(e)  → m3-int-infix(e,dict,ln),
 is-Cond(e)   → m3-int-cond(e,dict,ln),
 is-Let(e)    → m3-int-let(e,dict,ln),
 is-Rec(e)    → m3-int-rec(e,dict,ln),
 is-Lamb(e)   → m3-int-lamb(e,dict,ln),
 is-Appl(e)   → m3-int-appl(e,dict,ln)

m3-int-const(mk-Const(k))=                              (23)
 (u := k;
  m3-push(u))

m3-int-var(mk-Var(id),dict,ln)=                         (24)
 (let n = dict(id);
  ep := cp;
  FOR i = 1 TO ln-n DO
      ep := s-EP((cStg)(cep));
  u := s-VR((cStg)(cep));
  m3-push(u);
  ep := cp)

m3-int-infix(mk-Infix(e1,o,e2),dict,ln)=                (25)
 (m3-int-expr(e1,dict,ln);
  m3-int-expr(e2,dict,ln);
  m3-pop(u);
  m3-pop(w);
  u := cu (cases o: ADD→+,SUB→-,...) cw;
  m3-push(u))

m3-int-cond(mk-Cond(t,c,a),dict,ln)=                    (26)
 (m3-int-expr(t,dict,ln);
  m3-pop(u);                                        ÷
  IF cu
    THEN m3-int-expr(c,dict,ln)
    ELSE m3-int-expr(a,dict,ln))

m3-int-let(mk-Let(id,d,b),dict,ln)=                     (27)
 (m3-int-expr(d,dict,ln);
  m3-pop(u);                                        ÷
  m3-int-Block(b,dict + [id→ln+1],ln+1))

m3-int-rec(mk-Rec(g,d,b),dict,ln)=                      (28)

  -- see appendix, part A.

m3-int-lamb(mk-Lamb(id,d),dict,ln)=                     (30)
 (let lfct : make-lbl(),                                .1
      lbyp : make-lbl();                                .2
  GOTO lbyp;                                            .3
  lab(lfct):                                            .4
     m3-int-Block(d,dict + [id→ln+1],ln+1);             .5
     GOTO cra;                                          .6
  lab(lbyp):                                            .7
  u := mk-FCT(lfct,cp);                                 .8
  m3-push(u))                                           .9

m3-int-Block(b,dict,ln)=                                (31)
 (LET ptr ∈ Ptr be s.t. ptr ∉ dom cStg;                 .1
  Stg := cStg ∪ [ptr → mk-DSA(cp,cep,cra,cu,<>)];
  p,ep := ptr;                                          .3
  m3-int-expr(b,dict,ln);                               .4
  m3-pop(u);                                        ÷   .5
  ep := s-EP((cStg)(cp));                               .6
  ra := s-RA((cStg)(cp));                               .7
  p  := s-CP((cStg)(cp));                               .8
 ----------------------
 | Stg := cStg∖{ptr};  |                                .9
 ----------------------
  m3-push(u))                                           .10
```

```
m3-int-appl(mk-Appl(f,a),dict,ln)=
 (let lret : make-lbl();
  m3-int-expr(a,dict,ln);
  m3-int-expr(f,dict,ln);
  m3-pop(u);                                   ÷
  IF is-FCT(cu)
    THEN (br := s-BR(cu);
          ep := s-EP(cu);
          m3-pop(u);
          ra := lret;
          GOTO cbr;
          lab(lret):
          I)
    ELSE ERROR)
```

end-of-definition.

Comments: The lines marked ÷ are strictly speaking not required due to the (provable) property that -- at these points -- the top of the *TL* and the *u* working register does contain identical *VAL*ues.

3. COMPILING ALGORITHMS & ATTRIBUTE SEMANTICS

In this section we shall arrive at a specification of SAL in terms of the combination of two separate definitions: a compiling algorithm which to any SAL construct specifies its translation,not into the meta-language,but into actual ('physically existing') machine code; and a suitably abstracted definition of the target machine architecture,i.e. its semantic domains (working registers,condition code,storage,input/output,etc.) and instruction repertoire: formats and meaning. The structure of the section is as follows: in subsect.3.1 we give the pair of definitions: target machine,TM,and the compiling algorithm from SAL to TM.The latter is directly derived from the last,concrete definition of SAL in sect.2.4. In subsect.3.2 we then restate the compiling algorithm of sect.3.1.2,but now in terms more familiar to affecionados of attribute semantics.And in sect.3.3 we give a similar attribute semantics definition of a compiling algorithm from SAL into TM.This latter algorithm is based on the separation of activation and temporary stacks first shown in the abstract machine of sect.2.2. The purpose of showing the attribute semantics is to demonstrate,finally,how such are formally derivable from denotational semantics definitions.The reason why we state two independent attribute semantics definitions is to illustrate the distinctions between synthesized & inherited attributes,and their relation to questions about single- & multi-pass compilers.The latter will be discussed in sect.4.

3.1 A Target Machine & a Compiling Algorithm

3.1.1 The Target Machine, TM

V.1 Syntactic Domains

```
(1)  Code = Ins*
(2)  Ins  = Sim|St |Lim|Ld |Fct|Jmp|Cjp|Mov|Adj|
            Pck|Unp|Pr | ...
(3)  Sim :: Adr (INTG|BOOL|...)
(4)  St  :: Adr Reg N1
(5)  Lim :: Reg (INTG|BOOL|Lbl|...)
(6)  Ld  :: Reg N1 Adr
(7)  Fct :: Reg Op (Reg|Adr)
(8)  Op   = ADD|SUB|MPY|DIV|AND|OR|NOT|XOR|LOW|
            LEQ|EQ |NEQ|HI |HEQ|...
(9)  Jmp  :: (Lbl Reg)
(10) Cjp  :: Reg Cmp (Lbl|...)
(11) Cmp   = TRUE|FALSE|ZERO|NOTFCT|...
(12) Pr   :: (Reg|QUOT)
(13) Adj  :: Reg INTG
(14) Mov  :: Reg Reg
(15) Pck  :: Reg  Reg Reg
(16) Unp  ::  Reg Reg  Reg

(17) Reg   = N1
(18) Adr  :: Base Displ
(19) Base  = Reg
(20) Displ = INTG
(21) Lbl   ⊂ TOKEN
```

V.2 Semantic Domains

```
(22) Σm   = REF  →m (STG|REG|OUT|...)
(23) STG  = LOC  →m VAL
(24) REG  = N1   →m VAL
(25) VAL  = INTG|BOOL|Lbl|LOC|FCT
(26) LOC  = INTG
(27) FCT :: Lbl LOC
(28) OUT  = VAL*
```

-- leaving a number of machine components undefined.

Global State Initialization:

```
(29) dcl S := [i → undefined|-2↑s<i<2↑s] type STG,
(30)     R := [i → undefined|-2↑r<i<2↑r] type REG;
```

V.3 (Micro-Program) Elaboration Functions

```
(31) type int-code: Code      → (Σm → Σm)
(32) type int-insl: Ins  N1   → (Σm → Σm)
(33) type int-ins:  Ins       → (Σm → Σm)
(34) type eval-adr: Adr       → (Σm → Σm LOC)

int-code(c)=                                              (31)
 (trap exit(lbl) with
   (let c' = c⌢<mk-Lbl(ERROR)>;
    let i = (Δj∈ind c')(c'[j]=lbl);
    int-insl(c',i));
  int-insl(c,1))

int-insl(c,i)=                                            (32)
 if i > l c
  then I
  else (int-ins(c[i]);
        int-insl(c,i + 1))

int-ins(ins)=                                             (33)
 cases ins:
  mk-Lbl(lbl)     → I,
  mk-Sim(a,k)     → (let ea : eval-adr(a);
                      S := cS + [ea → k]),
  mk-St(a,r,n)    → (let ea : eval-adr(a);
                      for i=0 to n - 1 do
                        S := cS + [(ea+i)→(cR)(r+i)]),
  mk-Lim(r,k)     → R := cR + [r → k],
  mk-Ld(r,n,a)    → (let ea : eval-adr(a);
                      for i=0 to n - 1 do
                        R := cR + [(r+i) → (cS)(ea+i)]),
  mk-Fct(r,o,ar) → (let v : if is-Adr(ar)
                              then
                               (let ea : eval-adr(ar);
                                (cS)(ea))
                              else (cR)(ar);
                     cases o:
                      ADD → R := cR + [r → (cR)(r)+v],
                      SUB → R := cR + [r → (cR)(r)-v],
                      ...
```

```
                        HI → R := cR + [r → (cR)(r)>v],
                        ...)),
mk-Jmp(l)       → exit(l),
mk-Cjp(r,c,l) → if cases c:
                        TRUE     → (cR)(r),
                        FALSE    → ~(cR)(r),
                        ...
                        NOTFCT → ~is-FCT((cR)(r)),
                        ...
                        ZERO     → (cR)(r)=0,
                        ...
                    then
                      (is-Lbl(l)→exit(l),
                       T          →exit((cR)(l)))
                    else I,
mk-Adj(r,i)     → R := cR + [r → (cR)(r)+i],
mk-Mov(r1,r2) → R := cR + [r1 → (cR)(r2)],
mk-Pck(r,l,a) → if is-Lbl((cR)(l))
                    ∨ is-LOC((cR)(a))
                    then
                      (let f:mk-FCT((cR)(l),(cR)(a));
                       R := cR + [r → f])
                    else
                      exit(mk-Lbl(ERROR)),
mk-Upk(l,a,r) → if is-FCT((cR)(r))
                    then
                      (let l':s-Lbl((cR)(r)),
                           d':s-LOC((cR)(r));
                       R := cR + [l → l',a → a'])
                    else
                      exit(mk-Lbl(ERROR)),
mk-Pr(rq)       → (let q : is-Reg(rq) → (cR)(rq),
                                   T       → rq;
                    Out := cOut⌢<q>),
...
```

```
eval-adr(mk-Adr(b,d))=                                   (34)
  (let il : (cR)(b);
   if is-LOC(il) ∨ is-INTG(il)
    then (let  ea = d + il;
          if -2↑s < ea < +2↑s
           then return ea
           else exit(mk-Lbl(ERROR)))
    else exit(mk-Lbl(ERROR)))
```

end-of-definition.

3.1.2 The Compiling Algorithm

Having now had time to digest and understand the target machine, TM, architecture, i.e. the semantics of the machine language, independently of SAL, we now turn to the specification of what *Code* to generate for each SAL construct. We are seeking a definition, *c-prog* & *c-expr*, etc., which again is to be understood/read in just one, the compiling phase (way). *DICT*ionaries are used as before, and so is *LN*. An extra (compile-time) object is passed to any macro invocation of *c-expr*. It represents the current *stack* index to the target machine realization of the *TL*s of *DSA*s. Since storage cannot (in general) be reclaimed when a *Block* body *VAL*ue has been computed, and since in this version we have decided to stick with the merge of the control information of the activations (*CP*,*EP*,*RA*) not only with local *Var*iable (*VR*) (and thus parameter (*PM*≡*VR*)), but also with temporaries (*TL*), we shall have to set aside, in linear storage, the maximum amount of storage cells needed in any expression elaboration, and let that be the over-cautious realization, at this stage, of *TL*. To that end a crude compiler function, *depth*, is defined. It computes the number of temporaries, *de*, needed to compute any expression, but takes into account that embedded *Lets* & *Recs* lead to new activations for which separate stacks, *TL*, are (to be) set aside. We say that *depth* is crude since optimizing versions are easy to formulate, but would, in this example, lead to an excessive number of formulae lines. The disjoint *DSA*s of the previous (IV) definition are now mapped onto a linear ('cell') storage. Each 'new' *DSA* realization consists of 4 + *de* cells: *CP*, *EP*, *RA*, *VR*, *TL*.

VI Compiling Algorithm

VI.1 Compiler Domains

VI.1.1 Syntactic Domains -- as in I.1

VI.1.2 Compiler Components

```
(1)  Σc    =  REF →m Lbl-set
(2)  DICT  =  Id  →m LN
(3)  LN    =  N0
(4)  Lbl   ⊂  TOKEN | ERROR
```

VI.2 Auxiliary Compiler Functions

```
(5)  dcl ls := {ERROR}  type Lbl-set;

(6)  type make-lbl:        → (Σc → Σc Lbl)
(7)  type depth:      Expr → N1
```

```
make-lbl()=                                               (6)
  (let l ∈ Lbl be s.t. l ∉ c ls;
   ls := c ls ∪ {l};
   return l )
```

```
depth(e)=                                                 (7)
 cases e:
  mk-Const( )        → 1,
  mk-Var( )          → 1,
  mk-Infix(e1,,e2)   → max(depth(e1),depth(e2))+1,
  mk-Cond(t,c,a)     → max(depth(t),depth(c),depth(a))+1,
  mk-Let(,d,)        → depth(d),
  mk-Rec(,,)         → 1,
  mk-Lamb(,)         → 1,
  mk-Appl(f,a)       → max(depth(f),depth(a))+1
```

VI.3 Translator Specifications

VI.3.1 Global Constant Definitions

```
(8)   let p          = 0,
(9)       ep         = 1,
(10)      ra         = 2,
(11)  vr,pm,u,j      = 3,
(12)      top        = 4,
(13)      br         = 5,
(14)      t          = 4,
(15)      error      = ERROR;
```

VI.3.2 Compiling Specifications

```
(17)     Φ                → (Σc → Σc Ins*)
(18)     Φ          STK → Ins*
(19-27)  Φ  DICT LN STK → (Σc → Σc Ins*)
```

where: Φ stands for the syntactic category name i.e.: *c-prog* ⊃ Φ=*prog*, *c-expr* ⊃ Φ=*expr*, etc.. And: $STK = N_1$.

```
c-const(mk-Const(k),stk)=                                 (18)
  <mk-Sim(mk-Adr(p,stk),k),
   mk-Lim(u,k)>
```

```
c-prog(e)=                                              (17)
 (let lexit : make-lbl();
  let de = depth(e);
  <mk-Lim(p,0),
   mk-Lim(ep,0),
   mk-Lim(top,t+de)>⌢
   c-expr(e,[],0,t)⌢
  <mk-Ld(u,1,mk-Adr(p,t)),
   mk-Pr(u),
   mk-Jmp(lexit),
   error,
   mk-Pr(ERROR),
   lexit>)

c-var(mk-Var(id),dict,ln,stk)=                          (20)
 (let n = dict(id);
  let lloop : make-lbl(),
      lload : make-lbl();
  <mk-Lim(j,ln - n),
   lloop,
   mk-Cjp(j,ZERO,lload),
   mk-Ld(ep,1,mk-Adr(ep,ep)),
   mk-Adj(j,-1),
   mk-Jmp(lloop),
   lload,
   mk-Ld(u,1,mk-Adr(ep,vr)),
   mk-St(mk-Adr(p,stk),u,1),
   mk-Mov(ep,p)>)

c-infix(mk-Infix(e1,o,e2),dict,ln,stk)=                 (21)
  (c-expr(e2,dict,ln,stk)⌢
   c-expr(e1,dict,ln,stk + 1)⌢
  <mk-Ld(u,1,mk-Adr(p,stk + 1))
   mk-Fct(u,o,mk-Adr(p,stk)),
   mk-St(mk-Adr(p,stk),u,1)>)

c-cond(mk-Cond(t,c,a),dict,ln,stk)=                     (22)
 (let lalt : make-lbl(),
      lout : make-lbl();
   c-expr(t,dict,ln,stk)⌢
  <mk-Ld(u,1,mk-Adr(p,stk)),
   mk-Cjp(u,FALSE,lalt)>⌢
   c-expr(c,dict,ln,stk)⌢
  <mk-Jmp(lout),
   lalt>⌢
   c-expr(a,dict,ln,stk)⌢
  <lout>)

c-let(mk-Let(id,d,b),dict,ln,stk)=                      (23)
  (c-expr(d,dict,ln,stk)⌢
  <mk-Ld(u,1,mk-Adr(p,stk))>⌢
   c-block(b,dict + [id → ln+1],ln+1,stk))

c-rec(mk-Rec(g,d,b),dict,ln,stk)=                       (24)

  -- see appendix, part B.

c-lamb(mk-Lamb(id,d),dict,ln,stk)=                      (25)
 (let lfct : make-lbl(),
      lbyp : make-lbl();
  <mk-Jmp(lbyp),
   lfct>⌢
   c-block(d,dict + [id → ln+1],ln+1,stk)⌢
  <mk-Jmp(ra),
   lbyp,
   mk-Lim(u,lfct),
   mk-Pck(u,u,p),
   mk-St(mk-Adr(p,stk),u,1)>)

c-appl(mk-Appl(f,a),dict,ln,stk)=                       (26)
 (let lret : make-lbl();
   c-expr(a,dict,ln,stk)⌢
   c-expr(f,dict,ln,stk + 1)⌢
  <mk-Ld(u,1,mk-Adr(p,stk + 1))>⌢
  <mk-Cjp(u,NOTFCT,error),
   mk-Unp(br,ep,u),
   mk-Lim(ra,lret),
   mk-Ld(pm,1,mk-Adr(p,stk)),
   mk-Jmp(br),
   lret>)

c-block(bl,dict,ln,stk)=                                (27)
 (let dbl = deptk(bl);
  <mk-St(mk-Adr(top,p),p,t),
   mk-Mov(p,top),
   mk-Mov(ep,top),
   mk-Adj(top,t + dbl)>⌢
   c-expr(bl,dict,ln + 1,t)⌢
  <mk-Ld(u,1,mk-Adr(p,t))>⌢
  <mk-Ld(p,t - 1,mk-Adr(p,p)),
   mk-St(mk-Adr(p,stk),u,1)>)

c-expr(e,dict,ln,stk)=                                  (19)
 (is-Const(e) → c-const(e,stk),
  is-Var(e)   → c-var(e,dict,ln,stk),
  is-Infix(e) → c-infix(e,dict,ln,stk),
  is-Cond(e)  → c-cond(e,dict,ln,stk),
  is-Let(e)   → c-let(e,dict,ln,stk),
  is-Rec(e)   → c-rec(e,dict,ln,stk),
  is-Lamb(e)  → c-lamb(e,dict,ln,stk),
  is-Appl(e)  → c-appl(e,dict,ln,stk))

                                         end-of-definition.
```

3.2 An Attribute Semantics

By an attribute semantics definition of a source language is normally understood a set of (usually concrete, BNF) syntax rules defining the source language's character string representations; an association of so-called attributes to each syntactic category (i.e. distinct rule definiendum); and to each pairing of a left-hand side definiendum (or: non-terminal) with a right-hand side definiens alternative, a set of action clusters, one per attribute associated with non-terminals of either the left- or the right-hand sides. The action clusters are usually statement (sequences), and their purpose is to assign values to the attributes. The meaning of such an attribute semantics definition is as follows: consider a source text and its corresponding ('annotated') parse tree. To each tree node allocate a(n attribute) variable corresponding to each of the attributes of the node category. Then compute the values of these according to the attribute semantics definition action clusters. Two extreme cases arise: the value of an attribute is a function solely of the attribute values of the immediate descendant-, or ascendant-node(s). We say that the attribute is synthesized, respectively inherited. Obviously non-sensical attribute semantics definitions can be constructed for which their computation for arbitrary or certain parse trees is impossible - e.g. due to circularity. Some such possibilities, e.g. that of circularity, can, however, be statically checked, i.e. without recourse to parse trees. Historically attribute semantics originated with E.T.Irons' work on ALGOL 60 compilers - and we still find that the technique is mostly used in compiling algorithm specification,including statically checkable context condition/constraint testing.In contrast hereto: to specify the semantics of a source language one usually introduces a parse tree 'walking' function which in addition to the local attributes,also work on,i.e.manipulate,global objects,thus effecting desired computations.It appears,however,that this brings us almost right back to ULD-like definition styles,and we shall not illustrate such renditions further.Instead we shall exemplify combined inherited/synthesized and just plain inherited attribute semantics-style compiling algorithms (this,and the next sect.).We first choose the same basic realization as up till now,but, for sake of notational variety,and perhaps also your increased reading ability,express the compiled target code in free form.Hence the meaning is intended to be identical,down to individual computation sequences.The reader will otherwise observe a close resemblance between this,and the immediately preceding definition.In fact their only difference is one of style.Either could equally rightfully be called an attribute semantics.

Annotation: A concrete, BNF-like grammar is given below.To each category is then associated a small number of attributes.The *d*epth attribute,*d*,computes, as did the *depth* function (VI.7),the *max*imum length of the *T*emporary *L*ist - and does so bottom-up;hence it is a synthesized attribute.The *st*ac*k*,*l*evel *n*umber & *dict*ionary attributes:*stk*,*ln*,*dict* are all passed down from the parse tree root,and are thus inherited.Finally the *code* attribute is synthesized and stores the generated *Code-text* strings.We have not shown a formal (say BNF-) grammar for these strings,but really ought to have done.Subsect.3 finally gives the actual action cluster rules for each grammar rule/production.

Note: Note also our distinction,in VII.3 formulae between *italisized* and *scriptized* formulae text parts.The latter denotes *Code-text* to be generated, the former auxiliary quantities whose values are to be resolved in the *code* attribute computation process.Thus in e.g. VII.8.4 *cde* is to be computed and its *scriptized* numeral representation then to be inserted.Similarly for lines VII.8.10,10.5 & 10, where appropriately *scriptized* unique label identifiers are to be inserted in lieu of the *italisized label* identifiers.The result of a parse tree computation is finally accumulated in *code* of the root node.

VII Synthesized & Inherited Attribute Semantics Compiling Algorithm

VII.1 Concrete BNF-like Grammar

```
(1)    Prog  ::= Expr
(2.1)  Expr  ::= k
  .2         ::= id
  .3         ::= ( Expr + Expr )
  .4         ::= if  Expr  then  Expr  else Expr
  .5         ::= let id = Expr ; Block  end
  .6         ::= rec  g  = Lamb ; Block  end
  .7         ::= Lamb
  .8         ::= apply  Expr  (  Expr  )
(3)    Block ::= Expr
(4)    Lamb  ::= fun ( id ) =  Block  end
```

where we have abbreviated the classes of identifiers,constants and operators to just id, k and +.

VII.2 Node Attributes

(5)	Prog	*code*	*type Code-text*	*synthesized*
(6)	Expr Lamb	*code*	*type Code-text*	*synthesized*
		ln	*type* N_0	*inherited*
		dict	*type Id* $\rightarrow N_0$	*inherited*
		stk	*type* N_1	*inherited*
		d	*type* N_1	*synthesized*
(7)	Block	*code*	*type Code-text*	*synthesized*
		ln	*type* N_0	*inherited*
		dict	*type Id* $\rightarrow N_0$	*inherited*

VII.3 Action Cluster Rules

```
(8)     Progp ::= Expre
   .1   let lexit : make-lbl();
   .2   codep := "R[p] := 0;
   .3             R[ep] := 0;
   .4             R[top] := t + cde;
   .5            "~ccodee~"
   .6             Out := cR[u];
   .7             goto lexit;
   .8             lerr:
   .9             Out := ERROR;
   .10            lexit:
   .11           ";
   .12  lne   := 0;
   .13  dicte := [];
   .14  stke  := t;

(9)     Expre ::=  k
   .1   de    := 1;
   .2   codee := "S[cR[p] + cstke] := k;
   .3             R[u] := k;
   .4            ";

(10)    Expre ::=  id
   .1   let lloop : make-lbl(),
   .2       lload : make-lbl();
   .3   de    := 1;
   .4   codee :=  R[j] := clne - cdicte(id);
   .5             lloop:
   .6             if cR[j]=0 then goto lload;
   .7             R[ep] := cS[cR[ep] + ep];
   .8             R[j] := cR[j] - 1;
   .9             goto lloop;
   .10            lload:
   .11            R[u] := cS[cR[ep] + vr];
   .12            S[cR[p] + top] := cR[u];
   .13            R[ep] := cR[p];
   .14           ";

(11)    Expre ::=( Expr^1    +  Expr^2    )
   .1   de      := max(cde^1,cde^2) + 1;
   .2   lne^1,lne^2 := clne;
   .3   stke^1      := cstke;
   .4   stke^2      := cstke + 1;
   .5   dicte^1,dicte^2 := cdicte;
   .6   codee := ccodee^1~
   .7            ccodee^2~
   .8            "R[u] := cS[cR[p] + cstke];
   .9             R[u] := cR[u] + cS[cR[p] + cstke];
   .10            S[cR[p]  + cstke] := cR[u];
   .11           ";
```

```
(12)   Expre  ::= if Exprt then Exprc else Expra
  .1  let lalt : make-lbl(),
  .2        lout : make-lbl();
  .3  de                    := max(cdt,cdc,cda) + 1;
  .4  lnt,lnc,lna           := clne;
  .5  stkt,stkc,stka        := cstke;
  .6  dictt,dictc,dicta := cdicte;
  .7  codee := ccodet~"
  .8             R[u] := cS[cR[p] + cstke];
  .9             if cR[u] then goto lalt;
  .10          "~ccodec~"
  .11            goto lout;
  .12            lalt:
  .13          "~ccodea~"
  .14            lout:
  .15            ";

(13)   Expre  ::= let id = Exprd ; Blockb  end
  .1  de         := cdb;
  .2  lnd     := clne;
  .3  lnb     := clne + 1;
  .4  stkd    := cstke;
  .5  dictd   := cdicte;
  .6  dictb   := cdicte + [id→clne + 1];
  .7  codee   := ccoded~"
  .8             R[u] := cS[cR[p] + cstke];
  .9           "~ccodeb~"
  .10            ";

(14)   Expre  ::= rec g = Lambd  ;  Blockb  end
```

-- details found in appendix, part C.

-- is brought there, together with correspon=ding level IV and VII solutions for reasons of enabling easy cross-reference

```
(15)   Lambe  ::= fun ( id ) = Blockb   end
  .1  let lfct : make-lbl(),
  .2        lbyp : make-lbl();
  .3  de     := 1;
  .4  lnb    := clne + 1;
  ..
  .6  dictb := cdicte + [id→clne + 1];
  .7  codee := "goto lbyp;
  .8             lfct:
  .9           "~ccodeb~"
  .10            goto cR[ra];
  .11            lbyp:
  .12            R[u] := lfct;
  .13            R[u] := mk-FCT(cR[u],cR[p]);
  .14            S[cR[p] + cstke] := cR[u];
  .15            ";

(16)   Expre  ::=  Lambl
  .1  de     := cdl;
  .2  lnl    := clne;
  .3  stkl   := cstke;
  .4  dictl  := cdicte;
  .5  codee  := ccodel;

(17)   Expre  ::=  apply  Exprf  ( Expra )
  .1  let lret : make-lbl();
  .2  de              := max(cdf,da) + 1;
  .3  lnf,lna         := clne;
  .4  stkf            := cstke;
  .5  stka            := cstke + 1;
  .6  dictf,dicta := cdicte;
  .7  codee := ccodea~"
  .8          "~ccodef~"
  .9            R[u] := cS[cR[p] + (cstke+1)];
  .10           if NOTFCT(cR[u])
  .11             then goto lerr;
  .12           R[br] := s-Lbl(cR[u]);
  .13           R[ep] := s-LOC(cR[u]);
  .14           R[ra] := lret;
  .15           R[pm] := cS[cR[p] + cstke];
  .16           goto cR[br];
  .17           lret:
  .18           ";

(18)   Blockb  ::=  Expre
  .1  lne    := clnb + 1;
  .2  dicte := cdictb;
  .3  stke   := t;
  .4  codeb  := "S[cR[top] + p ] := cR[p];
  .5            S[cR[top] +ep] := cR[ep];
  .6            S[cR[top] +ra] := cR[ra];
  .7            S[cR[top] +vr] := cR[u];
  .8             R[p]    := cR[top];
  .9             R[ep]   := cR[p];
  .10            R[top] := cR[top] + (t+cde) ;
  .11         "~ccodee~"
  .12            R[ep] := cS[cR[p] + ep];
  .13            R[ra] := cS[cR[p] + ra];
  .14            R[u]  := cS[cR[p] + t];
  .15            R[p]  := cS[cR[p] + p];
  .16            S[cR[p] + cstke] := cR[u];
  .17         ";
```

end-of-definition.

3.3 Another Attribute 'Semantics'

The concrete BNF grammar given in 3.2 for SAL is both bottom-up and top-down analyzable,or more precisely: the corresponding language can be syntactically parsed with respect to this (one) grammar both bottom-up and top-down. That didn't matter very much in section 3.2,since attribute variable value computations still required the presence of the entire parse tree before any *Code-text* could be generated.In this section we present an attribute semantics specification of another compiling algorithm,which,based on a top-down parse process, is capable of generating *Code-text* simultaneously with parsing. Again we shall not (here) argue how we choose a/the solution - design rules are given in [53].Instead we ask you to recall the twin stack abstract machine of section 2.3. Now all *DSA* realizations fit exactly into four (*t*) positions: (*CP*, *EP*,*RA*,*VR≡PM*) with temporaries allocated to a global,contiguous stack, *STK*s direct implementation. Since SAL is simply applicative (it permits e.g. no GOTOs) this poses no special problems as concerns correct indices into stack tops.The *STK* has been realized in 'core' "below" the activation stack: think of the target machine addressing being "wrapped around" zero address to maximum available core storage address - and you get a scheme which was very common in the earlier days on mono-processing. One crucial,final note:to cope with known *Code-text* to be "delay" generated (after unknown,variable length *Code-text* corresponding to subtree source texts yet to be top-down recognized) has been generated,a global 'attribute' (also) called *code*,is introduced.It is treated as a stack.Push corresponds to concatenation, pop to taking the head off - leaving the tail. Pushing occurs for all *Code-texts* known when recognizing the initial prefix string, as one does in top-down analysis, of a composite expression: if, let, rec, apply, (& fun. Popping of one part occurs when any expression has been completely analyzed: k, id, fi, end, end, end,), end respectively.

VIII Inherited Attribute 'Semantics' Compiling Algorithm.

VIII.1 Syntactic Domains -- as in VII.1, but:

```
(2.4) Expr ::= if Expr then Expr else Expr fi
```

VIII.2 Node Attributes

```
(5)  Expr   ln    type N0          inherited
     Lamb   dict  type Id ->m N0   inherited
     Block
```

VIII.3 Global Attribute

```
(6)  Prog   code   type Code-text   stack
            print  type Code-text   output
```

VIII.4 Attribute Rules

```
(7)    Progp ::= Expre
  .1   let lexit : make-lbl();
  .2   print "R[p]    := 0;
  .3         R[ep]   := 0;
  .4         R[top]  :=  ;
  .5         R[stk]  := -1;
  .6         ";
  .7   code := <"R[u] := cS[-1];
  .8             Out  := cR[u];
  .9             goto lexit;
  .10            lerr:
  .11            Out  := ERROR;
  .12            lexit:
  .13            ">;
  .14  lne  := 0;
  .15  dicte := [];

(8)    Expre  ::=  k
  .1   print "S[cR[stk]]  := k;
  .2         R[u]  :=  ;
  .3         R[stk] := cR[stk] + 1;
  .4         "⌢h c code;
  .5   code := t c code;

(9)    Expr   ::=  id
  .1   let lloop : make-lbl(),
  .2       lload : make-lbl();
  .3   print "R[j] := clne - (cdicte)(id);
  .4         lloop:
  .5         if cR[j]=0 then goto lload;
  .6         R[ep] := cS[cR[ep] + ep];
  .7         R[j]  := cR[j] - 1;
  .8         goto lloop
  .9         lload:
  .10        R[u] := cS[cR[ep] + vr];
  .11        S[cR[stk]]  := cR[u];
  .12        R[stk] := cR[stk] - 1;
  .13        R[ep]  := cR[p];
  .14        "⌢h c code;
  .15  code := t c code;

(10)   Expre ::= ( Expr1 + Expr2 )
  .1   lne1, lne2     := clne;
  .2   dicte1, dicte2 := cdicte;
  .3   code := <"">⌢
  .4            <"R[u]  := cS[cR[stk]];
  .5              R[u]  := cR[u] + cS[cR[stk] + 1];
  .6              R[stk]:= cR[stk] + 1;
  .7              S[cR[stk]] := cR[u];
  .8            ">⌢ccode;

(11)   Expre ::= if Exprt then Exprc else Expra fi
  .1   let lalt : make-lbl(),
  .2       lout : make-lbl();
  .3   lnt, lnc, lna        := clne;
  .4   dictt, dictc, dicta  := cdicte;
  .5   code :=  "R[u] := cS[cR[stk]];
  .6             R[stk] := cR[stk] + 1;
  .7             if cR[u] then goto lalt;
  .8             ">⌢
  .9            <"goto lout;
  .10            lalt:
  .11            ">⌢
  .12           <"lout:
  .13            ">⌢ccode;

(12)   Expre ::= let id = Exprd ; Blockb end
  .1   lnd   := clne;
  .2   lnb   := clne + 1;
  .3   dictd := cdicte;
  .4   dictb := cdicte + [id -> clne + 1];
  .5   code  := <"R[u]    := cS[cR[stk]];
  .6              R[stk] := cR[stk] + 1;
  .7              ">⌢
  .8             <"">⌢ccode;

(13)   Expre ::= rec g = Lambd ; Blockb end

   -- details found in appendix, part D.

(14)   Expre ::= Lambd
  .1   lnd   := clne;
  .2   dictd := cdicte;

(15)   Lambe ::= fun ( id ) = Blockb end
  .1   let lfct : make-lbl(),
  .2       lbyp : make-lbl();
  .3   lnb   := clne + 1;
  .4   dictb := cdicte + [id -> clne + 1];
  .5   code  := "goto cR[ra];
  .6             lbyp:
  .7             R[u] := lfct;
  .8             R[u] := mk-FCT(cR[u],cR[p]);
  .9             S[cR[stk]] := cR[u];
  .10            R[stk] := cR[stk] - 1;
  .11            ">⌢ccode;
  .12  print "goto lbyp;
  .13        lfct:
  .14        ";

(16)   Expre ::= apply Exprf ( Expra )
  .1   let lret : make-lbl();
  .2   lnf, lna       := clne;
  .3   dictf, dicta   := cdicte;
  .4   code := <"">⌢
  .5            <"R[u] := cS[cR[stk] - 1];
  .6              if NOTFCT(cR[u])
  .7                then goto lerr;
  .8              R[br] := s-Lbl(cR[u]);
  .9              R[ep] := s-LOC(cR[u]);
```

```
    .10            R[ra]  := lret;
    .11            R[pm]  := cS[cR[stk]];
    .12            R[stk] := cR[stk] - 2;
    .13            goto cR[br];
    .14            lret:
    .15          ">~ccode;
(17)    Blockb  ::=  Expre
    .1  lne   := clnb + 1;
    .2  dicte := cdictb;
    .3  print "S[cR[top]+ p] := cR[p];
               S[cR[top]+ep] := cR[ep];
    .5         S[cR[top]+ra] := cR[ra];
    .6         S[cR[top]+vr] := cR[u];
    .7         R[p]             := cR[top];
    .8         R[ep]            := cR[top];
    .9         R[top]           := cR[top] + t;
    .10        ";
    .11 code := <"R[ep] := cS[cR[p] + ep];
                 R[ra] := cS[cR[p] + ra];
    .13          R[u]  := cS[cR[p] + t];
    .14          R[p]  := cS[cR[p] + p];
    .15          S[cR[stk]] := cR[u];
    .16          R[stk]     := cR[stk] + 1;
    .17        ">~ccode;
```

end-of-definition.

Attribute semantics definitions received their purifying, individualizing treatment from Knuth, Lewis/Stearns/Rosenkrantz, Wirth/Weber and others; Irons started the whole thing [61-75].

4. COMPILER STRUCTURES

From the compiling algorithm specifications of section 3 (especially 3.2-3) we can now read properties other than just the source text input vs. target machine code output itself. Thus the compiling algorithm determines first level structures of the compiler itself. Such as: "is it to, ar can it, be a single-pass compiler?". "What information is primarily, and when is it, put in the *DICT*ionary?". "How is the dictionary realizable: as part of the intermediate text of a multi-pass compiler, with the *dict*ionary components 'scattered' over this, 'local' to e.g. the *Expr* bodies; or necessarily as a 'global' component, 'disjoint' (as you might have first understood it above) from any intermediate text or parse tree?".

Single- & Multi-Pass Compilers

If all attributes can be computed in a synthetic manner then a single-pass compiler based on a bottom-up parse can always be realized. This is so since any deterministic language can always be so (in fact LR(K)) parsed. Similarly, if the language can be top-down (e.g. LL(K)) parsed (possibly using some recursive descent method), and a compiling algorithm given by a purely inherited attribute 'semantics', then a single-pass compiler is again possible. If, however, as e.g. suggested by our first SAL attribute 'semantics' compiling algorithm (3.1-2), some attributes, like the local, *Tempo*rary *List stack* pointer, and the block/body *l*evel *n*umber, and *dict*ionary, are inherited, while others, the maximum local stack *d*epth and the generated *code*, are synthesized, then a multi-pass compiler with at least two passes cannot be avoided. If the inherited and synthesized attributes of such a compiling algorithm solely derive from constants emanating from respectively the root and leaves, then a two-pass compiler can result. This is in fact the case with the VI & VII specifications. The exact minimum number of logical, i.e. 'inherently' required, passes, then is a function of the semantics and syntax of the language - with the semantics property eventually showing up in the intricate web-like relationships between synthesized & inherited attributes. Of course: silly, unnecessarily complicated, attribute semantics, i.e. such involving non-intrinsical combinations of inherited & synthesized attribute value computations, would then indicate a higher ('minimum') number of passes than strictly required. Only calm scrutiny, a careful analysis and a complete mastering of the language semantics & specification tools will eventually lead to optimal realizations. So what is then the difference between the two compiling algorithms: VII & VIII? One leads to a two-pass-, the other to a single-pass compiler for one and the same language (semantics). Is not the minimum pass compiler always to be preferred? Well, the gain in compilation speed in the latter has been gotten at the expense/sacrifice of slower execution speed, since - as is usually the case with pure, stack-oriented execution (especially such fixed in the hardware) - since, a temporary stack index, *R[stk]*, must now be dynamically adjusted: at the worst once per 'popping', and once per 'pushing'. This being in contrast to the fixed-offset addressing possible by our two-pass compilation, which - in turn - causes possibly excessive storage to be (pre-)allocated.

Compiler Object Realizations

Whilst the purpose of 'mapping' the denotational semantics into successively lower-order, increasingly more concrete/intricate semantics definitions, was one of eliminating higher-order, functional objects -- as well as the run-time presence of elaboration routines -- we now suddenly see the re-appearance, in e.g. the attribute semantics definitions, of higher-order (albeit simple domain) objects: the functional *DICT*ionaries, and even the (non-functional, but) varying (*flex*) string length (*Code-text*) objects. The input/output relationships of a compiler has been specified. Now we must object refine the abstractly described compiler objects, and operation decompose the likewise implicitly specified primitive operations on these. In fact, we must also take issue, at long last, with the internal realization of abstract SAL programs. But note this: nothing has been lost in post-poning this decision till now. On the contrary: we may now be able to design exactly that internal representation which best suits the single- or multi- (here: double-) pass compilers' code-generation parse-tree walking algorithm. The techniques of 'mapping' such abstractions into concrete implementations using methods akin to those of this papers' specialized, run-time structure-oriented ones, will not be further dealt with here, instead we refer to [2,3,26].

5. COMPILING CORRECTNESS

Time has finally come to take issue with the problem of correctness. In this section we shall illu=

strate only one such proof. We prove that the development I → II is correct. Subsequent development stages are proved using essentially the same technique, but becoming, first increasingly more cumbersome (to report & read), and with III → IV also somewhat more complex. [57] is a good reference, displaying the current 'minimum' complexity, and exhibiting the principal issues involved when going to 'larger' languages.

Correctness Criterion:

(∇) (∀*env* ∈ *ENV*, ∀*env1* ∈ *ENV1*)
  (*env* = *retr-ENV(env1)*)
  ⊃ (∀*e* ∈ *expr*)(*eval-expr(e)env*
   = *retr-VAL(m1-eval-expr(e,env1)))*

Annotation: For all such abstract, *env*, and concrete, *env1*, environments which correspond, it shall be the case that evaluating any expression, *e*, using the abstract interpreter on *env* shall yield the same value as is retrievable from evaluating that same expression *e* using the more concrete interpreter on *env1*.

The statement of this criterion, as well as its actual, detailed proof, is new. No proof of correctness was reported in connection with [33]. The structure of ∇ can be pictured:

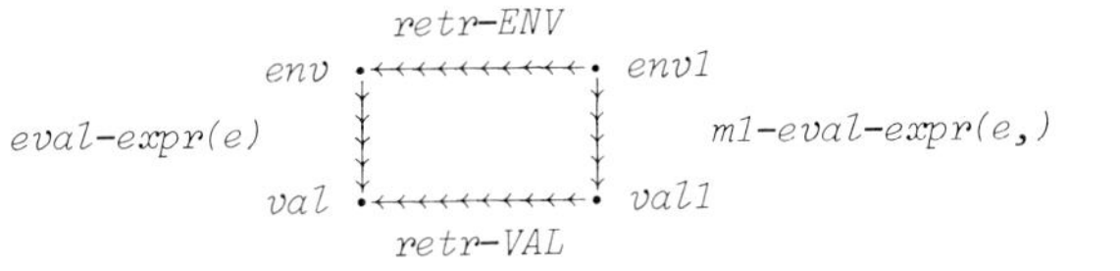

and is derived from the general idea of 'simulation' of one program by another (executing one algebra on another). [76,77] as reported by Landin & Burstall [28], and (independently) used by McCarthy & Painter [27]. Notable other references are [29,30, 32,34,35].

Proof of Correctness: Our task of proving that *m1-eval-expr* (in the sense of the criterion above) does the same, to any expression, as *eval-expr*, i.e. delivers comparable results, can be broken into two steps. Firstly we plan the proof. We look for a strategy, a proof technique, which, with the least amount of effort, will safely bring the proof home. Secondly we carry through the actual details of all parts of the proof, as structured in the first step above. The strategy to be followed here is that of: proof by structural induction [78], that is: since the criterion calls for all expressions, we naturally look for a way of only proving it for a finite set of representative examples. The selection of these is guided by the structure (and alternatives) of the syntactic domain abstract syntax, and by the corresponding structure and alternatives of the elaboration functions. The structure of the semantic domains here play a lesser role (than might otherwise be the case -- for e.g. III → IV). The abstract syntax for expressions determined the major structure of the elaboration functions, as is natural for denotational semantics definitions. Therefore we shall now structure the proof according to the cases of alternative syntactic categories, and by induction due to the recursive definition of *Expr*. We leave it to the reader to decipher the use of formulae nos.

case 1: *e* = *mk-Const(k)*

1. *eval-expr(mk-Const(k))env* I.17.2
2. = *k*
3. *m1-eval-expr(mk-Const(k),env1)* II.11.3
4. = *k*
5. *retr-VAL(k)* II.8.3
6. = *k* QED.

case 2: *e* = *mk-Var(id)*

0. assumption: *env* = *retr-ENV(env1)* Thm
1. *eval-expr(mk-Var(id))env* I.17.3
2. = *env(id)*
3. *m1-eval-expr(mk-Var(id),env1)* II.11.5
4. = *look-up1(id,env1)*
5. *env(id)* = *retr-VAL(look-up1(id,env1))* Lm,QED.

case 4: *e* = *mk-Cond(t,c,a)*

0. assumption: *env* = *retr-ENV(env1)* Thm
1. *eval-expr(mk-Cond(t,c,a))env* I.17.
2. = if *eval-expr(t)env* .8
  then *eval-expr(c)env* .9
  else *eval-expr(a)env* .10
3. *m1-eval-expr(mk-Cond(t,c,a),env1)* II.11.
4. = if *m1-eval-expr(t,env1)* .12
  then *m1-eval-expr(c,env1)* .13
  else *m1-eval-expr(a,env1)* .14
5. induction, hypothesis 0,Thm
 .1 *eval-expr(t)env* ~ *m1-eval-expr(t,env1)*
 .2 *eval-expr(c)env* ~ *m1-eval-expr(c,env1)*
 .3 *eval-expr(a)env* ~ *m1-eval-expr(a,env1)*
6. *m1-eval-expr(t,env1)* ∈ *BOOL*
7. *eval-expr(t)env* = *m1-eval-expr(t,env1)* 5.1,6.
8. subcase 1
 .0 *eval-expr(t)env* = *true* asm
 .1 *eval-expr(mk-Cond(t,c,a))env*
  = *eval-expr(c)env* mls
 .2 *m1-eval-expr(mk-Cond(t,c,a),env1)*
  = *m1-eval-expr(c,env1)* 8.0,5.1,mls
 .3 8.1=8.2 follows from 5.2 QED.
9. subcase 2 -- as 8. QED.

case 5: *e* = *mk-Lamb(id,d)*

0. assumption: *env* = *retr-ENV(env1)* Thm
1. *eval-expr(mk-Lamb(id,d))env* I.17.17
2. = *eval-fun(mk-Lamb(id,d))env*
3. *m1-eval-expr(mk-Lamb(id,d),env1)* II.11.21
4. = *mk-CLOS(mk-Lamb(id,d),env1)*
5. *retr-VAL(mk-CLOS(mk-Lamb(id,d),env1))*
 .1 = *eval-fun(mk-Lamb(id,d))(retr-ENV(env1))* II.8.2
 .2 = *eval-fun(mk-Lamb(id,d))env* 0.

QED follows from 2.=5.2

case 6: *e* = *mk-Appl(f,a)*

0. assumption: *env* = *retr-ENV(env1)*
1. *eval-expr(mk-Appl(f,a))env* I.17.21
2. = (*eval-expr(f)env*)(*eval-expr(a)env*)
3. *m1-eval-expr(mk-Appl(f,a),env1)* II.11.
4.1 = (let *clos* = *m1-eval-expr(f,env1)*, .23
 .2 *arg* = *m1-eval-expr(a,env1)*; .24
 .3 *apply1(clos,arg)*) .25
5. induction, hypothesis 0,Thm
 .1 *eval-expr(f)env* ~ *m1-eval-expr(f,env1)*
 .2 *eval-expr(a)env* ~ *m1-eval-expr(a,env1)*
6. *eval-expr(f)env* ∈ *FUN* ⊃ asm
7. (∃*mk-Lamb(id,d)*,∃*env'* ∈ *ENV*) I.18
  (*eval-expr(f)env* = *eval-fun(mk-Lamb(id,d)env)*
 -- considering only a 'good' case

```
8.    m1-eval-expr(f,env1) ∈ CLOS ⊃                   6.,5.1
9.    (...,∃env1' ∈ ENV1)                              7.,8.
 .1      (env' = retr-ENV(env1'))
 .2     ∧(m1-eval-expr(mk-Lamb(id,d),env1')
         = m1-eval-expr(f,env1)
10.   m1-eval-expr(id,d),env1')
 .1   = mk-CLOS(km-Lamb(id,d),env1')          II.11.21
 .2   = m1-eval-expr(f,env1)                        9.
 .3   = clos                                        4.1
11.   apply1(clos,arg)                              10.
 .1   = apply1(mk-CLOS(mk-Lamb(id,d),env1'),arg)
 .2   = (let env1"=<mk-SIMP(id,arg)>⌢env1' II.12.3
         m1-eval-expr(d,env1"))                     -.4
12.   (eval-expr(f)env)(eval-expr(a)env)
 .1   = (eval-fun(mk-Lamb(id,d))env')(eval-...} 7.
 .2   = λx.(let env" = env' + [id→a];}..-expr(a)env)
            eval-expr(d)env")(eval-expr(a)env)
 .3   = (let env" = env' + [id→eval-expr(a)env];
         eval-expr(d)env")
13    env" = retr-ENV(env1")              follows from:
 .1      retr-ENV(env1') = env'                    9.1
 .2     ∧ env1" =<mk-SIMP(id,arg)>⌢env1'           11.2
 .3     ∧ env"  = env' + [id→eval-expr(a)env]12.3
 .4     ∧ arg   = m1-eval-expr(a,env1)             4.2
 .5     ∧ retr-ENV definition                   II.7
 .6     ∧ eval-expr(a)env = retr-VAL(arg)          5.2
14. induction,hypothesis:
 .1   eval-expr(d)env" ~ m1-eval-expr(d,env1")Thm
15.   QED then follows
```

case 7: *e = mk-Rec(g,mk-Lamb(id,d),b)*

```
0.    assumption: env = retr-ENV(env1)
1.    eval-expr(mk-Rec(g,mk-Lamb(id,d),b))env
2.     = (let env'=env+[g→eval-fun(mk-Lamb(id,d)env
          eval-expr(b)env')
3. m1-eval-expr(mk-Rec(g,mk-Lamb(id,d),b),env1)
4. =(let env1'=<mk-REC(g,ml-Lamb(id,d))>⌢env1;
    m1-eval-expr(b,env1'))
5. env1' = retr-ENV(env')                 follows from:
 .1    env' = env+[g→eval-fun(mk-Lamb(id,d)env']
 .2 ∧ env1'= <mk-REC(g,mk-Lamb(id,d))>⌢env1
 .3 ∧ env  = retr-ENV(env1)
 .4 ∧ retr-ENV(env1')
6. (5) ⊃ eval-expr(b)env'
         =retr-VAL(m1-eval-expr(b,env1'))     QED.
```

Comments:

asm: assumption, Thm: theorem (∇), Lm: Lemma,which states:

```
(env = retr-ENV(env1))
⊃ (∀id∈dom env)
     (env(id)=retr-VAL(look-up1(id,env1)))
```

The lemma is (e.g.) proved by induction on the length of *env1* .Two cases form the basis step:the *SIMP*le and the *REC*ursive header.We leave that part of the overall proof as an exercise.

6. CONCLUSION

We have shown the systematic derivation,from a denotational semantics definition,the definition,in a number of increasingly concrete,more detailed, run-time-oriented styles,of a Simple Applicative Language featuring both a block-structure and the procedure concept.Hence we were able to illustrate how run-time structures such as DISPLAYs could be orderly developed,eventually proven correct.The various definition styles were basically those current during the 1960's,and we have thus shown how they relate.A number of other,semantics definition styles were not so exemplified.Notably the axiomatic method.As is shown e.g. by Scott ,Ligler [79] and Donahue [22] one can indeed (elegantly) derive axiomatic (+ 'surface property') semantics from that of a denotational semantics. [32] shows an early demonstration of this possibility. .We leave it to the reader to uncover those semantic definition methods which we do not believe can be meaningfully incorporated in a stepwise development method such as based on object refinement and operation decomposition.

ACKNOWLEDGEMENTS

The current authors' interest in programming language semantics dates back (only) to 1970,his first 'challenger' then being J.Backus with whom he spent nearly two,very fruitful years.To Dr.Jean-Paul Jacob goes many thanks for providing an opportunity to lecture on the topic in South America in July/August 1972.To Prof.Lotfi Zadeh for further opportunities to tighten the understanding during lectures at Berkeley.But to the outstanding colleagues at the IBM Vienna Lab. (during more than two years,73-75) goes my most sincerest gratitude.It was here that programming language semantics was studied most seriously,and with an aim towards its use as a basis for the practical development of correct compilers. In particular I wish to acknowledge: P.Lucas,H.Bekić,C.B.Jones & W.Henhapl for their daily vigilance, and Dr.K.Walk and particularly Prof.H.Zemanek for providing such outstandingly fitting working conditions.It is the authors' dearest wish that the fine work that has hitherto come out of the Vienna Lab. may also in the future be furthered there.

REFERENCES & BIBLIOGRAPHY

General:

[1] D.Bjørner: "Programming Languages: Linguistics and Semantics",these proceedings,a Tutorial.

[2] --: "Software Abstraction Principles" & "Abstract Software Specifications",Techn.Monograph,resp.Rept.,Techn.Univ.Denmark,Fall 76.

[3] --: "Systematic Program Derivation" & "... Techniques",Techn.Monograph,resp.Rept.,Techn. Univ.Denmark,Fall 76.

Abstract Syntax:

[4] J.McCarthy: "Towards a Math.Sci.of Computation", in: 'Information Processing' (ed.C.M.Popplewell),Proc.2nd IFIP Conf.,North-Holland Publ., pp 21-28,1963.

[5] P.Lucas & K.Walk: "On the Formal Definition of PL/I",Ann.Review in 'Automatic Programming', Pergamon Press,vol.6,pt.3,pp 105-152,1969.

[6] D.Bjørner: "META-IV: A Formal Meta-Language for Abstract Software Specifications",Techn. Rept.,Techn.Univ.Denmark,Fall 76 (subm.for publ).

Comparative Semantics Definitions:

[7] J.W.deBakker: "Semantics of Programming Lan=

guages",in:'Advances in Information Systems Science',vol 2 (ed.J.T.Tou),Plenum Press,N.Y., 1969.

[8] P.Lauer & C.A.R.Hoare:"Consistent & Complementary Formal Theories of the Semantics of Programming Languages",IBM Vienna Lab.Techn.Rept. TR25.121,1971 & TR-44 Univ.of Newcastle upon Tyne,Comp.Lab.,1973.

[9] M.Marcotty,H.F.Ledgard & G.V.Bochmann:"A Sampler of Formal Definitions",ACM Comp.Surv.,vol 8,no.2,pp 191-276,1976.

Procedure Implementation Techniques:

[10] E.W.Dijkstra:"Recursive Programming",Numer. Mathematik,pp 312-318,1960.

[11] --:"An Algol 60 Translator for the X1",Ann. Review in'Automatic Programming',1962.

[12] D.Gries:"Compiler Construction for Digital Computers",J.Wiley & Sons,N.Y.,1971.

[13] W.Henhapl & C.B.Jones:"A Run-Time Mechanism for Referencing Variables",Information Proc. Letters,vol.1,no.1,pp 14-16,1971.

[14] C.B.Jones & P.Lucas:"Proving Correctness of Implementation Techniques",in:'Semantics of Algorithmic Languages',(ed.E.Engeler) Springer Lecture Notes in Mathematics,vol.188,N.Y., pp 178-211,1971.

Denotational Semantics (see also refs.in: [1])

[15] P.Landin:"The Mechanical Evaluation of Expressions",Computer Journal,vol.6,no.4,pp 308-320, 1964.

[16] C.Strachey:"Towards a Formal Semantics",in: 'Formal Language Description Languages for Computer Programming' (ed.T.B.Stell Jr.) Proc. IFIP Working Conf.,Vienna,North-Holland Publ., pp 198-220,1966.

[17] D.Scott & C.Strachey:"Toward a Mathematical Semantics for Computer Language",in:'Computers and Automata',(ed.J.Fox) Polytechnic Inst.of Brooklyn,Micriwave Res.Inst.,Symp.Series XXI, pp 19-46,1971.

[18] D.Scott:"Mathematical Concepts in Programming Language Semantics",Proc.AFIPS SJCC,vol.40, pp 225-234,1972.

[19] --:"Data Types as Lattices", To the Memory of Christopher Strachey,SIAM J.Comput.,vol.5,no. 3,pp 522-587,1976.

[20] R.D.Tennent:"Mathematical Semantics of SNOBOL 4",Conf.Rec.of ACM.Symp.on:'Principles of Programming Languages',Boston,pp 95-107,1973.

[21] --:"The Denotational Semantics of Programming Languages",CACM,vol.19,no.8,pp 437-453,1976.

[22] J.E.Donahue:"Complementary Definition of Programming Language Semantics",Springer Lecture Notes in Comp.Sci.,vol.42,1972.

[23] J.Stoy:"The Scott-Strachey Approach to Mathematical Semantics",Lecture Notes,MIT,1974.

[24] H.Bekić,D.Bjørner,W.Henhapl,C.B.Jones & P.Lucas:"A Formal Definition of a PL/I Subset", Pts 1 & 2,IBM Vienna Techn.Rept.TR25.139,December 1974.

Denotational Semantics Applications:

[25] C.B.Jones:"Formal Definition in Compiler Development",IBM Vienna Techn.Rept.TR25.145, Feb.1976.

[26] D.Bjørner:"Systematic Compiler Specifications", Techn.Monograph (draft),Techn.Univ.Denmark, Fall 1976.

[27] J.McCarthy & J.Painter:"The Correctness of a Compiler for Arithmetic Expressions",in:Amer. Math.Soc.Proc:'Math.Aspects of Comp.Sci.', Proc.Symp.Appl.Math.,vol.19,pp 33-41,1967.

[28] P.Landin & R.M.Burstall:"Programs and their Proofs:An Algebraic Approach",in:'Machine Intelligence' (ed.D.Michie),Edinburg Univ.Press, vol.4,pp 17-44,1969.

[29] R.W.Weyrauch & R.Milner:"Program Correctness in a Mechanized Logic",Proc.1st USA-Japan Comp. Conf.,pp 384-390,1972.

[30] FLockwood Morris:"Advice on Structuring Compilers and Proving them Correct",ref 20.,pp 144-152,1973.

[31] --:"The next 700 Programming Language Descriptions",unpubl.ms.,Univ.of Essex,Comp.Ctr.1970.

[32] P.Lucas:"On Program Correctness and the Stepwise Development of Implementations",Proc.Convegno di Informatica Teorica,Pisa Univ.,1972.

[33] J.C.Reynolds:"Definitional Interpreters for Higher-Order Programming Languages",ACM Proc. 25th Nat.Conf.,Boston,vol.2,pp 717-740,1972.

[34] J.A.Goguen,E.Wagner,J.B.Wright,J.Thatcher: "Initial Algebra Semantics",IBM Res.Rept.RC 5243,Ths.J.Watson Res.Ctr,Yorktown Heights, N.Y.,1975.

[35] --:"A Junction between Computer Science and Category Theory",ibid,RC4526,1973.(Known as the ADJ series.)

First-Order Functional Semantics

[36] J.McCarthy et al.:"LISP 1.5,Programmer's Manual",MIT Press,Cambridge,Mass.,1962.

[37] M.J.Gordon:"Models of Pure LISP",Ph.D.Thesis, Experimental Prgr.Res.Grp.,Rept.no.31,Theory of Comp.Grp.,Univ.of Edinburg,1973.

[38] PL/I Definition Group of the (IBM) Vienna Lab.: "Formal Definition of PL/I",ULD III version I, Techn.Rept.TR25.071,Dec.1966.

[39] --:"...",ULD III version II,Techn.Repts:TR25. 074/081/080/084/086/083/082,April '67 - June '68.

[40] --:"...",ULD III version III,Techn.Repts.TR25. 095/096/097/098/099,April - June 1969.

[41] J.C.Reynolds:"GEDANKEN -- A Simple Type-less Language based on the Principle of Completeness and the Reference Concept",CACM,vol.13, no.5,pp 308-319,1970.

[42≡40,43≡5]

[44] P.Wegner:"The Vienna Definition Language", ACM Comp.Survey,vol.4,no.1,pp 5-63,1972.

[45] E.Neuhold:"The Formal Description of Program=ming Languages",IBM Systems Journal,vol.10, no.2,pp 86-112,1971.

[46] A.Ollongreen:"Definition of Programming Lan=guages by Interpreting Automata",Academic Press,1974.

[47] P.Lucas,P.Lauer & H.Stigleitner:"Method and Notation for the Formal Definition of Program=ming Languages",IBM Vienna Lab.,Techn.Rept. TR25.087,June 1968.

[48] P.Lauer:"Formal Definition of ALGOL 60",ibid, TR25.088,Dec.1968.

[49] K.Zimmermann:"Outline of a Formal Definition of FORTRAN",ibid,Lab.Rept.,LR25.3.053,June 1969.

[50] ECMA TC10 / ANSI.X3J1 (European Comp.Manuf.As=soc./Amer.Nat.Stand.Inst.):"PL/I BASIS/1-12, Feb.1975,346 pg.

[51] D.Beech:"On the Definitional Method of Stan=dard PL/I",ref 20,pp 87-94.

Compiler-Compilers:

[52] P.D.Mosses:"Compiler Generation Using Denota=tional Semantics",in:'Math.Found.of Comp.Sci.' Springer Lecture Notes in Computer Science, vol.45,pp 436-441,1976.

[53≡26]

[54] F.Weissenböck & W.Henhapl:"A Formal Mapping Description",IBM Vienna Lab.Techn.Note,TN25. 3.105,Feb.1975.

[55] H.Bekić:"Formale Übers.Entw." (Course Notes, Techn.Univ.Vienna),IBM Lab.Vienna,Spring 75.

[56] --,H.Izbicki,C.B.Jones & F.Weissenböck:"Some Experiments with using Formal Definitions in Compiler Development",IBM Vienna Lab.,Lab. Note,LN25.3.107,Dec.1975.

[57≡25]

[58] A.Ansted & B.Lysdal:"The Definition & Deve=lopment of a PASCAL-based Macro-Processor", Dept.of Datalogy,Univ.of Copenhagen,Summer 1975.

[59] L.Jensen:"The Definition & Realization of a Procedure-oriented Language for the PDP/11", ibid,Fall 1975.

[60] P.G.Howalt:"Studies of the Procedure-Concept, and its Formal Realization",ibid,M.Sc.Thesis, Winter 1976/77.

Attribute Semantics

[61] E.T.Irons:"A Syntax Directed Compiler for AL=GOL 60",CACM,vol.4,pp 51-55,1961.

[62] --:"The Structure and Use of the Syntax Di=rected Compiler",in:'Ann.Review in Automatic Programming',vol.3,Pergamon Press,pp 207-227, 1963.

[63] N.Wirth & H.Weber:"EULER - A Generalization of ALGOL and its Formal Definition",Pts.1 & 2, CACM,vol.9,nos 1-2,pp 13-23,89-99,1966.

[64] D.E.Knuth:"Semantics of Context-Free Languages", Math.Sys.Thery,vol.2 & 5,pp 127-145 & 95,1968 & 1971.

[65] --:"Examples of Formal Semantics",ref 14,pp 212-235.

[66] P.M.Lewis II,R.E.Stearns:"Syntax Directed Transductions",JACM,vol.15,no.3,pp 464-488,1968.

[67] -- & D.J.Rosenkrantz:"Attributed Translations", J.Comp.& Sys.Sci.,vol.9,pp 279-307,1974.

[68] L.Petrone:"Syntax Directed Mapping of Context Free Languages",Proc.IEEE SWAT,9th Ann.Symp. on Automata & Switch.The.,pp 160-175,1968.

[69] R.E.Stearns & P.M.Lewis II:"Property Grammars and Table Machines",Inf.& Control,vol.14,pp 524-549,1969.

[70] B.Lorho & C.Pair:"Algorithms for Checking Con=sistency of AttributeGrammars",IRIA Colloq. on 'Proving & Improving Programs',Arc et Se=nans,Rocquencourt,Le Chesnay,France,1975.

[71] D.Neel & M.Amirchahy:"Semantic Attributes and Improvement of Generated Code",ACM Nat.Cong., 1974,pp 1-10.

[72] G.V.Bochmann:"Semantic Evaluation from Left to Right",CACM,vol.19,no.2,pp 55-62,1976.

[73] W.T.Wilner:"Formal Semantics Definition using Synthesized and Inherited Attributes",in:'For=mal Semantics of Programming Languages' (ed. R.Rustin),Prentice Hall,1972.

[74] K.Kennedy & S.K.Warren:"Automatic Generation of efficient Evaluators for Attribute Gram=mars",ref 71,pp 32-49.

[75] D.Bjørner:"On the Definition of Higher-Level Language Machines",ref 17,pp 106-136.

Compiler Correctness Proof Techniques [27-30]

[76] R.Milner:"Program Simulation:An Extended For=mal Notion",Memos 14 & 17,Univ.of Swansea, Dept.Comp.Sci.,1971.

[77] --:"An Algebraic Definition of Simulation be=tween Programs",Stanford Univ.,Comp.Sci.Dept., CS-205,1971.

[78] R.M.Burstall:"Proving Properties of Programs By Structural Induction",Comp.J.,vol.12,no. 1,pp 41-48,1969.

Relationship to Axiomatic Semantics [22]

[79] G.Ligler:"Surface Properties of Programming Language Constructs",ref 70,pp 299-323.

General on Semantics:

[80] R.Milne & C.Strachey:"A Theory of Programming Language Semantics",Chapman and Hall,1976.

-- and the references of [1] of these proceedings.

APPENDIX:

In this appendix we treat the case of the postponed realization of recursion. The solution can be seen to transpire as the result of a 'special' merge of the *m3-int-lamb* & *m3-int-Block* elaboration functions, etc., -- such that the correct environment pointer is stored in the *FCT*-denotation.

Part A:

```
m3-int-rec(mk-Rec(g,mk-Lamb(id,d),b),dict,ln)=
 (let lfct : make-lbl(),
      lbyp : make-lbl();
  GOTO lbyp;
  lab(lfct):
     m3-int-Block(d,dict + [g → ln+1,id → ln+2],ln+2);
     GOTO cra;
  lab(lbyp):
  LET ptr ∈ Ptr be s.t. ptr ~∈ dom c Stg;
  u := mk-FCT(lfct,ptr);
  Stg := cStg ∪ [ptr → mk-DSA(cp,cep,cra,cu,<>)];
  p,ep := ptr;
  m3-int-expr(b,dict + [g → ln+1],ln+1);
  m3-pop(u);
  ep := s-EP((cStg)(cp));
  ra := s-RA((cStg)(cp));
  p  := s-CP((cStg)(cp));
  ----------------------
  | Stg := cStg\{ptr}; |
  ----------------------
  m3-push(u))
```

Part B:

```
c-rec(mk-Rec(g,mk-Lamb(id,d),b),dict,ln,stk)=
 (let lfct : make-lbl(),
      lbyp : make-lbl();
  <mk-Jmp(lbyp),
   lfct>⌢
   c-block(d,dict + [g → ln+1,id → ln+2],ln+2,stk)
 ⌢<mk-Jmp(ra),
   lbyp,
   mk-Lim(u,lfct),
   mk-St(mk-Adr(top,p),p,t-1),
   mk-Pck(u,u,top),
   mk-St(mk-Adr(top,u),u,1),
   mk-Mov(p,top),
   mk-Mov(ep,top),
   mk-Adj(top,t+db)>⌢ where db = depth(b),
   c-expr(b,dict + [g → ln+1],ln+1)⌢
  <mk-Ld(u,1,mk-Adr(p,t)),
   mk-Ld(p,t-1,mk-Adr(p,p)),
   mk-St(mk-Adr(p,stk),u,1)>)
```

Part C:

```
(14)   Expre  ::= rec g = Lambλ  ;  Blockb  end
  .1   let lfct : make-lbl(),
  .2          lbyp : make-lbl();
  .3   de       := 1;
  .4   lnd      := clne + 2;
  .5   lnb      := clne + 1;
  .6   dictd := cdicte + [g →ln+1,id →ln+2];
  .7   dictb := cdicte + [g →ln+1];
  .8   codee := "goto lbyp;
  .9               lfct:
  .10           "⌢ccoded⌢"
  .11              goto cR[ra];
  .12              lbyp:
  .13              R[u] := lfct;
  .14              R[u] := mk-FCT(cR[u],cR[top]);
  .15              S[cR[top] + p ] := cR[p];
  .16              S[cR[top] +ep] := cR[ep];
  .17              S[cR[top] +ra] := cR[ra];
  .18              S[cR[top] +vr] := cR[u];
  .19              R[p]    := cR[top];
  .20              R[ep]   := cR[top];
  .21              R[top]  := cR[top] + (t+cde);
  .22           "⌢ccodeb⌢"
  .23              R[ep]   := cS[cR[p]+ep];
  .24              R[ra]   := cS[cR[p]+ra];
  .25              R[u]    := cS[cR[p]+t];
  .26              R[p]    := cS[cR[p]+p];
  .27              S[cR[p + cstke]:= cR[u];
  .28           ";
       where: Lambλ  ≡ fun ( id ) = Blockd  end
```

Part D:

```
(13)   Expre  ::= rec g = Lambλ  ;  Blockb  end
  .1   let lfct : make-lbl(),
  .2          lbyp : make-lbl();
  .3   lnd    := clne+2;
  .4   lnb    := clne+1;
  .5   dictd := cdicte + [id →clne+2,g →clne+1];
  .6   dictb := cdicte + [ g →clne+1];
  .7   print "goto lbyp;
  .8          lfct:
  .9          ";
  .10  code := <"goto cR[ra];
  .11             lbyp:
  .12             R[u] := lfct;
  .13             R[u] := mk-FCT(cR[u],cR[top]);
  .14             S[cR[top]+ p ]:= cR[p];
  .15             S[cR[top]+ep]:= cR[ep];
  .16             S[cR[top]+ra]:= cR[ra];
  .17             S[cR[top]+vr]:= cR[u];
  .18             R[p]   := cR[top];
  .19             R[ep]  := cR[top];
  .20             R[top]:= cR[top]+ t ;
  .21          ">⌢<"
  .22             R[ep]  := cS[cR[p]+ep];
  .23             R[ra]  := cS[cR[p]+ra];
  .24             R[u]   := cS[cR[p]+t];
  .25             R[p]   := cS[cR[p]+p];
  .26             S[cR[stk]] := cR[u];
  .27             R[stk]     := cR[stk]+1;
  .28          ">⌢ ccode;
       where: Lambλ  ≡ fun ( id ) = Blockd  end
```

Erratum:

Interchange lines III.(16).29 & -30.

Postscript:

The author graciously acknowledges the devoted & meticulous help of Dr.Torkel Jensen in pointing out a serious flaw in an intermediate version. The error being the 'traditional',but certainly thereby not excusable result of un-proven compressions from formulae otherwise informally argued correct.

E. Morlet and D. Ribbens, (Eds.), International Computing Symposium 1977.

PROGRAMMING : FROM CRAFT TO SCIENTIFIC DISCIPLINE

Professor Dr. Edsger W. Dijkstra
Burroughs Research Fellow
Plataanstraat 5, NL-4565 Nuemen.
THE NETHERLANDS

In response to the software crisis and to the lack of clear guidance in the design of programming languages, "programming methodology" emerged in the second half of the sixties, with the avowed purpose of discovering what would be involved in the design of sizeable high-quality programs. The recognition that high-quality implied correctness and that correctness could be proved in theory and might be provable in practice then became a major driving force. The proper roles of intuition and of formal discipline were reassessed, thereby re-shaping the nature of the programmer's task and his way of working. After a general survey of this development and an indication of its significance, some of its consequences will be discussed, because it is certain to have great impact upon our educational practices in computing science and software engineering, on the constitution of our work force, on the division of intellectual labour and on the management of software development projects.

When, in the late sixties, I coined the term "Structured Programming" I made a few serious mistakes. One mistake has been that I did not make it a registered trademark. Another mistake has been that I introduced the term without giving a definition for it. My only excuse is that I had foreseen that the term, just the term, mind you, would spread like wildfire, and would become one of the most overworked buzzwords of the computing scene in the seventies (to such an extent, as a matter of fact, that since a number of years I myself have stopped using the term altogether). I would like to use this opportunity to explain why I did not define it and, yet, introduced it. Such an explanation seems a good introduction for a description of what has roughly happened since then : to give you a feeling for the significance of the development in programming during the last eight years is the main purpose of this talk.

x x

x

For reasons that I shall mention in a moment, several of us felt that the activity of computer programming had not only the potential, but also a great probability of changing drastially. Whether the change would be so slow as to be called "evolution" or so abrupt as to be called "revolution" was something we did not venture to predict. But the nature of the change itself was clear enough and we needed a name to label the development that, we felt, was about to occur. Hence I coined the term "Structured programming": I felt that it captured my observations and my hopes very nicely.

In the mid-sixties we observed what was then known as "the software failure" or "the software crisis". Its emergence was no surprise, its occurrence had been predicted. In not much more than ten years the power of commonly available computers had increased by a factor of thousand, and our programming ability had not increased in proportion. Besides that, the logically simple, sequential machines of the fifties had been replaced by much more complicated pieces of equipment, complicated by such features as multi-level stores and asynchronously active peripherals. It was very clear that the programming task was outgrowing our programming capacities and the emergence of the software crisis was, as said, no surprise. The problem, however, was that very little could be done about it, as long as its existence was hardly admitted or even denied : it is vain to urge a world to try to improve its programming habits as long as that world pretends that its programming habits are perfectly adequate. In this respect the conference on "Software Engineering", sponsored by the NATO Science Committee and held in Garmisch, Germany, in October 1968 was the great turning point : here the existence of the software crisis and the urgency of the situation was openly admitted by such an impressive collection of representative authorities, that this admission was sure to have its impact and to help create the climate in which a change in our programming habits could be discussed. This conference was one of the main reasons why we felt that for the expected change the time to happen at last had come.

Another reason was the fate of a number of committees trying to design a new and better programming language, such as the SHARE Committee designing PL/I and IFIP Working Group 2.1 trying to design a successor for ALGOL 60. I --and many share this opinion, although perhaps for different reasons -- consider both efforts, each in their own way, as most unsuccessful. It was already during the design phase of those languages that many of the people originally involved became very doubtful as to whether things were developing in the right direction. Inexperienced as they were, they first blamed the committee mechanism, and the joke of the season was to define a camel as a horse designed by a committee. But on closer inspection it was discovered that not all the blame could be put on the committee mechanism, for there was a profounder reason : we did not know the nature of the programmer's task well enough.

Each tool shapes its users, and each programming language reflects, in its capacity as a tool, a picture of the programmer and his task. A rather intuitive, not very explicitly described but commonly accepted picture of the programmer and his task had given rise to FORTRAN and ALGOL 60. The failure to achieve striking improvements upon them was a direct consequence of the fact that our view of the programmer and his task had insufficiently evolved. The "typical programmer" still seemed to be the professional physicist or engineer who, for some technical computation, would write as a nonprofessional programmer a three-page program in an afternoon, i.e. very much the same prospective user that had inspired FORTRAN and ALGOL 60 some ten years earlier. Hence, for instance, the paralyzing stress on the requirement that the new language should be "easy to learn"; in practice this meant that the new language should not be too unfamiliar, and too often "convenient" was confused with "conventional". More and more people began to feel that tuning those designs to the supposed needs of the non-professional programmer was ..... for lack of any idea how a truly professional programmer would look like! We knew how the nonprofessional programmer could write in an afternoon a three-page program that was supposed to satisfy his needs, but how would the professional programmer design a thirty-page program in such a way that he could really justify his design? What intellectual discipline would be needed? What properties could such a professional demand with justification from his programming language, from the formal tool he had to work with? All largely open questions. In an effort to find their answers a new field of scientific activity emerged in the very late sixties; it even got a name : it was called "Programming Methodology".

x x

x

Programming methodology was in its infancy a rather vague and diffuse subject. More stress was certainly given to program correctness than to execution efficiency. In some minds this has created the impression that programming methodology did not care about efficiency, but his impression is wrong. In the sorry state of the art that could be observed in those days it was not the inefficiency that seemed most alarming : most alarming seemed that all sizeable programs seemed to be bug-ridden. Efficiency of computer programs had already been such a fashionable topic for so many years, that the balance seemed to need some redressing. When programming methodology first focussed its attention on the problem of program correctness, it did so because many of us felt that that was a relevant concern that for too long a time had not received the attention it apparently deserved.

I called programming methodology in its infancy vague and diffuse. In spite of the fact that Naur [1], Floyd [2], and Hoare [3] had already published their articles, we used in the beginning hardly the cruel and uncompromising expression "proving the correctness of a program". For at least yet another year their articles stood on the shelf reserved for interesting academic exercises without much practical significance. It was the time when people could make four different programs for the same problem and then could ponder for hours or days on the question which of the four versions they liked best. That was an exploratory activity that encountered little appreciation and even evoked criticism. The practitioners -- the programmers of "the real world"-- could not see much significance in all those aesthetic exercises, the theoreticians -- the mathematicians and logicians -- saw no depth and, therefore, no significance in them either.

The fact that, as an alternative to the quantifiable efficiency, we turned to easthetic criteria has not without justification been qualified as an exaggerated preoccupation with "programming style".

Yet, all those experiments with little programs have not only been valuable, they were at that stage even necessary! Programming at that time was still an intuitive craft, and before the decision to adopt and to further develop a formal discipline can be taken, it should have been established with sufficient evidence that such a formal discipline is needed and that its further development is indeed worth the effort. And in order to prevent the formalization from becoming an end in itself, it should be sufficiently clear what it should achieve.

The exploratory stage, during which the notions of "simplicity" and "elegance" absorbed so much of our attention has had one very important effect. By the time that formal techniques became more general adopted, we had, for "aesthetic reasons" stripped our programming vehicles, removing many of the usual bells and whistles whose presence would only have encumbered the formal treatment. The beauty of some of the programs we had discovered was an incentive to look for correctness proofs of comparable beauty and the circumstance that our most beautiful programs were often by all the usual standards also very efficient gave us the encouraging feeling that the whole made sense.

In short I think that the infancy of programming methodology, with its stress on aesthetic criteria, has not been wasted. As craftsmen that to a certain extent had become artists as well, we had already developed into better intuitive programmers; at the same time the subject matter worth of formal treatment had been filtered out. And, finally : the fact that we talked about "the beauty of a program" in very much the same way as in which mathematicians refer to "the beauty of a proof" provided an emotional link between two at that time rather disjoint cultures, a link that may very well have had a decisive influence.

x x

x

In the above I have tried to sketch the emotional and intellectual climate of the infancy of programming methodology. I have done so in the hope that it will assist you in getting some appreciation of the significance of its later achievements, an appreciation I would like to transmit to you without fully going into the technicalities that would take a full semester to cover.

We should remember that, when all this started, programs were almost exclusively considered from the point of view of what would happen when the program would be executed by a computer. It was only via the class of possible computations that could be evoked under control of a program that such a program could be appreciated. Textbooks on programming used to begin with a few chapters devoted to the description of the average computer architecture and the global characteristics of the machine's major components. Efforts at the formal definition of the semantics of programming languages were almost exclusively so-called "operational definitions", i.e. in terms of the properties of the possible computational histories. The quality of a program was very often equated to run-time efficiency, a notion which is, of course, highly implementation-dependent.

Yet, for progress it was necessary that the close tie to the process of program execution be loosened. One reason for this necessity was that as long as the tie was so close, characteristics of machines as they happened to exist, whether desirable or not, tended to pervade the thinking about programming : the way in which the properties of the IBM/360 had pervaded the design of PL/I was a warning not to be ignored. Another reason --although that one was perhaps discovered only later-- was that program correctness and cost of execution are two so important concerns, that the programmer who has to give full attention to both of them, should be given the mental tools to <u>separate</u> these two concerns.

Two concurrent developments made it possible to loosen the tie between a program and the corresponding class of computational histories. I have already mentioned them both.

The one development consisted of the many, many programming experiments made during the infancy of programming methodology. As the problem of programming language design was one of the major incentives for these numerous programming experiments, many of these experiments were performed in tentative, unimplemented (and often yet incomplete) programming languages : the purpose of the experiments was very often to explore the consequences of a yet untried language feature.

The fact that these experiments were mostly carried out in unimplemented languages loosened the tie between the programs and their executions. The other development was the discovery and application of the papers by Naur [1], Floyd [2], and Hoare [3], which dealt with the possibility of proving program correctness by means of a formal discipline. Such a formal discipline may have been inspired by what happens during program execution via a computer, by the time that the formal discipline is applied it can be used "in its own right" so to speak.

This second development was a necessary complement to the first one : it is all right to push the class of possible computational histories to the background of one's awareness, but this is only possible provided we have an alternative technique for coming to grips with what a program "means" : Naur and Floyd gave a proof technique, Hoare was the one who stressed most clearly that these proof rules could be regarded as axioms. This was an important discovery : from now onwards the proof rules need no longer be regarded as summarizing properties of computers, but they could be regarded as axioms, as postulates, as a functional specification for computing engines that those engines had better satisfy if they were to be useful engines. The discovery was important for its psychological side-effect : while in the past it was regarded as the purpose of our programs to instruct our computers, a shift to the opposite view could now take place, viz. that it is the purpose of our machines to execute our programs. Or, to put it in another way, logic which up to that moment had mostly been a descriptive science, fraught with metaphysics, now also admitted to be regarded as a prescriptive science, almost as a discipline of engineering.

x x

x

The transition from the vague and emotional terms as "understandable", "clear", "readable" to the uncompromising and crual notion of "a formal correctness proof" marks for Programming Methodology the transition from infancy to adolescence. It was a slow and sometimes painful process, like all processes of mental growth. From the people involved it required a greater agility in the propositional calculus and a greater familiarity with various induction patterns than most of them originally possessed. Younger computing scientists are free to laugh in either amazement or contempt, but I am not ashamed of confessing in public that five years ago, I was thorougly familiar with the logical connectives "and" and "or" but certainly not with the implication, which I, therefore, tended to avoid, programming around it by replacing "a   b" by the more familiar "b or non a".

Besides this inherent cause that made the growth process a slow one, there was an external, and rather accidental one. Floyd's paper [2] was given greater publicity than Naur's earlier one [1]; we must conclude that Naur's paper was published ahead of its time. In contrast to Naur's paper that deals with programming, Floyd's paper had immediately been associated with mechanical verification --or even : discovery-- of formal proofs of the correctness of programs. As a sad result, Programming Methodology has for quite some years been in danger of being killed in its youth by the superstition that underlies so much of the Artificial Intelligence activity, viz. that everything difficult is so boring that it had better be done mechanically.

I called the growth process, besides slow, also painful --like every adolescence, for that matter-- . For some time during its adolescence, programming methodology indeed had a very difficult time. This was when the first correctness proofs started to circulate : some of them were, indeed, appalling, even distressingly so. I was repelled by them, and at one occasion I declared, full of disgust, with emphasis that such formal techniques "were not my cup of tea". Those present at that occasion take a special delight in reminding me of it. For some time it indeed looked as if formal correctness proofs were totally unfit for human design and for human consumption.

Thank goodness there were also a few beautiful programs with beautiful correctness proofs hanging around and, as a result, Programming Methodology survived its adolescence without committing suicide.
The point is that those convincing examples were very inspiring because "length of formal correctness proof" was immediately accepted by all people involved as an objective and relevant yardstick for "quality". Its objectivity caused among those people a greater unity of purpose than eloquence or money could ever have achieved. This unity of purpose was so welcome that programming methodology survived its first disappointing experiences with formal correctness proofs, until it had been discovered that many of those early proofs, indeed, had been unnecessarily ugly and cumbersome.

x x

x

The first proofs were very cumbersome because, for lack of any theorems, they were built upon the axioms themselves. In the meantime a few general, but very powerful and useful theorems have been discovered and proved, and we have gained much experience in their effective exploitation.

A second cause for improvement was the discovery that the existence of such theorems and the ease with which they are formulated and used depends on the programming language used. The combinatorial freedom of the flowchart language that was used by Floyd in his fundamental article [2] creates problems with the satisfactory solution of which people are still struggling today [4]; by adhering to a more strict sequencing discipline, these problems can be made to disappear.

A third cause for improvement was the discovery --in retrospect not very surprising-- that besides a formal theory about one's programming language and its constructs, one also needs a certain amount of formal theory about the subject matter of the computation. For instance : while proving the correctness of a parser it is not enough to have axioms about the relevant programming language constructs such as the operations on strings. Besides those one needs a certain amount of theory about sentences generated according to, say, a BNF-grammar; one may even be expected to need some theorems about the specific grammar of the language in question. In the beginning we often did not clearly separate those two different aspects of our proof obligations, thus confusing the issue.

A fourth improvement was perhaps the most spectacular. For many years the whole correctness issue had been posed in the following form "Given a program and given the specification of what its execution should achieve, can you prove that the program meets these specifications?"
The attention was thus focussed on "a posteriori" verification of given programs. It was then observed, however, that for different programs meeting the same specifications, the corresponding correctness proofs could greatly differ in complexity! And as a result, our picture of the programmer's task changed : it was no longer sufficient to design a correct program, in addition the program should be designed in such a way that its correctness could, indeed, be established. The simplicity of the corresponding correctness proof became thus an important aspect of program quality. But when this message was taken to heart, the programme's task and his way of working changed radically. For, how does one develop a program that admits a nice correctness proof? Well, by developing the program and its correctness proof hand in hand. In actual fact the correctness proof is often even developed slightly ahead of the actual program text : as soon as the next step in the correctness proof has been chosen, the next refinement of the program is made in such a way that the chosen step in the correctness proof is applicable to it.
Instead of seeking for a proof to go with a given program, we now construct a program to go with a chosen correctness proof! The later construction process is so well understood that we are now entitled to talk about a calculus for the formal derivation of programs[5.]

Let me repeat. We are trying to find a "matching pair", consisting of a program and a proof and "matching" in the sense that the proof establishes that the program meets its specifications. Given a program, finding a matching proof may be very hard; given a proof, finding a matching program is almost trivial. This is not the place to ponder about a mathematical or psychological explanation of this phenomenon. I have repeated and described the phenomenon in other words because of its drastic social impact. Here I use the term "drastic social impact" because it is bound to cause a change in a traditional division of labour.

x x

x

Ten years ago, before the above had been understood, a tradition of "software production" had already established itself. It was regarded as the programmer's task "to produce programs", and the management of "software production" was organized under that assumption in close analogy to more traditional production processes such as those of cars, TV-sets or washing machines. This view of "software production" has had a few severe consequences.

1) In analogy to the production line worker, for "programmer productivity" the measure "number of lines of code produced per month" became among managers accepted. Doubts about its adequacy and significance have been voiced. It has been remarked that the adoption of this measure of programmer productivity is certain to encourage the production of insipid code. It has also been remarked that "code" is no end in itself, but only a means, and that rather than talking about the lines of code "produced" we should refer to the lines of code "used", and that, therefore, this "productivity measure" books the number of lines on the wrong side of the ledger. But large organizations have a great inertia, and the number of lines of code "produced", no matter how inadequate, is still in use as a grading criterion for programmers.

2) In analogy to the production line, software managers have tried to reduce software production costs by resorting to cheaper labour, which, in each given environment, means less educated people. The results of these tactics are only too well known.

3) In analogy to the production line, completely independent groups for "quality assurance" have been installed: the people from "quality assurance" had to certify the software "products". Little it was understood, however, how impossible their task was. They could hardly do any better than to "certify" after the successful run of a set of test cases, no matter how inadequate they were for "certification". Also the results of this are only too well known.

So much for the traditional division of labour in the process of software production. This tradition has to be broken because it is based on a false assumption. The tradition will be broken because the modern way of developing programs is so dramatically more effective. In future we shall see in retrospect that today's traditional way of software production was the result when a craft was applied, where a scientific discipline was needed.

x x

x

In the last decade programming has made the transition from craft to scientific discipline. It has been a development not unlike the one that took place in medieval painting in Europe. Before the discovery of the relevant rules of projective geometry, painters had only intuitive ideas about perspective. It was the old and experienced craftsman-painter who, on the average, was most successful in rendering the proportions well. But each new painting was in this respect an experiment that involved a certain risk, and, whenever a craftsman-painter had been exceptionally lucky, he had created a work of art that would become famous for its geometrical perfection. But within a few decades the old craftsmen had been superseded by a next generation of painters, mostly pupils of a certain Albrecht Dürer : these youngsters just knew the rules of perspective and produced without risk and with absolute confidence in this respect perfect paintings. Not only that they could do it, they knew that they could do it, they knew how they did it and could teach it to their successors. A next area of human endeavour had shown itself to be amenable to mathematical treatment, and a craft had been replaced by a scientific discipline. But whenever a craft is replaced by a scientific discipline, the old members of the guild feel themselves threatened, and quite understandably so.

I used the term "drastic social impact" because today's "programming guild" encompasses -- depending on how we count-- between 500.000 and 1.000.000 people, for the majority of whom it is totally unrealistic to expect that they can still acquire a scientific attitude. For them the recent developments in programming poses a serious problem, and their existence presents a serious barrier to the more wide-spread adoption of the newer programming techniques. In view of these conflicts it is very hard to predict how, when, and where the old programming tradition will be broken first. I shall just give you a few observations and leave the extrapolation to you.

When in 1968 the software crisis was for the first time openly admitted, a quite well-known professor of computing science waved the idea of correctness proofs away as being "idyllic", to another one the idea of correctness proofs caused "mental hiccups" [6].

As late as 1972, the suggestion that programming was so difficult that it deserved scientifically educated programmers has been waved away : with a reference to the then current intellectual calibre of "the average programmer" the suggestion was waved away as obvious nonsense.

Three years later, however, an International Conference on Software Reliability, where formal techniques played a predominant role, was held at Los Angeles and attended by about a thousand people.

Another year later, in 1976, a draft proposal for an advice to the U.S. government draws attention to the for them alarming circumstance that "by an accident of history, the United States has more inertia (and local vested interests) in current software practices than the rest of the world." It points out the danger for the USA that in the practice of software development they be overtaken by nations that in this respect are yet more flexible.

So much for my few observations : I gladly leave to you to guess the now, the when, and the where of the breakthrough.

The conclusion that successful computer programming will eventually require a reasonable amount of scientific education of a rather mathematical nature is not too welcome amoung the guildmembers : they tend to deny it and to create a climate in which "bringing the computer back to the ordinary man" is accepted as a laudable goal, and in which the feasibility of doing so is postulated, rather than argued. (This is understandable, because its infeasibility is much easier to argue). They create a climate in which funds are available for all sorts of artificial intelligence projects in which it is proposed that the machine will take over all the difficult stuff so that the user can remain uneducated. I must warn you not to interpret the fact that such projects are sponsored as an indication that they make sense : the fact of their being sponsored is more indicative for the political climate in which this happens.

I am convinced that all these projects will fail, and that, the more ambitious they are, the more miserably they will do so. Hence I consider these projects as rather foolish, and for programming as a scientific discipline worth teaching, as rather harmless rearguard actions. As a bit pathetic, even.

In the meantime these projects can still do a lot of harm. They can do so by their false promises, pretending that the sophistication of their future systems, combined with decreasing hardware costs, makes it economically attractive to forsake our educational obligations to the next generation. Needless to say, falling into that seductive trap would be the cultural blunder of the decade.

In another respect I sometimes fear that the harm has already been done. There is a wide-spread folklore that in particular correctness proofs for computer programs are intrinsically so long, tedious, boring, uninteresting and prone to error, that the mechanization of their verification is a must. The assumption, however, is wrong : correctness proofs for programs can be -- and should be!-- just as beautiful, fascinating and convincing as any other piece of mathematics. But the rumour to the contrary is constantly spread by the advertizing campaigns for the mechanical verification systems. The fact that the most outstanding feature of most artificial intelligence projects seems to be the heavy advertizing campaigns deemed necessary for this support, should install into our minds a healthy mistrust and suspicion.

(1) Naur, P., "Proof of Algorithms by General Snapshots", BIT 6 (1966) pp. 310-316.

(2) Floyd, R.W., "Assigning Meanings to programs", Proceedings of a Symposium in Applied Mathematics 19 (ed. Schwartz, J.T.), Providence, Rhode Island : American Mathematical Society, 1967, pp. 19 - 31.

(3) Hoare, C.A.R., "An Axiomatic Basis for Computer Programming", Comm. ACM 12, 10 (Oct. 1969), pp. 576 - 583.

(4) Manna, Zohar and Waldinger, Richard J., "Is "sometime" sometimes better than "always"? Intermittent assertions in proving program correctness." Stanford Artificial Intelligence Laboratory Memo AIM-281 / Computer Science Department Report No. STAN-CS-76-558, June 1976.

(5) Dijkstra, Edsger W., "Guarded Commands, Nondeterminacy and Formal Derivation of Programs" Comm. ACM 18, 8 (Aug. 1975) 453 - 457.

(6) Naur, P. and Randell, B., "Software Engineering", Report on a Conference Sponsored by the NATO Science Committee, January 1969.

Burroughs Research Fellow

E. Morlet and D. Ribbens, (Eds.), International Computing Symposium 1977.

TYPES AND RELATED CONCEPTS

Reiner Durchholz
Gesellschaft fuer Mathematik und Datenverarbeitung (GMD)
St. Augustin, Germany
January 1977

Contents

Abstract : In most DBMS discussions "types" are mentioned in important contexts. It therefore appears to be essential to develop some precise meaning associated with this word. This paper proposes such a meaning and discusses several related concepts. After a glimpse at the colloquial use of the word, the difference between set and type is worked out. The paper proceeds to discuss aspects of type descriptions. As an illustration the type concept proposed here is applied to the CODASYL DDL. Other well-known concepts usually related to the type concept - instance, population, consistency constraint, integrity constraint - are discussed. Finally a more generalized concept, called coherence, is recommended, which seems to be more pertinent to a changing environment as is the case with data base management systems.

1. INTRODUCTION

In the discussions about DBMS the word "type" has been used very often and it seems from its uses, that the associated semantics is somewhat ambiguous. Because there are interpretations of the word "type" which make reference to the more important concepts for DBMS, it is quite necessary to make its meaning more precise.

The CODASYL DDL /C2/ will be taken for examples. However throughout this paper, CODASYL sets will be called "cosets" for better distinction from mathematical sets, according to a suggestion in /N2/.

2. THE WORD "TYPE" IN COLLOQUIAL USE

The following explanations for the word "type" are taken from the Random House Dictionary /R1/:

1. a number of things or persons sharing a particular characteristic, or set of characteristics, that causes them to be regarded as a group, more or less precisely defined or designated ; class ; category.
2. a thing or person regarded as a member of a class or category :
"This is some type of mushroom".
3. Informal. a person, regarded as reflecting or typifying a certain line of work, environment, etc. : "a couple of civil service types".
4. a thing or person that represents perfectly or in the best way a class or category ; model.

Basically, there are two ways to interpret "type". One way is to look at it as a class or set of things and the other is, to take it as a representative of such a class. For our technical use we better adopt only one of these views. I propose to agree upon the "class" interpretation and to call any member of such a class an "instance" of that type.

3. SETS AND PROPORTIES

We now have to consider the somewhat loose expression "sharing a particular set of characteristics" from explanation 1 above. What kind of characteristics is admitted ? If there is no restriction on the choice of characteristics, then any set is a type, because all members of the set and only the members of the set share the characteristic of being member of this set.

This characteristic appears to be trivial, but should trivial characteristics be excluded from the definition of the type concept ? If yes, what is the criterion for triviality ? A triviality can be hidden most cunningly behind some distracting ornament. The set $\{2,3\}$ can be characterized e.g. by

" set of all things belonging to $\{2,3\}$ ",
" set of all things that are number 2 or number 3 ",
" set of all things for which does not hold : the thing is not number 2 or number 3" or
" set of all prime numbers not greater 3".

Which of these characteristics are the trivial ones ?

Sets and characteristics are therefore equivalent in the sense, that any characteristic defines a set (the set of things sharing the characteristic) and any set defines a characteristic (the property of being element of the set). However there will be several characteristics which define the same set. So each set defines a c l a s s of characteristics of which the "trivial" one ("... is element of the set") is a distinguished representative. We have therefore an equivalence between sets and classes of characteristics in the stronger sense of a one-to-one mapping.

4. THE CONCEPT OF TYPE

With the feature of the distinguished "trivial" property we have indeed no restriction for sets considered as types. The question is however, whether this is the desired concept. We may assume, that the same set is considered a type in one context and is not in another one. Think for instance of a blood bank, where donors or recipients of blood are considered as instances of types characterized by blood-groups, whereas an applicant for a job is considered as an instance of a type of people with certain capabilities.

It seems therefore sensible to associate with the concept of type a reference to a communication situation. We may assume that, given a communication situation, it is also given which sets are to be considered as types. Or, the other way round : a description of a communication situation is complete only if it specifies the types to which the communication partners may refer. In case there is a fixed language (called *type definition language*, TDL for short) in which the communication partners can specify types, the expressive power of this language defines what can be a type in this communication situation. In addition, and more significantly for the present issue, it also defines the concept of type for all communication situations for which this language is given as the means to specify types.

We call the set of all types specificable in the language between communication partners a *type system*. Any element of a type system is a *type* with respect to the type system. Mind that only idioms like "t is a type for communication situation c", "t is a type definable by language l " or " t is a type from type systems s " are well-defined. To be a type therefore is not a unary predicate but a binary relationship between a set and a communication situation, a language or a type system.

The idea, that the concept of type includes a reference to a communication situation is clearly expressed in /BR/: "The definition of a particular entity type is part of the data analyst's job", although it is restricted to entity types and to a particular reference system (system's analyst. In /DR/ the type concept was introduced as in the present paper, except that only a TDL was considered as a reference system, not a communication situation nor a type system.

5. SCHEMA AND SCHEMATIC TYPE DEFINITION LANGUAGE

If the very syntactical appearance of a type definition makes evident features common to the instances of the type described, then we will call the type definition a *schema*. A TDL mainly dealing with schemas will be called *schematic*.

This of course does not pretend to be a precise definition, nor is it intended to be made more precise. Instead, we will allow for such vague wordings as "mainly schematic", "more schematic", "schematic language element" and so on. In the DDL of CODASYL e.g. the definition of an aggregate type is very schematic, the DUPLICATES clause however is a non-schematic language element.

A schema looks much like a description of a representative instance of the type, where all those parts that vary through the type are replaced by a description of the range of variation.

Another good intuitive explanation of a schema is the following: Represent all instance of a type on transparent foils in some normalized manner; put all these foils upon each other; look through the package: what you see is a schematic representation of the type. Parts, which are common to all instances, are sharply outlined, all other parts are more or less fuzzy. This is only to help communication situation. More generally, it also defines the imagination and would of course require more elaboration if need be.

The proposed use of the word "schema" is somewhat in contrast with the usage now common in the DBMS-world. However, it brings it back to its colloquial meaning. "Schema" is such a general word, that it should not be misused as a technical term in a largely distorted way. Implied is the suggestion, that in our technical terminology we replace the word "schema" by "type description", excepth when we m e a n "schematic type description".

6. DESCRIPTION OF TYPES

There is a variety of ways in which types can be described.

If the type is finite and not too large, its instances can be explicitly written down, e.g. (Monday, Tuesday, Wednesday, Thursday, Friday, Saturday, Sunday).

In a more abstract way, any algorithm which accepts or rejects any given data construct can be regarded a type definition.

For practical purposes, we are mainly interested in the possibilities to describe types by combining types already obtained, ultimately "built-in" types.

One such operation is the set-theoretic union of types. This is a very powerful operation, which is difficult to handle because it affords checking of alternatives. It is therefore quite rightly neglected in the TDLs of most DBMS. In the sense of section 5, unions will also cause non-schematic language elements.

The following example is given to show the power of the union: Let the singleton set 12-34-56 be the (degenerate) type with one instance 12-34-56. If we make a proper selection of such one-instance types and join them all together, we can obtain a type of the calendar dates of a century. In fact, any finite type can be given as the union of singleton types.

A very common and very convenient operation is the Cartesian product of types. For instance in the DDL of CODASYL the description of a type of aggregates is formed by composition of the type descriptions of the immediate components, from which the instances of the type to be described are built. Basically this relates to the Cartesian product of the latter types. Look for instance at the following example:

```
03 X OCCURS 1 TIMES
   04 A PICTURE IS "X99"
   04 B PICTURE IS "9(5)"
```

This means, that the instances of the type described are constructed by composition of a n y instance of type "X99" under name A with a n y instance of type "9(5)" under name B.

The Cartesian product is the kind of type generation which is most characteristic for the TDLs of existing DBMS. The description of a more complex type is composed out of descriptions of less complex types right in parallel to the composition of instances of the more complex types from instances of the less complex types. This is an exemplary case where the structure of the instances of a type is reflected in the syntax of the type description. The Cartesian product is therefore particularly well suited for schematic TDLs.

The less complex types, the instances of which are the immediate components of the instances of the more complex types will be called <u>constituent types</u> (of the more complex types). Unfortunately this term has a potential for misunderstanding: A c o n s t i t u e n t t y p e i s n o t p a r t o f t h e m o r e c o m p l e x t y p e.

The composition takes place at the instance level, not at the type level : A type of trousers and a type of jackets may be constituent types of a type of suits. That is, each instance of the type of suits (i.e. each suit) is composed out of an instance of the type of trousers (a trouser) and an instance of the type of jackets (a jacket).

The Cartesian product, although it is very convenient to handle, is not powerful enough in those cases, where the entire product is too large for the intended purpose. The Cartesian product can be seen as the "full relation" or the "all-relation" over the constituent types, and in the cases considered one wants to "shoot holes" in it, that is, to make exceptions. Whether it is more convenient to make exceptions or to build the relation from smaller ones by set union depends upon the number and the pattern of the holes.

As an example we consider the calender-date type again. It can be described (in a fancy language) by

```
(("01:31" * "01:12") -
 ("29,30,31" * "02") -
 ("31" * "4,6,9,11") * "00:99"
```

(We are not concerned here with the exceptions of the leap-year).

The same type can also be described with unions:

```
(("01:28 * "01:12) U
 ("29" * "02") U
 ("29,30" * "01,03:12") U
 ("31" * "1,3,5,7,8,10,12")) * "00:99".
```

Here both methods are about equally convenient.

Finally it should be indicated , that there are other cases of type construction for which the Cartesian product is insufficient, e.g. if each instance of a type is a set which is required to have as members exactly one instance from each of a number of given types. If the given types overlap, this is significantly different from the cartesian product.

7. TYPES IN THE DDL OF CODASYL

With generalized DBMS we have a perfect case where a seperate language in which to specify types is given. This language is mostly called "data description language": With one DBMS fixed it is therefore clear, what a type is. It should be kept in mind however, that a type for one DBMS might not be a type for another DBMS.

The word "data description language" is one of those unfortunate choices of words of which our field abounds. If a description is understood as an identification within some given context, then it is by no means data that is described by DDL statements, but a data type. Therefore a better word would be "type description language". We will however see later on, that the DDL of CODASYL for instance actually does more than just describe types. (see section 9).

To illustrate the concept of type we shall inspect the types definable with the DDL of CODASYL. In the report of June 73 /C2/ the only types mentioned, which are specifiable in DDL, are record types, coset types and certain data item types. (The report of 71 /C1/ was a little bit different, but by no means more consistent about this.) The latter type even receives a special distinction as the word TYPE is used in the DDL syntax. Unfortunately this does not contribute to conceptual clarity because one tends to imply, that in all other cases where TYPE is not mentioned, the language does not deal with types.

That this implication is wrong is of course clear for records and cosets, but it is less obvious for other data constructs the DDL speaks about, for instance data items with PICTURE, data aggregates or areas. Consider for instance

```
PICTURE IS "X99".
```

This describes the set of all strings of characters, the last two of which are digits. Clearly this is a type. Similarly the DDL statement for an aggregate

```
03 X OCCURS 1 TIMES
   04 A PICTURE IS "X99"
   04 B PICTURE IS "9(5)"
```

specifies a type of aggregates, not a single one.

With "area" we come to a more controversial subjact. Although the report characterizes an area as "a named collection of records" (p. 2.5 of /C2/, one can argue that the area is an abstract location within which records are stored. This argument is supported by the choice of the word "area" itself.
But however the area concept is drawn up, there is the fact, that records in an area are considered to be aggregated into a set (RECORD OF AREA). In any case there does exists a data construct which is a set of records - independent of whether it is considered to b e an area or only s t o r e d within an area.

For easy reference I will use the word "area" for this construct. The area becomes a different one, when one of its records is delected or changed or when a new record is added. The AREA entry of the DDL describes all possible outcomes of such changes, that is, a type of areas.

If one follows the construction of a DDL schema step by step one realizes, that with each step a data construct type is described. The description in each step includes descriptions of types the instances of which are components of of the instances of the type to be described ("constituent types", see section 6). For instance a data aggregate type is described by writing down types of each of its immediate components in proper sequence.

The last step of schema construction is putting together the entire schema itself. It is only consequent to consider the entire schema too as a description of some type. It describes all possible data bases (for this communication situation), that is, it is a data base type description. I have some reservations to dwell on this point too long, because it seems so obvious and simple. On the other hand I have seen often enough hesitation to accept this view, so that I would like to put some emphasis on it.

I shall now turn to another point which is liable to cause confusion. Above we have considered several cases of types which have not been identified as such in the CODASYL report. Let us now ask the other question, whether the record types and coset types as defined in the report are actually types. We have seen that - given a communication situation or a type definition language - a type is a set. The identity of a set is given by its elements. Two sets are equal if they have the same elements.

Now how about two record type descriptions which are identical except for the record name? In this case any record that satisfies one description also satisfies the other one. Consequently both type descriptions describe the same record type. But this is not what we want, because in several contexts the type of a record instance must be uniquely given. Actually this is the case, because upon retrieval of a record, say by data-base-key, also its type is known (in system communication location RECORD-NAME, cf. /C1/, p. 201). We must conclude from this, that the designation of the type of a record is included in the record as one of its components. The record is therefore not only just a collection of data items and data aggregates, as the report pretends (p. 2.5 of /C2/), but includes also the type designation.

This brings the solution to our problem of record type identity. If the record type designation is considered part of the record instance, then any two RECORD entries describe two different record types, because they are required to have different record type designations ("record names" in the DDL). A similar observation holds for coset types. Therefore if, and only if, we consider the type designation to be part of the instances, we can agree with the words "record type" and "coset type".

8. TYPE, POPULATION AND INSTANCE

Sometimes one wants to speak of the set of instances of one type which are present in the data base. More precisely, which are components of one instance of the data base type. This set will be called a population of the type. Mind that the concept of population makes reference to a component type and a data construct. The complete idiom should be : p is the population of type t within data construct d.

The population of a record type (in the data base) for instance is the set of all record instances of this type that occur in the data base.

Populations of coset types have received special attention in /N1/ and /N2/. A coset population defines a function from its member records to its owner records. This functional property however is not a property of the coset instance nor of the coset type, but of the coset population. That is, it cannot be decided by inspection of single cosets nor of the coset type, whether the function condition is satisfied in the data base, but the whole coset population must be checked. The coset population appears therefore as a data construct by itself and the function condition is a type specification on this data construct. Let us call the coset population "coset function". (This is not a very good word for it, because it is not a function on cosets, but it is intended for temporary use only.)

We now have coset functions as data constructs and coset function types. Of course there is also a coset function population. But in the CODASYL DDL this is degenerate. A data base has one coset function instance only. It is perfectly well conceivable, that a modified DDL allows for several instances of one coset function type within one data base.

There is also another well-known case of a degenerate population in the CODASYL DDL. This is the SYSTEM-owned coset, which is also called singular, because the coset population has one occurence only (/C2/, p. 2.28/).

9. TYPE AND INTEGRITY CONSTRAINT

When type description languages are discussed, very often the word "integrity constraint" or "consistency constraint" is used. For instance for the set of relations produced by normalization it is said, that certain integrity constraints must hold. In the CODASYL DDL the SOURCE clause is considered to establish an integrity constraint, as well as does the coset membership type AUTOMATIC/MANDATORY.

What is the nature of such conditions ? Their net effect is, that they exclude all those data bases from the data base type defined by the entire schema which violate these conditions. Obviously they are type specifying conditions and in fact it is hard to see why - apart from being concerned with different levels of aggregation - PICTURE IS "X99" should be a basically different kind of condition than SOURCE IS F OF OWNER OF S.

Of course it would be helpful to know what makes people look for a distinction between type condition and consistency constraint.

One reason can certainly be seen in the fact, that the main constructive principle for TDLs of current DBMS is type composition with Cartesian products. As discussed in section 6 (Description of types) this leads to basically schematic TDLs. When the need for more sophisticated types became more and more apparent, additional language elements have been invented, which are non-schematic (e.g. DUPLICATES, SOURCE, AUTOMATIC). These language elements have been recognized as being something special, or even alien, although it was not realized what sort of speciality this was. In any case it seemed appropriate to give them a special generic name (i.e. "integrity constraint").

This can be quite acceptable if the choice of the name is acceptable (which I doubt in this particular case). However two things should be observed. Firstly, the property of being more or less schematic is concerned with the *language* and not with the type system given by the language. Therefore the distinction appears to be somewhat circumstantial if the main interest is the semantics of the DBMS.

Secondly, this distinction should not obscure the fact, that non-schematic language elements are parts of the type description as well as are schematic language elements.

This last statement brings us directly to another supposed reason for the distinction, which is more fundamental but less acceptable. It is partly the non-relization that e.g. the CODASYL DDL deals with more component types and more complex ones than is inidicated explicitly and that the entire schema defines a data base type. Partly it is an incorrect assumption about the type that is affected by a particular statement.

As an example for the latter case the SOURSE clause specifies an identity condition for data items across a coset occurrence. It therefore describes the coset type, not the record type. Nevertheless it appears as part of the record entry, i.e. in the record type description.

The "consistency constraint" AUTOMATIC/MANDATORY is an example for the former case. It establishes a condition between the population of a record type and the population of a coset type. We have seen earlier, that these populations are not recognized as data constructs, not to mention a still higher construct which comprises both.

10. CONSISTENCY, PERSISTENCY AND COHERENCE

In this section I want to abandon the simplistic view of types adopted so far and give a short overview of a more general viewpoint.

The generalization is in the two directions. One is, that the state of the data base is not only defined by the data constructs stored, but also by various other things as for instance currency status indicators or the KEEP status /CJ/. We will not be concerned here with the question what goes into the data base state, but simply talk of s t a t e s.

The second generalization is based on the assumption, that the real interest is not in the admissible states, but in the states that are reachable by all possible changes affected through the DBMS. In fact it does not make much sense to admit states which are not reachable. On the other hand no state should be reachable that is not admissable.

Reachable states are defined by initial states and transition rules. A transition may be envisaged as a pair of states (old state , new state). A transition rule then is equivalent to a set of such pairs of states. We call such a set a <u>coherence</u> and a description of a coherence is called <u>coherence statement</u>.

There are special coherences which are particularly interesting for the purpose of perspicuous coherence descriptions. These are those, where the transition to the new state does not depend on the old state. They have the form S * F (with * for the Cartesian product), where S is the set of all st ates or at least comprises all "initial" states and F. Coherences of this kind we call <u>consistencies</u>. A coherence which is not a consistency we call a <u>persistency</u>.

An example for a consistency statement is the PICTURE clause, because it allows transition to any of the data items of the type specified, regardless of the former state. The coset membership clauses however are persistency statements, except for the combination AUTOMATIC/MANDATORY which can be rendered as a consistency. (That e.g. AUTOMATIC/OPTIONAL is not a consistency condition can be seen from the fact, that for the object record population any state of coset membership can be reached by suitable REMOVEs.) Furtheron, the condition on the marital status, that a married man can never become a bachelor again is a persistency condition. Another example of a persistency condition is associated with the idea of a stack. This is a list with the persistency rule, that for any transition the list must be left unaltered or truncated or extended by one entry only.

The overall coherence statement for a data base is expected to be composed out of several "smaller" coherence statements. It makes the overall statement easier to handle and to survey if as much as possible of the complexity is broken down to consistency statements. Consistency statements differ from type statements formally only. The consistency concept is basically the type concept integrated into the coherence concept.

11. RELATION TO TYPES IN PROGRAMMING LANGUAGES

The type concept has been, and currently still is, widely discussed for programming languages (see e.g. the discussion on abstract data types). At first glance, the data base viewpoint and the programming language viewpoint of types seem to be incompatible. Type declarations for data bases support a "static view", under which the objects are classified into types according to inner properties, mostly of a structural kind, properties that make no reference to their behaviour under certain operations. In programming languages types are defined by the way they behave under operations. Particular importance with respect to type membership is attributed to "well-behaviour" under an operation, that is, whether the operation is defined at all for the given object. This leads to an emphasis on the set of operations that are defined for a type. On the other hand the set of operations does not define a type under all circumstances. In particular, when subtypes are provided, the same set of operations may be defined on several types. (e.g. i n t e g e r s can be considered the subtype of r e a l s on which ENTIER is the identity.)

The differences between the two views however vanish on closer examination of the somewhat fuzzy wording "inner properties, mostly of a structural kind". The "structural" or "inner" properties become apparent only when the object is operated upon, in particular when it is decomposed. If one regards composition and decomposition to be just operations among others, these "inner" properties are transformed to "outer" or "behavioural" properties. In fact, there is no sense in postulating "inner" properties which cannot be detected by any operation. So the distinction between the views turns out to be a matter of emphasis only : in the data base context composition and decomposition operations play a prominent role. Consequently the interest is focussed on types characterized through these operations.

As the jargon and symbolism of data base people prefers to see structured objects over seeing a "part-of"-relation between unstructured objects, the close connection of the views, in fact their identity except for terminological variations, may have been overlooked at times. As a parenthetical remark, a similar kinship may be detected between classical data structures and the more recent propositions to use "unstructured" data.

Acknowledgement : The considerations on the type concept are a partial result of the efforts on IMC (Information Management Concepts) undertaken jointly by the DAGS project group. I am indepted to my colleagues for their support during the preparation of the paper. Further I want to acknowledge the very helpful and clarifying discussions which have been held within IFIP-WG2.6 (Data Bases).

References

/BR/ Brown, A.P. G. : Modelling a real world system and designing a schema to represent it. IFIP-TC2 Special Working Conference "A technical in-depth evaluation of the DDL", Namur, January 1975.

/C1/ CODASYL Data Base Task Group : Report April 71.

/C2/ CODASYL Data Description Language Committee Report June 73.

/CJ/ CODASYL COBOL Journal of Development, 1976.

/DR/ Durchholz, R. ; Richter, G. : Concepts for Data Base Management Systems. In Data Base Management Systems, J.W. Klimbie and K.L. Koffeman (eds.), North Holland Publishing Company, 1974.

/N1/ Nijssen, G.M. : Data Structuring in the DDL and Relational Model. In Klimbie, Koffeman (eds.) : Data Base Management, Cargese (Corsica) April 1-5, 74, North Holland Publishing Company 1974.

/N2/ Nijssen, G.M. : DDL illustrated with data structure diagrams. IFIP-TC2 Special Working Conference "A technical in-depth evaluation of the DDL", Namur, January 75.

/RA/ The Random House Dictionary, College Edition 1968.

E. Morlet and D. Ribbens, (Eds.), International Computing Symposium 1977.

CONCEPTS FOR THE COEXISTENCE APPROACH TO DATA BASE MANAGEMENT

Eckhard Falkenberg

Siemens AG - ZT ZFE
Hofmannstraße 51
D - 8000 München 70
Fed. Rep. of Germany

The idea providing coexistence of various data models and data manipulation methods within one data base management system imposes new requirements on the design of such systems. The most important task is to find a suitable architecture and a common basis for any arbitrary data model and data manipulation method. Within the gross architecture, three levels of data base interfaces are provided, namely various external interfaces, a central interface, and an internal interface. As a common basis for any external or internal interface, the use of a semantically complete and unique form of data - the deep structure of data - at the central interface is suggested, together with a data manipulation method which corresponds to the deep structure, and which incorporates descriptive and procedural elements. Transformations from a deep structure into various semantically equivalent surface structures of data are shown.

TABLE OF CONTENTS

1. INTRODUCTION

For several years there was a debate among data base researchers as to which data model and which data manipulation method is most suitable for data base management. There is no absolute answer to that question, for although a particular data model and data manipulation method may be favorable for some classes of data base applications, it is never suitable for all. Even within a particular application, different data base users may prefer different views of the universe of discourse and different methods of handling it. Moreover, as far as machine efficiency is concerned, it is impossible to find a data structuring and accessing method which is optimal for all classes of applications.

Data base researchers are therefore now considering the best methods of achieving coexistence of different, arbitrary data models and data manipulation languages within one and the same data base management system (DBMS) (NIJSSEN, ref. 24, 25, 26).

Compared with standard DBMS, the coexistence approach imposes some new requirements on the design of DBMS. First of all, new thought must be given to a modular architecture, one aim being minimization of total expenses. As regards data models, one very important point is the possibility of transforming one view of data into any other which is semantically equivalent. In the case of data manipulation it is useful to search for a set of concepts which can serve as a common basis for any data manipulation language. Furthermore, various other aspects of data base management, such as consistency and privacy, have to be reviewed critically as a consequence of the coexistence principle.

The purpose of this paper is to outline concepts which were designed to meet some of the requirements imposed by the coexistence approach to data base management.

2. GROSS ARCHITECTURE

Coexistence means that within the DBMS there is an arbitrary number of different user interfaces in parallel. These interfaces are termed external data base interfaces, and each one consists of an external schema designed according to a particular data model, and a corresponding data manipulation language. There should be no restriction on the choice of data model or data manipulation language. A user group should be able to choose an external interface which, from the point of view of the users, is easy to learn, easy to comprehend, and easy to use, and which is also adapted as far as possible to the particular application problems of these users.

On the other hand, we have, in principle, one physical data base. For this we need an internal schema which describes the physical structure, and we need an accessing and manipulation facility on that physical level. This interface is termed the internal data base interface. The main criterion for the internal interface is machine efficiency. If, in the course of time, the access characteristics of the data base application change, and if machine efficiency is diminished as a result, the physical data base may be reorganized in accordance with a new and improved internal schema.

Assuming we have n external interfaces, we could provide n direct mappings from the external interfaces to the internal interface. There are, however, several disadvantages in doing so. Direct mapping is usually very complicated, due to the high conceptual distances between external interfaces and internal interface. These complicated mappings have to be performed n times. If the application evolves in such a way that a number of external interfaces need to be modified, all the corresponding mappings to the internal interface have to be changed as well. If the internal interface needs to be redefined, due to efficiency considerations, all n mappings have to be altered.

2.1. Three Kinds of Data Base Interfaces

In order to avoid these disadvantages, to separate the problem-oriented aspects at the external interfaces from the efficiency-oriented aspects at the internal interface, and to minimize the total expenses of mappings, it is necessary to introduce another interface between the external interfaces and the internal interface. This is called the central data base interface. The resulting gross architecture is shown in fig. 1.

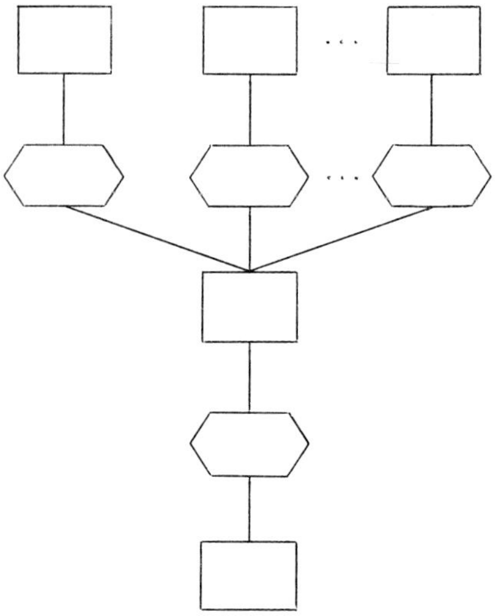

Fig. 1: Three kinds of data base interfaces

As far as schemas are concerned, this architecture is equivalent to other proposals (e.g. ANSI/SPARC, ref. 2; NIJSSEN, ref. 24, 26). We have several external schemas, one central or conceptual schema and one internal schema. In addition to this we suggest that the same trinity be provided for data manipulation. The advantages of doing so are analogous to those gained by providing the three kinds of schemas.

2.2. Requirements Imposed on the Central Data Base Interface

The requirements imposed on the central data base interface are critical, due to its pivotal position within the architecture. The most important points are the following:

Semantics:

It is self-evident that semantics must be preserved through the various mappings. The consequence is that the concepts at the central interface have to be chosen such that a formalized and precise definition of semantics can be provided and a unique interpretation of the expressions at the external interfaces can be given using expressions at the central interface. The power of the concepts at the central interface has to be sufficient to allow any data model and data manipulation language at the external interfaces.

Transformability:

To minimize the total expenses of mappings, the concepts at the central interface must be chosen in such a way that the mappings between the external interfaces and the central interface become as simple as possible.

Stability:

Assuming that the total application-specific universe of discourse is not changed, the following must be true: Whenever existing external interfaces are modified or dropped, whenever new ones are added, or whenever the internal schema is altered, the central interface has to remain stable. This assures that only the necessary and wanted changes have to be performed. Interfaces which do not require modification must not be affected by a change in some other interface.

Evolvability:

If the universe of discourse itself changes in the course of time, the reprogramming costs must be kept as low as possible. This means that the concepts at the central interface have to be chosen in such a way that changes in the universe of discourse will involve as few as possible modifications to the central schema.

In the following two sections we will consider how the requirements imposed on the central interface can be fulfilled.

3. CHOICE OF A SUITABLE DATA MODEL FOR THE CENTRAL DATA BASE INTERFACE

At the central interface, a formalized and precise definition of semantics is required. In the case of the data model at the central interface, this means that it must be possible to represent all the semantically relevant elements of a universe of discourse with all essential detailed points of their structure. These elements are known as elementary facts (other terms: e.g. elementary messages, ref. 33; elementary sentences, ref. 26; relationships, associations, ref. 16,18,30). What we need at the central interface is a unique and complete representation of each single elementary fact of the universe of discourse. Unique means that an elementary fact can be represented in only one particular way by means of the data model. Complete means that all the structural characteristics of an elementary fact can be represented by means of the data model.

Since there is a strong resemblance to the concept of deep structure, as developed by linguists (e.g. CHOMSKY, ref. 9), we call a data structure which fulfils the above conditions a deep structure of data (or conceptual data structure) (FALKENBERG, ref. 15). Our approach is to use the deep structure of data at the central interface, while at the other interfaces particular surface structures of these data may be chosen. By using this approach, the semantic equivalence of the data at the various interfaces can be guaranteed in the simplest possible way, because there is only one authoritative instance where the semantics of data are defined, namely at the central interface.

The process of transforming a surface structure into its deep structure is termed conceptualization of data (SCHANK, ref. 27), its reverse being deconceptualization of data. These points are illustrated in fig. 2.

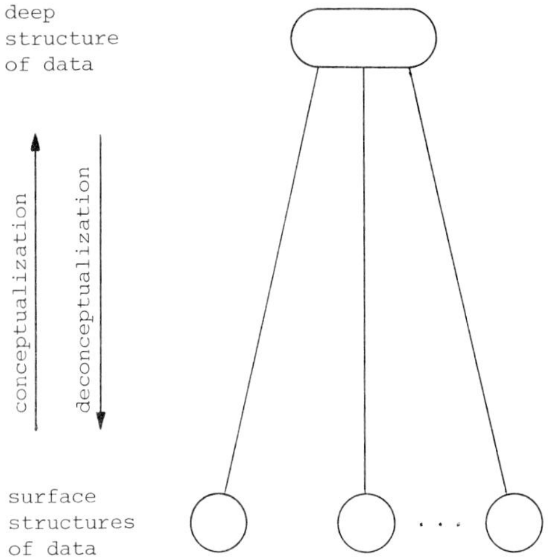

Fig. 2: Deep structure and surfaces structures of data

The process of conceptualization eliminates all those aspects of data structures which are irrelevant for the deep structure, i.e. those which have nothing to do with the semantics of data. The main aspects which have to be eliminated in order to reach the deep structure of data are the following:

- Organization and encoding of data at the physical storage media
- Access paths
- Notational distinctions, like the distinction between graphical, tabular, or character-string notation
- Aspects of designation, synonyms
- Representational aggregations of elementary facts

The transformations from the central schema to the various surrounding schemas are, according to our approach, processes of deconceptualization, i.e. these aspects of aggregation, designation etc. have to be added to the deep structure to perform the data transformation. A simpler data transformation principle with the same claim to universal applicability is hardly imaginable.

Looking at the various existing data models, we can classify them by considering how far they fulfil the conditions of a deep-structure data model.

3.1. Surface-structure Data Models

Let us first consider the two best-known data models, the CODASYL/DBTG data model (ref. 10), and CODD's relational model (ref. 12, 13).

By the DBTG data model, particular representational aggregations of elementary facts can be defined. There are two kinds of aggregations, record occurrences and CODASYL-set occurrences. A record occurrence is, in general, a hierarchical aggregation of elementary facts, where in most cases the record identifier represents the radix of that hierarchy. A CODASYL-set occurrence contains one owner record and n member records. Beyond that, a CODASYL-set occurrence aggregates n elementary facts of the same type. Each one of these elementary facts is given by a pair, set up by the radix of the owner record and the radix of a member record.

CODD's relational model uses a simpler and more restricted aggregation method. There is only one kind of aggregation, namely n-tuples of relations. Considering first-normal-form relations, the main restriction on the aggregation is that in one n-tuple all aggregated elementary facts have to be of different type, i.e. repeating attributes are not allowed. There is an additional restriction in the case of third-normal-form relations, where it is not permissible for an elementary fact to be represented several times.

Since both data models involve the aspect of fixed representational aggregation of elementary facts, we must regard them as surface-structure data models. Another data model of that kind is the entity set model by SENKO et al. (ref. 31), where the aggregation structure is very similar to third-normal-form relations.

Bearing in mind the principle of providing the deep structure of data at the central interface, the data models referred to above are all suitable for external interfaces, some of them may be used for the internal interface, but none of them is adequate for the central interface.

If, in spite of this, we were to apply such a surface-structure, aggregation-oriented data model at the central interface, we would have to face various disadvantages. First of all, it would be more difficult to guarantee the semantic equivalence of the data at the various interfaces, and the problem of data transformation would become more complicated. In addition to this, there would be a lack of stability and evolvability, because evolution events might necessitate modification or redefinition of the aggregation structure (attribute migration), so that the corresponding manipulation functions relating to the aggregation structure would no longer be valid.

There is a class of data models based on the principle of defining the reference of data aggregates (e.g. records, n-tuples) to the real world. The usual interpretation of data aggregates using real-world concepts is, roughly speaking, the following: A data aggregate is a description of an <u>object</u> belonging to the real world. This object has a number of <u>attributes</u> which are represented by the items of the data aggregate. There may exist also <u>relationships</u> between objects represented as linkages between the corresponding data aggregates (e.g. CODASYL-sets). Varieties of this kind of data model are developed e.g. by BENCI et al. (ref. 3), MOULIN et al. (ref. 23), SCHMID/SWENSON (ref. 28), SUNDGREN (ref. 33).

At first sight, these data models seem to be deep-structure-oriented. But since the starting point was the data aggregate and the distinction between attributes and relationships is thus dependent on the aggregation structure, these models show the same disadvantages as the aggregation-oriented data models, namely they are lacking in transformability, stability, and evolvability. They cannot be considered as true deep-structure data models.

3.2. Deep-structure Data Models

During recent years a number of data models have been developed which display more characteristics of an ideal deep-structure data model.

One example is the binary relational model (e.g. ABRIAL, ref. 1; BRACCHI et al., ref. 7; SENKO, ref. 30), where an elementary fact is always defined as an element (pair) of a binary relation. Any universe of discourse can, in fact, be modelled with binary relations, but in the case of modification of the types of elementary facts, due to some evolution event, the restriction to binary relations often results in an unnecessary and complicated restructuring of the universe of discourse. This means that the binary relational model shows a lack of evolvability which can be avoided by allowing n-ary relations (n greater 0) which are <u>semantically irreducible</u> (FALKENBERG, ref. 18, 19; HALL et al., ref. 20; NIJSSEN, ref. 26). To avoid misunderstandings, this concept has nothing to do with third normal form. A semantically irreducible relation represents a single type of facts, while a third-normal-form relation is, in general, an aggregation of several types of elementary facts, and thus semantically reducible.

The question which arises now is, what are the basic concepts of a deep-structure data model? The first and most obvious approach is to use the concepts of predicate logic (BILLER/ NEUHOLD, ref. 5; MEYER/SCHNEIDER, ref. 22; STEEL, ref. 32). This approach is quite successful, but does not fulfil all the requirements of a deep-structure data model. In particular, a unique representation of elementary facts is not always possible. For example, we assume that the two expressions

P1 (O1,O2),
P2 (O2,O1),
where
O1 = person A
O2 = person B
P1 = is superior to
P2 = is subordinate to

represent one and the same fact. To state this assumption formally, we need an additional semantic rule, saying that P1 is the inverse predicate of P2. From the point of view of an ideal deep structure, such a semantic rule is only a makeshift solution.

We can avoid such makeshift solutions by introducing the concept of role. In the above example, the object O1 (person A) plays the role R1 (is superior to), while the object O2 (person B) plays the role R2 (is subordinate to). The elementary fact is defined in our example as the set of object-role pairs:

$\{(O1,R1),(O2,R2)\}$

Thus we have a unique representation of that elementary fact.

Generally speaking, the deep structure of an elementary fact can be defined as a set of n pairs (n greater 0). Each pair is either an object-role pair or a pair of an elementary fact and a role. In the latter case we speak of nested elementary facts.

This deep-structure data model we call the object-role model, due to its basic concepts. It is represented in a more comprehensive way elsewhere (FALKENBERG, ref. 16, 18; NIJSSEN, ref. 26). In the present paper we only wish to demonstrate the relevance of that model for the central interface. We do this by showing how a central or conceptual schema, designed according to the object-role model, can be transformed into internal or external schemas, structured in accordance with some surface-structure data models.

3.3. Data Transformation Examples

As a demonstration example we have chosen the following universe of discourse, written in a graph-like notation (fig. 3). Object types are represented by circles, roles by arrows, and the corresponding names - object type names and role names - are written at these circles or arrows. In addition to this there is an indication of how often an instance of a special object type may play a particular role. This set of possible occurrence frequencies is stated for each role and is put in brackets.

A machine-readable notation of this deep structure may be as follows:

Fact type No.	Object type names	Role names	Occurrence frequencies
1	person	is manager of	O-80
	person	is subordinate to	O,1
2	person	was born at	1
	date	is birthdate of	O-arb.
3	person	receives as salary per month	O,1
	money	is salary per month of	O-arb.
4	person	is coworker of	O-3
	hours	is time of cooperation per week	O-arb.
	project	has as coworker	O-50
5	person	is employed in	O,1
	institution	employs	1-arb.
6	institution	has as residence	1
	city	is residence of	O-arb.
7	institution	supports	O-arb.
	project	receives support from	O-arb.
8	money	is budget per year of	O-arb.
	project	has as budget per year	O,1
9	date	is start of	O-arb.
	project	started at	1
10	project	is parent project of	O-10
	project	is child project of	O,1

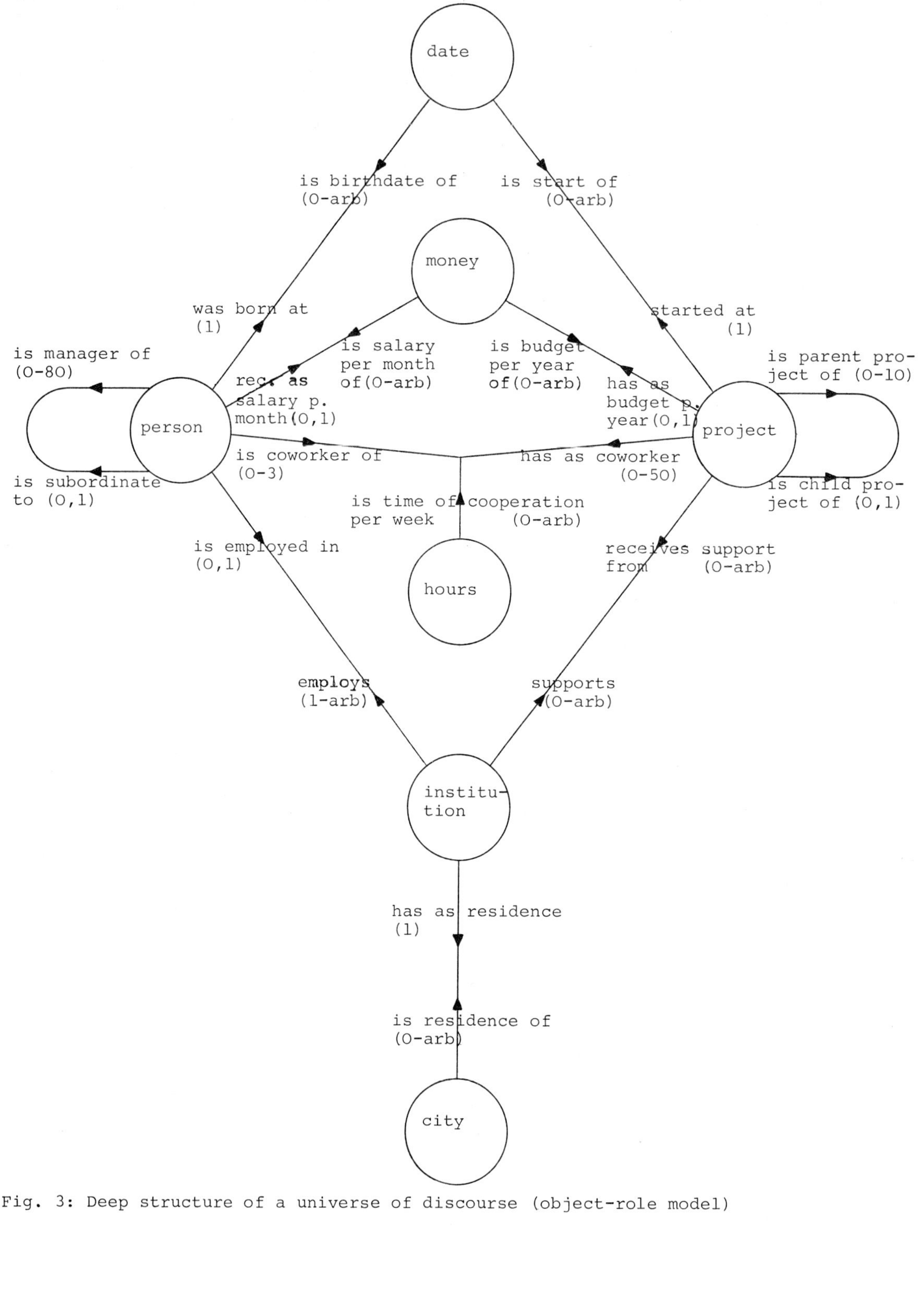

Fig. 3: Deep structure of a universe of discourse (object-role model)

We now transform this deep structure into various surface structures. We consider only external schemas, where we dispense with implementation-oriented aspects like access paths etc. Basically, for each transformation we have to define the wanted aggregation structure, together with the special designations and notations. For users working with a particular surface structure, this structure has to be intelligible from the point of view of their background. This means for instance, that not all designations used in the deep structure have to be taken over into the surface structure, and that various notational simplifications may be introduced.

In the first transformation example, we apply the DBTG data model for the specification of a surface structure. We define two record types, one of which aggregates fact-types Nos. 6,7,8,9,10, where the object type "institution" is taken as the radix. The aggregation is designated "institution-record" and is hierarchical. The second level of that hierarchy is realized by introducing a group which aggregates the fact-types Nos. 8,9,10 with the object type "project" as radix, this group being termed the "support-group". Since the set of possible occurrence frequencies of the instances of the object type "institution" in the role "supports" (fact-type No. 7) is unlimited (0-arb.), the group ist optional and repeating.

The other record type aggregates the fact-types Nos. 3,1,2,4 with the object type "person" as the radix, and it is termed the "employee-record". Since the possible occurrence frequencies assigned to the role "is coworker of" within the ternary fact-type No. 4 are from zero to three, this fact type requires special treatment. An optional and repeating group called the "cooperation-group" is introduced for it.

Furthermore, new and adequate designations are chosen for the record attributes, in such a way that the designations of the deep structure are simplified to some extent.

The remaining fact-type No. 5 is declared as a CODASYL-set type named "employment-set". The participating object types are "institution" and "person" which are the radices of the connected record types. The occurrence frequencies are (1-arb.) and (0,1), i.e. the owner of this CODASYL-set type is "institution-record", the member is "employee-record".

The result of the whole transformation process is shown in fig. 4, where a notation according to the feature analysis of GDBMS (CODASYL, ref. 11) is used.

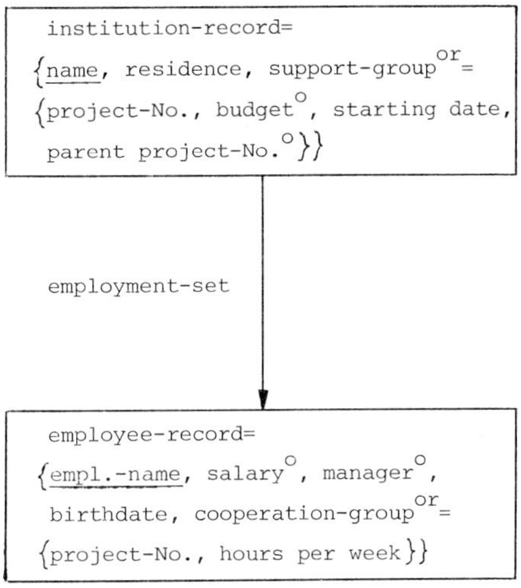

Key:

record identifiers underlined;

o optional groups or attributes;

r repeating groups or attributes;

Fig. 4: A surface structure of the universe of discourse according to fig. 3 (DBTG data model)

In the second transformation example we apply CODD's relational model to construct a surface structure. We define two relations. One is named "employee-relation" and aggregates the fact-types Nos. 3,2,1,4,5,6, while the other is called "project-relation" and aggregates the fact-types Nos. 7,8,9,10. In addition to this appropriate domain names are chosen. The result is shown in fig. 5.

employee-relation	(empl.-name, salary$^{\circ}$, birthdate, manager$^{\circ}$, project-No.$^{\circ}$, hours per week$^{\circ}$, institution$^{\circ}$, city$^{\circ}$)
project-relation	(project-No., support$^{\circ}$, budget$^{\circ}$, starting date, parent project$^{\circ}$)

Key:

primary key underlined;

$^{\circ}$ value may be omitted;

Fig. 5: A surface structure of the universe of discourse according to fig. 3 (CODD's relational model)

In the third transformation example we use the same data model, but we create a different aggregation structure. We construct five relations, namely "employee-relation", "project-relation", "coworkership-relation", "support-relation", and "residence-relation". The aggregated fact types are Nos. 3,2,1,5; Nos. 8,10,9; No. 4; No. 7; and No. 6, respectively. This surface structure is shown in fig. 6.

employee-relation	(empl.-name, salary$^{\circ}$, birthdate, manager$^{\circ}$, institution$^{\circ}$)
project-relation	(project-No., budget$^{\circ}$, parent project$^{\circ}$, starting date)
coworkership-relation	(empl.-name, project-No., hours per week)
support-relation	(project-No., institution)
residence-relation	(institution, city)

Fig. 6: A surface structure of the universe of discourse according to fig. 3 (CODD's relational model)

4. CHOICE OF A SUITABLE DATA MANIPULATION LANGUAGE FOR THE CENTRAL DATA BASE INTERFACE

The choice of a deep-structure data model at the central interface, and the dependence of data manipulation on the applied data model, means that at the central interface a manipulation language is needed which is oriented towards the deep structure of data. We call such a language a deep-structure manipulation language (or conceptual manipulation language).

Expressions of the various external, surface-structure-oriented manipulation languages have to be transformed into semantically equivalent expressions of the deep-structure manipulation language. These have to be mapped into the internal manipulation expressions.

4.1. Deep-structure Manipulation

The meaning of deep-structure manipulation and the way in which it differs from surface-structure manipulation can be illustrated by an example.

Let us take as a basis the universe of discourse as shown in fig. 3,4,5,6. We want to retrieve the set of birthdates of all those persons who work on projects which are supported by the institution A.

If we take the surface structure of fig. 5, according to CODD's relational model, and if we use the manipulation language SEQUEL (CHAMBERLIN/BOYCE, ref. 8), we have to write the following expression:

```
SELECT BIRTHDATE FROM EMPLOYEE-RELATION
WHERE PROJECT-NO. =
     SELECT PROJECT-NO. FROM PROJECT-
     RELATION WHERE SUPPORT = A
```

If, on the other hand, we take the surface structure of fig. 6, again using SEQUEL, we have to write:

```
SELECT BIRTHDATE FROM EMPLOYEE-RELATION
WHERE EMPL.-NAME =
     SELECT EMPL.-NAME FROM COWORKERSHIP-
     RELATION WHERE PROJECT-NO. =
          SELECT PROJECT-NO. FROM SUPPORT-
          RELATION WHERE INSTITUTION = A
```

The difference between the two syntactically different expressions whose intention, however, is identical, is a direct consequence of the different aggregations used in each case. Thus SEQUEL is a typical surface-structure manipulation language.

The corresponding deep-structure manipulation expression does not deal with aggregations at all, it deals only with objects and roles (compare fig. 3):

PRINT DATE WHICH IS BIRTHDATE OF PERSON WHO
IS COWORKER OF PROJECT WHICH
RECEIVES SUPPORT FROM INSTITUTION A

The keywords and marks have the following meaning:

PRINT	retrieval operator
WHICH or WHO	qualification operator
=====	object type name
-----	role name
═════	individual name (value)

A comprehensive description of this (descriptive) deep-structure manipulation language is given by the author elsewhere (FALKENBERG, ref. 18). Another example of such a manipulation language, but one which is restricted to binary facts, is FORAL (SENKO, ref. 30).

4.2. Descriptive and Procedural Manipulation

The question now arises as to what features should be provided within the deep-structure manipulation language to enable it to serve as a common basis for all external manipulation languages. In particular, it must be remembered that both descriptive and procedural languages may be used, as external manipulation languages. It is therefore not appropriate to use a purely descriptive language at the central interface. We could, on the other hand, use a purely procedural language, but, the mappings from the various descriptive external manipulation expressions to the central manipulation expressions would then become relatively complicated. In order to minimize the total cost of mappings it is therefore advisable to use a central manipulation language which incorporates both descriptive and procedural elements.

Contributions on this subject are available from data base researchers (e.g. BERILD/NACHMENS, ref. 4; DATE, ref. 14; HUITS, ref. 21), and also from developers of high-level algorithmic languages (e.g. SCHWARTZ, ref. 29; WITT, ref. 34). In this paper we do not intend to got into details on this matter, and we will merely illustrate a possible method of managing this problem, using an example.

The following possibility of integrating descriptive and procedural elements exists: Firstly, a set of objects, roles or elementary facts is specified in a descriptive way. Secondly, each element of this set is manipulated individually by means of a procedure. As components of this procedure, descriptive specifications may occur again.

As an example, let us consider the following retrieval problem, where the above universe of discourse is assumed (fig. 3): We want to know all projects which receive support from institution A and whose budget per year is less than twice the salaries per year of the coworkers of these projects. Of course, this retrieval problem can be managed in a purely descriptive way by using the sum function, but without using that function we can formulate the query in a half-descriptive, half-procedural fashion, where descriptive expressions of the kind used above are embedded within a procedure:

```
DECLARE MANPOWER-EXPENSES
FOR EACH PROJECT/X WHICH RECEIVES SUPPORT FROM
INSTITUTION A
DO
   MANPOWER-EXPENSES := Ø
   FOR EACH MONEY Y WHICH IS SALARY PER
   MONTH OF PERSON WHO IS COWORKER OF PROJECT/X
   DO
      MANPOWER-EXPENSES := MANPOWER-EXPENSES
      & MONEY/Y
   OD
   MANPOWER-EXPENSES := MANPOWER-EXPENSES . 24
   IF (MONEY WHICH IS BUDGET PER YEAR OF
   PROJECT/X) LESS THAN MANPOWER-EXPENSES
   THEN PRINT PROJECT/X
OD
```

The meanings of the keywords, symbols and marks are as follows:

DECLARE	declaration of a data variable; a data variable has to follow;
FOR EACH	one-element-at-a-time operator; a descriptive specification of a set of objects, roles, or elementary facts, and a do-loop have to follow; within this do-loop for-each statements may occur again;
WHICH or WHO	qualification operator (part of a descriptive set specification)
DO ... OD	begin and end of a do-loop
IF ... THEN	if-then-statement operators

LESS THAN	relational operator
PRINT	retrieval operator
/	reference-variable operator; a reference variable has to follow;
:=	assignment operator
&	arithmetic operator: addition
.	arithmetic operator: multiplication
.....	data variable
~	reference variable
=====	object type name
-----	role name
═════	individual name (value)

5. A UNIFIED DESIGN OF THE CENTRAL DATA BASE INTERFACE

So far we have outlined the modelling and manipulation principles relating to the central interface. We now wish to discuss briefly the question of how to provide a unified linguistic conception for all the functions required at the central interface, such as type definitions, definitions of semantic rules for consistency checks, privacy specifications, retrieval and update functions.

If we bear in mind the idea of using the deep structure of data at the central interface, we can interpret and analyze the essential characteristics of the data base management functions at this interface in the following way:

A type definition is a linguistic expression declaring the type membership of a set of elementary facts or objects.

A definition of a semantic rule contains linguistic expressions specifying the sets of elements to which the semantic rule applies. Furthermore, it is necessary to state what kind of rule it is and what the system has to do if the rule is violated.

A privacy specification contains linguistic expressions which define those elements of the universe of discourse which have to be protected against unauthorized access.

In a retrieval expression, the set of requested elements of the universe of discourse has to be specified. A possible manipulation of this set must also be defined.

Finally, update means to specify those instances of elementary facts which have to be inserted in or deleted from the universe of discourse.

The common feature of all these data base management functions is the necessity of specifying sets of elements of the universe of discourse. These sets may be empty, one-element, or multiple-element sets. A linguistic expression which specifies a definite set of elements of the universe of discourse is known as a signification.

On this basis a unified design of the central interface can be performed in the following two steps:

Firstly, we have to design a signification language which refers to the chosen data model, in our case to the object-role model which allows the definition of the deep structure of data.

Secondly, we have to design function-specific operators and constructs which are used in connection with significations, or where significations are embedded. For instance, in the above example of a simple print statement, the retrieval operator is followed by a signification of a set of objects. In the other example of a for-each construct, various significations are embedded within this construct.

The uniformity of such a design is achieved by the application of one and the same signification language for all data base management functions.

A more comprehensive description of the signification approach permitting a unified design of any data base interface, also using a surface-structure data model, is given by the author elsewhere (FALKENBERG, ref. 17, 18). Other authors have used a similar approach on the basis of a particular surface-structure data model (e.g. BOYCE/CHAMBERLIN, ref. 6). We emphasize again, however, that for the central interface, and within the framework of the coexistence approach, it is advisable to consider the deep structure of data with all its consequences.

6. SUMMARY

In this paper we have tried to work out some suitable concepts for the coexistence approach to data base management. As far as the architecture is concerned, we consider it advisable to introduce three levels of schemas and of corresponding data manipulation languages. The intermediate level, the central data base interface, has to fulfil various important requirements. In particular, semantics have to be defined formally and precisely at that interface. Other requirements are transformability, stability and evolvability.

We propose the use of a deep-structure data model and a corresponding deep-structure manipulation language at the central interface, because all the requirements referred to can be fulfilled most simply in this way. A specific deep-structure data model, the object-role model, and a suitable deep-structure manipulation language which contains both descriptive and procedural elements, are described. A solution of the data transformation problem is illustrated on the basis of the object-role model. Management of this problem is an essential prerequisite for the coexistence approach.

Finally, we have shown how it is possible to achieve a unified design for all data base management functions, in particular for those at the central interface. The key for such a unified approach which simplifies the design of the central interface is the concept of signification.

ACKNOWLEDGEMENTS

It was G.M. Nijssen, Control Data Brussels, who convinced the author of the benefits of the coexistence approach to data base management in many helpful discussions. The author wishes to thank him as well as K. Hahne, A. Schütt, C. Vavra, and E. Wildgrube, Siemens AG Munich, for valuable suggestions of improvement.

REFERENCES

(1) Abrial, J.R., "Data semantics", in Klimbie, J.W., and Koffeman, K.I. (eds.), "Data base management", North-Holland, Amsterdam (1974), 1-59

(2) ANSI/SPARC, "Status report SPARC/DBMS", February 1975

(3) Benci, E. et al., "Concepts for the design of a conceptual schema", in ref. 25, 181-200

(4) Berild, S., and Nachmens, S., "Some practical applications of CS4 - a DBMS for associative data bases", Proceedings IFIP-TC-2 Working Conference on "Modelling in data base management systems", Nice, January 1977

(5) Biller, H., and Neuhold, E.J. "Semantics of data bases: the semantics of data models", Technical report 03/76, Institut für Informatik, University of Stuttgart

(6) Boyce, R.F., and Chamberlin, D.D., "Using a structured english query language as a data definition facility", IBM-Report RJ 1318, December 1973

(7) Bracchi, G., Fedeli, A., and Paolini, P., "A multilevel relational model for data base management systems", Klimbie, J.W., and Koffeman, K.I. (eds.), "Data base management", North-Holland, Amsterdam (1974) 211-225

(8) Chamberlin, D.D., and Boyce, R.F., "Sequel:a structured english query language", Proceedings ACM-SIGFIDET Workshop (1974)

(9) Chomsky, N., "Aspects of a theory of syntax", M.I.T. Press, Cambridge, Mass. (1965)

(10) CODASYL, "DDL journal of development", Report, June 1973

(11) CODASYL System Committee: "Feature analysis of generalized data base management systems", Technical Report, May 1971

(12) Codd, E.F., "A relational model of data for large shared data banks", Communications of the ACM, Vol. 13, No. 6, June 1970, 377-387

(13) Codd, E.F., "Further normalization of the data base relational model", Courant Computer Science Symposia 6, Data Base Systems, Prentice-Hall, New York, May 1971

(14) Date, C.J., "An architecture for high-level language data base extensions", Proceedings SIGMOD (1976), 101-122

(15) Falkenberg, E., "Deep structure of data", Working paper IFIP WG 2.6 (Data Bases), January 1977

(16) Falkenberg, E. "Concepts for modelling information", in ref. 25, 95-109

(17) Falkenberg, E., "Significations: the key to unify data base management", Information Systems, Vol. 2, No. 1 (1976), 19-28

(18) Falkenberg, E., "Structuring and representation of information at the interface between data base user and data base management system", Doctoral thesis, University of Stuttgart, June 1975 (English and German)

(19) Falkenberg, E., "Semantical irreducibility", Working paper IFIP WG 2.6 (Data Bases), January 1976

(20) Hall, P., Owlett, J., and Todd, S., "Relations and Entities", in ref. 25, 201-220

(21) Huits, M.H.H., "Requirements for languages in data base systems", in Douque, B.C.M., and Nijssen, G.M. (eds.), "Data base description", North-Holland (1975), 85-109

(22) Meyer, B., and Schneider, H.-J., "Predicate logic applied to data base technology", Lecture notes of the Advanced Course on Data Base Languages and Natural Language Processing (1975), Freudenstadt

(23) Moulin, P. et al., "Conceptual model as a data base design tool", in ref. 25, 221-238

(24) Nijssen, G.M., "A gross architecture for the next generation database management systems", in ref. 25, 1-24

(25) Nijssen, G.M. (ed.), "Modelling in data base management systems", North-Holland, Amsterdam (1976)

(26) Nijssen, G.M., "On the gross architecture for the next generation database management systems", Presentation at the IFIP Congress 77, Toronto (forthcoming)

(27) Schank, R.C., "Identification of conceptualizations underlying natural language" in Schank, R.C., and Colby, K.M. (eds.), "Computer models of thought and language", Freeman, San Francisco (1972)

(28) Schmid, H.A., and Swenson, J.R., "On the semantics of the relational data model", Proceedings of the ACM-SIGMOD Conference, San Jose, California, May 1975

(29) Schwartz, J.T., "On programming: an interim report on the SETL project", Lecture notes, Courant Institute of Mathematical Sciences, New York University

(30) Senko, M.E., "DIAM as a detailed example of the ANSI/SPARC architecture", in ref. 25, 73-94

(31) Senko, M.E. et al., "Data structures and accessing in data-base systems", IBM Systems Journal, Vol. 12, No. 1 (1973) 30-93

(32) Steel, T.B. jr., "Data base standardization: a status report", in Douque, B.C.M., and Nijssen, G.M. (eds.), "Data base description", North-Holland (1975) 183-198

(33) Sundgren, B., "An infological approach to data bases", Urval No. 7, Stockholm (1973)

(34) Witt, J., Personal communication on the programming language JOKER, Siemens AG Munich

E. Morlet and D. Ribbens, (Eds.), International Computing Symposium 1977.

BEYOND APL - An Interactive Language for the Eighties

by

W.K. G i l o i

Department of Computer Science

University of Minnesota

In the paper, we first identify requirements and formulate postulates for a high-level programming language that shall function as an 'implementation' language for interactive programming systems. Subsequently, it is discussed to what extent APL fulfills these postulates. The unique assets of APL as an interactive language are recognized as well as its severe deficiences. From this discussion it becomes evident how a language should be structured that preserves the advantages yet remedies the shortcomings of APL. The concept of such a language, preliminarily dubbed BEYOND APL, is outlined. BEYOND APL is not a modified or extended APL. Rather, it is conceived as a compiler language into which the most valuable features of APL are carried over, yet which moreover posseses a data type 'pointer' as well as an inhomogeneous list structure in addition to homogeneous, rectangular arrays, a modern control structure tailored for interactive use, and a clean procedure concept.

1. Requirements for an Interactive General-Purpose Language.

1.1. The Characteristics of Interactive Systems.

Interactive systems can be found in a broad variety of computer applications. To mention a few, we may present the following list, which is not claimed to be exhaustive

- General purpose time sharing systems (commercial, scientific, or educational)
- Transactional systems (e.g. banking, seat reservation, catalog ordering, data acquisition and inventory control, hospital admission, etc. etc.)
- Interactive information systems and data banks
- Systems for computer aided human activities
- Control and command systems.

The first three types of interactive systems have become rather ubiquitous whereas the realm of computer aided human activities, under which label we subsume such areas as computer aided design, computer aided instruction, computer aided delivery of health care, etc., has not yet been developed to its full potential.

One of the problems raised by the diversity of interactive systems is to identify the 'end user' of such systems. In the case of transactional systems, for example, the end user very often is just a keyboard operator. The other extreme is the realm of computer aided human activities, where the end user may be a highly specialized engineer, physician, educator, or psychologist. However, there is a common denominator for this variety of end users, given by the fact that they need not necessarily have any working knowledge of programming. The exception from this rule is the end user of general purpose time-sharing systems who certainly must possess a certain proficiency in a high-level programming language. However, the days of time sharing used for solving simple numerical problems (e.g., time sharing for educational use with BASIC as the programming language) are numbered, as this kind of computer access will be more and more replaced by the use of "intelligent" terminals which have enough computing power to allow for edition, debugging, and execution of sophisticated numerical programs without the assistance of a host computer /1/.

After an identifying criterion for the end user has been established, the question may be raised who is the designer and the implementer of an interactive system? In general purpose systems, this usually is the system programmer.

The design of an application system in the area of computer aided human activities, however, requires first of all a very profound knowledge of the respective field of application. Systems programmers or computer scientists in general will not share this knowledge with the application expert. Conversely, an expert in the application field can readily acquire enough programming skill to implement a system that will perform adequately, even if it may turn out to be, from a computer science point of view, not the best possible system.

The question is how to transfer computer science concepts and know-how into such application systems. As long as we do not have truly interdisciplinary curricula, where an education is offered in computer science as well as in an appropriate application science, the only possible contribution from the side of the computer scientists to the development of an application system may be to provide appropriate tools in terms of hardware, data models and organizational concepts for data bases, and languages. To be more specific, what the application programmer needs is not a "universal" data base management system -- which is intended to be everything to everybody -- but building blocks which he can use for the construction of his own, tailored data structures; it is not some "ultimate" programming language but a language that must have, in addition to the constructs required for interactive computing, the syntactic flexibility if not extensibility to enable the application programmer to define, within the given syntactic framework of such an 'implementation' language, an appropriate language for the end user of his system.

Summarizing this discussion, we see a symbiosis of three groups of persons being concerned with interactive computer systems

- The system programmers who provide the application programmers with basic tools for the implementation of application systems.
- The application programmers who design and implement application systems.
- The end users, that is, the everyday users of the application systems.

The system programmer is proficient in language concepts, data structures, data models, and data base management concepts, but also in the valid concepts for achieving software modularity and portability. The application programmer will have some working knowledge in high-lvel language programming. The end user is trained in the use of a particular system.

1.2 The Four Postulates for an Interactive Language.

In order to constitute a proper tool for the application programmer of interactive systems, a high-level 'implementation' language should satisfy the following four postulates.

(1) The language shall exhibit syntactic simplicity and flexibility, in order to be a useful tool for the casual user and to allow for the implementation of especially tailored 'end user languages'.
(2) The language should support data independence in order to be general, modular and portable.
(3) The language should provide transparency in order to facilitate for the casual user the testing and debugging of his application programs.
(4) The language should provide adequate control constructs for interactive computing as well as complete and minimal tools for the implementation of data structures.

The validity of the first postulate is self-evident though not always recognized. Data independence is the attempt to separate the logical representation of data from their physical representation such that program requests to data are only governed by the logical structure but not by the physical access modes. Transparency is one of the most important properties of an interactive language. That is, the user must be provided with insight into the state of the program during its execution. Besides of having adequate tracing facilities at his command, he should be enabled to halt program execution at any arbitrary instant, either manually or by programmed 'stops', and to interrogate the current program status and the current values of the variables at such a breakpoint. Furthermore, it should be possible during a program stop to type in expressions and have them executed with the current values of the referenced variables.

Interactive programs differ from ordinary batch programs in the way that the user can exercise a certain influence on the program execution during run time. Basically, there exist two techniques by which this can be accomplished, viz., program flow modification and dynamic procedure (or blocks) declaration. The more commonly used technique is program flow modification, simply because it is in most programming languages the only possibility offered. The major disadvantage of this approach is that the user cannot act spontaneously but only in response to a prompting by the system. The dynamic declaration of program blocks or procedures, on the other hand, allows the user a certain spontaneity of 'attentions'.

In this approach, a program block or procedure is not executed at the instant of call, but execution is deferred until an attention from the user (issued by activating an interactive input device) is received. Finally, an implementation language should provide the tools which are necessary and sufficient for the implementation of all given data structures.

2. An Evaluation of APL as Interactive Language

2.1 APL Information Structure and Operators

It is a mandatory feature of an interactive language that the user be permitted to build up data structures dynmically. Furthermore, a certain liberalism with respect to declarations is at least helpful. In APL, this principle is carried to the extreme that there are no name-attribute declarations at all, i.e., everything is dynamic. This requires that the language has 'attribute examining' capabilities, i.e., that the data are self-descriptive. The value of a variable may be considered as a pair (structure, data), with the two components of the pair being separate information entities /2/. Consequently, we find in APL operators which transform solely a structure without affecting the data, operators which transform solely the data without affecting their structure, and operators which operate on both, the data as well as the structure of their argument. As structures are restricted to rectangular, homogeneous arrays, they are completely defined by a dimension vector. Data are internally stored in the form of a data vector; i.e., the internal 'canonical' data structure is the linear list. Consequently, there may exist an empty structure but no unstructured set of data. Besides of interrogating the value of a variable, the programmer can separately reference the two information items of a value, the dimension vector (representing a structure) or the data vector (representing a set of data). New structures are created either as a result of an operation or by a value-generating statement. In the value-generating statement, the programmer specifies a structure, by specifying a dimension vector, and a set of data, either by specifying a data vector of by referencing another variable in which the data of the referenced variable are used to fill the specified structure. A variable is created on the first assignment of a value to its name.

The APL syntax is of extreme simplicity. As mentioned above, there are no name-attribute declarations. Furthermore, there is only one precedence rule calling for the execution of an expression from right to left (in order to preserve the prefix notation of monadic operators so common in mathematics). Of course, the user can always specify a different order of execution by using parentheses. APL features a host of monadic or dyadic operators. Monadic operators can be arbitrarily concatenated, provided the domain of the concatenated operator equals the range of the operator it is concatenated to. The syntactic simplicity of APL allows the novice programmer to learn the language by using it, for he does not have to learn a great number of complicated and rather arbirarily defined syntactic rules before he can undertake his very first steps in programming.

The set of APL operators can be partitioned into three major classes, namely /2/

SCALAR OPERATIONS
I/O OPERATIONS AND QUERY FUNCTIONS
STRUCTURE OPERATIONS.

Structure operations have rectangular, homogeneous arrays as their operand(s). We subdivide the class of structure operations or 'functions' (in the APL terminology) in the following subclasses

ARRAY FUNCTIONS
GENERATOR FUNCTIONS
SELECTION FUNCTIONS
RELATIONAL FUNCTIONS
CONVERSION FUNCTIONS.

A classification of the existing APL operators into these five subclasses is given in Table 1 (for a formal description of all APL operators, see /3/).

Array functions as well as generator functions create new values. Selection functions have the fact in common that they first select a certain subarray from a given structure and, subsequently, restructure that subarray. Hence, they generate new structures but not new data. Of course, the selected subarray may be the original structure itself. Relational functions form equivalence classes or orderings by introducing relations between two sets. Conversion functions perform conversions between number systems or between data type classes. APL distinguishes only two data type classes : Numbers and characters.

CLASS	FUNCTION	CHARACTERIZATION
ARRAY FUNCTIONS	REDUCTION	Generates new array with reduced rank
	INNER PRODUCT	Generalization of the matrix product
	OUTER PRODUCT	Special form of a cartesian product
	MATRIX INVERSION	Questionable primitive function of APL
GENERATOR FUNCTIONS	INDEX GENERATOR	Generates vector of index numbers
	DEAL	Generates vector of random numbers
SELECTION FUNCTIONS	INDEXING	Selection of a subset and restructuring
	RESHAPE	Creation of a structure
	CATENATION	Union of two ordered sets
	LAMINATION	Union of two ordered sets
	TAKE	Selection of a subset
	DROP	Selection of a subset
	COMPRESSION	Selection of a subset
	EXPANSION	Selection of a subset and augmentation
	REVERSAL	Restructuring of a set
	ROTATION	Restructuring of a set
	TRANSPOSITION	Selection of a subset and restructuring
RELATIONAL FUNCTIONS	INDEX OF	Intersection of two ordered sets
	MEMBERSHIP	Intersection of two ordered sets
	GRADE UP	Reordering of a set
	GRADE DOWN	Reordering of a set
CONVERSION FUNCTIONS	ENCODE	Conversion of number representations
	DECODE	Inverse conversion of number representations
	EXECUTE	Conversion of character strings into program statements (and subsequent execution)
	FORMAT	Conversion of numbers into character arrays

Table 1 Classification of Structure Functions of APL

Some of the structure functions are dyadic (e.g., inner and outer product, catenation, membership and 'index of'). Generator functions are niladic. All other structure functions are monadic, some of them parameterless, others requiring the specification of a parameter value. In the case of dyadic structure functions or monadic functions for which an array may be specified as parameter value, certain conformity conditions, linking the two structures, must be satisfied. Of course, the argument value and the parameter value must also be in the domain as defined by the nature of the operation. Since the language has no name-attribute binding, domain and conformity tests can only be performed on the actual data, i.e., they must be carried out during program execution as part of each operation in an expression. These tests often consume more time than the execution of the operation itself. This, of course, creates a tremendous overhead, leading to the effect that APL (when executed on a von Neumann machine) is very slow. The slowness of the interpretative program execution of APL can be somehow mitigated by furnishing the hardware processor with microprogrammed routines for the basic APL operations. Nevertheless, the price in terms of slowness of execution to be paid for the extremely dynamic character of APL is high, maybe too high.

Summarizing this part of the discussion, we may state that APL satisfies perfectly the postulate calling for syntactic simplicity and flexibility. Through the introduction of structures and data sets as separate information items, data independence is furthered. However, it must be added that the only data structure of APL is the multidimensionally and linearly ordered homogeneous set /4/, represented by rectangular, homogeneous arrays. Many practical applications necessitate the construction of inhomogeneous data structures. It is a deficiency of the language that it does not comprise an inhomogeneous structure.

2.2 The Major Shortcomings of APL.

Besides of the lack of an inhomogeneous data structure and the slowness of execution, we have to list among the deficiencies of APL its crude control structure and certain shortcomings of its procedure concept. The APL control structure is comparable with that of FORTRAN, i.e., the only control construct available is the computed GOTO. Control constructs for structured programming do not exist.

APL comprises procedures of the function type but not genuinely procedures of the statement type /5/. APL procedures or, in the APL terminology, 'defined functions' may have zero, one, or two arguments. Deviating from the common concept of procedures of the function type, a defined function need not necessarily assign a value to its name. Consequently, such a 'function without explicit result' (in the common terminology a contradiction in itself) cannot be invoked as part of an expression. The lack of a value assigned to its name, on the other hand, does not make it a procedure of the statement type but rather a hybrid construct that has no output parameters, and whose number of input parameters is restricted to in maximum two. Results can only be produced through a change of the values of non-local variables. A procedure concept that is based on the use of "implicit parameters' /6/ and the creation of side effects certainly is not a clean concept and may give rise to dangerous pitfalls.

The lack of a 'multiadic' function has been recognized by several authors (e.g. /7/) as probably the most severe shortcoming of APL. As a makeshift measure, one can have any arbitrary list of input, output, or transition parameters if this list is passed into a defined function as a character string. Internally, this string must then be analyzed, and the substrings representing names or expressions must be converted by the aid of the EXECUTE operator into real names or expressions. This approach gives the user the almost unlimited freedom to define his particular problem oriented language in which arbitrary keyword operators are introduced as APL function calls and parameter lists are declared as character strings. In this way, it is possible to change the regular call by value mechanism of APL into a call by name parameter passing. Along the same line, arbitrary control constructs can be introduced /8/ or even name-attribute declarations /9/. However, whereas this offers a great potential for experimentation, it cannot really be recommended for production-type programming systems, for the use of the EXECUTE operator has the dangerous effect of destroying the name integrity /2/.

It is a most important question whether the same degree of transparency can be achieved in a compiled language as in an interpreted language.

In fact, this is possible if a special 'post processor' is provided that can be activated by the user during a program suspension by invoking an EVALUATE operator, applied to an arbitrary expression. As a result, the expression is evaluated with the current values of the variables occurring in it, and the obtained value is returned. Of course, such a device adds some overhead (e.g., the name table must be kept during the life time of the program), but this is a small price to pay for the tremendous gain in insight it offers to the user.

3. Beyond APL.

3.1. The General Concept of an Improved APL-Type Language.

From the above discussion, it becomes evident what steps should be taken to remedy the shortcomings of APL. These are

- Introduction of a modern control structure
- Introduction of a cleaner and less restrictive procedure concept
- Introduction of an inhomogeneous data structure
- Introduction of name-attribute declarations.

Declarations are a necessary prerequisite for an inhomogeneous data structure. However, one must carefully consider the question which attributes to declare. Static array dimensions would imply to abolish such extremely useful operations as, e.g., CATENATE, TAKE, DROP, etc. Therefore, it is of utmost importance to keep the dimensions of structures dynamic. On the other hand, there is no particular advantage in the approach to keep the data type and even the structure type of a language dynamic, as exercised in APL. Data type and structure type declarations, in connection with a compiled rather than an interpreted program execution eliminates all run-time domain tests and the bulk of the run-time conformity tests (the tests for 'rank conformity'). In a language with the information structure of APL, the hence created data objects will be descriptors for the data entities rather than memory locations. Data access is accomplished through a standardized memory access function which has the dimension vector as parameter /10/. Hence, a test for dimension conformity causes hardly any considerable overhead, as the dimension vector must be looked up in the descriptor anyway in order to execute the memory access function. Another parameter of the memory access function is the data type tag of a structure, also stored in the descriptor.

Finally, the dimension vector implies the structure type of its data entity and, hence, data entities in BEYOND APL remain to be self-descriptive (through their descirptors). Consequently, it is still possible to have the query functions of APL, to which a function is added that is missing in APL, namely a function which yields a code value identifying the data type of its argument variable.

The principle of internally representing data entities through their descriptors need not be restricted to rectangular, homogeneous arrays. For example, inhomogeneous linear lists can readily be implemented by representing each list element or <u>record</u> individually by a descriptor and linking these descriptors through pointers. A descriptor for the entire list may be added as the head element of the thus created linked list. Additionally, the introduction of a data type <u>pointer</u> provides the programmer with the necessary building blocks for the construction of arbitrary data structures such as trees, hierarchical lists, etc.

3.2. Variables, Structures, Data Types, Declarations.

In general, variables have as their value a structured set of data. Variables may be indexed. An indexed variable represents a subset of the value of the variable. BEYOND APL comprises the following structure types

SCALAR
ARRAY
LIST

SCALARs can be of one of the following data types

NUMBER
CHARACTER
LOGICAL
IDENTIFIER

ARRAYs are rectangular and homogeneous. Conversely, LISTs need neither be rectangular nor homogeneous; however, the records of a LIST are rectangular and homogeneous ARRAYs.

Variables are declared as to their structure type and data type. SCALARs and ARRAYs have only one single structure and data type declaration, whereas a LIST requires a list of such declarations, one for each record. A variable of structure type ARRAY can be indexed as in APL. A LIST is indexed by specifying a record designator and an array index list.

The record designator can be either a record index (an ordinal number indicating the position of the record in the LIST), or, alternatively, a record name. This alternative is introduced to increase the readability of BEYOND APL statements. Of course, record names are local to their LIST.

LISTs may be filled by entering entire records or subsets of records at the time. Moreover, it is possible to enter a 'cross section' or 'row' of the whole LIST. To this end, the following types of constants are introduced
(1) NUMERICAL/LOGICAL CONSTANT: Numbers, represented as in APL.
(2) CHARACTER CONSTANT: Characters, inserted between quotes (cf. APL)
(3) INHOMOGENEOUS VECTOR CONSTANT: List of components which are of type (1) or (2).
Generally, a list (in a declaration, an array indexing, an inhomogeneous vector constant, etc.) consists of a string of elements separated by semicolons. As a LIST may be non-rectangular, we need a syntactic form for a nil element, for which the APL notation'' (two quotes without a blank in between) may be adopted.

Before any operation can be performed on a LIST, the LIST must be dimensioned. As in the case of an array structured variable, a dimension can only be declared for a value but not for a name and, thus, the dimension of a variable is that of its current value. Consequently, though a variable is created through a name-attribute declaration (and not, as in APL, through the initial assignment of a value to its name), it must be initialized by assigning a value before any operation can be performed on it. To this end, a device is needed for creating a constant of the structure type LIST, e.g., in the form of an empty LIST. This is accomplished through an extension of the APL structuring operator (dyadic) (cf. the following section for the extension of APL operators to LISTs).

Data of the type IDENTIFIER are character strings which must represent valid names. If the value or an element of the value of a variable A is of data type IDENTIFIER, e.g., a character string representing the name of another variable, say B, then the referencing of A or of the component of A, respectively, returns the value of B. E.g.: Let A be a matrix of data type IDENTIFIER whose rows are the character vectors 'A1'; 'A2'; 'A3'. Let the variables A1, A2, A3 have the constant values 1 2 ; 3 4 5 ; 6, respectively.

Then we have constructed an ordered tree, as depicted by the following diagram. Note that the terminal nodes can be accessed by the appropriate indexing of A. E.g., we have
(A 2) 3   A2 3   5.

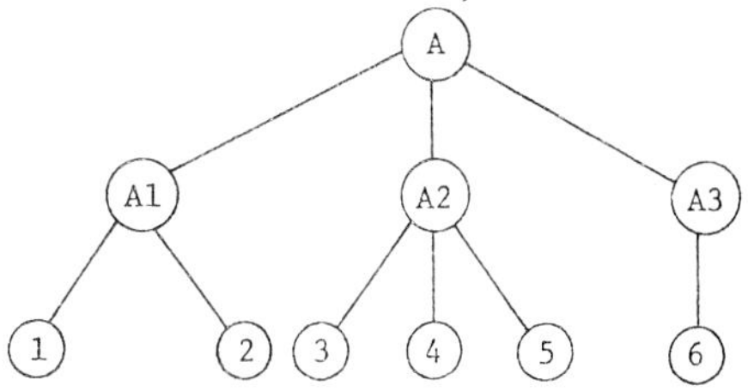

The reader will readily recognize that in the same manner more general, hierarchical structures can be built (e.g., cycle-free graphs). The data type IDENTIFIER differs from a data type POINTER as found in other languages (e.g., PL.I) inasmuch as a value of type IDENTIFIER does not represent a memory allocation but a name, in connection with a substitution mechanism by which the reference of a variable of type IDENTIFIER is replaced by the reference of its value which, of course, must hence represent another name.

3.3. Operators

As in APL, we find in BEYOND APL scalar operators, I/O operators, query functions, and structure operators. The scalar operators are the same as in APL, except for the ROLL function of APL which does not exist in BEYOND APL. The set of APL query functions, the monadic RHO and the monadic COMMA, has been augmented by the monadic use of REPRESENTATION ( ), a function that yields the data type code of its argument. Query functions can only be applied to arguments of the structure type ARRAY. I/O operators are
(i) The pseudo variables and ' (quad and quote-quad) for interactive use as in APL, i.e., terminal output and prompting of inputs.
(ii) Keyword commands for input from and output to files, printer output, etc. Structure functions are the same as in APL with the exception that in BEYOND APL one will not find EXPAND and the GENERALIZED TRANSPOSITION. These functions have been abolished for the sake of streamlining the operator set and eliminating illogical features. An array operation not included in APL, the MATRIX ROW PRODUCT, has been added.

All relational functions and the following selection functions

TAKE, DROP, COMPRESSION, REVERSAL, ROTATION, TRANSPORTATION

can also be applied on LISTs. The general scheme of the functions extension is to write instead of a single parameter a list of parameters with as many elements as is the number of records in the LIST. Moreover, the introduction of the structure type LIST necessitates the existence of special LIST operators, viz.

LIST INDEXING
LIST CATENATION
LIST COMPRESSION.

LIST INDEXING has already been discussed. LIST CATENATION allows the user to add a new record to an existing LIST. LIST COMPRESSION enables him to delete records from a LIST. The reader will have recognized that the set of APL data structures and operators is a proper subset of the set of structures and operators of BEYOND APL, with a few unsystematic or illogical features of APL /2/ being corrected in BEYOND APL. E.g.: The meaning of the two arguments of the function MEMBERSHIP has been interchanged in order to eliminate the existing inconsistence of the APL MEMBERSHIP function.

3.4. Procedures and Control Constructs

BEYOND APL encompasses two types of procedures: Functions and subroutines. BEYOND APL functions correspond with the APL 'defined function' with the proviso that there is always a value assigned to the function name. Hence the APL construct of a 'function without explicit result' does not exist.

BEYOND APL subroutines are external procedures of the statement type.

A subroutine may have an arbitrary number of parameters, declared as input or output of a certain data and structure type. Transitional parameters are those which are declared as input as well as output. The regular parameter passing mechanism, viz. 'call by reference', can be changed into a 'call by name' if explicitly declared as such. If no declaration is given, the default is the 'call by reference'. The scope rules are governed by the common nesting scheme, where an invoked subroutine inherits the access rights of the invoking program, unless variables of the subroutine are declared as local and thus shaded against the environment of the invoking program.

At present, we have no unconventional ideas to offer concerning the control structure of BEYOND APL. What we envision is a modern control structure that may be inspired by the thorough discussion of this topic in /11/. Consequently, we will probably have IF...THEN...ELSE, FOR..., CASE... . The REPEAT-UNTIL and WHILE constructs may be combined into the 'Dahl's clause' /11/ which is of the form LOOP...WHILE...REPEAT. For an interactive language, we deem it necessary to have an event-driven construct. Following a suggestion by Zahn /12/, this construct may be given the form

```
BEGIN UNTIL  event  OR...OR  event_n ;

                 statement list_0 ;
END;

THEN  event_1        statement list_1 ;
                .
                .
                .
      event_n        statement list_n ;

FI;
```

4. Conclusion and Acknowledgement

Abrams recognizes in his criticism of APL /7/ the procedure concept and the control structure as the two most severe deficiencies of APL. His conclusion, however, is to leave APL untouched until someone comes up with solutions to these problems as ingenious as was Iverson's notion of ordered set operations. We want to emphasize that BEYOND APL is not proposed as an improved version of APL. Rather, we want to carry over into a compiler language the valuable features of APL, namely its information structure, supporting so well transparency and data independence, as well as its unique set of operators on ordered sets. In order to remedy one of the shortcomings of APL viz. to have rectangular, homogeneous arrays as the only structure type, we introduce the inhomogeneous LIST of arrays as a natural extension. In our opinion, procedure concepts and control structures of high-level languages have become well-understood topics. Therefore, it is a rather straightforward task to devise a modern control structure and procedure concept for such a language. For the APL user, BEYOND APL will have the bonus that it includes the basics of APL as a subset, except for a few inconsistent and unimportant operators, the computed GOTO, and the 'function without explicit result'.

We consider the data type IDENTIFIER as the greatest asset of BEYOND APL, as it allows us to implement in a most simple and straightforward way any kind of data structure.

The author is gratefully indebted to his colleagues, Messrs. Dr. Donald Boyd, Dr. William Franta, Dr. Kurt Maly, and Helmut Berg, all with the University of Minnesota, for many discussions and valuable contributions to the concept of BEYOND APL.

References

1. Giloi W.K.: Interactive Systems: Patterns and Prospects; Proc. IBM Internat. Symposium on Interactive Systems (Bad Homburg, Germany 1976)

2. Giloi W.K.: APL as a General-Purpose High-Level Language - Potential Problems, Pitfalls, and Possibilities: University of Minnesota, Dept. of Comp. Science Tech. Report 75-19 (Second, revised edition, 1976)

3. Giloi W.K.: Programmieren in APL, Verlag Walter de Gruyter, Berlin - New York 1976

4. Giloi W.K., Berg H.: A Uniform, Algebraic Description of Data Structures; University of Minnesota, Dept. of Comp. Science Tech. Report 76-15 (1976)

5. Wegner P.: Programming Languages, Information Structures, and Machine Organization; McGraw-Hill, London 1971

6. Wirth N.: Systematic Programming; Prentice Hall, Englewood Cliffs 1973

7. Abrams P.S.: What's Wrong With APL?; APL 75 Congress Proceedings (Pisa 1975), ACM Publ., 1-8

8. Giloi W.K., Hoffmann R.: Adding a Modern Control Structure to APL Without Changing its Syntax; APL 76 Congress Proceedings (Ottawa 1976), ACM Publ.

9. Giloi W.K.: The Description and Simulation of Concurrent Hardware Processes in APL; Proc. Int. Symposium on Parallel Pro cessing (Erlangen 1976)

10. Abrams P.S.: An APL Machine; Standord University SLAC Report N°3, Feb. 1970

11. Knuth D.E.: Structured Programming With GOTO Statements; Stanford University Tech. Report STAN-CS-74-416

12. Zahn C.T.: A Control Statement for Natural Top-Down Structured Programming; Proc. Symposium on Programming Languages, Paris 1974 (see also /11/).

E. Morlet and D. Ribbens, (Eds.), International Computing Symposium 1977.

VERY HIGH LEVEL LANGUAGES : SOME ASPECTS OF THE EVOLUTION OF LANGUAGE DESIGN

Philippe Jorrand

Maître de recherche au CNRS
Laboratoire d'Informatique
Université de Grenoble. France

Abstract : The evolution of Computer Science research is currently concentrated in two complementary domains. One, on the technological side, shows a growing importance of microprocessors as building blocks in designing and architecturing computer systems. The other, on the application side, shows the need for highly reliable means for using these computer systems. The focus here on the second of those two domains where, in the great majority of the cases, the access means which are designed have the characteristics of languages.

Starting with some insight into the basic motivations which have been underlying the historical evolution of language design, we then characterize the state of the art in that domain. Behind the words "very high level languages" two aspects can be isolated which represent the main lines of efforts :

(1) High level data models and abstract data types constitute an attempt to build data description tools which are free of irrelevant, machine level, representation details. The efforts in that direction are related with all the activities in the area of program verification and make use of results obtained in a variety of other domains like, for example, data bases and automatic theorem proving.

(2) Aggregate operations, associative referencing, non determinacy and non procedural description of problems constitute a set of attempts for building control and environment structures which are adapted to a variety of problem areas by ignoring part or all of the control and environment details when they are irrelevant. Relational data base query languages can be chosen here as examples, but problem solving languages and systems, especially designed for artificial intelligence applications, have also put a very strong emphasis on such aspects.

For characterizing the evolution towards very high level languages, we describe the first of these two aspects and, in conclusion, we indicate some foreseeable implications of these efforts on the design of future linguistic devices for accessing the resources of a computer system.

I. A VIEW OF THE EVOLUTION OF LANGUAGE DESIGN

Accessing the resources of a computer system is done, in the great majority of the cases, through a language. That language is used for specifying the nature of the data involved in a representation of the problem to be solved, its internal organization and, in some form, the logical or functional relations of that data with the results to be obtained.

If one considers, from on historical point of view, the evolution of language design and of the various linguistic mechanisms which permit such communication with a machine, one notices that very soon, as soon as the definition of FORTRAN by John Backus (it was in 1954), a fundamental move has been started inside computer science research : the ultimate goal to achieve is to provide economical means of expressions which have to be natural to the problem area, which should permit to build and use with ease and reliability a representation of the concrete application area, without forgetting some rigor and discipline imposed by the usage of a computer system.

For that purpose, a first requirement rapidly emerged ; it must be possible to abstract from constraints which are specific of the own structure and behavior of the computer and which are completely irrelevant to the problem to be solved by the computer. This has been the starting point for the design of "high level" languages, as opposed to "low level" ones like machine or assembler languages.

FORTRAN has been the first such attempt to design a high level language. Then, mostly after Algol 60 /45/, a growing inflation of languages occurred and two schools have appeared. There were the tenants of special purpose languages and those of general purpose languages, both tendancies having their obvious respective advantages and drawbacks. But the increasing number of languages rapidly worried the implementors, in search for practical well suited compiling tools.

This is where the idea of "compiler compilers" originated, with much help from the development of formal language definition mechanisms. However, if compiler compilers have brought a great improvement in the construction of the syntax analysis part of compilers, they remained very poor in the semantic analysis and code generation parts, and they seemed very soon to have reached a kind of dead end.

This has been one of the reasons for an attempt to go along another alternative for language architecture. The aims were to get away from a large number of independent languages, thus suppressing most of the implementation difficulties, while keeping the respective advantages of special purpose and general purpose languages and eliminating their drawbacks. The idea stemmed from a very simple remark: since the user of a language is the person who knows best the nature of the objects and operations he needs for a "good" representation of his problem area, he should also be the person in charge of defining those objects and operations. In order to enable him to perform that definition activity, definition tools should be provided in the language itself which would then be called an "extensive" language /7/.

The general architecture of an extensible language comes then as a direct consequence of that idea. From a systematic study of the "fundamental" elements used in constructing programs, which appear more or less explicitly behind most languages, a "base language" should be built.

Then, two "extension mechanisms" should be designed: one in the syntactic dimension and the other in the semantic dimension. Their purpose is to permit combinations, in their respective domains, of base language elements, or of already defined "extended" elements, in order to construct new elements of a "higher level". Those new elements, thus obtained by extension, can then be used for writing programs, almost analogously to the way a variable can be used once it is declared /34, 49, 50, 60/.

Unfortunately, most efforts for designing completely such an extensible language have failed, for two reasons. The first reason is a practical one. The original objective was to design extension mechanisms for enabling an application user to define, in fact, his own language. But that user will not, in general, be also a compiler writer, although he is expected to write, in some implicit way, translation rules for expressing the meaning of extended language constructs in terms of lower level or base level constructs. Such an enterprise requires, in general, skills that the application user does not have. That ambiguity has been, from the start, one of the main troubles encountered by extensible language designers.

The second reason is a deeper one and reaches the essence of extensibility itself. Designing extension mechanisms is in fact the same as designing a formal language definition tool covering syntax and semantics and having a very peculiar property: it must be possible to automate completely the construction of implementations for languages whose definition is given with that formalism. We are then back into the compiler-compiler problem mentioned above, which has not yet received any satisfactory solution.

However, at that same time, it has been recognized that the construction of programs required the development of some rigorous methodology /17/. In that context, one very useful result came out of these efforts for designing extensible languages: the basic idea in an extensible language is precisely that of defining objects or operations in terms of more elementary objects or operations, themselves built in terms of even more elementary ones, etc.

down to the lowest level of the base language which provides access to the representation on a computer /35/. This is quite analogous to the idea of layers of abstraction, which can best be applied when the language which is used provides tools for that purpose. Especially in the domain of data, extensible languages have started the move towards mechanisms for describing rigorously, in terms of elementary concepts, the organization and the properties of the data used in a program. That subject, now known as "abstract data types" or "user defined types" is one of the main domains of activity in the design of the next generation of languages: the very high level languages /38/. We shall study it in section II under its various angles: the description of data structures, for the representation at the machine level, the description of data models, for machine independent data organization, and the description of data types, for abstraction and verification purposes.

A much less explored area is that of co - trol and environment structures in programming languages, although the evolution of the tools available for these features follows a direction parallel to that of data description tools and obeys to the same motivations. In the same way as the linear organization of the memory should not appear in the organization of the data at the application programming level, the essentially sequential behavior of the central processing unit should be the basis neither for organizing the actions to be performed in a specific application, nor for setting the way in which pieces of data are accessed. There are even cases where the notion itself of an algorithm can be eliminated. In that area, extensible languages have not made a significant contribution and most of the results currently obtained for very high languages come from languages designed for programming artificial intelligence applications /4, 54/.

For lack of available space, those questions will not be presented with more details in that paper, although they cover a whole spectrum of research topics which are of the same importance for the design of languages than the description of data: control and access structures adapted to the use of high level data organizations /21, 22/, non determinacy /20/ back tracking /4, 29, 31/, "non procedural" languages /38/, first order logic as a programming language /6, 12, 37/, program synthesis /3, 43/, etc.

In conclusion, we summarize the results obtained in trying to design higher levels of expressions in programming languages, we mention a number of yet unresolved problems and suggest some possible directions for future work in the area of very high level languages.

II. HIGH LEVEL DATA DESCRIPTION

In the design of programming languages, the description of data has long been considered, in the majority of language proposals, less important than the description of the actions to be performed on that data. This situation is now changing and most current language designers have recognized that describing the data is essential for the description of the algorithms themselves, which have to input data, to computer data, to organize data and to output data.

But, when considering that problem of data description, one is faced with several different ways of attacking it :

- first, the structure of the data, as it is organized in the memory of the machine, has to be chosen. That choice may be, in some cases, made automatic. But, in most cases, it will still have to be explicitely written in the program. Thus, a mechanism is needed for describing data structures.

- second, since the memory organization of the data is not, in general, relevant at the application level, it should only be considered as a (hidden) representation of some higher level model of that data.
  For example, one dimensional arrays of n-tuples are data structures which can be used to represent models of data organization like n-ary relations. Therefore, it must be possible to describe also machine independent data models. Both the data structure and the data model mechanisms could be available in one given language, thus providing a 2-level data description facility. However, most existing languages provide only one of them.

- third, since data models and data structures provide a framework for organizing the data, they already establish a number of implicit rules for accessing, modifying and using that data. For example, an array of integers may be indexed, but not used as a sequence of bits, a set of characters may be used for iteration over its elements, but not concatenated with a character string, etc. But although a given data model or data structure may have been chosen because its properties are "close enough" representations for these of the objects actually involved in the application area, these properties are not, in general, specific enough. Sometimes, they may even be completely irrelevant. This is why, independently of the data structure or data model chosen for representation purposes, a last level of abstraction is required for describing the rules which must be obeyed when using the data. That part, which constitutes the data type, specifies the way in which the application programmer actually views the data he uses and it constitutes the basic information against which uses of the data can be checked by an automatic program verification mechanism known as type checking.

Thus, we shall consider the data description problem in very high level languages under three angles :

- data structures;
- data models;
- type checking and data types.

1. Data Structures

For organizing the data in storage, two notions must be clearly recognized : the notion of value and the notion of storage object /40/.

The characteristic properties of a value are the following :

- it is immutable (a value cannot "change");
- it is storable (a value can become the contents of a storage object);
- it is returnable (operators may produce values as results, and any result returned is always a value).

These of a storage object are :

- it is referable (a reference value is used for "naming" a storage object or its components
- it is constructible and deletable (special operators return references to newly created storage objects and others may destroy them)
- it is changeable (a value may be "assigned" to its contents).

It must be noted that these two notions are related: references are values used for handling storage objects and values may be stored into and retrieved from storage objects.

If we consider, on that basis, most recent classical language proposals containing features especially designed for describing data structures, we can identify a common general approach which constitutes the main source of inspiration for very high level language designers on that subject.

a. Description of Values

For describing values, a number of different primitives are first provided and symbols are associated with them in the language, like:

integer, real, boolean, character

They correspond to sets of elementary values having specific memory representation conventions and which may well not be disjoint.

Then, some operators, drawn from set theory, are provided for constructing more elaborate - or more restricted - kinds of values. Some possibilities are:

- the subsetting, like in Pascal /33,61/ where the notion of scalar may take the form of "subranges" or of enumerations of symbols for representing ordered sets of values:

```
        1..10
(mond, tues, wed, thur, fri, sat, sun)
        mon..fri
```

- the cartesian product, which may also take different forms. For example, in Algol 68 /58/, where the notion of data structure is covered by the notion of "mode", it is called a structure:

```
struct (int A, bool B)
```

describes values which are structures with two components ("fields, in Algol 68). If x is such a value, then it has two "selectors": A is attached to its integer part and B is attached to its boolean part.

In Pascal where that notion is called record, one may write:

```
record day   : 1..31;
       month : 1..12;
       year  : integer

end
```

- the sequence, often called vector or array:

  [1:N] int

  describes, in Algol 68, values composed of N integers which can be individually accessed by means of indexing. In Pascal, there is also the notion of file:

  file char

  describes sequences of character components, only one of them being accessible at any given time. The other components are accessible by progressing sequentially through the file.

b. Description of storage objects

A storage object, which may be used for storing and retrieving values, can also be described in a systematic way, by telling the kind of reference value which is able to give access to it.

In many classical languages, like FORTRAN, Algol 60 or COBOL, such description is implicit in the declaration of variables. More elaborate languages, like PL/1 /48/, Pascal or LIS /14/, allow, in addition to that, explicit description of such reference or pointer values. In PL/1, it is only possible to say that it is a POINTER. In Pascal or Algol 68, the description is more precise, since it also tells the kind of value that can be stored into it. For example, in Algol 68:

ref [2:11] int

describes the reference values which give access to storage objects able to contain arrays of 10 integers numbered from 2 to 11. Furthermore, in LIS, the notions of index types and of references to domains allow an even more complete specification of the set of storage objects over which a reference value may range:

```
TYPE ELEMENT = PLEX SUCC, PRED: REF POOL;
                    CONTENTS   : INTEGER;

               END;

POOL: DOMAIN OF ELEMENT;

FREE, OCCUPIED: REF POOL;
```

ELEMENT is a data structure description for PLEXes (structures, in LIS terminology) with three components: SUCC and PRED, which are references to storage objects allocated in the DOMAIN called POOL, and an INTEGER called CONTENTS. FREE and OCCUPIED are also references able to range over objects allocated in the domain POOL, which are themselves only able to contain ELEMENT values. That ability to describe the kind of values storable into a given kind of storage objects gives an opportunity to broaden the description of values themselves, by using the union facility. For example, in Algol 68, saying that the contents of a storage object are described by:

struct (int A, union (int, bool) B)

tells that they are structured values composed of an integer called A and either an integer or a boolean called B. In Pascal, an even more elaborate way of achieving that is provided through the variant facility of records, also available in LIS for PLEXes.

c. Declaration of Data Structures

Thus, starting with some choice of elementary kinds of values (integer, real, ...) and using data structuring operations (subsetting, cartesian product, sequence, reference, union, ...) it becomes possible to build an image of the organization of every piece of data in storage by combining those elements in any suitable way. For example, in Algol 68, one may write:

ref struct (int I, [1:15] struct(int A, bool B)J,
ref union (int, bool)K)

But this is not yet powerful enough:

- it would be convenient to associate a symbol with a given data structure for identifying it;

- some pieces of data, like binary lists or trees, have a recursive structure whose depth may change at various points in time during execution.

This is where the need for a data structure declaration mechanism appears. Most classical languages, including PL/1, do not have such a feature, since they have not, in fact, clearly isolated the notion of data structure. But it is present in Algol 68, Pascal, LIS, most, if not all, of the tentative extensible languages /34, 50, 60/, and it must of course be retained for very high level languages. For instance, in PASCAL, one may declare:

```
type card = array [1..80] of char
type card = male, female)
type person = record name, firstname: alfa;
                     age: integer;
                     married: boolean;
                     father, child, sibling:
                            ↑ person;
```

```
case s: sex of

        male: (enlisted, bold:
                     boolean);
      female: (pregnant:boolean;
               size: array [1:3]
                     of integer)

end
```

(the case is an example of using the variant facility in records and ↑ person describes pointers to storage objects able to contain a "person" value).

In Algol 68:

```
mode bintree = struct (int value,
                       ref bintree son1,son2)
```

It must be noticed that, since we describe data structures, a recursive definition has to go through a pointer or a reference in order to be able to perform an allocation using a finite amount of memory space (as it is also the case in the above example of domain in LIS).

2. Data Models

The description of data structures is the necessary ground on which more abstract ways of looking at the data can be built. A first step in the direction of abstraction is to choose data structuring devices which no longer rely upon actual storage requirements, but upon a more mathematically oriented model of data. This is why, at that level, we no longer talk about data structures, but about data models, although that distinction may not always be made very clear in a number of languages. Algol 68, with its notion of procedures as values, Pascal with its notion of sets both tend to put data structures and data models at the same level. Other classical high level languages do not include that notion of data model and, conversely, a number of very high level language proposals do not describe data at a level lower than the data model.

Furthermore, some possible data models are not (yet) included, in their full generality, in programming languages but are studied in the context of data bases: a junction between the work in language design and the data models developed for data bases would then certainly be very fruitful.

Finally, if a language enables such machine independent data organization, we must solve the problem of finding a way to map this into data structures in storage.

a. Description and Use of Data Models

Data models are based upon simple mathematical notions: sets, relations and functions. We consider here the ways in which they can be described and constructed and, for each case, the main utilisations which can be made of them.

The most elementary data model is the set, which has been used in a number of very high level language proposals. In the construction of data models, there are essentially two ways of looking at sets, which are respectively analogous to the value and storage object concepts that we encountered in describing data structures /40/.

First, a set can be viewed as an immutable finite collection of occurrences of homogeneous values. This is the way sets are viewed in Pascal and also in SETL /52/. For example, in Pascal, one may declare:

```
type primary = (red, yellow, blue);
     color   = set of primary;
var  hue1, hue2: color
```

The variables hue1 and hue2 take as values sets of type color. It is possible to build sets, to return sets as results of expressions (union, intersection, difference) and to test for equality, inclusion or membership:

```
hue1:=[red]; hue2:=[ ];
hue2:=hue2 + [succ(red)];
if hue1 <= hue2 then ...
```

However, in Pascal, only scalar values may be elements of sets. This is not the case in SETL where, for example, sets may be members of sets, like in the result of the power set operation:

pow ({a,b}) has a result which is

$$\{ \underline{nl}, \{a\}, \{b\}, \{a,b\} \}$$

where nl is the empty set.

But sets may also be considered as some high level image of storage objects. They are then viewed as hosts for a dynamically varying number of homogeneous values. It is possible, in that case, to insert or delete elements from a set, to empty a set, in addition to the operations that can be performed on sets viewed as values. For example, in VERS2 /21, 22/, one may write:

```
DECL E : SET (INT); ...
ADD 5 TO E;
DEL 3 FROM E;
IF I∈E THEN ...
FOR I∈E DO ...
```

Statements with a similar flavor can also be written in LEAP /26/:

```
set XSET, YSET, ZSET;
    XSET    {a,b,c,d} ; YSET   XSET;
put e in XSET;   ZSET ← XSET - YSET
```

It is clear that languages like VERS2, LEAP (and SAIL /27/) and SETL, which make extensive use of such features, can be considered of very high level: they permit the specification of algorithms in a procedural fashion, with a minimum attention to the problem of detailed data structure design /19/.

This can go even further, when the notion of set is extended to cover also the notion of relation. In mathematics, the term relation may be defined as follows: given sets D1, D2, ..., Dn (not necessarily distinct), a relation R is a set of n-tuples each of which has its first element from D1, second element from D2, etc. The sets Di are called the domains and n is the degree of R. A domain, or a set of domains, whose values uniquely identify a n-tuple of a relation is called a key of the relation. Finally, a domain can be identified by a name called (in Codd's terminology) a role name /9, 10, 11/.

That idea of relational organization of data is currently essentially exploited in the data base area /5/. However, a number of languages have already included it, most of the times with simplifications or restrictions. For example, in LEAP and in SAIL, there is the notion of triple (a, o, v) denoted by:

$$a \otimes o \equiv v$$

meaning that the "attribute" a of "object" is the "value" v. In fact, a set of tuples with same attribute represents a binary relation. For example, we may have:

a = parent
o = John
v = Peter

This means that in the binary relation called "parent", there is the 2-tuple ⟨John, Peter⟩ .

In LEAP and SAIL, that data organization is known as the associative store. It is indeed the presence of such data models which opens the way to associative access to data items: it becomes possible to access data not only through the classical identifier or naming convention, but also by telling properties of the desired data item(s). Such facilities are present in languages like LEAP and SAIL where we may access the x ('s) such that his parent (their parents) is (are) called Richard:

$$\text{parent} \otimes x \equiv \text{Richard}$$

But associative access has mainly reached its highest degree of sophistication in relational data base query languages. For example, Codd has developped two query facilities respectively based upon the relational calculus /11/ and upon the relational algebra /10/. The language based upon the relational calculus, called ALPHA, is essentially a form of the first order predicate calculus, whereas the relational algebra is a collection of operators (like projection, union, interaction, ...) which operate on whole relations and yield new relations as results.

Given the following relations /5/, represented here in an array format (columns are domains and lines are n-tuples), respectively called PRESIDENTS and YEAR-ELECTED:

PRESIDENTS

NAME	PARTY	HOME-STATE
Eisenhower	Rep	Texas
Kennedy	Dem	Mass.
Johnson	Dem	Texas
Nixon	Rep	Calif.

YEAR-ELECTED

PRES	YEAR
Eisenhower	1952
Eisenhower	1956
Kennedy	1960
Johnson	1964
Nixon	1968
Nixon	1972

we may want to access the party of the president elected 1960. In the relational calculus, this will be written:

```
    RANGE       PRESIDENTS      P
    RANGE       YEAR-ELECTED    Y
GET W P.PARTY =∃Y (P. NAME=Y.PRES∧Y.YEAR=1960)
```

This means that, P and Y being variables declared as ranging over the relations PRESIDENTS and YEAR-ELECTED respectively, we get in W the value of the PARTY domain of the 3-tuple P which is such that its NAME domain is the same as the PRES domain of a 2-tuple Y which has a YEAR domain equal to 1960.

In the relational algebra, the same desired value would be the result of the following expression:

```
(PRESIDENTS [NAME=PRES] YEAR-ELECTED)
        [YEAR = 1960]    [PARTY]
```

That expression is evaluated in the following way: from the relations PRESIDENTS and YEAR-ELECTED, first build a degree 4 relation over the domains (NAME, PARTY, HOME-STATE, YEAR), whose 4tuples (there are 6 of them) are formed, in the obvious way, from the tuples in the original relations which have same president name (this is the join operation). Then, restrict that relation to these tuples (only one here) having YEAR = 1960, and project the result over the PARTY domain.

There have been many other query languages based upon the relational approach, using as well the relational calculus as the relational algebra /2, 5, 46, 47/.

However, the relational approach has not yet reached the same generality and sophistication in the programming language environment as it has already reached in the data base environment. This is certainly one of the lines of efforts which has to be followed, since it should bring a whole new range of facilities, especially for controling the global consistency of data, which is a problem almost never approached by programming languages. Other mathematically oriented models of data are also worth considering for that purpose /18, 23, 24, 25, 36, 59/. One of them, the data semantics model developed by Abrial, seems to be, in particular, a very interesting candidate for data organization in programming languages /1/.

Finally, a third kind of abstraction that we must consider here with data models is that of functions. If we start from the notion of relation, we may define a (partial) function in the following way:

> a partial function F from set A into set B is a binary relation with domains D1 A and D2 $\subseteq$ B such that :
>
> $\forall a \in D1, \exists b \in B$, b unique, such that $(a,b) \in F$

D1 is called the domain of F and D2 its range.

In a language like SETL, the notion of maps is an example of such a way of considering functions in programming. Thus, in addition to the usual, algorithmic fashion of describing functions by the procedure mechanism available in most languages, very high level languages also provide more mathematically oriented ways of describing them. However, in view of introducing a maximum knowledge about the functions of a program into the compiler (for checking purposes) the description of the functions must be given in a form which tells their respective domains and ranges.

This has been accomplished in Algol 68, although the data descriptions available in that language remain at the data structure level. In that language, functions are considered as values and, as such, it is possible to mention explicitly their modes: the mode of a procedure (representing a function) tells that it is a procedure, indicates the respective modes of its parameters and the mode of its expected result:

proc (int, bool) struct (bool X, int V)

is the mode of procedures which take an integer and a boolean parameter and return a structured value with a boolean X and an integer Y.

b. Mapping Data Models into Data Structures

The design of machine independent, mathematically oriented, very high level linguistic tools for expressing algorithms and organizations of data must be supported by the development of practical methods for translating these tools into working computer programs. The intelligent choice of implementation level representation for high level data models is here the central problem.

For example, let us assume that two sets A and B are used in a given program. The elements of A are initialized and then A is exclusively used for membership tests, whereas B is very frequently used for adding or deleting elements from it. Another family of sets, U, V, W, ..., are all subsets of one same set S and are essentially used within union, intersection, complement, ... operations. Although A, B, U, V, W, ... are all sets, they should have different representations:

- A should be represented by a hash table
- B should be represented as a list structure,
- U, V, W, ... should be bit strings.

The problem of automatic selection of data structures is currently a quite active research area /41, 42, 53, 57/. Some results have been obtained, especially in the framework of LEAP, SAIL and SETL. One of the basic techniques which are used is that of performing a static analysis of the program, constructing a flow graph of the program and then performing symbolic (also called abstract) /15, 16, 55/ evaluation of the program. This general technique, also used for more classical global optimization, permits here to build a model of the potential contents of all the sets and high level data models, and to partition them into various classes, according to the operations which are applied to them.

Such an analysis must also identify those sets and high level data which are used within the same expression or assignment statement: since the cost of converting between representations is usually high, they should have the same representation.

In addition to that static analysis, it may also be necessary to rely upon additional information provided by the users like, for example, the average size of a given set.

All that information is then used for evaluating cost functions and minimizing them. For that purpose, the system has access to a library of representations for sets, relations, ..., with space and time cost functions attached to each kind of representation.

It is clear that quite a similar problem exists for relational data bases. It still is an open research question whether the relational model can be implemented to form an efficient and operationally complete data base management system /5/.

Furthermore, even for programming languages, automatic optimization techniques for choosing data structures may often be inadequate. This is why some language designers have found it necessary to provide also means of choosing explicitly in a program the data structures felt to be best suited for representing data models. This is the case in SETL, where the writing of a program can be composed of two parts /19/:

- the algorithm is first stated in the very high level style of SETL. The program can then be tested and debugged by executing it at that level, using the standard general data structures.

- the second step is to construct a <u>representation section</u> which describes the data structures required for efficient execution of the program. The program itself is thus unchanged and if an error is introduced at that stage, it is guaranteed to be localized within the representation section.

3. Type Checking and Data Types

Telling the data structure or the data model associated with some object X used in a program may first appear simply as a good programming practice, which it is. But a compiler may take advantage of the existence of such descriptions for partially checking the correctness of programs. Saying, by means of a declaration, that X is organized accordingly to some data structure or data model D has tow consequences at the compiler level:

(1) It implies a <u>representation</u> for X, which will be obtained directly if D is a <u>data structure</u>, or indirectly, may be by means of an optimization technique, if D is a <u>data model</u>. Thus the compiler knows how to allocate space for X, how to perform assignment to it, and how to access it or parts of it.

(2) It defines a <u>rule</u> for using X. That rule can be stated as follows: X may be used by <u>operations</u> belonging to a set of operations implied by D, and only by those operations. A description of that rule is called the <u>type</u> of X.

Thus, choosing a data structure or a data model for an object X defines also the <u>data type</u> of X. For example, if P has been declared, in Algol 68, as having the mode:

<u>proc</u> (<u>int</u>, <u>real</u>) <u>struct</u> (<u>int</u> A, <u>bool</u> B)

the compiler is informed that the following operations, among others, may be applied to P:

f1: <u>call</u> P with 2 parameters: an integer and a real
f2: <u>select</u> the A field of the result of calling P.
f3: <u>select</u> the B field of the result of calling P.
f4: use the result of f2 as an <u>integer</u>.
f5: use the result of f3 as a <u>boolean</u>.
etc.

For example, it is correct to write:

<u>if</u> B <u>of</u> P (1, 3.14) <u>then</u> ...

Finally, given a use of an object X as operand (or parameter) to some operation f, the compiler is able to check whether f belongs to the set of operations associated with the type of X. That verification is called <u>type checking</u>. Most high level languages are designed in such a way that it is possible to perform that type checking <u>statically</u>. This has a number of advantages, like the possibility of completely checking the program before attempting to execute it, and an increased run time efficiency. That question has been particularly well treated in Algol 68:

- every named <u>object</u> (identifier, constant, ...) has a statically known mode (i.e. a type);

- every <u>expression</u> has a statically deduceable mode for its result (this is where the necessity of modes for procedures appears).

That property can be viewed in the following way: it is possible, in Algol 68, to "interpret statically" a program by performing operations on the modes instead of on the actual values manipulated at run time. For example:

```
at run time :      1 + 2          3
at compile time:int + int        int

at run time :   B of P (1, 3.14)  true or false
at compile time:B of proc (int, real)
                struct (int A, boolB)(int,real)

    B of            struct (int A, bool B)

                 blood
```

We may talk about concrete interpretation at run time and about abstract interpretation at compile time. That idea of abstract interpretation of programs is currently considered as a very important one for the design and implementation of very high level languages. Global optimization, choice of data structures for representing data models, interval analysis, etc., are in fact applications of that same idea /15, 16/.

However, as we have said earlier, the type of an object described by a data structure or a data model may not always provide a set of operations which are well suited for representing the properties of interest to a specific application area. Since we are interested here in describing objects through a notion of data type viewed as a statically known set of applicable operations, that remark suggests to start from the operations themselves:

(1) from the properties of interest of the objects in the application area, establish a set of relevant operations, by telling their names and various rules for using them. That first step introduces all the information required for type checking, if we consider now a type as actually built upon a set of operations. This is called the abstract type.

(2) choose an implementation, usually in terms of procedures, for these operations. For that purpose, it may be required to choose also a representation, in terms of data structures or data models, for the objects which will be of the abstract type. This representation can in fact be viewed as a means of retaining necessary information for the procedures which implement the operations introduced at the abstract type level.

In addition, that 2-level description must be done in such a way that the abstract type information, which is the only one of interest to a user and to the type checker, is the only "visible" part of the type definition. The representation and implementation parts may be changed without affecting the type itself, provided that they remain "correct" representation and implementation of the abstract level.

That general approach to data type definition is used in most current very high level procedural language proposals with, in most of the cases, a number of further refinements /8, 13, 28, 30, 39, 51, 56, 62/.

One of the simplest such mechanisms is the cluster mechanism of CLU /39/:

```
istack: cluster (n: integer)
        is push, pop, top, empty;
        rep=(tp:integer, stk: array [1..n]
                               of integer);
        create=oper () returns (cvt);
          s:rep; s.tp:=0; returns (s); end
                                     create
        push=oper (s:cvt, v: integer)
                             returns (cvt);
          s.tp:=s.tp + 1; s.stk [s.tp]:=v;
          return (s); end push;
        pop = oper (s:cvt) ...
          .
          .
          .
        end istack
```

It only tells, at the abstract type level, the names of the operations. Then, at the implementation level, it describes a representation for stacks of integers (structured object with an integer tp and an array stk) and, one by one, the procedures implementing the operations plus a mandatory "create" procedure activated when a new "istack" is constructed. In that part, the abstract type (istack) is conventionally called cvt and its concrete representation (the structure) is called rep. If S is then declared as being an "istack":

S: istack (50)

the compiler is able to check that it is used only through the operations push, pop, top and empty.

A much more elaborate scheme is proposed in Alphard /62/:

```
form istack (n: integer)=

 beginform

  specification requires n > o;
                let istack = <...xj...>
                 where xj is integer;
                invarriant o ≤ length
                 (istack)  n;
                initially stack = nullseq;
                function  .
                          .
                          .
                          top (s:istack)
                           returns x: integer
                           pre o ≤ length (s) ≤ n
                           post x = last (s'),
                          .
                          .
                          .
  representation unique v: vector (integer,1,n),
                        sp:integer init sp ← o;
                 .
                 .
                 .
                states mt when sp = o,
                       normal when o < sp < n,
                       full when sp=n,
                       err otherwise;

  implementation
         .
         .
         .
      body top out (x=s.v [s.sp])=
               normal, full:: x   s.v [s.sp] ;
               otherwise:: FAIL;
        .
        .
        .
 endform
```

A form, which is used here to define the type of a stack of integers, contains:

(1) a specification part, which constitutes the user's and type checker's sole source of information about the form;

(2) a representation part, which describes the concrete representation and related properties of an object of this type;

(3) an implementation part, which contains procedural definitions of the functions that can be applied to an object.

Not all the details of that mechanism are described here. We only briefly mention how the operations are defined.

In the specification part, the name of every function is introduced, together with types telling its domain and range, and with pre and post conditions, in Hoare's style /32/, expressed in terms of predicates on an "abstract representation" associated with the type being described (here, that abstract representation is a sequence, introduced in the let clause). Thus, if Aj is a use of an operation and y is an object of the type being described, we have :

$$\text{pre } (y) \{Aj\} \text{ post } (y)$$

pre and post being here the conditions associated with the specification of Aj. This tells that : if pre (y) holds before Aj is executed, then post (y) will be guaranteed to hold afterwards.

Then, together with other formal indications provided in the representation and implementation part, this allows a verification of the consistency of the form itself, by deducing whether the specifications are correctly represented and implemented.

Other aspects of the description of abstract types are approached, in various ways, in a number of proposals /8, 28, 30, 44, 56/. Most of them are still open research problems, like:

- types as parameters,
- relations between operations,
- validity conditions for operation calls,
- influence of all that on program structure,
- etc.

Furthermore, a unifying ground for all these aspects of the notion of type still has to be found. There are currently hopes that the idea of abstract interpretation could bring some light in that area /15, 16, 57/.

III. CONCLUSION

The evolution of language design is directed towards the construction of language features which provide higher levels of abstraction; they permit to write programs without paying attention to unnecessary details. This has been presented here in the area of data description. The same is true for control structures: aggregate operations /21, 22/ introduce various ways of implicitly performing iterations over sets or relations for achieving specific operations; non determinacy permits, among other things, to to specify that any one of several possible control pathes may be taken at some points in a program; with non deterministic execution and backtracking /4, 12, 29, 31, 37, 54/ it is possible to specify that a given result may be obtained by trying several alternatives in the values of some input parameters; some combinations of values will yield a "correct" answer, whereas others will reach a dead-end in execution, thus triggering an "undoing" of every operation back to the "wrong" choice of parameter values; etc. Here again, there is not much of unifying linguistic framework behind all those facilities.

Furthermore, most research on elaborate tools for abstract data definition is being made in language projects which are independent of those which propose those high level control structures. It is certainly possible now to start designing a really "very high level" language. It would have more than two "levels" :

- the "highest" level would permit to describe the relevant nature of the objects involved, their relations with each other, may be in terms of first order logic or analogous expressions, and to state the properties of the desired results, together with "rules of the game" for getting to it. This would mainly come from ideas in Prolog /12/, Planner /31/ and other languages of similar flavor. At that level, a program could already be executed.

- the next level would then permit a more precise description of the properties of the data, analogous to the specification part of an Alphard form /62/. That description would be essentially used for writing procedures providing, in a specific application, deterministic implementations of some of the otherwise non deterministic general mechanisms called at the highest level.

- the further levels could then cover the representation and implementation levels of Alphard - like languages and, even further down, the implementation level of LIS /14/.

REFERENCES

/ 1/ ABRIAL, J.R., "Data Semantics" North Holland 1974

/ 2/ ADIBA, M., DELOBEL, C. and LEONARD, M., "A unified approach for modelling data in logical data base design" IFIP-TC-2 Working Conference 1976

/ 3/ BERT, D., "Problem Specification and Algorithmic Programming" U. of Grenoble To be published

/ 4/ BOBROW, D.G. and BERTRAM RAPHAEL, "New Programming Languages for Artificial Intelligence Research" ACM Computing Surveys, Vol. 6, N° 3 September 1974

/ 5/ CHAMBERLIN, D.D., "Relational Data Base Management Systems" IBM Research, RJ 1729 February 1976

/ 6/ CHANG, C.L., LEE, R.C.T, "Symbolic Logic and Mechanical Theorem Proving" Academic Press, New York 1973

/ 7/ CHEATMAN, T.E., FISCHER, A. and JORRAND, Ph., "On the Basis ELF - An extensible Language Facility" AFIPS FJCC, Vol. 33 December 1968

/ 8/ CLEAVELAND, J.C., "Pouches : a programming Language Construct encouraging Redundancy" UCLA, ENG. 7555 July 1975

/ 9/ CODD, E.F., "A relational Model of Data for large shared Data Banks" CACM, Vol. 13, N° 6 June 1970

/10/ CODD, E.F., "Relational Completeness of Data Base Sublanguages" Data Base Systems, Prentice Hall, New York 1971

/11/ CODD, E.F., "A Data Base Sublanguage founded on the Relational Calculus" ACM-SIGFIDET Workshop on Data Description, Access and Control November 1971

/12/ COLMERAUER, A., et al, "Un Système de Communication homme-machine en français" Université d'Aix-Marseille Octobre 1972

/13/ CONFERENCE ON DATA: Abstraction, Definition and Structure SIGPLAN Notices, Vol 8, N° 2 March 1976

/14/ COUSOT, P., "The Systems Implementation Language LIS. An Introduction" IRIA June 1976

/15/ COUSOT, P. and COUSOT, R. "Abstract Interpretation: a unified lattice model for static analysis of programs by construction or approximation of fixpoints" Symposium on principles of programming languages, Los Angeles January 1977

/16/ COUSOT, P. and COUSOT, R., "Static Determination of dynamic Properties of Programs" Programming Symposium, Paris. Springer-Verlag lecture notes in Comp. Sc. April 1976

/17/ DAHL, O.J., DIJKSTRA, E.W. and HOARE, C.A.R., "Structured Programming" Academic Press, New York 1972

/18/ DATE, J.C., "An Introduction to Data Base Systems" Addison-Wesley 1975

/19/ DEWAR, R. and SCHWARTZ, J.T. "Data Structure Specification in the SETL Language" New York University August 1976

/20/ DIJKSTRA, E.W., "Guarded Commands, non Determinacy and formal Derivation of Programs" CACM, Vol 18, N° 8 August 1975

/21/ EARLEY, J., "Relational Level Data Structures for Programming Languages" Acta Informatica, Vol 2, N° 4 1973

/22/ EARLEY, J., "High Level Operations in automatic Programming" Symposium on very high level languages, SIGPLAN Notices, Vol 9, N° 4 March 1969

/23/ ELCOCK, E.W., et al, "ABSET, a programming Language based on Sets: Motivations and Examples" Machine Intelligence 6 1971

/24/ ENGMANN, R., "Set theoretic Concepts in Data Structures and Data Bases" Technische Hogeschool Twente, Nr. 111 January 1976

/25/ FEHDER, P.L., "The Representation-independent Language" IBM Research, RJ 1121 and RJ 1251 November 1972 and July 1973

/26/ FELDMAN, J.A. and ROVNER, P.D., "An Algol based associative Language" CACM, Vol 12, N° 8 August 1969

/27/ FELDMAN, J.A., et al "Recent investigations in SAIL - An Algol based Language for Artificial Intelligence AFIPS FJCC, Vol 41 1972

/28/ FLON, L. and HABERMANN, A.N., "Towards the Construction of verifiable Software Systems" SIGPLAN Notices, Vol 8, N° 2 March 1976

/29/ FLOYD, R., "Special Classes of C.F. Languages and their Recognizers" NATO - Summer School, Villars de Lans September 1966

/30/ GUTTAG, J., "Abstract Data Types and the Development of Data Structures" SIGPLAN Notices, Vol 8, N° 2 March 1976

/31/ HEWITT, C., "Description and theoretical Analysis of Planner" Ph.D., MIT 1972

/32/ HOARE, C.A.R., "An axiomatic Basis for Computer Programming" CACM, Vol 12, N° 10 October 1967

/33/ JENSEN, K. and WIRTH, N., "Pascal, User's Manual and Report" Springer-Verlag 1976

/34/ JORRAND, Ph., "Contribution au Développement des Languages extensibles" Université de Grenoble Janvier 1975

/35/ JORRAND, PH; and BERT, D. "On some basic Concepts for extensible Programming Languages"
ICS, Venice
April 1972

/36/ KERSCHBERG, L., KLUG, A. and TSICHRITZIS, D., "A Taxonomy of Data Models"
CSRG, U. of Toronto, TR CSRG-70
May 1976

/37/ KOWALSKI, R., "Logic for Problem Solving"
U. of Edinburgh, A.I. Memo 75
March 1974

/38/ LEAVENWORTH, B. (Ed.), "Proceedings of a Symposium on very high Level Languages"
SIGPLAN Notices, Vol 9, N° 4
March 1974

/39/ LISKOV, B., "An Introduction to CLU"
in /51/
August 1975

/40/ LOMET, D.B., "Objects and Values : the Basis of a Storage Model for Procedural Languages"
IBM Journal of R. and D., Vol 20, N° 2
March 1976

/41/ LOW, J.R., "Automatic Coding: Choice of Data Structures"
Stanford A.I. Lab. Memo 242
August 1974

/42/ LOW, J.R. and ROVNER, P., "Techniques for the automatic Selection of Data Structures"
University of Rochester
Technical Report TR4

/43/ MANNA, Z., and WALDINGER, R., "Towards Automatic Program Synthesis"
CACM, Vol 14, N° 3
March 1971

/44/ MORRIS, J.H., "Types are not Sets"
Symposium on Principles of Programming Languages"
October 1973

/45/ NAUR, P., et al., "Revised Report on the algorithmic Language Algol 60"
CACM, Vol 6, N° 1
January 1963

/46/ PIROTTE, A., "Explicit Description of Entities and their Manipulation in Languages for the relational Data Base Model"
MBLE, Brussels, R 336
September 1976

/47/ PIROTTE, A. and WODON, P., "A Comprehensive formal Query Language for a relational Data Base : FQL"
MBLE, Brussels, R283
December 1974

/48/ PL/1 Language Specifications
Order N° GY33-6003-2, IBM U.K.
1970

/49/ SCHUMAN, S.A. and JORRAND, Ph. "Definition Mechanisms in extensible Programming Languages"
AFIPS FJCC, Vol 37
December 1970

/50/ SCHUMAN, S.A. (Ed.), "Proceedings of a Symposium on Extensible Languages"
SIGPLAN Notices, Vol 6, N° 12
December 1971

/51/ SCHUMAN, S.A. (Ed.), "New Directions in Algorithmic Languages"
IFIP Working Group 2.1
August 1975

/52/ SCHWARTZ, J.T., "On Programming : An Interim Report on the SETL Project"
New York University
1973

/53/ SCHWARTZ, J.T., "Automatic Data Structure Choice in a Language of very high Level"
CACM, Vol 18, N° 12
December 1975

/54/ SHAPIRO, B.A., "A Survey of Problem Solving Languages and Systems"
Maryland University, TR-235
March 1973

/55/ SINTZOFF, M., "Calculating Properties of Programs by Valuations on Specific Models"
ACM Conference on Proving Assertions about Programs
SIGPLAN Notices 7, 1

/56/ SINTZOFF, M., "Composing Specifications of Information Structures"
August 1975

/57/ TENENBAUM, A., "Type Determination for very high level Languages"
New York University
October 1974

/58/ van WIJNGAARDEN, A. et al., "Revised Report on the algorithmic Language Algol 68", U. of Alberta, TR 74-3 March 1974

/59/ WARREN, H.S., "Data Types and Structures for a Set theoretic Programming Language" IBM Research, RC 5567 August 1975

/60/ WEGBREIT, B., "Studies in extensible Languages" Harvard University, ESD-TR-70-297 May 1970

/61/ WIRTH, N., "The Programming Language Pascal" Acta Informatica, Vol 1, N° 35 1971

/62/ WULF, W.A. et al., "Abstraction and Verification in Alphard in /51/ August 1975

E. Mortlet and D. Ribbens, (Eds.), International Computing Symposium 1977.

THE EVOLUTION OF RELATIONAL DATABASE MANAGEMENT TECHNOLOGY

W.E. King
IBM San José Research Laboratory
San José, CA.
U.S.A.

ABSTRACT

Since Codd's now classic papers in 1970 <1,2,3,4>, considerable international research has been directed toward developing database management systems which provide the user with a relational, or more informally, a tabular model of the data in a database. While much has been written concerning the potential advantages of relational database management, the central theme is the same that justified Fortran over machine or assembly language; namely, that the higher the level of a database language, the better it is for most users. Advantages cited include simplicity 5 (fewer lines to write, fewer decisions to make), and data independence <6, 7> (isolation from changes in the techniques used to store the data). Of course, these advantages are realizable only if they can be obtained with adequate performance in a realistic environment. This paper will trace the evolution of database technology in the past six years by examining relational database systems which have been developed during this time.

We have chosen to limit the discussion to relational systems which have been strongly influenced by Codd's work and therefore have omitted earlier work <8, 9, 10>. Also, the list of systems chosen for this discussion is not all inclusive; other excellent work has been done but is less well known to this author. The final caveat is that we will not focus on novel hardware-based systems but will limit the discussion to software implemented on conventional general purpose computers. The systems to be discussed are :

1. RDMS (Relational Database Management System) implemented in PL/1 on the MULTICS System at MIT <11, 12>.

2. REGIS (Relational General Information System) implemented in PL/1 on the TSS System at General Motors Research <13>.

3. XRM (Extended Relational Memory) implemented in BAL on the VM/370 System at the IBM Cambridge Scientific Center <14>.

4. INGRES (Interactive Graphic Relational System) implemented in 'C' on the UNIX System at the University of California at Berkeley <15>.

5. Query-By-Example implemented in PL/1 on the VM/370 System at the IBM T.J. Watson Research Center <18>.

6. PRTV (Peterlee Relational Test Vehicle) implemented in PL/1 on the VM/370 System at the United Kingdom Peterlee Scientific Center <16>.

7. System R implemented in PL/1 and an IBM system programming language on the VM/370 system at the IBM San Jose Research Laboratory <17>.

Specifically, we will examine relational systems from the following viewpoints :

1. Data Sublanguage. Codd's original idea was for a predicate calculus - like language and later he proposed the relational algebra. More recently, standalone languages have been developed which provide the power of the calculus and algebra without requiring the mathematical sophistication of either. Other research efforts have developed graphical languages using two-dimensional syntaxes and examples of the required data. Yet another direction is to provide relational capabilities in the common programming languages, e.g., COBOL, PL/1. We will examine the type(s) of language interface provided by each system.

2. Data Storage and Accessing Techniques. Various techniques for data accessing are well-known (multi-lists, inverted files, B-trees, hashing, etc.) but the key to database performance lies in choosing appropriate techniques. Because relational systems exhibit a collection of access patterns (sequential, associative, associative sequential), involving either a single relation or several relations simultaneously, these systems usually supply more than one accessing technique. Perhaps the key determiner of performance of any given technique is how the data are clustered on the physical medium.

The databases of interest here are much larger than the main electronic memory available and therefore must be moved between main memory and the secondary storage devices. This can be automatically controlled by the operating system itself or the movement can be under the explicit control of the database system.

We will examine the accessing techniques provided by each system, how data is physically clustered, and how data is moved from secondary to main storage.

3. Translation and Optimization Techniques. In supporting the high level relational languages, the system must translate the high level language onto the lower level accessing techniques provided. This translation process involves first parsing the input data statement, accessing system catalogs to find how and where the data is stored, checking the authorization of the user for the request, selecting a particular set of techniques for satisfying the report, and finally performing the required actions. We will focus on the techniques used for satisfying the request. Of principal interest are techniques for processing requests involving a single table, and techniques for processing "join" or multi-table requests. In addition, we will examine global optimization techniques which can be applied to sequences of requests.

4. Transaction Concurrency. A database system which supports simultaneous users accessing shared data must provide some facility for controlling the user's access to the shared data. This control is necessary to insure both the physical integrity of the data (pointers are correct, the indexes are consistent with the data) and logical integrity (the user is allowed to see only "valid" (data). To insure isolation between users, systems either serialize transactions (sequences of user requests) or provide a mechanism to allow users to control their interactions with others (locking). While this topic is not particular to relational systems, it does represent a major portion of concurrent access systems and therefore is of interest. In particular we will focus on the type of isolation provided by the system, if locking is used on the unit of locking, and on the technique used to handle the deadlock problem.

5. Database Recovery. Techniques must be provided to insure against catastrophic loss of data due to either system or user malfunction. System malfunction includes loss of DASD due to hardware malfunction, loss of (virtual) memory contents, an error in the database system itself, etc. User malfunction may occur if the user abnormally aborts the transaction, etc.

Several other areas could also be discussed including authorization mechanisms <20> , and techniques for supporting relational views <21, 22> , etc. We omit detailed discussion of these topics because they are not supported in enough systems for any trends to have emerged.

The paper examines the various systems for the specific techniques used in each area. To the extent possible common examples are used to illustrate the various approaches. Because the various systems have different design goals and constraints (size of implementation effort, support of application programming vs query environment, etc.), which are not always explicitly stated, our purpose will not be to evaluate the designs but to describe the various alternatives chosen.

REFERENCES :

1. Codd, E.F. "A Relational Model for Large Shared Data Banks". Comm. ACM 13, 6 (June 1970), 377-387.

2. Codd, E.F. "Relational Completeness of Database Sublanguages". In Courant Computer Science Symposia, Vol. 6 : "Data Base Systems", G. Forsythe, Ed., Prentice-Hall, Engelwood Cliffs, N.J., 1971, pp. 65-98.

3. Codd, E.F. "A Data Base Sublanguage Founded on the Relational Calculus". Proc. 1971 ACM-SIGFIDET Workshop on Data Description, Access and Control, Nov. 1971, ACM, New York, pp. 35-68.

4. Codd, E.F. "Relational Algebra". In Courant Computer Science Symposia, Vol. 6, "Data Base Systems", May 1971, Prentice-Hall, New York.

5. Halstead, M.H. "Software Physics Comparison of a Sample Program in DSL Alpha and Cobol", IBM Research Report RJ 1460, San Jose, Calif., Oct. 1974.

6. Date, C.J. and Codd, E.F. "The Relational and Network Approaches : Comparison of the Application Programming Interfaces", Proc. 1974 ACM-SIGMOD "Debate Data Models : Data Structure Set versus Relational", May 1974, ACM, New York, 1974.

7. Date, C.J. An Introduction to Data Base Systems. Addison-Wesley, Reading, Mass., 1975.

8. Levien, R.E. and Maron, M.E. "A Computer System for Inference Execution and Data Retrieval", Comm. ACM 10, 11 (Nov. 1967), pp. 715-721.

9. Childs, D.L. "Feasibility of a Set-Theoretical Data Structure - A General Structure Based on a Reconstituted Definition of Relation", Proc. IFIP Congress 1968, North-Holland Publ. Co., Amsterdam, The Netherlands, pp. 162-172.

10. Feldman, J.A. and Rovner, P.D. "An Algol-Based Associative Language", Comm. ACM 12, 8 (Aug. 1969), pp. 439-449.

11. Goldstein, R.C. and Strnad, A.L. "The Macaims Data Management System", Proc. 1970 ACM-SIGFIDET Workshop on Data Description and Access, Nov. 1970, ACM, New York, pp. 201-229.

12. Stewert, J. and Goldman, J. "The Relational Data Management System : A Perspective", Proc. ACM-SIGMOD Workshop on Data Description, Access, and Control, May 1974, ACM, New York, 1974, pp. 295-320.

13. Whitney, V.K.M. "RDMS : A Relational Data Management System", Proc. Fourth International Symposium on Computer and Information Sciences (COINS IV), Dec. 1972, Plenum Press, New York, 1972.

14. Lorie, R.A. "XRM - An Extended (n-ary) Relational Memory", IBM Scientific Center Report G320-2096, Cambridge, Mass., Jan. 1974.

15. Stonebraker, M., Wong E. and Kreps, P. "The Design and Implementation of INGRES". ACM Transactions on Database Systems, Vol. 1, N° 3 (Sept. 1976), pp. 189-222.

16. Todd, S.J.P. "The Peterlee Relational Test Vehicle - A System Overview", IBM Systems Journal, Vol. 15, N° 4 (1976), pp. 285-308.

17. Astrahan, M.M., et al. "System R: Relational Approach to Database Management". ACM Transactions on Database Systems, Vol. 1, N°2 (June 1976), pp. 97-137.

18. Zloof, M.M. "Query by Example", Proc. AFIPS National Computer Conference, May 1975, Vol. 44, AFIPS Press, Montvale, N.J., 1975, pp. 431-438.

19. Shu, N.C., Housel, B.C. and Lum, V.Y. "Convert : A High Level Translation Definition Language for Data Conversion", Proc. ACM-SIGMOD Conference, May 1975, ACM, New York, 1975, p. 3. (Comm ACM) 18, 10 (Oct. 1975) pp. 557-567.

20. Griffiths, P.P. and Wade, B.W. "An Authorization Mechanism for a Relational Database System". ACM Transactions on Database Systems, Vol. 1, N° 3 (Sept. 1976), pp. 242-255.

21. Stonebraker, M. "Implementation of Integrity Constraints and Views by Query Modification". Proc. ACM SIGMOD Conf., San Jose, Calif., May 1975, pp. 65-78.

22. Chamberlin, D.D., Gray J.N. and Traiger, I.L. "Views, Authorization, and Locking in a Relational Data Base System", Proc. AFIPS National Computer Conference, May 1975, Vol. 44, AFIPS Press, Montvale, N.J., 1975, pp. 425-430.

E. Morlet and D. Ribbens, (Eds.), International Computing Symposium 1977.

BRAINS AND PROGRAMS

B. Meltzer

University of Edinburgh

In the last 25 years or so many computer programs have been written which modelled cognitive activities of various kinds, such as : interpreting scenes, understanding natural language text, proving mathematical theorems, writing programs, acting sensibly in the real world (with the help of sensory and motor peripherals), forming concepts and theories, etc. These programs and the active field of studies associated with them are of much interest to both computer science and our understanding of the mind.

There is no sharp dividing line between such programs and 'ordinary' programs such as ones for solving equations or calculating payrolls, say. But the dimension along which they differ is what is interesting. For all such activities and tasks depend for their possibility on the possession and use of knowledge : knowledge about subject-matter, knowledge about how to do things, interpret things and solve problems. And it is the location and representation of such knowledge in good accessible and exploitable form which is the crucial issue. Let me illustrate :

One may write a program in Algol, to invert a matrix. This may be a very clever and efficient program, but it will be so because the writer has used his knowledge of linear algebra, of numbers and of efficient ways of operating with numbers to design it. But that body of knowledge is in his head, not in the program. If, however, we designed a program which incorporated some of this knowledge and used it to do the inversion of the matrix, then we would have written a 'more cognitive' program. Of course, even in such a case the programmer will have used still other knowledge - namely, of the programming language and efficient ways of coding in it. One could then imagine a still more 'cognitive' program, which would have a representation of this knowledge too, and so be able itself to generate the program for matrix inversion.

So, compared with ordinary programs, 'cognitive' programs are characterised by the possession of much knowledge, and since most of this must be of a general kind, they will be more versativle than the former. For example, one of those I have mentioned might be able not only to invert a matrix but solve polynomial equations with numerical coefficients.

The programming languages that have been developed for the writing of such programs are therefore different from the more standard languages. I shall very briefly review their evolution.

Since they are concerned with the representation of knowledge of all kinds, rather than with doing arithmetic, they must have a good, easy-to-use, flexible way of writing all kinds of symbolic structures. Also, one cannot generally forecast in advance the storage needs arising in any particular run of the program: for example, one does not know what the length or amount of search involved in proving a mathematical theorem will be; so storage register sets cannot be fixed in advance.

These needs were met by the first list-processing languages developed in the 1950's and 1960's like IPL.V at Pittsburgh, LISP at Boston and, later, POP at Edinburgh. These used nested lists of symbols, the basic operations being construction of lists and selection of symbols from lists. Available storage registers were allocated during run-time as required, while register contents no longer needed by the program were erased by a 'garbage collector'.

These languages were a great advance, but left much to be desired. They were still deterministic in the sense that the program-writer had in effect to specify the order in which the "instructions" or function calls had to be carried out by the interpreter or compiler. Thus, for example, in any part of the program, if any sub-routine or function was called it could only be some definite named one. But one wants, for flexibility and generality, the ability to choose one appropriate to the needs of the task in hand.

For this purpose one needs to use variables. Suppose, for example, at some point in a program for understanding children's stories, it has to find out whether John goes to school. Among a great many other items in its database it might have the following two (written here in LISP)

> (IMPLIES (BOYX) (GOSCHOOL X))
> (BOY JOHN)
> Now the program would first look up the database for an item
> (GOSCHOOL JOHN)

and, on not finding it, see whether any final item in an IMPLIES list starts with GOSCHOOL, and try to match the latter with (GOSCHOOL JOHN). In this case it succeeds by identifying the variable X with JOHN, so making the second item (BOY JOHN); the search in the data base for this assertion would be successful, thus achieving the original goal of recognising that John went to school.

This example, though simple, shows clearly the main features of the more modern languages of artificial intelligence like MICROPLANNER, developed at Boston, and PROLOG, developed at Marseilles.

Firstly, they are goal-directed : when the program is running, the computation may be and generally is determined by some overall goal or sub-goal. Secondly, they involve search in a database. Thirdly, they make extensive use of pattern-matching of symbolic structures containing variables (the above example of a single variable being matched against a single constant being an extremely simple one). Essentially, subroutine invocation is by pattern matching.

The knowledge of the program is in the database, where items may be of two kinds: facts or procedures. Although my simplified notation disguised this, the children's story example contained both : (BOY JOHN) is a mere assertion of fact, while (IMPLIES (BOY X) (GOSCHOOL X)) is interpreted by the program as : "if you want to establish that something goes to school, try establishing that it is a boy". In Winograd's famous language understanding program assertions played a minor part; most of the knowledge whether of syntax or semantics or of the world of discourse was in procedural form. There is little doubt that our own knowledge is of both kinds. To take an example from Winograd's stimulated robot world, if the robot was asked to put block A on block B, a procedure in the database would immediately check whether the top of B was clear and if not do something about it. You or I would do the same - we would not first do a logical deduction from some item of general knowledge like "no two things can occupy the same space at the same time". But on the other hand, if somebody asked us why the top of block B had had to be clear, we could give the right answer, while Winograd's robot would have no idea. Clearly there is here the not very well-understood issue of the trade-off between efficiency and generality.

The features of modern programming languages I have been describing, namely assertional plus procedural databases, goal-direction, search and pattern-matching, have resulted from studies of the problems of modelling particular cognitive tasks like board games, I.Q. analogy tests, question-answering, proof, etc. When one reflects on these features, it is not surprising that the languages of artificial intelligance seem to be evolving into some kind of system of approximate representation of human mental activities in so far as we understand them. What is the next stage in this evolution?

In my view, shared with probably many others in this field of research, it will come from schemes of representation wich take into account some of the more 'global' aspects of knowledge, which appear to be responsible for the apparent speed and immediacy of much of our thinking, especially of the commonsense type. As Minsky put it, the latter - so far from being some kind of search through a space of possibilities of not much structure - proceeds in a much more direct way by the use of large, largely ready-made, well-organised "chunks" of knowledge which handle situations on the basis of expectations.

Take his example of seeing a room. Just before you enter a room, you usually know enough to expect a room rather than, say, a landscape. You can usually just tell by the character of the door. The recognition of the door will trigger immediately a room "frame", as he calls it. If it is not a certain particular room that is expected, the frame might contain a representation of the following structure :

CEILING

LEFT WALL   CENTRE WALL   RIGHT WALL

a b c   FLOOR

If it is a particular room that is expected, the frame might contain other components, e.g. a piano in the far right-hand corner.

The cognitive system for processing the input visual data has a headstart in that it can fit the internally generated representations of lines, vertices, areas, etc. immediately to the appropriate parts of the frame. More to the point still, the frame itself can direct the processing, both by selecting what to process and how much of it - for example having established there is a straight edge corresponding to ab in the structure, it need not bother to "look at" bc.

Minsky summarises his notion of a frame as follows :
"When one encounters a new situation (or makes a substantial change in one's view of the present problem) one selects from memory a substantial structure. This is a remembered framework to be adapted to fit reality by changing details as necessary.

A frame is a data-structure for representing a stereotyped situtation ... A frame may be thought of as a network of nodes and relations. The "top levels" of a frame are fixed, and represent things that are always true about the supposed situation. The lower levels may have many terminals - "slots" that must be filled by specific instances or data."

I would expect in the not too distant future this fundamental aspect of cognition, which is already being experimented with in interesting natural language and vision programs, becoming part of the facilities of working and tested programming languages.

Some of my audience, hard-headed computer engineers and scientists, may be getting a bit restive at what might be considered the rather loose way I have switched in this talk to and fro between brain processes and computer programs, as if they were much the same sort of thing, so I propose to end by giving my view of the relationship between artificial intelligence and the psychology of thinking. It is not an entirely simple one.

Essentially, artificial intelligence is concerned with possible working models of cognitive activities. The natural question to ask is : do the programs do these things in the same way as human beings? In a sense one could say no, since the human brain system is not made up of transistors, condensers, magnetic stores, etc. But this is really trivial, since we would surely agree that the same Fortran program working on two differently designed digital electronic computers would-as far as the "brainy" part of the activity is concerned - be doing the task in the same way. So any comparison we make of an AI program with a human mental process must be made at some higher level than physical processes like flow of electric current, or even more "abstract" processes like movement of signal pulses from one bit register to another. But doing this kind of comparison of program with mental process is a difficult and subtle matter.

Firstly, it is not easy to specify what the "level" of comparison is, although in special cases one can get a feel for what it may be. For instance, one of the landmarks in earlier developments was Samuel's program for playing draughts, or "checkers" as the Americans call it. It evaluated potential moves by means of a weighted sum of a few numerical terms, each of which corresponded to some preselected features of the resulting board configuration.

Such features might be (though I do not remember Samuel's choice) the taking of an opponent's piece or the making of a King, etc. The program improved its performance by altering the weightings of the features according to its experience in playing against human opponents. Now at one level one could say that it is most unlikely that this is the way people decide what is a good move at draughts, for it is unlikely that we compute numerically figures of merit in this way. But at a higher level it is probably right to say that we do make judgments based on a few preselected features of the board configuration. On the other hand it is also probably that in improving our game by learning from experience we introduce new features to take into account in making this judgment.

But the great snag in making the kind of comparison we are considering is that so much of the processes that must be involved in our thinking and cognition take place below the level of consciousness. We would therefore, often, be able to make the comparisons only indirectly, e.g. by seeing whether an "unconscious" sub-routine in some other related, perhaps simpler, cognitive activity comes to the consciousness on introspection. (The notable Pittsburgh School of artificial intelligence led by Newell has made systematic study and analysis of protocols of human subjects).

However, my view is that ultimately artificial intelligence will make its main contribution to human psychology not by immediately providing accurate simulations of our mental activities, but by eliciting features and principles which apply to cognitive systems in general, whether they be machines or men, or for that matter dolphins or extra-terrestrial living beings. The advantage of studying these processes in programs rather than in human subjects is, firstly, that they are there so much more accessible for examination and, secondly, they are infinitely more amenable to experimentation.

I have already indicated how such general features are emerging and exhibiting themselves in the evolution of programming languages. Further development of this kind should provide human psychology with the same kind of boost as did the study of the chemistry of dead matter for this century's spectacular advances in our knowledge of the chemistry of life.

E. Morlet and D. Ribbens, (Eds.), International Computing Symposium 1977

CONCEPTUAL SCHEMAS, ABSTRACT DATA STRUCTURES, ENTERPRISE DESCRIPTIONS *

Michael E. Senko

Mathematical Sciences Department
IBM Thomas J. Watson Research Center
Yorktown Heights, New York 10598

This paper relates recent work on conceptual schemas in the data base area to work on abstract data types in computer science. It then suggests that a "real world association between two objects" be used to compare data models. An improved conceptual schema level for DIAM II is used as an example of this approach. This level is compared in detail with other proposed models for the conceptual schema.

INTRODUCTION

In recent years, both the "data base" and the "computer science" communities have been using abstraction techniques to simplify their areas of interest. In this paper, I will first use a philosophic approach to discuss and relate the use of abstract levels in the two areas. I will then discuss technical work on the abstract level that most concerns the data base community - the "conceptual schema" or the "enterprise description"**. Finally, I relate the abstract level work in the data base and computer science areas in more technical terms.

LEVELS OF ABSTRACTION

Abstract levels have been used as a problem solving technique in many areas. Informal use of the technique is found in everyday life - for example, in the construction of organizational hierarchies. More formal use appears in the physical sciences, in the data base area, and in the computer science area (for proving that programs meet assertions).

In the program proof area, the approach has been to build from the "bottom up" in the sense that the "computer-oriented" researcher starts with either machine instructions or procedural language statements as components and attempts to conceive of useful, ***well-defined*** higher level components (e.g. stacks, queues) that can be used in his proofs. If he can prove that certain sets of machine or procedural instructions meet his assertions about the components, then he can move his proofs to a higher level of abstraction and use the components to to prove things about even larger program components.

This "bottom up" approach is not the only way to deal in levels of abstraction - in fact, many problem solving systems seem to work "top down". The "top down" approach has appeared in structured programming; but the components that are used are ***ad hoc*** in the sense that they differ from application to application. In contrast, the physical sciences and data base research have worked to specify sets of components that cover all applications and which, therefore, have a general, long term viability for use in problem solving and teaching.

In the physical sciences, research started by designing a set of components and rules of interaction to describe the real world at a gross level of approximation. For example, an early level consisted of the components, earth, air, fire, and water. As time passed, this level was improved by noting where its properties deviated from the properties of the real world and changing the model to reduce the deviations. A better level was called the "periodic table". Its components are "elements" and their interactions are described by "valence rules". Even though this periodic table level is not a completely accurate representation of the real world (there are some chemical compounds it does not predict), it continues to be the basis for most work in chemistry.

---

*This work has been partially supported by the National Science Foundation under Grant MCS76-03142 A01, through a University of Maryland subcontract.

** The term "enterprise description" has been proposed by C.W. Bachman (1976) as a term whose component words have more meaning than "conceptual schema" for most users. (The term "enterprise" meaning, in general, any worthwhile undertaking.)

In addition to defining a gross level of abstraction for discussing large problems in a simple fashion, the physical scientists have defined a series of levels of greater detail which allow them to discuss smaller, special problems with greater accuracy. These levels include one that uses electrons and nuclei, and a second that uses protons and neutrons in the nuclei.

The work on abstract levels in the data base systems area has similarities and differences with to respect to the work in physics. Since the major application of data base systems has always been the description of real world resources - like physics, the anchor point of its levels has been the real world. In effect, the starting data base level - the conceptual schema or enterprise description - tries to be a close match to the complex real world behavior of resources in an enterprise.

There is, however, some problem in following the lead of physics in improving the definition of this anchor level. Physical measurements of the real world are relatively reproducible and uninfluenced by the model that the physicist is using. Therefore deviations between experiments and the model stand out in an unquestionable way. The physicist cannot easily force the real world to fit his model. He must acknowledge the deviations and try to change his model to remove the deviations. In fact, physicists are quite comfortable with the notion that models are imperfect and must be changed to fit the real world.

The situation in data base systems is different.Information about resources in the real world can be ***forced*** to fit almost any model. (For example, we have great experience with forcing information to fit into punched cards and onto magnetic tapes.) Deviations are complex and hard to spot and again we can force them to fit the the model. (For example, a small change in a corporation, a change in number of employees from 999 to 1000, requires a rather large change in a punched card model - the addition of a column to the first field on the card. Essentially all the boards have to be rewired.) Although the fact that the real world and the model don't behave similarly causes a lot of work, few people have questioned the model.

Similar differences between data base models and the real world continue to the present day, we can sense them in the inability of models to gracefully follow the evolution of the real world - much unnecessary reprogramming must still be done. Nonetheless since a model seems so simple, concrete, and consistent while the real world seems so complex, vague, and inconsistent, we tend to prefer to use the model as our standard.

For example with regard to mathematical models, one frequently hears that we should use a model because it is based on a mathematical theory - rather than that we should use a model because it provides a particularly good and efficient fit to the evolution of a real world enterprise. This situation is rather pernicious because it affects the quality of data base discussion. The ***precision*** of mathematical discussion carries with an aura of ***accuracy***. However, any physical scientist or statistician will tell you that the concepts are dangerously different. (It is better to be generally accurate than to be precisely wrong.) Accurate discussion in the data base area demands an attention to assumptions and consequences that is more often found in new science than in what Kuhn (1962) calls "normal science".

The question that data base researchers are facing then is how to discover a good model for the real world resources of an enterprise - a conceptual schema. And how to tie it back to the solid foundation of computer instructions created by researchers in computer science.

A "REAL WORLD" FOR DATA BASE SYSTEMS

The portion of the "real world" that we seek to describe in data base systems is somewhat different from the portion described by physics. It is a much more complicated task to describe an enterprise than it is to describe a few properties of physical matter. In both mathematical and physical theories, there are many objects to talk about - but many of the objects are, ***for all practical purposes,*** alike. And they tend to fall into a very small number of classes - the integers, the electrons, etc. In an enterprise, the number of interesting objects is not 10 ** 23, nor is it infinite, but there are thousands of ***significantly different*** interesting objects. Since we must have different names to distinguish different objects, we must have a more powerful naming structure for naming objects and their relationships to other objects. The single letter symbols used for objects and classes in mathematics and physics are simply not adequate.

It is also true that the behavior of the objects in enterprises tends to be much less mathematically predictable than the behavior of objects in physics. The system is much more a repository of facts based on observation of the real world than it is a basis for complex calculations which will predict new states of the real world. In a sense, data base systems lie at the far end of a spectrum which starts with models of simple physical matter with predictable states and goes through the complex models (like the weather prediction model) with less predictable states.

With ***simple matter,*** the input is simple and evaluation of equations will predict its behavior for many intervals of time. In the case of ***weather prediction,*** the importance of equations and the importance of input is almost equal. For each cycle of prediction, much new observational data must be entered. In the case of ***data base systems,*** essentially all the useful information in the model must be entered and the output is usually some simple selection of the contents of the model. Here again is a reason why physical models tend to be viewed as imperfect and data models are viewed as being "perfect". Physical models support prediction which can be and is checked, data models simply have to return some subset of the information that was entered in the form the data model specified in the first place.

THE CONCEPTUAL SCHEMA IN A SYSTEM DESCRIPTION

The beginnings of the notion of a conceptual schema can be traced back to the early notion of machine independence. In particular, the idea involves removing as much of the knowledge of the details of the computing process as possible from the description of a problem solution. Over a period of time, attention has been directed to the definition of a logical level that provides the best possible interface to the data base system user in terms of efficient use of his time. Among the properties found desirable were:

(1) Faithful representation of real world relationships. For example, the model should not exhibit computer-oriented relationships like the undefined relationships between fields in records, some of which imply spurious relationships between real world entities.

(2) Simplicity of concepts required to accessing the user's information.Understandibility for users. In effect, the user's accessing language should possibly have some of the non-procedural behavior of natural language.

(3) Stability of the user's programs to changes in stored data structures underlying the conceptual level. This property is often called "data independence".

(4) Stability of the user's programs to changes in the real world that do not concern his programs. In effect, a small change is the real world should not require sweeping changes in the conceptual schema (enterprise description).

(5) Ability to have one place to maintain a particular "fact". (For example, an employee's address should not have to be maintained in many different places in the conceptual structure. If there were many physical copies of the "fact" for computer efficiency, then the user should be able to tell the system to change the fact only once and the system should maintain the copies automatically.)

In Figure 1, we present the DIAM II "Double Funnel" diagram to indicate where the conceptual schema fits into the levels of abstraction for data base system description. On the left, we have the DIAM II terms (Senko (1976)) for the levels, and on the right, we have the ANSI SPARC terms (ANSI (1975)) for the same levels.

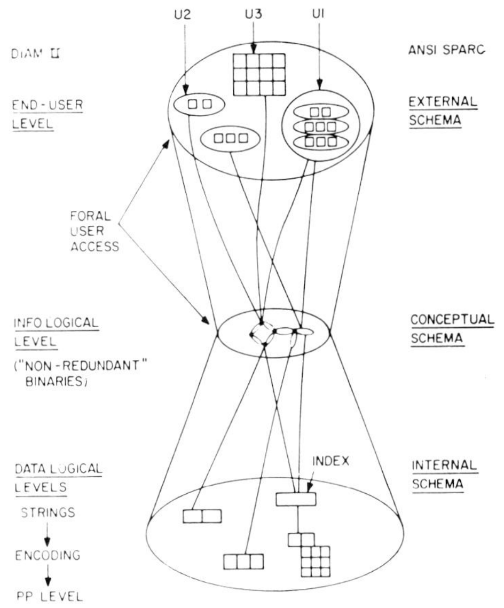

Figure 1 DIAM Funnel Diagram

The "conceptual schema level" provides a non-redundant, data-independent level from which the internal and external levels are mapped. It also provides a place for controlling system integrity and multiple user data sharing. The funnels opening upward and downward indicate that a data base system will describe and support a wider variety of data structures at its external and internal levels. The upper End-User Level is designed to support many (possibly redundant) data structure views for the End-User.

These views are designed to provide:

(a) end-user efficiency

(b) compatibility with data structures of existing systems (FORTRAN, COBOL, DBTG DML, IMS DL/I, etc.)

Similarly, the three DIAM II internal model levels provide a general set of file organizations to support efficient use of the computer.

AN APPROACH TO THE CREATION OF A GOOD CONCEPTUAL SCHEMA

In the study of conceptual schemas, we must first realize that each proposal for a conceptual schema has properties that are open to testing and comparison to analogous properties of other proposals. There are, first of all, the "qualitative" properties of the model. For example, Steel (1975) has proposed that the conceptual model be used only by experts and that it be a descriptive model. In his work he has used the language of formal logic as a basis.Conversely, I have felt that the conceptual model should be a communication medium for all users of the system and that it should have a very readable descriptive language along with a user oriented accessing language. Users will have to decide which set of qualitative properties best fulfills their needs.

Then there are the "quantitative" properties. For example, "how simple is the model relative to other proposed models", "how stable are programs addressed to it when changes occur in the real world", etc. Discussions on questions of this nature have appeared in the data base literature (Bracchi (1976), Schmid and Swenson (1975), Senko (1975), Sundgren (1974), etc.) and more are beginning to appear. In the following sections, I will make some personal comments on the unique aspects of a few early proposals.

EARLIER WORK ON CONCEPTUAL MODELS

The Information Algebra (CODASYL (1962)) was an early attempt to define an abstract level for the data processing area. The model contained the concept of entity as a thing that has reality and the concept of bundling (or joining of records on equal values of keys). It used the relatively complex hierarchic record as an information structure. Since a fact can be accessed in a variety of ways depending on the hierarchic record structure selected - and different hierarchic structures would be selected for different transaction loads, the information structure was relatively unstable to change. Although the Information Algebra recognized and talked about the real world, it did not make a very clear separation between a conceptual level and a data processing level.

Langefors (1966) contributed to the area by noting that separate abstract levels should be used in describing computer implementations of information systems. In his information level, he introduced the concepts of "elementary messages" which were binary "entity - property" relationships. An important aspect of Langefors' logical level was that it considered "time" as a special property of each elementary message. This foreshadowed the direction of recent work on conceptual structures.

Mealy (1967) contributed "Another Look at Data". This paper was more philosophic in tone than the earlier papers; it discussed three realms - "the real world itself, ideas existing about it in the minds of men, and symbols on paper or some other storage medium." Mealy's information structure consisted of binary "data maps" between entities and properties and binary "structural maps" between entities and entities.

Emphasis on Networks, Hierarchies and Flat Files for the Conceptual Model

In 1969, Bachman published a paper on data structure diagrams (Bachman (1969)) which were, in essence, a network structure for the conceptual level. These diagrams were an abstraction from the physical access path structures of the Integrated Data Store data base system. Nijssen (1975) related the CODASYL sets of Bachman's level to set notions in mathematics.

In 1969 and 1970, much discussion in the United States was focused on the separation of "logical" and "physical" levels. Both GUIDE-SHARE (1970) and Meltzer (1969) published on the topic of data independence - that is, the separation of the logical (conceptual) level from the physical level. In both cases, the conceptual level structure was assumed primarily hierarchic records - although extensions to networks were considered.

At about this time, some work on the specification of ***functions*** of data base systems was begun in the Information Sciences Department of IBM Research. In looking over the various possibilities for a "data independent level", we "overlooked" the use of binary associations. We did, however, study networks, hierarchic structures, and the flat file entity set model proposed by C. Davies (1967).

In reviewing these latter three possibilities, we decided that networks and hierarchies both had obvious access path dependence built into their naming structures and that they required quite complex data description facilities. Considering the more regular and homogeneous nature of the entity set model and the appearance of "less" access path dependence in its structure, we selected a form of the entity set model for a data independent level (or conceptual schema). Codd provided a mapping between hierarchic structures and the flat file structure of the entity set model and first published these conclusions as a relational data model (Codd (1970)).

The properties of this model were improvements over the network and hierarchic models in the areas mentioned above, but there were still problems. First of all, Codd indicated that relational language operations could produce results that were not meaningful in the real world. Also, there were problems with the representation of semantics of the real world as noted later in a paper by Schmid and Swenson (1975). Finally, the level was not "cannonical" in the sense that it gave no guidance on how one could achieve the desirable property of having only one place in the model to store a particular fact.

Some improvements on this situation were made by a further publication out of the Information Sciences Department on the Data Independent Accessing Model (DIAM) (Senko (1973)). This model gave Role Name Identifier Attribution (RNIA) rules for achieving one location for a fact in its data-independent "entity set model" level.

The DIAM paper also went deeper into the question of naming for the many kinds of objects that would be found in large data base systems. In particular it talked about "entities" in order to point out that a particular "entity" might have more than one name in the system (for example, a "person" might have an "employee number" and "social security number") and that the system should have a means for correlating information about the same entity - even though the information was stored under two or more different names.

Finally, it indicated that there were two separate functions to be performed by names associated with fields in a description. One function was to indicate the set of values that could be used in the field to stand for real world things (for example, employee numbers to stand for employees). Since this name would be used when the same set of values appeared in another description, it could be used to make connections to other descriptions (files) (for example, on the basis of employee numbers appearing in both files). The second function was to indicate how this field described the identifier ofthe record (whether a color was a color hair or a color of eyes). The terms used for these two separate functions were "Entity Name Set Name" and "Role Name". The requirement for these two names has more recently been recognized in the relational literature (McLeod (1976), Hall (1976)).

The paper also gave specific parameterizations for three abstract levels of a very general internal model for achieving efficient search and processing stored data structures. We will come back to these when we relate data structure abstractions between the data base and the computer science communities.

At the 1974 IFIPS TC-2 Working Conference in Cargese, Corsica, B. Sundgren presented a paper (1974) extending and detailing the earlier work of Langefors. A particular feature of this paper was the clear separation specified between an "infological level" and a "datalogical level." The infological level, like the conceptual schema, is to describe the enterprise in user-oriented terms. The datalogical level is for describing the computer oriented implementation of the infological level. This paper continued and extended the concepts of elementary messages and the use of time as a special variable.

Increased Emphasis on Binary Fact Forms for the Conceptual Schema

In another paper at the Working Conference, Abrial (1974) brought together the concepts of the logical level of data systems and the semantic networks of artificial intelligence in taking a step that returned to the use of binary associations. The step was a partial one because he still used n-ary relations at his network nodes - nonetheless, he emphasized the use of binary association networks. One difficulty with the model was that it still used a relatively primitive structure for "naming" objects. Another problem was that the accessing language was still quite procedural in character. For some purposes, this was, however, a useful feature of the paper - it provided the reader with a bridge to the traditional procedural languages of computer science.

At a later IFIPS TC-2 conference, a paper by Bracchi, Fedeli, and Paolini (1976) compared the properties of an n-ary conceptual level with the properties of a binary level. They pointed out that the n-ary schema still mixed logical and physical notions (a n-ary still has some properties of a record) and that this created difficulties in the areas of optimization and reorganization. For these and other reasons, they proposed a rather pure binary modelling approach for the conceptual schema of their multilevel model.

A BASIS FOR RELATING DIFFERENT CONCEPTUAL MODELS

The various conceptual models differ in how they categorize their basic elements. To indicate the differences, we will start with a very simple basic structure and relate the various categorizations to it. Our basic element will be an association between two entities as shown at the top of Figure 2.

On the bottom, we have a template for associations of a particular type. In essence, the entity that fills the position of ENTITY 1 must be drawn from the entity set named ENTITY-SET-NAME1. ENTITY 2 must be drawn from an entity set named ENTITY-SET-NAME2, and the type of association is named, "association-name". (ENTITY-SET-NAME1 may be the same as ENTITY-SET-NAME2.)

```
          ENTITY 1___________ENTITY 2
                 association

          An Association Occurence


ENTITY-SET-NAME1________________ENTITY-SET-NAME2
           association-type-name

             An Association Type
```

Figure 2

To start, we need a detailed set of parameters for one model to provide an illustration. On the other models, we will then need only to discuss unique features. At the 1975 IFIP TC-2 Working Conference (Wepion, Belgium), a paper on DIAM II (Senko (1975)) presented such a detailed set of parameters for a binary conceptual schema. In papers given at the following year's conference (Senko (1976)) and at VLDB I (Senko (1975a)), the parameters remained the same, but some of the names changed. In the following, some of the names are again changed for further clarification.

<u>DIAM II Parameters for Fact Types (Association Types)</u>

```
FACT TYPE

   ATTRIBUTE-NAME1 attribute-name1
                         OF entity-set-name1

             ⎧ 1 ⎫
     FUNCTION⎨   ⎬   [ NICNAME nicname ]...
             ⎩ M ⎭

     [ VIA attribute-name-v ... ]

   ATTRIBUTE-NAME2 attribute-name2
                         OF entity-set-name2

             ⎧ 1 ⎫
     FUNCTION⎨   ⎬   [ NICNAME nicname ]...
             ⎩ M ⎭
```

For example:

```
FACT TYPE

   ATTRIBUTE-NAME1 PROJ-OF-EMP OF EMPLOYEE

     FUNCTION M NICNAME PROJECT

     VIA EMP-PROJ-OF-EMP PROJ-OF-EMP-PROJ

   ATTRIBUTE-NAME2 EMP-OF-PROJ OF PROJECT

     FUNCTION M NICNAME EMPLOYEE
```

The DIAM FACT TYPE that corresponds to the "association type" in Figure 2 is drawn as:

```
                  ATTRIBUTE-NAME1 -->
ENTITY-SET-NAME1_______________ENTITY-SET-NAME2

                  <-- ATTRIBUTE-NAME2
```

For example:

```
               PROJ-OF-EMP -->
EMPLOYEE______________________________PROJECT

               <-- EMP-OF-PROJ
```

To discuss the fact type parameters, it is best to start with the concept of "Context" which gives DIAM II's conceptual model and its accessing language, FORAL II, natural-language-like properties.

In natural language, one interprets names on the basis of some known context - for example, the name "JOHN" has very little meaning until we interpret it in the context of a particular family. At the start of a FORAL II statement, Context is immediately established at some Entity Set and (until the context is changed) all names in the statement are interpreted as names for attributes of ***that*** Entity Set. The reason we have one attribute name leading from each entity set is because this again corresponds to usage in natural language. We use different names for the same fact when it is used to provide attributes for the two different possible contexts.

For example, when we are in the Context of EMPLOYEE, then the above fact will give an attribute of EMPLOYEE - in particular, the projects of the employee (the ones he works on), that is, PROJ-OF-EMP. However, if we are talking in the context of projects, then exactly the same fact gives us the attribute of project, employees of the project - that is, EMP-OF-PROJ. Each fact in DIAM II is symmetrical in the sense that the user can follow the association in either direction. Its interpretation as a attribute, as in natural language, depends on the user's context.

FUNCTION specifies how many attribute values there can be for each entity name - one or many.

The DIAM naming structure, like English, allows us to use short names for attributes. For example, when we are talking about employees, we generally say their "projects" rather than "projects of the employees". In effect, we use the name of the entity set at the other end of the attribute as a short nickname for the attribute. We can do the same for any one attribute that leads from one entity set to a second. This is the reason for the parameter, NICNAME. In fact, we can give a short names to any attribute of a particular context. The only restriction is that each name stands for only one attribute leaving the context.

Finally the VIA parameter allows us to define attributes in terms of paths through the network. (Since the paths are symmetrical, the path needs to be defined in only one direction.) VIA is particularly useful in defining Many-to-Many associations such as the association between employees and projects.

DIAM II Parameters for Entity Sets

To discuss the parameterization of Entity Set Name, we need to say something about entities and names. One can find the term "entity" defined in dictionaries using terms like, "object", "thing", "concept", etc. Although all the terms are talking about essentially the same kind of something, each term carries a slightly different connotation of concreteness or abstractness. Such definitions tend to end up being circular because something like "concept" will be defined using "entity". A better definition is:

An ***Entity*** is something that is so important that it ***will normally*** be given a ***Name***.

A ***Name*** is an ***Entity*** that stands in place of "itself" or "another Entity".

This pair of definitions are an improvement over most, and the reader may find that becoming comfortable with them helps in reading the data base research literature. The little proviso, "***will normally***", is put in to avoid infinite recursion of names. The starting set of entities of interest will all have "names". However, since these "names" are also entities, they should supposedly have "names" ***ad infinitum***. We put a stop to this in one of two ways. Either we say that an Entity stands for itself and therefore provides its own name - or, in the other cases, "names" simply won't be "named".

If we understand that many entities (employees, for example) cannot be stored and processed inside of computers, then we can recognize that we need to store something in the computer that will stand for each entity of interest - we will call it an Entity Name. We can now discuss the DIAM II parameterization of Entity Set.

```
ENTITY-SET-NAME entity-set-name

   [SYNONYM synonym]...

   PREFERRED-ENTITY-NAME-BASIS
                          { entity-set-name      }
                    IS    {                      }
                          { attribute-name-1...  }

   [CONSISTENCY-GENERATE procedure-name]
```

```
[[ALTERNATE-ENTITY-NAME-BASIS

                    IS  attribute-name-1...

[CONSISTENCY-GENERATE procedure-name ]]...
```

For example:

```
ENTITY-SET-NAME  EMPLOYEE  SYNONYM  EMPLOYEES

   PREFERRED-ENTITY-NAME-BASIS

                    IS  EMP-NO-OF-EMPLOYEE

   ALTERNATE-ENTITY-NAME-BASIS

                    IS  SSN-OF-EMPLOYEE
```

The parameter ENTITY-SET-NAME allows us to assign a name to each of the entity sets in the type description. SYNONYM allows us to assign additional names. The PREFERRED-ENTITY-NAME-BASIS allows us to tell how the preferred name for each of the entities in the set is formed and assigned.

One way of forming a name for an entity is to use names of one or more entities that are associated with it. In our example, an entity from the set "EMP-NO" associated by the attribute "EMP-NO-OF-EMPLOYEE" will be used in the system to stand each entity in the set EMPLOYEE.

It is also possible to use a combination of attributes. For example, the Entity Names for "DATE" are normally formed from entities associated by the attributes, DAY-OF-DATE, MONTH-OF-DATE, and YEAR-OF-DATE. For purposes of later discussion, we will call this kind of name a "compound entity name" and the kind formed from a single name like "EMP-NO", an atomic entity name. These terms have no formal standing in the DIAM II parameterization.

If the entities in an entity set are to be used as names for themselves, the the entity-set-name will itself appear again after the "IS". For example, if the user wanted employee numbers to stand for themselves, then the name of the entity set might be "EMP-NO" and "EMP-NO" would also appear after the "IS" for that entity set definition. When entities in sets such as "EMP-NO" act as "names" for themselves or for entities in other entity sets, we will say that the sets are playing the role of "entity name sets".

There may be more ways than one of naming entities from a particular entity set. (Employees,for example, might be named by both employee numbers and social security numbers.) ALTERNATE-ENTITY-NAME-BASIS allows us to define these other ways. When this paramenter is used, a table will exist in the system for correlating all the names for the same entity (for example, each employee's social security number with his employee number).

Finally, CONSISTENCY-GENERATE is used to tell the system how to check that a particular name for an entity is valid and if a new entity is to be described to the system, how to generate a name for it. (There are many standard procedures for consistency checking - the COBOL PICTURE clause, table comparison, range comparison, etc.)

Use of this parameterization with entity sets named by other entity sets gives the diagram in Figure 3 with the upper-case names representing ***sets of entities***. The asterisks adjacent to an entity set indicate the attributes that are used to name the entity set. The "A" indicates an "alternate entity name" for employees.

The diagram also contains the name "DEPT-MGR" in parentheses. This indicates that department managers are a subset of employees. We have not given the parameters for specifying subsets in earlier papers, but we will discuss them later in this paper.

Most of the associations do not need to be named because we can use NICnames for them. In the case where there are two associations between sets of entities (for example, between employees and departments), we have given the second association line a lower-case name which conveys it meaning.

Use with most entity set providing names for themselves gives the diagram in Figure 4 where most of the upper case names can be considered to represent ***sets of names*** for entities.

Entity Sets vs. Entity Name Sets

The diagrams in the two figures are capable of representing exactly the same universe of real world entities and real world associations. The one in Figure 3, however, requires substantially more names. There are, nonetheless, some compensating advantages. For example if the employee identifier is not tested in a program, then the program need not be changed when the employee identifier is changed from "EMP-NO" to Social Security Number (SSN). In addition, a class of employees who had a SSN but did not have an employee number could be easily recorded.

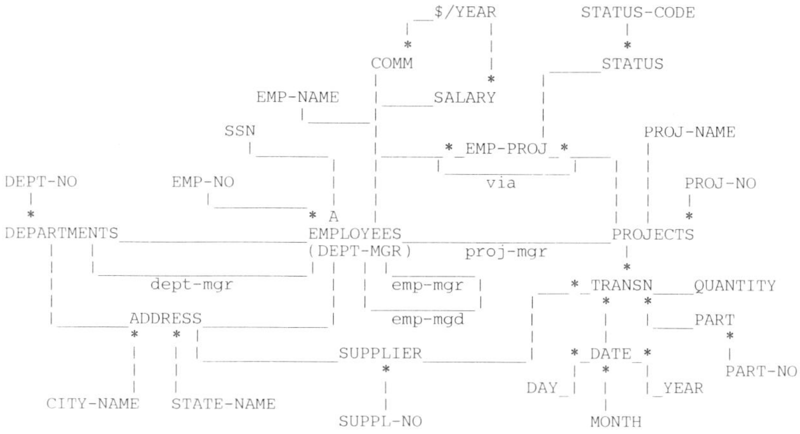

Figure 3 DIAM II Type Diagram - Mainly Entity Sets

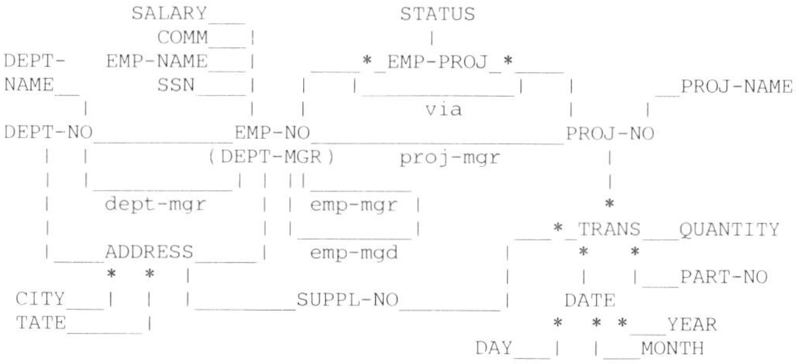

Figure 4 DIAM II Type Diagram - Mainly Entity Name Sets

We said "mainly" in the captions of the two figures because it is difficult to know in Figure 3 whether "QUANTITY" is an entity set or an entity name set. In Figure 4, "DATE" clearly is an entity set because its name is composed of the names DAY, MONTH, YEAR. There are researchers that argue for one extreme or the other with regard to Entity Sets or Entity Name Sets. (With careful study, it is often possible to find both types of sets in their diagrams.) In deciding on a conceptual model it seems best to allow both types and let the user, on the basis of his knowledge, choose which representation is best - on a set by set basis.

The above is the kind of discussion that will allow us to improve conceptual models on the basis of their properties. What we have done is compare two possible models with regard to two properties - "number of names" and "stability in the face of an identifier change". At this point in time, each researcher will give a different weighting to the two factors when he makes an overall evaluation, but as the discussion continues with more and more examples, it should be possible to develop a technical concensus.

At first glance, such a discussion may seem trivial. However, when you consider the number of instructions that would have to be rewritten in a large installation if the employee identifier was changed and we used the second diagram - or the increased size of the catalog, if we used the first - then it is possible to see that such discussions have far-reaching consequences.

English-Oriented User Languages for the Conceptual Schema

Earlier in the article, we suggested that the user's language for the conceptual model should have some of the non-procedural character of natural language.

Moving away from file and record oriented representations to binary associations means that the user does not have to mention the artificial terms, files and records, in his language statements. This simplifies the user's language. Even though it remains simple and unambiguous, it appears much more like a natural language. For example, the following is a statement from the FORAL II (Senko (1976a)) language for the DIAM II system.

```
output
DEPT-NO
     (where for EMP-NO,
            count PROJ-NO greater-than 3)
     print
     DEPT-MGR,
     average SALARY_of_EMP-NO_of_DEPT-NO,
     EMP-NO
for ADDRESS
     print
     SUPPL-NO.
```

For those departments where some employee works on more than three projects, the statement will print the department number, the department manager, the average salary of employees of the department, the employees, and the address of the department with any suppliers who have the same address. The lowercase names are reserved words for the system.FORAL programs call also be written by touching the nodes and lines of the diagram with a light pen (Senko (1977)).

RELATING CONCEPTUAL MODELS

In defining a conceptual model, the researcher must decide on a set of basic categories for the elements of the model. Much of the character of the model then depends on the number of categories and the meaning that the researcher assigns to each category. In the following, we will try to relate the categorizations of the various models. We will use the elements in Figure 2 as a starting point.

In Figure 2, there are four basic categories, "associations", "association types" (or association sets), "entities", and "entity sets". These categories, by themselves, are of use to us only for philosophical discussion because we cannot store them in a computing system. Even disregarding computers, we cannot honestly talk about the individuals in any of the categories because we have not defined a process for naming the individuals. We only reach solid and interesting ground when we define a process for naming the individual entities, entity sets, etc. In a sense, this what we have done in the DIAM II parameterization above. To actually compare models, we will really be more interested in the categories of names that they use and this is what we will emphasize in the next section.

Name Categories - The General Primitives of the Model

In the DIAM II information structure, we use three different types of names - Entity Set Names, Attribute Names and Entity Names. Since DIAM II uses three types of names, we will call it a "three category model".

Flat file models also seem to be "three category models" because they use File Names, Field Names and Values. However, there is general agreement that a name correlated with a field can perform two different functions - it can be the name for the domain of values for the field - or it can be the name for the role the values play in the record. When one considers both domain names and role names, flat file models are in reality four category models. Hierarchic models have names for both files and different kinds of segments within the files and, therefore, are "five category models" (although here again certain shortcuts which lead to ambiguity can appear to reduce the number of categories).

The above numbers are the numbers of basic categories in the models - researchers generally break these down into additional categories with slightly different meanings. There are a number of reasons for these additional categories, but a prevalent one seems to be that the categories suggested are "natural". "Natural" may mean that the researcher is using categories from his previous experience with natural language or with some data processing language. There is also often a tendency to feel that more categories imply a better definition of the problem.However, this is the case only when the categories themselves are well-defined and not overlapping.

The difficulty with having many categories is that they make the system more complicated and harder to understand. In addition, they may make it more difficult for the system to follow the evolution of the real world. Very frequently, evolution of "the real world" or "a user's point of view" may make it necessary to change an element from one category to another. When this happens, work is required to change to the new category, and even worse, the user's programs may have to be changed.

For example, in natural language, we often categorize things into "objects" and "attributes", requiring us to have two categories of names, "names for objects" and "values for attributes". If we have a single "employee file" then "employee" is obviously an "object" and "department" is obviously an "attribute".

Unfortunately, if we then create a "department file", we must change "department" to an object. Worse yet, suppose there is a user who wishes to retain a view that includes only the employee file - how should "department" be described in the conceptual schema - as an "object" or an "attribute ?"

In DIAM II, all lists of names or values are considered to be lists of Entity Names so no change has to be made in this case. This seems "unnatural" to many researchers and they have defined more categories in their models. We will now discuss some of these models.

Abrial's Model

The DIAM II conceptual model is a modification of Abrial's model (1974) and so it is not surprising that the two models are quite similar.

Abrial's associations are bidirectional and he calls them, "relations". He calls the directions, "access functions". (Access functions ⟷ DIAM II "attributes" and "access function names" ⟷ "attribute names".)

For consistency checking, the model requires a specification of the cardinality of the set that should appear at the end of an access function. DIAM II's FUNCTION parameter is very close, but not equivalent to the "cardinality specification".

Finally for the special case association where an entity set at one end of an association contains only one entity, Abrial specifies a new category of association called a "property". In DIAM II, this would be handled without adding a category by using the name of the property as an attribute name and entity set name. The entity name would then perhaps be, "Yes", if the property was present. There would be no association between "Yes" and any entities that did not have the property.

The main difference between the two models occurs in the naming of "entities". Abrial's "Category" ⟷ "Entity Set", and his "Object" ⟷ "Entity". In naming, however, the system assigns all "Objects" unique "internal names" which cannot be known by the user. (These internal names could conceivably be used to relate two different external names (EMP-NO, SSN) for the same entity. However, Abrial does not define such a mechanism.)

If the user wants to assign an atomic name like "JOHN" to an object, he may do so. This name is an "external name". However, if the user wishes to assign a compound name having the components, DAY-OF-DATE, MONTH-OF-DATE, YEAR-OF-DATE, to an object category called "DATE", he will find no obvious mechanism for doing so. This type of object still has an internal name, but it is not allowed to have an external name. Since the user has no way of knowning what attributes will give him a unique key to the relation, this creates a problem in maintenance. If one would look into what Abrial calls the generator function for the category, he might be able to decipher it and discover what is meant to be the key, but the key for this type of object is not obvious as it is for all entity sets in DIAM.

Finally, the internal name seems like a good idea until one tries to think how he would maintain it over a distributed data base system. In spite of a few difficulties, this model represented a major step forward. There are many features of the paper that are well worth reading.

Bracchi's Model

The parameterization of Bracchi's model (1976) is not as detailed as the two models discussed above. For example, entities, names for entities, and alternate names for entities are not yet strongly distinguished. In addition, parameters have not yet been given to aid in consistency checking. However, where parameters do exist, there is a very close relationship between them and the parameters of DIAM II.

Bracchi's Binary Logical Association" ⟷ "Association Type". It is also symmetrically bidirectional, but he does not specifically give different names to the two attribute directions.

His "Concepts" ⟷ "Entities", and his "Sets of Concepts" ⟷ "Entity Sets". For purposes of discussion, he distinguishes Sets of Concepts that are named by atomic names (Fundamental Domains) from those that have compound names. He calls these latter Sets, "Internal Sets of Concepts", but immediately points out that they do not differ from Sets of Concepts with atomic names. On this point, Bracchi's model and DIAM II essentially equivalent.

A very interesting aspect of his paper is the careful path of reasoning by example he follows to conclude that his binary model offers advantages over n-ary relational and network models.

Much of the discussion in recent years has compared the properties of n-ary relation models with binary association models. The basic n-ary model is a "four category model" in the sense that it uses Relation Names, Domain Names, Role Names and Values. Many of the proponents of n-ary relations have reconized that, as a rule, an n-ary relation will contain a number of basic facts mixed up in an indistinguishable manner. This leads to an unclear presentation of the semantics of the real world. And to certain difficulties in maintenance transactions because many maintenance transactions desire to change, not a complete n-tuple of a relation, but a single basic fact (for example, "change John's weight to 178"). As we have noted, some proponents are retaining the four category model but improving it by accentuating its binary nature.

Schmid and Swenson's Model

The starting point of Schmid and Swenson's model (Schmid (1975)) is the n-ary relation, but they quickly find certain semantic difficulties with the pure model. Here again, there is some careful reasoning by example. For example, they point out that there is not semantic difference between inter- and intra-relational functional dependencies. They also point out that relational theory gives no indication about the way in which the world should be represented by collections of relations. In effect, there is no guidance for achieving the desirable property of one location for a fact.

Schmid and Swenson's "objects" ⟷ "Entities or Entity Names" and "object types" ⟷ "Entity Sets". They do not distinguish strongly between "things" and "names for things".

Their "Relationship Instance" ⟷ "Association", and their "Relationship" ⟷ "Association Type".

It is interesting to note that although they define a relationship as an n-tuple, that is (ir(obj1,....objn)), all the examples of relationships that I could find in their paper were binary. In fact, if one looks at the figure they provide of their model, it looks very much like our Figure 3.

Although they imply that their model is n-ary, it seems - actually - to be a binary association model in n-ary clothing. This is particularly implied when they point out that an identifier of an object may be formed by concatenating keys of objects with which it is related. On this point again, they are roughly equivalent with Bracchi's model and DIAM II. Their point of departure is that they define a large number of categories of objects and relationships.

They first divide "relationships" into two categories, "characteristics" and "associations". This division is similar to the one frequently found between "properties" and "associations" in other systems. It is exemplified by the pairs, EMPLOYEE - CAR and EMPLOYEE - WEIGHT. In the first pair, both entities are obviously "objects" and therefore of similar stature. In the second, WEIGHT is not an "object" (or at least, appears not to be the kind of independent entity we think of as an object in English). They believe that there is an important fundamental difference between the two types of relationships.

They call the first type, "an association" and the second "a characteristic". They then go on to give a precise set of criteria for distinction between characteristics and associations. Unfortunately, a few paragraphs later, they say that the same relationship may be regarded as either an association or a characteristic depending on the user's point of view.

In DIAM, we have recognized that this distinction is hard to make and depends on point of view. Even though natural language makes the distinction, we have felt that it has no place in the supposedly "point of view independent" conceptual schema.

Schmid and Swenson do make the point that making such a distinction might help in formulating consistency rules for update and insertion. However, personally it seems that it would be better to treat the problem in the context of the consistency rules for update and insertion rather than indirectly in the data structure definition where the distinction is point of view dependent and therefore not fundamental.

The paper then goes on to categorize objects into "independent objects" (like employee) and "characteristic objects" (like weight). "Complex independent objects" are independent objects with all their characteristics and characteristics of characteristics, etc. A "simple independent object" has no characteristics. There other categories which, like these, seem to be more for purposes of discussion than to be "required naming categories" in their model. They also discuss "repeating" and "non-repeating" characteristics which are equivalent to the FUNCTION parameter above. The paper concludes with an excellent discussion of the semantics of insertion and deletion.

Hall, Owlett, and Todd's Model - Irreducible N-aries

While Schmid and Swenson have moved to emphasize more semantics in their model, Hall, Owlett, and Todd (1976) seem to emphasize mathematical form. They recognize that most n-aries contain more than one basic fact, and therefore suggest a formal method for reducing the n-aries to basic facts. In the process of this reduction, they, however, seem to throw away the concepts of "primary keys" which in many systems give some hint of the semantics of the relation.

Their "Entities" ⟷ "Entities", their "Entity Domains" ⟷ "Entity Sets". At this point, they depart from the other models because they are not satisfied with their naming procedures. In particular, they do not wish to require the user to invent a set of unique names for each entity set (for example, employee numbers), and yet they are worried that any set of attributes will not give unique identification either. They solve this problem by assigning a "surrogate" to each entity. "Surrogates" are a collection of unique objects which act as the representatives of the objects in the outside world. A surrogate could be something like Abrial's internal identifier, but they imply that it could be something else - for example, a row in a table, etc. Unfortunately, they do not give a mechanism for guaranteeing that a set of columns in a table will give unique identification. (This is the same problem as guaranteeing that a set of attributes will give unique identification.) In effect, there may be some difficulty for the user to determine how to access a surrogate that he is interested in since unique atomic external names are not considered. If these problems could be solved, then the surrogate could be used to correlate information about an entity in the same way that the Preferred and Alternate Entity Names in DIAM are used.

Since their way of dealing with associations is somewhat table oriented, it is a little difficult to translate into our earlier terms. One way to think of it, however, is to consider that they have defined a special class of entity sets called "relations". Each element in such a set is called an "n-tuple". Each "n-tuple entity is related to each of its "values" by a "selector" ⟷ "association-type-name". (A role name in DIAM I terms.) The "sets of values" ⟷ "Entity Name Sets". There is no interconnection between the special class entities, these connections must be made by program.

The major innovation in the model is its recognition that n-aries should be reduced to the size of basic facts. They indicate a mathematical process for doing this, but it may be that one needs to know the basic binary network of the problem to get a good decomposition. They believe that irreducible n-aries have advantages over pure binaries. We will address this issue in the following sections.

SOME DISCUSSION POINTS

Asymmetry in Many-to-One and One-to-Many Relationships

The question is what kind of properties does this additional category give the four category systems with regard to the three category systems. In the first place, it makes the accessing language a little more complex. The user must use different kinds of language statements to move between associations than he uses when moving inside of associations. For example, a relational user can simply ask for any attributes that the "primary key" is many-to-one with (for example, `DEPT.ADDRESS`), but to get attributes that are many-to-one with the primary key, he must go to a different syntax form where he indicates a match to another relation (usually with a construct like - `"DEPT.DEPT-NO = EMP.DEPT-NO"`). At least in the binary language FORAL II (Senko (1976a)), there is no syntax distinction. For example, one could write the query:

```
output
DEPT-NO
      print
      ADDRESS,
      EMP-NO.
```

In this case (as in natural language), the user doesn't have to treat the two types of associations differently.

"Excess Entity Sets" or "Excess Name Categories" ?

Another discussion deals with what is perjoratively called the "excess entity set" (Hall (1976)). The entity so called often appears in the representation of a many-to-many relationship - for example, employees with projects. This argument is illustrated in Figure 5.

```
      ___* EMP-PROJ ____
      |        *        |
      |        |        |
   EMP-NO   PROJ-NO   STATUS

      BINARY REPRESENTATION


EMP-PROJ
 ______________________________
|         |           |        |
| EMP-NO  | PROJ-NO   | STATUS |
|_________|___________|________|

IRREDUCIBLE N-ARY REPRESENTATION
```

Figure 5

It is said that to give the property, STATUS, to the relationship between EMP-NO and PROJECT, in the binary approach that the user must create the "excess entity" EMP-PROJ. It is also said that the "excess entity" is unnatural and has no meaning in the "real world". Of course, to handle the same problem using irreducible entities, the user must create an irreducible n-ary (which is not an entity ?). This "nonentity" somehow is considered to be more natural and to have more meaning in the "real world".

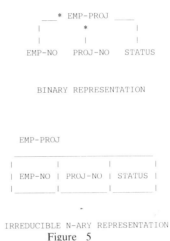

In a more technical sense, it can be seen that both forms in Figure 5 require the same number of names, four each. So that there is in no sense an "excess" in the binary form in terms of names, the final thing that the user must wrestle with. The irreducible n-ary form does, however, call for a heterogeneous set of constructs at the Conceptual Level. Some things are set of entities and others are sets of something different, irreducible n-aries. Whether these latter constructs are more "natural" than entities is a matter of opinion. In refering to Figure 6, we get some additional properties.

```
          ___* EMP-PROJ  ____________
          |       *     |___         |
          |       |       |          |
EMP-NO    PROJ-NO    STATUS    START-DATE

          BINARY REPRESENTATION


    EMP-PROJ
   ____________________________
  |         |          |        |
  | EMP-NO  | PROJ-NO  | STATUS |
  |_________|__________|________|

    EMP-PROJ1
   __________________________________
  |         |          |             |
  | EMP-NO  | PROJ-NO  | START-DATE  |
  |_________|__________|_____________|

      IRREDUCIBLE N-ARY REPRESENTATION
```

Figure 6

In Figure 6, we have added a second property, START-DATE. The addition of this property causes a greater divergence in how the two representations seem to work. In the binary case, the property is added easily to the "excess entity" EMP-PROJ, which looks even more real. In the irreducible form however a new "excess irreducible n-ary" must be created. The number of names required to handle the change in Figure 6 differs. Pure binaries require only five whereas irreducible n-aries require six. On this technical basis, binaries seem to be simpler. A second consideration is the way in which EMP-PROJ relates STATUS and START-DATE in the binary form. In this case, they are clearly seen to be related by being properties of one "real world" entity. In the n-ary form, it is not clear whether they are related or not, one needs some additional information to find out. In this sense, the binaries have more semantic content.

Many-to-Many Relationships - Associations that Evolve to Become Entities

Another issue in the model area is whether the associations should be "functions" or not. That is, in an association, should at least one of the attributes have only a single value for each entity in the set being described. In systems that have some background from "record oriented representations", it is difficult to represent many-to-many relationships and therefore there has been a bias against using them in models. This bias, for example, exists in n-ary relational models. One must create a new relation to represent the many-to-many relationship. In DIAM, we must do the same thing, but this can be disguised from the user by the VIA function so he can talk simply about employees and projects, for example. This is not an exciting solution, but it does seem to be a feasible one.

A more interesting problem is concerned with the possibility of a association acquiring attributes of its own and therefore evolving to become an entity. In DIAM, this can be handled by defining a new entity with a new name that fits in between the two old entities. New associations are then defined to attach this new entity to the old ones. The old association is then defined in terms of the new ones by a VIA operation. When FORAL is used and Context is changed by moving over the VIA, then the Context resides also at the new entity. this way old programs can be preserved if the meaning of the name assigned to the attribute has not changed.

Subsets - Unions

In DIAM as in most systems, it is relatively easy to declare subsets of entity sets and give them names. Essentially, what one does is give the qualifications on the members of the entity set which allow them to become members of the named subset. For example, for the "DEPT-MGR" subset mentioned above, we would simply declare that department manager is an employee where "department managed exists". This declaration would be done as a phrase in a user language so it could be substituted for DEPT-MGR in the users program statements.

There has also been some question of how a system would deal with "unions" of existing sets. Whenever one talks about things like this, it is important to know how the naming mechanism will operate. That is, when one defines a union in his program, exactly how will the name of the union be read and interpreted. For example, one conceivable way this could be done in DIAM is to in effect declare a new "Entity Set" whose elements were members of other entity sets. This seems simple enough, but there is a catch - if the sets are not disjoint, how do you correlate entities from the old that are the same ? You, of course, must construct a table relating their names. Any system must be prepared ask the user to do when he calls for a "union".

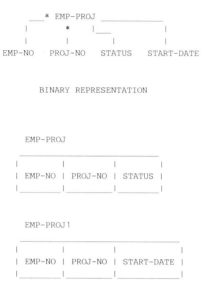

Time

In the sections above, we have discussed the importance of having a conceptual schema that evolves through time, but we have said nothing about how such a schema should treat ""time"". There has been some discussion of this problem in the writings of Langefors (1966) and Sundgren (1974) and more recently in the work of Bubenko (1976). One paper that gives some detailed operations is that of Falkenberg (1975) which is based on a paper by Bruce (1972).

These authors discuss models which use time intervals. In effect, each entity and each association is considered to have a beginning time. They may then have an ending time or they may be valid for all time (for example, a person's birthdate). Unlike existing systems where "facts" disappear into father and grandfather files never to be seen again, A system like this simply accumulates facts. As a start to providing such capabilities in a DIAM system, we must define a parameter to add to both the entity set and the fact type specifications. The parameter is simply:

```
TIME GIVEN BY entity-set-name
```

The entity set then defines the time interval and the representation of time. It is assumed that each association and entity set will have both a beginning and ending time (the last may be infinite time).

The final requirement is one on the accessing language rather than the conceptual schema. The accessing language must have relations which can compare intervals of various kinds. Falkenberg gives a listing of operations proposed by Bruce. If FORAL would include such relational tests, then DIAM would be further improved.

CONCLUSIONS ON CONCEPTUAL MODELS

In the above, we have reviewed a number of conceptual models and discussed their properties. It is still a matter of personal opinion as to which properties of which models are best. Like physics, we still can improve.

With regard to my own model, I feel that the addition of subset capability and the new FORAL languages has improved it and now it is, perhaps, ninety-five percent accurate - an improvement of five percent.

DATABASE ABSTRACTIONS AND COMPUTER SCIENCE ABSTRACTIONS

The character of abstractions is different in the data base and computer science areas.

The real world of concern for computer scientists includes machine instructions, operating systems and procedural language compilers - computer scientists have been mainly concerned with abstractions for dealing with procedures and have been less concerned with abstractions dealing with general types of data structures.

As we have mentioned, the real world for data base systems covers the general representation of resources and their interaction. Data base researchers are mainly concerned with abstractions with respect to data structures; they have been somewhat, but less, concerned with discussing underlying procedures for the manipulation of these data structures.

Although the data base real world in a sense covers computing systems, data base researchers have addressed computing systems in much less detail than the computer scientists. This is one reason why the two areas have different notions of the term, semantics". In the data base area, we are concerned with a "semantics" that closely corresponds with the term in use in natural language. The constructs of our models have "semantic" content in so much as they correctly mirror the behavior of the real world resources. The constructs in computer science have correct "semantics" if they faithfully mirror the intended behavior of particular program functions like "stacks", "queues" etc.

The "Conceptual Level" which we have been discussing has no parallel in computer science discussions. It is in a sense, one or two levels of abstraction above the levels of buffers, loops, and queues that occupy computer science discussions (for example, see Flon and Haberman (1976)). Nonetheless, the goals of abstraction in the two areas are similar - to remove as much of possible of implementation oriented detail from the specification of data structures and data processing procedures. We can best relate the two areas by starting with the conceptual level and talking about about its implementation in terms of the DIAM multilevel system.

In our specifications of Fact Types and Entity Sets at the Conceptual Level of DIAM, we have tried to define a complete set of concepts for describing the real world of resources. These concepts are as completely free of implementation detail as we can make them. The operations for processing these concepts are mainly the operations of set theory expressed in a notation called FORAL (which is designed to unambiguous and yet have more the familiar character of natural language).

Of course, computers cannot directly deal with these concepts and their processing - they must be given some indication in computer terms as to how these conceptual structures are to be efficiently stored and processed. This is the purpose of the lower levels of abstraction in DIAM. In what follows, we will consider only the next lower level of DIAM, the Access Path" or "String Level". Its relationship to the Conceptual Level is shown in Figure 7.

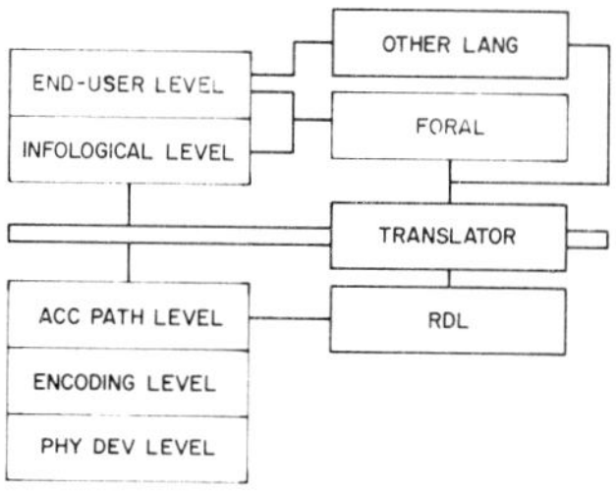

Figure 7 The DIAM II Mulltilevel Model

In particular, at this next level, given some knowledge of the kinds of transactions that the system is to process at the conceptual level (specified mainly in terms of disguised set operations), we wish to specify at the string level a set of access path which will allow the computer to store and search efficiently for the required information.

Computer scientists are working on this problem with a slightly different set of assumptions. Both Low (1974) and Schwartz (1975) contain discussions of the selection of data structures for set processing in the languages, SAIL and SETL respectively. In particular, their problem is simpler because they use fewer and simpler data structures - for example, simple one level lists, bitstrings, and hash tables. On the other hand, their problem is more difficult because their sets are of unknown and dramatically varying size. In the data base area, the main sets we are concerned with are the "files" stored on random access devices. Thse sets are relatively large, but stable, in size. To gain efficiency in accessing them, we use rather complex file organizations - access methods, indexes, interconnected lists, etc.

It turns out, as has been shown in DIAM, that these complex file organizations can be described in a general abstract way at DIAM's "string (or access path) level" by a sets of "strings" which contain intensionally defined, ordered subsets (or lists) of "Entity Names" from the conceptual level. an actual system, the enterprise administrator would look at the enterprise and design a conceptual structure which would adequately describe the enterprise, and the data base administrator would look at the transactions and specify some arbitrary set of strings, encodings and physical access methods to provide for efficient execution of the transactions. A DIAM system search path optimization algorithm would then have the responsibility for selecting an efficient accessing path for each FORAL transaction statement and compiling the appropriate Representation Dependent Language program for accessing the stored data. It would be interesting to "prove" that a search path compiling algorithm does indeed translate from conceptual level processing statements to appropriate "string level" processing statements.

It is at the access path level where the abstractions of the data base area meet the abstractions of the computer science area. In effect, the processes for maintaining and searching strings are very close to similar processes for queues, buffers, and stacks. These latter functions are really methods of different efficiency characteristics for operating on sets. If you always want the last element added to a list, then a stack is efficient - if you always want the first element added to a list then a FIFO queue is most efficient. In data base systems, we generally want some arbitrary element in the list based on the contents of the element, so our searching algorithms and file structures are usually more complex.

We can now relate the abstract data types of computer science with the abstract data levels of data base research. There are many different definitions of abstract data types (for example, see Parnas (1976)). A frequently appearing definition, however, portrays them as special purpose entity with defined representation and behavior. (Behavior means that the operations on the type are specified.) It is generally implied that the programmer-user will be deeply involved in the specification of the abstract data types for his problem - that is the special data representation and the operations to access and process the representation. There is no general set of data types, representations, or operations that are considered to cover the area of interest of computer science.

In contrast, in the data base area,for example, in DIAM, it is conceived that Fact Types and Entity Sets provide the only abstract data types that are required, and that a language like FORAL (there are many other data base languages) provides all the operations required for dealing with the abstract data type. In addition, many of the aspects of a general implementation of the abstract data type are specified by the lower abstract levels of a system like DIAM. The details of such an implementation have not been coded or proved in the exact way that certain implementations have in the computer science area, but it is expected that similar techniques can be used. In effect, it does seem possible to relate the work in the two areas and that each has something to contribute to the other.

REFERENCES

J. R. Abrial, (1974) Data semantics, in Data Base Management, J.W. Klimbie and K.L. Koffeman, eds., North-Holland Publishing, Amsterdam. pp 1-60.

ANSI/X3/SPARC Study Group on Data Base Management Systems, (1975) "Interim report", FDT Bulletin of ACM SIGMOD 7, No. 2, pp 1-140.

C. W. Bachman, (1969) Data structure diagrams, SIGBDP: Data Base 1, No. 2.

C. W. Bachman, (1976) Private Communication, to be presented at Data Base Workshop, National Bureau of Standards, Gaithersburg, Md. (January, 1977).

G. Bracchi, P. Paolini and G. Pelagatti, (1976) Binary logical associations in data modelling, in Modelling in Data Base Management Systems, G.M. Nijssen ed., North-Holland Publishing, Amsterdam, pp 125-148.

B. C. Bruce, (1972) A model for temporal references and its application in a question-answering system, Art. Intell., Vol 3.

J. Bubenko, (1976) The temporal dimension in information modeling, Research Report RC-6187, IBM Research, Yorktown Heights, New York.

CODASYL Development Committee, (1962) An information algebra, phase I report of the language structure group, Comm. ACM 5, No. 4, pp 190-204.

E. F. Codd, (1970) A relational model for large shared data banks, Comm. ACM, 13, No. 6, pp 377-387.

C. T. Davies, (1967) A logical concept for control and management of data, Report AR-0803-00, IBM, Poughkeepsie, New York.

E. Falkenberg, (1975) Design and application of a natural language oriented data base language, Lecture notes prepared for Advanced Course on "Data base languages and natural language processing, H-J. Schneider ed., Technical University Berlin.

GUIDE-SHARE Data Base Requirements Group, (1970) Database management systems requirements, GUIDE International, Chicago, Ill.

L. Flon and A. N. Haberman, (1976) Toward the construction of verifiable software systems, Conference on Data: Abstraction, Definition, and Structure, ACM SIGPLAN Notices, Vol. II, or ACM SIGMOD FDT, 8, No. 2, pp 141-148.

P. Hall, J. Owlett, and S. Todd, (1976) Relations and entities in Modelling in data base management systems ed. G.M. Nijssen North Holland, Amsterdam. pp 201-220.

T. Kuhn, (1962) The structure of scientific revolutions, The University of Chicago Press, Chicago, Ill.

B. Langefors, (1966) Theoretical analysis of information systems, Studentlitteratur, Lund, Sweden (1973) 4th edition Auerbach, Philadelphia, Pa.

J. R. Low, (1974) Automatic coding: choice of data structures, The University of Rochester, Department of Computer Science, Technical Report No. 1.

D. McLeod, (1976) High level domain definition in a relational data base system, ACM SIGMOD FDT, 8, No. 2, pp 47-57.

H. S. Meltzer, (1969) Data base concepts and architecture for data base systems, Presented to SHARE Information Systems Research Project, available from IBM Corp., San Jose, California.

G. H. Mealy, (1967) Another look data, Fall Joint Computer Conference 1967 pp 525-534.

G. M. Nijssen, (1975) Set and CODASYL set or coset, in Data Base Description, B.C.M. Douque and G.M. Nijssen, eds. North-Holland Publishing, Amsterdam. pp 1-70.

D. L. Parnas, J. E. Shore, and D. Weiss, (1976) Abstract types defined as classes of variables, Proceedings of Conference on Data: Abstraction, Definition, and Structure, ACM SIGPLAN Notices, Vol. II or SIGMOD FDT, vol. 8, No. 2, pp 141-148.

H. A. Schmid and J. R. Swenson, (1975) On the semantics of the relational model, Proceedings of the SIGMOD 1975 Conference ACM, New York pp 211-223.

J. T. Schwartz, (1975) Automatic data structure choice in a language of very high level, Comm. ACM 18, No. 12, pp 722-728.

M. E. Senko, E. B. Altman, M. M. Astrahan, and P. L. Fehder, (1973) Data structures and accessing in data base systems, IBM Systems Journal, 12, No. 1, pp 30-93.

M. E. Senko, (1975) The DDL in the context of a multilevel structured description: DIAM II with FORAL, in Data Base Description, B.C.M. Douque and G.M. Nijssen, eds., North-Holland Publishing, Amsterdam. pp 239-257.

M. E. Senko, (1975a) Specification of stored data structures and desired output results in DIAM II with FORAL, Proceeding of the International Conference on Very Large Data Bases, ACM, New York. pp 557-571.

M. E. Senko, (1976) DIAM as a detailed example of the ANSI SPARC architecture, in Modelling in Data Base Management Systems, ed. G.M. Nijssen, North-Holland Publishing, Amsterdam. pp 73-94.

M. E. Senko, (1976a) FORAL II for DIAM II, information structure and query-maintenance language, Working document, IBM Research Yorktown Height, New York.

M. E. Senko, (1977) FORAL LP for DIAM II: FORAL with light pen, a language primer, IBM Research Report, IBM Research, Yorktown Heights, New York.

T. B. Steel, Jr. (1975) Data base standardization: a status report, in Data Base Description, B.C.M. Douque and G.M. Nijssen, eds. North-Holland Publishing, Amsterdam. pp 183-198.

B. Sundgren, (1974) Conceptual foundation of the infological approach to data base, in Data Base Management, J.W. Klimbie and K.L. Koffeman, eds. North-Holland Publishing, Amsterdam.

E. Morlet and D. Ribbens, (Eds.), International Computing Symposium 1977.

FROM PROGRAMMING EDUCATION TO PROFESSIONAL PRACTICE

by

E. MILGROM and R.M. SIMPSON

Université Catholique de Louvain
Unité d'Informatique

and

Y.D. WILLEMS and P. VERBAETEN

Katholieke Universiteit te Leuven
Afdeling Toegepaste Wiskunde en Programmatie

Following their continuing experience in computer science education, the authors have felt the need for a precise delineation of what is programming and what is a programmer, which would be accepted by university and industry alike.
They propose such a definition, explore its consequences and present some conclusions concerning the education and the roles of professional programmers and "computer scientists".
In addition, they remove a number of misconceptions that have been clouding the issues in the computing community for quite some time, principally: the relation between programming and problem-solving, the importance of programming languages, and the role of methodology.

I. ALGORITHMS, PROGRAMMING and PROGRAMMERS.

1. From problem to computer solution: 3 steps.

To avoid misunderstanding, we would like to agree on a common terminology. We distinguish three different stages when solving a problem by means of a computer:

- discovering the solution;

- constructing the algorithm;

- preparing for computer execution.

There are some difficulties with this classification, and the boundaries are not as clearly defined as the above enumeration seems to imply. Still, we would describe the three stages as follows.

1.1. From problem to solution.

First, there is the discovery of the solution (for the given problem). This highly creative process, also known as "problem-solving", is based on intuition and experience. Somebody has used the term "eureka experience" to describe the moment when the spark of invention flashes up. We do not want to elaborate on this stage: we agree that it is necessary, we doubt whether it can effectively be taught, and we will argue that it lies outside the realm of programming as we understand it.

To illustrate this point, consider the following example: in a programming test, one would explain to the student the main idea of the logarithmic search method, telling him that, at every step, the number of entries to be searched can be cut in half. This informal description of the problem also gives away the "trick" to be used. We believe that finding this trick is another matter altogether, and does not belong to a programming test.

1.2. From solution to algorithm.

In this section, we will assume that a solution has been discovered, and we will investigate the process of formalizing that solution, of constructing an algorithm. By algorithm we mean: an "unambiguous description of a method which can be used to solve any problem in a given class". The keywords here are "unambiguous", and "description".

We feel that the construction of such a description can be viewed as an activity separate from finding the solution. An activity which also contains creative aspects, certainly not to be ignored, but which can be analyzed more rigorously, and which can be taught. We will return to this point below.

It may come as a surprise to some people that constructing an algorithm turns out to be a non-trivial task. It often takes years of experience for a teacher to recognize this fact and to dare to "give away the trick" when preparing a programming assignment.

One of the difficult points seems to be the correct sequencing of the different actions, keeping in mind the information available at each moment in time. As Dijkstra states it [4]: "on the one hand we have the algorithm, a finite text, a timeless, static concept; on the other hand we have the corresponding happenings that may be evoked by it, dynamic concepts, happenings evolving in time".

Another difficulty has to do with the concept of (abstract) data structure. The underlying data structure is usually only implied in the informal description of an algorithm. It has to be made very explicit when constructing the algorithm. We suspect this is a point Wirth wanted to stress when he entitled his recent book "Algorithms + Data Structures = Programs".

A further difference between the informal solution and the algorithm is the very precise flow of control, the sometimes painstaking bookkeeping necessary when implementing loops, conditionals and so forth.

Finally, there is the need for an unambiguous notation, a "language". We mention this point with some reluctance, because we feel that it has received too much emphasis in the past. Indeed, many courses on programming are nothing other than detailed explanations of all the features of a programming language. It is clear, however, that an "algorithm description language" is needed. Whether this language should be directly amenable to computer execution is a debatable point. We do feel, however, that many details in current programming languages have more to do with the limitations of available computers than with the essence of unambiguous algorithm description. This point will be addressed in the second part of this paper.

1.3. From algorithm to computer output.

The third step is the one in which the computer comes into focus. The two previous steps can be viewed completely independently from its existence, although, of course the usefulness of a complete, unambiguous description is enhanced by the availability of an automaton to execute it correctly and speedily. To arrive at the point of automatic execution, one faces the issues of machine readability, machine translatability, and machine (or job) control.

This step involves "coding": the translation of the algorithm into machine-acceptable form, a process which includes the conversion from "abstract" data structures into "concrete" ones.

Other aspects of this activity involve communication with an operating system, access to information stored in files, interpretation of diagnostics, etc. These tasks could be made much easier if a clear model of the operating system were available, a model which gives a feeling for available features.

2. Programming.

At this point, we can be clear about what we consider to be "programming": we view it as the second and third steps in the complete problem-solving process. It involves the construction of an algorithm, its translation into a program, and getting that program to run.

We have not included the discovery of a solution within our definition of programming. This is a rather important distinction, which in our minds explains a great deal of the current confusion over the term "programmer". On the one hand, some people indicate that only Ph.D.'s in computer science can claim the title of "programmer". On the other hand, many industrial organizations place "programmers" at the bottom of their hierarchy and employ people with 1 or 2 years' vocational training beyond high school.

Both the more academically-oriented readers and the more practically-inclined ones might take exception to our definition: the former will most certainly want to include the discovery of a solution in the programming activity, while the latter frequently want to restrict it to the coding aspect.

Nevertheless, we hope that all will agree that the construction of algorithms lies at the heart of computing and forms the basis for many other functions in the fields of data processing, software engineering or computer science. It is thus very important that this basic skill be taught very carefully to all the people involved in these fields.

3. Beyond programming: "Computer Science".

However, more is needed to tackle the problems where computers are currently utilized. Many relevant topics are taught in computer science departments to people who wish to go beyond programming. We think now of such subjects as compiler construction, operating systems principles, data base concepts, etc...

Other skills seem to be of particular interest to the industry, for instance: the management of a team of programmers, defining problems in a dialogue with prospective users, forecasting the resources needed to complete an assignment, identifying the sensitive parts of a project, and so on. In these areas, experience still plays the major role and this is gained primarily on the job, not from formal courses. We attempt to address this dilemma in the third section of the paper.

II. TEACHING PROGRAMMING

Now that we have presented our frame of reference, we can address ourselves to the question of teaching programming to novices. (The problem of teaching experienced programmers - "remedial programming" in the words of B. Huntington Snark [9] - is a very different matter altogether)

1. Programming is not difficult: it is different

A first point which should be made is that programming, even though it is not a difficult endeavour, is, for most people, rather different from their other intellectual activities. Therefore, we feel that it takes, on the average, a long time to get acquainted with and accustomed to. A few people do grasp the essence very quickly, and they manage to exhibit seemingly age-old familiarity with the subject a few days after their first contact. Most people, however, have to overcome quite a number of mental blocks (some of them rather unexpected), before actually feeling at ease in the world of programming.

2. Small steps teaching strategy

It is, therefore, essential that the student be brought to first understand a small number of immediately applicable notions; then, he should be given enough time to acquire practice and experience with these basic notions, before going on with more sophisticated matters. It is our belief, moreover, that the time span needed to really grasp some of the very elementary notions is often underrated.

A simple example is the use of vectors (one-dimensional arrays): students believe very quickly that they understand all about vectors; it seems a very useful concept, which they yearn to use at every opportunity. One sees, however, that beginners seldom realize that it is not always necessary first to store 10000 numbers and then process them sequentially later on. Most teachers will certainly agree with our finding that beginners (and even some experienced programmers) tend to overlook this point. We feel that this is the symptom of a deeper lack of understanding, namely a failure to grasp the time-sequential nature of a given process: for these people, the relation between sequential time-instants and the availability of data items is still unclear.

Summarizing this point, we strongly advocate proceeding in cautiously small steps, interspersed with long assimilation stretches: the learning steps must be short because they involve getting familiar with powerful notions which are entirely novel to most people.

3. Programming languages considered harmful

A common misconception is that teaching programming is the same as teaching the features of one or more programming languages. One cannot escape the impression that many authors are campaigning to promote their own pet language constructs for teaching purposes. We claim that there has been too much emphasis on programming languages, and not enough on the essence of programming. The consequences of such a misplaced emphasis are disastrous:

- many of the best recommendations appear to be applicable only to pet programming languages that are unavailable or unacceptable on commercial installations;
- people outside the academic world remain unconvinced that there is any more to be learned about programming than what is in the language manuals;
- there is a fallacious notion that programs written in a "good" language are, almost by necessity, "good" programs;
- students are forced to dig for concepts which are hidden behind the syntactic wall and the extraneous detail of the programming language and of its compiler(s): this adds to the difficulty of understanding the concepts.

4. The languages of programming

As was said earlier, we consider that the programming activity involves two main tasks:

- construction of an algorithm (not to be confused with discovery of a solution)
- transformation of an algorithm into a working program, or coding.

Of course, one needs a language to describe algorithms, and one needs a language to write programs which are to be submitted to a computer. We disagree with the general trend, which insists that one should use the same language for both purposes.

On the contrary, we feel that a very strong point can be made for the use of different notations during the different phases of the programming activity. Graphical and symbolic notations such as flow-charts, decision tables, sketches, and formulae can be very helpful at some points or in some cases. In a certain sense, the importance given to correct indentation of programs illustrates the need to return to a graphical representation of structure which some (much maligned) flow-charts convey even more explicitly.

Nevertheless, one could use an existing programming language as an algorithm description language, as long as one remembers that its practical limitations (due to the language itself or to its available compilers) should not unduly interfere with the presentation of the important programming concepts.

5. Organization of programming education

Learning to program involves:

- understanding certain programming concepts;

- becoming familiar with the details of a program execution environment.

The first part is certainly suitable matter for a well-prepared set of lectures, but skilled teachers are needed to convey the message properly. We can't, therefore, agree with the practice - encountered in many colleges and universities - of letting the most junior and less experienced teaching staff bear this responsibility.

We think that it is useful to divide the exposure to the concepts of programming into at least two stages: fundamental and advanced concepts. This is true, whatever the bias of the teacher may be. Indeed, one will never manage to present a set of concepts which would be called "fundamental" simultaneously by a FORTRAN-oriented teacher, by an APL-oriented teacher and by an Algol 68-oriented teacher [8]. However, all will probably agree that, whatever their personal ordering of concepts may be, some concepts must be presented first, and others may follow later.
The point we wish to stress here, is that the chosen fundamental concepts must be presented with the utmost care, lest they reinforce the mental blocks some students inevitably exhibit against the programming activity.

There are a few notions, often thought advanced, which are sufficiently "universal" in the programming world that students should be made to pay attention to them at a very early stage.
Among these notions are generalization and optimization.

- Generalization is the idea that one can sometimes solve a larger class of problems with an algorithm (or a slight variation of it) than one first expected.

- Optimization is the notion that one can sometimes solve a problem using less resources than one first needed.

We don't claim that beginners will be able to construct "optimal" algorithms and programs, but we certainly believe that they should constantly bear in mind that programming involves developing a critical sense with respect to one's own production.

The second part of the teaching must relate to the environment in which programs (not algorithms) are executed. This implies getting to know the myriad of rules relating to a given programming language, a specific compiler and a particular installation. If the concepts have been presented in a successful way, there is no need to teach this second part by means of lectures (in the conventional sense). This part can best be covered in exercise sessions, whereby small groups of students are induced to solve simple problems (whose solutions are given informally), following all the steps to the execution of their programs. What help is necessary should be provided by a set of manuals and a special consulting service, geared to the needs of these students.

6. The role of methodology

One should not, of course, ignore the contributions of current research in the field of programming methodology. The question is rather how to make use of the proposed methodology in teaching programming.

Let us consider, for instance, the technique of stepwise refinement [11], which is used in several texts as a tool for simultaneously discovering a solution and constructing the corresponding algorithm. As said earlier, we believe one must seperate these two activities. Besides, one can doubt whether the person who shows a neatly logical development actually used this same development to get to his neat result (see, for instance, Naur [7] on this subject).

A second point is that no method is going to make a difficult task really easy. The least one can hope for is that the method should not add to the intrinsic difficulty of the task.

The third point is that programs resulting from a series of refinements can still be incorrect [5]!

What, then, is the role of stepwise refinement in a programming course?

Firstly, it does provide a set of guidelines which help to organize one's thoughts. One should not, however, "elevate good heuristics into bad dogma" ([1]): the thinking process is not necessarily defective if it does not proceed in a strictly hierarchical way!

Secondly, although the development of a program need not always proceed in orderly steps, the final presentation should exhibit the modular structure aimed at by stepwise refinement.

Thirdly, it turns out that stepwise refinement is an extremely useful tool to explain and document algorithms. Indeed, if we accept the idea that an algorithm is a precise description of a solution of a problem, it can very well happen that this precise description may not be easy to understand: one uses stepwise refinement, therefore, as a pedagogical device to facilitate the understanding of an algorithm by building it up piecewise.

Another methodological technique is that of correctness proofs for programs. Current literature on the subject indicates that it is possible to formally prove the correctness of small to medium-size programs, but it is clear that the effort involved in the proof grows faster than the size of the programs. Besides, even for small programs, it sometimes happens that deriving the proof requires a considerable amount of skill (e.g. if arrays are involved). While it may be true that only those capable of providing a formal correctness proof of a program really understand that program, it is certainly unrealistic to hope that, in the near future at least, the majority of programs will be written together with their correctness proofs! However, a spin-off of this technique has been the growing awareness that trying to establish invariant relations which hold at a few crucial points of a program is, in itself, a powerful tool which helps avoiding gross logic errors (e.g. with respect to special or border cases).

We therefore recommend that students be encouraged to express clearly (albeit informally) the relations which must hold between the input data, between the values of important variables at the main points of their programs, and between the expected results. These relations are then to be included in the algorithm and the resulting program as comments.

This could be used as a starting point for making the students aware of the need for documentation. Just as stepwise refinement is used to explain an algorithm, documentation has to be provided in order to enable others to understand a program: we find that students are receptive to this point, be it only because they expect to be graded on basis of their work!

7. Results of programming education

We should now be able to guess, with some accuracy, what can and what cannot be expected of an average student who has been successfully exposed to a programming education scheme designed along the lines of what has been said above.

7.1. What cannot be expected

- a vast improvement of the problem-solving capability;
- the ability to discover solutions;
- the ability to construct program proofs.

7.2. What can be expected

- the ability to transform a fuzzily expressed solution of a problem into an algorithm and then into a working program, and to make intelligent assumptions concerning incomplete specifications;
- the ability to keep an eye on possible optimizations and generalizations;
- an awareness of invariant relations;
- the ability to learn new programming languages;
- the ability to adequately document one's programs;
- a working knowledge of a model of a computer and of its software system.

In short, we feel that it is quite possible that not one out of hundred students will produce a program that, say, Dijkstra would recognize as his own. However, they should, on the average, be able to construct satisfactory medium-size programs and to proceed to more complex endeavours as time grants them a larger share of experience.

We are fairly confident that the points mentioned above are realistic aims. We base this belief on the preliminary results of an introductory programming course organized along the lines presented earlier at the Université Catholique de Louvain; this course is discussed in more detail in the Appendix.

III. THE REAL WORLD.

1. Is there a difference ?

We hope that, to the reader, the above question will be a rhetorical one. It should be obvious that there exists a large gap between programming in a teaching environment and programming in the real world:

- A first point has to do with the type of the problems. One very often hears the remark that the "toy" problems used in education are too "neat", too well-defined, and too easily amenable to an elegant solution.

- Second, there are differences in scale: the problems to be solved are more elaborate, the number of people involved in the projects is larger, more time is needed.

- The previous point has a profound influence on the work environment: people usually work as a team, have to adhere to time schedules (and should be able to forecast time requirements), people have to manage (and be managed), people have to communicate (and document).

2. Should there be a difference ?

To no one's surprise, the educational institutions are confronted with the criticism of academism, and are accused of producing "useless" graduates. Very often, this criticism is used to advocate a teaching environment which simulates the "real world".

We feel it necessary to object strongly to this view. The primary purpose of education is to "concentrate" a very time-consuming experience into a short but logically coherent framework. It is obvious that physics is not being taught in the same way and in the same sequence as it was developed. As a matter of fact, the more a branch of science has matured and developed, the wider the gap between its historical evolution and the teaching sequence.

In the case of computer science, part of the trouble lies in the novelty of the field. Still, it does seem pointless to want to simulate in the universities an environment that already exists. This may be the place, then, to push for a traineeship program, allowing students to gain some on-the-job experience during their education.

Another important point we want to make is that no agreement has been reached on the ideal working environment: we have all heard about experiments with novel organization schemes, such as "chief-programmer teams" and other similar approaches.

We feel that it should be our objective to give students a solid background which will enable them to operate and develop in a number of different and rapidly changing environments. In most fields, it is commonly accepted that an incoming graduate will need a working-in period to operate successfully and to achieve professional growth.

3. From education to real world.

As a concluding point for this paper, we would like to mention a problem encountered by computer science graduates when they attempt to embark on a professional career. When one scans the job advertisements for computer personnel, one is dismayed by the rather narrow wording of the qualifications which are required, at least in Europe. How come industry seems to need mostly "senior programmers with experience in DOS-VS1" or "system analysts trained in the use of VSAM"? Could it be that the requirements of industry are at a purely technical level, and that computer science graduates are overqualified or wrongly qualified? Industry seems to think that computer science education is too theoretical, yet if we were to teach to fulfill the immediate needs of the real world, we feel that industry would soon castigate us for failing to prepare people capable of handling the rapid changes which occur in that world!

Let us therefore conclude by quoting a remark made by M.E.Hopkins, (from IBM Corporation, no less) at a conference on programming and computer science education [6]:

> "Certainly, you must listen to the people from government and industry when they tell you what they want. But at the end, you must teach what you believe in and,most important, what you know. It is only by teaching what you believe in and what you know that you ever really impart a true sense of discipline and prepare people for all the things that no one really knows are going to happen. But it certainly will. We all know, in computing, whatever can go wrong - will go wrong, and in the real world if we try to teach what banks want today it will certainly not be what they want tomorrow. ... Let the computer science professors teach what they know, what they feel deeply and, I think, you will have done great service to everybody at the end. I do not think it is possible to be practical all the time."

REFERENCES

[1] Abrahams, P., "Structured Programming Considered Harmful", SIGPLAN Notices, 10, 4, April 1975, pp. 13-24.

[2] Dijkstra, E.W., "A Short Introduction to the Art of Programming", EWD 316, Technische Hogeschool Eindhoven, 1971.

[3] Courtin, J. et Voiron, J., "Introduction à l'algorithmique et aux structures de données", Grenoble, 1974-75.

[4] Courtin, J. et Voiron, J., "Traduction des schémas de programmes en Fortran", Grenoble, 1974-75.

[5] Henderson, P. and Snowdon, R.A., "An Experiment in Structured Programming", BIT 12, 1, Jan 1972, pp 38-53.

[6] Hopkins, M.E., in [10], p 210.

[7] Naur, P., "An Experiment in Program Development", BIT 12, 3, March 1972, pp 347-365.

[8] Peck, J.E.L., in [10], p 215.

[9] Snark, B.H., "Diverse Approaches to Teaching Programming: Three Reports", in [10], pp 93-105.

[10] Turski, W. M. (ed), "Programming Teaching Techniques", Proceedings of the IFIP TC-2 Working Conference, North-Holland, 1973.

[11] Wirth, N., "Program Development by Stepwise Refinement", C.A.C.M. 14, 4, April 1971, pp 221-227.

Appendix

Yet another introductory programming course

We present here a few salient features of an introductory programming course given since September 1975 at the Université Catholique de Louvain.

1. Background

The course is given to about 450 undergraduates, mostly first-year students, from the departments of engineering, of mathematics, of physics and of agronomy. More than 80% of these students have had no previous experience with computers or programming: they are truly unspoilt beginners in the field. A small number have been previously exposed to a conventional FORTRAN course: we consider them as potential trouble makers, since some of them have already acquired what we think are bad programming habits.

The "client" departments impose the following constraints:

(a) that the students should be able, after successful completion of the course, to write simple FORTRAN programs, and
(b) that the course should extend only over 7 two-hour lectures and 7 two-hour exercise sessions.

It should be noted that there is no way to modify these constraints, since the teaching staff for the programming course is considered as only providing a service. If it fails to do so according to the client departments' wishes, the latter might well decide to organize their own programming courses. One is far from the situation of, say, Stanford, where the computer science department has managed to impose AlgolW as teaching language.

2. Limited extent of the course

In accordance with the small steps teaching strategy, and its corollaries, it was deemed preferable to present a small number of concepts, and to make sure that these concepts were understood, rather than to attempt to cram together the sum of what everybody wanted the students to know. There will be plenty of opportunity later, for the students who wish to do so, to get to know what wasn't taught in the introductory course.

3. Languages

Similarly to what had been done previously at the Université de Grenoble [2,3], it was decided to separate algorithm construction from coding. The authors of the course designed, for this purpose, their own algorithm description mini-language (MILA) which contains, in an admittedly subjective form, the constructs they felt were needed to illustrate the following concepts:

- objects: constants and variables (simple and array), types;

- actions: assignment, input and output statements, expressions;

- combination of statements: sequences, loops, conditionals, procedures;

- simple assertions as comments;

- memory allocation: static (compile time) and dynamic (execution time);

- generalization and optimization.

(The authors of the course readily admit their own bias toward Algol and Pascal-like languages).

Sufficient time is spent in the first lectures to introduce the notions of:

- the computer as an automaton, with a processor having an instruction repertoire, a memory and input-output devices;

- an algorithm as a description of a sequence of actions to be executed in order to achieve a goal;

- the construction of an algorithm as a stepwise process, proceeding by successive refinements of the initial statement of a solution.

This last point is illustrated by an example (the building of a brick wall), which enables one to introduce successively, and in a single lecture:

- statements,
- combination of statements,
- simple assertions,
- variables,
- data.

A number of lectures are then spent exploring the possibilities of this first set of basic concepts with various examples of algorithm construction. The other concepts are introduced one by one in the remaining lectures.

4. Practice

The exercise sessions are organized in groups of about 25 students, who are given the opportunity:

- to construct algorithms in MILA;

- to translate their algorithms into FORTRAN;

- to run their programs on a computer.

The following aids are provided to help the students:

- one or more assistants,

- a manual describing rules to translate MILA algorithms into FORTRAN programs,

- a FORTRAN reference manual written especially for the course,

- a dozen interactive display terminals connected to the University's IBM 370 computer, which provides the students with CMS virtual machines,

- a guide to the CMS commands the students need to know.

5. Results and conclusions after one year of experience

1. The constraints have been respected, and the students are able to write simple, but non-trivial FORTRAN programs.

2. The method teaches the principles of programming and algorithm construction by means of lectures, while leaving the tedium of getting familiar with a programming language and a programming environment to the exercise sessions. According to one of the teachers who also participated in an earlier course (of the traditional "teach FORTRAN" variety), the new method does work better than the previous one. It is, however, too early to give quantitative indications about the improvement.

3. It would not be difficult to change the programming language, since the course itself would not be modified.

4. The course can be readily adapted to a different student population by changing the problem area covered in the exercise sessions.

E. Morlet and D. Ribbens, (Eds.), International Computing Symposium 1977.

PROBLEM SPECIFICATION AND ALGORITHMIC PROGRAMMING

D. BERT
Attaché de Recherche CNRS
Laboratoire d'Informatique
38041 - GRENOBLE-CEDEX

At present, programming languages are seeking the possibility to describe the problem to be solved, rather than the algorithm which solves the particular problem. Such languages are called specification languages or very high level languages. The first task is to verify whether the specifications are coherent; the second is to find an algorithm which corresponds to the specifications. In order to answer this second point, we shall take some results known from program synthesis ans we shall compare them and try to bring out a strategy for the implementation of specifications, applicable to a very high level language.

1. INTRODUCTION

In the field of artificial languages, research is more and more oriented towards the design of specification languages, rather than algorithmic languages. In other words, the universe of the objects is described (these universes can also be predefined : integers, real numbers, and so on) and particular sets of this universe are expressed by means of functions and predicates [10].

For example, let N be the set of positive integers, provided with the usual operations; we are interested in the following set :

$$D(a,b) = \{(q,r) \in N^2 \mid a = bq+r \wedge 0 \leq r < b\}$$

where $a \in N$ and $b \in N - \{0\}$.

An other example could be this one :
let $I_k = [1,k]$, $k \in N \wedge k > 1$;
let $C = I_k \times I_k$;
the set : $R(k) = \{X \in C^k \mid Q(X)\}$
where $X = \{(x_i,y_i)\}$, $(x_i,y_i) \in C$, $1 \leq i \leq k$
and $Q(X) = (\forall(i,j) \in I_k^2 \wedge i \neq j)$

$$(x_i \neq x_j \wedge y_i \neq y_j \wedge x_i + y_i \neq x_j + y_j \wedge x_i - y_i \neq x_j - y_j)$$

We recognize, of course, in D(a,b) the quotient-remainder set of the integer division of a by b and in R(8) the set of the solutions of the eight queens problem.

These sets have a general form which is expressed by :

$$F(x) = \{y \in E \mid P(x,y)\}$$

where x is a parameter of F
and E the initial set of which F is subset. We suppose, as usually, that E can be built with basic sets (integers, booleans, etc...) and constructors (cartesian product, union, etc...).

We can ask the following questions about these sets :
- membership : $z \in F(a)$
- mapping on all the elements $(\forall z \in F(a))(\phi(z))$
- selection of an arbitrary element : let $z \in F(a)$

The first problem is easily solved :

$$z \in F(a) \iff z \in E \wedge P(a,z)$$

as long as the predicate P is computable. The second (or third) problem is more difficult to resolve because it is necessary to find a sequence of simple actions which lead to the result and this invention must be automatic if we want to compile a specification language.

We shall not give an entirely automatic method for translating specifications into deterministic and efficient algorithms ; it is not possible currently. The aim of this paper is to show :

- the processes to obtain algorithms from specifications;
- the influence of the specifications on efficiency;
- the optimisations that are possible to use.

In conclusion, we shall see that the reasoning on the specifications can give different algorithms from those obtained directly from these specifications, even after optimisation. Therefore, different specifications of the same problem lead to different algorithms ; and modification of specifications is important in order to obtain efficient algorithms. The efficiency reason underlies the transformation of programs or specifications, but it can happen only "a posteriori". We shall give, however, a transformation principle driven by efficiency.

2. SPECIFICATION PROGRAMMING

Given a set specified by a predicate :
$F(x) = \{y \in E \mid P(x,y)\}$ where x,y may be vectors of variables, we must find either some element or all the elements of the set F.

2.1. Enumerating

A trivial, but correct if terminated program exists, satisfying the specification F(a). It consists in enumerating all the elements of E with a variable and an enumerating function :

```
y := y0; {y0 ∈ E}
while ¬ P(a,y)
do y := enumerate(E) od;
```

The loop is ended, either when we have found an element of F(a), or when the whole E set has been enumerated. We shall use also an algorithmic notation close to the loop statements of Alphard [12]:

```
first y ∈ E suchthat P(a,y)
then S1(y) co exit action for success co
else S2    co exit action for failure co
```

Here the enumeration of E is provided by two functions : init and next, which update the y variable and yield a boolean result : true if a next element exists, false otherwise. The semantics of "first" is equivalent to :

```
begin bool b ;
b := init(y) ;
while b do
    if P(a,y)
    then begin S1(y); goto ℓ end
    else b := next(y)
    od ;
S2 ; ℓ:
end
```

Particularly, the predicate :
$(\exists y \in E)(P(y))$
can be programmed

```
first y ∈ E suchthat P(y) then true else false
```

as long as the set E is finite and P is a boolean procedure.

This means that the program can loop indefinitely when the set is unbounded, as we might expect. We shall that we can draw from the properties of the E set (total, partial order, ...) or from the fact that we can determine a bounded subset $E' \subset E$ such as $(\forall t \in E - E') \neg P(a,t)$, which leads to a stop test.

The first principle for generating such a program is to express specifications in order to make clear the enumeration bounds as well as the relations between the enumeration variables.

Example : to find an element of the D(a,b) set, we can modify the formulation to avoid enumerating N^2 because there is a relation between q and r :

$D(a,b) = \{(q,r) \in N^2 \mid 0 \le a - bq < b \wedge r = a-bq\}$
or again
$D(a,b) = (\{q \mid bq \le a < b(q+1)\}, a - bq\}$

It is sufficient therefore to determine q and to deduce r from it. We can then choose the increasing enumeration : $q_0 = 0$, $q_1 = 1, \ldots$ and a stop test exists with $q = a$, since for $b > 0$, $(\nexists q)(q > a) \wedge (0 \le a-bq)$. The deduced program is :

```
D1 : q := 0;
     while ¬(b * q ≤ a ∧ b * (q+1) > a)
     do q := q+1
     until q > a;
     if q ≤ a then (q,a-b * q)
     else no solution fi ;
```

We would have been able to enumerate from a to 0, in the same way. If the compiler which produces this program accepts advice, we can suggest that the D(a,b) set has always an element (and one alone) and that the error test is useless, which leads to the more reasonable algorithm :

```
D2 : q := 0;
     while ¬(b * q ≤ a ∧ b * (q+1) > a)
     do q := q+1 od ;
     (q, a - b * q)
```

2.2. Invariant reinforcement

Studying more precisely this kind of program, we note that it matches to the synthesis of conjunctive goals :
"find x such that $P(x) \wedge Q(x)$ [4] [9].
In our case : find y such that $y \in E \wedge P(a,y)$. The stop test is P(a,y) whereas the loop invariant is $y \in E$. Now, it is well known that it is better to have a strong invariant and a weak stop test to get an efficient program. This means that enumerating is "the most general solution" of the invariant $y \in E$ and to strengthen the invariant is equivalent to restricting the enumerated set. This explains why the programs deduced by using the § 2.1 method are among the most inefficient.

Can we strengthen the invariant predicate from specifications ? Generally yes. Take the above examples :

a) D(a,b);
The predicate which determines q is :

$$0 \le q \le a \wedge q * b \le a \wedge (q+1) * b > a$$

By taking the first two terms as invariant and the third as test, we get an almost "classical" program :

```
D3 : q := 0;
     while (q+1) * b ≤ a
     do q := q + 1 od;
     (q, a - b * q)
```

The verification conditions are provided :

$$q = 0 \supset q * b \le a \wedge 0 \le q \le a$$
$$(q+1) * b \le a \{q := q+1\} q * b \le a \wedge 0 \le q \le a$$

It would have been possible to take the first and the third conjuncts for invariant and the second for test, with a decreasing enumeration:

```
D4 : q := a;
     while q * b > a
     do q := q - 1 od ;
     (q,a - b * q)
```

b) R(k) ;

If we decompose Q(X) into four predicates :

$P_1(X) \equiv \forall(i, j), i \neq j, x_i \neq x_j$;

$P_2(X) \equiv \forall(i, j), i \neq j, y_i \neq y_j$;

$P_3(X) \equiv \forall(i, j), i \neq j, x_i + y_i \neq x_j + y_j$

$P_4(X) \equiv \forall(i, j), i \neq j, x_i - y_i \neq x_j - y_j$

we can try the invariant : $X \in C^k \wedge P_1(X)$, which leads to enumerate a smaller number of solutions in the body of the loop (usual program of the eight queens).

Another "toy" example is that of the greatest element of an array T; the specification is :

Max : T(z) such that

$z \in [1,n] \wedge (\forall k)\ (k \in [1,n])\ (T(z) \geq T(k))$

If we take $z \in [1,n]$ as invariant and $(\forall k)\ (k \in [1,n])(T(z) \geq T(k))$ as exit test, we get the following program written with first :

```
T(first z ∈ [1,n]
  suchthat (∀k) (k ∈ [1,n])(T(z) ≥ T(k))
  then z else skip)
```

The stop condition can be transform into "exists": $\neg[(\exists k)(k \in [1,n])(T(z) < T(k))]$
Hence the program :

```
Max 1 :
T (first z ∈ [1,n]
  suchthat ¬(first k ∈ [1,n]
             suchthat T(z) < T(k)
             then true else false)
  then z else skip)
```

Of course, this program is inefficient because it is built with two nested loops and the run time is proportionnal to n^2. The reinforcement of the invariant can be obtained by one of the splitting methods shown in [4]. These are heuristics which add new variables, used as controlled variables in the loops. Here, we shall take the specification :

T(z) such that
$z \in [1,j] \wedge (\forall k)\ (k \in [1,j](T(z) \geq T(k)) \wedge (j=n)$

with j = n as test and the first part of the predicate, quoted I(z,j) as invariant. For the while program, we must find :

. z_o such that $I(z_o,1)$

. z' such that

$j \neq n \wedge I(z,j)\ \{z:=z';\ j:=j+1\} I(z,j)$

which are initialisation and loop body :

```
Max 2 : T(z := z_o ; j := 1 ;
          while j ≠ n
          do z := z' ; j := j+1 od ;
          z )
```

With the second specification, we get only one loop.

2.3. Loop body synthesis

Thus, when we have choosen conjunctive goals from the initial specifications, the program is :

```
y := y_o {I(a, y_o)};
while ¬A(a,y)
do y := y' {I(a,y')} od ;
{A(a,y) ∧ I(a,y) ⊃ P(a,y)}
```

Now, the choice of y_o and y_1 is posed.

In the D(a,b) example, the enumerating of the integers gives y' : y+1 or y' : y-1 following the enumerating sense. For the ordered sets, the enumerating is led by the order of the elements and we may seek y' such that for each components y_j, we have $y'_j \geq y_j$ or $y'_j \leq y_j$ and $y' \neq y$. That is called the "range strategy" by Manna [4].

An other technique used for the combinatory problems is backtracking or non deterministic choice. These strategies are connected to the existence of a termination function t which permits, if it exists, to pass from a program state to another state "nearer" to the solution.

This function t is, in a classical way, a mapping of the space of the program states onto the positive integers. If t is strictly decreasing inside a loop, we may be sure that the loop will terminate [5]. The other alternatives to prove termination are connected to that one [7]. There are two main methods to go nearer the solution :

- to restrict the space of the solutions at each step (case of the enumerating of finite sets);
- to find a "distance" to the solution and to make it decrease.

In the Max 2 program, the distance to the solution is immediately provided by the quantity n-j. This second method is often connected to the data structure and the loop induction is then the "structural induction".

So the assignement y := y' will have the following general form :

```
y := if q_1(a,y) then y'_1
     orif q_2(a,y) then y'_2
     ...
```

The y'_i are determined with respect to t and I because we must have :

$t(y'_i) < t(y) \wedge I(a,y'_i)$

The order of the tests is irrelevant. For the program to be complete, we must verify :

(1) $\forall$ y such that I(a,y), $\bigcup_i q_i(a,y) \cup A(a,y)$.

If moreover $\bigcup_i q_i(a,y) \supset \neg A(a,y)$, we can do without the stop test by the guarded - commands formalism.

We have here several unknown variables binded each others. The method introduced by Dijkstra [5] is to find a priori some values y'_i fulfiling $I(a,y')$ and to deduce from them, by symbolic computation, the "weakest preconditions" which provide the q_i tests with the notation :

$$wp(y:=y'_i,\ I(a,y)) \equiv (\exists y'_i)\ I(a,y'_i)$$

where y'_i depends on the old y value, that is to say we can write, if the predicate is always true:

$$(\exists y'_i(y))\ I(a,y'_i(y)) \equiv q_i(a,y).$$

Example : Synthesis of the loop body of Max 2.

1. We set $z_o = 1$ since $z_o \in [1,1]$;
   $I(1,1)$ is true because $\forall k \in [1,1]\ T(1) \geq T(k)$.

2. For $j \neq n$, the weakest precondition is :
   $$wp(\{z:=z';\ j:=j+1\},\ I(z,j))$$
   $$\equiv (\exists z' \in [1,j+1])\ I(z',j+1)$$

Let us derivate $I(z,j) \wedge wp$ for $z' = z$:

$$(\exists z \in [1,j])(\forall k \in [1,j])\ T(z) \geq T(k) \wedge$$
$$(\exists z'=z)(\forall k \in [1,j+1])T(z') \geq T(k)$$
$$\equiv (\exists z \in [1,j])(\forall k \in [1,j])T(z) \geq T(k) \wedge T(z) \geq T(j+1)$$
$$\equiv I(z,j) \wedge T(z) \geq T(j+1)$$

from where the first piece of the loop body :

```
z := if T(z) ≥ T(j+1) then z ;
j := j+1
```

But the predicate :
$\forall(z,j)$ suchthat $I(z,j)$, $T(z) \geq T(j+1) \vee j = n$
is not always true.
Therefore, we must imaginate an other assignement to the couple (z,j).
Let $\{z := j+1\ ;\ j := j+1\}$;
with $I(z,j) \wedge (\forall k \in [1,j+1])\ T(j+1) \geq T(k)$
$\equiv I(z,j) \wedge T(j+1) \geq T(z)$

and finally :

```
z := if T(z) ≥ T(j+1) then z
     orif T(z) ≤ T(j+1) then j+1 ;
j := j+1
```

Now, the condition (1) is verified :
$\forall(z,j)$ such that $I(z,j)$
$T(z) \geq T(j+1) \vee T(z) \leq T(j+1) \vee j=n$
and the whole program is :

```
Max 2 : T(z:=1; j:=1 ;
          while j ≠ n
          do z := if T(z) ≥ T(j+1) then z
                  orif T(z) ≤ T(j+1) then j+1;
             j := j+1
          od ; z)
```

It is interesting to note that first, the search was centered on the conjunction of an invariant and a test, whereas for the guarded commands, it is centered on the invariant and the variant function. The second approach, although similar to the first is more difficult because it tries to resolve the halting problem.

Let us examine again the eight queens problem ; the deduced program (§ 2.2) is the following :

$$X := X_o\{X_o \in C^k \wedge P_1(X_o)\}\ ;$$
$$\underline{\text{while}}\ \neg(P_2(X) \wedge P_3(X) \wedge P_4(X))$$
$$\underline{\text{do}}\ X := X'\ \{X' \in C^k \wedge P_1(X')\}\ \underline{\text{od}}\ ;$$

X is then a k-tuple of pairs such that the first element of each pair are all distinct. The X' choice can be done by systematically enumerating the k-tuples. The optimisation that we know for the eight queens problem is based on the fact if the first i terms of a k-tuple infirm one of predicates P, all the k-tuples builded from these i terms will also infirm this predicate. If we go on with that example, we see that it is not always possible to strengthen the invariant. Given the program :

$$X := X_o\ \{X_o \in C^k \wedge P_1(X_o) \wedge P_3(X_o) \wedge P_4(X_o)\};$$
$$\underline{\text{while}}\ \neg P_2(X)$$
$$\underline{\text{do}}\ X := X'\ \{P_1(X') \wedge P_3(X') \wedge P_4(X')\}\ \underline{\text{od}}\ ;$$

An element X_o is : (1,1) (2,1) (3,1) ... (k,1).

We can find a variant function with the number of equality conflicts of the P_2 predicate; for example, in the position X_o, the number conflict (X_o) is C_k^2. It is tempting then to try a loop body with k alternatives :

$$\underline{\text{if}}\ eq\ (couple_i)\ \underline{\text{then}}\ couple_i := couple'_i$$
$$\{\neg eq(couple'_i)\}$$

with $eq(couple_i) \equiv (\exists j)\ y_i = y_j$.

At every step in the loop we have
$conflict(X') < conflict(X)$.
Unfortunately, the precondition gives :
$wp(couple_i := couple'_i, \neg eq(couple'_i))$
$\wedge\ conflict(X') < conflict(X)$
$\equiv eq(couple_i) \wedge (\exists couple'_i) \neg eq(couple'_i)$.
Now it is easy to show by an example that :

$$R \equiv (\forall X)\ (P_1(X) \wedge P_3(X) \wedge P_4(X))$$
$$(((\exists\ couple_i \in X)(eq(couple_i) \supset (\exists couple'_i)$$
$$\neg eq(couple'_i)) \wedge P_1(X') \wedge P_3(X') \wedge P_4(X'))$$
$$\vee\ P_2(X)$$

is not always true.

The settling strategy of such a program can be :

- to perform backtracking, if choices are actually nondeterministic ;
- to find other alternatives to complete the R predicate, in that case modifying the conflict variant function.

But it does not seem that we obtain an efficient eight queens program in this way (or else somebody would already have found it).

2.4. Specification deduction by cases

It is sometimes useful to deduce new specifications to obtain new programs. A fruitful category of specifications is the case study, in the manner of the LISP functions [3] and called also generic functions [8].

The principle is to suppose a decomposition in the space of the values of the input parameter vector x. This decomposition may be structural :

- e.g. if x is a linear list, we may have :

$$x = \underline{nil} \vee$$
$$x = \underline{cons}\ (x_1,x_2) \text{ with } x_1 = hd(x) \wedge x_2=t\ell(x)$$

or algebraic :

- e.g. if x is the vector (x_1,x_2), we may have :

$$x_1 < x_2 \vee x_1 < x_2 \vee x_1 = x_2$$

It must be noticed that the algebraic decomposition is not systematic at all and comes from the invention. The steps of the synthesis are : let a specification be S(x) and relations on x be $R_1(x)$, $R_2(x)$,... We study successively :

$$S(x) \wedge R_1(x),\ S(x) \wedge R_2(x),\dots$$

and for each case, knowing the properties of the domain of x and of the functions used in the specification, we must obtain two kinds of computation rules :

- the terminal predicates, quoted $R_i^t(x)$, for which an algorithmic function gives immediately the solution :

$$R_i^t(x)\quad \{y := f_i(x)\}\quad S(y)$$

- the non-terminal predicates : $R_i^r(x)$, for which the result is characterized by the initial specification :

$$R_i^r(x)\quad \{y := g_i(x')\}\ S(y)$$

where x' is specified as $S(h_i(x))$; g_i and h_i are algorithmic functions.
The synthesis of f_i, g_i, h_i can be made by the symbolic evaluation of the specification, but the discovery of subgoals identical to the initial goal requires a non easily automatic induction step.

The algorithmic solution of this problem is a recursive function ϕ such that :

$$\text{true } \{y := \phi(x)\}\quad S(y) \qquad (2)$$

built in the following way :

$$\begin{aligned}\phi(x) = &\ \underline{if}\ R_1^t(x)\ \underline{then}\ f_1(x)\\ &\ \underline{orif}\ R_2^t(x)\ \underline{then}\ f_2(x)\\ &\ \dots\\ &\ \underline{orif}\ R_1^r(x)\ \underline{then}\ g_1(\phi(h_1(x)))\\ &\ \underline{orif}\ R_2^r(x)\ \underline{then}\ g_2(\phi(h_2(x)))\\ &\ \dots\end{aligned}$$

By the inference rules given by Hoare, proposition (2) is well verified. As for guarded-commands, we must have :

$$(\forall x)\quad \bigcup_i R_i^t(x) \cup \bigcup_i R_i^r(x)$$

The alternative choice may be non deterministic ; if g_i is the identity function, we can transform the program into iterative program :

$$\begin{aligned}\phi(x) = &\ \underline{while}\ \neg \bigcup_i R_i^t(x)\\ &\ \underline{do}\ \underline{if}\ R_1^r(x)\ \underline{then}\ x := h_1(x)\\ &\qquad \underline{orif}\ R_2^r(x)\ \dots\\ &\ \underline{od}\\ &\ \underline{if}\ R_1^t(x)\ \underline{then}\ f_1(x)\\ &\ \dots\end{aligned}$$

The detection of sub-goals identical to the initial goal gives recursive specifications which produce iterative (or recursive) programs, whereas precedently, it was enumerating or existence of conjunctive goals.

For D(a,b), we can consider two cases :

$$\begin{aligned}D(a,b) = &\ a < b \Rightarrow (0,a)\\ &\ a \geq b \Rightarrow (1+q',\ r') \text{ with } (q',r')=D(a-b,b)\end{aligned}$$

The recursive program, with a,b input parameters and q,r result parameters, is :

```
D5 : Div(a,b,q,r) =
       if a < b then q := 0 ; r := a
       orif a ≥ b then begin
                Div (a-b,b,q',r') ;
                q := q'+1; r := r'
                end
```

This method of synthesis by cases or generic functions proceeds on the contrary of that of the loop body synthesis (§ 2.3) since in the former the preconditions are deduced from the statements on the variables, whereas in the latter the modification functions are deduced from the different cases. In the both methods, the termination problem is : given an input vector x, will the exit condition of the loop (A(x,y)) or of the recursivity ($\bigcup_i R_i^t(x)$) always be reached ? A very interesting result has recently been obtained by Sintzoff for iterative non-deterministic systems [13] : given such a system Σ which terminates if the goal Q is reached, it is possible to build a system Π "equivalent" to Σ (that is to say, ending if Σ ends, with same result) and always terminating. This construction is based on the resolution of a recursive equation of predicates and is connected to the fixpoint semantic.

2.5. Optimisation

A very important point is the optimisation of synthetised programs. Many papers have already been published in this area and we can content ourselves with classifying roughly optimisation techniques in three categories :

- the usual optimisations of algorithmic lan guages [1] ;
- the optimisations connected to the universe properties, that is to say set and operation properties [11] ;
- the optimisations by transformations of programs [6] [14] [2].

The example D(a,b) shows that the transformations coming from logical deductions give good results. In D2, we get :

- $q = 0 \supset b * q \leq a$
- $b * q \leq a \wedge \neg(b * q \leq a \wedge b * (q+1) > a)$

  $\supset b * q \leq a \wedge b * (q+1) \leq a$

  $\supset b * (q+1) \leq a$
- $b * (q+1) \leq a \;\; \{q := q+1\} \;\; b * q \leq a$

These three propositions indicates that $b * q \leq a$ is an invariant of the program and can be taken off the stop test to obtain algorithm D3. This transformation is connected to the formal research of invariants [7] [15].
The next optimisation of D3 consists in eliminating expensive operations by changing the variables.
With $r = a - b * q$, we get :

$q := 0 \Rightarrow r := a$
$q := q + 1 \Rightarrow r := r - b$
$(q+1) * b \leq a \Rightarrow r \geq b$

wich gives the D6 algorithm :

```
D6 : r := a ; q := 0 ;
     while r ≥ b
     do  q := q + 1 ; r := r - b  od
     (q,r)
```

We note that D6 is the usual program of the division of integers.

The optimisation of D5 gives, with q_1 le number of calls to Div :

```
D'6 : q1 := 0 ;
      while a ≥ b
      do a := a-b ; q1 := q1 + 1 od
      q := 0 ; r := a ;
      while q1 ≠ 0
      do q := q+1 ; q1 := q1 - 1 od
      (q,r)
```

of course, $q_1 = q_{final}$, thus :

```
D"6 : q := 0 ;
      while a ≥ b
      do a := a - b; q := q+1 od ;
      (q,a)
```

3. CONCLUSION

The first point was to give a very simple algorithm from specifications. Next, we have tried to see how to obtain more efficient programs, either by modifying the specifications, or by transforming the program using the most powerful means. We may wonder if there is not a close relation between logical transformations of programs and the deduction of specification; that is to say, given specifications S1, let A1 be the deduced algorithm and A1' the optimised program; in another way, let S2 be the new specifications of S1, from which we obtain the A2' optimised program, the question is "what is the relation between A1' and A2' ?" For the D(a,b) set, we have obtained the same program, but in the general case, it seems that the nature of the algorithms is connected to the nature of the specifications [14]. We can quote another classical example : the gcd problem. The first specification is the following :

$$(1) \quad gcd(a,b) = \max \{g \in N \mid \exists (m,n) \in N^2 , \; gm = a \wedge gn = b\}$$

This specification, directly developped, gives programs computing divisors (or multiples) of a and b, because of the variables m and n. In another way, the recursive specification :

$$(2) \quad gcd(a,b) = \begin{cases} a = b \Rightarrow a \\ a > b \Rightarrow gcd(a-b,\ b) \\ a < b \Rightarrow gcd(a,\ b-a) \end{cases}$$

leads to the well known iterative algorithm by substractions and all its variants. It is not possible to pass from the divisor-program to the substraction-program, but it is relatively easy to pass from the specification (1) to the specification (2), and we may consider that to be automatic by folding and unfolding [3].

The last point of this conclusion is that there is not a single method to get over the specification-programming step. We must use a lot of techniques (programs synthesis, automatic deduction, invariants search, program transformation, symbolic evaluating, and so on) of which most are in the research area. That is why this paper tries to clarify and simplify the problem in order to advance very high level programming.

4. BIBLIOGRAPHY

[1] Allen, F.E. and Cocke, J - A catalogue of optimizing transformations. Design and optimisation of compilers. Prentices Hall 1972

[2] Arsac, J. - Program transforms as a programming tool. Institut de Programmation, Université de Paris VI, 1976

[3] Burstall, R.M. and Darlington, J. - Some transformations for developing recursive programs. Proc. Int. Conf. on Reliable Software, Los Angeles, California, april 1975

[4] Dershowitz, N. and Manna, Z. - On automating Structured Programming. Colloques IRIA, Proving and Improving Programs.Arc et Senans,7.75

[5] Dijkstra, E. - Guarded Commands, Nondeterminacy and Formal Derivation of Programs. C. ACM 18, 8, august 1975

[6] Gerhart, S.L. - Knowledge about programs : a model and case study. in [3].

[7] Katz, S. and Manna, Z. - Logical Analysis of Programs - C. ACM, 19, 4, april 1976

[8] King, P.R. - Program Synthesis using Generic Functions. New directions in Algorithmic Languages, WG 2.1., ed. IRIA, 1975

[9] Manna, Z., and Waldinger, R. - Knowledge and Reasoning in Program Synthesis. Artificial Intelligence 6, 1975

[10] Pair, C. - Some proposals for a very high level language on a variable universe, in [8]

[11] Schwartz J.T. - Automatic Data Structure Choice in a Language of Very High Level. C. ACM, 18, 12, Dec. 1975

[12] Shaw, M., Wulf, Wm. A., London R.L. - Abstraction and Verification in Alphard. Iteration and Generators - Carnegie-Mellon University, august 1976

[13] Sintzoff, M. - Iterative methods for the generation of successful programs. MBLE Research Lab. Brussels, dec. 1976

[14] Wegbreit, B. - Goal Directed program transformation. Third ACM Symposium on principles of Programming Languages. Atlanta, Georgia, 1976

[15] Wegbreit, B. - The Synthesis of loop predicates. C. ACM, 17, 2, Feb. 1974

E. Morlet and D. Ribbens, (Eds.), International Computing Symposium 1977.

SOLUTIONS AND THEIR PROBLEMS

Dennis de Champeaux
Mirror Co
Vakgroep Bedrijfsinformatica en Accountancy
University of Amsterdam
Amsterdam, Holland

0. Abstract

Recent developments in the problem solving techniques: search, reduction and pseudo reduction (where sub-problems are interdependent) are discussed.
An algorithm is given for pseudo reduction and it is compared with other approaches. Some ideas are suggested how to improve automatically an operator tool box and how to improve a heuristic function, using solutions of simple problems.

Contents

1. Overview

(In Nepal all paths and bridges are liable to disappear or change at no notice due to monsoons, Acts of Gods, etc./ from the legend of a Nepal map)

The terminology of natural language suggests that problems of different types can be distinguished.
There are yes/no questions about logical truth, empirical truth, and modal truth; which-, what-, who-questions about entities that fulfil certain characteristics; when-, where-, why-questions about time, location, reasons and motives of events; how questions about constructions, and possibly still other types. These different questions do not correspond to absolute distinctions in the sense that they require different techniques to solve them.
For a while it has been popular in A.I. to transform how-questions into yes/no questions and solve them with the resolution technique.

These days however, graph searching techniques are more powerful hence there is a tendency to translate problem solving into graph searching. A natural interpretation of graph searching is finding an answer to a how-problem where the start state must be transformed into a goal state using a set of actions, and where the nodes in the graph correspond to the collection of states and the actions to the edges.

We will discuss recent developments in this problem solving paradigm. In section 2 some distinctions are made in the how-problem family. In section 3 several techniques are outlined. In section 4 some ideas are given suggesting what to do next in this field. Finally in the appendix an algorithm is given to handle pseudo reduction which deals with conjunctive interdependent sub-problems.

2.0. Distinctions

Since what lives under the heading of 'problems' is a wide and heterogenous family we must first make some distinctions and throw out pathologies in order to limit ourselves to a sub-family which can be dealt in the current stage of formalizations.

2.1. Fuzzy versus clear problems

At the moment fuzzy problems are beyond the capability of any formalizable strategy. The situation is gravest where the goal of a problem is only losely formulated (or known), as in some areas of political decision making, inductive generalisation, or the writing of a good survey article.
But even where the goal is perfectly well known and describable, when the

knowledge about the topic to be modeled is incomplete one has a fuzzy problem and the solution construction process is doomed to failure. Yet a formalized strategy need not be at a loss in this case, as is pointed out in /6/, which suggests a global plan that neglects all sorts of inaccessible details (when there is a reasonable chance that they can be dealt with, step by step, during the execution stage).
As we will see later this approach is also valuable where the problem solver has complete knowledge about the topic at hand. For the sequal we will exclude the fuzzy problems and so concentrate on those whose goal as well as topic is well known and formalizable.

2.2. Plan versus algorithm solutions

Our next task is to discriminate between those problems for which a solution can be found in the form of a plan, and those more difficult problems which can only be tackled with an algorithm.
With "plan" we mean a simple sequence of actions (also called operators), in contrast to an algorithm which, apart from actions, is composed out of case distinctions and/or recursions (possibly replaced by loops). At first one might think that this distinction runs parallel to the separation of problems into a specific topic, solvable by a plan, or a general topic, solvable only by a algorithm.

Fig. 1

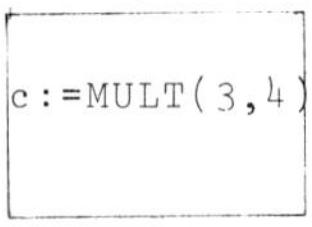

Example of a solution in the form of a plan for a specific problem: assign to c the product of 3 and 4, where, among other operators, MULT is available which multiplies arbitrary arguments.

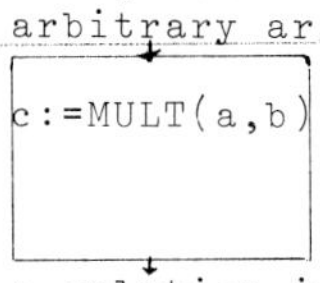

Example of a solution in the form of a plan for a non-specific problem, where the same operator MULT is available.

continued

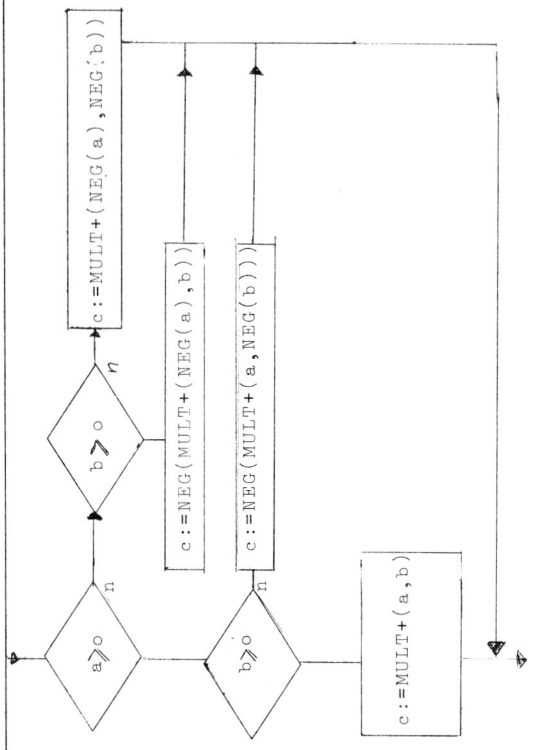

Example of a solution in the form of an algorithm, containing case distinctions, for a non-specific problem, using the operator MULT+, which produces a product under the restriction that its arguments are positive, and the operator NEG, which switches the sign of its argument.

The examples in fig. 1, however, show that this hypothesis isn't correct. On the other hand there are specific problems for which it is easier (for human problem solvers) to design an algorithm, capable of handling a broader task, and of which the original problem is a special case.

In order to instruct somebody to do the repetitive task T, say 15 times, one is unlikely to offer the plan: "do T T T T T T T T T T T T T T T". Instead there is the convention to write in this case the ellipsis "do $T_1 \ldots T_{15}$", which is a shorthand notation for the algorithm "repeat T fifteen times".

In the same spirit, if one wants to instruct a computer to do a certain task, say 15000 times, one is not advised to do this in the form of a plan.

Automatic algorithm generation can be seen as plan generation augmented with the capability of recognizing cases which lead to simpler sub-problems and the capability of recognizing a sub-problem P_2 as being of the same 'form' but 'intrinsically simpler' than a previously generated sub-problem P_1, thus introducing a loop (or a recursion).

If we denote the problem of realizing the goal g starting from the situation s by (s,g), then the criterion "(s_2,g_2) is intrinsically simpler than (s_1,g_1)" looks something like:
$s_1 \models s_2$, (meaning that s_2 can be inferred form s_1), $g_1 \models g_2$, and there is also a well-ordered relation R with $R(s_1,g_1) > R(s_2,g_2)$ ensuring only a finite cycling through the loop at execution time.

Obviously these conditions can only be satisfied if somewhere between p_1 and p_2 there has already been generated a case distinction which can lead out of the potential loop.
Automatic algorithm generation would thus need a theorem prover (which can be seen as an instrument to construct plans; e.g.: which sequence of actions, inferences, must be performed starting from some axioms and the negated theorem in order to reach the goal, a contradiction). Since it is not yet generally clear how to perform the case recognition task and how to obtain the well-ordering relation and since all general purpose theorem provers are still quite weak, until now only a few simple algorithms have been synthesized automatically (see / 7/ and /9 /).

For the remainder of this paper we will exclude problems which can only be solved by an algorithm, whether for an essential or practical reason.

2.3. Explicit versus implicit goals.

As we assumed in 2.1. the goal of a problem is clearly described. Still we have to distinguish between a description which indicates a specific element in the state space that must be reached and a description which formulates a criterion that must hold in an element of the state space.
Notice that if one represents a state as a conjunction of first order predicate calculus non-negative literals, such an implicit goal, described by a criterion, becomes a meta predicate, which expects an argument from a certain subclass of the first order, well formed formulas. And in fact the explicit goal description then becomes a special case when we introduce from the is-clan the predicate "≙" and reformulate the problem by: "find a state x for which ≙(x, $state_{goal}$) holds".
A well known problem with an implicit goal is to find a 'best' solution, using an optimum criterion, among a set of solutions; but as we shall see there are techniques which automatically produce, under certain conditions, a'best' solution when they solve a problem.

Some of the techniques in the next section apply only to problems with an explicit goal.

3.0. Techniques

In this section we outline the basic technique, search, a more specific one, reduction, and a specific recent technique, pseudo reduction. With the exception of recent developments the first two techniques are more fully described in /10/.

3.1.0. Search

Search is simply an orderly trying out of actions of states to obtain the sequence of actions which connects the initial state with a goal state. If the goal state is explicitly given one has the option to work from both sides, bi-directionally; otherwise the search is called uni-directional. Bi-directional search can lead to exponential savings in comparison to uni-directional search as is shown in /12/. Uni-directional search can be done in two modes: depth first, where alternatives at a choosing point are remembered for the purpose of trying them in a later stage when a previous choice has lead to a failure; and breadth first, where all alternatives at one level are tried and their results remembered before the next level is entered.
Depth first search has the advantage that it is easy implementable (in a language allowing recursion) by using the stack. Breadth first search has the advantage that it will always end up, given enough resources, with a shortest solution path if there is one.
This property makes breadth first search a candidate for the title of general plan generator. This title is supported by the fact that theorem proving can be pushed in a uni-directional breadth-

first search framework. In practice however this technique gets lost in the exponentially exploding search spaces.

3.1.1. Heuristic search

The power of the search technique improves dramatically when knowledge about the search space is available which can be expressed as a function that assigns to every state in the search space a number estimating the nearness to the goal. Uni-directional and bi-directional search combined with a heuristic function, guiding the effort, can still end up with a shortest solution path when certain conditions hold for the heuristic functions(/10/ ,/ 3/).
An other theoretical result is that an ordering of heuristic functions can be defined, which can then be interpreted as ordering the estimation quality, and leads to provable differences in performance of two estimators of different quality (/10/, /4 /).

The power of such a heuristic function can be demonstrated by a bi-directional program working on the 24-puzzle, having a search space of magnitude 10^{25}, where it solves with a path of length 340 (fig. 2) the intuitively most difficult problem.
On the other hand this technique can no longer claim to be a general plan generator as a consequence of the topic sensitive heuristic, which until now was always cooked up by a programmer.
In section 4 we will sketch an approach describing how to get them automatically.

3.2.0. Reduction

This technique applies only to those cases where an additional operator is available (or can be constructed) which assigns to a problem specification one or more sequences of sub-problems.
Each sequence has the property of being composed of at least two sub-problems which constitute a solution to the original problem and are independent of each other in the sense that a solution of one does not affect a solution of an other. In fig. 3 an example is depicted of a problem P for which it is sufficient to solve either Q_1 and Q_2 or to solve R_1, R_2 and R_3.
Ordinary search strategies are necessary for deciding which sequence to pick if more than one is produced by the reduction operator, and they are also necessary for those sub-problems which do not decompose further.

Fig. 2 Example of the performance of a bi-directional heuristic 24-puzzle search program.

startnode

B	24	23	22	21
20	19	18	17	16
15	14	13	12	11
10	9	8	7	6
5	4	3	2	1

goalnode

1	2	3	4	5
6	7	8	9	10
11	12	13	14	15
16	17	18	19	20
21	22	23	24	B

front length 75
nodes visited 6896
nodes expanded 2671
solution path length 340 (177+163)
solution time 1130 CPU seconds (C.D.C.)

Fig.3 Example of an AND/OR-tree where a reduction operator working on the problem P produces two reductions.

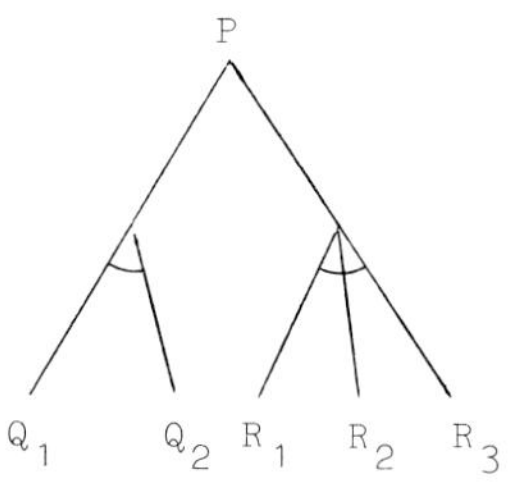

The standard example problem which is completely solvable with repeated reduction is the Tower of Hanoi. In logic a trivial reduction of U⊨V1&V2 is:
U⊨V1 and U&V1⊨V2, or alternatively
U⊨V2 and U&V2⊨V1.
A regular search problem can in fact be transformed into reduction.
The problem of going from s to g (s,g) can be reduced to solving each element of the sequence $(s,t_1)\ldots(t_i,t_{i+1})$ $(t_{i+1}, t_{i+2})\ldots(t_n,g)$, but in general it is not obvious how to obtain the intermediate stepping stones $t_1,\ldots,t_n$ if reduction of effort would result from this particular order.
An analogus reduction would be obtained if a particular sequence of ac-

tions $\{A_i\}_{i=1}^n$ could be found leading to effort reduction by solving $(s,p_1)...$ $(A_i(p_i),p_{i+1})...(A_n(p_n),g)$, where p_i is a state in which the action A_j can be performed leading to $A_j(p_j)$.

Observe that although these sub-problems are independant in the above mentioned sense, a subproblem is still unspecified because its start state is not known until the previous sub-problem in the sequence is solved.

In /13/ a method is given how under an easily satisfiable condition such a sequence of actions can be constructed. The condition is that every action has associated with it a hierarchy of its preconditions (which must hold in order that the action can be performed). A precondition has a lower criticality than a second precondition if constructing a state in which the low critica- lity precondition holds, does not af- fect the truth of the second precondi- tion. The sequence of actions is then constructed by an ordinary search which pays attention only to preconditions of highest criticality. If this search is succesfull then this method can be re- peated on each sub-problem by lowe- ring the criticality level.

A facility which can be considered as returning to a higher abstraction level, for finding an alternative action se- quence, is necessary for coping with sub- problems which turn out to be unsolva- ble. This method can also be used for creating plans that ignore details, as mentioned in section 2.1.

3.2.1. Pseudo Reduction

Where the goal of a problem is a con- junction, reduction of it to finding solutions for each element of the con- junction is only allowed when the sub- problems are independent of each other. Since the reduction technique is quite strong it is attractive to apply it also to conjunctive goals which are 'weakly' dependent by supplementing the technique with 'watchdogs' that signal conflicts in proposed sub-pro- blem sequences. Such a pseudo reduction technique can be considered to employ AND/OR/& -pseudo-graph's, where the & stands for graph parts which are po- tentially dependent. In fig. 4 two examples are given of such AND/OR/&- pseudo-graphs. In Appendix 1 we give an algorithm explaining how one might run around in such a graph. Several implementations have been constructed which must be considered as special cases of this algorithm.

In fact a direct implementation of the algorithm without a strong heuristic cannot be advised because of the high- ly explosive growth rate.

Fig. 4 Two examples of AND/OR/&-pseudo- graphs. The nodes represent problem spe- cifications. The situation is shown af- ter reductions of two levels have been completed, assuming that the subproblem Q is irreducible.

= OR-splitting
= AND-splitting
= &-splitting
(see the appendix for more details)

O pseudo redu- ces to P&Q. P pseudo redu- ces to R&S.

O pseudo redu- ces to P & Q P reduces to R AND S.

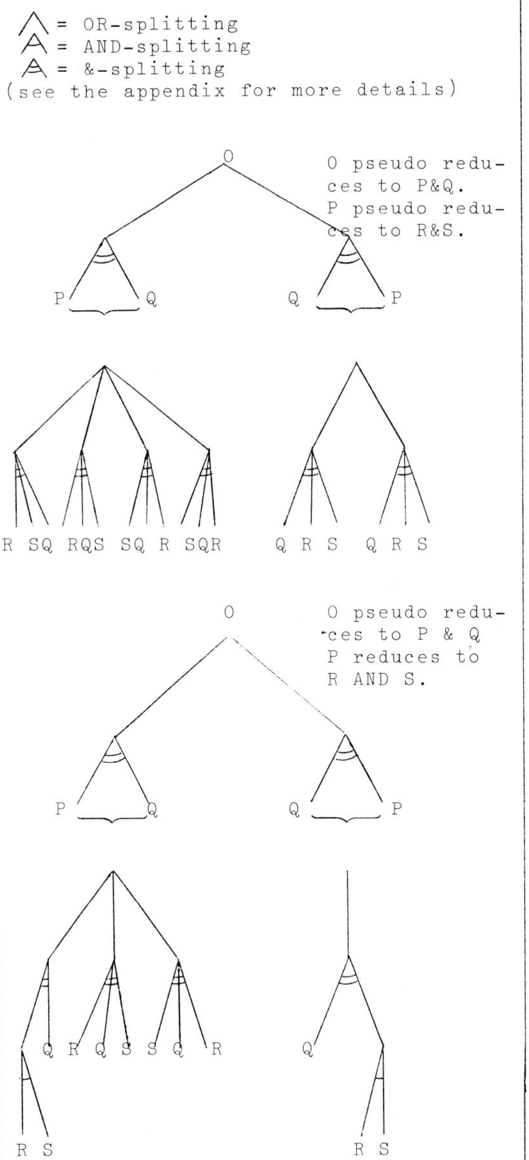

In /15/ and /16/ an essentially depth first approach is described to tackle the growth rate. The implementation easily facilitates switching of attention from one branch to nearby branches in the graph. Indeed, too easily because in /16/ it is reported that the program can get into a loop. Another appraoch is given in /14/. The trick used here boils down to making no commitments about the linearity of plans which still need refinement unless a conflict has arisen. Thus, plan construction follows many branches of the graph in parallel. A limitation of the implementation of this approach is that OR-nodes which do not result from pseudo reduction cannot be handled (see also the appendix).

4.0. Next issues.

The backbone of the technique we have discussed in the former section is heuristic search. At present every thing seems to be allright since we know a lot about it and even: "The problem of efficiently searching a graph has essentially been solved and thus no longer occupies AI researchers. This one core area, at least, seems to be well under control". (from /11/). On the other hand application of heuristic search presupposes 1) a nice representation of the problem space, 2) a good set of operators and 3) a strong heuristic function. The adjectives 'nice', 'good' and 'strong' indicate that these topics are not under control at all. A complicating factor is that these issues are strongly related with other core areas of AI.

4.1. Nice representations

In order to get a grip on this issue we will formulate it in category terminology[1]. A representation is a category C in which the objects are state descriptions (problem specifications are also possible, but let's not make it too complicated) and in which the morfisms are the operators.
It is reasonable to assume $HOM(C,C)=\{ID_C\}$ and for representation of the 'real world' that $HOM(C_1,C_2)\neq\emptyset \Rightarrow HOM(C_2,C_1)=\emptyset$.
A representation transformation from C to D can then be considered as two covariant functors $F:C\rightarrow D$ and $G:D\rightarrow C$ such that $FG=ID_D$, and F is full (thus $F(HOM_C(C_1,C_2))=HOM_D(FC_1,FC_2)$).
Such a transformation makes sense with respect to a problem P in C when FP is solvable in D, since one can 'pull back' the solution with G.

"1) Just skip freightening technicalities".

But now we have the question how we get a nice category D in which P is easier to solve than in C.
One way is 'forgetting' morfisms in C. To go from N.Y. to L.A. one can get rid of the operator 'move one meter'. An other way is 'forgetting' objects. To construct a bridge we can throw out microscopic descriptions. A third way combines the former two. A question however is whether other general options are still remaining. Emphasis is given in /1 / and / 2/ on different languages that might be used for the representation. Certainly one might switch representation within one syntax by mapping one universe of discourse into another basket of concepts, especially when 'completely other' types of operators are active in the second universe. Still it seems probable that we (human problem solvers) have only a limited collection of ad-hoc transformations of this type available (although some people have the capability to recognize (once in x centuries) a new fruitful transformation). Therefore it looks premature to automatize this aspect of intelligence. Even more problematical is the question whether representation switching by human problem solvers is done by changing the syntax of the language used for the representation. Such ad-hoc tricks may be necessary however, for automatic problem solvers since we have not yet found a general purpose representation (just think about the procedural-declarative debates). But if several representation languages are hanging around one is seduced into thinking about a single underlying general purpose language and so...

4.2. Good operators

Good operators are characterized by contradictory features. They must take 'big' steps leading to a short solution path without using overly strict preconditions leading to a wide applicability. It is also important to have only a few operators such that the fan out of search graphs is small. As was already suggested in section 3.2.0. a compromise can be found by making packages of operators for which the highest criticality of preconditions is equal (this thus presupposes not only a relative rank-ordering of the preconditions of an operator but also an absolute interoperator ordering).
The hierarchy induced on these packages can then be employed by first plugging in the package of highest order and in case of (partial) failure, by resorting to a lower level package.

Although for many years it was 'forbidden' to suggest automatic learning within AI as a device to obtain more than trivial improvements, it seems to us that enough fundamental structures about the search paradigm have now been developed to enter a second round. More specifically, one might attempt to automatize the synthesis of big step operators. In /8/ a very general scheme is mentioned (intended for all kinds of learning) that for the generation of new sequences (of say operators) relies on cross over, inversion and random mutation of parent sequences. Random mutation is a dirty word especially since the ultimate check on the usefulness of new sequences comes from a survival of the fittest mechanism that needs, in order to fight combinatorial explosion, an unbounded (practically infinite) amount of time. Perhaps it is sufficient to guide the random mutations by paying attention only to those sequences that actually appear in solution paths of simple problems. Remarkable sequences are then those where the preconditions of a subsequent operator are inferrably satisfied as a consequence of the preceding operators. Less remarkable but still interesting are those sequences where all preconditions (the few the better) can be pushed to the front of the sequence. But in the end, we have to admit, a hypothesized sequence must prove its usefullness in practice before being co-opted by an operator package.

4.3. Strong heuristics

Even if a problem solver can augment dynamically its assortment of operators it is still faced with the decisions to be made in those choice situations where more than one operator apply. Since one has good results in settling these decisions by using externally provided heuristic functions, it would be desirable to automatize the adaption of a heuristic function by evaluating right and wrong decisions based on it. (Automatic creation of a heuristic function is adaptation of the heuristic $h \equiv 0$.)

The input of a heuristic function is commonly a state to be judged, and the output is an estimation of the path length to a goal using this particular state. Unfortunately, a state description is a 'voluminous thing'. Another point is that we do not need an estimation of the distance to a goal; instead it is sufficient to know whether one comes nearer to a goal. A simple transformation shows that a distant function is equivalent to a direction function. Let h be a heuristic function, let P and Q be states, where Q can be reached in one step from P. Then we can define the function D1 with:

$h(Q)=h(P) + D1(P,Q)$.

We can rewrite D1 as a function D2 of four arguments:

$D2(Q-P, P-Q, P,Q)= D1(P,Q)$,

in which Q-P denotes the difference between the two states, e.g. some literals when states are described using the predicate calculus, and which corresponds to the add-list of the operator used to transform P into Q; in the same way P-Q corresponds with the delete list.

(Observe that we can reconstruct h from D2 up to an arbitrarily unimportant constant). But now we approximate D2 with a function d:

$d(Q-P, P-Q) = D2(Q-P, P-Q, P, Q)$.

We can interpret this d as an estimate of improvement as we go from P to Q. Since the arguments of d are 'small things' there is the reasonable hope that a program can generate its own d-function in a specific problem area, by using a clever, externally provided, training sequence, which leads from simple problems solvable by breadth first search ($h \equiv 0$), to more difficult ones.

5. Conclusion.

Problem solving using search and reduction technique has reached a plateau. Recent efforts in this field relate to constructing solutions where the goal is a conjunction of interdependent subproblems. Future hills to be climbed concern automatic adaptation of operator packages and automatic improvement heuristic functions.

Appendix

In order to handle AND/OR/&-pseudo graphs we will employ the same trick as was done in /5/, we will squeeze them into ordinary OR-graphs. After this transformation we simply turn loose on it the A* algorithm of /10/. Instead of associating a state with a node, as is the custom in the search technique, we associate with a node a problem specification. Since pseudo reduction has to deal with interacting subproblems we will be careful in our description of problem specifications (given in pseudo BNF).

problem_0 specification = regular problem_1 | &-problem_4;

regular problem_1 = simple problem_2 | AND-problem_3;

simple problem_2 = terminal problem_5 | reducible problem;
AND-problem_3 = conjunction of independent simple problems_2;
$\text{\&-problem}_4$ = ordered sequence of regular problems_1;

$\text{terminal problem}_5$ = solved problem_6 | unsolved and irreducible problem;
solved problem_6 = a triple consisting of start state, goal state and an operator which transforms the start state into the goal state.

The right hand sides above without a subscript are terminals. We will elaborate on the 'reducible problem' in the sequel while describing the successor function Γ ; the other two must be obvious.

Remark: A peculiarity of the &-problem is that the sub-problem in its ordered sequence may be partially unspecified, e.g. when the dependency is the consequence of variables that are shared by these sub-problems. Solutions of each sub-problem may restrict a variable and these restrictions have to be compatible. Therefore we will specify in the sequel a strict order, left to right, how to deal with these sub-problems. A problem thus gets in a unique way possibly more specified.

A node is called a solution node if it is:

1) a solved problem, or
2) an AND-problem with only solved problems in its conjunction, or
3) an &-problem with only solved problems in its sequence (or inside AND-problems of its sequence) with the additional property that the start state associated with an element in the sequence holds in the goal state of the preceding element (except for the first element).

A node is called a failure node if:

1) it contains an unsolved and irreducible problem, or
2) it is an &-problem which contains adjacent solved problems, not preceded by reducible problems (or AND-problems containing reducible problems) for which the start state of the second one doesn't hold in the goal state of the preceding problem.

To facilitate the description of the successor function Γ working on nodes we will assume that with each reducible problem is connected a level number (to be explained in the sequel); and that a reducible problem reduces only to atmost two OR-related sub-problems, two AND-related sub-problems or two &-related sub-problems.

Now we are ready to describe the successor function Γ.

Let n be the node to be expanded, let r be the left most occurring reducible problem of lowest level in n (if there is not such a r then $\Gamma(n)=\emptyset$).

We distinguish several cases:

A) If r reduces to $s_1 \vee s_2$ then $\Gamma(n)$ consists out of the two nodes obtained by substituting s_1 respectively s_2 for r.

B) If r reduces to $s_1 \wedge s_2$ then

B1) in case n=r then $\Gamma^2(n)=\text{AND}(s_1, s_2)$;

B_2) in case n=AND(...,r,...) then $\Gamma^2(n)=\text{AND}(\ldots,s_1,s_2,\ldots)$;

B_3) in case $n=\&(\ldots,r_{i-1},r,r_{i+1},\ldots,r_k)$ then

$$\Gamma(n)=\bigcup_{j=i}^{k}\{\&(\ldots,r_{i-1},s_1,r_{i+1},\ldots,r_j,s_2,r_{j+1},\ldots,r_k)\}\cup\bigcup_{j=i}^{k}\{\&(\ldots,r_{i-1},s_2,r_{i+1},\ldots,r_j,s_1,r_{j+1},\ldots,r_k)\};$$

B_4) in case $n=\&(\ldots,r_{i-1},\text{AND}(\ldots,r,\ldots),r_{i+1},\ldots,r_k)$ then

$$\Gamma(n)=\bigcup_{j=i}^{k}\{\&(\ldots,r_{i-1},\text{AND}(\ldots,s_1,\ldots),r_{i+1},\ldots,r_j,s_2,r_{j+1},\ldots,r_k)\}\cup\bigcup_{j=i}^{k}\{\&(\ldots,r_{i-1},\text{AND}(\ldots,s_2,\ldots),r_{i+1},\ldots,r_j,s_1,r_{j+1},\ldots,r_k)\}.$$

C) If r reduces to $s_1 \& s_2$ then

C1) in case n=r then $\Gamma^2(n)=\{\&(s_1,s_2)\}\cup\{\&(s_2,s_1)\}$;

C2) in case $n=\&(\ldots,r_{i-1},r,r_{i+1},\ldots,r_k)$ then

$$\Gamma(n)=\bigcup_{j=i}^{k}\{\&(\ldots,r_{i-1},s_1,r_{i+1},\ldots,r_j,s_2,r_{j+1},\ldots,r_k)\}\cup\bigcup_{j=i}^{k}\{\&(\ldots,r_{i-1},s_2,r_{i+1},\ldots,r_j,s_1,r_{j+1},\ldots,r_k)\};$$

C3) in case n=AND(...,r,...) then:

$$\Gamma(n)=\{\&(s_1,\text{AND}(\ldots,s_2,\ldots))\}\cup\{\&(s_2,\text{AND}(\ldots,s_1,\ldots))\};$$

(Remark: The second parts in C1, C2 and C3 can be suppressed when r reduces to an <u>ordered</u> $s_1 \& s_2$)

C4) in case n=&(...,AND(...,r,...),...) then performe first C3 and next C2.

Observe that insertion of say s_2 somewhere to the right of s_1, as happens in B3, B4 and C2 may result in a sequence that can be simplified by replacing s_2 and an adjacent subproblem c by AND (s_2,c) under the provisio that s_2 and c are independent.

Finally the levels of s_1 and s_2 are equal to the level of r plus one.
Since we assume that reduction of n to m (thus $m \in \Gamma(n)$) requires a non- negative cost $l(n,m)$, we can define for a node n the function $\hat{g}(n)$ as the current known minimal cost of reducing the original problem s to n. As usual we presuppose that we have available a function $\hat{h}$, where $\hat{h}(n)$ is an estimation of reaching a solution node by expanding n.
And thus we define $\hat{f}(n)=\hat{g}(n)+\hat{h}(n)$.
Next we describe a modified A^*algorithm:
Step 1: $W:=\{s\}$; $F:C:=\emptyset$.
Step 2: Select $n \in W$ for which $\hat{f}(n)$ is minimal, resolve ties arbitrarily, but in favor of solution nodes; $W:=W-\{n\}$.
Step 3: If n is solution node then exit with solution.
Step 4: If n is a failure node then $F:=F \cup \{n\}$ and go to step 12.
Step 5: $V:=\Gamma(n)$; $C:=C \cup \{n\}$.
Step 6: Select $x \in V$ and $V:=V-\{x\}$.
Step 7: If $x \in F$ then go to step 11.
Step 8: If $x \in W$ then [if $\hat{g}(n)+l(n,x) < \hat{g}(x)$ then { redirect the pointer to n} ; go to step 11] .
Step 9: If $x \in C$ then [if $\hat{g}(n)+l(n,x) < \hat{g}(x)$ then { redirect the pointer to n; $C:=C-\{x\}$; $W:=W \cup \{x\}$}; go to step 11] .
Step 10: $W:=W \cup \{x\}$; provide a pointer to n and store $\hat{g}(x)=\hat{g}(n)+l(n,x)$ also at x.
Step 11: If $V \neq \emptyset$ then go to step 6.
Step 12: If $W \neq \emptyset$ then go to step 2.
Step 13: Exit without solution.
The conclusion out of all this mess is that pseudo reduction is only feasible when a high priority can be given to the recognition in an early stage of failure nodes, otherwise the generator of successor nodes swamps the memory.
It is not clear whether the trick used in /14/ of not making commitments about the ordering of sub-problems is the answer. In particular it is not clear whether the "Resolve Conflicts" component of the program described in /14/ allows arbitrarily often 'undoing' of sub-goals (as sometimes is necessary and permitted by this algorithm).

References

IJCAI4 referes to: Advance papers of the fourth international joint conference on artificial intelligence, 1975, AI lab, 545 Technology Square, Cambridge Mass. 02139, USA.

1) Amarel, S., On representations of problems of reasoning about actions, In Machine Intelligence 3, Ed Michie D., Edinburgh, 1968;
2) --, Representations and Modelling in Problems of Program Formation, in Machine Intelligence 6, Ed Meltzer/ Michie, Edinburgh, 1971;
3) Champeaux, D.de and Sint, L. An Improved Bi-Directional Heuristic Search Algorithm, IJCAI4 and Journal ACM, in press;
4) --, An Optimality Theorem for Bi-Directional Heuristic Search Algorithm, The Computer Journal, in press;
5) Chang, C.L. and Slagle, J.R., An Admissible and Optimal Algorithm for Searching AND/OR Graphs, Artificial Intelligence 2, 1971;
6) Chien, R.T. and Weissman, S., Planning and Execution in incompletely Specified Environments, IJCAI4;
7) Green, C. and Barstow, D., Some rules for the automatic synthesis of programs, IJCAI4;
8) Bookreview by F. Hayes-Roth about Holland, J.H. Adaption in Natural and Artificial Systems, Ann Arbor 1975, which appeared in Sigart 53, August 1975.
9) Manna, Z. and Waldinger, R., Knowledge and Reasoning in Program Synthesis, IJCAI4;
10) Nilsson, N.J., Problem-Solving Methods in A.I., 1971, McGraw-Hill;
11) Nilsson, N.J., Artificial Intelligence, IFIP74,(778-801);
12) Pohl, I., Bi-directional and Heuristic Search in Path Problems, Clearing house for Federal Scientific and Technical Information, Springfield, Virginia 22151, 1969;
13) Sacerdoti, E.D., Planning in an Hierarchy of Abstraction Spaces, IJCAI3, 1973;
14) Sacerdoti, E.D., The Nonlinear Nature of Plans, IJCAI4;
15) Tate, A., Interacting goals and their use, IJCAI4;
16) --, Interplan, memorandum MIP-R-109, Machine Intelligence Research Unit, University of Edinburgh, 1974.

Careful typing was done by Anya Kooijman.

E. Morlet and D. Ribbens, (Eds.), International Computing Symposium 1977.

A COMPARISON OF MODULA WITH OTHER SYSTEM PROGRAMMING LANGUAGES

Jiri Hoppe
Institut für Informatik
Eidg. Technische Hochschule
Zürich, Switzerland

A comparison is made between Modula and some other programming languages. Especially considered are concepts for modularity, synchronizing, representation of parallel activities and I/O handling.

Introduction

The great proliferation of appplications of micro and minicomputers in all branches of our life has increased the need for a high level language for real time (RT) programming. In many countries of the world a number of languages have been developed for this purpose such as PEARL [3] in Germany, CORAL [4] and RTL in England, Concurrent Pascal [7] and CS4 in the USA.

A project was undertaken at the ETH Zürich to investigate the techniques of multiprogramming as well as to develop a new language that can be used to write an operating system for a small computer without coding in assembly language. One of the results of this project was a new programming language called MODULA [1,2].

This paper attempts to compare MODULA with some other system programming languages.

Systems written in sequential languages and most of the programs written in real time languages basically consist of two parts: of a basic operating system (host operating system, supervisory system) - mostly written in assembly language - and of the actual program.

It seems that such a concept is not suitable for real time programming on small computers. There are the following difficulties:

a) There is hardly enough memory in small computers to accommodate a standard basic operating system.
b) A general basic operating system offers a great number of comfortable functions at the expense of having low speed and using a large core memory. Unfortunately, a particular RT system generally needs only a fraction of such functions. When writing a particular system in a good RT language only a minimal basic system should be used in order to achieve efficiency and to save memory.
c) Any changes in the hardware configuration not only require a rewriting of the basic OS, but also quite often involves changes in the compiler of the language in which the system is written. This generates problems when such a language should be used operationally. It is not to be expected that a system programmer be able to adapt a compiler when a new device is added to the system.

Considering the above mentioned problems we conceived MODULA in another way than most of the existing languages for system programming. We wanted the language to be suited for writing programs down to the lowest level of programming. This would enable writing the whole operating system in a high level language and to omit the dangerous assembly part.

Using MODULA we need no basic operating system. The only part which is written in assembly language is a very short NUCLEUS about 100 words long, which implements only primitives for synchronization and process scheduling. This NUCLEUS may be considered as an extension of the hardware and could even be incorporated as a microprogram in some computers. All other parts of an operating system written in MODULA - even drivers - can be written in this high level language. This gives us entire independence of the hardware configuration and allows writing efficient programs which are tailored to the particular program.

All other languages mentioned above require more or less a large basic operating system written in a assembly language (e.g. the kernel of Concurrent Pascal needs 4k). The communication between the program written in RT language and the outside world is done by calls to the basic OS. Some of the languages specify exactly the format of such calls (e.g. Pearl). Some other languages (e.g. Corall) lay down no fixed conventions. The calls are implementation dependent.

We tried to define a small but powerful language, free of ambiguous or complicated concepts, a language which can be defined on a few pages and therefore can be well understood by any programmer. We tried to represent all actions in the computer by similar concepts in the language, so that every programmer realizes the actual flow of the program. For example, we omitted any "on condition" construct as used in Pearl for interrupt control. We can express it in MODULA by two parallel processes communicating together: one main process and another process which controls the interrupt.

Likewise, we did not introduce any dangerous concepts such as goto's and pointers. According to our experience the absence of goto's forces the programmer to think of his program thoroughly which results in better structured and more efficient programs.

Although they are very efficient, pointers offer no security as they allow the program to by-pass any access rule or synchronizing concept. Up to now, the question of introducing pointers into MODULA is still open since we are looking for a concept which could replace them. The aim is to find a concept that offers both high efficiency and full security.

Modules

The concept of a module gave the name to the language MODULA. The idea of modularity exists in nearly all system programming languages. It is represented by modules in PEARL, by modules and bricks in RTL, and by classes in Concurrent Pascal.

Modules are used to divide a large program into a number of small parts which can be defined, checked, and tested one at a time independently of each other.

In contrast to modules in other programming languages (Pearl, RTL) the module in MODULA is not a unit of compilation or element of a library. The essential purpose of a module is the control of access to all entities declared or used in a module. All data and procedures declared in a module are strictly local unless they are exported or imported by means of two lists. The define list exports local data and procedures for use in external modules. Exported data are read only. The use list allows external data to be used inside of a module.

There is a close relationship between the class of the Concurrent Pascal and the module of MODULA. Both of them are used to define types with associated operators. Let us compare these two concepts.

Consider the following class definition:

```
type C = class
           var x,y:T;
           procedure p(U);
             begin ... end;
           procedure entry q(V);
             begin ... end;
         begin S
         end
```

This is expressed in terms of a module as follows:

```
module M;
  define R,q,s;
  type R=record x,y: T end;
  procedure p(var r:R; U);
    begin ... end p;
  procedure q(var r: R; V);
    begin ... end q;
  procedure s(var r:R);
    begin S end s;
end M
```

Using class C we can create several instances of the data structure, each consisting of the components x and y ;

```
var a,b: C
```

Thereby the initialisation statement S is implicitly invoked once for a and once for b . An invocation of procedure q , applied to a is expressed conveniently as

```
a.q(v)
```

In the case of the module structure, the two variables are declared as

```
var a,b: R
```

and the call as

```
q(a,v) .
```

Initialization must be stated explicitly as s(a) and should be never forgotten if we try to simulate class by module.

The principal advantage of the class notation appears, if there are several instances of variables of a class. However, in most operating systems there exists only one instance of each class variable (e.g. only one driver for one device). In this case a module notation would be equally useful. The implementation of a module is simpler, since no code is needed to create a new instance and to initialize it. The code produced by the compiler does not contain any indication of the structure of a particular module. This structure is used at compile time only.

The other advantage of a module is the possibility of exporting several types or variables. This feature makes the use of a module more flexible than use of a class, where only one type can be exported.

Processes and tasks

In principle there are two representations of parallel activities in a language: processes (in Concurrent Pascal, MODULA) and tasks (in Pearl, RTL). In [3] a task is defined as a separable flow of control within the program system, regardless of its purpose or its reason. Hansen defines in [6] a process as a sequence of operations carried out one at a time. These definitions are very similar. Both the task and the process are defined as a sequence of operations and therefore the sequential parts of a program could be nearly the same if we use either processes or tasks. The difference lies both in their use and their interactions.

A process system in MODULA consists of a fixed number of processes. They run, after being started, autonomously and independently of other processes. No process is able to interfere with another process as the other processes are not known to him. The only interprocess communication should be done in well defined interface modules (monitors) via shared variables and signals. This concentrates all time dependent parts of a program to a small number of short routines and keeps the rest of the program strictly sequential. The result of this concentration is that the programmer need not know the rest of the system as no other process can interfere with his program.

We can represent two communicating processes in the following way

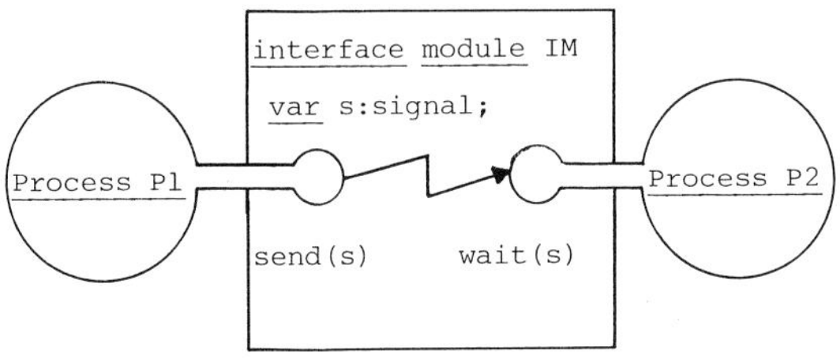

The interprocess communication is done in the interface module. Process P2 waits for the signal s . Process P1 enters the interface module and sends signal s , which resumes the process P2.

The task system can be represented by the following diagram:

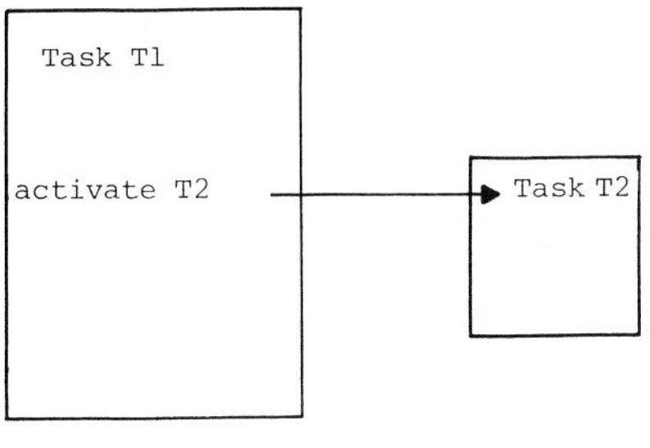

We can conceive of task as a kind of sleeping procedure, waked up (activated) by other tasks. In distinction to the processes which are mutually anonymous, the tasks know each other by names. The task communication is done by calls of scheduling operations to the named task. The task system is built up as a network of tasks. A running task T1 activates another task T2. After the activation both tasks run concurrently. When task T2 finishes its job, it waits for the next activation. The effect of the simultaneous activation of the same task by more then one other task is not defined in most systems and depends on the particular basic operating system. In many systems only the first activation is accepted, the other activations are ignored.

The task system allows the communication between tasks nearly everywhere in the program. This can cause some unpredictable time dependent effects, if the programmer is not aware of the exact structure of the rest of the system. In most of the task systems a great deal of unstructured handling of parallel activities is allowed: delay, suspension, or even termination. Although this seems to be very powerful, it is not secure and makes the verification of a program difficult. We chose processes as a concept of MODULA, because we agree with Brinch Hansen who says [6]: "Starting point of a theory of operating systems must be a process. This is the way our machine works, this is the way we think." The process is a neat representation of activities in a computer and can be well understood. It forces the programmer to write his program in a structured way.

The process allows, because of the simplicity of interprocess interaction, a much easier implementation than the task concept where the complicated task communication must be considered.

Synchronization

The choice and implementation of the synchronization primitives determines the efficiency and security of a RT language. Various synchronization primitives are contained in different RT languages: semaphores (PEARL), queues (Concurrent Pascal), messages (PLATON) or indirect synchronization by block structure (PEARL). Each synchronizing concept is used to solve a certain kind of problem in a direct, efficient manner. In MODULA, the concept of signal was chosen together with operations send and wait . They are used to exchange synchronizing signals between processes only. The signals correspond to the conditions, introduced by Hoare [8] or queues as they are used by Hansen in Concurrent Pascal [7]. The procedure call wait(s) delays the calling process until it receives the signal s . The procedure call send(s) sends the signal to the process, which is waiting for the longest time. If no process is waiting, send(s) has no effect.

We believe that the concept of signal sufficiently supports most applications, is easy to implement, and that the other "primitives" can be expressed in terms of signals.

For example a semaphore may be implemented inside of an interface module as follows:

```
interface module usesema;

 type semaphore = record s : signal;
                         busy : boolean
                  end;

 procedure P ( var x : semaphore );
   begin
     if x.busy then wait( x.s ) end;
     x.busy := true
   end P;

 procedure V ( var x : semaphore );
   begin
     x.busy := false; send ( x.s )
   end V;
   ...
 end usesema;
```

Although signals in MODULA may be used everywhere - even outside of an interface module - this feature should be used with care only. We can gain some efficiency, but we risk some time dependent errors. Outside of an interface module a signal may get lost if one process sends a signal before the other process reached the corresponding wait .

The most task oriented languages do not include any language structure for mutual exclusion (e.g. interface module, monitor). Such languages mostly use semaphores as only the concept of semaphores guarantee secure synchronization everywhere in the program.

The language Corall 66 does not include any standard synchronization concept. All synchronization is done by calls to the supervisory software.

It is interesting to compare the execution times of synchronization primitives in various RT languages. On the PDP 11/45 the primitives <u>delay</u> and <u>continue</u> of Concurrent Pascal are executed in about 600 usec. In MODULA for the PDP 11/40, the primitive of <u>wait</u> (equivalent to <u>delay</u>) is executed in 45 usec, the primitive <u>send</u> (equivalent to <u>continue</u>) in 34 usec. Taking into account the different execution times of instructions on these machines we see the current implementation of MODULA is about 40 times faster than that of the Concurrent Pascal as described in [7].

Input / Output

Most RT languages do not allow direct access to the peripheral devices. All I/O transfers are done by calls of standard procedures of the basic OS. The amount of the I/O support of the basic OS is rather different in various systems. Some systems offer drivers only which transfer data without any conversion or formatting (e.g. IO procedure of Concurrent Pascal). Some other (e.g. Pearl) offer a comfortable file system and a number of conversion routines (e.g. real number to character string).

In contrast to the other RT languages MODULA includes facilities for handling peripheral devices directly in the high level language. To achieve this two new features are included:

1) Access to the device registers. They are declared like normal variables with special access rules.

2) Waiting for an interrupt. We introduced a standard procedure DOIO which delays a process until an interrupt arrives from the designated device.

All the I/O handling must be done in a special kind of an interface module - in the device module. The mutual exclusion between CPU-processes and processes running in a peripheral device is guaranteed by setting the appropriate masking register or by increasing the hardware priority.

The consequence of the possibility of writing drivers in MODULA language is that the MODULA compiler cannot support any form of formatted I/O instructions or file system or even overlay system. All this features must be explicitly programmed out.

Keeping the overhead of an interrupt routine short is even more necessary than for synchronization primitives. In our implementation 8.2 usec are required after an interrupt to restart the device process. It takes 17 usec to return to the interrupted process. This means we are able to write an interrupt service routine with a total runtime length of only 50 usec.

Conclusion

MODULA seems to be a useful and simple language for implementation of small systems on minicomputers. In contrast to the other languages mentioned above MODULA allows writing programs down to the very low level of programming. Some problems are still unsolved: pointers, overlays etc.

Acknowledgement

I would like to thank Prof. N. Wirth, Dr. H.P. Frei and Dr. R. Schoenberger for many helpful suggestions.

References

[1] Niklaus Wirth: "MODULA: A language for Modular Multiprogramming", Institut für Informatik ETH, Bericht No. 18, March 1976, to be published in Software Practice and Experience, January 1977.

[2] ---: "The Use of MODULA and Design and Implementation of MODULA", Institut für Informatik ETH, Report No. 19, June 1976, to be published in Software Practice and Experience, January 1977.

[3] "PEARL" PDV Berichte, Gesellschaft für Kernforschung mbH, Karlsruhe, April 1973.

[4] "Official Definition of CORAL 66", Ministry of Defence, London 1970.

[5] "PLATON - Reference Manual", Aarhus 1975.

[6] Per Brinch Hansen: "Operating System Principles", Series in automatic Computation, Prentice Hall, Inc. 1974.

[7] ---: "Concurrent Pascal Report", Information Science, California Institute of Technology, June 1975.

[8] C.A.R. Hoare: "Monitors: An Operating System, Structuring Concept", Communications of the ACM, October 1974.

E. Morlet and D. Ribbens, (Eds.), International Computing Symposium 1977.

MORE FLEXIBLE AND POWERFUL CONTROL CONSTRUCTS FOR STRUCTURED PROGRAMMING

G. De Michelis, G.A. Lanzarone, C. Simone

Gruppo di Elettronica e Cibernetica
Istituto di Fisica - Università di Milano
Via Viotti 5 Milano (Italy)

Many well-known algorithms may not be expressed by means of only do-while statements. The use of newly introduced and more powerful control constructs (leave-like statements), however, gives rise to difficulties in top-down programming (specifically, the multi-level jumps problem, and the violation of the one-entry, one-exit rule).
In the paper, control constructs are analyzed on the basis of the expressive power of algorithms (which is founded on previous theoretical results) and are grouped into two main families (here called 'control structures' and 'control environments'). This analysis leads to the identification of objective criteria for designing an organic set of control constructs which allows flexibility in top-down programming and avoids the above mentioned difficulties. A choice for such a set is shown, and its advantages are illustrated by recoding some well-known algorithms.

1. INTRODUCTION

The increase in the number and size of programs and their range of uses has led to the necessity for a method of programming that permits the construction of programs that are readable, modifiable, verifiable and documentable.
Starting with Dijkstra's letter /7/, it has been emphasized by several authors that the principal reason for which these characteristics were missing from programs was the absolute liberty of the programmer to use jump instructions in program construction. The flow of control thus became very complicated with the resulting difficulty in finding the parts of the program implementing the desired functions.
The first proposal of eliminating the go to was shown to be inapplicable in practice because it relied only upon the fundamental schemes sequence, if-then-else, and while-do or repeat-until (which are very limited, especially as far as iteration is concerned) as alternative linguistic tools.
The proposal for the reintroduction of the go to in order to supplement the insufficiencies of the fundamental schemes in more complex situations /10/ doesn't improve the results since it is a purely syntactical solution that doesn't take into consideration the conceptual aspects related to algorithm construction.
To permit "top-down" programming /5/, which was a first method for interpreting control schemes as linguistic-conceptual tools, it is useful to have available iterative constructs more powerful than the fundamental ones.
Although several theoretical results have been obtained in the literature /3/, /11/ /1/, /13/, /16/ and much experience has been accumulated through the debate on the topic /7/, /20/, /10/, /14/ a useful synthesis between theoretical studies and empirical suggestions has not yet been attempted.
Thus, while various new constructs have been individually advanced (for instance in /9/, /2/, /8/), the lack of an organic and well-founded set of structured control constructs remains. The aim of this paper is to advance a proposal in this direction.

2. HIERARCHY OF ITERATIVE CONTROL CONSTRUCTS

The various iterative control constructs proposed up till now can be classified into two categories. Those of the first category, that we will call control structures, have the following characteristics: a single entry point, a single exit point and a precise and well-defined relationship between the predicate and the functional blocks. The constructs while-do and repeat-until belong to this category; so does their generalization (Figure 1), called scheme $\Omega_n (n \geq 1)$, /3/ which for each given n number of predicate blocks defines one and only one computational model (flowchart).

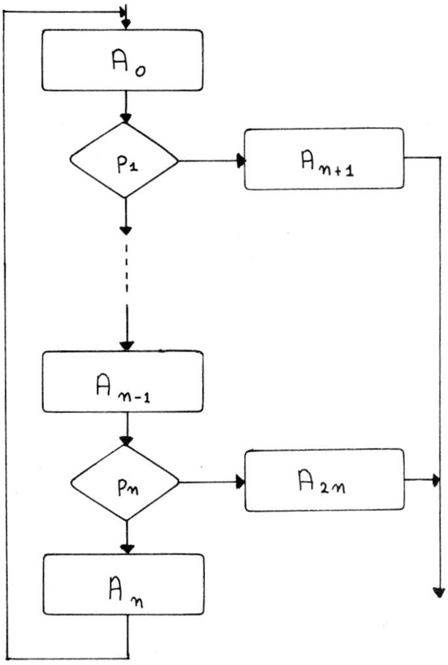

fig. 1

The constructs of the second category, which we will call control environments, are characterized by their relationship with the other parts of the program and no longer by their own internal structure. They are defined by the number of entry points and the number of exit levels, that is, the number of points to which all the paths that exit from the control environment converge. Thus, assuming only one entry point, the number n of exit levels characterizes each control environment, denoted by the symbol RE_n. Is is not possible to represent control environments with a flowchart, but only with a generic diagram of the type shown in Figure 2, where nodes B and C enclose an RE_2 environment, nodes A and D indicate another iteration containing it, and exits of level 2 into E_2.

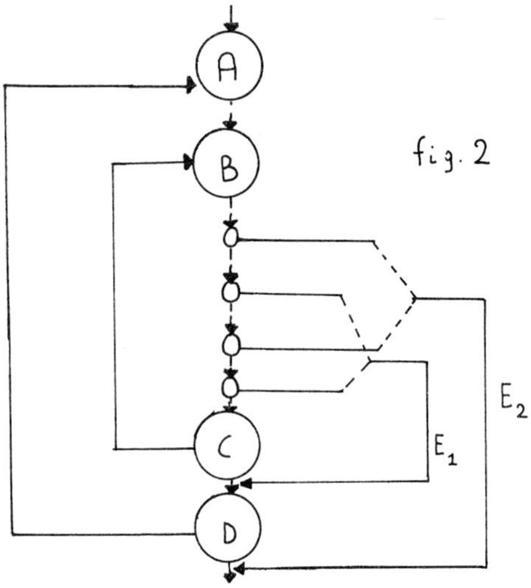

fig. 2

So, for a given n, an RE_n represents more than one computational model, i.e. different flowcharts, but with each having the same number of exit levels. Statements like do-forever, leave and Zahn's 'Event Indicator' /16/, /20/,/21/ may be used to implement the RE_n schemes. Let $\mathcal{G}(\gamma)$ indicate the class of programs that can be constructed using assignment and conditional statements, and the generic iterative construct γ. In the literature a series of results has been obtained that leads to the following classification:

(1) $\mathcal{G}(\Omega_1) \overset{f}{\subset} \mathcal{G}(\Omega_2) \overset{f}{\subset} \dots \overset{f}{\subset} \mathcal{G}(\Omega_n) \overset{f}{\subset} \dots \overset{f}{\subset} \mathcal{G}(BJ)$

(2) $\mathcal{G}(BJ) \overset{f}{\subset} \mathcal{G}(RE_1)$

(3) $\mathcal{G}(RE_1) \overset{f}{\subset} \mathcal{G}(RE_2) \overset{f}{\subset} \dots \overset{f}{\subset} \mathcal{G}(RE_n) \overset{f}{\subset} \dots \overset{f}{\subset} \mathcal{G}(RE)$

where the symbol $\overset{f}{\subset}$ indicates that the class on the right properly contains the class on the left, in the sense that no program of the latter is strongly equivalent to a program of the former. In addition, the class $\mathcal{G}(BJ)$ contains all the programs constructed with an Ω_k structure, for any k; so, it is a limiting class. Similarly, $\mathcal{G}(RE)$ is the limiting class with respect to control environments. The results relative to (1) are due to Böhm, Jacopini /3/ and

Kosaraju /13/, while (2) was shown by De Michelis, Simone /6/, and (3) where obtained by Kosaraju /13/.
As a conclusive result, we cite the theorem of Peterson, Kasami and Tokura /16/, which states: given any program (thus possibly containing go to statements), there exists a program belongin to the $\mathcal{P}(RE)$ class that is strongly equivalent to the given program. The theorem means that the availability of control environments with exits at any level allows the elimination of go to statements, without having to turn to auxiliary boolean variables or functions (but possibly with code duplication).
The above-given program classification leads to an ordering of control constructs based on their expressive power. The expressive power of a construct γ (its capacity to express algorithms), is given by the size of the program class $\mathcal{P}(\gamma)$. Thus, we have:

$$\Omega_1 < \Omega_2 < \dots < \Omega_n < \dots < BJ < RE_1 < \dots < RE_n \dots < RE$$

The concept of expressive power is useful only if it is possible to measure the size of a program class, that is, to decide if a given element does or does not belong to a given class. In our case, this procedure exists /6/; given any program P, it permits the construction of a program P', strongly equivalent to P, by means of the minimal expressive power construct. The expressive power concept thus constitutes a first correct evaluation criterion of control instructions. In fact, it can be confusing to compare, as has sometimes been done /8/, /9/, the applicability to top-down construction, or the readability, of two instructions that realize constructs of different expressive power.

3. THE PROBLEM OF MULTI-LEVEL EXITS

Control environments RE_n which, as has been seen, are the iterative constructs with maximum expressive power and permit the elimination of jump instructions, are not, however, very suitable for top-down programming, for two reasons. The first is that if during program construction a function is refined by means of an RE_n environment, it becomes necessary to consider the n interconnections between this part of the program and the other parts to which control may be transferred. As n increases, this tends to diminish the advantages of program construction through successive refinements. The second reason is that the use of environments with n exit levels may interfere with the readability and clarity of the program, since all the exit jumps from an environment are syntactically equal (they all interrupt the normal control flow), but can mean different things with respect to the algorithm that they are used for.
In fact, from the semantic point of view, following Clint and Hoare /4/, two types of exits can be distinguished from an iteration. The first occurs when the result that the iteration was to obtain is actually arrived at, and thus control must pass to the next block. This positive result was that foreseen by the algorithm.The other type corresponds to the negative situation: the iteration's execution cannot proceed because the necessary conditions are missing. Thus, an exceptional condition has occurred that was not foreseen by the algorithm and prohibits its continuation. The first case is known as a return jump, while the second is called an exit jump. It is evident that control environments RE_n, in whatever form they are realized, are not capable of representing this semantic difference. From the point of view of top-down programming, the RE_n environments ($n \geq 1$) don't represent conceptual model but only very powerful sintactical tools.

4. CRITERIA FOR CHOOSING AN ORGANIC SET OF CONTROL CONSTRUCTS

The preceding paragraphs indicate some characteristics required of a well-founded set of control constructs so that they also become conceptual models suitable for top-down programming.

1. Constructs must be representative of the main expressive power classes, each of them must be specialized to express a class or a coherent group of classes, and they must not overlap classes of very different expressive power.
2. The syntactic form of each construct must clearly indicate its expressive power.
3. Constructs must be able to express the most common programming situations,

from the simplest to the most complex. For this reason, it is better to have both control structures and environments, so as to be able to use the best linguistic tool in each circumstance, instead of using the most powerful tool in every case. This is a generalization of Knuth's remark: "it would be nicest if our language would provide a single feature which covered all simple iterations without going to a rather 'big' construct"/12/.

4. In partial constrast with point 3, constructs useful in top-down programming must have a single entry and a single exit point.
5. Combining one construct with another more powerful construct shouldn't have the 'side-effect' of destroying the characteristics of the first one. This has been discussed by Wirth with reference to Algol 60; specifically, referring to the combination of a <u>for</u> with a <u>go to</u> statement: "The whole purpose of the <u>for</u> clause is to proclaim to the reader: "the qualified statement is going to be executed once for every i=1,2,...,100. The jump, however, may sneakily cause this promise to be broken" /17/. But it has not yet been acknowledged that the same situation occurs when combining, for instance, a <u>while-do</u> with a <u>leave</u> statement.

All the structures satisfy (by definition) point 4 above, but only the RE_1 environment does. Because of this, and of point 5, the other environments are not to be included in the set of constructs chosen.

The problem remains of expressing the jumps out of iterations at a level higher than 1. The distinction between return jumps and exit jumps provides a key to a possible solution. Exit jumps are due to expentional conditions, and this fact, as indicated in point 2, has to be emphasized instead of hidden. The instruction that makes explicit the break in the control flow is exactly the typical jump, the <u>go to</u>. It will be allowed to represent this special case only.

Return jumps of a level higher than 1 seem, according to both practical programming experience and current literature, to arise from the expression of algorithms containing interacting components by sequential programming control constructs. In these cases, it would be convenient to have more specific linguistic tools that are suitable for expression of the interaction, such as <u>coroutines</u> (see /5/). This advantage can, for instance, be seen by comparing the two versions (shown in example 5 of section 6) of the "Quicksort" algorithm /12/, /21/, that is the only example to be found in the literature of a program belonging to an RE_n class ($n \geq 1$) with a return jump.

The above considerations motivate the proposal of the following set of control constructs as a basis for a language oriented toward top-down structured programming.

5. THE PROPOSED SET OF CONTROL CONSTRUCTS

On the basis of the last discussion and of criteria 1 and 5 of the previous paragraph, the three constructs chosen and their composition rules are described below.

a) A construct that expresses the Ω_n ($n \geq 1$) structures, as follows:

<u>loop</u>

a_1;

<u>when</u> p_1 <u>do</u> b_1 <u>and</u> <u>exitloop</u>;

a_2;

<u>when</u> p_2 <u>do</u> b_2 <u>and</u> <u>exitloop</u>;

....

a_n;

<u>when</u> p_n <u>do</u> b_n <u>and</u> <u>exitloop</u>;

a_{n+1};

where:

- p_i are conditions;
- the clause "<u>do</u> b_i <u>and</u>" is optional;
- the number of <u>when</u> clauses that can be contained inside a group "<u>loop</u>...<u>endloop</u>" is arbitrary;
- some, or all but one, of the a_i blocks and some, or all, of the b_i block may not be present - Any a_i or b_i blocks may be an Ω_n structure.

Execution of construct a) is as follows. The statements between <u>loop</u> and <u>endloop</u>

are executed sequentially. When a statement <u>when</u> p_i <u>do</u> b_i <u>and</u> <u>exitloop</u> is reached, if p_i is false, block a_{i+1} is executed; if it is true, block b_i (if present) is executed and control is transferred to the statement following <u>endloop</u>. When the clause <u>endloop</u> is reached (all p_i are false), control is transferred back to block a_1 and execution of the group is repeated.
Note that in the case n=1, the simple form

<u>loop</u>; a_1; <u>where</u> p <u>exitloop</u>; a_2; <u>endloop</u>

is obtained, which naturally solves the 'n+1/2' problem (see example 1 of section 6) and contains both the <u>while-do</u> and <u>repeat-until</u> statements as special cases. The idea of such an instruction is present in Wirth's previous proposal of

<u>repeat</u> <u>begin</u> S_1; <u>when</u> B <u>exit</u>; S_2 <u>end</u>

and in Dahl's recent proposal of:

<u>loop</u> ; S ; <u>while</u> $\overline{B}$: T ; <u>repeat</u>

(see /12/) Here it appears in a construct generalized to the whole class of Ω_m structures. A similar statement has been used in /15/.

b) A construct that expresses the RE_1 environment.
We adopt Zahn's 'event-indicator' statement /21/ as especially suitable for top-down programming, since it separates the iteration body from the actions to be performed after the exits. For the reasons previously discussed, however, we limit it in such a way that multi-level exits are not allowed, as is shown in the following specification:

```
until E1 or...or En do
  S0
repeat
then case
E1 : S1
.......
En : Sn
```

where $E_1 \ldots E_n$ are event identifiers, $S_1 \ldots S_n$ are blocks of any kind except for the <u>until</u> construct itself, and S_o is a block where all the E_i events specified in the declaration, and only they, must appear. If S_o is a block containing another <u>until</u> construct, the event identifiers declared in this latter one must be different from the previous ones and must not appear in the external construct (events are strictly local to the <u>until</u> construct in which they are declared). In any case, events must occur within a conditional statement, not inside an iterative construct.
Execution is as follows: S_o is repeatedly performed and the iteration can only be terminated by the occurrence of an event; when an event E_i occurs, execution of S_o is immediately interrupted, block Si (corresponding to event E_i) is executed, and then control passes to the statement following the whole <u>until</u> construct.
The above specification of the <u>until</u> construct is such that events of one construct cant't terminate execution of another construct containing it. Therefore, in our formulation, this construct strictly realizes the RE_1 environment (non-iterative version of the above construct aren't considered here, since the hierarchy of power classes is based on iterative constructs only).

c) An instruction to express exit jumps.
As previously discussed, we limit our treatment of RE_n $(n > 1)$ environments to express multi-level exits of the error type only, by using a <u>go to</u> statement.
We propose an instruction that explicitly associates with the verb <u>go to</u> the exceptional condition, as follows:

<u>on</u> p <u>go to</u> L

where p is an (error) condition, and L is a label.
Execution is as follows: if condition p is true, control is transferred to the statement labelled L; otherwise the next statement is executed.
In our syntax, while an event indicator can't occur within an Ω_m structure, the <u>on-go to</u> statement is allowed to fall within any Ω_m structure (construct a) or RE_1 environment (construct b), since its syntactic occurrence within an iterative construct corresponds to the break in the normal computation flow that is its intended purpose. The proposed syntax enforces this aspect, in oppositiom to a <u>leave</u>-like statement that "goes to without saying <u>go to</u>" /12/.
The <u>on-go to</u> statement is also a conceptual model in top-down construction, in that its use corresponds to the fact that the exceptional condition hadn't been foreseen by the algorithm, and has to be expressed where need for it becomes appearent, without any implications about the future treatment of the error.
In the following section, examples of use

of the proposed set of constructs are given, with the aim of showing that the (hopefully) better representation of the problems that they achieve is not related to their 'syntactic sugar', but to the fact that they are semantically (i.e. with respect to expressive power classes) founded.

6. EXAMPLES

1) The first example shows how construct a), illustrated in the previous section, expresses the loop performed "n and a half times" /12/ (this case is referred to as the 'exit in the middle construct' by Wirth /18/ and as 'imbedded termination of a repetition' by Zahn /21/; it is the Ω_1 structure in our terminology) without recurring to algorithm redesign as done in /18/.

The problem is the following /18/: construct a 'scanner', which scans an input sequence of characters, delivering as its result the next character, but skipping over blanks and comments (defined as any sequence of characters starting with a left bracket and ending with a right bracket). Wirth shows a common solution to the problem in the form of a flowchart which exhibits the loop structure with exit in the middle, then reformulates the problem so as to express the solution in terms of while...do statements only.

In our syntax, Wirth's flowchart (which belongs to the Ω_1 class) is simply expressed as follows:

```
loop
    loop
    next;
    when  x ≠ '␣' exitloop;
    endloop;
when  x ≠ '{' exitloop;
    loop;
    next;
    when x = '}' exitloop;
    endloop;
endloop;
```

2) Now we consider the 'table search' routine discussed by Knuth and Floyd /11/, Hopkins /10/ and Wulf /19/, and then built up in top-down fashion and extended by Zahn /21/. The problem (as stated by Zahn) is to find the first occurrence of x in a sequential table A and increment a counter variable associated with the matching table entry. If no match exists then a new table entry is to be created for x and the associated counter variable initialized to 1. To express a first version of the program we note that the fundamental structure of the algorithm belongs to the Ω_2 class; therefore, we use construct a), as follows:

```
loop
search_table_for_x;
when found do increment_count
         and exitloop;
when not_found do create_new_entry
              and exitloop;
endloop;
```

Then, deciding that the table is an array A, n is the index of the last entry and the counter variables are the elements of an array B, the program above is expanded to:

```
i:=o
loop
i:=i+1;
when A[i]=x do
              Match_index ← 1
              B Match_index  plus 1
              and exitloop;
when i=n do
         n plus 1
         A[n]← x
         B[n]← 1
         and exitloop;
endloop;
```

Note that in Zahn's version of the above program /21/ the use of the event-indicator construct (which is a construct of wider expressive power than that required by this algorithm) implies the falling of an event inside the for construct, whose nature is thus destroyed, becoming a loop with two exits (besides being redundant with the key-word repeat of the event-indicator construct).

Inserting a check for a possible table-overflow error: (overrun of the amount of storage allocated to arrays A, B [1:nmax]) into the program above (in the part do of statement when i=n, immediately before n plus 1) doesn't modify in this case the structure of the algorithm.

3) Let us now consider, as done by Zahn /21/, the above routine contained within a program which makes a table with frequency counts from the values of an input file. We write that as follows:

```
Initialize_table;
loop
Get_new_x_from_input_file
when end_of_input_file
   do print_table_with_counts and exitloop;
enter_x_in_table;
endloop;
```

If enter_x_in_table is the above table search routine without the check on table-overflow, there is no problem (we simply have an Ω_2 structure nested within an Ω_1 structure).

But if we add the error check, the algorithm now belongs to the RE_2 class, since it becomes a two-level exit environment. In our syntax, the whole program becomes:

```
   Initialize_table;
   Get_new_x_from_input_file;
   when end_of_input_file
    do print_table_with_ counts and exitloop;
   i:=o;
      loop
      i:=i+1;
      when  A[i] = x  do
                      Match_index <— 1
                      B Match_index plus 1
                      and exitloop;
      when i=n        do
                      on n = nmax goto  L
                      n plus 1
                      A [n]<- x
                      B [n]<- x
                      and exitloop;

      endloop;
   endloop;
L : print-partial-table-with-counts
```

With regard to his version of the program above, Zahn comments: "one of the nicer aspects of the until...then case statement is that the appropriate modifications to handle the table overflow situation are easy to make and tend to be additive rather than disruptive of the existing program logic". If the "additivity" refers to the syntax, this is true in our version too; no previous code has been rewritten, only a label and a statement on...goto have been added. What is more important is that the construct must not be semantically additive ; that is, it must be such as to point out to the programmer that the 'existing program logic' has changed. The program itself must be readable in this sense; in our version, the presence of the on...go to statement emphasizes the occurrence of an error condition and of the related multi-level exit from that environment.

In Zahn's version there is no such a priori visibility of this situation, due to the fact that his until-then case construct may be used to express either an Ω_n structure or an RE_1 environment or even an RE_n $(n > 1)$ environment.

4) This example is the 'tree search and insertion' scheme described by Knuth /12/ and coded by himself, using Zahn's event-indicator construct, exactly as follows:

```
loop until leaf replaced:
  if A[i]<x
  then if L[i]≠ o then i:=L[i]
    else L[i]:=j; leaf replaced fi;
  else if R[i]≠ o then i:=R[i]
    else R [i] := j; leaf replaced fi;
  fi;
repeat
A[j]:=x; L[j]:=o; R[j]:=o; j:=j+1
```

It is interesting to note that this example is not reported by Zahn, although, since it is an algorithm belonging to the RE_1 class, the event-indicator construct is, in our analysis, specifically appropriate to it.

5) This last example shows the two version of the 'quicksort' algorithm referred to in section 4, the first one coded with do forever-exit statements and the second one with coroutines.

5a)

```
   begin
   i:=m; j:=n; v:=A(j);
A: do forever
   if A(i) > v then
      begin
      A(j):=A(i);
   B: do forever
         begin
         j:=j-1;
         if i = j then exit A;
         if v>A(j) then begin A(i):=A(j);
                                  exit B;
                              end
         end;
   i:=i+1;
   if i=j then begin A(j):=v;
                     exit A;
                  end
      end
   end
```

5b)

```
begin
coroutine move i;
  repeat begin if A(i)>v then begin
                               A(j):=A(i);
                               resume move j;
                               end
           i:=i+1;
         end
  until i=j;
coroutine move j;
  repeat begin if v>A(j) then begin
                               A(i):=A(j);
                               resume move i;
                               end
            j:=j-1;
         end
  until i=j;
i:=m; j:=n; v:=A(j);
call move i;
A(j):=v;
end
```

7. REFERENCES

/1/ Ashcroft E., Manna Z. "The translation of goto programs into while programs" Information Processing 71, North Holland, Amsterdam (1972), 250-255

/2/ Bochman G.V. "Multiple exits from a loop without the goto" CACM 16,7 (1973), 443-444

/3/ Böhm C., Jacopini G. "Flow diagrams, Turing machines, and languages with only two formation rules" CACM 9,5 (1966), 366-371

/4/ Clint M., Hoare C.A.R. "Program proving: jumps and functions" Acta Informatica 1 (1972), 214-224

/5/ Dahl O.J., Dijkstra E.W., Hoare C.A.R. "Structured Programming" Academic Press (1972)

/6/ De Michelis G., Simone C. "Well formed programs optimal with respect to structural complexity" Proc. GI '75 Conference; Lecture Notes in Computer Science, Springer-Verlag (1975)

/7/ Dijkstra E.W. "Go to statement considered harmful" CACM 11, 3 (1968), 147-148, 538, 541

/8/ Evans R.V., "Multiple exits from a loop using neither GOTO nor labels", CACM 17,11 (1974), 650

/9/ Friedman D.P., Shapiro S.C. "A case for while-until" SIGPLAN Notices 9,7 (1974), 7-14

/10/ Hopkins M. "A case for the goto" SIGPLAN Notices 7,11 (1972), 59-62

/11/ Knuth D.E., Floyd R.W. "Notes on avoiding 'goto' statements" IPL 1,1 (1971),23-31

/12/ Knuth D.E. "Structured programming with goto statements" Comp. Surv. 6,4 (1974), 261-301

/13/ Kosaraju S.R. "Analysis of structured programs" Journal of Computer and System Science 9,3 (1974), 232-255

/14/ Leavenworth B.M. "Programming with (out) the goto" SIGPLAN Notices, 7,11 (1972), 54-58

/15/ McGowan C., Kelly J. "Top-down structured programming techniques" Petrocelli-Charter, N.Y. (1975)

/16/ Peterson W.W., Kasami T., Tokura N. "On the capabilities of while, repeat and exit statements" CACM 16,8 (1973) 503-512

/17/ Wirth N. "On the design of the programming languages" IFIP Congress '74 vol. 2, North Holland-American Elsevier (1974), 386-393

/18/ Wirth N. " On the composition of well-structured programs" Comp. Surv. 6,4 (1974), 247-259

/19/ Wulf W.A. "Programming without the goto" Information Processing '71, North Holland, Amsterdam (1972), 408-412

/20/ Wulf W.A. "A case against the goto" SIGPLAN Notices 7,11 (1972), 63-69

/21/ Zahn C.T. "A control statement for natural top-down structured programming" Proc. of the Symposium of Programming Languages, Paris, Springer (1974), 170-180

This research has been sponsored by Honeywell Information System Italia, in the frame of the Communication Programming Project.

E. Morlet and D. Ribbens, (Eds.), International Computing Symposium 1977.

THE FUNNEL, A NEW AND PRACTICAL PRESENTATION METHOD FOR PROGRAM BUILDING BLOCKS

Eduard Mumprecht

Institut für Informatik
Universität Zürich
Switzerland

The problem of designing and implementing Telecommunications Software often becomes tedious due to the lack of effective and consistent techniques that allow both representation and implementation of suitable program building blocks.
A module called "FUNNEL" is presented which has been derived from finite automata and shows various useful properties, among which are notably recursive aspects as well as process concepts. Other features are the compact graphical representation of a FUNNEL module, and as an important advantage, the ease of its direct implementation. An example of a network control program illustrates the feasibility of the methods described.

1. INTRODUCTION

Telecommunication software seems to belong to a program family that shows only little affinity to the other two areas being application programs and operating systems software. This can be seen by the fact that both operating systems theory and application software engineering do not offer consistent methods that would be useful for strightforward telecommunication software production. The techniques needed should cover design aids and implementation support for programs that deal with process communication and string handling problems. Neither the "structured programming" methods nor flow chart techniques alone will help much. The one being a verbal way of expression, the other useful for graphical representation of algorithms, these two are somehow incompatible with each other.

First we have a look at the taks that telecommunications software must deal with. All communication between two interlocutors is governed by protocols which are essentialy sets of precise rules that direct the exchange of messages across interfaces on different levels down to bit manipulation. Messages are formed according to some syntactical rules, and one colloquy can also be understood as a set of messages whose sequence and directions of transfer is managed depending on a syntax diagram. This property of protocols calls for graphical design method, whose results should be implementable straightforward.

Since a telecommunication program is merely a part of a distributed interprocess communication mechanism it shows characteristics of a real time process. It must be able to observe several external events at a time and to handle the arising situations in time. We need therefore elements for process management that are not offered by high level programming languages. Those in general hide all nonsequential mechanisms from the user.

The FUNNEL module is proposed here as a program building block which tries to combine clear and comprehensive graphical representation with ease of implementation. As a "device" ist shows recursive qualities as well as process concepts.

2. DERIVATION OF THE FUNNEL MACHINE

Any data processing device can be represented by some abstract machine in the mathematical sense. For our purposes we have chosen the mealy automation because of the following reasons:

- Its internal structure and behaviour can be expressed neatly by graphical methods.
- As a state machine it allows treatment of syntactical structures.

The finite state automaton in its intrinsic form however is more of theoretical interest. In order to meet our practical requirements we apply some modifications which are explained in the following paragraphs.

Step 1: The Mealy automaton

The transition function of a mealy automaton is invoked by the occurence of an input symbol that is fetched from outside by some implicit mechanism. (Fig.1) It yields for one part a successor state of the machine, for the other it emits an output symbol. Input and output symbols are atomic entities, that means one transition precisely handles one input symbol. In fact we have merely a finite transducer with limited capabilities.

Step 2: Explicit input and output functions

It now becomes desirable to have control facilities over an explicitely given function which fetches an input element from outside and places its symbolic representation in the input register (e.g. the former "input slot"). We also provide for specification of the output element generation instead of the direct emission of the output symbol associated with each transition. Thus a transition has the following functions: (see also Fig. 2)

T_s gives the succesor state

T_i triggers the input function

T_g selects and triggers output generator function

However this way transitions have side effects on preceding and succeeding ones. Consider the case where a transition has activities on both T_i and T_g. Obviously there is a time lag between input and output operations of one element cycle which makes it necessary to have a communication path between the input function and the set of output generators.

Step 3: Reduction to a feedback automaton

It then can be seen that there is no essential difference between a generator function and the input function from the transition's viewpoint. Both are triggerable procedures which perform some computation (Fig. 3). By this fact it is the next step that unifies input and output functions in a so called "action". A transition is now reduced to two functions:

T_s the successor state function

T_a the action function

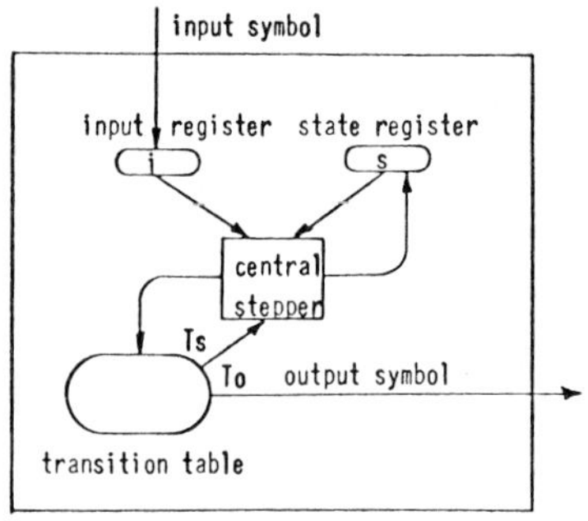

next.state = $T_s(s,i)$
output.symbol = $T_o(s,i)$

Fig.1: A Mealy Automaton

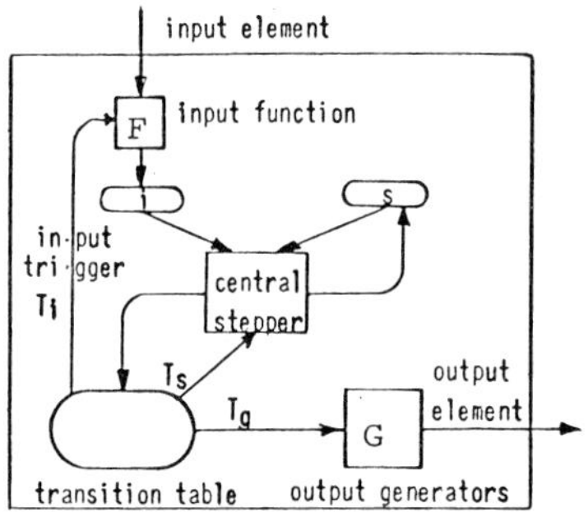

Fig.2: Extensions to the automaton

next.state = $T_s(s,i)$
input.trigger = $T_i(s,i)$
output.element = $G(T_g(s,i))$
i = F(last input.trigger,in.element)

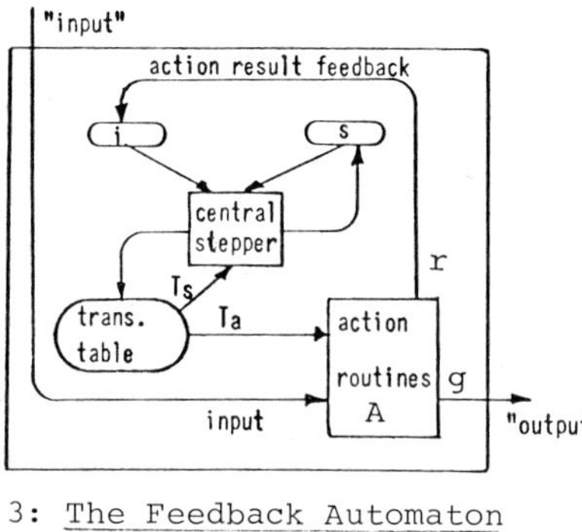

Fig.3: The Feedback Automaton

next.state = $T_s(s,i)$
Action A = $T_a(s,i)$
i = r(A("input"))
"output" = g(A("input"))

The input register that formerly has been fed by the input function now obtains its contents by a feedback from an action that just fetched some data from outside. Generally an action may be any computing procedure. The only requirement is its finiteness and its ability to return a feedback signal as a result of its operation. The input register is now called "result" register.

This feedback automaton shows a very condensed control structure which still bases on the mealy machine. But the generaility of the "action" makes it suitable to solve various practical programming problems.

<u>Step 4: The basic Funnel machine (Fig. 4)</u>
The Funnel machine in its intrinsic form is nothing else than our feedback automaton. It can be viewed as a transition processor that walks through a state graph and executes action routines as specified by the arcs. Its name is due to Dennis Birke [4] and indicates that the control flow passes repeatedly through a small pipe where only the registers "state" and "result" are affected.

<u>Step 5: The Funnel module</u>
An implementation of the Funnel machine results in a Funnel module and consists of two distinct parts (Fig. 5):

1. The substrate that is independent of the programming problem to be solved:
   a) a suitable data structure to hold the transition graph
   b) data elements for the registers "state", "result" and "action"
   c) a procedure that does the task of the "central stepper" (Funnel stepper)
2. The elements that make the Funnel machine running a particular task:
   a) a Funnel transition graph
   b) a couple of action routines

The funnel module as a program building block shows certain unique features:

- Since it is derived from a clearly arranged finite automaton, it allows to take full advantage of the consistent graphical methods of state machine theory. The graphs used have well defined properties and thus are suitable for proving correctness and completeness.
- An implementation of the Funnel machine has no undesirable reactions on the design phase at all.

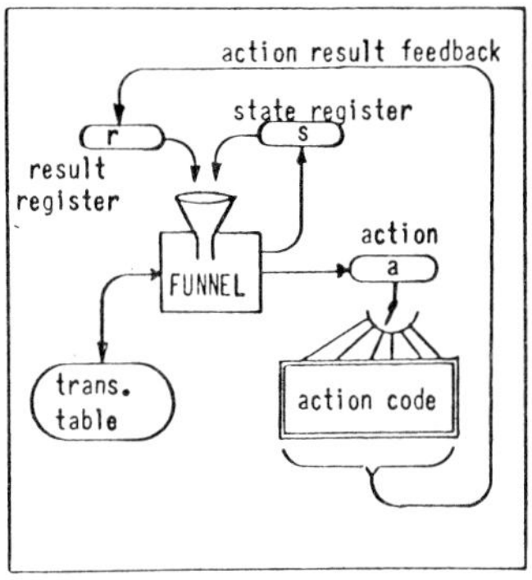

(a,s) = FUNNEL(s,r)
r = ACTION(a)

<u>Fig.4: The basic FUNNEL machine</u>

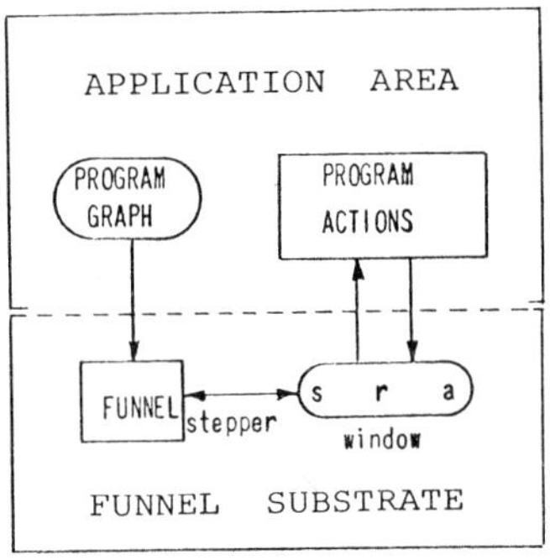

<u>Fig.5: The FUNNEL module</u>

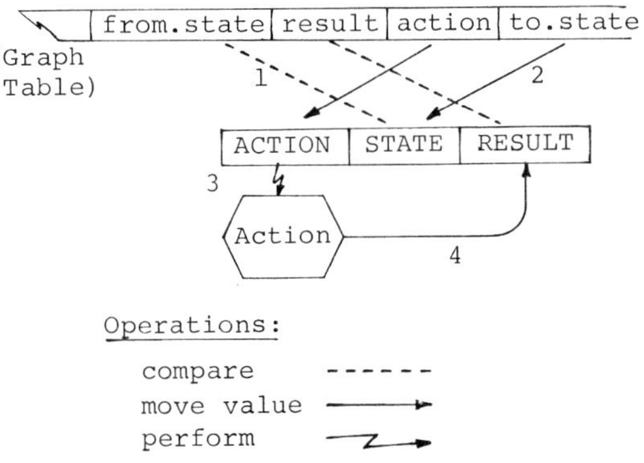

<u>Fig.6: The FUNNEL stepper algorithm</u>

3. PROPERTIES OF INTERNAL FUNNEL ELEMENTS

Storage of the transition table

The form of the Funnel transition function, (Action,State):= T_F(State,Result), shows two argument entries, so it seems suitable to organise the table as a matrix. But the usually low density of the transition graph leads to a sparse occupied matrix which might waste a pile of memory. The main advantage of a matrix however is the direct access to its elements by the two function arguments used as indices.

Another method is to store the graph in terms of its transitions, each of which is represented by a record with the four fields "from.state","result", "action","to.state". A search function then uses the left half of the records as key field to be compared against the function arguments. This way at a first glance seems to be less efficient than the full matrix solution, but the experience has shown, that the time consumed even by a linear table search procedure does not give raise to a visible performance degradation.

The Funnel stepper algorithm

When entering the funnel (Figs. 4 and 6), we find ourselves with the STATE register which identifies the node of the graph assumed to be the current state of the machine. The RESULT register contains some value representing the outcome of the previously executed action. We now go down into the table to find a transition which starts from the given STATE and is labelled with the same symbol as given in RESULT. Then we have this transition carried out by first updating the STATE register with the value of the transition's terminal node identifier and then perform the action which is associated with that transition. The action now must deposit some value in the RESULT register and pass control back through the funnel.

The verbal description of the FUNNEL stepper algorithm, which is essentially the same as going on in a mealy automaton, together with the sketch (Fig. 6) shows, that the functions used are rather primitive ones, available on hardware and microprogramming levels as well as with high level languages.

Additional Funnel features

- The "else" path

In order to function properly the stepper algorithm must be sure to find always a valid transition for any possible STATE - RESULT combination. That forces the graph table to be complete, i.e. missing transitions must be specified by some "error"-entries. It also makes it necessary to specify each transition per RESULT, although they might have been grouped together by one path. This disadvantage also appears in decision tables 5 , where the number of rules would become impractical to handle unless there is the possibility of giving a way out through the "else" rule.

The "else" path of Funnel allows it to proceed with a normal transition. In terms of a graph matrix the "else" option corresponds to a compression of empty columns for one row into an "else" column (Fig. 7a). For the search algorithm in the case of the record-wise stored graph it means that, upon failure on a missing transition, it must start a second scan through the table using a modified key. The "else" option however needs to have reserved one RESULT symbol as the "else" result.

- The "trap" option

Until here we are proud of having no "goto", since control strictly moves along the specified transitions. This is assured by the fact that the STATE register of the Funnel machine can only be altered by the Funnel stepper procedure which takes the appropriate value from a valid transition.

The "trap" option now opens the possibility for an action to deposit some value in the RESULT register which belongs to a reserved set of "trap" signals within the range of RESULT symbols. Because the table search would fail either way (with or without "else" option) the Funnel directly performs a predesigned action which then is believed to handle the event that caused the trap. This feature might be compared to the "ON unit" of PL/1.

If we insist on not having any "goto" function within Funnel, control flow will remain in the ending STATE of the last transition (which caused a trap) and proceed from there after the completion of the "ON"-action (Fig. 7b).

Otherwise if we allow the "ON"-action to modify the STATE register, the flow of control will make jumps that are not specified by the graph table.

- The "trace" option

Because of the narrow tube of the funnel it is easy to record each pass through the Funnel stepper. The trace information consists merely of the contents of the STATE and RESULT registers. This allows to keep long histories of control flow in a very concise format. (Fig. 7c)

Fig.7: FUNNEL Options

a) "ELSE"

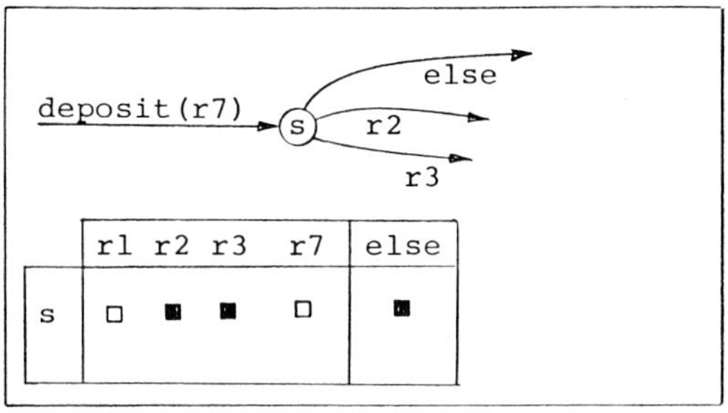

b) "TRAP"

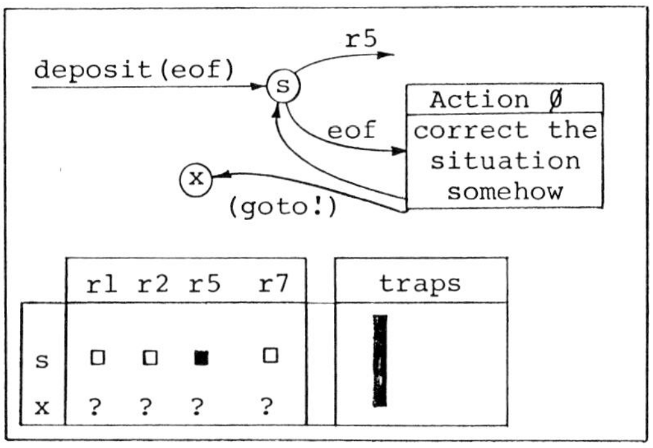

c) "TRACE"

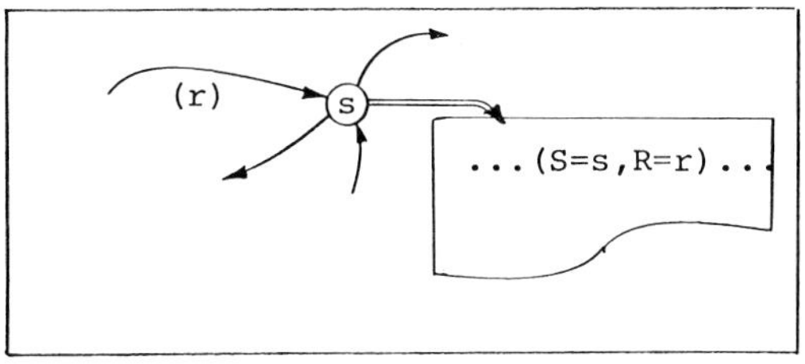

4. EXTERNAL FUNNEL PROPERTIES

The Subfunnel

When again considering Figure 5 we can also see the Funnel module as an interpretative system. The Funnel stepper is interpreting a Funnel graph by executing its associated actions. Thus the Funnel module is somewhat like an executable procedure. The stepper algorithm therein is embedded within an infinite loop, which only can be terminated if one action has a means to do an "exit". Once there exists a return path from a Funnel module block (being a do-while-exit structure) it satisfies all requirements stated earlier for single actions. This fact allows nesting of Funnels in the ways that an action of a surrounding Funnel module contains a complete Subfunnel module, which itself can contain further Subfunnels and so forth (Fig. 8).

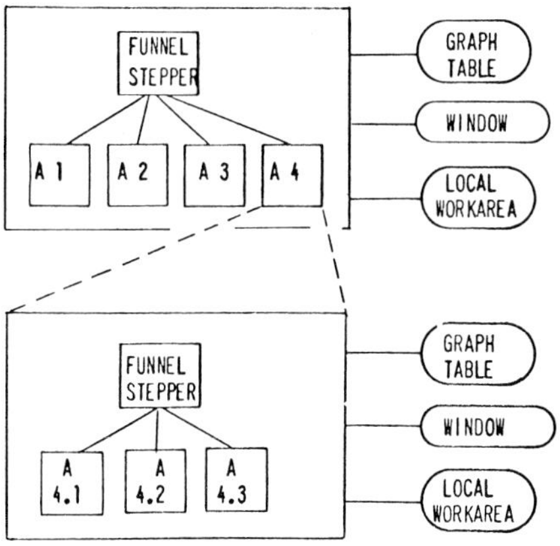

Fig.8: Subfunnel

Recursion

One important feature of a Funnel module can be derivated the following way: If the codes of the Funnel stepper and of the action routines are reentrant, and if the Funnel window (e.g. STATE and RESULT registers) and the actions local working area are allocated and stacked dynamically upon Funnel module activation, then we have full recursion capabilities with Funnel modules (Fig. 9).

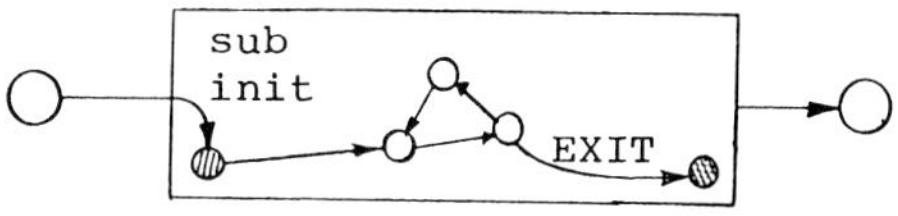

Fig.9: Reentrant or recursive Subfunnel

Co-process
If the window of a Subfunnel is allocated on static storage the STATE and RESULT register remain saved even when a (sub-)action does an "exit". The control flow in the subgraph then proceeds from the node which it would have reached anyway, when the action containing the Subfunnel is executed again (Fig. 10). This behaviour is similar to coroutine concepts where one wishes to leave a module for a short time without loosing local status and data.

One can thus model interacting processes in the frame of a purely procedural program by having a couple of static Subfunnels working together.

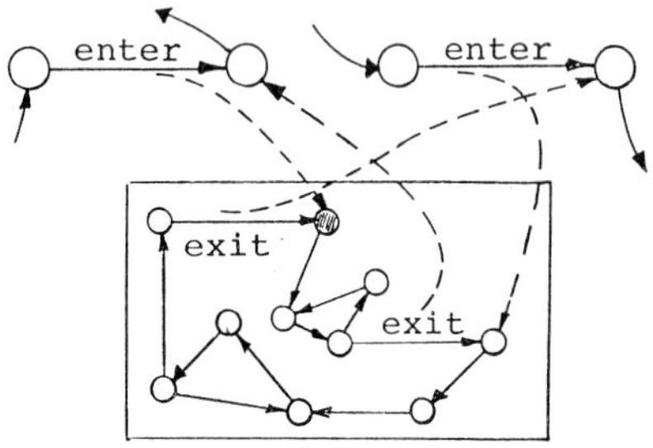

Fig.10: Coroutine type subfunnel

5. A SMALL DESIGN EXAMPLE

A terminal handler program for a TTY
An application program is to be connected to a Teletype terminal (Fig. 11). This requires a TTY protocol handler which communicates with the application program through a message queue interface and at the other side renders character service to the adapter. The protocol in a simplified form is given by a syntax diagram (Fig. 12) and illustrates the following events:

The user program can pass a text line to the terminal driver which in turn transmits it character by character to the adapter. At the end of the output line the TTY driver program automatically adds a "carriage return" sequence. However if the last character of the text message is the device control character "DC1", this text is considered to be a prompter which causes the terminal driver to attempt inputting characters from the TTY. Incoming text is gathered in a buffer and passed to the user program after receipt of an "end-of-line" code.

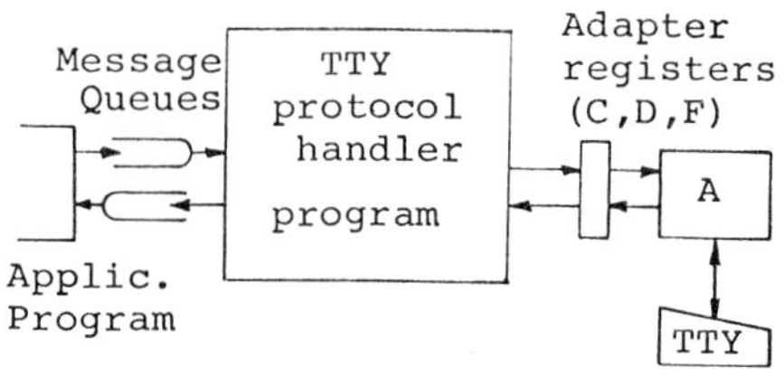

Fig.11: A terminal handler program

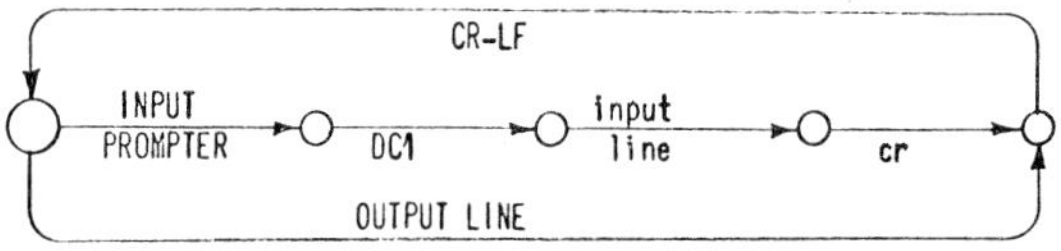

Fig.12: The Teletype protocol assumed

When implementing the TTY protocol handler as a Funnel module we have three main areas that are to be developed simultaneously:

1) a set of data structures
2) a set of actions that refer to and move data items of 1)
3) a Funnel graph that arranges the execution sequence of 2).

Figures 13, 14 and 15 represent those areas in concise form and so we guess, should be self-explaining. The iterative kind of the design process causes the three areas being subject in parallel to modifications. But it is always easy to check the consistence and completeness of the parts. If one action becomes too complex we describe it by means of a Subfunnel.

Data Elements

QA, QB	Message queues from and to the application program.
B, X, L	Text buffer with pointer to one character within, and message length variable.
C, D, F	Adapter registers "control", "data", "status flags".

Actions

Name	Operation description	Result range
MA	read message from QA into B initialize X and L	-
MB	write buffer contents B to QB	-
OUT	move character at B(X) to D initiate output operation by register C increment X	was last char
INA	initiate input operation through C	-
INB	move D contents to B(X) increment X	-
EXAM	wait completion of adapter cycle (if running at all) examine D and F registers	'break' 'CR' in D 'DCl' in D
CLB	clear B, X and L	-
CRLF	load a 'CRLF' sequence into B	-
BRK	write a "broken!" message to QB	-

Fig.14: Specification Tables for Data elements and actions

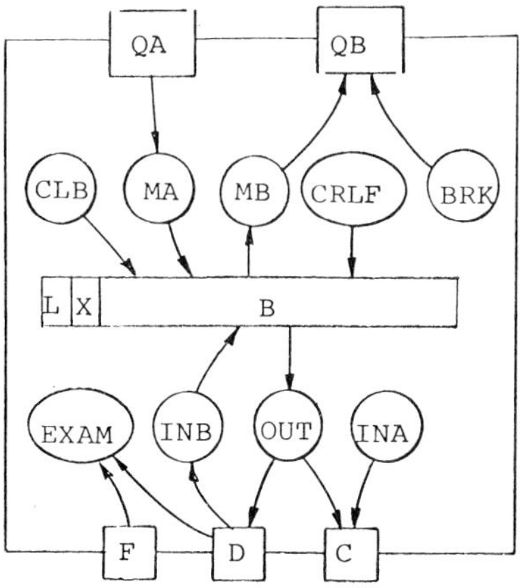

Fig.13: Data flow graph (data elements and action set) for the TTY handler Funnel module

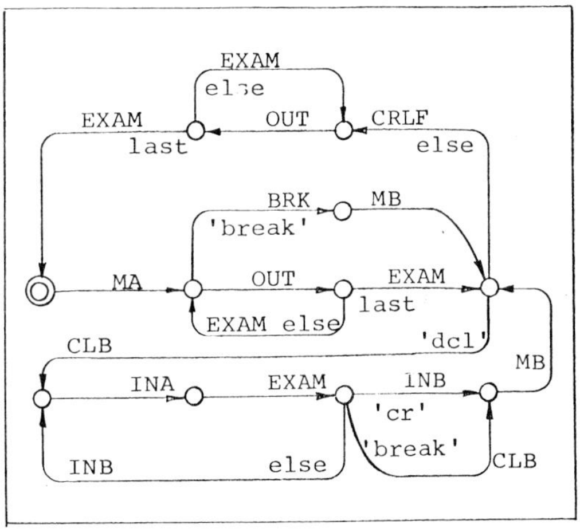

Fig.15: The Funnel transition graph for the TTY handler

6. CONCLUSION

The Funnel module as a program building block has been shown to be a concise and efficient representation method when dealing with telecommunications software and its implementation. Because of the nesting capabilities it is suitable as a design aid for complex problems, either faced with recursion or pseudoparallel processes. The main feature however is the ease of implementation of Funnel modules once the Funnel substrate exists.

Our experience was gained with working on a Burroughs B-1700 computer. The Funnel substrate implementation consists of about 300 program source lines and includes auxiliary functions (e.g. table loader etc.) in a Pascal-like language; the Funnel stepper has been microcoded.

7. REFERENCES

[1] M.A. Jackson, "Principles of Program Design", Academic Press Ltd. London, 1975

[2] I.Nassi, B. Shneiderman, "Flow Chart Techniques for Structured Programming", ACM Sigplan, Vol. 8, No. 8, Aug. 73)

[3] H. Ledgard, M. Marcotty, "A Genealogy of Control Structures", CACM, Vol. 18, No. 11, Nov. 75)

[4] D. Birke, "State Transition Programming Techniques and their Use in Producing Teleprocessing Device Control Programs", ACM/IEEE Second Symposium on Problems in the Optimization of Data Communications Systems, 1971

[5] R. Thurner, "Entscheidungstabellen-Benützerhandbuch PL/I"

[6] D. Bjorner, "Finite State Automation - Definition of Data Communications Line Control Procedures", AFIPS, FJCC, 1970

[7] P. Naur, "Control Record Driven Processing", Infotech State of the Art Report Structured Programming, p. 309

[8] A. Oliver, D. Neil, "Program Control via Transition Matrices - A Novel Application of Microprogramming, ACM Sigmicro,Vol. 7,No.1, March 76)

E. Morlet and D. Ribbens, (Eds.), International Computing Symposium 1977.

SEMANTIC APPROACH TO DESIGN OF CONTROLLER LANGUAGES AND HARDWARE

E Mark GOLD

Computer Science Department
University of Rochester
Rochester, New York

1. OVERVIEW

1.1. TOPIC

This paper proposes principles for the design of programmed controllers such as microprogram controllers for CPU's. Three example controller designs are constructured by the use of these principles. The last two are novel.

1.2. PROPOSED STEPS FOR CONTROLLER DESIGN.

Construct controller programming language
Choose machine code.
Design interpreter.

The interpreter is the resulting controller. This paper is primilarly concerned with the first step, language design :

1.3. PROPOSED STEPS FOR LANGUAGE DESIGN

The proposed approach to language design is general, not limited to the design of control languages. It proceeds from semantic (i.e. abstract) objects to concrete representation (machine code in the case of control languages) by choosing a sequence of representations which are successively more detailed, i.e. less abstract and more concrete. It will be shown that it is possible to choose and define the semantic universe of a control language before choosing its syntax.

Initially a model is proposed for the type of semantic object to be defined in the language. Then (semantic) primitive objects and (semantic) combinators are chosen. These generate the semantic universe : The semantic universe consists of the primitive objects and the constructed objects which can be constructed by repeated application of the combinators to the primitive objects.

The abstract concept of applying a specified sequence of combinators to specified objects, in order to construct a constructed object, will be called a semantic expression. The constructed object is the value of the semantic expression. A specified set of primitive objects and combinators generates a set of semantic expressions. The semantic universe consists of the values of the set of semantic expressions.

So the semantic expressions can be used as abstract representations of the objects of the semantic universe. We wish to specify a syntax, i.e. concrete (symbol string) representations for the objects of the semantic universe. This is obtained by first choosing an abstract tree representation for semantic expressions, and then choosing a symbolic linearization of the abstract trees. Three types of syntax will be introduced : The user syntax is a written form which is easy for humans to write and understand. The machine code is a storage representation chosen to be compact and easy to interpret. Assembly syntax is a mnemonic form of a machine code.

2. SHORT FORMS OF TERMINOLOGY

Terms being defined are underlined. If part of the underlined phrase is in parentheses, this means that the parenthesized part is optionally omitted in the text.

3. MODEL FOR PROGRAMMED CONTROLLERS

3.1 EXTERNAL INTERFACE

The purpose of a control language is to define control routines. In order to define "control routine" it is necessary to specify the type of controller which is being considered. In this paper it is assumed that the controller controls a device, the controller having 3 logical communication channels to the outside world : The macrocommand, microcommand, and

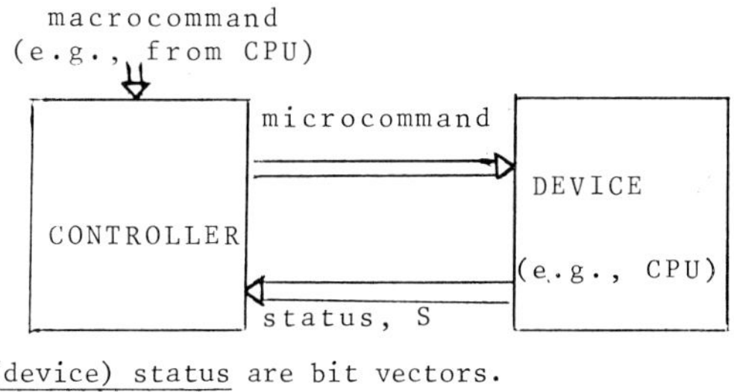

(device) status are bit vectors.

3.2 OPERATION

Each macrocommand codes a control routine.
The controller accepts a macrocommand, executes the control routine called by the macrocommand, accepts another macrocommand, etc., forever. The controller executes a control routine by alternately observing the device status and outputting a microcommand until the control routine terminates :

observe status	output microcommand
⋮	⋮
observe status	output microcommand
observe status	terminate

A (control) routine is a function which determines which microcommand to output, and when to terminate, as a function of its observations of the device status since the start of execution.

3.3. SYNCHRONIZATION

After the controller outputs each microcommand it must wait until the device has finished obeying it before the controller observes the device status and decides what to do next. The means for synchronization are not shown in the above figure and will not be discussed.

3.4. PROGRAMMED CONTROLLER

A (programmed) controller consists of a machine program and an interpreter. The machine program, written in machine code, is logically a set of declerations. Each decleration defines a control routine and binds a macrocommand (name) to it.

4. APPROACH USED FOR LANGUAGE DESIGN

4.1. LEVELS OF REPRESENTATION

In the approach to language design used here, one starts by defining a semantic universe of the semantic objects which the language will be used to define. One chooses a set of primitive (semantic objects) and a set of combinators. These generate constructered (semantic) objects. The semantic universe consists of the primitive and constructed semantic objects.
Next one chooses successively more concrete representations for the semantic objects. In the case of a control language, the semantic objects are control routines and functions which operate on them. The successive levels of representation which are constructed lead to specification of machine code.

The primitives and combinators can also be used to construct semantic expressions. These are also abstract objects, and are the most abstract level of representation for the semantic objects. The semantic objects are the values of the semantic expressions.
Abstract syntax is the next, somewhat less abstract level of representation. Namely, the semantic expressions are represented by (expression) trees. These are trees with labelled notes, the labels being (abstract) primitives and combinators.
The next level of representation, user syntax, is a symbolic (written) form. These representations are obtained by linearizing the expression trees and choosing literal (identifiers) to represent the primitives.
Control languages require 2 lower levels of concrete representation : Assembly syntax is a symbolic representation which can be efficiently coded for machine interpretation.
Machine code is the binary representation in the controller.

4.2. TYPES OF SEMANTIC OBJECTS

The objects of the semantic universe are of the following types :

Order 0 objects :	objects of the type the language will be used to define.
Order 1 objects :	order 1 functions, i.e., functions from order 0 objects to order 0 objects.
higher order objects:	higher order functions, which take functions as arguments and/or return functions as values

In the case of a control language the semantic objects are

order 0 objects :	(control) routines
order 1 functions :	control structures, or parametric routines which take routines as arguments
higher order functions :	e.g., parametric routines which take control structures as arguments

OBJECTS OF EACH REPRESENTATION LEVEL OF A CONTROL LANGUAGE

Sem Obj's	Sem Exp's	Abstract Syntax	User Syntax	Assembly Syntax	Machine Code
			Programs	Programs	Machine Programs
			each is a set of : Declarations	each is a set of : Declarations	each is a set of : Entry points
			each consists of : a Decl'd Ident a Syntactic Exp	each consists of : a Decl'd Ident a 1-Level Syntactic Exp.	each consists of : a label a Code Segm. (starting from Label)
Sem Universe contains : Sem Obj's	Sem Exp's	(Exp) Trees	Syntactic Exp's	1-Level Syn Exp's	Code segments
generated by: (Sem) Prim's	generated by: (Sem) Prim's	generated by: (Sem) Prim's Arg Selectors	generated by: Literal (Ident's) Parm(Ident's) Decl'd Ident's	generated by: Literal (Ident's) Parm(Ident's) Decl'd Ident's	generated by : Literal (Ident's) Parm(Ident's) Labels
(Sem) Comb's which produce: Constructed Obj's	(Sem)Comb's	Tree Constructors	Productions	Productions	Format

Abbreviations

arg	argument	obj	object
comb	combinator	parm	parameter
decl'd	declared	prim	primitive
exp	expression	sem	semantic
ident	identifier	syn	syntactic

In the 3 example control languages the primitive objects are order 0 and order 1, i.e. routines and control structures. The semantic universe for Control Language 1 is generated by the weakest combinator, which only allows order 0 objects to be constructed, i.e. routines. The combinators of Control Language 2 allow, in addition, the construction of order 1 functions, i.e. new control structures. The combinators of Control Language 3 also allow the construction of higher order objects.

4.3 CONTROL LANGUAGE; PROGRAMS

A language comprises all the levels of representation. The principal objects of the upper (abstract) 3 levels of a language are the semantic objects or their representations. In the case of a control language the principal objects of the lower 3 levels are programs. A (control) program is a finite set of declarations, each of which is of the form

declared identifier = syntactic expression

The syntactic expression is a symbolic or binary string which denotes, through many levels of indirection, a semantic object.

Note the semantic transition which takes place when we reach the syntactic levels of representation: At the syntactic level the objects are programs. A (control) program does not denote an element of the semantic universe. Rather, it denotes a symbol table, which binds declared identifiers to elements of the semantic universe.

4.4. TYPES OF IDENTIFIER

A syntactic expression is constructed from strings of symbols

literal (identifiers)	denote	primitive objects
declared identifiers	denote	constructed objects
parameter (identifiers)	denote	argument selectors
assembled according to production rules	denote	combinators

Declared identifiers can occur in syntactic expressions in the same places as literal identifiers. The parameter identifiers are one syntactic device for representing the combinators composition and local abstraction, defined below, which can be used to construct functions, i.e. parametric semantic objects. The parameter identifiers can occur in syntactic expressions in some or all of the places where literal identifiers can occur, depending on which combinators were used to generate the semantic universe.

Note the additional semantic transition which takes place when we reach the syntactic levels of representation : Semantic expressions are built up from the primitive objects, assembled by means of the combinators. Alternatively, we can say that semantic expressions are built up from primitive objects and argument selectors, assembled by means of a conceptually simpler set of combinators. In syntactic expressions the primitive objects are represented by literals and the argument selectors by parameters. Syntactic expressions are also allowed to include declared identifiers, which is an innovation at the syntactic levels of representation. Of course, the reason for this innovation is to provide a macro facility for recurring subexpressions. However, allowing a syntactic expression to include declared identifiers might make it possible for syntactic expressions to denote objects which were not in the original semantic universe. Allowing declared identifiers in syntactic expressions is equivalent to allowing nested use of the combinators. In control Languages 1,2 the semantic universe will be defined to be generated by arbitrarily nested use of the combinators, so syntactic expressions always denote objects of the semantic universe. The definition which will be given for the semantic universe of Control Language 3 will not allow combinator nesting, and it is possible for a syntactic expression (in a program which defines the declared identifiers) to denote an object which was not in the semantic universe. Actually, if we allow a program to contain recursive definitions of the declared identifiers then even the programs of Control Languages 1,2 can define semantic objects not in the original semantic universe.

4.5 USER VS ASSEMBLY SYNTAX

User syntax and assembly syntax differ only in the allowed depth of nesting of syntactic expressions. In assembly syntax all syntactic expressions are required to have precisely 1 level of nesting. This is possible because declarations have been introduced at the syntactic level of representation. So it is possible to introduce auxiliary declarations to name all nested subexpressions.

5. PRIMITIVES FOR CONTROL LANGUAGES

5.1 EXAMPLE LANGUAGES USE SAME PRIMITIVES

The semantic universes of the 3 example languages are generated from roughly the same primitives, using successively more powerful combinators. These primitives are, roughly,

order 0 primitives : '00...0'
'00...1'
.
.
.

order 1 primitives : SEQUENCE
CASE
LOOP

The primitives are abstract objects, although I must represent them syntactically in the text.

The order 0 primitives are the most elementary control routines : e.g., '10...1' denotes the routine "Regardless of the device status, output (the microcommand) '10...1' and terminate."

(continued ** next column)

**

The order 1 primitives have been chosen to make it possible to construct a wide variety of routines from the primitive routines. They are, roughly, the control structures which Dijstra proposes for "structured programming" :

Let arg.1,...,arg.n be routines. SEQUENCE (arg.1,...,arg.n) is the routine which consists of executing arg.1,...,arg.n in that order and terminating. CASE(arg.1, ...,arg.n) is a routine which first observes the device status, then chooses one of the arg.i to execute, then terminates. LOOP(arg.1,...,arg.n) is a routine which repeatedly executes the arg.i in some order, observing the device status before each execution in order to choose one of the arg.i or to terminate. The order 1 primitives have not been specified completely because they vary somewhat in the 3 example languages.

Higher order semantic objects are not used as primitives in the 3 example languages, but can be constructed in Control Language 3.

5.2 EXAMPLE OF REPRESENTATION LEVELS

Suppose that the only combinator is application. Then an example of a semantic expression is denoted by the English sentence

Apply SEQUENCE to arg.1, arg.2, where
arg.1 is OUTPUT '01...1'
arg.2 is the result of applying CASE
to arg'.1; arg'.2,arg'.3,
where arg'.1 is OUTPUT '11...1'
arg'.2 is OUTPUT '11...0'
arg'.3 is the result of
applying LOOP to arg'.1,
arg'.2

At the abstract syntax level this semantic expression can be represented by the tree

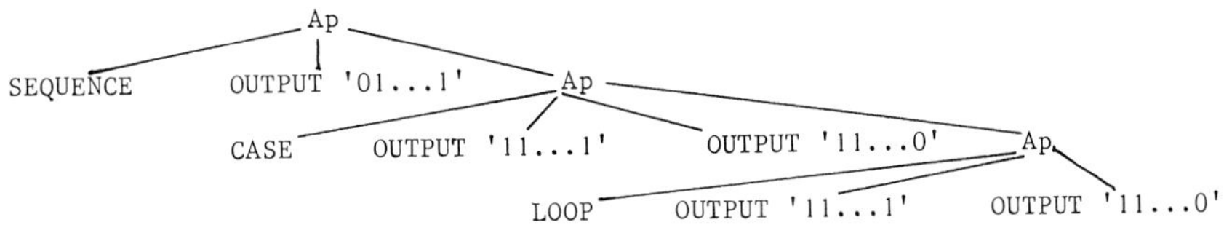

However, since there is only 1 combinator, the nonterminal labels carry no information. Therefore, I prefer to represent this semantic expression by the tree

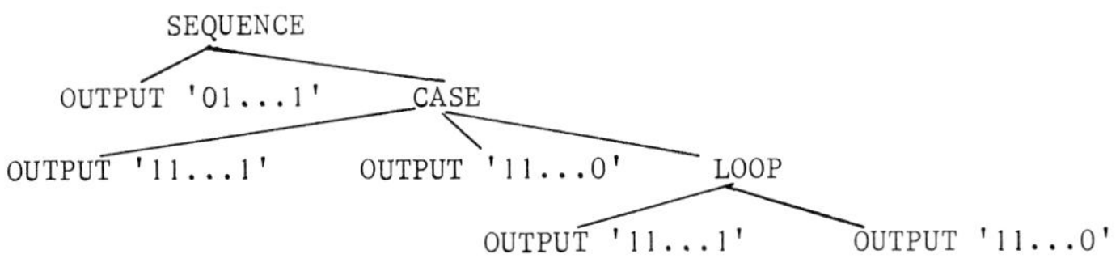

An abstract syntax tree has semantic objects as node labels, so the above figure is a representation of the actual tree. Namely, in the actual tree the label of the top node is the control structure denoted here by SEQUENCE, the label of its leftmost subnode is the routine denoted by OUTPUT '01...1', etc.

At the user syntax level we might choose to represent the semantic primitives by the following literal identifiers :

semantic primitive	literal identifier
OUTPUT '00...0'	'00...0'
OUTPUT '00...1'	'00...1'
.	.
.	.
.	.
meaning of SEQUENCE	SEQUENCE
.	.
.	.
.	.

Furthermore, we might choose to linearize the tree by means of functional notation. So a user syntax program which binds 'rout' to the value of the semantic expression denoted by the above abstract syntax tree might contain the declaration

```
rout=SEQUENCE('01...1',CASE('11...1','11...0',
            LOOP('11...1', '11...0')))
```

Alternatively, the program might contain the 2 declarations

```
rout1=CASE('11...1','11...0',LOOP('11...1',
                                  '11...0'))
rout=SEQUENCE('01...1',rout1)
```

However at the assembly syntax level we are only allowed expressions of depth 1. So an assembly syntax program to define rout must contain 3 declarations of the form

```
rout2 = LOOP('11...1','11...0')
rout1 = CASE('11...1','11...0',rout2)
rout  = SEQUENCE('01...1',rout1)
```

5.3 PRIMITIVES OF EACH EXAMPLE LANGUAGE

Control Language

	1.Application	2.Composition 3.Local-Abstraction
primitive routines	'00...0' '00...1' . . . '11...1'	'00...0' '00...1' . . . '11...1' NOOP

	1.Application	2.Composition 3.Local-Abstraction
primitive order 1 functions	Seq IfSdo Until¬Sdo (WhileSdo)	Seq.2 : Seq.8 Case.1 : Case.8 Loop.1 : Loop.8

The "Seq" form of SEQUENCE takes a list of arguments of any length. The "Seq.i" form takes 1 arguments.

In Control Language 1 the device status S is assumed to be a single bit. The routine

IfSdo(arg)

first observes S, then if S = 1 it executes arg, otherwise does nothing. The routine

Until¬Sdo(arg)

repeatedly executes arg, observing S after each execution, until S = 0. The routine

WhileSdo(arg)

is the same loop except that S is tested before execution of arg. WhileSdo is not a primitive of this language, but WhileSdo (arg) can be constructed by applying IfSdo and Until¬Sdo to arg. The machine code is such that WhileSdo appears to be a primitive control structure.

Control Languages 2,3 have the same primitives. S is assumed to be a bit vector. Case.n and Loop.n take n arguments. For example, the routine

Case.3(arg.1,arg.2,arg.3)

observes the first 2 bits of S (since 2^2 is the smallest power of 2 which is $\geqslant 3$), then executes

arg.S+1 if $S+1 \leqslant 3$
NOOP if $S+1 > 3$

and terminates.

Loop.3(arg.1,arg.2,arg.3)

repeatedly executes

Case.3(arg.1,arg.2,arg.3)

until $S+1 > 3$, then terminates.

5.4 REASONS FOR VARIATION OF PRIMITIVES USED

The primitive routine NOOP (do nothing) is included in Control Languages 2,3 because functions can be constructed in these languages. NOOP is a useful argument for the constructed functions.

The choice of primitives is influenced by feedback from the choice of machine code format. The following are examples of this influence :

Functions cannot be constructed in Control Language 1, so expressions can only have primitive functions. I decided to use a bit tag on each machine code instruction to determine if each of the primitive functions is to be applied. Therefore, it was desirable to choose a set of primitive functions which is small and such that all possible tag bit vectors are useful.

(continued * next column)

* Functions can be constructed in Control Languages 2,3. Declared functions can be used in expressions. So it was necessary to provide a large number of bit vectors to represent functions in machine code expressions. Therefore, a large number of primitive functions does not add much to program size. I choose the primitive functions to have fixed numbers of arguments. Then all functions had fixed numbers of arguments. That is, the number of arguments is determined by the function definition rather than the call. Presumably this makes more efficient use of space.

6. COMBINATORS FOR CONTROL LANGUAGES

6.1 COMBINATORS DISCUSSED IN THIS PAPER

application
composition
local-abstraction
abstraction

These combinators are defined below. The semantic primitives used to generate the 3 example control languages were specified in the last section. The combinators are as follows :

Control Language	semantic expressions formed by
1. Application Language	nested application
2. Composition Language	nested application and composition
3. Local-Abstraction Language	local-abstraction

These control languages are in order of increasing power in that more general types of semantic objects can be constructed. For comparison, an even more powerful language is

λ-Calculus	nested application and abstraction

Application is the action of applying a function to arguments. Nested application allows the construction of semantic expressions which can be represented by application trees of the form

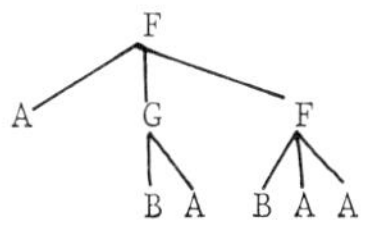

In the case of the 3 example control languages, the primitive objects are order 0 and order 1. To be meaningful, the nonterminal labels of an application tree must be order 1 functions and the terminal labels must be order 0 objects. Therefore, the objects constructed by nested application, i.e. the values of semantic

(continued at ** next column)

** expressions denoted by application trees, are order 0 objects. That is, the constructed objects of Control Language 1 are all routines. Nonprimitive functions can't be constructed.

Composition combines functions to construct new functions. More precisely, if F is a function of several parameters, then composition allows functions to be substituted for some of these parameters, or argument values to be substituted for some of the parameters, or the parameters to be reordered and/or equivalenced. Nested application and composition allows the construction of semantic expressions which can algorithmically be converted to semantic expressions which have the same value and which can be represented by composition trees of the form

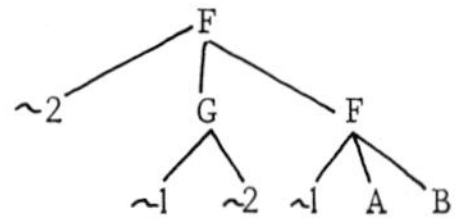

where ~1, ~2,... denote argument selectors. This tree denotes a function f of 2 parameters. f(arg.1,arg.2) is defined to be the value of the semantic expression denoted by the application tree which results if ~1 is replaced by arg.1 and ~2 by arg.2.

Composition trees are a generalization of application trees in that argument selectors are allowed at the terminal nodes. Since the primitive objects of the example languages are order 0 and order 1, the constructed objects will be order 0 if there are no argument selectors in the composition tree, order 1 if there are argument selectors. That is, Control Language 2 can define new control structures as well as new routines.

Local-abstraction, introduced here, will mean the following generalization of nested application and composition : a local-abstraction tree is allowed to have argument selectors at the nonterminal nodes, e.g.

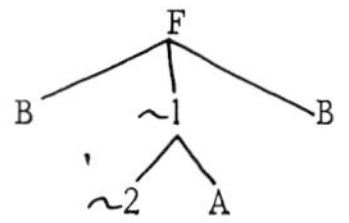

A single (unnested) use of local-abstraction produces a semantic expression denoted by a local-abstraction tree. The local-abstraction tree above denotes a semantic expression, the value of which is a function f of 2 parameters. f is at least of order 2 since the domain of ~1 is functions of at least order 1. f is not well defined because the domain of (~1, ~2) is not obvious.

Thus, Control Language 3 can construct higher order objects from its order 0 and order 1 primitives, but the semantic vagueness of the λ-calculus is creeping in. Nested local-abstraction allows the construction of pure nonsense, but I do not allow it at the semantic expression level. However, it is introduced automatically at the user syntax level, as is discussed below.

Abstraction is not truly a combinator in the sense of this paper since it edits semantic expressions rather than operating on their values. Abstraction is the action of constructing a parametric expression, the value of which is a function, by replacing some of the semantic objects in a semantic expression by argument selectors. For instance, the λ-calculus expression

(λF,A) [F(A, G(B,A), F(B,A,A))]

denotes a function with 2 parameters. An alternative notation, using distinguished parameter identifiers, is

~1(~2, G(B, ~2), ~1(B, ~2, ~2))

Thus, nested application followed by a single abstraction is the same as local-abstraction. However, since abstraction operates on semantic expressions rather than their values, nested application and abstraction is more powerful (and more difficult to interpret) than nested local-abstraction, as is discussed below.

6.2 DISADVANTAGES OF THE λ-CALCULUS

The λ-Calculus is appealing because nested application and abstraction are the most powerful combinators known. However, λ-Calculus expressions are not suitable for interpretation by low level hardware. Landin's (1964) SECD machine and McGowan's contour model machine show that a complex display is required to specify ths dynamic environment. Furthermore, despite the heroic efforts of Dana Scott (1970-2) the semantic denotation of the λ-calculus is obscure. For an introduction to the λ-calculus see Landin (1966).

6.3 USER SYNTAX

The abstract syntax trees of sect. 6.1 have 2 types of node label : primitive objects denoted by A,B...,F,G,...and argument selectors denoted by ~1, ~2,... . Besides literal and parameter identifiers, a syntactic expression in a program can also contain previously declared identifiers a,b,...,f,g,... . Since user and assembly syntax are not the principal topics of this paper (see title), I will usually use functional notation to linearize abstract syntax trees.

User syntax examples are

Application Language Program

```
begin

   a = F(B,B,A)
   b = F(A, G(B,A), a)
   .
   .
   .
```

```
end

   Composition Language Program

begin

      f = F(~1,A,~2)
      a = G(B, f(A,B))
      g = f( ~1, f(a,~1))
        .
        .
        .
end

   Local-Abstraction Language Program

begin

      f =~1(~1)
      a = f(f)
        .
        .
        .
end
```

Suppose that in each syntactic expression of a user syntax program we repeatedly replace all declared identifiers by their definitions. Suppose that the declarations are not recursive. It can be shown that in the Application Language and in the Composition Language this substitution process will terminate. Now each syntactic expression contains only literals and parameters, no declared identifiers. This shows that, barring recursive declarations, allowing declared identifiers in syntactic expressions does not increase the definitional power of these 2 languages.

However, in the above Local-Abstraction program if we try to substitute the definition of "f" for f in the definition of "a" the result is not a well formed syntactic expression, since this language does not allow the application of local-abstraction expressions, i.e. nested local-abstraction (application is a special case of local-abstraction).

So the definitional power of the Local-Abstraction Language <u>is</u> increased by allowing syntactic expressions to contain declared identifiers in user syntax programs. This increases the definitional power of the Local-Abstraction Language to the point where it becomes possible to construct well known nonsense of the λ-Calculus, such as "a" in the above program.

6.4 ASSEMBLY SYNTAX

Assembly syntax is the same as user syntax except that syntactic expressions are required to have a depth of nesting of precisely 1. In order to make composition possible it is necessary to generalize user syntax somewhat : if G is a function of n parameters then

F(..,G,..) means F(..,G(~1,..,~n) ...)

No ambiguity between application and composition results if the primitives are all order 0 and order 1.

The definitional power of assembly syntax is the same as user syntax, but auxiliary declarations must be used. For example, the following program defines "g" of the second example program above :

```
     begin
          f = F(~1,A,~2)
         a1 = f(A,B)
          a = G(B,a1)
         g1 = f(a,~1)
          g = f(~1,g1)
     end
```

6.5 LOCAL-ABSTRACTION VS ABSTRACTION

Let declared identifiers be replaced by their definitions in Local-Abstraction Language programs. The resulting syntactic expressions are just those obtainable by nested local-abstraction. Nested local-abstraction expressions are equivalent to those λ-Calculus expressions which satisfy the following constraint : whenever abstraction is performed on a subexpression <u>all</u> identifiers of the subexpression which are bound in the complete expression must be bound simultaneously in the subexpression.

That is, bound globals, which are bound in a larger context, are not allowed. For example, the λ-Calculus expression

$$(\lambda G)\ [F(A,\ \ (\lambda B)\ [G(A,B)])]$$

is not a nested local-abstraction expression because the global G of the subexpression $(\lambda B)\ [G(A,B)]$ is bound in the entire expression.

Each subexpression of a nested local-abstraction expression contains only identifiers which are free in the entire expression and local parameter identifiers. For this reason an interpreter for nested local-abstraction expressions only requires a display with 1 pointer.

6.6 SUMMARY : DEFINITIONAL POWER VS DISPLAY REQUIRED BY INTERPRETER

Let us consider control languages such that the primitives are order 0 objects (routines) and order 1 functions (control structures). The implications of the choice of combinators is as follows :

types of objects which can be constructed		display required by interpreter
	Application Language:	
routines		none
	Composition Language:	
routines control structures		1 pointer
	Local-Abstraction Language :	
routines control structures routine-valued high order garbage		1 pointer
	λ-Calculus	
routines control structures general high order garbage		array of pointers

Interpreters for the first 3 languages are presented in Sects. 8,9,10. These interpreters show that these languages can be interpreted with the displays stated in the above table.

7. THREE EXAMPLE CONTROL LANGUAGES

7.1 EXAMPLE ROUTINE DEFINED IN APPLICATION LANGUAGE

Application Tree :

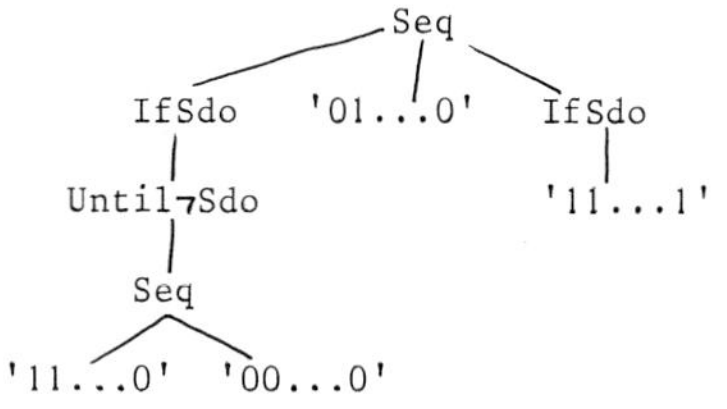

(continued at ** next column)

** User syntax :

```
Seq(
    IfSdo(Until¬Sdo(
     Seq('11...0', '00...0'))),
    '01...0',
    IfSdo('11...1'))
```

More Palatable User Syntax :

```
WHILE S = 1 DO
     OUTPUT 11...0
     OUTPUT 00...0
OUTPUT 01...0
IF S = 1  DO
     OUTPUT 11...1
```

Assembly Syntax (the machine code of Sect. 8.1 allows some functional nesting) :

```
   a = Seq('11...0','00...0')
rout = Seq(WhileSdo(a),
           '01...0',
           IfSdo('11...1')
```

More Palatable Assembly Syntax :

```
   a : OUT  11...0
       OUT  00...0
rout : WhileS DO a
       OUT  01...0
       IfS  OUT 11...1
```

7.2 EXAMPLE CONTROL STRUCTURE DEFINED IN COMPOSITION LANGUAGE

Composition Tree :

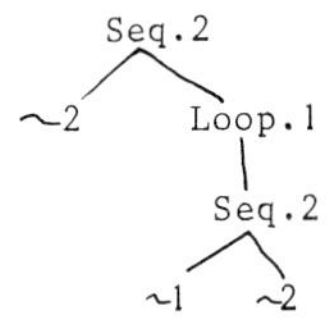

User Syntax :

```
exitmiddle = Seq.2( ~2, Loop.1(Seq.2(
                          ~1, ~2)))
```

More Palatable User Syntax :

```
exitmiddle(~1,~2) =
          ~2
          WHILE S=0  DO
          ~1
          ~2
```

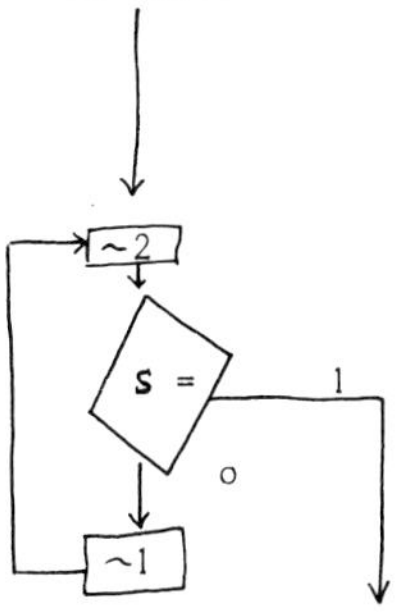

Assembly Syntax : f = Loop.1(Seq.2)

exitmiddle = Seq.2(~2,f)

7.3 OTHER USES FOR COMPOSITION

Thinking of the order 1 functions constructible by composition as being control structures suggests uses such as exit-in-the-middle. The order 1 functions can also be thought of as routine modifiers. This suggests the order 1 function Indivis(~1) which turns the device interrupts off before executing ~1 and on afterwards.

The order 1 functions can also be thought of as parametric routines which take routines as arguments. This shows that composition is useful for controlling data operations in a device with iterated memory such as a CPU : an order 1 function performs the operation. Its arguments are the access routines which determine on which registers the operation is to be performed.

7.4 USES FOR LOCAL-ABSTRACTION

Although order 1 functions constructible by composition are quite useful, I have found it difficult to propose interesting uses for the higher order functions constructible by local-abstraction.

The order 2 functions are parametric routines which take control structures as arguments. It is difficult to propose order 2 functions which provide useful families of routines because the control structures with which we are familiar are so disparate. Changing a control routine has drastic effects.

However, there are families of control structures which have roughly the same effect in their intended applications. E.g., we implement equivalent control structures in order to optimize resource utilization. This suggests the use of order 2 functions to provide alternative methods of error control or concurrent scheduling.

7.5 SPACE OPTIMIZATION

The example control languages were designed with the objective of minimizing program size at the expense of interpretation time. Therefore, means were sought to make it possible to name recurring patterns in order to avoid repetitions in the code.

One result of this objective was the decision to interpret (machine coded) syntactic expressions, rather than evaluate then (at compile time).

Another result was the interest in higher order combinators. The ultimate purpose of a control language is to define routines. The same routines (order 0 objects) are definable in all 3 example languages. The difference is that the higher order combinators allow higher order patterns to be named. The Application Language allows terminal subtrees of an expression tree to be named. The Composition Language allows nonterminal subtrees to be named. Local-Abstraction allows the naming of powerful higher order objects ranging from higher order functions on up into the incomprehensible.

8. EXAMPLE CONTROLLER 1 : APPLICATION

8.1 MACHINE CODE

Since Seq takes an arbitrary number of arguments, the number of arguments must be specified at the point of call. This could be done by and END instruction, but I guess that a continue/end tag bit on each (micro) instruction will reduce program size. Two more tag bits are used to determine if IfSdo and Until¬Sdo are to be applied to each instruction. Thus, the instruction format is

	E	I	U		ARG
No. bits :	1	1	1		n + 1

n = No. bits in microcommand

E : continue/end
I : IfSdo
U : Until¬Sdo
T : Terminal/nonterminal

The argument can be a microcommand (literal) or a label (declared identifier). A fourth tag bit T (Terminal/nonterminal) distinguishes between these 2 types of argument.

The user syntax program

```
rout =
     IF S=1 DO
          OUTPUT 11...1
     OUTPUT 01...0
     WHILE S=1 DO
          OUTPUT 11...0
          OUTPUT 00...0
```

can be coded as

		E	I	U	T	SUBR
		.	.	.	.	.
	rout :	0	1	0	1	11...1
fixed machine program (ROM)		0	0	0	1	01...0
		1	1	1	0	a
		.	.	.	.	.
	a :	0	0	0	1	11...1
		1	0	0	1	00...0
		.	.	.	.	.

8.2 INTERPRETER HARDWARE

The machine code can be interpreted by straightforward stack hardware :

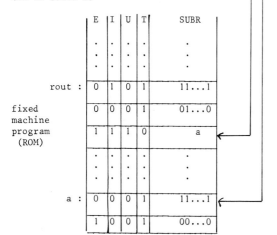

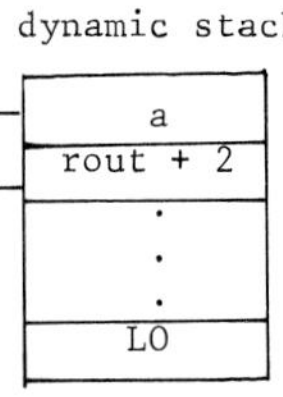

8.3 INTERPRETER OPERATION

When the stack is empty the next macrocommand is decoded to a label (ROM location) LO pushed onto the stack. If the stack is not empty the the stacktop label is executed and increased by 1 if E=0, or popped if E=1. An instruction with T=1 is a microcommand literal which is outputted. An instruction with T=0 is a label (subroutine call) which is executed by pushing it on the stack. Each instruction is executed 0 or more times, depending on the I and U tag bits and on the observed values of the device status S, which is assumed to be a single bit in this controller.

9. EXAMPLE CONTROLLER 2 : COMPOSITION

9.1 MACHINE CODE

The number of parameters of each (order 1) function is specified by its definition. So the number of arguments of a function call needn't be specified. The assembly syntax declaration: declared identifier = fnc(arg.1, arg.2, ...) can be coded as

	ROM
	.
lab:	fnc
	arg.1
	arg.2
	.

lab is label (ROM location) assigned to declared identifier

9.2 INTERPRETER HARDWARE

The rules of operation of the composition interpreter are such that the stacktop PROC can be a literal, a label, or a parameter. The lower PROC's can't be parameters or routine literals, the stackbottom PROC and any PROC pointed at by a DISP(-LAY) pointer must be a label.

ident	possible values
fnc	label, function literal
arg.1	label, function literal, routine literal, parameter
P	label, function literal, routine literal, parameter
P'	label, function literal
P''	label
LO	label (called by macrocommand)

dynamic stack

PROC DISP

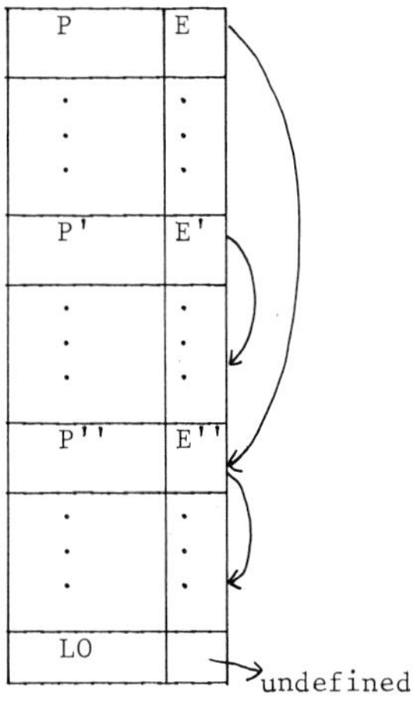

9.3 INTERPRETER OPERATION

old stack new stack

PROC DISP PROC DISP

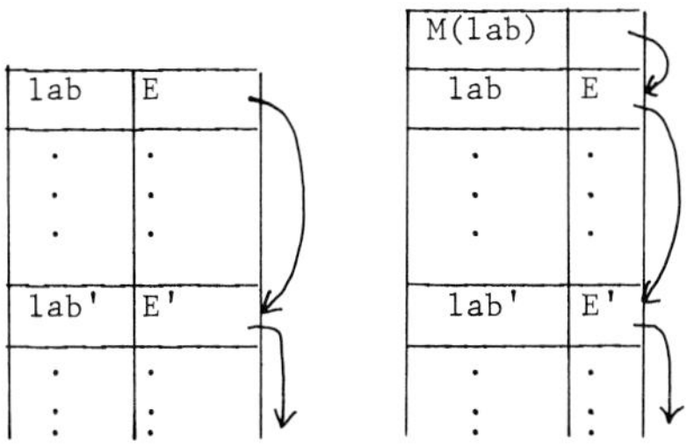

M is vector of ROM values, i.e. M(L) = ROM value at location L

M(lab) = fnc in ROM figure above

old stack new stack

PROC DISP PROC DISP

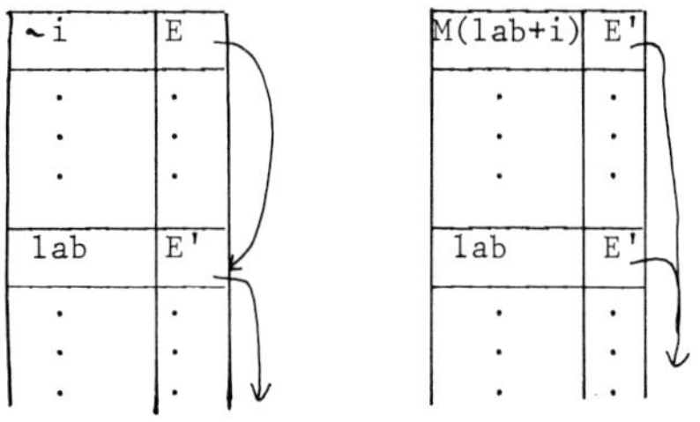

M(lab+i) = arg.i in ROM figure above

old stack new stack

PROC DISP PROC DISP

output '10...1'

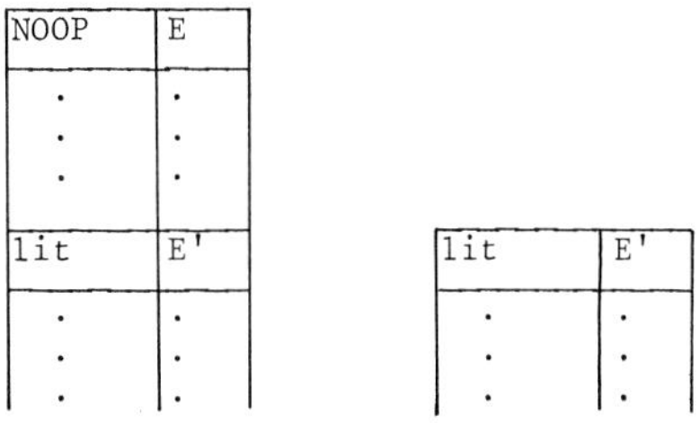

pop stack to topmost literal (necessarily a function literal : Seq.i, Case.i, Loop.i)

old stack new stack

PROC DISP PROC DISP

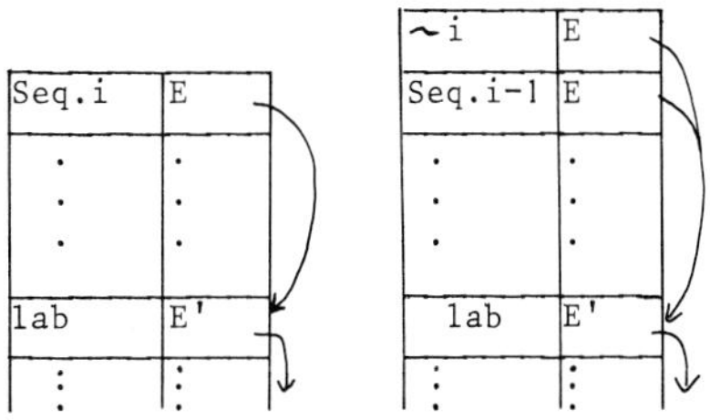

Seq.0 = NOOP

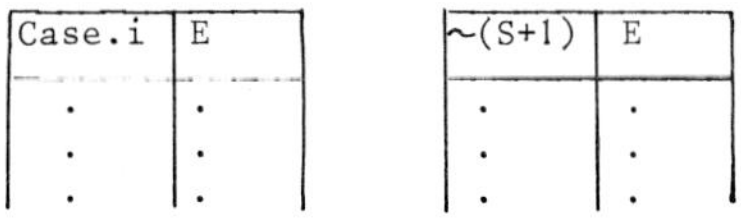

S is device status if S+1 ⩽ i, otherwise ~(S+1) means NOOP

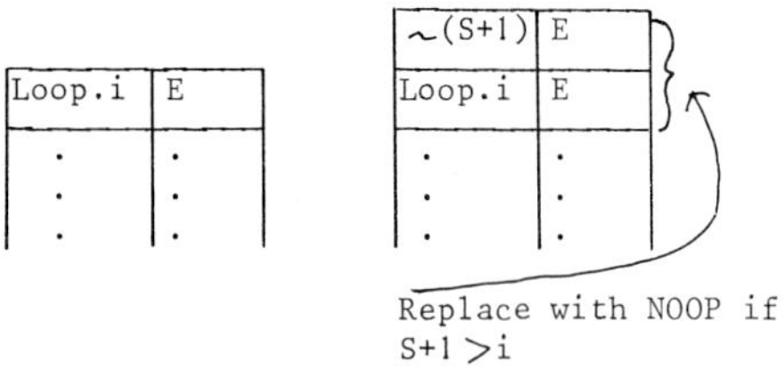

10. EXAMPLE CONTROLLER 3 : LOCAL ABSTRACTION

10.1 MACHINE CODE

The assembly syntax and machine code of the Local-Abstraction Language are the same as those of the composition language with the following generalization : in the declarations

assembly syntax

decl'd ident=fnc(arg.1, arg.2, ...)

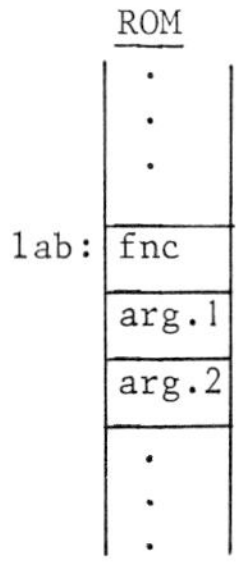

fnc is allowed to be a parameter identifier.

10.2 INTERPRETER HARDWARE

The hardware for the interpretation of local-abstraction code is the same as that for composition with the addition of a register which takes 3 values :

mode register

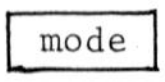

mode = "---","fnc","arg"

When the stacktop PROC is a parameter identifier, the mode register remembers whether it came from the fnc part or an arg.1 part of a code expression. The rules for updating the display are different in the 2 cases.

10.3 INTERPRETER OPERATION

old stack old   new stack new

PROC DISP MODE   PROC DISP MODE

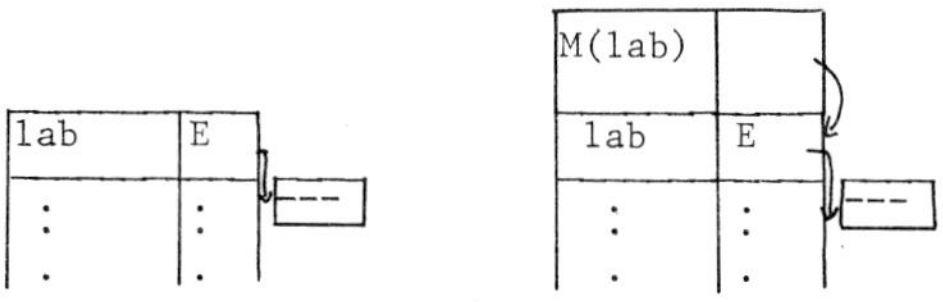

if M(lab) = label or (function) literal

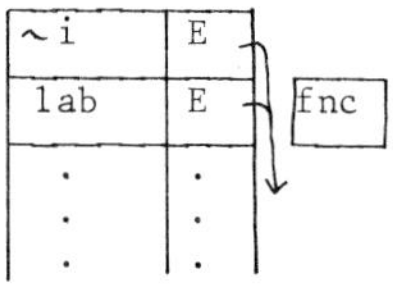

if M(lab) = ~i

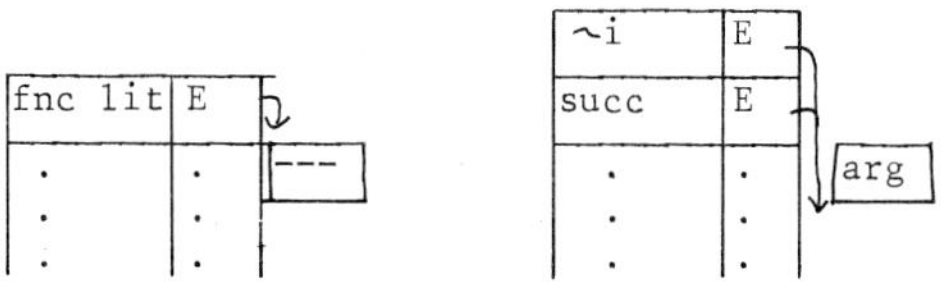

The choice of ~i and of the successor function literal are the same as in the composition interpreter.

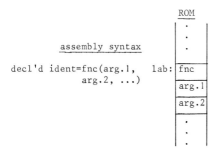

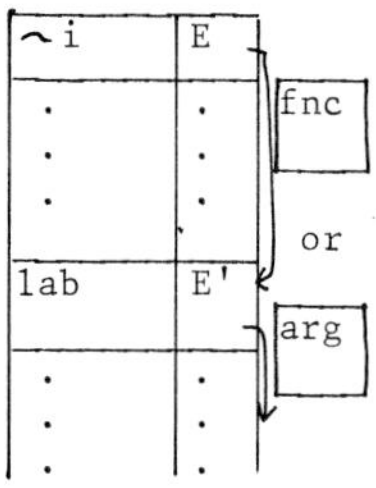

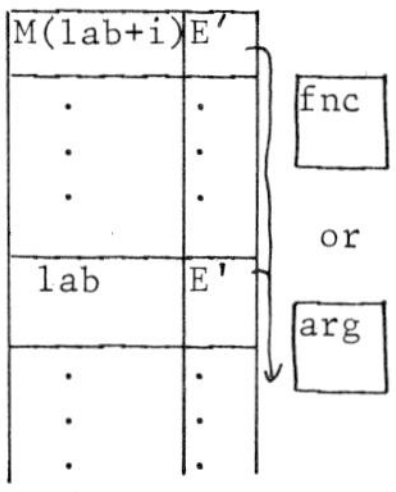

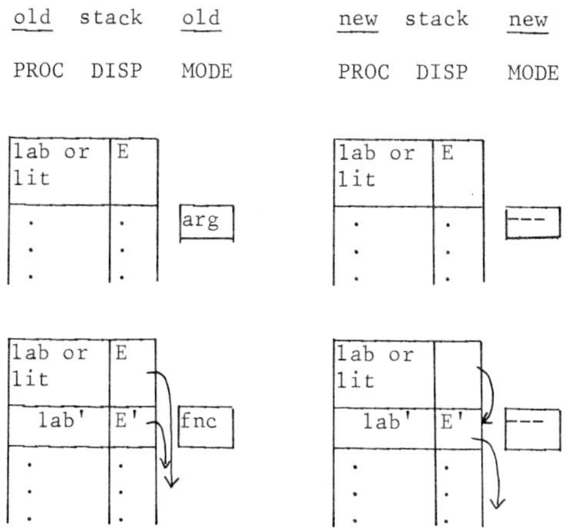

11. FEEDBACK FROM HARDWARE TO LANGUAGE DESIGN

11.1 FROM SEMANTICS TO HARDWARE TO SEMANTICS

This paper has shown examples of the use of linguistic analysis, starting with semantics, to design hardware. Conversely, when the hardware is proposed it suggests modifications of the language.

It has been shown in Sect. 5.4 that the choice of machine code influences the choice of primitives. Less obvious is the possibility of letting the interpreter design suggest modifications of the choice of combinators and additions to the primitives.

After the interpreter is designed it should be checked to see if the hardware is capable of performing operations which can't be programmed in the machine code. If so, then one seeks a semantic interpretation for these hardware operations and a means for calling then in the user syntax which makes them comprehensible.

11.2 EXAMPLE : USES FOR INITIAL ENVIRONMENT

Consider the hardware proposed for the Composition Language. The stackbottom PROC was called by the macrocommand which initiated the routine. The stackbottom DISP (-LAY) is not used because, to be meaningful, the macrocommand called a routine, i.e. and order 0 objects, and not a function. The following are possible uses for the stackbottom DISP :

one possibility is to allow macrocommands to be function calls with arguments. Then extra registers are needed to store the arguments of the initial parameter environment.

Alternatively, the stackbottom DISP can be predefined to indicate some environment, i.e.

~1 = NOOP, ~2 = NOOP, ~3 = NOOP, ...

At an insignificant hardware cost this gives meaning to ROM entry points which were previously meaningless if called by a macrocommand. Namely, if a macrocommand calls an (order 1) function, its arguments are all set to NOOP. This is the way SIMULA treats the "inner" parameter of its classes.

11.3 EXAMPLE : POSSIBLE OPERATIONS ON A HARDWARE STACK

The way in which hardware stacks are normally implemented makes it possible to perform many operations besides push and pop. For example, it is easy to pop to any indicated position on the stack. This suggests adding to the semantics the possibility of exit-in-the-middle through several levels of control nesting.

Arbitrary positions in the stack can easily be overwritten. I don't know what this would mean.

11.4 EXAMPLE : FROM COMPOSITION TO LOCAL-ABSTRACTION

When I originally considered the possibility of using high order combinators to reduce (micro-) program size, I rejected abstraction because of the complex display required for interpretation. I was pleased to find that composition expressions can be interpreted with a simple display.

It was obvious that the assembly syntax was capable of defining higher order functions if the functional part of assembly syntax expressions was allowed to be a parameter. I was surprised to find that the display of the composition interpreter was adequate to interpret these more general expressions. This observation led me to introduce the notion of local-abstraction and study its semantics and possible forms of user syntax. The results are in Sects. 6.2, 6.5.

12. CONCLUSION

This paper illustrates a semantics approach to the design of programmable hardware : first specify what you want to do, i.e. the semantic universe of abstract objects which are to be definable by the programming language. This semantic universe is defined by choosing primitive objects and combinators. Next, identify those primitive objects and/or combinators which are difficult to implement. Replace them with weaker (constrained) versions. Note that the syntax has not yet be chosen. The choice of syntax greatly influences the appearance of the language and the logic necessary for interpretation, but it does not seem to influence the complexity of the interpreter.

As an example of this approach, the design of a general purpose controller was considered. The primitive objects were taken to be single outputs and Dijkstra's control structures. These are easy to implement. Concerning the combinators one would like to use, the implementation of nested application requires a dynamic stack, but not much can be done without nested application. The implementation of abstraction greatly increases the amount of dynamic storage which is required. So abstraction was weakened to composition. It was found that the implementation of nested application and composition only requires a modest increase in stack width. Further consideration showed that composition could be generalized to local-abstraction with a neglegible increase in dynamic storage requirements.

When the syntax has been chosen and the interpreter designed, it is likely that not all the hardware capabilities will be accessible from the programming language. So the final step of the proposed design process is to augment the primitives and combinators in order to make the hardware capabilities accessible.

REFERENCES

Landin, P.J. (1964) "The Mechanical evaluation of expressions," Comp. J. 6, 4.

Landin, P.J. (1966) "A lambda-calculus approach," Advances in Programming and Non-Numerical Computation, Pergamon Press, 97-141.

Scott, D. (1970) "Outline of a Mathematical Theory of Computation," Proc. Fourth Annual Princeton Conf. on Information Sciences and Systems, 169-176.

Scott, D. (1971) "Lattice Theory, Data Types, and Semantics," New York University Symp. in Areas of Current Interest in Computer Science, ed. R. Randell.

Scott, D. (1972) "Lattice-theoretic models for various type-free calculi," Proc. Fourth International Congress for Logic, Methodology, and the Philosophy of Science, Bucharest.

E. Morlet and D. Ribbens, (Eds.), International Computing Symposium 1977.

EXTENSION OF PRECOMPILERS FOR EVALUATION OF PROGRAM TESTS

Marco Maiocchi

University of Milano - Gruppo di Elettronica e Cibernetica
Milano, Italy

The paper presents a proposal for the extension of the capabilities of the preprocessors (both macroprocessors and precompilers) for structured programming, in order to allow a quantitative measure of the coverage of a program exercise through its execution with test data, and then to allow a quality evaluation.

1. INTRODUCTION

From a theoretical point of view it is possible to design a program by means of structured programming and top down techniques and then to code it in any programming language, even not specifically designed for such techniques; but in practice many reasons discourage from following this way (e.g. it is difficult to respect boring code standards, the resulting code is almost not readable, problems arise about closeness to program documentation, etc.).

The need of programming languages directly supporting such techniques has to be connected to problems such as language diffusion, portability and programmers training. Therefore, preprocessors were developed which extend well-known and spread languages, such as FORTRAN and COBOL, and enable to use structured programming techniques.
These preprocessors usually insert in the existing language only the most common control environments of structured programming; by this way it is quite possible to avoid the use of jump instructions (both conditional and unconditional) set at disposal by the existing language (references for FORTRAN precompilers in Reifer /1/).

This paper presents a proposal to extend the use of such preprocessors in the range of program testing, in particular to evaluate execution covering. For this purpose precompilers have been already constructed (Fait /2/, Brown /3/, Stucki /4/ etc.): they accept as input a program to be tested and give as result the same program equipped with new instructions which enable to record the number of times that each instruction of the source program has been executed. The additional instructions are inserted in connection with the control instructions of the source program, on all the paths they may select. They perform the task of increasing appropriate counters.
Below are analyzed the proposed testing criteria, the benefits which come from the insertion of these facilities for testing in precompilers for structured programming, and a proposal on the structure and the characteristics of a system using these facilities.

2.TESTING PURPOSES

In the practice of the quality control of software products it is necessary to have at disposal criteria for defining test data and methods or tools for evaluating if the designed test data are or not sufficient in obtaining a reasonable quality of the product.
Two are generally the used criteria:

. functional coverage: the programmer compiles a "checklist", that is a list of (1) all user visible functionalities provided by the program ("user" can be a module of a higher level) and of (2) the set of corresponding test data which exercise that functionalities. The checklist is the result of the programmer's personal characteristics and consequently its quality depends on the programmer's own experience, cleverness

This research has been sponsored by Honeywell Information System Italy, in the frame of the Communication Programming Project.

or intuition. Therefore, even though the objectives of the functional coverage are clear, there is no guarantee of obtaining good program quality; this for the reason that such criteria are based on "abstract" elements rather than concrete.

topological coverage: the programmer plans the sets of test data with the purpose of exercising at least once "physical elements" of the program: instructions, control paths or others. Topological coverage presents the advantage that the list of the elements to be exercised is not abstract, but is constituted by the program itself; it presents the following risk, however: a program completely covered can provide functionalities different from those initially required.

The use of both criteria together can avoid risks: functional checklists can be used for controlling that a topological coverage provides a satisfactory functional coverage.

3. PREPROCESSORS AND COVERAGE

The aim pursued by the mentioned precompilers is to provide a quantitative evalation of the quality of tests designed to verify correct program running. In fact, knowing the number of times that each instruction of the program was executed, it is possible to know which of its parts have never been tested, which have been not much tested, which a lot; minimal covering request - that is each element has to be exercised at least once (e.g., each path between two conditional control instructions has to be executed at least once) - represents a limited but precise objective which provides a minimum warranty on program qualification. Obviously this tool is not used during program testing phases, but only during an initial evaluation phase of the designed tests; these are then suitable means to verify the correct running of the non-instrumented source program (consider, e.g., the case of regression tests of a product).

Therefore this tool is oriented to the programmer: knowing the internal structure of the program, he is able to evaluate which functions have not been tested, basing on not executed instructions; some products make this task easier (Fait /2/, Brown /3/, Stucki /4/) by printing information on instruction execution directly on the list of the source program.

4. THE PROPOSAL

The introduction of these facilities in the preprocessors for structured programming would contribute a lot to rationalize program testing and would offer some benefits such as:

. a preprocessor for structured programming has to examine the source program to translate it; therefore it results very cheap, as regards both execution time and dimension of the compiler, to instrument it so to record covering information;

. the use of structured programming techniques while writing programs draws the physical structure of the program nearer to the logical structure of the computation; this way it is easier to point out the functions to be tested, starting on the information about the parts of the program which have not been executed;

. the preprocessor for structured programming provides the translation of all those parts concerned with execution control, that is of all the parts which the instrumentation to record covering information is interested in: problems arising from the introduction of such new parts are therefore quite reduced.

Of course testing facilities should be requested on option.

The schema of fig.1 shows the use of the proposed preprocessor. Here the source program is supplied to the precompiler together with the request of instrumenting it for testing; it is translated into the existing language and then supplied to the compiler for this language, which gives the running program. Subsequent executions of this program with different input data produce the recording of information about the number of times that each instruction was executed and the sum of the executions related to several program runs. Finally, a printing program wich reads this information and an image of the source program gives a list where, beside each instruction, there is printed the number of times it was executed.

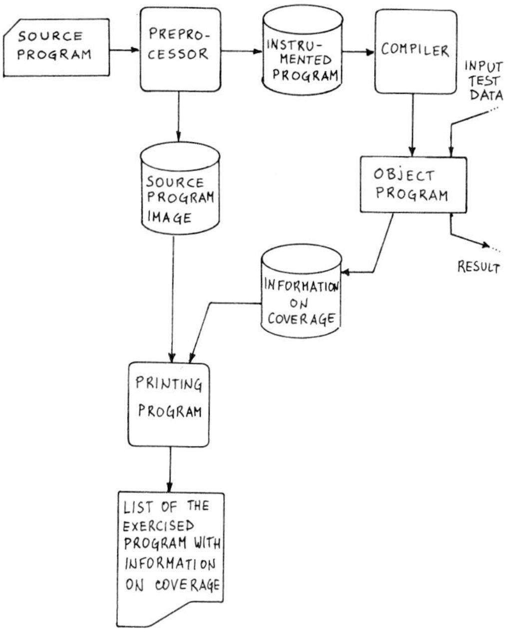

Fig.1

5. ANALYSIS OF INSTRUMENTING INSTRUCTIONS FOR FORTRAN

The proposal is obviously independent of the programming language; in particular it offers further benefits in the case of assembly languages: the exclusive use of standard control structures removes here the presence of indirect or modified jumps, which cannot be noted for the covering (as the point where the jump arrives is known only during the execution phase: a syntactical analysis cannot find out where instrumenting instructions are to be inserted). The instrumentation of a FORTRAN structured program will be analyzed here. When choosing the syntactical form of the source language, the proposal in Meissner /5/ will be followed.

Let's consider the following simple example of fig.2. The program computes the solutions of a quadratic equation of the form $ax^2+bx+c = 0$.

```
          READ (5,10) A,B,C
          DELTA = B**2 - 4.*A*C
          IF (DELTA.LT.0) THEN
            WRITE (6,20)
          ELSE
            X1=(-B-SQRT(DELTA))/(2.*A)
            X2=(-B+SQRT(DELTA))/(2.*A)
            WRITE (6,30) X1,X2
          ENDIF
          STOP
    10    FORMAT (3F7.3)
    20    FORMAT (1X,'NO SOLUTIONS')
    30    FORMAT (1X,F7.3,2X,F7.3)
          END
```

Fig. 2

A possible translation instrumentef for the testing is shown in fig. 3. Here, the array XX contains the counters of the instructions executions; the subroutine READXX initializes this array by reading, e.g. from a disk file, the values of the counters obtained in the previous program runs; the subroutine STORXX records, e.g. on disk, the values of the counters after the execution.

```
        COMMON XX
        DIMANSION XX(...)
        CALL READXX
        READ (5,10) A,B,C
        DELTA = B**2 - 4.*A*C
        IF(.NOT.(DELTA.LT.0))GOTO 10000
        XX(1) = XX(1) + 1
        WRITE (6,20)
        GOTO 10001
10000   XX(2) = XX(2) + 1
        X1=(-B-SQRT(DELTA))/(2.*A)
        X2=(-B+SQRT(DELTA))/(2.*A)
        WRITE (6,30) A,B,C
10001   CONTINUE
        CALL STORXX
        STOP
   10   FORMAT (3F7.3)
   20   FORMAT (1X,'NO SOLUTIONS')
   30   FORMAT (1X,F7.3,2X,F7.3)
        END
```

Fig. 3

Note that counters are updated just in two points, which correspond to the beginning of the two options in the if-then -else clause; by this way it is possible to know all the information concerned with covering of any other instruction.

Let's suppose to launch the program with the following input data:

A = 1 B = 4 C = -1

Through the final printing program, the following list may be obtained:

```
1        READ (5,10) A,B,C
1        DELTA = B**2 - 4.*A*C
1        IF (DELTA.LT.0) THEN
-           WRITE (6,20)
1        ELSE
1           X1=(-B-SQRT(DELTA))/(2.*A)
1           X2=(-B+SQRT(DELTA))/(2.*A)
1           WRITE (6,30) X1,X2
1        ENDIF
1        STOP
   10    FORMAT (3F7.3)
   20    FORMAT (1X,'NO SOLUTIONS')
   30    FORMAT (1X,F7.3,2X,F7.3)
         END
```

Fig. 4

This list shows clearly that all program instructions were executed once, except the instruction WRITE (6,20), which corresponds to the first option in the if-then-else structure.

6. INSTRUMENTING THE SINGLE CONTROL STRUCTURE

With reference to the control structures mentioned in Meissner /5/, a possible translation with testing instrumentation is reported below.

In the translation code, the parts indicated with trk, trk-i, etc. show the points where instructions to increase the counters are to be inserted, without any further detail on the characteristics of such instructions.

Analogous instrumentation can be inserted in preprocessors for different programming languages.

A. Basic selection.

Structure		Translation
IF(cond)THEN		IF(.NOT.cond)GOTO a
		trk-1
...		...
ELSE		GOTO b
	a	trk-2
...		...
ENDIF	b	CONTINUE

B. Basic case structure.

Structure		Translation
TEST (k)		IF(k.GT. .. .OR.k.LE. ..)GOTO a_n
		GOTO(a_1,a_2,..,a_i),k
CASE(...)	a_1	trk-1
...		...
CASE(...)		GOTO b
	a_2	trk-2
...		...
ELSE		GOTO b
	a_n	trk-n
...		...
ENDTEST	b	CONTINUE

C. Basic loops.

Structure		Translation
DO WHILE (cond)	a	IF(.NOT.cond)GOTO b
		trk
...		...
REPEAT		GOTO a
	b	CONTINUE
DO	a	trk
...		...
REPEAT UNTIL (cond)		IF(.NOT.cond)GOTO a

DO UNTIL version and REPEAT WHILE version are respectively analogous to the two presented above.

D. Extended IF structure.

Structure		Translation
IF (cond) THEN		IF(.NOT.cond)GOTO a_2
		trk-1
...		...
ELSEIF(cond)		GOTO b
THEN	a_2	IF(.NOT.cond)GOTO a_3
		trk-2
...		...

```
ELSE                GOTO b
                 an trk-n
  ...               ...
ENDIF             b CONTINUE
```

E. Extended CASE structure.

The translation is the same as in the previous case, from the point of view of the instrumentation.

F. Indexed DO loops.

```
      Structure             Translation

DO FOR ...           DO a ....
                     trk
  ...                ...
REPEAT             a CONTINUE
```

G. Exit.

```
      Structure             Translation

DO                 a trk-1
  ...                ...
  IF(cond)EXIT       IF(cond)GOTO b
                     trk-2
  ...                ...
REPEAT               GOTO a
                   b CONTINUE
```

H. Cycle.

```
      Structure             Translation

DO                 a trk-1
  ...                ...
  IF(cond)CYCLE      IF(cond)GOTO a
                     trk-2
  ...                ...
REPEAT               GOTO a
```

I. Event driven case.

```
      Structure             Translation

TEST k               ...
  ...                ...
  SELECT v1          IF(k.EQ.v1)GOTO a1
                     trk-1
  ....               ...
  CASE v1            GOTO b
                  a1 trk-i1
  ...                ...
ENDTEST            b CONTINUE
```

7. ALTERNATIVE PROPOSAL

The illustrated instrumentation and the resulting list show the executed instruction of a program; the coverage of the instructions may not correspond to the coverage of the paths between control instructions (e.g., it can be not easy to discover the coverage of the empty path of an if-then-else clause in which no else key and code are provided).
An alternative implementation could provide a printout only of the truth values assumed by any condition in the program; so the list

```
T       IF (cond) THEN
TF        IF (cond) THEN
            ....
          ELSE
            ....
          ENDIF
        ELSE
          ....
        ENDIF
```

shows that the outer IF THEN ELSE has been executed with the condition TRUE and the inner has been executed with both values TRUE and FALSE for the condition.

This kind of printout can obviously be composed with the previous one.

8. CONCLUSIONS

The use of such kind of tools has indicated some advantage in the program quality control:

. the effectiveness of test data can be indicated with a number, for example the percentage of the executed instructions;
. a relation between "quality level" (expressed, e.g., in terms of errors discovered in any product release) and percentage of exercised instructions can be achieved, on the basis of a statistical analysis.

Studies toward such a direction are on the way.

9. REFERENCES

/1/ D.Reifer,L.P.Meissner - Structured Fortran Preprocessor Survey -1975- UCID 3793

/2/ G.F.Fait,L.Ferri,G.A.Lanzarone- Un semplice strumento per misure automatiche nelle prove del software - 13th International Automation Conference - Human Engineering - 1974

/3/ Brown et al - Automated Software Quality Assurance - in Program test methods - Hetzel editor, Prentice Hall

/4/ L.G.Stucki - Automatic Generation of Self Metric Software - IEEE Symposium on Computer Software Reliability - New York , 1973

/5/ L.P.Meissner - Proposed Control Structures for Extending FORTRAN - FORWORD n.5, Oct.1975

Acknowledgments.
The author wishes to thank mr. G. Degli Antoni for many useful suggestions and comments and to mr. P. Grandi for his support in the implementation.

APPENDIX

A simple example of the result of covering check on the execution of a program is given below.

The example uses the FORTRAN precompiler ESF, implemented at the University of Milan. The precompiler was initially developed without instrumentation capabilities for testing: its further updating required less than a week to the programmer.

The program in the example reads three values, checks whether or not they can be the sides of a triangle and, in case, determines the kind of triangle.

Keywords TRACE, CODE, ACCEPT refer to the use of options of the precompiler; keywords DEBUG and DEBUGEND include the program portion to be instrumented; the number after the keyword DEBUG (20 in the example) indicates the dimension of the array to be reserved for to record information on coverage: generally, two array elements are needed for each condition present in the program.

The input to the precompiler is:

```
TRACE
CODE
ACCEPT
DEBUG 20
    INTEGER A,B,C,AB,AC,BC,FL
1   FORMAT()
2   FORMAT(' ','ERRORE')
3   FORMAT (' ','TRIANGOLO',I4)
4   FORMAT(' ','EQUILATERO')
5   FORMAT( ' ','SCALENO')
6   FORMAT(' ','ISOSCELE')
    READ 1,A,B,C
    PRINT 1,A,B,C
    AB=A+B
    AC=A+C
    BC=B+C
    IF AB.GT.C THEN
          IF AC.GT.B THEN
                   IF BC.GT.A THEN
                   FL=1
                   FI
          FI
    FI
    IF FL.NE.1 THEN
    PRINT 2,FL
    ELSE
    PRINT 3,FL
    FL=0
          IF A.EQ.B THEN
                   IF A.EQ.C THEN
                   PRINT 4
                   ELSE
                   FL=1
                   FI
          ELSE
                   IF A.EQ.C THEN
                   FL=1
                   ELSE
                            IF B.EQ.C THEN
                            FL=1
                            ELSE
                            PRINT 5
                            FI
                   FI
          FI
          IF FL.EQ.1 THEN
          PRINT 6
          FI
    FI
    DEBUGEND
    STOP
    END
```

A first its execution produces the following result:

```
          4          8          4
ERRORE          0
```

The corresponding coverage is indicated by the output of the printing program:

```
 1 TRACE
 2 CODE
 3 ACCEPT
 4      INTEGER A,B,C,AB,AC,BC,FL
 5 1    FORMAT()
 6 2    FORMAT(' ','ERRORE')
 7 3    FORMAT (' ','TRIANGOLO',I4)
 8 4    FORMAT(' ','EQUILATERO')
 9 5    FORMAT( ' ','SCALENO')
10 6    FORMAT(' ','ISOSCELE')
11      READ 1,A,B,C
12      PRINT 1,A,B,C
13      AB=A+B
14      AC=A+C
15      BC=B+C
16      IF AB.GT.C THEN
1  TIMES
17           IF AC.GT.B THEN
0  TIMES
18                  IF BC.GT.A THEN
0  TIMES
19                  FL=1
20                  FI
21           FI
22      FI
23      IF FL.NE.1 THEN
1  TIMES
24      PRINT 2,FL
25      ELSE
0  TIMES
26      PRINT 3,FL
27      FL=0
28           IF A.EQ.B THEN
0  TIMES
29                  IF A.EQ.C THEN
0  TIMES
30                  PRINT 4
31                  ELSE
0  TIMES
32                  FL=1
33                  FI
34           ELSE
0  TIMES
35                  IF A.EQ.C THEN
0  TIMES
36                  FL=1
37                  ELSE
0  TIMES
38                         IF B.EQ.C THEN
0  TIMES
39                         FL=1
40                         ELSE
0  TIMES
41                                PRINT 5
42                                FI
43                         FI
44                  FI
45                  IF FL.EQ.1 THEN
0  TIMES
46                  PRINT 6
47                  FI
48           FI
49 DEBUGEND
```

The list shows that only the IF instructions number 16 and 24 have been executed once with the condition true.

After several further runs, the last launch produces the result:

```
                5                  4                  4
TRIANGOLO    1
ISOSCELE
```

The list of the global coverage dued to all the runs is the following:

```
 1 TRACE
 2 CODE
 3 ACCEPT
 4      INTEGER A,B,C,AB,AC,BC,FL
 5 1    FORMAT()
 6 2    FORMAT(' ','ERRORE')
 7 3    FORMAT (' ','TRIANGOLO',I4)
 8 4    FORMAT(' ','EQUILATERO')
 9 5    FORMAT( ' ','SCALENO')
10 6    FORMAT(' ','ISOSCELE')
11      READ 1,A,B,C
12      PRINT 1,A,B,C
13      AB=A+B
14      AC=A+C
15      BC=B+C
16      IF AB.GT.C THEN
7  TIMES
17           IF AC.GT.B THEN
6  TIMES
18                  IF BC.GT.A THEN
5  TIMES
19                  FL=1
20                  FI
21           FI
22      FI
23      IF FL.NE.1 THEN
3  TIMES
24      PRINT 2,FL
25      ELSE
```

```
5  TIMES
      26    PRINT 3,FL
      27    FL=0
      28          IF A.EQ.B THEN

2  TIMES
      29                 IF A.EQ.C THEN

1  TIMES
      30                 PRINT 4
      31                 ELSE

1  TIMES
      32                 FL=1
      33                 FI
      34          ELSE

3  TIMES
      35                 IF A.EQ.C THEN

1  TIMES
      36                 FL=1
      37                 ELSE

2  TIMES
      38                        IF B.EQ.C THEN

1  TIMES
      39                        FL=1
      40                        ELSE

1  TIMES
      41                        PRINT 5
      42                        FI
      43                 FI
      44          FI
      45          IF FL.EQ.1 THEN

3  TIMES
      46          PRINT 6
      47          FI
      48    FI
      49 DEBUGEND
```

The list shows that each instruction has been executed at least once.

E. Morlet and D. Ribbens, (Eds.), International Computing Symposium 1977.

STRUCTURED PROGRAMMING IN COBOL - YET ANOTHER APPROACH

Václav Chvalovský
Lecturer

Institute of Computer Science, University
of Nairobi, P.O. Box 30197, Nairobi, Kenya.

Abstract

This paper aims at presenting an alternative approach to structured programming in COBOL, based on the thorough implementation of decision tables. The proposed technique makes extensive use of the relatively old idea of parsing of decision tables and modular programming and attempts to work out a general method of developing well structured and easily manageable programs in COBOL. Possible impact of advanced operating systems on the idea of structured programming in COBOL is also discussed here.

Aims and scope of the paper

This paper is devoted to the two seemingly different things, i.e. structured programming and decision tables and aims at showing that these two can be joined together for the sake of increasing programmer's productivity, improving programming discipline, making programs more flexible and manageable and last - but not the least - open to possible future amendments and updating at all. Since most of the above listed benefits are claimed to be the logical attributes of structured programming, it is possible to set the main objective being the structured programming with decision tables.

It is fair to mention at least the most decisive stimuli that altogether steered the idea of writing a paper of this kind.

First comes my own positive experience with decision tables that we have been using in ČKD PRAHA Co. to solve various data processing projects for more than 9 years, and on the basis of which I got the impression something has to be done to make the data processing world believe this is a technique to be thought of and counted on.

Secondly, the ever growing widespread criticism of commercial programmers and dissatisfaction with their efficiency as well as reliability of their products (although it is not all that bad as some people try to paint it) made me think of alternative ways of coping with this situation.

Finally, several important and well written contributions among which at least /1/, /8/, and /3/ should be mentioned (D. McCracken's recent article /3/ really does deserve our words of praise), have helped a lot in formulating of what is intended to become a kernel of the paper.

Before we get involved in describing the proposed methodology, it is necessary to outline its background, in other words, identify those elements it owes to both structured programming approach and decision tables.

Structured programming reviewed

Since I am neither aiming to explain the very basic principles of structured programming in this paper, nor do I think it is a brand new term for data processing professionals, I will mention only few following aspects of structured programming that have had definite impact on my previous work and this paper as well.

(1) We have done somewhat painful experience with modular programming in COBOL before finding ourselves in a situation when we had to trade off again between the pros and cons of this approach. Having spent a lot of time discussing these things, we arrived onto the decision that the only acceptable alternative for us was to adopt a stepwise program development approach, originally outlined by E. Dijkstra in /5/, and some time later well explained by N. Wirth in /10/, for each respective program module.

(2) Rather than spending too much time developing a GO TO less programming methodology, we have devoted ourselves to the idea of the top down design approach, viewing majority of our current projects as mostly hierarchical structures. It appears that a reasonable selection of control constructs automatically follows from this design philosophy.

(3) The idea of functional programming described by Dr. Bloom in /1/ had the most decisive impact not only on our work but eventually led to my writing of /9/ and to this paper as well.

Decision tables - structured programming view

I guess there is no need to spend much time describing decision tables technique because most of the people have already learned about it, if not used it for some time. Anyway, for those who feel they may like some kind of briefing about decision tables, references /4/ and /6/ contain enough details, certainly more than I am going to make use of in this paper. To assess decision tables from structured programming point of view, we should make a distinction between:

- their theoretical principles *) and
- various ways of their implementation.

*) Of the three possible formats of decision tables, i.e. limited tables, extended tables and mixed tables, only the first one is going to be used throughout the paper.

(1) As we know, every decision table has the four basic parts, called stubs:

- Condition stub;
- Action stub;
- Condition entries stub;
- Action entries stub, the last two being split into a finite number of the so called decision table rules, as shown in Fig. 1.

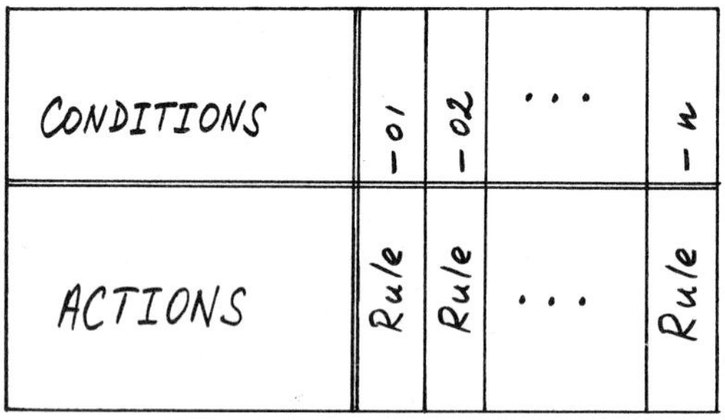

Fig. 1 Decision tables layout.

What is essential, however, is the main flow of control within a decision table, exposing the interaction among conditions and actions of the table (Fig. 2). In Fig. 2, symbols c_1 up to c_m stand for conditions, symbols a_1 up to a_n stand for actions, and finally r_1 up to r_o for rules. Symbols V is used to mean OR, and $\wedge$ represents AND. Finally, $\neg$ stands for NOT (in fact, it assumes an 'N' condition entry).

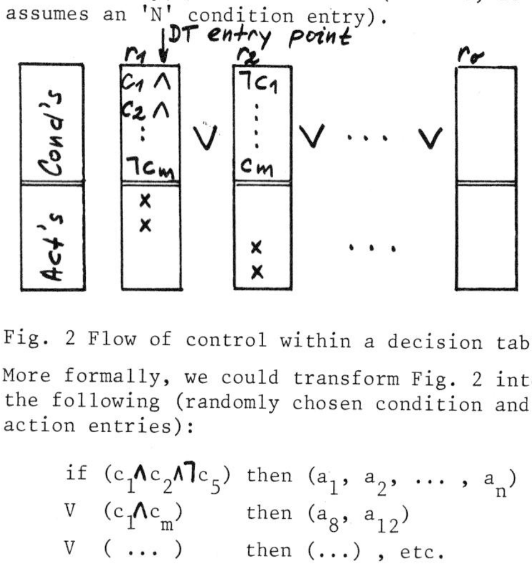

Fig. 2 Flow of control within a decision table.

More formally, we could transform Fig. 2 into the following (randomly chosen condition and action entries):

$$\begin{array}{lll} \text{if} & (c_1 \wedge c_2 \wedge \neg c_5) & \text{then } (a_1, a_2, \ldots, a_n) \\ V & (c_1 \wedge c_m) & \text{then } (a_8, a_{12}) \\ V & (\ldots) & \text{then } (\ldots), \text{ etc.} \end{array}$$

If we allow for a slight substitution, replacing conditional tests by a group symbol r_1^c up to r_o^c, and similarly action sets by r_1^a up to r_o^a, we get:

$\text{if}\left(r_1^c\right) \text{then} \left(r_1^a\right)$
$V\left(r_2^c\right)\text{then}\left(r_2^a\right)$, etc. (IF's are implied in front of every V, here and in the above as well).

From this, it is only a minor step toward the final notation in the form:

$$\text{CASE } r_i^c \text{ OF } (r_1^a;\ldots r_o^a) \quad *)$$

which is nothing else but one of the most rewarding decomposition statements in structured programming approach!

---

*) See for instance /10/, p.35.

To make a distinction between the original syntax of this statement that is:

$$\text{CASE } i \text{ OF } (s_1;\ s_2;\ \ldots\ ;\ s_n),$$

we may call our version of it a compound case statement, for it implies more logical steps to it. It is my view that the above analysis of a typical decision table format gives enough support to my claim of the close resemblance between decision tables and structured programming approach as far as the types of program decomposition are concerned. This leads to yet another conclusion, i.e. that programs developed using decision tables are themselves fairly well structured without even noticing any rules of structured programming.

(2) As it was mentioned before in the Review of structured programming, production of well structured program modules (structured coding) is only one part of the story for we have to extend structured design methodology as far as possible in order to be able to yield maximum benefits of it. This overall design philosophy, introduced as the top down approach before, can also be implemented and supported by means of decision tables, as will be shown in the final part of the paper.

To be able to do this, we had to dust off an old technique of parsing of decision tables, described by N. Chapin in /2/, and develop what may be called a complex procedure of coping with large and complicated problems using the decision tables hierarchy/network. We have already gained very favourable experience with this approach as it really does enforce the obvious advantages of structured programming.

Structured programming in COBOL - no decision tables used

In order to be able to assess properly all the potential benefits steming from the joint use of structured programming techniques in COBOL along with decision tables, it is useful to review what is relevant to COBOL from the whole structured programming theory and practice, we can hear a lot about all around these days.

I cannot but recall D. McCracken's contribution /3/ to DATAMATION again because he really did spend a word on behalf of COBOL programmers there. The truth is that despite the fact commercial like computer applications, using mostly COBOL world wide take as much as 80 per cent of the total computer time used, thus being the true "bread & butter jobs" for data processing centres, only a handful of people (certainly not academic ones) have cared so far what is going on in COBOL programming. This situation becomes even more ironical if we take into account all those features in COBOL (D. McCraken has listed most of them) which, if properly utilised, could result in producing true structured programs. I only wish someone undertook to estimate how much time, effort and money could have been saved, had the COBOL folk been trained and instructed how to use all those things with structured philosophy in mind.

It is indeed possible to develop a well structured COBOL program although I would favour in this case saying - a readable and easily manageable one. Let me recall the following items of a COBOL arsenal:

- PERFORM ... UNTIL ...
- IF ... THEN ... ELSE IF ... THEN ...
- GO TO ... DEPENDING ON ...
- avoiding the use of ALTER, unnecessary switches, etc.

Of these, however, IF ... THEN ... ELSE ... is not all that harmless, as it can turn in its opposite and become programmer's nightmare, if used too extensively (too deeply nested IF's may result in loosing the control over the ways our program is structured). More than that, I have personally come across several COBOL compilers which were fairly limited in the maximum possible size of an IF stack, allowing for instance only a dozen or so statements inside the IF's control, i.e. both TRUE and FALSE branches of the statement. Here, again, decision tables offer us a reasonable way out of this contradiction for they group all IF's in a manageable way.

Summing it up, one should accept possibility of producing a well structured coding within COBOL programs, adhering of course to the elementary programming discipline (for more detailed list of rules, see for instance /12/).

As I tried to maintain in the very beginning of this paper, this should be only one side of the coin because the main benefit from structured programming (or better - design philosophy) stems from applying like principles to overall system and program design. What we have learned so far was that COBOL itself does not have enough means to meet this goal efficiently. Saying this I do not mean COBOL has no such means because most of us have already gone through the era of modular programming which used to be almost a magic expression a few years ago.

No doubt, modular approach as such is a great thing and is fully justified but only having made use of it for sometime could we learn few lessons from it. Let me list them briefly.

(1) While apparently speeding up the process of developing individual program modules, we often happened to be in trouble linking them into one program and it took us considerable time sometimes to get such a program running smoothly;

(2) Trying to keep the run time core size of a program at minimum, we mostly had to design it with the modules resident on an overlay device thus adding one extra file to the program's requirements, plus the obvious time overhead spent swapping the modules between the core and an overlay peripheral;

(3) The most crucial problems of all were those connected with modules interface like intermediate files, common (linkage) sections, etc.;

(4) Apparently the most decisive objection against modular programming (or better one way of its implementation) arose at the very time we upgraded our computer installation and changed for a highly sophisticated operating system of third generation machines. At that time we found, we could no longer produce such programs for it would take us incredible time to work out appropriate run time job descriptions for them - in other words, such programs became suddenly unmanageable (!)

Frankly speaking, the last mentioned lesson made us modify our modular approach and follow somewhat different pattern of program development which may serve as an example of structured programming in COBOL without necessarily using decision tables. This approach implies observation of the following basic rules.

(1) Every project is broken down into the most elementary while still logical self-standing programs;

(2) All such programs are being coded individually, keeping in mind the above mentioned "rules of good conduct" to produce a well structured coding;

(3) Programmers debug their programs via terminals and VDU's thus accelerating their development. This single fact, i.e. them being capable of debugging such programs within few days has incredibly positive psychological impact on their overall efficiency and self-confidence;

(4) It is the team leader's responsibility to write a final job description for all participating programs, which becomes the sole means of their bootstrapping into one system's run. In this schema, all interim (linking and interface) data files become a part of operating system's filestore and are scratched once the system's run is over.

Structured programming in COBOL with decision tables

Even after having implemented the above schema we felt we were still a half way to reach our goals of applying a thorough top down design and programming approach. That was why we had to re-consider decision tables use to make them a part of our schema.

It has already been explained that decision tables can be treated as a properly structured piece of coding similar to that of the CASE decomposition. This condition holding, it is obvious that once being able to incorporate whole PROCEDURE DIVISION of a COBOL program into one or more (see decision tables networks further on) decision tables,we can get a truly structured program, avoiding possible problems with nested IF's, and so on.

However, since neither decision tables themselves can become a kind of panacea, it is necessary to adjust them a bit in order that they suit to this particular purpose, and also make them the exclusive tool of a COBOL program development. The complex task of making such a schema operational implies therefore several subgoals.

(1) Since decision tables are intended to be used mostly for complex and complicated decision - making situations within a program with numerous alternative solutions, it is inevitable to make use of extra facilities that should provide cover for wider range of cases. Amongst the most important ones are:

(1.1) Initiating rule, which makes it possible to perform most initiating actions in a PROCEDURE DIVISION, like opening files, setting various markers, zeroizing work areas, etc., before the decision table itself is entered (that is before the very first condition is tested).

(1.2) Actions sequencing facilitates programmer's job allowing him to order (or disorder) actions absolutely arbitrarily. By means of this, also the otherwise stringent decision tables format is a bit simplified.

(1.3) It is sometimes necessary to exit a decision table, if certain condition states hold without even doing any action. This is feasible by means of blank actions entries in any of the decision table rules.

(1.4) Although there are several advocates of the so called Action decision tables, that is tables with virtually no conditions, it should be born in mind that the same if not better effect can be reached by the proper use of the PERFORM statement, making such a piece of coding a subroutine.

Fig. 3 serves as an illustration of most of the features described above. The table in Fig. 3 is an example of a job's schedulling program for a workshop. Note that the whole COBOL PROCEDURE DIVISION neatly fits into one decision table. Letters 'A' and 'B', respectively in front of certain conditions introduce groups of dependant conditions (see for their peculiar entries - no 'N' entries are used).

JOBS-SCHEDULLING	1	2	3	4	5	6	7	8	9	10	11	12	13	14	15	16	17	18	19	20	21	ELSE
EOF = 1		N	N	N	N	N	N	N	N	N	N	N	N	N	N	N	N	N	N	N	Y	
ACAP-WH > ZERO		Y	-	Y	-	-	Y	-	-	Y	-	-	-	-	-	Y	-	-	-	-	-	
ACAP-WH = ZERO		-	Y	-	Y	Y	-	-	-	-	Y	-	-	-	-	-	Y	-	-	-	-	
ACAP-WH < ZERO		-	-	-	-	-	-	Y	Y	-	-	Y	Y	Y	Y	-	-	-	Y	Y	-	
BCAP-MH > ZERO		Y	Y	-	-	Y	-	Y	-	-	-	-	Y	-	-	-	-	-	-	-	-	
BCAP-MH = ZERO		-	-	Y	Y	-	Y	-	Y	-	-	-	-	Y	-	-	-	-	-	-	-	
BCAP-MH < ZERO		-	-	-	-	-	-	-	-	Y	Y	Y	-	-	-	Y	Y	Y	Y	Y	-	
CAP-WH NOT> -42.5		-	-	-	-	-	-	-	-	-	-	-	Y	Y	N	Y	Y	Y	Y	N	-	
CAP-MH NOT> -168.0		-	-	-	-	-	-	-	-	-	-	-	Y	Y	Y	Y	Y	N	Y	N	-	
WSHOP-NO NOT > 10		-	Y	Y	-	N	N	Y	Y	Y	Y	Y	N	N	N	N	N	N	N	N	-	
OPEN INPUT CAP-FILE	1																					
OPEN INPUT JOBS-FILE	2																					
OPEN OUTPUT JOBS-SCHEDULED-FILE	3																					
READ CAP-FILE AT END STOP "FAIL 1"	4		3	3	2			5	5	5	5	5	4	3	5	4	3	5	4	5		
READ JOBS-FILE AT END MOVE 1 TO EOF	5	2	4	4	3	2	2						5	4		5	4		5			
COMPUTE CAP-WH = CAP-WH - JOB-WH	6	3	5	5	4	3	3	6	6	6	6	6	6	5	6	6	5	6	6	6		
COMPUTE CAP-MH = CAP-MH - JOB-MH	7	4	6	6	5	4	4	7	7	7	7	7	7	6	7	7	6	7	7	7		
PERFORM WRITE-JOBS		1	1	1	1	1	1						1	1		1	1		1			
GO TO JOX001		5	7	7	6	5	5	8	8	8	8	8	8	7	8	8	7	8	8	8		
COMPUTE CAP-WH = CAP-WH + JOB-WH								1	1	1	1	1			1			1		1		
COMPUTE CAP-MH = CAP-MH + JOB-MH								2	2	2	2	2			2			2		2		
DISPLAY "LEFT", WSHOP-NO, SPACE, CAP-WH			2					3	3	3	3	3			3	2		3		3		
DISPLAY "LEFT", WSHOP-NO, SPACE, CAP-MH		2						4	4	4	4	4	2		4			4		4		
DISPLAY "NEEDS",WSHOP-NO, SPACE, CAP-WH													3	2					2			
DISPLAY "NEEDS",WSHOP-NO, SPACE, CAP-MH																3	2		3			
STOP "OTHER ERROR"																						4
CLOSE CAP-FILE																					1	1
CLOSE JOBS-FILE																					2	2
CLOSE JOBS-SCHEDULED-FILE																					3	3
STOP "END OF SCHEDULLING"																					4	

Fig. 3 Job schedulling decision table ('GO TO JOX001' statement branches to the first conditional paragraph of the generated program).

(2) Previous example was to some extent rather exceptional for far too often our program is too complex to fit into one decision table of a reasonable (manageable) size, in which case we should make use of the most rewarding thing with decision tables, i.e. a decision tables hierarchy/network.

The idea in behind setting up a hierarchy or network of decision tables is fairly simple. The whole problem (or better its proposed solution) is broken down into several logically self-standing fragments that are being controlled through one control decision table. Although there is hardly any general rule of problem decomposition into a set of decision tables (a couple of useful hints are mentioned in /2/), several important points are to be born in mind regarding mainly the ways tables are linked together and their contents.

(2.1) The best method of entering any decision table is via PERFORM statements. By means of it, it is secured that every table behaves itself as a closed and relatively independant piece of coding and that the control passes from one table to another absolutely smoothly.

(2.2) While not compulsory, it is nevertheless recommended to make maximum use of an ELSE rule, just for the purpose of linking the tables. A good rule of thumb is to cover for all more or less "positive" outcomes of a decision table in its ordinary rules and let any exceptional or simply "other" cases drop into an ELSE rule, which should call for yet another table to decode what happened, and proceed on.

(2.3) The most critical issue of table linkage is that of keeping trace of conditions states form a control table in all subordinated ones. As a general rule, those states should stay intact, that is no subordinate decision table is allowed to change states of the conditions external to it. In other words, even though we could under some circumstances (if we knew the way a decision table is translated into a COBOL source coding), selectively branch back to the table in command reaching its particular condition paragraph, this practice is strongly discouraged.

(2.4) Further to what we said under (2.1) about using PERFORM as a sole means of entering each individual decision table, also any other piece of coding (COBOL paragraphs and sections) external to the table should be entered exclusively via PERFORM. It implies that there should appear no 'GO TO's within a table attempting to go outside of it (a good decision tables preprosessor has to detect errors of this kind, flag them and reject such a table).

(2.5) It may happen that either of decision table actions ties to itself an individual condition which is otherwise irrelevant to all other actions. In such a case, it is better to enter this condition alone with its respective action inside an action stub area rather than complicate a condition stub area and add unnecessary rules.

A typical pattern of a decision tables hierarchy is shown in Fig. 4. Even without having to look at that model of a hierarchy, however, I would like to emphasize the idea that observing the above recommendations and rules does result in production of a well structured COBOL PROCEDURE DIVISION, with hardly any room left for idiocracies of today's programming.

But, as in the majority of like cases, "seeing is believing" that is to say, a real work is the best tutor. The most important thing with this proposed method is that we have to abandon the so far almost exclusive viewing of our programs as a sequence of individual steps. Instead of this, I would suggest that any program be treated as a more or less complex structure showing a variable degree of hierarchical relationships, where most of its procedures are condition(s) dependant.

(3) It is true to say that decision tables preprocessors (if available) not only support our proposed schema of structured programming with decision tables but also tremendously increase programmer's productivity while at the same time taking away of them the so much boring and sometimes nearly frustrating task of an actual coding. It is neither possible to explain in detail all obvious and already known advantages of using these preprocessors, nor describe methods of decision tables analysis and COBOL code generation.

Let me list the most important features of preprocessors at least.

(3.1) Decision tables preprocessors support the above model of setting up decision tables hierarchies/networks in the sense they can translate any such a schema and provide for necessary linkage;

(3.2) With a preprocessor, our programmer does not have to worry about his IF's getting out of control because these are well cared for in the generated code;

(3.3) The code generated on the basis of a table is "bug-free" in the sense that there can appear no formal errors (no missing commas, periods, etc.);

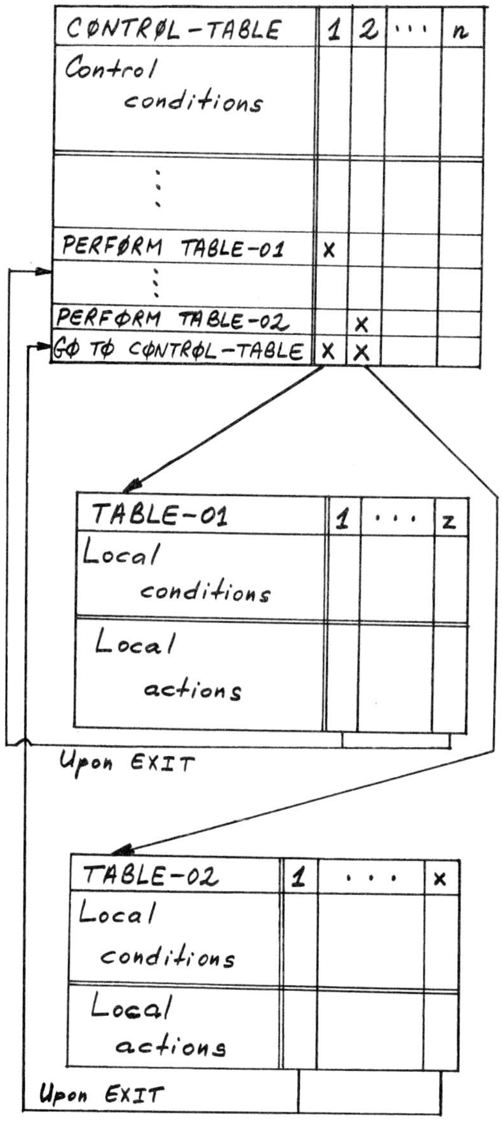

Fig. 4 An example of a decision tables hierarchy

(3.4) Most of the current preprocessors make every possible attempt to generate minimum amount of coding in both parts (condition tests, action paragraphs);

(3.5) Using a preprocessor, we can significantly accelerate development of COBOL programs;

(3.6) With a preprocessor, even less experienced COBOL programmers can develop reliable and efficient programs after a fairly short time;

(3.7) Once having his/her program generated by means of a preprocessor, our programmer does not in fact de-bug the actual procedural coding but his/her program's logic built in decision tables the program has been generated from. From my point of view, this seems to be the most promising outcome of the decision tables preprocessor that can only be matched (to some degree) by an on-line program testing via VDU's or terminals;

(3.8) As a practical result of (3.7) above, such programs are normally extremely easy to amend, most often it is sufficient to replace one line in a decision table by a correct one and get the whole loop of program generation, translation and a trial run repeated.

In place of a summary

The structured programming approach proposed in this paper is not the only possible one of its sort as most of us have learned a lot about other ways of coping with this problem. Either of these methods has its advantages and disadvantages, irrespectively of whether we like it or not. The method I have attempted to outline here could serve as a means of the gradual introduction of the structured programming discipline and methods without necessarily investing into development of new COBOL compiler facilities or learning a new language. From the practical computer user's point of view, such changeover should be strongly preferred and encouraged.

Acknowledgement

It would be impossible to write this paper without making use of the practical experience in the field of the DP staff in ČKD PRAHA Co. in Prague, Czechoslovakia, which has managed to build up, throughout the years, the best computer installation I have ever worked for.

The Institute of Computer Science at the University of Nairobi generously supported the idea of producing this paper, also in the form of an access to its computer facilities, and Miss Irene Karimi did all the typing as the matter of urgency.

References

/1/ Bloom: "The ELSE Must Go Too." Datamation 5(21), 1975.

/2/ Chapin, N.: "Parsing of Decision Tables." Communications of the ACM 8(10), 1967.

/3/ McCracken, D.: "Let's Hear It For COBOL." Datamation 5(22), 1976, pp. 240-242.

/4/ McDaniel, H.: "Applications of Decision Tables." New York, Auerbach Publishers Inc. 1970.

/5/ Dijkstra, E. - Hoare, C.A.R. - Dahl, O.J.: " Structured Programming." Academic Press, New York - London 1972.

/6/ Humby, E.: "Programs From Decision Tables." Macdonald and American Elsevier 1972.

/7/ Inmon, B.: "An Example of Structured Design." Datamation 3(22), 1976, pp. 82-91.

/8/ Neely, P.M.: "The New Programming Discipline." Software Practice & Experience 1(6), 1976, pp. 7-27.

/9/ Chvalovsky, V.: "Traditional/Modular/Structured/Functional/? Programming and COBOL Programmers." (unpublished paper).

/10/ Wirth, N.: "Systematic Programming: An Introduction." Prentice-Hall. Englewood Cliffs, N.J. 1973.

/11/ Mills, H.D.: "The New Math of Computer Programming." Communications of the ACM 1(18), 1975, pp. 43-48.

/12/ Kernighan, B.W. - Plauger, P.J.: "The Elements of Programming Style." McGraw-Hill Book Co., New York 1974.

E. Morlet and D. Ribbens, (Eds.), International Computing Symposium 1977.

SOME MEASURES OF INFORMATION ABOUT PROGRAM STATES

Andrew Arblaster

M.R.C. Social and Applied Psychology Unit
University of Sheffield
Sheffield, England

Some measures of information about the semantic state of programs are considered. A method for defining measures for a variety of data types is first discussed, then some measures of the relationship between tests and actions in conditionals are examined.

1. INTRODUCTION

This paper discusses some measures which can be applied to programs to help us to analyse the operation of the programs. The work described in section 4 of the paper was carried out first, though it is described here last. The reason for this is that parts 2 and 3 of this paper provide a general, and reasonably solid, base on which we can build the measures described in part 4 as a special case. However, it may be helpful in this introduction to say something of the way in which this investigation has developed.

The need for the measures described in part 4 became evident during the analysis of the performance of programmers in some experiments on programming language design by Sime, et.al. /6,16,25-28/. These measures, of the relationship between actions in a program and the value of predicates in conditional statements in the program, were therefore developed by the present author completely independently of any other work. The formal similarity of these measures to some measures which have been discussed in a quite different discipline, that of the philosophy of science, was then noticed. This philosophical work was done, for the most part, more than twenty years ago and its purpose was to provide measures of the "simplicity" of scientific hypotheses and of the strength of the support which various sets of evidence give to hypotheses. Kyburg /14/ gives a useful review of these ideas. However, since the use of these ideas in their original setting depends on a precise characterisation in some logical language of the evidence to be considered and of the hypotheses, and since such a characterisation of any scientific hypothesis and any scientific evidence is very difficult to come by, their use has been negligible. The suggestion in the present paper is that precise characterisation in logical terms of the operation of program is possible, and that modifications of the measures discussed by Kyburg can be of great value in the analysis of algorithms. For these reasons the original work has been integrated in this paper with some discussion of the way in which the work of the philosophers of science can be applied in this new field.

D and G, the measures originally developed, apply only to one data type, booleans. It was felt that an extension of the range of data types to which the basic measures could be applied would be very valuable, firstly to provide a general and reasonably rigorous base for the special measures of conditional structure, and secondly for direct application in cases where, during the development of a program, we may have incomplete information about the state of the data structures on which the program is operating. Such occasions are, for example, when

a. the program under development is unfinished in some respects,
b. the program does not satisfy the given specifications, so that it contains bugs or misconceptions,
c. the program is unfamiliar to us, and the documentation inadequate,
d. during the execution of a program the program itself may need to know how much information it has about the state of its own data structures - this is particularly the case in backtrack or nondeterministic programming, used in some advanced applications.

In cases like these we need a general measure of "how much we know about the state of the program".

The work described in parts 2 and 3 of this paper were therefore carried out, drawing some ideas from Kemeny /11/, which he developed in the context of work on the logic of science, and linking these to the ideas of Floyd /5/, Hoare /7/ and others on the characterisation of the operation of programs in logical terms.

2. DESIDERATA FOR BASIC MEASURES OF PROGRAM STATE

Measures of how much information we have available about the state of the variables of a program, possibly including a program pointer (the state vector, in McCarthy's /17/ terms) should be:-

a. applicable to as wide a range of data types as possible - not only the simple primitive data types used in most languages but also records, lists, subtypes and more complex structures.
b. as independent as possible of any programming language that the algorithm to which they are applied is written in.

c. independent of the machine on which the program is to be run, but able to take account of the structure of the machine or a particular implementation if such is desired.

For these reasons the measures will be developed relative to logical languages in which the effects of a computation can be described. Over the past dozen or so years many workers have developed characterisations of algorithms and data structures in terms of logical calculi, beginning with Floyd /5/ and Hoare /7/, and developed by Manna /18, 19/, Igarashi et al. /10/ and others. A rather different direction has been taken by Codd /3/, in which the description of large scale data bases in terms of logical calculi has been successfully undertaken.

3. DEVELOPMENT OF THE MEASURES

Floyd's method for the verification of algorithms, which is essentially similar to that of Hoare, is to attach assertions (propositions in some logical language) to the edges of a flowchart representation of the algorithms, or between statements in a conventional linear representation of the program. Some of the free variables of these assertions may be variables manipulated by the program. By using rules of verification of Igarashi et. al.'s weak logic of programs for each type of command in the program it can be verified that the assertion at each point in a program follows from those at all the immediately preceding points. The details of the method will not be described here - descriptions are given in /5, 10/. Our interest here is in finding a measure for how much an assertion tells us, and what effects program statements have on how much succeeding assertions tell us.

To ensure machine and implementation independence we will use a technique originally due to Kemeny /11/, who applied it to statements of scientific fact.

The basic idea is that instead of considering the indeterminate, and possibly infinite, number of states of any particular data structure we consider a finite number of these states, n. In this finite number we find those which are compatible with the assertion in which we are interested, and we normalise by dividing this by the total number of possible states. By varying n we obtain a family of functions of the assertion. Our measure of the assertion is therefore a function whose value is itself a function of n. We can use this measure function to compare the amount of information about the semantic state of a program which various assertions give us. We will now go into slightly more detail about how the measure functions can be defined, and what their properties are.

We assume a model-theoretical semantics for the formulae of the logical language in which we choose to make our assertions. Of course we may choose to use different logical calculi, depending on our needs, for any particular algorithm. The variables and constants of the logical language in use at any one time are to have values which may be assigned from ranges of individuals. The models (interpretations) of the logical language may have a finite or an infinite number of individuals. For example, an integer variable in the programming language under consideration may have, in a machine-independent algorithm, any of an infinite range of values. Relative to any particular implementation, however, only a finite number of values for the variable can occur.

We assign cardinal numbers to the finite models, and we call a model that assigns altogether n things to the various ranges for individuals an "n-model". We make the assumption that for all but a finite number of positive integers, n, the logical system under consideration has at least one, but only a finite number of n-models. (We can't say "for all n", since n must be at least as great as the number of individual constants in the logical language.) For any n, Mn denotes the number of n-models of the logical system L, and M_n^A denotes the number of n-models of L in which the assertion A is valid (true under the given interpretation). The value of m(A) is rational - valued function of n,

$$m : A \longmapsto M_n^A/Mn \ (n \in z^+),$$

where z^+ is the set of positive integers.

For this function the relation of "being greater than" is defined:

$$m(A_1) > m(A_2) \text{ if } \exists_{n_o}: (n > n_o \Rightarrow m(A_1) > m(A_2)).$$

the relations of "being equal to" and "being greater than" are defined similarly. The language L must be consistent, there must be no well formed formula provable in L which can be satisfied only in an infinite model (such a wff is called a statement of infinity), L must have finite number of different types of individual variable, L must have finite number of constants, and each constant must be of finite order. These conditions are necessary for the applicability of the measure - function, and together they are sufficient to ensure applicablity.

If we consider each model as a possible state of the world (program) and each assertion cuts down on the number of possibilities by eliminating the models in which it is not satisfied we get as a measure of the content of anassertion the number of models in which the assertion is not satisfied. If we normalise this by dividing by the total number of models (for a given n), we get as a measure of content the function c:

$$c : A \longmapsto 1 - m(A).$$

A topologically equivalent form of this content

measure is obtained by choosing an atomic sentence of the logical metalanguage as a unit. This function is:

$$s:A \longmapsto -\log_2 (m(A)).$$

The properties of c and s are somewhat different and one or the other may be used in any particular case depending on which properties are felt to be important in that case.

The properties of the three functions m, c and s may be summarised as follows, where "." signifies logical conjunction, "-" signifies negation and "v" signifies disjunction.

1. The values of m and c lie between 0 and 1, those of s lie between 0 and ∞.
2. Values of m and c are rational, those of s need not be.
3. m(A) is 0, c(A) is 1 and s(A) is infinite identically just in case A is a contradiction (or a statement of infinity, which has been explicitly excluded above).
4. m(A) is 1, c(A) is 0 identically just in case A is analytically true.
5. $m(\bar{A}) = 1-m(A) = c(A),\ c(\bar{A}) = 1-c(A) = m(A).$

   $s(\bar{A}) = s(A) - \log_2 (2^{(A)}-1)$
6. $m(AvB) = m(A)+m(B)-m(A.B),$

   $c(AvB) = c(A)+c(B)-c(A.B),$

   $s(AvB) = -\log_2 c(\bar{A}.\bar{B})$

   $= -\log_2 (1-2^{-s(\bar{A}.\bar{B})})$
7. $m(A.B) = m(A)+m(B)-m(AvB)$

   $c(A.B) = c(A)+c(B)-c(AvB)$

   $s(A.B) = -\log_2 c(\bar{A}v\bar{B})$

   $= -\log_2 (c(\bar{A})+c(\bar{B})-c(\bar{A}.\bar{B}))$

   $= -\log_2 (2^{-s(A)}+2^{-s(B)}-2^{-s(AvB)})$

   If there is only one individual range then
8. If A and B have no (extra-logical) constants in common, and if the two sets of constants are independent of each other (in the sense that the number of possible assignments to the elements of one set does not depend on what assignments have been made to the elements of the other set) then:

   $m(A.B) = m(A) \times m(B),$

   $s(A.B.) - s(A) + s(B).$

Note that this independence requirement can be fulfilled even in languages where the atomic sentences are not independent.

Here are two examples of how the measure-functions may be applied in this new setting.

Example 1.
Suppose a program manipulates integer variables i,j,k and the test shown in figure 1 occurs within it, with the associated assertions.

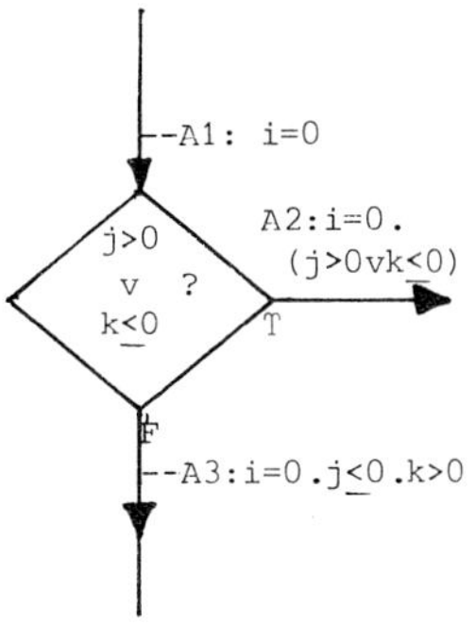

FIGURE 1

To be concrete, let us consider a range of four values for the integers, as would be appropriate for a two bit machine using twos complement arithmetic:

Bits	10	11	00	01
Decimal value	-2	-1	0	1

then

$m(A1)(4) = 0.25,\ c(A1)(4) = 0.75,$
$s(A1)(4) = 2.0$

That is, given this range, the measure of A1 is 0.25, the content of A1 is 0.75, and the amount of semantic information is 2.0. similarly,

$m(A2)(4) = 0.203,\ c(A2)(4) = 0.797,$
$s(A2)(4) = 2.3$

By knowing that the test is true we gain 0.3 units of semantic information.

$m(A3)(4) = 0.047,\ c(A3)(4) = 0.953,$
$s(A3)(4) = 4.4$

By knowing that the test is false we gain more information about the state of the program.
Varying n, we have:

$m(A1) = 1/n,\ c(A1) = 1 - 1/n,$
$s(A1) = -\log_2(m(A1))$

$m(A2) = (3n^2/4+1)/n^3,\ c(A2) = 1 - m(A2),$
$s(A2) = -\log_2(m(A2))$

$m(A3) = (n2/4 - 1)/n^3,\ c(A3) = 1 - m(A3),$
$s(A3) = -\log_2(m(A3))$

and, by the definition of the relation $>$ given previously, we have $m(A1) > m(A2) > m(A3)$. Similarly, $c(A1) < c(A2) < c(A3)$ and $s(A1) < s(A2) < s(A3)$.

Example 2.
Suppose that a program contains a triple as in figure 2,

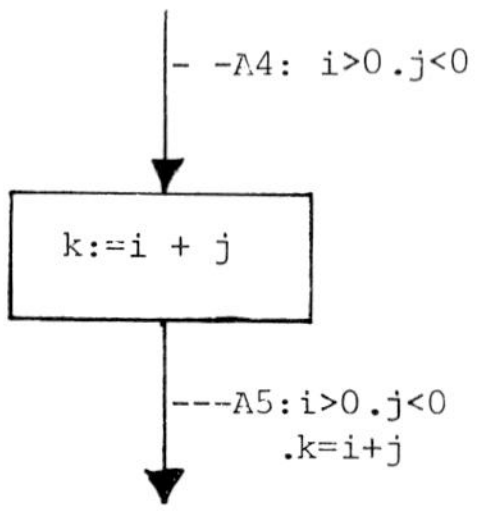

FIGURE 2

the program again manipulating integer variables i,j,k. In this case we need to add a new distinct value, undefined, to all ranges, corresponding to the setting of an overflow register or some similar condition. We also need to alter the definition of the operation "+" to take account of the possibility of an overflow.

$$m(A4) = (n^3 - 4n^2 - 3n)/4n^3, c(A4) = 1 - m(A4)$$
$$s(A4) = -\log_2(m(A4))$$

$$m(A5) = (n^2 - 4n + 3)/4n^3, \quad c(A5) = 1 - m(A5)$$
$$s(A5) = -\log_2(m(A5))$$

It should be noted that these measures can be applied to the higher-order meta languages discussed by Suzuki /29/, in work on automatic program verification. This is important because such higher-order metalanguages are necessary for many applications to realistic programs.

4. MEASURES ON CONDITIONAL STATEMENTS

We will now proceed to describe some measures particularly applicable to conditional statements. These measures were originally developed as an aid in analysing the results of some experiments on programming language design and teaching carried out by Sime, et.al. /6,16, 25-28/. The experiments were on the writing, debugging and comprehension of programs using various experimental microlanguages.

The microlanguages had varying syntactic structures but all contained tests of various predicates and all had simple actions which were equivalent to procedure calls. In this way it was possible to experiment on one linguistic feature only, the conditional structure of programs, without any other features to confuse the issue. This type of simple program is also very close in its operation to that of program schemata, which have been proposed as a formalisation of programming language semantics by Ianov /9/ and Luckham, et.al. /15/.

These experiments showed that in program writing one of the main problems programmers had was to choose a test which would be optimal in terms of how much information it obtained about the actions to be taken. In debugging and comprehension experiments two different and important problems were found, one being that of tracing through a program, given truth values for the predicates appearing in the program, and another being the task of discovering what the truth-values of the predicates must have been, given that a certain action or series of actions occurred.

For the analysis of these experiments and the programming skills involved it was necessary to have measures of the relationship between the result of a test and the actions which appear in the program. From a consideration of the way in which programmers went about writing programs, given the specifications, and from consideration of what conditions such measures should intuitively satisfy (Arblaster /1/), two measures were devised. One of the simplest of the experimental microlanguages will be used here to illustrate the way in which the measures work.

The syntax of the language in Backus Naur Form is:-

```
<P>::=IF <PREDICATE> THEN <S> ELSE <S>
<S>::=<P> | <ACT>
<ACT>::=FRY|ROAST|BOIL|GRILL|CHOP|PEEL
<PREDICATE>::=HARD|TALL|LEAFY|JUICY|GREEN
```

in this particular language programs are obeyed until an action is performed, then a new set of values for the predicates is read in and execution begins again. A simple program and its equivalent flowchart are shown in figure 3.

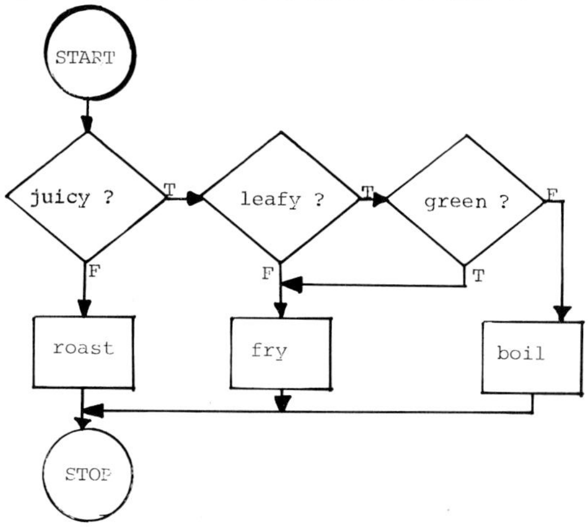

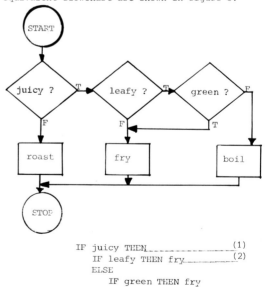

```
IF juicy THEN_______________(1)
   IF leafy THEN fry________(2)
   ELSE
      IF green THEN fry
      ELSE boil
ELSE roast
```

Figure 3

we allow assertions about the truthvalues of the predicates only, and we can identify each action with the set of values of the predicates which can cause that action to be obeyed. For example, in figure 3 the action fry is equivalent to an assertion that either juicy and leafy are both true or juicy and green are true and leafy is false. We can abbreviate this to: $(J.\bar{L}.G) \vee (J.L)$

We define a function D, which measures how necessary a test (T) is to the performance of an action (A):

$$D(T,A) = \frac{\dfrac{m(T.A.)}{m(T)} - \dfrac{m(\bar{T}.A)}{m(\bar{T})}}{\dfrac{m(T.A)}{m(T)} + \dfrac{m(\bar{T}.A)}{m(\bar{T})}}$$

This function takes values between -1 and +1, 0 indicating that the test is neutral with respect to the action.

We do not need the full generality of m in this case, since we can take n to be the number of predicates in the program. Then m(X) is the number of states of the predicates in which the assertion X is true, divided by the number of possible states of the predicates.

In figure 3 we can make the assertion that juicy is true (J) at point 1. The possible states of the predicates are: $(J.L.G), (J.L.\bar{G}), (J.\bar{L}.G), (J.\bar{L}.\bar{G}), (\bar{J}.L.G.), (\bar{J}.L.\bar{G}), (\bar{J}.\bar{L}.G), (\bar{J}.\bar{L}.\bar{G})$. fry, as we have seen, is equivalent to $(J.L) \vee (J.\bar{L}.G)$. Therefore $m(J.fry) = 3/8$, $m(J) = 0.5$, $m(\bar{J}.fry) = 0$, $m(\bar{J}) = 0.5$
so,

$$D(J,fry) = \frac{0.375/0.5 - 0/0.5}{0.375/0.5 + 0/0.5} = 1$$

indicating that J is totally necessary for fry to occur. D(J,roast) = -1, which indicates that roast cannot occur if juicy is true, and also showing that $\bar{J}$ is totally necessary for roast to occur. We can make the assertion (J.L) at point 2 in figure 3, and D(J.L,fry) = 5/7. $D(J.\bar{L},fry) = 0.2$.

It is possible that we might want to make assertions on other evidence than that contained in the program. For example, we might want to assume that leafy was true, to see what that might lead to, or we might have been told by a debugging aid that leafy was true. Then D(L,fry) = 1/3. Correspondingly, $D(\bar{L},fry) = -1/3$.

We need another measure, of the degree to which the result of a test is a sufficient condition for an action to be obeyed. We therefore define G as:

$$G(A,T) = \frac{\dfrac{m(A.T)}{m(A)} - \dfrac{m(\bar{A}.T)}{m(\bar{A})}}{\dfrac{m(A.T)}{m(A)} + \dfrac{m(\bar{A}.T)}{m(\bar{A})}}$$

Again, the values of G lie between -1 and +1. Some example values are:

$G(J,fry) = 2/3$, $G(J.L,fry) = 1$, $G(J.\bar{L},fry) = 1/4$, $G(J,roast) = -1$.

These measures can be used in the production of a program. Suppose we are given the specification of a problem in the form of a set of sets of values of predicates, together with a set of actions which must be called in the case of certain of these sets of predicates occurring and we have to produce a program to solve this problem. Such a problem is common in the use of limited entry decision tables where a program must be produced from a decision table specification. One difficulty in this type of problem is to choose an order for the tests which gives the least number of tests stored (Reinwald /22/, Schwayder /23/). We can use D as a heuristic for situations where an exhaustive search is not economic.

Our procedure is to take each of the tests, C1, C2 -Cn in turn and to determine the mean absolute D of each of the tests for the set of k actions.

$$V_j = \sum_{i=1}^{k} |D(Cj, Ai)| * m(Ai)$$

Choose the test which has the highest value to be the first test in the program, say Ch and repeat the process on the positive side of the test Ch for all state descriptions in which that test is true and for the conjuction of Ch and all other tests to give

$$V_{hj} = \sum_{i=1}^{k} |D(Ch.Cj,Ai)| * m(Ai)$$

Repeat the process until D and G for the series of tests is equal to 1 for an action, then plant a call for that action. Go on to the negative side of the last test and repeat the process until D and G for the conjunction of assertions and negations of the predicates in the tests is 1 for an action, plant a call to that action, and continue the process until all cases have been considered.

Here is an example:
Suppose we have a problem of the form:-

GRILL: All things which are tall and not leafy
FRY: All things which are leafy and not hard
ROAST: All things which are not leafy and not tall

BOIL: All things which are leafy and hard.

from this problem specification we can get the decision table

LEAFY	Y	N	N	Y
TALL	-	Y	N	-
HARD	N	-	-	Y
GRILL		X		
FRY	X			
ROAST			X	
BOIL				X

Now,

$V_L = 1,\ V_T = 1/2,\ V_H = 1/2$

So we choose leafy as the first test. Leafy is not a sufficient condition for either boil or fry so we continue with the state descriptions in which leafy is true.

$V_{L.T} = 0,\ V_{L.H.} = 1$

So the next test is hard. We find that leafy. hard is a sufficient condition for boil so we plant boil, delete those states where leafy. hard leads to boil from consideration, and go on to the ELSE part of the conditional controlled by hard. We find that leafy.hard is a necessary and sufficient condition for fry, plant fry and continue to the ELSE part of the leafy conditional. So far we have

```
IF leafy THEN
   IF hard THEN boil
   ELSE
ELSE
```

considering the state descriptions in which $\bar{L}$ is true,

$V_{\bar{L}.T} = 1,\ V_{\bar{L}.H} = 0$

So we choose tall as our next test. We find that $\overline{\text{leafy}}$.tall is necessary and sufficient for grill, so we plant grill and continue to the ELSE part of the tall conditional. Here we find that $\overline{\text{leafy}}.\overline{\text{tall}}$ is necessary and sufficient for roast so we plant roast, and we have

```
IF leafy THEN
   IF hard THEN boil
   ELSE fry
ELSE
   IF tall THEN grill
   ELSE roast.
```

Note that if we had used Pollack's /20/ rule of choosing the row with the minimum dash count to expand on we would have obtained the same program. It is easy to see that a dash represents a case where the column is an abbreviation for two columns and that in such a case the D for that test of combination of tests will be equal to zero. This will reduce the mean D for all actions under consideration. The "minimum dash count" rule is thus seen to follow from the use of this procedure.

If we have two tests for which the mean D is the same how should we proceed? One possibility is to consider n-tuples of tests and choose the n-tuple giving the highest mean D. If all the Vs are equal to 1 then we can look at the degrees of sufficiency. If we take the highest mean degree of sufficiency this corresponds to taking the lowest Y-N excess - as suggested by Press /21/ or Pollack /20/. If we choose the test Ck which gives the highest

$W_j = \text{MAX}_{i=1}^{k}\ (G(Cj,Ai))$ then we get the "maximum YN excess" rule.

Here is an example where the simple application of the procedure suggested breaks down. The problem is:

GRILL: All things that are juicy, leafy and green
FRY: All other juicy things
BOIL: All things that are leafy, green and not juicy.
ROAST: All other things that are hard
PEEL: All other things

this problem was suggested by Dr. L. Miller of I.B.M. as one which may possibly be easier to program using goto's than an algolic <u>if</u> ... <u>then</u> ... <u>else</u> structure.

The problem corresponds to the decision table:

JUICY	Y	Y	Y	N	N	N
LEAFY	Y	Y	N	Y	-	-
GREEN	Y	N	-	Y	-	-
HARD	-	-	-	-	Y	N
GRILL	X					
FRY		X	X			
BOIL				X		
ROAST					X	
PEEL						X

$V_J = 1,\ V_L = 1/2,\ V_G = 1/2, V_H = 3/8$

we choose juicy as the first test, and consider

$V_{J.L} = 1/2, V_{J.G} = 1/2, V_{J.H} = 0$

Leafy and green are absolutely symmetrical here, so we choose leafy at random.

$V_{J.L.G} = 1, V_{J.L.H} = 0$

We proceed until we have

```
IF juicy THEN
   IF leafy THEN
      IF green THEN grill
      ELSE fry
   ELSE fry
ELSE
```

Now we look at the negative side of the juicy conditional.

$V_{\bar{J}.H} = 3/4,\ V_{\bar{J}.L} = 1/2,\ V_{\bar{J}.G} = 1/2$

So we choose hard and eventually get for this side of the conditional

```
IF hard THEN
   IF leafy THEN
      IF green THEN boil
      ELSE roast
   ELSE roast
ELSE
   IF leafy THEN
      IF green THEN boil
      ELSE peel
   ELSE peel
```

here we store eight tests and the mean number of tests for each case, assuming that each combination of attributes is equiprobable, is three. However, if we choose

```
IF leafy THEN
   IF green THEN boil
   ELSE
      IF hard THEN roast
      ELSE peel
ELSE
      IF hard THEN roast
      ELSE peel
```

for the not juicy part of the conditional then we get a mean number of tests of 2.875 and we store seven tests. In this case the "minimum dash count" rule gives the same program as the simple procedure based on maximum D. The "minimum weighted dash count" mentioned by Humby /8/ also gives the less efficient program. Many programmers also find the less efficient program, particularly under time pressure.

After the measures just discussed had been devised it was noticed that they are formally similar to a measure proposed by Kemeny /12/ in the literature on the philosophy of inductive inference, which he calls "degree of factual support". This measure can be expressed as:

$$F(H,E) = \frac{\dfrac{m(H.E.)}{m(H)} - \dfrac{m(\bar{H}.E)}{m(\bar{H})}}{\dfrac{m(H.E)}{m(H)} + \dfrac{m(\bar{H}.E)}{m(\bar{H})}}$$

Where H is a scientific hypothesis and E is the evidence available to support it. This formal similarity suggests that we should be able to apply F to hypotheses and evidence about programs, particularly as a debugging aid.

As an example, suppose we are in a debugging situation in a program which manipulates four integer variables, I,J,K,L. We have as a hypothesis that $I < J$ and $K = L$. Let us fix an n of eight for possible values of integers, -4, -3, -2, -1, 0, 1, 2, 3. We have the evidence that $I = 0$ and $K = 1$.

What degree of factual support does this evidence give to this hypothesis?

$m(E)(8) = 64/4096, \quad m(H)(8) = 64/4096$

$m(\bar{H})(8) = 4032/4096 \quad m(E.H)(8) = 3/4096$

$m(E.\bar{H})(8) = 61/4096$

$F(H,E)(8) = .677$

This indicates that the evidence gives quite strong factual support to the hypothesis.

Suppose we find out that $J = 2$. Our evidence now is that $I = 0$, $J = 2$, $K = 1$. Now

$m(E)(8) = 8/4096 \quad m(E.H)(8) = 1/4096$

$m(E.\bar{H})(8) = 7/4096$

$F(H,E)(8) = .8$

- quite a large increase in support.

5. CONCLUSION

The measures discussed here have proved useful in the analysis of experimental programs, and some indication has been given of their more general applicability. In the earliest important publication on structured programming, Dijkstra /4/ considers the amount of information required to 'characterise the progress of a process'. He writes "Suppose that a process, considered as a time succession of actions, is stopped after an arbitrary action, what data do we have to fix in order that we can redo the process until the very same point?" We have gone some way in this paper towards quantifying Dijkstra's question.

Other avenues are now being explored. One is the application of similar measures to information contained in databases, using Codd /3/ as a basis. Another is the extension of work which has been done in the field of heuristic problem solving, where a measure of distance in the space of all possible states of a system is needed: ad hoc measures in finite state spaces have been used, for example by Burstall /2/, and the technique used in part 3 allows us to find measures in indefinite or infinite state spaces. A third possibility which is being explored is the development of measures which are directly applicable to the programming language itself, rather than to a logical semantic metalanguage, using Knuth's ideas about semantics as a basis /13/. This latter application has its roots in the observation that, for example,

A:=D*E + (A+B)*D*E

gives more information to a compiler than

A:= D*E + (B+C)*F*G,

information which may be used for optimisation of compiled code. The question is, what exactly do we mean by "information" in this sense? How much information?

The work presented here is therefore only a first sortie into what seems to be a very promising area.

6. REFERENCES

/1/ Arblaster, A.T. (1976) "A Semantic Measure Function for Conditional Statements" unpublished memo.

/2/ Burstall, R.M. (1969) "A Program for Solving Word Sum Puzzles", Computer Journal 12.

/3/ Codd, E.F. (1970) "A Relational Model of Large Shared Data Bases", C.A.C.M. 13.

/4/ Dijkstra,' E.W. (1968) Letter to the Editor, C.A.C.M. 11 pp.147-148.

/5/ Floyd, R.W., (1967) "Assigning Meanings to Programs, "Mathematical Aspects of Computer Science, Amer. Math. Soc. Symposium, Providence, Rhode Island.

/6/ Green, T.R.G. (1976) "Conditional Program Statements and their Comprehensibility to Professional Programmers", M.R.C. Soc. & App.Psych. Unit Memo 79.

/7/ Hoare, C.A.R. (1969) "An Aximomatic Basis for Computer Programming", C.A.C.M. 12, pp.576-583.

/8/ Humby, E., (1973) "Programs from Decision Tables", Macdonald/Elsevier, London/N.Y.

/9/ Ianov, I.I. (1958) "On the Equivalence and Translation of Program Schemes", C.A.C.M. 1, pp.8-12.

/10/ Igarashi, S., London, R.L. and Luckham,D.C. (1972) "Automatic Program Verification 1: Logical Basis and Its Implementation" AIM-200, Stanford and Acta Information 4, 1975.

/11/ Kemeny, J.G. (1953) "A Logical Measure Function, "Jour. Symbolic Logic, 18, pp.289-308.

/12/ Kemeny, J.G., and Oppenheim, P. (1952) "Degree of Factual Support", Philosophy of Science, 19, pp.307-324.

/13/ Knuth, D.E. (1968) "Semantics of Context-Free Languages", Mathl. Systems Theory, 2, pp.127-146.

/14/ Kyburg, H.E. (1970) "Probability and Inductive Logic, Macmillan, London.

/15/ Luckham, D.C., Park, D.M.R. Paterson, M.S. (1970), "On Formalised Computer Programs", Jour. Comp. & Sys., 4, pp.220-249.

/16/ Lukey, F.J., Green, T.R.G., Sime, M.E. and Arblaster, A.T. (1974) "An Experiment on Debugging", M.R.C. Soc. & App. Psych. Unit Memo 57.

/17/ McCarthy, J. (1964) "A Formal Description of a Subset of Algol", in Formal Language Description Languages, edited by T.B. Steel, North-Holland, 1966.

/18/ Manna, Z. and Waldinger, R.J. (1971) "Towards Automatic Program Synthesis" C.A.C.M. 14.

/19/ Manna, Z. (1969) "Properties of Programs and the first order Predicate Calculus", A.C.M. Symposium on the Theory of Computing.

/20/ Pollack, S.L. (1963) "How to Build and Analyse Decision Tables". RAND Corp.

/21/ Press, L.I., (1965) "Conversion of Decision Tables to Computer Programs", C.A.C.M. 8, pp.385-390.

/22/ Reinwald, L.T., & Soland, R.M. (1967) "Conversion of Limited Entry, Decision Tables to Optimal Computer Programs," 1 J.A.C.M. 13, 2, J.A.C.M. 14.

/23/ Schwayder, K., (1971) "Conversion of Limited Entry Decision Tables to Computer Programs", C.A.C.M. 14, pp.69-73.

/24/ Schwayder, K., (1974) "Extending the Information Theory Approach to Converting Limited Entry Decision Tables to Computer Programs", C.A.C.M. 17, pp.532-537.

/25/ Sime, M.E., Green, T.R.G., & Guest, D.J. (1973), "Psychological Evaluation of Two Conditional Constructions Used in Computer Languages", Int. Jour. of Man-Machine Studies 5, pp.105-113.

/26/ Sime, M.E., Green, T.R.G., and Guest, D.J. (1977) "Scope Marking in Computer Conditionals - a Psychological Evaluation", Int. Jour. Man-Machine Studies, 9 (in press)

/27/ Sime, M.E., Arblaster, A.T. and Green,T.R.G. (1977) "Reducing Programming Errors in Nested Conditionals by Prescribing a Writing Procedure". Int. Jour. Man-Machine Studies, 9 (in press).

/28/ Sime, M.E., Arblaster, A.T. and Green,T.R.G. (1977), "Structuring the Programmers Task", paper presented to 10th Annual Occupational Psychology Conference of the British Psychology Society.

/29/ Suzuki, N. (1974) "Automatic Program Verification 11", Stanford A.1 Lab. Memo AIM-255.

E. Morlet and D. Ribbens, (Eds.), International Computing Symposium 1977.

A CASE STUDY IN MODULAR DESIGN

Flaviu CRISTIAN

Ecole Nationale Supérieure d'Informatique
et de Mathématiques Appliquées

B.P. 53, 38041 GRENOBLE Cedex (France)

This paper describes a case study in the application of a design methodology for the production of modular programs. We introduce briefly this methodology and a set of tools designed for its application, and we apply it to the process of modular design of a complex program : the librarian. At the end, we present an overall view of the resulting program structure.

1. INTRODUCTION

Recent progress in programming methodology has fostered the development of appropriate programming tools. The work described in this paper was done in connection with the design of SESAME, a supporting system for the production of modular programs. This system, currently under development at the University of Grenoble, provides :

1) A compiler for a modular implementation language which is an extension of Pascal.

2) A processor which performs generation and linking of modules : the connector.

3) A file system specially designed for keeping and searching modules : the librarian.

The implementation and connection language are described in /2/, /8/, and shall be briefly presented in §3. This paper presents the overall design and the modular specification of the librarian, using the design methodology embodied in the SESAME project. This presentation is intended as a case study for the illustration of this methodology ; therefore, the description of the program will be restricted to its essential features.

The design and implementation of the librarian have been performed as a 3rd year student project at the Ecole Nationale Supérieure d'Informatique et de Mathématiques Appliquées de Grenoble (ENSIMAG) during the Academic year 1975-76.

2. DESCRIPTION OF A COMPLEX PROGRAM : THE LIBRARIAN

Since the librarian is essentially a data base management program, its structure will be best explained by presenting the data structures it has to manage.

2.1. The data structures managed by the librarian

The SESAME system provides two levels for the expression of algorithms similar to the two levels defined in /4/ : "programming in the small" : modules, and "programming in the large": connection programs. These two classes of objects, written in an appropriate source language, are the basic entities managed by the librarian. Let us call them source objects. By compilation and connection they generate executable binary objects. Since any large program is subject to frequent modifications, a facility is provided by the system to keep several versions of each source object. A natural structuring of the versions of an object is a tree-structure, as described in Figure 1 : a version, obtained by modifying an existant version is represented as a descendant of this latter.

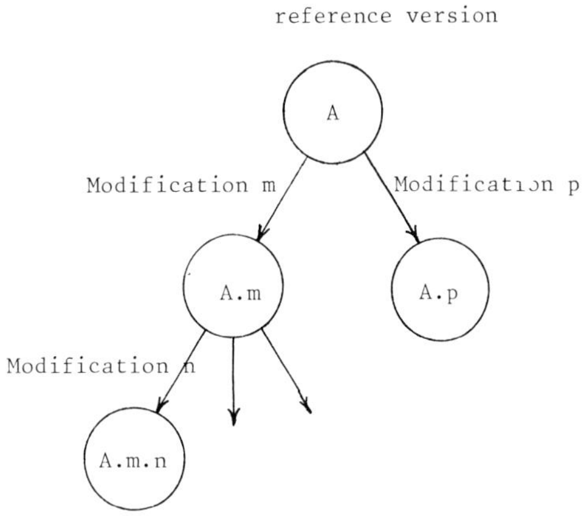

Fig. 1

The root of a version tree is called the reference version ; any version may become a reference version after deletion of its ancestors and cousins (see § 2.2). The following consistency rules must be enforced :

- the deletion of one version involves the deletion of its descendants.
- one only needs to keep a reference version and modification tree to reconstruct any version after accidental destruction.

Every source object may be parameterized and may therefore generate a class of binary objects (see § 3.2 and 3.5). As a consequence :

- The deletion of a source object involves the deletion of the binary objects generated from it.
- A binary object is uniquely defined by the values of its generation parameters (meta-variables, see § 3.2). Keeping track of these parameters, any binary object can be reconstructed.

Let us assume that a user wants to replace in the library a source module, A, by a functionally equivalent, but more efficient one, A'. This entails the replacement of the binary text corresponding to version A by the binary text corresponding to version A' in all module connections where A is involved :

- The modification (deletion) of a source object involves reinterpretation (deletion) of the connection programs using this source object. For the sake of simplicity, this constraint is only imposed on objects having the longest life : the reference versions. To every reference version is associated the list of connection programs which use this version.

The librarian has to manage a large number of small modules. The available file system is intended for efficient access to a small number of large data volumes. We had to build a bank of segments, simple and well suited to the librarian's needs.

If we say that all objects handled by a same set of operations belong to the same "type", we can regard the library as containing three types of complex objects. We shall briefly present these three types.

2.2. Source objects

For the user, a source object is composed of :

1) An identification name.
2) A segment containing the program specifications.
3) A segment containing the program text.

The operations defined on source objects are :

- creation of a reference version
- creation of a new version by modifying an old one with the text editor
- deletion in the tree of versions of a sub-tree referenced by its root
- replacement of a sub-tree, VERSION A, by another one, VERSION B (Fig. 2). If VERSION A is the reference version, VERSION B becomes the reference version
- access to documentation (items (2), (3))
- printing the descendance-tree of a version as well as documentation on the descendants (items (1), (2), (3)).

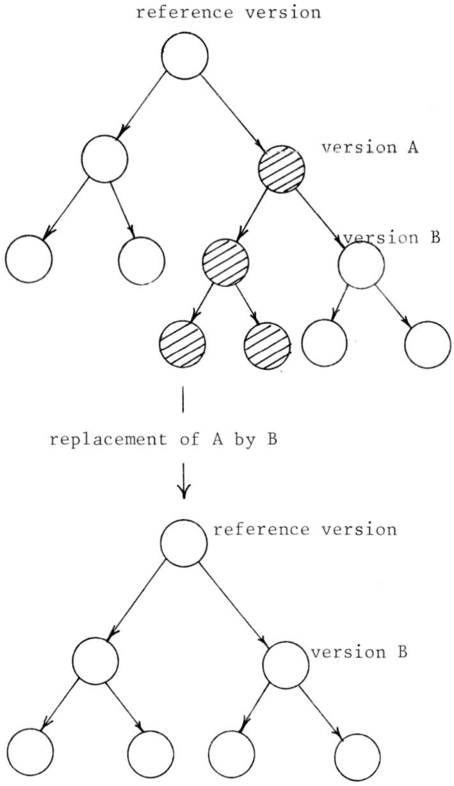

Fig. 2

Reference versions of a source object (roots of version trees) contain as an additional information the list of the connection procedures using this source object. One can

- add a connection procedure name at this list
- delete an element of the list
- access the documentation on the list of connection procedures using the object.

Similarly, the reference version of a connection procedure contains the list of the connected modules. One can access documentation about the modules connected by a connection procedure (for example their generation parameters, their specifications, etc).

As the set of operations defined on reference versions is not identical to the set of operations defined on simple versions, we distinguish two types of source objects : source objects belonging to the reference version type and source objects belonging to the version type.

2.3. BINARY OBJECTS

A binary object is composed of :

1) An identification name (the list of values of its generation parameters).
2) A segment containing the binary text.

The operations on this type of objects are :

- creation
- deletion
- access to documentation (items (1), (2)) about the list of binary objects generated from a source object
- copying the text of a binary object on a file or device.

3. MODULAR SPECIFICATION OF THE LIBRARIAN

3.1. The concept of module

The concept of module used here is the synthesis in a unique concept of notions which were for a long time developed independently :

a) Decomposition unit which may be produced (written, compiled) separately.
b) Implementation of "abstract types", not provided by the programming language used /9/, /7/.
c) Implementation of a set of protected objects, accessible only through a specified set of operations /10/, /5/, /6/.
d) A model for a class of parameterized objects, used as a (macro) generator.

3.2. Module patterns

One of the aims of the project is to allow users to build a library of modules, which may be linked together into systems. The users will not keep individual modules, which are bound to a specified environment, but module generators, which we call module patterns. Two kinds of parameters are introduced in a module pattern definition :

- Metavariables, which allow the user to adjust internal characteristics of a module according to a particular environment.
- Dummy procedures, to be implemented by the user of the module in other modules, allowing inter-module connection by linking a dummy name to a real procedure name.

3.3. An example of module pattern

The following program is the text of a module pattern, which implements parameterized objects belonging to a linear list type. This type is defined by the set of operations implemented as a set of external functions and procedures ; any data in the module can be accessed only through these external functions and procedures. The text contains undefined metavariables (for readability reasons metavariable names begin with "&") and dummy procedures supposed to be implemented in other modules. The bodies of some external procedure have been omitted.

```
pattern LIST (&NLE : integer ; &VAL : type) ;
{&NLE = number of list elements, &VAL = the type
 of information conserved in lists}
type POINTER = -1..&NLE-1 ; {-1 is nil}
     PAIR = record VAL : &VAL ;
                   NEXT : POINTER
            end ;
var ZONE : array [0..&NLE-1] of PAIR ;
    FREE : POINTER ; {references the list of free
                      pairs in zone}
    CURRENT : POINTER ; {references the current
                         list}
dummy procedure OVERFLOW ;{treatment of the
overflow-trap in ZONE}
ext function  CREATE-LIST (ELEMENT : &VAL) :
POINTER ;
var P : POINTER ;
begin if FREE = -1 then OVERFLOW
      else
      begin CREATE-LIST := P := FREE ;
            FREE := ZONE [P]. NEXT ;
            ZONE [P]. VAL := ELEMENT ; ZONE [P].
            NEXT := -1 ;
      end
end ;
ext procedure FREE-LIST (HEAD-OF-LIST : POINTER);
...
ext procedure CHAIN-ELEMENT (HEAD-OF-LIST :
              POINTER ; ELEMENT : &VAL) ;
...
ext function UNCHAIN-ELEMENT (HEAD-OF-LIST :
             POINTER ; ELEMENT : &VAL) : POINTER;
...
ext procedure OPEN-LIST (HEAD-OF-LIST : POINTER);
    {current list ← the list referenced by
     HEAD-OF-LIST}
...
ext function NEXT-ELEMENT : &VAL; {if end of cur-
    rent list then NIL else next element of the cur-
    rent list}
end LIST ;
```

3.4. The connection language - Connection programs

Modular programs are designed by the repeated decomposition of a problem into sub-problems, each being solved by a specific module. Each module is intended to implement an abstract type providing the type of objects which are considered necessary to solve such a sub-problem. On the other hand, a given module may need to be interpreted by a machine providing some types of objects which are not directly available in the implementation language ; in that case, these types of objects must be implemented by other modules.

A connection program allows a new abstract type to be built, starting from a set of existing module patterns, by specifying

1) The operations on the new abstract type.
2) The list of component modules implementing the types of objects which are necessary to build the new abstract type. These modules are created by assigning real values to the metavariables of module patterns. For example, if a list of integers is needed, the executable module managing this type of

list is created by interpreting the following declaration of the connection language

module : INTEGER-LIST = LISTS(1000, integer);

3) The list of connections to be set up between the component modules. For instance, the correspondence between the dummy name *OVERFLOW* in the preceding example and an external procedure *OVERFLOW-TREATMENT* implemented by the user in his error handling module *ERRORS* is set up by interpreting the following affectation of the connection language :

INTEGER-LIST. OVERFLOW := ERRORS. OVERFLOW-TREATMENT ;

3.5. Connection procedures

A connection procedure is a parameterized description of a connection program using metavariables and dummy names. Each connection procedure describes how a new abstract type is built up by interconnecting several modules. Metavariables and dummy procedures allow the user of this abstract type to adjust its program to a particular environment.

3.6. Example : construction of the bank of segments

In order to store the texts and specifications of the objects belonging to the library, we have built a simple bank of segments. We have used the following module patterns :

```
pattern LISTS (&NLE : integer ; &VAL = type) ;
{see the preceding example}

pattern VDAM (&NB, &TB : integer) ;
{manages the inputs and outputs on a fine in
Virtual Direct Access Mode, &NB + 1 = Number of
blocks of the disk, &SB = the size of a block}
type BUFFER-DISK = packed array [1..&TB] of
char ;
ext procedure READ-BLOCK (BLOCK : 0...&NB ;
var BUF : BUFFER-DISK) ;
  :
ext procedure WRITE-BLOCK (BLOCK : 0..&NB ;
var BUF : BUFFER-DISK) ;
  :
end VDAM ;

pattern BIT-STRING (&NB : integer) ;
{&NB + 1 = number of bits, in this example the
bit string is a map of free [0] and occupied
[1] blocks of the disk}
ext function ALLOW : -1...&NB ; {-1 is nil}
  :
ext procedure FREE (BIT : 0..&NB) ;
  :
end BIT-STRING ;
```

We represent a segment by a descriptor and a set of disk-blocks containing sequences of records, as in figure 3.

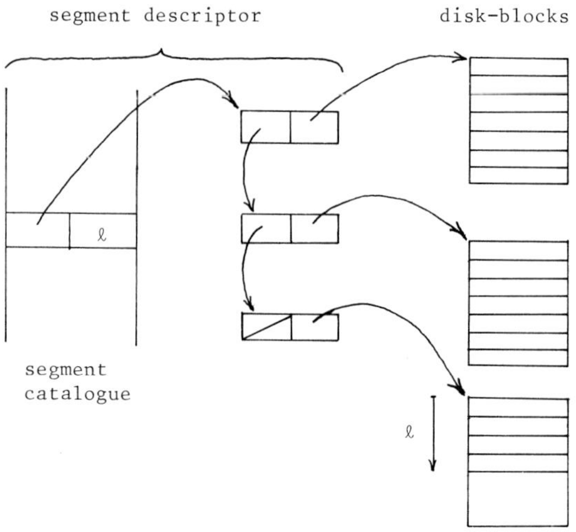

Fig. 3

We have to write a module pattern *CONTROL-SEGMENTS* managing the segment catalogue and using objects of the following types in order to build segments :

LISTS : construction of the segment descriptor
BIT-STRING : management of the free and occupied blocks
VDAM : input and output on the disk .
CONTROL-SEGMENTS : implements operations defined on segments :

- creation of a segment : a sequence of calls to *WRITE-RECORD* (space allocation for the records) followed by a call to *NAME-SEGMENT* (creation of an entry for the segment in the catalogue),
- deletion of a segment : call of *FREE-SEGMENT*,
- sequential reading of the records composing a segment : call of *OPEN-SEGMENT* followed by a sequence of calls to *READ-RECORD*.

This decomposition provides a structuring of the program managing the bank of segments into a "control module" (*CONTROL-SEGMENTS*) which decomposes each operation into a sequence of calls to "action modules" (Fig. 4).

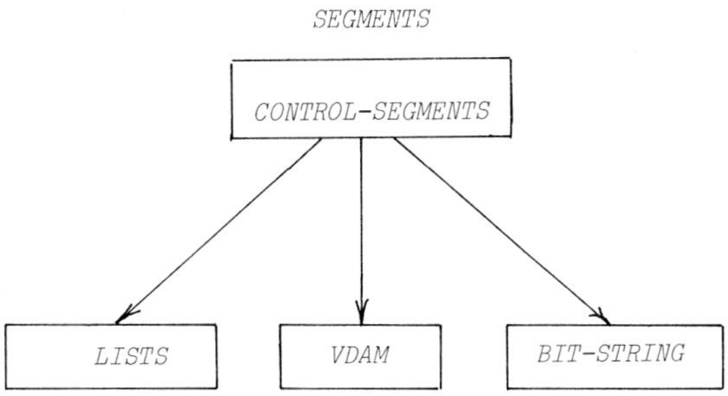

Fig. 4

A connection procedure describing the abstract type segment is given below :

```
connection-procedure SEGMENTS (&NSEG, &NB, &SB,
&SA, &NLE : integer) ;
{&NSEG = maximal number of segments, & NB = number
of available disk-blocks, &SB = size of a block,
&SA = size of an article, &NEL = number of list-
elements ; the component modules are : }
module : DISK-IO = VDAM (&NB, &SB) ;
module : BLOCKS-MANAGEMENT = BIT-STRING (&NB) ;
module : INTEGER-LIST = LIST (&NEL, integer) ;
module : ERRORS-TREATMENT = ERRORS ;
module : S-PILOTE = CONTROL-SEGMENTS (&NSEG) ;
{the list of intermodule connections : }
...
INTEGER-LIST.OVERFLOW := ERRORS-TREATMENT.
                         LIST-OVERFLOW ;
...
{the list of the procedures and functions
accessible from outside : }
ext proc S-PILOTE.WRITE-RECORD (var BUF :
packed array [1..&SA] of char) ;
ext func S-PILOTE.SEGMENT-NAME : -1..&NSEG-1 ;
{-1 is nil}
ext proc S-PILOTE.FREE-SEGMENT (SEGNAME :
0..&NSEG-1) ;
ext proc S-PILOTE.OPEN-SEGMENT (SEGNAME :
0..&NSEG-1) ;
ext func S-PILOTE.READ-RECORD (var BUF : packed
array [1..&SA] of char) : 0..1 ;
{if end of segment then 0 else 1}
connection-procedure-end ;
```

Let us assume that the disk space available to a user is composed of a hundred 4000 bytes blocks. If he needs a bank of at most 500 segments of 80 bytes records, he may generate it by the following declaration in the connection program describing his system :

```
module : SEGMENTS = BANK-OF-SEGMENTS (500, 100,
                    4000, 80, 1000) ;
```

A modification of the environment, e.g. a change in the number of available blocks &NB, may be catered for by reinterpretation of the connection procedure. This will ensure that the metavariable &NB is correctly updated in all modules in which it appears.

3.7. The overall structure of the librarian

The three types of objects presented in §2.1.1 - 2.1.3. are described respectively by the connection procedures *REFERENCE*, *VERSIONS* and *BINARY*.

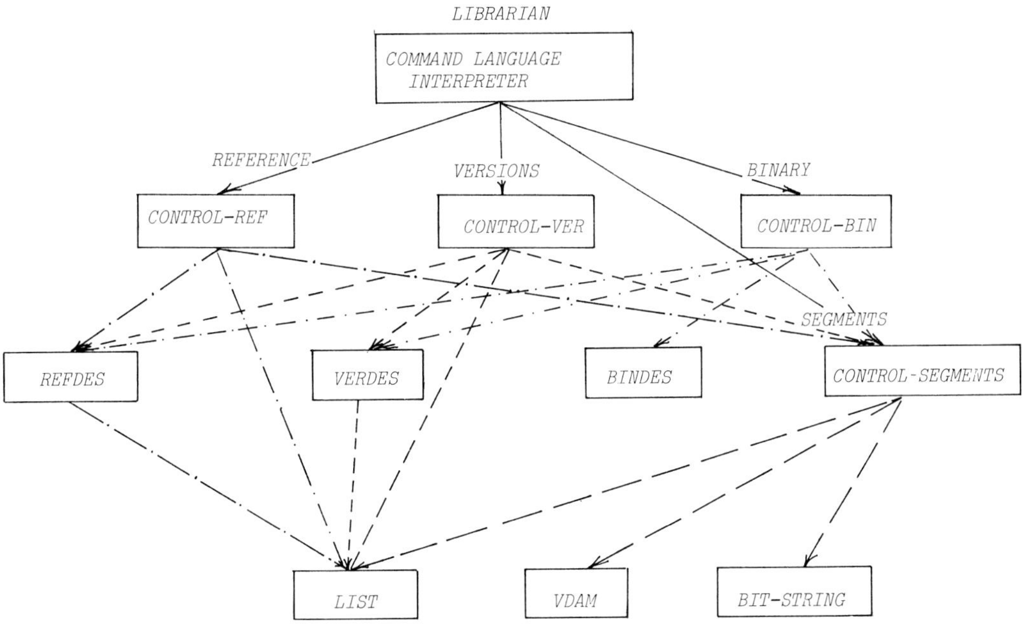

Fig. 5

The objects are accessed by the users of the librarian (compiler, connector, interacting users) through a simple command language.

Every object of the library is represented by a descriptor and one or two data segments. For example, to build a reference object we need a *REF*erence-*DES*criptor and two *SEGMENTS*, containing respectively the specifications and the text of the object. As the descriptor of a reference object contains the list of the binary objects generated from it, we need objects belonging to the type LIST to build *REF*erence-*DES*criptors. That is shown in Fig. 5 : the program managing the reference objects is structured in a "control module" : *CONTROL-REF* which decomposes each operation on a reference object into a sequence of calls to "action modules" implementing respectively objects belonging to the types *REFDES*, *LIST* and *SEGMENTS*. The connection procedure *REFERENCE* describes this structure.

Similarly, the connection procedures *VERSIONS* and *BINARY* describe the structures of the programs managing source versions and binary objects. The overall structure of the librarian is shown in Fig. 7. Each module implements a type of primitive object and connection procedures express the relations to be established between modules to build more complex types of objects.

4. CONCLUSIONS

The work presented here was influenced by the current trends in programming methodology which aim :

- to develop notations and tools to express and apply methods of decomposition, specification and structuring of programs,
- to experiment on relatively complex programs the design methods previously developed for small programs.

The main guideline of the SESAME project is that a software development methodology can only be applied if its underlying concepts are actually integrated in the available programming tools. The design and implementation of the librarian described in this paper was a test of the adequacy and effectiveness of the methods provided by SESAME. We hope to have demonstrated that the resulting structure of programs allows :
- an easy understanding of the main design decisions,
- an easy pinpointing and implementation of modifications introduced by specification or environment changes.

While the design of the librarian was conditioned by the concepts of modular decomposition, the experience gained in the process of its specification and implementation induced a useful feedback on the definition of the methodology. In particular, the notion of connection procedure, which allows the stepwise refinement process to be extended to intermodule connection programs, was introduced during the design of the librarian and integrated in the tools provided by SESAME.

Acknowledgements

I thank F. GAUDUEL for the constructive discussions and cooperation in this work.
I also thank the members of the SESAME project : S. KRAKOWIAK, J. MOSSIERE, J. MONTUELLE, J.L. CHEVAL, Ma. LUCAS for their advice during the design and implementation of the Librarian.

REFERENCES

/1/ BRINCH HANSEN P. : "Operating Systems Principles", Prentice Hall, 1973.

/2/ CRISTIAN F., KRAKOWIAK S., LUCAS Ma., MONTUELLE J., MOSSIERE J. : "Un Système d'Aide à l'Ecriture de Systèmes d'Exploitation", Congrès AFCET, Paris 1976.

/3/ CROCUS : "Systèmes d'Exploitation des Ordinateurs", DUNOD 1975.

/4/ DEREMER F., KRON H. : "Programming in the Large Versus Programming in the Small", IFIP WG 2.4, Working paper (Oct. 1974).

/5/ ENGLAND D.M. : "Capability Concept, Mechanism and Structure in System 250", International Workshop on Protection in Operating Systems, IRIA (Aug. 1974).

/6/ FERRIE J., KAISER C., LANCIAUX D., MARTIN B.: "An Extensible Structure for Protected Systems Design", International Workshop on Protection in Operating Systems, IRIA (Aug. 1974).

/7/ FLON L. : "Program Design with Abstract Data Types", Carnegie-Mellon University 1975.

/8/ KRAKOWIAK S., LUCAS Ma., MONTUELLE J., MOSSIERE J. : "A Modular Approach to the Structured Design of Operating Systems", MRI Symposium on Computer Software Engineering (April 1976).

/9/ LISKOV B., ZILLES S. : "Programming with Abstract Data Types", Symposium on Very High Level Languages, SIGPLAN Notices 9, 4 (1974).

/10/ PARNAS D.L. : "A Technique for Software Module Specification with Examples", CACM, May 1972.

E. Morlet and D. Ribbens, (Eds.), International Computing Symposium 1977.

VERIFICATION OF CONCURRENT SYSTEMS OF PROCESSES

J.Y. Cotronis P.E. Lauer

University of Newcastle upon Tyne,
Computing Laboratory,
Newcastle upon Tyne, NE1 7RU.
England.

R.J. Lipton has introduced a reduction method which permits a process assumed to be interruptible to be reduced to an uninterruptible process without affecting the behaviour of the rest of the system to which the process belongs. Demonstration of the adequacy of a system of reduced processes is considerably less complex than such a demonstration for systems involving unreduced processes. Reformulation of Liptons ideas in Special Petri net theory leads to the formalization of some informal aspects of Liptons method and permits a weakening of his reducibility conditions on processes without loosing any of his results.

0. MOTIVATION

It is often important for systems programmers to know whether programs which generate concurrent system behaviour (or, in brief "concurrent programs") satisfy certain criteria. These criteria may include the protection of shared resources, absence of deadlocks and the observation of capacity bounds. For the present we will call systems and programs for specifying their behaviour adequate provided they satisfy criteria of these three types.

Conventional debugging techniques are particularly inappropriate as an approach to generating satisfactory concurrent programs. The aim of these techniques is to verify that all possible processes generated by a program, rather than just isolated processes arising from sample test cases, work properly. Furthermore, these methods presuppose that repeated test runs of the program with one and the same test data always lead to an identical sequential process, or at least to identical end results. This assumption of reproducibility of test runs is often not satisfied in the case of concurrent processes which may give rise to non-determinism. Hence, there is increased urgency for devising more rigorous methods of certification.

To date, rigorous demonstration of the adequacy of concurrent programs has proved to be extremely difficult and tedious. The importance of adequate system behaviour and the tediousness of demonstrations of adequacy have spawned numerous attempts to automate part or all of such demonstrations. Existing automatic debugging and theorem proving techniques have so far been able to do little to alleviate the task of the systems programmer in convincing himself and others of the adequacy of his programs.

We have been engaged in an alternative approach to the problem of providing rigorous demonstrations of the adequacy of concurrent programs, which is based on a formal syntactic classification of programs and corresponding system structure and behaviour. We believe that syntactic methods are a most promising basis for practicable automation of the certification of program adequacy. Indeed the one established automated method enabling programmers to verify some aspects of the correctness of their programs is the syntactic error detection portion of a compiler, and several recent advances in language design have been motivated by the wish to increase the proportion of errors that can be detected by simple compile time checks. This was also the motivation for the work described in Lauer and Campbell [8] and Lauer [10].

Another alternate approach for improving the unsatisfactory situation confronting the systems programmer is the search for techniques permitting the reduction of more difficult problems to simpler and well understood problems, wherever possible. Thus many researchers have insisted that the only way to tackle the problem of concurrency is to find ways of reducing it to essentially sequential notions. In this spirit C.A.R. Hoare [4] defined notions like commutativity and semicommutativity between sets of "atoms" in a program, which he used to construct a sequential program from a parallel one.

R.J. Lipton [15,16] has contributed to this approach by introducing certain criteria which permit the reduction of some interruptible subprocesses of a system to equivalent uninterruptible subprocesses without effecting the overall behaviour of the system. Such reduction decreases the complexity of the verification problem of the system.

Lipton's reduction method does not presuppose that a routine R in a system of processes P is uninterruptible. This means that the execution of the routine could be interrupted and control passed temporarily to another routine in the system. P/R is then defined to be the system of processes obtained from P by reducing R to one indivisible action and is called the reduction of P by R.

A desirable result would be the following:

if P/R has the property Σ then
P has the same property Σ (1)

Thus, from an examination of the simpler system P/R, conclusions can be drawn about the more complicated system P. In his paper Lipton gives sufficient conditions on routines under which (1) is true for the properties of deadlock and determinacy.

In the present paper the notions which Lipton uses for his system of processes are formulated in terms of the theory of Petri-nets and equivalent results are obtained. By using Petri-nets weaker reducibility conditions on routines were found thus obtaining a larger class of routines to which the reduction method applies. Petri-net Theory is a powerful mathematical theory of parallel system description. A brief introduction to the theory will be given in the first section.

In the second section Lipton's systems of processes are described; also a general algorithm for finding the equivalent Petri-net from Lipton's systems is described. Similar work has been carried out by P.E. Lauer and R. Campbell in [8]. In that paper they first developed a high level language which is based on the concept of path expression introduced by Campbell and Habermann [1]; the path programs are a high-level means for generating systems of co-operating concurrent processes. They defined the syntax of such programs by means of formation rules and the semantics of these programs were determined by a set of transformation rules corresponding one-to-one to the formation rules. The iterative application of the transformation rules to a path program yields its corresponding simulating Petri-net, which is an equivalent mathematical system description of the system of processes generated by the program.

Lipton's results using Petri-net theory are obtained in section three and in section four these results are applied to various nets. Finally in section five weaker conditions on routines for the applicability of the reduction method are derived.

1. INTRODUCTION TO PETRI-NETS

A Petri-net is defined as a quadruple

$$N = (P,T,pre,post)$$

where P,T are non-empty disjoint sets and pre, post are binary relations with pre,post $\subseteq P \times T$. The elements $p \in P$ and $t \in T$ are called places and transitions respectively. In the figures we shall represent places by circles and transitions by squares. The physical interpretation of a place is a condition and that of a transition is an event.

A place p is called an input place of a transition t if $(p,t) \in$ pre and an output of t if $(p,t) \in$ post. A Petri-net is called a pure Petri-net if the input and output places of each transition are disjoint sets. A pure Petri-net may be represented algebraically by means of its incidence matrix C. C is defined as $C = (c(p,t))$ where $c(p,t)$ is an element of C and is defined as:

$$c(p,t) = \begin{cases} -1 & \text{if } (p,t) \in \text{pre} \\ 1 & \text{if } (p,t) \in \text{post} \\ 0 & \text{otherwise} \end{cases}$$

A marking M of a net N is a mapping $M: P \to \mathbb{N} \cup \{0\}$, where $\mathbb{N}$ is the set of natural numbers 1,2,.... M(p) is called the number of tokens on a place p. We say that a place p is marked if $M(p) \geq 1$. We represent a marking M by its corresponding vector M which is indexed by the set of places P. A transition t is called activated or enabled if all its input places are marked. The net can be used to simulate system behaviour in the following way: the holding of a condition in the system is represented by the existence of a token on the corresponding place of the net. The activity of the system consists of the "firing" of enabled transitions. A "firing" of a transition removes one token from each input place and adds one to each output place of the transition. The firing of a transition corresponds to the notion of the occurrence of the event associated with it.

If there is a sequence of firings of transitions which transform a marking M1 into a marking M2 we call M2 reachable from M1. The set of all markings reachable from M - including M itself - is denoted by [M]. A marking M is called live-1 if $\forall \tilde{M} \in [M] : |[\tilde{M}]| > 1$. i.e. every marking which is reachable from M can be transformed into another marking.

A transition t is called dead under a marking M, in symbols dead(t,M) if t cannot be activated. A marking M is called live-2 if there is no dead transition. A marking M is called dead if all transitions are dead under M. We say that a Petri-net deadlocks if there exists a sequence of firings which produces a dead marking.

A marking M is called safe if:

$$\forall \tilde{M} \in [M] : \forall p \in P : \tilde{M}(P) \leq 1$$

Let M be a marking and U,V sets of transitions such that $U \cap V = \emptyset$. Then beginning with M, the maximum number of firings of transitions in V without a firing of a transition in U is called the slack of U with respect to V under M; in symbols sp(U,V;M).

A marked net represents the set of all sequences of occurrences of events (firings of transitions) determined by the holding of the conditions as specified by the marking on the net.

The simple invariants of a net are all integer, positive solutions of $C'.x=0$ which cannot be obtained by addition of any other such solutions. C' is the transpose of the incidence matrix C. Invariants can be interpreted as complete systems of circuits.

A variant V is a solution of an inhomogoneous system of equations

$$C'.y=r \quad \text{where r is a compatible vector.}$$

Variants can be interpreted as incomplete systems of circuits.

Matrix (column) x is a characteristics vector if $\forall p \in P: x(p) \in \{0,1\}$.

2. NET THEORETIC FORMULATION OF LIPTON'S NOTION OF SYSTEMS OF PROCESSES

In this section we briefly describe Lipton's basic system of parallel processes and give equivalent definitions in terms of Petri-nets.

2.1 Description of Lipton's Systems

Lipton [15] implements a parallel system of processes using the bracket pair parbegin, parend as used by Dijkstra in [2]. The effect of parbegin S_1; S_2; ... S_x parend is to interleave components of the statements $S_1, S_2, \ldots S_x$ in some arbitrary order until no further execution is possible. With the aid of another bracket pair repeat, end it is possible to enter a process more than once.

```
parbegin
    repeat T1;T2; ... Tn end;
    repeat P1;P2; ... Pk end;
parend;
```

2.2 Petri-net Formulation of Lipton's Systems

We can now give the basic rules which will produce Petri-nets equivalent to Lipton's systems.

(i) First we "translate" each process of Lipton's system without representing the semantics of the statements in this process. We do that as follows:

(a) When we enter a process we start building up the net corresponding to this process by drawing a marked place.

(b) Then the next statement in the process will be "translated", into one transition which has the last place we drew as an input and a new one as output. Then we repeat (b) until we exhaust all statements in the process.

(c) If the process is in the bracket pair repeat, end we identify the marked place with the output place of the last transition.

(ii) We represent possible predicates involved in statements as places on the net and we translate the semantics of the statements which govern the state of these places (in section 2.4 we show how to do that mechanically for PV systems).

(iii) We perform steps (i), (ii) for all processes in the system.

(iv) We identify places in different processes which correspond to the same predicate.

(v) Finally we set the marking on places according to the initial value of the predicates they represent.

We demonstrate this algorithm in section 3.2 where we find equivalent nets for parallel systems.

Definition: Places which are obtained in step (i) of the algorithm will be called flow-of-control places.

Definitions: Transitions which are obtained in step (i) of the algorithm are called syntactical transitions. Sometimes when applying step (ii) of the algorithm we need to introduce some more transitions to model the semantics of a statement in Lipton's system as Petri-nets. These transitions are called semantical transitions and will be represented in nets by thick bars.

2.3 The Notion of Computation

According to Lipton a computation of a system of processes is a finite sequence of statements such that each statement is in turn able to execute.

In Petri-nets we will mean a possible finite sequence of firings of transitions.

2.4 PV Systems in Petri-Nets

A program P is a PV parallel program provided there is a distinguished subset of program variables $a_1 \ldots a_k$ called semaphores with integer values such that they can be used only in either of $P(a_i)$ or $V(a_i)$ operations with the following semantics:

$$P(a_i) \equiv \text{if } a_i > 0 \text{ then } a_i \leftarrow a_i - 1;$$
$$V(a_i) \equiv a_i \leftarrow a_i + 1.$$

In Petri-nets P and V operations together with their semantics will be represented by:

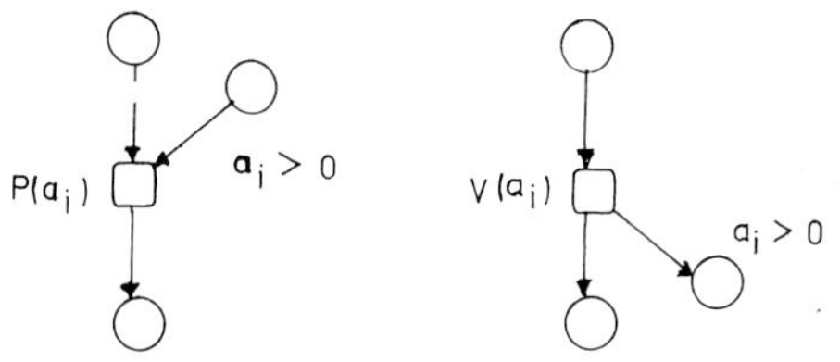

2.5 An Advantage of Petri-nets over Lipton's System

Once we have "translated" a system of processes into its Petri-net we can forget about the interpretation of the transitions and places. This is so because an unformalised aspect, the semantics of the statements of Lipton's model are formalised in net theory. In Lipton's model the co-ordination in the system is done by checking the current values of the predicates and updating these as determined by the semantics of the statements involved. So we have to refer to the semantics of the statements.

But in Petri-nets we have translated these semantics which are integrated with the rest of the system and the co-ordination is done mechanically as defined by firing rules and the marking on the net. We can also apply general theorems in Petri-net theory to infer if the net possesses certain properties, whilst in Lipton's model one has to check each system using specific arguments.

3. NET THEORETIC FORMULATION OF THE NOTION OF REDUCTION

In this section we give definitions of notions used by Lipton in terms of Petri-nets and we derive Lipton's main results.

3.1 Routines, Composite transitions, Reduction

Definition: Syntactical transitions $t_1 \ldots t_n$ in a Petri-net form a routine if there is a connected path (consisting of directed arcs) which starts at t_1 and terminates at t_n meeting all t_i s $(2 \le i \le n-1)$ and passing through flow-of-control places only.

Definition: Suppose syntactical transitions $t_1 \ldots t_n$ form a routine. Then by a composite transition of $t_1 \ldots t_n$ we mean the single syntactical transition we obtain if we identify these transitions. In this joining we bring together the transitions thus all places which are output places of some t_i $(1 \le i < n)$ and input places of some t_j $(1 < j \le n)$ disappear and all other places which were only input or only output places of some transition t_k $(1 < k \le n)$ become input or output place of the new syntactical transition.

Definition: Syntactical transitions $t_1 \ldots t_n$ will belong to the same process if the output place of t_i $(1 \le i < n)$ which is input place of t_{i+1} is a flow-of-control-place for every $i (1 \le i < n)$.

Definition: Suppose that $t_1 \ldots t_n$ is a routine in a Petri-net P. Then the reduction of P by $t_1 \ldots t_n$ (in symbols $P/t_1 \ldots t_n$) is the Petri-net formed when we replace $t_1 \ldots t_n$ by the composite transition of $t_1 \ldots t_n$. $P/t_1 \ldots t_n$ is simpler then P but do the two nets possess the same properties? One of the properties we are interested in preserving is halting (deadlocks). If P deadlocks we want $P/t_1 \ldots t_n$ to deadlock as well.

3.2 Restrictions on Reduction to Preserve Halting

Let us consider the PV system of processes EX1: (fig. 3.2.1.).

```
integer a,b (a=b=1);
parbegin
      repeat P(a); P(b); V(a); V(b) end;
      repeat P(b); P(a); V(b); V(a) end;
parend;
```

fig. 3.2.1: EX1

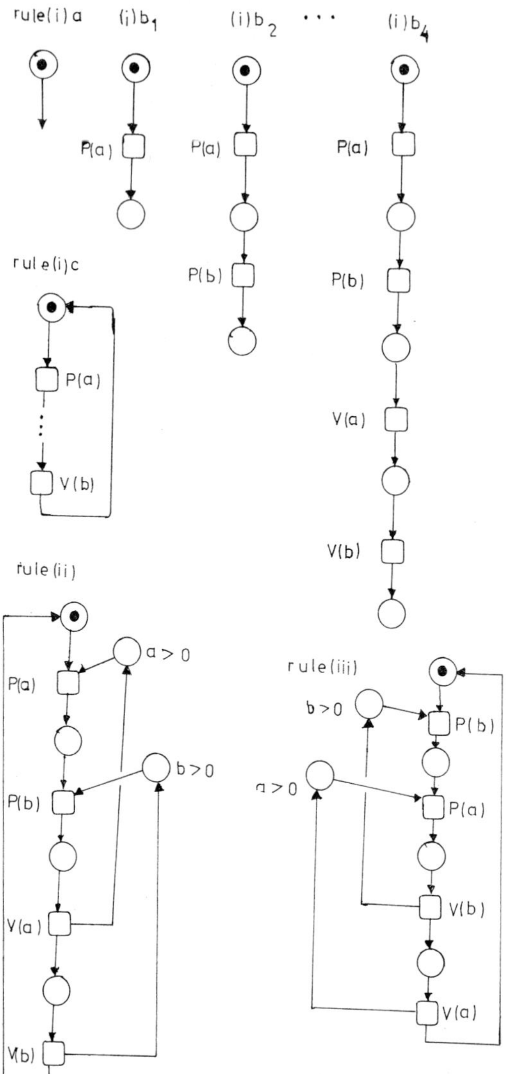

rule(iv-v)

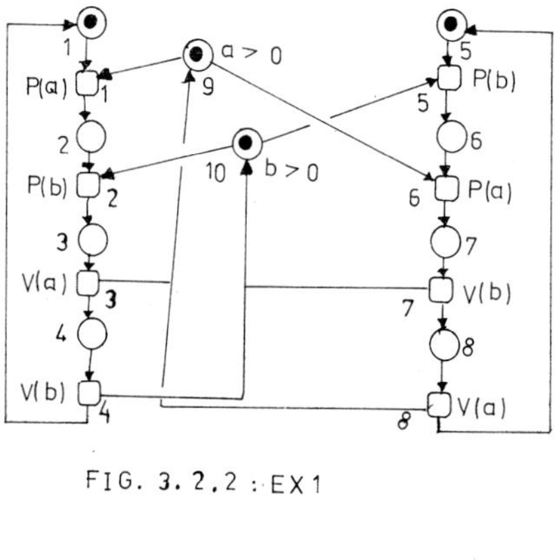

FIG. 3.2.2 : EX1

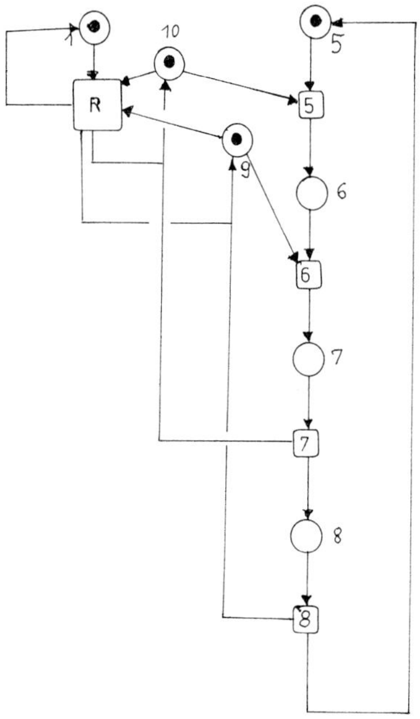

fig. 3.2.3: EX1/R

Figure 3.2.2 shows how we obtain the equivalent Petri-net using the steps of the rules given in sections 2.2, 2.4. This net deadlocks if we fire t_1 and t_4 or t_4 and t_1.

If we reduce the net by routine $t_1t_2t_3t_4$ we get the net in fig. 3.2.3. This net does not deadlock. R can fire or sequence t_5,t_6,t_7,t_8 can fire or any combination of R and $(t_5t_6t_7t_8)$ without getting a deadlock.

The mathematical theory of Petri-net explains this as follows:

Let V be a variant and γ a vector defined by $\gamma=C'.V$. Among the solutions y of the equation system $C'.y=\gamma$ we find all systems of directed paths leading from the transitions filling up V to the transitions emptying V. We shall call the set of these systems of directed paths Wv. Now we state Theorem 1 [12].

Theorem 1: A marking M under which each simple non-negative invariant is marked is not live if there exists a variant with max $M'(V-y)\leq 0$, $y\in Wv$. Going back to EX1, we first find all invariants of this net (fig. 3.2.4), (in terms of their characteristic vectors).

1	2	3	4	5	6	7	8	9	10	PLACES
1	1	1	1	0	0	0	0	0	0	
0	1	1	0	0	0	1	1	1	0	
0	0	1	1	0	1	1	0	0	1	
0	0	0	0	1	1	1	1	0	0	

fig. 3.2.4: Invariants of EX1

The invariants are all marked so we can apply Theorem 1. Let V be the characteristic vector:

(1 0 0 0 1 0 0 0 1 1).

Then we find all simple solutions of $C'.y=\gamma$ where $\gamma=C'.V=(-2\ -1\ 1\ 2\ -2\ -1\ 1\ 2)$. The solutions are shown in fig. 3.2.5 as characteristic vectors:

1	2	3	4	5	6	7	8	9	10	PLACES
1	0	0	0	1	0	0	0	1	1	(y_1)
2	1	1	1	1	0	0	0	1	1	(y_2)

fig. 3.2.5: Solutions of $C'.y=\gamma$

Then max $M'(V-y)=M'(V-y_1)=0$, $y\in Wv$.

This result is consistent with our observation that the net deadlocks. Now if we identify transitions $t_1t_2t_3t_4$ we eliminate a variant which causes a deadlock.

Thus we should not perform the reduction when it is possible to enter the routine but not exit it. (R1)

For our next example consider EX2, fig. 3.2.6.

```
integer x,y(x=y=0);
parbegin
        if x=1 then x←0;
        repeat if x=0 then x←1; y←x; P(y) end;
parend;
```

fig. 3.2.6: EX2

The Petri-net for EX2 is fig. 3.2.7. This figure shows the two processes together with the semantics of the statements in Lipton's system. To implement the semantics of y←x we needed to introduce four transitions to represent explicitly the four situations:

x=0 and y "changes" from 0→0,
y changes from 0→1
and x=1 and y "changes" from 1→1,
y changes from 0→1

which were implicit in Lipton's system. These four situations are represented by transitions s_1,s_2,s_3,s_4 respectively, but we shall refer to all of them by t_2.

This net deadlocks if we fire sequence $t_1t_4t_2$. But when we reduce the net by routine t_1,t_2 the net does not deadlock any more, fig. 3.2.8,

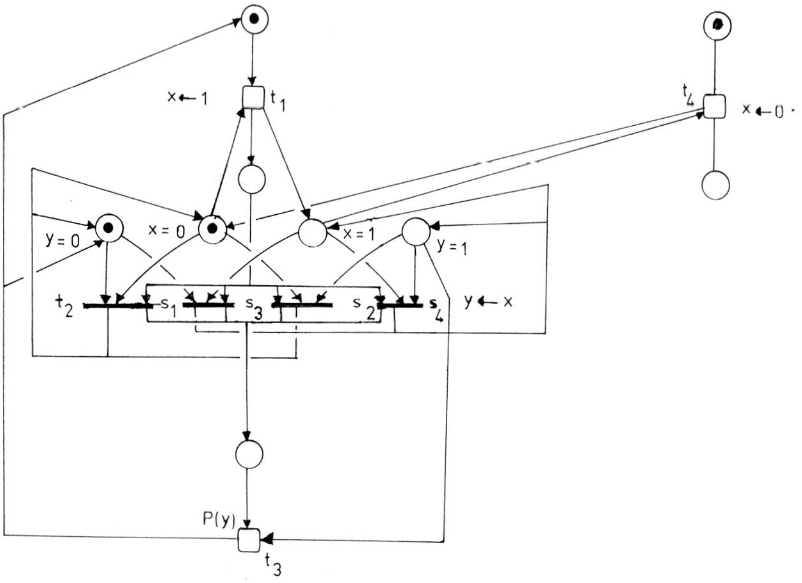

fig. 3.2.7: EX2

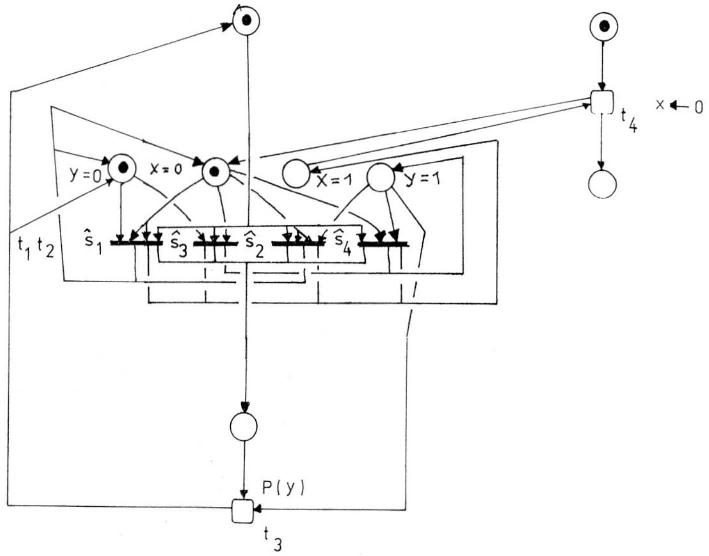

fig. 3.2.8: EX2/t_1, t_2

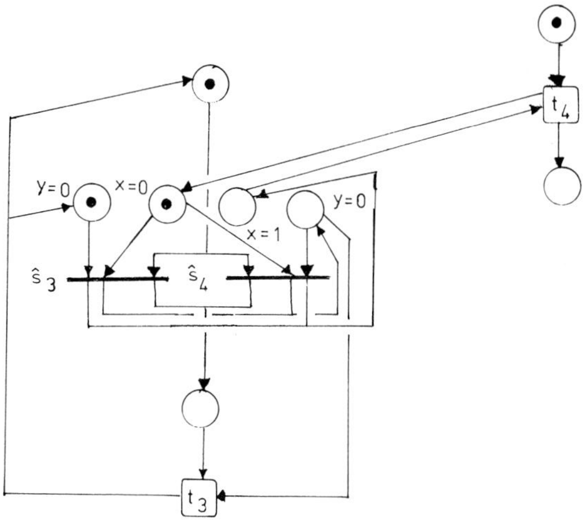

fig. 3.2.9: EX2/$t_1 t_2$ (abbrev)

3.2.9. This happened because the interruption of routine $t_1 t_2$ by t_4 in the sequence $t_1 t_4 t_2$ produced a deadlock. But when we regard $t_1 t_2$ as uninterruptible we eliminate this sequence and eliminate a deadlock. Our second restriction will be: The marking on the net when the routine is interrupted and when not must be the same.(R2)

Note: In fig. 3.2.8 we can eliminate the semantical transitions $\hat{s}_1, \hat{s}_2$ since they will never fire. To be enabled they require two markers on the place corresponding to predicate x=0 (since there are two input arcs from this place to transitions $\hat{s}_1, \hat{s}_2$) which is impossible. Thus the simpler net of fig. 3.2.9 is obtained.

3.3 Formalization of Restrictions

As an aid to formalise (R2) we use the notion of a mover:

Definition: Let t_1, t_2, t_3 be transitions of a Petri-net t_1 and t_2 not belonging to the same process as t_3 and α, β be finite sequences of firings (computations) of the same net. Then t_1 is a right mover provided: if $\alpha t_1 t_3 \beta$ is a computation then so is $\alpha t_3 t_1 \beta$ and the markers on the net after these two computations are the same. And t_2 is a left mover provided: if $\alpha t_3 t_2 \beta$ is a computation then so is $\alpha t_2 t_3 \beta$ and the marking on the net after the two computations are the same.

With respect to restrictions (R1) and (R2), Lipton defines a class of routines, the D-routines. A D-routine in Petri-nets will be a routine t_1 .... t_n such that when t_1 has fired t_n will eventually be able to fire and for some k ($1 \le k \le n$) $t_1 \ldots t_{k-1}$ are right movers and $t_{k+1} \ldots t_n$ are left movers.

Before we prove the main theorem we prove two lemmas:

Lemma 1: Suppose that $t_1 \ldots t_n$ forms a D-routine in P and α, β are computations in P and that $\alpha t_i \beta$ is also a computation for some i, $1 < i \le n$. Then $\alpha = \alpha_1 t_{i-1} \alpha_2$ where no firing of any transition $t_1 \ldots t_n$ is included in α_2.

Proof: For t_i to be enabled, t_{i-1} has been fired some other computation α_2 outside the routine might occur before t_i fires. So α is of the form $\alpha_1 t_{i-1} \alpha_2$.

Lemma 2: Suppose that $t_1 \ldots t_n$ forms a D-routine in P and α, β, $\alpha t_i \beta$ ($1 \le i < n$) are computations in P and $\alpha t_i \beta$ leads to deadlock. Then $\beta = \beta_1 t_{i+1} \beta_2$ where no firing of any transition $t_1 \ldots t_n$ is included in β_1.

Proof: Since no deadlock can occur before we exit the routine (def. of D-routines) it is possible for transitions $t_{i+1}, \ldots t_n$ to fire before the deadlock occurs. After t_i has been fired some computation outside the routine might occur until t_{i+1} fires and then the rest of the computation of β will follow until we reach a deadlock: so $\beta = \beta_1 t_{i+1} \beta_2$.

Theorem 2: Suppose that $t_1 \ldots t_n$ is a D-routine in Petri-net P. Then P deadlocks if $P/t_1 \ldots t_n$ deadlocks.

Proof: (i) if $P/t_1 \ldots t_n$ deadlocks then P deadlocks.

Every computation of $P/t_1 \ldots t_n$ is also a computation of P. So if there exists a computation C that produces a deadlock in $P/t_1 \ldots t_n$ the same computation produces a deadlock in P.

(ii) if P deadlocks then $P/t_1 \ldots t_n$ deadlocks.

Suppose α is a computation in P which leads to a deadlock. We first construct another computation β such that the markings on the net are the same after α,β are executed, and $t_1 \ldots t_n$ will always appear as "consecutive blocks" in β. More formally:

(by β_i we mean the ith firing of sequence β)

1) if $\beta_i = t_j$ $(1 \le j < n)$ then $\beta_{i+1} = t_{j+1}$ and
2) if $\beta_i = t_j$ $(1 < j \le m)$ then $\beta_{i-1} = t_{j-1}$.

If no firing of any t_i occurs in α then α is already in the desired form. We then set $\beta=\alpha$. So assume that same t_i fires in α. $\lambda_1 t_i \lambda_2$ where λ_1,λ_2 are computations in p. Applying lemmata 1,2 repeatedly we get:

$\alpha = \mu_1 t_1 \alpha_2 t_2 \ldots \alpha_n t_n \mu_2$ where again

μ_1 and μ_2 are computations in P and no occurrence of $t_1 \ldots t_n$ in any α_i $(2 \le i \le n)$.

Since, by definition of D-routines, $t_1 \ldots t_{k-1}$ and $t_{k+1} \ldots t_n$ are right and left movers respectively for some $1 \le k \le n$ we construct a computation δ

$$\delta = \mu_1 \alpha_2 \ldots \alpha_k t_1 \ldots t_n \alpha_{k+1} \ldots \alpha_n \mu_2$$

such that δ,α agree on the markings on the net. This argument can be repeated for μ_1,μ_2 until we form the desired computation β.

$$\beta = \beta_1 t_1 \ldots t_n \beta_2 \ldots\ldots \beta_{m-1} t_1 \ldots t_n \beta_m$$

where no occurrence of any transition $t_1 \ldots t_n$ is in any β_i $(1 \le i \le m)$.

Let g be the composite transition of $t_1 \ldots t_n$. Then

$$\gamma = \beta_1 g \beta_2 \ldots\ldots \beta_{m-1} g \beta_m$$

is a computation in $P/t_1 \ldots t_n$ and α,β,γ agree on the marking of the net.

Since for any computation in P which produces a deadlock there is one in $P/t_1 \ldots t_n$ which has an identical effect, i.e. produces a deadlock, $P/t_1 \ldots t_n$ will deadlock if P deadlocks. Q.E.D.

A Corollary of the above theorem is that reduction of D-routines also preserves <u>determinacy</u>. We say that a net is not determinate if there are sequences α,β which both lead to deadlock but do not agree with respect to the possible markings on the net.

<u>Corollary</u>: $P/t_1 \ldots t_n$ is not determinate if P is not determinate.

<u>Proof</u>: (i) Assume P is not determinate. Then there are sequences α_1,α_2 such that both lead to a deadlock but give rise to different markings on the net. As established in Theorem 2 there are sequences β_1,β_2 in $P/t_1 \ldots t_n$ such that (1) α_1 and β_1 agree on the marking
(2) α_2 and β_2 agree on the marking

Thus β_1,β_2 cause a deadlock but they do not agree on the markings on the net. Therefore $p/t_1 \ldots t_n$ is not determinate.

(ii) Using the same argument we can prove P is not determinate if $P/t_1 \ldots t_n$ is not.

<u>Theorem 3</u>: (1) The V operation is a left mover.
(2) The P operation is a right mover.

<u>Proof of (1)</u>: Suppose there are sequences α,β and transitions t_1,t_2 (belonging to different processes) such that t_2 is a V operation and $\alpha t_1 t_2 \beta$ is a computation.

Then (i) αt_2 is a possible sequence since t_1 does not have any input place in common with t_2 whence these could be in conflict.

(ii) $\alpha t_2 t_1$ is a computation since the firing of t_2 could not disable t_1. Furthermore $\alpha t_2 t_1$ produces the same marking as $\alpha t_1 t_2$.

(iii) Finally $\alpha t_2 t_1 \beta$ is a computation (since $\alpha t_1 t_2$ and $\alpha t_2 t_1$ produce the same marking) with the same effect on the net as $\alpha t_1 t_2 \beta$.

<u>Proof of (2)</u>: Again take sequences α,β, transitions t_1,t_3 (not belonging to the same process) such that t_3 is a P operation and $\alpha t_3 t_1 \beta$ is a computation.

(i) αt_1 is a possible sequence since the firing of t_3 does not mark any input place of t_1.

(ii) $\alpha t_1 t_3$ is another computation: if t_1,t_3 do not have place "$s>0$" as a common input place this is obvious. But even if they do, since $\alpha t_3 t_1$ is able to execute, $\alpha t_1 t_3$ can by symmetry.

(iii) $\alpha t_1 t_3 \beta$ has the desired properties. Argue as in (1iii).

4. APPLICATIONS

Consider EX3 (fig. 4.1). Its equivalent Petri-net is shown as fig. 4.2.

```
integer a,b(a=b=1);
parbegin
    repeat P(a); P(b); V(a); V(b) end;
    repeat P(a); P(b); V(a); V(b) end;
parend;
```

<u>fig. 4.1: EX3</u>

Suppose we want to make the maximum reduction by joining transitions 1,2,3,4 and 4,6,7,8. The invariants of EX3 are:

	1	2	3	4	5	6	7	8	9	10	PLACES
1)	1	1	1	1	0	0	0	0	0	0	
2)	0	0	0	0	1	1	1	1	0	0	
3)	0	1	1	0	0	1	1	0	1	0	
4)	0	0	1	1	0	0	1	1	0	1	

which are all marked since the intial marking is

$$M = (1\ 0\ 0\ 0\ 1\ 0\ 0\ 0\ 1\ 1)'.$$

So we can apply Theorem 1.

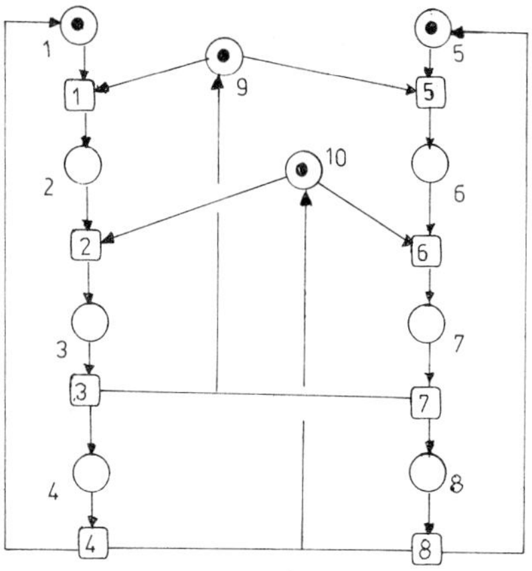

fig. 4.2: EX3

For this net to deadlock inside the routine 1,2,3,4 places 1,3,4,9,10 have to be unmarked and to deadlock inside the routine 5,6,7,8 places 5,7,8,9,10 have to be unmarked. So take V in theorem 1 to be the characteristic vector of places 1,3,4,5,7,8,9,10. Take V to be $(1\ 0\ 1\ 1\ 1\ 0\ 1\ 1\ 1\ 1)'$, $\gamma = C'.V = (-2\ 0\ 1\ 1\ -2\ 0\ 1\ 1)'$. The solutions of $C'.y = \gamma$ are:

y_1)	1	0	0	0	1	0	0	0	1	0
y_2)	2	1	1	1	1	0	0	0	1	0
y_3)	1	0	1	1	1	0	1	1	1	1

$\therefore \max M'(V-y) = M'(V-y_1) = 1 > 0,\ y \in W_V.$

Applying Theorem 3 we see that 1,2 and 5,6 are right movers and 3,4 and 7,8 are left movers. So both 1,2,3,4 and 5,6,7,8 are D-routines. Thus we can reduce the net to that of fig. 4.3.

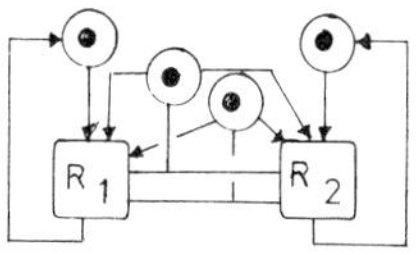

This net is very much simpler than EX3.

fig. 4.3: EX3/R_1R_2

For our next example consider EX4 in fig. 4.4:

```
integer a,b(a=0;  b=N>0);
parbegin
    repeat P(a);  if N-b>0 then b←b+1 end;
    repeat P(b);  if N-a>0 then a←a+1 end;
parend;
```

fig. 4.4: EX4

Its Petri-net is fig. 4.5:

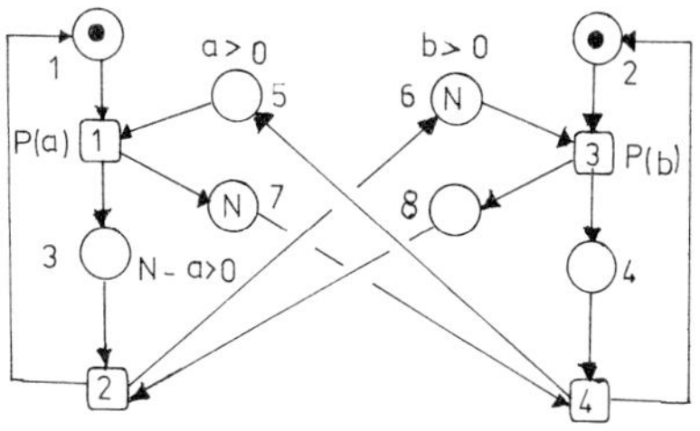

fig. 4.5: EX4

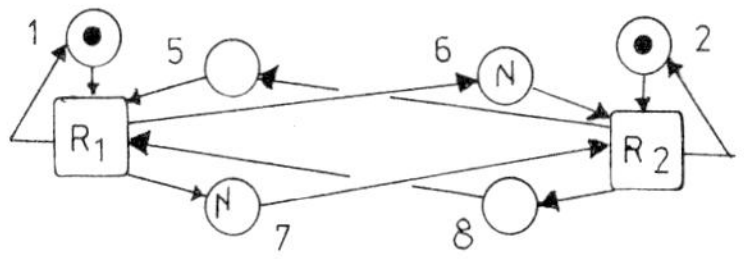

fig. 4.6: EX4/R_1R_2

The "N" on places 6,7 mean that there are N markers there initially.

The invariants of the net are:

1)	1 0 1 0 0 0 0 0	4)	0 0 0 0 0 1 0 1
2)	0 1 0 1 0 0 0 0	5)	1 1 0 0 0 0 1 1
3)	0 0 0 0 1 0 1 0	6)	0 0 1 1 1 1 0 0

which are all marked under the initial marking

$$M = (1\ 1\ 0\ 0\ 0\ N\ N\ 0)'$$

To be inside the routine 1,2 implies place 1 is empty. The only way we cannot exit the routine is for place γ to be unmarked. This means that place 6 must have N markers on it (the number of tokens on an invariant is constant) which implies that places 3,4,5 must all be empty of tokens since they belong to the same invariant (6) which had N markers on initially. But this is a condradiction since place 3 has to be marked since 1 is empty. So this net does not deadlock inside the routine 1,2. Similarly we can prove it does not deadlock inside 3.4. Also since 1.3 are right movers, 1,2 and 3,4 are D-routines. Thus we can reduce the net to that of fig. 4.6.

5. EXTENSIONS

In section 2.1 we made a distinction between places on a net by defining the flow-of-control places. This distinction was made apparent in the definition of routines and processes in section 3.1. But in Petri-nets there is no reason why we should make such a distinction.

In this section we allow transitions to form a routine if there exists a subnet on which the only output place of each transition t_i $(1 \le i < n)$ is the only input place of t_{i+1} $(1 < i \le n)$ (e.g. in EX5 we would exclude 1,3 and 2,4 but include 4,1 and 3,2).

Still we have to check if these routines are D-routines (if they satisfy (R1), (R2)) for the reduction by these routines to preserve halting and determinacy.

Consider EX5 in fig. 5.1 and its Petri-net in 5.2:

```
integer a,b(a=0, b=1);
parbegin
     repeat P(a); V(b) end;
     repeat P(b); V(a) end;
parend;
```

fig. 5.1: EX5

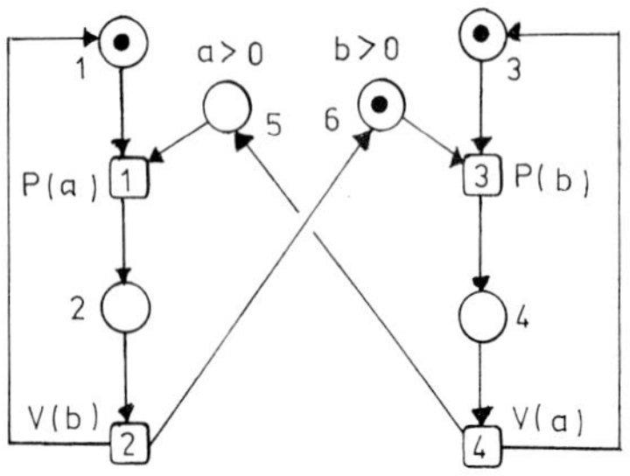

fig. 5.2: EX5 in P.N.

According to the new definition of routines we can consider all four transitions to form a routine in the order 3 4 1 2.

This net does not deadlock: 3 can fire, followed by 4 then 1 follows and finally we exit our routine by firing 2. So (R1) is satisfied.

(R2) is trivially satisfied since there is no transition which belongs to another "process".

So we can reduce the net to a single transition as shown on fig. 5.3:

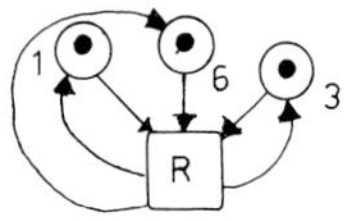

6. CONCLUSIONS

Petri-nets have a powerful theory for describing concurrent systems. It is possible to represent on these nets the syntax and sematnics of a large class of processes. This has the advantage that general theorems about Petri-nets can be applied without having to use specific arguments for each system when certain system properties are proven.

Lipton's reduction method is a useful technique for simplifying a net while preserving the properties of deadlock and determinacy.

An important aspect of the reduction method is that the reduction P/R cannot always be described in terms of the system in which P was described, for example if P is a PV system of processes, P/R need not be a PV system. This is not the case with Petri-nets. When we represent a system P_L in Lipton's model by a Petri-net (call this net P_{PN}) and apply the reduction P_L/R_L (R_L being a routine in Lipton's model) we can still represent this reduction in terms of Petri-nets.

Furthermore, we have established rules for the reduction method in Petri-nets so that we can reduce a system P_{PN} by R_{PN} (where R_{PN} is a routine in Petri-nets) and the following diagram commutes:

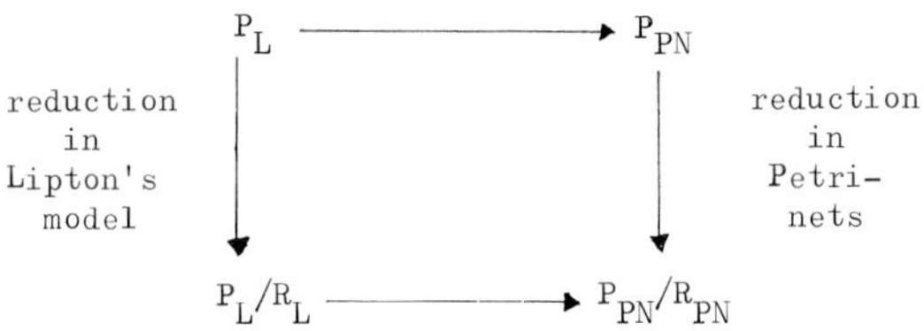

The Petri-net corresponding to P_L/R_L is the same as the net obtained from P_{PN} by applying the reduction rules.

We were also able to extent Lipton's definition of a routine by allowing transitions to form a routine although they belonged to different processes.

7. REFERENCES

[1] Campbell, R.H., Habermann, A.N., "The specification of Process Synchronisation by Path Expressions", University of Newcastle upon Tyne, Tech. Report Series (1974).

[2] Dijkstra, E.W., "Co-operation sequential processes, Programming Languages", pp.43-112, Edited by F. Genuys, 1068, Academic Press.

[3] Genrich, H.J., Lautenbach, K., "Synchronisations - graphen", Acta Informatica 2, pp.143-161 (1973).

[4] Hoare, C.A.R., "Program Correctness Proofs" Proceedings of the Joint IBM-University of Newcastle upon Tyne Seminar (1974): Formal Aspects of Computer Science.

[5] Holt, A.W., "Information System Theory Project", Applied Data Research Incorporated, Princeton, New Jersey, (1968).

[6] Holt, A.W., Commoner, F., "Events and Conditions", Applied Data Research, New York, (1970).

[7] Holt, A.W., "The Chinese Menu or the Axioms of Choise", Private Circulation.

[8] Lauer, P.E., Campbell, R.H., "Formal Semantics of High-level Primitives for Co-ordinating Concurrent Processes", Acta Informatica 5, pp.247-332 (1975).

[9] Lauer, P.E., "A Project to investigate a Design technique for Asynchronous Systems of Processes", University of Newcastle upon Tyne, (1975).

[10] Lauer P.E., "Abstract Tree Processors with Networks of state Machines as Control: Their Use in Programming Language Definition", University of Newcastle upon Tyne, Tech. Report Series, 87, also in proceedings of a Colloque sur les Arbres en Algebre et en Programmation, Universite des Science et Techniques de Lille, France. (1976).

[11] Lautenbach, K., "Dual Aspects of Process Co-ordination", GMD St. Augustin, (1974).

[12] Lautenbach, K., Schmid, H.A., "Use of Petri-nets for proving Correctness of Concurrent Process Systems", Information Processing, North-Holland Publishing Company, (1974).

[13] Lautenbach, K., "Exakte Bedingungen der Lebendigkeit für eine klasse von Petri-netzen", Ph.D. Thesis, University of Bonn, (1973).

[14] Lautenbach, K., "Liveness in Petri-nets", Submitted at Conference on Petri-nets and Related Methods, at M.I.T., (1975).

[15] Lipton, R.J., "Reduction: A new Method of Proving Properties of Systems of Processes" ACM Communications, (1975).

[16] Lipton, R.J., "A new Method of Proving Properties of Systems of Processes", Second ACM Symposium on Principles of Programming Languages. Palo Alto, California, (1975).

[17] Cotronis, J.Y., "Proof Methods for Asynchronous Systems of Processes", M.Sc. Thesis, University of Newcastle upon Tyne, (1975).

Acknowledgement

We would like to thank Roy Campbell for his valuable suggestions in our discussions.

E. Morlet and D. Ribbens, (Eds.), International Computing Symposium 1977.

AUTOMATIC DEADLOCK ANALYSIS OF PARALLEL PROGRAMS

Otthein Herzog
Abteilung Informatik
Universität Dortmund
Postfach 500 500
D-4600 Dortmund 50, F. R. G.

A new subclass of Petri nets, the "Control Structure Nets", is defined which contains Petri nets not belonging to known subclasses. The relationship to these subclasses is discussed and necessary and sufficient conditions for liveness are given. Furthermore it is shown how the semantics of the most important control statements of multitasking ("parallel") PL/I programs can be represented by Petri nets. Finally it is discussed how the liveness of Control Structure Nets is related to the absence of deadlocks in multitasking PL/I programs. By checking the Control Structure Nets representing such a program it can be proven at compile-time in polynomial time if this program is deadlock-free.

1. INTRODUCTION

In a programming language like PL/I there exists the facility of "multitasking": it is possible that a program which constitutes itself a task for the operating system may create separate task ("subtasks") which are independently executed, such that it is not possible to determine the relative ordering of the execution.

Programs of this type are also called "parallel programs". Unfortunately there is no syntactical connection between the statement initiating a subtask and the one at which is waited for the completion of this subtask. This gives a great deal of freedom in the design of control structures, but on the other hand mutual blocking ("deadlock") between the tasks of a parallel program may happen and could be only detected at execution-time if this type of error really occured. In order to discover potential deadlocks and other errors in the control structure of parallel programs during compile-time it is necessary to give a mathematical model of the semantics of the control structure and then to check this representation for these faults.

In this paper Petri nets are proposed in order to represent the semantics of the control structure of parallel programs: A new subclass of Petri nets, the Control Structure Nets, is defined which contains Petri nets not belonging to other known subclasses. Necessary and sufficient conditions for liveness are given.

Furthermore it is shown, how the most important PL/I control statements are represented by Petri nets and how the liveness of Control Structure Nets is related to the absence of deadlocks in multitasking PL/I programs. The results mentioned here are given in an informal way. Proofs as well as algorithms can be found in HERZOG /5/. A different approach which is more related to hardware requirements is treated in HERZOG and YOELI /6/.

2. PETRI NETS

The basic definitions of Petri nets are the following ones (PETRI /12/, LAUTENBACH /9/, HACK /3/, YOELI /14/):

Definition 1:

A Petri net $pn = (P,T; Pre,Post)$ consists of

- a finite non-empty set P called places,
- a finite non-empty set T called transitions,
- the relations Pre and Post, where $Pre \subseteq P \times T$, $Post \subseteq T \times P$, and $P \cap T = \emptyset$, and there exist no isolated places and transitions.

As usual, Petri nets are represented as graphs, where circular nodes represent places and square nodes represent transitions. The directed arcs between places and transitions are given by the relation Pre, and between transitions and places by the relation Post.

For a given transition t, every place p with $(p,t) \in Pre$ is called input place of t, and every place p with $(t,p) \in Post$ is called output place of t.

For a given place p, every transition t with $(t,p) \in Post$ is called input transition of p, and every transition t with $(p,t) \in Pre$ is called output transition of p.

The dynamical behaviour of a Petri net is started by an initial marking m_I, where m_I is a mapping from P into the set of nonnegative integers. In the graph, a marking m is represented in a place p by a corresponding number of dots ("tokens").

Definition 2:

A transition t is called enabled iff every input place of t holds at least one token.

If a transition is enabled, it may fire, decreasing the number of tokens on each input place by one and increasing the number of tokens on each output place by one. By the firing of a transition a new marking is defined (see fig. 1).

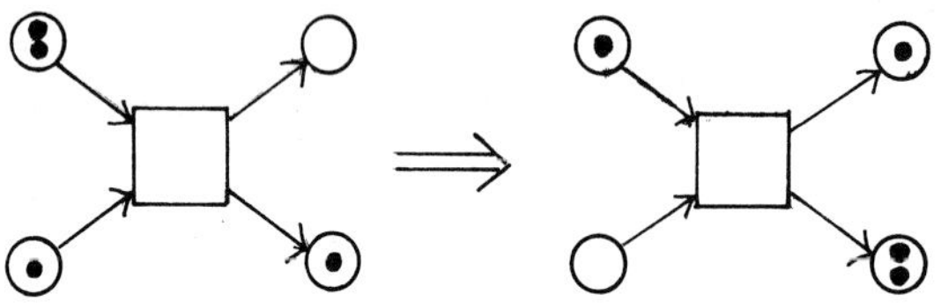

Fig. 1: The firing of a transition

Definition 3:

A marking m_k is called reachable from a marking m_o iff there exist transitions $t_1,\ldots,t_k$ and markings $m_1,\ldots,m_k$, such that the firing of transition t_i produces the marking m_i out of the marking m_{i-1} $(i=1,\ldots,k)$.

In this way the sequencing of processes is represented in a Petri net by some sequence of transition firings.

Definition 4:

Let pn = (p,T;pre,Post) be a Petri net.
A sequence of edges ("se") is defined as any series of edges $se=(e_1,\ldots,e_n)$, where
$e_i = (x_{i-1},x_i)\varepsilon Pre \cup Post$, $i=1,\ldots,n$, and
$x_o \neq x_n, x_o, x_n \varepsilon P$.

A directed path ("pa") is defined as a sequence of edges, where no edge is contained twice.

A directed simple path ("sp") is defined as a directed path where no vertex is contained twice.

A directed circuit ("ct") is defined as a directed path where no vertex except the start vertex is contained twice.

The set of vertices of a path pa is denoted by V(pa).

3. CONTROL STRUCTURE NETS

In this section, the new subclass of Control Structure Nets is defined and some of their properties are discussed. Furthermore the necessary and sufficient conditions for liveness of Control Structure Nets are given (HERZOG /5/, HERZOG and YOELI /6/).

3.1 The definition of Control Structure Nets

Definition 5:

A transition t is called SIGNAL transition ("S-transition") iff
there exist at least two output places of t.

A transition t is called RECEIVE transition ("R-transition") iff
there exist at least two input places of t.

A place p is called DECIDER place ("D-place") iff there exist at least two output transitions of p.

A place p is called UNION place ("U-place") iff there exist at least two input transitions of p.

A place is called START place iff there exists no input transition of p.

A place p is called HALT place iff there exists no output transition of p.

Definition 6:

A Control Structure Net csn = $(P,T;Pre,Post;m_I)$ is defined by

1. (i) P,T,Pre,Post as in definition 1.
   (ii) There exists exactly one START place p_I and at least one HALT place p_F.
   (iii) For every place p there exist the paths $sp_I = (p_I,\ldots,p)$ and $sp_F = (p,\ldots,p_F)$.
2. Under the initial marking m_I the START place is the only marked place and $m_I(p_I)=1$.
3. Let s be a S-transition with the output places p,p', let r be a R-transition with the input places q,q', and let p_F,p_F' be two HALT places.
   (i) Then there exist two directed sequences of edges se and se' ("task paths") where se = (p,...,q) se' = (p',...,q') or se = $(p,\ldots,p_F)$, se' = $(p',\ldots,p'_F)$ and $V(se')\cap V(se') = \emptyset$ (se and se' are said to "belong to s".) or
   (ii) then there exists a R-transition r on a task path and either p or p' is input place of r, where r is the only output transition of p respectively p'. (see fig. 2)
4. Let r be a R-transition with the input places q,q', and let s be a S-transition with the output places p,p'.
   (i) Then there exists a pair of directed simple paths ("simple task paths") sp = (p,...,q), sp' = (p',...,q') or
   (ii) then there exists a task path containing r and there exists a S-transition s which is input transition of an input place of r.

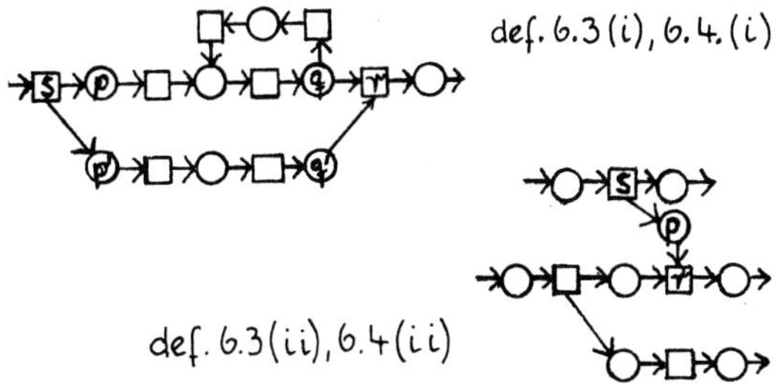

Fig. 2: Examples for definition 6.3 and 6.4

5. Let s be a S-transition with task paths. Then there exists exactly one output place of s at which each main task path starts.

6. Let s be a S-transition with the output places p and p', let $tp_1 = (p,\dots)$, $tp_2 = (p,\dots)$, $tp' = (p',\dots)$ be task paths.

   (i) Let $\bar{s}p = (\bar{p},\dots)$ be a directed simple path and let $\bar{p}$ be a D-place on tp_1; furthermore let $V(\bar{s}p) \cap V(tp_1) = \{\bar{p}\}$ and $V(\bar{s}p) \cap V(tp_2) = \emptyset$ or $\{p\}$.

   Then tp_1 and tp_2 are main task paths and $V(\bar{s}p) \cap V(tp') = \emptyset$

   (ii) Let $\hat{s}p = (\dots,\hat{p})$ be a directed simple path and let $\hat{p}$ be a U-place on tp_1; furthermore let $V(\hat{s}p) \cap V(tp_1) = \{\hat{p}\}$ and $V(\hat{s}p) \cap V(tp_2) = \emptyset$ or $\{\hat{p}\}$.

   Then tp_1 and tp_2 are main task paths and $V(\hat{s}p) \cap V(tp') = \emptyset$.

   (see fig. 3)

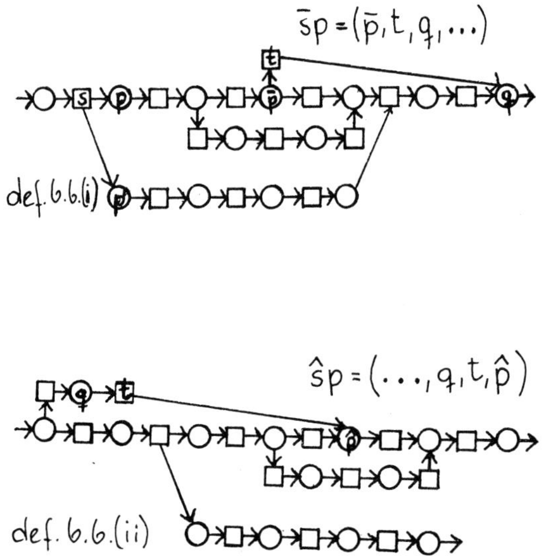

Fig. 3: Example for definition 6.6

The following fig. 4 shows an instance of a Control Structure Net.

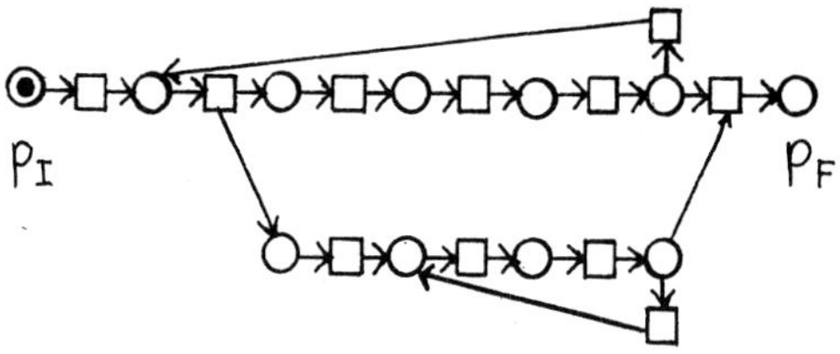

Fig. 4: A Control Structure Net

3.2 The relationship among the known subclasses of Petri nets

Theorem 1:

Let

SM:= {sm | sm is State Machine and sm is not Marked Graph (/3/, /7/)}
MG:= {mg | mg is Marked Graph and mg is not State Machine (/2/, /7/)}
SMMG:= {smmg | smmg is State Machine and Marked Graph}
FCN:= {fcn | fcn is Free Choice Net and fcn∉SM,MG, efcn∉SM,MG,SMMG,FCN (/4/)}
EFCN:= {efcn | efcn is Extended Free Choice Net and efcn∉SM,MG,SMMG,FCN (/4/)}
PNRC:= {pnrc | pnrc is Petri Net with Regulation Circuits and pnrc∉SM,MG,SMMG,FCN,EFCN (/9/)}
SPN:= {spn | spn is Simple Petri Net and spn∉SM,MG, SMMG,FCN,EFCN,PNRC (/1/)}
CSN:= {csn | csn is Control Structure Net (/5/)}
GPN:= {gpn | gpn is General Petri Net without restrictions, gpn∉SM,MG,SMMG,FCN,EFCN,PNRC,SPN}

Then it holds:

1. CSN∩SM,MG,SMMG,FCN,SPN,GPN ≠ ∅
2. CSN∩PNRC = ∅
3. There exist Petri nets pn∈SM,MG,SMMG,FCN,EFCN, SPN,GPN such that pn ∉ CSN.

Fig. 4 shows a Control Structure Net csn, csn∈GPN, csn∉SM, MG, SMMG, FCN, EFCN, PNRC, SPN.

Using the results of HACK/3/ and LAUTENBACH/10/ the following fig. 5 shows the relations among the subclasses of Petri nets.

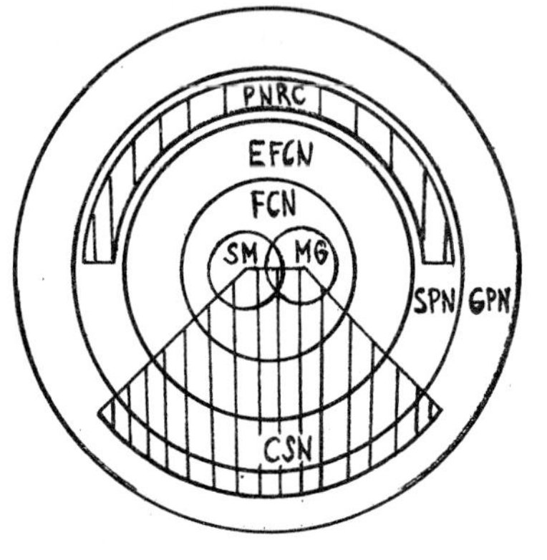

Fig. 5: Relations among the subclasses of Petri nets

3.3 Properties of Control Structure Nets

By definition 7 and 8 two different kinds of directed circuits are distinguished: loops and synchronization circuits (fig. 6 and 7).

Definition 7:

Let csn be a Control Structure Net and $\bar{p},\hat{p}$ places. A directed circuit ct = $(\hat{p},\ldots,\bar{p},\ldots,\hat{p})$ is called loop iff
There exists a U-place $\hat{p}$ and a D-place $\hat{p}$ on ct and if there exist the directed simple paths $sp_I=(p_I,\ldots,\hat{p})$, $sp_F=(\bar{p},\ldots,p_F)$, such that $V(ct)\cap V(sp_I)=\{\hat{p}\}$, $V(ct)\cap V(sp_F)=\{\bar{p}\}$.

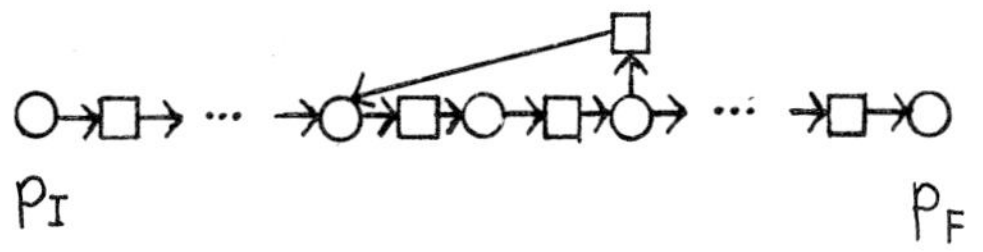

Fig. 6: Example for definition 7

Definition 8:

A directed circuit ct is called synchronization circuit ("sct") iff

(i) there exists a S-transition s, a task path tp belonging to s and a R-transition r with the input places q,q', such that
$q \in V(tp)$, $q \notin V(ct)$
$q' \in V(ct)$, $q' \notin V(ct)$

(ii) there exists a directed simple path $sp_I=(p_I,\ldots,q)$, such that $V(ct)\cap V(sp_I)=\emptyset$.

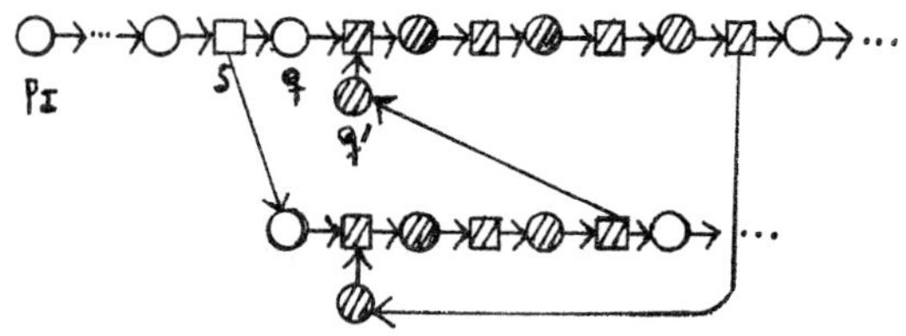

Fig. 7: Example for Definition 8

It is obvious that, in contrast to loops, synchronization circuits like the one in fig. 7 may prevent the firing of R-transitions.

Now alternative directed simple paths are defined. If there exists an alternative simple path asp in respect to a directed simple path sp then there exists a D-place on asp and sp where a token has to "choose" the subsequent subpath ("conflict").

Definition 9:

Let csn be a Control Structure Net and sp=(p,...,p') a directed simple path.
A directed simple path asp=(p,...,p') is called directed alternative simple path in respect to sp iff

(i) there exist a D-place $\bar{p}$ and a U-place $\hat{p}$ on sp and asp,

(ii) there exists a simple directed subpath $(\bar{p},\ldots,\hat{p})$ of asp which is not contained in sp,

(iii) the directed subpath $(p,\ldots,\bar{p})$ and $(\hat{p},\ldots,p')$ are identical for both paths.

ASP_{sp} := {asp | asp is directed alternative simple path in respect to sp} ∪ {sp}

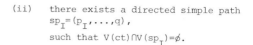

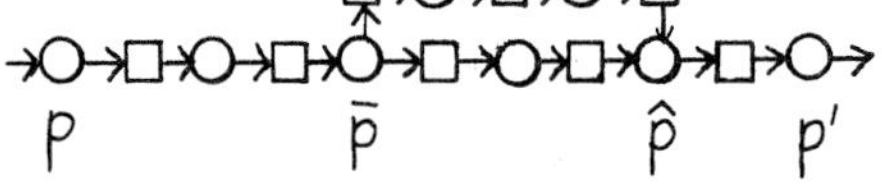

Fig. 8: Example for definition 9

Finally the last definition states the important property of a Control Structure Net, the "liveness" which is very closely related to the absence of deadlocks in parallel programs.

Definition 10:

Let csn = $(P,T;Pre,Post;m_I)$ be a Control Structure Net, let r be a R-transition with an input place q, where there exists either a simple main task path mtp = $(\ldots,q)$ or a task path tp = $(\ldots,q,r,\ldots)$.

A Control Structure Net csn is live iff

for any R-transition r and for any marking m which is reachable from the initial marking and where $m(q) \geq 1$; there exists a marking m' which is reachable from m, such that each input place of r marked under m'.

Now, the four conditions for liveness of a Control Structure Net are given which are expressed only in terms of paths, synchronization circuits and loops. Thus these conditions are independent of the existence of special markings (except the fixed initial marking).

This means that these conditions are only derived from the graph of a Control Structure Net, i.e. from the statical structure of a concurrent system which allows to conclude for a dynamical property like liveness.

The first condition assures liveness if there exist certain alternative paths, the second, if there exist synchronization circuits, and the third and fourth are provided for the case of the existence of loops.

Theorem 2:

Let csn = $(P,T;Pre,Post;m_I)$ be a Control Structure Net, let r be a R-transition with the input places q,q', where there exists either a simple main task path mtp = $(\ldots,q)$ or a task path tp = $(\ldots q,r,\ldots)$.

A Control Structure Net csn is live iff the following four conditions are satisfied:

Condition 1:

For any R-transition r there exists a S-transition s with the output places p,p' and there exist the directed simple paths $sp_I=(p_I,\ldots,s,p,\ldots q)$, $sp_I'=(p_I,\ldots,s,p',\ldots q')$, and for any asp ASP_{sp_I} there exists a S-transition $\underset{\sim}{s}$ on $a\underset{\sim}{s}p$ with an output place $\tilde{p}$ and a task path $\tilde{tp} = (\tilde{p},\ldots q')$, and if there exists a directed simple path $\underset{\sim}{sp} = (\bar{p},\ldots)$ such that $\bar{p}$ is a D-place and $\bar{p} \in V(\tilde{tp})$, then there exists a S-transition s on $\bar{sp}$ with an output place $\tilde{\tilde{p}}$ and a task path $(\tilde{\tilde{p}},\ldots,q')$.

Condition 2:

For every synchronization circuit sct there exists a R-transition r, $r \in V(sct)$ with the input places q,q', where $q \notin V(sct)$, $q' \in V(sct)$, and there exists a S-transition s with the output places p,p' and the simple paths $sp_I=(p_I,\ldots,s,p,\ldots,q)$, $sp_I' = (p_I,\ldots,s,p',\ldots q')$, such that $V(sp_I) \cap V(sct) = \emptyset$, $V(sp_I') \cap V(sct)=\{q'\}$, and for any $asp \in ASP_{sp_I}$ there exists a S-transition $\underset{\sim}{s}$ on $a\underset{\sim}{s}p$ with an output place $\tilde{p}$ and a task path $\tilde{tp} = (\tilde{p},\ldots,q')$, such that $V(\tilde{tp}) \cap V(sct)=\{q'\}$, and if there exists a directed simple path $sp = (\bar{p},\ldots)$, such that $\bar{p}$ is a D-place and $\bar{p} \in V(\tilde{tp})$ then there exists a S-transition $\tilde{\tilde{s}}$ on $\bar{sp}$ with an output place $\tilde{\tilde{p}}$ and a task path $\tilde{\tilde{tp}} = (\tilde{\tilde{p}},\ldots,q')$, where $V(\tilde{\tilde{tp}})\ V(sct) = \{q'\}$.

Condition 3:

For every loop lp and for any R-transition r on lp, and for any input place q of r, there exists a S-transition s on lp with a task path $(p,\ldots,q)$ belonging to s.

Condition 4:

For every loop lp and for any S-transition s on lp and for any task path tp = $(p,\ldots,q)$ belonging to s, which does not meet lp and where $p \neq q$, and for any R-transition r on tp and for any input transition q' of r, $q' \notin V(tp)$, there exists a S-transition s' on lp with a task path tp' = $(p',\ldots,q')$.

4. THE REPRESENTATION OF PARALLEL PROGRAMS BY CONTROL STRUCTURE NETS

In this section it is shown by examples of PL/I control statements (IBM/8/) how the semantics of these statements can be represented by Petri nets. It should be mentioned here that there exist no PL/I statements which perform semaphore operations on event variables.

In general a control statement is modelled as a transition, an input place of which carries the label of this statement.

The flow of control through a parallel program is represented by the flow of tokens in the corresponding Petri net.

- The start of a parallel program is represented by a START place followed by a transition (fig. 9 (i)),

the end as a HALT place (fig.9(ii)).

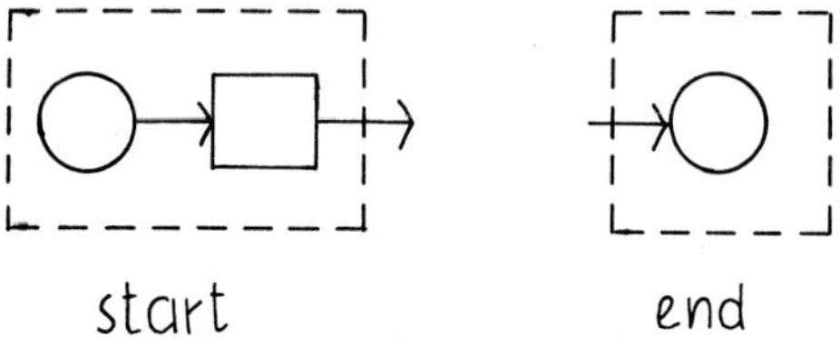

Fig. 9: Representation of start and end of a program

- The GOTO statement is represented as a place followed by a "simple" transition. The output place of this transition is the place carrying the label denoted by the GOTO statement (fig.1o).

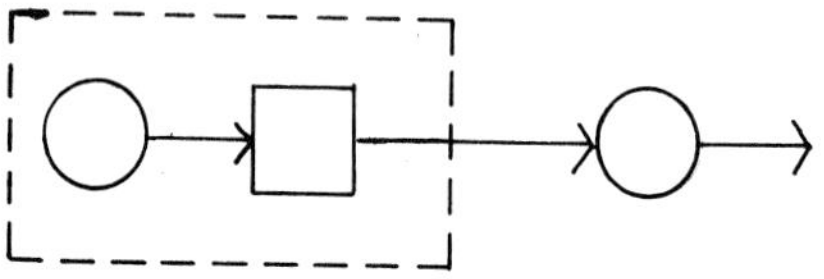

Fig. 1o: Representation of the GOTO statement

- At the execution of an IF statement the value of a logical expression is checked and according to the result of the test, either a sequence of statements a_1 or another one, a_2, is executed. This is modelled in the Petri net as shown in fig. 11, where the transitions a_1 resp. a_2 represent the two sequences of statements.

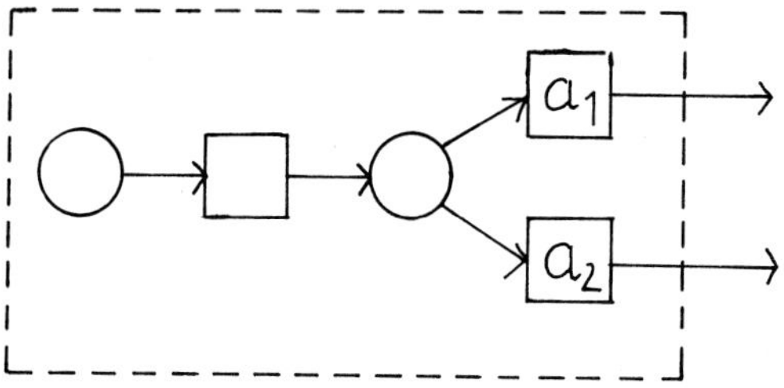

Fig. 11: Representation of the IF statement

- By a CALL statement with EVENT, PRIORITY or TASK option or by a READ, WRITE, DELETE or REWRITE statement with EVENT option, a separate flow of control for the initiated subtask is established. This is represented by a S-transition s (fig.12).

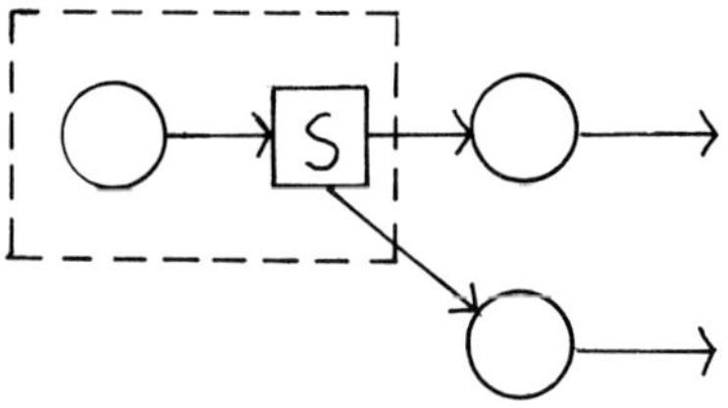

Fig. 12: Representation of the call of a subtask

- When a WAIT statement is reached during execution of a task, the execution of this task will be delayed until the event variables specified in the WAIT statement will have the value '1' B. This statement is represented by a R-transition (fig.13). The input place p_o represents the label of this statement whereas the input places $p_1, \ldots, p_k$ represent k specified event variables.

The transition can only fire if it is reached by the control flow (p_o is marked) and if all the event variables are set to '1' B ($p_1, \ldots p_k$ are marked).

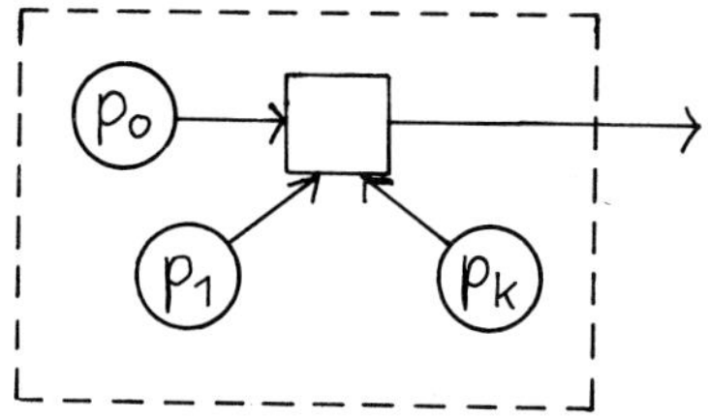

Fig. 13: Representation of the WAIT statement

- The value assignment to event variables assigned to subtasks by the EVENT option is modelled as shown in fig. 14(i): The event variable is represented by the last place of the subtask. The representation of a COMPLETION statement setting the value of an event variable to '1' B is given in fig. 14(ii).

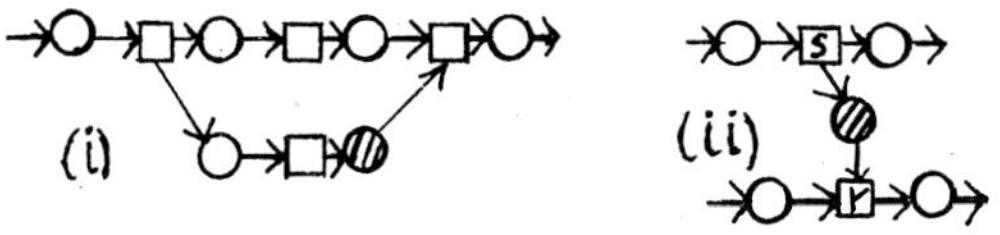

Fig. 14: The representation of value assignment to event variables

Every control statement not mentioned here is representable by a combination of the given ones. Fig. 15 shows the representation of the following multitasking PL/I program:

```
P: PROCEDURE OPTIONS(MAIN);
   DECLARE (EV1, EV2) EVENT;
   SUB: PROCEDURE;
        .
        .
        .
   S1:  WAIT(EV2);
        :
   END SUB;
        :
M1:IF p THEN M2:CALL SUBTASK EVENT(EV1);
M3:...
   :
M4:COMPLETION(EV2) = '1'B
   :
M5:WAIT(EV1);
   :
END P;
```

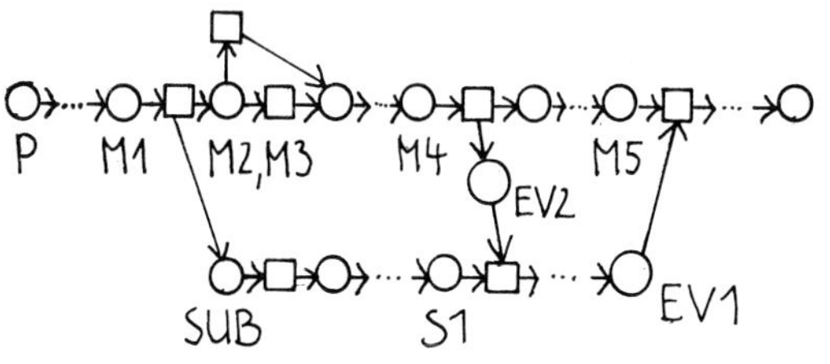

Fig. 15: Representation of the PL/I program above

On the background of parallel programs the definitions of section 3 can be explained now: Definition 6.1 and 6.2 clearly reflects that a parallel program has exactly one start and perhaps several exits in different tasks.

In definition 6.3 and 6.4 it is stated that there exist task execution paths (the "task paths") of a task calling a subtask and of the subtask which have no statements in common. The second case could be that a S-transition represents a COMPLETION statement.

By definition 6.5 it is required that the calling task ("main task") continues after the initiation of the subtask and by definition 6.6, GOTO's from one task into another one are forbidden.

Clearly the loops of definition 7 correspond to programs loops, and the synchronization circuits model the awkward business that the assignment of '1'B to an event variable specified in a WAIT statement can only be reached if this WAIT statement is already succesfully executed.

By alternative simple paths in definition 9 the conditional jump is covered and by definition 10 it is required that every event variable specified in a WAIT statement must get the value '1'B, when the control has reached this WAIT statement.

Condition 1 of THEOREM 2 can be explained as follows: For each execution path of a multitasking program leading to the control input of a R-transition, the event variable inputs of this R-transition must receive a token by a preceding completion of a task or by a COMPLETION statement.

The condition 2 states about the same for one R-transition on a synchronization circuit, but in addition the paths leading to this R-transition must be disjoint to this circuit.

The conditions 3 and 4 have no equivalent in multitasking PL/I programs as they are obtained by the fact that the test of a place representing an event variable removes the token from it. On the contrary the test of an event variable in a program does not destroy the value.

Hence the checking of a multitasking PL/I program for deadlocks can be done as follows:

The control statements of the program have to be translated into a Petri net according to the given representations.

In the case that there results a Petri net which does not happen to be a Control Structure Net, the places and transitions which cannot be reached from the START place (because of unconditional jumps) have to be removed in order to assure connectedness (definition 6.1 (iii)). The same has to be done with outgoing arcs of transitions representing GOTO's from one task into another one. Then the resulting net will be a Control Structure Net which has to be checked only for conditions 1 and 2 of theorem 2. As there exist algorithms (READ and TARJAN/13/) which allow to find an elementary circuit or a simple path in a graph within the time O(m+n), where m is the number of vertices and n the number of edges, it has been possible to develop algorithms working in polynominal time (HERZOG/5/).

If the conditions 1 and 2 of THEOREM 2 are satisfied it is proven at compile-time that the checked program is deadlock-free. If one of the conditions fails to be fulfilled, it can be stated only, that there exists an interpretation of the Control Structure Net which leads to a deadlock. This is caused by the data dependence of tests which are not incorporated in the Petri net model. Nevertheless this proposed approach seems to be a step toward automatic proving the semantics of parallel programs.

5. REFERENCES

/1/ COMMONER, F.: Deadlocks in Petri Nets.- Applied Data Research Inc., CA - 72o6 - 2311 (1972)

/2/ GENRICH, H.J., LAUTENBACH, K.: Synchronisationsgraphen.- Acta Informatica 2 (1973), p. 143 - 161

/3/ HACK, M.T.: Analysis of Production Schemata by Petri Nets.- M.I.T. Project MAC, TR - 94 (1972)

/4/ HACK, M.H.T.: Extended State-Machine allocatable Nets (ESMA), an Extension of Free Choice Petri Nets Results.- M.I.T. Project MAC, Computation Structure Group Memo 78 - 1 (1974)

/5/ HERZOG, O.: Zur Analyse der Kontrollstruktur von parallelen Programmen mit Hilfe von Petri-Netzen.- Abteilung Informatik, Universität Dortmund, Bericht Nr. 24/76 (1976)

/6/ HERZOG,O., YOELI,M.: Control Nets for Asynchronous Systems, Part 1.- Technion - Israel Institute of Technology, Computer Science Department, TR - 74 (May 1976)

/7/ HOLT, A.W., COMMONER, F.: Events and Conditions.- Applied Data Research Inc., New York (197o)

/8/ IBM: OS PL/I Checkout and Optimizing Compilers: Language Reference Manual.- GC 33-ooo9-3 (1974)

/9/ LAUTENBACH, K.: Exakte Bedingungen der Lebendigkeit für eine Klasse von Petri-Netzen.- Berichte der Gesellschaft für Mathematik und Datenverarbeitung Nr. 82 (1973)

/1o/ LAUTENBACH, K.: Lebendigkeit in Petri-Netzen.- Gesellschaft für Mathematik und Datenverarbeitung, Institut für Informationssystemforschung, Internal Report o2/74-4-1 (1975)

/11/ ORE, O.: Theory of Graphs.- Providence (1962)

/12/ PETRI, C.A.: Concepts of Net Theory.- In: Proceedings of Symposium and Summer School "Mathematical Foundations of Computer Science", High Tatras, Sept. 3-8, 1973, p. 137 - 146

/13/ READ, R.C., TARJAN, R.E.: Bounds on Backtrack Algorithms for Listing Cycles, Paths, and Spanning Trees.- Networks 5 (1975), p. 237 - 252

/14/ YOELI, M.: Petri Nets and asynchronous Control Networks.- University of Waterloo, Ontario, Res. Report CS-73-o7 (1973)

E. Morlet and D. Ribbens, (Eds.), International Computing Symposium 1977.

USING AUXILIARY VARIABLES IN PARALLEL PROGRAMS VERIFICATION

R. DEVILLERS and G. LOUCHARD

Université Libre de Bruxelles, Faculté des Sciences,
Laboratoire d'Informatique Théorique, Bruxelles, Belgium

The need for formal proofs is much more crucial for parallel processes than for sequential ones. In this connection, S. Owicki has developed an interesting method for proving partial correctness of parallel programs. The same technique may also be used to exhibit the behaviour characteristics of non-terminating processes.
In this paper, we check this technique's efficiency by applying it to a problem we already used to compare various synchronisation techniques. That enables us to analyse the power of the method. We also make some comments on its applicability and some suggestions for future work.

1. INTRODUCTION
OWICKI'S AXIOMATIC PROOF TECHNIQUES

While the interest of correctness proofs for sequential programs has long been recognised, the need for such proofs for parallel programs is even much more crucial. Indeed, if several processes are executed in parallel, their results can depend on the unpredictable order in which actions from different processes are executed, and then the mistakes may not be detected during program testing, since the particular interactions in which the errors are exhibited may not occur.
In this connection, S. Owicki has developed in her thesis [1] (see also [2] and [3]) an interesting axiomatic technique for proving partial correctness of parallel programs. She uses a generalisation of Hoare's sequential deductive system [4], based on the same simple algol-like language plus two special statements for parallel processing:
parallel execution:

$\underline{\text{cobegin}}\ S_1//S_2//\ \ldots\ //S_n\ \underline{\text{coend}}$

which starts the parallel execution of S_1, S_2, ... and S_n

and synchronisation:

$\underline{\text{await}}\ B\ \underline{\text{then}}\ S$

where the evaluation(s) of the Boolean expression B and - when B is or becomes true - the execution of the (purely sequential) statement S are indivisible operations.

The axioms and inference rules for this language, GPL, are then

A0 consequence:

$$\frac{\{P'\}\ S\ \{Q'\},\ P \vdash P'\ ,\ Q' \vdash Q}{\{P\}\ S\ \{Q\}}$$

A1 assignment:

$\{P^x_E\}\ x:=E\ \{P\}$

A2 null:

$\{P\}\ ;\ \{P\}$

A3 composition:

$$\frac{\{P_1\}\ S_1\ \{P_2\},\{P_2\}\ S_2\ \{P_3\},\ldots,\{P_n\}\ S_n\ \{P_{n+1}\}}{\{P_1\}\ \underline{\text{begin}}\ S_1;\ldots;S_n\ \underline{\text{end}}\ \{P_{n+1}\}}$$

A4 alternation:

$$\frac{\{P \wedge B\}\ S_1\ \{Q\},\{P \wedge \neg B\}\ S_2\ \{Q\}}{\{P\}\ \underline{\text{if}}\ B\ \underline{\text{then}}\ S_1\ \underline{\text{else}}\ S_2\ \{Q\}}$$

A5 iteration:

$$\frac{\{P \wedge B\}\ \ S\ \ \{P\}}{\{P\}\ \underline{\text{while}}\ B\ \underline{\text{do}}\ S\ \{P \wedge \neg B\}}$$

A6 synchronisation:

$$\frac{\{P \wedge B\}\ S\ \{Q\}}{\{P\}\ \underline{\text{await}}\ B\ \underline{\text{then}}\ S\ \{Q\}}$$

A7 parallel:

$$\frac{\{P_1\}\ S_1\ \{Q_1\},\ldots,\{P_n\}\ S_n\ \{Q_n\}}{\{P_1 \wedge\ldots\wedge P_n\}\ \underline{\text{cobegin}}\ S_1//\ldots//S_n\ \underline{\text{coend}}\{Q_1 \wedge\ldots\wedge Q_n\}}$$

provided $\{P_1\}\ S_1\ \{Q_1\},\ldots,\{P_n\}\ S_n\ \{Q_n\}$ are "interference-free"

The main point in this schema is that the "interference-free" property does not concern the dynamic behaviour of the execution but the static properties of the proof. Its precise definition is:

for each component T of S_i and each assignment or $\underline{\text{await}}$ statement T' of S_j $(i \neq j)$, where neither T nor T' is a proper component of an $\underline{\text{await}}$ statement, $\{pre_i(T) \wedge pre_j(T')\}\ T'\ \{pre_i(T)\}$ and $\{Q_i \wedge pre_j(T')\}\ T^j\{Q_i\}$ can be proved,
i.e. T' does not interfere with the proof of $\{P_i\}\ S_i\ \{Q_i\}$ (determined by its pre- and post-condition functions).

In fact, a supplementary condition has to be realised in order to apply these rules:

the assignments and the evaluations of a Boolean in a $\underline{\text{if}}$ or $\underline{\text{while}}$ must be indivisible or, what is generally more realistic, if memory reference is indivisible and if they are not part of a $\underline{\text{await}}$ statement, they must each contain at most one reference to a shared variable (it is always possible to split the state-statements in order to do that).

When devising a proof for a parallel program, it is sometimes necessary to augment artificially the program by introducing "auxiliary variables", i.e. variables which only appear in assignment statements with an auxiliary variable as left side.
These auxiliary variables do not affect the flow of control or the values of the other variables but they may occur in the proofs, i.e. in the pre- and post- conditions. Then, to get back to the original program, a new axiom is necessary

A8: $\dfrac{\{P\}\ S'\ \{Q\}}{\{P\}\ S\ \{Q\}}$

where S is a "reduction" of S' with respect to a set AV of auxiliary variables
and P and Q do not contain free variables from AV
i.e. S is deduced from S' either by
- suppressing an assignment "x:=E", where x∈AV
- replacing a "begin S end" by "S"
- or replacing an "await true then x:=E" by "x:=E", provided the condition mentioned about assignments is verified.

Owicki also translated her schema in the context of a more structured language, RPL, very similar to the conditional critical sections of Hoare [5] and Hansen [6].
In RPL, synchronisation is given by statements

with r when B do S

where r is a "resource", collection of variables which may be used in B and S (in conjunction with "local variables" and "resource variables" protected by another with); execution of S can only begin if B is true and no other process executes a critical section for the same resource.
In this context, the induction rules A6 and A7 are modified to give

A6' critical section:

$$\frac{\{P \wedge B \wedge I(r)\}\ S\ \{Q \wedge I(r)\}}{\{P\}\ \underline{\text{with}}\ r\ \underline{\text{when}}\ B\ \underline{\text{do}}\ S\ \{Q\}}$$

A7' parallel:

$$\frac{\forall 1 \leq i \leq n:\ \{P_i\}\ S_i\ \{Q_i\}\ \text{is "Einmischungsfrei"}}{\{P_1 \wedge \ldots \wedge P_n \wedge I(r_1) \wedge \ldots \wedge I(r_m)\}}$$

$\underline{\text{resource}}\ r_1(\ ),\ \ldots,\ r_m(\ ):$

$\underline{\text{cobegin}}\ S_1 // \ldots // S_n\ \underline{\text{coend}}$

$\{Q_1 \wedge \ldots \wedge Q_n \wedge I(r_1) \wedge \ldots \wedge I(r_m)\}$

where Einmischungsfreiness informally means that
- $I(r_j)$ contains only variables of r_j and variables which are not changed in the parallel statement which declares the resource
- if {P'} T {Q'} is a line in the proof of the parallel statement, all free variables in P' and Q' are

either unchanged in the parallel statement
or local to the process containing T
or protected by a critical section.

The reduction process has also to be slightly modified.

As already noted by Owicki and by Gries [7], these techniques, and especially the introduction of auxiliary variables (which typically record the history of the processes), may be very useful not only to prove the "result" of a parallel program but also to exhibit its behaviour, even if it is non-terminating.
We have tried to apply these techniques to a rather intricate problem we treated in a precedent paper [8].

2. THE PROBLEM

The problem we considered in [8] concerns a policy for sharing a finite buffer between several groups of producers-consumers, where the consumers of a group may only treat the messages created by the producers of the same group.
In order to avoid the messy behaviour where slow consumers of a group cause the invasion of the buffer by messages from their producers, and hence block the work of the other groups, it is decided that
- for each group, a certain number of frames (the identity of which is not fixed) is reserved, which is supposed to be adequate for a normal workload
- the residual frames may be used as a common pool, ready to absorb the production peaks of the various groups.

Buffer of Nb frames:

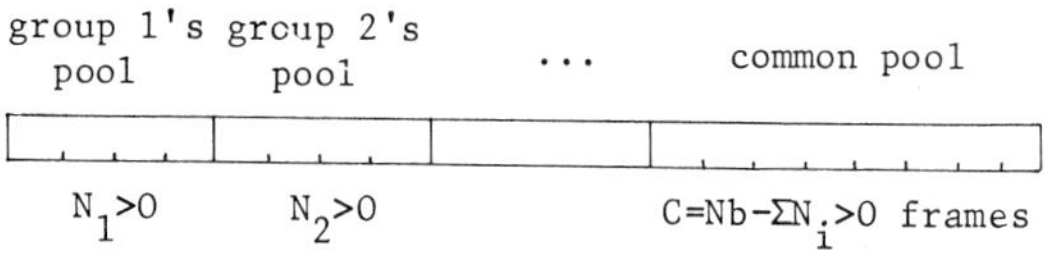

Dijkstra, who introduced this problem in [9], devised a rather simple solution but the details of its behaviour were not entirely satisfactory. Then, we tried to improve the parallelism, to discharge the processes of administrative work and to compare in this context various synchronisation methods. We derived four solutions, using respectively conditional critical sections, semaphores, path expressions and monitors; we also gave hints in order to convince the reader of the adequacy of the solutions.
We shall here construct the proof for two of them in the light of Owicki's method. The other two may be treated similarly but it would be too lengthy to include them here.

3. CONDITIONAL CRITICAL SECTIONS

With slight modifications in order to conform the program to Owicki's notations, this first solution is:

```
begin integer f; integer array N, m[1:n];
      initialise f to C, N[i] to N_i
            and m[i] to 0;
      resource r[1](m[1]),...,r[n](m[n]),rc(f):
      cobegin...//each producer of each group
                //each consumer of each group
                //...coend
end
```

where the program of a consumer of group i is:

```
while true do
begin with r[i] when m[i]>0 do
  begin pick up a full frame of type i;
        collect the message from the frame;
        release the frame;
        m[i]:=m[i]-1;
        if m[i]≥N[i] then with rc do f:=f+1
  end;
  consumption of the message
end
```

and the program of a producer of group i is:

```
while true do
begin production of a message;
  with r[i] and rc when m[i]<N[i]∨f>0 do
    begin if m[i]≥N[i] then f:=f-1;
          m[i]:=m[i]+1;
          pick up a free frame;
          place the message in the frame;
          attach the frame
    end
end
```

Some remarks are in order:

(i) Producers and consumers are non terminating processes; this is not annoying because what interests us here is the behaviour of the processes (their cooperation), and not the value of the variables at the end.

(ii) We have used here a slight extension of the original with when statement since we accept synchronisations concerning several resources simultaneously; this is not a hard problem; a statement "with r_1 and r_2...and r_p when B do S" can be translated in GPL very similarly to a simple with:

```
begin await B∧¬ busyr_1∧¬ busyr_2 ∧...∧¬ busyr_p
  then busyr_1:=busyr_2:=...:=busyr_p:=true;
  S;
  await true then
  busyr_1:=busyr_2:=...:=busyr_p:=false
end
```

where $busyr_i$ is a new variable (initially false) associated to resource r_i.

(iii) Informally, m[i] counts the number of existing group i's messages and f counts the number of free frames in the common pool. We want to prove about this program assertions like:

$$\sum_i (m[i]-N[i])_+ \leqslant C$$

(where $(x)_+$ means $\max\{x,0\}$)

meaning that the number of frames from the common pool attributed to the various groups never exceeds C, the dimension of this common pool;
such an invariant is not of the form $I(r_1)\wedge I(r_2)\wedge\ldots\wedge I(r_m)$, as required by the axioms A6' and A7'; hence it does not seem possible to use the RPL version of Owicki's method, unless we extend it, which does not seem that easy; fortunately, it will not be very difficult to prove such assertions by returning to the original GPL formulation.

(iiii) In order to shed light on the behaviour of the program, we shall introduce some auxiliary variables:

- λ will count the number of free frames in the buffer,
- mp[i] will represent the same quantity as m[i], except in its critical section when manipulations are made on m[i].

The solution with its proof outline then appears, with the invariant

$$I=\{f+\sum_k(mp[k]-N[k])_+=C\wedge\lambda=f+\sum_k(N[k]-mp[k])_+\wedge f\geqslant 0\wedge\lambda\geqslant 0$$
$$\wedge\forall k:(mp[k]\geqslant m[k]\geqslant 0)\wedge(\neg busy[k]\vdash m[k]=mp[k])\}$$

```
begin integer f,λ;integer array N,m,mp[1:n];
      Boolean busyf;
      Boolean array busy[1:n];
      initialise f to C, λ to Nb, N[i] to N_i,
            m[i] and mp[i] to 0,
            busyf and busy[i] to false;
      {I∧¬ busyf∧f>0∧(∀k:m[k]=0∧¬ busy[k])}(3.1)
      cobegin...//each producer of each group
                //each consumer of each group
                //...coend
end
```

consumer of group i:

```
integer inter;
{I} while true do
{I} begin {I} await ¬ busy[i]∧m[i]>0 then
              {I∧¬ busy[i]∧m[i]=mp[i]∧m[i]>0}
              busy[i]:=true;
      {I∧m[i]>0∧m[i]=mp[i]∧busy[i]}
      pick up a full frame of type i;
      collect the message from the frame;
      release the frame;
      inter:=m[i]-1;
      {I∧m[i]>0∧m[i]=mp[i]∧busy[i]
        ∧inter=m[i]-1}
      m[i]:=inter;
      {I∧m[i]=mp[i]-1∧busy[i]}
      if m[i]≥N[i]
      then begin
            {I∧m[i]=mp[i]-1∧m[i]≥N[i]∧busy[i]}
            await ¬ busyf then busyf :=true;
            {I∧m[i]=mp[i]-1∧m[i]≥N[i]
              ∧busy[i]∧busyf}
            inter:=f+1;
            {I∧m[i]=mp[i]-1∧m[i]≥N[i]
              ∧busy[i]∧busyf∧inter:=f+1}
            await true then begin f:=inter;
                   λ:=λ+1;mp[i]:=mp[i]-1 end;
            {I∧m[i]=mp[i]∧m[i]≥N[i]∧f>0
              ∧busy[i]∧busyf}                    (3.2)
```

```
            busyf:=false
          end
      else {I∧m[i]=mp[i]-1∧m[i]<N[i]∧busy[i]}
        await true then begin λ:=λ+1;
                              mp[i]:=mp[i]-1 end
        {I∧m[i]=mp[i]∧m[i]<N[i]∧busy[i]};(3.3)
      {I∧m[i]=mp[i]∧busy[i]}
      busy[i]:=false
{I} end
{false}
```

producer of group i:

```
integer inter;
{I} while true do
{I} begin {I} production of a message;
     {I} await ¬ busy[i]∧¬ busyf
               ∧(m[i]<N[i]∨f>0) then
     {I∧¬ busy[i]∧m[i]=mp[i]∧(m[i]<N[i]∨f>0)
       ∧¬ busyf} busy[i]:=busyf:=true;
     {I∧m[i]=mp[i]∧(m[i]<N[i]∨f>0)
       ∧busy[i]∧busyf}
     if m[i]≥N[i]
     then begin
            {I∧m[i]=mp[i]∧f>0∧busy[i]∧busyf}
            inter:=f-1;
            {I∧m[i]=mp[i]∧f>0∧inter=f-1
              ∧busy[i]∧busyf}
            await true then beginf:=inter;
                  mp[i]=mp[i]+1;λ:=λ-1 end
            {I∧m[i]=mp[i]-1∧mp[i]>0
              ∧busy[i]∧busyf}
          end
     else
       {I∧m[i]=mp[i]∧m[i]<N[i]∧busy[i]∧busyf}
       await true then begin mp[i]:=mp[i]+1;
                             λ:=λ-1 end
       {I∧m[i]=mp[i]-1∧mp[i]>0∧busy[i]∧busyf};
     {I∧m[i]=mp[i]-1∧mp[i]>0∧busy[i]∧busyf}
     inter:=m[i]+1;
     {I∧m[i]=mp[i]-1∧inter=mp[i]∧mp[i]>0
       ∧busy[i]∧busyf}
     m[i]:=inter;
     {I∧m[i]=mp[i]∧m[i]>0∧busy[i]∧busyf}  (3.4)
     pick up a free frame;
     place the message in the frame;
     attach the frame;
     {I∧m[i]=mp[i]∧m[i]>0∧busy[i]∧busyf}
     await true then busy[i]:=busyf:=false
{I} end
{false}
```

Interference-freeness is very easy to check; indeed, one can use a particular result of Owicki who shows that if two parallel statements are protected by what would correspond to critical sections for a same resource, it is always possible to add auxiliary variables such that their pre- and post- conditions become incompatible; these auxiliary variables are in fact simply indicators for the various critical sections activity. As the assertions only use the invariant I and protected variables, there is no problem.

The invariant shows that

there is never overflow of the common pool:

$$\sum_k (m[k]-N[k])_+ \leq C$$

nor overflow of the total buffer:

$$\lambda \geq 0$$

nor underflow of the private pool:

$$m[k] \geq 0$$

no frame is "lost"

as $f+\sum_k (mp[k]-N[k])_+ = C$

and $mp[k]=m[k]$

outside its critical sections.

Another important point to examine about parallel programs is the possibility of deadlock; in this connection, Owicki and Gries devised a sufficient condition for non blocking:
if S is a statement which contains the await and cobegin statements

A_j: <u>await</u> B_j <u>then</u> ...

T_k: <u>cobegin</u> $S_1^k // \ldots // S_{n_k}^k$ <u>coend</u>

not occuring in another cobegin statement, then, if we define

$$D(S)=[\bigvee_j (pre(A_j) \wedge \neg B_j)] \vee [\bigvee_k (\bigwedge_i [post(S_i^k) \vee D(S_i^k)] \wedge [\bigvee_i D(S_i^k)])],$$

D(S) = false implies that no complete blocking may occur.
Unfortunately, this test is only concerned with complete blocking (where no progress is allowed at all for the active processes) and not partial (but permanent) blocking. In our case, taking into account the possibility of adding the indicator auxiliary variables already mentioned, one gets

$$D(\text{our program})=\{I \wedge \neg busyf \wedge f=0 \wedge (\forall k: \neg busy[k] \wedge m[k]=0 \wedge m[k] \geq N[k])\}$$

which is trivially false if there is at least one frame in the buffer.
That means that, if the buffer is not void, either a consumer or a producer can work.

This property is rather weak but a better information can be (informally) obtained from the assertions of the proof about the harmonious cooperation of the processes inside each group. Indeed,

- when entering the cobegin statement, the precondition (3.1) shows that if $N[k]>0$, as we assumed, we have $\forall k$: $m[k]<N[k]$ and at least one producer of each group may start; even if it is not the case, as $f>0$ at least one producer may start;
- when a producer of group i ends its work, the assertion (3.4) shows that $m[i]>0$, so that a consumer of the same group may start;
- when a consumer of group i ends its work, the assertions (3.2) and (3.3) show that

  $$m[i] \geq N[i] \wedge f>0$$

  so that a consumer of the same group and another producer may start

```
or
  m[i]<N[i]
```

so that a producer of the same group may start.

We have supposed here that memory references were the only indivisible operations, besides the await statements. We then had to split the original assignments "m[i]:=m[i]±1" and "f:=f±1", with the introduction of the intermediate variable "inter", in order to have at most one reference to a shared variable.

4. PATH EXPRESSIONS

The next solution we shall examine uses the path expression technique of Campbell and Habermann [10]:

```
declarations:
  type frame; ...
  endtype;
  type sharedpool;
variables:
  queue L; queue array P[1:n];
  integer f; integer array m,N,w,fg[1:n];
paths:
  path return,detach end;
  path add1f,distr end;
  path{(eadd1f,add1w);cdistr} end;
  path{signal;cadd1f} end;
  path sub1-i,add1-i end;                  \
  path attach-i,pick-i end;                 |
  path {cattach-i;cpick-i} end;             |
  path test-i,distr-i,test2-i end;          >  i=1,2,...,n
  path {signal-i;cdistr-i} end;             |
  path {(sub1fg-i,sub1w-i);cadd1-i} end;   /
operations:
  procedure cpick-i(fullframe);
            pick-i(fullframe);
  procedure pick-i(fullframe);
            fullframe:=full frame of P[i];
  procedure cattach-i(fullframe);
            attach-i(fullframe);
  procedure attach-i(fullframe);
            P[i]:=P[i]vfullframe;
  procedure return(freeframe);L:=Lvfreeframe;
  procedure detach(freeframe);
            freeframe:=free frame of L;
  procedure cadd1-i;add1-i;
  procedure add1-i;m[i]:=m[i]+1;
  procedure sub1-i;
            begin m[i]:=m[i]-1;
                  if m[i]≥N[i] then signal
                  else signal-i end;
  procedure signal;null;
  procedure signal-i;null;
  procedure cadd1f;add1f;
  procedure add1f;begin f:=f+1;eadd1f end;
  procedure eadd1f;null;
  procedure cdistr;distr;
  procedure distr;if f>0 then
            begin integer j;j:=0;
                  for j:=j+1 while f>0∧j≤n
                      do test2-j
            end;
  procedure test2-i;while w[i]>0 and f>0 do
                  begin f:=f-1;
                        sub1w-i
                  end;
  procedure cdistr-i;distr-i;
  procedure distr-i;
            if w[i]=0 then fg[i]:=fg[i]+1
                      else sub1w-i;
  procedure sub1w-i;w[i]:=w[i]-1;
  procedure add1w(i);w[i]:=w[i]+1;
  procedure test-i;if fg[i]>0 then sub1fg-i
                               else add1w(i);
  procedure sub1fg-i;fg[i]:=fg[i]-1;
initialisation:
  initialise L to the whole buffer
             P[i] to a void queue
             m[i] and w[i] to 0
             fg[i] and N[i] to N_i
         and f to C
  endtype;
program:
  sharedpool B,
  cobegin ...//each producer of each group
             //each consumer of each group//...
             //while true do cadd1f
             //while true do cdistr-i
             //while true do cdistr
  coend
where
Consumer of group i:
  while true do
  begin frame fram;
    B.cpick-i(fram);
    collect the message from fram;
    B.return(fram);
    B.sub1-i;
    consumption of the message
  end;
Producer of group i:
  while true do
  begin frame fram;
    production of a message;
    B.test-i;
    B.cadd1-i;
    B.detach(fram);
    place the message in fram;
    B.cattach-i(fram)
  end;
```

This algorithm may seem quite complicated; one can find the details of its elaboration in [8]. Let us simply mention that:

- L is the queue of the free frames of the buffer,
- P[i] is the queue of the frames used by group i's processes,
- w[i] is the number of waiting producers of group i,
- fg[i] counts the number of free frames in group i's pool;

some of the procedures have been artificially introduced in order to respect the restriction that a procedure may appear in at most one path; the other ones handle the queues and distribute the frames.

It should be highly interesting to dispose of a

direct translation of Owicki's technique in the context of the synchronisation paths (an attempt to apply Hoare's methods for data types to path expressions may be found in [11]) but we have again chosen to go back to the GPL formalism. Some of the translation rules are:

when <u>path</u> $p_1, p_2, \ldots, p_m$ <u>end</u>

  p_i becomes <u>await</u> ¬ busy <u>then</u> busy:=<u>true</u>;
    p_i;
    busy:=<u>false</u>

  where busy is initialised to false

when <u>path</u> $p_1; p_2; \ldots; p_m$ <u>end</u>

  p_i becomes <u>await</u> sp_i <u>then</u> (if i>1)
    p_i;
    sp_{i+1}:=<u>true</u> (if i<m)

  where the sp_i are initialised to false

when <u>path</u> $\{p_1; p_2; \ldots; p_m\}$ <u>end</u>

  p_i becomes <u>await</u> $ns_i>0$ <u>then</u>
      $ns_i:=ns_i-1$; (if i>1)
    p_i,
    <u>await</u> <u>true</u> <u>then</u>
    $ns_{i+1}:=ns_{i+1}+1$ (if i<m)

  where the ns_i are initialised to 0

Moreover, one can reinsert the artificial procedures in their calling processes.

Then, an interesting phenomenon occured, which shows again that formal proofs may be much more profitable than simple informal hints for proof. Indeed, while we have showed in [8] that the general behaviour of the program was correct, some particular aspects of this behaviour arised when we tried to apply Owicki's method to it, which were not required and appeared troublesome. More precisely, we wanted to show as in §3 that $f+\sum_k(mp[k]-N[k])_+=C$, with mp[k] near m[k] and $(N[k]-mp[k])_+$ near fg[k], being equal most of the time; and we failed. Two possibilities were then open: either we did not introduce the "good" auxiliary variables or the property was false. In fact, the latter was true: if the distributing processes have granted more than N_i frames to group i but if most of the producers of this group do not enter quickly caddl-i after test-i, when their consumers will return a frame, they will see that m[i]<N[i] (and not that fg[i]=0) and will thus return the frames to the private pool instead of the common pool; a group may thus unduly block some frames from the common pool.
The problem arises from a discrepancy between m and fg; the solution we chose then was to replace them by a common variable (of course the level of parallelism is slightly restricted). The program is now:

```
Declaration:
  type frame; ...
  endtype;
  type sharedpool;
variables:
  queue L; queue array P[1:n];
  integer f;integer array m,N,w[1:n];
paths:
  path return, detach end;
  path add1f,distr end;
  path {(eadd1f,add1w);cdistr} end;
  path {signal;cadd1f} end;
  path attach-i,pick-i end;                 )
  path {cattach-i;cpick-i} end;             ) i=1,...,n
  path test-i,distr-i,test2-i end;          )
  path {(add1-i,sub1w-i);go-i} end;         )
operations:
  procedure cpick-i(fullframe);
            pick-i(fullframe);
  procedure pick-i(fullframe);
            fullframe:=full frame of P[i];
  procedure cattach-i(fullframe);
            attach-i(fullframe);
  procedure attach-i(fullframe);
            P[i]:=P[i]vfullframe;
  procedure return(freeframe);L:=Lvfreeframe;
  procedure detach(freeframe);
            freeframe:=free frame of L;
  procedure signal;null;
  procedure cadd1f;add1f;
  procedure add1f;begin f:=f+1;eadd1f end;
  procedure eadd1f;null;
  procedure cdistr;distr;
  procedure distr;if f>0 then
            begin integer j;j:=0;
                  for j:=j+1 while f>0∧j≤n
                      do test2-j
            end;
  procedure test2-i;while w[i]>0 and f>0 do
                  begin f:=f-1;
                        m[i]:=m[i]+1;
                        sub1w-i
                  end;
  procedure distr-i;
            if m[i]≤N[i]∧w[i]>0 then sub1w-i
            else begin m[i]:=m[i]-1;
                   if m[i]≥N[i] then signal
                 end;
  procedure sub1w-i;w[i]:=w[i]-1;
  procedure add1w(i);w[i]:=w[i]+1;
  procedure test-i;if m[i]<N[i] then add1-i
                                else add1w(i);
  procedure add1-i;m[i]:=m[i]+1;
  procedure go-i;null;
initialisation:
  initialise L to the whole buffer
             P[i] to a void queue
             m[i] and w[i] to 0
             N[i] to N_i
         and f to C
  endtype;
program:
  sharedpool B;
  cobegin ...//each producer of each group
             //each consumer of each group//...
             //while true do cadd1f
             //while true do cdistr
  coend
```

where Consumer of group i:

```
while true do
begin frame fram:
   B.cpick-i(fram);
   collect the message from fram;
   B.return(fram);
   cobegin
      consumption of the message//
      B.distr-i
   coend
end;
```

and Producer of group i:

```
while true do
begin frame fram;
   production of a message;
   B.test-i;
   B.go-i;
   B.detach(fram);
   place the message in fram;
   B.cattach-i(fram)
end;
```

We shall now translate this program in GPL in order to apply Owicki's method.
Besides the variables of the original program, we have used:

- busy indicators and signal counters in order to respect the paths:

  busy[i], busyf, busyP[i] and busyL

  signalf, ndistr, ngo[i] and nfull[i]

- intermediate variables to split the Boolean expressions and assignment statements with more than one reference to a shared variable:

  inter and interB

- various auxiliary variables to describe the history and the behaviour of the processes:
  fp counts the number of frames of the common pool which are logically considered free,
  λ counts the number of frames of the whole buffer which are logically considered free,

mp, ff, wp are the same as m, f and w except during modifying phases,
markadd1f takes into account the delay between entering add1f and updating f,
cph1, cph2, cph3, cph4, cph5 mark various phases in the consumers and take into account other delays; the number of consumers will be nc,
pph1, pph2, pph3, pph4, pph5 mark various phases in the producers, for the same reason; the number of producers will be np,
#P[i] and #L are the dimensions of the queues P[i] and L, respectively,
nbef[i] counts the number of times a group i's producer has passed test-i,
naft[i] counts the number of times a group i's producer has passed go-i.

In order to shorten the paper, we shall only mention here the main pre- and post- assertions; the reader will easily find the other ones. We shall also replace the notation "await true then begin S end" by [S], to notify that S is indivisible.
The invariant of the program will be now:

$$
\begin{aligned}
I=\{\, & fp+\sum_k (mp[k]-N[k])_+ = C \wedge \lambda = fp+\sum_k (N[k]-mp[k])_+ \\
\wedge\ & fp = ff+signalf+markadd1f \\
\wedge\ & \forall k: \#P[k] = nfull[k] + \sum_{j\in groupk} cph1[j] + \sum_{j\in groupk} pph1[j] \\
& = mp[k]-ngo[k]-\sum_{j\in groupk} cph5[j] - \sum_{j\in groupk} pph5[j] \\
\wedge\ & \#L = N - \sum_k nfull[k] - \sum_j cph2[j] - \sum_j pph2[j] \\
& = \lambda + \sum_k ngo[k] + \sum_j cph3[j] + \sum_j pph3[j] \\
\wedge\ & \forall k: mp[k] = nfull[k] + ngo[k] + \sum_{j\in groupk} cph4[j] + \sum_{j\in groupk} pph4[j] \\
\wedge\ & \forall k: wp[k]>0 \vdash mp[k] \geq N[k] \\
\wedge\ & \forall k: nbef[k] = naft[k]+wp[k]+ngo[k] \\
\wedge\ & signalf \geq 0 \wedge 1 \geq markadd1f \geq 0 \\
\wedge\ & f+1 \geq ff \geq f \geq 0 \wedge (\neg\, busyf \vdash f=ff) \\
\wedge\ & \forall k: (|mp[k]-m[k]| \leq 1 \wedge |wp[k]-w[k]| \leq 1 \\
& \quad \wedge mp[k] \geq 0 \wedge m[k] \geq 0 \\
& \quad \wedge wp[k] \geq 0 \wedge w[k] \geq 0 \\
& \quad \wedge \neg\, busy[k] \vdash mp[k]-m[k] = wp[k]-w[k] = 0) \\
\wedge\ & \forall k: \#P[k] \geq 0 \wedge nfull[k] \geq 0 \wedge ngo[k] \geq 0 \\
& \quad \wedge naft[k] \geq 0 \wedge nbef[k] \geq 0 \\
\wedge\ & \forall j: cph4[j] = cph1[j]+cph5[j] = cph2[j]+cph3[j] \\
& \quad \wedge (1 \geq cph1[j], cph2[j], cph3[j], \\
& \qquad cph4[j], cph5[j] \geq 0) \\
\wedge\ & \forall j: pph4[j] = pph1[j]+pph5[j] = pph2[j]+pph3[j] \\
& \quad \wedge (1 \geq pph1[j], pph2[j], pph3[j], \\
& \qquad pph4[j], pph5[j] \geq 0)\}
\end{aligned}
$$

The program with its proof outline can then be written:

```
queue L;queue array P[1:n];
integer f,ff,fp,λ,#L,signalf,
      markadd1f,ndistr;
integer array m,N,w,mp,wp,#P,
            ngo,nfull,nbef,naft[1:n],
            cph1,cph2,cph3,cph4,cph5[1:nc],
            pph1,pph2,pph3,pph4,pph5[1:np];
Boolean busyf,busyL;
Boolean array busy,busyP[1:n];
initialise L to the whole buffer;
           P[i] to a void queue;
           f,ff,fp to C;λ,#L to Nb;
           signalf,markadd1f,ndistr,m[i],mp[i],
```

```
          w[i],wp[i],#P[i],ngo[i],nfull[i],
          nbef[i],naft[i],cph1[j],cph2[j],
          cph3[j],cph4[j],cph5[j],pph1[j],
          pph2[j],pph3[j],pph4[j],pph5[j] to 0;
          N[i] to N_i;
          busyf,busyL,
          busy[i],busyP[i] to false;
{I∧f>0∧¬ busy∧¬ busyL
  ∧∀k:(m[k]=0∧¬ busy[k]∧¬ busyP[k])}
cobegin...//each producer of each group
          //each consumer of each group//...
          //add1f//distr
coend {false}
where
consumer j of group i:
frame fram;integer inter;Boolean interB;
  while true do {I}
  begin
    await nfull[i]>0 then
          [nfull[i]:=nfull[i]-1;
          cph1[j]:=cph2[j]:=cph4[j]:=1];
    await ¬ busyP[i] then busyP[i]:=true;
    a frame is extracted from P[i] to be attri-
    buted to fram and when extraction occurs one
    executes indivisibly:
     [#P[i]:=#P[i]-1;cph1[j]:=0;cph5[j]:=1];
    busyP[i]:=false;
    collect the message from fram;
    await ¬ busyL then busyL:=true;
      fram is attached to L and when attaching
      occurs one executes indivisibly:
      [#L:=#L+1;cph2[j]:=0;cph3[j]:=1];
    busyL:=false;
    cobegin consumption of the message
      //begin await ¬ busy[i]
              then busy[i]:=true;
          {I∧m[i]=mp[i]∧w[i]=wp[i]}
          interB:=m[i]≤N[i];
          if interB∧w[i]>0
          then {I∧w[i]=wp[i]∧m[i]=mp[i]
                ∧m[i]≤N[i]∧w[i]>0}
            begin inter:=w[i]-1;w[i]:=inter;
              [ngo[i]:=ngo[i]+1;wp[i]:=wp[i]-1;
              cph3[j]:=cph4[j]:=cph5[j]:=0
              {I∧w[i]=wp[i]∧m[i]=mp[i]
                ∧ngo[i]>0}]
            end
          else {I∧w[i]=wp[i]∧m[i]=mp[i]
                ∧(m[i]>N[i]∨w[i]=0)}
            begin inter:=m[i]-1;m[i]:=inter;
              {I∧w[i]=wp[i]∧m[i]=mp[i]-1
                ∧(mp[i]>N[i]∨w[i]=0)}
              if m[i]≥N[i]
              then {I∧w[i]=wp[i]∧m[i]=mp[i]-1
                    ∧mp[i]>N[i]}
                [signalf:=signalf+1;fp:=fp+1;
                λ:=λ+1;mp[i]:=mp[i]-1;
                cph3[j]:=cph4[j]:=cph5[j]:=0
                {I∧w[i]=wp[i]∧m[i]=mp[i]
                ∧m[i]≥N[i]∧signalf>0}]
              else {I∧w[i]=wp[i]∧m[i]=mp[i]-1
                    ∧mp[i]≤N[i]∧w[i]=0}
                [mp[i]:=mp[i]-1;λ:=λ+1;
                 cph3[j]:=cph4[j]:=cph5[j]:=0]
                {I∧w[i]=wp[i]∧m[i]=mp[i]
                  ∧m[i]<N[i]∧w[i]=0}
            end;
```

```
              {I∧w[i]=wp[i]∧m[i]=mp[i]}
              busy[i]:=false
            end
      coend {I}
  end;
add1f:
  integer inter
  while true do {I}
  begin await signalf>0 then
      [signalf:=signalf-1;markadd1f:=1]
      await ¬ busyf then busyf:=true;
      {I∧f=ff}
      inter:=f+1;
      [f:=inter;ff:=ff+1;markadd1f:=0];
      {I∧f=ff}
      busyf:=false;
      [ndistr:=ndistr+1{I∧ndistr>0}] {I}
  end;
distr:
  integer k,inter;Boolean interB;
  while true do {I}
  begin await ndistr>0 then ndistr:=ndistr-1;
      await ¬ busyf then busyf:=true;
      {I∧f=ff}
      if f>0 then
      begin k:=1;
        while f>0∧k≤n do
        begin await ¬ busy[k]
                  then busy[k]:=true;
          {I∧f=ff∧m[k]=mp[k]∧w[k]=wp[k]}
          interB:=f>0;
          while interB∧w[k]>0 do
          begin inter:=f-1;f:=inter;
            inter:=m[k]+1;m[k]:=inter;
            inter:=w[k]-1;w[k]:=inter;
            [ngo[k]:=ngo[k]+1;
            fp:=fp-1;mp[k]:=mp[k]+1;
            λ:=λ-1;ff:=ff-1;wp[k]:=wp[k]-1
            {I∧f=ff∧m[k]=mp[k]∧w[k]=wp[k]
              ∧ngo[k]>0}];
            interB:=f>0
            {I∧f=ff∧m[k]=mp[k]∧w[k]=wp[k]}
          end
          busy[k]:=false;k:=k+1;
        end
      end {I∧f=ff};
      busyf:=false {I}
  end;

producer j of group i:
  frame fram;integer inter;
  while true do {I}
  begin production of a message;
    await ¬ busy[i] then busy[i]:=true;
    {I∧m[i]=mp[i]∧w[i]=wp[i]}
    if m[i]<N[i]
    then begin inter:=m[i]+1;m[i]:=inter;
           [ngo[i]:=ngo[i]+1;nbef[i]:=nbef[i]+1;
            mp[i]:=mp[i]+1;λ:=λ-1
           {I∧m[i]=mp[i]∧w[i]=wp[i]∧ngo[i]>0}]
         end
    else begin inter:=w[i]+1;w[i]:=inter;
           [ndistr:=ndistr+1;wp[i]:=wp[i]+1;
            nbef[i]:=nbef[i]+1
           {I∧m[i]=mp[i]∧w[i]=wp[i]∧ndistr>0}]
         end;
    busy[i]:=false;
```

```
    await ngo[i]>0 then
          [ngo[i]:=ngo[i]-1;naft[i]:=naft[i]+1;
           pph3[j]:=pph4[j]:=pph5[j]:=1];
    await ¬ busyL then busyL:=true;
    a frame is extracted from L to be attributed
      to fram and when extraction occurs one
      executes indivisibly:
      [#L:=#L-1;pph2[j]:=1;pph3[j]:=0];
    busyL:=false;
    place the message in fram;
    await ¬ busyP[i] then busyP[i]:=true;
    fram is attached to P[i] and when attaching
      occurs one executes indivisibly:
      [#P[i]:=#P[i]+1;pph1[j]:=1;pph5[j]:=0];
    busyP[i]:=false;
    [nfull[i]:=nfull[i]+1;
     pph1[j]:=pph2[j]:=pph4[j]:=0
    {I∧nfull[i]>0}]
  end
```

As in §3, the interference-freeness results from the fact that, besides the invariant I, the assertions only use local variables and protected shared variables.
The main characteristics of the behaviour of the processes may be extracted from the invariant. For instance, it appears that

$\#L \geqslant \lambda \geqslant fp \geqslant ff \geqslant 0$ and $0 \leqslant \#P[k] \leqslant mp[k]$
$\#L = \lambda$ if none of the producers-consumers are in phase 3
and all of the ngo-signals have been swallowed
$\lambda = fp$ if $\forall k: mp[k] \geqslant N[k]$
$fp = ff$ if all the signalf-signals have been absorbed by add1f
and add1f is not in the marked phase
$\#P[k] = mp[k]$ if none of the producers-consumers are in phase 5
and all of the ngo-signals have been swallowed
$ff = f$ outside its critical section
$mp[k] = m[k]$ outside its critical section

The harmonious cooperation of the various processes may be informally demonstrated from the assertions, in the same manner as in §3.

5. CONCLUSIONS

Owicki's technique appears to be very powerfull to prove behavioural properties of parallel programs. The main problem is to find the "good" auxiliary variables and the adequate invariant to exhibit the desired behaviour of the various processes. This may be tedious but one gets a better insight on the parallelism. In fact, a high level of parallelism is payed by an increased complexity in the algorithms and especially in the proofs.
It can be mentioned that solutions with monitors and semaphores present about the same level of difficulty as the solutions with critical sections and path expressions, respectively. The need arises however of disposing of adequate translations of Owicki's formalism in the context of the various synchronisation mechanisms.
The problem of partial blocking should also be more completely examined in the lights of this formalism.
We intend to follow this "path" in future work on the subject.

ACKNOWLEDGMENTS

We are much indebted to David Gries who introduced us in Owicki's technique with a talk on [7] (during the first meeting of the Computer Science Metatheory and Theories Belgian Contact Group, April 1976).

BIBLIOGRAPHY

[1] S.S. Owicki, *Axiomatic proof techniques for parallel programs*, Ph.D.thesis, Cornell University (July 1975).

[2] S.S. Owicki and D. Gries, An Axiomatic Proof Technique for Parallel Program I, *Acta Informatica*, vol.6, n°4, pp.319-339 (1976).

[3] S.S. Owicki and D. Gries, An Axiomatic Proof Technique for Parallel Program II, in preparation.

[4] C.A.R. Hoare, An axiomatic Basis for Computer Programming, *CACM*, vol.12, n°10, pp.576-580 (1969).

[5] C.A.R. Hoare, Towards a Theory of parallel Programming, in International Seminar on Operating System Techniques, Belfast, Northern Ireland, 1971; and *Operating Systems Techniques*, pp.61-71, edited by C.A.R. Hoare and R.H. Perrot, Academic Press, New York, 1973.

[6] P.B. Hansen, A comparison of two synchronizing Concepts, *Acta Informatica*, vol.1, pp.190-199 (1972).

[7] D. Gries, An Exercice in Proving Properties of Parallel Programs, submitted to CACM.

[8] R. Devillers and G. Louchard, Improvement of parallelism in a finite buffer sharing policy, *The Computer Journal*, vol.19, n°3 (1976).

[9] E.W. Dijkstra, Information Streams sharing a finite Buffer, *Information Processing Letters*, vol.1, pp.179-180 (1972).

[10] R.H. Campbell and A.N. Habermann, The Specification of Processes Synchronization by Path Expressions, *Lecture Notes in Computer Science*, vol.16, Springer-Verlag (1974).

[11] L. Flon and A.N. Habermann, Towards the Construction of verifiable Software Systems, *Sigplan notices*, vol.8, n°2, pp.141-148 (1976).

E. Morlet and D. Ribbens, (Eds.), International Computing Symposium 1977.

PARSING LANGUAGES DESCRIBED BY SYNTAX GRAPHS

A. Celentano

Istituto di Elettrotecnica ed Elettronica
Politecnico di Milano
Milan, Italy

Syntax graphs and extended BNF, in which regular expressions are allowed as right hand sides of grammar rules, can be used instead of context-free rules to describe the syntax of programming languages in a more clear and natural way. In this paper an extension of LR algorithms is presented, which allows to construct parsers for languages defined in such a way, which are smaller and faster then parsers constructed for context-free grammars. Semantics can be added to regular expressions, and the parsing algorithm can be modified to allow performing actions at each point of the parsed rule.
Some suggestions for the implementation are also given, which essentially consist of a proper choice of data structure for representing the states of the parsing automaton.

1. INTRODUCTION

Syntax graphs and extended BNF notation, in which regular expressions are allowed as right hand sides of grammar rules, are often more clear and natural ways for describing the syntax of programming languages, instead of context-free productions.

In particular I am concerned with regular expressions built up with three operators, represented by the metasymbols |, [...] , {...} :

1. $A ::= \alpha(\beta_1 | \beta_2 | \cdots | \beta_n)\gamma$ (selection)

which means that exactly one of the alternatives, separated by |, must be selected (round brackets mean that selection has higher priority than concatenation, and are metasymbols).

2. $A ::= \alpha\{\beta\}\gamma$ (iteration)

which means that the part enclosed in braces can be repeated zero or more times.

3. $A ::= \alpha[\beta]\gamma$ (option)

which means that the part enclosed in square brackets can be omitted.

All of these operations can be combined among them, and nested at any level; so, for example, the rule

EXPRESSION ::= [+|-] TERM {(+|-) TERM}

defines an expression as a sequence of one or more terms divided by plus or minus operators, the first term being optionally preceded by a plus or a minus.

As an alternate representation, I shall consider syntax graphs constructed by terminal nodes, represented by ◯ , which are labeled with terminal symbols, nonterminal nodes, represented by ▭ , which are labeled by nonterminal symbols, and directed edges between nodes, reflecting the concatenation of symbols in the corresponding regular expression; I'll introduce also branch nodes and gathering nodes , represented by

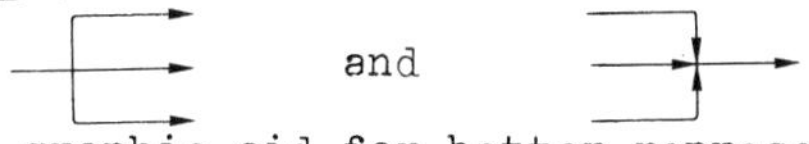

as a graphic aid for better representing the graphs.
With these conventions the above grammar rule can be pictorially described by this graph:

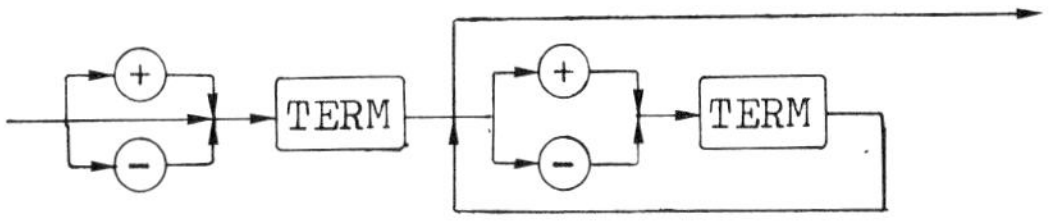

A path through the graph, from the entry point to the exit point, is a particular instance of the nonterminal EXPRESSION and corresponds to a particular value of the associated regular expression in extended BNF. I shall consider in the following the two notations as equivalent.

For grammar's symbols, the following conventions hold: nonterminal symbols are represented by words in uppercase letters, terminal symbols by words in lower case letters or operators, regular expressions over nonterminal and terminal symbols by greek letters.
The empty string is represented by ε .

2. LR PARSERS FOR EXTENDED CONTEXT-FREE GRAMMARS

Regular expressions and syntax graphs are normally adopted in top-down parsers, in particular recursive descents (Amman/4/, Gries/9/); a limitation of bottom-up parsers is that they require the grammar be described by context-free productions; the parsing algorithm is in fact requested to find a sequence of stack symbols and input symbols which match the right hand side of some appropriate production, and substitute them with the corresponding left-hand side (reduce action); selections, options and iterations make difficult to do the matching, mainly in LR parsers, in which the length of the stack string to be replaced is no more fixed.

A certain number of transformations can be found, which translate rules in extended BNF into context-free productions:

i) if the grammar contains the rule

$$A ::= \alpha(\beta_1 | \beta_2 | \dots | \beta_n)\gamma \qquad (a)$$

replace it with the rules

$$\begin{aligned} A &::= \alpha B \gamma \\ B &::= \beta_1 \\ B &::= \beta_2 \\ &\vdots \\ B &::= \beta_n \end{aligned} \qquad (a')$$

where B is a new nonterminal symbol.

ii) if the grammar contains the rule

$$A ::= \alpha\{\beta\}\gamma \qquad (b)$$

replace it with the rules

$$\begin{aligned} A &::= \alpha B \gamma \\ B &::= B\beta \\ B &::= \varepsilon \end{aligned} \qquad (b')$$

iii) if the grammar contains the rule

$$A ::= \alpha[\beta]\gamma \qquad (c)$$

replace it with the rules

$$\begin{aligned} A &::= \alpha B \gamma \\ B &::= \beta \\ B &::= \varepsilon \end{aligned} \qquad (c')$$

Other transformations are possible, for example replacing the rule (a) with the rules

$$\begin{aligned} A &::= \alpha\beta_1\gamma \\ A &::= \alpha\beta_2\gamma \\ &\vdots \\ A &::= \alpha\beta_n\gamma \end{aligned} \qquad (a'')$$

without adding new symbols. I shall consider these transformations as equivalent. In the same way I shall consider equivalent the structures generated by the rules (b) and (b'), even if they are different (Fig. 1); the former structure can't be generated by context-free grammars: since it is usually adopted to represent lists, one can think that an implicit left association of the list's elements is assumed.

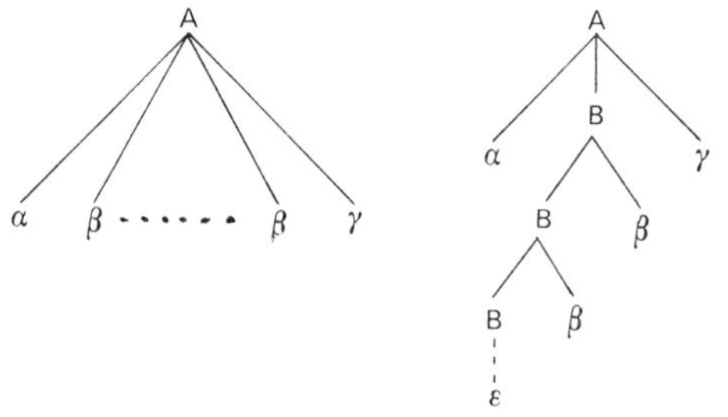

Figure 1

A first solution to the problem of constructing LR parsers for Extended context-free grammars is thus to convert the rules in pure context-free form, and use the derived grammar for the parsing.

LR algorithms can also be extended to work with regular expressions. (DeRemer /7/, Early/8/). In Madsen/10/ selections and iterations are considered: for each rule $A ::= \alpha$, α can be split into δ_1, $\delta_2, \dots, \delta_n$ such as $\alpha = \delta_1 \delta_2 \dots \delta_n$ and each δ_i represents a selection, an iteration or simply a sequence of grammar symbols. The parsing automaton is constructed following the algorithms for normal LR parsers, with the following additional rule: if a state contains an item in the form $A ::= \delta_1 \delta_2 \cdots \delta_i \, \delta_{i+1} \cdots \delta_n$, the corresponding table is completed with a descrittion of δ_i (that is the alternative or iteration or sequence involved).

When performing a reduction according to the rule $A ::= \alpha$, if α' is the instance of α actually read, then $\alpha' = \delta_1' \delta_2' \dots \delta_n'$, where δ_i' is an instance of δ_i.
The popping of the stack can be split into popping first δ_n', then $\delta_{n-1}', \dots$, and finally δ_1' according to the informations stored in the LR table which, after each pop action, appears on the stack's top. Since iterations and selections can be nested, each δ_i and δ_i' must eventually be split in a similar way.

In this paper a different approach is taken, which allows the construction of efficient and small LR parsers for grammars described in extended BNF or by syntax graphs (for practicality I shall consider only SLR(1) parsers).

The main difference with the method described in Madsen/10/ is that selections iterations and options are checked during the scan and not at the moment of reduce actions. Besides being simpler, this methos allows an easy insertion of semantic actions at various points of a rule (as usually in top-down parsers), and not only at the end (as usually in bottom-up parsers), giving more freedom to the compiler writer.

A price must be paid for this simpeer approach: a limitation is imposed on the form of right-hand sides of the rules. Expressions in which a symbol closes more than one optional or iterative part are not allowed (e.g. $A ::= \alpha\{\beta\{\gamma\}\}\delta$), since these situations request some major inspection on the string to be parsed than performed by this algorithm. An extention can be made in order to remove this limitation, and a sketch will be given later, but much of the simplicity of the approach is lost. Moreover, the constraint doesn't seem too heavy for programming languages (the description of PASCAL, Wirth/12/, fits this form) and little local changes are sufficient to convert these rules into a suitable form. Furthermore, for practical reasons, I shall consider the rule $A ::= \alpha_1|\alpha_2|\ldots|\alpha_n$ as n distinct rules $A ::= \alpha_1$, $A ::= \alpha_2, \ldots,$ $A ::= \alpha_n$.

3. CONSTRUCTION OF LR(0) STATES

The reader is assumed to be familiar with LR concepts as treated in Aho/2/ and DeRemer/6/. The concept of item is extended to deal with regular expressions: an item is a grammar rule with a distinguished position (a dot) in the regular expression wich constitutes its right hand side; to consider an item at a certain point of the parse means that an instance of the part which precedes the dot has been scanned. Some additional rules are necessary for constructing the LR(0) set of states, which are described by DeRemer/7/ and Early/8/:

a) if a state contains an item of the form

$$A ::= \alpha.(\beta_1 | \beta_2 | \ldots | \beta_n)\gamma$$

replace it with the n items

$$A ::= \alpha(.\beta_1 | \beta_2 | \ldots | \beta_n)\gamma$$
$$\vdots$$
$$A ::= \alpha(\beta_1 | \beta_2 | \ldots |.\beta_n)\gamma$$

meaning that the next input symbol can match the start symbol of each of the alternatives.

b) if a state contains an item of the form

$$A ::= \alpha.[\beta]\gamma \quad \text{or} \quad A ::= \alpha.\{\beta\}\gamma$$

replace it with the two items

$$\begin{matrix} A ::= \alpha[.\beta]\gamma \\ A := \alpha[\beta].\gamma \end{matrix} \quad \text{or} \quad \begin{matrix} A ::= \alpha\{.\beta\}\gamma \\ A ::= \alpha\{\beta\}.\gamma \end{matrix}$$

meaning that an instance of β can be found on the input stream or not.

c) if there is an item of the form

$$A ::= \alpha\{\beta\}.\gamma$$

add to the state the item

$$A ::= \alpha\{.\beta\}\gamma$$

meaning that the part between braces can be repeated.

Thise transformations are made providing that no item is added twice to the same state. In the following I shall adopt a shorthand notation for the states, representing items constituted by the same rule with dots in different positions as a single item with many dots, each dot marking the parsed part in the separate items; for example, the rule (a) will result in placing in the state the item

$$A ::= \alpha(.\beta_1 |.\beta_2 | \ldots |.\beta_n)\gamma$$

This notation is not introduced only for saving space, it reflects the representation of items when using graphs, and a possible representation of data for the implementation.

The closure of a state is taken following the algorithms for normal LR parsers. In the same way new states are added to the machine moving dots across symbols and the LR(0) set of state can be constructed in the same way as for context-free grammars.
The GO TO graph shows the connections between the states; due to the rules (a), (b) and (c) above, unlike usual LR parsers, edges with different labels can enter in the same state in the GO TO graph. When this happens, all the symbols labeling such edges are last symbols of a selection, and from that point on the actions performed by the parser are the same independently from the past history.

It is time now for a complete example. Let us consider the following grammar, whose syntax graphs are in fig. 2 :

$$\begin{aligned} &\text{EXPRESSION} ::= \text{TERM } \{(+|-)\text{ TERM}\} \dashv \\ &\text{TERM} ::= \text{FACTOR } \{(*|+)\text{ FACTOR}\} \qquad (1) \\ &\text{FACTOR} ::= \text{id} \end{aligned}$$

This well known grammar can be described by these context-free rules:

```
HEAD ::= EXPR ⊣
EXPR ::= TERM
EXPR ::= EXPR ADOP TERM
TERM ::= FACTOR
TERM ::= TERM MULOP FACTOR                 (2)
FACTOR ::= id
ADOP ::= +
ADOP ::= -
MULOP ::= *
MULOP ::= ÷
```

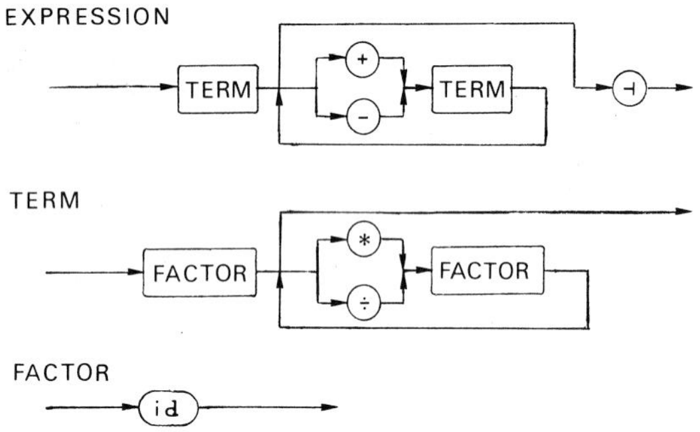

Figure 2

```
0: EXPRESSION ::= .TERM {(+|-) TERM}⊣
   TERM ::= .FACTOR {(*|÷) FACTOR}
   FACTOR ::= .id
1: EPRESSION ::= TERM {(.+|.-) TERM}.⊣
2: TERM ::= FACTOR {(.*|.÷) FACTOR}.
3: FACTOR ::= id.
4: EXPRESSION ::= TERM {(+|-) .TERM}⊣
   TERM ::= .FACTOR {(*|÷) FACTOR}
   FACTOR ::= .id
5: EXPRESSION ::= TERM {(+|-) TERM}⊣.
6: TERM ::= FACTOR {(*|÷) .FACTOR}
   FACTOR ::= .id
```

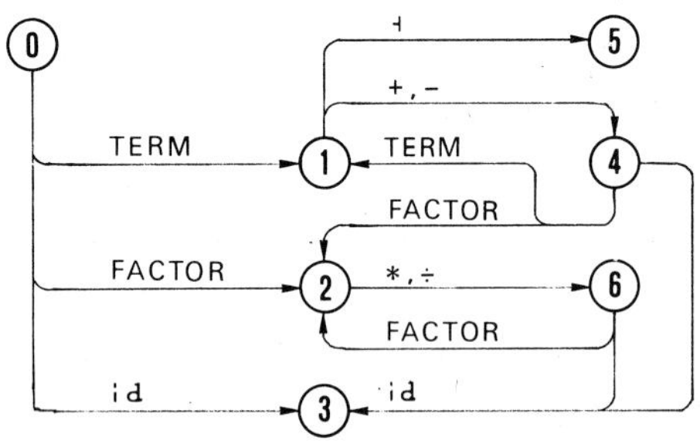

Figure 3

The one reported is not the only way to describe the same language as generated by (1), but it seems the most immediate one and in effect it is used for many languages as Algol 60 (on the opposite, syntax graphs of fig. 2 are used to describe expressions in PASCAL).

In fig. 3 and 4 the sets of states and the GO TO graphs for the two grammars are given.

```
 0: HEAD ::= .EXPR ⊣
    EXPR ::= .TERM
    EXPR ::= .EXPR ADOP TERM
    TERM ::= .FACTOR
    TERM ::= .TERM MULOP FACTOR
    FACTOR ::= .id
 1: HEAD ::= EXPR .⊣
    EXPR ::= EXPR .ADOP TERM
    ADOP ::= .+
    ADOP ::= .-
 2: EXPR ::= TERM .
    TERM ::= TERM .MULOP FACTOR
    MULOP ::= .*
    MULOP ::= .÷
 3: TERM ::= FACTOR .
 4: FACTOR ::= id .
 5: HEAD ::= EXPR ⊣.
 6: EXPR ::= EXPR ADOP .TERM
    TERM ::= .FACTOR
    TERM ::= .TERM MULOP FACTOR
    FACTOR ::= .id
 7: ADOP ::= + .
 8: ADOP ::= - .
 9: TERM ::= TERM MULOP .FACTOR
    FACTOR ::= .id
10: MULOP ::= * .
11: MULOP ::= ÷ .
12: EXPR ::= EXPR ADOP TERM .
    TERM ::= TERM .MULOP FACTOR
    MULOP ::= .*
    MULOP ::= .÷
13: TERM ::= TERM MULOP FACTOR .
```

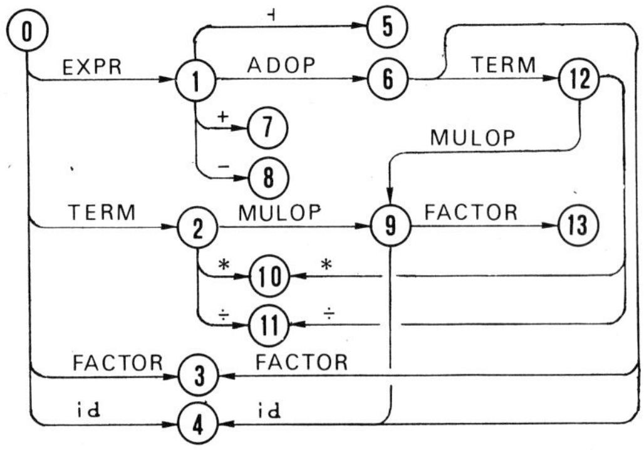

Figure 4

A first comparison between the two machines shows that the number of states decreases when using extended BNF. But the number of states is not always a good measure for comparing two LR parsers: sometimes the number of transitions is a better comparison element. Also in this case our parser is better than the original one, even if the ratio is not so good as for states number.

While the rules for deriving the set of states require little changes to adapt to regular expressions, more is to be said about the construction of the parsing automaton, due to the problem of matching the handle during the parse. Given a regular expression ϱ, let ϱ^f be the expression obtained from ϱ removing all iterative and optional parts (if no selection is in ϱ then ϱ^f is the shortest instance of ϱ). I shall call ϱ^f the <u>fixed part</u> of ϱ.

Let us for the moment consider only a particular form of regular expressions in which the fixed parts of alternatives in a selection are all of the same length; that is, whenever a rule is of the form $A ::= \alpha(\beta_1 | \beta_2 | \cdots | \beta_n)\gamma$ the number of symbols in the fixed parts of $\beta_1, \ldots, \beta_n$ are the same. Later I shall drop this constraint, introducing a slight modification in the parsing algorithm.

In LR parsers for context-free grammars, four kinds of actions are associated to states and transitions: <u>shift actions</u>, which put on the stack the input symbol* and the next state, <u>reduce actions</u>, which are associated to <u>complete items</u> (items of the form $A ::= \alpha.$) which pop the handle out from the stack, replacing it with its left hand side and the associate state, <u>accept actions</u>, which identifie final states, and <u>error actions</u>, which report syntactic errors, eventually trying a correction or a recovery.
A fifth kind of action must be added to an LR parser in order to work with extended BNF, that is <u>pop actions</u>, which pop some symbols out from the stack without replacing them.

The modified SLR(1) parser works as follows: while shift actions are to be performed, the parser acts as a normal SLR(1) parser; this means that nor a right hand side of some rule has been recognized, nor an optional or iterative part has been scanned.
If a pop action is to be performed, this means that the parser has completed the scanning of an optional or iterative part. Due to the rules (b) and (c) of the transformation algorithm on LR(0) states, the parser is in the same state in which it would be if the optional or iterative part had not been included in the input stream; if this part (their associated states) is popped from the stack, when the right hand side of the rule has been completely parsed, only an instance of its fixed part would be on the stack, representing a valid sequence of symbols for that production, so the match is succesful.

Moreover, if the pop action regards an iterative part, the parser is resetted to the state it was in before scanning the iterative part (due to the rule (c)), so more occurrences of the iteration can be parsed. Popping them at each iteration results again in having at at the end into the stack the sequence of states associated to an instance of the fixed part of the rule.

On the assumption that all the fixed parts in selections be of the same length, the reduce action must not investigate the stack's contents, since it involves a fixed number of elements.
For grammar (1) the reduce actions reduce according to the instances:

EXPRESSION ::= TERM
TERM ::= FACTOR
FACTOR ::= id

4. CONSTRUCTION OF THE PARSING AUTOMATON

A correspondence can be found between the connections between states, that is the movement of the dots across symbols in items, and the parsing actions to be performed; I shall represent the parsing automaton as a directed graph (DeRemer /6/), whose nodes represent the states, and edges represent the transitions, and are labeled with grammar symbols, and an action is associated to each transition:

a) if the state Q" is obtained from the state Q' by moving the dot across a symbol X in a right hand side of some item of Q' (and consequently an edge exists in the GO TO graph from the state Q' to the state Q" which is labeled X), and the symbol X is not followed by] or } (that is it is not the last symbol of an option or iteration), then a transition exists in the parsing machine form the state Q' to the state Q", which is labeled X, and a shift action is associated to this transition.

b) if the state Q' has a complete item

* In effect input symbols are a redundant information, and only states must be recorded into the stack (Aho/2/).

A ::= α. a transition exists from the state Q' to a dummy state, the transition is labeled with all symbols which belong to FOLLOW(A) (*), and a reduce action is associated to it which reduces according to the fixed part of the parsed rule.

c) if the state Q' is obtained from the state Q' as in case (a), but the symbol X is followed by] or } then a transition exists from the state Q' to the state Q", labeled X, and a pop action is associated to this transition, which pops the part enclosed in square brackets or braces from the stack (**).

It can be shown that these actions are consistent with the transformations on the grammar's rules described in section 2. E.g. when the parser for the extended context-free grammar performs a pop action, the parser for the derived context-free grammar announces a reduction according to one of the rules introduced in cases (b') and (c').

In fig. 5 the parsing automaton for the grammar (1) is shown; in fig. 6 the parse of the sentence id*id*id⊣ is illustrated.

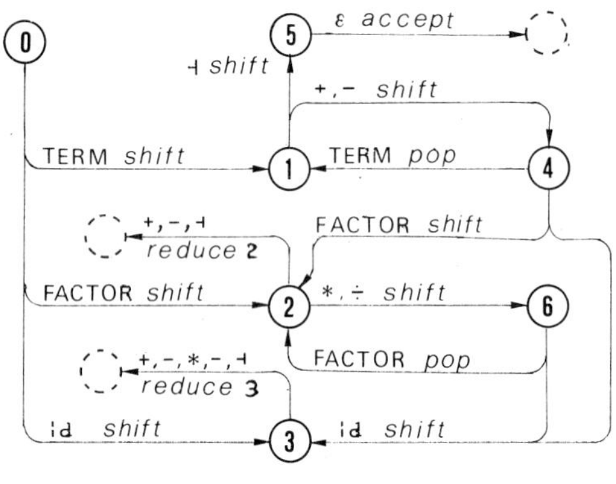

Figure 5

(*) FOLLOW(A) is the set of all terminal symbols that can follow the nonterminal A in some derivation of some sentence of the language (DeRemer/6/).

(**) By this way pop actions are performed during the scan of the last symbol of the option or iteration, so they must pop one symbol less; reduce actions are performed one step after the scan of the last symbol of the rule, so no ambiguity arises when the last part of the rule is optional or iterative.

stack	input
0	id * id * id ⊣
0 3	* id * id ⊣
0 2	* id * id ⊣
0 2 6	id * id ⊣
0 2 6 3	* id ⊣
0 2	* id ⊣
0 2 6	id ⊣
0 2 6 3	⊣
0 2	⊣
0 1	⊣
0 1 5	

Figure 6

Till now I have supposed to base the algorithms on extended BNF description of the grammar. The same rules are valid adopting a notation with syntax graphs. With this notation items are represented by <u>graphs</u> with <u>distinguished nodes</u> (I shall use arrows pointing to the nodes). To have a distinguished node is equivalent to having a dot in front of the corresponding symbol in the regular expression (fig. 7). Moving a dot across a symbol is equivalent to moving the arrow in the graph along all edges which leave the old distinguished node. Since square brackets are represented by edges which bypass the optional part, while iterations are represented by edges folding back to the beginning of the iterative part, and selections are represented by couples of branching nodes and gathering nodes, the rule (a), (b) and (c) of the statesconstruction algorithm (section 3) are consistent with this representation. A sequence of shift moves corresponds to a path along edges; considering an item at a certain point of the parse means that a suffix of the stack's contents spells out one of the paths from the

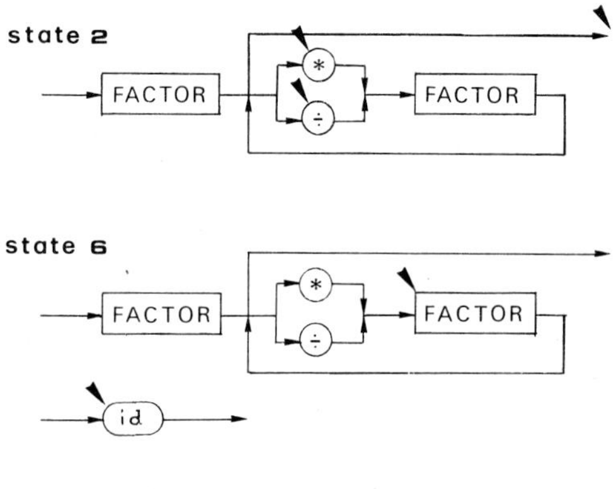

Figure 7

entry point of the graph to the distinguished nodes. Pop actions mean that the paths must skip optional and iterative parts, and reduce actions mean that the stack contains a sequence of states associated to symbols which spell out one of the shortest paths between the entry point and the exit point of the graph.

5. PERFORMING SEMANTIC ACTIONS

Even if the algorithm effectively recognizes all the sentences of the language and detects all the syntactic errors, a certain amount of information is lost if one reports only reduce actions as output for driving semantic routines, since optional parts are not reported, alternatives are not selected and iterations are not counted.

In LR parsers semantics are associated to rules, and actions are performed when a reduction is executed; in this case actions can (an sometimes must) be associated also to pop and shift actions, where this means that a certain part of a rule has been recognized, and a subsequent reduce action won't report any information about this part.

Suppose we have the rules

$A ::= \alpha B \gamma$ <action 0>
$B ::= \beta_1$ <action 1>
$B ::= \beta_2$ <action 2>
⋮
$B ::= \beta_n$ <action n>

each semantic action is performed when the corresponding rule is used in a reduction. Expressing the rules in extended BNF, actions must be transported into the selection part of the unique rule

$$A ::= \alpha(\beta_1 | \beta_2 | \ldots | \beta_n)\gamma$$

since no rule is associated to $\beta_1 \ldots \beta_n$.

Actions can be represented in this way:

$A ::= \alpha(\beta_1$<action 1>$|\ \beta_2$<action 2>$|$
$\ldots |\ \beta_n$<action n>$)\gamma$<action 0>

This scheme is similar to the one adopted for top-down parsers, in which actions are scattered along the right hand side of a rule. In our case, if actions are associated only to the recognition of options and iterations (that is when performing pop actions), the scheme is not different from an usual LR parser (pop actions are a particular kind of reductions in which the string popped from the stack is replaced by the empty string), and a good modularization of the compiler can be mantained.

In the final scheme of the parser, the grammar is represented with syntax graphs in which <u>semantic nodes</u> are introduced, represented by ⟨   ⟩ ; e.g. considering the translation of an expression into reverse Polish , the representation by syntax graphs is in fig. 8.
During the construction of the parser semantic nodes are skipped when moving arrows along edges, but the code for performing the inclosed action is associated to the transitions in the parsing machine.

The major advantage of this parser with respect to usual LR parsers is that the parser itself is more compact and faster. This derives from the fact that syntax graphs don't contain some productions, gathering selections and iterations into a single rule. In practice the productions that are eliminated are single productions, and many algorithms exist that lead to the same result operating on normal LR parsers (Aho/3/, Pager/11/) but such transformations request no semantic action be associated to single productions since no traces remain of them after the transformation; working on a description of the grammar in which actions can be dispersed along the rules doesn't request such a limitation.

6. EXTENTIONS

Now I shall drop the constraint that the fixed parts in selections be of the same length. After the scan of an alternative sometimes no trace remain of which alternative has been matched; for example if the alternatives are consituted by a single symbol all the transitions across the alternatives are between the same states of the parsing automaton (see fig. 3). Moreover, since the reduce actions must not test that the stack symbols match the right hand side of the rule (this is guaranteed by the LR parsing algorithm), it is not necessary to examine the stack's contents, and all the paths through the graph are considered equivalent.

If we drop the above limitation, the reduce actions can't know how many symbols must be popped out from the stack. Some informations must be added to shift actions which are performed at the end of selections, so that fictitious reductions are performed (as we were dealing with context-free grammars), which replace the alternative with a dummy symbol. The reduce action at the end of the rule must be modified in

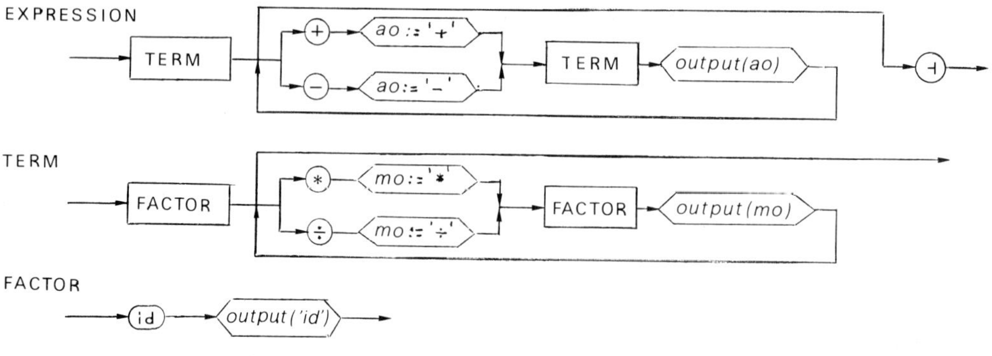

Figure 8

order to consider selections as composed by a unique symbol. But in this case it is perhaps better to transform the grammar rewriting the rule according to the transformation i) of section 2. Since this case has prooved to be not frequent in practice (the grammar's description is clear only if selection is used carefully, and not whenever possible) the previous limitation can be mantained without loss of generality.

Also the limitation imposed at the beginning of this paper can be dropped if the algorithm is modified to add look-ahead to pop actions. Only a sketch will be given here, for further extents see Celentano/5/.

Suppose a rule $A ::= \alpha[\beta[\gamma]]\delta$ is in the grammar. After the scan of β is completed, the pop action must be performed only if the incoming symbol starts an instance of δ, while a shift action must be performed if the incoming symbol starts an instance of γ; moreover, when an instance of γ has been scanned, the subsequent pop action must pop the instances of both β and γ, that is of the part enclosed in the most external pair of brackets currently crossed. The parsing machine can be modified by introducing look-ahead states which, according to the next input symbol, perform the right parsing action. The method described in this paper is in effect a particular case of the general method in which look-ahead states can be eliminated since the pop actions are associated to all the incoming symbols (delaying error checking), and can be anticipated during the scan of the last symbol of the option or iteration. The situation is in a certain sense similar to the difference between LR(0) and LR(1) parsers: in the former case the reduce actions are performed regardless of the next symbol, and can be performed immediately after the scan of the last symbol of the rule.

7. IMPLEMENTATION

The only suggestion about the implementation I shall give here concerns with the representation of items and states, since the parsing machine doesn't differ greatly from usual SLR(1) parsers.

The grammar being described by a set of graphs, all the structures normally adopted for representing graphs can be used (if the implementation language allows pointers, as PASCAL or Algol 68, such structures can be efficiently constructed). This representation allows to insert actions directly, associating to semantic nodes pointers to the entry points of the routines which implement the actions.

In usual LR parsers, items are represented by a pair of numbers (production number - dot's position), and dots are moved by incrementing the latter element of the pair. In this case items are constituted by graphs with a number of distinguished nodes, so it seems natural to represent them with a set of pointers, the first pointing to the entry point of the graph, the subsequent to the distinguished nodes. Nodes must be marked to specify the beginning and the end of options and iterations, so that appropriate pop actions can be generated. When encountering semantic nodes proper subroutine calls can be associated to the parsing action.

The parsing automaton can be realized as a set of tables (Aho/2/) but, due to the flexibility of this scheme that allows (and sometimes requests) performing semantic actions at various points of the the parse, a program notation is perhaps better (Aho/1/); the parsing tables are coded as a sequence of if...then...else or case constructs.

8. CONCLUSION

The major advantage of LR parsers with respect to LL (recursive descents) is that a larger class of languages can be parsed, and that efficient algorithms exist that construct automatically the parser given the set of rules.

Extending LR algorithms to work with syntax graphs gives more freedom in designing new languages and compilers, bypassing some often heavy and useless translation into context-free form. Moreover, the opossibility of having a unique representation for bottom-up and top-down parsers allows to perform meaningful comparisons between different kind of parsers.

9. REFERENCES

/1/ Aho A.V.,Johnson S.C.:"LR Parsing" Comp. Surveys 6 pp. 99-124

/2/ Aho.A.V.,Ullman J.D.: "The theory of parsing, translation and compiling", Prentice-Hall (1973)

/3/ Aho A.V.,Ullman J.D.: "A technique for speeding up LR(k) parsers" SIAM J. Comp. 2 pp. 106-127

/4/ Amman U.: "The method of structured programming applied to the development of a compiler" in Gunther et al. (eds.) "ICS 73", North-Holland (1974)

/5/ Celentano A.: "A simple approach to LR parsing of extended context-free grammars" to appear

/6/ DeRemer F.L.: "Simple LR(k) grammars" CACM 14 pp. 453-460

/7/ DeRemer F.L.: "Lexical analisys" in Bauer F.L. and Eickel J. (eds.) "Compiler construction", Springer Verlag (1974)

/8/ Early J.: "An efficient context-free parsing algorithm" CACM 13 pp. 94-102

/9/ Gries D.: "Compiler construction for digital computers", John Wiley and Sons (1971)

/10/ Madsen O.L.,Kristensen B.B.: "LR parsing of extended context free grammars" Acta Informatica 7 pp. 61-73

/11/ Pager D.: "On eliminating unit productions from LR(k) parsers" Techn. rep., Information Science Program, University of Hawaii, Honolulu, Hawaii (1974)

/12/ Wirth N.: "The programming language PASCAL" Acta Informatica 1 pp. 35-63

E. Morlet and D. Ribbens, (Eds.), International Computing Symposium 1977.

PROJECT LILA : THE ELL(1) GENERATOR OF LILA, AN INTRODUCTION

J. Lewi, K. De Vlaminck, J. Huens, M. Huybrechts

Applied Mathematics and Programming Division
Katholieke Universiteit Leuven
Heverlee (LEUVEN), Belgium

LILA is an acronym standing for Language Implementation LAboratory. It has been developed at the Computer Science Department of the Katholieke Universiteit Leuven (K.U.Leuven). LILA is both a software writing tool to construct translators for different machines and a pedagogical aid in a course on compiler construction. It is extensively being used as a compiler writing system in a joint project between the Katholieke Universiteit Leuven and the development department of Siemens Oostkamp (Belgium). Within this project, a compiler for PLL (a PL/1-like language) and for ATLAS (a language for automatic testing) are being implemented.

1. INTRODUCTION

LILA has been developed as an attempt to augment the reliability of translators[☆] and to minimize the cost of their construction.
The need for constructing translators (compilers and interpreters) of all kinds exists in many applications. There is an increasing demand for special-purpose languages, i.e., programming languages that have a reasonably low level of complexity and that are well-tuned to a given application. Special-purpose languages already exist in a number of fields such as operating systems, microprogramming, tool cutting, computer graphics, automatic test equipment. For each language a number of compilers for different computers have to be built.

Translator writing is a very complex and time consuming activity. The ideal translator should satisfy a number of requirements such as *reliability*, *modular design* and *efficiency*. A translator must be *easy to maintain* and to *modify*. It must be *well-documented* and *easily transportable*.
LILA has been developed as a tool for designing translators, helping the translator writer to follow the above software engineering principles. The use of LILA reduces the complexity level of the translator design up to a great extent and forces the user to structure his translator in a modular way.

☆In this paper, 'translator' will be used as a general term for a program that maps an input set into an output set. Compilers and interpreters are considered special cases of translators where the input and output sets consist of character strings.

LILA also produces very reliable and well-structured programs and it facilitates the writing of portable translators. Experiments have proven that flexibility in modifying an implementation is one of the major advantages of LILA. This aspect is even indispensable when implementing a language whose definition is not yet frozen.

LILA is the base on which a project-oriented course on compiler construction (Lewi [1973]) is built. In this course the accent is put on software engineering aspects, such as *modular design*, *reliability*, *flexibility*, *portability* and *documentation*. Due to LILA, these aspects can be investigated using non-trivial examples. Through a language implementation project, the student can turn into practice the concepts and principles studied in courses on structured programming, theory of programming languages, data structures, graph theory, etc.

2. THE STRUCTURE OF LILA

LILA consists of a *control system* and a number of *generators* each of a given type. The translator writer is able to divide his translator into logically separate modules (phases). A module is produced by LILA by selecting one of the generators and by feeding it with the appropriate generator input. The generated modules are then linked together. The interfaces between them are partially system-defined and partially user-defined.

Each generator input consists of the syntax of the input language, the description of the translation process (by means of semantic actions and attributes) and the description of the interfaces between the different modules of the translator. This method of describing a translation process is called *syntax-directed*. The generator input is compact, readable, easy to modify and to correct. The input itself serves as an excellent documentation of the translator.

The generated modules are well-structured and indented PL/1 programs. In these programs, a number of comments are inserted that indicate where each piece of text is originated from. A piece of text may be a semantic action, a global routine, an attribute declaration or it may be inserted by the generator itself.

Other comments are related to the nodes of the syntax tree of the syntax rules in the generator input. This is exhaustively described in Lewi [1976b]. All these comments make the generated programs readable. It makes the use of LILA very flexible in the sense that generated modules may be optimized by hand and even modules may be hand-coded.

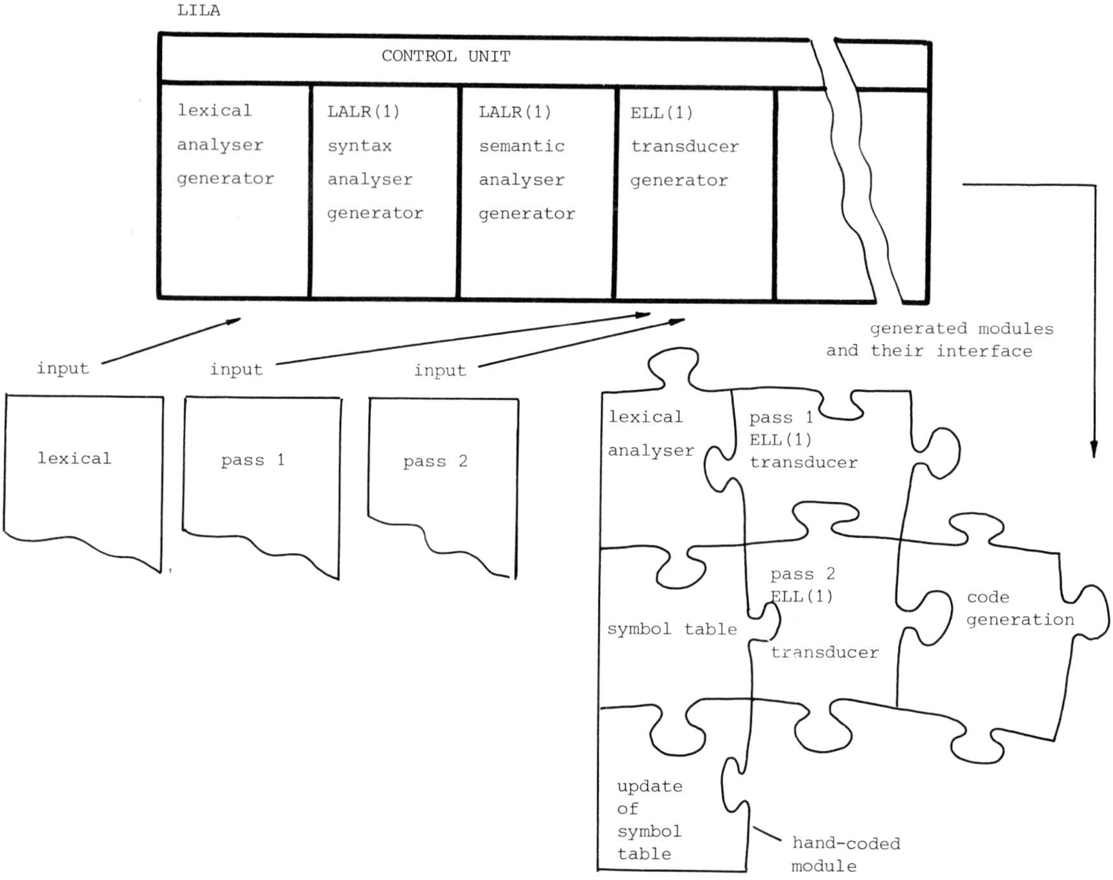

3. THE EXTENDED CONTEXT-FREE SYNTAX

The kernel of the ELL(1) generator in LILA is the ELL(1) parser *generator* which produces recursive descent parsers from an input syntax of the *extended context-free* (ECF) form. The ECF syntax formalism is derived from the context-free (CF) syntax mechanism on which a number of metasyntactical symbols (n, ☆, +, ☆n, +n, ε, (,)) are superimposed.

More precisely, an extended context-free syntax is a quadruple <VT, VN, A_0, P> where

(1) VT is the set of *terminal symbols*

$$VT = \{s_1, s_2, \ldots, s_i, \ldots, s_n\}$$

(2) VN is the set of *nonterminal symbols*

$$VN = \{A_0, A_1, A_2, \ldots, A_j, \ldots A_m\}$$

$$VT \cap VN = \phi$$

(3) A_0 is the *start symbol* of G.
$A_0 \in VN$

(4) P is a *finite set of rules*. Each rule has the general form $A_j = e_j$ where A_j belongs to VN and e_j is an ECF expression, defined by the definition scheme given below. This scheme shows how ECF expressions are composed of smaller modules, called ECF subexpressions. To each ECF subexpression corresponds a language and to each composition rule for ECF expressions corresponds a composition rule for languages.

Axiomatic rules

(1) ϕ is an ECF expression. (This rule is only given for reasons of mathematical completeness).
It denotes the empty set.

(2) ε is an ECF expression.
$L(\varepsilon)$ denotes the set containing the empty string.

(3) s_i (for all i, $1 \leqslant i \leqslant n$) is an ECF expression.
$L(s_i)$ denotes the set $\{s_i\}$.

(4) A_j (for all j, $i \leqslant j \leqslant m$) is an ECF expression.
$L(A_j)$ denotes the set defined by the ECF expression which is the right part of the ECF syntax rule $A_j = e_j$. Thus $L(A_j)=L(e_j)$. This process is recursive since for the calculation of $L(e_j)$, again rule (4) of the definition scheme may be involved.

Composition rules

Suppose e, e_1 and e_2 are ECF expressions defining the languages L(e), $L(e_1)$ and $L(e_2)$ respectively.

(5) $e_1|e_2$ is an ECF expression.
$L(e_1|e_2) = L(e_1) \cup L(e_2)$

(6) $e_1.e_2$ is an ECF expression.
$L(e_1.e_2) = L(e_1).L(e_2)$. In the sequel, the product set operator '.' will be implicit.

(7) e^n is an ECF expression.
$$L(e^n) = L(e)^n = \underbrace{L(e)\ L(e)\ \ldots\ L(e)}_{n\ \text{times}}$$

(8) $e^{\star}$ is an ECF expression.
$$L(e^{\star}) = L(e)^{\star} = \bigcup_{i=0}^{\infty} L(e)^i$$

(9) e^+ is an ECF expression.
$$L(e^+) = L(e)^+ = \bigcup_{i=1}^{\infty} L(e)^i$$

(10) $e^{\star n}$ is an ECF expression.
$$L(e^{\star n}) = \bigcup_{i=0}^{n} L(e)^i$$

(11) e^{+n} is an ECF expression.
$$L(e^{+n}) = \bigcup_{i=1}^{n} L(e)^i$$

(12) (e) is an ECF expression.
$L((e)) = L(e)$

From the above definition, it follows that a CF syntax is a special case of an ECF syntax. Clearly, by superimposing the metasyntactical symbols $\{n, +, \star, +n, \star n, \varepsilon, (,)\}$ on the CF syntax mechanism, no additional power is added, in the sense that the class of ECF languages is identical with the class of CF languages. However, the extensions are very important for three reasons :

(1) In many cases, recursive definitions of language features can now be described by iterative ones, giving rise to very efficient top-down parsers of the type ELL(1).

(2) A necessary, but not sufficient condition of an ECF syntax to be ELL(1) requires that the syntax must not be left-recursive. In many cases, left recursivities can be easily removed by introducing iterative definitions, see (1).

(3) More compact and readable syntaxes can be written.

4. THE ELL(1) PARSER GENERATION SCHEME

Given an ECF syntax $G = <VT, VN, A_0, P>$. A top-down parser of the type ELL(1) can be produced from G in a mechanical way by applying the generation scheme given below. The parser modules are described in an Algol-like language.

Axiomatic rules

ECF subexpression		*ELL(1) parser module*
(1) ϕ	→	ℓ : *goto* ℓ *co* this (academic) program accepts the empty set *co*
(2) ε	→	*skip*
(3) s_i for all i $(1 \leqslant i \leqslant n)$	→	*if* in = s_i *then* read *else* error
(4) A_j occuring in the right part of an ECF rule for all j $(0 \leqslant j \leqslant m)$	→	A_j *co* call of the routine definition for A_j, see rule (13) *co*

Composition rules

Suppose [P(e)] represents the ELL(1) parser module for a regular expression e.

(5) $e_1 \mid e_2$	→	*if* in $\in$ DIRSYMB (e_1) *then begin* [$P(e_1)$] *end* *else begin* [$P(e_2)$] *end*
(6) $e_1 e_2$	→	[$P(e_1)$] ; [$P(e_2)$]

(7) e^n →

for i *from* 1 *by* 1 *to* n
do begin
P(e)
end

(8) $e^{☆}$ →

while in ∈ FIRST(e)
do begin
P(e)
end

(9) e^+ →

repeat
P(e)
until in ∉ FIRST(e)

(10) $e^{☆n}$ →
$n \geqslant 0$

for i *from* 1 *by* 1 *to* n
while in ∈ FIRST(e)
do begin
P(e)
end

(11) e^{+n} →
$n \geqslant 1$

i := 1
repeat
P(e)
i := i+1
until in ∉ FIRST(e) ∨ i > n

(12) (e) →

P(e)

(13) $A_j = e_j$ →
for all j $(0 \leqslant j \leqslant m)$
where $A_i \in VN$ and e_j is an ECF expression

proc void A_j = *void* :
begin
P(e_j)
end

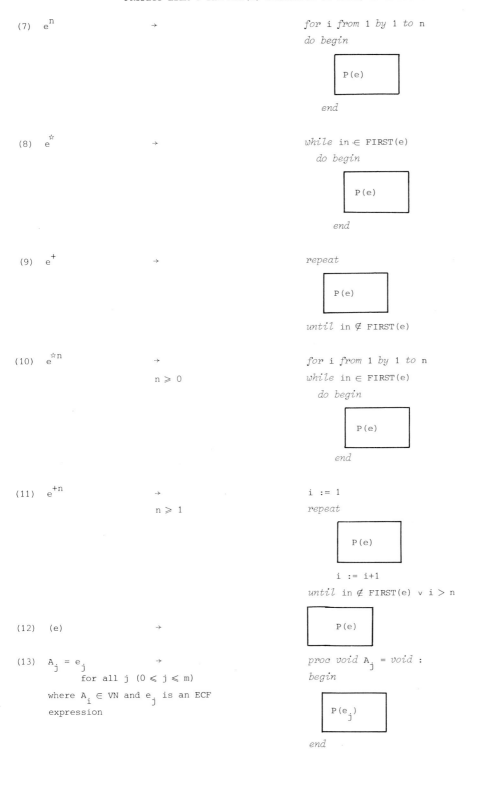

The ELL(1) parser for L(G) is activated by the call of a routine named program, defined below. It contains the environment of the routines defined by the above generation scheme :

proc void program = *void* :

begin

char in := *co* first symbol in the input string *co*;

proc void read = *void* : *co* the next symbol in the input string is put in the variable 'in' (the reader is moved one symbol to the right). *co*;

proc void error = *void* : *co* this routine provides for error diagnostics, produces appropriate error messages and performs error recovery. This is explained in detail in Lewi [1976a,d]. *co*;

proc void stop = *void* : *co* the input string has been parsed. Some appropriate actions can be performed *co* ;

| $P(A_0 = e_0)$ | ; |

| $P(A_1 = e_1)$ | ; |

⋮

| $P(A_j = e_j)$ | ; |

⋮

| $P(A_m = e_m)$ | ; |

A_0 *co* call of the routine definition for A_0 *co*;

stop

end

The above generation scheme is part of the ELL(1) documentation on the ELL(1) generator. This documentation, see Lewi [1976a], consists of a number of successive generation schemes. Starting from a very elementary scheme, five new ones are derived by successively adding new generation features, such as attribute handling, error recovery mechanism. Thanks to the simplicity and transparency of these generation schemes, the implementation of the ELL(1) generator resulted in a very reliable program.

5. THE ELL(1) CONDITIONS

The parsers produced by the above generation scheme must be deterministic. Therefore, two classes of conditions must be fulfilled. In rule (5) of the generation scheme, DIRSYMB (e_1) represents the set of all symbols that are representative for the choice of the alternative $P(e_1)$. Clearly, DIRSYMB (e_1) and DIRSYMB (e_2) must be disjoint. This is the first ELL(1) condition. In rules (8), (9), (10) and (11), FIRST (e) represents the set of all symbols that may start e^x, where x stands for one of the monadic operators ☆, +, ☆n and +n. Clearly, FIRST (e) and FOLLOW (e^x) must be disjoint sets. This is the second ELL(1) condition.

More precisely, an ECF syntax G is said to be ELL(1) if for each syntax rule $A_j = e\ (0 \leqslant j \leqslant m)$, the following two conditions hold (ELL(1) is a natural extension of LL(1), see Griffiths [1976]) :

(1) for each ECF subexpression of the form $e_1 | e_2$ in e :

$$\mathrm{DIRSYMB}(e_1) \cap \mathrm{DIRSYMB}(e_2) = \phi$$

(2) for each ECF subexpression of the form e_1^x in e, where x stands for one of the monadic operators ☆, +, ☆n and +n :

$$\mathrm{FIRST}(e_1) \cap \mathrm{FOLLOW}(e_1^x) = \phi$$

The exact definitions of FIRST, EMPTY, FOLLOW and DIRSYMB can be found in Lewi [1976a]. The ELL(1) conditions of the LILA input syntax are exhaustively checked by the system. All values of FIRST, EMPTY, FOLLOW and DIRSYMB can be printed on request. If the ELL(1) conditions are not satisfied, precise error indications are produced.

6. THE SKELETON OF THE LILA INPUT FOR THE GENERATION OF UNIT CONVERSION

The ELL(1) generator of LILA is designed in such a way that it can be used in a flexible way, i.e. transducers with different characteristics can be produced by it.
In Lewi [1976b], it is illustrated how one can generate, e.g. interpreters, lexical analysers, syntax-semantic analysers, one-pass and multi-pass compilers.

As an illustration of one of the possible uses of LILA, a language called *unit conversion* (see Cohen [1973]) is implemented. A program in the language consists of a number of commands which may be assignment statements and questions about conversion factors of previously defined units.
An example of a program is :

```
CM = 0.01 ☆ M,
INCH = 2.54 ☆ CM,
FEET = 0.3048 ☆ M,
HOW MANY INCH IN FEET ? ,
YARD = 0.9144 ☆ M ,
HOW MANY INCH IN YARD ? ,
HOW MANY FEET IN YARD ? ,
SQINCH = INCH ☆ INCH ,
SQFEET = FEET ☆ FEET ,
HOW MANY SQINCH IN SQFEET ? ,
CUINCH = INCH | 3 ,
M2 = M ☆ M ,
M3 = M | 3 ,
HOW MANY SQINCH IN M2 ? ,
HOW MANY CUINCH IN M2 ☆ M ? ,
HOW MANY M/S IN (SQFEET/YARD)/S ?
#
```

The implementation of unit coversion illustrates one particular use of the ELL(1) generator. The generated program is a two-pass translator; it consists of a *lexical analyser* and a *syntax-semantic analyser*. The role of the first pass consists in grouping the characters in the input string into elementary constructs and setting up the appropriate tables. This pass produces tokens. Each token has two fields : a *class field* specifying to which class (e.g. identifier, number) the construct belongs, and a *specification field* holding e.g., an index to a table where additional information is stored.
The sequence of tokens, output of the lexical analyser, together with the tables of information form the input of the syntax-semantic analyser. The syntax analysis only considers the class field of the tokens, whereas the specification field is used in the semantic actions.
The syntax-semantic analyser is an interpreter and produces answers to the questions in the source program.

The LILA input for the generation of the translator for unit conversion consists of three main parts. Each input part is subdivided into a number of sections and each section is headed by a LILA job control statement starting with ++. The skeleton of the LILA input is given below.

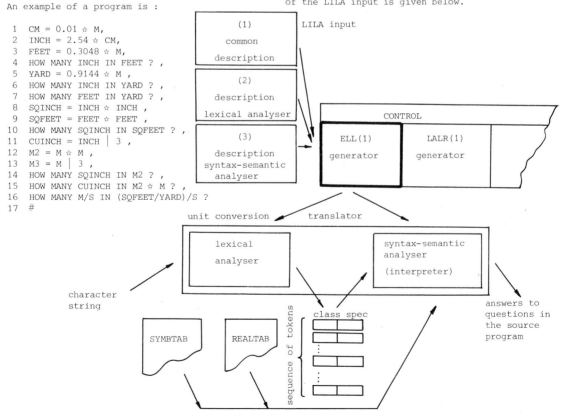

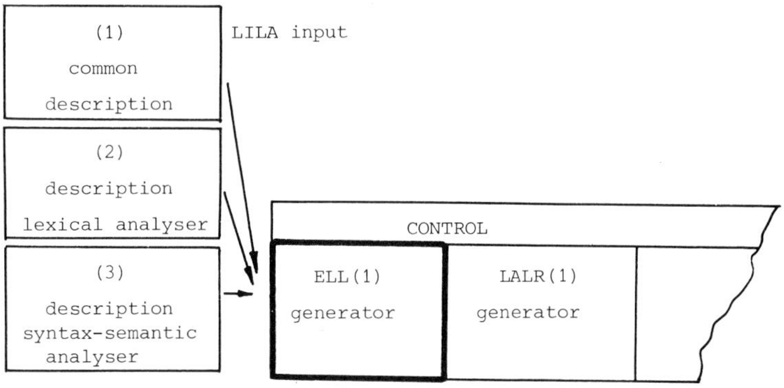

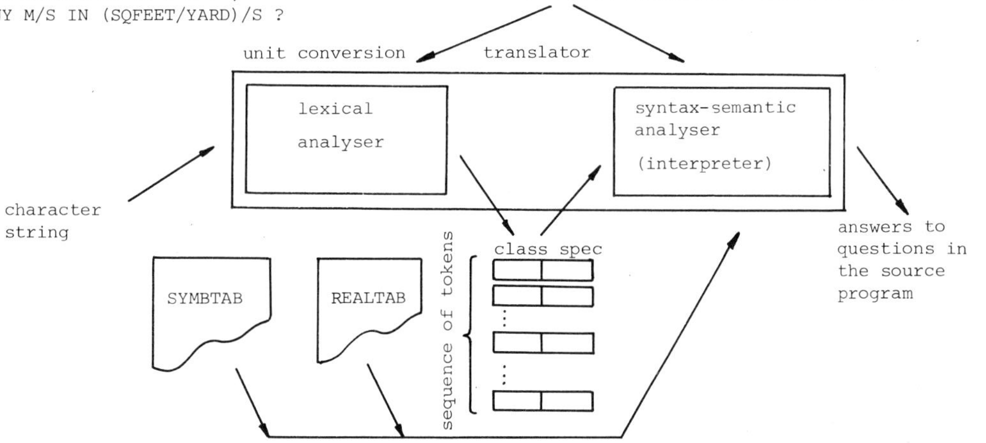

(1) LILA input common to lexical and syntax-semantic analyser

This input defines the interface between the two translator modules.

++ DEFINE TABSPEC
This part defines the table interface. It contains the specifications, in the form of PL/1 declarations, of the data (e.g., tables) that are common to both the lexical and syntax-semantic analyser.
The destination of these data is specified in TABDEST by means of IN and OUT instructions. TABDEST is information that is local to the LILA input of each translator module (see (2) and (3)).

++ DEFINE VOCABULARY
This part defines the token interface. It contains the list of all class fields of tokens appearing in the output of the lexical analyser. This vocabulary is at the same time the set of terminal symbols of the ECF syntax in the LILA input for the syntax-semantic analyser (see (3)).

(2) LILA input for the lexical analyser

++ NAME EXECUTE ELL(1) OPTIONS(INPUT(CHAR),...)
The CHARACTER input version of the ELL(1) generator in LILA is called. The input of the lexical analyser will be a string of simple characters. A detailed description of the possibilities in the option list is given in Lewi [1976c].

++ DEFINE SYNTAXRULES
First, the definition of begin and end markers for the nonterminal symbols are given, together with the definition of a stop marker for the syntax rules.
Then follows a number of ECF syntax rules in which names of semantic actions are inserted.

++ DEFINE SEMANTICROUT
The definitions of the semantic actions are given. Each action starts with # followed by the name of the action followed by a number of PL/1 statements and, possibly, declarations.

++ DEFINE GLOBALINFO
This part contains a number of PL/1 declarations (variables, files, tables, etc...) that are global to the semantic actions.

++ DEFINE TABDEST
This part is described in (1) under the heading TABSPEC. As an example, OUT(SYMBTAB, REALTAB) indicates that both tables will be saved on secondary storage (disk) at the end of the lexical analysis.

++ DEFINE HEADING
This part mainly contains a number of PL/1 statements and/or declarations that will appear in the head of the generated program such that they will receive the lowest block number. One of the purposes of this input part is to localise the specifications of the table lengths.

(3) LILA input for the syntax-semantic analyser

++ NAME EXECUTE ELL(1) OPTIONS(INPUT(TOKENS),...)
The TOKEN input version of the ELL(1) generator in LILA is called. The input of the syntax-semantic analyser is a sequence of tokens.

++ DEFINE SYNTAXRULES
This part has been discussed in (2).

++ DEFINE SEMANTICROUT
In the semantic actions, one has access to the specification field of a token by simply writing α.SPEC, where α is the name of the class field of that token. α is an element of VOCABULARY.

++ DEFINE GLOBALINFO
This part has been discussed in (2).

++ DEFINE ATTRIBUTES
This part consists of a PL/1 declaration defining the attributes used in the semantic actions. In the present ELL(1) generator version, to each nonterminal, the same set of attributes is associated. Access to the attribute,e.g. LENGTH, of the nonterminal E is simply written as E.LENGTH.

++ DEFINE TABDEST
This part has been discussed in (1) under the heading TABSPEC. As an example, IN(SYMBTAB,REALTAB) means that both tables will be taken from secondary storage at the start of the syntax-semantic analyser.

++ DEFINE ERRORSYNCHRO
This part specifies the appropriate information for the error recovery mechanism within the syntax-semantic analyser. A detailed discussion of this subject is given in Lewi [1976d].

++ DEFINE HEADING
This has been described in (2).

7. UNIT CONVERSION

Unit conversion is described in Cohen [1973]. This example is choosen since it is short, compact and at the same time nontrivial. It is representative for a great number of compiler generator features dealed with by LILA. An exhaustive documentation of this and many other examples can be found in Lewi [1976b].

```
 1         ++DEFINE TABSPEC OPTIONS(PRINT)
 2         DCL     1 SYMBTAB(0 : MAXSYMBTAB) ,
 3                   2 ALPHA CHAR(8),
 4                   2 UNITS,
 5                     3 MASS BIN FIXED,
 6                     3 LENGTH BIN FIXED,
 7                     3 TIME BIN FIXED,
 8                     3 CONV BIN FLOAT,
 9                   2 DEFINED BIT(1) ;
10         DCL REALTAB( MAXREALTAB) BIN FLOAT ;
11         ++DEFINE VOCABULARY OPTIONS(PRINT)
12         ,
13         IDENTIFIER
14         =
15         HOW
16         MANY
17         IN
18         ?
19         -
20         +
21         *
22         /
23         |
24         NUMBER
25         )
26         (
27
28
29
30         ++COMMENT

                    LEXICAL ANALYSIS

           ++
31         ++STEP1 EXECUTE ELL(1) OPTIONS(INPUT(CHAR),FILE(LEXAN),GENERATE,SYNCHRO)
32         ++DEFINE SYNTAXRULES OPTIONS(PRINT)
33         START='<' END ='>' STOP='.' ;
34         <PROGRAM> =  INIT
35              ( <LET> INITBUF
36                  ( <LET> BUF
37                  | <DIG> BUF
38                  )*7 <NOLETDIG> OUTIDENTIFIER
39              | <DIG> INITBUF
40                <DIG> BUFDIG *
41                  ( <.> BUFDIG
42                    <DIG> BUFDIG
43                    <DIG> BUFDIG *
44                  | &
45                  )
46                  ( <LET>
47                  | <NOLETDIG>
48                  ) OUTNUMBER
49              | <,>     OUTSYMBOL
50              | <=>     OUTSYMBOL
51              | <?>     OUTSYMBOL
52              | <->     OUTSYMBOL
53              | <+>     OUTSYMBOL
54              | <*>     OUTSYMBOL
55              | </>     OUTSYMBOL
56              | <|>     OUTSYMBOL
57              | <(>     OUTSYMBOL
58              | <)>     OUTSYMBOL
59              | < >     READ
60              )* <#> FINAL  .
61         <LET>=<A>|<B>|<C>|<D>|<E>|<F>|<G>|<H>|<I>|<J>|<K>|<L>|<M>|<N>|<O>|<P>|<Q>|<R>|
62               <S>|<T>|<U>|<V>|<W>|<X>|<Y>|<Z>.
63         <DIG>=<0>|<1>|<2>|<3>|<4>|<5>|<6>|<7>|<8>|<9>.
64         <NOLETDIG>=<,>|<=>|<?>|<+>|<->|<*>|</>|<|>|<)>|< >|<(>|<#>.
65         ++DEFINE SEMANTICROUT OPTIONS(PRINT)
66         #READ *
67         IF CARDINDEX > 80
68            THEN DO ;
69                    GET FILE(SYSIN) EDIT (CARD) ( A(80)) ;
70                    PUT EDIT(LINENUMBER,CARD)(SKIP,F(7),X(3),A(80));
71                    CALL OUT('LINENUMBER',LINENUMBER) ;
72                    LINENUMBER = LINENUMBER + 1 ;
73                    IN = SUBSTR(CARD,1,1) ;
74                    CARDINDEX = 2 ;
75                END ;
76            ELSE DO ;
77                    IN = SUBSTR(CARD,CARDINDEX,1) ;
```

```
              CARDINDEX = CARDINDEX + 1 ;
         END ;
#INIT
    DO I = 1 TO MAXSYMBTAB ;
         SYMBTAB(I).UNITS.MASS = 0 ;
         SYMBTAB(I).UNITS.LENGTH = 0 ;
         SYMBTAB(I).UNITS.TIME = 0 ;
         SYMBTAB(I).UNITS.CONV = 0.0;
         SYMBTAB(I).DEFINED = '0'B ;
    END ;
    /*   INITIALIZATION OF THE FIRST THREE ELEMENTS OF SYMBTAB  */
    SYMBTAB(1).ALPHA = 'KG' ;
    SYMBTAB(1).UNITS.MASS = 1 ;
    SYMBTAB(1).UNITS.CONV = 1.0;
    SYMBTAB(2).ALPHA = 'M' ;
    SYMBTAB(2).UNITS.LENGTH = 1  ;
    SYMBTAB(2).UNITS.CONV = 1.0 ;
    SYMBTAB(3).ALPHA = 'S' ;
    SYMBTAB(3).UNITS.TIME = 1  ;
    SYMBTAB(3).UNITS.CONV = 1.0 ;
    SYMBTAB(1).DEFINED = '1'B ;
    SYMBTAB(2).DEFINED = '1'B ;
    SYMBTAB(3).DEFINED = '1'B ;
    /*   INITIALIZATION OF LINENUMBER    */
    LINENUMBER = 1  ;
    /*   READ FIRST CHARACTER   */
    CALL READ ;
#INITBUF
    BUFFER = IN ;
    CALL READ ;
#BUF
    BUFFER = BUFFER || IN ;
    CALL READ ;
#OUTIDENTIFIER
    IF BUFFER = 'HOW' |
       BUFFER = 'MANY' |
       BUFFER = 'IN'
         THEN CALL OUT(BUFFER,0) ;
         ELSE CALL OUT('IDENTIFIER',SEARCHSYMBTAB(BUFFER));
#BUFDIG
    IF LENGTH(BUFFER) = 8
         THEN CALL ERROR(1) ;
         ELSE BUFFER = BUFFER || IN ;
    CALL READ ;
#OUTNUMBER
    CALL OUT ( 'NUMBER',SEARCHREALTAB(BUFFER)) ;
#OUTSYMBOL
    CALL OUT(IN , 0) ;
    CALL READ ;
#FINAL
    CALL OUT ( '--|',0) ;
    /*   PASS INFORMATION TO NEXT PASS   */
    SYMBTAB(0).UNITS.MASS = LASTNAME ;
    SYMBTAB(0).UNITS.LENGTH = LASTREAL ;
++DEFINE GLOBALINFO OPTIONS(PRINT)
 DCL BUFFER CHAR(8) VARYING ,
         CARD CHAR(80) ,
         CARDINDEX BIN FIXED INIT(81) ,
         LASTNAME BIN FIXED INIT(3) ,
         LASTREAL BIN FIXED INIT(0) ;
 DCL LEXOUT FILE RECORD SEQUENTIAL ENV(FBS RECSIZE(4)),
         TOKENS FILE STREAM PRINT;
 OUT : PROCEDURE ( STRING , NUMBER ) ;
    /*   OUTPUT OF A TOKEN   */
    DCL STRING CHAR(*) ,
         NUMBER BIN FIXED ,
         1 TOKEN ,
              2 CODE BIN FIXED ,
              2 SPEC BIN FIXED ;
    TOKEN.CODE = LOOKCODE(STRING) ;
    TOKEN.SPEC = NUMBER ;
    WRITE FILE(LEXOUT) FROM ( TOKEN) ;
    PUT FILE(TOKENS) SKIP EDIT(STRING,NUMBER)(A,COL(20),F(5));
 END OUT ;
 SEARCHSYMBTAB : PROCEDURE ( STRING) RETURNS(BIN FIXED ) ;
    /*   FILL IN A SYMBOL IN SYMBTAB  */
    DCL STRING CHAR (*) ;
    DO I = 1 TO LASTNAME ;
         IF SYMBTAB(I).ALPHA = STRING
              THEN RETURN(I) ;
    END ;
    IF LASTNAME ¬= MAXSYMBTAB
```

```
               THEN DO ;
                        LASTNAME = LASTNAME + 1  ;
                        SYMBTAB(LASTNAME).ALPHA = STRING ;
                        RETURN(LASTNAME) ;
                    END ;
               ELSE DO ;
                        CALL ERROR(3) ;
                        RETURN(1) ;
                    END ;
      END SEARCHSYMBTAB ;
      SEARCHREALTAB : PROCEDURE ( STRING) RETURNS( BIN FIXED ) ;
          /*   ENTER A NUMBER IN REALTAB  */
          DCL STRING CHAR(*),
               X BIN FLOAT ;
          GET STRING(STRING) LIST(X) ;
          DO I = 1 TO LASTREAL ;
               IF REALTAB(I) = X
                    THEN RETURN (I) ;
          END ;
          IF LASTREAL ¬= MAXREALTAB
               THEN DO ;
                        LASTREAL = LASTREAL + 1  ;
                        REALTAB(LASTREAL) = X ;
                        RETURN(LASTREAL) ;
                    END ;
               ELSE DO ;
                        CALL ERROR(2) ;
                        RETURN(1) ;
                    END ;
      END SEARCHREALTAB ;
      ERROR : PROCEDURE ( I ) ;
          DCL Z(3) LABEL ;
          PUT SKIP EDIT('*** ERROR ***')(A(14)) ;
          GO TO Z(I) ;
          Z(1) : PUT SKIP EDIT('NUMBER '|| BUFFER || ' TRUNCATED')
                        (COL(20),A) ;
                    RETURN ;
          Z(2) : PUT SKIP EDIT( 'OVERFLOW IN REALTAB ')(COL(20),A) ;
                    STOP ;
          Z(3) : PUT SKIP EDIT(' OVERFLOW IN SYMBTAB ')(COL(20),A) ;
                    STOP ;
      END ERROR ;
    ++DEFINE TABDEST
      OUT(SYMBTAB,REALTAB)
    ++DEFINE HEADING
    #BEGIN PARAMETERS: PARAM ;
          DCL PARAM CHAR(100) VARYING,
              (MAXSYMBTAB,MAXREALTAB) BIN FIXED ;
          GET STRING(PARAM) LIST(MAXSYMBTAB,MAXREALTAB) ;



    ++COMMENT

                         SYNTACTICAL SEMANTICAL ANALYSIS

    ++
    ++STEP2 EXECUTE ELL(1) OPTIONS(INPUT(TOKENS),FILE(SYNAN),SYNCHRO)
    ++DEFINE SYNTAXRULES OPTIONS(PRINT)
      START='<' END ='>' STOP ='.' ;
      <PROGRAM>             = INIT <C>
                              ( <,> <C>
                              )* FINAL .
      <C>                   =
                <IDENTIFIER> <=> <E> ASSIGN
              | <HOW> <MANY> <E> <IN> <E> <?> PRINTRESULT
      <E>                   =
                <->.<T> MINUS
              |  <T> TRANS_ET
                   (
                        <+> <T> ADD
                   |
                        <-> <T> SUBTRACT
                   )* .
      <T>                   =
              <F> TRANS_TF
                   (
                        <*> <F> TIMES
                   |
                        </> <F> DIVIDE
                   )*.
    <F>                     =
```

```
238                  <3> TRAN3_FS
239                      ( <|> <S> POWER
240                      )*.
241          <S>            =
242                  <IDENTIFIER> TREATIDEN
243                  | <NUMBER> TREATNUMBER
244                  | <(> <E> <)> TRANS_SE .
245          ++DEFINE SEMANTICROUT OPTIONS(PRINT)
246          #ASSIGN
247              SYMBTAB(IDENTIFIER.SPEC).UNITS.MASS = E_1.MASS ;
248              SYMBTAB(IDENTIFIER.SPEC).UNITS.LENGTH = E_1.LENGTH ;
249              SYMBTAB(IDENTIFIER.SPEC).UNITS.TIME = E_1.TIME ;
250              SYMBTAB(IDENTIFIER.SPEC).UNITS.CONV = E_1.CONV ;
251              SYMBTAB(IDENTIFIER.SPEC).DEFINED = '1'B ;
252          #PRINTRESULT
253              IF E_2.MASS = E_3.MASS &
254                 E_2.LENGTH = E_3.LENGTH &
255                 E_2.TIME = E_3.TIME
256                  THEN PUT SKIP EDIT((E_3.CONV/E_2.CONV))(X(20),E(20,5)) ;
257                  ELSE PUT SKIP EDIT('NO CORRESPONDING DIMENSIONS ')(X(20),A) ;
258          #MINUS
259              E.MASS = T_1.MASS ;
260              E.LENGTH = T_1.LENGTH ;
261              E.TIME = T_1.TIME ;
262              E.CONV = - T_1.CONV ;
263          #TRANS_ET
264              E = T_2 ;
265          #ADD
266              IF E.MASS = T_3.MASS &
267                 E.LENGTH = T_3.LENGTH &
268                 E.TIME = T_3.TIME
269                  THEN E.CONV = E.CONV + T_3.CONV ;
270                  ELSE CALL ERROR(1) ;
271          #SUBTRACT
272              IF E.MASS = T_4.MASS &
273                 E.LENGTH = T_4.LENGTH &
274                 E.TIME = T_4.TIME
275                  THEN E.CONV = E.CONV - T_4.CONV ;
276                  ELSE CALL ERROR(1) ;
277          #TRANS_TF
278              T = F_1 ;
279          #TIMES
280              T.MASS = T.MASS + F_2.MASS ;
281              T.LENGTH = T.LENGTH + F_2.LENGTH ;
282              T.TIME = T.TIME + F_2.TIME ;
283              T.CONV = T.CONV * F_2.CONV ;
284          #DIVIDE
285              T.MASS = T.MASS - F_3.MASS ;
286              T.LENGTH = T.LENGTH - F_3.LENGTH ;
287              T.TIME = T.TIME - F_3.TIME ;
288              IF F_3.CONV = 0.0
289                  THEN CALL ERROR(2) ;
290                  ELSE T.CONV = T.CONV / F_3.CONV ;
291          #POWER
292              IF S_2.MASS = 0 &
293                 S_2.LENGTH = 0 &
294                 S_2.TIME = 0
295                  THEN DO ;
296                          F.MASS = F.MASS * S_2.CONV ;
297                          F.LENGTH = F.LENGTH * S_2.CONV ;
298                          F.TIME = F.TIME * S_2.CONV ;
299                          F.CONV = F.CONV ** S_2.CONV ;
300                      END ;
301                  ELSE CALL ERROR(3) ;
302          #TRANS_FS
303              F = S_1 ;
304          #TREATIDEN
305              IF SYMBTAB(IDENTIFIER.SPEC).DEFINED
306                  THEN DO ;
307                          S.MASS = SYMBTAB(IDENTIFIER.SPEC).UNITS.MASS ;
308                          S.LENGTH = SYMBTAB(IDENTIFIER.SPEC).UNITS.LENGTH ;
309                          S.TIME = SYMBTAB(IDENTIFIER.SPEC).UNITS.TIME ;
310                          S.CONV = SYMBTAB(IDENTIFIER.SPEC).UNITS.CONV ;
311                      END ;
312                  ELSE CALL ERROR(4) ;
313          #TREATNUMBER
314              S.MASS = 0 ;
315              S.LENGTH = 0 ;
316              S.TIME = 0 ;
317              S.CONV = REALTAB(NUMBER.SPEC) ;
318          #TRANS_SE
319              S = E ;
```

```
#FINAL
    /*   PRINT ALL TABLES  */
    PUT PAGE EDIT('SYMBTAB','*******')(A,COL(1),A) ;
    DO I = 1 TO SYMBTAB(0).UNITS.MASS ;
         PUT SKIP EDIT(SYMBTAB(I).ALPHA,
                   SYMBTAB(I).UNITS.MASS,
                   SYMBTAB(I).UNITS.LENGTH,
                   SYMBTAB(I).UNITS.TIME,
                   SYMBTAB(I).UNITS.CONV,
                   SYMBTAB(I).DEFINED)
                   (A(8),F(8),F(8),F(8),E(20,5),X(3),B(1));
    END;
    PUT PAGE EDIT('REALTAB','*******')(A,COL(1),A);
    DO I = 1 TO SYMBTAB(0).UNITS.LENGTH ;
         PUT SKIP EDIT(REALTAB(I))(E(20,5)) ;
    END ;
#INIT
    PUT PAGE EDIT ('ANSWERS TO THE QUESTIONS')(A);
++DEFINE GLOBALINFO OPTIONS(PRINT)
 ERROR : PROCEDURE ( I ) ;
    DCL I BIN FIXED ;
    DCL Z(4) LABEL ;
    PUT SKIP EDIT(LINENUMBER,'*** ERROR ***')(F(10),A) ;
    GO TO Z(I) ;
    Z(1) : PUT SKIP EDIT('NO CORRESPONDING DIMENSIONS FOR + OR - OPERATO
 R')(COL(20),A) ;
              STOP ;
    Z(2) : PUT SKIP EDIT('ATTEMPT TO DIVIDE BY 0 ')(COL(20),A)  ;
              STOP ;
    Z(3) : PUT SKIP EDIT('EXPONENT MUST BE A NUMBER')(COL(20),A) ;
              STOP ;
    Z(4) : PUT SKIP EDIT('ATTEMPT TO USE  AN UNDEFINED IDENTIFIER')
              (COL(20),A) ;
              STOP ;
 END ERROR ;
++DEFINE ATTRIBUTES OPTIONS(PRINT)
    DCL  1 MASS BIN FIXED,
         1 LENGTH BIN FIXED,
         1 TIME BIN FIXED,
         1 CONV BIN FLOAT ;
++DEFINE TABDEST OPTIONS(PRINT)
  IN(SYMBTAB,REALTAB)
++DEFINE ERRORSYNCHRO OPTIONS(PRINT)
    'HOW'      '?'  'C'
    '('        ')'  'S'
++DEFINE HEADING OPTIONS(PRINT)
#BEGIN PARAMETERS: PARAM ;
    DCL PARAM CHAR(100) VARYING ,
         (MAXREALTAB,MAXSYMBTAB) BIN FIXED ;
    GET STRING(PARAM)LIST (MAXSYMBTAB,MAXREALTAB) ;
    GET STRING(PARAM)LIST (MAXSYMBTAB,MAXREALTAB) ;
```

PROJECT LILA : THE ELL(1) GENERATOR OF LILA, AN INTRODUCTION

```
 1     CM = 0.01 * M,
 2     INCH = 2.54 * CM,
 3     FEET = 0.3048 * M,
 4     HOW MANY INCH IN FEET ?,
 5     YARD = 0.9144 * M,
 6     HOW MANY INCH IN YARD ?,
 7     HOW MANY FEET IN YARD ?,
 8     SQINCH = INCH * INCH,
 9     SQFEET = FEET * FEET,
10     HOW MANY SQINCH IN SQFEET ?,
11     CUINCH = INCH | 3,
12     M2 = M * M,
13     M3 = M | 3,
14     HOW MANY SQINCH IN M2 ?,
15     HOW MANY CUINCH IN M2 * M ?,
16     HOW MANY M / S IN ( SQFEET / YARD ) / S ?
17         #
```

ANSWERS TO THE QUESTIONS
```
                         1.20000E+01
                         3.60000E+01
                         3.00000E+00
                         1.44000E+02
                         1.55000E+03
                         6.10237E+04
                         1.01600E-01
```

SYMBTAB
****
KG	1	0	0	1.00000E+00	1
M	0	1	0	1.00000E+00	1
S	0	0	1	1.00000E+00	1
CM	0	1	0	1.00000E-02	1
INCH	0	1	0	2.54000E-02	1
FEET	0	1	0	3.04800E-01	1
YARD	0	1	0	9.14400E-01	1
SQINCH	0	2	0	6.45160E-04	1
SQFEET	0	2	0	9.29030E-02	1
CUINCH	0	3	0	1.63871E-05	1
M2	0	2	0	1.00000E+00	1
M3	0	3	0	1.00000E+00	1

REALTAB
****
```
     1.00000E-02
     2.54000E+00
     3.04800E-01
     9.14400E-01
     3.00000E+00
```

8. REFERENCES

Cohen, J. [1973]. Syntax-directed unit conversion. Information Processing Letters 2, p. 100-102, North-Holland.

Gries, D. [1971]. Compiler Construction for Digital Computers. Wiley, New York.

Griffiths, M. [1976]. LL(1) Grammars and Analysers. In : Compiler construction, an advanced course. Lecture Notes in Computer Science 21, Springer-Verlag.

Knuth, D.E. [1967]. Top-down syntax analysis. Lecture Notes. International Summer School on Computer Programming, Copenhagen, Denmark.

Knuth, D.E. [1968]. Semantics of context-free languages. Math. Systems Theory J. 2, No. 2, 127-146.

Lewi, J., De Vlaminck, K., Huens, J. and Huybrechts, M. [1976a]. Project LILA, The ELL(1) generator, basic principles. Report CW 5. Applied Math. and Progr. Div. Katholieke Universiteit Leuven.

Lewi, J., De Vlaminck, K., Huens, J. and Huybrechts, M. [1976b]. Project LILA, The ELL(1) generator, primer. Report in preparation.

Lewi, J., De Vlaminck, K., Huens, J. and Huybrechts, M. [1976c]. Project LILA, User's manual. Report in preparation.

Lewi, J., De Vlaminck, K., Huens, J. and Huybrechts, M. [1976d]. Project LILA, The ELL(1) generator, Error recovery. Report CW 8. Applied Math. and Progr. Div. Katholieke Universiteit Leuven.

Lewi, J., De Vlaminck, K., Huens, J. [1976e]. Project LILA, FIGDRAW and PICO-ALGOL, an experience with LILA in a course on compiler construction. Report CW 4. Applied Math. and Progr. Div. Katholieke Universiteit Leuven.

Lewi, J. [1975]. Notes on the course of compiler constrcution.

OTHER LITERATURE

Ganzinger, H. [1976]. MUG1-Manual. Report nr. 7608, Technische Universität München.

Bauer, F.L. and Eickel, J. (eds.) [1976]. Compiler Construction, An advanced course. Lecture Notes in Computer Science, 21. Springer-Verlag.

Blaizot, L. [1973]. DELTA, système de description de langages et de traducteurs par attributs. IRIA, Rapport de Recherche no. 20.

Bochmann, G.V. and Lecarme O. [1972]. Un système d'écriture de compilateurs. Documents de travail 27, 30, 40, 44. Université de Montreal.

Bochmann, G.V. [1973]. Semantic evaluation from left to right. Comm. ACM 19:2, 55-62.

Bouckaert, M., Pirotte, M. and Snelling, M. [1973]. SOFT : a tool for writing software. MBLE Research Laboratory Brussels, R212.

Branquart, P., Cardinael, J.P., Lewi, J., Delescaille, J.P. and Vanbegin, M. [1976]. An optimised translation process and its application to Algol 68. Lecture Notes in Computer Science 38. Springer-Verlag.

Fang, I. [1972]. FOLDS, a declarative formal language definition system. Stanford University CS-72-329.

Koster, C.H.A. [1971]. A compiler-compiler. Mathematisch Centrum Amsterdam, report 127.

Wilhelm, R. [1976]. Syntax und Semantikspezifikation in der Eingabesprache für einen Compiler Compiler. Abteilung Mathematik an der Technischen Universität München, Bericht Nr. 7301.

E. Morlet and D. Ribbens, (Eds.), International Computing Symposium 1977.

COMPUTER WORK FOR LITERARY PRODUCTION
A PARTICULAR APPLICATION FOR BIBLICAL STUDIES

E. de Borchgrave R. F. Poswick

Concordance de la Bible
MAREDSOUS - BREPOLS
B 5642 Denée (Belgique)

The main purpose of this article is to inform newcomers to the field of computer-assisted literary text processing, particularly those who intend to start a major project, of the options available to them and by the same token of the long-range implications of their initial choices.

INTRODUCTION

The analysis is based on the experience gained by our group at the Abbey of Maredsous in a specific area, but its conclusions are believed to be independent from the subject matter. It should also be pointed out that we are a very small team operating under rather stringent economic constraints, a circumstance which has made us cost-conscious even though we are not profit-motivated and has led us to put more emphasis on efficiency than on elegance for its own sake.

This pragmatic and production-oriented approach is perhaps the only original aspect of our contribution to a field which is almost as old as the computer itself and which has by now become fairly well established. Indeed, everyone today is aware of the ever-increasing use of computers to various aspects in the literary and linguistic studies. Specialized periodicals now make available basic information on large-scale surveys and main trends in the literary studies aided by modern technology, for example "Computers and the Humanities", or "Revue" (L.A. S.L.A., Liège). In particular in the field of religious literature, we would like to mention Fr BUSA, S.J., a genuine pioneer in the field /1/. Many other projects are now being carried out and the results of those already finished have been published. In addition, computer typesetting and photocomposition combined with automatic production of data banks has now come to existence.

Generally speaking, such enterprises demand large teams, access to equipments and adequate financing. Despite our limited means, we set the ambitious goal of analysing, producing a data bank of publishing materials related to Biblical Study, our first published result being "La Table pastorale de la Bible" /2/. Our next one, under compilation at present, is an exhaustive analytical and multilingual index of the Bible in French, Hebrew, Greek, Latin and English.
We hope that an account of our modest experience, incidentally confined to religious literature, can be of some use and interest for those wishing to begin using computers in text processing or any other literary or editing endeavour. We trust our account will provide some assistance to those who, like ourselves, put high priority on cost aspects and the need for efficiency. As we are limited by space, this paper will confine itself to presenting a global, rather than detailed, view of some opportunities made available by the computer.

A first section, Preparing the data, will deal firstly with input problems such as encoding, organisation of files, and secondly with problems of lemmatisation (nominalized forms).
A second section, Using the data, will examine three types of application. A first type is the publishing of texts from a data bank. A second type is the creation of various work-instruments. This second type may be divided into two levels : the production of tools such as indices, concordances, frequency lists, etc, as well as more elaborated products of higher analysis such as syntactic, linguistic, semantic, stylistic analysis, etc. A third type will discuss photocomposition. Before concluding, a last section will briefly mention computer programming.

SECTION 1 : PREPARING THE DATA

Our work is an attempt to solve effectively the problem of dealing with a vast quantity of data and the time involved in collating it. In our particular case, we found ourselves confronted with a "corpus" /3/ of more than 850.000 literary elements, namely the words of the Bible. Putting these in rigorous alphabetical order, selecting appropriate keywords, choosing a significant yet brief context which allows us to situate each element, the construction of a vast network of cross-references, are among the many problems we had to face, the moment we considered preparing an index of Biblical themes and ideas which would serve as a sort of concordance or topical resource work. The problems loomed larger since we were bound by economic consideration.

The suggestion to resort to computer usage arose early in the project. Investigation quickly proved that the method would be useful, provided it was applied thoroughly and continuously from the input encoding stage down to the final printed book.

Just over two years after our initial introduction to the COBOL language, a volume of 1.214 two-columned pages was electronically produced via photocomposition. This was only some ten or twelve hours after committing the last stage of the work to magnetic tape. There was need for no further, and possibly faulty, proof reading. The printed, bound volume was on sale two months later /2/.

1.1. Encoding

Before one is in a position to make full use of the innumerably variegated possibilities of a computer, one laborious and burdensome yet indispensable task has to be gone through, namely transforming the data to be used in a machine readable form. It is a matter of a long encoding operation, relatively simple in its basic conception (one literary symbol per machine bit configuration), but one which needs to be well thought out, for on this first operation will depend the extent to which it will be possible to use the data to the full. There is no need to dwell here on the "hardware" side of the operation in which technical progress is constantly being made : punched cards, disketts, magnetic tapes, etc. Whatever technique one's economic situation makes most practical, one will always have to type the entire text to be processed /4/. If maximum flexibility for the future is to be retained, on the other hand, what will matter is the way in which the coding has been done at the outset.

An easy and rapid use of the data contained in the text being encoded demands a very careful study of its reference system. This must take account of the references contained in the source document, or those habitually used for a given text, but all the while producing them in a systematic structure (generally a numeric one) easily fed into the machine. For every literary work (choice of contexts, comparisons, etc), it soon becomes clear that one must divide the text into short portions. We are tempted to say : into segments as small as the meaning or any material accident of textual transmission will permit. Each corpus and each text constitutes here a unique and specific case which has to be submitted to a preliminary close scrutiny.

From this stage onwards, one must anticipate all the elements which could ultimately affect the techniques of typographic composition : for instance the problems caused by accents in French, breathing marks, accents and other diacritical indications in Greek, vocalization and musical accentuation in Hebrew, etc. For our part, we have chosen to represent these diacritical marks either in numeric codes or in special signs preceeding the letter in question. Upper-case letters required by grammatical position of the word have been automatically generated through programming by a special sign whilst those required by proper-names have received a special code at the encoding. All punctuation signs should be incorporated while encoding if one wishes to obtain a text or a portion thereof typographically correct. In short, every graphic change, especially every typographic change in a given text, can have its importance and thus constitutes one indispensable information (e.g. use of italics in a text to show it is a variant from another manuscript than that which serves as a basis for the edited text; a text quoted from another work; a passage in regular script but in foreign language, etc). A selection of special and sufficiently mnemonic characters allows one to combine and retain, while encoding, those various indications whitout being always obliged to resort, at least for modern languages, to the additional stage of transcription of the data upon encoding sheets before keyboarding.

Once the entire text has been encoded, recorded on magnetic tape and revised on print-out from the tape, we have worked out what we have called a vertical text : we take every individual word of the recorded text and we create a file of one record per word.Each record is designed to contain the maximum possible information concerning the word in question, and can be enriched indefinitely according to the stages of literary or statistical analyses of the text. The basic structure of a record in this vertical file is as follows : nine bytes for the reference; three bytes for locating the element in the segment; one for the graphic shape of the word (first letter upper-case, all lower-case, all upper-case, etc); 31 bytes for the original shape of the word; two for punctuation signs; one for typographic indications (italics, regular script, change of face, etc); one for the treatment of figures; two giving the length of the word. Before feeding up this file with new elements, especially during the process of lemmatisation (of which we will speak later), several corrective programs are already at work. Experience shows that re-reading of listings overlooks ordinarily some 10 % of the errors which are bound to occur at the encoding and which are ranging between 10 % and 20 % of the entire text - depending on the difficulty of the text and the quality of the punching. One will avail oneself with profit of the computational abilities of the computer for producing frequency lists sorted on occuring forms : it is among the rarest occurrences (one or two according to the volume of the corpus processed) that one will find almost all the erroneous or suspect forms. Thanks to the reference accompanying each of the elements, one is able to make quickly any correction by substitution, insertion or suppression. This first stage, probably the most laborious in time, can be considered complete once the text is deemed "formally correct". It is evident that there still remains a number of grammatical or semantic mistakes (singular for plural, present for past, etc) which can have escaped the attention of the person who has revised the listing of the continuous text, and which cannot be perceived by the machine at this level of processing.

1.2. Lemmatisation

A second stage is then required in order to have on hand a text completely responding to any further demand in the field of a polyvalent use from a electronic processing. This is the stage of lemmatisation or affixing nominalizations. Grammatical custom inherited from the past requires that one regroup the different forms of a same word under one single form, designated as a lemma (example : 'DRIVE' for 'drives', 'drove', 'driving', 'driven'). This lemma serves as a basis for further use such as the production of concordances, comparison of texts, automatic lemmatisation of any other text, contents analysis, etc. At this point, we must concede that the traditional regrouping under a lemma is conventional, and thus arbitrary. In one language, for a noun, one distinguishes only the alteration singular/plural (house/houses); in another one, there is a series of alterations showing the case (nominative, genitive) which is represented in the first language by several other elements (rus, lat. = the country; ruri, lat. = in the country). The computer allows to provide several levels of lemmatisation.

But again, one must start from the classic conception of a dictionary and integrate it into the basic work, as one does for the system of reference. This must be done for each language processed according to its own, traditionals norms. A sorting of all the forms occurring in the text will provide a preliminary concordance of forms on the basis of which, thanks to the contextual situation of each form, one will be able to select the proper lemma. The forms will receive an identification number in the alphabetical order. Once the lemmas are selected by the researcher, they will be recorded and also provided with an individual identification number. Thence forward, forms and lemmas will be used solely on the basis of this numerical identification which is always made according to a strict alphabetical classification. At this level, one of the most important difficulties is the processing of homographs, homonyms and words really polysemical. These need to be analysed in their contexts, a labour best carried out by human hands. This method seems to be the most realistic and swiftest of all. It is much less burdensome than designing analytical programs, grammatical or other, which will still demand further verification and a prohibitive amount of machine time. All the informations resulting from this lemmatisation constitute a new series of data consisting of about 40 bytes which then complete the vertical file.

Two important remarks have to be made at this level we still consider as being a part of a correct and complete storing of the data.

1° We must emphasize that the entirety of the above described work of lemmatisation needs to be done only once on a relatively extended corpus for a given language. In effect, based on our first lemmatised vertical text - namely the 850,000 elements found in the Bible of Maredsous -, one creates automatically a Dictionary of French forms and lemmas. This dictionary itself designed to allow the storing of information added at each new processing, serves also as an instrument for automatic lemmatisation of any new corpus of texts in the same language. It is sufficient to read in parallel the newly 'verticalised' elements and the dictionary forms in order to select non-existent or ambiguous forms which require direct analysis. In all ambiguous cases, the program facilitates the researcher's work in that it fixes the most probable lemma from all statistical information gathered in the course of previous processings. The researcher has only to check, on the basis of the context in which the ambiguous form is located, whether the lemma automatically assigned by program is accurate. He corrects it only if the automatic assignation proves incorrect.

The development of this dictionary allows for enrichment at each stage via inclusion of new material : classes of words, expressions, elements of verification from the classic dictionaries of the language in question. From the Biblical corpus, one obtains immediately a dictionary of about 30,000 forms corresponding to somme 14,000 different lemmas. This universal and literary stock of language allows one to lemmatise automatically from 65 to 89 % of a new literary text, depending on its nature.

2° A second important remark requires that we deal again with the vertical conception of our files. This disposition of the text is the best available for numerous supple uses, foreseen and unforeseen. With the assistance of this corrected vertical text, we can easily reconstruct a 'horizontal' text for various purposes: be it a partial or entire reconstruction of the original text in order to produce a continuous text in a typographical and faultless presentation; or be it selected segments which could serve as a basis for the automatic choice of small connecting contexts allowing the full meaning of a given word to emerge. This small context (about 60 characters) provides the researcher at all levels of the work with guide-lines that leave him free from constant recourse to the original text, barring only very exceptional cases. This allows for an economy of labour and a gain in time.

At the end of these two stages, we must add that the record format we have adopted allows us, by means of certain differentiated or complementary codes, to process similarly languages as much different as French, Latin, Greek or Hebrew. Hence a great economy in programming is possible because the algorithms remain the same.

SECTION 2 : USING THE DATA

Having on magnetic medium our texts in lemmatised vertical files according to the two elaborating stages described above, we stand before a work which allows us nearly unlimited applications.

The previous two stages are undeniably long. But we must emphasize the fact that this process is much less long and considerably more reliable than any former method which required transformation of a manuscript text to a printed shape : yet, in spite of the reduction of effort, we find ourselves now not with a closed text, but with one open to all conceivable investigative techniques and editorial productions.

On the other hand, we must also draw attention to the increasing number of centres and teams who were at work, these past few years, on these long and demanding labours, applying various linguistic sciences to various literary works which constitute mankinds cultural patrimony. All these efforts have not yet been unified, methodology is not yet perfect; there is some waste. Yet numerous texts are already encoded and will become accessible via computer methodology in the near future.

The universality of technology allows us to exchange data while reducing out time considerably and favouring the development of a spirit of cooperation and complementarity among the different work centres (a result not to be underestimated given the chauvinistic tendency of 'academism' in traditional universities).

Within our sphere of interest - that of the Bible in the various cultural forms in which it has been transmitted - we are pleased to be able to use the work of the Revised Standard Version Bible of Zondervan Publishers /5/. For the Greek text, we have the excellent recorded text of the Thesaurus Linguae Graecae of the University of California at Irvine /6/. As for the Latin Vulgate text, we have the text of Rev. Father Boniface FISHER and Dr OTT of the University of Tübingen /7/. We share also in the benefits of the work being done on the Greek language by L.A.S.L.A. at the University of Liège /8/. In the modern language section, we have also gained access to the Jerusalem Bible (in French) via a paper tape system in Photon typographic composition /9/. We call your attention to these acquisitions, because we believe the editors and publishing houses have not yet measured the latent possibilities made available by computer techniques.

The work so far completed here and there opens, through its several directions, a new type of market for the international exchange of literary data. This type makes possible an overthrow in the near future of the traditionally separate functions of publication and circulation.

We must now consider the field of applications. They are numberless, even for the most fertile imagination. We are tempted to classify the possibilities into two large types : 1) preparation of text editions; 2) preparation of work-instruments. A possible third type could be added, but we think unnecessary to isolate it since it concerns developing research on the basis of original data with interactive computer usage. When we speak of type of application, we are mainly concerned with editorial activity based on the data encoded and processed.

2.1. Editing

We have the possibility, on the basis of our lemmatised vertical text, to produce in part or in whole a printed edition of the data in the most useful form. Subtitles, notes, etc, can be added when desired.

One could also raise the question whether, in the field of critical or integral editions of the classic authors, no new method can be proposed to researchers, which could eliminate the need for each new generation to begin anew this kind of work.

2.2. Creation of tools

2.2.1. Basic level

There are two categories of instruments. There are those classified as tables, which include concordances, frequency lists, inverse indices, references tables, etc. The numerous combinations made available by the sorting process allow us to offer to the public all the working tools desirable. For an edition in the classical way, one must choose among the possible instruments those which are of universal interest. But one must increasingly call the public's attention to the fact that the only truly universal instrument is the very text, as it can be processed and consulted from its shape on storage medium. To this end, the access to the magnetic files must be simplified and larger numbers of people taught to make use of their possibilities. Nearly all centres interested in literary data or documentation are familiar with these instruments /10/. One appreciates especially the computer's speed and accuracy in manipulating great masses of data.

2.2.2. Higher level

We have also the instruments which proceed from a more detailed analysis of texts : syntactic, linguistic, semantic, contents analyses, as well as those arising from the text's different matrices (sociological, psychological, political, structural, etc...). There is a vast area, which the limit set on this paper will not allow us to pursue, yet which can provide at every time one or several instruments which will bring us to a closer understanding of the text. In order to give an idea of such possibilities, we would like to say a word here about an application of comparison of texts. Our project is the publication of a comparative and exhaustive concordance of the Bible using the different language versions as it can be found in three French translations, an English translation, and a Latin translation as well as the Greek and Hebrew versions. This requires that for each word of a given version of the Bible, one must give the corresponding or equivalent word in each of the other versions. It is easy to compare two versions in the same language by parallel reading to see if they use the same word in the same place. When the corresponding words are not the same (which is always the case when two different languages are compared), it becomes more difficult to recognize automatically which word in one version corresponds to which one in the other. If the computer can recognize two physically identical configurations, it cannot recognize semantic identities.

We believe we have found and set in motion a process which allows to automatize to a large extent the identification of these equivalents /11/. For two versions of the same language, one must recognize synonyms automatically; for two versions of different languages, one must recognize linguistic or translational equivalents automatically. The principle is simple and the method effective : one applies to a large corpus a series of calculations to discover the proportions of co-occurrences in context. In the same segment, one attributes a priori identity to a word in version A with all possible words which one finds in the identical reference segment in version B. Within the whole of the corpus, the "significant" identities will clearly emerge through higher occurrences from those insignificant identities. We cannot give here the details of this procedure which is in reality somewhat complex, since the level of minimum occurrence necessary to establish a workable identity varies from one word to another according to its frequency in the corpus. Very rare occurrences (hapax) and very frequent occurrences offer some particular difficulties. Another complication arises in the case of complex equivalences, where the nature of one language renders in one word what another expresses in several words.

Co-occurrence or certain words makes it possible to suspect this kind of phenomena, but there is always a limit where direct intervention by the researcher is necessary.

This offers a suitable opportunity to emphasize that we believe that our use of the computer, which we think is in conformity to its nature as well as its possibilities and limits, is always aiming to automatize all processes which can be done that way perfectly and reliably, but never the whole work. To attempt the latter in the literary field is a harmful utopia. Those who believe in fully automatic translation projects are sadly in error /12/.

We note further that all these processes presuppose the processing of long texts. The longer the text, the more performing are the methods and the more paying is the work.

It is a matter of course that many other applications of this type could be set in motion.

2.3. Computer typesetting and photocomposition

We must now turn to the admirable technique of electronic photocomposition and the great services it is called upon to render in the field of publishing.

To plan a literary work via computer, one must know from the very beginning the way one wishes to present the work to the public, and one must provide from that moment all the information needed for automatic typographic composition (complete spelling, diacritical marks, punctuation signs, editorial rules, typographic variants, etc). This is a new way of thinking for the investigator accustomed to deliver to his editor an often illegible hodge-podge for correction which, since the base is poor, provides only a mediocre result.

The computer team must care for the possible ways towards the presentation of the final results. They must call on the advice of graphic artists who are sufficiently familiar with typography to preserve all the possibilities of composition available into the encoded and processed data /13/.

The photocomposition process starts as soon as a work is judged ready for publishing, assuming of course that one can recognize the exact nature of the different codified data which one wishes to publish (in the case of a dictionary for instance : keywords, cross-references, localizations, quotations, etc). Provided that all data of whatever nature may be localized, it is very easy to insert at the head of each series the typesetting commands which correspond to the lay-out previously designed (page lay-out, choice of type face, justification, etc). Since the magnetic tape contains together both the literary data and the typesetting process control, the text can be electronically composed either directly on cathode-ray tube on the basis of which impressions are made on films and then offset, or indirectly by transcodification onto paper tape intended to control machines whose functioning is either genuinely electronic or still mechanical (monotype system, for example, which is still one of the most frequently used in the printing industry).

One can thus collate great dictionaries and lexica swarming of references in a few hours and without the risk of introducing new errors, since the data are submitted to this process only when they are perfectly correct. There is no longer a need for proof reading and amendments involving new manual data entry. One must only verify that pages and columns are in their proper order when put on film.

Further, the longer the volume, the more effective will be the operation which will be beyond comparison with the fatigue and the delays encountered in conventional text composition.

Typographic quality is equal to that of traditional processes. As a complementary remark however, we would say that if one deplores the bad quality sometimes presented in cases of often illegible photographic reproductions of computer's outputs, one must admit also that typographic refinement is far from desirable for the publication of lists and other work instruments. This will become increasingly true in proportion to the investigators increasing possibilities to have access to the data on computer.

SECTION 3 : COMPUTER PROGRAMMING

Only a word remains to be said about programming. Acquisition of a computer language is fairly easy today with high-level languages, i.e. problem-oriented or machine-independent languages. A rudimentary knowledge of the machine is sufficient for the specialist in literature to learn a computer language well enough to carry out even complicated tasks. But even beyond a certain apprenticeship, practice is indispensable to manage a computer efficiently.

Experience alone teaches one how to save writing time and how to make more performing programs. Imagination and logic allied with precision and accuracy which leaves nothing to chance, are the qualities required for a programmer. Are they not the same qualities required for the meticulous scholarly researcher ? Is it not a suitable discipline for the literary investigator who is now and then a bit too quickly satisfied with vague impressions and formulas ?

Programming and computer technology have, however, other secondary requirements, heavier than one might imagine. We think especially of maintaining the files, documentation and programs. This presupposes a real organisation allowing permanent access to all the files and the procedures useful for processing the data. These tasks are in danger of neglect. In case of accident, changing personnel, exchange of programs between different organisations, a total or partial loss of the potential provided by the computer is liable to result.

CONCLUSION

We can certainly say that continual progress in computer technology opens a new era in the field of literary study and publication as well as in the diffusion of knowledge in general.

The main contribution of the computer resides in the preparation of tasks and in the compilation of a series of intermediary work instruments, which no investigator has until now been able to produce without the risk of toiling on an endless work.

But, from the point of view of the data processing and the profit-earning research as well, this contribution is worthwhile only if the processes are applied to large literary data sets and if one considers doing the work as a part of the whole process of publication and diffusion, i.e. if one creates data banks.

Speed of processing and accessing, security of data sets, are the self-evident advantages of computerized handling of literary data.

The diverse means of access to these present and coming data banks, will be, as we believe, a new pillar of our future culture.

ACKNOWLEDGEMENTS

We would like most particularly to thank IBM-BELGIUM for its helpful encouragement, the direction and the staff of Brussel's C.G.E.R. Computer Centre for allowing us to use hardware facilities, and BREPOLS (Turnhout - België) publishing house as the manager of the work now in the making.

REFERENCES

/1/ See especially : D. DESTOBBELEIR and E. PERSONS, Actes du Colloque : "L'utilisation des ordinateurs et la recherche en sciences humaines " (Bruxelles, 25-27 février 1971), Archives et Bibliothèques de Belgique, n° 5 et 6, Bruxelles, 1971 (= Revue (L.A.S.L.A.) 1971, 1-2-3); the review Computers and the Humanities (edited at

Queen College, Flushing, N.Y. USA) where the Annual Bibliography Reviews and Directory of Active Scholars offer good panorama in this domain; for Busa's bibliography, see note n° 10.

/2/ G. PASSELECQ & F. POSWICK, Table pastorale de la Bible, Index analytique et analogique, Paris, Lethielleux, 1974, 1214 p.

/3/ By "corpus", we mean a collection of literary texts assembled into a logical unity functioning on a principle of textual similarity (author, culture, nature). The Bible is a "corpus" assembling, according to different traditions, from twenty-four to seventy-three books or documents.

/4/ So far, technical research has not reached, it seems, a successful stage concerning a useful system for optical reading which allows a presentation of printed matter of all kinds to an optical head.

/5/ This text is used in "The Layman's Parallel Bible", Zondervan Bible Publishers, Grand Rapids, Michigan, USA, 1973.

/6/ Thesaurus Linguae Graecae Newsletter, n° 4, December 1975, University of California, Irvine, California, USA.

/7/ B. FISCHER, The Use of Computers in New Testament Studies, with special reference to textual criticism, The Journal of Theological Studies, vol. XXI, part. 2, 1970, pp. 297-308; Dr WILHELM OTT, Transcription and correction of texts on paper tape experiences in preparing the Latin Bible text for the Computer, Revue, 1970, n° 2, pp. 51-56.

/8/ For the work of Prof. DELATTE and associates (L.A.S.L.A., Université de Liège, Belgium), see the series Revue, especially : S. GOVAERTS & J. DENOOZ, Codification d'un texte latin sur cartes mécanographiques IBM 80 colonnes, Revue, 1974, n° 3, pp. 1-22.

/9/ We refer to classic composition on TTS 8 channels 25/4 mm paper tape with use of 6 channels. Software : PD8L of 32K for a composition on Pacesetter Photon (13 corps, 8 polices) developped by MAURY-PRINTER at Malesherbes (France). Paper tape are transcoded by IBM-2671.

/10/ P. TOMBEUR, Les méthodes et les travaux du Centre de traitement Electronique des Documents (CETEDOC), Bulletin de Philosophie Médiévale, Louvain 1968-1970, 10-12, pp. 141-174; P. BICHARD-BREAUD, Traitement automatique des données biographiques, Analyse et Programmation, Onomasticon Arabicum, 5, IRHT, CNRS, Paris, 1973; R. BUSA, Der Index Thomisticus, IBM Nachrichten, 228, Dezember 1975, pp. 317-324 and Revue (L.A.S.L.A.), 1976, 6, pp. 1-45; G. PIGAULT, Documentation automatique et recherche en Sciences religieuses, Mémoires du CERDIC, 6, Strasbourg, 1975.

/11/ D. HIRSCHBERG has been perfecting the algorithms (private communication of 28/08/76).

/12/ See B. VAUQUOIS, La traduction automatique à Grenoble, Doc. de linguistique quantitative, 24, Dunod, Paris, 1975; but above all see the wise and sensible remarks of Lydia HIRSCHBERG and R. MICHEA in the Report of G. GOUGENHEIM, Problèmes de la traduction automatique, Klincksiek, Paris, 1968.

/13/ A. H. PHILLIPS, Computer Peripherals & Typesetting, HMSO, London, 1968;
P. TRABAND, La photocomposition et l'ordinateur à l'Imprimerie Nationale, in : L'Art du Livre à l'Imprimerie Nationale, Paris, 1973, pp. 285-295.

E. Morlet and D. Ribbens, (Eds.), International Computing Symposium 1977.
© North-Holland Publishing Company, 1977

MICROPROCESSOR BASED PARALLEL COMPUTERS AND THEIR APPLICATION TO THE SOLUTION OF CONTROL ALGORITHMS

D. Al-Dabass

Control Systems Centre
The University of Manchester
Institute of Science & Technology
Sackville Street, Manchester
England

The small size of single-chip microprocessors enable some 1000 of these devices to be packed within one cubic foot. This represents perhaps more processing power per unit volume per £ than any other known processor. This paper considers ways of tapping this processing power for the solution of problems involving a large number of similar computations and investigates their efficiency. The application of these methods to control problems is illustrated by analysing Bellman's dynamic programming algorithm along the lines proposed for operating these microprocessor clusters.

1. INTRODUCTION

The need to solve very large problems at moderate speed on the one hand, and relatively smaller problems at very high speed on the other, has lead to the development of special purpose parallel processing computers over the past decade. Problems in the first category include weather forecasting, and the manipulations of very large matrices, such as those found in linear programming. The second class of problems mainly involves real-time algorithms in computer control, such as filtering in object tracking and data processing and control in phased array radar.

Two types of parallel processors have dominated the scene: the associative processor and the array processor. While both of these processors fall within the general category of single instruction stream/multi-data steam architecture, they differ considerably in the way they handle these data streams. In the associative processor memory is accessed by content rather than by address. A common register is compared with all memory words simultaneously, either one bit or one byte at a time, and when a match is found the address of the corresponding memory location is saved for subsequent processing. This parallel operation on all words is achieved by associating separate arithmetic and logic hardware with each memory word. Examples of this machine are the Goodyear STARAN Rudolph [11], Raythean RAP, and ICL DAP. In the array type machine the processing elements are much more sophisticated and each has a whole memory area allocated to it. Although in general all elements execute the same instruction stream generated by the control unit, local control is usually provided to disable execution according to local tests. Communication is usually limited to the four neighbouring elements, although the more recent machines have additional but limited communication along the diagonal paths. Examples of array processors include the Illiac IV, Barnes [3], PEPE, Crane [6], the Cannon and Mulder type Mulder [8] and the 3-dimensional computer, Rudberg [10].

All these computers are special purpose not only in operation but in their use of specially designed processing elements. The appearance of the general purpose single-chip microprocessor must eventually lead to the development of parallel computers based on these devices due to their low cost, small size and increasing power. In this paper possible configurations for using large numbers of these devices to form the basis for more powerful and cost effective parallel computers will be considered. To illustrate the use of the proposed configurations Bellman's dynamic programming algorithm will be analysed with a view to solving it on such machines.

2. PARALLEL ORGANISATIONS

Two distinct phases of operation are recognised when considering parallel processing organisations. The first is the computation phase when each element is processing its share of the work loads, and the second is the overhead phase when the individual results are collected and cross-communicated among the processors memories. Overhead is the more important of these two phases as it ultimately determines the minimum achievable parallel processing time, Al-Dabass [1] and careful considerations have to be given to reduce its effect. Theoretically the overheads can be reduced to a minimum by having as many communication buses as there are processors, and memory areas, so that all data transfers among memories can be carried out in parallel. This, however, is prohibitively complex in practice even for a small number of processors and leads to simpler and more practical arrangements which may be divided into single and multiple bus systems.

2.1 Single Bus Systems

In this scheme each processor memory area is provided with switching logic to connect it to either its own processor or to a common bus, Figure 1. During the computation phase each memory/processor pair form an isolated computing unit working in parallel with all other pairs. During the overheads phase the memory areas are

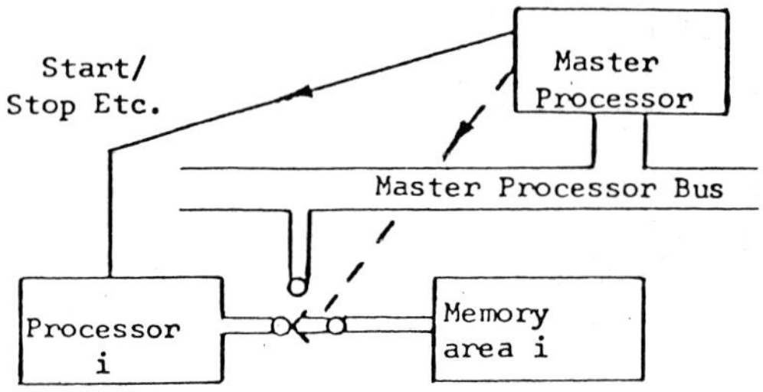

Figure 1

switched to the common bus which enables a master processor to perform all cross-transfer of data between memory units.

(i) Multiple and Single Instruction Streams: The program for the processor may be resident in the processor's own memory, thus enabling the processors to have different programs. This creates a Multi-Instruction stream, Multi-Data stream (MIMD) organisation. The programs in these memory areas are fed by the master processor during the development and initialisation stages, using the common bus system.

In applications where all processors execute the same program access to a single copy of the program is required to avoid duplicating the same instruction stream in every processor memory. This can be provided by a switching logic triggered by the instruction fetch signal to switch all processors to a common instruction bus, Figure 2.

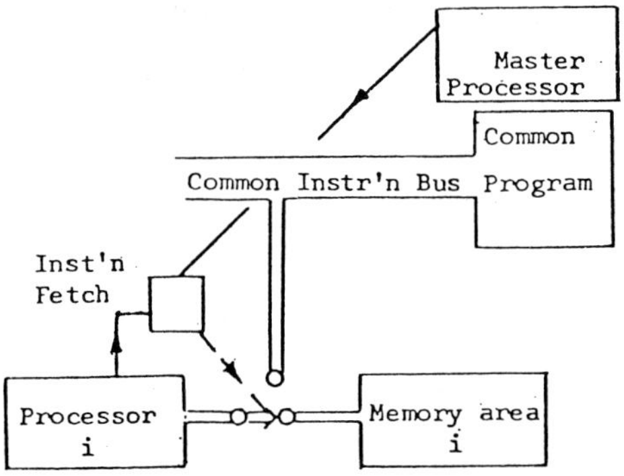

Figure 2

(ii) Multiple and Single Data Areas: Similarly, the processors may either have different data areas in their memories or be able to access a common data area. This again avoids memory wastage in applications requiring the processors to access the same data. The common bus can be used for this purpose by employing a queueing unit (which itself can be microprocessor based) to which the processors place a request to access the comon data via the common bus (i.e. become masters of the common bus), Figure 3. To avoid conflict and the inevitable

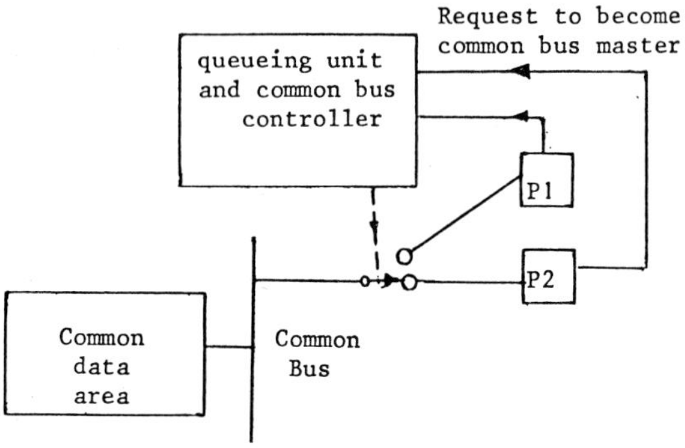

Figure 3 : Access to common data area.

waiting time great care is needed in programming the indivudal processors. An obvious scheme is to sequence access with computation so that only one processor may access the data area while the remaining processors are performing the computation in each access/compute cycle, Figure 4. Note that no waiting time is necessary if the total access time by all processors is less than or equal to one compute cycle. To avoid waiting time when this is not the case multiple copies of the common data area, together with a multi-bus system, are needed.

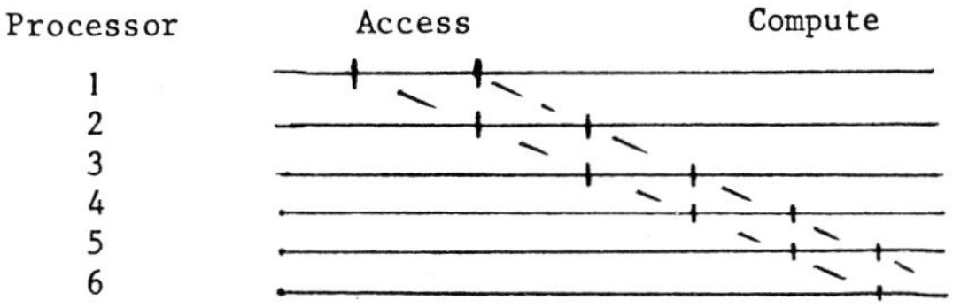

Figure 4 : Overlapping access to the common data area with computation.

2.2 Multi-Bus Systems

The need for a multi-bus system arises when two types of limitations are met. The first is due to overheads when no more time reduction can be achieved by simply adding more processors. The second is due to the waiting time to access a common data area during the computation phase of parallel processing. These multiple bus systems can be of a nested structure, in that each bus in the system can itself be divided into multi-data buses for the access of multiple data areas in parallel.

(i) Multi-Bus Systems to Reduce Overheads: During the overheads phase of parallel computation a master processor performs the data transfer among processors. In general the time spent in performing these overheads increases with the number of processors used and a limit is soon reached, beyond which no further reduction in computing time is achieved. To overcome this limitation more than one master processor can be used by dividing the system into minor clusters and performing the overheads on those in parallel, Figure 5. Note the extra switch provided for the master in each cluster which enables it to perform the data transfer among memory areas in its own cluster. This switch also disconnects all the submasters from the bus lines during the program development stage when the overall master and all memories simply resemble a conventional single processor computer. It is also used when the overall master executes the inter-cluster overheads by cross-transferring data among clusters.

(ii) Multi-bus Systems to Eliminate Waiting Time: It was seen above how access to the same copy of common data caused waiting time by some of the processors in the cluster. This can be reduced or eliminated by having more than one copy of the data and to assign one group of processors to every copy, Figure 6. The size of each group is determined by the ratio of compute time to access time in the sequential access described above. The minor common bus is segmented into sections so that each group of processors and their common data area communicate through one section of the bus in parallel. A queueing unit and a bus-section controller is assigned to each group as in the single bus case.

(iii) Common Features and Flexibility: It is clear that the above two methods of multi-bus organisation are very similar. In both cases the common bus is divided into sections thus allowing the units attached to each section to work in parallel. The devision of computing units (each unit being a processor/memory pair) into groups is a natural extension to the larger division into minor clusters. The switching logic to access the common data area can be made identical to that used in the minor common bus (Figure 5) by adding a switch similar to the one used by the master in each cluster. This similarity can be extended to form a concept which ensures a perfectly flexible structure. Starting with a computing unit, consisting of a processor, two memory areas and a queueing unit, a parallel organisation can be formed which is completely flexible in the sense that the number of clusters, groups and processors within each group can be changed under program control from the overall master to suit the problem being solved, Figure 7. In this arrangement switch A severs the common bus into the required number of clusters and groups. The queueing unit is also disconnected so that only the requisite

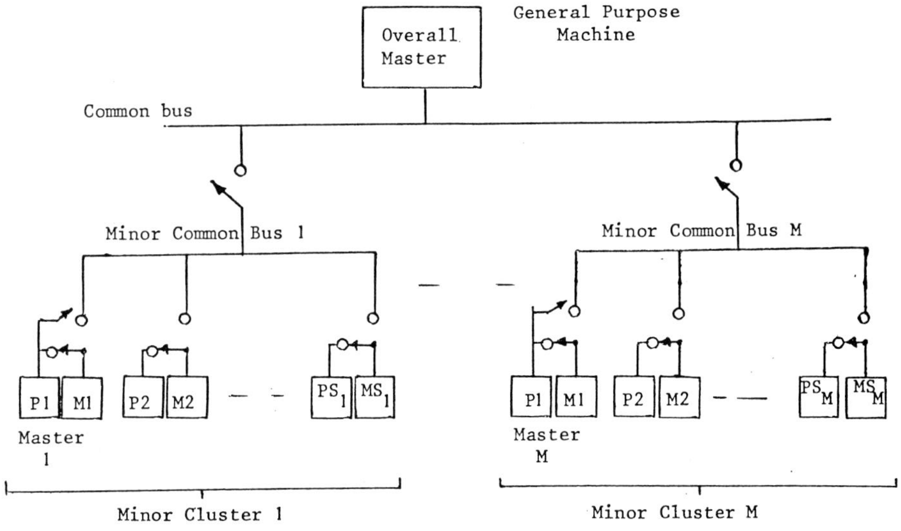

Figure 5 : Multiple Clusters and Bus Systems.

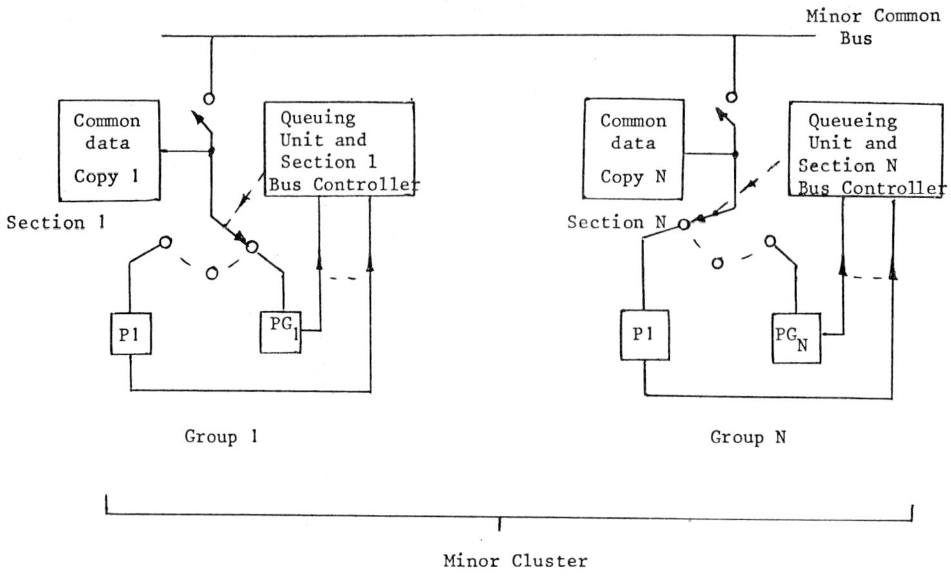

Figure 6 : Multi-Data Buses.

number of processors are affected. Switch B connects the processor to the common bus during access to common memory. This is required for 3 main reasons: (i) to access common data, (ii) to access common program during single-instruction stream operation, and (iii) to perform overheads when the processor is acting as the master in the associated cluster. Note that the queueing unit controls this switch during queued access to common memory requested by the processor, as described earlier. Switch C merely connects the local memory to the common bus after the computing phase of parallel processing has ended.

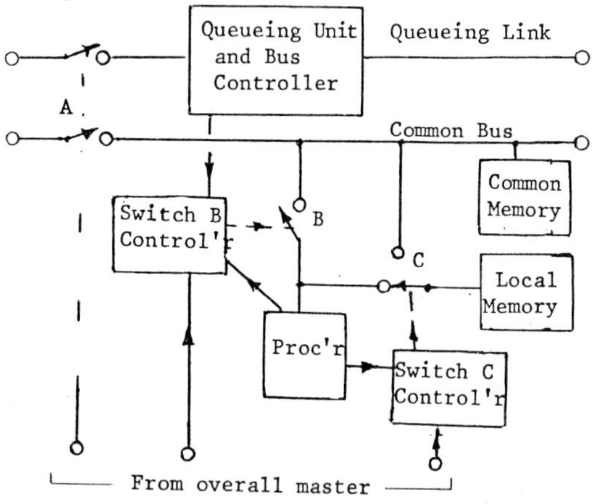

Figure 7 : Basic Computing Unit.

3. APPLICATION TO THE SOLUTION OF CONTROL ALGORITHMS

To assess the efficiency of the above organisations the dynamic programming algorithm, Bellman [4] will be used. Many methods for solving this algorithm on parallel computers have been proposed (Casti, [5]; Al-Dabass, [2]). The parallel states method proposed by Larson and his group will be used. This method has recently been extended by the present author so that whole regions of the discrete state space can be allocated to each processor.

3.1 Problem Statement

Consider the discrete time system given by

$$x(i+1) = f(x(i),u(i),i) \tag{1}$$

where x is the n-vector state variable, u is the m-vector control and f is an n-vector function. It is required to find the sequence of control functions $u^*(i)$ vs. $x(i)$, $i = 1,\ldots,N$, which will minimise the performance measure,

$$J_N[x(0)] = \sum_{i=1}^{N} H(i) \tag{2}$$

subject to the usual constraints of admissible state and control sets and H(i) is the measure of performance at stage i. Using the principle of optimality, the optimum value of the performance index for a sequence of k stages is given in terms of that of (k-1) stages by (* indicates optimum):

$$J_k^*[x(o)] = \min_{u(o)} \left(H(1) + J_{k-1}^*[x(1)]\right) \qquad (3)$$

and the procedure is started with 1 stage optimisation simply given by:

$$J_1^*[x(o)] = \min_{u(o)} (H(o)) \qquad (4)$$

where x(1) is related to x(o) and u(o) by equation (1), and the time index is always relative to the general k-stage sequence.

To solve the problem on a digital computer the variables x and u are restricted within specified ranges and quantised into a finite number of discrete values. If Q_x and Q_u are the number of discrete values in each variable of x and u, then the total number of discrete values are Q_x^n and Q_u^m respectively. The solution involves 3 sets of nested loops: m loops to iterate over all values of u, n loops for all values of x, and one outer loop for all stages (see figure 8).

Evaluate eqn. 3, compare with last value and save minimum	m nested loops (iterate over all control values Q_u^m)	n nested loops (iterate over all state values Q_x^n)	stage loop

Figure 8 : The general dynamic programming method.

3.2 Parallel Solution Using Multiple Copies of J_{k-1}^*

Consider the case when each processor is provided with its own copy of the J_{k-1}^* results (Figure 9). Let t_e be the time to evaluate equation (3) for any given state and control value, compare its result with the previous value and save the minimum of the two. The total single processor time t_s for all state and control values for one stage of optimisation is therefore:

$$t_s = t_e . Q_u^m \times Q_x^n \qquad (5)$$

To solve the problem on a parallel processor consisting of s processors, divide the points in the discrete state space Q_x^n equally among the processors so that the computing time t_c on any one processor is

$$t_c = \frac{t_e . Q_u^m . Q_x^n}{s} \qquad (6)$$

Overheads: The master processor transfers the results of each processor to main memory first. The total number of data transferred is Q_x^n for

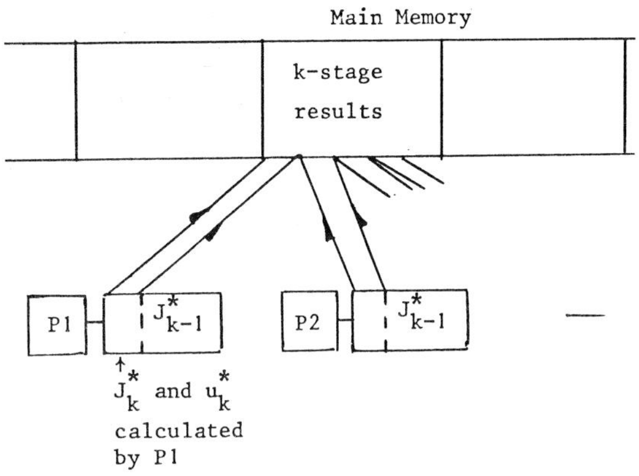

Figure 9 : Separate copies of J_{k-1}^* for each processor.

the J^* function, and the same number for each variable in the control vector u^*, a total of $(1+m)Q_x^n$. If t_t is the transfer time for each point, then the total transfer time is $(1+m)Q_x^n t_t$.

The J_{k-1}^* table in each processor memory is only a small portion of the total table as there are constraints on the available control. This portion is made up of the region allotted to the processor, Q_x^n/s, plus an additional fraction of the state space, say α, giving a total of $(\frac{1}{s} + \alpha)Q_x^n$. The $\frac{1}{s}$ part can be updated by the processors themselves in parallel, thus taking $Q_x^n t_t/s$. The α part has to be updated by the master processor in serial thus taking $\alpha Q_x^n \, s \, t_t$ for all s processors. The total overheads are therefore:

$$t_o = (1+m + \frac{1}{s} + \alpha s)Q_x^n t_t \qquad (7)$$

The total parallel processing time is made up of equations (6) and (7), or

$$t_p = \frac{t_e Q_u^m Q_x^n}{s} + (1 + m + \frac{1}{s} + \alpha s)Q_x^n t_t \qquad (8)$$

or as a fraction of single processor time (equation 5),

$$\frac{t_p}{t_s} = \frac{1}{s} + (1 + m + \frac{1}{s} + \alpha s)t_t (t_e Q_u^m)^{-1} \qquad (9)$$

Graph 1 curve a shows a typical plot of this formulae for a 2-input system each quantised in ten steps, i.e. m = 2 and Q_u^m = 100, the evaluation time t_e set to 1 mS, the transfer time t_t to 10μs, and the fraction α of state space, fed to update the J^*_{k-1} table, is set to 0.1.

A more efficient method is to relate the J^*_{k-1} table to the portion of the state space handled by each processor. This will eliminate the s parameter from the α term (now designated α_1) in the equation which becomes;

$$\frac{t_p}{t_s} = \frac{1}{s} + \left(1 + m + \frac{1}{s} + \alpha_1\right) t_t \left(t_e Q_u^m\right)^{-1} \qquad (9a)$$

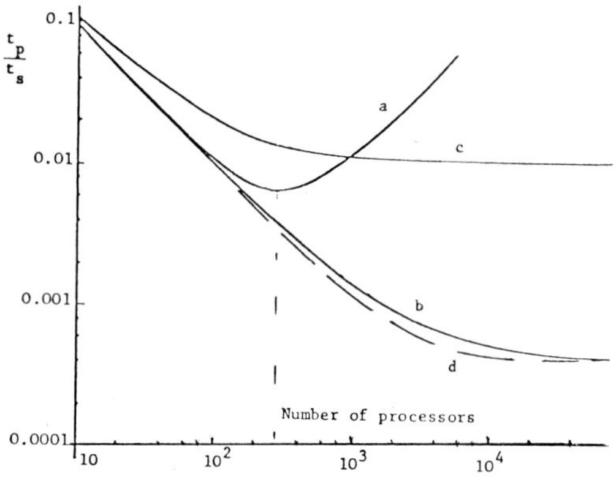

Graph 1 : Parallel processing time vs. number of processors

Curve b shows the relation for $\alpha_1 = 1$ and is a vast improvement over the other method. Note however that the α term in both methods is a convenient simplification. In practice the size of the J^*_{k-1} table is a more complicated function of the processor's own region.

<u>Idle Factor</u>: This is the fraction of processing power left idle while the master is performing the overheads, and is indicative of the efficiency of the method of using the parallel organisation. In this case it is given by (see Figure 10)

$$I = \frac{(s-1)\tau_2}{s(\tau_1+\tau_2)} \qquad (10)$$

which, when substituting the parameters shown, becomes:

$$I = \frac{s-1}{s + \dfrac{\left(1 + Q_u^m \frac{t_e}{t_t}\right)}{1+m+\alpha s}} \qquad (11)$$

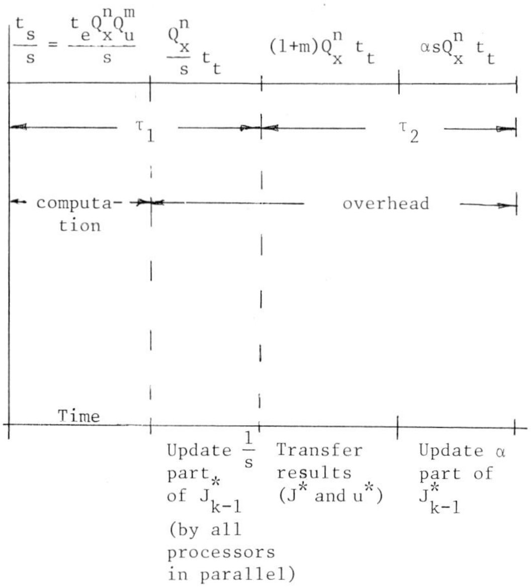

Figure 10 : Using separate J^*_{k-1} copies.

Graph 2 curve a shows a plot of this factor for the same parameter values used in graph 1. Note that the idle factor corresponding to the minimum parallel time is 0.5 and is consistent with the intuitive idea that the best way of operating the ststem is when the processing power is equally divided between computations and overheads, Al-Dabass, [1]. Curve b shows the case of decreasing α portion which is more efficient than the other case, as expected.

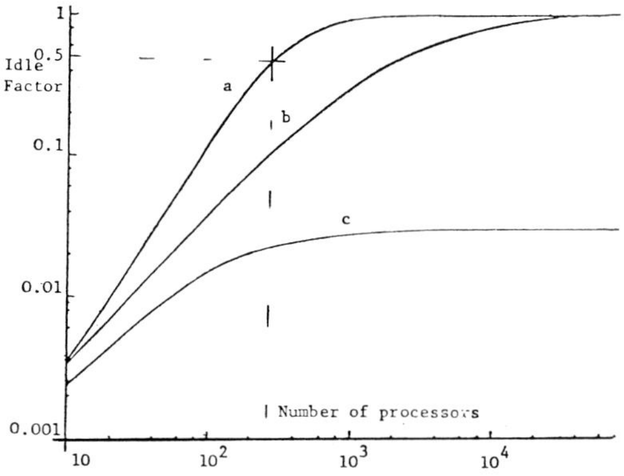

Graph 2 : Idle factor vs. number of processors

The formula for this is obtained by removing the s from the α parameter of the above equation to become:

$$I = \frac{s-1}{s + \dfrac{(1+Q_u^m t_e/t_t)}{1+m+\alpha_1}} \qquad (11a)$$

3.3 Solution Using a Common Copy of J^*_{k-1}

Although there are advantages, such as completely free access, in using a separate J^*_{k-1} copy in each processor, these may be outweighed by the waste in memory space and the time needed to update these copies. The limited access in using a common copy inevitably leads to waiting time and thus has to be taken into consideration when assessing the efficiency of this method.

Let t_w be the waiting time associated with every single evaluation of the recursive equation so that the computing time for each processor is now, (see equation 6):

$$t_c = \frac{(t_e+t_w)Q_u^m Q_x^n}{s} \qquad (12)$$

The overheads now only involve transferring the J^* and u^* results (see equation 7),

$$t_o = (1+m)Q_x^n t_t \qquad (13)$$

giving a total time of

$$t_p = \frac{(t_e+t_w)Q_u^m Q_x^n}{s} + (1+m)Q_x^n t_t \qquad (14)$$

and dividing by equation 5 to get it as a fraction of single processor time,

$$\frac{t_p}{t_s} = \frac{(1+t_w/t_e)}{s} + (1+m)t_t(t_e Q_u^m)^{-1} \qquad (15)$$

The overheads term is constant in this case and may give a lower minimum processing time than in the last case. There is, however, a limit to this minimum which is given by the overhead terms. Moreover, the waiting time t_w is an increasing function of the number of processors and a more accurate way of representing it is by replacing the fraction t_w/t_e by a linear function of s, say ws, where w is the waiting time per extra processor as a fraction of the evaluation time t_e. Substituting this in equation (15) gives:

$$\frac{t_p}{t_s} = \frac{1}{s} + w + (1+m)t_t(t_e Q_u^m)^{-1} \qquad (16)$$

The waiting factor w increases the minimum parallel processing time as can be seen in graph 1, curve c. The waiting factor w was set to 0.01 to obtain the curve, which represents 1% increase in t_e for every extra processor in the system.

Idle Factor: This method should yield a smaller idle factor, given in general by equation (10). Substituting the parameters shown in Figure 11 gives:

$$I = \frac{s-1}{s + \dfrac{(1+ws)Q_u^m . t_e}{(1+m)t_t}} \qquad (17)$$

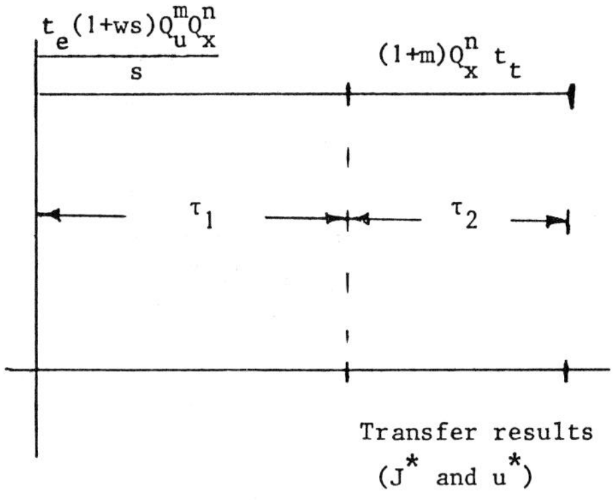

Figure 11 : Using common J^*_{k-1} copy.

Graph 2 curve c shows a plot of this factor with w set to 0.01. It is clearly seen that this method is more efficient than the separate copies method, as the processing power left idle is very much reduced.

3.4 Progessively Increasing Workload

In both of the last two methods the workload was divided equally among the processors and the master processor carried out the overheads after all the processors finished their work load. Another, and perhaps better, way of processing the algorithm is to give the first processor to be be serviced the smallest load and the last processor the largest load. The workload should be distributed so that the load for the next processor to be serviced is equal to the workload and overheads of the previous processor, Figure 12.

It can be shown that the parallel processing time in this case is given by:

$$\frac{t_p}{t_s} = \frac{h}{1-(1-h^2)(1+h)^{-s}} \qquad (18)$$

where s is the number of processors and h is the overhead per processor as a fraction of the workload and is assumed to be constant (see Figure 12):

$$h = \frac{t_{o1}}{t_{c1}} = \frac{t_{o2}}{t_{c2}} = \ldots = \frac{t_{os}}{t_{cs}} \qquad (19)$$

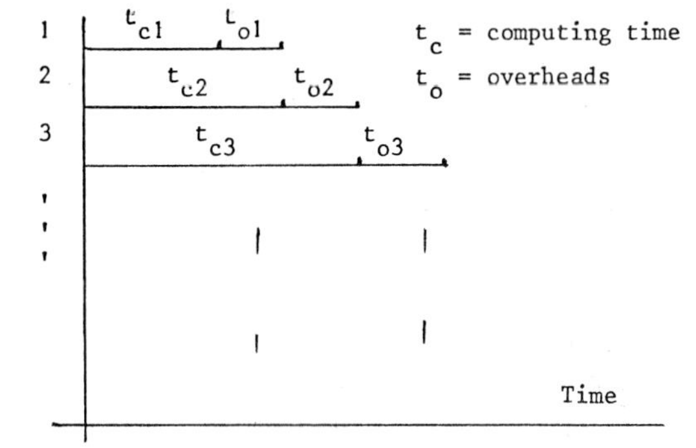

Figure 12 : Progressively Increasing Workload.

For the case where separate copies of J^*_{k-1} is kept in every processor the overheads carried out by the master for every processor is:

$$t_{oi} = (1+m+\alpha_1)q_i\, t_t \qquad (20)$$

where the region surrounding the processor's own region q_i to make up the portion of the J^*_{k-1} stored in processor i, is now assumed to be a linear function of q_i and related to it by the constant α_1. The computing time t_{ci} is the time to evaluate the workload $Q^m_u\, q_i$ plus the time to update the J^*_{k-1} portion corresponding to processor i own region q or

$$t_{ci} = Q^m_u\, q_i\, t_e + q_i\, t_t \qquad (21)$$

Dividing t_{ci} by t_{oi} gives the overhead parameter h to be

$$h = \frac{1+m+\alpha_1}{1+Q^m_u\, t_e/t_t} \qquad (22)$$

Graph 1 curve d gives a comparison between this and the equal workload methods. The advantage of this method is only marginal, e.g. at 10,000 processors this method is 20% faster than the equal workload method.

For the case when all processors access the same copy of J^*_{k-1} the α_1 and $q_i\, t_t$ overhead terms disappear from equations (20) and (21), and t_e is replaced by $t_e(1+ws)$ to include the waiting time during access. The overhead factor in this case becomes:

$$h = \frac{1+m}{(1+ws)Q^m_u\, t_e/t_t} \qquad (23)$$

The parallel time is given by adjusting equation (18) to account for the waiting time during access,

$$\frac{t_p}{t_s} = \frac{h(1+ws)}{1-(1-h^2)(1+h)^{-s}} \qquad (18a)$$

For the same parameter values as before this equation gives practically the same parallel time as the equal workload case given by curve c graph 1, e.g. for 1000 processors t_p/t_s works out to be 0.0112 against 0.0113 for the other method. Typical processor-workload graphs for the two methods are shown in Figure 13, and explains the closeness of the results of the two methods. The difference between the two methods is due to the overheads being distributed along the diagonal workload instead of being separated from it as in the equal workload method. This produces smaller parallel time under certain conditions as shown in graph 1 curve d.

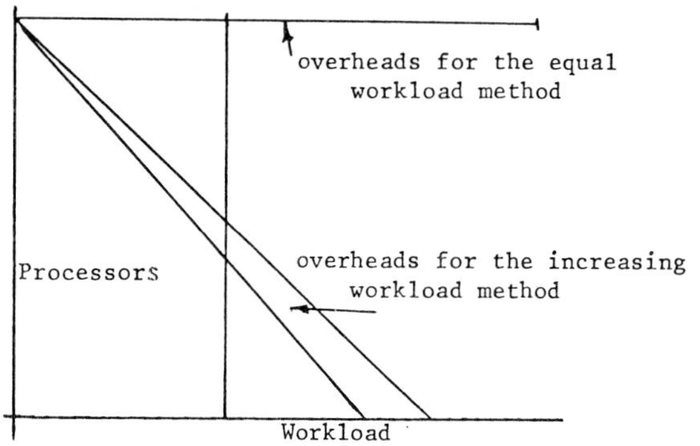

Figure 13 : Workload and overheads for the two methods.

3.5 Multi-Bus Systems

In all the cases discussed above a lower limit to the parallel processing time is soon reached where the addition of further processors does not yield any reduction in time. This is primarily due to the use of a single master processor to carry out the overheads. The use of multiple masters working in parallel through a multi-bus system is an obvious solution to this problem. This is expected to reduce the processing time limit by a factor which is nearly equal to the number of masters employed. There may be extra overheads involved, such as co-ordinating the masters in the overall system, but these are expected to be small compared with the other overheads.

4. CONCLUSIONS

A number of alternatives were considered for co-ordinating a large number of microprocessors for a parallel processing computer and led to the formulation of a basic computing unit. A large number of these basic units can be easily configured into different parallel organisations under control from the overall master without any additional hardware. They can be divided, for example, into multiple clusters whose sizes can be varied according to the overheads of the problem being solved. They can be organised into a single instruction stream/multi-data stream computer; and, by reducing the memory associated with each processor to a single word, they can be extended to work as an associative processor. However, considerable work is needed to fully verify these apparent advantages. Simulation may be an economic method of carrying out this investigation and effort is now being directed to this area.

Applications have a direct influence on computer architecture and any new proposals for parallel computers must be tested against several applications. To this effect the dynamic programming algorithm solution on the proposed parallel organisations was considered in detail. There does not seem to be much difference between the equal and progressively increasing workload methods, although more detailed investigation of the latter may uncover areas in the parameter space where this method is superior. The difference between the common and separate ccpy methods of the J^*_{k-1} table is a simple trade-off between memory space and execution time. The decreasing size and price of memory makes the storage problem of dynamic programming much less acute now than it was a decade ago, and is expected to get even easieras Very LSI and Ultra LSI technologies become common practice enabling some 1000K bytes of memory to be mounted on a single card, and opening new areas of application to dynamic programming.

5. FUTURE WORK

Another application area, and one where modern control theory has met with success, is estimation, Tam and Moore [12]. Detail investiation of the solution of the adaptive estimation problem on parallel processors should provide feedback for more efficient parallel organisations on the one hand, and satisfy the practical need for solving the relevant algorithms in real-time.

When considering high level languages for parallel computers, the explicit appraoch has the advantage of involving the programmer in organising the workload among the processors. A parallel DO loop is perhaps the simplest and most needed command in this case. The implicit method has the merit that any programs written for a conventional processor can be run on the parallel machine without any change, Rammamoorthy et al [9]. The compilers needed, however, are more complicated and may require very long compilation time. To avoid this the compilers themselves may be written to run on the parallel machines to reduce compilation times. The implicit approach can even be extended to the hardware organisation, where the conventional CPU may employ a number of microprocessors to carryout multiplications in parallel, for example. In this case the microprocessors are hardwired to execute a microprogram in the main CPU control memory and, as such, are transparent to the user. The parallel configurations proposed here can then be placed under microprogram control in this case, rather than the usual program instructions.

ACKNOWLEDGEMENTS

The author wishes to thank the Science Research Council for the Fellowship to carry out this work. He would also like to thank Dr. G.C. Barney, Dr. D. Bell and Dr. D. Rutherford (Control Systems Centre) for many stimulating discussions which proved to be a constant source of inspiration during the preparation of this paper.

6. REFERENCES

[1] Al-Dabass, D., 1976: "An Evaluation of the Effectiveness of Multiprocessor Clusters in Real-Time Applications", IFAC/IFIP International Workshop on Real-Time Programming, Paris.

[2] Al-Dabss, D., 1976a: "Two Methods for the Solution of the Dynamic Programming Algorithm on a Multiprocessor Cluster", Report No. 347, Control Systems Centre, UMIST.

[3] Barnes, G.H. et al, 1968: "The ILLIAC IV Computer", IEEE Trans. on Computers, Vol. C-17, No. 8

[4] Bellman, R.E. and Dreyfus, S.E., 1962: "Applied Dynamic Programming",Oxford Univ. Press.

[5] Casti, J., Richardson, M. & Larson, R., 1973: "Dynamic Programming and Parallel Computers", Journal of Optimisation Theory & its Applications, Vol. 12, No. 4.

[6] Crane, B.A. et al, 1972: "PEPE Computer Architecture", 6th Annual IEEE Computer Soc. International Conf., San Francisco, Calif., pp. 57-64.

[7] Flynn, M.J., 1966: "Very High Speed Computing Systems", Proc. IEEE, 54, No. 12,pp.1901-1909.

[8] Mulder, M.C., 1971: "A Real-time Computer to Implement Filtering and Control Algorithm", Proc. of the 4th Hawaii Intern. Conf. on System Science, pp.733-735.

[9] Ramamoorthy, C.V., Park, J.H., Li H.F., 1973: "Compilation Techniques for Recognition of Parallel Processable Tasks in Arithmetic Expressions", IEEE Trans. on Computers, Vol. C-22, No. 11, pp. 986-998.

[10] Rudberg D.A. and Hanna, W.A. 1975: "The Three Dimensional Computer: A Multiple Array Processor ", Comput. & Elect. Eng. Vol. 2, pp. 141-148.

[11] Rudolph, J.A. 1972: "A Production Implementation of an Associative Array Processor - STARAN" FJCC Proceedings, p. 229.

[12] Tam, P.K.S. and Moore, J.B. 1975: "Adaptive Estimation Using Parallel Processing Techniques", Computers and Electrical Engineering, Vol. 2, pp. 203-214.

E. Morlet and D. Ribbens, (Eds.), International Computing Symposium 1977.

GOSPEL: A TIME-SHARING APPROACH TO CONTINUOUS SYSTEM SIMULATION (*)

A. Brini, R. Ferrari, T. Montagna, M. Montagni, G. Perna, J. Szanto

CISE, Computing Service, Milano (Italy)

This paper describes the GOSPEL system, operating in the Time Sharing environment of Honeywell 6000 computers. GOSPEL is an application-oriented system which allows engineers or scientists to easily model and investigate the dynamic behaviour of systems mathematically described by differential equations.
The system is interactive at any level, during the simulation program preparation, the simulation program execution and the output-data investigation. GOSPEL provides a CSSL-like language whose main features are: macro capability allowing easy user-extension of the language, array capability, scalar and vectorial integral operators, a package of integration routines including Gear's algorithm for stiff systems, a large set of simulation oriented functional operators. Other features are: the possibility of inserting FORTRAN source subroutines and functions in the model description; access to system or user FORTRAN libraries, as well as access to user and system Macro-definition libraries; automatic function generation from tabular functions of one, two or three independent variables; a large set of diagnostics; interactive output reports; the possibility of stopping a simulation session at any moment and saving the current status from which to restart in a subsequent session.
After the description of these features, some significant examples conclude the paper.

1. GENERAL DESCRIPTION

GOSPEL is an interactive subsystem which runs under the Time Sharing System of GCOS on Honeywell 6000 computers, and allows the implementation of continuous system simulation programs. The SCi recommendations /1/ have been followed as concerns the language syntax and the structure of problem description.
GOSPEL has been implemented to provide the designer with a useful and easy-to-use tool to model and evaluated the behaviour of physical systems described by differential equations.

The digital computer simulation of a system consists of three phases:
- construction of a simulation program to compute the system's behaviour;
- execution of the simulation program with the eventual input data;
- output data inspection for system evaluation.

The GOSPEL subsystem supervises and cohordinates the three phases and provides an integrated set of functions and utilities which assists the user.

During the first phase a powerful problem-oriented language allows the user to easily prepare the problem description, i.e. to describe the model of the dynamic system to be simulated, and to specify the test sequence for the model. The problem description is processed by a Macro Processor, which expands the macro instructions (if any); the expanded description is translated by a Translator into a set of Fortran subroutines, which are then compiled by a Fortran Compiler. During this phase the user is greatly helped by the interactive 'editing' and 'file management' functions combined with on-line diagnostics.

During the next phase, the subroutines produced during phase one are linkage-edited with a library of functional and utility subroutines, to build an executable program. Execution of this program allows to compute the model behaviour, following the specifications given in the input description. At run-time the user may input on-line values of variables and parameters required by the program; he may also monitor the evolution of selected variables, and break processing at any time. The history of the variables of the simulation program may also be saved onto a mass storage file, for subsequent, more detailed inspection.

This inspection is performed during the third phase, after the simulation program execution is over: an interactive module is available to scan the output file, allowing selective proces-

(*) This work has been sponsored by Ente Nazionale per l'Energia Elettrica (ENEL), to which the authors are grateful for allowing the publication of the paper.

sing of variables of groups of variables; the reports, in graphic or tabular form, may be directed either to the central (or remote) line printer or to a terminal.

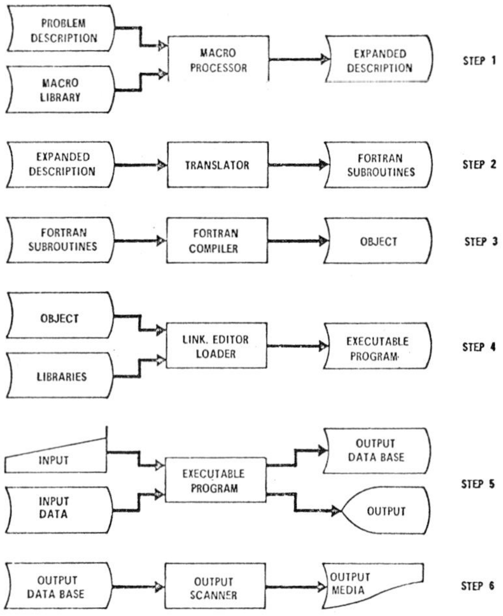

Fig. 1

Figure 1 shows in detail the steps performed during execution of phase one, two and three. Each step corresponds to an executive module of the GOSPEL subsystem. Execution of these modules and inter-module communication are supervised and cohordinated by a Control Module, which communicates with the user by means of an interactive control language. The user's commands may start execution of sequences of modules, or ask for file editing and file management functions, giving high flexibility to the subsystem.

2. THE SIMULATION PROGRAM

The generation of a suitable simulation program is the main goal of GOSPEL. Usually people who don't use CSSL languages have to write the whole program, i.e. they must prepare not only a mathematical, procedural problem code, but also the selected integration method, I/O routines for data input and output document preparation, and organize them for a proper execution. GOSPEL relieves the user from this heavy burden; it only requires a problem-oriented description of the model, together with proper specification of input/output and execution modalities. Following this description and user requests, GOSPEL generates a set of Fortran subroutines and organize them to form a complete program.

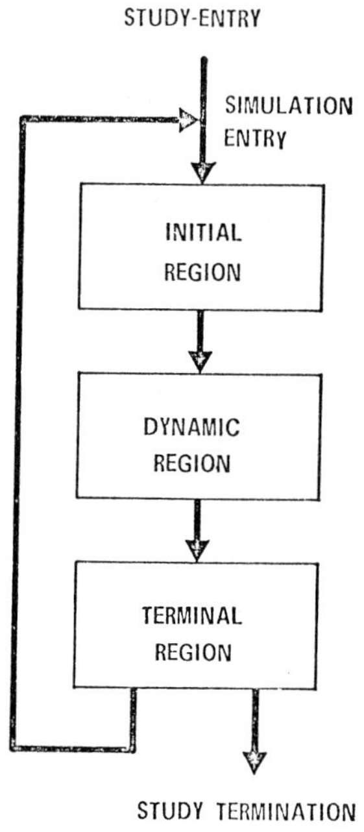

Fig. 2

The typical structure of a simulation program produced by GOSPEL and executed at step 5 is described in fig. 2. A simulation study (a Study) may consist of one or more simulation runs. By simulation run (Simulation) we mean the solution of the differential and algebraic equations describing the mathematical model over the entire range of the independent variable.

In the Initial Region optional scan of the results of preceding Simulation is allowed; in this case the Output Scanner has to be engaged. After output scanning has been exhausted, if terminal conditions have not been met or forced by the user, initial functions are performed. These functions consist of:

- initial values set up;
- input of on-line variables;
- initial computations;
- initializing calls to integration and derivative routines.

The Dynamic Region is repeatedly executed until End of Simulation conditions are met. Inside

this Region, computations tests, dynamic updating of parameters and control variables take place; these functions are performed each so called 'Communication Interval'. The output is performed every Print interval, which is a multiple of the Communication interval. There are two kinds of output: terminal and mass storage directed. At every Communication interval, control is given to the integration procedure which, by means of a user-chosen algorithm and repeated calls to the derivative section, updates the state variables. Exit from the Dynamic Region is determined by end of Simulation conditions being reached.
The Terminal Region, finally, is entered at the end of each Simulation and establishes whether a new Simulation has to be initiated or the entire Study has to be ended, due to terminal conditions having been met.

Since the problem description is very simple and concise, it is very easy to modify it and start again with a new study, if the results of the preceding study indicate that some refining is necessary, or at user's will anyway.

3. THE TIME-SHARING ENVIRONMENT

The TSS environment fully enhances the intrinsic flexibility of GOSPEL. The user may continuously monitor the status of the session (i.e. after each step shown in fig. 2) and act accordingly.

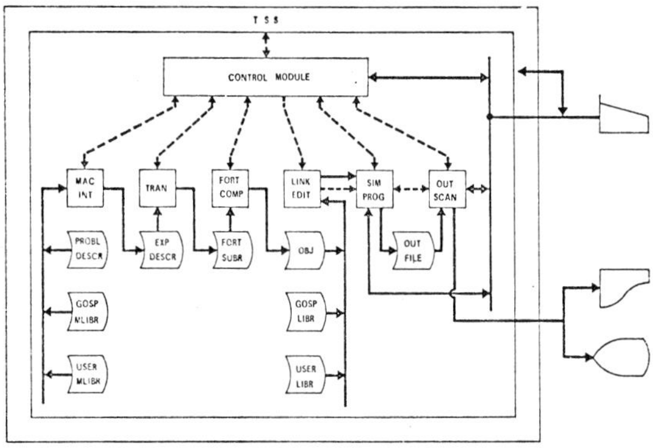

Fig. 3

Fig. 3 shows the structure of GOSPEL with reference to the TSS environment. Each step of fig. 2 is performed by a module; the Macro Processor, the Translator and the Output Scanner were appositely designed for the GOSPEL subsystem, while the Fortran Compiler and the Linkage editor-loader are standard TSS facilities. The simulation program is not a permanent module, but it is tailored on the model description being produced in steps 1 to 4. A Control Module cohordinates the executive modules and provides the interface with the user through an appropriate command language. Some commands direct the preparation of the simulation program; they allow to stop after each step or to perform some steps in sequence. After each step or step sequence intermediate results may be inspected and modified eventually. Other command perform GOSPEL utility functions, like user's Fortran and Macro library handling, session and file status monitoring, etc. Beside the proper GOSPEL commands, all the standard TSS commands are supported, thus giving the user access to all the TSS facilities and resources (file management, editing, etc.).
Interactivity is also provided during execution of the simulation program. Data may be input at run-time and on-line output is also available to allow monitoring of user-selected variables.
When the Output Scanner is engaged either at the beginning of a run during a study or at the end of it), a wide range of commands is available to obtain various forms of output reports, which may be directed to the central site (or remote) line printer or to the user's terminal.

4. CONCLUDING REMARKS

GOSPEL subsystem provides an interactive CSSL-type simulation language available to time-sharing users. Main features of GOSPEL are:

- Interactive development and updating of the problem description; availability of intermediate results during processing of the problem description; large use of macro and program libraries; optional retention of working and output files.
- A Macro Processor, particularly suited for string manipulation, providing conditional statements, nested and recursive Macro calls, multilevel Macro definition and redefinition.
- A Translator consenting nested integration of scalar and vectorial variables and single precision problem description.
- An integration package including modern numerical methods for resolution of stiff systems beside classical integration algorithms.
- Tabular functions of 1, 2, 3 independent variables, with possibility of selecting the interpolation algorithm.
- On-line input and output; possibility of changing

control variables and parameters at run time or in the course of a Simulation.

- A diagnostic file collecting diagnostics for later examination.

5. BIBLIOGRAPHY

(1) "The SCi Continuous System Simulation Language (CSSL)", SIMULATION 9, pp. 281-303, Dec. 1967.

(2) L. Beretta et al., "A Package For The Numerical Solution Of Ordinary Differential Initial Value Problems", ENEL Internal Report, Aug. 1973.

(3) "TSS General Information Manual", Honeywell Information Systems Inc.

(4) A. Brini et al., "GOSPEL: An Interactive Language For Continuous System Simulation", SCSC 1976, Washington, USA.

(5) A. Brini et al., "GOSPEL un linguaggio interattivo per la simulazione di sistemi continui", Congresso AICA 1976, Milan, Italy.

EXAMPLES

Example 1: bouncing ball

This example simulates the behaviour of an elastic ball whose displacement is both top and bottom limited.

Fig. E1.1 shows the system, along with the involved state equations. The problem description is reported in fig. E1.2. The derivative block contains a set of FORTRAN statements encased between the 'PROCED' and 'ENDPRO' structural statements.

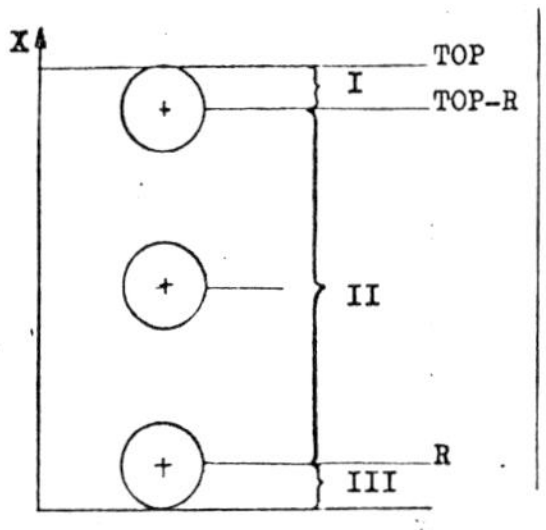

I: FOR X≥TOP-R

$$\ddot{X}=-G-(D/M)\dot{X}+(K/M)*((TOP-R)-X)$$

II: FOR R<X<TOP-R

$$\ddot{X}=-G-(D/M)\dot{X}$$

III: FOR X≤R

$$\ddot{X}=-G-(D/M)\dot{X}+(K/M)*(R-X)$$

A UNIQUE EQUATION MAY BE WRITTEN: $\ddot{X}=-G-(D/M)\dot{X}+FF$

WHERE:

$FF=(K/M)*((TOP-R)-X)$ I)

$FF=\emptyset$ II)

$FF=(K/M)*(R-X)$ III)

Fig. E1.1

```
LISTH /EXAMPLE/BOUNCE

08/25/76    16.20

10/DER
20*
30* BOUNCING BALL
40*
50*-------------------------------------------------------------
60* INTEGRAL EQUATIONS
70*
80 XD=INTEG(XD0,FF-G-(D/M)*XD)
90 X=INTEG(X0,XD)
100*------------------------------------------------------------
110* FORCING TERM DEFINITION
120*
130 PROCED(FF=X,R,K,M,TOP)
140  FF=0.0
150  IF(X.LE.R)FF=(K/M)*(R-X)
160  IF(X.GE.(TOP-R))FF=(K/M)*((TOP-R)-X)
170 ENDPRO
180*------------------------------------------------------------
190* PARAMETER DEFINITION
200*
210 CONSTANT TOP=4.0,G=9.81,R=0.5,M=10.0,K=12500
220 ONLINE X0,XD0,D
230*------------------------------------------------------------
240* CONTROL STATEMENTS
250*
260 ALGORITHM IALGOR=2
270 CINTERVAL CINT=0.08
280 NSTEP NSTP=800
290 MAXTIME TMAX=4.0
300*************************************************************
310/OUT
320 TITLE BOUNCING BALL
330 PLOT T,X,0.0,4.0

READY
```

Fig. E1.2

```
PLEASE ENTER THE FOLLOWING VALUES:
X0 ?
=3
XD0 ?
=15
D ?
=7

BOUNCING BALL

-
          RUN =  1

T          = 0.                     IALGOR   =   2
CINT       = 0.80000000E-01         NSTP     = 800
TMAX       = 0.40000000E 01         NWRT     =   1

************************************************************

T                  X                 0.                0.40000E 01

0.                 0.30000000E 01
0.80000000E-01     0.38815896E 01
0.16000000E 00     0.29927205E 01
0.24000000E 00     0.18899115E 01
0.32000000E 00     0.78627745E 00
0.40000000E 00     0.15767859E 00
0.48000000E 00     0.11125479E 01
0.56000000E 00     0.20520261E 01
0.64000000E 00     0.28861990E 01
0.72000000E 00     0.36049205E 01
0.80000000E 00     0.34553309E 01
0.88000000E 00     0.27869836E 01
0.96000000E 00     0.21094266E 01
0.10400000E 01     0.14045625E 01
0.11200000E 01     0.72829216E 00
0.12000000E 01     0.25596144E 00
0.12800000E 01     0.87453941E 00
0.13600000E 01     0.14847080E 01
0.14400000E 01     0.20056247E 01
0.15200000E 01     0.24370916E 01
0.16000000E 01     0.27839760E 01
0.16800000E 01     0.30508799E 01
0.17600000E 01     0.32421601E 01
0.18400000E 01     0.33619365E 01
0.19200000E 01     0.34141049E 01
0.20000000E 01     0.34023487E 01
0.20800000E 01     0.33301505E 01
0.21600000E 01     0.32008035E 01
0.22400000E 01     0.30174211E 01
0.23200000E 01     0.27829475E 01
0.24000000E 01     0.25001661E 01
0.24800000E 01     0.21717088E 01
0.25600000E 01     0.18000643E 01
0.26400001E 01     0.13875854E 01
0.27200001E 01     0.93649684E 00
0.28000001E 01     0.45102775E 00
0.28800001E 01     0.47143474E 00
0.29600001E 01     0.90852166E 00
0.30400001E 01     0.12553906E 01
0.31200001E 01     0.15224884E 01
0.32000002E 01     0.17139816E 01
0.32800002E 01     0.18339675E 01
0.33600002E 01     0.18863409E 01
0.34400002E 01     0.18747852E 01
0.35200002E 01     0.18027830E 01
0.36000002E 01     0.16726273E 01
0.36800002E 01     0.14904316E 01
0.37600003E 01     0.12561397E 01
0.38400003E 01     0.97353524E 00
0.39200003E 01     0.64525015E 00
0.40000000E 01     0.37091912E 00
    ***END-OF-STUDY PROCEDURES***

COMMAND
-DONE
SYSTEM ?BYE
**COST:  $   1.52 TO DATE:  $ 2507.74= 13%
**ON AT 10.450 - OFF AT 10.539 ON  08/26/76
```

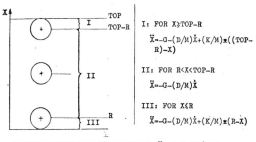

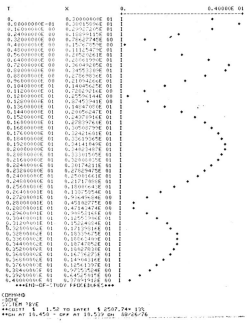

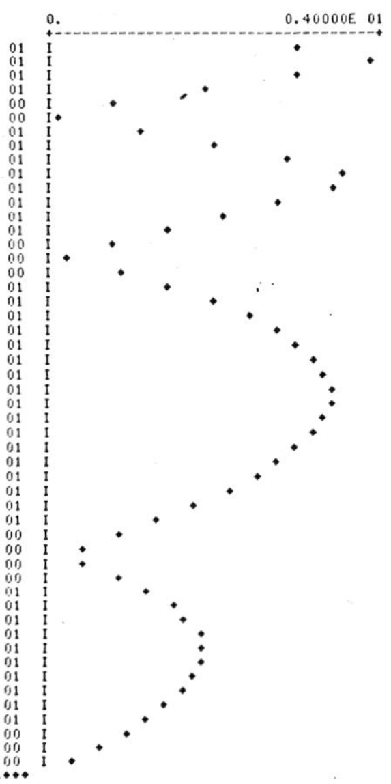

Fig. E1.3

On-line input for some parameters and control variables is achieved by using the 'ONLINE' control statement. The stiffly-stable Gear algorithm is chosen, due to the problem stiffness. Multiple simulation runs are obtained by setting the the control variable ENST = .FALSE. in the terminal block.
The block/OUT contains the output specifications.
On-line plotted output of displacement is shown in fig. E1.3.

Example 2: L-transform control loop

This example investigates a system described in the Laplace transform domain. Fig. E2.1 shows the block diagram of the system. The plant has a second order model and is controlled by a device having one pole and one zero. The feedback network contains a time constant. Standard functional operators available in GOSPEL libraries are used to describe the system model (see fig. E2.2).
Fig. E2.3 shows the off-line terminal printout obtained using the Output Scanner.

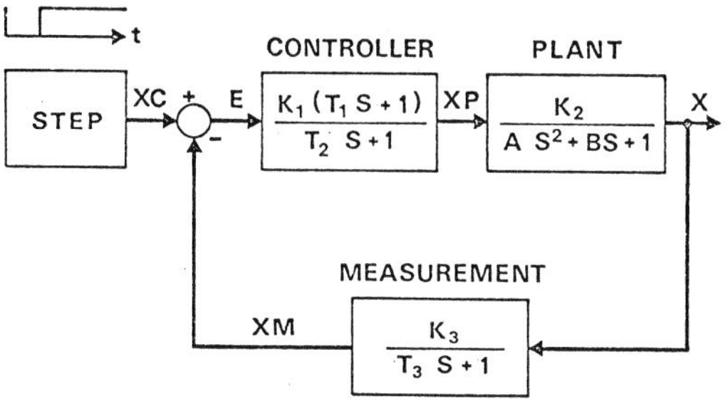

Fig. E2.1

```
LISTH

08/27/76     14.67

10/DER
20*
30* CONTROL LOOP
40*
50*-------------------------------------------------------------
60* DEFINE PRESET VARIABLES
70*
80 CONSTANT K1=0.3,K2=20.0,K3=0.33
90 CONSTANT TA1=0.1,TA2=0.03,TA3=0.01
100 CONSTANT A=0.0003,B=0.029,TZ=0.01
110*------------------------------------------------------------
120* MODEL DESCRIPTION
130*
140*
150* OUTPUT OF FIRST ORDER LAG IS MEASUREMENT
160*
170 RPOUT=REALPL(TA3,X,0.0)
180 XM=K3*RPOUT
190*
200* FORCING FUNCTION
210*
220 XC=STEP(TZ)
230 E=XC-XM
240*
250* SECOND ORDER PLANT DEFINITION
260*
270 OUTCPX=CMPXPL(A,B,XP,0.0,0.0)
280 X=K2*OUTCPX
290*
300* CONTROLLER OUTPUT
310*
320 OUTCTR=LEDLAG(TA1,TA2,E,0.0)
330 XP=K1*OUTCTR
340*------------------------------------------------------------
350* DEFINE CONTROL VARIABLES
360*
370 CINTERVAL CINT=0.005
380 MAXTIME TMAX=0.15
390 ALGORITHM IALGOR=9,JALGOR=0,KALGOR=2
400 ONLINE ENST,EPS,JALGOR
410************************************************************
420/OUT
430 PREPARE XC,E,X,XM
440 TITLE CONTROL LOOP SIMULATION
450************************************************************
460/TER
470 ENST=.F.
480************************************************************

READY

*
```

Fig. E2.2

```
COMMAND
-OUTPUT

          ***OUTPUT MODULE***

CONTROL LOOP SIMULATION
::::::::::::::::::::::::::::::::::::::::::::::::::::::::::::::::::::

NR. OF RUNS =      2

**TOUTPUT RUN=2
 PRINT OPTIONS :
 HEADER : OFF LINE OUTPUT INSPECTION
 VARIABLES : X,XM,XC

CONTROL LOOP SIMULATION
::::::::::::::::::::::::::::::::::::::::::::::::::::::::::::::::::::

OFF LINE OUTPUT INSPECTION

*** RUN :   2 OF    2 ***
```

T	X	XM	XC
0.50000000E-02	0.	0.	0.
0.10000000E-01	0.	0.	0.
0.15000000E-01	0.67866151E 00	0.34766309E-01	0.10000000E 01
0.20000000E-01	0.21564270E 01	0.20879882E 00	0.10000000E 01
0.25000000E-01	0.36938438E 01	0.51765831E 00	0.10000000E 01
0.30000000E-01	0.47164403E 01	0.87338396E 00	0.10000000E 01
0.35000000E-01	0.49051580E 01	0.11650683E 01	0.10000000E 01
0.40000000E-01	0.42491954E 01	0.13055458E 01	0.10000000E 01
0.45000000E-01	0.30149122E 01	0.12608511E 01	0.10000000E 01
0.50000000E-01	0.16353518E 01	0.10582069E 01	0.10000000E 01
0.55000000E-01	0.55752581E 00	0.77303118E 00	0.10000000E 01
0.60000000E-01	0.97991217E-01	0.50128171E 00	0.10000000E 01
0.65000000E-01	0.35158364E 00	0.32725097E 00	0.10000000E 01
0.70000000E-01	0.11782208E 01	0.29755389E 00	0.10000000E 01
0.75000000E-01	0.22658040E 01	0.40916207E 00	0.10000000E 01
0.79999999E-01	0.32432453E 01	0.61420285E 00	0.10000000E 01
0.84999999E-01	0.38035835E 01	0.83273806E 00	0.10000000E 01
0.90000000E-01	0.37970901E 01	0.10083685E 01	0.10000000E 01
0.94999998E-01	0.32669112E 01	0.10721435E 01	0.10000000E 01
0.99999998E-01	0.24203471E 01	0.10168344E 01	0.10000000E 01
0.10500000E 00	0.15498827E 01	0.86841872E 00	0.10000000E 01
0.11000000E 00	0.93313980E 00	0.68063912E 00	0.10000000E 01
0.11500000E 00	0.74530810E 00	0.51571283E 00	0.10000000E 01
0.12000000E 00	0.10110927E 01	0.42378247E 00	0.10000000E 01
0.12500000E 00	0.16084712E 01	0.42782682E 00	0.10000000E 01
0.13000000E 00	0.23190354E 01	0.51842820E 00	0.10000000E 01
0.13500000E 00	0.29052362E 01	0.65927784E 00	0.10000000E 01
0.14000000E 00	0.31877573E 01	0.80086291E 00	0.10000000E 01
0.14500000E 00	0.30982942E 01	0.89730831E 00	0.10000000E 01
0.15000000E 00	0.26927846E 01	0.92074397E 00	0.10000000E 01

Fig. E2.3

E. Morlet and D. Ribbens, (Eds.), International Computing Symposium 1977.

PROGRAM RESTRUCTURING ALGORITHMS FOR GLOBAL LRU ENVIRONMENTS

Domenico Ferrari
Politecnico di Milano, Milano, Italy
and University of California, Berkeley, California, U.S.A.

Makoto Kobayashi
University of California, Berkeley, California, U.S.A.

In several existing virtual-memory systems, the memory hierarchy is managed by a policy of the global LRU type. Two algorithms for restructuring programs to be executed in such an environment are described. The principles forming the bases of these algorithms, which try to tailor the referencing behavior of programs to the one expected by the global LRU policy so as to improve their paging performance, are stated in general terms. The results obtained in a series of experiments on the reference strings generated by a real program under various inputs confirm the expectations about the practical applicability and the performance improvements of the new algorithms.

1. THE GLOBAL LRU ENVIRONMENT

The choice of the policy for the automatic management of a virtual-memory system's memory hierarchy is an important part of the design of such systems. Besides being well-suited to the referencing behaviors of the programs to be executed on the system, the policy must be economic to implement, and the overhead caused by it must be tolerable. These implementation and overhead considerations have non-negligibly influenced the design of the memory policies to be incorporated into the existing systems. As pointed out by Oliver /1/, some variations of the global LRU policy have been adopted in several multiprogrammed virtual-memory systems just because of their relative simplicity of implementation, and even in spite of the fact that they are inherently prone to thrashing.

The global LRU policy may be described as follows. In a multiprogrammed system, the primary memory usually contains, at any given time, several programs. If the system has a virtual memory, those in primary memory are not, generally, complete programs, but portions of programs. When the program which is running references an information item (instruction or datum) which is not in primary memory, that item must be fetched from another memory where it is stored, and brought into primary memory, where the central processing unit (CPU) can access it. This event is called a <u>fault</u>. Due to the physical characteristics of the secondary memory devices where the complete programs reside, a large number of adjacently stored information items must be transferred to primary memory together with the needed item. The complex of these items is called a <u>page</u> or a <u>segment</u>, depending on the way virtual memory is implemented /2/. For simplicity, we shall assume a paged implementation throughout this paper. When the primary memory is full, the loading of a new page must be preceded by the selection of the page to be replaced among those in primary memory, and by its unloading if the page selected is not an identical copy of its parent page in secondary memory. Since all pages have the same size and can be placed anywhere in primary memory, this selection is not subject to size constraints.

The global LRU replacement algorithm keeps a list of all the pages in primary memory, sorted according to their recentness of reference, and replaces, whenever this is necessary, the least recently referenced page. Thus, the amount of primary-memory space allotted to each process is time-variant, and depends on the referencing behaviors of the other processes which share the system's resources with it. A global replacement policy like the one just described is not concerned with the degree of multiprogramming, that is, the number of processes simultaneously present in memory, which is to be controlled by an additional mechanism. This mechanism must contain suitable provisions for avoiding the often catastrophic collapse of system performance called <u>thrashing</u>, which is caused by an overcommitment of a critical resource, usually of the primary memory /3/.

Variations of the global LRU policy have been implemented, because of their simplicity, in several systems, including Multics, CP-67 and VM/370. For the purposes of our discussion, we summarize the policies implemented in the latter two systems as follows /4/. A circular list, containing the so-called "use bits" of the pages present in primary memory at any given time is kept by the operating system. Each page has a use bit, which is turned on whenever the page is referenced.

A pointer to the list is advanced to the next entry every time a page fault is generated by the running process. If the use bit pointed to is on, it is turned off and the pointer is advanced immediately to the next entry. If the use bit is off, the corresponding page is replaced by the needed page, to which the same use bit will be related until its replacement by another page. This is the environment to be considered in this paper.

2. IMPROVING PERFORMANCE BY PROGRAM RESTRUCTURING

Several studies have recently shown that the performance of virtual-memory systems and of the programs running on them can often be effectively improved by the technique of program restructuring /5/. Restructuring a program means modifying the relative positions of its parts in the virtual address space. If the parts to be rearranged (called *blocks* in the sequel) are substantially smaller than the pages, the performance of the restructured program may drastically differ from that of the original one. By an appropriate rearrangement, it may be possible to reduce considerably, for instance, the total number of page faults generated during an execution of the program, or its mean primary memory-space demand, or some other index of the same type. Certain restructuring procedures may be completely, or almost completely, automated, and in fact some automatic restructuring tools have recently appeared on the market. The most successful among the methods which have been proposed so far is based on the knowledge of a program's dynamic behavior. One possible implementation of the method consists of recording a *block reference string*, that is, the sequence of references issued by the program to its blocks during an execution, and extracting from it the *restructuring graph*, which is then clustered to determine how the program's blocks should be distributed among the pages /5/. In order for this clustering to achieve the desired results, the nodes of the (non-directed) restructuring graph are to represent blocks, and the label of each edge the strength of the connection between the two corresponding blocks, in other words, the desirability that the two blocks be put into the same page. The labels on the edges of the restructuring graph are computed by a *restructuring algorithm*. Various restructuring algorithms have been devised and experimented with. A particularly successful class of such algorithms is the one based on the *tailoring* philosophy /5, 6/. This philosophy consists of exploiting, in the design of the algorithm, the knowledge of the memory policy (or policies) under which the programs to be restructured will have to run. Their referencing behaviors are made closer to those the policy expects, and may be viewed as being tailored to the policy.

In Section 4, two restructuring algorithms which try to tailor programs to the global LRU-like policy described in Section 1 are presented. The next section discusses the principles used in the design of the two algorithms.

3. CRITICAL-SET AND MINIMUM-SET RESTRUCTURING ALGORITHMS

Two classes of tailoring algorithms have been particularly investigated in the recent past: the *critical-set algorithms*, whose ultimate objective is to reduce the page fault rate of a program, and the *minimum-set algorithms*, which are aimed at reducing the mean size of a program's resident set. The concept of resident set is crucial to the understanding of both classes of algorithms. The *resident set of pages* of a program at a given virtual time t of its execution, $R_p(t)$, is the set of the program's pages which reside immediately before time t in primary memory. It is useful to introduce a similar definition at the level of blocks. The *resident set of blocks* at time t, $R_b(t)$, is the set of those blocks which are *certainly* going to be in memory immediately before time t. The identity of all the blocks that will be in memory at time t cannot be determined from a block reference string if, as is the case in a restructuring procedure, the program's layout has not been specified. However, for a number of policies, the set of blocks which will surely be in memory at any given time can be identified. Assuming that the policy being dealt with satisfies this condition, $R_b(t)$ can be determined from the block reference string being considered, and used in the construction of the restructuring graph as follows.

When the next reference is to a block which is not included in $R_b(t)$, we say that a *block fault* occurs, or that the reference is *critical*. Not all block faults become page faults when blocks are assigned to pages, but all page faults derive from block faults. In order to reduce as much as possible the number of block faults which become page faults, we increase by a fixed amount (usually 1) all the labels of the edges connecting the critically referenced block to each of the blocks in $R_b(t)$. In fact, if any of these pairs of blocks is assigned to the same page, there cannot be a page fault at time t. Non-critical references are ignored. The one we have just described is the basis of the critical-set algorithms /5,7/.

The minimum-set algorithms also assume that $R_b(t)$ can be determined from a block reference string. However, at each new reference, they increment the labels of the edges connecting each pair of blocks in $R_b(t)$, so as to reduce the mean size of the resident set of pages.

The two classes discussed above contain restructuring algorithms which are generally not optimum. First of all, these algorithms only consider connectivity information for pairs of blocks, while pages often contain more than two blocks. Furthermore, the clustering algorithms which produce the new layout from the restructuring graph are not guaranteed to yield an optimum clustering.

4. THE CPSI AND MPSI RESTRUCTURING ALGORITHMS

We have seen in the previous section that a critical-set or minimum-set algorithm can be easily implemented whenever the policy under which the programs will have to run allows us to determine the sequence of resident sets of blocks $R_b(t)$ from the given block reference string. But does the LRU-like policy described in Section 1 satisfy this requirement? The answer is no. As already observed in Section 1, for global policies the composition of the resident set (of blocks or pages) of a program is a function of the dynamic behaviors of the process being considered and of the other processes, hence unpredictable and varying from run to run.

However, Bard /4/ has proposed and successfully experimented with a method for determining, in an approximate way, certain indices of program behavior, including the sequence of the resident sets of pages. The method is based on a single parameter, the <u>page survival index</u> (PSI), which summarizes the influences of the rest of the workload on the process being considered. The execution of a program is usually suspended when (a) a page fault is generated, or (b) the completion of an I/O operation must be waited for, or (c) the time quantum assigned to the process expires. The value of the PSI represents the mean number of such interruptions that a page of the program can survive (that is, remain in primary memory) without being referenced. High values of the PSI correspond to situations of low paging activity and vice versa. The probability that an unreferenced page is "stolen" by another process increases with the number and duration (in real time) of the interruptions . However, the PSI method takes only the number, which is determined by the process itself, and not the durations, which depend on the other processes, into explicit account. As observed above, the effect of the other processes is concisely though approximately expressed by the value of the PSI. Thus, the composition of the resident set of pages may be roughly estimated from the page reference string by applying the PSI method: a page which is in primary memory will remain there unreferenced for a number of interruptions equal to the value of the PSI and will disappear immediately after the last of these interruptions. Often, a string does not contain any information about I/O operations; in this case, the interruptions caused by them will have to be ignored or artificially recreated in some way.

It is easy to see that the PSI method can also be used to estimate the sequence of the resident sets of blocks by applying it to a block reference string. For a page to be unloaded from primary memory, it is necessary that all of its blocks be unreferenced for at least a number of interruptions equal to the value of the PSI. Thus, when the PSI method is applied to a block reference string, all pages containing blocks being in the estimated $R_b(t)$ will necessarily belong to the estimated $R_p(t)$.

Having reached the above conclusion, the design of a critical-set and of a minimum-set restructuring algorithm intended to tailor programs to the PSI policy (shown by Bard to be an acceptable approximation of a global LRU-like policy as far as the behavior of a single process is concerned) is straightforward. If the block referenced at virtual time t is denoted by r_t, the <u>critical PSI (CPSI) algorithm</u> will consist of incrementing, whenever $r_t \notin R_b(t)$, the labels of all edges connecting r_t to the members of $R_b(t)$. Similarly, the <u>minimum PSI (MPSI) algorithm</u> will simply increment at every time t a new reference is issued the labels of the edges connecting all the pairs of members of $R_b(t)$.

5. EXPERIMENTAL RESULTS

A number of experiments have been designed and implemented to analyze the performance of the CPSI and MPSI algorithms. A trace-driven simulator of a PSI environment, which is able to simulate the running of a program under a number of different values of the PSI in just one pass over a reference string, has been constructed. Programs which compute the labels of the restructuring graph using the CPSI and MPSI algorithms, as well as other restructuring algorithms against which the new ones had to be compared, were also implemented. A hierarchical clustering program already employed in a number of previous experiments (see /5, 7/) has been used to produce the layouts of the restructured programs. Our experiments were performed on block reference strings generated by a PASCAL compiler running on a CDC 6400 while compiling five different programs /8/. To gather these strings, the compiler's code was partitioned into 139 blocks, corresponding to its 139 procedures. The strings do not include data references.

Under each of the five inputs, the PASCAL compiler was restructured using a non-tailoring algorithm like the nearness method (NM)/9/, the critical working set (CWS) and the minimum working set (MWS) algorithms /5/, which try to tailor programs to a working-set policy (a window size of 50 ms was assumed), and the two new algorithms. Then, the non-restructured version and the various restructured ones were run in the simulated PSI environment, and the values of such indices as the total number of page faults and the mean resident-set size were computed. It was unfortunately impossible to repeat the same tests in the global LRU environment which the PSI method tries to approximate. Even if a system incorporating this policy had been available, the design of such experiments for a real-life situation would have been extremely difficult because of the workload control problem, and the use of some artificial load would have probably been required.

The results obtained for two inputs to the compiler are plotted in Figure 1 and Figure 2, respectively. Those for the other three inputs were similar to those presented in these figures and have therefore been omitted. The diagrams are of the type called "paging characteristic" by Bard /4/: they show, in semi-logarithmic scale, the relationship between the number of page faults and the mean resident-set size for various values of the PSI. The CPSI and MPSI algorithms have been applied assuming a PSI equal to 13, a value which Bard's measurements of a CP-67 system /10/ have shown to be reasonable. However, the reader will notice that these diagrams suggest qualitative conclusions which are valid in a wide range of values of the PSI and not only for PSI = 13. The main conclusions may be summarized as follows:

(a) the non-restructured program is normally outperformed by its version restructured according to the nearness method, which is not a tailoring algorithm; for PSI = 13, the relative improvement of the number of page faults is about 63% in Figure 1 and 24% in Figure 2, that of the mean resident-set size is about 8.5% in Figure 1 and 1.7% in Figure 2;

(b) The layouts suggested by the tailoring algorithms CWS, MWS, CPSI and MPSI clearly outperform those obtained by NM and, *a fortiori*, the original ones; for PSI = 13, the relative improvements of the numbers of the page faults and of the mean resident-set size over the performance of the original program are about 80.3% and 17.6% (CWS), 74.5% and 15.1% (MWS), 81.8% and 14.3% (CPSI), 78% and 13.4% (MPSI) in Figure 1, 75.2% and 12.9% (CWS), 68.4% and 7.6% (MWS), 79.6% and 15% (CPSI), 70% and 9.9% (MPSI) in Figure 2; thus, for PSI = 13 and for both performance indices, the critical-set algorithms produce better results than the minimum-set ones, and the tailoring algorithms (CPSI and MPSI) tend to slightly outperform the other two; however, the differences are so small that changes in the value of the PSI cause also these relative rankings to vary;

(c) as the mean resident-set size (and the value of the PSI) increases, the differences in performance among the various layouts of the program tend to decrease; in the limit, when there are no space constraints, the number of page faults equals the number of pages accessed at least once by the program and does not depend on the layout.

The influence of the PSI value used in the restructuring procedures was further investigated by applying the CPSI and MPSI algorithms with various values of the PSI and comparing the performances of the layouts obtained. The paging characteristics of these layouts for CPSI and reference string 2 (the one whose performance is shown in Figure 1) are reported in Figure 3. The results for PSI = 8 and PSI = 13 are very close to each other over the 8 to 20 range of PSI values during execution. As should be expected, the former are slightly better for PSI equal to 8 or 9, but become worse for higher values. The curve for PSI = 25 shows a considerably poorer performance for PSI $<$ 12, a lower page fault rate and a larger resident set for PSI $\geq$ 13. That obtained with PSI = 50 is even worse than the original one for PSI $\leq$ 14 but becomes better for higher values of the execution PSI.

Thus, if we know that the actual PSI in our system is normally comprised in a certain range, we may restructure our programs assuming a value of the PSI slightly lower than the mean of the two extremes of that range, without worrying about the sensitivity of the results to PSI variations at execution time, at least as long as these vatiations are not too large.

In the experiments reported on above, I/O operations were not considered among the sources of interruptions. Quantum time was set at 400 ms throughout the experiments, since a previous experiment had shown that quantum expirations had little influence on the two performance indices.

6. CONCLUSION

Two restructuring algorithms which try to tailor the behavior of programs to a global LRU environment have been presented. Their design has been derived in a straightforward way from the principles of critical-set and minimum-set algorithms stated in Section 3. Their performance was found to be excellent but not appreciably better than that of other tailoring algorithms like CWS and MWS. The fact that the two new algorithms do not provide substantially better performance is probably to be attributed to the near-optimality of the results achieved by CWS and MWS, which is also due to the fortunate choice of the window size used when applying them. Since this is not guaranteed to be always the case, the use of the CPSI or MPSI algorithms (whose cost of implementation and usage is comparable to those of CWS and MWS) would seem to be safer when restructuring programs to be executed in a global LRU environment.

ACKNOWLEDGMENTS

The authors are indebted to David Ching and Edwin Lau, who recorded the reference strings used in the experiments. They also gratefully acknowledge the support of the National Science Foundation grant DCR74-18375 and of the Computer Center of the University of California at Berkeley.

REFERENCES

/1/ N.A. Oliver, Experimental data on page replacement algorithm, AFIPS Conf. Proc. 43 (NCC 1974), 179-184.

/2/ P.J. Denning, Virtual memory, Comp. Surveys 2,3 (Sept. 1970), 153-189.

/3/ P.J. Denning, Thrashing: its causes and prevention, AFIPS Conf. Proc.33 (FJCC 1968), 915-922.

/4/ Y. Bard, Characterization of program paging in a time-sharing environment, IBM J. Res. Develop. 17, 5 (Sept.1973) 387-393.

/5/ D. Ferrari, The improvement of program behavior, Computer 9,11 (Nov. 1976).

/6/ D. Ferrari, Tailoring programs to models of program behavior , IBM J. Res.Develop. 19,3 (May 1975), 244-251.

/7/ D. Ferrari, Improving locality by critical working sets, Comm.ACM 17,11 (Nov.1974), 614-620.

/8/ D. Ferrari and E. Lau, An experiment in program restructuring for performance enhancement, Proc. 2nd Int. Conf. on Software Engineering, San Francisco, Calif. (Oct.1976), 203-207.

/9/ D.J. Hatfield and J. Gerald, Program restructuring for virtual memory, IBM Sys.J. 10,3 (1971), 168-192.

/10/ Y. Bard, Application of the page survival index (PSI) to virtual-memory system performance, IBM J.Res. Develop. 19,3 (May 1975), 212-220.

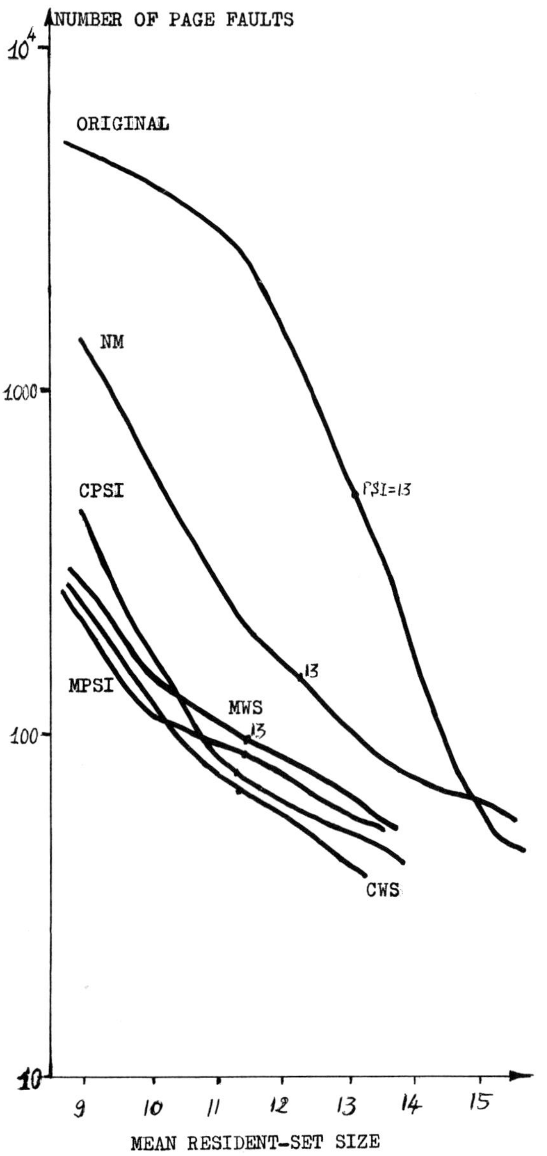

Figure 1. Paging characteristics of reference string 2.

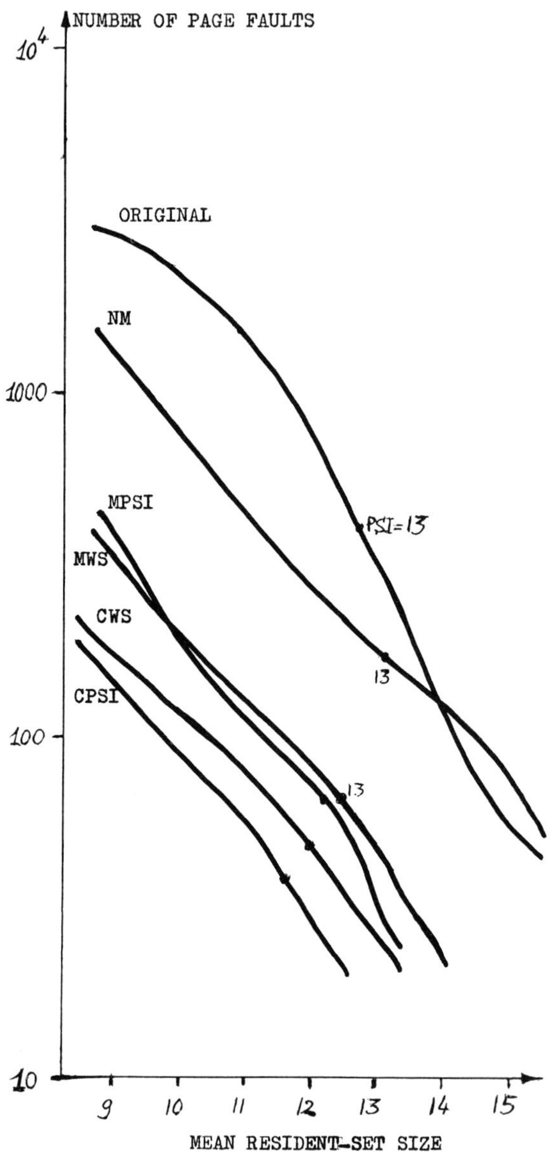

Figure 2. Paging characteristics of reference string 4.

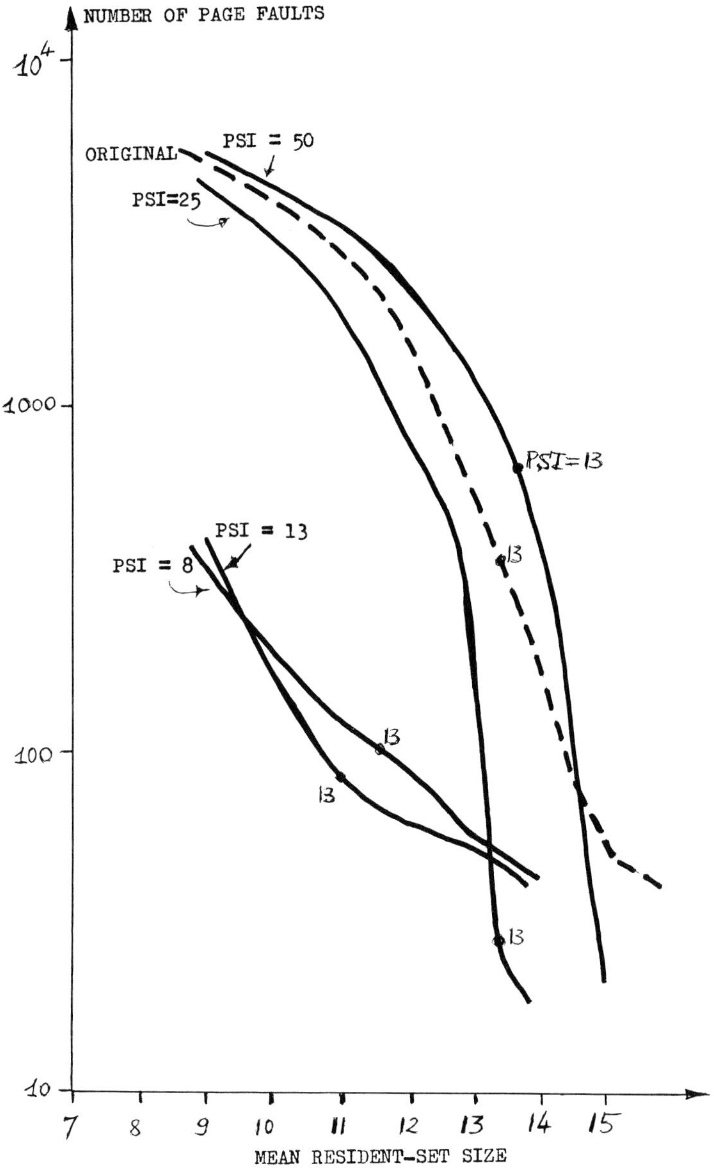

Figure 3. Paging characteristics obtained applying CPSI with various values of the PSI (reference string 2).

E. Morlet and D. Ribbens, (Eds.), International Computing Symposium 1977.

A PREDICTIVE TOOL FOR THE IMPROVEMENT OF PROGRAM BEHAVIOUR

P. RIBEYRE P.Y. SAINTOYANT
Ecole Nationale Supérieure d'Informatique
et de Mathématiques Appliquées
B.P. 53, 38041 GRENOBLE Cedex, France

This paper describes a set of tools used for the prediction and improvement of program behaviour in a segmented virtual memory. Three components are presented : a method for measuring the inter-segment dynamic reference pattern, a clustering algorithm for the improvement of locality, and a model and simulator of program behaviour.

1. INTRODUCTION

The work reported in this paper was performed as a 3rd year student project at the ENSIMAG (Ecole Nationale Supérieure d'Informatique et de Mathématiques Appliquées de Grenoble), in cooperation with CII-HB in Paris. The aim was to develop a predictive tool for the improvement of program behaviour by clustering in a segmented virtual memory ; the interest of prediction is to be able to evaluate the expected benefit without any modification of the programs under study. Thus, the project involves three main parts : measurements on program activity, clustering algorithm, model and simulator of program behaviour. A few options had been initially chosen : dynamic measurements, same inputs for clustering and simulation, simplicity of the model. The investigation was conducted with a HB 64 computer /1/, which is a segmented virtual memory computer.

2. OBSERVATION OF A PROGRAM

When studying program behaviour in relation with the virtual memory, it is natural to consider a program as a sequence of references to segments. It is possible to build a matrix containing all the references between all the segments of a given program, or of a phasis of this program (a phasis being a subset of segments where a chain of references between any two segments can be found). The problem of the validity of such a matrix is quite important and delicate. First we had to choose between a static matrix (obtained for instance during the linkage) and a dynamic one (resulting from the actual execution). These two matrices present important differences : for instance, the elements of the static matrix are generally rather small (lower that ten), while we can find in the dynamic one some elements in the range of one thousand, or even ten thousands. But these two matrices have the common property of being very sparse (more than 90 % of their elements are null). A first conclusion is that the dynamic matrix is more appropriate to study the behaviour of the program. Anyway, we have to deal with another problem : can we consider that the dynamic matrix is fit for the description of the program activity ? Indeed, the transition from the sequence of references to the matrix involves a certain reduction of data that we cannot ignore. It is obvious that ten references between 2 given segments happening in a range of one hundred references, and ten other happening in a range of ten thousands have not the same meaning in relation with virtual memory management. Nevertheless we have used a simple matrix, directly obtained from the time series of references, and the results, as it will be seen later, seem to prove that this approximation was correct. Anyway, it is possible, for the future, to think of more sophisticated methods.

We reach now the practical problem : how to build the matrix ? Two measurement methods have been developped and will be presented below :

a) Hardware Method

The first method uses a hardware monitor and allows to collect all the references between two code segments corresponding to an explicit call. Thus we obtain by this way the whole chronicle of calls with which we can build the matrix using a special program. However a few lacunas exist : we can neither know the size of the segments (necessary for simulation), nor collect the references to data segments. In fact, the main interest of this method is to check the data obtained with the software method.

b) Software Method

We have also used a software monitor (Implementor's Instrumentation). The principle is then to collect a couple of segments (calling-called) when a segment miss occurs. The data is richer than with the hardware method, but the matrix that we can build is biased, because every reference does not cause a miss, and because the virtual memory management algorithm favours some segments. Several solutions exist in order to reduce this bias. It would have been possible to modify the memory management algorithm. Our action was only to reduce the user memory size, which implies an increase of the miss ratio. Of course the execution of a program with a strongly reduced memory is longer but the time remains reasonable.

The software monitor gives us directly the matrix of code-code references, and also the code-data matrix. To build the data-data matrix, we suppose that if there is a link x between the code segment S and the data segment T_1, and a link y between S and another data segment T_2, then it exists an link (x+y) between T_1 and T_2.

3. THE CLUSTERING ALGORITHM

3.1. The case for clustering

Any program has a logical structure, defined by the programmer,when he divides the code in subroutines or procedures, or when he structures the data (for example in Fortran local data or common blocks). According to the machine he uses, the influence of the programmer may be more or less important. With a paged virtual memory (VM), he must specify completely all the pieces of data or code composing any given pages. In the case of the segmented VM of the HB 64, each simple unit defined by the programmer (for example a subroutine) becomes a segment ; thus we can see that the problem is quite different. Anyway this logical structure is exactly represented by what we have called the static matrix.

The important differences existing between the static and dynamic matrices can suggest that a program has an other structure, that we can call the dynamic structure, revealed by the execution. The aim of clustering is, on examination of the dynamic matrix, to substitute a new division to the one specified by the programmer.

In order to explain precisely the principles of clustering, we shall tell a few words about the program behaviour in a VM environment. Let us remind that the Working-Set W (t,T) is the set of segments referenced in the interval of time (t,t-T). Denning, and other authors /2,7/ have shown that the working-set has a few important properties, and particularly the property of locality. If we consider the sequence S of references to segments generated during the execution of a program, we can divide it into subsequences S_1, S_2, ..., S_n such that :

i) S_i and S_{i+1} are very similar

ii) S_i and S_{i+k} are weakly correlated as k becomes large.

It is almost obvious that a very local program will have a good behaviour in VM because :

a) If the locality is strong, it means that there exists a range of values of T such that, for a given t, W(t,T) is constant or has very small variations. Then during the time T, the references are located in a rather small subset of segments, and the number of segment faults will be small, which implies that the execution will not be slowed down by the processing of segment faults.

b) If we are now interested in the consumed memory size, a strong locality implies that the working-set size will be small.

We know that the best (but not implementable VMM) algorithm is the algorithm knowing the future working-set. We have the possibility to improve any VMM algorithm by making some clusterings of segments. Indeed, if we know that the call to the segment S_a is followed with a strong probability by the calls to the segments (S_i, S_{i+1}, ..., S_{i+n}) it may be interesting to bind the segments S_a with the segment S_i, in order to avoid a few segments faults. Thus, we try to approximate the Working-set W(t+T,T) where t is the time when a segment fault occurs.

By this process, we only make use of the existing locality without improving it. It would be possible, and certainly better to break, before clustering, the initial segments in smaller ones (with the programmer's help), but this way has not yet been explored.

Clustering can provide improvements in two different directions :

- minimizing the fault ratio, for a given memory size
- minimizing the necessary memory size for a given maximum fault ratio.

This double action appears on the curve representing the fault ratio as a fonction of the memory size (Figure 1), on which we can see a leftwards shift.

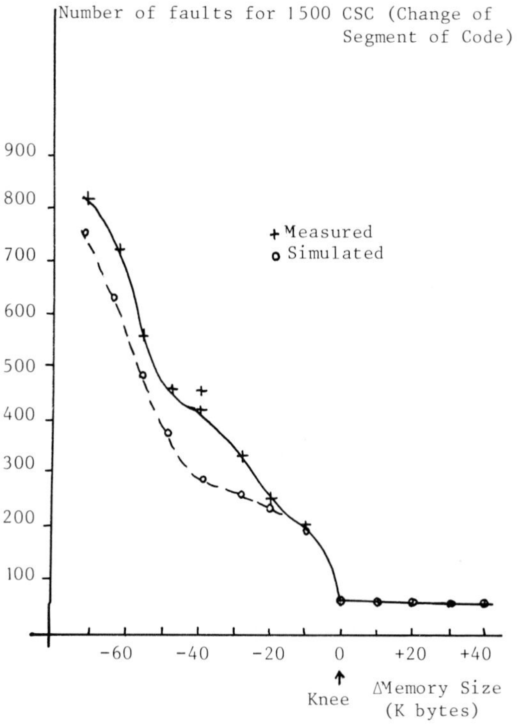

Figure 1

The actual implementation is composed of the following operations :

i) execution of the studied programs and measurements
ii) clustering algorithm
iii) binding of segments pointed out in the phase ii)
iv) linkage.

3.2. The algorithms

Many clustering techniques have been studied /4,5,6/. Most of them work in a paged environment ; therefore the size of a cluster is fixed. Anyway, a program is always divided in blocks, a block being a segment or any piece of code or data. Then, a matrix holding the references between the selected blocks is built, the element (i,j) containing the number of references from block i towards blocks j. We must note that the notion of reference may be quite different from the notion of call.

We can give a geometrical interpretation of the clustering. Initially the non-null elements of the matrix are scattered anywhere, and the aim is to bring them in the neighbourhood of the main diagonal, by reordering the rows and columns. A candidate for clustering will be then represented by a square submatrix, containing very few zeros.

In fact, only a few algorithms are directed by this principle. Some others use data analysis techniques, and some others graphs techniques.

Our algorithm can be divided in to two distinct parts :

i) pseudo-diagonalization
ii) search of groups in the modified matrix.

We see that, if we move a row, we must to move also the corresponding column, thus the matrix must be symmetrical.

In phase i) we sweep the matrix diagonal by diagonal, starting from the outside one (which holds only one element). When we find an element larger than Min (a parameter that may be zero) in the cell (i,j), we try to bring closer the rows (and columns) i and j. For this purpose, we test the displacements of row j towards the rows i-d, i-d+1, ..., i-1, i+1, ..., i+d where d is a parameter. For example we can pass from the state (1,...,i-d,...,i,...,j,...,N) to the state (1,...,j,i-d,...,i,...,j-1,j+1,...,N). Of course we test also the displacements of row i towards the rows close to the row j. We now have to explain how to test a displacement. We have tried to define a coefficient describing the state of the matrix, this state being represented by a N-vector, where N is the size of the matrix. Two coefficients have been defined, and give two different versions of the algorithm. In the first one called "band", we compute the sum of the elements in a band of width 2 ℓ (ℓ is a parameter), centered on the main diagonal. In the second one, called "center of gravity", we compute the difference between the coordinates of the center of gravity of the superior triangular matrix (we must remember that the matrix is symmetrical). After having tested all the displacements for a selected element, we keep the best on and we go on sweeping the matrix. The algorithms stop when reaching the limit diagonal D (D being a parameter).

In phasis ii) we try to find the best clusters or groups. A group is evaluated by its coefficient R = sum of inside references/sum of inside and outside references, that must be maximized. So we start from a 1×1 submatrix and we expand it as long as R increases. There is no limit to the size of a group and some segments may remain isolated.

We have not tested all the possibilities of combinations between the different parameters, but nevertheless we can give some observations on the algorithm. Concerning the cost, we can show that it depends on N^4, and on d. This cost may seem high, but we must note that generally N is of the order of 20 or 30. The first results seem to point out that the "band" version, with d=l=N-D=2 is the best one. Anyway, a comparison with other algorithms is impossible, for no published result gives an evaluation of the cost.

4. A MODEL OF PROGRAM BEHAVIOUR

Our model had to follow a few constraints. It had to be simple, accurate (for a good prediction), and had to use the same data than the clustering algorithm (i.e. the reference matrix). Many models exist in the litterature /2,9/ but they consider always a paged environment, and they do not usually distinguish between code and data, while the system GCOS 64 makes the distinction for considerations of protection. Thus, we had to build a new model.

Our model considers two subspaces in the space of the segments of a program : the subspace of code segments, and the subspace of data segments. This subspace is also partitioned into as many subspaces as there are code segments : each code segment has only one associated data subspace, that may be shared with other code segments. We regard a program as a sequence of references to code segments, and the execution of a given code segment as a sequence of references to data segments belonging to the corresponding subspace. The activity ot the program is described by (n+1) stochastic processes, where n is the number of code segments :

- a process ρ describing the movements in the code subspace
- n processes ρ_i, each ρ_i describing the movements in the data subspace D_i associated to the code segment S_i.

The problem of the termination of the processes has been solved in two different ways. The processes ρ_i end when reaching an absorbing state, and the process ρ ends after a given number of references, which allows to control the time of simulation.

To be able to use this model, we had to make an important hypothesis : we assume that the model is markovian, that is to say that the state of a process depends only on its previous state. We must note that this hypothesis is consistent, because the property of locality may be obtained without using a process with memory, and we can also see that it is consistent with the principle of the clustering technique.

We can do some important statistical observations on this model :

i) the markovian models are homogeneous : the state of a process depends only on its initial state and on the transition matrix.

ii) the processes are regular, i.e. they have only one class of final states.

iii) the processes are ergodical, thus we can ensure the convergence of the transient means towards the statistical mean.

Beside this model we have built a simple random number generator, and two modules of memory management (LRU and FIFO).

During the development and tuning phases, we have performed many measurements on the model in order to study its behaviour. We can obtain the number of faults, the working-set for several window sizes, the activity and inactivity count. Our model is discrete and does not involve physical time. Thus, our time unit is the CSC (Change of Segment of Code). Therefore, the activity count is the average time (in CSC) of residence in main memory, the inactivity count is the average time of residence in secondary memory.

5. RESULTS

In only six months, we did not have enough time to make a complete and precise study of the model and the clustering algorithm. All the results which we shall present have been obtained by using the measurements on phases 2 and 3 of a Cobol compiler, these phases being part of the syntactic analyzer. We have tried to answer the following questions :

1) When does the model reach a stable behaviour (problem of convergence) ? We can see in figure 2 that the permanent regime is reached for 1400 CSC.

2) Does the model give a good evaluation of the actual fault ratio ? The comparison between the fault ratios observed on the actual system, and on the model shows a good adequation for memory sizes greater than the size corresponding to the knee of the curve, and less good for other sizes (figure 1). Nevertheless, the two curves tend to be closer when we reduce the parameter H, which defines the probability of the absorbing state in a data subspace. But of course the simulation time increases when H decreases.

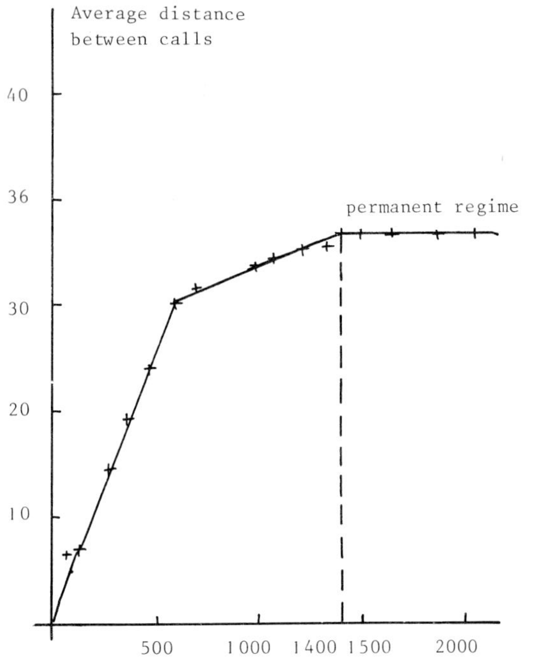

Figure 2

3) How does the model react to a variation of memory size ? The general aspect of the curve of the figure 3 representing the fault number as a fonction of memory size is typical, and presents the same remarkable points as real programs.

4) What is the expected gain ? The study of the gain in number of faults (shown in table 4, where the memory size zero corresponds to the knee) points out a leftwards shift of the parachor curve. The gain in memory is about 10 K in the interesting zero (near the knee).

5) Is the prediction accurate and fast ? The curve on figure 4, as well as the table on figure 5, shows that the gain strongly depends on memory size. But the important point is that the three curves : predicted LRU gain, predicted FIFO gain, and observed gain are very close.

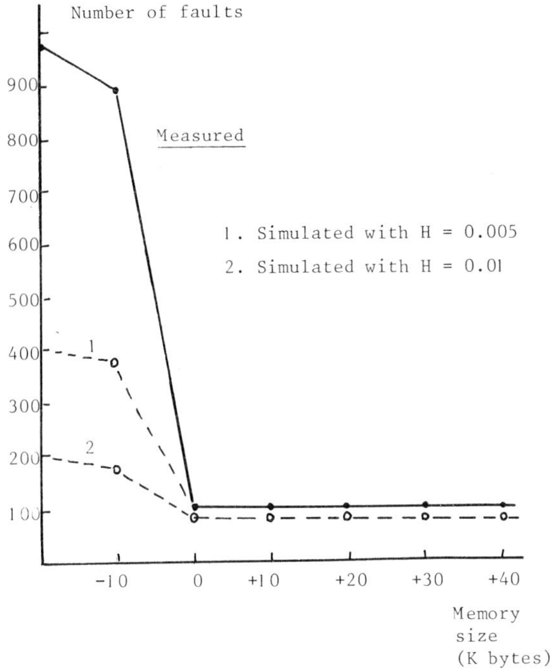

Figure 3

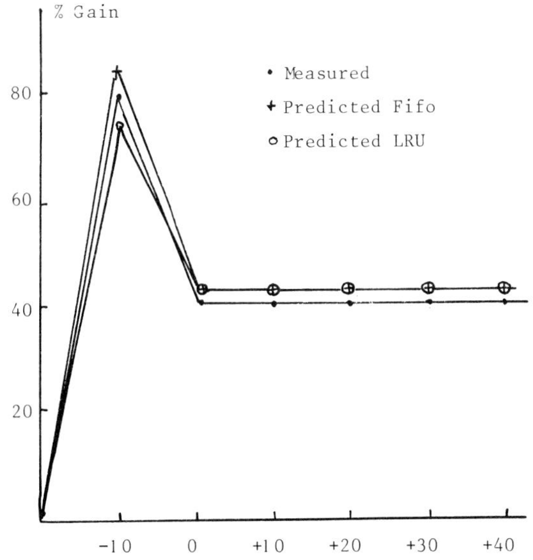

Figure 4

Memory Size	-20K	-10K	0	+10K	+20K
Gain (measured)	5 %	80 %	40 %	40 %	40 %

Figure 5 : Gain in number of faults

Knowing that the model is adequate, and that the algorithm gives satisfactory results, it is now possible to deal with the problem of performance. The question is : is it worth to simulate the programs that we want to cluster ? We have established a comparison between the actual implementation of clustering and the simulation. We observed an important gain both in elapsed time and in programmer time.

Indeed, the simulator is very easy to use. The user has only to create a few cards for the parameters, and he can know very quickly what will be his gain for the memory sizes he has selected. If these results are good enough, he can realize the bindings, and a new linkage, which are long and complex operations. Without simulator, he would have to do many measurements, which is costly for small memory sizes. Thus, the interest of the simulator is clearly demonstrated.

6. CONCLUSIONS

The first results seem to show that the tool we have presented satisfies the initial goals. However we can indicate a few possible improvements :

- We could use the chronicle of calls to build the matrix. With this method, we cut the chronicle in equal sequences and we assure that there is a link between all the segments belonging to the same sequence. Thus, we suppress the bias created by the software monitor, but we cannot collect references (now this notion is different from the notion of call) to data segments.

- It would be possible to introduce in phasis 2 of the clustering a limit for the size of a cluster, in order to avoid too large groups.

- We have supposed that the behaviour of a program was data independant. We could perhaps think of several measurements performed with different data, and a merge of the matrices.

We must also mention an important drawback of the model which overestimates the fault number, because it introduces what we call "ghost sequences" : if we have a link A-B and a link B-C, the simulator will create the sequence A-B-C which may never appear in the actual program.

We can wonder whether the results will remain valid in a multiprogrammed environment. All our experiments have been made with a single program in memory. We can think that the answer is positive, because the observed leftwards shift of the parachor curve implies a decrease in the memory size, which improves multiprogramming performance.

As a conclusion, we can say that the tool we have implemented has reached a good level of performance, but that some improvements are possible, to make it still more efficient, and to head for a completely automatic tool (generation of cards for binding and linkage).

ACKNOWLEDGMENTS

We thank M. DE RIVET and M. PINET, of CII-HB, for their guidance and support during this investigation, and Professor S. KRAKOWIAK for his help in the preparation of this paper.

7. REFERENCES AND NOTES

/1/ Architecture of series 60/64.
T. ATKINSON, Honeywell Computer Journal, 1975.

/2/ A study of program locality and lifetime functions.
P.S. DENNING, K.C. KAHN, CACM SIGOPS Austin 11/75.

/3/ A multifactor paging experiment.
R.F. TSAO, L.W. COMEAU, B.H. MARGOLIN
Statistical Computer Performance Evaluation
Academic Press 1972.

/4/ Adaptation automatique des programmes en milieu paginé.
G. MORISSET, Thèse Université Paris VI 1975.

/5/ Optimization of program organization by cluster analysis.
T. MATSUDA, H.S. HIUTA, K. NOGUCHI
Information Processing 1974.

/6/ Program restructuring for virtual memory.
D.J. HATFIELD, J. GERALD,
IBM Syst. J. 1971.

/7/ The working set model for program behaviour.
P.J. DENNING, CACM 1968.

/8/ Projet Mac TR 103.
A. SEKINO, MIT, Sept. 1972.

/9/ Evaluation of Markow program models in virtual memory systems.
R.P. BOGOTT, M.A. FRANKLIN
Software Practice and experience 1975.

E. Morlet and D. Ribbens, (Eds.), International Computing Symposium 1977.

THE VARIANCE OF CONDITIONAL WAITING TIME FOR THE M/G/1 QUEUE

by

Arne Nilsson
Lund Institute of Technology, Sweden

Abstract

Different well-known scheduling algorithms for time-shared computer systems are studied. Especially the mean and variance of conditional response times are determined for the M/G/1 queueing system structure. By numerical examples it is shown that the variance of conditional response time is a good additional measure for the performance of time-sharing systems.

1. Introduction

Most scientist of today have to work with a computer now and then. Even the non-scientist of our modern society are often - if not directly - at least via punched cards and/or datafiles in rather close contact with those powerful computing machines. This evolution has clearly created a need for us to understand and even predict the behaviour of the complex computer systems. In this paper we will analyze a special class of computer systems - from a queueing theoretical point of view - and try to determine some suitable parameters for describing the efficiency of the time-shared computer systems.

2. Definitions and Preliminaries

When we want to study a computer system we are faced with the problem of trying to sort out the important parts of the system for performing a pertinent analysis and/or synthesis. Here we are especially interested in time shared systems and therefore we are concerned with a collection of remote terminals from which users may gain simultaneous access to a collection of computing resources referred to as a computer system. Figure 2:1 shows a typical configuration for this computer system.

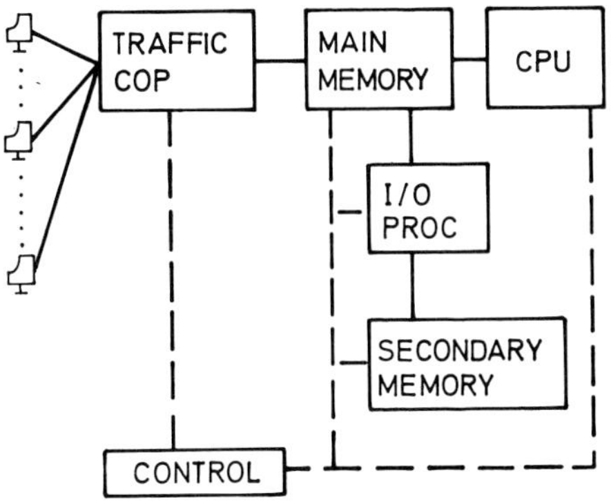

Fig 2:1 Computer System
(- denotes data flow, - - - denotes control)

We see that the resources include the terminals themselves, the communication lines connecting the terminals to the computer system, the traffic handler, a so called COP, controlling the flow of traffic between the users and the computer system. The main memory and secondary memory devices e.g. drums, discs, etc., are also typical resources in the computer system as are the various types of I/Ø media which may be present. Lastly, the most important resource of them all: the Central Processing Unit (CPU) whose processing capacity most certainly will be a dominant factor if we try to determine the processing capacity of the computer system. Quite obviously a number of conflicts may arise in this system when many user programs compete for resources, and it is the intention to study a subclass of these conflicts in this paper, namely those arising when users (jobs, programs) compete for access to the CPU.

2.1 The Queueing Structure

Kleinrock/5/ studied time-shared systems as a class of feedback queueing systems and the same approach will be used in this paper.
These systems consist of a single resource, the CPU, the server, and a system of queues in front of the server, see figure 2:2.

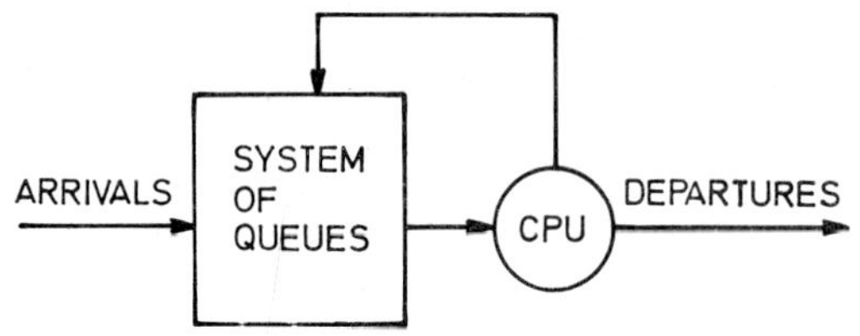

Figure 2:2 Feedback queueing system

The server has the option of sending back a job to the queues when this job has been given some amount of service. Whenever the server becomes idle a customer is brought from the queues into the server. The selection determining which customer to pick is made according to a rule that is commonly called the scheduling discipline.
The scheduling discipline plays an important part in the analysis of time sharing systems, as we will soon see. Therefore, let us now define the class of scheduling disciplines that we will allow. "Any disciplines that do not use information about an individual customer´s service requirement or some measure of that service need," will be acceptable to us. The strategy adopted in most time sharing configurations is to let the jobs themselves prove that they are short and therefore should be given immediate attention. This operation is accomplished through the following strategy:

A new job is given a quantum of service as soon as possible. If the job is finished during that quantum it will depart from the system and so, obviously, it was a short job (unless the quantum size is foolishly chosen). If the job needs more service, it will not finish during the first quantum, it will be sent back to the system of queues and after some appropriate time, once again be given access to the server, where it will receive a second quantum of service. Should the job finish during this second quantum it leaves the system (the job was almost short), if not it will again be sent back to the queues and it will have to wait for further quanta. Let us introduce the notation

q_n=quantum of service that a job gets when it arrives at the server for the n.th time

In order to make the future analysis easier we are going to assume infinitesimal quanta, i.e. $q_n \to 0$. This situation is often called processorsharing.
Whenever a job is transferred from the queues to the server, or from the server to the queues, the program has to be moved from the queueing media into the core, and vice versa. The time it takes to perform this transfer is usually called swap-time. Swap-time has in most studies of time sharing systems been neglected and we choose to do the same here.
How do we then measure the quality of a time sharing system? In fact, what kind of parameters would we like to know or even like to control? The most used parameter has so far been the conditional mean response time (and/or the conditional mean waiting time), defined through

$T(x) \triangleq$ average response time for a customer requiring x seconds of processing

and

$$W(x) \triangleq T(x) - x$$

In this paper we will also study the variance of the response time for a customer requiring x seconds of processing. This quantity will be denoted $\sigma^2(x)$.

2.2 The M/G/1 Queue

We will analyse our feedback queueing system under the assumption that it is an M/G/1 queue.
This means that the arrival process is Poisson, with mean arrival intensity denoted λ, and that the service time distribution is arbitrary (General). We assume that a customer has a service requirement $\tilde{x}$ that is a stochastic variable, where

$$P(\tilde{x}<x)=B(x)$$

The n.th moment of service time distribution will be denoted by $\overline{x^n}$ and is computed as (the mean is denoted $\overline{x}$)

$$\overline{x^n}=\int_0^\infty x^n\, b(x)dx$$

where b(x) is the density function of the service time. Often we will also need to work with the Laplace transform $B^*(s)$ of the service time distribution.

$$B^*(s)=E\{e^{-s\tilde{x}}\}=\int_0^\infty e^{-sx}b(x)dx$$

The load on the system will be denoted ρ and thus $\rho=\lambda\overline{x}$. When we study an M/G/1 queue and want to obtain numerical results, we have to specify the service time distribution. In this paper we will often choose B(x) as an Erlang-r distribution, and/or an H_2-distribution, i.e.

$$b(x)=\begin{cases} r\mu\frac{(r\mu x)^{r-1}}{(r-1)!}e^{-r\mu x} & \text{Erlang-r} \quad r=1,2,\ldots \\ \alpha\mu_1 e^{-\mu_1 x}+(1-\alpha)\mu_2 e^{-\mu_2 x} & H_2 \quad 0\leq\alpha\leq 1 \end{cases}$$

The reason for this particular choice of service time distribution is that we will then get the opportunity to model a fairly large class of service time distributions. We can see that the Erlang-1 distribution is the same as the exponential distribution, thus we have also incorporated the classical M/M/1 system among the systems that we are especially interested in.

3. Mean Conditional Response Time

In this section we will present results for T(x) for some wellknown scheduling algorithms, namely FCFS (actually this one is a poor candidate for a scheduling algorithm), FB, LCFS-PR, and RR. The results have all been published elsewhere e.g. by Estrin /4/, Kleinrock /5,6,7,9/, McKinney /10/, and Schrage /14/, which means that we are just going to list them here.

3.1 FCFS - scheduling

For an FCFS system we know that the average waiting time, W, is given by the Pollaczek-Khinchine formula, Kleinrock /8/.

$$W=\frac{\lambda\overline{x^2}}{2(1-\rho)} \tag{3.1}$$

and the mean waiting time is independent of the service required. We can therefore conclude that

$$T(x)=\frac{\lambda\overline{x^2}}{2(1-\rho)}+x \tag{3.2}$$

3.2 FB - scheduling

For a system working under FB-scheduling (Foreground- Background), it can be shown that Coffman /2/, and Schrage /14/.

$$T(x)=\frac{W_x+x}{1-\rho_x} \tag{3.3}$$

where

$$W_x=\frac{\lambda\overline{x_x^2}}{2(1-\rho_x)} \tag{3.4}$$

and

$$\overline{x_x^n}=\int_0^x y^n b(y)dy+x^n(1-B(x)) \tag{3.5}$$

and

$$\rho_x=\lambda\overline{x_x} \tag{3.6}$$

3.3 LCFS - PR - scheduling

The Last - Come - First - Served - Pre-emptive - Resume scheduling produces the response time

$$T(x)=\frac{x}{1-\rho} \tag{3.7}$$

3.4 RR - scheduling

The popular and widely used scheduling algorithm Round-Robin generates the same response function as does LCFS-PR. Sakata /13/ was perhaps the first to study the M/G/1 queue under RR, and he found that the solution for the average response time was independent of the form of the service time distribution (dependent only on the mean service time). He found by using a rather complicated method that equation (3.7) is valid also for RR.
This certainly indicates that one should look for a complementary measure for the performance of scheduling algorithms.

3.5 A Numerical Example

Let us illustrate the behaviour of W(x)=T(x)-x for the scheduling algorithms and let us choose an M/M/1 system, i.e.

$$B(x)=1-e^{-\mu x} \qquad x\geq 0 \tag{3.8}$$

We then get with $\rho=\lambda/\mu$

$$W_{FCFS}(x)=\frac{\rho}{\mu(1-\rho)} \tag{3.9}$$

$$W_{RR}(x)=W_{LCFS-PR}(x)=\frac{\rho x}{1-\rho} \tag{3.10}$$

$$W_{FB}(x)=\frac{\rho}{\mu}\cdot\frac{1-e^{-\mu x}-\mu x e^{-\mu x}}{(1-\rho(1-e^{-\mu x}))^2}+\frac{\rho(1-e^{-\mu x})x}{1-\rho(1-e^{-\mu x})} \tag{3.11}$$

Equations (3.9) - (3.11) are drawn in figure 3:1, where $\mu=1$ and $\rho=0.75$. We note the extreme fairness of the scheduling disciplines RR and LCFS-PR, the total ignorance of service requirement x by FCFS, and a tendency to favour short jobs that is inherent for FB-scheduling.

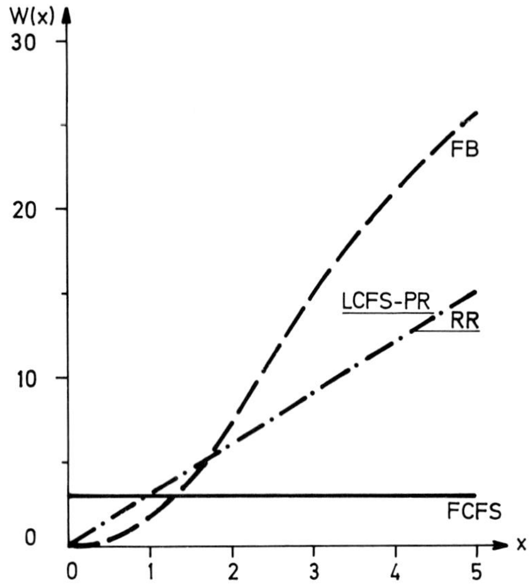

Fig 3:1 Average conditional waiting time for the system M/M/1, ρ=0.75 and μ=1.

4. The Variance of Conditional Response Time

In the previous section we presented results for T(x) and W(x) for the well-known scheduling algorithms FCFS, RR, FB and LCFS - PR. We found that the mean conditional response time was not a sufficiently good indicator for the system performance. A fact that was illustrated by the mean conditional response time for RR and LCFS - PR. Naturally we would like to have a better measure of system performance and a good candidate for that measure would then be the variance of conditional response time. Of course the ultimate goal would be to determine the conditional distribution function of response time i.e.

$$S(y|x)=P(\tilde{y}\leq y|\tilde{x}=x) \tag{4.1}$$

where $\tilde{y}$ is the response time. Often, however, $S(y|x)$ is hard to determine especially for the RR - algorithm and therefore we will be quite satisfied if we can obtain the variance of conditional response time

$$\sigma^2(x)=\mathrm{Var}\{\tilde{y}|\tilde{x}=x\} \tag{4.2}$$

In the rest of this section we will determine $\sigma^2(x)$ for the scheduling algorithms under interest when as usual the queueing structure is of the type M/G/1. At least we will try to push the analysis as far as possible for general service time distributions. In some cases, however, we have to restrict the allowed service time distribution somewhat. When we present the results it will often be convenient to work with Laplace-transforms and especially the transform for $S(y|x)$ namely

$$S^*(s|x)=\int_0^\infty e^{-sy}dyS(y|x) \tag{4.3}$$

4.1 FCFS - scheduling

If the scheduling discipline is FCFS the general theory for M/G/1 queues /8/ tells us that

$$S^*(s|x)=\frac{s(1-\rho)}{s-\lambda+\lambda B^*(s)}e^{-sx} \tag{4.4}$$

Which easily gives us that

$$\sigma^2(x)=\frac{\lambda\overline{x^3}}{3(1-\rho)}+\left(\frac{\lambda\overline{x^2}}{2(1-\rho)}\right)^2 \tag{4.5}$$

4.2 FB - scheduling

Schrage /14/ has shown that under FB-scheduling

$$S^*(s|x)=W_x^*(s+\lambda-\lambda G_x^*(s))\exp\{-x(s+\lambda-\lambda G_x^*(s))\} \tag{4.6}$$

where

$$G_x^*(s)=B_x^*(s+\lambda-\lambda G_x^*(s)) \tag{4.7}$$

and

$$W_x^*(s)=\frac{s(1-\rho_x)}{s+\lambda-\lambda B_x^*(s)} \tag{4.8}$$

This gives that

$$\sigma^2(x)=\frac{3W_x^2}{(1-\rho_x)^2}+\frac{\lambda\overline{x_x^3}}{3(1-\rho_x)^3}+\frac{2W_x}{(1-\rho_x)^2}x \tag{4.9}$$

4.3 LCFS - PR - scheduling

The transform $S^*(s|x)$ can, under LCFS-PR scheduling, be determined by using a busy period analysis. This analysis is straight forward and the result is

$$S^*(s|x)=\exp\{-x(s+\lambda-\lambda G^*(s))\} \tag{4.10}$$

where $G^*(s)$ is determined through

$$G^*(s)=B^*(s+\lambda-\lambda G^*(s)) \tag{4.11}$$

$\sigma^2(x)$ is then readily computed and the result is

$$\sigma^2(x) = \frac{\lambda\overline{x^2}}{(1-\rho)^3}x \qquad (4.12)$$

4.4 RR - scheduling

Before we start with the analysis for RR-scheduling we should note that the results obtained for FCFS, FB and LCFS-PR are valid for general service time distributions. When the scheduling discipline is RR we know of only one system, the M/M/1 queue, for which the variance of conditional response time has been published, Coffman /3/. The result obtained by Coffman et. al. is

$$\sigma^2(x) = \frac{2\rho x}{\mu(1-\rho)^3} - \frac{2\rho}{\mu^2(1-\rho)^4}(1-e^{-\mu(1-\rho)x}) \qquad (4.13)$$

$\sigma^2(x)$ for the systems $M/E_r/1$ and $M/H_2/1$ has been found by this author /12/ by using a generalization of the method employed in /3/. The method used in /12/ is most easily illustrated by an analysis of the $M/E_2/1$ system.
For this system the service time distribution is Erlang-2, and we know that this distribution can be looked upon as consisting of two independent exponential stages. Conceptually the service mechanism in the $M/E_2/1$ queue can therefore be depicted as

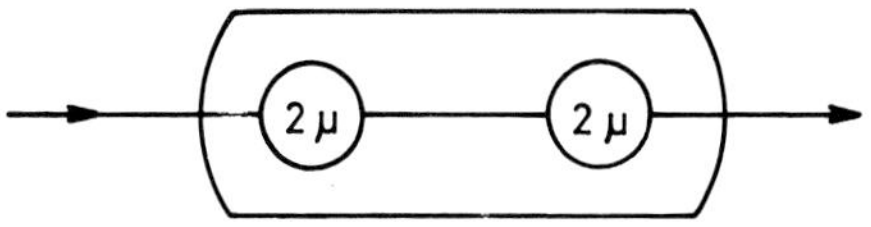

It is known Muntz /11/ that the state-probability $p(n_1,n_2)$ defined by

$$p(n_1,n_2) \underline{\underline{\Delta}} P(n_1 \text{ customers in stage 1, } n_2 \text{ customers in stage 2})$$

can be expressed as

$$p(n_1,n_2) = (1-\rho)\binom{n_1+n_2}{n_1}\left(\frac{\rho}{2}\right)^{n_1}\left(\frac{\rho}{2}\right)^{n_2} \qquad (4.14)$$

where

$$\rho = \lambda/\mu$$

Now let $w_{n_1,n_2}(x)$ be a random variable that corresponds to the waiting time experienced by a customer with service requirement x, and who, upon arrival finds n_1 customers in stage 1, and n_2 customers in stage 2. Our objective is to find the variance of conditional response time, this, however, must be equivalent to finding the variance of the conditional waiting time.

Let us define

$$W^*_{n_1,n_2}(s|x) \underline{\underline{\Delta}} E\{e^{-sw_{n_1,n_2}(x)}\} \qquad (4.15)$$

If we could find $W^*_{n_1,n_2}(s|x)$, we can easily determine $W^*(s|x)$ - the Laplace transform of the conditional waiting time, since

$$W^*(s|x) = \sum_{n_1}\sum_{n_2} W^*_{n_1,n_2}(s|x)p(n_1,n_2) \qquad (4.16)$$

A relation for $W^*_{n_1,n_2}(s|x)$ can be derived in the following way. Let Δx be a differential element of (service) time. The tagged customer must spend $(n_1+n_2+1)\Delta x$ seconds in the system before he has received Δx seconds of service. Neglecting terms of the order $\sigma(\Delta x)$, we may write

$$W^*_{n_1,n_2}(s|x+\Delta x) =$$

$$= (1-(\lambda(n_1+n_2+1)+2\mu(n_1+n_2))\Delta x)\cdot$$

$$\cdot e^{-s\Delta x(n_1+n_2)}W^*_{n_1,n_2}(s|x)+$$

$$+\lambda(n_1+n_2+1)\Delta x\; W^*_{n_1+1,n_2}(s|x)+$$

$$+2\mu n_1\Delta x\; W^*_{n_1-1,n_2+1}(s|x)+$$

$$2\mu n_2\Delta x\; W^*_{n_1,n_2-1}(s|x) \qquad (4.17)$$

Rearranging and taking the limit $\Delta x \to 0$ we obtain

$$\frac{\partial}{\partial x}W^*_{n_1,n_2}(s|x) =$$

$$= -(\lambda(n_1+n_2+1)+(s+2\mu)(n_1+n_2))\cdot$$

$$\cdot W^*_{n_1,n_2}(s|x)+\lambda(n_1+n_2+1)W^*_{n_1+1,n_2}(s|x)+$$

$$+2\mu n_1\; W^*_{n_1-1,n_2+1}(s|x)+2\mu n_2\; W^*_{n_1,n_2-1}(s|x) \qquad (4.18)$$

In order to gain more information from this equation it is convenient to introduce the generating function

$$f = f(z,y,s|x) \underline{\underline{\Delta}} \sum_{n_1}\sum_{n_2} W^*_{n_1,n_2}(s|x)\cdot$$

$$\cdot\binom{n_1+n_2}{n_1}z^{n_1}y^{n_2} \qquad (4.19)$$

This generating function will satisfy the following partial differential equation

$$\frac{\partial f}{\partial x}-(z(2\mu y-s-\lambda-2\mu)+\lambda)\frac{\partial f}{\partial z}-$$

$$-(y(2\mu y-s-\lambda-2\mu)+2\mu z)\frac{\partial f}{\partial y}=(2\mu y-\lambda)f \qquad (4.20)$$

This equation can probably be solved, but we are, however, interested only in determining $\sigma^2(x)$ and because of this we choose to attack the equation in another way. We note that

$$W^*(s|x)=(1-\rho)f(\frac{\rho}{2},\frac{\rho}{2},s|x) \qquad (4.21)$$

$\sigma^2(x)$ can obviously be determined through the second and first derivatives of $W^*(s|x)$ and thus through the same derivatives of the generating function f. If we differentiate the partial differential equation once and twice with respect to s and perform some other manipulation - complicated, but rather straight - forward - we will find that

$$\int_0^\infty \sigma^2(x)e^{-sx}dx=$$

$$=\frac{6\mu\rho+2\rho s}{(1-\rho)^2 s^2(s^2-s(\lambda-4\mu)+4\mu^2-4\mu\lambda)} \qquad (4.22)$$

This Laplace transform of $\sigma^2(x)$ can be inverted an we easily find that

$$\sigma^2(x)=\frac{3\rho x}{2\mu(1-\rho)^3}$$

$$-\frac{6\mu\rho+2\rho s_1}{(1-\rho)^2 s_1^2(s_1-s_2)}(1-e^{s_1 x})-$$

$$-\frac{6\mu\rho+2\rho s_2}{(1-\rho)^2 s_2^2(s_2-s_1)}(1-e^{s_2 x}) \qquad (4.23)$$

Where s_1 and s_2 are roots to the equation

$$s^2-s(\lambda-4\mu)+4\mu^2-4\mu\lambda=0 \qquad (4.24)$$

The linear term of $\sigma^2(x)$ can be written as

$$\frac{\lambda\overline{x^2}}{(1-\rho)^3}x \qquad (4.25)$$

This happens to be the same kind of linear term as was found for the M/M/1 system. As stated above $\sigma^2(x)$ has been found for the systems $M/E_r/1$ and $M/H_2/1$ and the result can be expressed very concisely by the following formula

$$\int_0^\infty \sigma^2(x)e^{-sx}dx=\frac{2\rho}{(1-\rho)^2 s^3}\;\frac{1-\hat{B}^*(s)}{1-\rho\hat{B}^*(s)} \qquad (4.26)$$

where

$$\hat{B}^*(s)=\frac{1-B^*(s)}{s\overline{x}} \qquad (4.27)$$

This expression is probably valid for any M/G/1 system, in spite of the fact that it has only been proven for the above mentioned queueing systems. From equation (4.26) we will find that the linear term of $\sigma^2(x)$ is the same as equation (4.25). This result can, however, also be established for general service time distribution /12/. Remember that equation (4.26) was found for the systems $M/E_r/1$ and $M/H_2/1$.

4.5 Numerical Examples

We will now demonstrate through some examples that the variance of conditional response time does provide us with a good complementary measure of system performance. In fact the results obtained in section 4.4 clearly shows that

$$\sigma^2_{RR}(x)\leq\sigma^2_{LCFS-PR}(x) \qquad (4.28)$$

Where equality holds only for x=0. Figure 4:1 and 4:2 show $\sigma^2(x)$ as a function of the load ρ with x as a parameter for the systems M/M/1 and $M/E_2/1$.

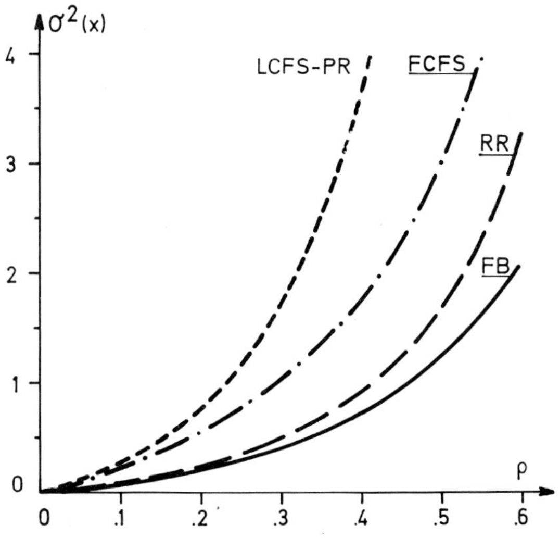

Fig 4:1 Variance of conditional response time M/M/1. $\overline{x}$=1. x=1.

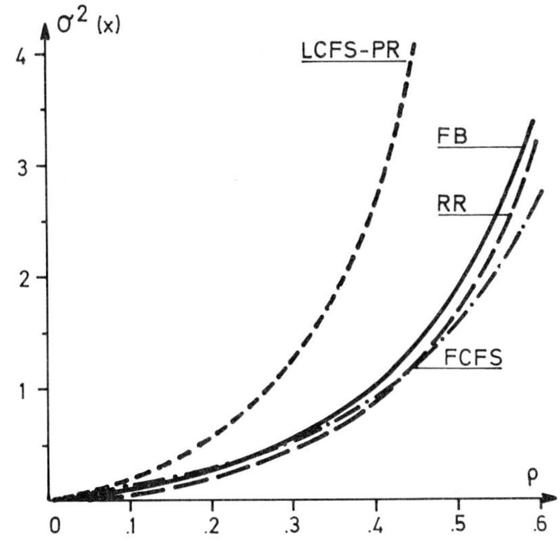

Fig 4:2 Variance of conditional response time. $M/E_2/1$. $\bar{x}=1$. $x=1$.

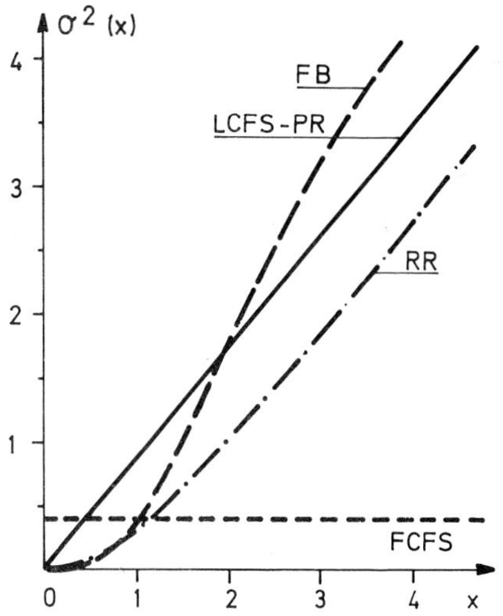

Fig 4:4 Variance of conditional response time. $M/E_2/1$. $\rho=0.25$. $\bar{x}=1$.

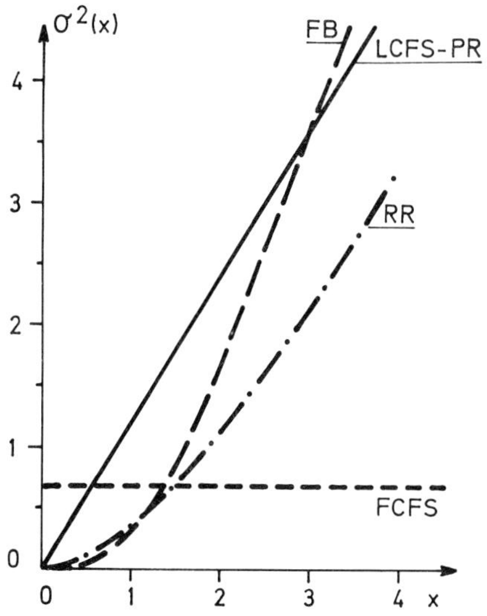

Fig 4:3 Variance of conditional response time. M/M/1. $\rho=0.25$. $\bar{x}=1$.

We note that for the region of the load showed FB does produce the smallest $\sigma^2(x)$. Referring to equation (4.9) we see that when the load increases $\sigma^2(x)$ must increase more rapidly for FB than it does for the other algorithms. Also of interest is the fact that $\sigma^2 RR(x)$ is less than $\sigma^2 FCFS(x)$ for values of the load up to approximately 0.5. This is a fact that is not so easily seen in the paper by Coffman et. al /3/.
Figures 4:3 and 4:4 show the dependence between $\sigma^2(x)$ and x when the load ρ is held constant. Once again we see that the RR - algorithm produces a smaller variance than does FCFS as long as the service requirement x is below some value. Clearly it seems that if we combine the effect of W(x) and $\sigma^2(x)$ then the RR - algorithm should be favoured.

4.6 Baskett´s Conjecture

In a contribution to the Seventh Hawaii International Conference on System Sciences, 1974, F. Baskett /1/ presented a conjecture (we hasten to point out that it was phrased as a hypothesis regarding the functional form) for the variance of time spent in an M/G/1 queue operating under RR - scheduling this conjecture was that

$E\{\tilde{y}^2\}$=(second moment of time spent in the system)=

$$=\frac{\overline{x^2}}{(1-\rho)^2(1-g(c_b)\rho)} \quad (4.29)$$

Where $g(c_b)$ is some positive decreasing function of the coefficient of variation of the service time. By using the result obtained in equation (4.26) we can show that this conjecture is false, e.g. an $M/E_2/1$ system will give us the following

$$E\{\tilde{y}^2\} = \frac{\overline{x^2}}{(1-\rho)^2}\ \frac{1-5\rho/24-\rho^2/96}{(1-3\rho/8)^2} \quad (4.30)$$

which happens to be impossible to transform into equation (4.29). If we, however, form the same kind of function as Baskett did, namely

$$f(E\{\tilde{y}^2\},\rho)=\frac{1}{E\{\tilde{y}^2\}(1-\rho)^2} \quad (4.31)$$

and plot this quantity as a function of ρ we will find that for $M/E_2/1$ $f(E\{\tilde{y}^2\},\rho)$ is very close to a straight line. This indicates that Baskett's conjecture is a very good one.

5. Conclusions

We have derived formulas for the variance of conditional response time for the M/G/1 queue under RR - scheduling. We note that this variance increases as $(1-\rho)^{-2}$ rather than $(1-\rho)^{-3}$ as in the case of LCFS - PR and $(1-\rho)^{-4}$ at least for large x as for FB. Furthermore we have managed to show that $\sigma^2(x)$ does provide us with an additional good measure for the performance of time-sharing systems.

6. References

/1/ Baskett, F., "The Variance of the Waiting Time for the M/G/1 Queue Under Processor Sharing," Proc. of the Seventh Hawaii International Conference on System Sciences, January, 1974.

/2/ Coffman, E.G., Jr., and Kleinrock, L., "Feedback Queueing Models for Time-Shared Systems," JACM, (October 1968) 15:549-576.

/3/ Coffman, E.G., Jr., Muntz, R.R., and Trotter, H., "Waiting Time Distribution for Processor-Sharing Systems," JACM, (January 1970) 17:123-130.

/4/ Estrin, G., and Kleinrock, L., "Measures, Models and Measurements for Time-Shared Computer Utilities," Proc. of 22nd National Conference of the Association for Computing Machinery, sponsored by the Association for Computing Machinery, August 29-31, 1967, Washington, D.C., (1967) pp. 85-96.

/5/ Kleinrock, L., "Analysis of a Time-Shared Processor," Naval Research Logistics Quarterly, (March 1964) 11:59-73.

/6/ Kleinrock, L., "Time-Shared Systems: A Theoretical Treatment," JACM, (1967) 14:242-261.

/7/ Kleinrock, L., "A Selected Menu of Analytical Results for Time-Shared Computer Systems," in Systemprogrammierung, R. Oldenburg Verlag, Munich, Germany, (1972) pp. 45-73.

/8/ Kleinrock, L., Queueing Systems, Volume I: Theory, John Wiley and Sons, New York, 1975.

/9/ Kleinrock, L., Queueing Systems, Volume II: Computer Applications, John Wiley and Sons, New York, 1976.

/10/ McKinney, J.M., "A Survey of Analytical Time-Sharing Models," Computing Surveys, (June 1969) 1:105-116.

/11/ Muntz, R.R., "Network of Queues Models: Application to Computer System Modeling" UCLA - course notes, 1973.

/12/ Nilsson, A., "Analysis and Synthesis of Time - Shared Computer Systems," PhD thesis, Department of Telecommunication Systems, Lund Institute of Technology, 1976.

/13/ Sakata, M., Noguchi, S., and Oizumi, J., "An Analysis of the M/G/1 Queue under Round Robin Scheduling," Operations Research (1971) 19:371-385.

/14/ Schrage, L.E., "The Queue M/G/1 with Feedback to Lower Priority Queues, " Management Science (1967) 13:466-471.

E. Morlet and D. Ribbens, (Eds.), International Computing Symposium 1977.

ANALYSIS OF A FOREGROUND-BACKGROUND SYSTEM WITH TWO LEVELS OF PRIORITY AMONG FOREGROUND JOBS

J.J. Dumont
(chercheur agréé de l'IISN)
Inter-University Institute for High Energies
ULB-VUB, Brussels

G. Latouche
Laboratoire d'Informatique Théorique
Faculté des Sciences, ULB, Brussels

A particular queueing process with three levels of priorities is considered as a model of a foreground-background system. A foreground job (class 1 or 2) has preemptive delay priority over background jobs. The mean number of type 1 and 2 jobs at instant of service completion are derived, as well as a measure of the loss of efficiency due to preemptions. The results are discussed in the framework of the system which motivated this analysis.

1. INTRODUCTION.

In a typical timesharing system, the main goal of the operating system is to share the resources, specially the central processor, as fairly as possible between all the running jobs. In some systems, the normal or background jobs may be interrupted by privileged jobs which must be serviced as soon as possible; consider for instance jobs affected to on line control of real time devices.
If the background job is interrupted immediately ('preemptive resume' priority rules, /3/), the system suffers usually an overhead cost associated with each preemption. On the other hand, if the background job is allowed to run until completion ('head of the line' priority rule, /3/), there is a cost for delaying the service of the privileged (or foreground) job. An intermediate policy, called 'preemptive delay' /2/, consists in introducing a delay d : the arrival of a foreground job causes a limit of d units of time to be placed on the amount of time the background job is allowed to run without preemption. If the background job is completed in less than d seconds, the foreground job is serviced as in the head of the line policy; otherwise the background job is preempted as in the preemptive resume policy.
In section 2 we define formally a queueing process with two different priority classes of foreground jobs and one class of background jobs.
In sections 3 and 4 we determine the long run average number of foreground jobs at the end of foreground job services (respectively $\overline{n}_1$ and $\overline{n}_2$).
In section 5 we study the efficiency of the system in function of d.
The results are discussed in section 6.
Our interest for this model comes from a practical problem encountered at our installation, where the scheduling is according to the preemptive resume policy. The system is usually filled with timesharing jobs, which may be interrupted by priority jobs belonging to two different classes. As two jobs cannot be present simultaneously in core, the arrival of a priority job necessarily imply a dead time due to swapping, which is by no means negligible compared to the running time of the lower priority jobs. Our purpose is to analyze the system in the case where the priority rule would be preemptive delay and to find a value of the delay compatible with the real time constraints, but keeping low the loss of efficiency.
Obviously, the mathematical model is only an approximation to the real system. Nevertheless, its analysis provides us with useful information on the effect of such a change of scheduling on the foreground jobs as well as the system as a whole.

2. DESCRIPTION OF THE MODEL.

We consider a system with three types of jobs; type 1 jobs have a non preemptive priority over type 2 jobs; both type 1 and type 2 have a preemptive delay priority over type 3. Type 1 and type 2 jobs will be known as 'foreground' jobs, type 3 as 'background' jobs.
We shall assume that type 1 (type 2) jobs arrive according to a Poisson process with parameter λ_1 (λ_2); their service times are random variables with distribution function G_1 (G_2).
We make no assumption on the arrival process of background jobs, but rather that

$$\rho = \lim_{t \to \infty} P \text{ (at time t the system contains at least one background job)}$$

is known. Moreover, the service times of background jobs are random variables with negative exponential (μ) distribution. If, upon arrival of a foreground job, the system contains no foreground job and at least one background job, the foreground job is delayed until either the current service is completed or d units of time have elapsed, whichever is smallest. At the end of the delay, the foreground job begins its service, if the background job was interrupted (delay = d), its service will resume when the system contains no more foreground job. We define a busy period to be the interval of time from the moment a foreground job arrives and the system contains no other foreground job until the first moment when the system contains again no foreground job.
Let D be the delay incurred by a foreground job that initiates a busy period. We have

$$H(x) = P(D \le x) = \begin{cases} 1-\rho & x = o \\ 1-\rho\, e^{-\mu x} & o < x < d \\ 1 & d \le x \end{cases}$$

$$\delta = E(D) = \frac{\rho}{\mu}(1 - e^{-\mu d})$$

$$\Delta^2 = E(D^2) = \frac{2\rho}{\mu^2}(1 - \mu d e^{-\mu d} - e^{-\mu d})$$

Let S_i ($i = 1, 2$) be random variables with distribution function G_i and $\overline{S}_i$ be the sums of the two independant random variables : S_i and D.
We define

$$F_i(x) = P(\overline{S}_i \le x)$$

$$\gamma_i = E(S_i)$$

$$\psi_i = E(\overline{S}_i)$$

$$\rho_i = \lambda_i \gamma_i$$

$$g_i(s) = \text{L. S. T. of } G_i(x)$$

$$f_i(s) = \text{L. S. T. of } F_i(x)$$

Obviously,

$$\psi_i = \gamma_i + \delta.$$

3. EMBEDDED MARKOV CHAIN.

Consider the sequence $t_1, t_2, \ldots, t_n, \ldots$ where $t_n > o$ is the nth epoch of completion of a foreground job, of either type 1 or type 2.
Let $n_i(k)$ = number of jobs of type i in the system at $t_k + o$ ($i = 1, 2$)

$$P_{i,j;m,l}(k) = P\,[n_1(k+1) = j,\ n_2(k+1) = l \mid n_1(k) = i,\ n_2(k) = m] \quad i,j,m,l = 0, 1, \ldots$$

It appears that those probabilities are independant of k and therefore the states $(n_1(k), n_2(k))$ form an ergodic Markov chain provided that steady state conditions are satisfied.
The probabilities

$$P_{ij} = \lim_{k \to \infty} P\,[n_1(k) = i,\ n_2(k) = j]$$

exist and are the unique solution to the system

$$P_{ij} = \sum_{m=o}^{\infty} \sum_{l=o}^{\infty} P_{ml}\, P_{m,i;l,j} \qquad (i,j = 0, 1, \ldots) \quad (1)$$

It is easy to see that

$$P_{o,i;o,j} = \frac{\lambda_1}{\lambda_1 + \lambda_2} \int_o^{\infty} \pi_{i,j}(t)\, d F_1(t) + \frac{\lambda_2}{\lambda_1 + \lambda_2} \int_o^{\infty} \pi_{i,j}(t)\, d F_2(t) \quad i,j \ge 0 \qquad (2)$$

$$P_{i,i;l,j} = \int_o^{\infty} \pi_{i,j-l+1}(t)\, d G_2(t) \quad i \ge 0,\ l \ge 1,\ j \ge l-1$$

$$P_{m,i;l,j} = \int_o^{\infty} \pi_{i-m+1,j-l}(t)\, d G_1(t) \quad m \ge 1,\ i \ge m-1,\ j \ge l \ge 0$$

where

$$\pi_{i,j}(t) = \frac{(\lambda_1 t)^i}{i!} \frac{(\lambda_2 t)^j}{j!} e^{-(\lambda_1 + \lambda_2)t}.$$

Let $P(z_1, z_2) = \sum_{i=o}^{\infty} \sum_{j=o}^{\infty} P_{ij}\, z_1^i z_2^j$.

From (1) and (2), one gets

$$P(z_1, z_2) = \{z_1 - g_1(\alpha(z_1, z_2))\}^{-1} \times \Big\{P(o,z_2)\Big(\frac{z_1}{z_2} g_2(\alpha(z_1, z_2)) - g_1(\alpha(z_1, z_2))\Big) + P(o,o)\, z_1\Big(\frac{\lambda_1}{\lambda_1 + \lambda_2} f_1(\alpha(z_1, z_2)) + \frac{\lambda_2}{\lambda_1 + \lambda_2} f_2(\alpha(z_1, z_2)) - \frac{1}{z_2} g_2(\alpha(z_1, z_2))\Big)\Big\}$$

where

$$\alpha(z_1, z_2) = \lambda_1(1-z_1) + \lambda_2(1-z_2).$$

To have an explicit form for $P(z_1, z_2)$ one has to determine $P(o,o)$ and $P(o,z_2)$.

A. <u>P(o,o).</u>

$P(o,o)$ is equal to $P_{o,o}$: the probability that, at completion of a foreground job, the system contains no foreground job. If steady state conditions are satisfied, $P_{o,o}$ is equal to the ratio of the mean number of times the event ($n_1 = o$, $n_2 = o$) occurs during a busy cycle divided by the mean number of foreground jobs served during a busy cycle (a busy cycle is equal to a busy period plus the interval of time until the arrival of a new foreground job).
Obviously,

$$P_{o,o} = \frac{1}{1 + (\lambda_1 + \lambda_2)\, E\,(\text{length of a busy period})}$$

As type 1 job have a non preemptive priority over type 2 jobs, the length of a busy period is the same as if the rule was 'first come first served', therefore, by the usual argument,

E (length of a busy period) =

δ + E (service of 1st foreground job)

+ E (time to serve the foreground jobs arriving during that 1st service or during the delay)

+ ...

$$= \xi + (\lambda_1 + \lambda_2)\, \xi \frac{1}{\lambda_1 + \lambda_2}(\rho_1 + \rho_2) + (\lambda_1 + \lambda_2)\, [(\lambda_1 + \lambda_2)\, \xi \frac{1}{\lambda_1 + \lambda_2} \times (\rho_1 + \rho_2)] \frac{1}{\lambda_1 + \lambda_2}(\rho_1 + \rho_2) + \ldots$$

$$= \frac{\xi}{1 - \rho_1 - \rho_2} \qquad (4)$$

where

$$\xi = \delta + \frac{\lambda_1 \gamma_1 + \lambda_2 \gamma_2}{\lambda_1 + \lambda_2} \qquad (5)$$

Eventually, one gets

$$P_{o,o} = \frac{1 - \rho_1 - \rho_2}{1 + (\lambda_1 + \lambda_2)\delta}$$

Observe that the necessary and sufficient condition for the busy period to have a finite positive mean (hence, for steady state conditions to be satisfied) is

$$1 - \rho_1 - \rho_2 > o$$

or (6)

$$\rho_1 + \rho_2 < 1,$$

which is to be expected.

B. $P(o, z_2)$.

From Rouché's theorem (see /1/, p 152), one can prove that for all z_2 such that $|z_2| < 1$, there exists a unique z_1 such that

$$|z_1| < 1,$$

$$z_1 - g_1(\alpha(z_1, z_2)) = 0, \qquad (7)$$

that we shall denote by $\zeta(z_2)$. Moreover, as $\rho_1 < 1 - \rho_2 < 1$ (see (6)), we have

$$\lim_{z_2 \to 1} \zeta(z_2) = 1.$$

As $P(z_1, z_2)$ is an analytic function for $|z_1| \le 1$, $|z_2| \le 1$, any root of the denominator has to be a root of the numerator and one gets from (3), replacing z_1 by $\zeta(z_2)$:

$$P_{(o,\, z_2)} = P_{o,o} \{z_2 - g_2(\beta(z_2))\}^{-1} \times$$
$$\{\frac{\lambda_1}{\lambda_1 + \lambda_2} z_2 f_1(\beta(z_2)) + \frac{\lambda_2}{\lambda_1 + \lambda_2} z_2 f_2(\beta(z_2))$$
$$- g_2(\beta(z_2))\}$$

where

$$\beta(z_2) = \lambda_1 (1 - \zeta(z_2)) + \lambda_2 (1 - z_2).$$

In particular,

$$P_{o,.} = \lim_{z_2 \to 1} P_{(o,z_2)} = P(n_1 = 0,\ n_2 \text{ takes any value})$$

$$= P_{oo}\left(1 + \frac{\lambda_2 \xi}{1 - \rho_1 - \rho_2}\right).$$

The proof of this last equation involves only algebraic manipulation when one observes from (7) that

$$\zeta'(1) = \frac{\lambda_2 \gamma_1}{1 - \rho_1}.$$

4. DETERMINATION OF $\bar{n}_1$ AND $\bar{n}_2$.

Let $\bar{n}_i = \lim_{k \to \infty} E(n_i(k)) \qquad (i = 1, 2)$

One has

$$\bar{n}_i = \frac{\partial P(z_1, z_2)}{\partial z_i}\Big|_{z_1 = z_2 = 1} \qquad (i = 1, 2).$$

As $\zeta''(1) = \dfrac{\lambda_2^2 E(S_1^2)}{(1 - \rho_1)^3}$,

one gets after lengthy but simple calculation the following results :

$$\bar{n}_1 = \frac{\lambda_1 P_{o,o}}{1 - \rho_1 - \rho_2}\left(\xi + \frac{\lambda_1 \varkappa}{2(1 - \rho_1)}\right) \qquad (8)$$

$$\bar{n}_2 = \frac{\lambda_2 P_{o,o}}{1 - \rho_1 - \rho_2}\left[\xi + \frac{\lambda_1}{2(1 - \rho_1)} + \frac{(\lambda_1 + \lambda_2)\varkappa}{2(1 - \rho_2)(1 - \rho_1 - \rho_2)}\right], \qquad (9)$$

where ξ was defined in (5),

$$\varkappa = (1 + (\lambda_1 + \lambda_2)\delta)\left[\Gamma^2 + P_{o,o}\Delta^2 + 2 P_{o,o}\delta \frac{\rho_1 + \rho_2}{\lambda_1 + \lambda_2}\right]$$

and $\Gamma^2 = \dfrac{1}{\lambda_1 + \lambda_2}(\lambda_1 E(S_1^2) + \lambda_2 E(S_2^2))$

5. MEASURE OF THE EFFICIENCY.

As was mentionned in the introduction, the reason why one would introduce a delay d in the preemptive priority rule is to decrease the inconvenience resulting from preemptions. The best achievement would be provided by the limiting case where d is equal to infinity (head of the line policy); but this may increase exceedingly the time a foreground job has to wait before being serviced.

In any particular system, a trade off between overall efficiency and foreground jobs response time may be obtained by choosing a value of d depending on the system parameters and requirements.

The variation of $\bar{n}_1$ and $\bar{n}_2$ may be considered as a measure of the effect of d on the foreground jobs response time. To measure the efficiency, we consider the following quantity :

η = long run average number of preemptions per unit of time

η is equal to the mean number of preemptions during a busy cycle divided by the expected length of a busy cycle, or :

$$\eta = \frac{P\,(\text{busy cycle begins with a preemption})}{E\,(\text{length of a busy cycle})}$$

$$\eta = \frac{\rho\, e^{-\mu d}}{\frac{1}{\lambda_1 + \lambda_2} + E\text{ (length of a busy period)}}$$

$$= \frac{\rho\, e^{-\mu d}}{\frac{1}{\lambda_1 + \lambda_2} + \frac{\xi}{1 - \rho_1 - \rho_2}} \quad \text{(see (4))}$$

Or $\eta = \rho\,(\lambda_1 + \lambda_2)\, P_{o,o}\; e^{-\mu d}$.

6. DISCUSSION.

The number of free parameters in the model being quite large, a complete discussion of the behaviour of such a system would be rather lengthy. Therefore, we restrict ourselves to the analysis of three variables which are most important when estimating the system performance, namely : η, $\bar{n}_1$ and $\bar{n}_2$. We study their variation in function of the delay d and the class 1 jobs arrival rate λ_1, which may be used as a representation of the priority jobs loading.
Moreovere, ρ is an important parameter, first because at our installation it is usually fluctuating and it may be an oversimplification to consider it a constant of the system; more generally, it should be noted that ρ is strictly speaking not independent of d but rather a decreasing function. It turns out that for our purposes this does not constitute a flaw in our model, as we show below.
For the fixed parameters, we have chosen the values measured in our installation :

$\lambda_2 = .05$
$\gamma_1 = 1.4$
$\gamma_2 = 4.8$ (times are expressed in seconds)
$\mu = 1.$
$E(S_1^2) = 4.8$
$E(S_2^2) = 33.5$

Figures 1 to 3 give respectively the variation of η, $\bar{n}_1$ and $\bar{n}_2$ in function of d for $\lambda_1 = .1$ and different values of ρ. It appears that the shape of the functions and therefore the conclusions which one can draw are qualitatively not affected by a particular choice of ρ, hence, it is a good approximation to assume ρ is constant if the preemption cost is small compared to the cycle time.
Figures 4 to 6 show the behaviour of the same variables η, $\bar{n}_1$ and $\bar{n}_2$ in function of λ_1, with d as parameter and $\rho = .8$. At first sight, it might be surprising that $\bar{n}_2$ is a decreasing function of λ_1 for small values of λ_1, but this may well be understood if one remembers that the increase of the number of class 1 jobs also increases the total number of end of service points.

The comparison of these figures reveals the advantages of the preemptive delay policy in the special case of our system :
from figures 2 and 3, it appears that the $\bar{n}_i$ vary relatively little for reasonable values of d, while the loss of efficiency is largely reduced (fig. 1). Figures 5 and 6 confirm that $\bar{n}_i$ depend only slightly on d in the full range of λ_1. Figure 4 indicates that the gain of efficiency is less important for extreme values of λ_1. More generally, the preceding discussion shows that the model presented in this paper may actually be useful for practical applications. However, in each particular case, a new sensitivity analysis of the crucial parameters should be done.

7. REFERENCES.

1. LARS V. AHLFORS, 'Complex Analysis', Mc Graw-Hill (1966).
2. E.G. COFFMAN, 'On the Tradeoff Between Response and Preemption Costs in a Foreground-Background Computer Service Discipline', IEEE Transactions on Computers C-18, 942-947 (1969).
3. N. JAISWAL, 'Priority Queues', Academic Press (1968).

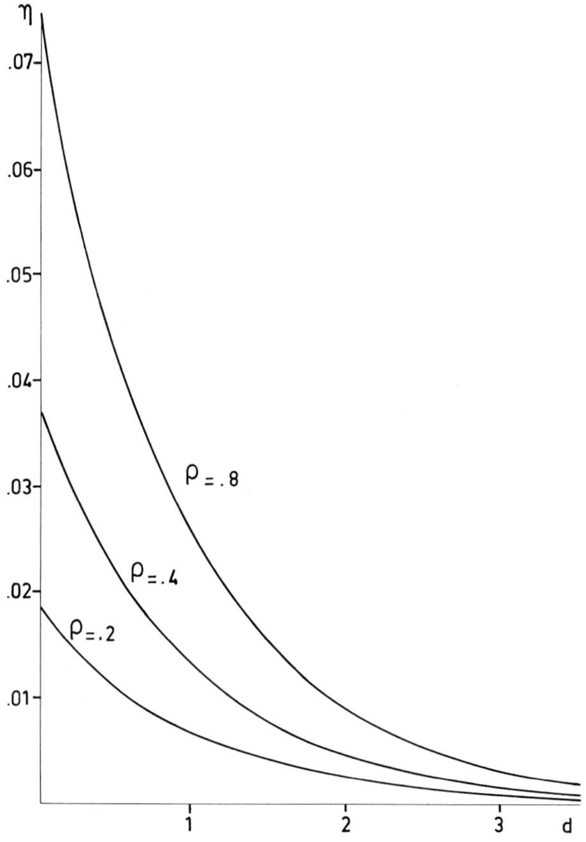

Fig.1

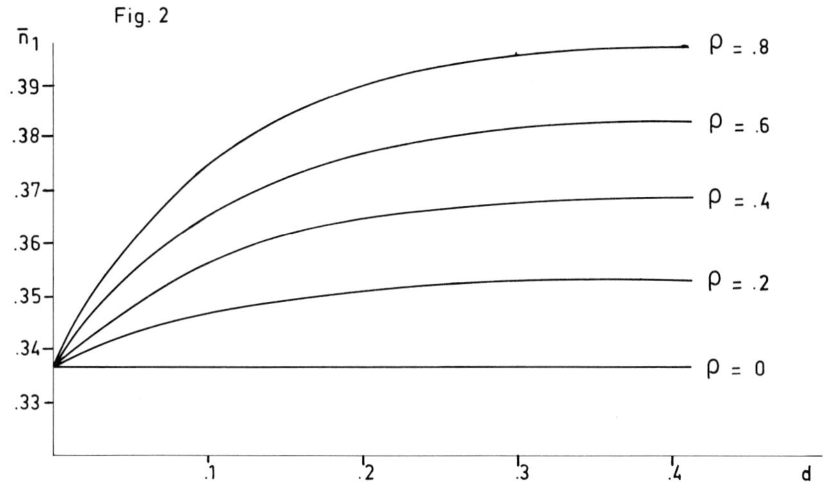
Fig. 2
$\bar{n}_1$
.39
.38
.37
.36
.35
.34
.33
ρ = .8
ρ = .6
ρ = .4
ρ = .2
ρ = 0
.1
.2
.3
.4
d

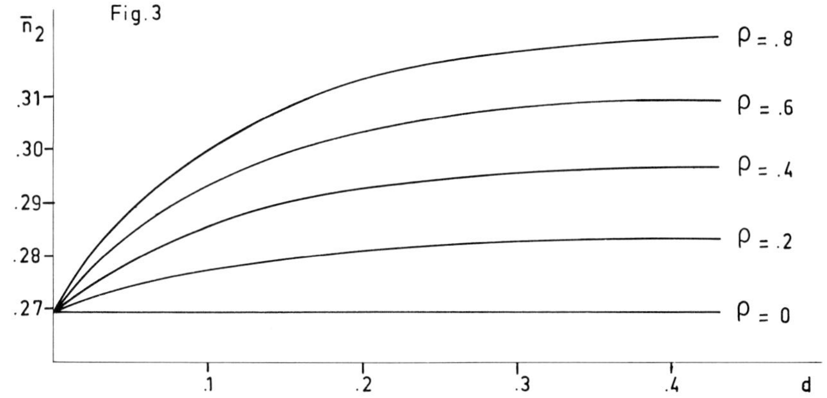
Fig. 3
$\bar{n}_2$
.31
.30
.29
.28
.27
ρ = .8
ρ = .6
ρ = .4
ρ = .2
ρ = 0
.1
.2
.3
.4
d

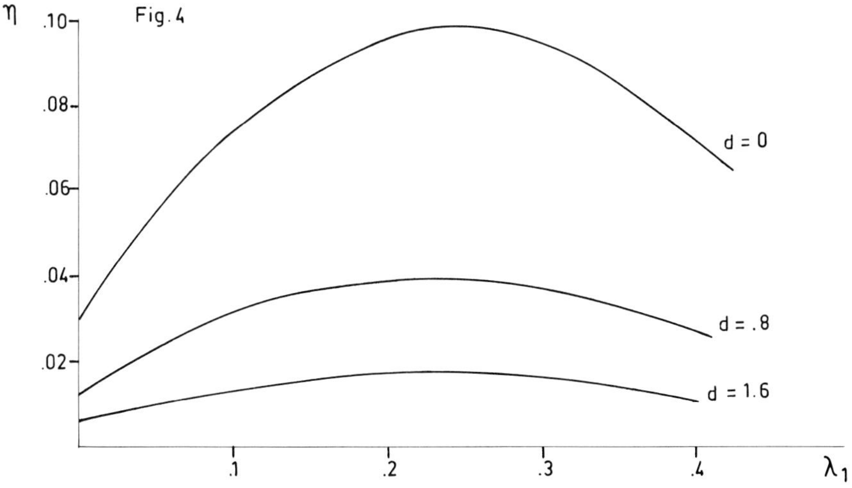
Fig. 4
η
.10
.08
.06
.04
.02
d = 0
d = .8
d = 1.6
.1
.2
.3
.4
λ_1

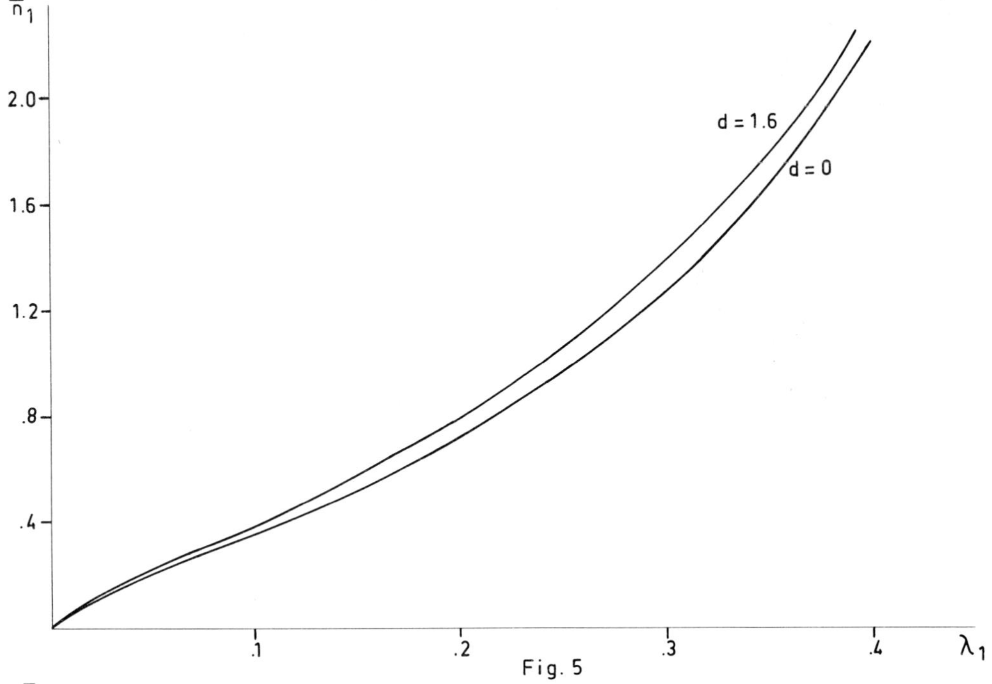
$\bar{n}_1$
2.0
1.6
1.2
.8
.4
d = 1.6
d = 0
.1
.2
.3
.4
λ_1

Fig. 5

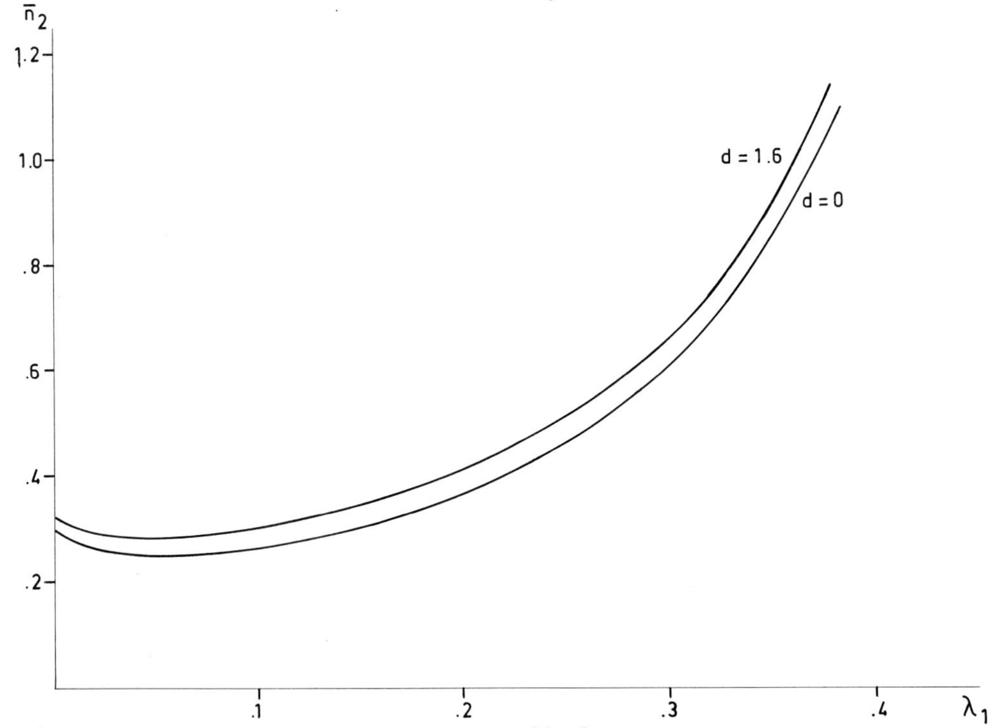
$\bar{n}_2$
1.2
1.0
.8
.6
.4
.2
d = 1.6
d = 0
.1
.2
.3
.4
λ_1

Fig. 6

E. Morlet and D. Ribbens, (Eds.), International Computing Symposium 1977.

OPTIMAL PARTITIONING OF A FINITE BUFFER BETWEEN TWO PAIRS OF PRODUCER-CONSUMER

Guy LATOUCHE

Université Libre de Bruxelles, Faculté des Sciences,
Laboratoire d'Informatique Théorique, Bruxelles, Belgium

We consider two pairs of producer-consumer sharing a finite buffer. In order not to let any pair block the other, the buffer is partitioned. Each time a message enters the buffer, the system gets a reward. Under Markovian assumptions for both production and consumption processes, we determine the partition that maximise the long term average reward per unit of time. The optimal solution and a measure of its efficiency are analysed.

1. INTRODUCTION

We consider a system of two producers: P_1 and P_2 and two consumers: C_1 and C_2; C_1 consumes only messages from P_1 and similarly for (C_2, P_2). Producers and consumers correspond through a unique buffer of size N ($N < \infty$).

When C_i (i=1, 2) gets a message, he becomes busy for a random interval of time and removes the message from the buffer. This is repeated until C_i finds no message in the buffer in which case he becomes idle until the arrival of a new message.

P_i(i=1, 2) wakes up at random intervals of time. If, upon awakening of P_i, the buffer is not full, the producer generates instantaneously a message and enters it in the buffer; otherwise, we assume that the message is 'lost'. This description of the abstract model may represent different situations: for instance, suppose the producer examines the buffer before sending a message, if the buffer is full, the producer waits for a new interval of time; a second example would be the case where a message that cannot enter the buffer is processed in another way, possibly less efficient or more expensive; third, we may assume that the time needed to generate a message is a random variable, if the buffer is full when a message is ready, the message is actually lost. In fact, what is important from the point of view of the abstract model is that the interval of time between two submissions of messages has the same distribution whether the messages enter the buffer or not.

It is an unfortunate event when a message cannot enter the buffer and therefore we assume in our model that whenever a producer is able to enter a message in the buffer, the system as a whole gets some reward. This is equivalent to the assumption that the system suffers some cost when a producer awakens uselessly (or when a message is lost).

If the two pairs (C_1, P_1) and (C_2, P_2) were allowed to share the whole buffer, one of the pairs could block the other by continuously filling the buffer. To prevent this event, we assume that the buffer is partitioned into two parts: n places ($0 \leqslant n \leqslant N$) will be reserved to (C_1, P_1), the other (N - n) places will be reserved to (C_2, P_2).

The problem is to find an optimal value for n. The criterion we choose is to maximise the long term average reward per unit of time.

As we show in section 2, it is very easy to determine the optimal n if all intervals of time have distribution negative exponential.

We define a measure of the efficiency of the optimal solution; in sections 3 to 5 we derive (analytically or numerically) properties of the optimal solution and the efficiency.

To conclude this introduction, let us mention that the problem of buffer sharing has already received some attention (see [1] to [4] for instance). The emphasis in these papers has been put on defining algorithms to implement such a scheme, not on the determination of the actual partitioning.

2. STOCHASTIC MODEL

We assume that the interval of time between two awakenings of producer P_i (i=1, 2) is a random variable with distribution negative exponential (λ_i) and that the interval of time during which consumer C_i becomes busy when receiving a message is a random variable with distribution negative exponential (μ_i). Moreover, all random variables are mutually independent.

Let $p_{ij}(n)$ = P[i messages from P_1 and j messages from P_2 in the buffer, in steady state|n]

$$p_{i\cdot}(n) = \sum_{j=o}^{N-n} p_{ij}(n)$$

$$p_{\cdot j}(n) = \sum_{i=o}^{n} p_{ij}(n)$$

The expected reward per unit of time in steady state is obviously

$$r(n) = \lambda_1 b_1(1-p_{n\cdot})+\lambda_2 b_2(1-p_{\cdot N-n}).$$

The problem is to find $\tilde{n}$ such that r(n) is maximum.

Clearly, for any fixed n, the system behaves as two independent M/M/1 queues with finite capacity. Hence,

$$p_{i\cdot}(n) = \rho_1^i \frac{1-\rho_1}{1-\rho_1^{n+1}} \qquad i = 0, 1, \ldots, n$$

$$p_{\cdot j}(n) = \rho_2^j \frac{1-\rho_2}{1-\rho_2^{N-n+1}} \qquad j = 0, \ldots, N-n$$

and

$$p_{ij}(n) = p_{i\cdot}(n)p_{\cdot j}(n)$$

where

$$\rho_i = \frac{\lambda_i}{\mu_i} \qquad i = 1, 2.$$

Moreover,

$$r(n) = \lambda_1 b_1 \frac{1-\rho_1^n}{1-\rho_1^{n+1}} + \lambda_2 b_2 \frac{1-\rho_2^{N-n}}{1-\rho_2^{N-n+1}} \tag{1}$$

Theorem 1

a. If $\lambda_1 b_1 \leqslant \lambda_2 b_2 \dfrac{(1-\rho_1)(1-\rho_2)\rho_2^N \log_2}{(1-\rho_2^{N+1})^2 \log\rho_1}$

then $\tilde{n} = 0$

b. If $\lambda_2 b_2 \leqslant \lambda_1 b_1 \dfrac{(1-\rho_1)(1-\rho_2)\rho_1^N \log\rho_1}{(1-\rho_1^{N+1})^2 \log\rho_2}$

then $\tilde{n} = N$

c. otherwise,

$$\tilde{n} = \lfloor\tilde{x}\rfloor \text{ or } \lceil\tilde{x}\rceil$$

where $\tilde{x}$ is the unique solution ($\in(0,N)$) of the equation

$$\lambda_1 b_1 \frac{(1-\rho_1)\rho_1^x \log\rho_1}{(1-\rho_1^{x+1})^2} - \lambda_2 b_2 \frac{(1-\rho_2)\rho_2^{N-x} \log\rho_2}{(1-\rho_2^{N-x+1})^2} = 0,$$

$\lfloor x\rfloor$ and $\lceil x\rceil$ are the usual 'floor' and 'ceiling' functions ([5], p.37).

Comments

i. This theorem is easy to prove when one observes that

$$(1-\rho_1^x)(1-\rho_1^{x+1})^{-1}$$

and

$$(1-\rho_2^{N-x})(1-\rho_2^{N-x+1})^{-1}$$

are concave functions.

ii. If we define

$$r(-1) = r(N+1) = -\infty,$$

$\tilde{n}$ may be characterised as follows: it is the unique integer in {0, 1, ..., N} such that

$$r(\tilde{n}-1) < r(\tilde{n}) \geqslant r(\tilde{n}+1).$$

iii. Although there is no explicit form for $\tilde{n}$, it is very easy to compute.

Moreover, as we shall mention later, it is not very difficult to derive properties of $\tilde{n}$ or $r(\tilde{n})$, either analytically or numerically.
One can show for instance, and it is intuitively obvious, that $\tilde{n}$ is an increasing function of b_1 and a decreasing function of b_2.

3. ASYMPTOTIC BEHAVIOUR OF $\tilde{n}/N$

Let us define by

$$\nu(N) = \frac{\tilde{n}}{N}$$

the proportion of the buffer size devoted to the set (C_1, P_1).

It is interesting to note that the limit

$$\nu = \lim_{N\to\infty} \nu(N)$$

always exists and does not depend on b_1 and b_2, except in the special case $\rho_1 = \rho_2 = 1$.

Theorem 2

If $\rho_1 = \rho_2 = 1$,

then $\nu = \lim_{N\to\infty} \nu(N) = \dfrac{b_1-\sqrt{b_1 b_2}}{b_1-b_2}$;

if $\rho_1 < 1 < \rho_2$ or $\rho_2 < 1 < \rho_1$,

$$\text{then } \nu = \frac{\log\rho_2}{\log\rho_2-\log\rho_1} \tag{2}$$

otherwise,

$$\nu = \frac{\log\rho_2}{\log\rho_2+\log\rho_1} \tag{3}$$

We shall only prove the theorem for $\rho_1 = \rho_2 = 1$ and $\rho_1 < \rho_2 < 1$.

In the other cases, the proof follows the same pattern.

a. For demonstration purpose, let us introduce the following function:

$$r(x;N) = \lambda_1 b_1 \frac{1-\rho_1^{Nx}}{1-\rho_1^{Nx+1}} + \lambda_2 b_2 \frac{1-\rho_2^{N(1-x)}}{1-\rho_2^{N(1-x)+1}}$$

$$N = 1, 2, \ldots \quad x\in[0,1]$$

For any N and $x = \frac{n}{N}$ (n integer), we have

$$r(\tfrac{n}{N};N) = r(n) \qquad \text{(see (1))}.$$

$r(x;N)$ would be the reward function if the proportion of the buffer size allocated to each pair (C_i, P_i) could be any real number in [0, 1], instead of multiples of $\frac{1}{N}$ only.

b. $\rho_1 = \rho_2 = 1.$

In this case, the function $r(x;N)$ becomes

$$r(x;N) = \mu\left(\frac{b_1 Nx}{Nx+1} + \frac{b_2 N(1-x)}{N(1-x)+1}\right)$$

and its first derivative with respect to x,

$$r'(x;N) = \mu N \frac{N^2(b_1-b_2)x^2-2N((N+1)b_1+b_2)x+(N+1)^2 b_1-b_2}{(Nx+1)^2(N(1-x)+1)^2}$$

is equal to 0 for

$$x = x(N) = \frac{(N+1)b_1+b_2-(N+2)\sqrt{b_1 b_2}}{N(b_1-b_2)} ;$$

as

$$x(N) \leqslant \nu(N) < x(N) + \frac{1}{N}$$

and

$$\lim_{N\to\infty} x(N) = \frac{b_1-\sqrt{b_1 b_2}}{b_1-b_2} ,$$

the theorem is proved for $\rho_1 = \rho_2 = 1$.

c. $\rho_1 < \rho_2 < 1.$

In this case, we have

$$r'(x;N) = N\alpha \frac{\rho_1^{Nx}}{(1-\rho_1^{Nx})^2} - N\beta \frac{\rho_2^{N(1-x)}}{(1-\rho_2^{N(1-x)+1})^2}$$

where

$$\alpha = -\lambda_1 b_1(1-\rho_1)\log\rho_1 > 0$$

$$\beta = -\lambda_2 b_2(1-\rho_2)\log\rho_2 > 0 .$$

Let

$$\bar{x} = \frac{\log\rho_2}{\log\rho_2+\log\rho_1}$$

be the unique solution of $\rho_1^x = \rho_2^{1-x}$ and let $\rho = \rho_1^{\bar{x}} < 1$.

We have $\lim_{N\to\infty} r'(\bar{x},N)$

$$= \lim_{N\to\infty} N\rho^N\left(\frac{\alpha}{(1-\rho_1\rho^N)^2} - \frac{\beta}{(1-\rho_2\rho^N)^2}\right) = 0.$$

If we define

$$a_N = \frac{\rho_1^{Nx}}{(1-\rho_1^{Nx+1})^2}$$

$$b_N = \frac{\rho_2^{N(1-x)}}{(1-\rho_2^{N(1-x)+1})^2}$$

and

$$\gamma = \frac{\rho_1^x}{\rho_2^{1-x}} ,$$

we observe that if $x < \bar{x}$,

$$\frac{a_N}{b_N} > \gamma^N \frac{(1-\rho_2\rho^N)^2}{(1-\rho_1\rho^N)^2}$$

and

$$\gamma > 1;$$

therefore, $\lim_{N\to\infty} \frac{a_N}{b_N} = \infty$

and for all $x < \bar{x}$, there exists $N(x)$ such that for all $N \geqslant N(x)$, $r'(x,N) > 0$.
Similarly, if $x > \bar{x}$, then $\lim_{N\to\infty} a_N/b_N = 0$ and for all $x > \bar{x}$, there exists $N(x)$ such that for all $N \geqslant N(x)$, $r'(x,N) < 0$.

If we denote by $x(N)$ the value of x such that $r'(x;N) = 0$, for all ε, there exists $\bar{N}(\varepsilon)$ such that for all $N \geqslant \bar{N}(\varepsilon)$, $x(N) \in (\bar{x}-\varepsilon, \bar{x}+\varepsilon)$. (Choose $\bar{N}(\varepsilon) = \max\{N(\bar{x}-\varepsilon), N(\bar{x}+\varepsilon)\}$).
Therefore, for all ε, there exists $\tilde{N}(\varepsilon)$ such that for all $N \geqslant \tilde{N}(\varepsilon)$, $\nu(N) \in (\bar{x}-\varepsilon, \bar{x}+\varepsilon)$. (Choose $\tilde{N}(\varepsilon) = \max\{\bar{N}(\varepsilon/2), 2/\varepsilon\}$).
This proves that

$$\lim_{N\to\infty} \nu(N) = \bar{x}.$$

FIG. 1 _ $V = \lim_{N\to\infty} \frac{\tilde{n}}{N}$ as a function of ρ_1, and ρ_2

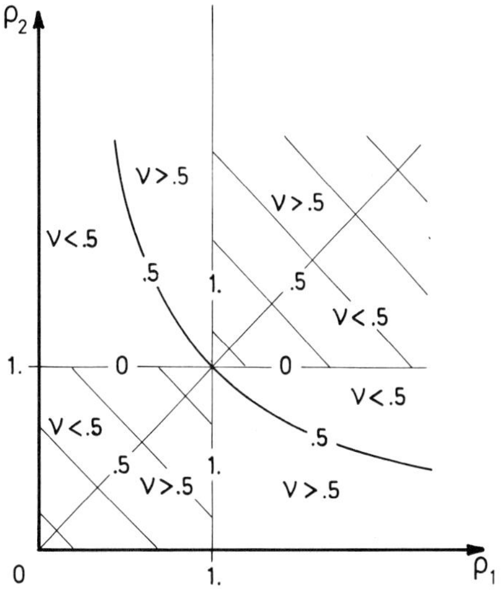

Comments

i. The shaded area on figure 1 indicates those values of (ρ_1,ρ_2) for which ν is given by (3).

ii. We have indicated on figure 1 the regions where $\nu < .5$ or $\nu > .5$.
It appears that

$$\nu > .5 \quad \text{iff} \quad |\log\rho_1| < |\log\rho_2|$$

in other words, the pair (C_i, P_i) for which ρ is closest to 1 will (asymptotically) receive the greatest share of the buffer, the distance from ρ to 1 being measured as $|\log\rho|$.

iii. In particular, if $\rho_2 = 1$, $\nu = 0$ for all $\rho_1 \neq 1$: it is obvious that $\tilde{n}$ increases if N increases; however, if $\rho_2 = 1$, $\tilde{n}$ increases at a slower rate than N.

iv. These asymptotic results give some information on how $\tilde{n}$, for a fixed N, depends on ρ_1 and ρ_2.
For instance, numerical investigations show, as can be conjectured from figure 1, that for a given value of ρ_2, $\tilde{n}$ is a unimodal function of ρ_1, the maximum being around $\rho_1 = 1$.

v. The rate of convergence of $\nu(N)$ to ν depends not only on ρ_1 and ρ_2 but also on b_1 and b_2.

4. $\tilde{n}$ AS A FUNCTION OF b_1 AND b_2

Obviously, $\tilde{n}$ depends on b_1 and b_2 only through the ratio $B = \lambda_1 b_1/\lambda_2 b_2$.
Numerical computations show that, with a very good degree of approximation,

$$\tilde{n} \doteq \min\{N, \max\{0, \lfloor c_1 \log B + c_0 \rfloor\}\}$$

for some c_1 and c_0.
In other words, if B is very small, $\tilde{n}$ is 0;
if B is very large, $\tilde{n}$ is N;
in the interval of values of B where $\tilde{n}$ goes from 0 to N,

$$\tilde{n} \doteq \lfloor c_1 \log B + c_0 \rfloor \qquad (4)$$

and it seems to us this last relation is not obvious at all.

The approximation (4) is very good if $|\log\rho_1|$ and $|\log\rho_2|$ are large enough or if $|\log\rho_1|$ is close to $|\log\rho_2|$; it is slightly less good otherwise. Figures 2 and 3 show examples of good approximations; figures 4 and 5 are examples of the worst cases we have observed.
In each case, the dashed line is the least squares approximation for the points marked by a '⊢' and defines the values for the corresponding c_1 and c_0.

It appears from the examples we examined, that c_1 and c_0 are unimodal functions of ρ_1; the maximum being around $\rho_1 = 1$. This confirms the remark iv in the preceding section. c_1 is also a unimodal function of ρ_2, with maximum around $\rho_2 = 1$; but c_0 is minimum for ρ_2 close to 1.

5. EFFICIENCY

The expected reward per unit of time is at most equal to $(\lambda_1 b_1 + \lambda_2 b_2)$, therefore, one might define the efficiency η of the system as follows:

$$\eta = \frac{r(\tilde{n})}{\lambda_1 b_1 + \lambda_2 b_2} .$$

η is essentially a function of ρ_1, ρ_2, B and N.

Figures 6 to 9 present η as a function of ρ_1 and ρ_2 for different values of N and B: we have drawn the curves $\eta = .1, .2, \ldots, .9$.
Figure 10 presents η as a function of B for some values of ρ_1 and ρ_2.

One observes that the efficiency is best when N is large; or when B is either very big or very small: this means that one of the b_i's is much larger than the other; the corresponding producer-consumer will get enough places in the buffer for η to be reasonnably good.

If B is close to 1, η is very small as soon as one of the ρ_i's is large.
On the other hand, if both ρ_1 and ρ_2 are smaller than 1, the efficiency is rather good even for B close to 1 and N not very large (see fig. 8 for instance).

Surprisingly, as one sees clearly on figures 7 and 9, the efficiency is not always a monotonous function of ρ_1 - all other parameters being constant; the same is true, of course, for η as a function of ρ_2.

6. CONCLUSIONS

The problem of partitioning a finite buffer among two pairs of producer-consumer is easy to solve, analytically as well as numerically.
This enables us to study the optimal solution $\tilde{n}$ and the efficiency as functions of the parameters. For instance, we have shown that in the range of values of b_1/b_2 for which $\tilde{n}$ goes from 0 to N, $\tilde{n}$ may be closely approximated through a linear function $\log(b_1/b_2)$.

Dijkstra proposes in [3], in the case where there is an arbitrary number (say M) of pairs producer-consumer, to partition the buffer into (M+1) areas: area i (i=1, ..., M) being devoted to the ith pair, area (M+1) to be shared by all pairs. We intend to investigate the problem of optimal partitioning in this context. Moreover, it is usually assumed - and we plan to do so in further work on the subject - that no message is lost when a producer finds a filled buffer but rather that the producer waits until it can enter its message.

BIBLIOGRAPHY

[1] R. Devillers and G. Louchard, "Improvement of Parallelism in a Finite Buffer Sharing Policy", *The Computer Journal*, vol.19, n°3 (1976).

[2] L.W. Cooprider, P.J. Courtois, F. Heymans and D.L. Parnas, "Information Streams Sharing a Finite Buffer: Other Solutions", *Information Processing Letters, vol.3, n°1,* (July 1973).

[3] E.W. Dijkstra, "Information Streams Sharing a Finite Buffer", *Information Processing Letters, vol.1* (1972), pp. 179-180.

[4] P.B. Hansen, "Concurrent Programming Concepts", *Computing Surveys, vol.5, n°4* (December 1973), pp. 223-245.

[5] D.E. Knuth, "*The Art of Computer Programming*", Addison-Wesley, 2nd edition (1969).

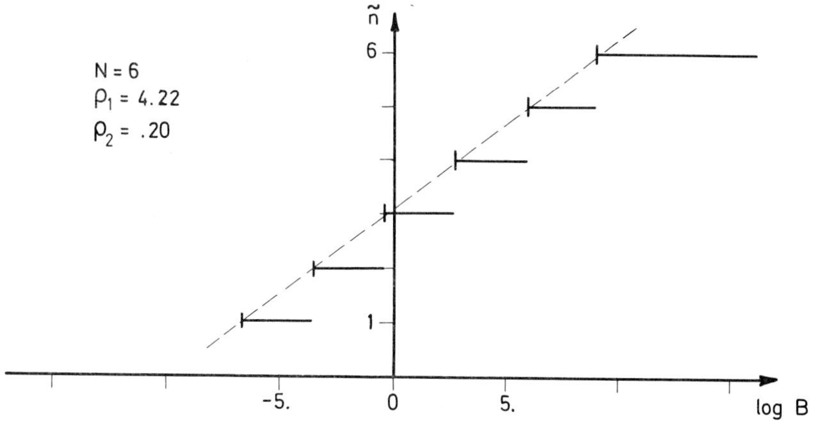

FIG. 2 _ ñ as a function of $B = \lambda_1 b_1 / \lambda_2 b_2$ ($c_1 = .32$, $c_0 = 3.12$)

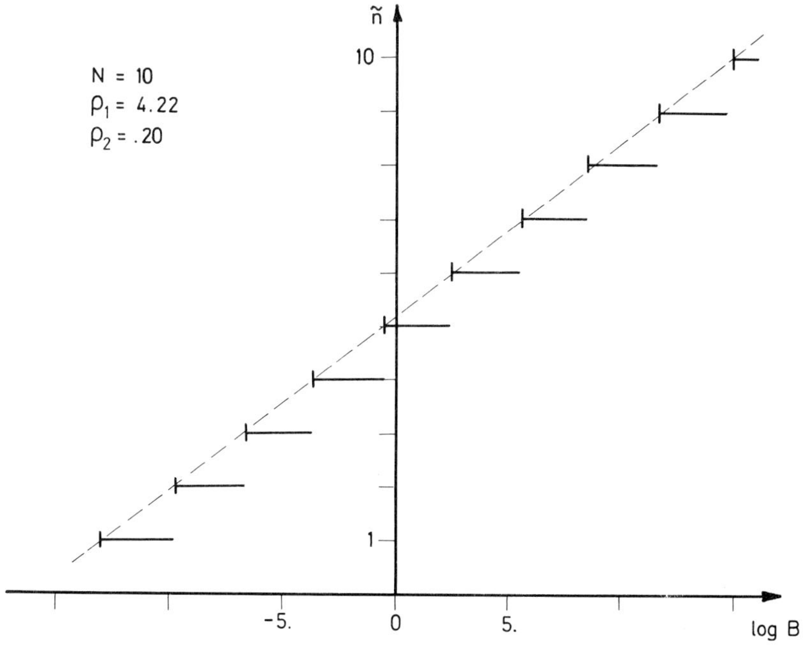

FIG. 3 _ ñ as a function of $B = \lambda_1 b_1 / \lambda_2 b_2$ ($c_1 = .32$, $c_0 = 5.20$)

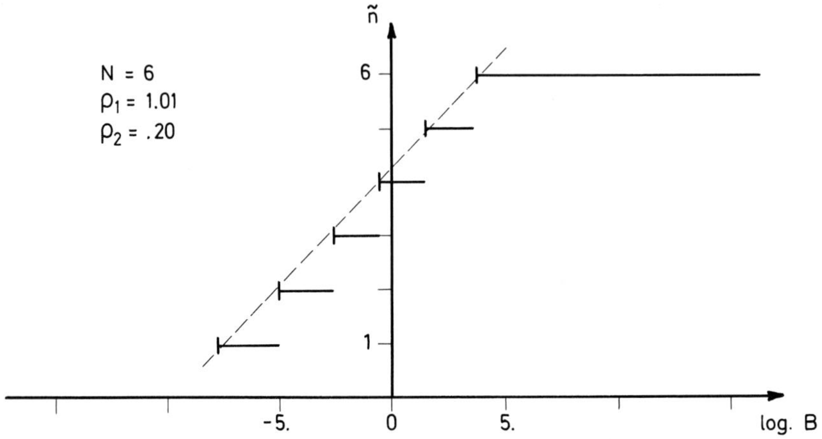

FIG. 4 _ $\tilde{n}$ as a function of $B = \lambda_1 b_1 / \lambda_2 b_2$ ($c_1 = .44$, $c_0 = 4.29$)

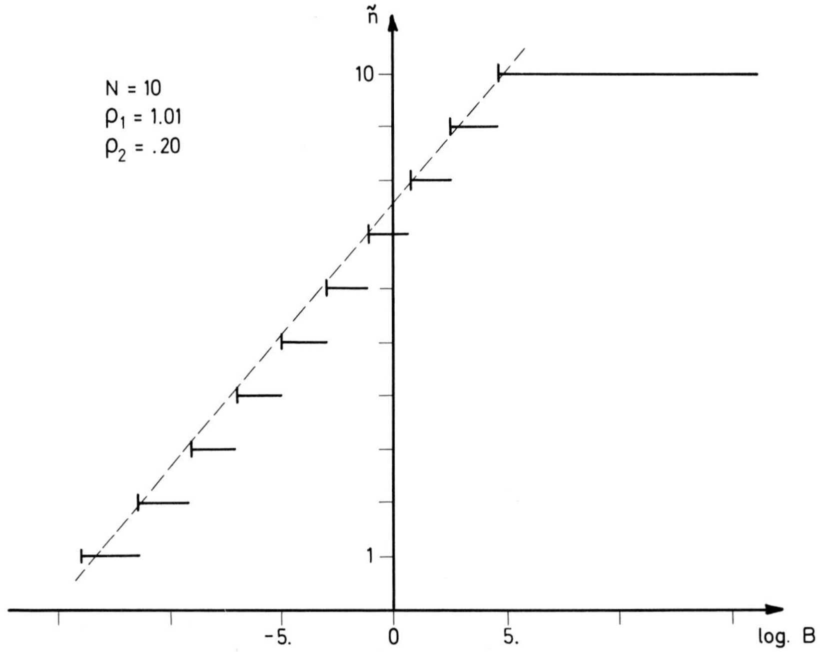

FIG. 5 _ $\tilde{n}$ as a function of $B = \lambda_1 b_1 / \lambda_2 b_2$ ($c_1 = .49$, $c_0 = 7.60$)

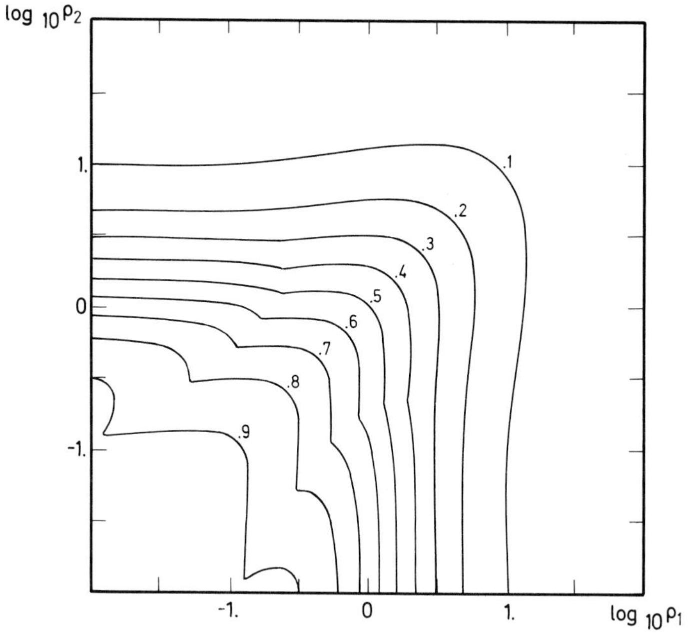

FIG. 6 – Contour map of the efficiency as a function of ρ_1 and ρ_2 ; N=2, B=1

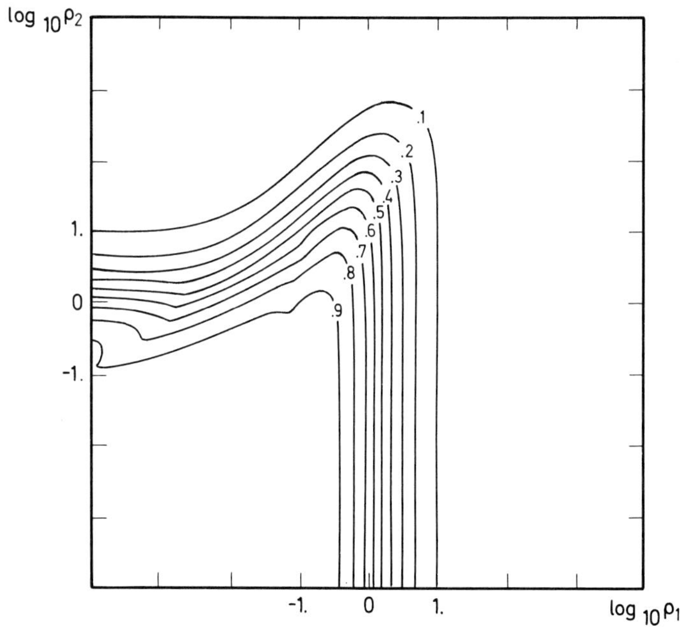

FIG. 7 – Contour map of the efficiency as a function of ρ_1 and ρ_2 ; N=2, B=100

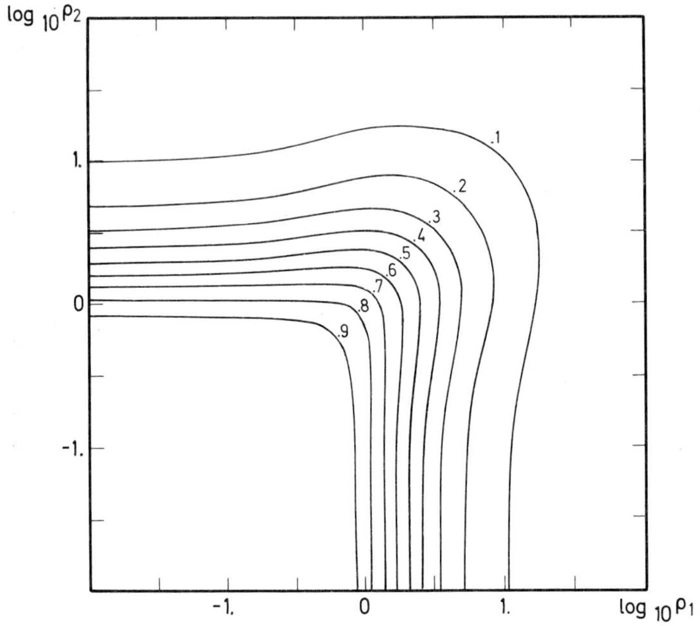

FIG. 8 _ Contour map of the efficiency as a function of ρ_1 and ρ_2 ; N=6, B=1

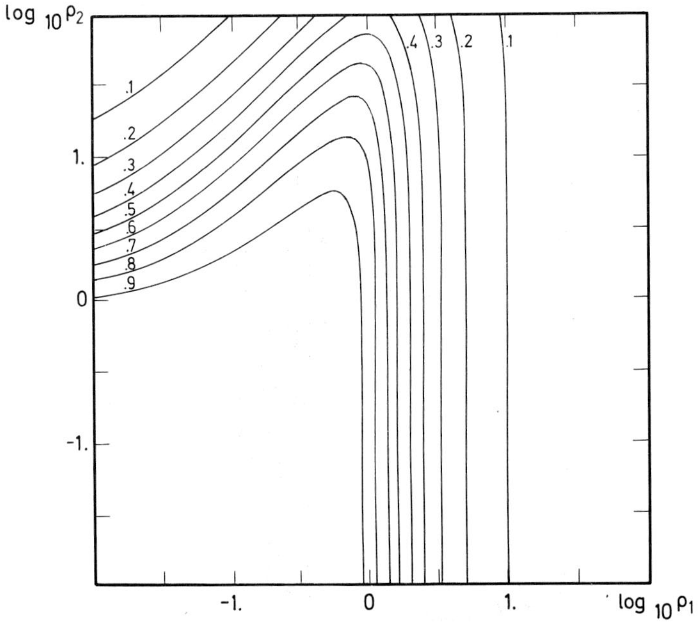

FIG. 9 _ Contour map of the efficiency as a function of ρ_1 and ρ_2 ; N=6, B=100

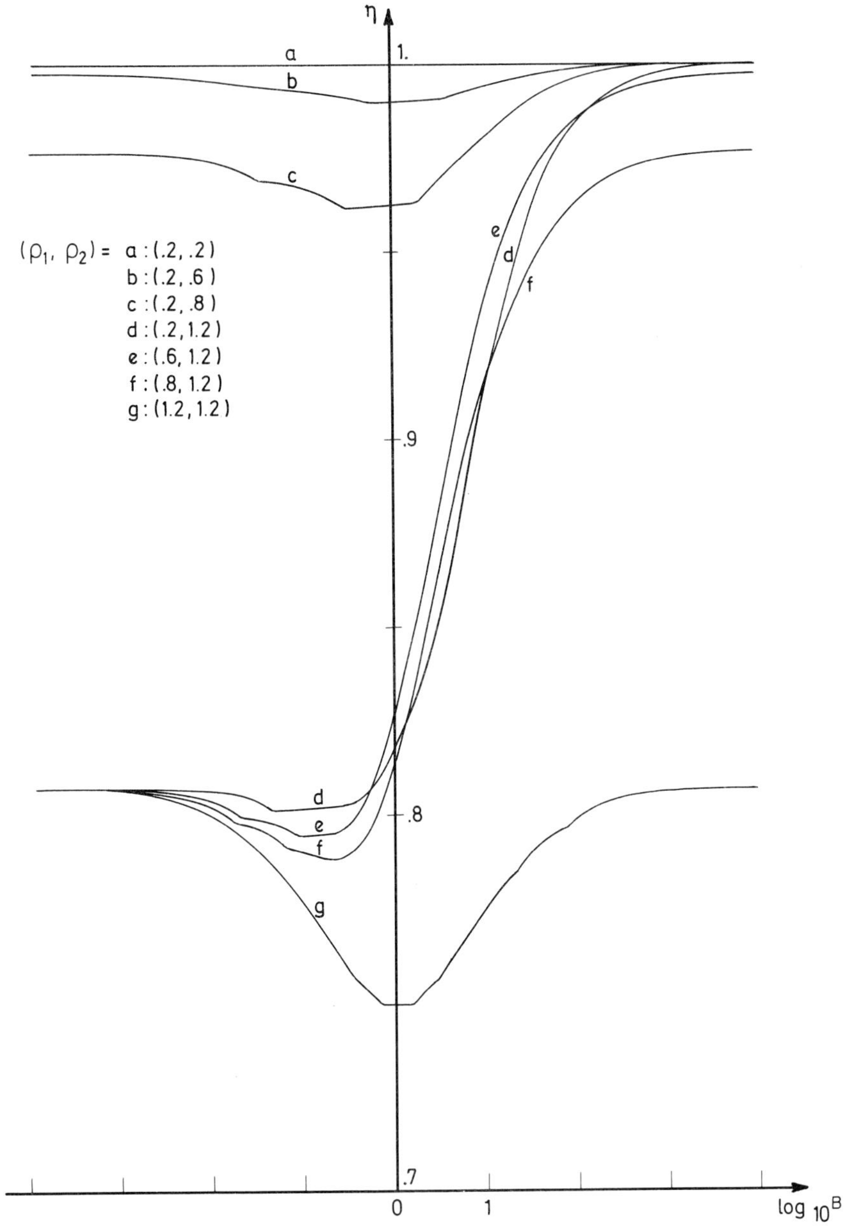

FIG. 10 _ Efficiency as a function of $B = \lambda_1 b_1 / \lambda_2 b_2$; different values of ρ_1 and ρ_2 (N = 10)

Publié avec le concours de la Fondation Universitaire de Belgique.

E. Moilet and D. Ribbens, (Eds.), International Computing Symposium 1977.

A CLOSED FORM EXPRESSION OF THE PAGE FAULT RATE FOR LRU PAGING ALGORITHM IN A MARKOVIAN REFERENCE MODEL OF PROGRAM BEHAVIOR

C. GLOWACKI

Université Libre de Bruxelles, Faculté des Sciences
Laboratoire d'Informatique Théorique, Bruxelles, Belgique

In this paper, we propose a closed form expression of the page fault rate for LRU paging algorithm in a Markovian reference model of program behavior. This is a generalization of the well-know King's formula and allows us to calculate the page fault probability faster than with the algorithm of Franklin and Gupta.

1. INTRODUCTION

The 'Markovian reference models' are based on the knowledge of a matrix p the elements of which give the probabilities of referencing one page from another one. These Markovian models are very adequate to take into account the dynamic change of localities during program execution and have been used by several authors to calculate the page fault probability for some paging algorithms. Franklin and Gupta [2] give an algorithm to evaluate page fault probabilities, but no closed form expression.
Courtois and Vantilborgh [1] propose an approximation of the page fault rate when p is "nearly completely decomposable".

In this paper, we propose a closed form expression for LRU paging algorithm. This allows us to calculate the page fault probability faster than with the algorithm of Franklin and Gupta.

We shall also show that our result is a generalization of King's formula [4] for the independent reference model.
This last model has been studied by several authors to calculate the page fault rate of several paging algorithms [3][4][5].

2. MODEL

Consider a program consisting of a set $N = \{1,2,\ldots,n\}$ of n pages.
As the program runs, it generates a sequence $r_1,r_2,\ldots,r_k,\ldots$ of references to its pages at instants $t_1,t_2,\ldots,t_k,\ldots$ respectively.
The stochastic process in the Markovian reference model is characterized by a stochastic transition matrix

$$p = (p_{ij}) \qquad i,\ j \in N$$

p_{ij} is the probability to reference page i from page j.
We assume that p is an irreducible stochastic matrix.
Thus, there exists only one column vector

$$\gamma \equiv \begin{pmatrix} \gamma_1 \\ \vdots \\ \gamma_n \end{pmatrix}$$

such that

$$\gamma = p\gamma$$

with

$$\sum_{i=1}^{n} \gamma_i = 1$$

The program is to be executed in a system with m, $1 < m < n$ page frames of main memory. We use a particular paging algorithm called 'least recently used' (LRU). Under LRU, the page selected for replacement is the one that has not been referenced for the longest time.
In order to study the paging behavior of a program executing under LRU, it is only necessary to observe the evolution of a m-uple

$$(j_1,j_2,\ldots,j_m)$$

which are the m most recently referenced pages.
If the last reference to j_ℓ occurs before the last reference to j_k, then ℓ is smaller than k.
We say $(j_1,\ldots,j_m)$ is a memory state.
Q is the finite set of memory states.

3. EVALUATION OF PAGE FAULT RATE

Let F(LRU) be the long run expected page fault rate.
Let $P(j_1,j_2,\ldots,j_m)$ be the long run probability of having a $(j_1,j_2,\ldots,j_m)$ memory state immediately before a reference to a page.

The following expression holds:

$$F(LRU) = \sum_{q\in Q} P(j_1,\ldots,j_m)$$
$$\times \text{Prob [a reference to page i, } i\in N\setminus\overline{q}]$$
$$= \sum_{q\in Q} P(j_1,\ldots,j_m).(1-p_{j_1j_m} \ldots p_{j_mj_m})$$
$$= \sum_{q\in Q} P(j_1,\ldots,j_m).D(q)$$

with

$$D(q) = 1-p_{j_1j_m} - \ldots p_{j_mj_m}$$

and

$$\overline{q} = \{j_1,j_2,\ldots,j_m\}$$

Evaluation of $P(j_1,j_2,\ldots,j_m)$

Let us describe the chronology of events which conduct to configuration $(j_1,\ldots,j_m)$ at time t_K^-. We now consider t_{k_i} : the epoch of the last reference to page j_i before t_K^- $i = 1,2,\ldots,m$.
We have

$$t_K = t_{k_m+1}$$

At t_{k_1}, page j_1 is referenced.
Between $t_{k_1}^+$ and $t_{k_2}^-$, only pages $j_2,\ldots,j_m$ are referenced.
At t_{k_2} page j_2 is referenced.
Between $t_{k_2}^+$ and $t_{k_3}^-$, only pages $j_3,\ldots,j_m$ are referenced.
At t_{k_3}, page j_3 is referenced.
...
At $t_{k_{m-1}}$, page j_{m-1} is referenced.
Between $t_{k_{m-1}}^+$ and $t_{k_m}^-$, only page j_m is referenced.
At t_{k_m}, page j_m is referenced and we have memory state $(j_1,\ldots,j_m)$.
Therefore, we may write

$$\begin{aligned}
&\text{Prob[memory state is } (j_1,j_2,\ldots,j_m) \text{ at } t^-_{k_m+1}] \\
&= \sum_{n_1+\ldots+n_m=k_m} \text{Prob}[r_{n_1}=j_1] \\
&\times\text{Prob}[r_{n_1+n_2}=j_2 \text{ and } r_\ell\in\{j_2,\ldots,j_m\}, \\
&\qquad \ell=n_1+1,\ldots,n_1+n_2-1 \mid r_{n_1}=j_1]\ldots \\
&\times\text{Prob}[r_{n_1+\ldots+n_{m-1}}=j_{m-1} \text{ and } r_\ell\in\{j_{m-1},j_m\}, \\
&\qquad \ell=n_1+\ldots+n_{m-2}+1,\ldots \\
&\qquad \ldots,n_1+\ldots+n_{m-1}-1 \mid r_{n_1+\ldots+n_{m-2}}=j_{m-2}] \\
&\times\text{Prob}[r_{n_1+\ldots+n_m}=j_m \text{ and } r_\ell=j_m, \ell=n_1+\ldots+n_{m-1}+1, \\
&\qquad \ldots,n_1+\ldots+n_m-1 \mid r_{n_1+\ldots+n_{m-1}}=j_{m-1}] \qquad (1)
\end{aligned}$$

Consider the matrix

$$p_i(q) = \begin{pmatrix} p_{j_{i+1}j_{i+1}} & \cdots & p_{j_{i+1}j_m} \\ & & \\ p_{j_mj_{i+1}} & \cdots & p_{j_mj_m} \end{pmatrix}$$

and the vector

$$v_i(q) = \begin{pmatrix} p_{j_{i+1}j_i} \\ p_{j_{i+2}j_i} \\ \\ p_{j_mj_i} \end{pmatrix}$$

We have

$$\begin{aligned}
&\text{Prob}[r_{n_1+\ldots+n_{i+1}}=j_{i+1} \text{ and } r_\ell\in\{j_{i+1},\ldots,j_m\}, \\
&\qquad \ell=n_1+\ldots+n_i+1,\ldots,n_1+\ldots+n_{i+1}-1 \\
&\qquad \mid r_{n_1+\ldots+n_i}=j_i] \\
&= (p_i(q)^{n_{i+1}-1}\, v_i(q))_{(1)}
\end{aligned}$$

$(v)_{(1)}$ is the first element of column vector v.
Moreover from (1), we may write

$$\begin{aligned}
&\text{Prob[memory state is } (j_1,\ldots,j_m) \text{ at } t^-_{k_m+1}] \\
&= \sum_{n_1+\ldots+n_m=k_m} (p^{n_1-1}\delta_o)_{(j_1)} \\
&\qquad \times \prod_{i=1}^{m-1} [p_i(q)^{n_{i+1}-1}\, v_i(q)]_{(1)}
\end{aligned}$$

where column vector δ_o is defined to be

$$(\delta_o)_{(i)} = \text{Prob}[r_1=i] \qquad i=1,\ldots,n$$

Thus, for long run probability we have

$$\begin{aligned}
P(j_1,\ldots,j_m) &= \sum_{n_1+n_2+\ldots+n_m=\infty} (p^{n_1-1}\delta_o)_{(j_1)} \\
&\qquad \times \prod_{i=1}^{m-1} [p_i(q)^{n_{i+1}-1}\, v_i(q)]_{(1)} \\
&= \lim_{n_1\to\infty}(p^{n_1-1}\delta_o)_{(j_1)} \\
&\qquad \times \prod_{i=1}^{m-1} \sum_{n_{i+1}=1}^{\infty} [p_i(q)^{n_{i+1}-1}\, v_i(q)]_{(1)} \\
&= \gamma_{j_1} \prod_{i=1}^{m-1} [(I-p_i(q))^{-1} v_i(q)]_{(1)} \qquad (2)
\end{aligned}$$

indeed, as p is irreducible, we have

$$\lim_{n_i\to\infty}[p_i(q)^{n_{i+1}-1}\, v_i(q)]_{(1)} = 0 \qquad i=2,\ldots,n$$

According, the long run expected page fault rate becomes

$$F(LRU) = \sum_{q \in Q} \gamma_{j_1} \prod_{i=1}^{i=m-1} [(I-p_i(q))^{-1} v_i(q)]_{(1)} \cdot D(q) \quad (3)$$

From (2) the following expression holds:

$$P(j_1,\dots,j_m) = \frac{\gamma_{j_1}}{\gamma_{j_2}} [(I-p_1(q))^{-1} v_1(q)]_{(1)} \times P(j_2,\dots,j_m)$$

It is thus possible to obtain these probabilities recursively

$$P(j_k,\dots,j_m) = \frac{\gamma_{j_k}}{\gamma_{j_{k+1}}} [(I-p_k(q))^{-1} v_k(q)]_{(1)} \times P(j_{k+1},\dots,j_m)$$

$$P(j_m) = \gamma_{j_m}$$

<u>Remark</u>

The independent reference model of program behavior is a special case of the Markovian reference model.
In that case we have

$$p_{ij} = \beta_i \qquad i,j = 1,2,\dots,n$$

where

$$\sum_{i=1}^{n} \beta_i = 1 .$$

It is obvious that

$$\gamma_{j_1} = \beta_{j_1}$$

and

$$[(I-p_i(q))^{-1} v_i(q)]_{(1)} = \frac{\beta_{j_i}}{D_i(q)}$$

with

$$D_i(q) = 1 - \sum_{k=i}^{m} \beta_{j_k}$$

Therefore (2) and (3) may be written as

$$P(j_1,\dots,j_m) = \frac{\prod_{k=1}^{m} \beta_{j_k}}{\prod_{k=2}^{m} D_k(q)}$$

$$F(LRU) = \sum_{q \in Q} \frac{\prod_{k=1}^{m} j_k}{\prod_{k=2}^{m} D_k(q)} \cdot D_1(q) \quad (4)$$

(4) has been obtained by W.F. King III, (3) is thus a generalization of King's formula.

4. EXAMPLE

This example has been inspired by a stochastic matrix given in Franklin and Gupta [2].
Consider the 5 × 5 page transition matrix

$$p = \begin{pmatrix} .9 & .1 & .0 & .0 & .0 \\ .0 & .3 & .0 & .9 & .2 \\ .1 & .0 & .5 & .0 & .7 \\ .0 & .6 & .0 & .1 & .0 \\ .0 & .0 & .5 & .0 & .1 \end{pmatrix}$$

Table 1 gives the probability and the page fault rate for some states, those with non zero probability, for m equal 2 to 4

m=2			m=3			m=4		
m.s.	Prob (m.s.)	Prob (p.f.)	m.s.	Prob (m.s.)	Prob (p.f.)	m.s.	Prob (m.s.)	Prob (p.f.)
(1,2)	0.2459	0.1	(4,2,1)	0.2108	0.1	(5,4,2,1)	0.2108	0.1
(4,2)	0.2108	0.1	(5,2,1)	0.0351	0.1	(3,5,2,1)	0.0351	0.0
(5,2)	0.3551	0.7	(5,4,2)	0.2108	0.1	(3,5,4,2)	0.2108	0.1
(1,3)	0.0492	0.5	(3,5,2)	0.0351	0.7	(1,3,5,2)	0.0351	0.6
(5,3)	0.1721	0.	(2,1,3)	0.0492	0.5	(4,2,1,3)	0.0422	0.5
(2,4)	0.1639	0.	(1,5,3)	0.1721	0.0	(5,2,1,3)	0.0070	0.0
(3,5)	0.1230	0.2	(5,2,4)	0.1639	0.0	(2,1,5,3)	0.1721	0.0
			(1,3,5)	0.1230	0.2	(3,5,2,4)	0.1639	0.0
						(2,1,3,5)	0.1230	0.0
page fault rate=0.1194			page fault rate=0.1194			page fault rate=0.0843		

m.s. = memory state.
Prob(m.s.) = probability of having ... as memory state.
Prob(p.f.) = probability of having a page fault.

Table 1

5. CONCLUSION

For a program of n pages which is to be executed in a system with m page frames of main memory, it is possible to show that to calculate the page fault rate of LRU paging algorithm, the algorithm of Franklin and Gupta requires the inversion of a matrix of order $\frac{n!}{(n-m)!}$.

The approximate number of multiplications needed to calculate the page fault rates with this algorithm for all m, 1 < m < n, is

$$\sum_{m=1}^{n-1} \frac{1}{3} \left(\frac{n!}{(n-m)!}\right)^3$$

Because it is possible to obtain the memory states probabilities recursively, the approximate number of multiplications needed to calculate the page faults rates with our algorithm for all m, 1 < m < n is

$$\sum_{m=1}^{n-1} \frac{n!}{(n-m)!} \left(\frac{m^3}{3m!} + m + 3\right)$$

Table 2 sums up these approximate numbers for some values of n and for both algorithms.

	general case	n=5	n=10	n=15	n=20	n=25
Franklin and Gupta	$\sum_{m=1}^{n-1} \frac{1}{3} \left(\frac{n!}{(n-m)!}\right)^3$	6.5×10^{5}	1.8×10^{19}	8.4×10^{35}	5.4×10^{54}	1.4×10^{75}
ourselves	$\sum_{m=1}^{n-1} \frac{n!}{(n-m)!} \left(\frac{m^3}{3.m!} + m + 3\right)$	2.0×10^{3}	7.0×10^{7}	4.0×10^{14}	9.0×10^{19}	7.0×10^{26}

Table 2. Approximate number of multiplications

ACKNOWLEDGMENT

The author wishes to thank P.J. Courtois and H. Vantilborgh of MBLE Research Laboratory for suggesting the subject of this paper.

REFERENCES

[1] Courtois P.J. and Vantilborgh H., A Decomposable Model of Program Paging Behaviour. *Acta Informatica 6, 2* (1976).

[2] Franklin M.A. and Gupta R.K., Computation of Page Fault Probability from Program Transition Diagram. *Comm. Ass. Comp. Mach. 17, 4, 186-191* (1974).

[3] Gelenbe E., A Unified Approach to the Evaluation of a Class of Replacement Algorithms. *IEEE Trans. Computers, C-22, 6, 611-618* (1973).

[4] King III W., Analysis of Demand Paging Algorithms. *Proceedings IFIP Congr. 71.1, 485-491*, North-Holland, Amsterdam, 1972.

[5] Vantilborgh H., *On Random Partially Preloaded Page Replacement Algorithms.* MBLE Res. Rep. R202, Brussels (1972).

E. Morlet and D. Ribbens, (Eds.), International Computing Symposium 1977.

A DESIGN OF A COMMUNICATION SUPERVISOR FOR A LOCAL NETWORK EMPLOYING MONITORS

J. van den Bos

Informatica
Faculty of Science
University of Nijmegen
Nederland

COMPLEX is a software system which governs communication between the central computer in a star-network and a large scientific computer, connected to each other via a moderately high-speed link. COMPLEX performs the basic I/O transfers on the half-duplex link. On top of that it makes the single physical link appear like a large number of logical channels through which user programs running under multiprogramming operating systems on both computers may communicate. Internally it operates on a packet basis while at the same time allowing users to communicate on a message basis. COMPLEX itself runs as a user program. Other user programs submit requests for data transfer through an operating system component which interfaces with COMPLEX. In addition COMPLEX provides utility functions such as support for satellite computer graphics, and COMLNK, a versatile fileshipping and remote job entry package, Van den Bos[1].
The general design follows a top-down modular approach throughout the package. To control access to critical sections of the program a construct closely resembling the monitor concept has been employed.
The communication multiplexer has been implemented for an IBM/370 running under MVT or VS2, connected to a PDP11/45 running under UNIX. The nature of the link is relatively unimportant because the I/O is isolated in a low-level module which can easily be replaced. Although the implementation has been done for specific computers, the design is such that it may easily be extended to other computers and operating systems.

1. INTRODUCTION

Data communications networks are becoming increasingly important for data processing. A special case of these networks is a local network where the computers are characterized by the following:

a. most computers are small- to medium-size machines used for special purposes: data acquisitions, experiment monitoring etc.
b. there is usually one large, high-performance, general-purpose computer.
c. distances between computers are not in excess of approximately 1 km.
d. data communication rates range from 100 bps (bits per sec) to one million bps.

This situation frequently arises when the small computers want access to the processing power and data base of a large machine, while themselves handling, usually very efficiently, their special-purpose function. A local network of this kind may also be characterized by distributed processing, here meaning that every system is doing what it knows best, while at the same time for a diversity of tasks relying on other computers (mostly the large general-purpose machine).

As described this situation occurs at our university where many PDP computers are handling various scientific experiments. One of the (larger) PDP machines, belonging to our department, is used for a variety of tasks among which interactive computer graphics plays an important role.

These PDP computers are (very) loosely coupled into a star-network (see Fig.1) of which our machine forms the center.

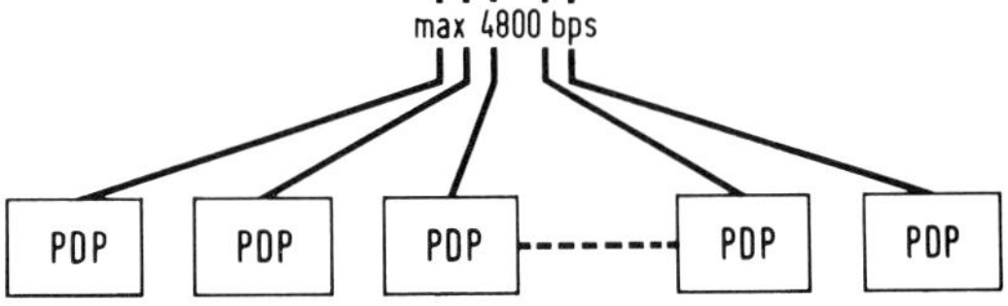

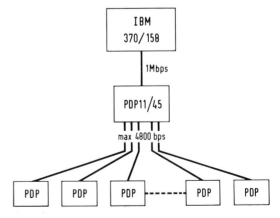

Fig. 1. Faculty of Science Computer Network

Other machines may communicate with the central machine on a dial-up basis (bit rates up to 4800 bps) through the IPCP communication package, Klok[2] designed by our group. In this manner they are capable of utilizing the greater processing power and storage capacity of the central machine. The central machine itself is connected via a 1 Mbps connection to a large IBM/370-158 computer. Through this connection the users of the other PDP machines may indirectly access the resources of the large machine. At the same time it has enabled our department to set up the central computer with graphics terminals (Vector General 3D and Tektronix 4015) as a so-called graphics satellite, where a program running on the large machine, supported by software in the central PDP, controls the graphics devices. This has made it possible to run applications that use vast amounts of CPU power (number crunchers) or a large data base, while delegating specific graphics functions such as display buffer management and interrupt handling, to the PDP machine.

Eventually the need arose to transport files back and forth between PDP and IBM, to have large source code and other text files printed or punched at the IBM installation and to submit jobs to the IBM computer from the PDP. Since both computers are controlled by multiprogramming operating systems (MVT & VS2 on the IBM and UNIX on the PDP) it was also judged worthwhile to allow communication between several programs on either machine to proceed at the same time, so that for example one program could be doing file transfer, while others were doing satellite graphics. Following the initial design of COMLNK, Van den Bos[1], a single-user system which offers file transfer and remote job entry services, COMPLEX has been designed to fulfill all these desires and requirements.

2. DESCRIPTION OF COMPLEX

The following description mostly deals with the IBM part of the design, however a conscious effort has been made to make the software on the PDP side as much as possible a mirror image, subject to limitations imposed by the operating system.

COMPLEX consists of two components: COMVISOR running in problem program mode and a system routine, SVCCOM, running in supervisor mode. COMVISOR executes all link I/O and supervises and schedules message routing. SVCCOM accepts read (CGET) and write CPUT) requests from other IBM user programs which it enqueues on COMVISOR's request queue. In addition it moves data from user program buffers to the COMVISOR I/O buffer or vice versa. SVCCOM is primed by an initialization call of COMVISOR through which the address of a communication area in COMVISOR is passed that contains an event control block (comecb), the I/O buffer and pointers to the I/O request queue (CCQ) and the write queue (Wq). SVCCOM saves the pointer to this area so that on subsequent calls it may access the contents of it.

If there is no useful message traffic COMVISOR ('C') exchanges DUMMY messages with its counterpart on the PDP, 'c'. This exchange of DUMMY messages is repeated once every 2 seconds until either side has an action message, this then will replace the DUMMY message. This ritual is followed to ensure communication on a ping-pong basis.

2.1 Protocol

Because of the special nature of the network we decided not to adapt one of the standard protocols, although our approach resembles the highest level protocol in ARPANET. Our protocol is simple and relies on the fact that the physical connection has a very low error rate ($<10^{-10}$).

2.1.1 GENERAL

The way communication takes place depends on who is looking at it. From the user point of view, all communication is done on a message basis. At this level, called logical level, the user simply submits a request to read or write a message of arbitrary length (limit:$2^{15}-1$ bytes). On a read the requestor will also be informed about the actual length of the message after completion of the transfer. It is important to note that on the logical level, message headers etc. do not exist unless the user has implemented some protocol at his own level. At the physical level, i.e. the level on which I/O is done in COMPLEX all transfers take place on a packet basis. Except when short messages have to be transmitted this packet has a fixed length of 1000 bytes. It holds all or part of one logical message or an internal COMPLEX message.

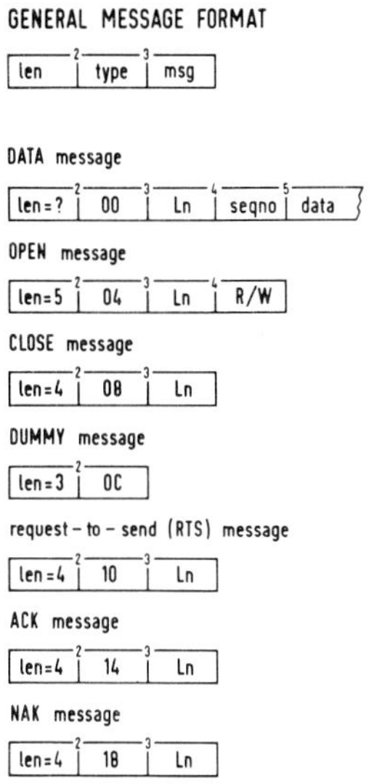

Fig. 2. Internal Message Types

The message in the physical packet contains three fields, a length field, a type field and the message field, msg. There are 7 different types of messages: OPEN, RTS, DATA, CLOSE, ACK, NAK and DUMMY (see fig. 2). Each message with the exception of DUMMY and, in some cases, NAK, carries a logical channel number as part of the msg field. This field, Ln, forms the connection between sender and receiver. Ln further subdivides into two 4-bit fields (nibbles) the first one of which identifies the IBM program, the second one the program in the central computer.

Adopting the terminology of Van den Bos [1] we distinguish between a data communication function and data communication transactions. The former is a complete logical operation such as a logical read. A transaction is a single message, possibly with a reply such as an acknowledgement. A series of logically related transactions constitute a data communication function. On the physical level a data communication function always starts with an OPEN message (see section 2.5) from one side, followed by a request-to-send (RTS) from the other side. This transaction serves to initialize queues and pointers in COMPLEX. The next transaction consists of a DATA packet, acknowledged by an ACK (or in the case of problems by a NAK). This type of transaction (DATA and ACK) is repeated until the logical request is satisfied. The data communication function then terminates with a CLOSE message, possibly followed by a DUMMY message.

2.1.2 ERROR CHECKING

Error checking is done by means of a cyclic redundancy check (CRC). If a hard I/O error develops or a bad CRC occurs a NAK will be immediately returned, if possible with the logical channel number in it. Errors will be logged and if a certain error limit is reached the link will be closed and COMVISOR will be terminated.

2.2 Accessing shared queues by means of monitors

Every data communication function corresponds with an entry in the channel communication queue, CCQ. This queue contains, as a function of the logical channel number Ln, IOflags, user buffer address and length, an event control block, the sequence number of the DATA message and a pointer to the head of a chain of operating system control blocks. The access to this queue is shared (both read and write) between COMVISOR and SVCCOM. Since SVCCOM, following a user request, may asynchronously add information to this queue access to CCQ has to be controlled.

Every packet that is to be written is initially queued on a so-called write queue, Wq. It basically consists of a pointer to the CCQ-entry as well as a pointer to the message itself. Again, since both SVCCOM and COMVISOR may put entries in this queue, Wq has to be considered a critical resource.

In order to synchronize access to CCQ and Wq we defined two monitors as described in Hoare[3]. CCQ and Wq are queue variables local to the corresponding monitor. The CCQ monitor consists of some local variables and a collection of procedures with access to CCQ. Every external routine invoking one of the procedures has to enter via the monitor. The monitor ascertains that at any time only one caller is active inside, and therefore delays additional callers until the active one has exited. The same type of simple monitor is used for Wq, but here the number of local procedures is considerably smaller.

Various implementation schemes for monitors have been considered. We could have embracketed the monitor code with an ENQ, DEQ system call pair, or possibly with WAIT and POST. We chose, however, to put the monitors inside a system routine which can only be accessed through a supervisor call. The routine runs with interrupts disabled to achieve the desired effect, unless a monitor caller suspends itself to wait for completion of some operation, in which case the caller releases the resource (i.c. the CCQ) to allow other callers to enter. In this way we feel we kept monitor overhead to an absolute minimum, thus ensuring a minimal delay for waiting accessors.

2.3 IBM-read (PDP-write)

To understand what happens when an IBM program wants to read from some PDP program assume that a user calls SVCCOM by means of a CGET macro. SVCCOM creates an entry for this user in the CCQ, in the process doling out a logical channel number, Ln. C in the meantime has a 'read' outstanding on the link. At some time c will receive a request from a Unix program to write to a specific IBM program. It (c) enqueues this request on its ccq and sends an OPEN message to C. C will wake up and read and interpret the message. If this OPEN matches an outstanding request on the CCQ it activates the CCQ-entry, returns an RTS (request to send) message to c and goes into a wait for reading. The RTS contains the logical channel number to be used for this communication. In response c will now send a DATA message in the form of packets of 1000 bytes, each of which will be acknowledged (ACK message) by C. C checks whether the corresponding CCQ entry is active and, through an SVCCOM call, puts the message packet-by-packet in the user buffer. This proceeds until either c indicates the last packet (seqno=255) or the user buffer is full. In either case C sends a CLOSE message, posts CCQecb, waits for comecb to be posted by SVCCOM (indicating that it is ready to return to user), and deletes the request from the CCQ. The user call to SVCCOM will now exit, while C waits for another read from the PDP.

It is also possible that c sent an OPEN before any CGET's were issued. In this case a partially filled out CCQ entry will be created by C. C inspects the logical line number Ln in the OPEN message. As mentioned earlier the first four bits of Ln indicate the IBM program desired. If this Ln-pgm is a standard one[1] COMVISOR will start it. When the CGET from this program materializes, SVCCOM searches the CCQ for a matching request, if found, missing information such as user buffer will be filled in. Also the CCQ entry will be activated and an RTS message will be queued on the Write queue (Wq). C sends c an RTS and subsequently waits for a reply from c. The remainder is exactly as sketched above for a C-initiated message exchange.

----

[1] A standard program is a program the JCL of which is available to COMVISOR through an input dataset which contains JCL dataset names as a function of the first nibble of Ln.

2.4 IBM-write (PDP-read)

Next assume that a user calls C through a CPUT macro. SVCCOM queues this request on the CCQ, keeping it inactive; subsequently it waits for completion of the write request via a wait(CCQecb). C now sends an OPEN with the logical channel number in it to c, and waits for a reply. At some time c returns an RTS message. This causes C to activate the CCQ entry. It then sends the first packet of data. After each send C waits for an ACK message. If it receives a NAK instead it will retransmit the packet. If an ACK is received then if the entry is active bufad and len in the CCQ will be updated and a new DATA message will be sent. This goes on until either the user buffer is empty or a CLOSE message is received from c. In the first case C sets the sequence number in the DATA message to 255 (X'FF') which value serves as a last-message indicator. It also inactivates the corresponding CCQ entry. When it receives a CLOSE message C posts the CCQecb, waits for comecb to be posted by SVCCOM (indicating that it is ready to return to user), deletes the CCQ entry, and sends a DUMMY message to c. The user call to C will now exit, while C waits for another read from the PDP.

Action may also commence at the PDP side. A PDP program may want to receive a message from an IBM program. This request will be translated by c into an OPEN message. On receipt C will create a CCQ entry, inspect the logical channel number, Ln, and start the corresponding program. Eventually this will cause a CPUT to be issued by said program. SVCCOM will complete the CCQ entry with bufad and length, and it will activate it. Furthermore the first DATA message will be queued on the Write queue (no RTS is necessary in this case!). As sketched before, SVCCOM enters a wait (CCQecb) until the CPUT request has been carried out to completion. In the meantime C goes through the steps described above.

2.5 Summary

```
        READ                    WRITE

□ CGET                    □ CPUT
           ← OPEN         OPEN →
  RTS →                            ← RTS
           ← DATA         DATA →
  ACK →                            ← ACK
           ← DATA         DATA →
  ACK →    .              .        ← ACK
  .        .              .        .
  .        .              .        .
  .        ← DATA         DATA →   .
  CLOSE →                          ← CLOSE
           ← DUMMY        DUMMY →
  DUMMY →                          ← DUMMY
```

2.6 Complications

With several programs requesting message exchange from C or c it will in fact seldom happen that the sequence as depicted in the summary will take place uninterruptedly. Due to the likelihood of transmission errors it seems particularly important that DATA messages be acknowledged. Under this regime the following sequence would be possible:

```
OPEN1  →
            ← OPEN2
RTS2   →
            ← DATA2
ACK2   →
            ← RTS1
DATA1  →
            ← ACK1
DATA1  →
            ← CLOSE1
DUMMY  →
            ← DATA2
ACK2   →
            ← DATA2
CLOSE  →
            ← DUMMY
```

However not every sequence is possible. Tentatively we seem to have the following rules:

- a NAK always refers to the directly preceding message from the other side
- no DATA may be sent until the ACK for the preceding DATA message has been received
- a read must be followed by a write and *vice versa*

In order to allow for general and more efficient interleaving several messages could be packed in a packet. We decided against making this generalization mainly because we felt it would distract from the simplicity and straightforwardness in the design of COMPLEX and therefore could be a potential source of problems.

REFERENCES

1. J. van den Bos and H.J. Thomassen: 'COMLNK - A file transport and job entry utility for a communication link', Software-Practice and experience 1977, 7, no. 1
2. P.F. Klok and H. Klaver: 'IPCP - Inter PDP Communications Package', Informatica/Computer Graphics Group Report, Un. of Nijmegen, October 1975
3. C.A.R. Hoare: 'Monitors: An operating system structuring concept', CACM 1974, 10, pp 549-557

OPTIMAL AND SUB-OPTIMAL CONFIGURATIONS FOR COMPUTER NETWORKS

Alan Pearman
Lecturer

School of Economic Studies,
University of Leeds,
England.

The paper undertakes a preliminary investigation of the likely opportunity cost of the sub-optimal solution of certain combinatorial problems. In particular, it considers a formulation of the network optimisation problem which is appropriate for computer network modelling at certain levels of abstraction and concludes that heuristic algorithms can reasonably be expected to provide satisfactory solutions to problems of this type.

1. INTRODUCTION

The development during the last decade of systems such as the A.R.P.A. network gives some indication of the potential benefits available through the linking together of spatially separated computer units in networks. The optimal specification of such systems, however, poses many complex and interdependent problems in areas such as routing, queuing, choice of link capacities, etc. Although, ultimately, it is necessary to consider the strength and nature of such interdependencies, many useful initial insights can be obtained by examining the relevant problem areas independently.

This paper concentrates on the question of network configuration and consequently makes rather simplistic assumptions about the nature of the other problem elements. Its main concern is with an examination of the opportunity costs of sub-optimisation in choice of network configuration. The reason for such an examination is that optimal network selection is so computationally intractable a problem that it is usually necessary to resort to the use of heuristic techniques. Heuristic algorithms yield a solution, the quality of which is a monotonic increasing function of the time for which they are allowed to run. They also, in general, fail to provide any guarantee of the closeness of the best solution located to the global optimum. This is particularly so when solving combinatorial problems of the network type.

It will be argued here that the appropriate criterion to apply when considering the application of heuristic search strategies to a class of problems is the expected opportunity cost of sub-optimality. This cannot, in general, be evaluated for combinatorial problems of realistic size, but it is possible to gain some indication in relative terms by extrapolating the results of an examination of smaller systems. In turn, this provides information about which type of heuristic strategy is most likely to be successful in solving problems of the type in question.

Of fundamental importance in determining the likely opportunity cost of sub-optimality in the solution of any combinatorial problem is the shape of the frequency distribution of objective function values of feasible solutions. No clear picture emerges from the literature as to what shape(s) might reasonably be expected. What evidence exists is contradictory. In this paper, complete enumeration and random sampling techniques are used to examine a number of network problems under various assumptions. The conclusion reached is broadly that, because of the nature of the evaluation process, network problems are significantly more likely than most spatial combinatorial problems to be susceptible to effective solution by heuristic algorithms. The implications of this finding for choosing between heuristic search strategies are also examined.

2. BACKGROUND

One of the many important problems associated with the planning of computer networks is the specification of an appropriate network topology. This problem, however, has proved particularly resistant to the development of optimising techniques, [see, for example, Kleinrock /6/, section 4.2.5]. So also have closely related network problems in the fields of geographical analysis and transportation planning [see, for example, Scott /11/, chapter 6]. As a result, a number of heuristic design procedures have been suggested. Examples in the field of computer networks include, notably, Frank /4/ and /3/.

For the purpose of examining the optimal network topology problem, it is neither necessary nor practical to use a model which represents the full detail of the proposed computer system. In this paper, a very simple series of models is employed in order to permit concentration on topological aspects. It is assumed that a computer facility exists at each node of a potential network and that, in general, each node both sends work to and receives work from all the other computers. It is also assumed that both the capacity of the computers themselves and the capacity of the one type of link which can be constructed between nodes is adequate to meet all the demands which may be imposed. There is thus no possibility of congestion, nor any question of link capacity selection, although it would not be impossible to incorporate such phenomena in a rather more complex model. The precise specification of the matrix of computer-to-computer flows to be fed through the system varies from example to example and will be discussed in more detail later. All the original nodes may be connected together by straight line links whose costs, both of construction and use, are proportional to their lengths. However, the formation of new nodes is not permitted. If links intersect in a spatial sense, no extra junction is created. Each existing node, however, is assumed capable of acting as a cost-free transmission site, thus permitting the indirect routing of flows. The objective, therefore, becomes in the first instance to minimise the annual cost in use of satisfying the demand for inter-computer communication while not exceeding a capital budget on link construction cost. Again, it would be relatively simple to reformulate the problem to allow for, say, an annual hiring cost ceiling for transmission lines rather than an initial construction cost limit, or some other cost objective. The one selected is merely chosen for its simplicity as part of an exploratory study. Optimality is thus sought in terms of a simultaneous choice of topology and routing pattern where, because of the absence of congestion, each flow will use the shortest possible series of links between its origin and its destination node.

In attempting to optimise such a system, the crucial problem is the interdependence between link investment decisions. It is, in fact, impossible to evaluate an investment in any single link. This is because the flow volume over any one link will depend significantly on the configuration of the remaining links. Different configurations will produce different flow patterns and hence impute different values to the link in question. It is therefore necessary to evaluate complete network topologies, not individual links. However, the number of different topologies rises exponentially with n, the number of nodes. For large n, it is of the order of 2 raised to the power $\frac{1}{2}n(n - 1)$. The network optimisation problem is thus a combinatorial problem of a marked ferocity. Branch-and-bound techniques can handle systems of up to ten nodes or so, if particularly simplistic assumptions are made about evaluation procedures [see Boyce /1/]. Beyond this order of magnitude, however, heuristics must be employed.

3. THE CHOICE OF PERFORMANCE CRITERION

It is a general weakness of heuristic algorithms, especially as applied to combinatorial problems, that it is not normally possible to know whether the best solution located at any stage is globally optimal, nor how far removed from global optimality it is. It is thus very difficult to allocate an appropriate amount of scarce computer time to the problem in question.

It is the contention of this paper that there are two major factors which should be taken into account when fixing an allocation of time for a heuristic algorithm to "solve" a given problem. One will clearly be the nature of the algorithm itself and existing experience with its use. More fundamental, however, since it may well influence choice of algorithm, is the nature of the set of all feasible solutions to the problem in question. It is primarily with this latter consideration that this paper is concerned.

The allocation of an increment of computer time to the heuristic solution of a given problem represents a trade-off, implicit or explicit, between the expected marginal improvement in the quality of the best solution located at any stage and the opportunity cost of the computer time, i.e., its expected value in its next best alternative use. A fundamental influence on the value of the expected improvement is the shape of the frequency distribution of objective function values of members of the set of feasible solutions. More precisely, it is likely to be reflected in the skewness of the frequency distribution. A number of authors, e.g., Wilde /14/, have pointed out that, on the basis of straightforward random sampling, a solution within the best x per cent of all feasible solutions can be found with probability y $(0 < y < 1)$ by taking a sample of a size z where $y = 1 - (1 - x)^z$. The size of z, however, is not, alone, an adequate criterion for judging random sampling or any other heuristic technique. It makes its assessment of quality of solution with reference to the large number of relatively inferior and possibly quite unacceptable solutions in the main body of the objective function frequency distribution. But what is important is the opportunity cost of sub-optimality and this is not reflected in the main part of the distribution, but in the nature of its upper tail (maximisation problems) or of its lower tail (minimisation problems).

The distributions A and B in Figure 1 represent frequency distributions of objective function values for all feasible solutions to two hypothetical minimisation problems. The shaded portions of the two distributions contain in

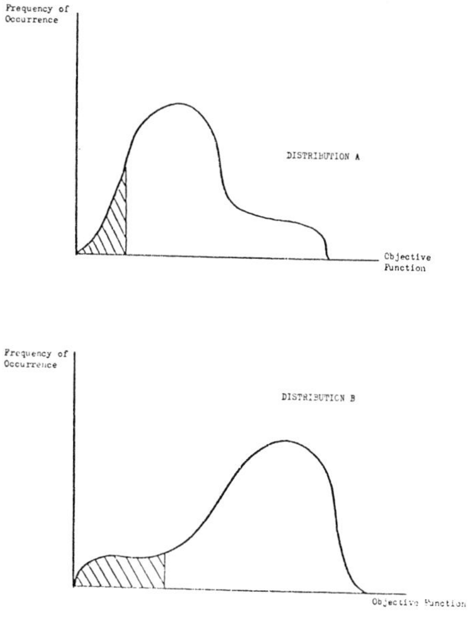

FIGURE 1. The frequency of occurrence of objective function values for two hypothetical minimisation problems.

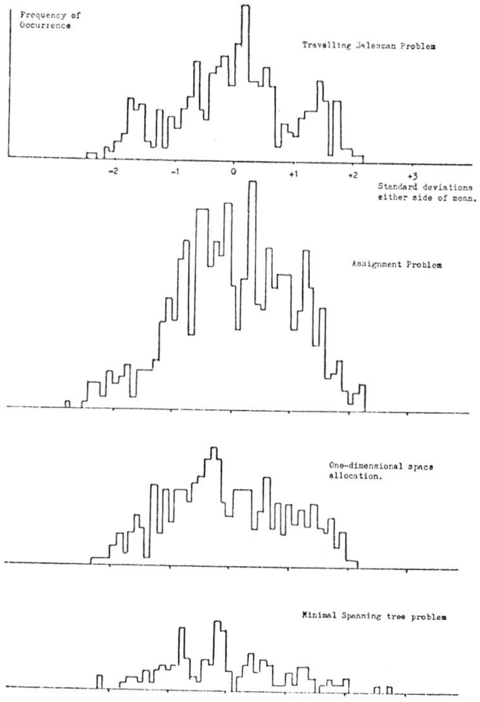

Figure 2. Frequency Distributions for four combinational problems (see also Figure 4).

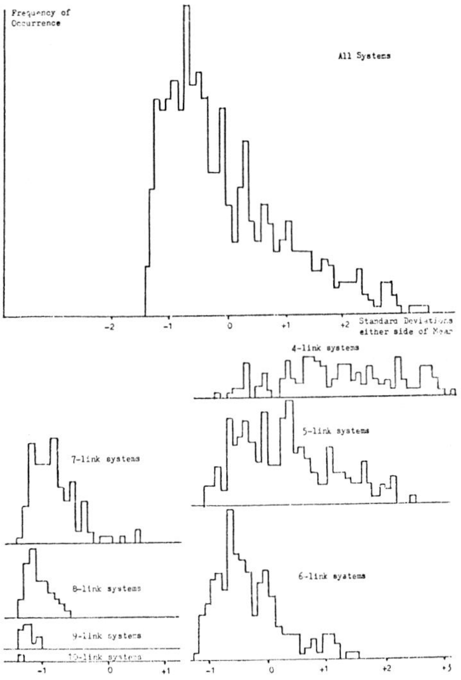

Figure 3 Objective function frequency distribution for basic five-node network problem

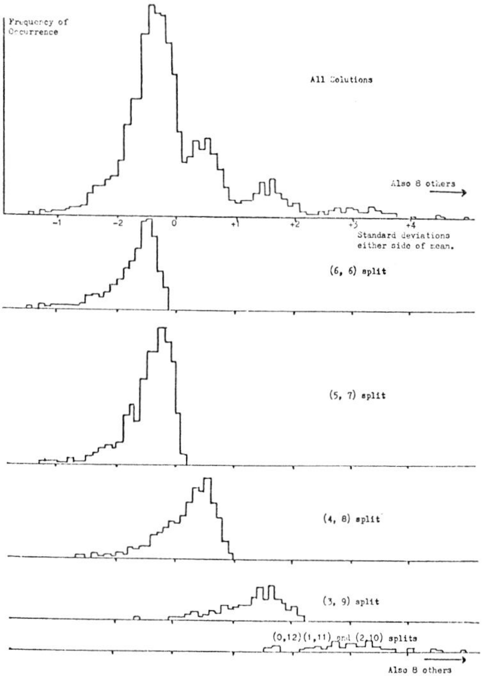

Figure 4. Disaggregation of Quadratic Integer Assignment Problem.

each case the top ten per cent of all solutions, but clearly, the expected opportunity cost of sub-optimality is significantly greater in Problem B than in Problem A. This is because Problem B exhibits significant negative skewness. Ceteris paribus, a given heuristic is much more likely to provide a satisfactory solution for Problem A than for Problem B.

A significant piece of information, therefore, in developing heuristic search techniques should be the anticipated shape of the frequency distribution of feasible solutions. This will influence both the type of strategy employed and the computer time allocation. Clearly, there are other important influences, such as the precise nature of the relationship between local optima and the global optimum. These will be particularly important in comparing individual algorithms. However, the question of frequency distribution shape is fundamental and it is surprising to find that it appears to have been afforded relatively little attention in published sources and also that opinions about its likely shape for various spatial combinatorial problems are not unanimous. The balance of opinion appears to be towards favouring a Normal curve pattern /̄ Siemens /12/; Scott /9/; Heller /5/_7, but others lean towards positively skewed distributions /̄ Kühner and Harrington /7/_7.

4. EMPIRICAL INVESTIGATIONS

The results reported in this paper are an attempt to fill, in part, this gap in the understanding of spatial combinatorial problems, with particular reference to network optimisation. The approach adopted was essentially empirical and took the form, in the first instance, of selecting a number of small and simple combinatorial problems for comparison with the network optimisation problem. For each problem, a number of examples was created at random, all feasible solutions were computed, and the corresponding frequency distributions constructed. Such a simplistic approach appears inevitable since, in practice, there is a major difficulty in determining the shape of the distribution for any given problem. The problem itself must be complex, for otherwise heuristic procedures would not be under consideration. Clearly, however, determining all feasible solutions is going to be computationally even harder than finding a single optimal solution. All that can be done, it seems, is to analyse small and simple problems and trust that conclusions based on such miniatures can legitimately be extrapolated to larger problems. Although there are dangers in this process, it is also true that by stripping a problem of all but its bare essentials, the chance of gaining some understanding of fundamental relationships is increased. It is implicit in the analysis that conclusions about the expected opportunity cost of sub-optimality for small problems might reasonably be extrapolated to problems of more realistic size.

In addition to the network optimisation problem, five other spatial combinatorial problems were examined. These are listed in Table I together with the number of feasible solutions generated. Although some of the solution sets are quite small, it should be borne in mind that combinatorial problems increase in size exponentially and often it would have been impracticable to examine even the next largest possible example. An illustration of this is afforded

Problem	Number of Feasible Solutions
Travelling Salesman Problem	360
Assignment Problem	720
Minimal Spanning Tree Problem	125
Quadratic Integer Assignment Problem	2,048
One Dimensional Space Allocation Problem	360

TABLE I: Problems Examined and the Number of Feasible Solutions

by the network optimisation problem. For a five-node system there are 728 feasible configurations. For six and seven-node systems, the corresponding figures are 26,704 and 1,866,256.

The five problems selected are well-known. Only a brief description of each is given here, together with references where a more detailed account is available.

(1) Travelling Salesman Problem: Given n cities, find the shortest circuit which visits each city once and once only, returning to the starting point. /̄ Further details in Scott /11/, pp. 85-91_7.

(2) Assignment Problem: n tasks must be assigned to n assignees such that one and only one task goes to each assignee. Each task/assignee pairing has an associated cost. Find the n pairings which together minimise total cost. /̄ Further details in Scott /11/, pp. 59/60_7.

(3) Minimal Spanning Tree Problem: Given n nodes, find the (n - 1) links shortest in total length which link all n nodes together into a single system /_ further details in Scott /11/, pp. 68-70_/.

(4) Quadratic Integer Assignment Problem: Given n locations and an interaction cost between each pair, split the n into two subsets such that the sum of the two interaction cost totals for locations within each subset is minimised. /_ Further details in Scott /9/, pp. 15/ 6_/.

(5) One-dimensional Space Allocation Problem: Given a corridor with n rooms down one side and an interaction volume between each pair of rooms, arrange the rooms along the corridor so as to minimise the sum of the interaction costs /_ further details in Simmons /13/_/.

Figure 2 shows a typical frequency distribution of objective function values for each one of the five problems. In each case, the original measurements have been standardised by subtracting the mean objective function value and dividing by standard deviation. Of the five problems, numbers (2), (3) and (5) generate approximately symmetrical frequency distributions. (4) generates a slightly positively-skewed distribution, implying the existence of a fair number of good sub-optimal solutions. (1) presents some problems. It is not clear why the travelling salesman problem, which in mathematical structure is closely related to the assignment problem, should exhibit a bunching of the solution values into groups. It may, for instance, reflect local optimality properties of the problem. This is a matter which is presently under more thorough investigation. Overall, however, a preliminary conclusion may be drawn that, at least for such small, randomly generated problems, there is evidence to suggest good solutions to combinatorial problems will exist in numbers at least as high as would be implied by a Normal type of frequency distribution, and perhaps more so.

It is now possible to start to investigate network optimisation in the context of the evidence of the other five combinatorial problems. Initially, a series of five-node networks was generated, the nodes of the networks being randomly placed in a 100 x 100 grid. The flow demands were assumed to be unity between each pair of nodes, irrespective of the distance separating them through the network. A typical example of the frequency distributions corresponding to this sort of problem is illustrated in Figure 3, together with a series of disaggregations by number of links. Objective function values have again been standardised.

Thus it may be concluded, again bearing in mind the simplicity of the network problem generated, that problems of this type appear to have objective function frequency distributions with a marked positive skewness. There is a better than Normal number of good sub-optimal solutions, or, equivalently, the expected opportunity cost of sub-optimality is low relative to the other combinatorial problems examined. This basic characteristic is substantially maintained even if capital cost ceilings on the total investment in links are imposed. It is also interesting to note that skewness is at its most marked in the subsets of systems with large numbers of links (notably seven and eight-link systems). In terms of this fundamental aspect of the structure of its solution set, therefore, the network optimisation problem appears to offer a relatively good field for the application of heuristics, recalling always that matters such as the local optima/global optimum relationship will also have a significant influence.

The reason why the network optimisation problem exhibits positive skewness is hypothesised to be that there is a degree of flexibility in the evaluation of the objective function which is not present in all combinatorial problems. This is because the evaluation phase is a two-stage one, consisting firstly of the choice of topology and then a use decision, what route each flow will take through the system. This decision is taken in the light of knowledge about the network structure and reflects a degree of flexibility in use not always available. The body which determines routing will always be biased toward low user cost solutions which will bias the user cost distribution towards positive skewness. This hypothesis is lent support by the fact that capital cost, which reflects only a link choice decision, is approximately normally distributed in these problems, as one might expect given the random nature of their generation. Further, there is no evidence of asymmetry in the four-link system subset objective function values, where no user choice of route can be employed. However, asymmetry increases markedly as the number of links increases and with it the discretion in route choice enjoyed by the network user.

Of the problems discussed earlier, only the quadratic integer assignment problem exhibited a degree of positive skewness. This example, however, serves to illustrate the necessity for caution in interpreting results of frequency distribution examination. The skewness here is caused not by a two-stage evaluation procedure, but by the structure of the problem itself. Figure 4 shows the frequency distribution for a quadratic integer assignment problem disaggregated according to whether the n nodes are split (12,0), (11,1), (10,2), etc. It illustrates that the skewness here arises from the fact that, in most randomly generated problems of this type, the best solutions are likely to lie in the large subsets of (6,6) or (7,5) splits, rather than in one of the more extreme ones. It is the relative quality of these large subsets as a whole, rather than any feature of the evaluation process, which gives the overall frequency distribution its shape. Indeed, the individual subsets indicate significant negative skewness. The implication may be drawn that here is a problem for which a two-stage heuristic solution procedure is desirable. First, estimate the rough order of division of the n nodes which seems likely to prove optimal. Then search the relevant subsets carefully since, within each subset, the opportunity cost of sub-optimality can be expected to be high. In contrast, the disaggregation of the network optimisation problem does not show up a similar situation. Here, all subsets by size of system have minima of about the same order. Most, although not all, of the skewness results from the skewed shape of the individual subsets.

There is thus some evidence to support the hypothesis that combinatorial problems with two-stage evaluation procedures will have positively skewed distributions of objective function values and will therefore be relatively amenable to solution by appropriate heuristic search strategies. It seems worthwhile, then, to look at some variations on the very basic network problem initially examined to see whether flexibility in use continues to have its hypothesised influence on distributions of objective function values.

5. MORE DETAILED INVESTIGATION OF THE NETWORK PROBLEM

The number of directions in which it would be desirable to test further in order to examine the sensitivity of the objective function frequency distribution to changes in underlying assumptions is considerable. Here, only a limited number of variations will be investigated.

The first variations tested assumed a more complex pattern of flow demand than the uniform inelastic demand of the basic model. Firstly, a model was constructed where random non-uniform weights, W_i, were associated with each of the nodes of the network and internode demand, F_{ij}, then computed on the basis of the relationship $F_{ij} = W_i W_j/1000$. Applying the same mode of analysis as before, the resulting frequency distributions were of the type shown in Figure 5. Introducing the extra dimension of non-uniform demand clearly does not affect the underlying pattern.

An alternative adjustment to the basic model is to permit internodal flow demand to vary with distance through the network, D_{ij}. To examine this possibility, a gravity model formulation was employed to estimate F_{ij} according to $F_{ij} = 10000\ D_{ij}^{-2}$. The introduction of elastic flow demand, however, complicates the evaluation process. It is no longer possible to work in terms of minimising cost in use, since the amount of use will vary depending on the set of D_{ij}'s in the topology under test. Instead, the concept of change in consumer surplus is used as a criterion. This measures the change in the excess of benefit over cost enjoyed by the users of the network relative to the position in a base network, which is here taken to be the complete, ten-node system. Removing links will diminish consumer surplus vis à vis this base. The objective becomes to minimise the loss in consumer surplus, which means that objective function values on the right of Figure 6 correspond to the more desirable topologies. Again, therefore, the introduction of elastic demand does not nullify the underlying skewness first identified in the basic model.

In addition to these two major changes in demand specification, another, related item which should be investigated is sensitivity to a less random distribution of the original nodes. This is clearly difficult to undertake in the context of systems as small as five nodes. There are also many different types of non-randomness which might be considered. Here, just one particularly extreme form was considered. This consisted of placing one node in one corner of the 100 x 100 grid and the remaining four clustered together in the opposite corner. The basic uniform inelastic demand model was used. As might be expected, such extreme assumptions tend to generate somewhat strange distributions. Nevertheless, as Figure 7 shows, the essential positive skewness remains.

It is an inevitable weakness of the type of exhaustive frequency distribution analysis undertaken here that the size of combinatorial problem which can be examined is severely limited. While it is feasible to examine a five-node system, even an extension to six nodes would increase more than thirty-fold the volume of computation required. One possibility here is to employ statistical sampling. The exponential growth of the problems as n increases soon ensures that any moderate-sized sample is a minute fraction of the total population. However, this should not affect the representativeness of the sample distribution obtained and so this approach was attempted. Figure 8 shows how the distribution of Figure 3 was approximately by a ten per cent random sample, scaled up for direct comparison with the original distribution. Figure 9 shows the distribution of objective function values obtained from random uniform inelastic demand problems of six and seven nodes. Again, the characteristic skewness is evident.

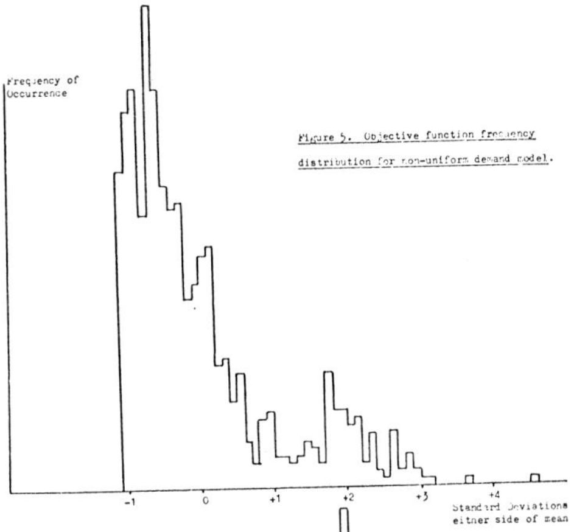

Figure 5. Objective function frequency distribution for non-uniform demand model.

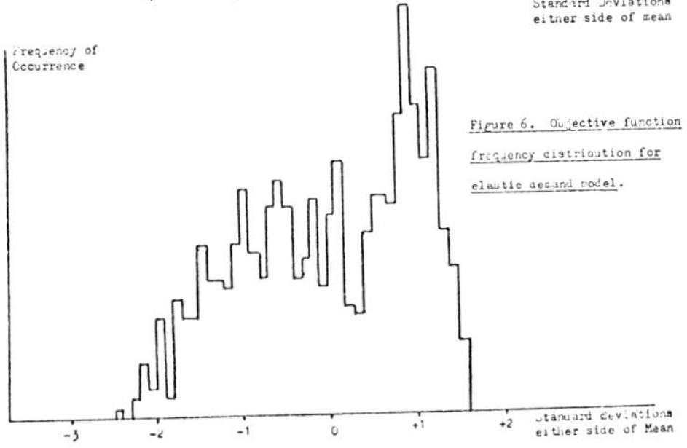

Figure 6. Objective function frequency distribution for elastic demand model.

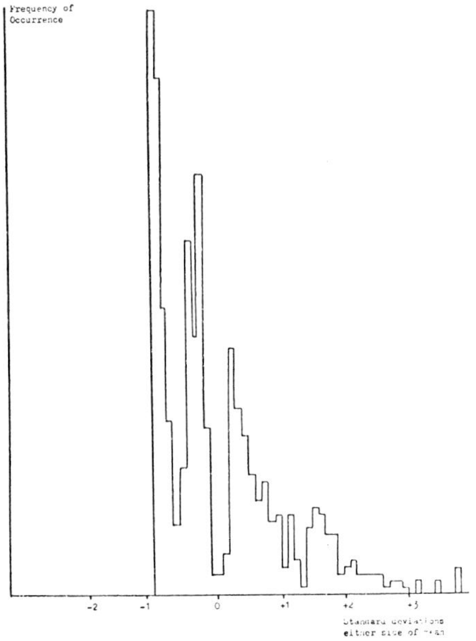

Figure 7 Objective Function frequency distribution for non-random system

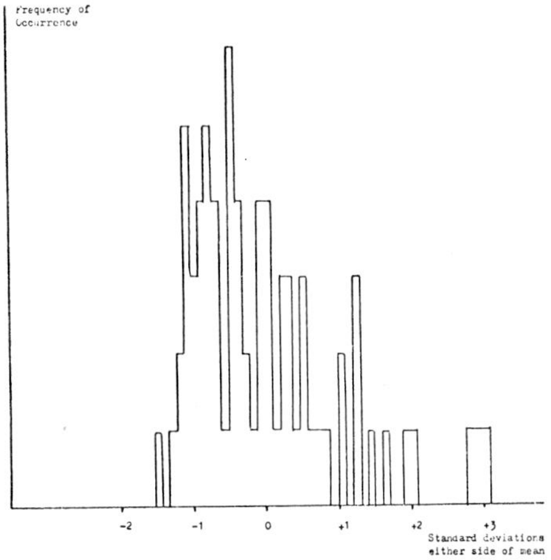

Figure 8 Objective function frequency distribution for basic five node problem estimated by a 10% sample

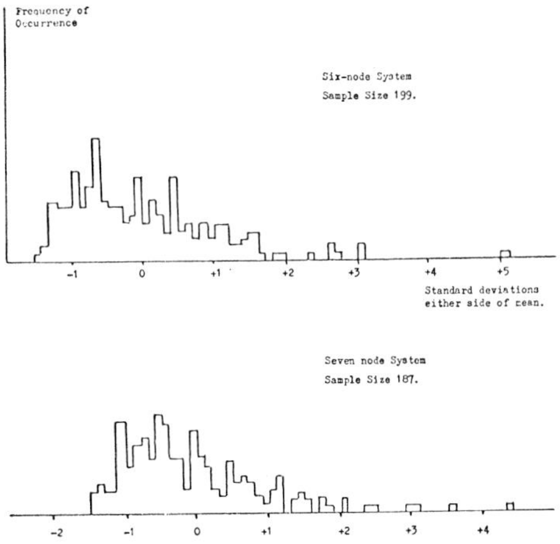

Figure 9. Frequency Distributions from random samples

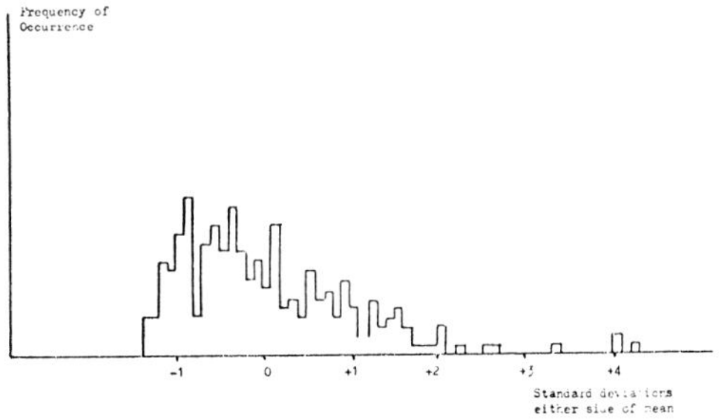

Figure 10 Frequency distribution of objective function values for double node-connection network

Finally, one rather more specialised variation on the original basic model was considered. This was concerned with the desire to maintain service in the event of link failure. It was necessary to exclude all topologies where the cutting of one link would cause the system as a whole to lose its unity. All nodes, therefore, would be required to be connected to at least two other nodes. All four-link and the majority of five link topologies would be excluded by the addition of such a constraint, as would a minority of the systems with a larger number of links. Given the arguments advanced in the previous section about the effect of route choice on skewness of distribution, it could reasonably be hypothesised that the addition of this extra connectivity constraint should not nullify the basic expectation of positive skewness. Figure 10 illustrates the resulting distribution for the original model of Figure 3 after the imposition of the connectivity constraint and confirms the existence of a positively-skewed distribution.

6. CONCLUSION

This paper has sought to show that, because of the inherent nature of their frequency distributions of objective function values, some spatial combinatorial problems are potentially more susceptible than others to satisfactory solution by heuristic search. It is hypothesised that situations where the pattern of use of a system is not solely determined by its structure, but where a degree of flexibility in use exists, will be more likely to exhibit the phenomenon of a positively skewed distribution and ceteris paribus to be satisfactorily solved in a heuristic fashion. Such a conclusion is in one sense fundamental but, equally, must be seen in the context of a requirement for additional information about the local and global optimality properties of the problem in question.

It has been demonstrated for a series of small trial problems that the optimisation of computer network topologies is a spatial combinatorial problem which appears to be particularly rich in good sub-optimal solutions. Such a finding is certainly in agreement with some practical experience [see Davies and Barber /2/, p. 456].

The implications for the types of heuristic search strategies which should be considered for application to the computer network problem are also of some consequence. Until relatively recently, combinatorial heuristic search strategies have tended to be problem-specific creations with little common core of theory. To some extent, the very nature of heuristic procedures makes this inevitable. However, recent work has started to consider more seriously relationships between heuristic methods and the problems to which they are applied [see, for example, Müller-Merbach /8/]. The findings of the present paper suggest that the best type of heuristics to apply to a computer network problem are those which are relatively straightforward. In preference to attempting rather complex series of hill-climbing changes from a few random initial solutions [as, for example, in Scott /10/], it is likely to be a more cost-effective use of computer time to sample the distribution of feasible solutions more generously, but to have only very simple adjustment procedures, if any. The opportunity cost of good sub-optimal topologies is such as to make it preferable to use computer time on other aspects of system specification. It is unlikely that any exceptionally good solution will be missed as a consequence.

REFERENCES

/1/ Boyce, D.E., Farhi, A. and Weischedel, R. Optimal Subset Selection. Multiple Regression, Interdependence and Optimal Network Algorithms, Lecture Notes in Economic and Mathematical Systems, No. 103, Springer-Verlag, New York, (1974).

/2/ Davies, D.W., and Barber, D.L.A., Communication Networks for Computers, John Wiley, London,(1973).

/3/ Frank, H. and Frisch, I.T., Planning Computer-Communication Networks in Abramson, N., and Kuo, F.F. (eds.) Computer-Communications Networks, Prentice-Hall, Englewood Cliffs, New Jersey, (1973).

/4/ Frank, H., Frisch, I.T. and Chou, W., Topological considerations in the design of the A.R.P.A. Computer Network, A.F.I.P.S., Conference Proceedings, Vol. 36, pp. 543-549, (1970).

/5/ Heller, J., Some numerical experiments for an M x J flow shop and its decision theoretical aspects, Operations Research, Vol. 8, pp. 178-184, (1960).

/6/ Kleinrock, L., Scheduling, queueing, and delays in time-shared systems and computer networks in Abramson, N., and Kuo, F.F. (eds.) Computer-Communications Networks, Prentice-Hall, Englewood Cliffs, New Jersey, (1973).

/7/ Kühner, J., and Harrington, J.J., Mathematical models for developing regional solid waste management policies, Engineering Optimization, Vol. 1, pp. 137-256, (1975).

/8/ Müller-Merbach, H.,
Heuristic methods: structures, applications, computational experience in Cottle, R.W., and Krarup, J., Optimisation Methods, English Universities' Press, London, (1974).

/9/ Scott, A.J.,
Combinatorial Pricesses, Geographic Space and Planning, Department of Town Planning, University College, London, Discussion Paper Series, No. 1, (1968).

/10/ Scott, A.J.,
The optimal network problem: some computational procedures, Transportation Research, Vol. 3, pp. 201-210, (1969).

/11/ Scott, A.J.,
Combinatorial Programming, Spatial Analysis and Planning, Methuen, London, (1971).

/12/ Siemens, N., Marting, E.H., and Greenwood,F.
Operations Research, Free Press, New York, (1973).

/13/ Simmons, D.M., One dimensional space allocation: an ordering algorithm, Operations Research, Vol. 17, pp. 812-826, (1969).

/14/ Wilde, D.J., Optimum Seeking Methods, Prentice-Hall, Englewood Cliffs, New Jersey, (1964).

TERMINAL ACCESS TO HOST COMPUTERS THROUGH RPCNET

L. Lazzeri L. Lenzini

CNUCE, Instituto del CNR, Pisa, Italy

A. Springer

IBM Centro Scientifico, Pisa, Italy
(On Leave From IBM Scientific Center, Cambridge, Mass. USA)

RPCNET, a network under development in Italy, is architected in three layers, an innermost packet switcher, an intermediate layer of interface functions which provide "logical channels", and an outer layer of network "application" programs that use these channels to communicate with each other. This paper describes a pair of "applications" that support connection between terminals and host computers that have interactive services. Of special importance are the relationships between the various components of the applications and the interface functions of RPCNET. In particular, the protocol used between the two applications is described in terms of the RPCNET logical channel and in terms of an idealized terminal.

INTRODUCTION

RPCNET is implemented on a number of computers and operating systems at various locations in Italy (Lenzini /1/). RPCNET is intended to provide a machine independant method of communicating between "applications" via "logical channels" maintained by the network. The architecture of RPCNET is structured in three well defined layers, the innermost packet store and forward "common network", the next outer "interface function" layer which supports "logical channels", and the outermost layer of network "application" programs that use the logical channels to communicate with each other. The "common network" provides transmission of packets on a full-duplex basis, and routing and reconfiguration facilities. The "interface functions" build upon the common network a "logical channel" facility which provides error detection of lost packets, and disassembly and reassembly of messages longer than packet length. From the viewpoint of the applications layer, the interface function layer provides an "access method" called RNAM (REEL Project Access Method) for using logical channels. From the viewpoint of the inner two layers, the application layer consists of programs that communicate with each other using the network services. But since applications also must take part in network error recovery, and since most users of the system do not normally write applications, the application layer is normally the only portion of concern to the user. By contrast, programmers of systems programming caliber would use the RNAM access method in developing network applications. Applications under development include file transfer functions and interconnection facilities between terminals and host interactive computers.

The RPCNET applications of interest in this paper are called the terminal and the host applications. For any particular interconnection of a terminal to an interactive host through RPCNET, there will be a terminal application and a host application maintaining the connection. The applications illustrate two approaches to implementation of network interconnections, from the viewpoint of the host computers of the network. The first approach is to not modify the host system code, and the second normally requires such modification. The IBM System/7 host application interfaces to a System/7 emulator of the 2703 communications control unit. Thus the System/7 appears to the interactive computer to be a 2703 with start-stop terminals. The operating system can interface to terminals via the network if it has software to access terminals via the 2703. By contrast, there are host and terminal applications which reside in the VM/370 operating system control software, and which are essentially additions to the VM/370 "access method" for communicating with terminals. This paper will primarily discuss the System/7 implementation and the features that are common to both the System/7 and VM/370 applications.

Several interfaces were involved in the design of the host and terminal applications. The two applications communicate via an RPCNET logical channel, using a protocol based upon an idealized terminal interface which the application uses to connect to a real terminal.

THE APPLICATION STRUCTURES

Figure 1 illustrates the logical separation of the various application components and their interconnection via RPCNET. The terminal application is made up of a line driver that maps a real terminal into an idealized terminal (here called a virtual terminal or VT; see Zimmerman /2/ and Bozzetti /3/), a network command processor, and a module for communicating with the host application via the RPCNET logical channel. The protocol by which such communication is carried out is called a virtual terminal protocol, or VTP. For the System/7 it was necessary to implement a line driver for the 2741. By contrast, the VM/370 terminal application could use the "access methods" already provided for the terminals supported by VM/370.

The host application maps the virtual terminal protocol into actions meaningful to the host computer. In the case of the System/7, the application maps the virtual terminal protocol into 2703 emulator actions. In the VM/370 case, the mapping is into a virtual console for the virtual machines, at a level where both the VM control program and the user virtual machine access the virtual console. Thus in essence, code has been added to the "terminal access method" of VM/370 so that the RPCNET virtual terminal is accomodated.

THE LOGICAL CHANNEL CHARACTERISTICS

RPCNET provides an interconnection facility which is most easily thought of as a half duplex channel with a limited "break message" facility that provides a full duplex capability. As far as the host and terminal applications were concerned, a full duplex facility was easier to work with. The main features of RPCNET of interest here are that the logical channel provided effectively a full duplex facility, with error detection in case of loss of messages or out of sequence messages between the components. In addition, loss of connection was checked for. The application must accomplish error recovery when a message is lost. Out of sequence messages (message n+1 arriving before message n) appear to the user of RPCNET as message n+1 (first received) followed by loss of message n. Thus error recovery is the same as for both loss and out of sequence. The most convenient error detection scheme provided by RPCNET from the viewpoint of the applications under discussion here is the ability of the sender to detect that a sent message was lost. It is normally the sender who can most easily recover in the case of message loss.

It is worth noting that the first implementation of RPCNET was intended to insure that message loss occurred only with the loss of a network node containing the message. Also, the first routing algorithm minimized out of sequence messages. Thus although the error recovery is necessary, it is seldom invoked except to prevent "hang conditions" in the rare case of a crash of a node holding a message relevant to the host and terminal interconnection.

The RPCNET logical channel allows only one operation to be specified at a time. Relevant to this discussion are the SEND, RECEIVE, BREAK and TESTLC operations. SEND is used to send a message, and the message will be buffered at the receiving side (given sufficient storage) until a matching RECEIVE is done by the application there. Due to the nature of the half duplex logical channel, it is necessary to "change direction" before a receiver can send and a sender can receive. The sender is in charge of changing direction. A BREAK can send a message (restricted in length to fit within a common network packet) from an application which is in receive state to one that is in send state. The break message is received in an asynchronous fashion, and no special operation of the receiver is necessary. Because the half duplex nature of the basic logical channel tremendously complicated the protocol, for the extended functions we desired for the applications, the terminal side was always kept in receive mode, and the host side was always kept

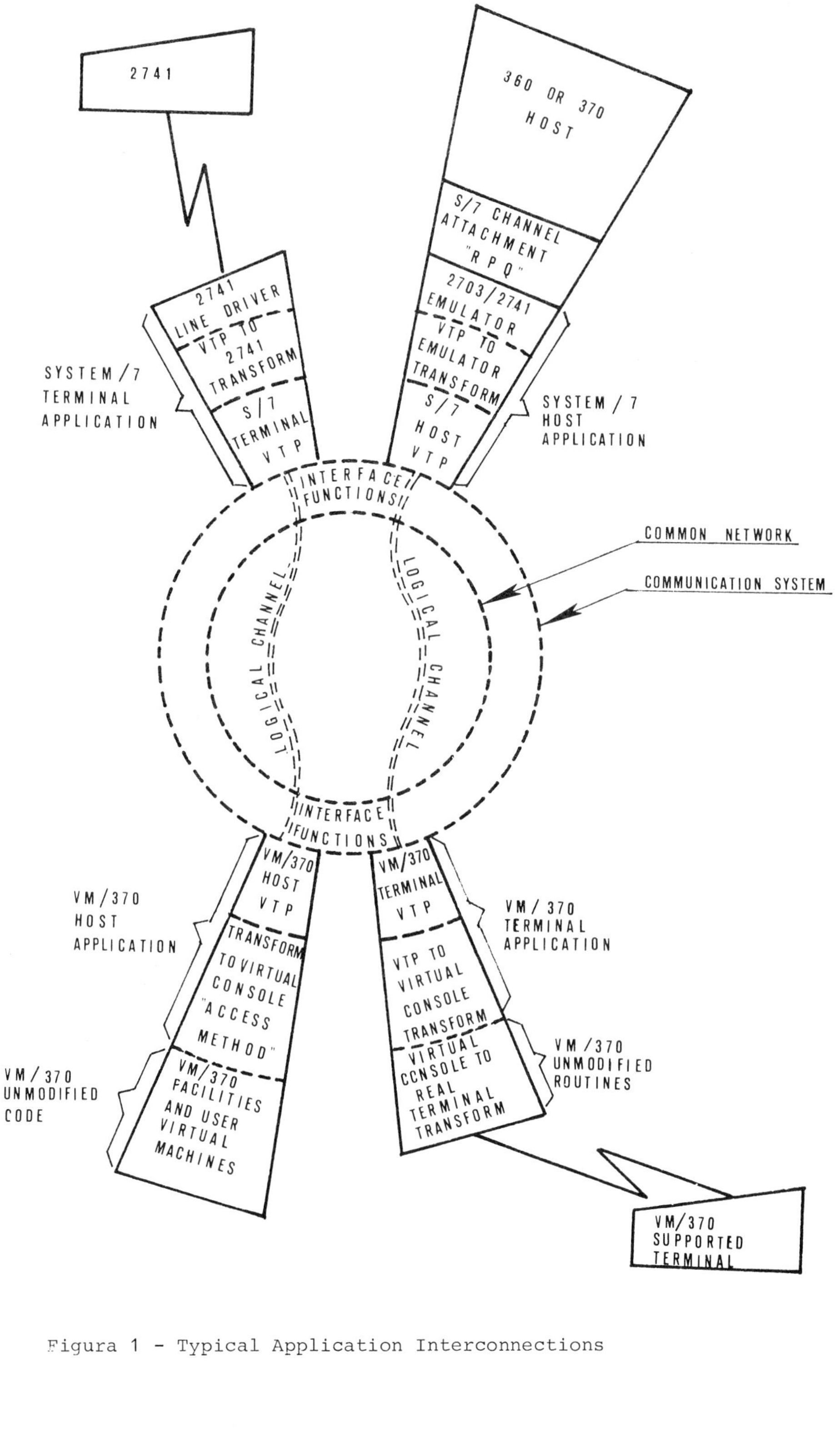

Figura 1 - Typical Application Interconnections

in send mode. This produced only minor restrictions on the terminal side, which has to stop its current RECEIVE in order to send its messages by BREAK.

The TESTLC operation is used by an application to control certain aspects of the logical channel error detection mechanism. In effect it requests that RPCNET verify whether sent messages have arrived at the other end of the logical channel. When any message is sent, there are three possible error detection options. The first is no error detection, the second is definite response (definite asknowledgement of successful receipt or of loss), and the third is exception response. A SEND sent by definite response does not end until an acknowledgement is received. The other two response forms allow the SEND to end as soon as the message leaves the network node. In the case of exception response, an asynchronous branch to the sending application is made (or it is scheduled as a task) upon detection of message loss.

Other functions for controlling the logical channel of interest here are those used for making and breaking connections (forming and deleting logical channels) between applications. When an application wants to connect to another, it does a BIND operation. An application wishing to be connected to by a "bind request" will do an INVITE operation. Typically, the host application of the System/7 will have as many INVITEs in action as there are free ports (emulated terminals) available for connection to its host. When a user of a terminal requests connection to a host, a BIND is done, and if there is a corresponding INVITE at the System/7 or VM/370 requested, then the connection is made. Since the "direction" of the logical channel is initially not as desired, the terminal application does a send with change direction to turn the channel around.

At any time, either application can do an UNBIND to break the connection. This is normally done either at the request of the terminal user, or when the host computer "crashes".

THE VIRTUAL TERMINAL

Figure 2. illustrates the states in which a virtual terminal can be. The write state is when the terminal is writing to the terminal user, and the read state is when the user can type input on the terminal. The prepare state is used to watch for asynchronous attentions or the disconnection of the terminal. (These may also be detected if they end a read or a write.) The prepare, the write and the read are haltable by the program driving the VT. The VT concept as implemented in the System/7 is not particularly sophisticated, but it provided a conceptual interface that was both practical to implement and fertile for providing the basis of the application to application protocol.

The virtual terminal character set, in the System/7 implementation, was the same as the 2741 character set. But the 7-bit PTTC code was mapped into an 8-bit PTTC code, and could have been further mapped into a standard interchange code. However space and other constraints prevented this. Also almost all network users work with 2741 or 2741-compatible terminals. The virtual terminal did not involve the control characters peculiar to the 2741 (circle c and circle d). The attention (break) of the 2741 is reflected as an ending condition of the prepare, read or write commands of the VT. The reverse break accepted by some 2741 terminals was generated as needed if a halt stopped a read operation.

It is worthwhile noting that the basis of the application designs for the VM/370 host and terminal applications were constrained by the nature of the virtual console. It turned out that it was considerably more convenient to map a virtual console of VM/370 into a virtual terminal than vice versa. The application to application protocol design is based upon the concept of the virtual terminal as outlined here. However, it was not necessary to have a recognizable virtual terminal interface in the VM/370 implementation, as long as the application used the virtual terminal protocol when communicating with either System/7 application.

OPENING AND CLOSING A TERMINAL/HOST SESSION

The behavior of the two applications when contacting each other is illustrated in Figure 3. There is a state diagram for each application, indicating how the BIND and INVITE operations are used. The BIND operation actually has four options, bind request, accept, reject, and reject-and-reset. The bind request option sends a request to a specific node/host of the network for a specific application, in this case the host application. If the host application exists and has an INVITE operation in effect, then the INVITE is

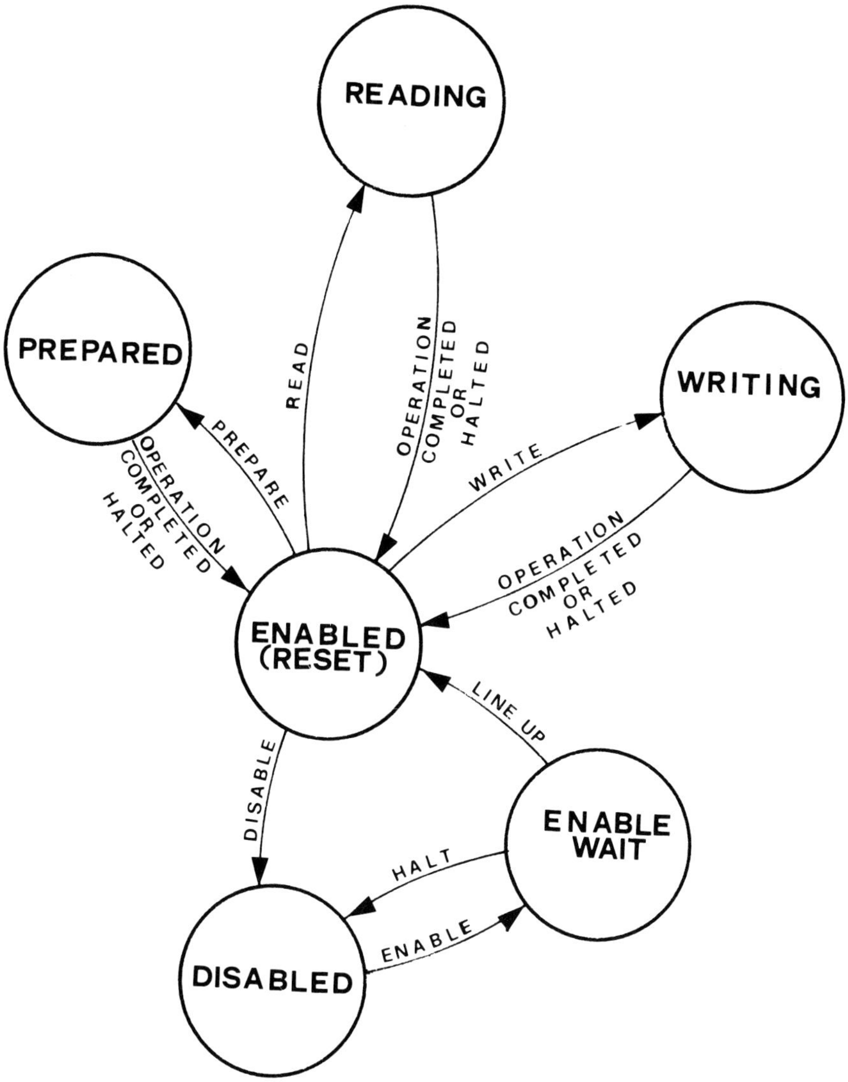

A line down, not shown, sends any state into the DISABLED state.

Figure 2 - Virtual Terminal State Transitions

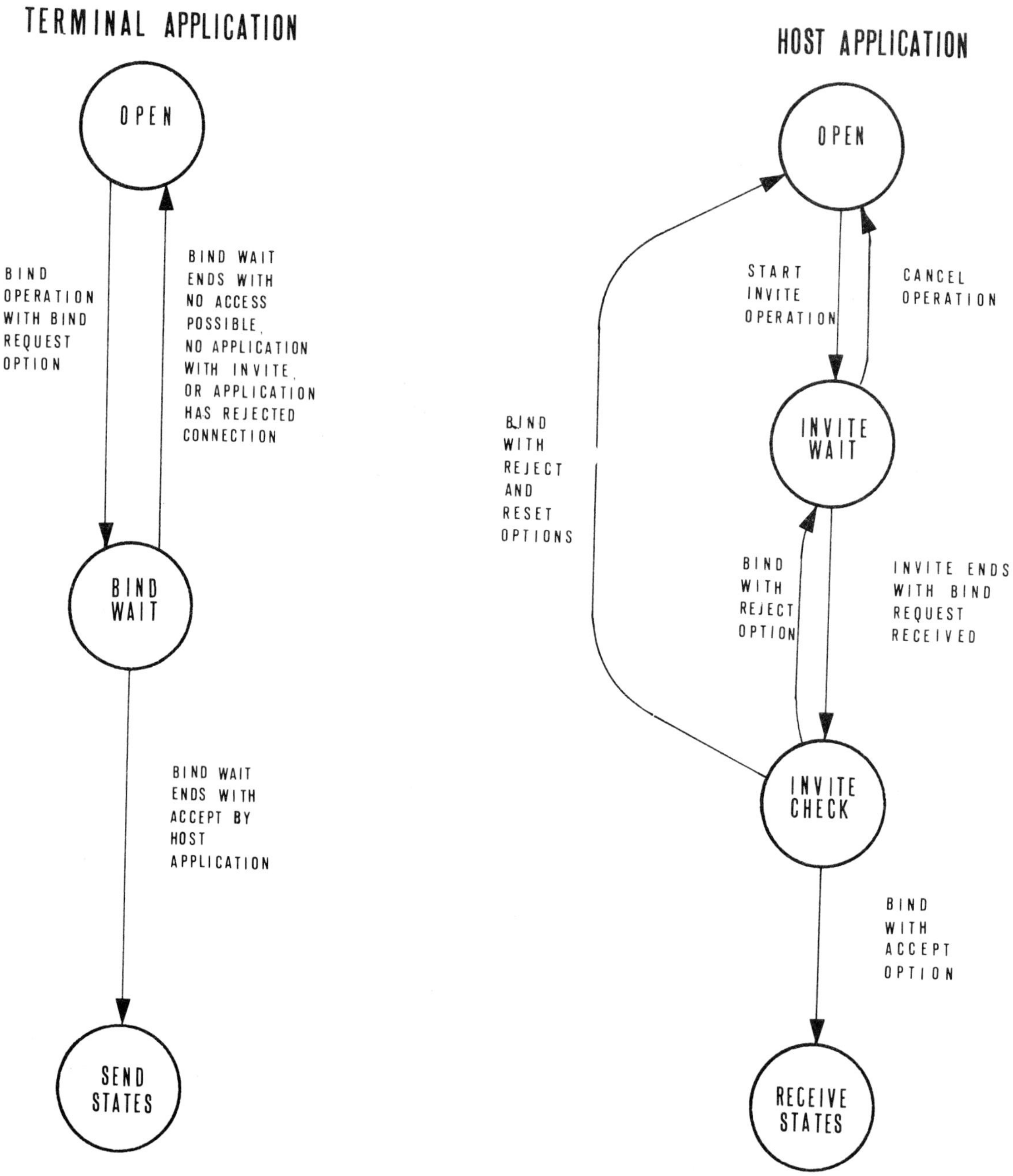

Figure 3 - Typical States For Connection Making

ended with an indication that a bind request arrived. A bind message can be sent with a bind request or with a bind with the accept option. The bind message used by the terminal and host applications is described later in this section. After inspecting the results of the INVITE, the host application may accept the bind request, or reject it. If it is accepted, a bind message is sent by the host application. Finally, the terminal bind request operation ends, with an indication of the success or failure of the connection making attempt. After inspecting the returned bind message, if the bind was successful, the terminal application can end the session by doing an UNBIND.

The bind message is one byte long. Bit 0 indicates the sender type with a value of 0 for a System/7 application, and 1 for a VM/370 application. Bits 1 and 2 designate the character code to be used. 00 designates EBCDIC, 01 designates ASCII, 10 designates PTTC/EBCD and 11 designates PTTC/Correspondance. The bind message can be up to almost a packet in length, allowing considerable expansion.

It is assumed by the host application that the terminal is already "enabled"; this assumption could be changed if desired. It would then be necessary to have an "enable" message to be sent from the host application. An acknowledgement of it would be sent when the terminal became enabled.

Read, write, halt, attention and related activities proceed until one of four situations arise, signalling the end of the session. If the terminal is disconnected, or the host goes down (but the front end processor stays up, for example), or if the host does a disable, the session is ended. In addition, behavior of the network itself can end the session, as when access is lost between the applications due to network failure.

SESSION MESSAGES

This section describes the message formats, and succeeding sections describe the use of the messages. The message formats shown in Figure 4 are those used by the two applications once connection has been established. All the messages are "data" with respect to the RPCNET facilities that support "logical channels". These messages compose the elements of the VTP. The first byte reflects the four classes of messages in bits 0 and 1. A value of 00 designates terminal and host action messages such as read, write, halt, attention, and acknowledgements thereof. A value of 01 designates terminal and host oriented control messages such as type-ahead control. A value of 10 designates a network oriented action message such as the "do TESTLC" message. A value of 11 designates network oriented control messages such as disable, host down, or terminal down. Bit 2 of the first byte indicates which application is the sender. A value of 0 designates the host, and 1 designates the terminal. Bits 3-7 are used to further distinguish the messages.

```
 byte 1   byte 2   byte 3...
00000000 n------n            halt n
00000001 n------n            read request n
00000010 n------n data...    write request n
00000011 m------m            acknowledge attention m

00100000 n------n            acknowledge write or halt n
00100001 n------n data...    read reply n
00100010 n------n m------m   write n ended by attention m
00100011 m------m            attention m

01100000 XY00CCCC            write ahead mode control
   XY=00 no write ahead; no message save
   XY=01 no write ahead; message saved for error recovery
   XY=10 write ahead allowed
   CCCC= count of messages the host application can write ahead

10100000                     do TESTLC

11000000                     host down
11000001                     disable

11100000                     terminal disconnected


00100100 n------n iiiijjjj data...
```

This is a multiple packet read reply form. It designates packet i out of j packets for the message.

```
00000100 n------n data...
```

This is a write request that does not have to be acknowledged. It can be sent in write-ahead mode, to minimize the number of write acknowledgements.

FIGURE 4. VTP MESSAGE FORMATS

READ, WRITE AND HALT PROCESSING

The host application does not need a queue for messages. It needs only a counter to record the number of unprocessed attentions and a variable to hold the latest attention sequence number. The terminal application will need queues for both input and output to communicate with the host application. The output queue is to hold items delayed because the current RECEIVE could not be cancelled since it was busy receiving a message. The input queue holds read, write and halt requests from the host. There is a second queue between the terminal and the input queue. It is used for processing terminal application control messages, and is otherwise empty.

The host application assigns numbers sequentially and cyclically running from 0, 1,..., 255, 0,... to read, write and certain halt requests of the host computer. A halt is assigned a number if it halts a read or a write, otherwise it is not counted and is ignored. Notice of each such halt, read or write is sent to the terminal application where each is enqueued for presentation to the terminal handler. As each is processed by the terminal handler, it is acknowledged by a message sent back to the host application. The message contains the message number assigned by the host application originally. The acknowledgement mechanism is necessary to prevent the host from flooding the network or the terminal application with a series of write messages. The acknowledgement messages are of several sorts: normal write or halt acknowledgement, write ended with attention, and read reply (which includes the data that was requested to be read from the terminal).

ATTENTION PROCESSING

Successive attentions are designated in the message formats by successive attention numbers, running cyclically from 0,1,..., 255, 0,... The terminal application assigns the sequence numbers for attentions.

When an attention is presented to the host computer by the host application, a message acknowledging the attention is returned to the terminal application.

Two messages designate an attention, one normal (not interupting a read or write) and one ending a write. Attentions ending a read are not included in the attention mechanism described here, since by convention they are designated by a read reply message that lacks a "new line" character as its last character.

One message is used to designate that an attention has been presented to the host. Such presentation is done by ending the current (if there is one) or the next read, write or prepare with an appropriate attention indication.

No more than two attentions can be sent from the terminal to the host at any time which have not yet been acknowledged. Some change of this figure is possible. Note that attentions ending a read are not counted in this figure.

USER TERMINAL APPLICATION COMMANDS

For the System/7 terminal application, several commands are proposed. They control connection to the host application as their main function. There are also other facilities that could be supplied by the same mechanism.

The terminal application is kept in a "read command" state with respect to the terminal, once the terminal is connected and enabled, until a host begins controlling the terminal. When the host initiates a read, a terminal command can be entered, after which the host read will be restarted. The terminal command is recognized as such by its special initial character, which will be called an escape character. It is only recognized if it is the first character of a line. When the host is in control, but no read is up, a special "double" attention is used to escape to the terminal application, which starts a read.

The initial escape character is the ">" ("greater than") character, and can be changed to some other character by the user. Some terminals may print a different character than >. However, the user can recognize what the initial escape character is since it is used in terminal application messages as a prefix character.

Terminal commands are recognized by their initial escape character. If the next character is also the escape, the first is removed, and the remainder of the message is treated as a line intended for the host. If the first character is the escape, but the second is not, the line is assumed to be an attempt to enter a terminal command. If it ends with an attention, the line is ignored and the read restarted, allowing the user to correct mistakes. An error message is typed if a command line does not have the correct syntax.

The first and only command allowed from a newly connected terminal is the "on" command which identifies the user and supplies information to recognize the terminal character code. Its syntax is:

>on name

where "name" is any alphabetic name of eight characters or less. The corresponding command for disconnecting is:

>off

This is almost equivalent to physically disconnecting the terminal (turning power off and hanging up the data set), except that the user remains connected to the terminal application.

The command to connect to a host is:

>begin hostname

where "hostname" designates the location of a host application. Only one host application connection can be maintained for a specific terminal at any one time. The command to disconnect from a host is:

>end

The command to specify a new escape character is:

>ne c

where "c" represents the new escape character.

To test the connection to the host do:

>test

The result is a "do TESTLC" message sent from terminal to host application.

The following command is used to ask if access is available to the specified host, as far as the network is concerned:

>q host

If the command has the following form, it is treated as a comment and no operation is performed:

> any characters

Note that the first character after the escape is a blank, followed by any desired character string. Also a line that consists of exactly the single escape character is treated in this fashion.

There are two commands to allow the terminal user to control the type-ahead mode, one to turn it on and one to turn it off:

>ta

>nta

Currently the user does not have control over the amount of messages that can be sent ahead.

Extensions could include local character editing of lines such as VM/370 has. An extension of the >q request could ask for the presence of specific terminal users. A message facility to other terminal users of the network would also be possible. There are message facilities of RPCNET, not described here, upon which this message facility or a more elaborate "mail box" facility could be constructed.

OPERATIONAL STATUS

As of December 1976, the various layers of RPCNET were either under test or operational for both the System/7 and the System/370 versions. The applications described here were in the planning stages (System/7) or a first version had been written (VM/370). For the System/7, certain components, such as the System/7 terminal driver and the 2703 emulator have been coded and used in a prototype virtual-terminal-like interconnection in Pisa (Lazzeri /4/). The virtual terminal protocol is a variation of a similar protocol in use in an experimental network connecting four IBM Scientific Centers in the United States (Springer /5/). Thus the current design is an outgrowth of previous experimental work.

References

/1/ L. Lenzini and G. Sommi, Architecture and Implementation of RPCNET, Proceedings of the Third ICCC Conference, Toronto, 1976

/2/ H. Zimmerman, Proposal for a Virtual Terminal Protocol, Reseau Cyclades, IRIA, Rocquencourt, France

/3/ M. Bozzetti and A. Le Moli, Some Consideration About Virtual Terminals, European Informatic Network, EIN/MILANO/760115/01, Milano, Italy

/4/ L. Lazzeri and L. Lenzini, Interactive Terminal Access in RPCNET, Proceedings of IFIP_IIASA Workshop on Computer Networks, Vienna, September 1975.

/5/ A. Springer, The NET7 Network Facility, Internal Document, IBM Cambridge Scientific Center, September 1975

E. Morlet and D. Ribbens, (Eds.), International Computing Symposium 1977.

A DISTRIBUTED STRATEGY FOR RESOURCE ALLOCATION IN INFORMATION NETWORKS

G. Bucci S. Golinelli
Centro di Studio Operatore-Calcolatore, CNR, Bologna, Italy

In this paper the problem of resource allocation in distributed computer systems is investigated on the basis of a new approach which leaves individual subsystems the freedom to make their own choices instead of imposing a centralized solution. Presented and evaluated is an algorithm for file allocation in information networks with numerical results obtained through algorithm application.

1. INTRODUCTION

The basic idea underlying the development of geographically-distributed computer systems is that, as computer hardware cost decreases, it becomes more and more attractive to put intelligence, i.e. logic and programs, where it is needed [1,2,3].
It is a common practice that, in single computer installations, intelligence is not simply directed toward problem solving, but toward enhancing the processing throughput as well. This is equivalent to saying that modern computer systems carry out two different kinds of activities: (1) operation activities and (2) decision-making activities. Roughly speaking, compilers, assemblers, application programs, etc., are instances of software components which implement activities of the first type whereas schedulers, resource managers (including human operators), etc., implement activities of the second type. These latter activities result in a self-optimization process.

Unlike multiprocessing systems, distributed systems are formed through a more or less loose-coupling of (possibly) autonomous subsystems, each of which is assigned to perform a specific subtask of the global system task. Cooperation among such units must ensure achievement of the objectives for which the system is built. Apart from this specific need for cooperation, each unit behaves not unlike a single computer installation. Thus, it is possible to conceive a distributed system as a set of units which, besides being loaded with a fraction of the total workload, autonomously perform local self-optimization to improve system performances.

Actually, these concepts of loose-coupling, local autonomy and self-optimization are the key words of a paper by T.C. Chen, who pioneered this topic of distributed intelligence [1].

For the sake of exposition let us consider an information system implemented as a hierarchically-distributed system, with a tree-like topological structure: a central computer, some first-level computers and (possibly) some second-level computers.

High-level computers will exercise some control over their subordinates; this will not, however, be global. Subordinates will follow the guidelines given by higher level computers, but will autonomously decide (where and) how to process their inputs.

Decisions taken by each unit will depend on both the current resource allocation and the workload. Subordinates have their decisions influenced by higher level(s). In this way, coordination originates at the top level and descends to lower ones. To exercise coordination, top level does not need an exact knowledge of lower-level operations, nor need it know how they adhere to coordination rules. Indeed a high-level computer needs only a high-level description of what comes up from lower levels. The system reacts to workload changes by adopting a possibly different division of work and a different resource allocation.

It must be said that, in spite of the tremendous growth of distributed systems observed in recent years, little attention has been given to the issues of local autonomy and adaptation [4], as the interest of scientists and designers has been focused on the development of methods and techniques for optimal resource allocation under given operating conditions. This is the case of the work done by Chu [5], Casey [6] and other authors [7,8,9].

To assume that workload will never change is quite an abstraction. Levin and Morgan, who call this approach "static", have developed a method for dynamic resource allocation in computer networks [10,11]. Their solution leads to an optimization process extended over several periods of time. However, neither pays any attention to the decentralization of decision activities.

In this paper we try to give a solution to the resource allocation problem, which allows local units to retain their autonomy of decision within a given limit. The solution is obtained for the optimal file allocation in a distributed information system, and is applied to Casey's model, giving the same results as in [6].

The solution presented strongly relies on the work done by Masarovic et al. on the coordination of hierarchical systems. For this reason we must first give a synthetic view of this theory [12].

2. THEORY OF HIERARCHICAL SYSTEMS

A system is said to be hierarchically structured when the following conditions are satisfied:

1. the system consists of a family of interacting subsystems;
2. each subsystem is a decision-making unit;
3. decision units are arranged in levels, in such a way that units at a certain level, while controlling or influencing those at lower levels, are, in turn, controlled or influenced by those at higher levels.

A decision-making unit is a (sub)system whose input-output relationship can be given implicitly by a decision problem; a hierarchical system as defined above will be referred to as a multilevel, multigoal system. A basic property of multilevel, multigoal systems is that higher level units condition but do not completely control the goal-seeking activities of the lower level units, as the lower units are given some freedom of action to select their own decision variables. In other terms, a hierarchical structure consists of a suitable division, among the system units, of the effort needed to attain the overall system goal.

From the above definitions the following categories of hierarchical system units can be recognized (see Fig. 1).

1. single-level, single-goal systems;
2. single-level, multi-goal systems;
3. multi-level, multi-goal systems.

Attention will be given to two-level systems like that of fig. 2.

2.1 Resource management in a single computer installation

Consider a single-computer system in which, because of multiprogramming, users' jobs compete to acquire system resources such as storage, processing unit, i/o channels, etc.

To make this system work, decisions must be taken to allocate resources to individual jobs. Such activity, called the resource management task, is normally performed by either a system program (operating system), the operator, or both. In any case, performance of this task can be considered as the activity of a decision-making unit. Let us, therefore, denote with w a measure of computer input or workload, and with y a measure of computer performance.

A relationship will exist between workload and computer performance which will depend on resource strategies. Usually a resource management strategy allows intervention on some parameters, by which one can tune the system to a given workload in order to improve system performances. Let us call these parameters control variables and denote the set with m. (Notice that the system manager must, at least, decide whether or not a given resource has to be included in the system at time of configuration; such a decision will be expressed through a binary variable).

Then, we can write

$$y = P(m,w)$$

P being called the outcome function.

By introducing an evaluation function the resource management task can be formulated as an optimization problem. The evaluation function, G, is a measure of the cost necessary to achieve a given performance, that is

$$G(m,y) = G(m,P(m,w)) = g(m,w)$$

The function g, depending only on the workload and control variables, will be referred to as the cost function.
Now, as far as the resource management task is concerned, a computer system can be seen as a decision-making unit whose decision problem can be stated as follows:

find a control variable $\hat{m}$ in M such that

$$g(\hat{m},w) \leqslant g(m,w) \qquad (1)$$

for all w in W and m in M, where W is the set of all possible workloads and M is the set of all feasible values of control variables m.

2.2 Resource management in a computer network

The arguments developed previously can be applied to each node of a computer network. In the following, symbols with subscript "i" refer to the subsystem at node i, symbols without subscript refer to the global system.
We shall name the local control variable m_i and the local workload w_i; w_i is the workload generated locally in the region directly served by system i. Since each network node is connected to some other network node, its outcome function and, hence, its cost function will depend on m_i and w_i; it will, therefore, be influenced in some way by what is going on in the rest of the network. If, for instance, nodes are allowed to decide whether or not to process the local workload by themselves, the total workload at a certain node i would be the sum of its local workload plus an exchange workload, i.e., the portion of workload which is generated elsewhere and routed to node i.
The influence of the rest of the network on the outcome and cost functions of node i are taken into account by introducing a new variable u_i named "interaction variable".

We then write

$$y_i = P_i(m_i,w_i,u_i)$$
$$g_i = g_i(m_i,w_i,u_i)$$

In the preceding example, u_i could be defined as the amount of exchange workload at node i.

Since the interaction variable must reflect the influence of the rest of the network, u_i is, normally, a function of local workload and decision variables at any network node, that is

$$u_i = K_i(m,w)$$

where m and w are the two vectors, $m \equiv \{m_1, m_2,\ldots,m_n\}$, $w \equiv \{w_1, w_2,\ldots,w_n\}$ which define the global decision and workload.

In the preceding example, K_i would give the exchange workload at node i as a function of global workload and individual decisions of the remaining network nodes, and would also reflect network configuration and routing algorithms.

The local optimization problem (1) may now be formulated as follows:

find a control variable $\hat{m}_i$ such that

$$g_i(\hat{m}_i,w_i,u_i) \leqslant g_i(m_i,w_i,u_i) \qquad (2)$$

for all m_i in M_i, all w_i in W_i, and all u_i in U_i, where U_i is the set of all possible values of interaction variables.

Considering the network as a global system, an overall outcome function can be defined as follows:

$$Y = P(m,w)$$

where $Y \equiv \{y_1, y_2,\ldots, y_n\}$ is a vector denoting the global performance. We can also introduce an overall evaluation function and an overall cost function:

$$G(m,Y) = G(m, P(m,w)) = g(m,w)$$

In the decision problem the global resource management task consists of minimizing the overall cost function, that is:

find a control vector $\hat{m}$ such that

$$g(\hat{m},w) \leqslant g(m,w) \qquad (3)$$

for all w in W and all m in M.
Where $M=M_1 x M_2 x\ldots x M_n$ and $W=W_1 x W_2 x W_3 x\ldots x W_n$ (x: cartesian

product).
At this point it should be clear that the global resource management task in a computer network can be thought of as a single-level, multi-goal system made up of the decision-making units as defined by (2), whose interactions are given by the exchange function K_i.

2.3 Coordination

The global resource management task presents conflicts if the overall optimum control vector $\hat{m}$ given by (3) is different from the vector whose components are the local optimum variables given by (2).

A prime reason for the existence of conflicts is due to local decision interactions; in fact, any network node, while solving the local optimization problem (2), does not know which actions will be taken by the other nodes, hence it ignores the value the interaction variable U_i will assume.

There are two ways to overcome these conflicts:

1. Entrusting the global resource management task to just one decision-making unit within the network. We call this solution "centralized approach".
2. Introducing a new decision-making unit (coordinator) whose goal is to hierarchically coordinate the local computer systems, which are still entrusted with decisions regarding local resources.
   This solution has been called "hierarchically-distributed approach".
   Notice that this unit need not be physically defined through a specific computer system.

Previous work [5,6,9] on resource allocation in distributed systems, belongs to the centralized approach. In this paper we shall try to attack the same problem under the distributed approach.

Another departure from previous work on the same subject is that we will approach the resource allocation problem not as an optimization but as an on-line adaptive problem, that is, as the problem of changing the control vector so that network performance is adapted to the evolution of workload and network structure. From this viewpoint the coordinator has to influence the local units in such a way that they select control variables which result in an improvement of the overall performance.
The improvement is measured by comparing the performance given by selected control vector $\hat{m}$ with that given by the previous vector $\tilde{m}$. This coordination mode is called "on-line coordination for improvement".

The overall decision problem (3) is stated as follows:

find a control vector m such that

$$g(\hat{m}, w) < g(\tilde{m}, w) \tag{4}$$

for all w in W and m in M^f

$\tilde{m}$ will be called the reference vector, whereas we will denote with M^f the subset of M in which m is sought.

Let us now focus on the decision problems (2).
They must be stated as on-line adaptive problems and modified in order to allow the coordinator to influence the local decisions.

First of all, we generalize the local cost functions g_i by introducing an additional variable β_i, which represents a generic cost parameter by which the coordinator can influence the local units.
Let B_i be the set of all the values β_i may assume, and similarly U_i the set of all feasible values of interaction variables u_i, then coordinator will select a subset of $U_i x B_i$, and local unit i will solve its decision problem assuming that u_i and β_i are in this subset.
Hence the coordinator can somehow control the local decision by selecting a suitable subset of $U_i x B_i$. Formally, if γ is the input provided by the coordinator the local decision problems are now stated as follows:

find a control variable $\hat{m}_i$ such that

$$g_i(m_i, w_i, u_i, \beta_i) \leq g_i(\tilde{m}_i, w_i, u_i, \beta_i) \tag{5}$$

for all w_i in W and all (u_i, β_i) in U_i^γ x B_i^γ and m_i in $M_i{}^f$
U_i^γ x B_i^γ is the subset of U_i x B_i which is given by the coordinator

through the coordination variable γ in order to influence the local units. This subset may, for instance, be an estimated range.

We now give a result about the applicability of this coordination mode.
First let us denote with ρ an integer function such that for any pair (m,m') the integer $\rho(m,m')$ is precisely the number of components in which m and m' differ. A pair (m,m') in M^f, with $\rho(m,m') = K>0$, is said to be ρ-connected if there is a sequence $\{m^0, m^1, \ldots, m^k\}$ in M^f, where $m^0=m$ and $m^k=m'$, such that

$$\rho(m^{i-1}, m^i) = 1 \text{ for } i=1, 2, \ldots, k.$$

A set M is said to be ρ-connected if any pair of elements in M is ρ-connected.
We can now give the following proposition [12].

Proposition 2.1

Let $\hat{m}$ be the vector $\{\hat{m}_1, \hat{m}_2, \ldots, \hat{m}_n\}$ where $\hat{m}_i$ $(i=1, 2, \ldots, n)$ is a solution of local problems (5). Suppose the following assumptions are satisfied:

(i) Reference vector $\tilde{m}$ is in M^f, and M^f is ρ-connected.

(ii) Each local cost function is in "balance" with the overall cost function, that is, for each index i, two functions, η_i and h_i, exist such that:

$$g_i(m_i, w_i, K_i(m,w), \eta_i(m,w)) + h_i(m,w) = g(m,w).$$

(iii) The functions K_i, η_i, h_i do not depend on local control variable m_i.

(iv) The sets U_i^γ and B^γ are given by:

$$U_i^\gamma = \{u_i | \; u_i = K_i(m,w) \text{ for all } w \text{ in } W \text{ and } m \text{ in } M^f\},$$

$$B_i^\gamma = \{\beta_i | \; \beta_i = n_i(m,w) \text{ for all } w \text{ in } W \text{ and } m \text{ in } M^f\}.$$

If there exists at least one index j for which

$$g_j(\hat{m}_j, w_j, u_j, \beta_j) < g_j(\tilde{m}_j, w_j, u_j, \beta_j)$$

for all w_j in W_j and (u_j, β_j) in $U_j^\gamma x B_j^\gamma$ then:

$$g(\hat{m},w) < g(\tilde{m},w) \quad \text{for all } w \text{ in } W.$$

In other words, this proposition states that, as long as the assumptions are satisfied, the control variables which improve at least one cost function for any w_i in W_i and (u_i, β_i) in $U_i^\gamma x B_i^\gamma$ while not worsening any other cost function, will, at same time, improve the overall cost.

Notice that, since by assumption (iv) sets U_i^γ and B_j^γ are given as functions of set M^f, actually the coordinator influences the local units by selecting a set M^f in which the improving control vector is looked for.
From now on, we will suppose that M^f is a subset of feasible control vectors which satisfies assumption (i).

3. FILE ALLOCATION IN AN INFORMATION NETWORK

We now turn our attention to the well-known problem of file copies allocation in a distributed information system.
Transactions with the multiply-located file give rise to two different kinds of traffic: (i) query traffic and (ii) update traffic.
An update message is assumed to be transmitted to every copy of the file, whereas a query is sent to a single copy.
The file allocation problem is a particular aspect of the management task.
The control variable m_i reduces to a binary variable taking the value 1 or 0, whether or not a copy of the file is allocated to node i.
We can now introduce an overall cost function $g(m,w)$ which depends on the allocation and global volume of query and update traffic. The costs which are to be included in the overall cost are: communication costs for query and update traffic and file storage costs.
The file allocation problem consists in finding an allocation $\hat{m}$ which meets some satisfactory requirement for a given range of update and query traffic.
We decompose the file allocation problem into several interacting subproblems. Each subproblem matches with a particular network node and depends on some

parameters which can be used for coordination. The file allocation problem and the resulting subproblems will be stated as improvement problems so we can use results of "on-line coordination for improvement" given in 2.3, in order to decompose the overall problem in such a way that a local improvement yields an overall improvement.

Let us first introduce the following notation. For any allocation vector we define

$$m[m_i=0] \equiv \{m_1, m_2, \ldots, m_{i-1}, 0, m_{i+1} \ldots m_n\}$$

that is, $m[m_i=0]$ denotes the vector one obtains by setting the value of component m_i in m to zero. Similarily, we define $m[m_i=1]$.

We also define m^i to be the vector one obtains by removing m_i from m, that is

$$m^i \equiv \{m_1, m_2, \ldots\ldots, m_{i-1}, m_{i+1}, \ldots\ldots, m_n\}$$

for the workload we define

$$w^i \equiv \{w_1, w_2, \ldots\ldots, w_{i-1}, w_{i-2}, \ldots\ldots, w_n\}$$

We now suggest a decomposition of the overall cost function $C_{tot}=g(m,w)$ into local cost functions $C_i^! = g_i(m_i, w_i, u_i, \beta_i)$ for each network node i, so that the costs are in "balance", that is, condition (ii) and (iii) of 2.1 are met(.).

Let $A_i(m^i,w)$, $Z_i^0(m^i,w)$ and $Z_i^1(m^i,w)$ be three functions which fulfil the following equations for n=1, 2,...n.

$$\begin{aligned} A_i(m^i,w) + Z_i^0(m^i,w) &= g(m[m_i=0], w) \\ A_i(m^i,w) + Z_i^1(m^i,w) &= g(m[m_i=1], w) \end{aligned} \qquad (6)$$

We define the local cost functions as follows

$$C_i^! = Z_i^0(m^i,w)\,\bar{m}_i + Z^1(m^i,w)\,m_i \qquad (7)$$

where $\bar{m}_i=1-m$.

Local cost functions (7) may be written in the form $C_i^!=g_i(m_i,w_i,u_i,\beta_i)$, as requested by the given model of hierarchical systems by defining u_i and β_i as follows:

$$\begin{aligned} u_i &= K_i(m,w) = m^i \\ \beta_i &= \mathcal{M}_i(m,w) = w^i \end{aligned} \qquad (8)$$

In fact, using (8), one can write

$$Z_i^0(m^i,w) = Z^0(m^i,w_i,w^i) = Z_i^0(u_i,w_i,\beta_i)$$

likewise

$$Z_i^1(m^i,w) = Z_i(u_i,w_i,\beta_i)$$

Therefore (7) becomes

$$C_i^! = Z_i^0(u_i,w_i,\beta_i)\,\bar{m}_i + Z_i^1(u_i,w_i,\beta_i)\,m_i = g_i(m_i,w_i,u_i,\beta_i)$$

We now prove that the suggested decomposition meets the "balance" condition. Of course one can write

$$g(m,w) = g(m[m_i=0],w)\,\bar{m}_i + g(m[m_i=1],w)\,m_i$$

then from eq. (6)

$$g(m,w) = A_i(m,w) + Z_i^0(m^i,w)\,m_i + Z_i^1(m^i, w)\,m_i$$

From the previous definition of g_i, u_i and β_i it is seen that

$$g(m,w) = h_i(m,w) + g_i(m_i,w_i,K_i(m,w), \beta_i(m,w)) \qquad (9)$$

where

$$h_i(m,w) = A_i(m^i,w) \qquad (10)$$

Now, relation (9) reflects condition (ii) whereas (8) and (10) show that functions $K_i(m,w)$, $\mathcal{M}_i(m,w)$ and $h_i(m,w)$ do not depend on the local control variable m_i as required by condition (iii).

The solution to the local improvement problem (5) when the local cost function is (7), is readily obtained by observing that m_i is a binary variable and that the costs for $m_i = 0$ and $m_i = 1$ are, respectively, $Z_i^0(U_i,w_i,\beta_i)$ and $Z_i^1(u_i,w_i,\beta_i)$. This solution can be stated as follows:

| $-\tilde{m}_i = 0$
| If $Z_i^1(u_i,w_i,\beta_i) < Z_i^0(u_i,w_i,\beta_i)$ for all (u_i,β_i) in $U_i^\gamma \times B_i^\gamma$ and all w_i in W_i
| then $\hat{m}_i = 1$ else $\hat{m}_i = 0$

(.) Note that this decomposition is applicable whenever the control vector is a binary vector.

$-\tilde{m}_i = 1$
If $z_i^0(u_i, w_i, \beta_i) < z_i^1(u_i, w_i, \beta_i)$ for all (u_i, β_i) in $U^\gamma \times B^\gamma$ and all w_i in W_i
then $\hat{m}_i = 0$ else $\hat{m}_i = 1$

From now on we suppose that U_i^γ and B_i^γ are defined as requested by condition (iv) of 2.1, so that the coordinator will coordinate local units by selecting a ρ-connected subset M^f of feasible control vectors. Then, using relations (8) to change the variables u_i, β_i into m^i and w in local decision rules, the latter can be restated as follows:

$-\tilde{m}_i = 0$
If $z_i^1(m^i, w) < z_i^0(m^i, w)$ for all m^i in M^f and all w in W, then $\hat{m}_i = 1$ else $\hat{m}_i = 0$
$-\tilde{m}_i = 1$
If $z_i^0(m^i, w) < z_i^0(m^i, w)$ for all m^i in M^f and all w in W, then $\hat{m}_i = 0$ else $\hat{m}_i = 1$

Let us put the preceding rules in a more convenient form. First we consider the difference $z_i^0(m^i, w) - z_i^1(m^i, w)$ and decompose it into two terms F_i and C_i'' so that F_i collects all the terms depending on m^i, that is:

$$F_i - C_i'' = z_i^0(m^i, w) - z_i^1(m^i, w) \qquad (11)$$

where C_i'' does not depend on m^i.

F_i is a function of m^i so that

$$F_i = F_i(m^i, w)$$

Finally, the local decision rules can be stated as follows:

$-\tilde{m}_i = 0$
If $C_i'' < a_i^0 \leqslant \min_{m \in M^f} F_i(m^i, w)$ for all w in W
then $\hat{m}_i = 1$ else $\hat{m}_i = 0$
$-\tilde{m}_i = 1$ (12)
If $C_i'' > a_i^1 \geqslant \max_{m \in M^f} F_i(m^i, w)$ for all w in W
then $\hat{m}_i = 0$ else $\hat{m}_i = 1$

Note that decision rules are very simple: the coordinator will supply a term, a_i^0 or a_i^1, which is compared only with C_i'', a term which depends only on local aspects of costs. C_i'' reflects the autonomy of each network node.

Let $\hat{m}$ be the vector whose components are given by rules (12); $\hat{m}$ is functionally dependent on the set M^f and the reference vector $\tilde{m}$, so we write:

$$\hat{m} = T(M_f, \tilde{m}) \qquad (13)$$

Now proposition 2.1 can be stated as follows:

Proposition 3.1

Let $\hat{m} = T(M^f, \tilde{m})$ if $\rho(\hat{m}, m) \geqslant 1$ then $C_{tot}(\hat{m}) < C_{tot}(\tilde{m})$

The condition $\rho(\hat{m}, \tilde{m}) \geqslant 1$ is only sufficient for global cost improvement; in fact, if $\hat{m}$ is identical to $\tilde{m}$ (that is $\rho(\hat{m}, \tilde{m}) = 0$), it is still possible that an allocation m' exists in M^f such that $C_{tot}(m') < C_{tot}(\tilde{m})$.
When $\rho(\hat{m}, \tilde{m}) = 0$, M^f is said to be non-coordinating.
We are now in a position to summarize the stages into which a coordination step can be divided:

1 - The coordinator is given a forecast of query and update rates from each network node.
2 - A "coordination strategy" is chosen; that is, the coordinator selects a subset M^f
3 - The coordinator calculates the terms a_i^1 and a_i^0 and communicates them to each corresponding network node
4 - The local decision-making units decide by decision rules (12) whether or not to have a file copy and communicate their decision to the coordinator
5 - The coordinator verifies whether the global cost has decreased by comparing the old allocation vector, $\tilde{m}$, with the new one, $\hat{m}$.

3.2 Optimal file allocation

In the following, a procedure is outlined which achieves the optimum allocation vector by implementing the on-line coordination mode through iterative application of coordination steps. The workload is assumed not to change between two iteration steps.

The generic h-step of the iterative procedure can be described as follows:

1. $\tilde{m}^h = \hat{m}^{h-1}$;
2. Select a subset M_h^f of feasible allo-

cation vectors;

3. $\hat{m}^h = T(M_n^f, \tilde{m}^h)$;

4. If $\rho(\hat{m}^h, \tilde{m}^h) > 1$ go to 1 else go to 2;

Iteration stops (at point 2) when every admissible set M_h^f is non-coordinating.

The initial reference allocation vector $\tilde{m}$ is selected arbitrarily. Since the workload w is fixed, the sequence of allocation vectors $\hat{m}^1, \hat{m}^2, ..$ is such that the corresponding sequence of global operative costs is monotone decreasing, that is:

$$C_{tot}(\hat{m}^h) < C_{tot}(\hat{m}^{h-1}) \quad h = 1, 2, ..$$

The main problems to solve in implementing the above procedure are:

(i) approximate evaluation of the minimum and maximum of F_i in M^f (terms a_i^0, a_i^1 of (12).

(ii) The choice at each coordination step of a suitable M_h^f from all those admissable.

(iii) The development of a method for checking stopping conditions. Namely, testing of every admissible M^f could become computationally too expensive when the network has many nodes.

The solution to the first problem depends upon the exact form of function F_i; thus it varies for each different model of the distributed information network.

The choice of M^f can be performed by adopting one of the following 4 strategies.

1) Adding a maximum of n file copies to $\tilde{m}^h$;
2) deleting a maximum of n file copies to $\tilde{m}^h$;
3) adding just one file copy at node i;
4) deleting just one file copy from node i.

We have proved [13] that if all the sets M_i^o, for i=1,2,..,n, which can be obtained through strategies 3 or 4 are non-coordinating, then any admissible M^f is non coordinating. This property constitutes a practical guide to verify the stopping condition.

We have also proved that the file allocation m^s which results from the iterative procedure meets Casey's definition of local minimum.

Implementation of the above iterative procedure yields an algorithm whose general mechanism is similar to Casey's monotone decreasing path-tracing procedure. In comparing the two algorithms we should note that the one presented here permits taking more than one step at a time along a monotone decreasing path, and that this path can move indifferently "forward" or "backward", that is, adding or removing file copies. Moreover, the allocation attained by the given algorithm is "local optimal" for an entire range of possible workloads.

We now turn to the details of Casey's model.

4 - CASEY'S MODEL

Casey [6] considers a computer network information system in which a copy of a data file may be multiply-located. Transactions with the file fall into one of two classes: (1) query traffic between a node and the file, and (2) update traffic. An update message is assumed to be transmitted to every copy of the file, whereas a query is communicated only to a single copy. Every node may communicate with every other node over communication links. This communication may entail routing through intermediate nodes.

The volume of query and update traffic emanating from node i are denoted with the symbols q_i and r_i, respectively. The couple (q_i, r_i) is our local workload w_i.

Costs for shipping information between any two nodes are assumed to be linear with the amount sent, hence they are completely defined by d_{jk} and d'_{jk}, where the coefficient d_{jk} and d'_{jk} are the costs of a unit of communication from node j to node k for a query and an update transaction, respectively. The storage cost of the data file at node k will be denoted by σ_k.

Let us define set I as the index set of network nodes having a file copy, that is:

$$I \equiv \{ i / m_i = 1 \text{ and } 1 \leqslant i \leqslant n \}$$

Since there is a direct two-way correspondence between the allocation vector m and allocation set I, we will use either notation just as a matter of convenience. We also define set I~X as the index set

I with the elements which are common to set X removed; that is:

$$I \sim X = I - [I \cap X]$$

The overall cost function for Casey's model can now be written as:

$$C_{tot}(I) = \sum_{j=1}^{n} \left[\sum_{k\,I} r_j \, d'_{jk} + q_j \min_{k\,I} d_{jk} \right] + \sum_{k \notin I} \sigma_k \qquad (14)$$

From (14) it is easy to obtain the expression of F_i and C''_i for this model. In fact, the index set corresponding to allocation vector $m[m_i = 0]$ is $I \sim \{i\}$, and the one corresponding to $m[m_i = 1]$ is $I \cup \{i\}$, so from equations (11) and (6) we have

$$F_i - C''_i = C_{tot}(I \sim \{i\}) + C_{tot}(I \cup \{i\}) \qquad (15)$$

Substituting from (14)

$$F_i - C''_i = \sum_{j=1}^{n} \left[- r_j d'_{ji} + q_j \left(\min_{k \in I \sim \{i\}} d_{jk} - \min_{k \in I \cup \{i\}} d_{jk} \right) \right] - \sigma_i$$

Since F_i must collect all the terms depending on the allocation vector m (allocation set I) we finally have:

$$C''_i = \sigma_i + \sum_{j=1}^{n} r_j \, d'_{ji}$$
$$F_i = \sum_{j=1}^{n} q_j \left(\min_{k \in I \sim \{i\}} d_{jk} - \min_{k \in I \cup \{i\}} d_{jk} \right) \qquad (16)$$

The local decision rules (12) for Casey's model are completely defined by (16).

We have proved elsewhere, [13], that, when M^f is chosen as previously suggested the minimum (maximum) of F_i is found by evaluating F_i only for those allocation vectors which have the largest (lowest) number of file copies. This allows a fast and efficient computation of a_i^0 and a_i^1 in decision rules (12).

We also proved that, if the global cost of a given allocation cannot be improved by adding a file copy at a certain node i, neither can the global cost of any allocation whose index set includes it be improved by adding a file copy at the same node i.

We would point out that this result can improve the efficiency of Casey's monotone-decreasing path-tracing procedure. In fact, by virtue of this result all those paths which correspond to paths discharged at some previous level, can be discharged at any level without inspection.

5. IMPLEMENTATION EXPERIMENTS

We now discuss some results obtained using a computer program which implements the algorithm described in 3.2.

Before presenting the program it is important to state the following.
The algorithm presented in 3.2 is an adaptive procedure, that is, one which, starting from a given point, seeks system performance improvement. In the real world, the application of any such procedure would give rise to an endless process, since the conditions under which any system operates (i.e., topology, workload, tariffs, etc.) are subject to change. To terminate the program, the conditions under which the system operates are assumed not to change, and the adaptive procedure starts by considering an arbitrary initial reference vector. Because of these assumptions the process of on-line improvement leads to an optimization process. In other words, because of the way it has been implemented, the algorithm leads to an objective, i.e. a (local) optimal file allocation, which is not a proper objective for an adaptive procedure.

The algorithm, plus some additions relevant to programming, is repeated in fig. 3.

The allocation $\hat{m}$ found when the program stops, may either be the optimal or a local optimal allocation in the sense explained by Casey[6].
The program has been used with the ARPA network example given in [6]. The network has 19 nodes; the ratio Update/Query traffic has been assumed equal for each node. Experiments have been made, as in [6], for the 5 cases of Update/Query ratio equal to: .1, .2, .3, .4 and 1. (with the following main results).

1. The procedure always finds a local minimum, whatever the initial reference vectors and the strategies employed to select M^f.
2. When the procedure ends with a local

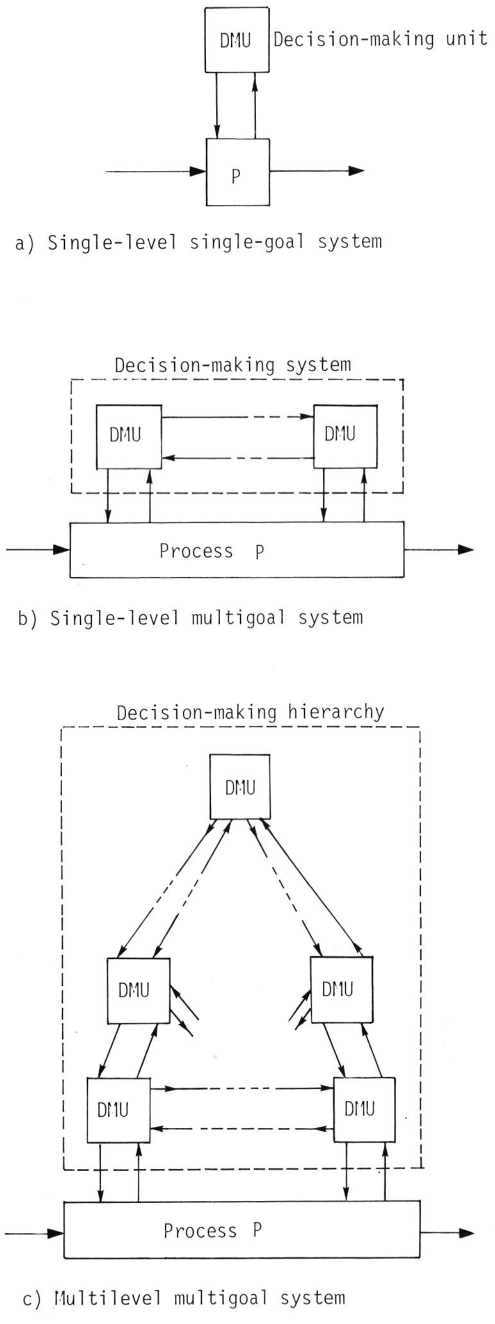

Fig.1 - A classification of decision-making systems.

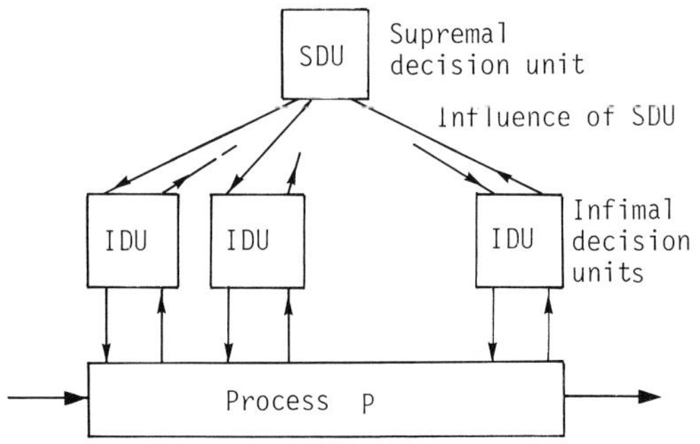

Fig.2 - A two-level organizational hierarchy

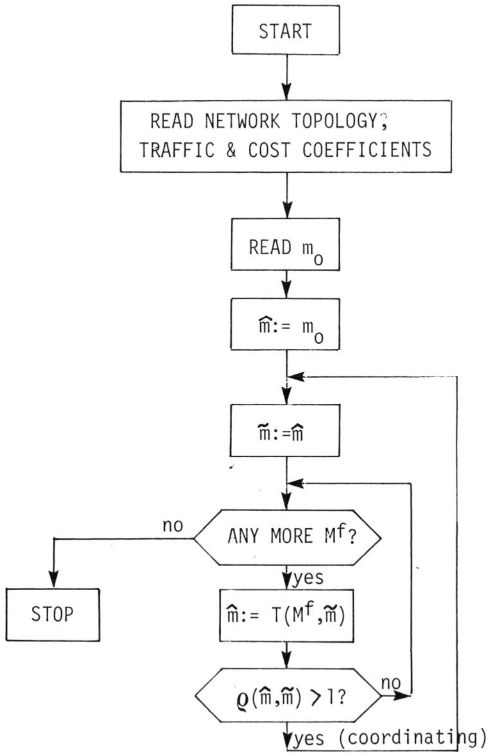

Fig.3 - Flow chart of the 'on-line improvement' procedure.

minimum, the corresponding allocation always differs from the optimal one by no more than one index.

3. Achievement of the optimal allocation depends on both the initial reference vector and the choice of M^f.
4. We found that the strategy which more often leads to the optimal allocation, is that which adds or deletes just one file per interaction step. Starting with all m_i's equal to 1 (that is, with a file copy at each node) and allowing this strategy, the procedure leads to 4 optimal allocations out of the 5 cases, whereas by adding or deleting as many allocations as possible, the procedure finds only one optimal allocation out of 5 cases.
5. For the experiments done, the procedure gave better solutions when the initial reference vector required more deletions than additions of files. In fact, starting with all m_i's equal to zero and allowing only one change per cycle, the procedure gave only 1 optimal allocation out of 5.

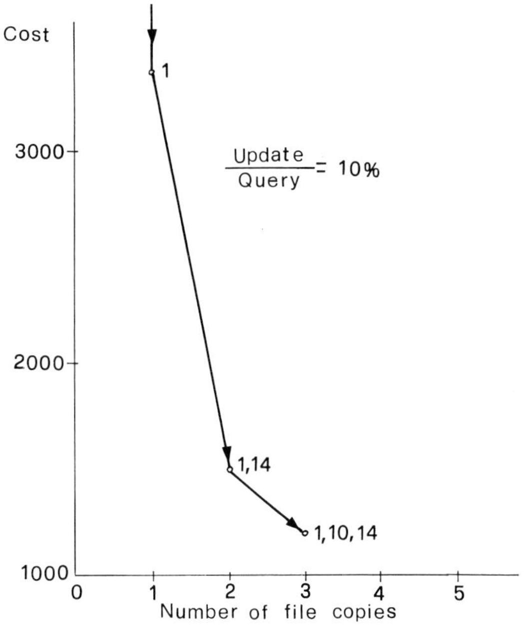

Fig.5

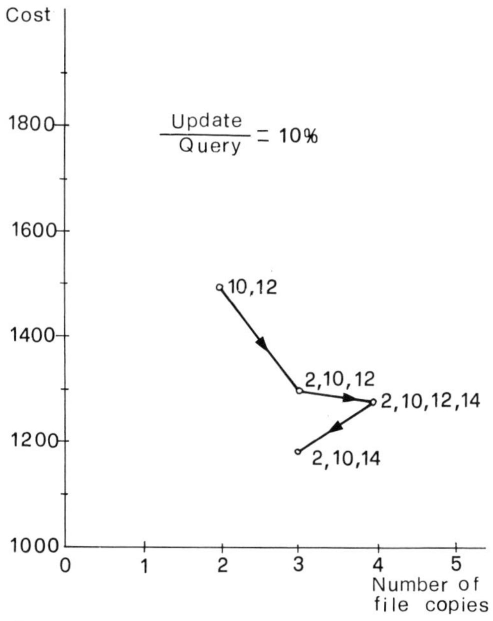

Fig.4

Fig. 4 shows the path followed by the procedure for the case Update/Query=.1, starting from the initial allocation 10, 12, and ending with the optimal allocation 2,10,14, which gives rise to a cost of .1176 10^6.
Fig. 5 shows the path followed starting from the initial allocation with all m_i's zero. In this case the final allocation 1, 10, 14 is not the optimal one as it costs .1203 10^6.

Compared with Casey's algorithm, ours does not perform a check for all possible paths to the optimal solution. Fig. 5 shows that this property may be a drawback, since it is possible to follow a path leading to a local minimum. On the other hand, when the network has a large number of nodes, which prohibits carrying out exhaustive testing, this property is very important as it allows us to find a (local) minimum in a very short number of tries.
Finally, let us say that the program of fig. 3 can be easily modified to encompass any change in the operating conditions of the information network.

CONCLUSIONS

We have presented a new approach to the problem of the resource management task in a (distributed) computer system. This approach has been applied to the well-known file allocation problem.
A computer program based on this approach showed its applicability and brought out some advantages with respect to previous known methods.
What we have reported here are the first results of our on-going experiments.

Further research is, however, needed to treat other, more complex problems not yet dealt with.

REFERENCES

[1] Chen, T.C., "Distributed Intelligence for User-Oriented Computing", Proc. FJCC, 1972, p. 1049-1056.

[2] Abramson, N., Kuo, F., "Computer Communication Networks", Prentice Hall, 1973.

[3] Streeter, D.N., "Centralization or Dispersion of Computing Facilities", IBM Sys. J., n.3, 1973, p.283-301.

[4] Kochen, M., Deustch, K.W., "Decentralization by Function and Location", Management Sc., v.19, n.8, 1973, p. 841-856.

[5] Chu, W.W., "Optimal File Allocation in Multi-Computer information Systems", IEEE Trans. on Comp., v.C-18, 1969, p.885-889.

[6] Casey, R.G., "Allocation of Copies of a File in Information Networks", Proc.SJCC, 1972, p.617-625.

[7] Feldman, E., Leher, F.A., Ray, T.L., "Warehouse Location under Continous Economies of Scale", Management Sc., v.12, n.9, 1966, p.670-684.

[8] Belokrinitskaya, L.B., Spivakoskii, S.I., Trakhtengerts, E.A., "Distribution of Functions between Central Processors and Peripheral Computers", Automatika i Telemekanika, n.1, 1972 p.161-170.

[9] Chang, S.K., "Data Base Decomposition in a Hierarchical Computer System", IBM Res. Rep., RC 5345, 1975.

[10] Levin, K.D., Morgan, H.L., "Dynamic Model for Distributed Data-Bases", Wharton School, Univ. of Pennsylvania, 1974.

[11] Levin, K.D., Morgan, H.L., "Optimizing Distributed Data Bases-A Framework for Research", Proc. NCC, 1975, p.473-478.

[12] Mesarovich, M.D., Macko, D, Takahara, Y., "Theory of Multilevel Systems", Academic Press, 1970.

[13] Bucci, G., Golinelli, S., "A New Approach to Resource Management in Distributed Computer Systems", in printing.

E. Morlet and D. Ribbens, (Eds.), International Computing Symposium 1977.

THE RELATIVE MERITS OF DISTRIBUTED COMPUTING SYSTEMS

F.E. Taylor,B.Sc.,M.Sc.,Ph.D.
Senior Consultant

The National Computing Centre Limited

MANCHESTER
U.K.

Distributed computing systems have a number of advantages and disadvantages when they are contrasted with centralised systems. The distributed systems philosophy is a flexible philosophy, as yet relatively undeveloped. This paper begins by defining the philosophy in its narrower sense, and then contrasts the distributed computing philosophy with the alternative centralised systems philosophy. It goes on to explore some of the advantages which can be expected from the use of distributed computing techniques, and the relative cost of various degrees of distribution. A later Section investigates the relationship further and outlines the total cost of a distributed system with that of a non-distributed system, as a function of the degree of distribution and performance/cost ratio of distributed system components. Finally, possibly future trends and directions are examined and some problem areas highlighted.

1. A DEFINITION OF "DISTRIBUTED COMPUTING"

Distributed systems, as the very phrase implies, involve the processing or storage of information within two or more system components. This implies either concurrent processing and/ or storage of information, or its handling using on-line links so that the various system components can communicate with each other - under normal circumstances via some form of on-line communications link. (It should perhaps be pointed out that under abnormal circumstances some distributed systems fall-back or resort to off-line communications links).

Until recently, computing systems subdivided into the relatively large and expensive mainframe systems, and the somewhat low-powered small computer systems - initially developed for dedicated applications such as process control. Differing architectures for the two types of system meant that problems were encountered when links were considered, and only a small number of interlinked systems appeared which interconnected the small real-time computers of the 1960's, to the much larger contemporary dp and scientific mainframes.However, a revolution has occurred during recent years.

The new philosophy has only become feasible in the last year or two, through the emergence of low cost but relatively powerful - small computers, based on developments in design and construction which enable new equipment to pack many more discrete computing circuits into a smaller space than hitherto, at a low unit cost per element.

As a result of the wide range of devices and equipment, and the ingenuity of suppliers and users, distributed systems have appeared in several forms. At one extreme, the traditional centralised single processor or on-line system mentioned above involves transporting all user tasks to and from non-intelligent terminals, or terminals with intelligence restricted to communication functions. At the other end of the spectrum, wholly distributed systems consist of a number of interlinked terminals and associated 'intelligence' (matched to user needs), sited at or near to the point of user activity, but without a mainframe processor. Between these two extremes, a wide range of systems involve the partial distribution of processing power/data storage. These subdivide into several types depending on the balance between the remote units accessible to users and the central system (Fig.1). Many current systems are concerned with the distribution of <u>processing power</u>, CHANDLER/1/, although systems are being increasingly used for the <u>physical</u> distribution of data stored at or near the user environment, especially in multi-tier systems involving three or more conceptual levels. In many commercial environments, partially distributed systems appear to offer the best cost/ performance ratios.

The majority of distributed systems involve on-line data communication between the elements; however one noteworthy distributed system operating within the UK by the distribution department of a large food manufacturer successfully uses off-line cassette-based communication between the distributed visible record computers and a third generation mainframe.

The design of the communications network is largely governed by the functions of the system components - BLOCH/2/ has examined a number of possibilities, and concludes that a partially-interconnected solution is desirable in most instances. The more complex

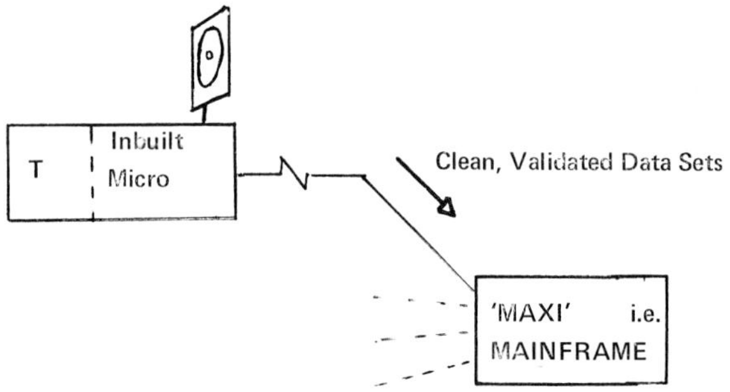

1 INTELLIGENT TERMINAL SYSTEMS

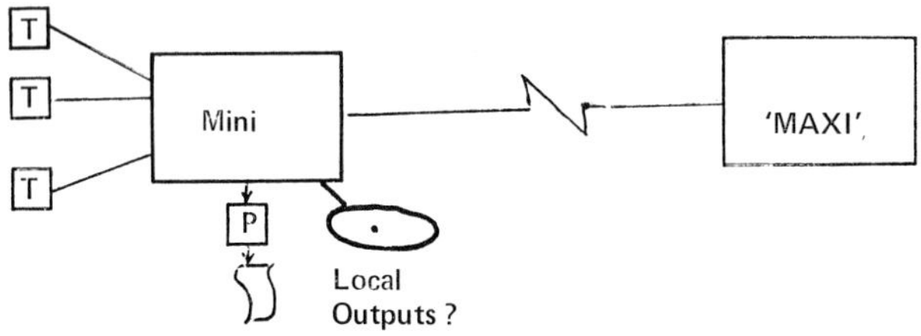

2. 'MINI/MAXI'

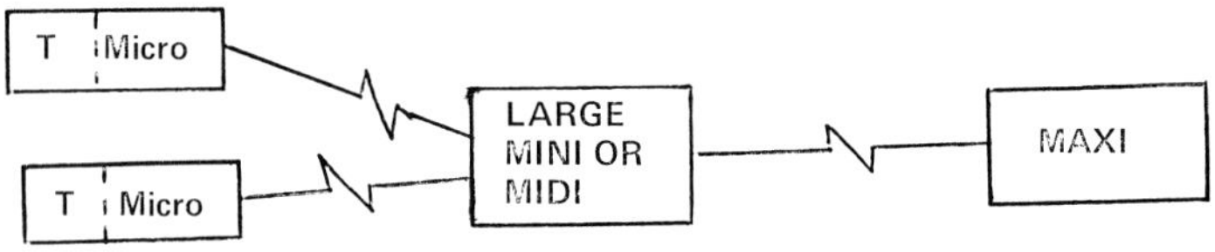

3. MULTI–TIER – COMBINATION OF 1 and 2

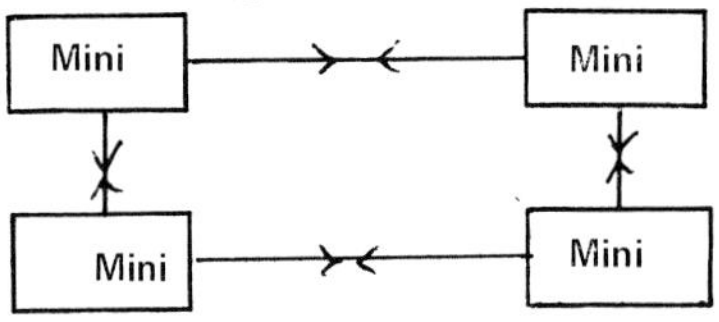

4. MULTI–MINI

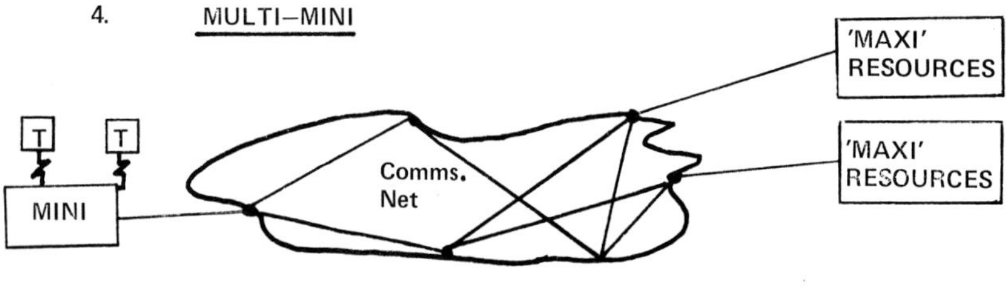

5. MINI SYSTEM WITH GATEWAY TO MULTIPLE 'MAXI' RESOURCES – EXTENSION OF 2.

FIG.1 SOME CLASSES OF DISTRIBUTED SYSTEMS.

possibilities are considered in depth by DAVIES and BARBER/3/.

The general term 'distributed systems' /4/ includes the following configurations:-

.1 Intelligent terminal systems

These are basically centralised systems, supported by the processing power of intelligent terminals, used for such tasks as data editing and some validation. This reduces the load on the central computer and the data transmission facilities, and, on occasion, provides better response for the user. (The intelligence of the terminal can also enable varying emulators and/or more efficient data transmission procedures to be used, although this is a communications function - FUJORAS/5/.)

With some backing store (e.g.cassette or disc), the terminal can also be used for other functions. For example, in the event of central computer or line failure, data can still be entered and held in the backing store for later transmission. It may also be possible to hold a stripped down version of a main file to provide more thorough data validation or limited local enquiry facilities, although systems capable of such processing fall within the next two classes.

.2 Mini-maxi systems

In these systems one or more small computers at the point(s) of action are linked to a maxi mainframe which handles all non-trivial tasks. In one example, a series of minis with their own files are dedicated to a particular local application (e.g. on-line order entry and stock control at a warehouse); master files are held at the central location with relevant 'slave' copies kept at the local sites. The mini deals with the local transactions, passing summarised information to and from the central computer, which aggregates the information received. On occasion, the mini-maxi relationship can usefully extend over more than one level to form a hierarchy; such as microprocessors acting as factory control or data collection devices, or as a user-system interface, linked to a large mini or "midi" computer (the smallest size of fully supported mainframe sold by the traditional suppliers). This leads to the next class.

.3 Multi-tier systems

Multi-tier systems fall effectively within the types already described, but involve more than two basic types of system elements. Many potentially feasible distributed systems which concentrate computing power in several medium to large processors (perhaps on a regional basis) fall within this category.

.4 Multiple Mini Systems

Multiple mini systems perform some jobs at the point of action and pass others to other locations on a load-sharing, overload, or 'centre of competence' basis - i.e. in the latter two instances only in exceptional circumstances.

.5 Resource Sharing Systems

When large computers share resources for standby, overload-sharing or other irregular use, they come under the heading of resource sharing systems. However, when tasks are regularly passed to a 'centre of competence' they become networking systems.

Distributed processor systems involving several interlinked computing components at one location are not, strictly speaking, within the writer's use of the term 'distributed systems'. Such distributed processors, are however a subset of distributed systems - normally involving high speed local communication links, rather than the slower speed remote links which link the more familiar geographically distributed systems considered in this paper.

In summary, the following is one definition of such distributed systems:-

"Distributed processing is a new system design philosophy which involves the processing and/or storage of data by means of two or more similar types of system component within the same system, interconnected via on-line communications links." (See also DOWN/6/)

It is necessary to say that there need to be two or more similar system components - since the connection of one processor to one store would be nothing more than a conventional processing system!

2 DISTRIBUTED SYSTEMS CONTRASTED WITH RESOURCE SHARING NETWORKS

In this section a distinction will be drawn between networking and distributed networks and distributed systems.

In a network a number of computers (generally large machines) are interconnected by data communications links to provide powerful and flexible shared processing and storage, with any terminal (user) able to access authorised facilities at any centre. Although developed mainly for academic and research applications, a few large organisations are now implementing such networks.

One of the best known examples is the ARPA network, originally developed for the coordination of defence projects in the USA. At the time of writing it links more than 50 host computers to several hundred terminal users, using a packet-switched network with alternative routing facilities.

Individual computers in such a network may have special facilities (e.g. a unique database, a particular operating system, application software, or special peripherals) making them suitable for certain types of work. Users can thus have access to a range of facilities which could not otherwise be economically provided by a single computer centre. If one machine is overloaded or goes out of operation work may be transferred to others in the network - literally "resource sharing". For commercial dp, the scope for this type of resource sharing and work transfer is limited - one reason being that the large files particular to one system may not be easily transferable to another location.

One example presently being implemented is a large network for the British Steel Corporation, which will transport particular types of tasks such as scientific calculations, program testing, etc. to an appropriate, specialised resource.

In summary, networking systems are concerned with the efficient transportation of user tasks to the most suitable resource within a number of interlinked, large scale processing resources, in other words taking the user tasks to a large resource. Whilst a small number of jobs may be processed at the point of activity (especially where a host or larger computer is located), the bulk of the work is likely to be transported to other sites.

In contrast, distributed systems are concerned with processing work at the point of user activity, using capabilities specifically devoted to those tasks and able to perform them economically and efficiently, in other words taking the processing resource to the task. Transfer of relatively simple work to other centres is the exception rather than the rule; normally only the more complex or sophisticated jobs are transmitted to a remote point for processing.

3 THE RELATIVE MERITS OF DISTRIBUTED COMPUTING SYSTEMS

3.1 Systems Efficiency

The d.c. philosophy theory has evolved from and is wholly dependent on very powerful minicomputers, microcomputers and intelligent terminals based on microcomputers which have become available in the last two or three years. Continuing the advance of the technology combined with growing market volumes, has led to a steady and significant reduction in the price of such components. The development of a wide range of cost/effective system components - has allowed discrete modular sub-systems to be closely matched to user requirements at a particular location, and to be dedicated to processing a small number of tasks. This avoids the overheads associated with centralised systems, and the dedication of small computers (minicomputers or microcomputers) to processing particular tasks results in higher machine efficiency in terms of cost per unit of work done than that associated with a multi-programming, multi-tasking central processing resource. This results from the lowered number of context changes, leading to better utilisation of the distributed processing resources than centralised resources - shown schematically in Fig.2.

One UK system achieves a high efficiency within its system components by allocating tasks to appropriate components. Data validation is carried out by intelligent terminals; whilst routine dp is carried out by a series of small dp mainframes, linked in turn to one large mainframe which processes overload, complex technical and centralised administrative tasks. (See Case History 4 of Appendix 2 of /6/.)

Expanding these comments a little, the development of complex general purpose operating systems for multiprogramming and multi-tasking, capable of handling different types of workloads within large and expensive processing units, has resulted in a significant amount of the "raw" processing power being used

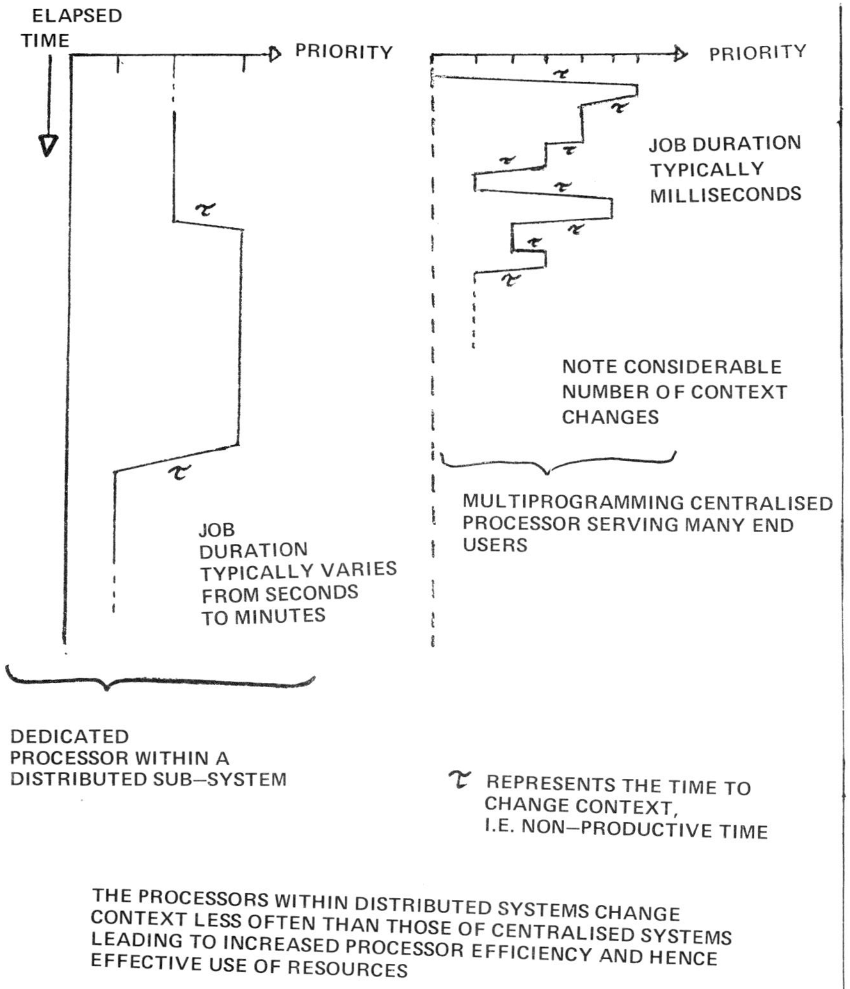

FIG.2 TYPICAL ACTIVITY/TIME PLOTS FOR PROCESSORS WITHIN ALTERNATIVE CENTRALISED AND DISTRIBUTED CONFIGURATIONS

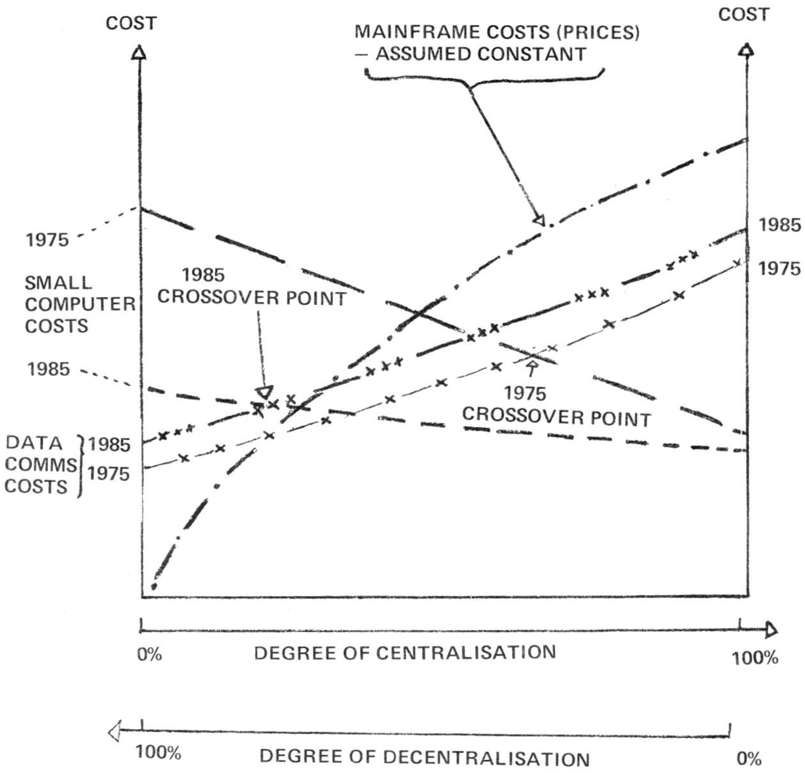

FIG. 3 FUTURE TRENDS : A QUALITATIVE REPRESENTATION OF THE INFLUENCE OF PROBABLE COST–TRENDS ON SYSTEM DESIGN PHILOSOPHY

for operating systems overheads rather than for user task processing. In the extreme, when such an operating system is overloaded in an on-line situation, a state can be reached in which all the machine power is devoted to housekeeping and none to user-task processing - a phenomenon known as "thrashing"!

3.2 Reliability

Distributed systems can be designed to have greater availability than centralised systems at lower cost. The use of several subsystems for processing can provide a considerable amount of 'fail-soft' capability or 'graceful degradation'

Indeed, duplication of critical subsystems at any particular location can give an availability closely approaching 100%. This arises as a consequence of the very high reliability of today's small computing systems - many running for several thousands of hours between system failures. To cover occasional failure, in non-duplicated systems, standby offline communications links or alternatively additional communications equipment can be incorporated to provide a "fall-back" facility.

A large wholesale food distribution company in the UK use a distributed system based on some ten identical configurations within their warehouses. In the event of any one failing, data is taken to the nearest operable system by car, for entry into the system at an alternative location.

The data communications links to a remote facility are much less critical within a distributed system than within a centralised system, since local users can still process a number of tasks within the capability of their equipment.Indeed the dependence upon communications links decreases as the degree of distribution increases.

3.3 Security Against Deliberate Threats

The distribution of intelligence can increase the apparent vulnerability of a system to deliberate attempts to breach security, e.g. to expose, modify,destroy or delay information in an unauthorised manner. /7/.

Further, the dispersed intelligent devices can theoretically be programmed to penetrate the system security built into other system components, e.g. by 'trying' passwords which are systematically cycled until access is obtained.

However, careful attention to system design can considerably reduce these risks. The following points are important:

.1 The location of information - the distribution of information, i.e. its handling within local files, access to which can be restricted to local users, greatly reduces the risk associated with centralised systems, where access by a large number of remote users must be carefully controlled, and the unauthorised 'masquerading' of one user as another may be difficult to detect.

.2 Access control - the use of the established techniques such as multiple passwords, cycled or changed frequently, in association with badge readers can be programmed into intelligent devices as an initial task - indeed the presence of the intelligence can allow more comprehensive controls to be used than when non-intelligent terminals are used as out stations.

One such control, or rather countermeasure, is encryption/decryption of communicated and/or filed data. These processes can be carried out by the 'intelligence' within a distributed subsystem.

.3 Threat Monitoring - routines following established procedures for checking the number of attempts to access and cut off attempts after a certain number of tries, and similarly monitor attempts to access unauthorised files, can be operated locally, and in the event of a threat, an alarm raised either locally or remotely.

The planned use of intelligence and storage within user environment can therefore reduce the security risks associated with distributed systems, in comparison with the risks associated with corresponding alternative centralised systems.

3.4 System Costs

Examination of the basic costs elements involved in implementing any processing system are those of hardware; communications - if on-line techniques are involved; software and systems implementation; and systems management.

This section will consider the effect of distribution on these cost elements.

If one considers hardware first, one finds that the cost of the hardware element within distributed processing systems is likely to be lower than the cost of an alternative centralised mainframe. This is a consequence of two factors - the first being the advantages accruing from processor dedication, already outlined; and the much higher performance/cost ratios of mini and micro computers, accruing from their advanced state of development, in comparison with mainframe processors.

The first factor which amends this argument relates to system utilisation in terms of The ratio of time devoted to user tasks, to total time - already discussed in Section 3.1. The efficiency of a collection of dedicated minicomputers relative to a 'maxi' or large mainframe may well be 95%:30%. Next, let us assume that Grosch's well-known "law" is true. This states that 'performance is proportional to the square of the cost'. Thus, if one doubles the expenditure on a processor, one should get four times the computing power. Within a given size and type of processor this is roughly true, and this "law" leads to an economic argument for centralising computing power. However, differences in application and relative performance within processor types radically modifies this statement.

Grosch's law states the following:

$$P = K \cdot c^2 \quad \ldots\ldots \text{E1}$$

This can be alternatively stated as

$$c = K'\sqrt{P}, \text{ where } K' = \frac{1}{\sqrt{K}} \quad \ldots\ldots \text{E2}$$

Then, to acquire a user capability P_u one finds that :

For one 'maxi' computer, the power acquired is P_{mx}

which is :- $P_u \times \frac{100}{30}$ or $3.33\,P_u$

$$C_{mx} \text{ will thus be } K'\sqrt{3.33\,P_u} \quad \ldots \text{E3}$$

If one now considers an alternative acquisition of three minicomputers, each with a power equal to one third of the total required (P_u /0.95) then one finds for one minicomputer -

$$C_{mn} = K'\sqrt{P_u/0.95 \times 3} \quad \ldots\ldots \text{E4}$$

and for three minicomputers

$$3.C_{mn} = 3.K'\sqrt{P_u/0.95 \times 3} \quad \ldots\ldots \text{E5}$$
$$= \sqrt{3}\,.\,K'\sqrt{P_u/0.95}$$

The relative cost of the configurations will thus be :

$$\frac{\text{Minicomputer}}{\text{Mainframe Configuration}} = \frac{(E5)}{(E3)}$$

$$= \sqrt{3}\,.\,K'\sqrt{\frac{P_u}{0.95}} \times \frac{1}{K'\sqrt{3.33\,P_u}}$$

$$= \frac{\sqrt{3}}{\sqrt{3.33 \times 0.95}}$$

$$= 0.974$$

The second factor which modifies this argument still further is the fact that development of minicomputers in terms of performance/cost ratio is well ahead of that of large mainframes. To quote an example, a contemporary large minicomputer (costing approximately £1000 per month) benchmarked by a leading UK organisation was recently shown to have equivalent power to a large 1960's medium-large mainframe, which would still cost £10K per month to rent. These figures are regarded as conservative - i.e. a performance/cost ratio 10:1 in favour of minicomputer systems.

Grosch's law for minicomputers will thus modify to -

$$P = 10\,K\,c^2 \quad \ldots\ldots \text{E1 - modified}$$

$$c = \frac{K'}{\sqrt{10}} \cdot \sqrt{P} \quad \ldots\ldots \text{E2 - modified}$$

When this factor is applied to the figures presented above, one finds that -

$$\frac{C_{mini}}{C_{maxi}} = \frac{0.974}{\sqrt{10}} = 0.308$$

illustrating that, in such situations, minicomputer configurations have indeed got a significant cost/advantage. The likely future increase in minicomputer performance/cost ratios, in combination with a likely rise in communication costs, both favour an increasing distribution of intelligence, as shown qualitatively in Fig. 3.

The cost of communications facilities within distributed processing systems are always less than those of the alternative centralised systems, since some data is by definition always processed locally. At the lowest level, validation of datasets reduces communications traffic, since bad datasets need not be transferred to and from a remote location for validation and subsequent reporting back. The magnitude of the economic benefits accruing from the local processing of data depend upon the elimination of the need for data communication links; although some links are s still essential for transmitting control information.

Some of the advantages associated with the implementation of systems and software, for distributed systems, result from the use of a number of very similar modules, when these are replicated on identical or similar mini or micro computers. In such cases the costs of preparing similar application systems for several sites are greatly reduced. Further, the use of a number of less complex system software implementations than with one multitask ng multiprogramming centralised machine yields other cost savings in many instances, and shortens the lead time for system implementation. In the majority of distributed systems, system implementation is comparatively straightforward since subsystems may be easily isolated for commissioning, and testing.

Systems management costs vary according to both the degree of distribution and corresponding simplification of the implemented systems compared with a non-distributed system. Costs also vary according to the distribution or centralisation of systems and programming, and the diagnosis and handling of faults - a topic mentioned in the next section.

3.5 Flexibility

The distributed approach offers several advantages during the implementation phase. First of all, distributed systems can be developed on a progressive basis, e.g. particular components can be added to a system as they are required. In some cases, existing system components such as existing third generation mainframes can be incorporated into the system and the shortcomings of such components can be complemented. For example, a large UK construction company has added regional minicomputers to a third generation mainframe. These have been configured to act as data entry and data validation sub-systems, for use by that company's work measurement staff. As a consequence, clean datasets are received by the mainframe for processing, with a consequential benefit in terms of faster invoicing, and corresponding faster cash in-flow.

Further, powerful minicomputers with on-line resources can be used to complement the absence of such features within a third generation mainframe.

Secondly, as systems are essentially modular, component parts carefully chosen and closely matched to particular needs can be installed to meet immediate requirements and often enhanced to match changing user needs.

Thirdly, systems can be reconfigured and systems components resited or even replaced and sold in a bouyant second-hand market. Also the philosophy can keep pace with changing information processing requirements. For example, distributed approach allows speedy reconfiguration, since each system consists of a number of interlinked, essentially modular subsystems, which can be replaced, enhanced or even removed, without substantially disturbing the rest of the system. Furthermore, general purpose components which need no longer fulfil their earlier role, can be used elsewhere by modifying the associated software.

The fourth major advantage results from the second and third - the risk of obsolescence associated with many highly expensive centralised systems is therefore greatly reduced, and in most cases removed entirely, since the system can keep pace with changing requirements, can be implemented progressively, and therefore the risk associated with any particular subsystem can be greatly reduced, and obsolescent or superseded components can be replaced and in some cases sold in the marketplace.

4 FUTURE DEVELOPMENT OF THE PHILOSOPHY

Many companies have already applied the philosophy of distributed systems most successfully. However, constraints are applied by the available technology, and research into certain problem areas and subsequent developments will make the philosophy both more effective and economic, and should accelerate its rate of application. For example, the increasing requirements for interconnection of system components generate a need for standards such as standardised operating dialogues for handling data communications, databases, and the control and progression of the various jobs within the system.

The future of the philosophy, as yet relatively undeveloped, depends very much upon the development of standards for the interlinking and interconnection of the similar and dissimilar components which are a fundamental part of any distributed system; as much as development in any one area such as hardware or portable software. In other words, the sucoess of distributed computing depends upon the interconnection, interworking and interchangeability of components. To give an example, many distributed systems necessarily use data communications protocols originally developed for linking non-intelligent terminals to large centralised mainframes. This currently has the advantage that it does not involve any changes to the teleprocessing software within the interconnected processors, but it has the distinct advantage of a low net rate of user data transfer. There is a clear need for agreed, standard, efficient, high-level communication protocols FUJORAS/5/;BSI/11/matched to the requirements of distributed systems.

Complementary standares are clearly required for entities such as hardware interfaces TAYLOR/8/;IEEE/9/ (which will widen the choice of components and source of supply of peripherals) and for portable software which can be run on widely differing processors. Some standards already exist in ebryo form, such as the various sets of ANSI standard COBOL, but they are not widely available for all minicomputers, and there is a need to propagate some existing standards which are not yet in widespread use.

Interest has been expressed in distributed Data Base Management Systems which will allow one logical data base to be physically and geographically distributed across a range of processing and storage systems. PARRY/10/. Distribution of such systems, which conceptually involve the routing of all accesses to one data record, to one unique record necessarily involve complex communication problems, and indexing and transaction recording problems. One well known authority believes that there are considerable problems associated with centralised data bases, and it will take time before distributed data bases become practicable. When software implementations appear, standards will again be all important, and means for auditing and certification of implementations which should interconnect will be extremely important.

This paper has examined the merits of distributed systems relative to centralised non-distributed systems. Whilst each particular information processing system must be considered individually, and the relevance of this philosophy determined, it is believed that the philosophy appears to offer considerable advantages for many organisations. Indeed, in many cases involving the use of on-line techniques, it can offer greater flexibility and greater cost-effectiveness than any other form of information processing.

BIBLIOGRAPHY

(1) CHANDLER, A.; 'The Exploitation of Computer Power by the User', Computer-Aided Design Centre (UK) Report - December 1974.

(2) BLOCH, C.; 'The Impact of Distributed Processing or Communication Systems', Minicomputers and Small Business Systems - proceeding of Minicomputer Forum 1976 - published by ONLINE Ltd., U.K., Nov.1976.

(3) DAVIES, D. and BARBER, D.;'Communications Network for Computers' - published by John Wiley, 1974

(4) 'In Your Future' - Distributed Systems' - EDP Analyser, August 1973

(5) FUJORAS, R.; Canadian Communications Research Centre Reports, as follows:

'Data Terminal Standards and Protocols' - Report 1275, April 1975

'Data Terminal Technology Present and Future'; Volumes 1 and 2 - April 1975

(6) DOWN, P.J., and TAYLOR, F.E., 'Why Distributed Computing' - NCC Publication - November 1976

(7) 'Where Next for Computer Security?' - NCC, UK - December 1974

(8) TAYLOR, F.E.; 'Towards Standard Interfaces for Minicomputers' - Minicomputers and Small Business Systems - proceedings of Minicomputer Forum 1976 - published by ONLINE Ltd. UK - November 1976

(9) 'The IEEE Standard Interface for Programmable Digital Instrumentation' - IEEE Standard 488-1975 - published by the IEEE (USA)

(10) PARRY, D.; 'Distributed Data Base Management Systems', Proceedings of ONLINE Conference on DBMS's - April 1976

(11) 'UK Proposal for a Structure for a Standard High Level Protocol' - Paper N1350 of ISO Committee TC97 SC6 - submitted December 1976

E. Morlet and D. Ribbens, (Eds.), International Computing Symposium 1977.

BALANCED INTERNAL MERGE SORTING

Eero Peltola
Academy of Finland
Helsinki, Finland

Hannu Erkiö
Department of Computer Science
University of Helsinki
Helsinki, Finland

A new algorithm for 2nd order (2-way) straight merge sorting is presented. This algorithm is called balanced, because it merges sequences whose lengths are equal or differ by unity. The algorithm can be generalized to higher order merge sorting. The balanced 2nd order and 3rd order merge sort algorithms as well as the corresponding standard (unbalanced) straight merge sort algorithms are analyzed theoretically and experimentally in their worst and best cases. The analysis shows only slight differences in the sort times of balanced and unbalanced algorithms of the same order, although the balanced algorithms usually require fewer key comparisons, especially in the worst cases. As expected, the 3rd order merge algorithms are faster than the 2nd order ones, but are somewhat longer.

1. INTRODUCTION

A new algorithm for straight internal merge sorting is given in this paper. This algorithm is called balanced, because it merges sequences whose lengths are equal or differ by unity. Although only 2nd order (often called "2-way") merge sorting is described in detail, the generalization of the principle to merge sorting of higher order is straightforward. In section 2 we discuss the characteristics of the method and in section 3 we give the algorithm itself. In later sections we analyze the number of key comparisons needed by the method and give some experimental results concerning the sort times of the algorithm. In the theoretical and experimental analyses the method is compared with standard unbalanced merge sorting.

2. STRAIGHT INTERNAL MERGE SORTING

Internal merge sorting consists of combining repeatedly two or more ordered sequences of records into a single ordered sequence. If we know nothing about the original order of the records to be sorted, we must start with trivial "ordered sequences" of just one record each. Along with the merge process the sequences are lengthened and their number is decreased until all the records are in one sequence in the desired (ascending or descending) order.

For simplicity, we assume that the records to be sorted consist only of integer keys that are stored in a vector A[1:n], where n is the number of the records. Furthermore, we consider merge sorting in the simple form which uses an extra working area of equal size, say B[1:n]. The merge sort is said to be of order r, if normally r sequences are interleaved in every individual merge. We examine only straight merge sorting where the length of a merged sequence is totally determined by n and r, as opposed to so-called natural merge sorting where the length of each merged sequence depends on the number of consecutive records originally in the correct order.

In a straight merge sort n and r also determine the number of passes: $p = \log_r n$ consecutive merge passes are needed to sort n records by an rth order merge sort. For example, three passes are needed to sort 8 records by the well-known 2nd order straight merge sort. The merge process can be described by a merge tree as in Figure 1, where the integer in each node represents the length of the sequence after a merge or initially.

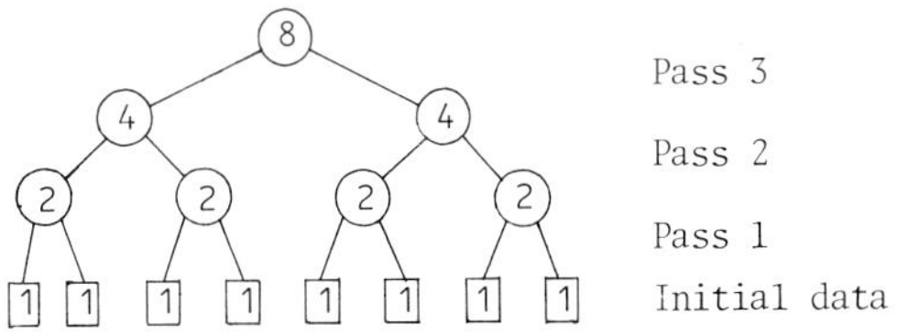

FIGURE 1: A Merge Tree Describing the 2nd Order Straight Merge of 8 Records (the integers in the nodes represent the length of the sequence after a merge or initially)

The algorithms usually given for 2nd order straight merge sorting (e.g. Knuth [1]) handle sequences in which there are exactly 2^{i-1} records in each sequence in pass i, except the last sequence whose length may vary from 1 to 2^{i-1} records depending on the value of n. Figure 1 represents a special case where the lengths of all sequences in each pass are strictly equal. A more general merge tree is given in Figure 2 for n = 13. Intuitively the merge process described by the merge tree of Figure 2 can be considered in some sense "unbalanced" with respect to the lengths of the sequences in one merge pass. In fact, Woodrum [2] states that the maximum number of key comparisons in the 2nd order straight merge sort is minimized when the subsequences are always of lengths $\lfloor n/2 \rfloor$ and

$\lceil n/2 \rceil$. The merge tree describing this balanced merge process is given in Figure 3 for n = 13.

Unbalanced and balanced merge sorts of higher order are also easily described by merge trees. Figures 4 and 5 represent unbalanced and balanced 3rd order merge sorts, respectively, when n = 13.

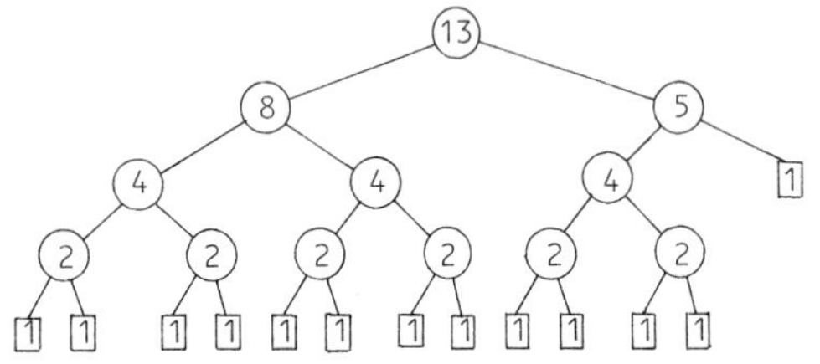

FIGURE 2: A Merge Tree Describing Unbalanced 2nd Order Merge When n = 13

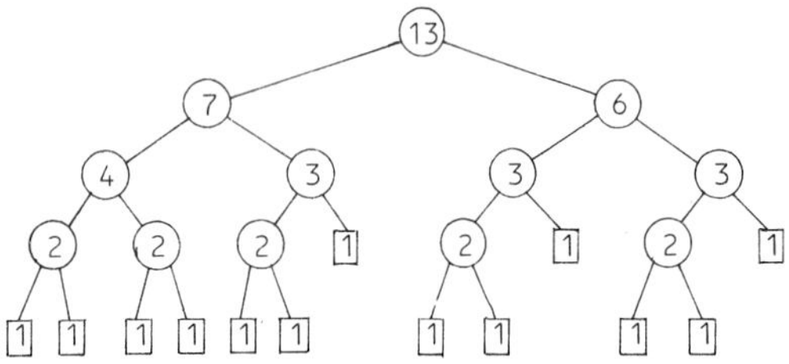

FIGURE 3: A Merge Tree Describing Balanced 2nd Order Merge When n = 13

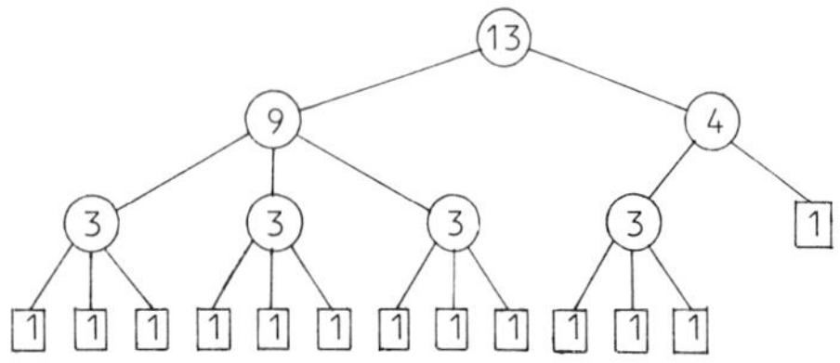

FIGURE 4: A Merge Tree Describing Unbalanced 3rd Order Merge When n = 13

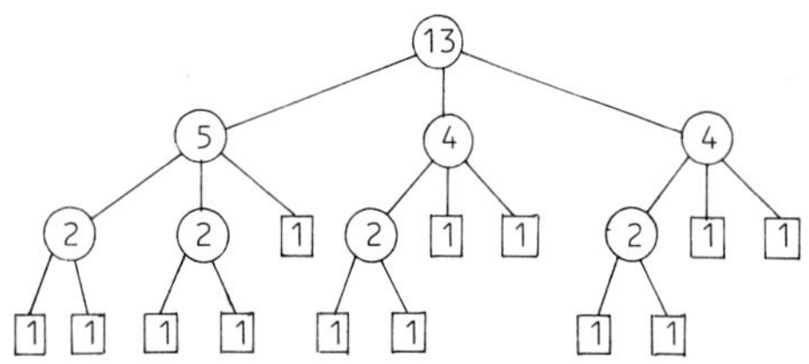

FIGURE 5: A Merge Tree Describing Balanced 3rd Order Merge When n = 13

We find that with certain values of n an unbalanced 3rd order merge actually degenerates to a 2nd order merge even in the last pass. A balanced 3rd order merge sort, on the other hand, is always genuinely of order 3, except in the first pass, which consists of merging pairs of records when $3^k < n < 2 \cdot 3^k$ and pairs and/or triplets of records when $2 \cdot 3^k \leq n \leq 3^{k+1}$.

Woodrum [2] presents both a recursive and a non-recursive merge sort algorithm in APL. The latter algorithm is actually an implementation of the recursive one with explicit recursion stacks. It is, however, possible to write an algorithm for balanced straight merge sorting without any recursion bookkeeping. Such an algorithm is given in the next section for the 2nd order case. The algorithm can be easily generalized to higher order merge sorting.

3. BALANCED 2ND ORDER MERGE SORT ALGORITHM

There are no great differences between the straight merge sort algorithms presented in the literature so far. In 2nd order merge sorting the main variations concern the initialization of the sort and the location of the sequences to be merged. Instead of starting the sort with sequences of just one record the original records can be ordered into sequences of some given length (say, 4-10 records), e.g. by straight insertion, thus avoiding the relatively large overhead involved in merging several very short sequences.

The main characteristic of our balanced merge sort algorithm is the method used to select the locations of the sequences. The sequences merged in pass i are formed by records with index distance d_i. The values of d_i are determined so that

$$d_1 = 2^k \quad (2^k < n \leq 2^{k+1}) \quad \text{and} \quad d_{i+1} = d_i/2$$

for i = 1,2,...,k. The records A[1], A[2],..., A[n] then initially form d_1 sequences of 1 or 2 records each so that there are always at least one and at most d_1 sequences of length 2, namely

$(A[1], A[1+d_1])$,

$(A[2], A[2+d_1])$,

. . .

$(A[n-d_1], A[n])$,

the remaining records forming $0...(d_1-1)$ sequences of length 1. In the first pass we order the 2-element sequences by exchanges instead of merging them. The subsequent passes are true merge passes. In every pass the end of each sequence is very easily determined using n because of the arrangement of sequences. The following example describes the method.

Example

Initial data:

13 87 22 61 28 70 97 75 53 36 54 49 65

After pass 1:

13 36 22 49 28 70 97 75 53 87 54 61 65

After pass 2:

13 36 22 49 28 70 54 61 53 87 97 75 65

After pass 3:

13 36 22 49 28 61 53 70 54 75 65 87 97

After pass 4:

13 22 28 36 49 53 54 61 65 70 75 87 97

Our balanced 2nd order merge sort algorithm is given below as an (extended) Algol procedure. For generality the lower and upper bounds of the vectors A and B are given in the procedure as parameters ℓ and u. During one pass the records are transferred from the vector A[ℓ:u] to B[ℓ:u] or vice versa. Besides the principles described above, we have made one practical modification: the first pass is implemented so that the process always ends with the sorted records in the vector A.

```
procedure balancedmerge2(A,B,ℓ,u);
value ℓ,u; integer ℓ,u;
integer array A,B[*];
begin
    integer n,d,e,i,j,w;
    Boolean atob;
    procedure mergepass2(s,t,ds,dt);
    value ds,dt; integer ds,dt;
    integer array s,t[*];
    begin
        integer i,j,k,m,si,sj;
        label next;
        for k:=ℓ+dt-1 step -1 until ℓ do
        begin
            i:=m:=k; % m points to output area t
            j:=i+dt; % i,j point to input area s
            si:=s[i]; sj:=s[j];
      next: if si ≤ sj then
            begin
                t[m]:=si; m:=m+dt; i:=i+ds;
                if i ≤ u then
                begin
                    si:=s[i];
                    go to next
                end;
                i:=j; si:=sj;
                  % i-sequence is exhausted
            end else
            begin      % si > sj
                t[m]:=sj; m:=m+dt; j:=j+ds;
                if j ≤ u then
                begin
                    sj:=s[j];
                    go to next
                end
            end;
% remainder of last sequence is moved to
% output area
            t[m]:=si; i:=i+ds;
            while i ≤ u do
            begin
                m:=m+dt; t[m]:=s[i]; i:=i+ds
            end
        end for k
    end of mergepass2;
    %
    %  the body of balancedmerge2
    %
    n:=u-ℓ+1; atob:=false; i:=d:=1;
    for i:=i+i while i < n do
    begin
        d:=i;  atob:= ¬atob;
    end;
    % first pass: initial sequences are
    % ordered by exchanges
    if atob then
    begin  % records are exchanged and
           % moved to area B
        for i:=u-d step -1 until ℓ do
        if A[i] > A[i+d] then
        begin
            B[i]:=A[i+d]; B[i+d]:=A[i]
        end else
        begin
            B[i]:=A[i]; B[i+d]:=A[i+d]
        end;
        j:=ℓ+d-1;  % sequences of one element
                   % are moved
        for i:=u-d+1 step 1 until j do
            B[i]:=A[i];
        atob:=false
    end else
    begin  % atob=false: records are exchanged
           % in area A
        for i:=u-d step -1 until ℓ do
        if A[i] > A[i+d] then
        begin
            w:=A[i]; A[i]:=A[i+d]; A[i+d]:=w
        end;
        atob:=true
    end;
    % remaining merge passes
    while d ≥ 2 do
    begin
        e:=d÷2;
        if atob then mergepass2(A,B,d,e)
                else mergepass2(B,A,d,e);
        atob:= ¬atob;
        d:=e
    end while
end of balancedmerge2;
```

4. ANALYSIS OF STRAIGHT MERGE SORT ALGORITHMS

The number of record transfers in a straight r^{th} order merge sort of n records is approximately $n \cdot \log_r n$ and it does not depend on the initial order of the records. The number of key comparisons is not given so simply, because the initial order of the records is significant. In this section we analyze the numbers of key comparisons made by balanced and unbalanced merge sort algorithms. Both the best and worst cases are considered for 2nd order and 3rd order merge sorts. The worst case in a merge sort appears when in every merge the sequences being merged take part in the merge as long as possible, i.e. the sequences are exhausted almost at the same time. On the other hand, the best case is obtained when the sequences are exhausted as quickly as possible one at a time. Finally, higher order merge sorts are briefly discussed.

4.1. 2nd Order Straight Merge Sort

The number of key comparisons made by straight merge sort algorithms can be derived by utilizing merge trees. The number of key comparisons made by our balanced 2nd order merge sort algorithm in its worst case, $B_2^W(n)$, is found to be (cf. Knuth [1], Woodrum [2])

$$B_2^W(n) = \sum_{k=1}^{n} \lceil \log_2 k \rceil = n\lceil \log_2 n \rceil - 2^{\lceil \log_2 n \rceil} + 1$$

$$= ne_1 - 2^{e_1} + \sum_{i=1}^{t} 2^{e_i} + 1 \qquad (1)$$

where

$$n = \sum_{i=1}^{t} 2^{e_i} \text{ and } e_1 > e_2 > \dots > e_t \geq 0 \qquad (2)$$

Thus the algorithm makes as many comparisons as are made in binary insertion. The number of key comparisons made by our algorithm in its best case, $B_2^B(n)$, is given by the expression

$$B_2^B(n) = \sum_{i=1}^{t} 2^{e_i - 1} e_i + \sum_{i=1}^{t} 2^{e_i}(i-1) \qquad (3)$$

The number of key comparisons made by an unbalanced straight 2nd order merge sort algorithm is given in its worst case by (cf. Knuth [1])

$$U_2^W(n) = \sum_{i=1}^{t} 2^{e_i}(e_i+i-1) - 2^{e_t} + 1 \qquad (4)$$

and in its best case by

$$U_2^B(n) = \sum_{i=1}^{t} 2^{e_i - 1} e_i + \sum_{i=1}^{t} 2^{e_i}(i-1) \qquad (5)$$

The difference between the numbers of key comparison made by the unbalanced and balanced 2nd order merge sort algorithms in their worst cases is

$$U_2^W(n) - B_2^W(n) = 2^{e_1} - 2^{e_t} - \sum_{i=2}^{t} 2^{e_i}(e_1 - e_i + 2 - i) \qquad (6)$$

It is easily seen that this difference is greater than or equal to zero. Equality is obtained if and only if $n = 2^k - 2^j$ for some $k > j \geq 0$. Correspondingly the maximum difference

$$2^k - k - 1 = n - \log_2 n + 2$$

is obtained when $n = 2^k + 1$ for $k > 1$. Thus for these values of n the unbalanced algorithm makes almost n comparisons more than the balanced one. On the other hand in their best cases both the algorithms make the same number of key comparisons.

4.2. 3rd Order Straight Merge Sort

As stated earlier the number of key comparisons made by balanced and unbalanced 3rd order merge sorts can be determined by analyzing the corresponding merge trees. The situation is, however, more complicated than in 2nd order sorting because of variations in the order of individual merges in the unbalanced merge as shown in section 2. The number of key comparisons made by the balanced 3rd order merge sort algorithm in its worst case, $B_3^W(n)$, is

$$B_3^W(n) = \sum_{i=1}^{t} a_i 3^{e_i}(2e_1+a_1) - (2a_1+\tfrac{1}{2})3^{e_1} + \tfrac{3}{2} \qquad (7)$$

where

$$n = \sum_{i=1}^{t} a_i 3^{e_i}, \quad a_i = 1 \text{ or } 2 \ (i = 1,2,\dots,t)$$

$$\text{and } e_1 > e_2 > \dots > e_t \geq 0 \qquad (8)$$

The number of key comparisons for the unbalanced 3rd order merge sort algorithm in its worst case, $U_3^W(n)$, is given by the formula

$$U_3^W(n) = \sum_{i=1}^{t} a_i 3^{e_i}(2e_i - \tfrac{3}{2} + \sum_{j=1}^{i} a_j) - a_t 3^{e_t}$$

$$- \tfrac{1}{2} \sum_{i=1}^{t} a_i + a_t + t \qquad (9)$$

As in the 2nd order merge sorts, both the balanced and unbalanced 3rd order merge sort algorithms require exactly equal number of key comparisons in their best cases:

$$B_3^B(n) = U_3^B(n) = \sum_{i=1}^{t} a_i 3^{e_i}(e_i + \sum_{j=1}^{i} a_j - \tfrac{1}{2}(a_i+1)) \qquad (10)$$

Unlike the 2nd order case the difference $U_3^W(n) - B_3^W(n)$ is not always nonnegative. Our calculations for n = 1...10000 show that the balanced algorithm usually makes fewer comparisons than the unbalanced one. The difference between the two algorithms in this respect is, however, almost negligible.

5. EXPERIMENTAL SORT TIME RESULTS

In order to compare the actual sort times of the balanced and unbalanced merge sort algorithms we have coded them in (Extended) Algol and run them on a Burroughs B6700 computer. The procedures have been made as compatible as possible so that the differences in sort times should be due to differences in the algorithms rather than differences in their implementation. We have also written and implemented algorithms to form the data for the best and worst cases of each merge sort algorithm.

The results are summarized in Table 1. There is a clearly perceptible difference in the efficiency of the 2nd order and 3rd order merge sort algorithms, as might be expected. On the other hand there are only slight differences between the results of balanced and unbalanced merge sort algorithms of the same order. The results indicate that the sort time mainly depends on the number of record transfers during the sort and that the influence of the differences in the number of key comparisons on the total sort time is quite small.

n	Worst case				Best case			
	2^{nd}order		3^{rd}order		2^{nd}order		3^{rd}order	
	b	u	b	u	b	u	b	u
100	39	41	33	33	34	37	28	26
500	261	272	207	206	227	241	177	162
1000	566	584	418	428	512	546	376	339

TABLE 1: Measured Sort Times (in milliseconds) of the Balanced (b) and Unbalanced (u) Merge Sort Algorithms

6. CONCLUSIONS

In this paper we have given a balanced 2nd order straight merge sort algorithm and shown how it can be generalized to higher order merge sorting. This algorithm makes the same number of key comparisons in the best case as the corresponding unbalanced one, but in the worst case it can make almost n comparisons less than the latter algorithm, depending on the value of n. The experimental results show, however, that this difference is not very significant when sort times are concerned. The 3rd order straight merge sort algorithms give significantly shorter sort times than the 2nd order algorithms. The sort time experiments were carried out on a specific computer, but on the basis of the operations involved in the algorithms we believe that the results on a different computer would be essentially similar.

7. REFERENCES

1. Knuth, D.E., The Art of Computer Programming, Vol.3, Sorting and Searching, Addison-Wesley, 1973.

2. Woodrum, L.J., Internal Sorting with Minimal Comparing, IBM Syst. J. <u>8</u>, 3 (1969), 189-203.

E. Morlet and D. Ribbens, (Eds.), International Computing Symposium 1977.

AN INSERTION SORT FOR UNIFORMLY DISTRIBUTED KEYS BASED ON STOPPING THEORY

W. JANKO

WIRTSCHAFTSUNIVERSITÄT WIEN
VIENNA, AUSTRIA

Summary. An algorithm is described which is an insertion sort producing a single linked list. The sorting method is based on stopping theoretical considerations. In comparison with alternative insertion sort algorithms the algorithm presented is similar in efficiency and global structure to an algorithm described in Janko [1]. However the expected number of comparisons and their variance is smaller in the algorithm presented.

1. THE METHOD

To explain the method, the problem of successful search is considered first. To do this we repeat shortly the basic considerations already given in Janko [1].

Let S denote a sorted set of keys, $S = \{s_i | i=1,2,\dots,n$ and $s_j \le s_{j+1}$ for $j=1,2,\dots,n-1\}$. d is called the distance function for ascending sorting order,

$$d(s_g,s_j) = \begin{cases} (s_g-s_j) & \text{for } s_j \le s_g, \\ n\bar{d}-s_j+s_g & \text{for } s_g < s_j \end{cases} \quad (g,j \in \{1,2,\dots,n\}),$$

$$\bar{d} = (s_{max}-s_{min})/(n-1) ,$$

where s_{max} is the largest key of S and s_{min} is the smallest key. Abbreviating $d(s_g,s_j)$ by d_{gj}, we consider d_{gj} to be a matrix element of the square matrix D.

Example.

$$S = \{s_1,s_2,s_3\} = \{5, 11, 25\},$$

$$s_{min} = 5,\ s_{max} = 25,\ \bar{d} = 10$$

$$D = \begin{pmatrix} 0 & 24 & 10 \\ 6 & 0 & 16 \\ 20 & 14 & 0 \end{pmatrix} .$$

Similarly it is possible to use d', the distance function for descending order,

$$d'(s_g,s_j) = \begin{cases} (s_j-s_g) & \text{for } s_j \ge s_g , \\ n\bar{d}-s_g+s_j & \text{for } s_g > s_j , \end{cases}$$

to build up a distance matrix D' for descending sorting order. It is easily verified that D' is equal to the transpose of D.

Scanning a circularly linked list sequentially (in sorting order) to find the key looked for is called sequential search. Let p_j be the pointer field associated with the key s_j and pointing to the next key s_{j+1} in sorting order. To access s_{j+1} using p_j and to compare s_{j+1} with a key searched for is called a <u>sequential search step</u>. Let z_{gj} denote the number of sequential search steps starting sequential search with s_j to find the key s_g. Z will be called the (square) matrix of sequential search steps and consists of the elements z_{gj}. In above example we get

$$Z = \begin{pmatrix} 0 & 2 & 1 \\ 1 & 0 & 2 \\ 2 & 1 & 0 \end{pmatrix} .$$

By analogy to the distance matrix we denote by Z' the matrix of sequential search steps assuming linkage in descending sorting order. The equality $Z' = Z^T$ is equally true.

Let Z_i denote the i-th row of Z and let D_i denote the i-th row of D. Obviously the set of elements of Z_i is equal to $\{0,1,\ldots,n-1\}$, $i=1,2,\ldots,n$ for $S = \{s_1, s_2,\ldots,s_n\}$ and considering successful search only. Let us assume that $(s_{i+1}-s_i) = \bar{d}$, $i=1,2,\ldots,n-1$, is valid for some key set S. We then call S an equidistant set of keys.

The sorting method presented is ideally suited for sorting equidistant sets of keys. Only in this case the equality relation

$$z_{gi} = d_{gi}/\bar{d}$$

is true for $g,i\varepsilon\{1,2,\ldots,n\}$. We then know exactly for some key s_g searched for and an arbitrary alternative key s_i, how many sequential search steps have to be performed to find s_g starting sequential search with s_i.

Similarly to the method already proposed in Janko [1], in the algorithm presented sequential search is combined with an alternative searching method. This alternative method consists in accessing the keys by chance in the sense of sampling. The probability p_j accessing s_j is n^{-1} for $j=1,2,\ldots,n$. We call this procedure a random search. One random search step consists of accessing one key s_j with probability n^{-1} and comparing s_j with the key searched for. It is equivalent to sampling from S with replacement. For every key s_j drawn, the distance d_{gj} can be calculated. Remembering that S is assumed to be equidistant, we can derive z_{gj}, the necessary number of sequential search steps.

Random search can therefore be considered as sampling with replacement from $Z_g = \{0,1,\ldots,n-1\}$. This means to generate observations X_j from a discrete and uniformly distributed population:

$$W(X_j=i) = \begin{cases} n^{-1} & \text{for } i\varepsilon\{0,1,\ldots,n-1\} \text{ and } j=1,2,\ldots \\ 0 & \text{for } i\notin\{0,1,\ldots,n-1\}. \end{cases}$$

To combine random search and sequential search optimally, we have to determine the stopping interval for drawing a discrete and uniformly distributed random variable at the opportunity cost of the number of sequential search steps which could be performed in the same time.

It is assumed that a sequential search step consumes the constant amount t_s of time units and a random search step consumes the constant amount of t_r time units.*

Using t_r time units consumed by a random search step we could perform t_r/t_s sequential search steps. These sequential search steps reduce the necessary search effort to find s_g by $c=t_r/t_s$ in terms of Z_g. c represents therefore the opportunity costs of one random search step. To minimize the total search time a stopping interval has to be chosen optimally. A stopping interval is characterised by an amount v; random search is stopped if $d_{gj} \le v\bar{d}$ for a key s_j randomly drawn. Stopping time is determined by the width v.

v is immediately derived by applying the transformation T(v) to the minimum

---

* It goes without saying that the measurement of time consumption has to use the same scale.

problem*

$$T(v) = \sum_{j=0}^{v} (v-j)w(j) = n^{-1} \sum_{j=1}^{v} j =$$

$$= \frac{v(v+1)}{2n}$$

and solving the equation

$$T(v) = c \ .$$

We get $v = -0.5 + \sqrt{0.25+2nc}$. As v needs not to be an integer we should chose [v] for practical purposes. Neglecting the effect of this truncation stopping a random search process is optimal whenever $d_{gj}/\bar{d} \le [v]$.

Furtheron we assume that c=1. This allows us to derive further results speaking simply of search steps. The total expected number of search steps is v. Simplifying we assume $v=\sqrt{2n}$. Random search is a Bernoulli process with the approximate expected waiting time

$$E(Y) = \frac{n-1}{\sqrt{2n}} \simeq \sqrt{\frac{n}{2}} \ .$$

The number of sequential search steps X is discrete and uniformly distributed in {0,1,...,[v]}. The expected value of search steps is therefore equal to

$$E(X) = \frac{[v]}{2} \simeq \sqrt{\frac{n}{2}} \ .$$

Using these considerations the approximate variance of the random variable Y of random search steps is derived from the variance of the geometric distribution,

$$\sigma_Y^2 \simeq \frac{n - \sqrt{2n}}{2} \ ,$$

and the approximate variance of the random variable X, the number of sequential search steps, is equal to the variance of a discrete and uniformly distributed random variable in $\{0,1,\dots,[\sqrt{2n}]\}$:

$$\sigma_X^2 \simeq \frac{n}{6} \ .$$

X and Y are independent random variables. The standard deviation of the number of total search steps Z=X+Y is therefore equal to

$$\sigma_Z = \left(\frac{2}{3} n - \sqrt{\frac{n}{2}} \right)^{0.5} \ .$$

So far we have derived the results for a successful search. Now we shall show that these results are valid for the insertion situation. Substituting S by $S = S-\{s_g\}$ where s_g denotes the key searched for gives us the key set for the associated insertion problem. Eliminating the zero elements from D and Z we get the distance matrix and the matrix of sequential search steps for the insertion problem. If we assume that we have to insert an element into a set of n mutually distinct elements the value of v remains unchanged. Above results are therefore approximate results for the insertion problem. Insertion sorting means successively inserting elements in sorted sublists until all elements are inserted. Therefore the approximate number of search steps in sorting is equal to the sum of the approximate number of search steps inserting a key s in sorted sublists with i=1,2,...,n-1 elements. The approximate expected number of random search steps in an insertion sort is therefore given by

---

* The maximum problem is treated in Randolph [4]. The minimum problem is easily derived (see Janko [3]).

$$E\left(\sum_{i=1}^{n-1} Y_i\right) \approx \sum_{i=1}^{n-1} \sqrt{\frac{i}{2}} \;.$$

Similarly

$$E\left(\sum_{i=1}^{n} X_i\right) \approx \sum_{i=1}^{n-1} \sqrt{\frac{i}{2}} \qquad \text{and}$$

$$E\left(\sum_{i=1}^{n} Z_i\right) \approx \sum_{i=1}^{n-1} \sqrt{2i} \;.$$

As every search step involves a key comparison the expected number of key comparisons using simple keys is of the order $O(n^{1.5})$. The expected variance of $\sum_{i=1}^{n-1} Z_i$ is equal to

$$\sigma^2_{\Sigma Z_i} = \sum_{i=1}^{n-1} \left(\frac{2}{3}\, i - \sqrt{\frac{i}{2}} \right) \approx \frac{n^2-n}{3} \;.$$

The standard deviation of the expected number of total search steps in the insertion problem is therefore of the order $O(n)$.

So far we have assumed that S is an equidistant key set. But usually it is not. Now let us assume, that the set of keys consists of n observations of a random variable S uniformly distributed in [a,b]. Without loss of generality we may assume a=0 and b=1. It is well known* that the absolute value of the difference $|s_i-s_j|$ of the keys s_i and s_j, where i and j are the rank of the keys in sorting order, is beta-distributed with $(|i-j|, n-|i-j|+1)$ degrees of freedom and the expected value is

$$E(|s_i-s_j|) = \frac{|i-j|}{n+1} \;.$$

The expected average distance $E(\bar{d})$ is equal to $E(\bar{d}) = \frac{1}{n+1}$. The expected distance of two neighbours in sorting order, s_i and s_{i+1}, is hence equal to $E(\bar{d})$. So the key set is <u>equidistant in its expectation</u> if it consists of random variables uniformly distributed in some real interval [a,b].

---

* See e.g. Wilks [5].

An interesting question which still remains open is

"Could we apply the method described even when the key set does not consist of uniformly distributed observations?"

The answer is positive. First, if the key set is assumed to consist of observations from a population continuously distributed according to F(s), applying the transformation F to the keys yields $F(s_1) \le F(s_2) \le \ldots \le F(s_n)$ which is equivalent to a sorted sample of n observations uniformly distributed in the unit interval.

But usually one or some of the following statements are true:

- F(s) is not known,
- the set of keys is not a random sample,
- transformation with F is extremely time consuming.

Now let $\hat{F}(s)$ denote the empirical distribution function

$$\hat{F}(s) = \begin{cases} 0 & \text{for } s \le s_1 \;, \\ \frac{i}{n} & \text{for } s_i < s \le s_{i+1} \;, \\ 1 & \text{for } s > s_n \;. \end{cases}$$

Using the transformation $\hat{F}$ the set of keys can be transformed to an equidistant set of values. If we approximate $\hat{F}$ by a piecewise linear function F^* we can estimate the value of $\hat{F}$ between two points by linear interpolation. Simulation, using $\sqrt{n}$ classes of equal width, gave reasonable results. Yet even this method seems prohibitively time consuming for internal sorting and searching and therefore only applicable in searching on peripheral devices. The quality of the approximation of $\hat{F}$ by F^* depends on the choice of the classes, the number of classes and the form of $\hat{F}$.

2. USING THE ALGORITHM

2.1. Remarks on the algorithms design

As it was mentioned above the sorting algorithm presented below is in its structure very similar to the algorithm given in Janko [2]. The main difference is the stopping criterion used in random search. The algorithm given in Janko [2] uses a fixed sample size for random search. In our algorithm the number of random search steps is a random variable. The expected value of this random variable is determined by the stopping interval width.

Therefore only the design of the part of the algorithm which performs the random search is considered in more detail here.

The variable IH is used to store $\bar{d}v$. We assume that the keys are stored in the array K and the associate pointers are stored in the array L.

Accessing keys randomly in the sense of sampling without replacement could be done accessing the keys in their initial order. Doing this we assume that the keys form initially a random permutation. The theoretical results for a random sample with replacement are asymptotically valid for a random sample without replacement.

Let the keys to be sorted be K(II), K(II+1),...,K(JJ). The value of $s_{max} - s_{min}$ is stored in M. A code which realizes above ideas assuming that K(J) has to be inserted into a sorted sublist containing K(1),K(2),.....,K(J-1) is the following:

```
      :
      :
110 JO=J-1
    IH=IFIX(-0.5+SQRT(FLOAT(JO*2+
   +0.25))*FLOAT(M)/FLOAT(JO)
    DO 160 KEY= 1,JO
       KDIFF=K(J)-K(KEY)
       IF(KDIFF) 140,205,150
140    KDIFF=KDIFF+M
150    IF(IH-KDIFF)160,205,205
160    CONTINUE
      :
      :Sequential search continues with the
       statement 205.
```

To accelerate random search it is useful to eliminate the calculation of the square root. This can be done, introducing an array TAB. TAB(I) holds these values of n, which lead to v=i+1 the first time for $n=1,2,...,n_{max}$. It is useful to correct the value of IH at the beginning of the insertion loop as relatively maximal and minimal keys arising during the sorting process are treated separately.

To avoid the execution of the statement 140 with an expected number of executions equal to $\sum_{i=1}^{n-1} \sqrt{\frac{i}{8}}$, it is sufficient, to check in a separate initialisation phase of random search if $d(s_j,s_{min}) \leq \bar{d}v$ is valid. If it is, we stop random search. If it is not, we know that only a value K(KEY) which is lower than K(J), the key to be inserted, can cause stopping of the random search process. Doing this is equal to perform one random search step in advance. The result of implementing the algorithm resulting from above considerations with the simple insertion sort given in Janko [1,2] is the algorithm SPGM.

2.2. Further remarks

It is possible to change this algorithm for descending sorting order. To reduce the expected number of key comparisons it is possible to use double circularly linked lists. A modified distance function has to be used in this case:

$$d(s_g,s_j) = \min\{(s_g-s_j),n\bar{d}-|s_g-s_j|\}.$$

The approximate optimal stopping interval can be derived using n/2 instead of n. The total number of search steps and comparisons is in this case approximately equal to $\sqrt{n}$. To reduce sorting time the different execution time of one random and one sequential search step should be taken into account calculating the optimal stopping interval.

If key comparisons are relatively inexpensive in comparison with the access time, simultaneous insertion of more than one key at a time is extremely favourable. This is the case in using the method described in an external sorting or searching process.

2.3. Time Tests

The tests were made using an IBM 113Ø. The execution time of the algorithm given here was compared with the execution time of the algorithm SPN given in Janko [1]. (Time comparisons with further sorting algorithms can be found there).

Sorting time in ms

n	SPN *	SPGM *
5	11	9.7
10	25.4	20
20	63.2	61
50	244	211
100	686	610
500	7370	5600
1000	21040	16000

*Floating point calculation were avoided in the time tests.

3. REFERENCES

[1] Janko,W., A List Insertion Sort for Keys with Arbitrary Key Distribution, ACM Transactions of Mathematical Software, Vol.2,No.2 (June 1976), p. 143-153.

[2] Janko,W., Algorithm 505, A List Insertion Sort for Keys with Arbitrary Key Distribution, ACM Transactions of Mathematical Software, Vol.2,No.2 (June 1976), p. 204-206.

[3] Janko,W., Stochastische Modelle in Such- und Sortierprozessen, Duncker & Humblot, Berlin, 1976.

[4] Randolph,P.H., Optimal Stopping Rules for Multinomial Observations, Metrica, Vol.14 (1968), p. 48-61.

[5] Wilks,S.S., Mathematical Statistics, Wiley, New York, 1963.

4. THE ALGORITHM

```
      SUBROUTINE SPGM(K,L,II,JJ,MIN)
C            **SAMPLE SEARCH SORT -
C SEQUENTIAL POLICY**AN INSERTION SORT
C TO BUILD UP A CIRCULARLY LINKED LIST
C IN ASCENDING SORTING ORDER.THE
C EXPECTED NUMBER OF ACCESSES AND KEY
C COMPARISONS IS OF ORDER O(N**1.5)
C (N=JJ-II+1).
C K         ARRAY OF KEYS.
C L         ARRAY OF POINTERS.
C IH        STOPPING INTERVAL.
C KDIFF     VALUE OF THE DISTANCE FUNCTION.
C M         DIFFERENCE OF MAXIMAL AND
C           MINIMAL KEY OF THE SORTED
C           SUBLIST.
C MAX,MIN   INDEX OF MAXIMAL AND MINIMAL
C           KEY OF THE SUBLIST SORTED IN
C           THE ARRAY K.
C TAB       ARRAY TO STORE THE VALUES OF
C           (I/√2+1/√8)**2-0.125 IN
```

```
C          TAB(I-1).
C MIN RETURNS THE ROCK OF THE LIST AFTER
C SORTING.THE ALGORITHM IS STABLE.
      INTEGER TAB(68)
      DIMENSION K(1),L(1)
      DATA TAB/3,6,1Ø,15,21,28,36,45,55,
     *66,78,91,1Ø5,12Ø,136,153,171,19Ø,
     *21Ø,231,253,276,3ØØ,325,351,378,
     *4Ø6,435,465,496,528,561,595,63Ø,
     *666,7Ø3,741,78Ø,82Ø,861,9Ø3,946,
     *99Ø,1Ø35,1Ø81,1128,1176,1225,1275,
     *1326,1378,1431,1485,154Ø,1596,1653,
     *1711,177Ø,183Ø,1891,1953,2Ø16,2Ø8Ø,
     *2145,2211,2278,2346,2415/
C INITIALISATION
      MIN=II
      MAX=II
      L(II)=II
      IF (JJ-II) 18Ø,18Ø,1Ø
   1Ø KMIN=K(MIN)
      KMAX=KMIN
      IRT=1
      ITAB=TAB(1)+II-1
      IH=JJ
      IA=II+1
C INSERTION LOOP
      DO 17Ø J=IA,JJ
C CORRECTION OF STOPPING INTERVAL WIDTH
         IF (J-ITAB)3Ø,2Ø,2Ø
   2Ø    IRT=IRT+1
         ITAB=TAB(IRT)+II-1
         IPOI=J-II
         IH=IFIX(FLOAT(IRT)*FLOAT(M)/
     *   FLOAT(IPOI))
C PROVISION FOR ARISING RELATIVELY
C MINIMAL AND MAXIMAL KEYS DURING THE
C SORTING PROCESS.
   3Ø    KJ=K(J)
         IF (KJ-KMAX)4Ø,6Ø,6Ø
   4Ø    IF(KJ-KMIN)7Ø,5Ø,9Ø
C KEY FOR INSERTION IS EQUAL TO THE
C RELATIVELY MINIMAL KEY.
   5Ø    KEY=MIN
         MIN=J
         GO TO 13Ø
C KEY FOR INSERTION IS LARGER OR EQUAL
C TO THE MAXIMAL KEY SORTED SO FAR.
   6Ø    I=MAX
         MAX=J
         KMAX=K(MAX)
         GOTO 8Ø
C KEY FOR INSERTION IS SMALLER THAN THE
C SMALLEST KEY SORTED SO FAR.
   7Ø    I=MAX
         MIN=J
         KMIN=K(MIN)
C INSERTION OF RELATIVELY MINIMAL AND
C MAXIMAL KEYS.
   8Ø    IPOI=L(I)
         L(I)=J
         L(J)=IPOI
         M=KMAX-KMIN
         GOTO 17Ø
C CHECKING FOR STOPPING WITH THE MINIMAL
C KEY.
   9Ø    KEY=MIN
         IF(IH-(KJ-KMIN))1ØØ,15Ø,15Ø
  1ØØ    JO=J-1
C RANDOM SEARCH
         DO 12Ø KEY=II,JO
            KDIFF=KJ-K(KEY)
            IF(KDIFF)12Ø,15Ø,11Ø
  11Ø       IF(IH-KDIFF)12Ø,15Ø,15Ø
  12Ø       CONTINUE
C SEQUENTIAL SEARCH
         KEY=II
         GOTO 15Ø
  13Ø    IPOI=KEY
         KEY=L(KEY)
         IF(KJ-K(KEY))16Ø,13Ø,13Ø
  14Ø    IPOI=KEY
         KEY=L(KEY)
  15Ø    IF (KJ-K(KEY))14Ø,13Ø,13Ø
C INSERTION
  16Ø    L(IPOI)=J
         L(J)=KEY
  17Ø    CONTINUE
  18Ø MIN=L(MAX)
      L(MAX)=Ø
      RETURN
      END
```

E. Morlet and D. Ribbens, (Eds.), International Computing Symposium 1977.

ALGORITHMS EMBEDDED IN FUZZY SETS

C. J. Hinde
Research Associate

Computer Applications Group
Department of Architecture
University of Bristol
England

This paper describes an approach to fuzzy algorithms based on the concept of an algorithm being a transformation of a situation in order to bring about another situation. An algorithm executed at a low level of 'existence' would bring about a low level or partial change, whereas an algorithm executed at a high level would bring about a high level or nearly complete change. The paper then discusses algorithms embedded in fuzzy sets where an algorithm is viewed as an ordered set of fuzzy instructions. Set theoretic manipulations may then be performed on the algorithm itself, usually by another higher order or meta-system.

I FUZZY SETS

Fuzzy sets [1,8] are a generalisation of conventional sets where the characteristic function may take on values other than those in the set {0,1}, Zadeh's [1] function takes values in the continuous closed interval [Ø,1]. Goguen [4] generalises this still further with a characteristic function which is a complete lattice; an example of such a function would be a normalised (or unnormalised) vector where the ordering function compares each element of each vector with the corresponding element of the other vector and is comparable only if every element of one vector is greater than or equal to the corresponding element of the other vector. The vector system was suggested by Capocelli and De Luca [5].

Many sets have members which are more typical of those sets than other members; it is very often a distortion of the data to classify an object in one set rather than another and it is this inherent ambiguity rather than a lack of knowledge which is the major difference between fuzziness and probability. For example a person's height may be known with almost absolute certainty and yet it may be difficult to classify that person into one and only one of the sets 'short', 'medium' and 'tall'. Other examples from the author's own problem domain of Computer Aided Architectural Design are the constraints imposed on a building design layout, such as 'room A should be "near" room B' cannot be interpreted as a definite positional constraint bu specifies a fuzzy relation between room A and room B; see also Zadeh [1Ø]. The set of rooms which should be "near" room A could be distilled out of this relation and would be a fuzzy set. Jardine and Sibson [2] discuss cluster analysis in general but draw examples from the field of biology analysing the distortion created if the objects are classified into disjoint sets with a characteristic function having a range {Ø,1}. Zadeh [3] discusses the implications of using fuzzy or linguistic variables more fully. A comprehensive set of papers on fuzzy sets together with an extensive bibliography may be found in Zadeh et. al. [8].

II FUZZY SET THEORETIC OPERATIONS

The operations associated with set theory have corresponding operations in fuzzy set theory, union and intersection, following Zadeh [1], are defined as:
where

$f^t_A(x)$ is the membership grade of x in the set A at time t

X is the universe

$C = A \cup B$ (union)

$$f^1_C(x) = \text{Sup}(f^0_A(x), f^0_B(x)) \qquad x \in X$$

$C = A \cap B$ (intersection)

$$f^1_C(x) = \text{Inf}(f^0_A(x), f^0_B(x)) \qquad x \in X$$

$C = \bar{A}$ (complement)

$$f^1_C(x) = 1 - f^0_A(x) \qquad x \in X$$

In addition there are operations which are possible in fuzzy set theory which have no equivalent in conventional set theory. These are mainly unary operations on the value of the characteristic function of the set and are called hedges. They can be arbitrarily defined to suit the particular user and the type of characteristic function employed. Some of these are illustrated below where f has a range [Ø,1].

INT(A,y) (intensify)

$$f_A^1(x) = f_A^0(x)^{1.\emptyset+y} \qquad \emptyset.\emptyset \le y \le 1.\emptyset$$

Intensify decreases the membership values of all members but decreases the lower valued members more than the higher valued members thus 'intensifying' the membership of the set.

DIL(A,y) (dilate)

$$f_A^1(x) = f_A^0(x)^{1/(1.\emptyset+y)} \qquad \emptyset.\emptyset \le y \le 1.\emptyset$$

is similar to INT(A,y) but increases the membership values of A but more so for lower valued members; INT(A,y) and DIL(A,y) are inverses.

CON(A,y) (contrast)

$$f_A^1(x) = \begin{cases} f_A^0(x)^{1.\emptyset+y} & \text{if } f_A^0(x) \le \emptyset.5 \\ f_A^0(x)^{1/(1.\emptyset+y)} & \text{if } f_A^0(x) > \emptyset.5 \end{cases} \qquad \emptyset.\emptyset \le y \le 1.\emptyset$$

Contrast separates the higher valued members from the lower valued members about f = Ø.5 thus increasing the contrast between low valued members and high valued members. Complete contrast would result in the set having a characteristic function with range {0,1}.

Zadeh [3,1Ø] and Chang [9] discuss these more fully.

III FUZZY ALGORITHMS

Before describing some formulations of fuzzy algorithms it is useful to distinguish between

i) algorithms which operate on fuzzy data e.g. fuzzy set manipulations as described in the preceding sections type α

ii) algorithms which operate fuzzily on fuzzy data type β

In section II of this paper union is defined as

$C = A \cup B$ (union)

$$f_C^1(x) = \text{Sup}(f_A^0(x), f_B^0(x)) * \rho \qquad x \in X$$

which completely defines $f_C^1(x)$ in terms of $f_A^0(x)$ and $f_B^0(x)$ giving an algorithm of type α, i.e. an algorithm which operates on fuzzy data.

In order to develop the type β algorithms it is necessary to invoke the notion of an algorithm being responsible for a change in its environment: or more formally a finite set of statements which transforms its initial situation into its final situation. Where the output variables are undefined prior to execution of the algorithm they become defined or partially defined; the values are perhaps changed or modified in some respect where they were previously defined.

By direct analogy, then, with membership values in fuzzy sets an algorithm executed with fuzzy level Ø.Ø would bring about no change in its environment- much the same as if it did not exist; conversely, an algorithm executed with fuzzy level 1.Ø would be executed with full effect on its environment. Intermediate valued algorithms would be executed with intermediate effects. In general a fuzzy statement could be formulated as

$$E^1 = E^0 + \delta E * \rho$$

where E^t is the environment at time t, δE is the desired change and ρ is the fuzzy level of the statement.

The definitions of union and intersection thus become

$C = A \underset{\rho}{\cup} B$ (fuzzy union)

$$f_C^1(x) = f_C^0(x) + (\text{Sup}(f_A^0(x), f_B^0(x)) - f_C^0(x)) * \rho$$

$C = A \underset{\rho}{\cap} B$ (fuzzy intersection)

$$f_C^1(x) = f_C^0(x) + (\text{Inf}(f_A^0(x), f_B^0(x)) - f_C^0(x)) * \rho$$

for ρ = 1.Ø the definitions of union and intersection degenerate to those in section II and for ρ = Ø.Ø there is no effect. For these definitions to hold, though, the lattice upon which f is defined must have a continuous set of points between $f_C(x)$ and $Sup/Inf(f_A(x), f_B(x))$ i.e a normalised n-dimensional vector would suffice with each element defined on the real line. Intuitively a fuzzy instruction is fuzzily well behaved if the following condition holds:

> let E be the environment and δE be the change in the environment after execution of a fuzzy instruction at fuzzy level ρ, then the instruction is said to be fuzzily well behaved iff $\rho_1 < \rho_2$ implies $\delta E_1 < \delta E_2$ for all δF_1, δE_2 and all ρ_1, ρ_2 where δE_1 is associated with ρ_1 and δE_2 is associated with ρ_2 and there exists some method for measuring δE.

With union and intersection defined as above there is still ambiguity remaining with expressions containing mixtures of union and intersection.

If the assignment statement $D = (A \cup B) \cap C$ is evaluated then the change is made only to D, however there are at least two ways of evaluating this expression.

i) $(A \cup B) \cap C$ is evaluated non-fuzzily (type α) and then the assignment to D is made fuzzily (type β).

ii) the expression is broken down and evaluated piecewise.This would probably be the case if the expression were to be changed from infix notation to postfix.

$$D \underset{\rho}{=} A$$

$$D = D \underset{\rho}{\cup} B$$

$$D = D \underset{\rho}{\cap} C$$

where $\underset{\rho}{=}$ is fuzzy assignment

In terms of type α algorithms the two are equivalent but type β algorithms yield different results.

fuzzy assignment is defined as follows

$C = A$ (fuzzy assignment)

$$f^1_C(x) = f^0_C(x) + (f^0_A(x) - f^0_C(x)) * \rho$$

which degenerates to

$$f^1_C(x) = f^0_A(x) \text{ for } \rho = 1.\emptyset$$

and

$$f^1_C(x) = f^0_C(x) \text{ for } \rho = 1.\emptyset$$

With union and intersection defined as type α the laws of association, commutation and distribution apply but do not hold for type β definitions. Order of evaluation is now important and $A \underset{\rho}{\cup} B \underset{\rho}{\cup} C \not\equiv A \underset{\rho}{\cup} C \underset{\rho}{\cup} B$. Watanabe [7] discusses some of the implications of logics that are order dependent and concludes that logics that are order independent are preferrable and easier to handle where they are applicable; however this is not always the case.

for an example of a piecewise evaluation of a fuzzy statement. let

$$f^0_A(x) = \emptyset.5$$

$$f^0_B(x) = \emptyset.7$$

$$f^0_C(x) = \emptyset.9$$

$$\rho = 0.5$$

$$f^0_D(x) = \emptyset.\emptyset$$

$$D = A \underset{\rho}{\cup} B \underset{\rho}{\cup} C$$

then

$$f^1_D(x) = \emptyset.6875$$

for

$$D = A \underset{\rho}{\cup} C \underset{\rho}{\cup} B$$

$$f^1_D(x) = \emptyset.6375$$

Most expressions of type β when executed repeatedly will tend to a limiting expression which depends not only on the equivalent type α expression but also on the value of ρ, assuming the expressions are evaluated piecewise. If union or intersection but not both are present on the right hand side and the left hand side is either absent from the expression on the right hand side or is the first literal then the expression converges to the equivalent type α expression.

for example

$$\lim_{n\to\infty} n \text{ times } (A = A \underset{\rho}{\cup} B) \equiv A = A \cup B$$

but

$$\lim_{n\to\infty} n \text{ times } (A = (A \cup B) \cap C) \not\equiv A = (A \cup B) \cap C$$

although the limit exists it depends on the value of ρ.

let

$f_A^0(x) = \emptyset.9$

$f_B^0(x) = \emptyset.5$

$f_C^0(x) = \emptyset.8$

$\rho = \emptyset.5$

then
$A = (A \cap B) \cup C$ implies

$f_A^1(x) = \emptyset.8$

and
$A = (A \underset{\rho}{\cap} B) \underset{\rho}{\cup} C$ implies

$f_A^1(x) = \emptyset.75$

which when repeated gives rise to the following sequence

$f_A^2(x) = \emptyset.7125$

$f_A^3(x) = \emptyset.7\emptyset3125$

$f_A^4(x) = \emptyset.7\emptyset\emptyset7812$

setting $f_A^n(x)$ to 0.7 yields $f_A^{n+1}(x) = \emptyset.7$ verifying a point of equilibrium at $f_A(x) = \emptyset.7$ for $\rho = 0.5$.

$\rho = 0.75$ yields the following sequence

$f_A^1(x) = \emptyset.75$

$f_A^2(x) = \emptyset.74\emptyset625$

$f_A^3(x) = \emptyset.7\emptyset\emptyset38$

$f_A^4(x) = \emptyset.74\emptyset\emptyset\emptyset24$

setting $f_A^n(x) = \emptyset.74$ yields $f_A^{n+1}(x) = \emptyset.74$ verifying a point of equilibrium at $f_A(x) = \emptyset.74$ for $\rho = \emptyset.75$

The concept of incomplete change may be extended into other fields such as arithmetic:

let a be a conventional floating point variable

$a = 1.\emptyset$ initially
$a \underset{\rho}{=} a + 4.\emptyset$
would change a to $3.\emptyset$ for $\rho = \emptyset.5$

However for a fuzzy variable A defined initially as

$\{\emptyset.5|\emptyset.5, 1.\emptyset|1.\emptyset, \emptyset.5|1.5\}$
the expression $A \underset{\rho}{=} A + 4.\emptyset$
would yield

$A = \{\emptyset.25\ \emptyset.5, \emptyset.5\ 1.\emptyset, \emptyset.25\ 1.5,$
$\emptyset.25|4.5, \emptyset.5|5.\emptyset, \emptyset.25|5.5\}$

which would probably be more useful in situations where fuzzy logic is applicable than the previous definition of fuzzy addition. The first fuzzy addition could, however, be used as a crude data smoothing device to keep a running average.

An interesting observation is that, whereas each instruction in a set of fuzzy instructions may be well behaved, the set as a whole may not be. This is illustrated by the evaluation of
$A = (A \underset{\rho}{\cap} B) \underset{\rho}{\cup} C$

with f^0 defined as before

$\rho = \emptyset.5$ implies

$f_A^1(x) = \emptyset.75$

but
$\rho = \emptyset.6$ implies

$f_A^1(x) = \emptyset.744$

and
$\rho = 0.75$ implies

$f_A^1(x) = \emptyset.75$

Difficulties arise if fuzzy instructions include GOTO statements or any statement which implies a transfer of control because a certain degree of parallelism is implied. If the transfer of control implied by a GOTO merely assigns (fuzzily the new instruction to a fuzzy program counter which then executes the least fuzzy (highest) instruction and then deletes that instruction from the set of active instructions replacing it with its successor, then management of the fuzzy program can be a fairly straightforward polling or multiplexing system.

Floyd [6] discusses non deterministic algorithms and uses the fuzziness as a guide to which instruction to execute next. The fuzzy program is searched as a tree in order to find an executable path through, see also Chang [9]. A non fuzzy program is distilled from the fuzzy program and executed. This non fuzzy program is regarded as a solution to the fuzzy program and is obtained by using the fuzz level of each instruction as an indicator of the usefulness of pursuing a particular path.

Capocelli and De Luca [5] discuss fuzzy logic in the context of decision theory but suggest making the decision non fuzzily, whereas if the decision is to perform some action it is argued in this paper that the actions under consideration should all be performed fuzzily thus eliminating the distortion, see Jardine and Sibson [2] which arises because of a {yes,no} decision. By employing fuzzy algorithms, as described, the range of the decision function can be mapped directly onto the fuzziness of the actions.

IV ALGORITHMS EMBEDDED IN FUZZY SETS

If an algorithm can be executed at various levels of effectiveness then a natural extension would be to describe the algorithm as a partially ordered fuzzy set of instructions, each member of which is a fuzzily executable statement.

If an algorithm is a partially ordered fuzzy set then the algorithm itself may be manipulated in the same manner as the data upon which it operates, as a fuzzy set. A simple example of a tracking system illustrates this.

Consider a tracking system with visual feedback which is able to detect the line to be followed in one or other of its eyes giving a fuzzy error signal *ERRORRIGHT* or *ERRORLEFT* depending on whether the line appears in its right eye or its left respectively. It also has a steering mechanism *TURNRIGHT* or *TURNLEFT*. A tracking algorithm could be described as follows

```
REPEAT UNTIL FINISHED
      BEGIN TRACKALG
         IF ERRORLEFT THEN TURNLEFT;
         IF ERRORRIGHT THEN TURNRIGHT;
      END;
```

which would work if the error signals and the steering mechanism were geared together correctly. If the error detection mechanism was too sensitive for the steering mechanism then the system would oscillate about the correct line to be followed. If the detection mechanism was not sensitive enough the algorithm would drift off course before returning to its correct line.

Clearly a second order correction algorithm could be applied in any tracking system, thus if *OLDERRORLEFT* and *OLDERRORRIGHT* are stored then the following algorithm could be applied

```
IF OLDERRORRIGHT ∧ ERRORRIGHT ∨
OLDERRORLEFT ∧ ERRORLEFT THEN
MORE(TRACKALG) ELSE
LESS(TRACKALG);
```

where LESS is defined as

LESS(A) (less)

$$f_A^1(x) = f_A^0(x) - (f_A^0(x))*\rho \qquad x \in X$$

and MORE is defined as

MORE(A) (more)

$$f_A^1(x) = f_A^0(x) + (1 - f_A^0(x))*\rho \qquad x \in X$$

MORE increases the membership level of the set and LESS decreases it, both according to the fuzz level at which they are called.

The two systems joined together give a complete algorithm as follows

```
REPEAT UNTIL FINISHED
      BEGIN TOTALSYS
        BEGIN TRACKALG
          IF ERRORLEFT THEN
          TURNLEFT;
          IF ERRORRIGHT THEN
          TURNRIGHT;
        END;
        BEGIN METASYS
          IF OLDERRORRIGHT ∧
          ERRORRIGHT ∨ OLDERRORLEFT ∧
          ERRORLEFT THEN
          MORE(TRACKALG) ELSE
          LESS(TRACKALG);
        END;
        OLDERRORLEFT = ERRORLEFT;
        OLDERRORRIGHT = ERRORRIGHT;
      END;
```

The assignment of *ERROR-* to *OLDERROR-* is removed from *METASYS* to avoid the fuzzy assignment that would result if *METASYS* was fuzzified.

A third or greater order system may be introduced to monitor the second order system and would require the same mechanism to operate it, thus algorithms to detect errors in other algorithms are written in a natural manner.

An example of a more complex nature is furnished by Uhr [11] who describes a parallel cognitive system where attention is directed to a particular 'sense' by increasing its activation or fuzz level. A Computer Aided Architectural Design system could be constructed in a similar manner where separate design sub-systems contribute information at various fuzzy levels and change the developing design accordingly. If a particular aspect of the building is deemed important the fuzz level of the relevant sub-system would be increased and the ensuing scheme would reflect the requirements of that aspect more strongly. As various values are assigned to the design the assignment would be made fuzzily according to the fuzzy level of the relevant sub-system.

For each sub-system the algorithm, in very broad outline, would be as follows

```
REPEAT UNTIL GOODENOUGH
      BEGIN DESIGN
        BEGIN PROCESS1
           :
           :
        END;
        :
        :
        BEGIN PROCESSn
           :
           :
        END;
      END;
```

where each process is performed in parallel and is of the form

```
BEGIN PROCESSi
  IF NOGOODi THEN IMPROVEi;
END;
```

The variable *NOGOOD*i and the procedure *IMPROVE*i are in general complex. *IMPROVE* could be a set of fuzzy instructions or even a fuzzy set of processes. Thus not only may each *IMPROVE* process change the developing design but may also influence the way in which the design is produced.

Although an algorithm would be unchanged in essence, small changes can be made by raising or lowering selected parts of the algorithm. This would be analogous to mutation in biological evolution whereas union and intersection would be more of a reproductive mechanism requiring two fuzzy sets for operation. Conventional algorithms usually require discrete changes which may have a considerable effect on the behaviour of the algorithm. Provided that the algorithm is 'well behaved' as defined in section III then by 'continuously' changing the levels of an algorithm there can be more delicate control of the algorithm. Coarse control effected by means of unions or intersections would at least ensure that the resultant algorithm had two respectable successful parents. Most processes which could be used to manipulate algorithms automatically could be implemented as fuzzy algorithms themselves and be organised to operate on algorithms embedded in fuzzy sets.

V CONCLUSIONS

Algorithm embedding in fuzzy sets not only gives a high degree of control over algorithms but also extends the concept of algorithm manipulation and development from discrete changes reminiscent of 'big switch' problem solving to continuous change. Section III of the paper developed fuzzy instructions so that all interesting instructions may be performed fuzzily. This was necessary for section IV where algorithm embedding was discussed, as a non fuzzy instruction can not be embedded in a fuzzy set. It is the author's opinion that fuzzy sets and fuzzy algorithms can model some parts of the real world more successfully than can conventional techniques and will be of use especially in the 'soft' sciences such as psychology e.g. see Kochen [12], social science and especially in the field of Computer Aided Architectural Design where the author has spent some time researching. Data in these fields is very often inherently ambiguous such as the concept of 'nearness' in architecture, 'rich' and 'poor' in social science, 'sane' in psychology. Complex control systems such as are employed in artificial intelligence systems need be defined less precisely and may modify their behaviour more easily to suit prevailing conditions.

VI REFERENCES

[1] Zadeh L.A.
'Fuzzy Sets'
Inf. and Contr. Vol 8, (1965)
p. 338-353

[2] Jardine N. and Sibson R.
'The construction of hierarchic and non-hierarchic classifications'
Comp. J. Vol 11, (1968)
p. 177-184

[3] Zadeh L.A.
'Complex Systems and Decision Processes'
IEEE Trans. on systems, Man and Cyber. SMC-3, (1973)
p.28-44

[4] Goguen J.A.
'L-Fuzzy Sets'
J. Math. Anal. and Appl. Vol 18 (1967)
p. 155-174

[5] Capocelli R.M. and
De Luca A.
'Fuzzy Sets and Decision Theory'
Inf. and Contr. Vol 23, (1973)
p. 446-473

[6] Floyd R.W.
'Non Deterministic Algorithms'
J. ACM. No 14 (1967)
p. 636-644

[7] Watanabe S.
'Modified Concepts of Logic,
Probability and Information based
on a Generalised Continuous
Characteristic Function'
Inf. and Contr. Vol 15, (1969)
p. 1-21

[8] Zadeh L.A., Fu K.S., Tanaka K. and
Shimura M.
'Fuzzy Sets and Their Applications
to Cognitive and Decision Processes'
Academic Press (1975)

[9] Chang C.L.
'Interpretation and Execution of
Fuzzy Programs'
in [8].
p. 191-218

[10] Zadeh L.A.
'Calculus of Fuzzy Restrictions'
in [8].
p. 1-39

[11] Uhr L.
'Towards Integrated Cognitive
Systems, Which Must Make Fuzzy
Decisions about Fuzzy Problems'
in [8].
p. 353-393

[12] Kochen M.
'Applications of Fuzzy Sets in
Psychology'
in [8].
p. 395-408

The work reported in this paper was
sponsored by the British Science
Research Council under grant no
B/RG/73993.

E. Morlet and D. Ribbens, (Eds.), International Computing Symposium 1977.

SOME BOUNDS ON QUASI-INITIALISED FINITE AUTOMATA

Paulo A. S. Veloso

Department of Systems and Computer Sciences
COPPE , Universidade Federal do Rio de Janeiro
Rio de Janeiro, RJ , Brazil

This paper deals with bounds on the number of states and on decision procedures for quasi-initialised finite automata. These parallel modular recognisers for regular languages are finite automata with the initial state replaced by a set of initial states. This restricted nondeterminism simplifies some decision procedures. Also, many - but not all - regular sets have quasi-initialised finite automata with substantially fewer states than their minimal finite automata.

1. INTRODUCTION

Multiple-entry finite automata were introduced by Gill /3/ as finite recognisers where any state can serve as an initial state. In this paper we consider quasi-initialised finite automata as a generalisation of both the multiple-entry finite automata and of the familiar finite automata of Rabin /5/, in that any state from a given set can serve as an initial state.

This apparently restricted nondeterminism in the choice for initial states of a qifa (short for quasi-initialised finite automaton) can be quite powerful. Indeed, we exhibit qifa's which are much simpler and have substantially fewer states than any fa (short for finite automaton) for the same language. This property is shared by many, though not by all, regular sets. Also, some decision procedures for qifa's are simpler than the corresponding ones for fa's.

Qifa's can be realised by parallel networks of distinctly initialised copies of a single fa, which is particulary appropriate for integrated circuitry implementation. They may also be used to model some aspects of routines with several entry points, such as storage saving, and of parallel processing, such as gain in speed.

2. QUASI-INITIALISED FINITE AUTOMATA

A quasi-initialised finite automaton (here abbreviated qifa) is a 5-tuple $M = < \Sigma,S,f,I,F >$ where Σ and S are finite nonempty sets (the alphabet and the state set, respectively, I and F are subsets of S (the sets of initial and of final states, respectively), and f is a function from $S\times\Sigma$ into S (the transition function). As usual we extend f recursively to a function $f : S\times\Sigma^* \to S$, so that each word $w\varepsilon\Sigma^*$ induces a function $f_w : S \to S$. The accepted set of a state $s\varepsilon S$ is $A(s) = \{w\varepsilon\Sigma^* / f(s,w)\varepsilon F\}$. The language recognised by M is $L(M) = \bigcup_{s\varepsilon I} A(s)$.

Two extreme cases of qifa's deserve mention. For $|I| = 1$ we have the familiar Rabin-Scott finite automata (fa's, for short), whereas for $I = S$ we have the mefa's (short for multiple-entry finite automata) of Gill /3/.

By a (k,n) qifa we mean a qifa with n states and k initial states. So, an n-state fa (resp. mefa) is a (1,n) (resp. (n,n) qifa). Now suppose that M is a (k,n) qifa with $I = \{s_1,\dots,s_k\}$. If we replace I by s_i we obtain an fa M_i for $A(s_i)$. A parallel recogniser for $L(M)$ can be obtained by connecting $M_1,\dots,M_k$ in parallel through an output logic OR. Due to its modular and parallel character this realisation scheme has several desirable features, among which are ease of design, implementation and maintenance.

Clearly, every qifa language is regular and conversely. Thus, qifa's are parallel modular recognisers for regular sets.

2.1. Remark

If a regular language has an n-state fa then it has a (1,n) qifa.

3. SOME PROPERTIES

Given two qifa's $M = < \Sigma,S,f,I,F >$ and $N = < \Sigma,T,g,J,G >$, with disjoint S and T, we form new two qifa's as follows. Their direct union is the qifa $M\vee N = < \Sigma,S\cup T,h,I\cup J, F\cup G >$ where for each $\sigma\varepsilon\Sigma$ $h_\sigma=f_\sigma\cup g_\sigma$. Their direct product is the qifa $M\times N = < \Sigma,S\times T,r,I\times J,F\times G >$, where for each $\sigma\varepsilon\Sigma$ $r_\sigma=f_\sigma\times g_\sigma$. The following property should be clear.

3.1. Lemma

If M is a (p,m) qifa and N is a (q,n) qifa then $M\vee N$ is a (p+q,m+n) qifa for $L(M)\cup L(N)$ and $M\times N$ is a (p.q,m.n) qifa for $L(M)\cap L(N)$.

We now generalise the concepts of reducedness and connectedness to qifa's. We call a qifa M reduced iff s=t whenever A(s) = A(t), i.e. distinct states have different accepted sets. We say that a qifa M is connected (resp. strongly connected) iff every state is reachable from some initial state (resp. from every other state). For the case $|I| = 1$, these notions become usual ones for fa's. Thus the next remark is not surprising.

3.2. Remark

If a regular set has a (p,m) qifa then it has a reduced connected (q,n) qifa with $q \leq p$ and $n \leq m$.

However, unlike fa's, reduced connected qifa's are not necessarily minimal. The following examples illustrate some pecularities of qifa's, when compared to fa's.

3.3. Examples

a) The minimal fa for $R = a^* + b^*$ has 4 states. By deleting its initial state one can obtain a (2,3) qifa for R. So, R has a qifa with fewer states than its minimal fa.

b) The minimal fa for $L = \{a\}^* - \{a^{140}\}^*$ has 140 states. But R has a (1,4x5x7=140), a (2,4+5x7=39), a (2,5+4x7=33), a (2,7+4x5=27), and a (3,4+5+7=16) qifa, all of which are reduced and connected. So, L has several reduced connected (2,n) qifa's, which are not minimal. (See 5.2).

c) $R(2,4) = (\lambda+a+ba^*ba^*b)(a+ba+bba^*ba^*b)^*$ has a (2,4) qifa but its minimal fa has $\binom{4}{1}+\binom{4}{2}=10$ states. Thus, R(2,4) has a qifa with substantially fewer states than its minimal fa (See 4.4).

d) a^*b^* has a 3-state fa but no (k,n) qifa with $n < 3$.

4. LOWER BOUNDS

The following alternative description of the language recognised by a qifa will be quite useful in the sequel.

4.1. Lemma

If $M = < \Sigma,S,f,I,F >$ is a qifa then $L(M) = \{w\varepsilon\Sigma^*/F\cap f_w(I) \neq \emptyset\}$.

Thus the language recognised by a qifa consists of all the words for which there is a path from some initial state to a final state. This shows that a qifa is really a nondeterministic fa (see e.g. Rabin /5/) of a special kind. For, all its transitions are deterministic, the only source of nondeterminism lying in the choice for the initial state. It is interesting to examine the power of this apparently rather restricted nondeterminism. We shall do this by applying a version of the well-known subset construction of Rabin /5/.

The fa-analogue of the qifa $M = < \Sigma,S,f,I,F >$ is the fa $N = < \Sigma,T,g,t,G >$, where $T = \{f_w(I)\subseteq S/w\varepsilon\Sigma^*\}$, t=I, $G=\{J\varepsilon T/J\cap F \neq \emptyset\}$ and $g(J,\sigma) = f_\sigma(J)$ for all $\sigma\varepsilon\Sigma$ and $J\varepsilon T$.

4.2. Proposition

The fa analogue of a (k,n) qifa M is a connected B(k,n) - state fa for L(M), where $B(k,n) = \binom{n}{1}+\ldots+\binom{n}{k}$.

Proof. Let $M = < \Sigma,S,f,I,F >$ and let N be its fa analogue. For any state J of N we have $0 < |J| \leq k$ and from 4.1, $A(J) = \bigcup_{s\varepsilon J} A(s)$. QED

Thus we have a bound on the saving of states we may expect to obtain in passing from fa's to qifa's. It is natural do ask - generalising the corresponding question of Gill/3/ for mefa's - whether this bound can ever be attained.

4.3. Proposition

Let R be a regular set over the alphabet $\Sigma=\{\sigma\}$.
a) If R has a (k,n) qifa with $k < n$ then R has an fa with at most $(B(k,n) - B(k-1,n-1) = B(k,n-1)+n$ states.
b) If R has an n-state mefa then R has an n-state fa.
Proof. Let M be a (k,n) qifa for R and N its fa-analogue.
a) If f_σ is onto then N has at most $\binom{n}{k}$ states. Otherwise, there exists a state s of M not in the image of f_σ, hence belonging to no state of N.
b) The states of N form a non-decreasing inclusion chain, so of lenght at most n. QED

So, for a single-letter alphabet the bound B(k,n) on the fa analogue can never be attained. However, over a binary alphabet there exist infinitely many regular sets (with bounded star-height) achieving this maximum saving of states.

4.4. Theorem

If the alphabet Σ has more than one symbol then for all $n \geq k > 0$ there exists a regular language R(k,n) over Σ (having star-height at most 2) with a strongly connected (k,n) qifa but with no fa with fewer than B(k,n) states. In particular R(n,n) is a mefa language with an n-state mefa and a minimal (2^n-1) - state fa.

Proof. Pick $a \neq b$ in Σ and consider a qifa $M = < \Sigma,S,f,I,F >$ with $S = \{1,\ldots,n\}$, $I = \{1,\ldots,k\}$, $F = \{1\}$, such that $f(1,a) = f(2,a) = f(n,b) = 1$, for $2 < s \leq n$ $f(s,a)=s$ and for $1 \leq t < n$ $f(t,b) = t + 1$. Clearly, M is a strongly connected (k,n) qifa and each A(s) is easily seen to have a regular expression with star-height 2 (see e. g. Ginzburg /4/). Call R(k,n) = L(M) and let N be the fa-analogue of M. We claim N is a reduced fa for L(M) having B(k,n) states. First, for any states J and K of N, $A(J) \subseteq A(K)$ iff $J \subseteq K$; because if $J \not\subseteq K$ then $b^{(n-t+1)} \in (A(J)-A(K)$, where $t = \max(J-K)$. Now, by induction on $0 < j \leq k$, one can show that any nonempty $J \subseteq S$ with $|J| \leq j$ is reachable from $\{1,\ldots,j\}$ in N (because if $t_1 < \ldots < t_i < \ldots < t_j$ then $\{t_1,\ldots,t_{i-1},(t_i-1),t_{i+1},\ldots,t_j\}$ is reachable from $\{t_1,\ldots,t_{i-1},t_i,t_{i+1},\ldots,t_j\}$ in N). QED

Hence the bound B(k,n) is attainable iff the alphabet has more than one symbol. For many regular sets a substantial saving in states is achieved in passing from fa's to qifa's . In the next section we will see that, even though the bound B(k,n) is not attainable over a single-letter alphabet, a considerable saving is still possible in this case. These languages are not mefa languages, though. Gill /3/ has shown that the mefa languages are exactly those regular sets R that are closed under suffix (i. e. $v \in R$ whenever $uv \in R$). For such languages, we cannot expect to economise states, in passing from mefa's to qifa's, as the next result shows (generalising theorem 3 of Gill /3/).

4.5. Proposition

Let $M = < \Sigma,S,f,I,F >$ be a connected (k,n) qifa for R. Then R is a mefa language iff $< \Sigma,S,f,S,F >$ is an n-state mefa for R.

Proof. The "if part" is obvious. Now, for any $t \in S$, we have $t=f(s,u)$ for some $s \in I$ and $u \in \Sigma^*$; thus $\{u\}A(t) \subseteq A(s) \subseteq R$, and R is closed under suffix. QED.

In order to have an idea of how much more complex than a qifa can an fa be, consider the case of the language R(2,4) of example 3.3.c. The state diagram of its minimal fa N is shown below with its final states underlined.

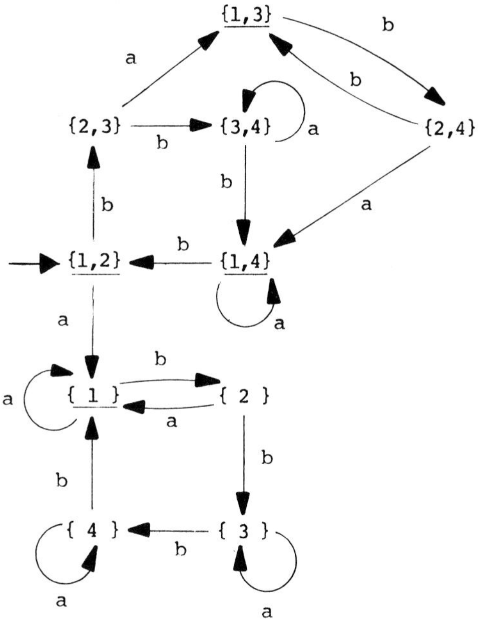

The state diagram of the (2,4) qifa M of theorem 4.4 consists of the singletons. Notice that this fact is perfectly general, showing that N is much more complex than M.

5. UPPER BOUNDS

Consider the alphabet $\Sigma = \{\sigma\}$. By a (τ,T)-fa over Σ we mean a $(\tau+T)$-state fa $M=< \Sigma,S,f,0,F >$ with $S = \{0,1,\ldots,\tau,\tau+1,\ldots(\tau+T-1)\}$, such that $f(\tau+T-1,\sigma) = \tau$ and, for $s < (\tau+T-1)$, $f(s,\sigma) = s+1$. It is easy to see that every connected fa over Σ is (isomorphic to) a (τ,T)-fa, where T is the length of its cycle (see e.g. Ginzburg /4/).

5.1. Theorem

Let R be a regular set over $\Sigma = \{\sigma\}$ with a (τ,T)-fa. For each factorisation $T=q_1\ldots q_k$ of T into pairwise relatively prime factors, R has a reduced connected $(k,k\tau+q_1+\ldots+q_k)$ qifa.

Proof

Let $M = < \Sigma,S,f,0,F >$ be a (τ,T)-fa as above. for each $j = 1,\ldots,k$ we construct a (τ,q_j)-fa $M_j = < \Sigma,S_j,f_j,0,F_j >$, wich will be reduced if M is, as follows. For $s < \tau$, $s \in F_j$ iff $s \in F$ and, for $\tau \leq s < \tau + q_j$, $s \in F_j$ iff s is not a remainder upon division by q_j of any state

$t \in (S-F)$ with $t \geq \tau$. One can see from 3.1. that $M_1 \vee \ldots \vee M_k$ is the desired qifa, since $\{\sigma^T\}^* =$

$= (\{\sigma^{q_1}\} \cap \ldots \cap \{\sigma^{q_k}\})^*$. QED

Thus, many regular sets over $\{\sigma\}$ have qifa's with fewer states than their minimal fa's. Some of them are given in the next corollary. (A similar result was obtained independently by Galil /2/).

5.2. Corollary

Let $m = q_1 \ldots q_k$ be the prime-power factorisation of $m > 0$. Then, the regular language $\Sigma^* - (\Sigma^m)^*$ has a $(k, q_1 + \ldots q_n)$ qifa but no fa with fewer than m states.

For the general case we can obtain a few somewhat loose upper bounds for qifa's by means of the bounds on the number of distinct derivatives ($D_u L = \{v \in \Sigma^* / uv \in L\}$) of a regular set of Brzozowski /1/. We first introduce the notion of a decomposition for a language in order to extend the correspondence between regular expression and fa's to qifa's.

A (k,n) decomposition for a language L is a set of k languages $L_1, \ldots, L_k$ having n distinct derivatives $D_w L_j$, for $w \in \Sigma^*$ and $j = 1, \ldots, k$, and such that $L = L_1 \cup \ldots \cup L_k$.

The next result shows that (k,n)decompositions correspond exactly to reduced connected (k,n) qifa's. This indicates the reason why reduced connected qifa's for a regular set may fail to be minimal and isomorphic. Namely, a regular set may have many decompositions.

5.3. Proposition

Let R be a regular language over Σ.
a) If $M = < \Sigma, S, f, I, F >$ is a reduced connected (k,n) qifa for R then $\{A(s)/s \in I\}$ is a (k,n) decomposition for R.
b) If $\{R_1, \ldots, R_k\}$ is a (k,n) decomposition for R then R has a reduced connected (k,n) qifa.

Proof
a) For each $s \in I$ and $w \in \Sigma^*$, $D_w A(s) = A(f(s,w))$.
b) Set $I = \{R_1, \ldots, R_k\}, S = \{D_w R_j / w \in \Sigma^*, j = 1, \ldots, k\}$, $F = \{T \in S / \lambda \in T\}$ and $f(T,\sigma) = D_\sigma T$; then $A(T) = T$. QED

5.4. Proposition

If the regular sets P and Q have respectively (p,m) and (q,n) qifa's then $P \cup Q$, $P \cap Q$, PQ and P^* have respectively $(p+q, m+n)$, $(p.q, m.n)$ $(p.q, m.2^n)$ and (k,r) qifa's, where $0 < k \leq r < 2^m$.

Proof. Remark 3.1 gives the first two bounds while the other two follow from those of Brzozowski /1/. QED.

Of course, a finite language with n words with lengths at most m has a $(1, 3+n(m-1))$ qifa, which is an fa.

6. DECISION PROCEDURES

We now examine some decision problems for qifa's. The questions of emptiness and finiteness of the language recognised by a qifa are similar to those for fa's considered by Rabin /5/. Of course the fa-analogue of 4.2 already gives positive answers to these questions. But, better bounds for the decision procedures can be obtained directly.

6.1. Theorem

Let $M = < \Sigma, S, f, I, F >$ be a (k,m) qifa for the language R, let $|F| = m$ and call $r = \max\{k, m\}$.
a) R is nonempty iff $I \cap F \neq \emptyset$ or M accepts some word w with length $|w| \leq (n+1)-(k+m) \leq (n-1)$
b) R is finite iff M accepts no word $\overline{w}$ with length $|w| > (n-1)$
c) R is infinite iff M accepts a word w with length $(n-1) \leq |w| \leq (n+1)+(n-r) \leq 2(n-1)$.
d) $R = \Sigma^*$ iff M accepts every word w with length $|w| \leq (n-1)$

Proof. It suffices to show one direction for each part. We consider a word $w = v_1 \ldots v_j \in R$ of length j and look at a trajectory

$$s_0 \xrightarrow{v_1} s_1 \xrightarrow{v_2} \ldots \longrightarrow s_{j-1} \xrightarrow{v_j} s_j,$$

with $s_0 \in I$ and $s_j \in F$.
a) If $R \neq \emptyset$ take w of minimal length in R then $s_1, \ldots s_{j-1}$ are (j-1) distinct states in $S-(I \cup F)$.
b) If $R \neq \emptyset$ is finite, take w of maximal length in R, pick $\sigma \in \Sigma$ and put $s_{j+1} = f(s_j, \sigma)$. Then $s_0, s_1, \ldots s_j, s_{j+1}$ are (j+2)distinct states.
c) If R is infinite, take w of minimal length among the words of R having length above (n-2). Then $s_1, \ldots, s_{j+1-n}$ are (j+1-n) distinct states in (S-I) and $s_{n-1}, \ldots, s_{j-1}$ are (j+1-n) distinct states in (S-F).
d) Follows from lemma 8 of Rabin /5/. QED

Two immediate consequences from this theorem are a lower bound on qifa's for finite languages (which is (m+2) if m is the length of the longest word), and a decision procedure for connectedness, as follows.

6.2. Corollary

A (k,n) qifa is connected iff every state is reached from some initial state by a word w of length $|w| \leq (n-k)$.

Finally, we consider the problem of deciding whether or not a qifa recognises a regular set given by an fa, as well as related inclusion problems.

6.3. Theorem

Let M be a (k,n) qifa with m final states and let R be a regular set with a p-state fa.

a) $L(M) \subseteq R$ iff every word w with length $|w| \leq np+1 - (k+m)$ accepted by M is in R.

b) $R \subseteq L(M)$ iff every word $w \in R$ with length $|w| \leq n+p-1$ is accepted by M.

c) M recognises R iff, for every word w with length $|w| \leq np-1$.

Proof. Follows from 3.1 and 6.2 (a,b). QED.

7. CONCLUSION

Our main results can be conveniently summarised as follows. Consider a regular language R over the alphabet Σ and let its minimal fa M have m states. By a minimal qifa for R we mean a (k,n) qifa N for R such that R has no qifa with fewer than n states and $k \leq j$ whenever R has a (j,n) qifa. A minimal qifa for R need not be unique to within an isomorphism; it must be reduced and connected but not conversely.

7.1. Bounds when $|\Sigma| > 1$

In general, $k \leq n \leq m \leq B(k,n)$ (2.1, 4.2) and, for the case of mefa languages, $k \leq n \leq m \leq (2^n-1)$ (4.5, 4.2). In either case the extremes are attained by infinitely many languages (4.4).

7.2. Bounds when $|\Sigma| = 1$

In general, $k \leq n \leq m \leq n + B(k,n-1)$ and, for the case of mefa languages, $k \leq n = m$ (4.3, 4.5). Also, if M is strongly connected then so is N and $n \leq q_1 + \ldots + q_k$ where $q_1 \ldots q_k$ is the prime-power factorisation of m (5.1, 5.2).

7.3. Decision procedures

L(N) is nonempty (resp. infinite) iff N accepts a word with length up to (n-k) (resp. between (n-1) and 2(n-1) (6.1). Further, in order to decide whether N is really a qifa for R it suffices to check all words with length below n.m(6.3).

Thus, even though qifa's appear to be similar to fa's, in that they recognise exactly the regular sets, their rather restricted nondeterminism in the choice of initial states permits considerable savings in number of states. In fact, we have shown the qifa nondeterminism to be practically as powerful as that of general nondeterministic fa's, in terms of number of states. Also, decision procedures for qifa's are quite similar to the corresponding ones for fa's, but they tend to be simpler in the qifa case.

Qifa's are very natural models for specifications given by a disjunction of conditions. Of course, this OR-case can be easily dualised to AND, and then to NOR and NAND, too. Finally, two natural implementation schemes for qifa's are parallel banks of copies of an fa and parallel routines with various entry points. In both cases the features of modularity and parallelism are apparently quite advantageous.

8. REFERENCES

/1/ Brzozowski, J.A., "*Derivatives of Regular Expressions*", J. ACM, 11 , 4 (Oct.1964), p.481-494.

/2/ Galil, Z. and Simon, J., "*A Note on Multiple-Entry Finite Automata*", J. Comput. System Sci, 12, 3(Jun.1976),p.350-351.

/3/ Gill, A. and Kou, L.T., "*Multiple-Entry Finite Automata*", J. Comput. System Sci., 9 , 1 (Aug. 1974), p.1-19.

/4/ Ginzburg, A., "*Algebraic Theory of Automata*", Academic Press, New York, 1968.

/5/ Rabin, M.O., and Scott, D., "*Finite Automata and Their Decision Problems*", IBM J. Res. Develop., 3 , 2 (Apr. 1959), p.114-125.

ACKNOWLEDGEMENTS

This paper is partly based on a dissertation written under Professor Arthur Gill's supervision,at the University of California, Berkeley, U.S.A. Financial support from the Brazilian National Council for Scientific and Technological Development (CNPq., T.C.14275) is gratefully acknowledged. Thanks are also due to Ms. S. Klajman for her patient typing.

E. Morlet and D. Ribbens, (Eds.), International Computing Symposium 1977.

BINOMIAL-EXPANSION ALGORITHMS FOR COMPUTING INTEGER POWERS OF SPARSE POLYNOMIALS*

Vangalur S. Alagar and David K. Probst
Department of Computer Science
Concordia University
Montreal, Canada

This paper presents three new algorithms for computing integer powers of sparse polynomials in one or several variables, and analyzes their computing time. It is shown that one of these algorithms is the best of a class of algorithms which contains what we believe are all major refinements of the binomial-expansion approach to the computation of integer powers of sparse polynomials. If the sparse polynomial has t nonzero terms in its representation, then the cost of computing the n-th power using this best algorithm is given by:

$$\frac{t^n}{n!} + t^{n-1}\left[\frac{1}{2(n-2)!} + \frac{1}{2^{n-2}(n-1)!}\right] + O(t^{n-2}),\ \text{for } n>2.$$

1. INTRODUCTION

In this paper we conduct a comparative study of a class of algorithms for computing integer powers of a class of multivariate polynomials. The computational model is the class of completely sparse polynomials in one or more variables with integer coefficients. We represent a polynomial $f(x_1,\ldots,x_r)$ in this class as a sum of monomials, where each monomial is of the form $c(\Pi\, x_i^{\alpha_i})$, $\alpha_i \geq 0$, c and α_i integers. A sparse polynomial may be characterized by the number of nonzero terms, t, in its representation. We say that a polynomial f is completely sparse to power n if f^k, fully expanded, for all k, $1 \leq k \leq n$, contains exactly the number of terms of the t-term multinomial expansion. This characterization is due to Gentleman [3].

Several algorithms for computing integer powers of sparse polynomials have been given recently by Fateman [2]. The purpose of this paper is to give better algorithms and better understanding of their computing time by considering a program family consisting of a wide range of possible refinements of the most successful of the general approaches considered by Fateman. We show that in this class of algorithms for computing an integer power of a symbolic polynomial, there exists one member which is far superior to the others.

According to Dijkstra [1] 'a program should be conceived and understood as a member of a family ...' or Parnas [4] 'the aim of the new design methods is to allow the decisions which can be shared by a whole family, to be made before those decisions, which differentiate family members'. Trees are good representations of program family structures. The root of the tree represents the problem to be solved and the terminal nodes represent the algorithms for solving the problem. Every node in the tree is the root of some subtree and the branches of this root are the possible design decisions at that point. Thus every path from the root to a terminal node represents a deliberate choice of a specific set of actions out of a possible family of other sets which could have been chosen as well. Such trees allow us to understand more clearly the relative costs of algorithms. Although cost functions as such are defined only for the algorithms (terminal nodes) themselves, analysis does indicate the relative costs of the various design decisions associated with different branching points. As consistently lowest-cost decisions give rise to the lowest-cost algorithm, we see why one algorithm is superior. Hence our practical goal would be to explore the possible design decisions, build up the program family tree, generate the algorithms and finally, analyze their costs to obtain sufficient understanding of their relative merits.

2. NOTATION AND ELEMENTARY RESULTS:

Following Fateman [2], we propose to analyze algorithms on the basis of the number of coefficient multiplications needed to produce the answer. Since the polynomials are either sparse or completely sparse, the number of like terms in the resulting polynomial is small or zero, and hence the cost of exponent comparisons is negligible. We denote the number of nonzero terms in a polynomial f by N(f)=t. The following results are useful for the analysis in section 4.

Result 1. Let N(f)= t. Then $N(f^n) = \binom{t+n-1}{n}$, $t \geq 2$. See [2] for proof. (2.1)

*This work is partly supported by NRC grant A3552.

Result 2. If f and g are two polynomials, then the cost of multiplying them is the cost of multiplying each term of f by each term of g, and then collecting like monomials in the result. In the sparse case, when the number of like monomials is small or zero, the cost is N(f). N(g). (2.2)

3. DESIGN DECISIONS

In this section we consider the four major design decisions which differentiate algorithms for computing integer powers of sparse polynomials.

3.1. General Approach:

Fateman [2] has considered repeated multiplication (RMUL), repeated squaring (RSQ), two kinds of multinomial expansion (NOMA and NOMB) and two kinds of binomial expansion (BINA and BINB) as means of computing integer powers of sparse polynomials. Of these six algorithms, BINB is the most efficient; the analysis suggests that binomial expansion is the most promising general approach. Yet BINA and BINB are only two of many possibilities here. For this reason we have investigated a program family consisting of a broad range of possible refinements of this approach. These refinements differ considerably in cost.

3.2. Splitting:

In binomial expansion the original polynomial f is split into two parts, f_1 and f_2. The way in which this splitting is done has a major impact on the algorithm's performance. Some of the splitting possibilities are: a) one term and the rest, b) as evenly as possible, c) as unevenly as possible, a power of two and the rest, and finally, d) as evenly as possible, a power of two and the rest. But we observe that when the size of f is a power of two, (b), (c) and (d) do not differ.

We must also choose whether to split the parts. If the polynomial is split only once, we have what we call a single-level splitting. Both BINA and BINB pursue a single-level splitting strategy, and this is appropriate when repeated multiplication is used to compute the powers of the subpolynomials. Our algorithms BINC, BIND and BINE use merge or recursion rather than repeated multiplication, and hence are committed to multilevel splitting.

BINA and BINB correspond to single-level versions of (a) and (b). We have investigated all the multilevel versions and show in this paper that a multilevel version of (b) is optimal for this problem. Cost analysis in section 4 shows that even splitting increases the cost of combining computed powers of subpolynomials but drastically reduces the cost of computing those powers. Moreover, the multilevel algorithms perform far better than the single-level algorithms.

3.3. Powers of Subpolynomials:

The central design decision of the binomial expansion family involves choosing the strategy for computing the powers of subpolynomials. The three major approaches are the following: 1) repeated multiplication, for which single-level expansion is appropriate, 2) recursion and 3) binary merge, both of which require multilevel expansion. These approaches are listed in order of increasing optimality.

Once the decisions about evenness and depth of splitting have been taken, the splitting process may be recorded in a binary tree. We call 'term group' one or more consecutive terms of a polynomial. The whole polynomial is placed in the root. We create new nodes by taking the term group in a node, and splitting it into two parts (according to the design decision), one of which becomes the left subnode and the other the right subnode. In the case of multilevel expansion, this process is repeated.

Examples:

single-level, one-and-the-rest splitting

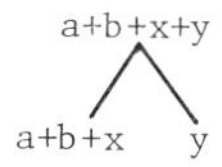

multilevel, as-even-as-possible splitting

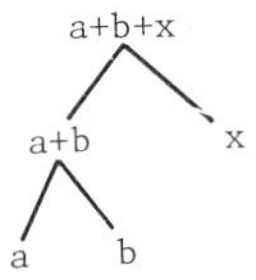

The idea of recursion is to compute the powers of the term groups of the subnodes by repeated application of the total algorithm to the subnodes. However, this causes the powers of some subpolynomials to be recomputed, leading to duplication of effort. The merge approach corrects this in an optimal way. We progress up the tree, in postorder, using the already computed powers of the subnodes to compute the powers of the father nodes. Either recursion or merge is better than repeated multiplication; hence, multilevel expansion is better than single-level expansion. Moreover, merge is better than recursion because it eliminates duplication of effort.

3.4. Combining Powers:

The final task is combining suitable powers in the binomial expansion. Since $f^n=(f_1+f_2)^n=\Sigma\binom{n}{r}f_1^r f_2^{n-r}$, the product $\binom{n}{r}f_1^r f_2^{n-r}$ may be computed either a) left to right (as in BINB) or b) by multiplying $\binom{n}{r}$ by whichever polynomial is smaller, and then this result by the remaining polynomial. It is easy to see that possibility (b) reduces the number of coefficient multiplications.

We can diagram the whole set of optimum design decisions in the following way:

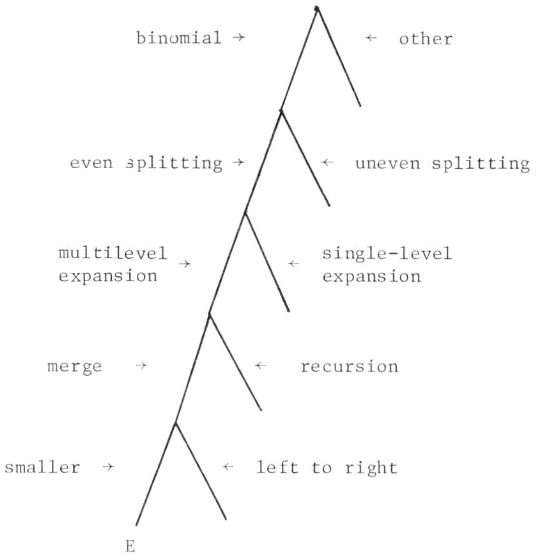

It would be possible, of course, to fill in the whole binomial-expansion subtree so that every binomial-expansion algorithm of which we are aware would be represented by a unique terminal node. There are many such algorithms. For example, if we decide on (some particular) uneven splitting, multilevel expansion, recursion and smaller, we obtain a very different algorithm than that which results from the choices: (the same) uneven splitting, multilevel expansion, merge and smaller. In the next section we present three general algorithms which we have investigated fully, and which we believe are both new and worthy of presentation. We also show (as the above diagram indicates) that E, the algorithm corresponding to the leftmost terminal node, is superior to its competitors for the simple reason that every design decision which characterizes it is optimum.

4. ALGORITHMS

We discuss below Fateman's BINB, which we analyze anew, and three algorithms which are all refinements of the binomial-expansion approach. Each of the three algorithms is superior to BINB. The algorithms will be described in terms of the program-family tree of section 3. For each algorithm, the input is a polynomial f with t terms which is completely sparse to power m and an integer n ($\le$ m). The output is f^n in each case. The cost of computing f^n is given as a function of t and n. For purposes of comparison, we need the following result:

No algorithm can compute $g=f^n$, the n-th power of an arbitrary polynomial, in fewer than $N(f^n)-N(f)$ multiplications. See [2] for proof. We denote the minimum cost function by

$$L(t,n) = N(f^n)-N(f) = \binom{t+n-1}{n} - t \qquad (4.1)$$

We also mention that only integer arithmetic is assumed in computing the cost.

4.1. Algorithm BINB:

This algorithm is due to the design decisions: binomial, even splitting, single-level expansion, repeated multiplication (some recursion) and left to right. The cost function as found in [2] is

$$F(t,n) = \binom{t+n-1}{n} + t\binom{t/2+n-1}{n-1} - 2\binom{t/2+n-1}{n}$$
$$- t/2(t/4-n-\log(t-1)+4) \qquad (4.1.1)$$

BINB uses a mixed strategy for computing powers of subpolynomials: recursion for the squares, and repeated multiplication for higher powers. After closely inspecting the steps in [2; p.152-153], we would itemize the total cost of this algorithm as follows:

Case I: Let $t=2^k$ $f=f_1+f_2$, $N(f_1)=N(f_2)=t/2$.

Step	Compute	Cost
1	f_1^2, f_2^2	$t^2/4 + kt/2$
2	$f_1^3,\dots,f_1^n$ $f_2^3,\dots,f_2^n$	$2.\frac{t}{2}\sum_{2}^{n-1}\binom{\frac{t}{2}+i-1}{t/2-1}$
3	$\binom{n}{1} f_2$	$t/2$
4	$\binom{n}{2} f_2^2,\dots$ $\binom{n}{n-1} f_2^{n-1}$	$\sum_{2}^{n-1}\binom{\frac{t}{2}+i-1}{t/2-1}$
5	$f_1^i \binom{n}{i} f_2^{n-i}$ $1\le i\le n$	$\sum\binom{t/2+i-1}{t/2-1}\binom{t/2+n-i-1}{t/2-1}$

Total Cost

$$F_1(t,n) = \binom{t+n-1}{n} - 2\binom{t/2+n-1}{n} + (t+1)\binom{t/2+n-1}{n-1}$$
$$- \frac{t}{2}(t/2 - \log_2 t + 1) - 1 \qquad (4.1.2)$$

Case II: When $t \neq 2^k$. Let $f = f_1+f_2$, $t_1=N(f_1) = \lceil t/2 \rceil$, $t_2 = N(f_2) = t-N(f_1)$. Itemizing the cost as before we get

$$F_2(t,n) = \binom{t+n-1}{n} - \binom{t_1+n-1}{n} - \binom{t_2+n-1}{n} + t_1\binom{t_1+n-1}{n-1} + (t_2+1)\binom{t_2+n-1}{n-1} + \varepsilon_2(t) \quad (4.1.3)$$

where $\varepsilon_2(t)$ is a polynomial in t of degree 2.

Comparing (4.1.1) and (4.1.2) we note that, for any n and any $t=2^k$, $F_1(t,n)>F(t,n)$. In the next paragraph, considering first the case when $t=2^k$, we show that replacing BINB's mixed strategy (which is predominantly repeated multiplication) by a pure recursive strategy yields a refinement having a considerably lower cost.

4.2. Algorithm BINC:

When $t=2^k$, the design decisions of this algorithm are binomial, even splitting, multilevel expansion, recursion and left to right.

The polynomial is split into two parts f_1+f_2, where $N(f_1)=N(f_2)=t/2$. We use the binomial theorem $f^n = \sum_0^n \binom{n}{r} f_1^r f_2^{n-r}$ to compute f^n. The powers of the subpolynomials are computed recursively using the design decisions of last paragraph.

Analysis of BINC. Let C(t,n) denote the cost of computing the n-th power of a t-term polynomial f. Writing f^n in the form

$$f_1^n + f_2^n + \sum_1^{n-1} \binom{n}{r} f_1^r f_2^{n-r}$$

we have

$$C(t,n) = 2C(t/2,n) + \sum_1^{n-1} Q_r, \quad (4.2.1)$$

where Q_r is the sum of costs itemized as follows:

Step	Cost
1) Compute f_1^r	$C(t/2,r)$
2) Compute f_2^{n-r}	$C(t/2,n-r)$
3) Compute $\binom{n}{r} f_1^r$	$\binom{t/2+r-1}{t/2-1}$ by (2.1)
4) Compute $\binom{n}{r} f_1^r f_2^{n-r}$	$\binom{t/2+r-1}{t/2-1}\binom{t/2+n-r-1}{t/2-1}$ by (2.2)

We obtain

$$C(t,n) = \binom{t+n-1}{n} - 2\binom{t/2+n-1}{n} + \binom{t/2+n-1}{n-1} - 1 + 2\sum_1^n C(t/2,r) \quad (4.2.2)$$

From C(t,n), we can find C(t,n+1) by using the formula:

$$C(t,n+1) = nt + \frac{t-1}{n+1}\binom{t+n-1}{n} + \sum_1^k 2^{r-1}\binom{t/2^r+n-1}{n} + \sum_1^k 2^{r-1}C(t/2^{r-1},n) \quad (4.2.3)$$

Using (4.2.3) and induction on n, we find that the general form of C(t,n) is a polynomial in n and t,

viz.,

$$C(t,n) = \sum_{i=1}^{n} a_i^{(n)} t^{n+1-i} + t\sum_{i=n+1}^{2n-1} a_i^{(n)} k^{i-n} \quad (4.2.4)$$

By inspection

$$a_1^{(n)} = 1/n!, \quad a_{2n-1}^{(n)} = 1/2(n-1)!$$

Exact analysis yields the following for n = 2,3 and 4:

$$C(t,2) = t^2/2 + t/2 + kt/2 \quad (4.2.5)$$

$$C(t,3) = t^3/6+5t^2/4+7t/12+t(k+k^2/4) \quad (4.2.6)$$

$$C(t,4) = t^4/24+t^3/3+65t^2/24-t/12 + t(31k/24+5k^2/8+k^3/12) \quad (4.2.7)$$

For an asymptotic analysis of the cost, we need the second coefficient $a_2^{(n)}$. We can find its magnitude by substituting (4.2.4) into (4.2.3) and then simplifying the resulting expression.

We obtain

$$a_2^{(n)} = \frac{1}{2(n-2)!} + \frac{3}{(n-1)!(2^{n-1}-2)}. \quad (4.2.8)$$

We also know $a_1^{(n)} = 1/n!$

Now we can compare the costs F(t,n), C(t,n) and L(t,n). First, considering the leading terms we have:

n	F(t,n)	C(t,n)	L(t,n)
2	$5t^2/8$	$t^2/2$	$t^2/2$
3	$t^3/4$	$t^3/6$	$t^3/6$
n>3	$\left[\frac{1}{n!} + \frac{2^{1-n}}{n(n-2)!}\right]t^n$	$t^n/n!$	$t^n/n!$

Next we find the absolute differences between F(t,n) and L(t,n) as well as between C(t,n) and L(t,n). We obtain

$$C(t,n)-L(t,n) = \frac{3}{(n-1)!}(t/2)^{n-1} + O(t^{n-2}/(n-2)!)$$

and

$$F(t,n)-L(t,n) = \frac{2}{n(n-2)!}(t/2)^{n} + \frac{n-1}{(n-2)!}(t/2)^{n-1} + O(t^{n-2}/(n-2)!)$$

Thus the relative deviations of C(t,n) and F(t,n) from the minimum cost are

$$[C(t,n) - L(t,n)]/L(t,n) = 3n/(2^{n-1}t)$$

and

$$[F(t,n) - L(t,n)]/L(t,n) = (n-1)t/2^{n-1}.$$

Thus, for large n and large t, C(t,n) approaches L(t,n) much more rapidly. Actual computation reveals that for all $n>2$ and $t\geq 16$, $L(t,n)<C(t,n)<F(t,n)$. Hence BINC is, so far, a better algorithm than BINB for computing powers of sparse polynomials.

4.2.1. When t is not a power of 2, we consider a balanced binary splitting of t. The rest of the design decisions are as before. For example if t=17, then the splitting scheme is shown below:

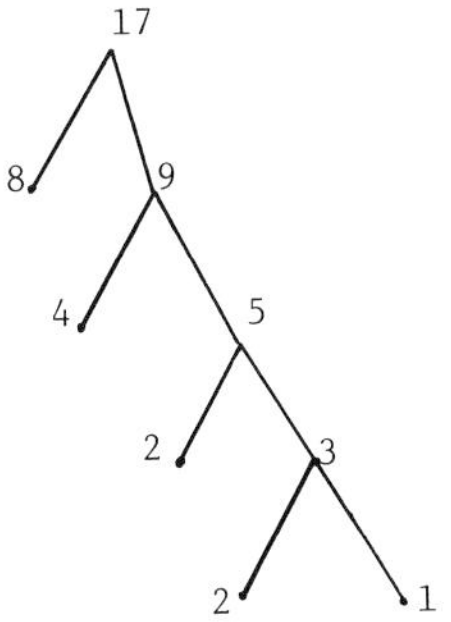

The description, therefore, is as follows:

Algorithm BINC: $(t \neq 2^k)$

1) split $f = f_1+f_2$, so that the splitting is as even as possible and $N(f_1) = 2^{k_1}$, for some integer k_1.
2) Compute $f_1^{\,r}$ for $1<r\leq n$ using BINC.
3) Compute $f_2^{\,n-r}$ for $0\leq r\leq n-2$ using BINC.
4) Compute $\binom{n}{r} f_1^{\,r}$
5) Compute $\binom{n}{r} f_1^{\,r} f_2^{\,n-r}$
6) Form $f^n = f_1^{\,n}+f_2^{\,n}+\sum_1^{n-1}\binom{n}{r} f_1^{\,r} f_2^{\,n-r}$

Analysis of BINC: Let S(t,n) denote the cost of computing the n-th power of f using BINC. We itemize the cost for each step:

Steps 2,3. $\sum_{r=2}^{n} C(t_1,r)$, $t_1=2^{k_1}$; $\sum_{r=2}^{n} S(t-t_1,r)$

Step 4. $\sum_{r=1}^{n-1}\binom{t_1+r-1}{r}$ by (2.1)

Step 5. $\sum_{r=1}^{n-1}\binom{t_1+r-1}{r}\binom{t-t_1+n-r-1}{n-r}$, by (2.2)

Hence the total cost is

$$S(t,n) = \sum_{r=2}^{n} C(t_1,r)+\sum_{r=2}^{n} S(t-t_1,r)+\sum_{r=1}^{n-1}\binom{t_1+r-1}{r} + \sum_{r=1}^{n-1}\binom{t_1+r-1}{r}\binom{t-t_1+n-r-1}{n-r} \qquad (4.2.1.1)$$

Let us suppose that the balanced binary multilevel splitting is $t=t_1+\ldots+t_p$, $t_i=2^{k_i}$. Let $t^{(o)}=t$, $t^{(i)}=t^{(i-1)}-t_i$, $i=1,\ldots,p-1$. Rearrangement yields:

$$S(t,n)=\sum_{0}^{p-2} S(t^{(r)},n-1)+\sum_{1}^{p} C(t_r,n)+\sum_{r=1}^{p-1} T_r,$$

where

$$T_r = 2\binom{t_r+n-2}{n-1} + \binom{t^{(r-1)}+n-2}{n} - \binom{t^{(r)}+n-2}{n} - \binom{t_r+n-1}{n} \qquad (4.2.1.2)$$

We have computed the cost according to BINC. The results support the conclusion that BINC performs better than BINB for $t>12$ and all values of n.

We now present two successive improvements compared with BINC, namely, the algorithms BIND and BINE. In contrast to BINC, both employ the design decision: smaller. BIND improves on BINC by employing an even-splitting strategy whether or not $t=2^k$, while BINE improves on BIND by replacing recursion with merge. We give the two refinements below in order of decreasing cost. Given the restriction to integer arithmetic, we have been unable to imagine improvements to BINE.

4.3. <u>Algorithm BIND</u>:

The design decisions of this algorithm are binomial, almost even splitting, multilevel, recursion and smaller. More formally, the description of BIND is as follows:

1) If t is even then $t_1=t_2=t/2$ else $t_1=(t+1)/2$, $t_2=t_1-1$.

2) $f=f_1+f_2$, $N(f_1)=t_1$; $N(f_2)=t_2$.

3) for r=2 to n compute f_1^r and f_2^r using BIND.

4) for r=1 to n-1

   a) multiply $\binom{n}{r}$ by whichever of $[f_1^r, f_2^{n-r}]$ has fewer terms.

   b) multiply this product by the remaining factor.

5) Add the terms of the binomial expansion.

Analysis of BIND: Let D(t,n) be the cost of computing the n-th power of a t-term polynomial. Then the costs are itemized as follows:

Step	Cost
3	$\sum_{r=2}^{n} [D(t_1,r) + D(t_2,r)]$
4(a)	$\sum_{r=1}^{n-1} \min[\binom{t_1+r-1}{r}, \binom{t_2+n-r-1}{n-r}]$
4(b)	$\sum_{r=1}^{n-1} \binom{t_1+r-1}{r}\binom{t_2+n-r-1}{n-r}$

The sum of the above costs yields D(t,n). We quote the results for $t=2^k$ so that we can compare F(t,n), C(t,n) and D(t,n). See Table 1 for other values of t and n. For the values n=2,3,4 we have

$$D(t,2) = t^2/2 + t/2 + kt/2 \quad (4.3.1)$$

$$D(t,3) = t^3/6+t^2+5t/6+t(5k/4+k^2/4) \quad (4.3.2)$$

$$D(t,4) = t^4/24+11t^3/36+53t^2/24+4t/9 +t(7k/4+3k^2/4+k^3/12) \quad (4.3.3)$$

For general n and $t = 2^k$,

$$D(t,n) = t^n/n! + t^{n-1}\left[\frac{1}{2(n-2)!} + \frac{1}{(n-1)!(2^{n-2}-1)}\right] + O(t^{n-2}). \quad (4.3.4)$$

The absolute differences of the various pairs of cost functions are as follows:

$$D(t,n)-L(t,n) = \frac{2}{(n-1)!}(t/2)^{n-1}+O(t^{n-2}/(n-2)!) \quad (4.3.5)$$

$$C(t,n)-D(t,n) = \frac{1}{(n-1)!(2^{n-1}-2)}t^{n-2}+O(\frac{t^{n-3}}{(n-2)!}) \quad (4.3.6)$$

Thus D(t,n) < C(t,n) for all n and t. Moreover for each n≥2 we have

$$\lim_{t\to\infty} \frac{D(t,n) - L(t,n)}{L(t,n)} = 0 \quad (4.3.7)$$

and

$$\lim_{t\to\infty} \frac{F(t,n) - L(t,n)}{L(t,n)} = n/2^{n-1} \quad (4.3.8)$$

These confirm that BIND is far superior to BINB.

4.4. Algorithm BINE:

The design decisions of this algorithm remain the same as in BIND but instead of recursion, we choose binary merge to compute the powers of subpolynomials. Let $f=f_1+f_2$.

Description:

1) Create a binary tree for the polynomial f:

   a) place f at the root

   b) place f_1, $N(f_1) = \lceil N(f)/2 \rceil$ in the left subnode.

   c) place f_2 in the right subnode.

   d) repeat steps (b) and (c) for the sub-polynomials until each term of f is one of the terminal nodes of the tree.

2) For each term of the original polynomial f, compute all powers from 2 to n. This completes the processing of terminal nodes.

3) For each interior node, both of whose subnodes have already been processed, compute all powers from 2 to n according to the following scheme:

   $(\text{node})^r = (\text{left subnode} + \text{right subnode})^r$, expanded binomially.

   i) For s = 1 to r-1 do

      a) multiply $\binom{r}{s}$ by whichever of $\{(\text{left subnode})^s, (\text{right subnode})^{r-s}\}$ has fewer terms.

      b) multiply the result in (a) by the remaining factor.

   ii) Add $(\text{left subnode})^r + (\text{right subnode})^r$ + the products computed in (i).

4) Compute the n-th power of the root according to the previous scheme.

Analysis of BINE:

Cost of step 2: t(n-1).

Cost of step 3: if the subnode sizes are

t_1 and t_2 and the power of the node sought is p, then the cost is

$$q_{p,i} = \sum_{s=1}^{p-1} \min\left[\binom{t_1+s-1}{t_1-1}, \binom{t_2+p-s-1}{t_2-1}\right] + \sum_{s=1}^{p-1} \binom{t_1+s-1}{t_1-1}\binom{t_2+p-s-1}{t_2-1}$$

Thus for processing all the interior nodes the cost is obtained by summing $q_{p,i}$ over all powers p from 2 to n and over all interior nodes i, i.e. $\Sigma_i \Sigma_p q_{p,i}$.

Cost of 4: the previous sum for the root and p = n.

As a particular case, let $t=2^k$ and let E(t,n) be the cost of computing the n-th power of f using algorithm BINE. We can show that

$$\Delta_n E = E(t,n) - E(t,n-1) = t + \sum_{i=1}^{k-1} \frac{t}{2^i} G(s,n) + G(t/2,n) - G(t/2,n-1) \qquad (4.4.1)$$

where $s = 2^{i-1}$, and G(s,n) gives the cost of computing the n-th power of a node whose subnodes are of size s. We use this to obtain E(t,n) for n=2,3 and 4.

$$E(t,2) = t^2/2 + t/2 + kt/2. \qquad (4.4.2)$$

$$\Delta_3 E = t + \sum_{i=1}^{k-1} \frac{t}{2^i}\left[s^3+s^2+2s\right] + (t/2)^3 + t/2.$$

Hence

$$E(t,3) = t^3/6 + 3t^2/4 + t/3 + 3kt/2. \qquad (4.4.3)$$

Similarly

$$E(t,4) = t^4/24 + 7t^3/24 + 29t^2/24 - 2t/3 + 11kt/4. \qquad (4.4.4)$$

In general

$$G(t/2,n) - G(t/2,n-1) = \binom{t+n-2}{n} - 2\binom{t/2+n-2}{n} + \binom{\frac{t}{2}+\frac{n-3}{2}}{\frac{n-1}{2}} \qquad (4.4.5)$$

We have taken n odd here but this has no effect on the leading terms. By induction we see that the leading coefficient in E(t,n) is 1/n!. The next coefficient, i.e., of t^{n-1}, obtained from (4.4.1) and (4.4.5) is $\frac{1}{2(n-2)!} + \frac{1}{2^{n-2}(n-1)!}$.

Hence

$$E(t,n) = \frac{t^n}{n!} + t^{n-1}\left[\frac{1}{2(n-2)!} + \frac{1}{2^{n-2}(n-1)!}\right] + O(t^{n-2}) \qquad (4.4.6)$$

Thus we have

$$D(t,n) - E(t,n) = \frac{t^{n-1}}{2^{n-2}(2^{n-2}-1)(n-1)!} + O(t^{n-2}) \qquad (4.4.7)$$

Hence, for all n and t, E(t,n) < D(t,n).

We give a representative segment of the cost table in Table 1. We quote the following other values as well. When t = 16 and n = 3, E(t,n) = 976 and F(t,n) = 1310. When t = 32 and n = 3, E(t,n) = 6480 and F(t,n) = 9278. Computed results show that for all n and t>4 the cost of algorithm BINE is significantly lower than that of any of the other algorithms.

5. CONCLUSION

We have considered the problem of computing integer powers of sparse polynomials. We have represented the family of algorithms for doing this as a tree in order to gain insight into the many choices involved. The binomial-expansion approach here is most likely optimal. Within this subfamily, we have discussed four algorithms, one previously published and three new. The main results are as follows:

There are a number of binomial-expansion algorithms which approach the theoretical lower limit for large t and large n, yet differ considerably in how closely and how rapidly they do so. This excess cost is a function most notably of the design decisions concerning polynomial splitting and subpolynomial powering. Even splitting is always to be preferred because of the substantial reduction in subpolynomial powering cost. Repeated multiplication is an expensive and inefficient way to compute the powers of subpolynomials. Recursion is a definite improvement, yet inferior to binary merge. The latter two also have the distinct advantage that, in the completely sparse case, no exponent comparisons whatsoever are required. Multiplication of the binomial coefficient by the smaller polynomial is an obvious improvement. Multilevel expansion is a mere consequence of using either recursion or merge.

We have analyzed these algorithms, using finite counting techniques and asymptotic analysis. For comparison purposes, the true costs have been tabulated, and the coefficients of the leading terms of the polynomial cost functions obtained analytically. The main result is that algorithm BINE has the least cost of all known algorithms belonging to the binomial-expansion family. We have tested the performance of BINE with a full implementation in PASCAL 6000.

TABLE 1

T	N	F	C	D	E	L
4	5	110	178	174	110	52
8	5	1254	1419	1364	1036	784
16	5	21870	18988	18412	16852	15488
17	5	28687	24403	23796	21948	20332
18	5	36664	31172	30320	28184	26316
19	5	46830	39282	38247	35823	33630
20	5	58558	49639	47714	45002	42484
21	5	73178	61715	59076	56034	53109
22	5	89846	75003	72462	69090	65758
23	5	110245	91200	88247	84545	80707
24	5	133270	114527	106632	102600	98256
25	5	161013	135572	128144	123688	118730
26	5	192060	160107	152932	148052	142480
27	5	228972	188307	181503	176199	169884
28	5	269974	221274	214134	208406	201348
29	5	318160	258144	251457	245243	237307
30	5	371338	300242	293740	287040	278226
31	5	433203	347865	341642	334456	324601
32	5	501086	401652	395528	387856	376960
4	6	162	290	284	164	80
8	6	2574	2923	2820	2140	1708
16	6	71462	62538	61084	57508	54248
17	6	98238	84484	82942	78617	74596
18	6	131020	113115	110830	105756	100929
19	6	174670	149296	146296	140473	134577
20	6	227198	196715	190672	184100	177080
21	6	295333	253107	246115	238660	230209
22	6	376143	323243	314274	305936	295988
23	6	478702	409016	397801	388580	376717
24	6	598838	532548	498956	488852	474996
25	6	748521	652920	621356	610067	593750
26	6	921984	797703	767598	755124	736255
27	6	1134722	970146	941871	928212	906165
28	6	1378956	1176437	1147714	1132870	1107540
29	6	1674418	1417035	1390442	1374181	1344875
30	6	2010833	1699647	1674210	1656532	1623130
31	6	2412970	2029322	2005249	1986154	1947761
32	6	2867502	2412504	2388784	2368272	2324752

6. REFERENCES

[1] Dijkstra, E.W., "*Structured Programming*" in Software Engineering Techniques, J.N. Buxton and B. Randell (eds.), NATO Science Committee,Brussels,(1970), p. 84-88.

[2] Fateman, R.J., "*On the Computation of Powers of Sparse Polynomials*", Studies in Appl. Math., 53 (1974), p. 145-155.

[3] Gentleman, W.M., "*Optimal Multiplication Chains for Computing a Power of a Symbolic Polynomial*", Math. Comp., 26 (1972), p. 935-939.

[4] Parnas, D.L., "*On the Design and Development of Program Families*", IEEE Trans. on Soft. Eng., SE-2, (1976), p. 1-9.

E. Morlet and D. Ribbens, (Eds.), International Computing Symposium 1977.

GRIN - A SIMPLE COMMAND LANGUAGE FOR GRAPHIC INTERACTION

G. Barta

CERN, Geneva, Switzerland

ABSTRACT

GRIN is a command language, the user interface part of a new graphics system for the display of vectors containing point coordinates. The system has a very simple, non-programming entry, with a full set of sensible defaults and an extremely tolerant dialogue, but there is room to expand for a more sophisticated user: as he uses fewer and fewer defaults, the flexibility and power of the system grow. This paper presents the dialogue aspect, concentrating on the command language and stressing man-machine communication; other parts of the over-all system prepare the data for display and perform the graphic functions themselves.

1. BACKGROUND

CERN, the European Organization for Nuclear Research, is a community of more than 600 European physicists, mostly visitors, supported by about 4000 other staff, carrying out theoretical and practical research in high-energy physics. To cope particularly with the analysis of the enormous quantity of experimental data, CERN has one of the largest computer installations in Europe -- three Control Data central processors and over 150 other computers.

The interactive element in CERN's computing is perhaps the fastest expanding one. Currently, about 100 terminals are connected to the Control Data machines by means of an exchange and three Hewlett Packard minicomputers acting as multiplexers (Bruins [1]); the vast majority are Tektronix graphic or alphanumeric displays working at 400 characters per second or more. Control Data's INTERCOM time-sharing supervisor [2] is the software base, together with CERN-written additions to handle the exchange and multiplexers and to extend the range of utilities available; they provide fast and flexible interaction with running user programs, as well as good editing, file handling, and job submission.

In volume, the principal computer load is the analysis and reduction of routine experimental results, which is largely a batch function. In addition, however, there are many areas of CERN's activity where interaction is far preferable; these run from on-line tryouts of the batch analysis programs, through data-base work, to on-line design of experimental set-ups and equipment. Most of these, as would still be expected in a scientific establishment, are carried on in FORTRAN, with the end-user generally writing his own programs (though of course extensive advisory services are available).

In this context, it is naturally a FORTRAN subroutine-callable graphics package that has proved most popular. A large part of CERN graphics is produced by *GD3* (Miller [3]), a very complete set of device-independent routines and a range of device-dependent postprocessors. The package has recently been partly rewritten and greatly extended, and includes notably facilities for scaling, for defining and calling symbols, for multiple character fonts, and for graphic input. Graphs are drawn using vectors of coordinates (FORTRAN arrays) in the X and Y directions separately -- the form in which most experimental data is presented.

There is, however, another area where GD3, FORTRAN, and conventional programming languages generally have not found favour: that of the theoretical physicist. While the "array" information structure is relevant also to the study of complex functions and relationships, the extra effort to learn the techniques of FORTRAN and conventional computing is not justified, whether by the quantity of data or the physicists' attitude.

Therefore theoretical physicists and computer scientists at CERN have collaborated to design and implement SIGMA (Hagedorn [4]), a totally interactive, interpretive language better suited to theoreticians' needs. SIGMA is oriented towards very simple graphic display, though with a range of options, and towards the handling of vectors and multi-dimensional rectangular arrays as single data objects, for instance as arguments to complicated functions. It fulfils its role very well, and is used around the world. If GRIN has a precursor, it is SIGMA, though the differences are fundamental -- it would be flattering to GRIN to compare the two.

2. THE PROBLEMS

2.1 A Dialogue which must work

There is nothing suitable in CERN for two classes of potential user:

- someone who would like to examine graphically information which he neither produced nor wants to change (the analysis of an experiment is often done by only one person in the group, but its results interest everyone); and
- someone whose knowledge of, or attitude towards, programming limits him to the classical FORTRAN mathematical program, but who nevertheless needs graphic display.

Programming languages, even SIGMA, are not suitable; still less the complicated calling sequences of GD3. A wide range of options for display must be provided, but combined with a very easy entry, without which any advantage over programming would be lost. GRIN is the dialogue part of a system designed to enable both classes of user to do graphic display without disproportionate effort.

2.2 Response without overloading the machine

Any approach which unites the functions of calculating the data and then displaying it tends to suffer from gigantism. Both involve significant effort: memory, execution time, access to secondary storage as well as programming. To combine them often produces a system that is too large, too slow, or both.

It seemed reasonable to try and provide, for those who did not necessarily require the two functions simultaneously, a facility to do display only, which would have to be faster and smaller than (for instance) SIGMA. GRIN separates the two functions: conventional programs (which already exist) can store their results without any display formatting; GRIN will then retrieve them for interactive graphics, without allowing further computation but providing a fast response.

3. GRIN - DESIGN AND CAPABILITIES

3.1 Principles

GRIN is not a programming language; it is a command language. It forms part of a larger system (Vandoni [5]) designed to solve the problems outlined above, and the fact that it is a command language implies notably that

- GRIN is not procedural, nor even "executable" in the normal sense;
- it consists of commands with arguments, not "language constructs";
- there is no clear distinction between syntax and semantics;
- the form of the dialogue is extremely simple and tolerant.

Commands have very few syntactic rules, and generally expect simply a series of arguments; the form of these arguments in turn does not impose many constraints. For example, punctuation is almost entirely ignored, on the basis of experience with other interactive systems. (A study by Williams [6] has shown that having to use punctuation slows human response down by up to 50%.)

3.2 Structure

The task of graphic display is divided up by GRIN into units called *frames*. Each frame provides information on the graphic environment and display options which are collectively known as the *setup conditions* (or simply *setup*) of that frame. These are concerned with such choices as whether and where to draw axes, how to scale the user's data to the physical display device, and whether to display in three dimensions and perspective. *Setup commands* serve to change these settings. Each frame contains in addition a set of commands called *pictures*, each of which is an instruction to draw one curve or plot one line of text. Each picture uses up to three *coordinate arrays* to provide the locations of the points on the curve in the X, Y and Z directions, and may include further options such as the texture of the line used to join the points. Figure 1 shows part of a frame definition: lines 3 to 11 contain some of the "setup conditions", and four "pictures" are shown at the end. *Items typed by the user are in lower case.*

There exist also *control commands* whose function is principally to organize the presentation of information on the screen and the definition of frames. They include commands to list defined arrays and frames, to provide on-line instruction and to switch from frame to frame.

3.3 Tolerance

It is normally clear from the keyword or the context, not only which of the three types of command is intended, but also what the significance of any arguments is supposed to be. There is thus no need to impose formal rules. GRIN almost always ignores punctuation, allows more than one command on a line, accepts abbreviations of commands (to a minimum of two characters), and is often able to interpret, and structure for itself, argument lists which do not follow a strict pattern.

Thus,

```
PRINT  1 10   0 25   A 0 5
       (a)    (b)    (c)
```

will print:

a) the first ten lines of the current frame definition;

b) line 25 of the definition of the "zero frame"; and

c) the first five lines of Frame A.

Another form of tolerance, especially in those commands (such as PRINT) which do not make irreversible changes, is as often to *ignore* incorrect or meaningless arguments as to diagnose them. It goes without saying that even a diagnosed error is followed by full recovery, with no loss of information beyond the current command line -- an essential part of a conversational system.

This type of tolerant behaviour has been found generally to evoke tolerance in turn from its users, especially from unsophisticated ones. Someone who is already far from confident in dealing with an intelligent, unfamiliar machine often reacts badly when brought face to face, not with his own stupidity, but simply with a lack of specialized knowledge.

```
 : print frameone 1 11 frameone 28 34

    FRAME FRAMEONE

 3 AXES              N        Y         Y
 4 BOX               N        Y         Y
 5 ERASE             Y
 6 GRID              N        N         N
 7 HARDCOPY          L
 8 LOG               L
 9 VIEWPORT          L
10 WAIT              N
11 WINDOW            L

PICTURES
--------
31 DRAW ZARRAY  YARRAY  XARRAY
32 ADD  ZARRAY2 YARRAY2
33 TEXT ∧ YPOSITION XPOSITION  'THIS IS A GRAPH'
34 CALL FRAMETWO

:
```

Figure 1

```
:

BASIC SETUP (POSSIBLE VALUES)                Z       Y       X

 3 AXES      (Y N - + VALUE(V) V,V L)        N       Y       Y
 4 BOX       (Y N)                           N       Y       Y
 5 ERASE     (Y N)                           Y
 6 GRID      (Y N)                           N       N       N
 7 HARDCOPY  (L Y N)                         N
 8 LOG       (L Y N)                         N       N       N
 9 VIEWPORT  (L D VALUE(V) D,V V,D V,V)      D       D       D
10 WAIT      (Y N)                           N
11 WINDOW    (L D POSVAL(P) P,P P/P P:P/P)   0,256   0,4096  0,4096

: log y yes

BASIC SETUP (POSSIBLE VALUES)                Z       Y       X

 3 AXES      (Y N - + VALUE(V) V,V L)        N       Y       Y
 4 BOX       (Y N)                           N       Y       Y
 5 ERASE     (Y N)                           Y
 6 GRID      (Y N)                           N       N       N
 7 HARDCOPY  (L Y N)                         N
 8 LOG       (L Y N)                         N       Y       N
 9 VIEWPORT  (L D VALUE(V) D,V V,D V,V)      D       D       D
10 WAIT      (Y N)                           N
11 WINDOW    (L D POSVAL(P) P,P P/P P:P/P)   0,256   0,4096  0,4096

:
```

Figure 2

4. GRAPHICS SETUP

4.1 Presentation

Figure 2 shows part of the *basic setup*, a "frame" (the "zero frame") which contains sensible defaults to be used in the absence of any other setup value. Each frame, in fact, only needs to specify those conditions whose value must be *changed*; the rest are marked *L* or LEAVE. (The only exceptions, AXES, BOX, and a few others, represent decisions which should be made for each frame independently: these have an "empty frame"-default which is not LEAVE.)

The setup values are passed from frame to frame, unchanged as long as LEAVE is specified; this means that a new value which applies to several frames need only be given once (for instance in the basic setup, as LOG is in Fig. 2), and it will be transmitted to other frames, such as that in Fig. 1, which have LEAVE for that value.

A feature of the presentation of setups to the user is also shown in Fig. 2 -- the optional display of the possible legal values for each keyword. This is done in a shorthand, though hopefully clearly: *L*, for instance, when typed in a setup command, can equally well be typed as LE, LEA, LEAV, or LEAVE. *D* is DEFAULT, *N* is NO, and *Y* is the coordinate direction, or YES, depending on the keyword. A *POS*itive *VAL*ue is an integer between zero and 9999, where a *VALUE* may be any real number.

4.2 Examples

In the following, examples are given of some setup commands with notes on their effect, concentrating on the simpler subset (lines 3 to 11 in any definition). No attempt is made to be exhaustive or detailed, whether with respect to options available or the results produced; the intention is to demonstrate the working of the dialogue. Abbreviations, parameter order, and punctuation are purposely varied, to show some of the mnemonic and shorthand devices possible.

AXES X:YES Y=1.0

- draw the X axis through the origin, or, if that is outside the screen, at YMIN (the minimum Y value); draw the Y axis at X = 1.0.

BOX X NO, Y YE; GRID X YES.

- draw horizontal (grid) lines through each major division of the Y axis, but only the two vertical strokes of the box through the end-points of the X axis.

ERAS NO; WAIT NO;

- do not erase the screen before drawing the pictures in this frame, nor wait for the viewer's go-ahead afterwards. This could be used, for example, when one image on the screen is to be built up by several frames.

LOG:=YES

- use a logarithmic scale for all coordinates.

VIEW,X(0-DEFAULT),Y(-100,0).

- the coordinates of the lower left corner of the display area (see WINDOW below) should be Y = -100, X = 0; and of the upper right corner Y = 0, X = XMAX, where XMAX is the largest value in all the X arrays in this frame.

WINDOW 2 : 6 / 9

- (exceptionally, the punctuation is necessary to distinguish these parameters from others which give the physical screen coordinates for the window) - set the display area to be square numbers two to six, out of nine representing the whole of the physical display screen. Squares are numbered from left to right, top to bottom. The VIEWPORT command above would now give the coordinates Y = -100, X = 0 to point *A* in the figure, and Y = 0, X = XMAX to point *B*; all display for this frame would take place in the top right "two thirds" of the screen.

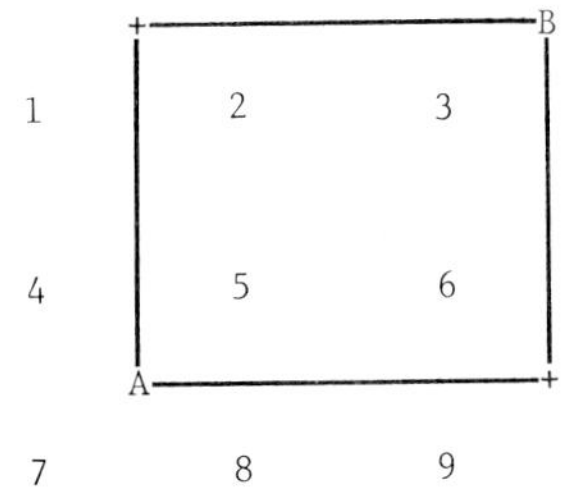

5. PICTURES

5.1 Definition

The setup conditions described above are static, that is to say they represent the status of the system at any moment but do not in themselves perform any display task. That is done by *picture commands*.

Picture commands, unlike setup or control commands, have no immediate effect when they are typed, except to be placed in the frame currently being defined. They are only interpreted to produce displays when their frame is *called*. The CALL statement starts the interpretation of the first picture in the called frame, which may contain further calls. The display process is initiated by a CALL from the "zero frame" (basic setup).

5.2 Editing

For convenience, the pictures in any frame are numbered from 31 on, thus placing all the lines of a definition in the same sequence: heading, then setup conditions, then pictures. This makes it easy to refer to the definition for scanning or comparison, using commands such as PRINT or SHOW. It also allows editing of pictures -- inserting and deleting them according to sequence. For instance, given the pictures in Fig. 1, the following would have the effect shown:

```
32  DRAW ...
```

- replace the ADD command with DRAW ...

```
33.5 ADD ...
```

- insert a new ADD command after TEXT

```
-33
```

- delete the TEXT command.

However, it is often not necessary to give line numbers at all: pictures typed without a number will be added at the end.

5.3 Coordinates

The DRAW and ADD picture commands in Fig. 1 specify the curves to be drawn using *coordinate arrays*. These are vectors, typically FORTRAN arrays, whose elements are taken three at a time (one from each array) to give the Z, Y, and X coordinates of successive points on the curve. Some other commands need a different coordinate specification (TEXT needs one point only, for the first character), but the form of the array arguments remains the same.

Unlike most other arguments in GRIN, the coordinate arrays are interpreted positionally. The concept of plotting the curve of a function *over* the range of the independent variable, i.e. $y(x)/x$, has determined the order of these two coordinates: extending the concept to Z results in "DRAW Z/Y/X" -- where punctuation (/) is unnecessary.

It is often useful to be able to plot several curves over the same independent variable, whose name should then not have to be repeated. Figure 1 shows an ADD command (32) which omits the name of the X array. To allow Y or Z arrays to be omitted, however, one needs a "place marker", so that the X array will not be misinterpreted as the Y array; the TEXT command following the ADD shows the use of the sign ∧ to show the repeated Z array. If this command were in a frame with the setup condition 3DIMENSIONS NO, the place marker for Z would not be necessary, since Z arrays are meaningless for two-dimensional display; in that situation, a picture with only two arrays is assumed to contain Y and X. For simplicity, this is the case in Figs. 3 to 5.

5.4 Examples

The examples in Figs. 3, 4, and 5 illustrate some of the possibilities of display commands in GRIN. One or two brief comments give an idea of the possible graphic results; reference [5] describes the graphics which GRIN commands help to define.

```
: print plotyear 1 plotyear 31 34

   FRAME PLOTYEAR
31 DRAW SEVEN4 WEEKS  DASH  LEGEND "1974"
32 DRAW SEVEN5        DOT   LEGEND "1975"
33 DRAW SEVEN6    DOT DASH  LEGEND "1976"
34 ANNOTATE BOTTOM RIGHT    "CURVES FOR THE YEARS:"

:
```

Figure 3

Frame PLOTYEAR draws three curves, representing the events (in whatever domain) over the three years 1974-1976. The LEGEND subcommands remember the texture of each line, together with the text provided, ready for the ANNOTATE command: this constructs a "legend" box, headed by the title given, in which a a sample of each line texture is listed with its corresponding LEGEND.

```
: print compare 1 compare 31 34

   FRAME COMPARE(TY,TX)
31 DRAW MAINCURVE    LEGEND "MAIN CURVE"
32 ADD ZEROCURVE TRANSLATE 10 SY"0" LE"0-CURVE SHIFTED BY 10"
33 ADD PEAKCURVE SYMBOL"ABCDEFGHIJKL" LE"PEAK CURVE, CLIPPED"
34 TEXT TY TX "COMPARISON OF THREE CURVES"

:
```

Figure 4

Frame COMPARE is defined with two *formal arguments* TY and TX, which allow the location of the title to be changed with each call. One MAINCURVE is plotted (the array expected is actually MAINCURV, since characters beyond 8 are accepted but ignored); two other curves should be added if possible, but the display area should not be expanded to accommodate them (this is the difference between DRAW and ADD). ZEROCURVE will be plotted with "0" at each point, and PEAKCURVE with letters of the alphabet (repeating "A" for the thirteenth point and so on); LEGEND will store these *symbols* instead of a line texture.

```
: print mainline 1 mainline 31 99

   FRAME MAINLINE(FORGOTX,FORGOTY)
31 CALL INTRODUCE
32 CALL STAGE1 WITH SOME ARRAYS TO PLOT
33 SETUP STAGE1
34 NUMBERS FORGOTY FORGOTX "STAGE1 FORGOT THESE" 1,2,3,4,5,6
35 SETUP STAGE2 "READY TO ADD SOMETHING TO STAGE 2"
36 CALL STAGE2
37 TEXT "THIS TEXT IS PRINTED AT THE START OF THE LAST CURVE"
38 SETUP MAINLINE
39 CALL FINISH

:
```

Figure 5

Frame MAINLINE shows how frame structures may be built up in GRIN. INTRODUCE is the frame called first, to start the sequence. Then comes STAGE1, for the first part of the plotting; if it leaves something out we can SETUP the same conditions as for the rest of STAGE1, and plot some NUMBERS accordingly. SETUP STAGE2 is redundant for STAGE2 itself, but affects the TEXT command afterwards, which uses the setup and the last coordinates given in STAGE2.

MAINLINE also demonstrates two features of picture format. First, comments written like text may be inserted almost anywhere after the initial command word; they clash only with true text strings or with the sign ∧, which they may not immediately follow. Secondly, when giving arguments in a CALL or DEFINE command (see below), it is not necessary to provide punctuation; but the frame heading formatted by GRIN gives the formal arguments enclosed in parentheses, as a mnemonic analogy with programming languages.

6. CONTROL COMMANDS

Commands available to control GRIN, which are not stored but have an immediate effect, are described below by means of simple examples. A few are omitted, among them END, which stops GRIN.

6.1 Screen handling

GRIN is designed primarily for the common cases where alphanumeric control dialogue takes place on the same screen as graphics; further, it is most suitable for a storage-tube type of display. The commands in this group control what appears on the screen, normally refreshed after every command.

REFRESH 8; 13; PAGE LINES=18,CHARS=80

- display 8 lines of the definition of the current frame, starting at line 13. REFRESH 0 would prevent any printing between commands. The screen is defined to have 18 lines of 80 characters each; in the PAGE command, only "C" or "L" is significant, and no punctuation is required.

REFRESH NOTEXT; SHOW FRAMEONE 20

- the (POSSIBLE VALUES) field in setup displays should not be printed. The SHOW command allows part of the definition of FRAMEONE, from line 20, to be shown for reference on the same screen as the current frame. FRAMEONE does not become the current frame, so its setup and pictures cannot be changed; it is given a special heading and indented to make this clear.

6.2 Frame handling

Some of the commands for manipulating frames may refer to the "zero" and "minus one" frames, using 0 and -1; as with SHOW, where these are also allowed, the context prevents any ambiguity with numeric values. The "minus one" frame is a reference to the absolute defaults built into the system; these cannot be changed and are the basis of the "zero frame".

DEFINE 0; SETUP MAINLINE; CALL COMPARE NY 1.0

- make the "zero frame" current (this causes the following SETUP and CALL to be interpreted immediately). NY and the one-component "array" with value 1.0 replace the arguments TY and TX in COMPARE (see Fig. 4). SETUP fetches the non-LEAVE values from MAINLINE into the basic setup.

COPY 0 BASIC; DE BASIC ARG1 ARG2; ELIMINATE OLD

- create BASIC as a copy of the basic setup, then make it the current frame, giving it two formal arguments. Delete OLD, which could be a frame or an array.

6.3 Arrays, and the outside world

Since GRIN has no calculating or progrmming facilities, it must be provided with data already prepared for display. This is normally stored in data structures or files, which are extensions of memory in that they provide rapid random access to permanently stored arrays. It is necessary also to store the frame definitions produced, to avoid tedious repetition in every session. These two needs constitute GRIN's contact with other computer systems and the outside world.

ACCESS ARRAYFILE MINE; NEWARRAY=1 2 3 FILEARRY 4 5; STORE NEWFILE THEIRS

- ACCESS is implementation-dependent, but is typically used to provide the name and owner of files containing prepared arrays for display. It is possible to define new arrays, like NEWARRAY, or to redefine or add to accessed arrays, but the = sign is necessary in order to show that the name is not a misspelled command. Names of existing arrays and numbers may be freely mixed, giving a type of "assignment" statement. A new data structure may be created with the STORE command; it will contain all currently defined arrays.

SAVE CURRENT MINE; FETCH LASTONE HIS

- SAVE and FETCH deal with files which contain mainly frame definitions, but include also local arrays -- which are often not STOREd elsewhere. The file on which SAVE makes a record of currently defined objects is written (or read by FETCH) once only straight through, so unlike ACCESS files it does not need to be randomly accessible; nor does it have to be in a format readable by any other system. Neither FETCH nor SAVE affect any current frames or arrays: FETCH ignores anything from the file which has a duplicate name.

7. CONCLUSION

The stage is now being reached where it is possible to solve some of the problems of man-machine communication in the machine rather than the man. Natural language dialogue may still be many years away, but with current software expertise and resources it is reasonable to expect computers to come and meet their users at least half-way. This principle is here applied to the user interface of a new graphics system designed for scientists but not necessarily programmers; a command language has been implemented which could make even a powerful graphics dialogue simple to learn and use. Its customers alone can judge whether GRIN has succeeded.

ACKNOWLEDGEMENTS

Carlo Vandoni of CERN initiated the project; the original design was done in collaboration with him. I am grateful for his continuing advice and support. He and Paul Burkimsher, of CERN and Brunel University, have also been working on the over-all system, which is described in Ref. [5].

REFERENCES

[1] T. Bruins, K.S. Olofsson, E.M. Palandri, B. Segal, H.J. Slettenhaar and H. Strack-Zimmerman, SUPERMUX, *A multi-host front end concentrator system for asynchronous consoles*, CERN 74-19 (CERN, Geneva, 1974).

[2] Cyber 70 and 6000 Computer Systems INTERCOM Reference Manual, Publication No 60307100 (Control Data Corp., Sunnyvale, Calif., 1975).

[3] R. Miller, *GD3*, CERN Computer Centre Program Library Long Write-up (CERN, Geneva, 1976).

[4] R. Hagedorn, J. Reinfelds, C. Vandoni and L. Van Hove, *SIGMA, a new language for interactive array-oriented computing*, CERN 73-5 (CERN, Geneva, 1973).

[5] C. Vandoni and G. Barta, *GRICS, a GRaphic Interactive Construction System*, report in preparation.

[6] B. Williams, T. Chen, D. Schultz and R. Johnson, *A terminal-oriented clinical record system*, Proc. Second Annual Conf. on Computer Graphics and Interactive Techniques, SIGGRAPH'75, Bowling Green, Ohio, 1975 (Computer Graphics 9, No. 1, Spring 1975), p. 115.

E. Morlet and D. Ribbens, (Eds.), International Computing Symposium 1977.

GPGS - GENERAL PURPOSE GRAPHIC SYSTEM

L.C. Caruthers
D. Groot*
E. Hermans*
A. van Dam
J. van den Bos

Informatica
Faculty of Science
University of Nijmegen
Nijmegen
Nederland

*Graphics Group
Rekencentrum
T.H. Delft
Delft
Nederland

Dept. Appl. Math.
Brown University
Providence, R.I.
U.S.A.

This paper describes the General Purpose Graphics System, a subroutine package for interactive and passive graphics. After discussing the design principles behind this system consisting of more than 100 subroutines, there follows a description of the facilities supported by this powerful yet easy to use, device independent package.

1. INTRODUCTION

GPGS is a subroutine package that provides interactive and passive graphics in easy to use form. This paper will describe how the design of GPGS specifies a package which is suitable for use with a wide range of graphics devices attached to large or small computers. The discussion will also cover how the several implementations of GPGS provide a uniform graphics interface for everything from simple programs to large graphic systems. By taking care of all the problems associated with operating systems, communications and the physical characteristics of devices, GPGS provides for the portability of graphics programs between devices and even between computer systems.

In 1972 common graphics hardware for the Universities of Nijmegen, Delft and Cambridge was recommended, and subsequently acquired. The desire for common software for these configurations lead to the design of the GPGS subroutines. The experience of building interfaces between the then existing device dependent subroutine packages supplied by the hardware manufacturers, in order to make the same picture on more than one device, made device independence a primary requirement for the new GPGS software. GPGS has been designed to replace and improve upon such packages as GSP, IBM [1] for the IBM 2250 and Calcomp's well known plotting subroutines. Among the three universities experience with device independent graphics had already been gained with the Cambridge GINO system. Rather than reimplement GINO, Woodsford[2], for the new hardware it was decided to design a new package with more facilities, especially for interactive graphics, than GINO and to give the subroutines a better packaging with different names.

Once the initial design of GPGS was completed in 1972, parallel implementations were begun on an IBM 370 with a PDP-11/45 as a satellite at Nijmegen and on a PDP-11/45 in stand-alone mode at Delft. These two assembly language implementations have been in more or less continuous development since then and have been in use by applications programs since the summer of 1973. Both implementations are now distributed by their respective developers. In 1974-75 the graphics group at the computing center at the University of Trondheim in Norway made an ANSI FORTRAN implementation based on the Delft PDP implementation. Furthermore, unauthorized versions of GPGS seem to exist in countries as far as Germany and India.

2. MAJOR DESIGN ISSUES

Over the course of its implementation the design of GPGS as given by the definitions of the subroutines in the Reference Manual, Groot[3], has gradually changed as a result of experience gained during the implementation. The major design decisions of GPGS therefore influenced both the initial specification and the changes that occurred with time. From the beginning our aims were twofold: first to make GPGS device independent so that a wide range of graphics devices would be easily accessible, and second not to burden an applications program with a superimposed data structure.

The main decision was to create a subroutine package instead of a graphics language or graphics extension to an existing language. A subroutine package is easier to design and implement, simpler for programmers to learn, and easily extended by adding more subroutines. The ease of implementation also allowed for more efficient assembler language implementations on different computer systems.

The limitation of a subroutine package, when compared with a language, is that you only have one type of syntax for expressing the graphics functions, a subroutine name followed by its easily forgettable arguments. On the other hand this simpler syntax makes the package easier for programmers to understand, especially because the syntax is that of a language they already know. FORTRAN linking conventions are frequently available from other high-level languages, so the choice of an applications language is not forced on the programmer. GPGS also provides a graphics interface for existing non-graphics programs or applications packages.

To make GPGS device independent it was decided that each implementation should be divided into a device independent part to be called by applications programs, and as many execution time loaded, device dependent device-drivers as there are devices for that implementation to support. To the applications programmer this means that he can write his graphics program once and use it with different graphics equipment without changing the source code or relinking his program. Since his program may run with a different device each time it is executed, the applications programmer should imagine that he is programming for a single idealized device. This idealized device draws pictures by moving a drawing mechanism from position to position. This characterization of graphics output devices applies to plotters, microfilm output, storage tube displays and moveable beam CRT refreshed displays. By designing GPGS to handle refreshed CRT's a design was achieved which was suitable for the simpler types of devices as well.

But if the applications program has no access to the internal GPGS data structure, how can it manipulate the display file of a refreshed CRT? For all graphics devices GPGS makes the applications program create ordered collections of picture elements called picture segments. For a refreshed CRT the picture segments are segments in a linear display file. Display picture segments can be created, extended and deleted, but not updated. Since picture segments have no internal structure to correspond to the applications data structure, GPGS allows the applications program to create a hierarchy of names to correspond to the data structure.

The device dependent display picture segments are built directly in response to the picture element creation calls from the applications program. If the applications program wants to make the same picture on several different devices, it can first create a device independent pseudo picture segment which can later be more efficiently used to make parts of display picture segments on possibly different devices.

The idealized device concept is also appropriate for describing the GPGS scheme for handling input from the user of a display device. The GPGS idealized device has the following single tools: refresh clock, alphanumeric keyboard, lightpen for picking, audible alarm; and at least one tool in each of the following classes of tools: dials (1-dimensional), tracking cross and tablet (2-dimensional), joystick (3-dimensional), function switches. Each single tool or class of tools has a format for returning integer and/or floating point data to the applications program. Those tools not available in hardware may be simulated in software by the device drivers.

GPGS uses the concept of an idealized device with real tools rather than a set of abstract tools, Foley[4], Trambacz [5], for all devices. The benefits of this approach are that when real hardware exists the applications program can use it directly, whereas with the abstract tool approach there will always be a layer of software mapping real tools into abstract tools. This extra indirectness is a conceptual burden for both the applications program writer and the console user, both of whom must figure out what the use of an actual hardware tool is going to mean to the program.

The subroutines included in GPGS were chosen to be just far enough removed (indirect) from the hardware to provide device independence and at the same time allow the applications programmer to (indirectly) control the hardware of an advanced CRT display. An additional guideline as to what features to include in GPGS was given by the desire to make the package general purpose. Thus those features required or extremely useful for a wide range of applications (2 and 3d windowing and clipping, transformations) were included. Those with more limited applicability like hidden-line removal, data structure, and animation, were not included.

When designing the subroutines themselves the key concept was simplicity, meaning that the subroutines should be easy to understand and to use. The name of a subroutine indicates what its function is and each subroutine has as few arguments as possible. GPGS supplies reasonable default values for any unspecified picture making conditions.

3. GPGS FACILITIES

The GPGS facilities are based on the activity cycle of interactive programs. First a picture is presented on a display, then input is received from the console user, which is used to make the next picture. In this section we will first describe how an applications program uses the facilities to build a picture, and second how the applications program obtains information from the console user.

For managing resources GPGS allows the initialization of several devices (NITDEV) or several buffers (NITBUF) before the corresponding releasing of any of the resources. To allow the applications programmer to designate which device or buffer is to be used there are routines for selecting (SELDEV, SELBUF) the device or buffer to be used. The selected device or buffer is then referred to as the 'current' device or buffer.

Once the resources have been initialized or selected, the applications programmer can begin making pictures. Picture segments are the GPGS unit of picture manipulation. The beginning of a picture segment is indicated to GPGS by an applications program call to the BGNPIC routine, which passes the unique picture segment identifying number to GPGS.

After BGNPIC the applications program calls picture element creation subroutines to fill the picture segment. A call to ENDPIC terminates the definition of a picture segment and serves as a command to make the picture segment visible.

Picture elements are passed to GPGS as cartesian coordinates in a 2 or 3 dimensional user coordinate space. Since the coordinate representation of an object only occupies a portion of the infinite coordinate space, GPGS must be told what part of the coordinate space is to be used for the picture. This is done by specifying a rectangle or box (window) to GPGS as high and low boundaries on each of the X, Y (and Z) coordinate axes.

Once the applications program has indicated the portion of the user coordinate space that is to be displayed, it may also specify a viewport, which is the portion of the display surface that the contents of the window are going to appear on. To provide a frame of reference for specifying viewport limits to GPGS, Normalized Device Coordinates are defined to have the range 0.0 to 1.0 along the side of the largest square area (cubic volume) that will fit on the display. If the display area is not square then the viewport specifications allowed for that device will have legitimate values outside the range of 0.0 to 1.0.

But what does this have to do with picture segments? A picture segment can have only one viewport, and preferably only one window. These viewing conditions must therefore be established for each picture segment before the creation of the picture segment is begun with BGNPIC.

Picture segments are built by the subroutine calls that pass picture elements and picture element attributes to GPGS. GPGS accepts line segments, character strings and circles as picture elements that can be specified by one call to GPGS. One attribute of a line segment is line type (solid, dashed, dotted, endpoint, or invisible) of the line. This attribute must be specified with each call to create a line segment. One attribute of a character string is the size of the characters, which unlike the line type of lines, is a global condition which is specified to GPGS by a separate subroutine, CSIZES. All character strings then are made with the same size until another call is made to CSIZES to change the character size.

A third kind of picture element attribute is one that is global within a picture segment and gets reset to a default value by each call to BGNPIC. These attributes include: blinking, intensity, colour, depth modulation, and lightpen sensitivity. For CRT displays these last attributes correspond to processing conditions of the display processing unit (DPU). Thus the call to request blinking picture elements would precede the subroutine calls to create the picture elements which will blink when they appear on the CRT display. So you can see that calls to set picture element attributes will be intermixed with the calls to create picture elements during the building of a picture segment.

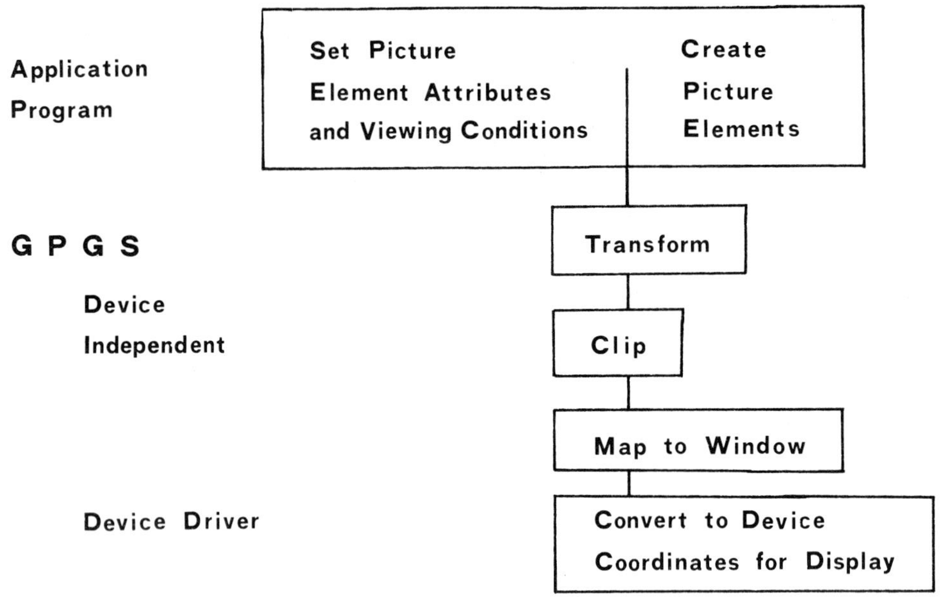

Fig. 1. Picture Processing Pipeline

Once pseudo picture segments have been created they can be used many times to build display picture segments. When the applications program calls the INSERT routine with the number of a pseudo picture segment, picture element attribute settings, names and picture elements are retrieved from the pseudo picture segment, passed back through the CPU processing pipeline and given to the currently selected device driver. During the inserting process all the references to lower level pseudo picture segments are resolved, so the result of an insert is always picture elements without the references.

Picture segments may be stored off-line in picture segment libraries which are controlled by the applications programmer much in the same way as the device and buffer resources. Indeed libraries can be thought of as extensions of buffers. They are particularly useful for making large pictures on small computers, saving display picture segments of standard menus or as a file of standard drawing symbols (picture parts) stored as pseudo picture segments.

To allow the applications program to find out the properties and status of its currently allocated resources, and to retrieve previously established attribute settings, GPGS has subroutines for returning execution environment information to the applications program. This information is sometimes very useful when used in conjunction with the GPGS error handling facility which will allow the applications program to specify one of its subroutines to receive control on the occurrence of an error condition.

The graphic output facilities of GPGS enable the applications program to make a picture on the display. But once the picture is made the applications program needs information from the console user to find out how the picture should be changed.

For easy identification by the applications program each tool is assigned a permanent integer identifier. To request information from the interactive console the applications program passes GPGS a list of the tools that it is willing to accept information from as a parameter of the INWAIT function subroutine. GPGS then looks at the interrupt queue, to see if the console user has used any of the tools; if he has, the information from that tool is returned to the applications program. If no tools have been used yet, then GPGS examines the time parameter which was also passed with the call to INWAIT. If the time is positive GPGS will return to the applications program, either when the time expires or the console user uses a tool. If the time is zero, information is returned from a tool only if the console user had used the tool prior to the call to INWAIT, otherwise GPGS returns without providing any tool information. If the time parameter is negative, INWAIT returns to the applications program only after the console user uses one of the tools in the list. Though not all implementations currently support it, INWAIT is designed to wait for information from more than one device at the same time.

When INWAIT returns to the applications program it gives back the information from only one tool. To allow the applications program to inquire as to the status of other tools, GPGS has the REATOL subroutine which has the tool number as input and returns information in the same format as INWAIT. On many kinds of display hardware there are program controllable mechanisms to assist in getting information from the console user. To allow the applications program to set various tools, GPGS has the routine WRITOL. WRITOL has the same parameter list as REATOL, but the information is going to the tool and not coming from it.

4. ACCOMPLISHMENTS

In this final section we will evaluate the success of the GPGS design and implementations in meeting design objectives. The discussion will examine how well device independence was achieved, how easy GPGS has been to use, the consequences of not having a data structure, the acceptance of the overall design, and the suitability of GPGS for writing programs in specific applications areas.

The decision to make a subroutine package instead of a language has proven to be a good one. This is largely seen in the fact that there are multiple implementations and that the subroutines are easily understood and used by applications programmers. Indeed the decision to make a new package and not to reimplement GINO is born out by the fact that the Trondheim group considered both the GINO and GPGS designs, and chose GPGS even though it meant making a separate implementation.

Device independence has been achieved. Programs that can make a plot on a plotter can make the same picture on a refresh CRT. But in order to allow this, the plotting program has been forced to abide by the same picture segment creation rules as a CRT program. In our experience in writing device drivers we have seen that a driver for a simple device like a plotter or printer is very easy to write, and that the driver for an interactive device, though much more work is certainly simpler than creating a whole new package and conversion interfaces for other devices. Making a new driver is usually a matter of modifying the lowest level of some existing driver. The table below shows the drivers implemented at the "home" installations of three GPGS implementations:

Devices Supported	GPGS Implementations		
	IBM370 Nijmegen	PDP11 Delft	FORTRAN Trondheim
Vector General	X	X	
Tektronix 4010---4015			
Buffered	X		
Unbuffered		X	X
Plotter			
Calcomp	X		
Tektronix		X	
Kingmatic			X
Printer		X	X

Table I: GPGS Device Support

The decisions to leave out a data structure and make a device independent picture representation optional have resulted in packages which take little memory space and which run quickly. With Tektronix 4014 (or 4015) driver the RT-11 version of GPGS is smaller than the nucleus of the batch version of the RT-11 operating system. Similarly the basic routines for making a picture on, and interacting with a CRT on console attached to a PDP-11 satellite of the IBM-370 requires about half again as much space as the FORTRAN I/O modules (IBCOM + FIOCS). For highly interactive (not much computation) applications programs on the IBM implementation, the CPU utilization and response time are comparable to that of text editing programs.

The final comments on the accomplishments of GPGS are on how "general purpose" GPGS has proven to be. That is, how easy it is to write applications programs. For computer-aided design programs, where a fairly low level interface is needed along with multiple devices (interactive and plotter), GPGS has proven to be ideal. For people who just want to make plots of their data GPGS is usable, but nonetheless a set of graph making routines to go on top of GPGS has been designed.

Applications that have proven to be unreasonable to attempt with GPGS have to do with a picture which must be changed in real-time in response to console user input. Due to the requirement that a picture segment must be completely rebuilt each time it is changed, even if the building of the next version of the picture is overlapped with the displaying of the previous version it is difficult to achieve real time animation with anything but the simplest of pictures. Where a device has transformation hardware, however, a program accessing this hardware through GPGS can produce real time motion of arbitrarily complex pictures.

Thus we have seen that GPGS has largely achieved its original design goals of being a device independent, easy to use subroutine package. GPGS provides applications programs with access to multiple graphics devices through the same subroutine calls. The GPGS design has proved to be implementable on small and large computers alike.

5. SAMPLE PROGRAM

```
C SAMPLE PROGRAM
      DIMENSION IBUF(2000),WIN(4),VP(4)
      DIMENSION IVIS(6)
      DIMENSION LTC(4),IDA(3),FDA(3)
      DATA WIN/0.0,1.0,0.0,1.0/
      DATA VP/0.0,1.0,0.0,1.0/
      DATA IVIS/1,1,1,1,1,1/
      DATA LTC/3,401,402,-1/
C
C INITIALIZE GPGS
      CALL NITDEV (3)
      CALL NITBUF (IBUF,2000)
      CALL WINDW(WIN(1))
      CALL VPORT(VP(1))
C
C DRAW BOX
    5 CALL BGNPIC(100)
      CALL LINE (0.2,0.5,0)
      CALL LINE (0.6,0.5,IVIS(1),1)
      CALL LINE (0.6,0.9,IVIS(2),2)
      CALL LINE (0.2,0.9,IVIS(3),3)
      CALL LINE (0.2,0.5,IVIS(4),4)
      CALL LINE (0.6,0.9,IVIS(5),5)
      CALL LINE (0.2,0.9,0)
      CALL LINE (0.6,0.5,IVIS(6),6)
C
C DISPLAY INSTRUCTIONS FOR THE USER
      CALL LINE (0.25,0.4,0)
      CALL CHAR ('THIS IS A BOX*.')
      CALL LINE (0.15,0.3,0)
      CALL CHAR ('LIGHTPEN LINE TO
     X DELETE IT
     X *N FUNCTION KEY 1: RESTORE
     X *N FUNCTION KEY 2: STOP*.')
      CALL ENDPIC
C
C PICTURE SEGMENT IS NOW VISIBLE
C WAIT FOR AN INTERRUPT
      IN=INWAIT(-1.0,LTC,IDA,3,FDA,3)
      GO TO (10,20,99), IN
C
C LIGHTPEN HIT: DELETE LINE
   10 JLINE=IDA(2)
      IVIS(JLINE)=0
      CALL DELPIC(100)
      GO TO 5
C
C FUNCTION KEY 1: RESTORE LINES
   20 DO 25 I=1,6
   25 IVIS(I)=1
      CALL DELPIC(100)
      GO TO 5
C
C FUNCTION KEY 2: STOP EXECUTION
   99 CALL RLSDEV(3)
      STOP
      END
```

REFERENCES

1. IBM - Graphics Subroutine Package (GSP) for FORTRAN IV, COBOL, and PL/I; form GC27-6932.

2. Woodsford, P.A. (Ed.), GINO, Computer Aided Design Group, Corn Exchange Street, Cambridge, England.

3. GPGS Reference Manual, Groot, D., Hermans E., Rekencentrum, T.H., Delft, and Caruthers, L.C., Patburg, J., Informatica, Faculty of Science, University of Nijmegen.

4. Foley, J.D., Wallace, V.L., The Art of Natural Man-Machine Communications, Proc. IEEE. 62, 4, pp.462-471, 1974.

5. Trambacz, U., Towards Device-Independent Graphics Systems, Computer Graphics (SIGGRAPH-ACM) 9, pp.49-52, 1975.

6. Caruthers, L.C., van Dam, A., General Purpose Graphics System, User's Tutorial, Graphics Group, University of Nijmegen, 1975.

E. Morlet and D. Ribbens, (Eds.), International Computing Symposium 1977.

SPECIFICATION AND DESIGN OF DIALOGUE SYSTEMS WITH STATE DIAGRAMS

Ernst Denert
SOFTLAB
Munich, Germany

A diagrammatic method for describing dialogue systems is presented. It uses the concept of the finite automaton in its graphical representation, the state diagram, adapted for top down design by hierarchical structuring of state diagrams. Not only man machine dialogues may be described but also communication with other computer systems. The use of state diagram hierarchies at different stages of software development, e.g. definition of the user interface, system specification and design, is discussed. Finally, a technique for implementing such diagrams is presented. It allows for an almost mechanical translation of a diagram into the programming language used to implement the system.

1. INTRODUCTION

A dialogue system (DS) is a computer system with which one or more partners - either human beings or other computers - exchange information. This communication serves two purposes:

(1) to raise the information potential of the dialogue system or the dialogue partners (DP) and/or
(2) to perform services like printing bills, tickets, etc.

The rules a man machine dialogue has to follow are much more formal than those for human conversation. Therefore, there is a need for a precise and comprehensible specification of these rules; precision is required by the computer, comprehensibility by the man. The method presented in this paper satisfies both aims. It provides a means for specifying the user interface of a dialogue system in a precise and comprehensible manner and to derive from it a system design which reflects the user interface directly.

Our method is based on a well known concept from theoretical computer science: the finite automaton. It consists of a finite set of states and a mapping which yields the successor state to the current state depending on a given input. This simple model in its graphical representation, the state diagram, is augmented so that it allows top down design through the possibility of building a hierarchy of state diagrams.

We consider not only man machine dialogues but also dialogues between the system and different types of dialogue partners. These dialogues have a star-shaped structure (fig. 1). Two DPs cannot communicate directly but only via the DS, i.e. we do not consider networks of a universal structure. It should be noted that in this context DP means one type of dialogue partner which may be a human being or some computer system. So, several users are considered to be one DP and it is assumed that each user has its own (virtual) dialogue system.

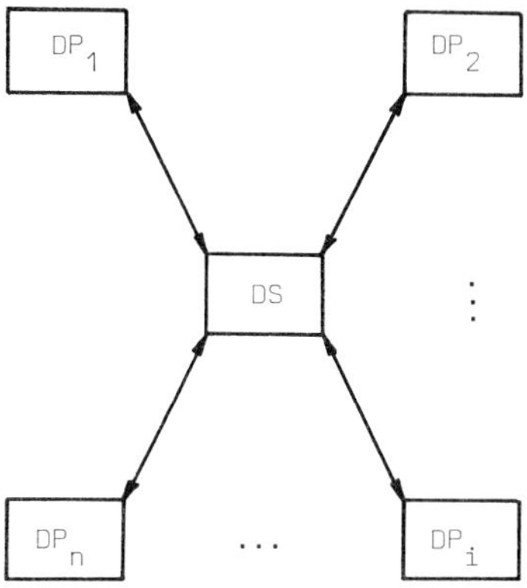

DS: Dialogue System
DP: Dialogue Partner

Fig. 1 Star-shaped dialogue structure

The state diagram method for dialogue specification originated in the computer graphics area where many rather different interaction devices have to be handled in order to get a manageable dialogue system, see /New 68/ and /StWa 71/. /Par 69/ proposes the use of state diagrams for describing the user interface of an interactive operating system.

Based on the ideas in these papers our concept develops them in the following ways:
- The notion of a "complex state" enables the widely accepted software engineering method of top down design (or stepwise refinement) for state diagrams.
- Our concept not only allows for modeling man machine communication but also interaction with other computer systems; i.e. it may be used for computer networks.

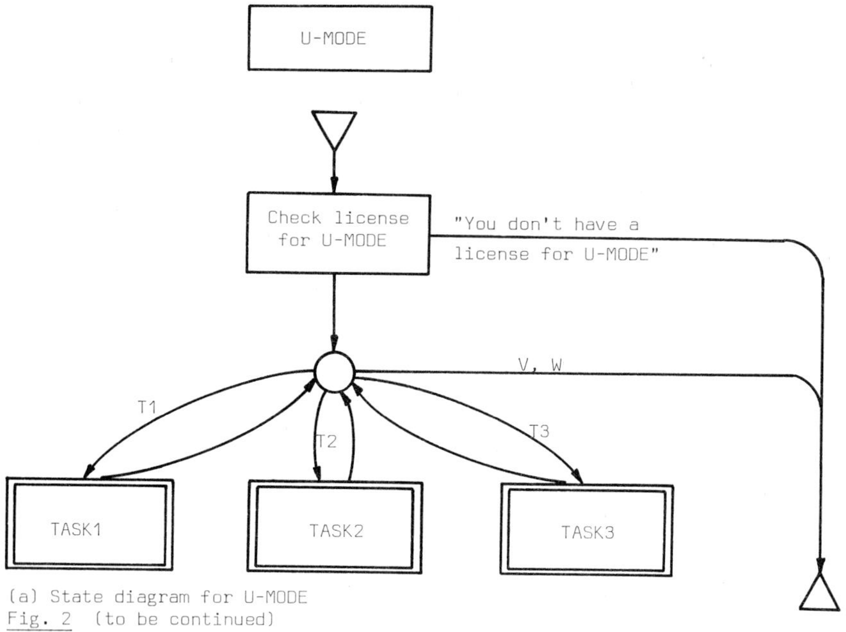

(a) State diagram for U-MODE
Fig. 2 (to be continued)

- So-called "interaction points" explicitly denote where an interaction between the DS and a DP takes place. This is important, among other things, because the load of a teleprocessing system heavily depends on the number of interactions it has to handle per second. Therefore, the design of a dialogue system should clearly reveal how many interactions a particular task requires.

State diagram hierarchies as presented in this paper have already been used in two very different software projects. The first one is an editor for a two-dimensional programming language, PLAN2D /De 75a/, for the manipulation of linked data structures. A PLAN2D program consists of complex line drawings which may be built up and modified with the PLAN2D editor, /De 75b/. This dialogue system is implemented on the ADAGE graphics system and utilizes some of its elaborate interaction devices (light pen, data tablet, analog dials, buttons and, of course, an alphanumeric key board).

The second project is a large teleprocessing system called START, which provides information and reservation services for travel agencies. The START system which is not yet implemented will serve about 1000 terminals in travel agencies. To accomplish this task it has to communicate with computer systems of several large companies in the public transport and mass tourism business. In the START system, state diagrams are used for the
- specification of the user interface,
- description of the dialogue with the other computer systems mentioned.

2. AN EXAMPLE

Fig. 2 shows two state diagrams where the second is a refinement of a part of the first one. A detailed discussion of the graphical symbols used for drawing state diagrams will be given in section 3. For the moment we only want to develop an intuitive understanding of the method to be presented.

The system described in the example always works in one of several modes (named U-, V-, W-Mode). When the user drives the system into U-Mode (Fig. 2a) it first checks whether he is authorized to do so. If not, the system forces an exit from U-Mode and sends him an appropriate message ("You don't have a license for U-Mode"). Otherwise, a so-called interaction point (IAP), depicted by a circle, is entered. Such a point symbolizes a wait for an interaction from a dialogue partner. Arrows emanating from an IAP define the set of states that can be reached from that IAP, the labels at the arrows determine the set of enabled interactions (input commands). Each other input is rejected.

Fig. 2a is to be interpreted as follows:
- Transactions T1, T2, and T3 drive the dialogue system into the states TASK1, TASK2, and TASK3, respectively. When the task is accomplished the system returns to the (single) IAP of the U-MODE diagram.
- The U-MODE can be left by using one of the transactions V or W, thereby switching to the V- or W-MODE.

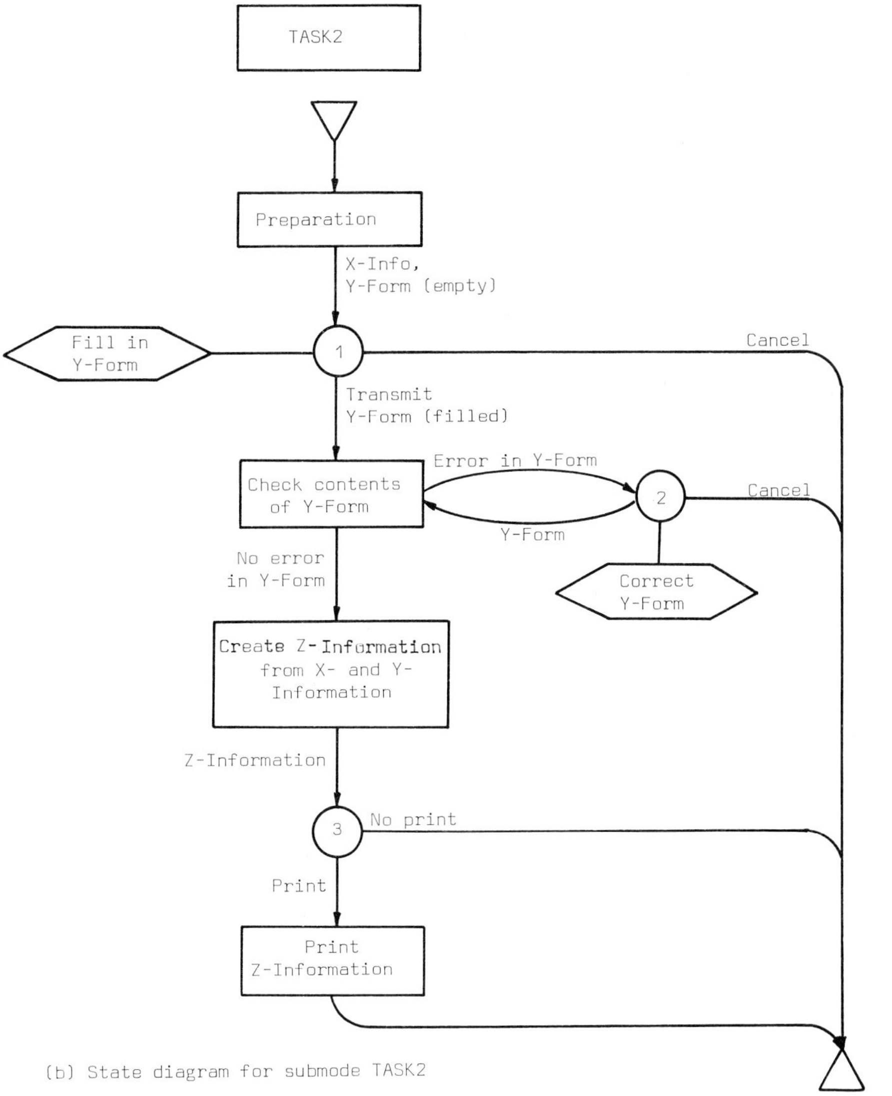

(b) State diagram for submode TASK2

Fig. 2 Part of a state diagram hierarchy

The difference between a simply and a doubly framed box is of major importance:

- A simply framed box denotes an action which is executed by the DS without further interactions with the user.
- A doubly framed box indicates that there exists a refining state diagram elsewhere, e.g. the TASK2 box in fig. 2a is refined by the TASK2 state diagram.

Fig. 2b shows this refinement in the TASK2 state diagram:

- After some "Preparation" the dialogue system displays the "X-Info" and the empty "Y-Form" on the screen and passes to interaction point 1 (IAP1). There it waits until the user has filled in and transmitted the "Y-Form". In addition, at this point the user may cancel TASK2.
- If errors are found in the "Y-Form" the system forces the user to correct them in IAP2, since the dialogue does not proceed until all errors are removed. Alternatively, in IAP2 the user again may cancel the whole process.
- Finally the output ("Z-Information") is created and displayed on transition to IAP3. Here the user has to decide whether he wants a hardcopy of the "Z-Information" (transmission of the print command) or not.

3. STATE DIAGRAMS AND STATE DIAGRAM HIERARCHIES

Basically, state diagrams (SD) are directed labeled graphs. The modes with their labels represent states and the edges (arrows) state transitions. The latter are labeled with input symbols so that the successor of the current state can be determined when an interaction occurs.

The symbols used for constructing state diagrams are shown in fig. 3; their meaning is as follows:

(a) Each SD contains exactly one initial state and one final state. They mark the points of entry and exit, i.e. they determine where the execution of a SD starts and stops. Furthermore, they are needed for embedding a SD which is a refinement of a complex state.

(b) A circle represents a special state termed interaction point (IAP). In such a state the system is waiting for an interaction, i.e. an input from a dialogue partner (man or machine). This DP is denoted by some abbreviation within the circle which may be omitted if no misunderstanding can occur (e.g. a SD describing a user interface deals with only one DP, the user). Notice that an IAP always describes an interaction with one and the same DP.

The explicit representation of IAPs supports the design of a teleprocessing system in some aspects:
- An IAP marks the point where the system may switch over to serve another user while it is waiting for a response from the DP of the IAP in question.
- The job which the dialogue system has to carry out between two IAPs is a clear candidate for a separate program unit.
- The number of interactions per second is an important performance characteristic of a teleprocessing system. In order to predict this figure it is necessary to derive the number of interactions that are needed for fulfilling the user's tasks. This can easily be done by simply counting the IAPs contained in a SD and its refining SDs.

(c) A simple state represents an action which is characterized by the text contained in the box and which is executed without further interactions. (This is not the whole truth: A simple state in a user interface SD may be refined for system design; then it may contain IAP's for interactions with other DPs, e.g. computers, operators, etc. but no more user interactions. But, considering a set of state diagrams for a special purpose (system specification, design), no further refinement for a simple state exists, i.e. it is at the bottom of the state hierarchy.)

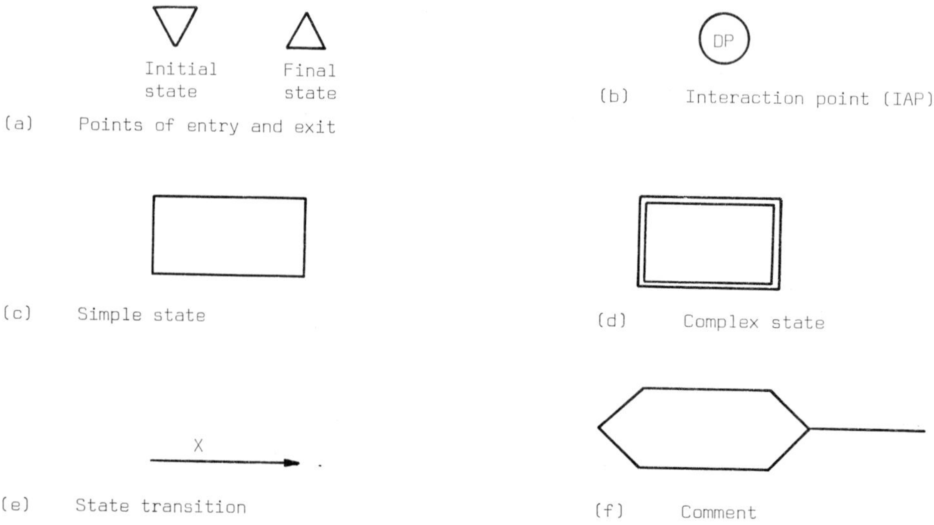

Fig. 3 Graphical symbols for the construction of state diagrams

(d) A complex state represents an action which is described by another SD identified by the name in the doubly framed box. It yields a simple, but nevertheless powerful means for designing and describing dialogue systems in a top down manner. In contrast to a simple state which is executed immediately the dialogue system may remain in a complex state for an arbitrary long period due to IAPs and inner complex states.

The embedding of a SD at the place of the complex state which it refines is discussed below.

(e) State transitions are depicted by arrows. Of all transition possibilities between the different kinds of states (a - d above) the following need special consideration:

- On transition to an IAP the DS always transmits a message to the DP; the arrow representing a transition is labeled with (a specification of) this message.
- All arrows emanating from an IAP must be uniquely labeled with permitted DP inputs in order to enable the system to select the desired transition. Inputs not corresponding to one of the transition labels are rejected.
- If there is more than one transition from a simple state they are labeled with predicates which can be somehow evaluated by the system and used to select one transition. Of course, exactly one predicate must evaluate to true. At most one of the arrows may be unlabeled, thereby stating that the corresponding transition has to be taken if none of the other predicates evaluates to true.
- All arrows pointing to a complex state are (conceptually) tied to the initial state of the refining SD.
- Arrows emanating from a complex state are (conceptually) connected with those arrows ending at the final state of the refining SD which are labeled identically.

(f) Comments are designated by a hexagonal box attached to its point of reference by a simple line.

Now, a state diagram hierarchy (SDH) consists of a set of states which may be arranged as a tree. Its leaves are the simple states whereas the complex states constitute its branch nodes.

4. STATE DIAGRAM HIERARCHIES FOR USER INTERFACE, SPECIFICATION AND DESIGN OF DIALOGUE SYSTEMS

We have seen how state diagrams can be developed top down using complex states. When appropriately designed the resulting state diagram hierarchy defines several meaningful levels of abstraction. The relations between these levels are formally defined by the rules for substituting complex states by their refining SDs.

In addition, we advocate another hierarchy viz. a hierarchy of SDHs. There are at least three levels in this second hierarchy:

(1) A SDH describing the user interface of a dialogue system.
(2) A SDH constituting the specification of the dialogue system, i.e. describing what the system does.
(3) A SDH for the design of the system, thereby stating how the system fulfills the specification.

Obviously, the most abstract level is the user interface. The specification is derived from it by some sort of refinement, and in a further step the design is obtained from the specification. We cannot give any formal rules for carrying out these refining steps. Instead, we should like to stress that they have to preserve the basic structure of the state diagrams, i.e. that the final design diagrams directly reflect the user interface diagrams. Taking this approach we accomplish Parnas' claim "that (user) interfaces should be an explicit article of attention for designers not an implication of the implementation decisions", /Par 69/.

Following are some remarks characterizing the above three levels of abstraction:

(1) SDHs for the user interface should, of course, contain only details relevant to the user who should not be bothered with implementation features. Especially, interaction points must solely designate interaction with the user, IAP's with other computer systems are not appropriate at this level.

(2) The specification of a dialogue system may involve interactions with other computer systems. Fig. 4 illustrates this point; it contains two IAP's each specifying an interaction between the DS and another system. Note that we introduce a somewhat formal notation for labeling the edges. "DS/SCS: Inquiry 1" means that the DS sends to SCS an inquiry 1. Therein lies some redundancy, since this label is attached to an edge pointing to an IAP with SCS which implies that some message is sent from DS to SCS. We accept this redundancy because we explicitly want to state sender and receiver of a message.

Fig. 4 further illustrates that a simple state in the user interface may become a complex state in the specification. In some cases, it also makes sense to refine an edge, i.e. to replace an arrow by a whole state diagram when developing the specification from the user interface.

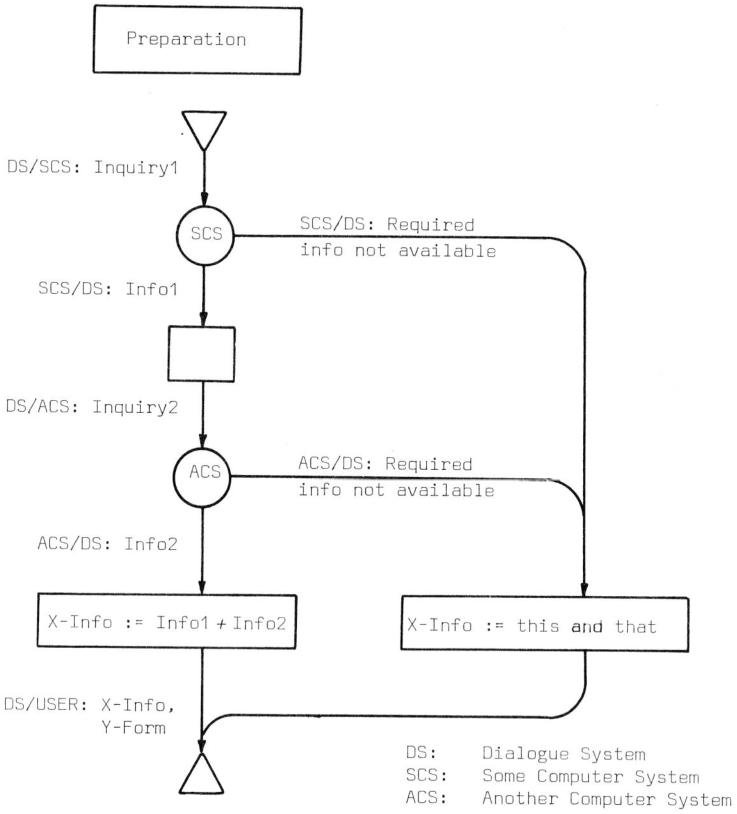

Fig. 4 Refinement of the user interface simple state "Preparation" (fig. 2b) for system specification purposes

If the action a simple states represents cannot be described sufficiently by the text in the simple framed box a more detailed specification may be given elsewhere either in some informal way or by an algorithmic notation. Such a refinement of a simple state must by no means contain an interaction with some dialogue partner.

(3) Part of the system design could evolve from enrichment of the specification with implementation dependent details, e.g. access to data structures, files, I/O devices etc. Considerably more experience with this level of refinement has to be gained.

5. IMPLEMENTATION OF STATE DIAGRAM HIERARCHIES

A SDH can easily be implemented by almost mechanical translation into some programming language using the following technique. The states are numbered in Dewey decimal notation, i.e. the states in a diagram are arbitrarily numbered and prefixed with the number of the refined state, if any. Consider fig. 5: The MAIN DIAGRAM has three states numbered 1, 2 and 3. The MODE A diagram has four states the numbers of which are prefixed with 2 (the number of the refined state MODE A) giving the state numbers 21, 22, 23, and 24.

The edge labels in both diagrams are considered to be predicates which are evaluated either from user inputs or from other data. Note that we do not distinguish between simple states and interaction points here, both are merely considered to be states.

Now, we implement the two diagrams in fig. 5 as given in fig. 6 guided by the following rules and using ALGOL 68 notation: A global integer variable **state** always holds the current state number. The structure of each diagram is translated into a *case*-statement with each case corresponding to one state. This *case*-statement is embedded in a infinite loop (*do...od*) which can only be left via the *out*-clause of the *case*-statement.

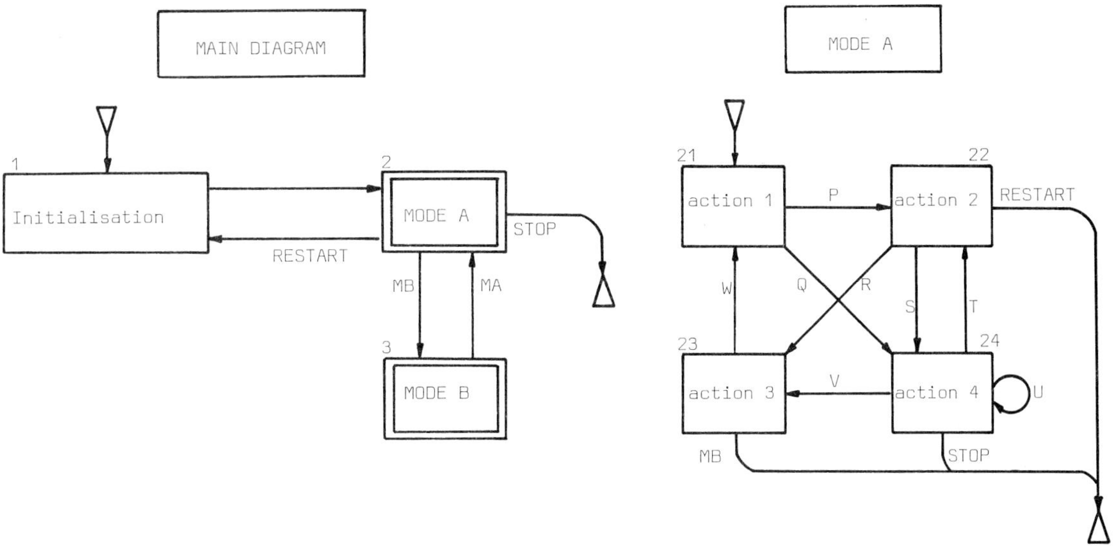

Fig. 5 SDH with state numbers in Dewey decimal notation

```
proc  MAIN DIAGRAM = void:
begin state := 1;
   do case state
        in (initialisation; state := 2)
           MODE A,
           MODE B
        out goto exit
      esac
   od;
exit:
end;

proc  MODE A = void:
begin state := 21;
   do case state - 20
        in (action 1; state := if P then 22 else 24 fi),
           (action 2; state := if RESTART then 1
                               elif R then 23 else 24 fi),
           (action 3; state := if MB then 3 else 21 fi),
           (action 4; state := if STOP then 0
                               elif T then 22
                               elif U then 24 else 23 fi)
        out goto exit
      esac
   od;
exit:
end;
```

Fig. 6 Implementation of the SDH of fig. 5 using ALGOL 68 notation

Let us consider a transition from MODE A to MODE B. Assume that the system being in MODE A somehow arrives at state 23 where it first executes ***action 3***. Then the input ***MB*** occurs and as a consequence the ***state*** variable gets the value *3*. The next execution of the case-statement evaluates the case selecting expression ***state-20*** to -17. Therefore, the out-clause is taken and the procedure ***MODE A*** is left via ***exit***. So, the next execution of the case-statement in the ***MAIN DIAGRAM*** procedure takes place resulting in the desired call of ***MODE B*** due to the value of ***state*** which is still *3* . This simple example should sufficiently illustrate the way of communication between the different levels in the state diagram hierarchy.

The example presented should have convinced the reader that the structure of a state diagram is transformed easily and almost mechanically in a program. Lacking a case-statement a language feature like the FORTRAN computed goto, the ALGOL 60 switch, or a PL/I label array may be used. Changes in a state diagram, e.g. inserting or deleting a state, cause only limited effort in changing the corresponding program. Due to the unique ***state*** variable no ambiguity concerning the state of the system can arise. This is especially useful for testing and debugging, because the ***state*** variable strongly helps in localizing an error.

6. CONCLUSION

We have presented a graphical method using state diagrams for describing dialogue systems which is both precise and comprehensible and which has proven its usefulness in two very different software projects. It not only allows for modeling man machine communication but also interaction with other computer systems, i.e. it may be used for computer networks. The notion of a complex state enables a top down design of state diagrams resulting in a state diagram hierarchy. Several SDHs each corresponding to another phase in a software project (user interface definition, system specification, system design) constitute a second kind of hierarchy which needs further investigation. Finally, an implementation technique was sketched. It offers a reliable and easily modifiable realization method for state diagram hierarchies.

Acknowledgement

The author gratefully acknowledges several fruitful discussions he had with colleagues at SOFTLAB, especially Ch. Floyd, U. Maiborn, and P. Schnupp.

References

/De 75a/ Denert, E., "PLAN2D - Konzept und Syntax einer zweidimensionalen Programmiersprache", Dissertation, TU Berlin, Fachbereich Kybernetik, Juli 1975

/De 75b/ Denert, E., "Eine Methode für Entwurf und Implementierung interaktiver Software-Systeme dargestellt am Beispiel des PLAN2D-Editors und des ADAGE-Graphics-Systems", TU Berlin, Fachbereich Kybernetik, Bericht Nr. 75-23, September 1975

/New 68/ Newman, W.M., "A System for Interactive Graphical Programming", Proc. SJCC 1968, pp. 47-54

/Par 69/ Parnas, D.L., "On the Use of Transition Diagrams in the Design of a User Interface for an Interactive Computer System", Proc. National ACM Conference 1969, pp. 379-385

/StWa 71/ Stack, T.R., Walker, S.T., "AIDS - Advanced Interactive Display System", Proc. SJCC 1971, pp. 113-121

E. Morlet and D. Ribbens, (Eds.), International Computing Symposium 1977.

TIME-DEPENDENT BLOCKING OF TERMINAL INPUT

E. Lopes Cardozo, Department of Physiology,
State University, Utrecht, Holland

Sometimes terminal input to a computer system has to be treated per character, rather than per line. In timesharing systems and computer networks this may result in a relatively high overhead. A technique is presented that blocks terminal input, independent of its logical structure.

INTRODUCTION

An increasing number of terminals are connected to computer systems of various kinds. This paper addresses a problem encountered with terminals that are used with character-oriented software.

In many timesharing systems terminal input is handled strictly one line at a time. The user enters a complete line and after pressing a special key (SEND or CARRIAGE RETURN), the system starts processing the line. Given a certain mean line length and typing speed this scheme results in a limited number of program activations per minute.

Some timesharing systems treat terminal input per character rather than per line. Each character typed is immediately processed by the system. Such a scheme has definite advantages for highly interactive programs (e.g. text editing, graphics, etc.) [3,4]. However, the program activation rate will be much higher, being equal to the character input rate rather than the line input rate. In timesharing systems where program activation requires swapping, this results in high system overhead.

Terminals may be connected to the host system via a front-end processor or even a packet-switching network [1]. In both cases the efficiency of the communication mechanism strongly depends on the mean message length. For example, when the ARPANET is used for single character transfers, line efficiency is less than 2 percent [2].

Both swapping overhead and datacommunication overhead can be reduced by blocking terminal input characters. However, a fixed block size can not be used. Each character can be the last one of a command, necessitating system response before any further input may be expected.

Some timesharing systems [5,6] partially solve the problem by requiring the running program to specify which characters should be considered command terminators. This reduces overhead for programs that do not use the character input facility, but leaves the problem unsolved for character-interactive programs. Moreover, this solution is not feasable for in-homogeneous networks.

TIME-DEPENDENT BLOCKING

A good solution to this problem should be 1) independent of the actual command structure and 2) transparant to user and program. The following technique, called Time-dependent Blocking, satisfies both requirements.

Terminal input characters are initially received by software, either in the timesharing monitor, the front-end processor or the terminal interface processor (TIP) connected to the packet switching network. The characters are accumulated in a buffer until either 1) the buffer is full or 2) there are no more characters received during a certain time. Use of the second condition is based on the assumption that the user does not expect system response as long as he is typing. Only when he stops typing, he may be waiting for system response.

The important parameter in the algorithm is the delay used to detect when the user stops typing. A long delay will yield unacceptable slow response for character-interactive programs, a short delay will give a low blocking factor and thus high system overhdad. The method is enhanced by requiring that certain characters always activate the program, e.g. CARRIAGE RETURN and non-printing control characters. It is possible to give the terminal user control over the delay. It is more elegant to let the system adapt the delay to the actual situation.

RESULTS

This technique was applied in a minicomputer (PDP/8) timesharing system [7,8], where each program activation involves a program swap of .3 seconds. Measurements were conducted while a trained typist was entering line-structured data via a display-terminal. The mean length of the lines that were entered was 19 characters. The internal buffer was 24 characters long. The resulting mean block lengths was determined. A large mean block length indicates that the program was activated only few times per line. A small block length indicates a high program activation rate. Note that this involves input which is in fact line structured and would in a line-oriented system result in just one program activation per line.

delay (seconds)	mean block length
.5	3.4
1.Ø	7.7

A delay of .5 second is acceptable, while 1 second is quite noticable for character-interactive programs.

As a rule, character-interactive programs have very short commands, often just one or two characters. It can be argued that people are less frustrated with a slow response to a long command than with a slow response to a short command. More generally, user frustration seems to depend on the number of wait-work-wait transitions per unit time. These considerations lead to an algorithm in which the delay is made a function of the number of characters accumulated so far (n).

delay=.2*n+.3

Short commands will get fair response with a delay of .5 to .7 second. Line input is allowed to accumulate full buffers; after the first few characters the delay is so long that a minor hesitation will not break the message. The following figures have been obtained with this algorithm.

delay (seconds)	mean block length
.2 * n + .3	8.7
.2 * n + .4	1Ø.2

In the last case (delay=.2*n+.4), over 2Ø pct. of the blocks were terminated because of overflow of our 24 character input buffer. A larger buffer will yield longer mean block length. Also, a number of blocks were terminated by non-printing control characters, mostly RUBOUT, which in our system is always handled by the user program. In systems where RUBOUT is treated by monitor software, the mean block length may approach the actual mean line length. In that case the excessive overhead normally associated with character-oriented protocols is effectively eliminated.

CONCLUSION

Character-interactive programs can introduce high overhead in timesharing and communication systems. The method presented here is able to block terminal input characters independently of the command structure used. It is based on the assumption that a terminal user will not expect reaction from the system as long as he is typing. A delay is used to detect at which moment the user has stopped typing. The value of this delay proved to be critical to the results of the method. With a fixed delay of .5 second overhead may be reduced by a factor 3 to 4, without penalizing interactive users.

Still better results were obtained when the delay is made a function of the number of characters accumulated so far. Measurements indicated that the mean block length may approach the actual line length. This means that only few additional program activations are performed as compared to line-oriented systems.

REFERENCES

[1] Cosel, B.P., et al., "An Operating System for Computer Resource Sharing", Proceedings of the Fifth Symposium on Operating System Principles (1975).

[2] Kleinrock, L., Naylor, W.E. and Opderbeck, H., "A Study of Line Overhead in the ARPANET". CACM 19,1 (jan. 1975)

[3] Bobrow, D.G., Burchfiel, J.D., Murphy, D.L. and Tomlinson, R.S., "TENEX, a Paged Timesharing System for the PDP1Ø", CACM 5,3 (march 1972).

[4] "Timesharing Computer Systems", Wilkes, M.V., MacDonald/American Elsevier 1972 (2nd ed.) pp 34.

[5] "Introduction to Programming 1", Digital Equipment Corporation, Maynard, Massachusetts.

[6] "ETOS System User´s Guide", EDUCOMP Corporation, Hartford, Connecticut.

[7] "MULTI8, a Realtime Foreground / Timesharing Background Operating System for a Minicomputer", Anthoni, J.F. (thesis), Delft, Holland, 1975.

[8] "MULTI8 System Manual", Lopes Cardozo, E., Westvries Computer Consulting B.V., Oostzaan, Holland, 1976.

E. Morlet and D. Ribbens, (Eds.), International Computing Symposium 1977.

DPL: A MATHEMATICAL COMPUTATION SYSTEM

R A Cowan
Executive Engineer

Computer Applications Division,
Post Office Research Centre,
Martlesham Heath, Ipswich, UK.

DPL (Direct Programming Language) is designed to enable users unfamiliar with computers to perform fairly complex mathematical calculations. To this end the system employs two dimensional notation and prompting. The basic philosophy behind and background to DPL are outlined, followed by a description of the language and how it is used. A brief account of the implementation, and future developments is given.

1. INTRODUCTION

This paper describes an interactive mathematical computation system, DPL ('Direct Programming Language'), the fundamental aim of which is to provide a range of calculation aids within a framework which is simple and intuitive for the inexperienced user. A comprehensive range of mathematical aids is provided, together with a graphics capability. The present implementation is for a PDP10 computer utilising Tektronix storage terminals, optionally in conjunction with a purpose built keypad. In order to make the system as mobile as possible it has been written in an intermediate macro language.

In the following sections we see how the basic consideration of simplicity has motivated the design of the system; sections 4 and 5 describe the language and system itself. Section 6 gives a brief outline of the implementation, and section 7 discusses future developments for the system, and provides an evaluation.

2. BACKGROUND

In the past ten years there have been many interactive systems designed to handle various aspects of mathematical computation (refer to Klerer[1], Smith[2], Petrick[3]). From JOSS (Shaw[4]), which came into daily use in January 1964, there has been a gradual refinement and expansion of facilities offered by numerical computation systems. The range of facilities available is diverse but we can broadly identify 3 areas which have received particular attention in recent years, namely

(a) handling different data types in a syntactically unified way (see APL(Pakin[5]), AMTRAN(Reinfelds[6]), ISLAND(Chau[7]), SPEAKEASY(Cohen[8])),

(b) increasing user interaction (Pakin[5], Chau[7], Cohen[8]),

(c) providing built in plotting and graphics facilities (Chau[7], Cohen[8]).

In designing and implementing DPL, attention has been expanded to three areas:

1. Use of the 'meta-expression'.
2. Prompting for undefined variables.
3. Use of 'standard' mathematical notation.

The 'meta-expression', a phrase used by Georges[9], refers to a generic or reusable expression. The effect when employed in an equation, as will be seen later, is to give statements such as 'A = B + C' an interpretation more closely approximating to their usual mathematical meaning. This feature has been used recently in OAS (Konapesak[10]) and proposed for CLIC (Georges[9]). It has been implemented in NAPSS and LCC (see Klerer[1]), and is evident in LG (Raymond[11]), a language for analytic geometry.

Automatic prompting for undefined variables is a central feature in DPL and although of considerable use does not appear to have been explored in previous systems. Several systems, however, have made use of 'standard' mathematical notation. Some, such as the Engineering Assistant (see Klerer[1]) and later versions of MADCAP (Morris[12]), use linear notation but with an extended character set (including such symbols as '∀' and '∃'), while others have provided 'two dimensional' notation, such as subscripts and exponents. The three mathematical computation languages incorporating 2D notation on input have all employed modified Friden flexowriters with a half-line-up and half-line-down facility. These had to be used off-line to prepare paper tapes which were subsequently batch processed.

MADCAP (Wells[13]) was the first system to introduce 2D notation: subscripts, exponents and an underline facility to signify division were available. A later version allowed special symbols such as sigma and integral to be formed by the combination of ordinary symbols juxtaposed (eg. sigma was two '<' signs, one above the other). Shortly after, Mirfac (Gawlik[14]) included a type face with special symbols ($\int, \Sigma, \Pi$) and an elementary subscripting/exponentiation facility. Finally, the Klerer-May system (Klerer[15]) employed 8 basic geometric shapes by means of which mathematical symbols could be synthesised. A later version of this system (see Klerer[1]) allowed use of a Selectric terminal with the same character set but an additional keypad with special symbols marked on it. Depressing a key caused the required symbol to be printed without the labour of typing all the key strokes individually to form the character.

3. DESIGN CONSIDERATIONS

In formulating the user interface for any interactive system the designer has always to reconcile the conflicting needs of experienced and inexperienced users. As already stated, the primary aim of DPL is to provide powerful computation facilites in an intuitive and simple framework. This has necessarily meant concentrating on the needs of the non-specialist, although considerable attention has been paid to allowing flexibility and succinctness appropriate to the experienced user.

The basic DPL system has arisen from elementary consideration of the way a mathematician or engineer specifies and solves mathematical problems. There are essentially two stages in arriving at the solution of a problem:

(i) statement of an environment, ie. relevant equations, data, and constraints

(ii) statement (implicitly) of what solution is to be found.

This process is mirrored in the way DPL can be used. Sets of equations, together with base data, are normally specified initially, and then followed by a request to DPL to compute the answers. If any variables during the computation are undefined, DPL prompts for the missing information. The response may be either a data value or an expression. If the response is an expression then an equation is formed, and this is stored in the user's workspace.

This scheme allows a steady progression from specification of a problem to its solution. Indeed, the user can request computation of expressions when the workspace is empty - in which case DPL will prompt for all information as needed. Additionally, the treatment of equations as stored definitions of variables, rather the more usual interpretation as immediate assignments, has the effect that a specific sequencing of equations is irrelevant, and any changes in equations are always automatically propogated through any expressions which ultimately reference the modified equations.

As well as providing this 'direct' approach to problem solution, notational familiarity has been a consideration in making the language palitable. To this end the syntax and conventions of standard mathematical text have been adhered to as far as possible. Subscripts, exponents and special symbols (including summation and integration) are allowed. Exponents, limits for integration, etc. can themselves be mathematical expressions with the restriction that they must be written on one line (ie. without subscripts, exponents, etc.). In addition, no declarations are mandatory, for example to define array sizes and names.

An interface is provided to allow the user to plot data using an existing plotting package, and a limited graphics capability has been implemented to allow users both to plot data and generate graphical displays.

A considerable effort has been made to assist the user in his general operation of the system, eg. any 2D block of information sent to DPL can be typed in any order - as long as the block appears correct on the printed page. It is also possible to recall the last line of information typed to the system in order to resend it to DPL perhaps with editing changes. Extensive error reporting is provided, together with a 'help' facility to give additional information when errors occur. Such matters, while relatively simple to implement, are of prime importance to the inexperienced user as unclear or unhelpful responses from any computer system can cause it to be abandoned very early.

4. DPL BASIC SYSTEM

The basic system represents essentially the 'desk-calculator' part of DPL, allowing the user to build up equations and data defining his problem, prompting as necessary, and providing editing, and basic computational facilities. All objects created by the user reside in a workspace, additional facilities being provided for listing and deleting selected objects from the workspace.

DPL operates interpretively: commands and equations are entered piece-meal by the user and obeyed as soon as they are typed. A '>' is displayed to indicate that DPL is waiting for information from the user, as can be seen in examples. For a detailed desciption of the DPL system see Cowan[16].

4.1 Equations

Equations are the means by which variables are defined and have the following syntax:

variable = expression

When the user types an equation to DPL, the equation is normally not executed immediately, but stored, thus providing a definition of the variable on the left hand side On subsequently evaluating an expression DPL examines all variables involved in the computation. If any are found to be 'undefined' (ie. which the user has not defined by means of an equation) then DPL prompts the user to supply the missing information Otherwise the expression on the right hand side is evaluated. The expression may itself contain variables and so the process continues recursively with termination of a particular level in the iteration occurring when all variables at that level are defined by the user as data values.

$$a = b + c + d$$

$$P_r = (B/pi)^{3/2} * e^{-r*B}$$

$$sumsq = \sum_{irx=1}^{num} xrs_{irx}^2$$

$$r = v_x^2 + v_y^2 + v_z^2$$

$$I = \int_{sin(pi*qfil)}^{cos(pi*a+omega)} w * e^{-w} dw$$

$$B = m/(2*k*T)$$

Fig 1. Simple DPL Equations

Expressions are made up of the following basic units: variables, numbers, operators, exponents, and functions; brackets can be used to group together parts of an expression. If a suitable graphics terminal is available, the user is able to type mathematical expressions in a form similar to standard textbook notation. Symbols for integration, summation, square root, etc are provided and the system gives as much help as possible to the user when for example positioning upper and lower limits in order to minimise typing. Optionally a teletype-like terminal may be used with the program in which case the mathematical notation reverts to an extension of that of FORTRAN or ALGOL type languages. Below we briefly describe the composition of the two dimensional form of the expression (see Fig 1).

Variables

The most important building block for mathematical expressions is the variable Variables can be scalar, vector, or matrix (see Fig 2).

<u>scalar</u> $x \quad y \quad limits$

<u>vector</u> $xvec_1 \quad yvec_j \quad Infoit_{n*2+3}$

<u>matrix</u> $xycont_{1,5} \quad M_{3+i,7+j*2}$

Fig 2. Examples of variable notation and referencing.

A SCALAR is written simply as a name (starting with a letter and followed by a string of letters and digits, of which the first 35 are significant). DPL distinguishes between upper and lower case characters when used in variables.

A VECTOR is written as a scalar, but with a subscript half a line down on the page.

A MATRIX is written as a scalar but with the two subscripts half a line down from the matrix name, and separated by a comma.

The maximum subscript size for a vector or matrix is 1023, and negative subscipts are not allowed. A subscript can itself be an expression, but must fit on one line (ie. no subscripts or exponents can be included). The accessing of variable elements consists of evaluation of any expressions specifying subscript values and then fetching the required element. The dimension of a variable is determined by context and so no dimension declarations are necessary, although a declaration of vector or matrix size may be given to provide for more efficient element processing.

Numbers

All numbers are represented internally in floating point form, and can be typed either in conventional integer or floating point notation.

Simple arithmetic operators

The usual arithmetic operators (+ - * /) are provided, and additionally factorial and square root.

Functions

The usual range of mathematical functions is provided (trig, logs etc), and are operated by taking a single argument in brackets and performing the specified operation on that argument.

Exponents

Exponents can be placed in the usual positions in expressions (typed half a line up), and must fit on one line, ie. no subscipts or superscripts are allowed in exponents.

The trigonometric functions, sin, cos, tan, when raised explicitly to the power '-1' are treated as specifying the corresponding arc-trig functions.

Sigma, Pi

These two operators are similar in format. Both require a lower limit of an equation (assignment), and an upper limit which is an expression. See Fig 3.

The lower limit must be a full line below the position of the operator itself, and the upper limit a full line above. DPL, however, helps the user position limits by automatically positioning the cursor when a special character is typed. The upper and lower limits must go on to one line only, ie. there can be no subscripts, exponents, etc. Precise horizontal positioning is not required, however, and limits need only be in the approximate area of the operator to which they refer.

Both operators have their usual mathematical meaning and specify looping. The lower limit specifies the first value of the dummy variable ('i' in Fig. 3a). DPL computes the values of the expression within the 'scope' of the sigma, storing the result. The dummy variable is then incremented by 1, and the operation repeated until 'i' is greater than the upper limit. All the partial sums calculated are then added together. The dummy variable is always local to the calculation, and any state it was in outside the scope of the evaluation is retained.

The increment for the dummy variable is normally 1, but can be changed by specifying the increment after the lower limit equation.

(a)

$$sum = \sum_{i=1}^{10} x_i$$

(b)

$$J_i = \sum_{j=3}^{lim} \sum_{k=1}^{dma} xload_{j,k} / mean_k$$

$$Prod = \prod_{j=low}^{high} \prod_{k=low}^{high} matdat_{j,k} + corr1$$

$$a = (n\sum_{i=1}^{n} x_i * y_i - \sum_{i=1}^{n} x_i \sum_{i=1}^{n} y_i) / (n\sum_{i=1}^{n} x_i^2 - (\sum_{i=1}^{n} x_i)^2)$$

$$b = (\sum_{i=1}^{n} x_i^2 \sum_{i=1}^{n} y_i - \sum_{i=1}^{n} x_i \sum_{i=1}^{n} x_i * y_i) / (n\sum_{i=1}^{n} x_i^2 - (\sum_{i=1}^{n} x_i)^2)$$

Fig 3. Usage of sigma and pi operators.

Integration

The integration operator requires a lower limit expression, and an upper limit expression. These specify the range of the integration. The variable of integration is specified in the standard manner, at the end of the integral. See Fig. 4.

$$I3 = \int_0^4 dummy^2 ddummy + \int_1^2 \log(avx) davx$$

$$I4 = \int_{omega*\cos(theta)}^{alpha*\cos(theta)} (\sin^2(x) - \log(x^2)) dx$$

Fig 4. Usage of integral operator.

There are several alternative integration routines provided, and the 'INTEGRATE BY' command allows the user to specify which routine he wishes to try.

Operator precedence

The order of execution of components of an expression, and the scope of sigma and pi operators, is governed by an operator precedence scheme. See Appendix I.

4.2 Basic commands

In general the following command syntax is used:

command-name argument

The format of an argument depends on the command involved, as is evident from the description of basic commands given below. Refer to Fig. 5. for examples.

```
>compute 1+2+3
        =6
>          10   2
>compute   Σ  j
          j=1
         =385
>list a
    a = b + c
>list all equations
    a = b + c
            num      2
    sumsq =  Σ   xrs
           irx=1     irx
    B = m / (2*k*T)
      •
      •
>delete all values
>
>edit a
>   a = b + c + d
>
>save file1
>
>delete all
CONTENTS OF WORKSPACE DELETED
>
>load file1
>
>find x near 3, sin(x) = 2/x

        =18.95526
>
>help commands
The available commands are summarised below:

Command Abriev  Argument
 name    iation

COMPUTE C       expression
      •
      •
```

Fig 5. Examples of DPL commands.

Note that '<' and '>' are syntactic brackets round basic language elements in the following description, and '[' and ']' indicate phrases which may be omitted.

COMPUTE <expression>

DPL evaluates the expression given as the argument. The user is prompted for any undefined variables.

LIST <variable specification>

'LIST' allows the user to list all, or selected parts, of the workspace. Data values, equations, and user defined commands (see later) may be listed. Undefined variables are not listed.

<variable specification> →
<list item>,<variable specification>

<list item> →
<variable name> | ALL EQUATIONS |
ALL VALUES | ALL COMMANDS | ALL

DELETE <variable specification>

Requesting deletion of a variable results in the variable being set 'undefined'. This results in DPL prompting the user to define the variable if it must be evaluated in some expression. The variable's characteristics, however, such as being scalar, vector, etc, still remain. This means that a variable which has been used in the context of, say, a vector, cannot be used as a scalar until the workspace is completely cleared.

'DELETE ALL' results in the whole workspace being cleared, ie. all variables and user commands are removed together with their characteristics.

EDIT <variable name>

The 'EDIT' command enables the user to change a previously defined variable. When the command is given, DPL types out the appropriate equation or variable value. The usual edit facilities can then be utilised to change the line, as if the user had just typed it.

SAVE <workspace name>

The 'SAVE' command allows the user to save on a disc file all the contents of his workspace. Both values and expressions (and user commands) are saved. The state of the workspace is unchanged.

LOAD <workspace name>

The 'LOAD' command loads from a disc file a previously saved DPL workspace. Any variables or user commands in the workspace prior to the load may assume new definitions if in the workspace file. Other variables remain in the workspace unchanged.

HELP [<name>]

When an error occurs additional information may be gained about the error and how to deal with it. Help on specific topics can be obtained by giving an argument to the command.

EXIT

Exit from DPL.

5. ELEMENTARY PROGRAMMING AND FILE FACILITIES

Whilst the basic system is sufficient for elementary calculations, it would soon be found to be inadequate by regular users; the ability to perform several commands in succession, perform loops, and generate subroutine-like constructs is clearly important in any flexible computation system. Whilst the emphasis in DPL is on small ad hoc calculations requiring little more than straightforward evaluation, facilities are provided for generating elementary programs namely, a looping feature and the ability to generate user-defined commands.

The box operator provides the facility of looping and operates on all commands to its right on a line. The upper and lower limits specified for the operator have the same form as for sigma and pi. See Fig. 6. The operator can be used in a variety of situations, for example tabulations can be generated by repeated execution of the 'TYPE' command.

Sequences of commands can be placed on one line (separated by ';') and saved as 'user defined' commands (by use of the 'COMMAND' command). They are executed in the same way as built-in commands without arguments.

Programming and mathematical analysis facilities are presently under active development, and the following description summarises the features currently implemented.

```
     10
>    □ type i, √i
    i=1
       1                    1
       2                    1.4142
       3                    1.7321
       4                    2
       5                    2.2361
       6                    2.4495
       7                    2.6458
       8                    2.8284
       9                    3
      10                    3.1623
>
>
>    max
>    □   type to data1 sx, cx
    jlim=min
 min=0
 max=30
 sx=sin(jlim)
 cx=cos(jlim*omega+phi)
 omega=2.5
 phi=0.5
>
>
>                     times
>command table1  =  □ type x, y, z
                     i=1
>
>                  high
>command tab2  =  □  tab3
                  i=low
>
>command tab3=type a,b; type c,d
>
>tab2
 low=1
 high=5
 a=sin(i)
 b=cos(i)
     0.8415               0.5403
 c=sin(i+0.5)
 d=cos(i+0.5)
     0.9975               7.074E-2
     0.9093              -0.4161
     0.5985              -0.8011
```

Fig 6. Examples of looping and command formation.

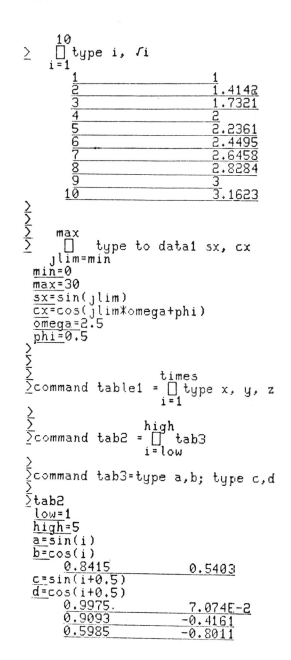

TYPE [TO <file name>] <list of expressions>

The evaluations of several expressions are typed on one line. Used in conjunction with the box operator, tables may be built up, and optionally directed to a file for storage or later plotting

READ [FROM <file name>] <list of variables>

DPL prompts for listed variables regardless of whether they are defined or not. The 'FROM' clause causes DPL to read the variable values from a disc file. If end of file is encountered before all the necessary variables have been read DPL resumes prompting for them at the terminal.

CLOSE <file name>

A file open for reading is released; a file which has been written to is closed.

TRACE

In a complicated computation with many equations and variables a confirmation of which equations are being executed is useful. With the trace set all equations are typed as they are executed. 'UNTRACE' turns off the trace.

DEFINE <system name> = <expression>

The user is able to define new values for system variables eg. the number of significant figures, accuracy required for numerical integrations.

FIND <variable> [NEAR <expression>] <expression>

'FIND' enables the user to employ the Newton-Raphson technique to find the root of an expression or equation given some starting approximation (supplied by the 'NEAR' clause).

CLEAR

Clear the terminal screen.

NEWPAGE

Pause for the user to indicate he is ready for a new page.

COMMAND <user command name> = <command list>

The list of commands specified is saved, and may subsequently be executed in one operation by typing the user command name given in the command.

<command list> -> <command> [<command list>]

SET <equation>

There is one situation where the straightforward use of the DPL equation does not provide the user with the effect that he may intend. For example, the user may wish to increment the value of a variable. If he uses a statement such as 'i = i+1' the desired effect will not be achieved as the equation will be set up as a definition of 'i'. The new definition, moreover, is directly recursive and any attempt to evaluate 'i' will quickly cause the execution stack to overflow. The general requirement is for a straightforward assignment with 'i+1' evaluated and the value assigned to 'i'. This may be achieved with the 'SET' command.

'SET' enables the ordinary FORTRAN assignment to be made, ie the RHS of the equation is evaluated and the value given to the variable on the left hand side.

6 IMPLEMENTATION

The method of implementation has been motivated by two requirements machine independence, and efficient run-time operation.

In order to make the implementation as portable as possible an intermediate macro language has been used to write the system. The intermediate language was implemented by means of the macro-processor STAGE2 (Waite[17]), and involved the writing of about 850 lines of macros to specify the translation of the intermediate language to PDP10 assembly language. The intermediate language includes reasonable control facilities (including IF THEN ELSE FI and DOWHILE DOEND statements), pointer and index variables, ability to define names as equivalent to sets of bits within words, and recursive and non-recursive subroutine calls. The programmer has explicit control over the execution and run-time stacks by means of specific statements in the intermediate language.

About 95% of the system is written in the intermediate language and the remainder consists of machine dependent routines to provide interfacing to the host operating system. All routines are loaded together when generating a new system. The effort required to generate a version of the program on a new target machine consists of rewriting the macros to generate code for the new machine providing routines for interfacing with the host operating system redefining the system parameter file which contains definitions of word lengths core size, etc., and redefining bit-definitions for the new machine.

When DPL is executing each statement or sequence of statements is translated one line at a time into a reverse Polish interpretive code block and in the case of equations, the symbol table is updated to reflect the state of the variable. Code blocks in practice form the interface between syntax analyis/code generation modules and the interpreter with its associated run-time system. This interface has been kept very clearly defined to enable the interpreter to be used as a flexible run-time system for experimentation with various DPL dialects.

When user's commands are executing, code blocks are created and deleted as the user is prompted to define variables or superceed existing variable definitions. Garbage collection is thus complicated by the dynamic way code blocks can be created while existing code blocks are still in part execution. Storage is divided into runtime and system stacks, fixed system locations and heap storage for code blocks.

The I/O system keeps track of positions of characters on the screen, position of the next line to be output , drawing of special characters, etc. Source buffers are headed by a character count and y-up/y-down information to give the extent of the source block on the screen, so enabling the I/O system to position output text to be non-overlapping.

As an aid to system debugging, a priviledged command allows selective type-out of specific system information, and as usual the program contains checks for internal logic errors.

7. CONCLUSION

This paper gives an overview of the DPL system as currently implemented. There are extensions planned in the areas of built in matrix and vector manipulation, with the emphasis on 'natural' notation. The user defined command facility is to be extended, to allow multi-line commands, and to increase the range of control structures within commands. The complexity of mathematical expressions analysed could be expanded, although it is doubtful that such a development would be of sufficient benifit to users, except for completeness. A very elementary graphics facility already exists and it is planned to extend this to enable graph plotting, and so hopefully provide a convenient and flexible facility for handling graphical data.

The prompting facility has proved to be very useful and flexible, and experience is indicating that it could be extended perhaps to include prompting for undefined commands and missing arguments to commands. Indeed, the possibility of having two alternative interfaces is under consideration: one would correspond to the present system, and the other would take prompting much further, including use of menus to prompt the user for commands, etc. The objective of such a scheme would be to enable novices to utilise a DPL-like system for arithmetic or mathematics without the need for a bulky manual and conventional protocol, thus attempting to reduce a major inhibition to the use of such a system.

ACKNOWLEDGEMENT

Acknowledgement is made to the Director of Research of the Post Office for permission to publish this paper.

REFERENCES

1. Klerer, M., and Reinfelds, J. (Eds.) (1968). Interactive Systems for Experimental and Applied Mathematics, Academic Press, New York.

2. Smith, L. B. (1970). A Survey of Interactive Graphical Systems for Mathematics, Computing Surveys, Vol 2, No 4, pp 261-301.

3. Petrick, S. R.(1971) Proc.2nd Symposium on Symbolic and Algebraic Manipulation, ACM.

4. Shaw, J. C. (1964). JOSS: A designer's view of an experimental on-line computer system, Proc. AFIPS 1964 FJCC, Vol 26, Pt 1, pp455-464.

5. Pakin, S. (1968). APL Reference Guide, Science Research Associates.

6. Reinfelds, J. A Concept by Concept Description of the AMTRAN language, SIGPLAN Notices, Vol 6, No 11, pp32-59.

7. Chau, A. Y. C., Davies, B.W., and Zacharov (1974). ISLAND -An Interactive Graphics System for Mathematical Analysis, Computer Journal, Vol 17, No 2, pp 104-112.

8. Cohen, S. SPEAKEASY, SIGPLAN Notices Vol 8, No 4, pp31-44.

9. Georges, J (1975). Design aspects of a language for interactive computing, Eurocomp Proceedings 1975.

10. Konopasek, M. (1975). An advanced question answering system on sets of algebraic equations, Eurocomp Proceedings 1975.

11. Raymond, J. (1976). LG: A Language for Analytic Geometry, CACM, vol 19, No 4 (April 1976), pp 182-187.

12. Morris, B. M., and Wells, M. B. (1972). The Specification of Program Flow in MADCAP6,

Proc. ACM Conf. (Aug 1972), pp755-762.

13. Wells, M. B. (1961). MADCAP: A Scientific Compiler for a Displayed Formula Textbook Language, CACM, vol 4, No 1 (Jan 1961), pp 31-36.

14. Gawlik, H. J. (1963) Mirfac: A Compiler Based on Standard Mathematical Notation and Plain English, CACM, vol 6, No 9, pp 545-547.

15. Klerer, M. and May, J. (1965). Two Dimensional programming, Proc 1965 FJCC, AFIPS, vol 27, part 1, pp 63-73.

16. Cowan, R. A. (1975) DPL Introductory Guide, Research Memorandum 75/R18/21, Post Office Corporation.

17. Waite, W. M. (1970) The Mobile Programming system STAGE2, CACM, vol 13, No 7, pp 415-421.

18. Clarke, K. E. and Woods, B. J. (1973) CUPID: An information display system which exploits the characteristics of the direct view storage tube, Datafair 73, Vol 2, pp 464-470.

Appendix I: OPERATOR PRECEDENCES

high precedence

exponents

- (unary)

functions

! (factorial)

√ (root)

* /

Σ Π ∫

\+ - (binary)

low precedence

Appendix II: WORKED EXAMPLE

A sample session is given below, illustrating the way DPL is used. The graphs in this example were plotted by a plotting package, CUPID (Clarke[18]), external to DPL. All typing by the computer is underlined.

The problem concerns the examination of reflections at a double optical boundary. Plots are generated of reflection, alpha, at wave numbers, k, between 1 and 100. Different reflection coefficients, N, are examined for each plot.

```
D P L
> Y = y / (2*(2+n+1/n)^2)                                  <-- set up basic equations
>
> y = 16*e^N + 2*(n-1/n)
>
> y = 16*e^N + 2*(n-1/n)^2* (cos^2(k*l) - sin^2(k*l)) + 4*root
>
> root = √(4*e^N + (n-1/n)^2*cos^2(k*l)) * √(4*e^N - (n-1/n)^2*sin^2(k*l)))
                                                                          ^
RIGHT BRACKET WITHOUT MATCHING LEFT BRACKET                   recall previous line
>
> root = √(4*e^N + (n-1/n)^2*cos^2(k*l)) * √(4*e^N - (n-1/n)^2*sin^2(k*l))@
>
```

```
.R CUPID

?DATA DAT2
?PLOT
```

Perform plotting

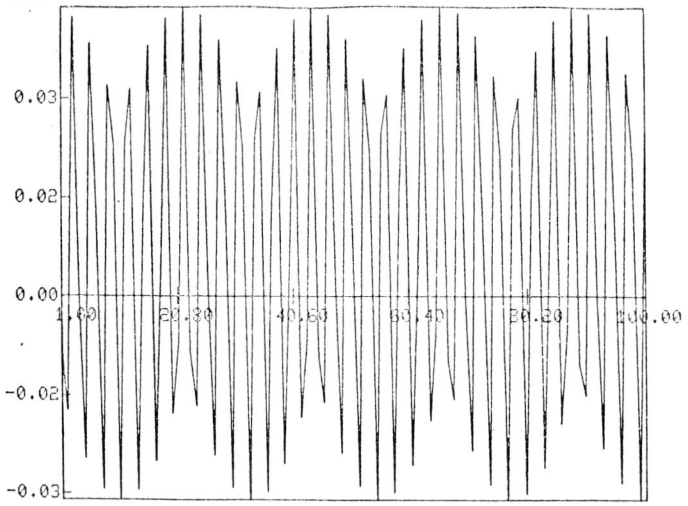


```
?

?BYE

EXIT FROM CUPID

.RUN DPL

D P L

>load mine
>edit command do

                   100
>command do  =  [] type to dat2 k, alpha
                   k=1
                   100
>command do  =  [] type to dat3 k, alpha
                   k=1
>list N
  N=0.1
>N=0.1 + (9.9/100)*k
>do
>exit

 BYE

.R CUPID

?DATA DAT3
?PLOT
```

reload works pace
change command 'do'
display edited line
list and redefine 'N'
generate final tabulation to file
perform plotting

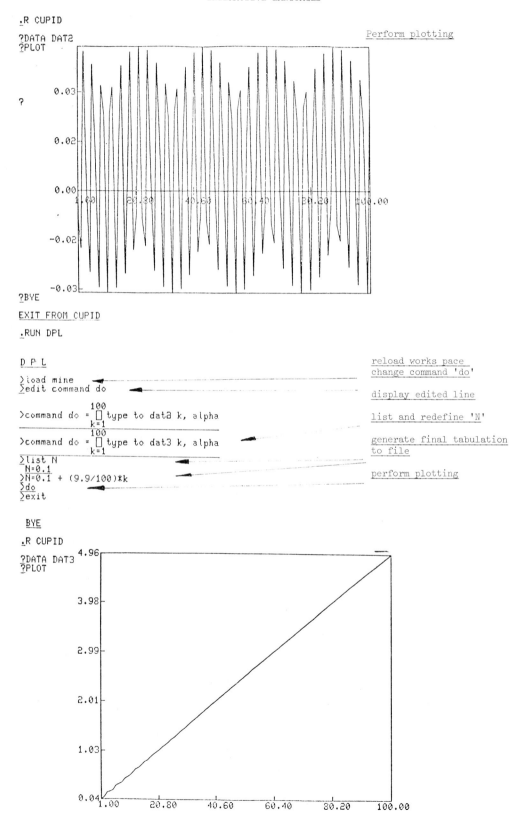

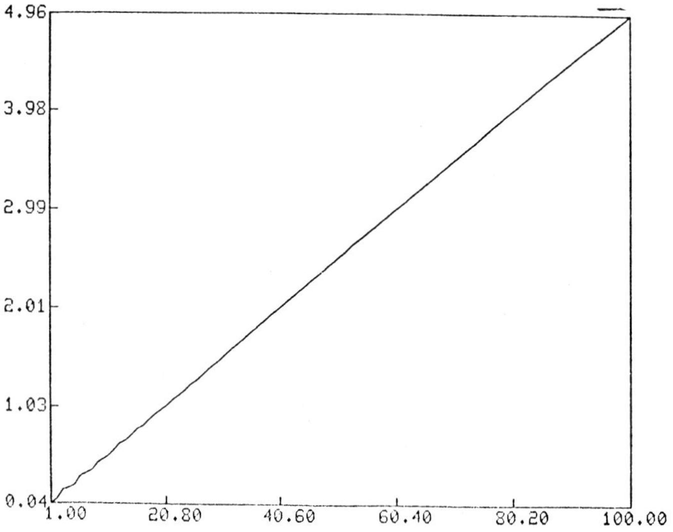

```
> alpha = 0.5 * ln(Y)
>
>   100
>    □ type to dat1 k, alpha
>   k=1
 e=2.7182818
 N= 10 - (9.9/100)*k
 n=1.5
 l=1
A DATA FILE ALREADY EXISTS CALLED dat1
SHALL I DELETE IT?
YES OR NO: yes
>
>save myfile
>
>exit

 BYE

.R CUPID

?DATA DAT1
?PLOT
```

basic equation

generate tabulation to file

prompting for undefined variables

save current workspace

perform plotting

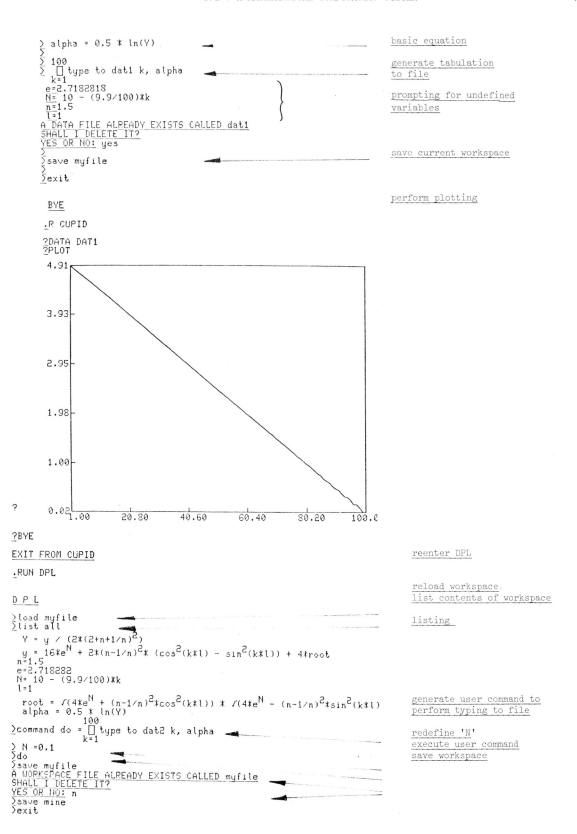

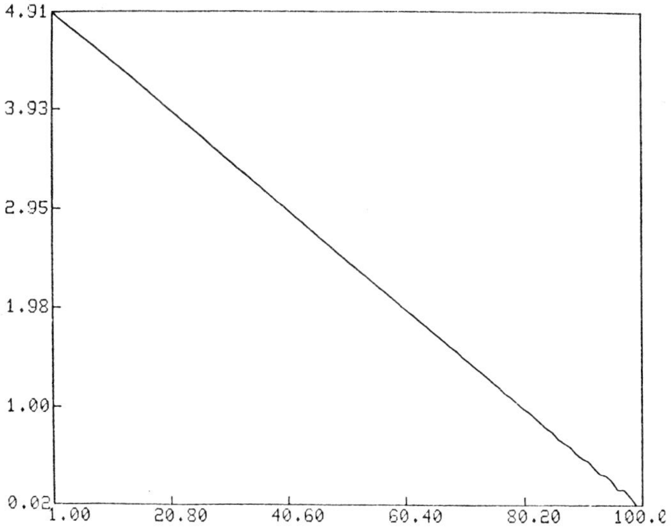


```
?

?BYE

EXIT FROM CUPID

.RUN DPL

D P L

>load myfile
>list all
  Y = y / (2*(2+n+1/n)^2)
  y = 16*e^N + 2*(n-1/n)^2* (cos^2(k*l) - sin^2(k*l)) + 4*root
 n=1.5
 e=2.718282
 N= 10 - (9.9/100)*k
 l=1
  root = √(4*e^N + (n-1/n)^2*cos^2(k*l)) * √(4*e^N - (n-1/n)^2*sin^2(k*l)
  alpha = 0.5 * ln(Y)
                  100
>command do =   □ type to dat2 k, alpha
                 k=1
> N =0.1
>do
>save myfile
A WORKSPACE FILE ALREADY EXISTS CALLED myfile
SHALL I DELETE IT?
YES OR NO: n
>save mine
>exit
```

reenter DPL

reload workspace.
list contents of workspace

listing

generate user command to perform typing to file

redefine 'N'
execute user command
save workspace

E. Morlet and D. Ribbens, (Eds.), International Computing Symposium 1977.

DISTRIBUTED CONTROL, MODULARITY AND DATA TYPES IN A SIMPLE PARALLEL LANGUAGE.

M. Bellia and G. Levi

Istituto di Elaborazione della Informazione
Istituto di Scienze della Informazione
Pisa, Italy

The paper introduces a language, based on a unique type of object, the functional unit, whose main activity is receiving and sending messages. Interaction among functional units is achieved by message exchanging.

The language has no imperative constructs and does not need an interpreter. A functional unit is activated by a message and the information on the computation state (control environment, storage state, etc.) is supplied through the message. The functional unit itself provides for its "interpretation" by performing some primitive operations. Such operations, apart from RECEIVE and SEND, are concerned with creation and deletion of functional units.

The language allows several functional units to be active at any given time. Functional units are responsible also for those control aspects which are concerned with concurrency.

Hence, control is not concentrated in an interpreter (or supervisor) state. It is distributed over a set of functional units which are mutually independent modules.

Our main concern is stressing that distributing control over several functional units can lead to semantically well-structured modular systems. As an example, a methodology is discussed in which the decomposition into modules is based on the concept of data type.

1. INTRODUCTION

Several related ideas have come out from different fields of computer science in the last few years. Research on operating system design has led to the concept of distributed system, i.e. collections of mutually independent modules cooperating in a non-hyerarchical environment. The concepts of class and data abstraction, originated from programming language and software engineering research, contributed to cut down the difference between active (procedures) and passive (data) objects. Finally, from the artificial intelligence field came the idea of knowledge distribution and some control constructs, such as "procedure call by pattern",which are based on associating procedural information to data. The formalism introduced in this paper was influenced by Hewitt's research on ACTOR's [1-4] , which is an attempt to define a language (or machine) acting according to the above mentioned concepts. Our aim was developing a very low-level formalism, having no primitive objects and only a limited number of basic operations, and still powerful enough to be used as a "machine language" for defining distributed computations.

2. THE FUNCTIONAL UNIT FORMALISM

The formalism is based on a single type of object the functional unit (fu), which is an active object whose main activity is receiving and sending messages. We will first consider a simplified class of fu's, whose form is the following:

```
(1) /RECEIVE 'pattern message'/
    /SEND ('output-message 1'......
              'output message n')/ .
```

Its behaviour is completely expressed in terms of the control primitives RECEIVE and SEND, and can be described as follows. Let us call system a set of functional units and assume that a fu is sent a message m. The fu performs a RECEIVE operation, which succeeds if and only if the incoming message "matches" its pattern message and fails otherwise. If the RECEIVE operation is successful, the fu performs a SEND operation, which consists in sending the n output messages in parallel to all the functional units in the system. A successful RECEIVE generally defines an environment for the fu, by assigning variables appearing in the pattern-message, in the fu's own storage. Outcoming messages are then "evaluated" within that environment.

Consider the following system consisting of two functional units, named F_1 and F_2, both having a single output message.

F_1: / RECEIVE (0 + =x) /
/ SEND (!x) /

F_2: /RECEIVE ((s =x) + =y)/
/SEND ((!x + (s!y)))/

Note that variable symbols identified by a prefix = (for instance, =x) are assigned a value in the fu's environment by a RECEIVE operation (1), while variable symbols identified by the prefix ! stand for their value in the environment. The above example can be interpreted as a procedure for computing the sum (+) on the nonnegative integers (defined by means of the constant 0 and the successor function s).

Assume the system is initially sent the message M_1

M_1: ((s(s 0)) + (s 0))

M_1 can only be RECEIVEd by F_2, which generates the environment
{(x,(s 0)), (y,(s 0))} and sends the message M_2 to the system.

M_2: ((s 0) + (s(s 0)))

(1) Matching between an incoming message m_i and a pattern message m_p is achieved by RECEIVE through first order unification, and the environment is exactly the most general unifier of m_i and m_p.

M_2 is RECEIVEd by F_2, which generates the environment {(x,0),(y,(s(s 0)))} and sends the message

M_3 : (0 + (s(s(s 0))))

M_3 is RECEIVEd by F_1, which generates the environment {(x,(s(s(s 0))))} and sends the message

M_4: (s(s(s 0)))

It is worth noting that the above system of functional units has no memory. In fact, fu's environments are only (locally) defined within a RECEIVE/SEND step. Since the only object which can be defined in our formalism is the functional unit, a mechanism is needed for defining functional units acting as (data or control) memory. The functional unit formalism is extended by allowing the use of three more primitives, DECLARE, DEFINE, and FREE, whose behaviour can be sketched in the following way. Assume each fu is allocated in a fu's symbolic storage, whose addresses are fu's names. In order to allocate a new fu we first need a name, that is a free address in the symbolic storage. This can be achieved by the primitive operation

/DECLARE ($=x_1$ $=x_2$..... $=x_n$)/

which when executed by a fu F, modifies the environment of F, by assigning to each (local) variable x_i a different free address. Values assigned to the x_i's can be used as names of new fu's to be allocated. The allocation can then be achieved by the primitive operation

/DEFINE (($name_1$ def_1)($name_2$ def_2)....
..... ($name_n$ def_n))/.

Assume that the def_i's are fu's definitions and the $name_i$'s are fu's names, possibly referenced through the value of a variable (for instance, !x) which must be local (2) to the fu F by which the

(2) Local variables are either variables occurring in the pattern message or variables occuring in a DECLARation.

allocation is executed. The allocation causes the n new fu's $name_1$, $name_2$ ..., $name_n$ to be added to the system of functional units. Disallocation is performed through the last primitive operation

/FREE $(n_1, n_2, \ldots\ldots, n_k)$/

which removes the fu's n_1 to n_k from the system and frees the corresponding names.

The general structure of a functional unit F is then the following,

/RECEIVE 'pattern-message'/
/DECLARE 'set of variables'/
/DEFINE 'set of name-definition pairs'/
/SEND 'set of messages'/
/FREE 'set of names'/

where one or more of the DECLARE, DEFINE, SEND and FREE operations can be omitted.

We are now able to define a computation in a system of functional units. The computation state σ_i is a pair of sets (M_i, S_i), where M_i is a set of messages, and S_i is a set of functional units. The initial computation state σ_0 is the pair (M_0, S_0), where M_0 is the set of "initial" messages. Given the state $\sigma_i = (M_i, S_i)$, the next state $\sigma_{i+1} = (M_{i+1}, S_{i+1})$ is obtained as follows.

Let A^i be the subset of S_i of all those functional units a^i_k which are <u>activated</u> by messages belonging to M_i. a^i_k is activated by a message m, if m can be RECEIVEd by a^i_k, i.e. if m "matches" the pattern message of a^i_k. σ_{i+1} is defined only if each a^i_k is activated by a single message. Let:

$m(A^i)$ be the set of messages <u>sent</u> by the activated fu's.

$d(A^i)$ be the set of functional units <u>defined</u> by the activated fu's.

$f(A^i)$ be the set of functional units <u>freed</u> by the activated fu's.

The next state σ_{i+1} is the the pair

$(m(A^i), d(A^i) \cup \{S_i - f(A^i)\})$.

Concurrency can be achieved in a system of functional units by letting several functional units to be active in the transition from state σ_i to state σ_{i+1}. Actually, this situation can arise either because a single message in M_i activates several fu's or because M_i contains several messages (possibly generated by a previous "parallel" SEND). Hence, multiple loci of control (active fu's) are allowed in a state transition. Moreover active fu's act as mutually independent modules. In fact, the behaviour of a functional unit in a transition depends only upon the set of messages M_i and does not depend upon the actual configuration of the system S_i.

It is worth noting that the language has none of the traditional language control constructs. In fact, there are no imperative constructs such as assignements and go-to's, and there are no applicative constructs such as arithmetic expressions and function composition. The primitive operations SEND and RECEIVE roughly correspond to procedure call and activation. However the language does not have argument evaluation rules and does not allow "returning" from a procedure. In other words the language has no interpreter and the control and data control operations must be provided by each functional unit. Therefore, a functional unit will receive all the needed control information within the message and the messages will usually contain a control field.

We will consider, as an example, the simulation of functions which "return" values. The control field in the pattern message can be handled as a"return link". The system,if provided with a message of the form ("function application""return-link"),must generate a message of the form ("return link"value of "function application").Note that this mechanism is similar to the continuation passing mechanism described in [5]. The mechanism is used in the example given in the next section, where also argument evaluation is shown to be performed within the function simulating fu.

3. AN EXAMPLE OF "PARALLEL" COMPUTATION: EVALUATION OF ARITHMETIC EXPRESSIONS

In order to show a meaningful example of parallel computation we will now define a system of functional units which is obtained by generalizing our first example, by first making the system $\{F_1, F_2\}$ work as a set of functions which can "return" values.

The functional units F_1 and F_2 are then modified as follows:

```
F1   /RECEIVE ((0 + =x) =ret)/
     /SEND ((!x !ret))/

F2   /RECEIVE (((s =x) + =y) =ret)/
     /SEND (((!x + (s !y)) !ret))/
```

Values are "returned" by the data structure itself (non-negative integers) which is also described by functional units:

```
F3   /RECEIVE (0 =ret)/
     /SEND ((!ret 0))/

F4   /RECEIVE ((s =x) =ret)/
     /SEND ((!ret (s !x)))/
```

Let us now define a functional unit, which allows the "evaluation"of expressions obtained by composition from the (prefix) binary operation +. "Argument evaluation"requires mechanisms to handle temporary control and data storage and to implement a specific evaluation rule. Functional unit F_5 works according to a parallel evaluation rule. Comments are inserted to explain the behaviour of temporarily DEFINEd functional units.

```
F5 /RECEIVE ((+ =x =y) =ret)/
   /DECLARE (=fu1 =fu2 =fu3)/  assign
      "new" fu names to local variables
      fu1,fu2,fu3.
   /DEFINE (          allocates two func-
      tional units named !fu1 and !fu3.
     (!fu1 /RECEIVE (!fu1 =x1)/ !fu1 is
               activated when x is evalu-
               ated, x1=value of expres-
               sion x.
           /DEFINE (   allocates func-
              tional unit !fu2.
               (!fu2 /RECEIVE (!fu2 !x1)/
                     /SEND ((!fu2 !x1))/
           )/ !fu2 sends a message which
              can activate both !fu2 it-
              self and !fu4,if defined.
           /SEND ((!fu2 !x1))/ the mes-
              sage can activate the
              looping state of !fu2 and
              !fu4,if defined.
           /FREE (!fu1)/) disallocates
              itself.
     (!fu3 /RECEIVE (!fu3 =y1)/  !fu3 is
               activated when y is evalu-
               ated, y1= value of expres-
               sion y.
           /DECLARE (=fu4)/
           /DEFINE (
               (!fu4 /RECEIVE (!fu2 =x2)/
                        !fu4 can be activ-
                        ated only when
                        both x and y have
                        been evaluated,
                        !x2=value of ex-
                        pression x.
                        !y1=value of ex-
                        pression y.
                     /SEND (((!x2+!y1)
                           !ret))/  mes-
                        sage to the adder.
                     /FREE (!fu2 !fu4)/)
           )/ disallocates both itself
              and ! fu2, to stop !fu2
              looping.
           /FREE (!fu3)/)
   )/
   /SEND ((!x !fu1)(!y !fu3))/ computes
      the values of expressions !x and
      !y to be"returned" to !fu1 and
      !fu3 respectively.
```

Figure 1 traces the behaviour of the system of functional units $S_0 = \{F_1,F_2,F_3,F_4,F_5\}$ with initial message m_1= ((+ (s 0)(+ 0 (s(s 0)))) output). Note that the "result" message can be received by any functional unit whose pattern message has the form (output =result).

The above example shows that a system of functional units does not possess an interpreter.All the tasks which are usually assigned to an interpreter are distributed over several independent modules. Each module is concerned with a specific semantic aspect (data type, primitive operations, evaluation rule, etc). Actually, in our example, functional units F_3 and F_4 can be thought of as defining the interpretation (eval) of the data of type "non-negative integer", (eval (0) = 0 and eval (s(x)) = s(x)). Functional units F_1 and F_2 define the interpretation of the "plus" operation on non-negative integers (eval (+(0,x)) = eval (x) and eval (+(S(x),y)) = eval (+(x,S(y)))). Finally, functional unit F_5 is concerned with the evaluation rule and its behaviour can be sketched as follows. F_5 activates two concurrent argument evaluation processes and creates two "continuation" functional units (!fu1 and!fu3), which are activated as soon as one argument evaluation process terminates. Since the value of the first argument cannot in general be used when !fu1 receives it, it is "stored" in a "constant" fu (!fu2), which goes on sending such a value, thus allowing it to "live" in the system as long as it is needed. The value of the second argument, received by !fu3, is "built-into" the functional unit !fu4, which can be activated by the message containing the first argument value and sends both values to the "plus" operation functional units. It is worth noting that temporarily DEFINED functional units are active (procedural) representations of what could be called "control and environment" information in an interpreted system (return and continuation links, intermediate local values, etc.). Note that functional units !fu2 & !fu4 are also responsible for the synchronization of the parallel evaluation processes.

If concurrency is allowed the problem arises of preventing a computation from being undefined. This situation occurs when a state σ_i contains several messages which can be RECEIVEd from the functional unit F (F is said to be multi-activated). In order to solve the above problem, a new functional unit F' can be associated to F: F can only be accessed through F', which transforms a set of concurrent messages into a set of sequential messages[3].

[3] F' can easily be defined if RECEIVE is extended to cope with more than one input message.

Therefore it is necessary to provide a "parallel" version of all those functional units which can be multi-activated. For instance, in our example, the data structure described by functional units F_3 and F_4 needs a different definition, if "concurrent accesses" to it are allowed. Since the corresponding functional units can be seen as resources usable by different processes, they must be able to sequentialize possible concurrent requests. The different tasks are still distributed over modules concerned with data structure semantics, but the semantics, related to parallelism, is different from the "sequential" one.

The aspects of our formalism which are worth to be emphasized,besides its ability to cope with concurrency, are the following

i) There is only one type of object, the functional unit, which is an active object. Hence both data and procedures are described by means of functional units.

ii) In an interpretation-oriented language, there is a unique locus of control (the interpreter) where knowledge about different semantic aspects is confusedly concentrated. In our formalism, knowledge distribution over several loci of control (modules) can be achieved. If our knowledge about a specific semantic aspect can be concentrated in a module, we get a decomposition of the system which can be considered well-structured from a semantic point of view.

In the next section we will consider an interesting approach to the decomposition into modules, which centers around the concept of data type.

4. DATA TYPES IN THE FUNCTIONAL UNIT FORMALISM

The behaviour of data types in the functional unit formalism can be explained in terms of some widely circulated ideas that have been recently settled, either as programming language features or as programming methodologies. We will refer to the concepts of class, of data driven programming and of data abstraction.

The class of SIMULA/67 [6,7] first introduced the idea of associating a set of procedures to data types. A class is a description of both the data type and of all the operations which can be applied to the data (instances) of that type. Classes are handled like blocks and are very similar to procedures.

A similar approach is taken in connection with a programming methodology, known as data driven programming [8]. According to such a methodology, which was mainly developed in connection with Artificial Intelligence languages, procedures are indirectly referenced through the data. One interesting referencing methodology which can be called type-driven programming [9] is through data type descriptors, which resemble SIMULA/67 classes.

The concept of data abstraction [10] was introduced in connection with top-down structured programming with the aim of defining suitable problem-oriented abstract machines. Data abstractions are motivated by the need of handling data and operations on data as implementation-independent objects. According to this methodology, a data type can be described at two different levels. At the first one, the specification level, the data type is specified by means of a set of axioms which describe implementation-independent properties of operations on the data type. At the second level, the implementation level, both the data type and the corresponding operations are implemented.

In the sequel we will show, by means of an example, how functional units acting as data types, can be developed according to the class/type-driven programming philosophy, which leads to emphasize the data type definition with respect to the standard procedure definition.

We will first consider "implementations" of data types, where each datum (instance) is a functional unit. An instance is identified by a typed pointer, which is a pair (instance-symbolic-name, type-tag) and is activated by messages of the form

((instance-symbolic-name type-tag) operation return).

When activated by such a message the instance must eventually provide for "packing" the result of the "operation" into a message to "return". The actual implementation (data representation, instance allocation and operations) is defined by a collection of "data-type" functional units. Let us consider, as an example, the definition of the data type "stack of integers", whith operations push, pop and top.

F_1 (structure definition and instance allocation for stacks of integers):

```
/RECEIVE (stackint ((=top integer)
    (=pop stackint)) instantiate =ret)/
/DECLARE (=instance)/
/DEFINE ( (!instance
          /RECEIVE ((!instance stack-
             int) =operation =return)/
          /SEND ((stackint (!instance
             stackint)((!top integer)
             (!pop stackint)) !oper-
             ation !return))/) )/
/SEND ((!ret (!instance stackint)))/
```

The pattern message of the functional unit F_1 shows the type-tag (stackint) and the data type structure, which is a "record" consisting of a pointer to an instance of type integer and a pointer to an instance of type stack of integers. It is activated only when a new instance has to be created as a result of a push operation and provides for the allocation of the new instance, SENDing back the instance typed pointer. Each instance has its typed pointer in the pattern-message and can be SENT any operation. The operations are described by a set of functional units, which play the role of the procedures defined within a SIMULA/67 class. Whenever an instance is SENT an operation, the instance simply sends itself (i.e. its name and value) to the "data-type operations" functional units.

F_2 (PUSH operation on stacks of integers):

```
/RECEIVE (Stackint (=instance
   stackint)((=top integer)(=pop
   stackint))(push (=z integer))
   =return)/

/SEND ((stackint ((!z integer)
   (!instance stackint))
   instantiate !return))/
```

F_3 (POP operation on stacks of integers):

```
/RECEIVE (stackint (=instance stack-
   int)((=top integer)(=pop stack-
   int)) pop =return)/

/SEND ((!return (!pop stackint)))/
```

F_4 (TOP operation on stacks of integers):

```
/RECEIVE (stackint (=instance
   stackint)((=top integer)(=pop
   stackint)) top =return)/

/SEND ((!return (!top integer)))/
```

Note the behaviour of F_2 which, when requested by an instance to create a new stack by pushing a new integer on it, sends an instantiation message to the functional unit F_1 which creates the new stack of integers.

A specific instance of the stack of integers (i.e. the empty stack of integers on which only the push operation is allowed) is needed to complete the data type definition:

F_5 (empty stack of integers):

```
/RECEIVE ((empty stackint)(push (=z
   integer)) =return)/

/SEND ((stackint ((!z integer)(empty
   stackint)) instantiate !return))/
```

The set of functional units $\{F_1,F_2,F_3,F_4,F_5\}$ is a definition of data type which resembles a SIMULA/67 class, in that it defines the structure of the new data type and all the operations which apply to the instances of that type. More operations could be added to our example, to cope with input/output (read and print) and with data type-tailored allocation and disallocation mechanisms.The computation of a system of functional units defined according to the above methodology is clearly type-driven. In fact, the application of a procedure P to an instance i can only be achieved by sending a message to i asking for an application of P. The instance i sends its value and the operation P to the "data-type" functional units which apply the procedure P to the instance, only if P is defined within the data type.A data type is not bound to be implemented as a record of typed pointers,but can be defined in terms of other previously defined data types.For instance, our stack of integers could have been implemented as a list structure.The operations on the stack would have been defined in terms of list operations. However, the new data type is protected, i.e. list operations could not directly be applied to instances of stacks, since such operations would not be expected by the stack functional units.

We now turn to a different description of data types, which is very similar to the "specification level" description of data abstractions. This description does not make reference to instances (i.e. specifically implemented data), but gives a set of functional units which specify properties of the abstract operations which characterize the data type. Data can only be considered to exist as parts of messages and are always tagged by their type. Consider the following set of functional units which characterize the data type "stack of integers".

```
F6 /RECEIVE ((empty stackint)(push (=z
      integer)) =ret)/

   /SEND ((!ret ((push (!z integer)
      (empty stackint)) stackint)))/

F7 /RECEIVE (((push =x =y) stackint)
      (push (=z integer)) =ret)/

   /SEND ((!ret ((push (!z integer)
      ((push !x !y) stackint)
      stackint)))/

F8 /RECEIVE (((push (=x integer) =y)
      stackint) top =ret)/

   /SEND ((!ret (!x integer)))/

F9 /RECEIVE (((push =x(=y stackint)
      pop =ret)/

   /SEND ((!ret (!y stackint)))/
```

Functional units F_6 and F_7 specify the abstract definition of stack of integers which is either the "empty stack" or is obtained by pushing an integer onto a stack of integers. Moreover they specify the functionality of push (push: stackint x integer → stackint). Functional units F_8 and F_9 specify the functionalities of top and pop

top: stackint → integer
pop: stackint → stackint

and embody the axioms:

top (push (x,y)) = x
pop (push (x,y)) = y

It is worth noting that the "abstract specification" set of functional units $\{F_6,F_7,F_8,F_9\}$ leads to computations on abstract stacks of integers which are exactly the same computations which would arise in connection with the "implementation level" set of functional units $\{F_1,F_2,F_3,F_4,F_5\}$. More precisely the "black-box" behaviours of the two sets cannot be distinguished. They are only different with respect to the data representations, which are functional units addressable by a typed pointer at the implementation level and are abstract descriptions appearing in a message at the specification level.

The operational equivalence between specifications and implementations, can be forced to hold for any data type. A top-down-like programming methodology can be based on such an equivalence. Whenever a new data type t is needed, it is first specified. All the functional units (possibly other data types) which make reference to t, must refer to its abstract specification. The resulting system can perform any computation which makes use of t. The actual implementation of t can be deffered, and any specification-equivalent implementation, will make the system work correctly.

5. CONCLUDING REMARKS

We mentioned that our formalism was deeply influenced by Hewitt's actors. Functional units behave like actors, as far as the RECEIVE-SEND mechanism in concerned. We have extended the set of primitive operations to cope explicitely with the creation and deletion of functional units. On the other hand, our formalism has no primitive objects acting as data, operations or control structures. In our belief, this should make easier a formal treatment of the behaviour of distributed systems and of their use in the implementation of algorithms.

One motivation of this paper was showing the relation between distributed systems and data types. It is worth pointing out that in our formalism the data type is a good pivot for structuring a high-level machine.

The machine can be simulated by systems of functional units acting as data type definitions. The operations that would appear in a standard interpreter are distributed over all the data types. On the other hand, the knowledge about a data type is concentrated in the set of functional units which are concerned with that data type. While in a standard interpreter modifying the implementation of a data type, would generally require the whole interpreter to be rewritten, in our distributed machine only the data type has to be redefined.

REFERENCES

1 Hewitt, C., Bishop, P. and Steiger, R., A universal modular ACTOR formalism for Artificial Intelligence. Proc. of 3rd IJCAI, Stanford, September 1973, pp. 235-245.

2 Hewitt, C. et al., Behavioral definition of nonrecursive control structures. Programming Symp., Paris, April 1974, in Lecture notes in computer science, 19, Berlin,Springer-Verlag, pp. 385-398.

3 Hewitt, C. and Smith, B., Towards a programmer's apprentice. IEEE Transactions on software engineering, SE-1 (1975), pp. 26-45.

4 Hewitt, C., Viewing control Structures as patterns of passing messages. M.I.T., Artificial Intelligence Laboratory Working Paper 92 (August 1976).

5 Sussman, G.J. and Steele, G.L. Jr., SCHEME. An interpreter for extended lamda calculus, MIT, AI Memo N. 349, (December 1975).

6 Dahl, O., Nyhrhaug, B. and Nygaard, K., The SIMULA/67 common base language Norwegian Computing Centre, Oslo 1970.

7 Ichbiah, J.D. and Morse, S.P., General concepts of the SIMULA/67 programming language. Annual Review in Automatic Programming, 6 (1971), pp. 65-93.

8 Sandewall, E., Ideas about management of LISP data bases. Proc. of 4th IJCAI Tbilisi, September 1975, pp. 585-593.

9 Aiello, L., Aiello, M., Attardi G. and Prini, G., Recursive data types in LISP: a case study in type driven programming. I.E.I. Technical Report B75-27, Pisa, December 1975.

10 Liskov, B. and Zilles, S.N., Specification techniques of Data Abstractions. IEEE Transactions on software engineering, SE-1 (1975), pp. 72-87.

$S_0 = \{F_1,F_2,F_3,F_4,F_5\}$ $M_0 = \{m_1\}$

m_1 activates F_5

$env(F_5)=\{(x,(s\ 0)),(y,(+\ 0\ (s(s\ 0)))),(ret,output),(fu1,F_6),(fu2,F_7),(fu3,F_8)\}$

F_5 allocates F_6 and F_8

F_6: /RECEIVE(F_6 =x_1)/
/DEFINE(
(F_7/RECEIVE(F_7 !x_1)/
/SEND ((F_7 !x_1))/))/
/SEND ((F_7 !x_1))/
/FREE (F_6)/

F_8: /RECEIVE(F_8 =y_1)/
/DECLARE(=fu4)/
/DEFINE(
(!fu4/RECEIVE(F_7 =x_2)/
/SEND(((x_2+y_1) output))/
/FREE(F_7 !fu4)/))/
/FREE(F_8)/

and sends m_2 = ((s 0) F_6) and m_3 = ((+ 0 (s(s 0))) F_8)

$S_1 = \{F_1,F_2,F_3,F_4,F_5,F_6,F_8\}$ $M_1 = \{m_2,m_3\}$

m_2 activates F_4
$env(F_4)=\{(x,0),(ret,F_6)\}$
F_4 sends m_4=(F_6 (s 0))

m_3 activates F_5
$env(F_5)=\{(x,0),(y,(s(s\ 0))),(ret,F_8),(fu1,F_9),(fu2,F_{10}),(fu3,F_{11})\}$
F_5 allocates F_9 and F_{11}

F_9:/RECEIVE(F_9 =x_1)/
/DEFINE(
(F_{10}/RECEIVE(F_{10} !x_1)/
/SEND((F_{10} !x_1))/))/
/SEND((F_{10} !x_1))/
/FREE(F_9)/

F_{11}:/RECEIVE(F_{11} =y_1)/
/DECLARE(=fu4)/
/DEFINE(
(!fu4/RECEIVE(F_{10} =x_2)/
/SEND(((x_2+y_1) F_8))/
/FREE(F_{10} !fu4)/))/
/FREE(F_{11})/

and sends m_5=(0 F_9) and m_6=((s(s 0)) F_{11})

$S_2 = \{F_1,F_2,F_3,F_4,F_5,F_6,F_8,F_9,F_{11}\}$ $M_2 = \{m_4,m_5,m_6\}$

m_4 activates F_6
$env(F_6)=\{(x_1,(s\ 0))\}$
F_6 allocates F_7
F_7:/RECEIVE(F_7 (s 0))/
/SEND((F_7 (s 0)))/
F_6 sends m_7=(F_7 (s 0))
and disallocates F_6

m_5 activates F_3
$env(F_3)=\{(ret,F_9)\}$
F_3 sends m_8=(F_9 0)

m_6 activates F_4
$env(F_4)=\{(ret,F_{11})\}$
F_4 sends
m_9=(F_{11}(s(s 0)))

$S_3 = \{F_1,F_2,F_3,F_4,F_5,F_7,F_8,F_9,F_{11}\}$ $M_3 = \{m_7,m_8,m_9\}$

Fig.1

m_7 activates F_7 $env(F_7)=\{\}$ F_7 sends $m_{10}=m_7=(F_7\ (s\ 0))$	m_8 activates F_9 $env(F_9)=\{(x_1,0)\}$ F_9 allocates F_{10} F_{10}:/RECEIVE(F_{10} 0)/ /SEND((F_{10} 0))/ F_9 sends $m_{11}=(F_{10}\ 0)$ and disallocates F_9	m_9 activates F_{11} $env(F_{11})=\{(y_1,(s(s\ 0))),(fu4,F_{12})\}$ F_{11} allocates F_{12} F_{12}:/RECEIVE(F_{10} $=x_2$)/ /SEND(((x_2 + (s(s 0))) F_8))/ /FREE(F_{10} F_{12})/ F_{11} disallocates F_{11}

$S_4=\{F_1,F_2,F_3,F_4,F_5,F_7,F_8,F_{10},F_{12}\}$ $M_4=\{m_{10},m_{11}\}$

m_{10} activates F_7	m_{11} activates F_{10} and F_{12}	
$env(F_7)=\{\ \}$ F_7 sends $m_{12}=(F_7\ (s\ 0))$	$env(F_{10})=\{\ \}$ F_{10} sends $m_{13}=(F_{10}\ 0)$	$env(F_{12})=\{(x_2,0)\}$ F_{12} sends $m_{14}=((0\ +\ (s(s\ 0)))\ F_8)$ and disallocates F_{10} and F_{12}

$S_5=\{F_1,F_2,F_3,F_4,F_5,F_7,F_8\}$ $M_5=\{m_{12},m_{13},m_{14}\}$

m_{12} activates F_7 m_{13} is lost $env(F_7)=\{\ \}$ F_7 sends $m_{15}=(F_7\ (s\ 0))$	m_{14} activates F_1 $env(F_1)=\{(x,(s(s\ 0))),\ (ret,F_8)\}$ F_1 sends $m_{16}=((s(s\ 0))\ F_8)$

$S_6=\{F_1,F_2,F_3,F_4,F_5,F_7,F_8\}$ $M_6=\{m_{15},m_{16}\}$

m_{15} activates F_7 $env(F_7)=\{\ \}$ F_7 sends $m_{17}=(F_7\ (s\ 0))$	m_{16} activates F_4 $env(F_4)=\{(x,(s\ 0)),(ret,F_8)\}$ F_4 sends $m_{18}=(F_8\ (s(s\ 0)))$

$S_7=\{F_1,F_2,F_3,F_4,F_5,F_7,F_8\}$ $M_7=\{m_{17},m_{18}\}$

m_{17} activates F_7 $env(F_7)=\{\ \}$ F_7 sends $m_{19}=(F_7\ (s\ 0))$	m_{18} activates F_8 $env(F_8)=\{(y_1,(s(s\ 0))),(fu4,F_{13})\}$ F_8 allocates F_{13} F_{13}:/RECEIVE(F_7 $=x_2$)/ /SEND(((!x_2 + (s(s 0))) output))/ /FREE(F_7 F_{13})/ F_8 disallocates F_8

$S_8=\{F_1,F_2,F_3,F_4,F_5,F_7,F_{13}\}$ $M_8=\{m_{19}\}$

m_{19} activates F_7 and F_{13} $env(F_7)=\{\ \}$ F_7 sends $m_{20}=(F_7\ (s\ 0))$	$env(F_{13})=\{(x_2,(s\ 0))\}$ F_{13} sends $m_{21}=(((s\ 0)+(s(s\ 0)))\ output)$ F_{13} disallocates F_7 and F_{13}

$S_9=\{F_1,F_2,F_3,F_4,F_5\}$ $M_9=\{m_{20},m_{21}\}$

m_{20} is lost m_{21} activates F_2 $env(F_2)=\{(x,0),(y,(s(s\ 0))),(ret,output)\}$
F_2 sends $m_{22}=((0\ +\ (s(s(s\ 0))))\ output)$

$S_{10}=\{F_1,F_2,F_3,F_4,F_5\}$ $M_{10}=\{m_{22}\}$

m_{22} activates F_1 $env(F_1)=\{(x,(s(s(s\ 0)))),(ret,output)\}$ F_1 sends $m_{23}=((s(s(s\ 0)))\ output)$

$S_{11}=\{F_1,F_2,F_3,F_4,F_5\}$ $M_{11}=\{m_{23}\}$

m_{23} activates F_4 $env(F_4)=\{(x,(s(s\ 0))),(ret,output)\}$ F_4 sends $m_{24}=(output(s(s(s\ 0))))$

Fig.1 (continued)

E. Morlet and D. Ribbens, (Eds.), International Computing Symposium 1977.

SPIP : A WAY OF WRITING PORTABLE OPERATING SYSTEMS

D. Thalmann B. Levrat

Centre Universitaire d'Informatique
Université de Genève
Genève, Suisse

An operating system compiler written in Pascal allows the programmer to write operating systems for a very general abstract mini-computer, and produces code for the mini-computer of his choice. This approach provides global optimization, good documentation and improved reliability of operating systems, as well as complete portability. One such portable operating system called S.O.S. has been written and runs on Nova and PDP-11 mini-computers.

1. INTRODUCTION

Writing software in assembly code for a minicomputer is very hard work. Addressing and register allocation problems hide basic algorithms and general conception.

An operating system written in assembly code is rarely well documented, modifications are hard to implement and are often a source of errors. Necessary improvements may result in an actual degradation. Furthermore, systems are not portable from one minicomputer to another.

We wanted to demonstrate that it is possible to use the power of a big computer and an appropriate high level language to generate an operating system for more than one minicomputer.

SPIP is in itself such a demonstration. Programmers can use it to write an entire operating system or a single module, to change a monitor request in a readable language, and to ensure much more reliability. The generator will produce an optimized code which will free the programmer from addressing and register allocation problems, hopefully providing increased efficiency.

SPIP is written in Pascal [4], and in the present implementation on our Univac 1108, it can produce operating systems for Nova and PDP-11 minicomputers.

The S.O.S. operating system is briefly described at the end of this paper. It has been completely written and runs on real machines.

2. SPIP PRINCIPLES

SPIP is an operating system compiler. The first step to be made to write an operating system in SPIP is to direct it to an abstract machine with a very rich instruction set : the λ-machine.

The object system produced by SPIP is an operating system directly ready for the minicomputer which has been chosen. A single option in SPIP allows the programmer to choose the object machine. At present, two options are implemented : option N for Data General Nova and option P for DEC PDP-11.

SPIP has 4 parts :

i) A compiler which accepts a SPIP language program and produces code : the λ-code. It is machine independent.

ii) A set of procedures which translates λ-code into optimized relocatable code for minicomputers. About 75% of these procedures are valid for all minicomputers.

iii) A link-program which produces absolute code for the minicomputer. This code is again optimized. The link program is minicomputer independent.

iv) A minicomputer simulator which enables the execution of absolute code on the Univac 1108.

2.1 The λ-machine

It is a 16-bit processor with :

- 30 16-bit word-registers : w_1 to w_{30}
- 10 8-bit byte-registers : b_1 to b_{10}
- 10 stacks : s_1 to s_{10}
- 10 queues : q_1 to q_{10}
- 10 lists : l_1 to l_{10}
- 30 tables : t_1 to t_{30}
- 1 memory, which can be addressed directly, indirectly, with index registers, or by page
- 1 interrupt system
- 1 input/output system with devices

Disc access is performed by using the logical units f_1 to f_{10}.

3. THE SPIP LANGUAGE : AN OVERVIEW

The SPIP language is a set of instructions for the λ-machine. 58 instructions and 18 macros are available. In the choice of these instructions, we were mainly influenced by two languages written by Wirth : PL360 [10] and Pascal [4].

3.1 The move instruction is the most important one; it is used to move information between different registers, devices, files, etc.

3.2 In addition to the 4 arithmetic operations, "and", "or", "exclusive or", "modulo" can be executed by the instruction :

arithmetic (<operand-1>,<operator>,
<operand-2>,<result>)

e.g.:

arithmetic (w1, or, w2, w3)
makes an "or" between w1 and w2 with the result in w3.

3.3 Instructions for the assembly of bytes into words, and shift instructions are available.

3.4 Memory access, indirect addressing, indexed addressing, and page addressing are allowed.

e.g.:

move (indirect w3, @245)
moves the contents of the location specified in w3 in location 245;

increment (ind 3 w4)
adds one to the contents of the location which has been specified by adding 3 to the contents of w4;

move (page w1 w2, output)
displays the contents of the location specified in w2 for the page specified in w1.

3.5 The processing of stacks and queues is analog to the processing of words and bytes.

e.g.:

move (s1, q2)
pops the operand off the stack s1 and pushes it onto the queue q2.

3.6 Table and list processing can be performed by the oper instruction. For tables, 3 functions are available : store (into), fetch (out), and look for (look); for lists, 4 functions are available : head, tail, cons and append (same as CAR, CDR, CONS and APPEND functions of LISP 1.5).

e.g.:

oper (into, t3, w2, s3)
pops the operand off the stack s3 and stores it in t3 [(w2)];

oper (append, l1, l2)
appends list l2 to list l1.

3.7 The prefix length enables to know the structure length.

e.g.:

move (length s1, w3).

3.8 The prefix address gives the location of an object.

3.9 Bit processing can be done by the instruction oper-bit.

e.g.:

oper-bit (on, bit3, w4)
sets bit 3 of w4.

3.10 Module definition has the form :

define-begin (<module>,<formal parameter list>)
<module body>
define-end

Modules can be used recursively and have value and variable parameters.

3.11 A vast set of program control structures is provided :

i) repeat-begin <instructions>
repeat-end (<condition>)

ii) while-begin (<condition>)
<instructions>
while-end

iii) loop-begin (<control word>,<first>,
<last>,<step>,up/down)<instructions>
loop-end

iv) if-begin (<condition>)<instructions>[otherwise <instructions>]
if-end

v) case-begin (<word or byte selector>)
of (<constant>) <instructions>
of (<constant>) <instructions>

:

[other-case <instructions>]
case-end

The SPIP language is a gotoless language.

3.12 Conditions make it possible to compare words, bytes, to test bits, interrupts and end-of-files.

e.g.:

if-begin (w1, lt, s7) ... if-end
We compare the contents of w1 with the last operand pushed onto stack s7; ("lt" means "less than").

while-begin (bit 4, w3, on) <instructions> while-end
While bit 4 of w3 is set, instructions are executed.

3.13 Type conversions (octal, decimal, binary and ASCII) are provided.

e.g.:

move (w3, decimal, output, octal)
displays the contents of w3 with the conversion from decimal to octal.

3.14 Input/output devices are operated by driver or in character mode. The complete ASCII set is available. The prefixes ctrl and shift can be used in front of a character.

e.g.:

move (ctrl 'C', output)

3.15 Disk file processing is admitted if the logical units are used; the instruction "move" is extended to the logical units. End-of-file processing, rewind, open and close instructions are included in the language.

Logical units are defined by :

attach (<logical unit>,<file name>, <properties>,<status word>)

The file name can be contained in a queue, properties allow files to be read- or write-protected, error codes are given by the status word.

e.g.:

attach (f3, 'scratch', read-write, w2)
In case of error, w2 can be tested as status word.

3.16 Disk access by sectors is provided by :

fetch-sector (<memory page word> <disk sector word>)
store-sector (<memory page word> <disk sector word>)

3.17 Facilities in interrupt processing are included in the SPIP language under the form of instructions :

i) save-processor and restore-processor

ii) case-interrupt of (<device>)
<instruction> ...
[othercase <instructions>]
case-end

iii) <interrupt condition>::= interrupt, <device>, on/off

iv) service-interrupt (<module>) defines a service module.

v) cause-of-interrupt (<word register>) moves device code in word register.

vi) interrupt (on/off)

vii) select-interrupt (<device>, on/off)

3.18 In addition, SPIP allows :

i) The definition of macro-instructions

e.g.:

macro (condition)
if-begin (↑1, ↑2, ↑3) need (↑4)
otherwise need (↑5)
if-end $

↑n represents the n-th argument;

and the use of :

e.g.:

condition (w1, lt, w3, m1, m2)
where m1 and m2 are module names.

ii) The definition of monitor requests :

e.g.:

request-begin ('STACKOUTWD', w1, w2/)

<<this request pops the word w1 off the stack of address w2>>

```
   if-begin (ind o w2, le, o)
      error-return(2) <<empty stack>>
   if-end
   arithmetic (w2, +, ind o w2, w3)
   move (ind 2 w3, w1)
   decrement (ind o w2)
request-end
```

Request is made by :

sos-request ('stackoutwd', w1, w3)

iii) The definition of overlays by :

overlay (name,<formal parameter list>)

iv) The definition of drivers.

Calls to requests or overlays are checked at compiling time. A control is provided at execution time on the minicomputer so as to avoid errors due to the bad use of a request.

To eliminate dangerous conflicts, we defined two levels of the SPIP language:

fundamental level :
(requests, overlays and drivers)
Disk access by logical units is forbidden.

secondary level :
(utilities, compiler, interpret)
memory addressing, interrupt instructions, and access to disk sectors are not allowed.

4. THE SPIP COMPILER

It accepts SPIP language instructions, parses them, and produces λ-code. λ-code is as independent of the computer as the compiler. The parsing method is top-down; globally, recursive descent is used, but instruction fields are checked against tables.

e.g.:

instruction oper-bit (on/off,<bit>,<word>) is defined in Pascal as :

```
with instr[26]do
  begin id:='oper-bit'; nparam:=3;
  p[1].kind:=gn2; p[1].lim2:=[off,on]
  p[2].kind:=gn1; p[1].lim1:=[bit 0..
                                bit 15];
  p[3].kind:=simples; p[3].lim:=[w1..
                                    w30]
  end;
```

In parser, we have :

```
   :
lookforinstruction; (*binary search*)
if nparam <> 0 then
  begin scanner;
  if sy <> leftpar then error (5)
    else repeat scanner; i:=i+1;
      checkfield (i);
      scanner;
      if not (sy in [comma rightpar])
        then error (7)
      until sy=rightpar;
```

The procedure checkfield (i : integer) checks if field[i].kind = p[i].kind, and if the range is correct.

The choice of this parsing method was mainly influenced by Wirth [8] and by the experience acquired by teaching courses on compiler construction (Thalmann [6, 7]).

4.1 Error Recovery

The parser can recover from errors by inserting, deleting, or modifying symbols. It is very important to give the user informations about the recovery; this facility is generally not provided with the present compilers.

For example, a programmer uses the instruction if instead of if-begin. The following lines are printed :

```
    :
move (5, w1)
if (w1, lt, w2) increment (w3) if-end
--- error(s) 1

DIAGNOSTICS BY SPIP
1 : DETECTED BY PARSER IN MOVE.
SYMBOL : IF
UNKNOWN INSTRUCTION
RECOVERY : 8 SYMBOL(S) SKIPPED.
RESTART AT INCREMENT.
```

4.2 Lambda-Code

The format can be defined by the following table :

	kind	subfield	variable field
instruction	'I'	instr. code	instruction field number
address	'A'	0	numerical address
number	'N'	0	value
character	'K'	0	ASCII code
string	'S'	0	string of fixed length for internal use (e.g. file name)
		1	ASCII code for each char., -1 to end
page	'P'	0	0 (followed by 2 words)
error	'E'	0	0 (followed by a word)
reserved word	'G'	1 2	ord (reserved word) 2 categories

```
                kind  subfield  variable field
object          'O'   dddocba   object number
                      with:
                            0   normal object
                            1   local object
                      a:    2   global structure
                            3   local global
                                structure
                      b:        indirect level
                      c:    1   address
                            2   length
                      ddd:      offset for indexed addressing
```

5. SEMANTIC ACTIONS

Relocatable code is produced from λ-code by a set of Pascal procedures. We can explain the mechanism by an example :

compose (S1, 'A', q2)

This instruction of the SPIP language pops a byte off stack S1, composes a word with it and with character 'A', and pushes the new word onto queue q2.

λ-code produced by the compiler is :

```
I     29      3
O     Ø      46
K     Ø     101
O     Ø      57
```

Two Pascal procedures, readlambda and interpretlambda, store information about instructions in records :

```
type ptrword =↑instrfield;
  instrfield = record subfield:integer;
                      obj:objects;
                 case kind of
                  'I','O','K','N':
                      (value:integer);
                  'P':(pt1,pt2:ptrword);
                  'G':(res1:gen)
                 end;
var instr:instrfield;
  field:array[1..10]of instrfield;
```

A procedure switch is called :

```
procedure switch;
  :
case instr. subfield of
  :
29:begin
   compose(pretreat(1),pretreat(2),
                          dest(3));
   if destin<>single then postreat(3)
   end;
   :
```

The pretreatment of fields 1 and 2 is made by function pretreat :

```
function pretreat(i:integer):varfield;
  :
with field[i] do
begin.
  :
if kind='K' then
begin needtemp (zwords,wbt,i,noindexed);
      enterint(value,wbt); obj:=wbt
end
                 else
if kind='O' then
begin if member(obj,stacks) or
         member(obj,queues) then
         oper(out,obj,wbt)
  :
```

The post-treatment of field 3 is made by function dest and procedure postreat :

```
function dest(i:integer):varfield;
  :
with field[i] do
begin
  :
if member(obj,strucs)then
  begin destin:=str;
  needtemp(component[obj],wbt,i,
                          noindexed);
  dest:=wbt; temp[i]:=wbt
  end
  :
procedure postreat(i:integer);
  :
with field[i] do
begin
  :
if member(obj,stacks) or
   member(obj,queues) then
   oper(into,obj,temp[i])
  :
```

We use the sequence as follows :

Semantic action (translation time)	Object code action (run time)
pretreat(1)	pops byte off the stack s1 by procedure oper(out,obj,wbt) and moves it in register r1 of the minicomputer
pretreat(2)	loads register r2 of the minicomputer with character 'A'
dest(3)	gets information for temporary use of register r3
compose( )	composes a word in register r3 with bytes in registers r1 and r2
postreat(3)	pushes the contents of r3 onto the queue q2 by procedure oper (into,obj,dt)

6. RELOCATABLE CODE AND ITS OPTIMIZATION

Relocatable code is generated with 4 program counters.

0 for constants, word and byte registers, and module addresses,
1 for main program instructions,
2 for modules,
3 for structures.

6.1 Optimization and Register Allocation

To minimize the frequency of storing, it is necessary to have a good algorithm of register allocation. Sethi [5] gives a set of rules in the case of arithmetic expressions and Ammann [1] has a good algorithm in the Pascal compiler.

SPIP uses the following rules :

i) Each register has a priority (integer number). The lowest priority is 0, the highest is maxprior.

ii) The more a register is available, the lower its priority.

iii) A register can be protected.

iv) When the contents of a λ-register is needed, if it is not in a real register, a load is performed. The register is protected and gets the maxprior priority.

v) When a value in a real register must be stored in a λ-register, priority is put on half of its value.

vi) Every nstep instructions generated, the priority of all the registers is decremented by 1.

vii) If all registers are protected and a register is needed, all protections are eliminated.

viii) A λ-word or byte register can be declared as fast; this will force its affectation to a real register. It is protected; if protection is removed, priority is set again to maxprior. Thus, it cannot be allocated, except if some fast registers compete; in this case, if a register must be allocated, the content is stored in the memory.

ix) A real register that is a loop control word has ploop start priority.

x) A real register that is a case selector has pcase start priority.

maxprior, nstep, ploop and pcase can be modified by the user.

To each register, a descriptor is attached :

```
type accudescriptor =
  record lambda:objects;
         indirect:boolean;
    indexed,value:integer
  end;
var virtual:array[accus] of
                     accudescriptor;
(*register allocation procedure is*)
procedure needaccu(var accu:accus;
                   indexac:boolean);
var prr:0..maxprior;
    address:location;
    ack,acd:accus;
begin
if indexac then
    acd:=firstindexaccu
        else acd:=firstaccu;
accu:=noacc; prr:=maxprior;
for ack:=acd to lastaccu do
  if not protected[ack] then
     if priority[ack]<=prr then
        begin
        prr:=priority[ack];
        accu:=ack
        end;
if accu<>noacc then
  with virtual[accu] do
     begin
     if fast[lambda].cond then
        begin
        fast[lambda].cond]:=false;
        outregis1(lambda,address,accu)
        end;
```

```
        clearoneaccuinf(accu)
        end
           else
        begin
        for ack:=acd to lastaccu do
          begin
          protected[ack]:=false;
          if fast[lambda].cond then
              priority[accu]:=maxprior
          end;
        needaccu(accu,indexac)
        end
end;
```

7. LINK PROGRAM

From relocatable code, absolute code is produced for the real minicomputer.

Words under counter 0 must stay in a memory block of maximum 256 words. This zone must be accessible from everywhere. Words under counter 1 and 2 stay in the next locations. Data structures can be stored in the next locations but overlap is allowed.

The rest of the memory (except the monitor) is available for dynamic use (stack for recursive modules and interrupts, list construction, overlays, file buffers).

7.1 Overlap

A structure s can overlap another structure s' or instructions when it is no longer possible to use the structure s' or the instructions.

e.g.:

```
title(example) move ('test program
                 07/12/76', output)
dimension(S1,20) clear(w2)
while-begin(w2,lt,20) decompose(w2,b1,b2)
    move(b2,output) move(b2,S1)
    increment(w2)
while-end
end.
```

Absolute code has the form :

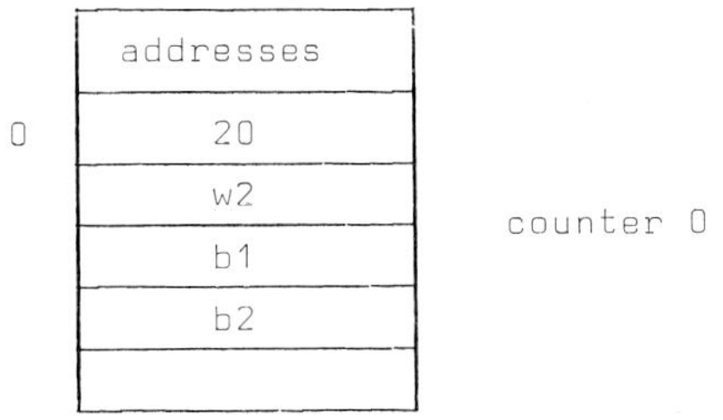

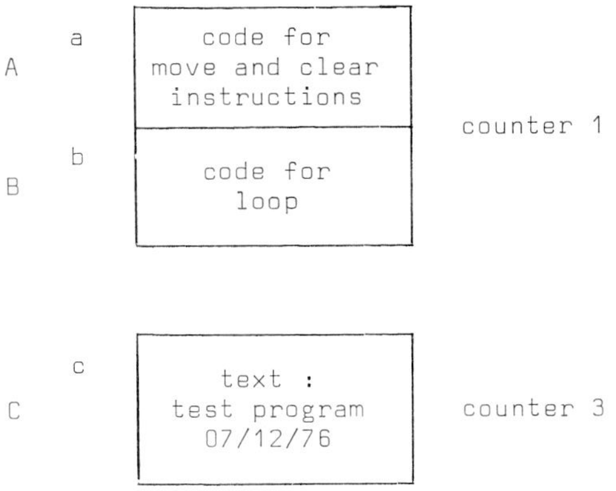

If zone A has more than 13 words (20 bytes for text + 3 control words), the address of S1 will be a (overlap of zone A), else c (overlap of zone C).

8. EXAMPLE OF AN OPERATING SYSTEM : S.O.S.

This single-user operating system allows the processing of files (create, read, write, delete, edit), the compiling in Pascal-S [9] and the execution by interpret.

S.O.S. handles 5 types of files :
X (system file in absolute binary),
O (system overlay file), S (file produced by SPIP), A (ASCII file : Pascal source or data file), I (S-code produced by Pascal-S compiler).

For the development of the file system, we used some ideas of Brinch Hansen [2, 3].

8.1 Job Control Language

CREATE (file, type, properties)
to create a file with type and properties.

FORMAT (file-1, file-2)
to produce a system file (X or O type) from a SPIP file (S type).

CHANGE (file, properties)
to change file properties.

COPY (file-1, file-2)
to make a copy of a file

DELETE (file)
to remove a file from the catalog and free all sectors.

READ (device, file)
to read information from device and copy into a file.

LIST (file, device)
to list a file on device.

APPEND (file-1, file-2, file-3)
to append file-2 to file-1 to build file-3.

EDITOR (file-1, file-2)
text editor.

PASCAL-S (input file, output file, listing)
Pascal-S computer.

INTERPRET (file)
to execute code produced by Pascal-S compiler.

Other commands are available to process the file by lines (ADD-NUMBERS, NO-NUMBERS, MODIFY, MERGE) and to have access to information structure (DUMP, PATCH, FILES).

The whole operating system is written in SPIP, monitor nucleus included; no instructions are written in assembly code.

9. CONCLUSION

The extension of SPIP to other minicomputers is very easy; only the code generation part has to be modified. But the greatest value of SPIP may well lie in the realm of providing systems for micro-computers.

APPENDIX : CHARACTERISTICS OF SPIP AND S.O.S.

SPIP machine : Univac 1108
language : Pascal (standard)

Program	Lines	Procedures	Total size in Kwords	Kwords used for stack*	Time to write
SPIP compiler	3200	63	38	16	3 months
Relocatable generator NOVA	5000	170	34	9	4½ months
PDP-11	5000	175	34	9	1½ months**
Link program	800	20	26	16	3 weeks
Simulator NOVA	1500	67	28	20	5 weeks
PDP-11	1900	95	29	20	2 weeks***

* included in total
** only about 1200 lines were rewritten
*** part of NOVA simulator was used

S.O.S.

program	lines	time to write
Pascal-S compiler	1500	2 weeks*
Interpret	400	3 days
Resident	1000	5 weeks
Editor	120	2 hours
Other utilities	900	2 weeks

* with use of N. Wirth's [9] Pascal-S listing.

REFERENCES

[1] Ammann U.
On code generation in a Pascal compiler. Berichte des Instituts für Informatik, report no. 13, April 1976.

[2] Brinch Hansen P.
Operating system principles. Prentice-Hall, 1973.

[3] Brinch Hansen P.
The SOLO operating system. Software - Practice and Experience 6, pp. 141-205 (1976).

[4] Jensen K. and Wirth N.
Pascal user manual and report. Springer Verlag, 1974.

[5] Sethi R. and Ullman J.
The generation of optimal code for arithmetic expressions. Journal of the ACM, 17, 4 (1970).

[6] Thalmann D. and Levrat B.
Un semestre pour écrire un compilateur : RALBOL. Proceedings of the IFIP 2nd World Conference on Computers in Education (1975).

[7] Thalmann D.
La construction des compilateurs. Vol. I-II. Federal Institute of Technology, Lausanne, 1976.

[8] Wirth N.
Algorithms + data structures = programs. Prentice-Hall, 1976.

[9] Wirth N.
Pascal-S. A subset and its implementation. Berichte des Instituts für Informatik, report no. 12, June 1975.

[10] Wirth N.
PL/360, a programming language for the 360 computers. Journal of the ACM, 15, 1, pp. 37-74 (1968).

E. Morlet and D. Ribbens, (Eds.), International Computing Symposium 1977.
© North-Holland Publishing Company, 1977

COMPARISON OF PERFORMANCE MEASUREMENTS OF A COMPUTER SYSTEM WITH A QUEUEING THEORY MODEL

Lester Lipsky[1]

Informatica
Faculty of Science
University of Nijmegen
Nederland

Anthony Ozorio, Al Begley, and Randy Coleman

Department of Computer Science
University of Nebraska
Lincoln, Nebraska 68588, USA

1. INTRODUCTION

There have been innumerable analyses made of untold numbers of computing systems based on either some simulation procedure, or of detailed measurements of the activities of the different components. There have been very few direct comparisons made, however, between experiment (the measurements) and theory (the simulation models). It is the purpose of this paper to describe one such comparison.

We describe measurements which were made on the IBM 360/65J which is at the University of Nebraska's Lincoln Computing Facility (LCF). The data was taken from the standard Systems Maintenance File (SMF) tape and some locally written software monitors.

The analytical model used in this paper is based on the theory of 'Closed Queueing Networks with Exponential Servers' as derived by Jackson[1], and Gordon and Newell[2]. Previous applications of this theory have been described by Lipsky[3], Bhandiwad and Williams[4], Boyse and Warn[5], and Lipsky and Church [6].

Section 2 of this paper describes the measurement of the CPU time spent by the computer on normal Batch jobs, as a function of the number of such jobs which are active in the system. The third section describes the detailed model which attempts to reproduce the data. The measurements and the model calculations are then compared. Given that the measurements and the model agree reasonably well, an attempt is made in section 4 to predict the effect on throughput of converting one megabyte of extended core storage (ECS) used by the system to high speed memory (a roughly two-to-one decrease in memory access time).

2. MEASUREMENTS

In an IBM 360 system such as that operated by the University of Nebraska's Lincoln Computing Facility (LCF), the number of batch jobs (user programs) which are active at any one time is not constant, even though the number of jobs which the system identifies as 'active' (in IBM terminology, 'active' or 'draining' initiators) may be. During very busy periods, the major reason for this variation in the number of active jobs is caused by the limited size of main memory. That is, when a given job is completed, it is not necessarily replaced immediately by another job. Instead, several new jobs, or none at all, may ultimately occupy the storage space previously held by the one completed. Some jobs which have already been initiated, may wait for space in main memory for extended periods of time before they can become active. For this reason, the data which is generated by the system (data on the SMF tape) does not reveal how much CPU time is used, as a function of the number of active jobs. The data which is generated indicates, instead, when a job enters the main memory (becomes active), when it leaves the main memory, and how much CPU time it used while there. What is not known is how the CPU time it used was distributed over its period of residence.

Let u(i) be the time that the ith job was loaded into the high speed memory, s(i) be the time the ith job left, and c(i) equal the amount of CPU time which the ith job used during its stay. Of course, c(i) will always be smaller than s(i)-u(i). Consider Figure 1, for example. During the time intervals (u(2)-u(1)) and (s(4)-s(2)), there was

----
[1] permanent Address: Department of Computer Science, University of Nebraska, Lincoln, Nebraska 68588, USA.

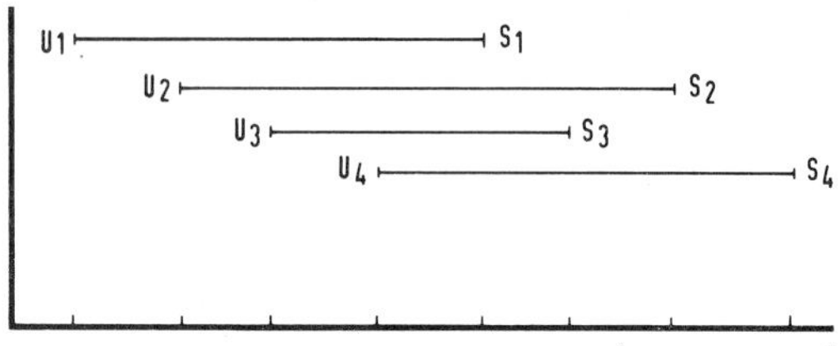

Fig. 1. Time Interval Diagram of Four Jobs Entering (u(j)) and Leaving (s(j)) the Main Memory of a Hypothetical Computer.

only one job active in the system, while during (u(3)-u(2)) and (s(2)-s(3)) there were two jobs active. We do not know how much CPU time job one used during the intervals (u(2)-u(1)) or (u(3)-u(2)), so we cannot say how much CPU time was used during those intervals.

Various assumptions can be made as to how the CPU time used by each job is distributed over its time of activity. For instance, it could be assumed that for each job the CPU time is distributed uniformly, irrespective of the other jobs in the system. This assumption would tend to be true for jobs which require very little CPU for each input or output request ('I/O-bound' jobs). If this were true, then the curve representing CPU time as a function of the number of jobs active would be linear. Curve 1 of Figure 2 is just such a function for the period 8 Dec 1975 to 12 Dec 1975 (Monday to Friday), for the hours 10:00 to 18:00.

A second assumption which could be made in the other extreme would be that each job uses the CPU in inverse proportion to the number of jobs in the system at that time. This case is true only for jobs which require a great deal of CPU time between I/O's ('CPU-bound', or 'Number Cruncher'). Such jobs would yield a productivity curve which was flat. The actual case measured, curve 2 of Figure 2, tends to that behavior, in that this curve is much flatter than curve 1, although it certainly is not horizontal.

Clearly, the true situation lies somewhere in between cases 1 and 2. In case 3, it was assumed that each job distributes its CPU usage in proportion to 1./sqrt(n), where 'n' is the number of active jobs in a given interval. It is this curve which is taken to be the 'measured' productivity when comparison is made with the analytic model in the succeeding sections.

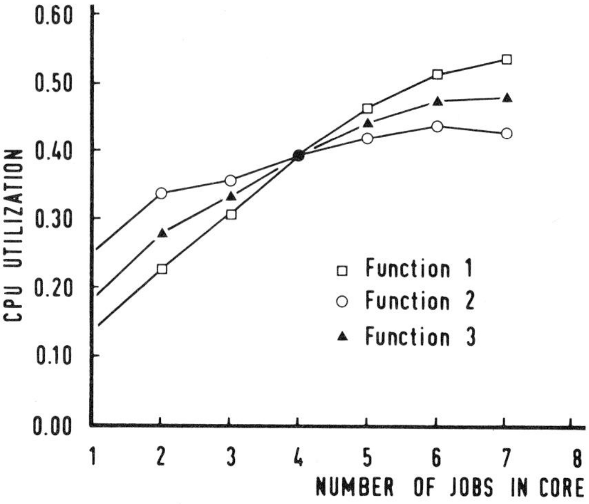

Fig. 2. 'Measured' CPU Utilization for the Period 8 Dec to 12 Dec, 1975, Assuming Three Different Distribution Schemes: Function 1 assumes that the CPU used by each job is uniformly distributed over the entire time it is in main memory. Function 2 assumes that the CPU used by each job is distributed in proportion to 1/n (n = no. of jobs in the system at any time). Function 3 assumes that the CPU used by each job is distributed in proportion to 1/sqrt(n).

Curve 3 indicates that productivity never reached 50 percent (the CPU utilization for seven jobs was 48.13 percent) during the week studied. The obvious question is 'why was this so low?'. The answer is that the various overhead functions kept the CPU busy the other half of the time. The general managing tasks of the operating system (IBM OS/MVT), the handling of the various card readers and printers, as well as the job queue (HASP), and the locally produced teleprocessing system which supports 130 remote CRT and typewriter terminals (NUROS), together used 50 percent of the CPU, as was measured by a software monitor which ran periodically during that time.

For purposes of comparison, data was also taken for the following week, 15 Dec to 19 Dec. The week of the 15th was the last week of the school term, and the students were desperately trying to complete their computer related assignments. During this time, the overhead programs were measured to be using approximately 55 percent of the CPU, most of the increase being due to the extra heavy load on NUROS, through which 80 percent of all batch jobs are submitted. Figure 3 shows the productivity

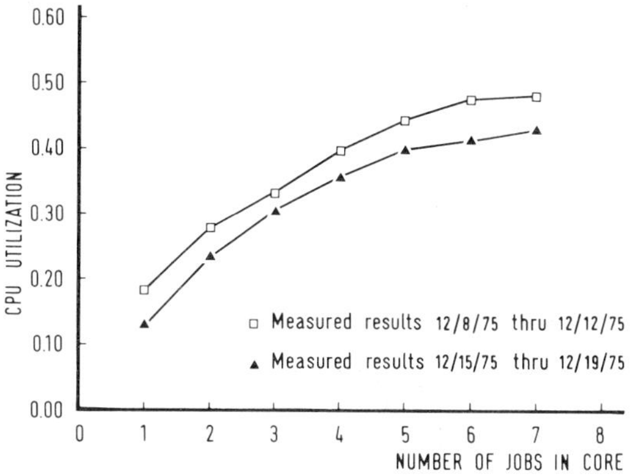

Fig. 3. 'Measured' CPU Utilizations for the Two Periods 8 Dec to 12 Dec, and 15 Dec to 19 Dec 1975.

curve for this week together with the comparable curve from the previous week (curve 3 of Figure 2). The difference between the two curves is clearly consistent with the 5 or 6 percent measured increase in overhead from one week to the next.

3. QUEUEING NETWORK MODEL

The model used for comparing with the data discussed in the previous section is described in detail in references [3], [4], [5] and [6]. Briefly, the model depends on knowing the mean service times, t(j), for each of the devices in the system, and the probabilities of accessing them. The mean CPU-task-time (the CPU-time a typical batch job needs before relinquishing control to perform an I/O - e.g. read or write to a disk unit) and the amount of CPU used by overhead functions are also needed. These parameters together allow the determination of the CPU productivity as a function of the number of batch jobs in the system.

The basic configuration of the LCF computer is shown in Figure 4. The system is made up of one IBM 360/65 CPU, three selector channels (direct data paths between the main memory and peripheral devices), six Memorex disks which are equivalent to IBM 3330's, and 16 older, slower IBM 2314 disks. All other devices such as tape drives are ignored. The time parameter for each device is listed in Table I. Based on data

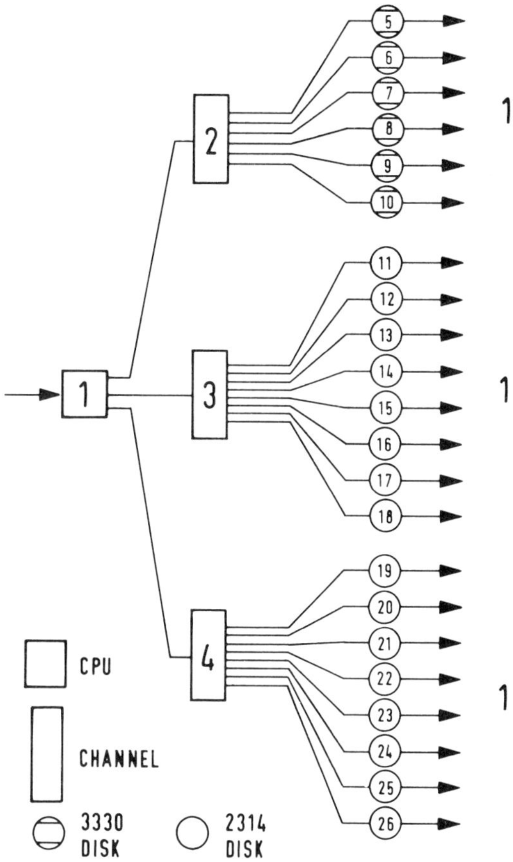

Fig. 4. Schematic Diagram of the Lincoln Computing Facility as Used in the Model.

available, it was assumed that 90 percent of all disk accesses went to the faster disks, which are on channel 2, and all disks on a given channel were equally utilized.

Table I: MEAN SERVICE TIMES FOR ALL INCLUDED IN MODEL.

DEVICE NUMBER	DESCRIPTION		SERV.TIME (SECONDS)
1	CPU		.009
2	SELECTOR CHANNEL	1	.010
3	"	2	.030
4	"	3	.030
5-10	3330 DISK		.027
11-26	2314 DISK		.070

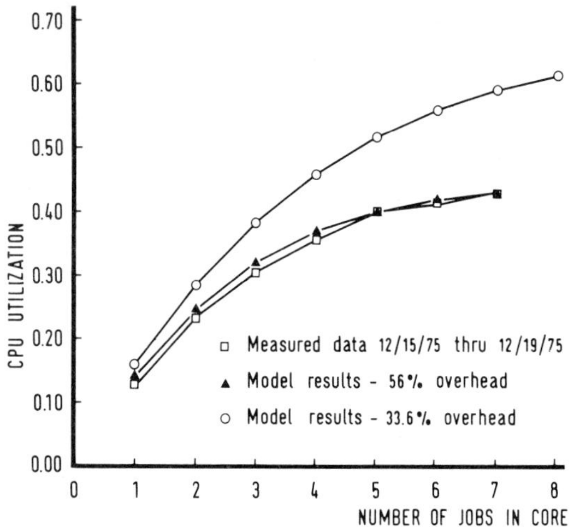

Fig. 5. CPU Utilization Curves, Both Measured and Calculated, For the Period 8 Dec to 12 Dec 1975.

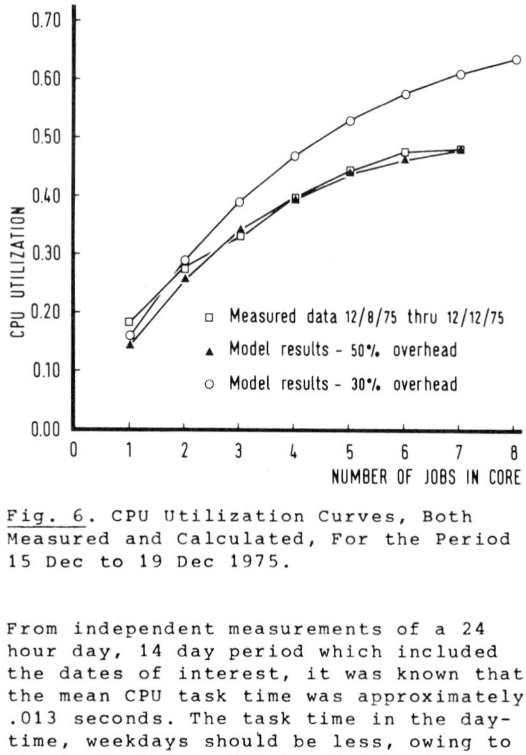

Fig. 6. CPU Utilization Curves, Both Measured and Calculated, For the Period 15 Dec to 19 Dec 1975.

From independent measurements of a 24 hour day, 14 day period which included the dates of interest, it was known that the mean CPU task time was approximately .013 seconds. The task time in the daytime, weekdays should be less, owing to the lack of long CPU-bound jobs in execution. How much less was not really known, so .009 seconds was chosen to provide a reasonable fit to the measured productivity curves. The accepted values of .50 and .56 for the overhead for the two five-day weeks under examination were also chosen so as to fit the data, but as mentioned previously, these numbers are consistent with short-period measurements which were made.

The results of the model calculations appear in Figures 5 and 6, together with the corresponding measured utilization curves from Figure 3. Clearly, the agreement is good, particularly in the region of 3 to 6 jobs, where the data is most reliable (over 90 percent of the time there were between 3 and 6 jobs active). The agreement is sufficiently close to encourage use of the model to predict the effects of potential changes to the system. One such change is discussed in the next section.

4. EFFECT OF A SYSTEM HARDWARE MODIFICATION

It is clear from the data presented here, that the system was saturated during the periods under investigation. The overhead was exceedingly large, greater than 50 percent. As much as 35 percent could be attributed to the remote operating system, NUROS. It is the case at the LCF that all of NUROS and parts of HASP and OS reside in ECS, a storage device which is treated in the same way as main memory, except that programs resident there take twice as long to execute as they would if they resided in main memory. A software monitor indicated that during periods of heavy teleprocessing, more than 40 percent of all CPU activity emanated from the ECS, almost all of which would be overhead.

If the ECS were replaced by memory which was as fast as the main memory, then the overhead might be reduced to 60 percent of its present value. A calculation with this modification was made, the results of which appear on Figures 5 and 6, together with the previous results. The figures show that throughput could be improved by as much as 20 percent if this change is implemented. Furthermore, since the system would then have two million bytes of main memory in one contiguous piece, less fragmentation would occur, and more jobs could be inserted, on the average. If it is assumed that this average would be one job more, then throughput improvement would be over 30 percent. Tables 2 and 3 summarize the expected percent improvements if the proposed change is made.

No. of Jobs	CPU Productivity Overhead=.5 (1)	CPU Productivity Overhead=.3 (2)	Measured Results for 8/12 1975 to 12/12 1975 (3)	Expected CPU Productivity Increase with 1 more job in core $P_{N+1}(2) - P_N(1)$ (4)	% Increase $P_{N+1}(4)/P_N(1)$ (5)
1	0.1468189	0.1602646	0.1822600	--	--
2	0.2584882	0.2883215	0.2782100	.1415026	96.4
3	0.3407357	0.3895929	0.3329200	.1311047	50.7
4	0.3989847	0.4687130	0.3968300	.1279773	37.6
5	0.4384289	0.5296831	0.4431200	.1306984	32.8
6	0.4638899	0.5759775	0.4761900	.1375486	31.4
7	0.4795573	0.6106022	0.4813100	.1467123	31.6
8	0.4887767	0.6361237	--	.1565664	32.6

Table II: MEASURED, CALCULATED AND PREDICTED PRODUCTIVITIES FOR THE PERIOD 8 DEC TO 12 DEC 1975.

No. of Jobs	CPU Productivity Overhead=.56 (1)	CPU Productivity Overhead=.336 (2)	Measured Results for 15/12 1975 to 19/12 1975 (3)	Expected CPU Productivity Increase with 1 more job in core $P_{N+1}(2) - P_N(1)$ (4)	% Increase $P_{N+1}(4)/P_N(1)$ (5)
1	0.1411664	0.1582996	0.1282600	--	--
2	0.2457344	0.2840268	0.2344400	.1428604	101.2
3	0.3197734	0.3826238	0.3063800	.1368894	55.7
4	0.3693993	0.4587849	0.3581900	.1390115	43.5
5	0.4006731	0.5166115	0.40050	.1472122	39.9
6	0.4191596	0.5597057	0.4142100	.1590326	39.7
7	0.4294349	0.5912102	0.4302200	.1720506	41.0
8	0.4348397	0.6138144	--	.1843795	42.9

Table III: MEASURED, CALCULATED AND PREDICTED PRODUCTIVITIES FOR THE PERIOD 15 DEC TO 19 DEC 1975.

5. CONCLUSION

It is generally difficult to examine the large amounts of data generated by systems programs or software or hardware monitors, and get a global view of how well a computer system is performing. It has been demonstrated here that one useful way of presentation is in the form of CPU Utilization curves. These curves are well suited for comparing the performances of different periods of time, and also in comparing with theoretical models. When the theoretical model agrees with the measured productivities, it can give insight as to why the system behaved the way it did, and also what it might do if specific changes are made.

REFERENCES

1. J.R. Jackson, 'Jobshop-like queuing systems with exponential servers', Management Sci. 10, 1, 131-142 (1963)

2. W.J. Gordon and G.F. Newell, 'Closed queueing systems with exponential servers', Oper. Res. 15, 2, 254-265 (1967)

3. Lester Lipsky, 'Use of queueing theory for modelling a computer system', Proceedings of SHARE XLIII p.602 (August 1974)

4. R.A. Bhandiwad and A.C. Williams, 'Queueing network models of computer systems', Proc. Annual Symposium on Computing Systems, Univ. Texas, Austin (Nov. 1974)

5. J.W. Boyse and D.R. Warn, 'A straightforward model for computer performance prediction', ACM Comp. Surveys 7, 2, 73-94 (1975)

6. Lester Lipsky and J.D. Church, 'Applications of a queueing network model for a computer system', ACM Comp. Surveys, To be published.

E. Morlet and D. Ribbens, (Eds.), International Computing Symposium 1977.

S O D A

A Flexible Scheme for Database/Program Interface

Paul Lindgreen Edith Rosenberg

A/S Regnecentralen, Copenhagen

The notion of a 'Sub Schema' or Local Data Description has been widely adopted as a useful interface between a data base and an application program to secure data independence. The present paper introduces a method for describing such an interface and outlines a set oriented DBMS that utilizes it in a convenient way. The method applies two fundamental principles: The declaration in the local data description of a number of record sets and the specification for each set of an individual list of field/variable associations. A record set is a concept similar to the well known Bachman/CODASYL set type, but simplified and generalized in several respects, resulting in a more convenient set of DBMS operations. The field/variable associations constitute a flexible mapping between the fields of a record and a set of variables in the program. This enables the programmer to refer to any combination of fields by means of local names.

1. INTRODUCTION

The problem of obtaining a satisfactory degree of data independence in a data base environment has been attacked in many different ways. A contribution to the solution of this problem appeared in the CODASYL DBTG proposal, [1]. Here, a common data base description - the 'Schema' - contains all the physical and a considerable part of the 'logical' information about the DB. The DB description is referred from a set of application oriented data descriptions - the 'Sub Schemas' - each one defining a mapping from a part of the DB onto an application program.

Still better - it seems - is the ANSI/SPARC proposal [2] in which the basic idea is the separation of the neccessary descriptions into three parts.

1) The 'Internal Schema' containing the physical description of the DB.

2) A set of 'External Schemas' each one bound to an application program and expressing the local view of the DB, with respect to the data structure as well as how to operate on them.

3) The 'Conceptual Schema' containing a description of that part of the information structure in an enterprise which is represented in the DB. Furthermore, this description serves as an unavoidable link in the connection between the internal and the external schemas.

Two elements of a solution of the data independence problem can be clearly recognized in most DB accessing schemes - including those mentioned above: A data base management system (DMBS) and a local data description.

A DBMS is necessary because the operations of a file system will refer to entities in the physical part of the DB description and because in most cases a certain amount of standardisation, check for logical errors and protection against misuse is to be desired.

A local data description is the source of information about the DB, necessary as well for the application program as for the DBMS. In this way the LD description is a common term for the CODASYL Sub Schema and for the ANSI/SPARC external schema.

The main purpose of a local data description (LD) is:

- to define the specific subset of a DB which the application program should operate on.

- to enable the application program to define a mapping from the physically bound storage structures of the DB to local data structures suitable for its own function.

- to allow the application program to refer to fields and other entities of the DB by means of locally declared names.

The importance of data independence was decisive for Regnecentralen when a series of large application programs operating on a common DB was to be implemented. As a base for the implementation a set of applicable tools were available, but also some constraints. Given were a rather advanced file system and a DB description system but no facilities on the LD level and no proper DBMS. Furthermore the programming languages were restricted to FORTRAN/ALGOL and to another non-COBOL language, all without the necessary facilities for describing data structures.

This resulted in the SODA system - a complex consisting of three parts: A local data description language, a compiler to read and check such a description and a DBMS that operates governed by a compiled LD description.

In this paper we shall not discuss the system as

a whole but emphasize two fundamental access principles and their implementation:

In SODA the relevant record types are declared as constituents of record sets and all records are accessed via such sets declared in the LD description. One current record is available from each set.

The record fields are accessed from a current record, not in the corresponding buffer, but in local variables associated with the relevant fields. The mapping between variables and fields is also specified in the LD description.

2. THE FILE SYSTEM AND THE DB DESCRIPTION BEHIND SODA

In order to give the reader a fair chance to understand the SODA accessing scheme and to distinguish between the general principles and the installation dependent details, we shall shortly outline the main features of the file system and the DB model behind the DBMS. For more details see ref. 3 and 4.

Physically, the records are stored in files and accessed one at a time by means of a set of standard procedures constituting a file system. At present the file system enables operations on three different file types: Ordinary sequential files, index sequential files and list files.

Records of the first file type can only be accessed sequentially, while records in an ISQ file, as probably well-known, can be accessed both sequentially and directly, since each record in the file is uniquely identified by keys and its physical address known by the file system.

The records in a list file are linked together in groups by means of pointer chains. Each chain starts in a so-called mother record, which must belong to an ISQ file or another list file. Access to the members of a record group - the daughter records - can only be accomplished sequentially and only after a previous access of the mother record. A record of a list file may be member of several uncorrelated groups, each one having its own mother record.

From the application point of view the records of the DB are organized in basic record sets or logical files. A logical file is a collection of records of one or more types associated with a certain physical file. More than one logical file may be associated with the same physical file, but the records can only be accessed according to the possibilities of the physical file. In the remaining part of the paper the term 'file' means 'logical file' unless otherwise stated.

The DB description contains the formal description of the physical files as it is necessary for the file system. Furthermore the DB administrator declares the potential record types and their organization in files. In this connection we shall not discuss the data description language - just point out a few elements and principles necessary for the understanding of the SODA accessing scheme.

Each record type of a file is declared to consist of a unique set of field types corresponding to the properties of the entity represented by the record. The field types are classified as attribute fields, key fields or relational fields.

The attribute fields correspond to the various attribute properties of the entities. Each record type of a file will have defined a set of attribute fields as its constituents, but these sets need not be exclusive. This means that a certain field type or group of field types may appear as constituents of several record types. An attribute field may be declared to represent numeric values of various types (integers, fixed or floating point numbers etc.) or alphanumeric values. They may be specified as simple fields, fixed length arrays or as singular groups or variable lengths repeating groups.

The key fields correspond to possible entity-identifying properties. Accordingly, every record type of a file which shall be accessed directly must have defined a set of key fields, the values of which identify the record in the file uniquely. The key values may be alphanumeric or numeric, but only simple key fields are allowed.

The relational fields correspond to relational properties of the one-to-many kind. With the present file system two kinds of relational fields must be considered: d-reference fields and m-reference fields.

A d-reference field is used in a mother record to contain the (physical) pointer value to the first record in the chain of records in a list file (or a dummy indication if the chain is empty). However, from the user's point of view it should be regarded as a 'key' to access a group of associated daughter records. In the DB description a d-reference field is specified by a reference to the list file containing the daughter records.

An m-reference field is used in records of a list file to contain a set of key values for a mother record. From a user's point of view m-references will only be relevant, if the records are connected in more than one chain, because it gives an access path from a mother record of one kind via a daughter record to a mother record of another kind, (see figure 1). The relational fields, in contrast to attribute fields, are automatically assigned by the file system when daughter records are inserted or connected in the chains of a list file.

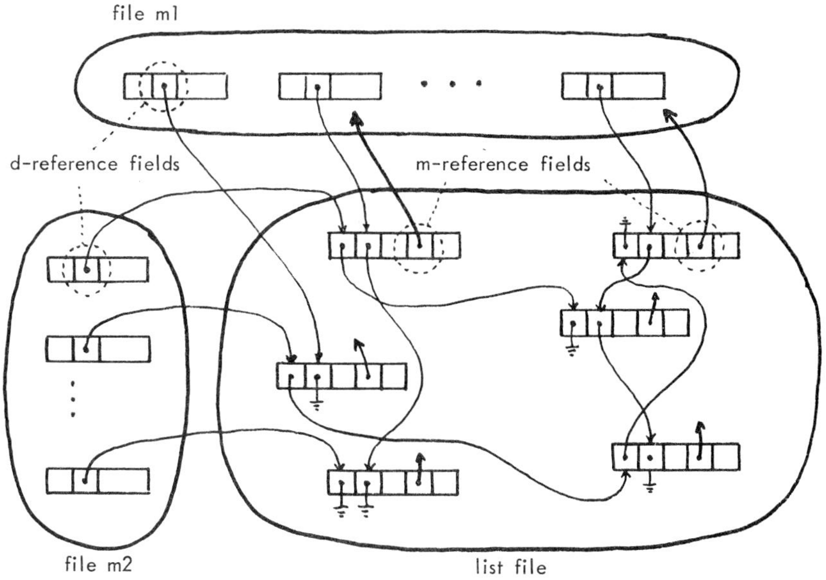

Fig.1. The records of a list file doubly connected to mother records of two other files.

3. THE SODA RECORD ACCESSING SCHEME

The name SODA means Set Oriented Database Access and this refers to the basic access principle: SODA enables an application program to interpret the relevant part of the DB as a collection of so-called record sets and to access fields of records belonging to such sets.

A record set in SODA is a collection of records of one or more types which are accessed in a unified way and which are common in some respect of interest for the application program. All record types that a given program wishes to access must be specified as members of record sets, but a given record type may be member of any number of sets.

A record set (RS) is declared in the LD description as shown in the following three examples:

```
s2: articles    = article_file
s3: spare_parts = article_file(r16,r18)
s5: sales_items = article_file(r12,r13,r16)
```

The set s2 with the local name 'articles' is declared to be equivalent with 'article_file' defined in the DB description. This implies that all the record types of the file are members of the RS. The set s3, on the other hand, is declared to be a subset of 'article_file' defined by the references to selected record types of the file. Also s5 is a subset partly overlapping s3 with r16 being a common record type for both sets. This could indicate that some of the parts are sold to customers and some are only used inside the enterprise.

For each set SODA maintains a current record - that is, a situation where it is possible to access the fields of the record. The same record type - in fact, even the same record - may be current in several sets at the same time.

The current record is provided by the DBMS either from the program itself by the operation CREATE or from the DB by the operations GET (direct access) or NEXT (sequential access). A current record can be inserted/transferred back to the DB by the operation PUT or it can be removed from the DB by DELETE.

The file reference in the RS declaration defines the potential record access possibilities, but in a usage statement associated with the declaration the actual list of intended DBMS operations on the set must be specified. This serves the documentation purpose as well as the formal check of field accesses as described in section 4.

In SODA two kinds of record sets are considered - singular and subscripted - just as the programmer must distinguish between simple variables and arrays.

A singular RS is a set where the records are accessed with a reference to the set only. The three sets declared above are typical examples of such singular record sets.

A subscripted RS is a set organized as a collection of subsets, each one identified by an index or subscript. Access to the records is performed inside one subset at the time. Therefore, not only a reference to the RS is neccessary before access can take place, but also the selection of an index.

Two quite different kinds of set-subscription have been implemented in SODA - namely subscription by mother records and subscription by dynamic value spectra. For a given set each of these subscriptions may be specified alone, but they may also be combined - in a way analogous to an array, that can be declared to be one-dimensional or multi-dimensional.

Subscription by dynamic value spectrum is specified in the RS declaration as a Boolean expression in values of record fields compared with variables or constants. The following declaration shows an example:

```
s6: special_customers = customer_file
    for which: balance > 1000
               and area_code = test_code
```

For given values of the involved variables the expression defines a subset of the RS consisting of those records for which the expression is true. In this way it is the change of values of the variables that constitutes the selection of an index. The corresponding subsets may then form a partition of the RS or they may be overlapping, depending on the variable values and the expression. The actual grouping of records in subsets is performed dynamically. Whenever a potential member record of the RS is accessed, the complete expression is evaluated to decide membership in the selected subset. In the example above an inverted file directed by the subexpression 'balance > 1000' might have improved the access speed, but the present file system do not comprise such facilities.

Subscription by mother records involves two sets - a mother set and a daughter set. The daughter set is the one that is subscripted by mother records, and the mother set is the one that contains these records. Subscription by mother records implies a partition of the daughter set where each subset is associated with a unique record of the mother set.

The following example shows a declaration of a daughter set.

```
s7: payments(s6) = pay_file(r28,r29)
```

The reference in s7 to the mother set s6 defines that the index to a subset of the daughter set is a record from s6. The selection of a subset is performed explicitly by activation of the DBMS operation NEWSET on the daughter set. The current record of the mother set at exactly that moment will define the subset now available for access.

In our implementation mother subscription requires that the daughter set records are stored in a list file and that this list file is connected to the file containing the mother records. At present the DBMS can only perform sequential access of the daughter records in a selected subset, because this is the only method supported by the file system. Not all the records of a given chain, however, need be members of the daughter set. In the s7-example above only the record types 28 and 29 will be delivered by the DBMS. Possible records of other types in the chain or those of type 28/29 which do not satisfy a possible subscription by value spectrum (not shown in the example) will appear to the program as non existing when the DBMS operations refer to s7.

The reader will observe a close resemblance between a mother-subscripted record set and the CODASYL DBTG set type [2]. They both serve as a mean to represent a 1:n-relation between entities in the user system, by way of one mother/owner record connected to any number of daughter/member records. However SODA and the DBTG proposal differ in several ways, both as regards the set definitions and the accessing of records.

The most important differences are:

- the mother record of a SODA RS is not regarded as a part of the set. It is available as the current record of the mother set, independent of the daughter set.
- the mother record types for a given set is defined by the reference to the mother set. Accordingly the mother records are not restricted to a single type as the owner record of a DBTG set is.
- the only way to access records in SODA is by reference to a record set. Accordingly, only the concept 'current record pr set' is relevant. However, this current record is established directly by the operations GET, NEXT or CREATE and is suppressed again upon a PUT or DELETE. Accordingly no FIND operation is needed as in the DBTG proposal.
- a record created as a member of a mother-subscripted set will automatically be connected to every of its mother records according to the m-ref fields of the DB description. Manual set-membership is not permitted since it may cause the integrity of the DB to be violated.

The examples pointed out above are the result of a very concious design philosophy for our system. We have tried to reduce the vast number of ad-hoc concepts and operation modes of the DBTG proposal and replace them by fewer, but more general principles. Our primary aim has been to reduce the complexity and simplify the logic of the application program, in order to reduce the costs of maintaining them. Admittedly, there are a few desirable DBTG features which are not implemented - for example direct access to records of mother subscripted sets and some of the protection facilities. However, this is not due to any lack in SODA, but because the file system or the DB description at present does not support a reasonable implementation.

4. THE SODA FIELD ACCESSING SCHEME

The fact that SODA maintains a current record for each RS still doesn't make the fields of the records accessible from the program, unless the concepts 'record' and 'currency of records' are defined in the programming language. In the design of SODA we have tried to find a solution which can be equally well applied, whatever the preferred programming language is.

A common principle for all programs, independent of the language in which they are programmed, is the execution of operations on variables. The contents of a variable may be changed either by the execution of an assignment statement, or as the result of an input operation invoked by the program.

When input is read from a DB, the problem arises that most file systems are not able to access less than a whole record, which is provided somewhere in a buffer area. It is then the task of the DBMS to make the relevant fields accessible from the program. To obtain this two addressing schemes can be applied: Either a set of variables are specially declared to be associated with the fields of interest and are located accordingly in the buffer, or the values of the fields are moved to and from ordinary variables by the DBMS. In this case the buffer is not touched directly by the program.

At first sight, the buffer addressing scheme may seem to be the most advantageous. No storage locations besides the buffer are required, and accordingly, no values have to be moved to and from such locations. However, there are two main drawbacks to this method:

The first one is that the possibility for concurrent programs to access records in the same file (multi-access) will be violated or made unnecessarily complicated if the programs are allowed to operate on the buffer.

Secondly not all programming languages allow of a convenient mapping of variables onto a (possibly otherwise declared) buffer area. The introduction of such methods would then require the necessary amendments to the language and their implementation in the compiler. To this can be added that the addressing of buffer variables will possibly be relative to a record base address. It means that if the same variable is referenced several times per record access, some of the gain from the stationary values will be lost by more laborious addressing.

The method with self-contained variables, on the other hand, will only occupy the buffer during the DB access and the period when the field values are moved. At other times the buffer could be used for access to the file from other programs. Furthermore, the variables can all be declared so that the advantage of direct addressing is obtained, and since ordinary variables only are used, no change of the programming language or the compiler is needed.

Especially in administrative data processing the transfer of values from fields in one record to fields in other records is a very common operation, requiring a lot of statements of the type MOVE A TO B scattered all over the program. Since the relevant field values by the second method must be moved anyway, it is an obvious idea to associate the same variable both to the field in the yielding and the receiving record and thereby saving half of the transfers.

For the reasons listed above we have chosen to implement the second method in SODA. The cost of this, besides the field value transfers, is that the field/variable mapping must be specified in all details in the LD description. However, this is quite natural, because the LD description must be regarded as a regular extension of the ordinary declarations of the program. Furthermore, since an LD language as well as an LD compiler was to be designed anyway, the effort to implement a flexible mapping scheme would not require modifications of existing compilers.

The mapping defining the field value transfers is specified in the LD description for each RS as a set of so-called field associations. They define the variables and the record fields which may be involved in a transfer during a DBMS operation on the RS.

The example in fig. 2 shows a list of field associations in a RS declaration:

The variable number refers to an entry in a table of variable declarations which is also a part of the LD description. These declarations are identical with ordinary variable declarations in the application program, except for the syntax. Both simple and subscripted variables as well as groups may be declared. Of cause, only variable types and kinds that are legal in the designated programming language may be used, but this is checked by the LD compiler. The declarations from the LD table are communicated to the ordinary compiler either as generated source text or as internal compiler tables. Thereby the application program can freely refer to the LD variables as if they were declared in the program itself.

The field number must refer to a field that is a constituent of at least one of the record types of the set. Only fields which are relevant for the program need be specified in field as-

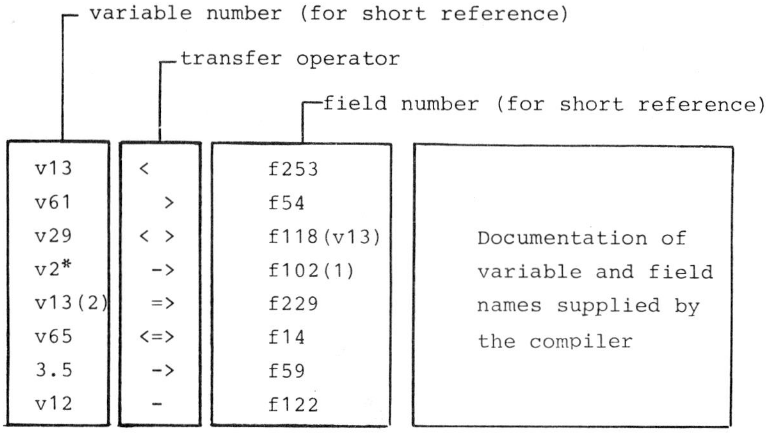

Fig. 2. A list of field associations in an RS declaration

sociations. For each association the LD compiler will supply and print the corresponding variable name from the declarations and the field name from the DB description. In this way full documentation is obtained with a minimum of manual description.

The type and kind of the fields and the variables must be compatible. For example, it is not permitted to move a numeric value to an alphanumeric location, or to specify a simple location as the receiver of an entire array. However, simple values may be moved to specified array elements, and values from array elements to simple locations. Also a whole array may be moved, but only to another array.

The elements of repeating groups should be associated with arrays of corresponding type and with a number of elements comprising the maximum number of occurences. The actual number of occurrences in a record can be obtained in a numeric variable associated with the repeating group itself.

The <u>transfer operator</u> defines the direction of the transfer as well as the DBMS operations which will activate the transfer.

The operator < (to be interpreted as an arrow) defines that upon a GET or NEXT operation the value of the specified field in the current record is moved to the variable. The same field may be moved to more than one variable, but a given variable may not be specified to receive values from more than one field unless the fields are exclusive with respect to the record type.

The operator > defines, that before a current record obtained by GET og NEXT is transferred back to the DB by PUT, the value of the specified variable is moved to the location of the field in the current record. The same variable may be moved to more than one field, but a given field may not be specified to receive values from more than one variable. The same holds for the operator -> except that it only becomes effective on a PUT following a CREATE operation.

Upon a CREATE operation standard values can be assigned to variables associated with fields of the created record. This is indicated by an asterisk following the variable number.

The transfer operators may be combined in an association. Thus, for example, the symbol <> will define a transfer both on GET/NEXT and on a following PUT, and the symbol => defines a transfer from variable to field on all PUT operations.

Moreover we should mention the operator - which is used in connection with a GET/NEXT operation to determine if the associated field is a member of the current record. If so the corresponding variable will have a non-zero value assigned. When the field is not present the assigned value becomes zero. This feature constributes to a simpler logic, when the program decides on the set of actions to be performed on the various record types.

What has been discussed so far concerns primarily attribute fields. A special case is the treatment of <u>key fields</u>, which, as mentioned in Section 2, are used in records that are accessed directly. The key values must be communicated to the DBMS when a GET or CREATE operation is activated. This is described by a set of field associations applying the special transfer operator = between variable and key field. The LD compiler will check that one, and just one, such association is specified for each key field of the records.

Also the access to relational fields is accomplished by means of field associations: The value of an <u>m-reference field</u> is communicated to the program applying the operator < as described above. When a daughter record is created, as mentioned in Section 3, it will automatically be connected to all of its mother records. This requires a corresponding set of field associations applying the symbol -> together defining the key values of the mother records.

The value of a d-reference field can be regarded as the 'key' to access a corresponding subset of a daughter set. Accordingly it must be specified in the declaration of the mother set that the value of the d-reference field is needed for such an access. This is done in an association as shown below. It is assumed to appear in the declaration of the mother set s6: (cf. examples in Section 3)

s7 <- f322

This association is partly redundant with the mother reference in the daughter set (s7), but it helps to document the use of the mother set. Furthermore it contains essential information in the case where a list file is connected to another file by more than one chain, as it is the case, in bill-of-material structures in production control systems, for example.

5. DISCUSSION AND CONCLUSION

The SODA accessing scheme was developed at a time when no DBMS was available, but where the file system had been in use for several years and had proved its value as the basic DB accessing tool in a number of application systems. Nearly every information structure in practice could be mapped onto the DB in a reasonable way and be described accordingly in the DB description. However, the lack of a less physical and more logical accessing scheme soon became obvious and caused many troubles during maintenance of the programs.

Accordingly, the primary goal in the development of SODA was to obtain a high degree of data independence. Also our intention was that the system should be applicable in connection with every reasonable programming language, without changes in the respective compilers. Furthermore, we wanted to remove from the application programs a number of tedious DB checking and control operations which could easily be standardized and performed by a DBMS. Finally we intended to enable the application programs to regard the records in the DB as organized in sets and to access the relevant fields via ordinary variables in the program.

This was accomplished in a DBMS with very few, but powerful operations that refer to declarations of record sets in a local data description. The information herein corresponds in principle to that contained in the Sub Schema of [1] or the External Schema of [2].
Our implementation is based on an existing file system and a given DB description methodology, but all the principles expressed in SODA could as well be realized if the local data description referred to a 'conceptual-like' schema like that of the ANSI/SPARC model, for example.

This could be illustrated by the principle of subscription by dynamic value spectrum explained in Section 3 of this paper. It is a direct implementation of the SELECTION operator defined formally in [5]. The information model evaluated there has exactly the properties covered by a schema of the 'conceptual' type.

The experience with SODA so far indicates great advantages in the design and construction of application programs. In particular the logic of the program becomes more straightforward, because the relevant part of the DB by means of the record sets can be regarded in a way that corresponds to the task of the program. Also, the removal of many statements defining detailed field value transfers has improved the quality of the programs considerably. The fact that information about these field value transfers must now be specified in the local data description has not caused any troubles, nor in any way costs comparable to the advantages. We regard the flexible possibilities of the field associations as the main reason for this.

6. REFERENCES

[1] CODASYL Database Task Group, April 1971 Report.

[2] Interim Report: ANSI/X3/SPARC: Study Group on Data Base Management Systems. Washington 1975.

[3] I. Borch, E. Rosenberg, J. Winther: Connected Files System. RC System Library 28-D5. Copenhagen 1972.

[4] V. Ambeck-Madsen, U. Ørding-Thomsen: DATABASE 80. RC System Library 21-V002.

[5] P. Lindgreen: 'Basic Operations on information as a Basis for Data Base Design'. Information Processing 74. North Holland Publ. Co. 1974.

E. Morlet and D. Ribbens, (Eds.), International Computing Symposium 1977.

A FRAMEWORK FOR DISTRIBUTED DATABASE SYSTEMS

Fabio A. SCHREIBER

Assistant Professor

Istituto di Elettronica - Politecnico

Piazza L. da Vinci 32 - 20133 - Milano - Italy

The main problems about Distributed Database Systems design are reviewed, and a multilevel structure is proposed for Distributed Database Management Systems following the philosophy of CODASYL and ANSI X3 proposals, in order to achieve a high level of data independence in the network environment. An example is given to show how the different problems could be solved in the framework of the proposed structure.

1. INTRODUCTION

The availability of commercially oriented computer networks has risen a growing interest in building Distributed Database Systems. Such systems in fact, allow a rather efficient and reliable implementation of those applications in which large amounts of data, originated and/or used over a wide geographical area, are to be shared by many users scattered, in turn, in several different locations.

For the scope of this work, we shall consider the following definition that, even if general, points out the main characteristics of a DDB:

> A Distributed Database (DDB) is a *set of files*, stored in different nodes of an information network, which are *logically related*, either by functional relations, or because being multiple copies of the same file, in such a way as to constitute a *unique collection of data*.

This definition covers all the possible cases, from the simple file duplication for reliability reasons or for communication traffic optimization, to the more complex case of file splitting, which can be obtained on the base of a partitioning due to the "quasi locality" of the data manipulation, yet to the necessity of sharing them in several occasions (e.g. large anagraphical systems). Centralized networks are enclosed in the definition as well. In this case some parts of the database, as the data structure information and possibly part of the data themselves, are stored in a single node called the "central node"; remaining data are distributed in the peripheric nodes.

Physical and logical independences, that is the application programs immunity to changes to the storage structure and to changes in the data model definition /1/ /2/ /3/, are still major goals to be achieved in the distributed environment as well as in the stand-alone one. Nay their importance is greatly enhanced since not only the storage media ad peripheral devices of the single computer can be changed, but entire nodal centers can be added to or taken away of the network, modifying in a substantial way its physical configuration and therefore that of the DDB. On the other hand, very high is the probability that the general logical view of data be subject to changes owing to the new requirements in the overall system. So, models have to be developed providing a frame in which to look for the solution of the design problems presented in the following, or at least of some of them, while assuring data independence.

2. MAIN DESIGN PROBLEMS

In this section we want to point out the main problems the designer of DDB and DDBMS is faced with when analysing and designing such systems, that is /4/:

- choosing the general architecture for the system; whether it have to be built from scratch or taking into account preexisting local systems;
- where to allocate how many copies of which files;
- how to retrieve and manipulate the remotely allocated and, possibly, splitted files.

These problems must be considered under several time, storage, integrity costraints many of which have great influence on the designer decisions.

The solution to the first question often depends on the dimensions of the machine involved in the system and on political factors. In fact, if the machines are medium or large size computers, provided by the manufacturer with standard software, it is unlike that the effort is worth of modifying the existing Database Management System and/or Operating System for fitting them on the distributed environment; it is then preferable to build a software system, running as a permanent user task, to manage the high level computer-computer communications and to interface the different DBMS, as in fig. 1.

The representation of fig. 1 is rather general and it is conceivable that the Network Interface will be integrated in future DBMS while the Transport Station will constitute the driver of the peripheral "network" in OS.

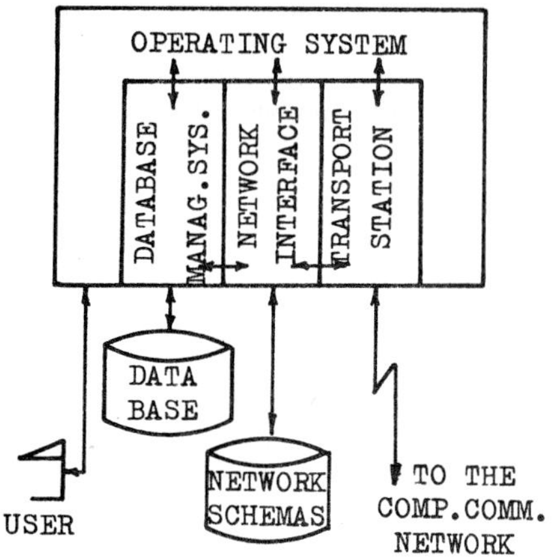

Fig. 1

This remark applies particularly to minicomputers which, in the actual trend, tend to substitute, connected in networks, the larger machines. In fact in such a case, the building of specialized software for a DDBMS can be considered a short-medium term solution since a wider knowledge of system-software building can be found for minicomputers even outside the manufacturer companies.

The problem posed by the second question was historically the first one to be investigated from a theoretical point of view. Starting from analogous problems found in Operational Research, W.W. Chu proposed a solution to the problem of the files allocation in a computer network to achieve a minimum for storage and transmission costs under the following costraints:

a) the access delay for each file be less than a fixed value;
b) the storage available at each node be less than a fixed amount;
c) in query mode, only one copy of a file is involved;
d) each file have an *availability* greater than a fixed value;

by availability meaning the amount of time the file can effectively "work", depending on the reliability of the nodes the files are stored in, on the reliability of communications links, on the maintenance times, etc.

Chu demonstrated that, under these assumptions and some additional costraints, the problem can be reduced to a zero-one integer programming one, which is easily solvable /5/ /6/.

R.G. Casey, basing himself on the work of Chu, states that the smaller is the update/query rate, the greater is the convenience to have multiple copies of the same file in the network, and proposes an algorithm for a quasi-optimal allocation /7/.

The work of Chu and Casey has been generalized by Levin and Morgan /22/ who take into consideration other parameters such as the dependency between programs and data files, developing also an algorithm for a dynamic optimum assignment and an adaptive model for organizing DDB in computer networks.

The problem then extends into a four dimensional space, locations, programs, and data being the independent variables, and the *amount* of access requests to a given file stored at location A by a program running at location B being the dependent variable. It may be that clustering and principal component analysis techniques applied to such a representation could prove useful in solving the problem in a more practical way.

The existence of more than one copy of a file in the network, however, even if convenient from an economical point of view, can cause serious troubles if a very tight spatial as well as time consistency /20/ must be kept among the information stored in all of them. Such is the case of a real time system in which both queries and updates are made on-line, as in a nation-wide reservation system.

Moreover, the methods to keep consistency always imply some locking algorithm, so a very careful study must be done to prevent deadlocks, the occurrence of which can be enhanced by the finite and possibly very different transmission times among the different copies and among them and their users. Synchronization algorithms have been proposed by Shoshani et al. /8/ for a parallel accessed database and more specifically by Holler /9/ for a multicopy file.

Besides being duplicated, a single logical (conceptual) file can be splitted into several physical subfiles following two main criteria /23/:

a - *horizontal splitting* - the records belonging to each subfile, while having all the same format as the logical record, are partitioned on the basis of some sorting principle;

b - *vertical splitting* - the records belonging to each subfile are constitued by subsets of the logical record (possibly with non empty intersections). The subsets are selected on the basis of the particular set of applications existing at each node.

These two criteria reflect the philosophy underlying the distributed system the database belongs to, that is wether the distribution is made either on topographic or on functional criteria. However the two kinds of partitioning can coexist at the same time on the same system.

Cost ans reliability are not the only reasons which lead to the proliferation of file copies in a DDB. If we consider, besides data and program files, also the directories and catalogs necessary in retrieving other files in a distributed environment, we can notice that in some cases the presence of a copy of a catalog file at every node is required by the functional architecture of the system /10/, /11/.

Such an architecture, besides all the already mentioned drawbacks for the multicopy files having to be tightly consistent, has the disavantage of requiring a lot of space. A method to overcome such disavantages is that of not keeping a network catalog at all! In this case each node keeps only the catalog of its own file. Would an access be required by a process for a file not enclosed in the local catalog, a request can be broadcasted to all the nodes and a positive answer waited for. If the file is stored in more than one location, a decision can be taken in a dynamical way as to which copy to enquire, while updating is made on all the copies. Once the node (s) is selected, the communication among the process and the file (s) can take place in the normal way.

An intermediate solution is to store the network catalog only in one node. If a file name does not appear in the local catalog of a node, a search is made in the central catalog. This is the way in which some centralized systems operate /12/.

The last problem, the man-system interaction philosophy, requires a careful study of data definition (DDL) and data manipulation languages (DML). These languages should reflect different levels of interaction and of description, allowing the user to choose the most convenient level for his scope.

A first distinction should be made wether the interaction is made in batch mode or in real time, since different interpretation mechanims must exist for the two cases.

As to the level at which data should be accessed it could be

- the *access method* level of each Operating System;
- the *access path* level to data in the network;
- a *logical (location independent) level*.

Each of these levels represents a higher degree of abstraction with respect to the preceeding one. However they all should be accessible in such a way as the experienced user could gain in efficiency by working at the lower levels, while the unskilled one could benefit by high level DDL and DML.

Works toward a definition of a Network Control Language, to be interpreted by a network monitor interfacing all the local systems, have been carried on mainly in France /13/, /14/.

Moreover, looking at languages allowing users to get information from the system, we can identify three actions that must be performed in sequence /10/:

- selecting the records to be processed;
- processing the records;
- producing an output report.

The first action is performed on the basis of some simple expression involving relational operators (=, > ,<) or of complex functions constituted by composing simple expressions by means of boolean connectives (AND, OR, NOT).

If the selection results in a large number of records which must be processed in the second phase, it would be much more convenient doing the processing in a distributed mode directly at the retrieval nodes, in order that only the results of the computations have to be transmitted back, with a high gain in communication efficiency.

The latter remark rises a fundamental question about the actual possibility of performing distributed computations and about which constraints this feature puts on splitting and allocating the files on the basis of the distributivity, associativity and commutativity of the required computations.

An example should clarify the last issue. Let us consider the existence of an hypothetical Distributed Information System having nodes in all the countries of the European Community, in which labour conditions in the different countries were recorded. The following enquiry could be issued at the EEC Headquartes in Bruxelles:

"Which is the average tax payed by software engineers over forty in the European Community?"

Let us suppose the "personnel" file, in which software engineers are recorded, be horizontally splitted in each country so that the averaging should be made on the records at each country and sent to the requesting node. The result obtained by averaging the partial averages, however, would be not correct; it is necessary to send the requesting node the total tax amount and the number of taxpayers fulfilling the requested features in each country and to do the average operation at it. On the other hand, would the request have been: "Which is the total tax amount of ....", the sum of the partial subtotals alone would have given a correct result, owing to the associativity of the addition. Moreover, if also a vertical splitting of the file occurs and ages are stored at one node while tax amounts are stored at another one, no partial distributed computation is possible, but all the software engineers over forty must be retrieved at one node and sent to the other one to make the computation. Even if it is possible to commutate the retrieval order (i.e. to send all the tax amounts payed by software engineers to the node at which ages are stored), obviously this would entail the transmission of much more information between the nodes so that also the commutativity of the enquiry expressions has to be carefully examined.

It is possible to conclude then that an extensive study should be made on the way of breaking complex enquiries and of distributing as much computation as possible, in order to achieve a minimum for data transmission volume. It must be noticed that in some limit case a reallocation or the creation of new copies of a file should be considered.

3. A MULTILEVEL MODEL

The problems presented in section two have emerged here and there, outside any formal consideration; here we propose a conceptual frame, inspired by the many works made in the effort of achieving physical and logical data independence /15/ /16/ /17/ /18/, in which the solutions to these problems can be looked for at the appropriate level.

Let us recall the main levels of description common to these models:

a. an abstract description, made in terms of some model (normalized n-ary relations, binary relations, network, hierarchic, etc.), of the logical structure of the whole database relevant to all the users of the database. This description is referred to as the Schema, the Conceptual Schema, the Common Schema, etc.

b. a description of the logical structure of the database, or of part of it, as seen by a particular user. This description is called the Subschema, the External Schema, the User Subschema, etc.

c. a description of the physical storage structure of the data composing the database. This is the Internal Schema, the Physical Mapping Model, etc.

Mappings between levels a and b provide the system with a decoupling between the global logical view of data and the data organization relevant to a specific application, then providing logical independence. A mapping between levels a and c provides the system with a decoupling between the logical and the physical representation of data, then providing physical independence.

Let us now notice the fact that a distributed database can be thought as the union of all the component databases, to each of which one of the above mentioned models can be applied. The components databases then constitute many partial views of the global system so that we can consider their *Local Conceptual Schemata* (LCS) like subsets of a main *Network Conceptual Schema* (NCS). This schema, which will be under the responsability of a Network Administrator, is to describe the data in a global view, no matter which node they are stored at (*).

Mappings exist between the NCS and each LCS in the network; they provide the system with logical data independence. This is very important since the global view of data could undergo very deep changes owing to the addition of new nodes with very different data organization requirements. Moreover, the models used in the description of the LCSs could be different from one to another; this is particularly true if the DDB is constitued by heterogeneous systems. To handle this case it is useful to insert an intermediate description level having the same function of Nijssen's Principal User Schemata /16/. This level, we call *Principal Local Schema* (PLS), will take into account the transformations and, possibly, the reorganization needed between the description model used for the NCS and those used in the different LCS. The latter can then be obtained by subsetting the PLSs. Finally the *External Schemata* (EXS) represent, at each node, the user's logical view of data.

All the problems related to the access process to the data, stored somewhere in the DDB (i.e. to find where they are resident, which routing policies are to be followed in query and in update mode, etc.) are the care of the Database Engineer who operates on the *Network Internal Schema* (NIS), while the truly physical storage organization problems are left to the *Local Internal Schema* (LIS) of each node.

A mapping, the *Network Node Mapping* (NNM), provides the system with a decoupling between the network physical view of data in NIS (i.e. how many copies and/or how many partitions exist for a file, where are they stored, etc.) and the actual storage parameters of the LIS of the computer in which they are resident. In NNM such problems as the routing strategies to be followed in query and updating mode must be solved, while in NIS the allocation, duplication, splitting, indexing problems have to be considered.

It must be noticed that changes in the storage structure of a computing center will affect only the LIS, while the addition of a new node in the network, entailing a relocation and a repartition of files, new routine policies, etc., will be relevant to both NIS and NNM.

The framework resulting from this discussion is presented in fig. 2.

In discussing the features of the NCS, of the NIS, and of the NNM, it seems very useful to ap

(*) Notice that the term network means hereafter "computer network", not a network data structure!

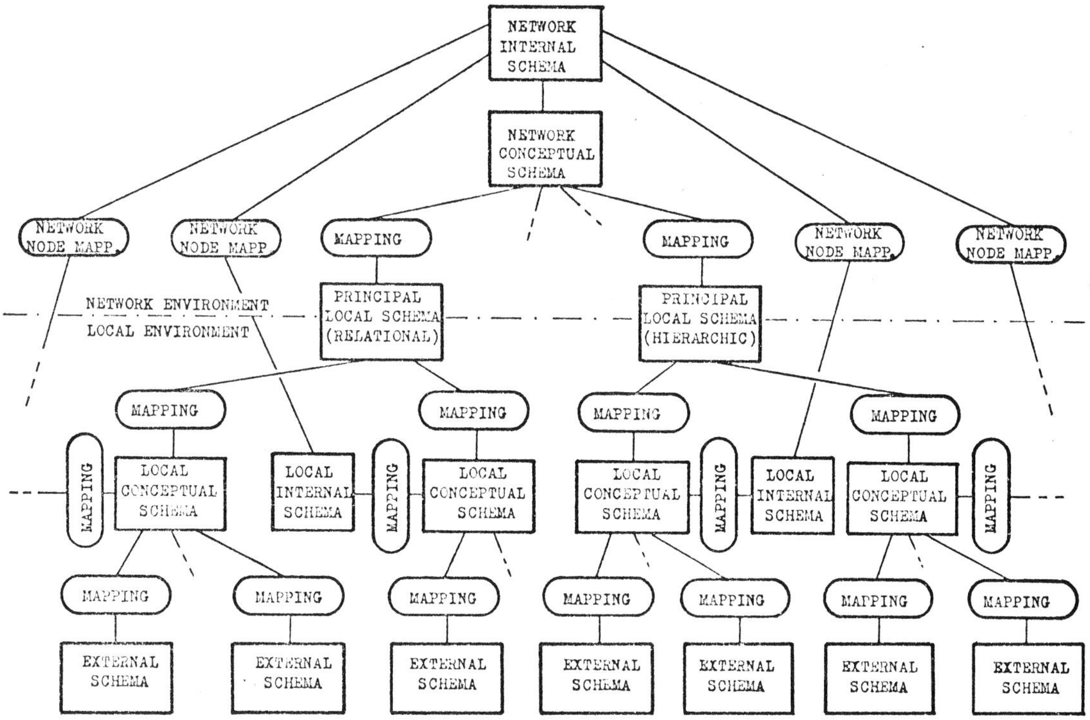

Fig. 2

ply a binary relations model, like the one proposed by Bracchi et al, /17/ /18/. In fact, in a system where one of the major goals is the flexibility in data description, the binary relation seems to represent the smallest meaningful and non arbitrary data unit.

Moreover, the NIS function is very similar to that of Bracchi's Schema File Subset, in which the elements of the Schema which are stored in the same System Physical File are indicated /17/. Transposing this function from the local to the network environment, in NIS all the relations are indicated which are stored at the same network node. Using binary relations and progressions of binary relations, we could attribute to each of them a function F giving the "weight" of that relation, for example as number of data items to be retrieved or as frequency of specified queries /18/. Such a function used at the NIS and NNM levels could guide the search for the optimal retrieval path in those cases in which the commutativity of the retrieval expression is relevant, as we saw for the example in section two. These two levels are involved also in the definition of a Data Definition Language in which a clear separation between the logical aspects of information and the access functions is achieved /18/.

In figure 3 the example of section two is used to give a concrete view of the proposed model. The symbology is drawn from Bracchi's work /17/ and we do not repeat its description owing to space reasons. The NCS and the LCSs are supposed

NETWORK CONCEPTUAL SCHEMA

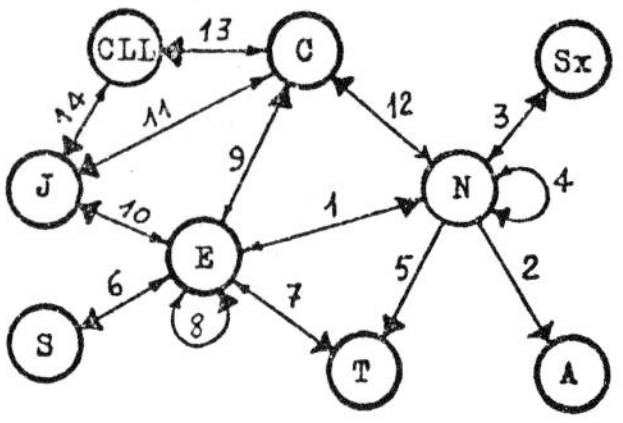

A = age
CLL= communitary labour laws
C = country
E = employee
J = job
N = name
S = salary
Sx = sex
T = tax

EUROPEAN COMMUNITY HDQ (ECH)
LOCAL CONCEPTUAL SCHEMA

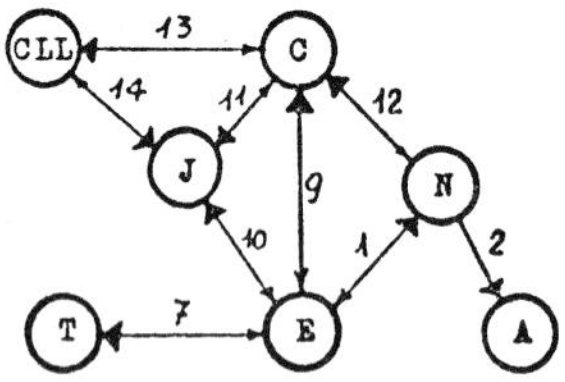

ANOTHER LCS

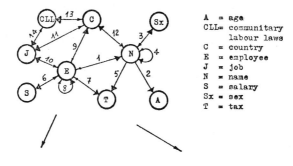

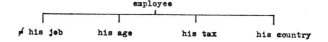

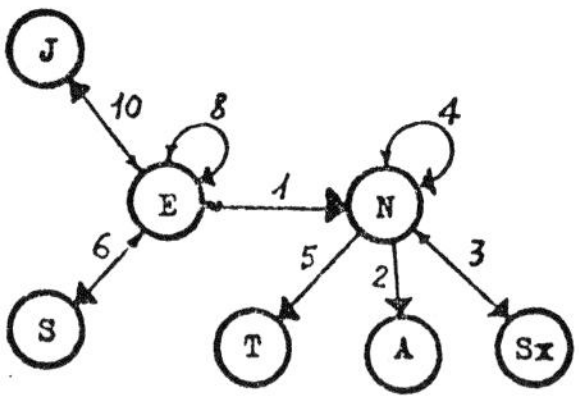

LOGICAL MAPPING MODEL

employee is (≠ his job= J; his age = A: 10^-, 1^+, 2^+; his tax = T: 10^-, 7^+; his country = C: 11^-)

TAX EVALUATION EXTERNAL SCHEMA

employee

≠ his job | his age | his tax | his country

NETWORK INTERNAL SCHEMA

(10^+, 10^-, 11^+, 11^-, 13^+, 13^-) ⟷ LIS(ECH)
(1^+, 1^-, 2^+, 5^+, 10^+, 10^-) ⟷ LIS(Bonn)
(1^+, 1^-, 7^+, 10^-) ⟷ LIS(Rome)
(1^+, 2^+, 3^+, 3^-; 10^-) ⟷ LIS(Milan)

QUERY IN COLARD

<u>for every</u> country <u>and</u> <u>for every</u> employee <u>such that</u> (his job = 'software engineer'<u>and</u> his age > 40) <u>then</u> <u>write</u> average tax

Fig. 3

all to be modelled as bidirectional binary relations sets, so that the PLSs are reduced to a mere subsetting. The EXS is supposed to be a hierarchic one and the Logical Mapping Model, that is the mapping between the LCS and the EXS, consists in a set of progressions of binary relations. The NIS binds sets of relations to the LIS of the site they are stored in.

We can notice that to reach the tax item in Bonn the progression (10^-, 1^+, 5^+) is needed, while in Rome the shorter equivalent progression (10^-,7^+) can be used. Moreover, for the Italian employer the data cannot be retrieved at a unique node since the Rome node lacks the relation 2^+ between names and ages, relation which is stored in Milan. So the NNM will have to decide the retrieval strategy, possibly on the basis of the "weight function" attributed to each relation.
Possible operating strategies in retrieving and manipulating the data using the COLARD query language /19/, in which the query has been rewritten in the example, are described in /17/.

5. REMARKS AND CONCLUSIONS

A framework to model DDB systems has been outlined. It is composed by several description stages which can be grouped in two main hierarchical levels:

- the description of the network relevant features (NCS, PLS, NIS, NNM);
- the description of the single component database systems (LCS, LIS, EXS).

Even if it may seem a "jumbo" and cumbersome structure, it is necessary to provide a full logical and physical data independence and to model as well heterogeneous systems as homogeneous ones.

The discussion of the possible solutions to the different problems in DDB organization and design has not been carried out in detail (and this cannot be the aim of a single paper indeed!), nevertheless we tried to show the appropriate levels at which to look for the solutions themselves.

A very last remark can be the following: while no problem is posed by the allocation of the data description and of the data manipulation algorithm in a stand-alone system, a choose has to be made as to where allocating NIS, PLS, NNM in the network. The solution can be a Network Management Node at which to keep description and algorithms relevant to the entire network. On the contrary, they could be duplicated in all the nodes of the network. Each solution has its pros and cons and must be considered in the frame of the problems outlined in section two.

5. REFERENCES

/1/ Date C.J., Hopewell P.: "*File definition and Logical Data Independence*", Proc. ACM-SIGFIDET Workshop, '71.

/2/ Date C.J. Hopewell P.: "*Storage structure and Physical Data Independence*", Proc. ACM-SIGFIDET Workshop, '71.

/3/ Collmeyer A.J.: "*Implication of data independence on the architecture of Database Management Systems*", Proc. ACM-SIGFIDET Workshop, 1972.

/4/ Schreiber F.A.: "*Distributed Databases: some problems still to be solved*", Proc. Convention Informatique; Paris, Sept. 1975.

/5/ Chu W.W.: "*Optimal file allcation in a multiple computer system*", IEEE Transactions on Computers, Vol. C-18, n.10, Oct. 1969.

/6/ Chu W.W.: "*Optimal file allocation in a computer network*", in Abramson and Kuo Ed., "*Computer Communication Network*", Prentice Hall, 1972.

/7/ Casey R.G.: "*Allocation of copies of a file in a information network*", Proc. AFIPS SJCC, May 1972.

/8/ Shoshani A. et al.: "*Synchronization in a Parallel-accessed database*", Communications ACM, Vol. 2, n. 11, Nov. 1969.

/9/ Holler E.: "*Koordination Kritisher Zugriffe auf werteilte Datenbanken in Rechnernetzen bei dezentraler Uberwachung*", Gesselschaft für Kernforschung M.B.M., Karlsruhe, KFK 1967, Apr. 1974.

/10/ Peebles R.W.: "*Design considerations for a Distributed Data Access System*", Wharton School of Finance and Commerce, University of Pennsylvania, Philadelphia, AD-775569 (Ph.D. Thesis), May 1973.

/11/ Chupin J.C., Seguin J.: "*A Network Direct Access Method*", Proc. European Workshop on Distributed Computer Systems, GMD Darmstadt, Oct. 1974.

/12/ Karl M.: "*The distributed Database of the information system of the German Police*", Proc. European Workshop on Distributed Computer Systems, GMD Darmstadt, Oct. 1974.

/13/ Chupin J.C.: "*Command languages and heterogeneous networks*," in C. Unger Ed., "Command Languages", North Holland 1975.

/14/ du Mastle J., Goyer P.: "*Some basic notions for computer networks command languages*", in C. Unger Ed., "Command Languages", North Holland 1975.

/15/ Bachman C.W.,: "*Trends in database management 1975*", Proc. NCC, 1975.

/16/ Nijssen G.M.: "*An evaluation of the ANSI*

DBMS *architecture and conceptual schema as in the Feb. 1975 report*", Working Paper for IFIP WG2. 6, May 1975.

/17/ Bracchi G., Fedeli A., Paolini P.: "*A multi level relational model for database management systems*", in Klimbie J.W. and Koffeman K.L. Ed., "Data Base Management", North Holland, 1974.

/18/ Bracchi G., Paolini P., Pelagatti G.: "*Data independent descriptions and the DDL specifications*", Doqué B.C.M. and Nijssen G.M. Ed. "Data Base Description", North Holland, 1975.

/19/ Bracchi G., Fedeli A., Paolini P.: "*A language for a relational database management system*", Proc. 6th Annual Princeton Conference, 1972.

/20/ Schreiber F.A.: "*Problemi posti dal progetto di Data Base distribuiti: II° - problemi di struttura e di comunicazione*", Automazione e Strumentazione, Vol. XXIV, n. 6, 1976.

/21/ Schreiber F.A.: "*Problems and models in Distributed Database systems*", Ist. di Elettronica, Politecnico di Milano, Lab. di Calcolatori, Internal Report n. 75-14, August 1975.

/22/ Levin K.D., Morgan H.L.: "*Optimizing distributed data bases-A framework for research*", Proc. of the National Computer Conference, 1975.

/23/ Giovacchini L., Schreiber F.A.: "*Some considerations on distributed management information systems*", Proc. of the International Symposium on Technology for Selective Dissemination of Information, San Marino, September 1976.

E. Morlet and D. Ribbens, (Eds.), International Computing Symposium 1977.

TO THE PROBLEM OF RECORD PLACEMENT IN INVERTED FILE SYSTEMS

Gunter Schlageter

Universität Karlsruhe
Institut für Angewandte Informatik
und Formale Beschreibungsverfahren
Postfach 6380, D-7500 Karlsruhe, Germany

Though much optimization is done in inverted file systems as to the directories, common inverted file organizations do not comprise any structuring techniques for the data file. The data file may be structured by appropriately allocating the records to the pages (clustering). In this paper it is shown that structuring the data file can reduce the necessary page accesses drastically. The problem of data file structuring is analysed, and it turns out to be a complex combinatorial problem. Heuristics for practical solutions are discussed together with implementational aspects. Some experimental results are presented.

1. INTRODUCTION AND BASIC NOTIONS

For the purposes of this paper we classify as an inverted file those file organizations in which all access path information is separate from the data and which permit, for a predefined set of attributes, the retrieval of all records with a given attribute value without accessing any records which do not have this attribute value. A typical organization is the following: for each selected attribute an index is maintained which contains, for each attribute value, a list of addresses pointing to the records which have this attribute value. We call the set of these indexes the directory as opposed to the data file which contains the user defined records. Attributes for which indexes are maintained are called inverted. Figure 1 shows a simple inverted organization where attributes D# and T are inverted.

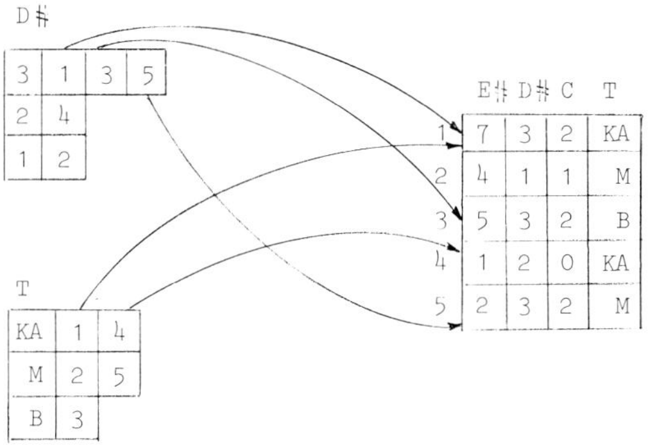

Figure 1: An example file with inversion of two attributes.

E·# = employee number
D # = department number
C = number of children
T = Town

We assume the principal implementation as shown in figure 2. The pointers in the indexes are logical pointers, which means that the corresponding record can only be found by the use of a logical-to-physical address-map. Given the logical pointer the address-map provides for direct access to the requested record. The logical pointers might be system-created identifiers or values of a user defined primary-key. The essential point is that any reorganization in the data file only concerns the address-map, whereas the indexes of the directory need not be touched.

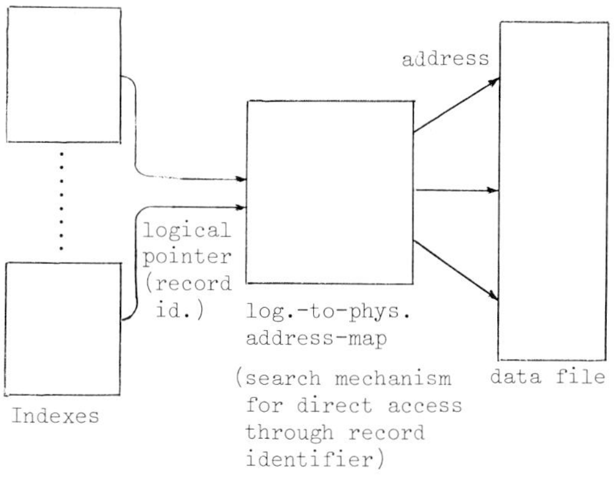

Figure 2: Principal implementation using logical pointers

In ideal random-access storage systems it is not of any interest how the records of the data file are arranged; virtually all available inverted file systems are implicitly based on this assumption. Incoming records are stored wherever place can be found, and the data file remains completely unstructured. In real life, however, databases must be stored on non-ideal secondary storage systems, and the distribution of the records over the storage medium can have strong effects on the system performance.

In the following we assume a paged memory system. The cost for answering a query depends essentially on the number of pages that must be transferred from secondary storage to memory in order to retrieve the specified set of records. For this reason it is a question whether the unstructured file organization of common inverted file systems is not rather a costly solution, in spite of the advantages of optimal storage utilization.

There are investigations that try to improve system performance by various optimizations in the directory /1, 3, 4, 8/ but, to the author's knowledge, there is only the paper of Rothnie and Lozano /5/ that points to the significance of data file structuring. There a particular heuristic file structuring method, called multiple key hashing, is discussed. In this paper, data file structuring is discussed from a more fundamental point of view; a rather general mathematical formulation of the problem is proposed and analysed. The problem turns out to be a complex combinatorial problem which, like a series of other combinatorial problems in computer sience, must be solved heuristically. Some heuristics are presented, and it is seen that remarkable reductions in the number of necessary page accesses can be achieved with simple structuring rules. Some implementational aspects and overall system considerations are discussed.

2. THE PROBLEM OF OPTIMAL DATA FILE STRUCTURING

We assume the data file to be represented as a relation in first normal form /2/. The n-tuples of the relation are called records. To each attribute A_i, $i = 1,\dots,n$, a known set of values $a_i = \{a_{i1},\dots, a_{ir(i)}\}$ is assigned. Thus a record $i \in M = \{1,\dots,m\}$, M the set of records, is an n-tuple $(b_{i1},\dots,b_{in})$, $b_{ij} \in a_j$.

The records are to be stored in a set $S = \{S_1,\dots,S_s\}$ of pages, each page comprising t records at most. The directories are not discussed here, but we only consider attributes that are inverted. It is of no major interest in the following discussion whether the values of inverted attributes are stored in the data file or not.

For the following problem analysis we consider <u>basic queries</u>, which are queries of the type

> "Give all records with a particular value of a specified attribute".

It is intuitively clear that the number of page transfers to memory is minimal if the accessed pages just contain the requested records, and are full. This is only possible for a rather restricted class of queries, since an optimal arrangement of the above type can be given for one attribute only. Nevertheless this approach may be a useful attack to the data file structuring problem, especially if one query type is of outstanding importance.

Notice that it is very unlikely that applications using other attributes only are markedly affected by the optimization relative to the one attribute, since, assuming statistical independence of the attributes, in their view the particular structured file is arbitrary anyways, and will show no essential change of its properties.

Figure 3 shows a data file, as it may exist in a conventional inverted system, and a structured version of this file. The structuring was done by the attribute A_1 (Fig. 3b). A query "Give all records with A_1 = 2" requires three page accesses in the unstructured file, but only one access in the structured version.

In general we do not want good performance for one restricted class of query but we want a good overall-performance. To improve overall-performance all attributes have to be considered. For instance, one can easily verify that, in order to answer all basic queries for the attribute values of A_1, A_2, A_3, and A_4, we need 26 page accesses in Figure 3b, but only 24 in 3c. Of course, the improvements achieved by data file structuring must be paid, and structuring may turn out to be useless for some system organizations and applications; this will be discussed later.

We now assume that a probability p_i' is given for each attribute A_i, $\sum_{i=1}^{n} p_i'=1$; p_i' is the probability for A_i to be referenced in a query. We further assume that the values $a_{ik} \in a_i$ are referenced with equal probability $p_{ik} = p_i = p_i'/\#a_i$. This assumption is not restrictive compared to the assumptions normally made in the analysis of file systems. In practice it will be difficult to get good estimates for p_i' and $\#a_i$, but to get the probabilities for the a_{ij} would hardly be possible. Finally, we assume that the measure for performance is the mean number z of page transfers necessary to answer a basic query. Then the problem is: find an allocation of records to pages such that the mean number z of page transfers per query is minimized.

Let f_{ik} be the number of pages containing records with value a_{ik} for the attribute A_i. Then, obviously,

$$z = \sum_i \sum_k p_{ik} f_{ik}$$

and with $p_{ik} = p_i$

$$z = \sum_i p_i \sum_k f_{ik} \qquad (1)$$

Note that the decisive weight is not the attribute-probability p_i' but the attribute-value-probability p_i.

We can interprete z as the mean file size, measured in number of pages, as seen by the programs issuing basic queries.

Lemma 1:

A lower bound for z is given by

$$z_{min} = \left\lceil \frac{m}{t} \right\rceil \sum_i p_i$$

(again t is the number of records a page can contain and m is the number of records in the file. $\lceil x \rceil$ denotes the smallest integer $\geq$ x.)

Proof: $\sum_k f_{ik}$ cannot be smaller than the number of pages n' containing records of the file. n' is minimal if all pages are full, except at most one page, which means $n' = \lceil m/t \rceil$. -

a)	b)	c)
1 2 3 4	1 2 3 4	1 2 3 4
3 1 4 2	1 4 1 3	3 2 3 4
2 2 2 3	3 1 4 2	1 4 1 3
3 1 2 3	2 2 2 3	2 1 3 4
2 3 2 3	2 3 2 3	3 1 3 4
1 4 1 3	2 1 3 4	2 2 2 3
2 1 3 3	3 1 2 3	2 3 2 3
3 1 3 4	3 2 3 3	3 1 2 3
3 2 3 3	3 1 3 4	3 2 3 3

Figure 3:
Example File and Two Structured Versions
a) unstructured file
b) structured version 1
c) structured version 2

z_{min} is achieved in the case that for each attribute no page contains more than one attribute value, the pages thereby being full (except at most one).

Though easily understandable, the objective function (1) is not useful. We introduce an equivalent objective function. Let again M be the set of records, S the set of pages, and $M_i \subset M$ the set of records allocated to S_i, such that $M_i \cap M_j = \emptyset$ for $i \neq j$.

Define the heterogeneity of page k to be

$$D_k = \sum_{i=1}^{n} p_i \#\{b_{ji} \mid j \in M_k\}. \qquad (2)$$

Then the objective function is

$$z' = \sum_{k=1}^{s} D_k. \qquad (3)$$

Lemma 2:

The objective functions (1) and (3) are equivalent. -

Proof:

$\#\{b_{ji} \mid j \in M_k\}$ indicates the number of different values of A_i for which page S_k must be accessed. Now

$$\sum_{k=1}^{s} \sum_{i=1}^{n} p_i \#\{b_{ji} \mid j \in M_k\} = \sum_{i=1}^{n} p_i \sum_{k=1}^{s} \#\{b_{ji} \mid j \in M_k\},$$

$$\sum_{k=1}^{s} \#\{b_{ji} \mid j \in M_k\} = \sum_{k=1}^{s} \sum_{g=1}^{\#a_i} \#\{b_{ji} \mid (b_{ji}=a_{ig}) \wedge (j \in M_k)\}$$

and by interchanging $\sum_{k=1}^{s}$ and $\sum_{g=1}^{\#a_i}$,

and noticing that the cardinality of the indicated set is either o or 1, we see

$$\sum_{k=1}^{s} \#\{b_{ji} \mid j \in M_k\} = \sum_{k=1}^{\#a_i} f_{ik} .$$

Thus the equivalence of (1) and (3) is shown. -

The formulation (3) of the objective function, based on the heterogeneity of pages, clearly shows the central problem, namely to allocate "related" records to a page; one would like that records which are frequently retrieved together be stored in the same page.

The file structuring problem now can be formulated:

> Find a partition $P = \{M_1, \ldots, M_s\}$ of the record set, such that
>
> (1) $\#M_k \leq t$
>
> (2) $\sum_{k=1}^{s} \sum_{i=1}^{n} p_i \#\{b_{ji} \mid j \in M_k\} \rightarrow \min.$

A look at other well-known combinatorial problems in the computer science area (scheduling in multiprocessor systems, segmentation in virtual computer systems, file allocation in computernetworks) destroys any hope to find a simple, efficient method for optimally solving this problem. Let us shortly compare the problem with the segmentation problem in virtual memory systems, where we want to pack code segments into pages so that the mean number of inter-page references during program execution is minimized. We chose this problem since it was discussed at length in the literature.

The graphical interpretation of the segmentation problem is obvious: nodes of the graph represent code segments, the arcs indicate possible control transfer between the code segments, and are weighted with the frequencies of control transfer. The problem is to collect the nodes to segments of at most page size such that the sum of the weights of the cut arcs is minimized.

In analogy we would define the records as the nodes of the graph. Each pair(r_k, r_j) of nodes is connected by an arc weighted with the distance d_{kj} defined as

$$\sum_{i=1}^{n} p_i \delta_i , \quad \delta_i = \begin{cases} o, & \text{if } b_{ki} = b_{ji} \\ 1 & \text{otherwise} \end{cases}$$

Unfortunately this model does not exactly represent the given file structuring problem, since the D_q values and the sum of the d_{kj} values in the pages are not an equivalent measure for heterogeneity.

This is seen by the following simple example: assume we have only one inverted attribute A, and assume we have a page S_1 with the A-values

3 3 3 1 1 1

and a page S_2 with the A-values

3 2 1 1 1 1

For S_1: $\Sigma d_{ik} = 9$

$D_1 = \#\{3,3,3,1,1,1\} = 2$

for S_2: $\Sigma d_{ik} = 9$

$D_2 = \#\{3,2,1,1,1,1\} = 3$

Obviously, the sum of the d_{ik}-values is an inadequate measure. The situation is characterized by the fact that the interesting property of a collection of records cannot be derived simply in an additive manner from the properties of pairs of records. In this respect the file structuring problem is clearly even worse than the segmentation problem.

3. PRACTICAL SOLUTIONS

The file structuring problem can be considered a special clustering problem, and much work was done on clustering in the context of document retrieval and library information systems /6/. In document retrieval systems we want to cluster documents with similar properties, where the properties of a document are expressed by a (normally weighted) term vector. The term vector indicates which terms, and perphaps with which frequency, occur in the document.

The given file structuring problem can be adapted to a clustering problem of the document retrieval system type, by representing each record by a binary vector of dimension $\sum_i \# a_i$, where each position indicates whether the record has a certain attribute value or not. Though this approach would guarantee good results as to file structuring, it is neither necessary nor desirable to pay the overhead for uncritically transferring document retrieval methods to our problem.

The main difference arises from the fact that clustering in document retrieval systems is a very critical step because retrieval is based on this clustering, i.e. the quality of the answer depends on the chosen clustering. In contrast, clustering in the data file of an inverted system is not done for file access and retrieval purposes, but ony for performance considerations. Thus there is much more freedom in considering trade-offs between clustering cost and retrieval cost, and even rather crude clustering techniques might be fully sufficient. We therefore do not further discuss clustering in document retrieval systems.

The file structuring problem is treatable with a variety of heuristics. Multiple key hashing, as introduced in /5/ can be understood as a heuristic solution, but which offers very useful additional features for retrieval. Most of the imaginable heuristics are unrealistic for practical purposes since we are normally dealing with very large data files. To this class of heuristics, which give good results but are hardly applicable in practice, belong all heuristics based on distance-checking between records. An example (heuristic 1):

> Choose a record r_i and select that record r_j for which d_{ij} is minimal. Repeat with r_j, and so forth, until the page capacity is reached.

Realize that heuristic 1 is not exceptionally good; but it is one of the simplest that is based on distance-checking for record pairs.

A very simple heuristic which is mostly at the same time feasible and tolerably good, is sorting the data file. The sort must be done according to the p_i-values, attribute with highest p_i first. Needless to say that normally sorting is rather far from the optimal solution, but

(1) the improvements obtained by sorting the data file are impressive enough, and

(2) physical file organization can be done in a way that the file does not lose locality properties very quickly as a result of updates: the records need not be sorted within the pages, and if we leave some initial free space in the pages new records can mostly be stored near related records; and, an important point, finding the proper insertion point is not too difficult.

Figure 4 gives an example for the effect of heuristic 1 and sorting. In this small example z is reduced from 4.04 to 3.06 by sorting. Since optimal values are not available, the results could be normalized as to z_{min}; in the example: the deviation from z_{min} (1.2) is reduced from 237 % to 155 %.

A_1	A_2	A_3	A_4
4	1	5	4
3	4	5	5
2	1	3	5
2	2	3	2
1	3	1	1
2	5	2	5
2	2	2	5
1	4	4	5
5	2	5	5
3	3	4	1
1	4	1	5
4	2	3	2
4	1	5	2
1	3	1	5
5	5	1	3
1	1	1	4
5	4	4	4
5	3	1	5
1	3	1	5
5	2	1	1
3	2	3	1
5	5	5	2
5	3	5	2
5	1	2	2
4	3	4	5
5	2	4	1
3	2	5	5
2	1	4	2
3	1	3	2
2	4	5	2

a)

A_1	A_2	A_3	A_4
4	1	5	4
4	1	5	2
4	2	3	2
2	2	3	2
2	2	2	5
2	5	2	5
2	1	3	5
2	1	4	2
2	4	5	2
3	4	5	5
3	2	5	5
3	2	3	1
3	1	3	2
5	1	2	2
5	5	5	2
5	3	5	2
5	3	1	5
1	3	1	5
1	3	1	5
1	3	1	1
1	1	1	4
1	4	1	5
1	4	4	5
5	4	4	4
5	2	4	1
5	2	1	1
5	5	1	3
4	3	4	5
3	3	4	1
5	2	5	5

b)

A_1	A_2	A_3	A_4
1	1	1	4
1	3	1	1
1	3	1	5
1	3	1	5
1	4	1	5
1	4	4	5
2	1	3	5
2	1	4	2
2	2	2	5
2	2	3	2
2	4	5	2
2	5	2	5
3	1	3	2
3	2	3	1
3	2	5	5
3	3	4	1
3	4	5	5
4	1	5	2
4	1	5	4
4	2	3	2
4	3	4	5
5	1	2	2
5	2	1	1
5	2	4	1
5	2	5	5
5	3	1	5
5	3	5	2
5	4	4	4
5	5	1	3
5	5	5	2

c)

Figure 4: An example data file and two structured versions.

a) unstructured file, $z = 4{,}04$
b) structured file, heuristic 1, $z = 2{,}96$
c) structured file, sorting, $z = 3{,}06$

Figure 5 gives some experimental results for randomly constructed data files.

$z_1 = \sum_{k=1}^{\#a_1} f_{1k}$ is the number of page accesses necessary to retrieve all records with value a_{11}, then all records with a_{12}, etc., where attribute A_1 is the attribute with the highest p_i-value. We see that heuristic 1 often results in a higher z_1 value, but a lower z value than sorting, as we would expect because of the distance-checking in heuristic 1. For instance, this "overruling" of attribute A_1 happens in page 1 of figure 4b, after record 4 2 3 2, when instead of 4 3 4 5 record 2 2 3 2 is selected. Heuristic 1 was slightly superior in all tested examples.

Some notes concerning the sort heuristic should be given here. At first we want to state a lemma that is rather surprising at first sight.

Lemma 3:

It is not possible to formulate conditions for the p_i-values such that sorting guarantees optimal file structuring, as long as $p_i > 0$, $i = 1,\ldots,n$, and $n > 1$. This is also true if the number of records per page is not fixed, but may vary between a lower and an upper bound.

Proof:

The proof can be given by one example: consider the record arrangement a

1 1
2 2
—
3 3
9 1

and arrangement b

1 1
9 1
—
2 2
3 3

Obviously b is superior to the sorted version a independent of the probability assignment. This example is easily extended to the situation where we have no fixed number of records per page, simply by putting a number of appropriate records between 1 1 and 9 1, such that 1 1 and 9 1 cannot be collected into the same page. To produce similar examples for $n > 2$ is straightforward. -

The deterioration of sorting compared to optimal structuring is the greater the more attributes must be considered, and the more the probabilities become equal. Since page boundaries are not considered, homogeneous portions of the file may be cut. In some cases it might be useful to look at the page boundaries on assigning the records to pages, thereby allowing a varying number of records, respectively a varying storage utilization, per page from the very beginning.

Another class of heuristics might be usefule in certain circumstances: define a set of cristallization points (similar to centroids in information retrieval) and assign each incoming record to that cristallization point to which it is most related. We just need a table showing all cristallization points and the pages containing the corresponding clusters. The set of cristallization points should be dynamic in order to prevent clusters from getting too large. The definition of the cristallization points requires some analysis of the data, unless we apply a clustering procedure which produces a set of identified clusters the cristallization points of which are then computed. Since it is difficult to

				random		sorting		heuristic 1	
exp	m	n	t	z_1	z	z_1	z	z_1	z
1	100	3	10	68	6.75	19	5.00	19	3.70
2	200	3	10	165	8.25	33	4.91	37	4.67
3	300	3	10	260	8.67	57	5.23	66	4.93
4	400	3	10	362	8.97	73	5.39	103	5.09
5	600	3	10	558	9.25	112	5.52	-	
6	800	3	10	755	9.46	155	5.72	-	
7	200	3	20	91	8.97	18	5.47	21	5.12
8	600	3	20	444	14.94	56	8.09	-	
9	1000	3	20	818	16.60	95	9.18	-	
10	1500	3	20	1392	13.81	167	7.62	-	
11	2400	4	40	1997	19.97	154	12.48	-	
12	2400	4	10	2299	23.01	326	14.62	-	
13	2400	4	20	2018	40.13	164	22.75	-	
14	3000	4	20	2515	50.13	196	27.20	-	

Figure 5: Some experimental results
probabilities p_i for the attributes:
exp 1-10 : 0.5, 0.3, 0.2; exp 11-14 : 0.4, 0.3, 0.2, 0.1

z = mean number of page transfers per basic query

$$z_1 = \sum_{k=1}^{\#a_1} f_{1k}$$

m = number of records
n = number of attributes
t = page capacity

give a set of cristallization points such as to avoid clusters comprising many pages, and since we have no additional structuring within the clusters, this method may be much inferior to the sorting heuristic; in effect, it could correspond to the sorting heuristic if sorting is restricted to a small subset of the inverted attributes.

4. COST CONSIDERATIONS

It is clear that the saving of page accesses for queries must be paid by the overhead for maintaining the file structure. We did not introduce a particular physical data file organization, so we cannot discuss the cost situation in detail.

At any rate, we have additional cost on update operations. On insertions the proper insertion point must be found, and provisions must be made for the case that the record cannot be placed near the ideal insertion point. The modification of attribute values can result in the deletion of the record and insertion of the modified record in a new place. As a consequence of the updates we have reorganization cost, either by reorganization in some intervals or by permanent ("on-line") reorganization. Permanent reorganization is found, e.g., in IBMs VSAM, reorganization in intervals is necessary if a file organization similar to conventional index-sequential systems is applied.

Strongly related to the cost question is the question of the stability of the query pattern over time. Reorganization may not only be necessary as a consequence of updates to the file, but also as a consequence of changes in the query pattern; in fact, a changing query pattern may require new file structuring, even if there is no update at all. It is not a simple matter to determine good reorganization points in general, and it is a more difficult problem, if the effects of performance deterioration due to update and due to a changing query pattern are not clearly separable. A separation is always possible, if the query pattern changes slowly enough to be treated as stationary compared to performance deterioration due to update.

Whether the additional reorganization cost is outweighed by the saving of page accesses cannot be said in general, of course; but without any doubt there is a large class of applications where data file structuring is valuable, in particular if the update/query ratio is small.

5. CONCLUSION

It is shown in this paper that for the important class of data organization, inverted files, performance improvements are achievable by data file structuring. The main idea is to place records which are often retrieved together as close one to the other as possible. A mathematical formulation of the problem shows that an optimal solution is out of discussion. However, very simple heuristics, like e.g. sorting the data file, give remarkable improvements. Some characteristics of possible heuristics are discussed, and experimental results are given. Further research is necessary, first of all to get some trade-offs as to the cost due to structuring and the saving for retrieval.

REFERENCES

[1] Cardenas, A.F., "Analysis and performance of inverted data base structures", CACM 18, 1975, 253.

[2] Codd, E.F., "A relational model of data for large shared data banks", CACM 13, 1972, 377.

[3] Inglis, J., "Inverted indexes and multi-list structures", The Computer Journal 17, 1974, 59.

[4] Härder, T., "Das Zugriffszeitverhalten von relationalen Datenbanksystemen", Dissertation, TH Darmstadt, 1975.

[5] Rothnie, J.B. and Lozano, T., "Attribute based file organization in a paged memory environment", CACM 17, 1974, 63.

[6] Salton, G., "Dynamic information and library processing", Prentice Hall, Inc.1975.

[7] Shneiderman, B., "Optimum data base reorganization points", CACM 16, 1973, 362.

[8] Vose, M.R., Richardson, J.S., "An approach to inverted index maintenance", The Computer Bulletin, 16, 1972, 256.

E. Morlet and D. Ribbens, (Eds.), International Computing Symposium 1977.

ON SAFEGUARDING STATISTICAL DISCLOSURE BY GIVING APPROXIMATE ANSWERS TO QUERIES*

Mohammad Inam ul Haq**

Department of Computer Science
State University of New York
at Stony Brook, New York U.S.A

1. INTRODUCTION

A statistical data base is a collection of personal records collected from public to use them to extract statistical summaries. The users of the data are allowed to ask only statistical questions about the stored data. The individuals about whom the information is collected are assured that their personal privacy would be safeguarded [1]. It has been shown in earlier papers that in order to accomplish this goal some of the queries about the data cannot be permitted [2,3,4,5,6]. For example, if a query is formed in such a way that it is specifically related to a particular individual then its answer can be either zero or one, and hence, if this query is permitted then it would disclose personal information about that particular individual. Obviously such queries cannot be permitted. It also then becomes necessary to assure that the answer to a restricted query cannot be computed from the answers of the other queries whose answers are known to a user; otherwise the user can perform the necessary computation to find the answer to the restricted query. This situation is referred to as statistical disclosure and has been discussed in detail in earlier papers [4,5]. It is asserted that if a single query cannot be permitted then many other queries have to be restricted to avoid statistical disclosure. And thus the number of restricted queries grows very rapidly. Hansen has described a method of access control in which the answer to a query is given within an approximation of m, where m is a predetermined positive number [3] i.e. the answer A_q of a query q would be selected between $A_q - m$ and $A_q + m$. This method has an advantage that significantly more queries can be permitted. But this method would only be effective if the exact answers of the queries cannot be determined. The main idea of this paper is to determine the necessary and sufficient conditions for the computation of the exact answer of a query from the answers of the queries whose answers are given within an approximation of m. The following definitions are needed and some of them are reproduced briefly from the earlier papers [4,5].

2. DEFINITIONS

A characteristic is a piece of information about a person. It has a name and a value. For example, (Name, Bernstein) and (Sex, Male) are characteristics. The group of persons about whom the information is collected are called data persons. A record is a set of characteristics collected about a data person. A data base is a set of records of all the data persons. A query, denoted by q, is a statistical question which can be asked about the data base. The answer to a query q, denoted by A_q, is the aggregate of all the data persons who have those characteristics in their records which are implied in the query q. A data base together with a procedure for limiting the access of the users to the data base for statistical purpose is said to be a statistical information retrieval system and will be referred to as 'system'. A query is

*This work was supported by National Science Foundation Grant #28177 while the author was a student in the Department of Computer Science.

**Author's new address: Department of Mathematics, The University of Engineering & Technology, Lahore, PAKISTAN.

called a permitted query if it is permitted by the system; otherwise it is called a restricted query. The answer to a query as given by the system within an approximation of m is denoted by A'_q. A set Q of queries is a dependent set if for all data bases, there exists a query $q_i \in Q$ such that the answer to the query q_i can be computed from the answers to other queries which belong to Q. In particular, a dependent set of queries is said to be in a family relation if there exists a query $q_i \in Q$ such that the equation $A_{qi} - \sum_{\forall qj \in Q-\{qi\}} A_{qj} = 0$ holds for all data bases. In this paper the notation $f_Q(A_q) = 0$ will be used to denote such a family relation. Obviously such relations are linear in A_q's. For example, consider the set $Q = \{q_1, q_2, q_3, q_4\}$. If the answer to the query q_1 is always equal to the sum of the answers to the queries q_2, q_3 and q_4, then the set Q is in a family relation.

A user's supplementary knowledge is a set of all the information about the data base which a user knows from a source other than the system. For example, he may know the exact answers of some of the queries, he may know the characteristics of some of the data persons and/or he may know some of the properties of the data base such as the family relation which hold among certain queries. A user may also know from his supplementary knowledge that the answer to a query is not greater than a certain number or/and is not smaller than a certain other number. The lower bound of a query q denoted by L_q is defined as the greatest non-negative number, n, such that $A_q \geqslant n$. Similarly the upper bound of a query q denoted by U_q is defined as the smallest non-negative number, n, such that $A_q \leqslant n$. If q is a permitted query then $L_q \geqslant A'_q - m$ and $U_q \leqslant A'_q + n$. Also $L_q \geqslant 0$ i.e. a user can always assume zero, the value of L_q, if no other positive number is known.

Exact disclosure is defined as: Exact disclosure occurs if the exact answer to a query can be computed from the information about the other queries known to a user, using the properties of the data base and the results obtained from the system, which is not possible without using these results. In other words if the exact answer to a query can be computed without using any result from the system then exact disclosure does not occur. However, if atleast a single result obtained from the system has to be used in computing the exact answer to the query then exact disclosure occurs.

The following theorems are based on the assumptions:

(a) a user is familiar with all the family relations which hold among certain queries.

(b) A user has the knowledge of m, where m is the approximation factor.

The following observations can be easily made:

i) The approximate answer to a query given by the system remains fixed at all times; otherwise a user can find the exact answer to the query which would be the median of all the possible answers of the same query by asking the query a great number of times.

ii) If the exact answer to a query is less than or equal to m, then the approximate answer would be selected between zero and $A_q + m$.

iii) A family relation that holds among a set Q of queries may not hold if in the relation the approximate answers are substituted for exact answers of those queries.

3. THEOREM I

There is an exact disclosure from a specific query q if and only if one of the following holds:

(i) $A'_q = L_q - m$

(ii) $A'_q = U_q + m$

Proof of if part: $A'_q - m \leqslant A_q \leqslant A'_q + m$ (1)

and $L_q \leqslant A_q \leqslant U_q$ (2)

Therefore if $A'_q = L_q - m$ (i.e. $A'_q + m = L_q$) then the user can conclude from assertions 1 and 2 that $A_q = L_q$. Hence, there is exact disclosure.

The same kind of argument can be given for the case when $A'_q = U_q + m$.

Proof of only if part: From assertions (1) & (2) $\text{Max}\ \{L_q, A'_q - m\} \leq A_q \leq \text{Min}\ \{U_q, A'_q + m\}$ Therefore, if there is an exact disclosure i.e. A_q is uniquely determined then the user has concluded from his computations that

either $L_q = U_q$ (3)

or $L_q = A'_q + m$ i.e. $A'_q = L_q - m$ (4)

or $A'_q - m = U_q$ i.e. $A'_q = U_q + m$ (5)

It is obvious that equation (3) cannot hold; otherwise A_q is known to the user from his supplementary knowledge and then it is not an exact disclosure which is a contradiction. Hence either equation (4) or equation (5) holds.Q.E.D.

Example:1 Let m = 5 and a user knows about a query q that $L_q = 100$. If $A'_q = 95$ then the condition (i) of the theorem is satisfied. Obviously, there is only one value of A_q (i.e. equal to 100) which can satisfy the assertions $A'_q - 5 \leq A_q \leq A'_q + 5$ and $A_q \geq L_q$. The same kind of argument applies if the user knows that $U_q = 100$ and $A'_q = 105$.

Consider now the general situation when the user of the system is permitted to ask all the permitted queries and hence, knows the approximate answers of all such queries. In addition, he may know the exact answers of some of the queries, lower or/and upper bounds of some of the other queries from his supplementary knowledge. Furthermore, he may be familiar with the family relations which hold among certain queries. The following theorem provides the necessary and sufficient conditions for exact disclosure in this general case.

4. THEOREM II

Let Q_k be the set of queries whose exact answers are known to a user. Let Q be a set of queries that contains a query $q' \notin Q_k$ and satisfying the family relation $f_Q(A_q) = 0$. There is exact disclosure if and only if one of the following holds:

(i) Either $A'_q = L_q - m$ or $A'_q = U_q + m$

(ii) $\forall q \in Q - \{q'\}$ implies that $q \in Q_k$

(iii) As d_q's vary from their L_q's to U_q's, the function $f_Q(d_q)$ vanishes uniquely at an extreme value, i.e. assumes values of which only one value which is an extreme value is zero.

Proof of if part: If condition (i) holds then there would be exact disclosure as shown in the proof of theorem I. If condition (ii) holds then all the quantities except A'_q are known in the linear relation $f_Q(A_q) = 0$. Hence, A'_q can be determined. If condition (iii) holds then for all $q_i \in Q$ there exists d'_{qi}'s such that $L_{qi} \leq d'_{qi} \leq U_{qi}$ and $f_Q(d'_{qi}) = 0$ i.e. d'_{qi}'s satisfy uniquely the family relation $f_Q(A_q) = 0$. Hence $d'_{qi} = A_{qi}$ for all $q_i \in Q$. In particular, A_q is known. Therefore, there would be exact disclosure.

Proof of only if part: Let there be an exact disclosure about q_1 but conditions (i), (ii), and (iii) do not hold. As condition (i) does not hold, from theorem I, the approximate answer of q_1, if permitted, would satisfy the inequality

$$L_{q1} - m \leq A'_{q1} \leq U_{q1} + m \qquad (6)$$

As condition (ii) does not hold, there exists a family Q which contains the query q_1 and another query q_2 such that A_{q2} is not known to the user.

$$\text{i.e. } \exists\, q_2 \in Q \text{ such that } q_2 \notin Q_k \qquad (7)$$

Condition (iii) does not hold implies that either the equation $f_Q(d_q) = 0$ does not have a solution at an extreme value of $f_Q(d_q)$ or if it has a solution, it is not unique. In the latter case, it is then possible to make a modification to the data base by changing the answers to the queries q_1 and q_2 within their lower and upper bounds and keeping all the information known to the user the same. Consequently, the user would claim the same answer to q_1 as before but that would be incorrect which would be a contradiction to the assumption that there is an exact disclosure. In the former case, there are two cases to be considered.

Case I: The equation $f_Q(d_q) = 0$ does not have a solution for any set of values of d_{qi}'s which lie between L_{qi}'s and U_{qi}'s respectively. This case does not arise since from the definitions of L_{qi}'s and U_{qi}'s there is a set of values A_{qi}'s which lie between L_{qi}'s and U_{qi}'s respectively which satisfy the equation $f_Q(d_q) = 0$.

Case II: The equation $f_Q(d_q) = 0$ has a unique solution for a set of values d_{qi}'s which lie between L_{qi}'s and U_{qi}'s respectively but $f_Q(d_q)$ does not attain its extreme value for this set of values. This situation is similar to as discussed earlier i.e. in this case, it is always possible to find another set of values of d_{qi}'s which lie between L_{qi}'s and U_{qi}'s such that $f_Q(d_q) = 0$. i.e. there would be another solution of the equation $f_Q(d_q) = 0$, which is a contradiction.

Therefore, the equation $f_Q(d_q) = 0$ has the only solution at an extreme value of $f_Q(d_q)$. This completes the proof of the theorem.

Example 2: Let m = 2 and $Q = \{q_1, q_2, q_3, q_4\}$ which satisfies the family relation $A_{q1} - \sum_{i=2}^{4} A_{qi} = 0$. Let $A'_{q1} = 14$, $A'_{q2} = 1$, $A'_{q3} = 2$ and $A'_{q4} = 3$. Therefore, $12 \leq A_{q1} \leq 16$, $0 \leq A_{q2} \leq 3$, $0 \leq A_{q3} \leq 4$ and $1 \leq A_{q4} \leq 5$. The values of the function $f_Q(d_q)$ ($\equiv A_{q1} - \sum_{i=2}^{4} A_{qi}$) vary from 15 to 0. Hence it has a solution at an extreme value. It can be easily verified that there is only a unique solution. Therefore by the theorem, there would be exact disclosure. i.e. the values of A_{qi} for i = 1 to 4 can be uniquely determined. These are in fact 12,3,4 and 5 respectively.

Example 3: Let the values of A'_{qi} for i = 2 to 4 be the same as in example 2 but $A'_{q1} = 13$. Therefore, $11 \leq A_{q1} \leq 15$ and the values of the function $f_Q(d_q)$ vary from 14 to -1. Hence, the equation $f_Q(d_q) = 0$ has a solution when $A_{q1} = 12$, $A_{q2} = 3$, $A_{q3} = 4$ and $A_{q4} = 5$ but it is not at an extreme value of $f_Q(d_q)$. Further this solution is not unique as there is another solution when $A_{q1} = 11$, $A_{q2} = 2$, $A_{q3} = 4$, $A_{q4} = 5$. Consequently, A_{qi}'s, i = 1 to 4 cannot be determined uniquely i.e. there would not be exact disclosure.

5. CONCLUSION

From the theorems proved in this paper it can be easily concluded that a method of access control in which the answers to queries are given by the system within some approximation, reduces but does not eliminate the chances for disclosure. However Turn and Shapiro[8] have pointed out that there is a limit to the amount a user will spend to find out personal information about a data person. The cost is basically dependent on the number of computations a user has to make to find the answers to those queries which are needed to obtain a personal disclosure. Obviously significantly more complexity is involved in this method compared to any other method in which the exact answers to queries are given by the system directly. Furthermore, this method has an advantage over the others at the cost of approximating the answers to the queries that significantly lot more queries can be permitted by the system.

6. ACKNOWLEDGEMENTS

I am very thankful to Professor Bernstein and Professor Heller for advising me in this work. I am indebted to my teachers namely Professor Kieburtz, Professor Tycko and Professor Gelernter for their sympathetic behaviour and continuous encouragement to me at all times. I am also thankful to Dr. Asghar Hameed, Professor of Mathematics, The University of Engineering and Technology, Lahore, for giving some useful suggestions.

7. REFERENCES AND BIBLIOGRAPHY

[1] Federal Statistics. Chapter 6, Vol I and Chapter 5, Vol.II.

[2] Fellegi, I.P., "On the question of statistical Confidentiality", Journal of the American Statistical Association, March 1972, Vol.67, Number 337, pp.7-17.

[3] Hansen, M.H., "Insuring Confidentiality of Individual records in data storage and retrieval for statistical purposes", AFIPS Conference Proceedings, 1971 Fall Joint Computer Conference, pp. 579-585.

[4] Haq, M.I., "Security in a Statistical Data Base", Proceedings of the American Society for Information Science, 1974 Annual Conference, Vol.11, pp. 33-39.

[5] Haq, M.I. "Insuring Privacy of an Individual from Statistical Data Base Users", AFIPS Conference Proceedings, 1975 National Computer Conference, pp.941-945.

[6] Hoffman, L.J. and W.F. Miller, "Getting a Personal Dossier from a Statistical Data Bank", Datamation, May 1970, pp.74-75.

[7] Reed, I.S., "Information Theory and Privacy in Data Banks", AFIPS Conference Proceedings, 1973 National Computer Conference, pp.581-587.

[8] Turn, R., and N.Z. Shapiro, "Privacy and Security in Data Bank Systems -- Measures of effectiveness, Costs and protector-intruder interactions", AFIPS Proceedings, 1972 Fall Joint Computer Conference, pp.435-444.

[9] Western, A., Privacy and Freedom, Atheneum New York, 1968.

E. Morlet and D. Ribbens, (Eds.), International Computing Symposium 1977.

D-GRAPHS: A CONCEPTUAL MODEL FOR DATA BASES

Herbert Weber
IBM Research Laboratory
San Jose, California 95193

Data bases are supposed to provide means for the representation of knowledge. An adequate representational schema must reflect both the purpose of the data base and consequently the way users and designers manipulate it and implementation aspects. The paper claims that now rather popular concepts based on a semantic net representation of knowledge meet neither one of the types of requirements. An alternate concept - the D-graph model - is proposed. It is based on the notions "abstractions" and "abstract data type." It does not emphasize the definition of new primitive semantic constructs but concentrates on a method for a proper specification and composition of primitives by providing means for a representation of declarative and procedural knowledge within the same framework. One may conclude from the results achievable with this method that choosing the right abstraction guarantees the correct modelling of semantics and makes the definition of integrity constraints superfluous.

1. INTRODUCTION

Data bases are symbolic representations of the knowledge human beings have about some parts of the reality (e.g., enterprises, large organizations). Since knowledge is an abstract concept possessed by an individual human being, for the specifications of a data base one needs some means:

(1) to express knowledge;
(2) to represent knowledge;
(3) to ensure a common understanding of the representation of knowledge among various human beings who share parts of this representation;
(4) and to manipulate the knowledge representation in order to reflect changes of the reality.

There is no disagreement that the knowledge expressible in a natural language (or in an abstracted field specific versions of a natural language) is the basis from which we start to construct symbolic representation. But, depending on the purpose of this symbolic representation, we can debate which representational tool should be chosen in order to construct adequate descriptions: texts, semantics nets [1], or data models [3,4].

Texts in a natural language are neither simple enough to allow the computations which are considered to be necessary on a data base nor are they sufficiently precise to serve as an easy understandable basis to communicate about the reality.

Current data base concepts provide the representation of knowledge in terms of primitives of a usually rather simple data model. Since different applications may require to express and represent different aspects of knowledge, one may debate which model provides the necessary representational capabilities in order to meet these requirements.

A more general and still rather formal concept to the representation of knowledge are semantic nets [1]. They have been developed in Artifical Intelligence to represent the meaning of natural language sentences. In recent years they gained some attractiveness as a basis for semantic schemata for data bases as well [5-11]. The rationales of the method may be briefly described as follows:

Symbols and connections among symbols are the primitives of semantic nets. The semantic net concept is based on the assumption that symbols have a meaning through human beings' ability to recognize their natural language word-sense meaning and through their connection to other symbols. This connection is called dependency, indicating that symbols involved in this dependency are in some way dependent upon each other.

<u>Example</u>

The connection of the symbol "SCHEDULE" with the symbols "ACTIVITY", "START", and "TERMINATION" characterizes a schedule as a listing of activities and their start and termination times.

In a graphical depiction of a semantic net, symbols are represented as nodes, dependencies as directed arcs.

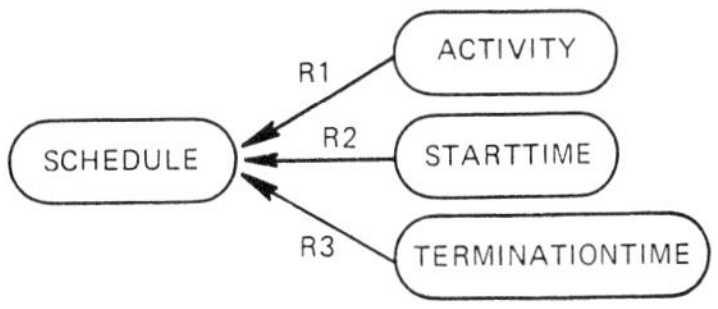

As we can see, the semantics of this representation are still rather vague. This semantic net represents a schedule in a very abstract sense. It does not indicate whether this is a schedule of a processor of a computer-system or a schedule for a transporation vehicle. In order to make the semantics more complete, one has to add other symbols and connect them to the exiisting graph.

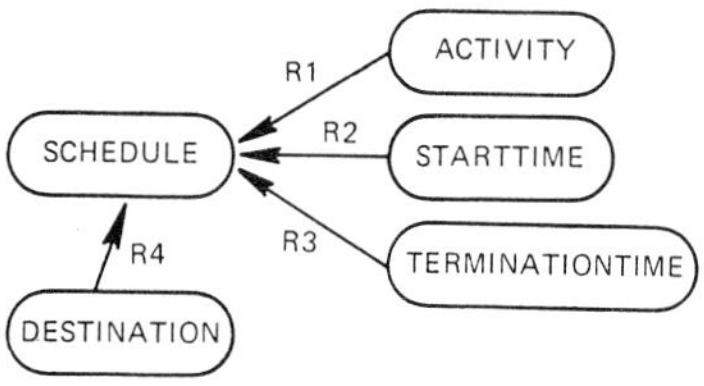

The connection of a symbol "DESTINATION" with the previously defined semantic net indicates - since processors can't have destinations - that it describes a vehicle schedule.

It is the general principle of the net-representation that its semantics could be made more specific by the connection of further symbols with the existing net. This "extendability" is the feature of the representational model to complete, modify, and correct the representation during its lifetime.

Although we agree that semantic nets may be considered as a basis for a data base semantic scheme, they lack in our opinion with respect to some very important requirements. We discuss therefore in the following chapter a number of requirements an adequate representational schema must meet and point out the deficiencies of semantic nets. Chapters 3 and 4 contain a proposal for an alternate schema which we hope will meet the requirements defined in Chapter 2.

2. ASSUMPTIONS AND REQUIREMENTS

Some basic assumptions about the purpose of data bases and the ways designers and users interact with a data base system will be specified now in order to define a realistic set of requirements for an adequate representational schema.

(1) The analysis of real phenomena and their description in a data base or in any other notation depends (as in other scientific fields like physics or engineering) on human beings' ability to master the complexity of the subject. The fundamental systems work by Simon [12] and Koestler [13] - among very many others - indicate that human beings' ability to develop representations is based to a large extent on their ingenuity in decomposing and describing complex phenomena in terms of subphenomena and their simultaneous simplification by ignoring facts of minor importance. A data base is therefore a representation of the hierarchical relationships between complex wholes and their constituent parts.

(2) Human beings (even well trained data base administrators) are unable to perceive and usually not interested to represent all aspects of a considered part of the reality. A data base is consequently not a complete representation but the result of a selective mapping of characteristics of the reality into the data base for a certain purpose. In order to make the data base usable for other purposes or to drop superfluous facts it becomes necessary to allow incremental changes of the representational schema. The creation and maintenance of a data base must therefore be considered as an evolutionary process.

(3) Due to the incompleteness of any representation and due to ambiguities in all possible notations (even in natural language) data bases never contain a universally valid description of the reality but rather the representation of facts which are only valid within a certain context.

(4) In most applications data bases are expected to be representations of characteristics of acting organizations. Possible actions will be specified in terms of possible changes of the representation. Due to the limited validity of representations, the possible changes of the same descriptive unit may be different in different contexts.

(5) Different human beings have different views of the reality (a different mental model in [14]). The common use of a data base by a number of users depends then on the mutual agreement about the information content of common parts of different mental models. It is highly improbable - and recent psycholinguistic research establishes some evidence [16] - that a total common understanding (i.e., the logical consistency) may be reached and recorded in a superschema. Data bases represent therefore rather a "union" of views than a uniform picture of the reality.

(6) The distribution of a data base over a number of computer systems in a communication network will be necessary in many applications. A central authority which guarantees the integrity of the entire data base and the compatibility among integrity constraints themselves contradicts the idea of distributed computing of independent users.

(7) In an increasing number of applications data bases will be interrogated and manipulated by nonprofessional programmers. High level user oriented languages for interrogation and manipulation purposes which support those users must be developed.

The basic assumptions listed above determine a number of very important requirements for an adequate representational schema

(i) Design and maintenance of a representational schema are very important and very difficult intellectual tasks. These tasks may be simplified if the representational schema suffices for the applicability of basic design principles. An adequate representational schema should therefore suffice for the description of hierarchical decompositions of usually rather complex real situations and for incremental changes of the decomposition hierarchy. It must then allow a hierarchical and highly modular structuring of data objects.

(ii) The correct deduction of the information content of the data base and its correct manipulation depend on an unambiguous representation. Since all possible notations lack with respect to this uniqueness criteria, an adequate representational schema must suffice for the explicit specification of contexts.

(iii) Representations are usually incomplete and therefore valid in a certain context only. Current concepts of data base management systems, on the other hand, provide universally applicable data base manipulations like insert, delete, and update. In order to preserve the meaning of data objects, it is very often necessary to specify a great number of exceptions for the applicability of those operations and the invocation of secondary operations. A knowledge representation in which a symbol may mean anything but those things which have been excluded explicitly is a misconception from our point of view. It is much more in accordance with systematic human thinking to specify tailored actions which reflect the meaning of individual data base objects since it is common practice to capture the reality in terms of semantic invariants and manipulations compatible with those invariants at the same time. An adequate representational schema is then expected to provide means to define context specific operations instead of integrity constraints.

(iv) The notion of a view refers not just to a subset of all data in the data base but to a particular mental model of a human being. Different views may prefer to look at the data base from different levels of detail or aggregation or may see different logical relationships among the data objects, etc. An adequate representational schema must suffice for the modelling of those coexisting views.

(v) Computer communication networks serve independent users in a coordinated fashion. They provide also means to distribute a data base over various locations in the net. In order to support the distribution of a data base, the representational model must be composed of independent modules connected by simple module interfaces.

(vi) Data bases will be interrogated and manipulated by nonprofessional programmers. Suitable representational models which support high level query language have already been developed [e.g., for the relational data model [17]). An adequate representational model, however, provides both support for high level query and manipulation languages.

In the light of the requirements specified above, we may now look at semantic nets again in order to be more specific about their deficiencies and the accordingly proposed modifications.

(1) Semantic nets are flat, i.e., they do not provide means to denote an entity which may be considered as a whole in another way than by enumerating all its components. They therefore fail to support the representation of hierarchical decompositions. This deficiency has been identified and an alternate hierarchical representation base been proposed in [18,19].

(2) The context of the description of an entity by a node symbol is defined by all the surrounding (i.e., directly connected) node symbols. Node symbols are therefore not independent modules of the net but rather components whose existence contributes to the meaning of all other components in the net. It is obvious that incremental changes may have unpredictable effects. This property may be acceptable for the representation of static (i.e., meaning keeping) texts but not for the representation of changing and acting organizations.

(3) Semantic nets do not provide means to represent context specific actions. They exclude the representation of procedural knowledge at all. It has however been shown that the analysis and description of acting organizations require the representation of their changing characteristics as well [20,21]. It is the main purpose of this paper to motivate the development of a representational schema which allows the simultaneous representation of declarative and procedural knowledge and to give an outline of its nature.

(4) Since semantic nets fail to provide means to represent information on different levels of detail and in different structural forms, they fail for the definition of different user views. The concept proposed in later parts of this paper is developed to offer an adequate view support.

(5) The nonmodularity of semantic nets hinders a simple distribution of the data base over various nodes in a computer communication network. The composition of the data base schema of selfcontained modules is therefore guaranteed in the concept defined below.

(6) The lack of semantic nets to provide means to represent information on different levels of detail is also the reason why they fail to support high level data base manipulation languages. The data and operation abstraction approach defined in the next chapter of this paper offers a solution to the problems described above.

3. ABSTRACTIONS

With the semantic net model in mind, we will now introduce our concept to build symbolic representations: abstractions. The primitives in our representational schema are -- as in semantic nets -- symbols and conceptual dependencies among symbols, e.g., the depiction below

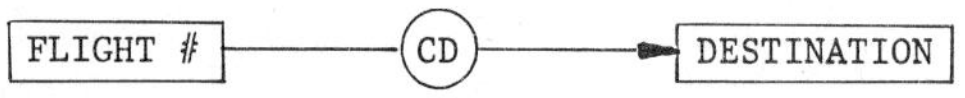

indicates that flightnumbers and destinations are related to each other. Instead of defining a fixed set of types of conceptual dependencies, we offer the opportunity to define arbitrary many. We require, however, that each new type will be explicitly specified in the representational schema. In other words, we expect the designer to specify the semantics of the links in the semantic network. With this specification a major deficiency of semantic nets (see Wood's in depth analysis in [22]) will be overcome.

In the concept dependencies characterize relationships but are considered as entities of their own right as well. They are compound entities of the somehow simpler dependent entities. Thus, dependencies are entities of higher order. They will be called abstract objects since they may be considered as more abstract than the components they link. An identifier which reflects the dependency (that may be a noun, a verb, a predicate, or the noun form of vers or predicates) must then be introduced to denominate the abstract object:

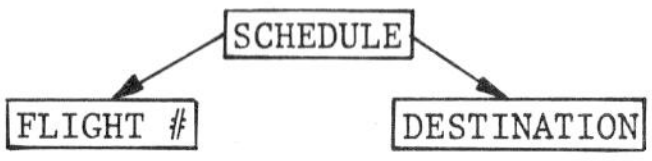

We will explain the concept and how it may suffice to define rather different abstract objects with the following examples.

3.1. Examples of abstractions

Classes of symbols. As a first kind of abstract object, we consider now classes of symbols. They are collections whose components may be identified by a common denominator. The symbols B707, B727, B747, DC10 constitute a collection of symbols. In order to simplify the communication about this collection, the term AIRPLANE may be introduced as an abstract representation of the entire collection and of the individual types of planes. In order to indicate the hierarchical relationship between individual plane identifiers and the class representing identifier, one may draw the following depiction

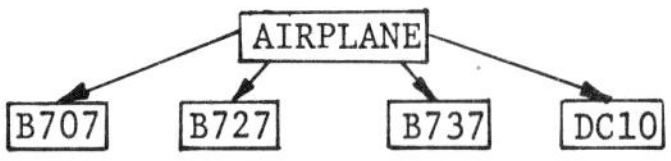

It is common practice in natural languages to use the same denominator to identify rather different things. Suppose the symbols CABIN, WING, ENGINE, WHEELS are brought together to form the abstract object AIRPLANE which may be depicted as follows:

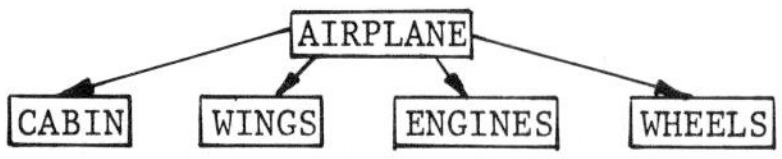

The identifier AIRPLANE now represents totally different things in the two different examples. The natural way to express the distinctiveness of the two from a data base point of view (since we intend to do something with the content of a data base) is to specify what one can do with this symbolic representation (i.e., retrieving and changing its information content).

It is obvious that one may add and delete components in the first example if certain preconditions (e.g., the added symbol is a legal plane identifier) hold:

IF CONDITION(X) DO ADD-PLANE(x)
IF CONDITION(X) DO DELETE-PLANE(x)

The symbol AIRPLANE, however, denotes in the second example not just a set of different components but an architecture of an airplane. Any change of the abstract object by component adding or deleting then changes this architecture concept as well. We would therefore prefer to keep the object unchangeable at all.

Dependencies among classes of symbols. The second kind of abstraction of great importance to the representation of knowledge we will consider here are dependencies among classes of symbols. As an example we choose the knowledge a data base should provide about flights given in the following verbal form:

(1) Every flight is uniquely determined by a flight number;
(2) The class of symbols used to denote flight numbers may be any natural number between x and y;
(3) Flights start at a certain start time;
(4) The class of symbols used to denote start times may be any of the time figures between 0:00 am to 12:00 pm.

The facts described above may be represented by an abstract object STARTTIME TABLE which denotes a functional dependency between the F# class and the ST-T class of symbols. The common way to identify functional dependencies (e.g., F#→ST-T) will be replaced by the previously introduced hierarchical depiction

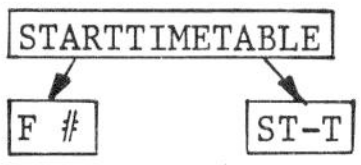

Despite its similar depiction, this time the drawn hierarchical relationship between the abstract object and its components is of a rather different nature. It does not represent a set inclusion relation as in the example above but the dependency between the two symbol classes F# and ST-T. Consequently, the way these two abstract objects will be manipulated makes all the difference between them. One may change the object by changes of its components F# and ST-T only.

IF CONDITION(F#) DO ADD FLIGHT(f#,st-t)
IS ADD(f#)
ADD(st-t)
IF CONDITION(F#) DO CANCEL FLIGHT(f#,st-t)
IS DROP(f#)
DROP(st-t)
IF CONDITION(F#) DO CHANGE STARTTIME(f#,$st\text{-}t_i$,$st\text{-}t_j$)
IS UPDATE($st\text{-}t_i \rightarrow st\text{-}t_j$)

The components F# and ST-T of the abstract object STARTTIME TABLE may be changed by simultaneous adds, deletes, and by updates of their components f# and st-t, respectively.

The operation specifications above automatically take care of the fact that primary key updates (e.g., flight number updates) may lead to unlegal states. They are consequently avoided.

Loop dependencies. The same abstraction principle may be applied in order to define an abstract object of yet another totally different nature. Suppose again a data base contains flight information. In order to assign unique starttimes to all destinations of a flight on its way back to its origin, one may define an abstract object FLIGHTSCHEDULE which represents a set of tuples composed of a location and starttime component (loc_i,$st\text{-}t_i$). One may represent this abstraction again by the following hierarchical depiction. (This example hopefully demonstrates clearly that this depiction concept differs drastically from traditional access path representations of data structures.)

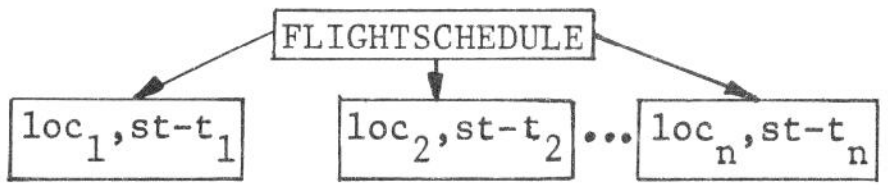

It is obvious that the way the abstract object will be manipulated determines its totally different nature.

```
IF CONDITION(LOC)
  DO CHANGE STARTTIME(loc_i,st-t_i,st-t_j)
  IS FOR k=i TO n DO
  FOR k=1 TO i-1 DO
  UPDATE(difference (st-t_i,st-t_j))
```

The specification of the CHANGE STARTTIME operation reflects the condition that the flight duration will remain constant (at least as long as it has not been changed by an authorized user).

A more detailed specification of relations and abstract objects which encompass relations as components may be found in [23].

3.2. The semantics of abstract objects

As we have shown in the previous examples, our notion of dependency differs somehow from the one in the semantic net concept. Here dependencies don't just represent associations among entities - but may be considered as entities of their own right. Their computer representation may be manipulated like any other data object (they may be inserted/deleted into/form a data base, and be changed in a way compatible with their semantics). We even took the standpoint that every dependency declared among entities is the representation of a higher order, i.e., more abstract, entity.

By taking a deeper look into the problem, we discover that our notion of dependency is in fact a notation for the kind of interactions among a whole and its parts, i.e., between an abstract object and its components. We have already made a very important assumption about these interactions. In our view, they are restricted to those between the abstract object and its components. The components are in no other "direct" interaction relationship to each other. This interaction pattern in fact may be represented by a hierarchical composition schema. The concept of dependency, or abstraction as it has been developed here, therefore corresponds to the notion of "nearly decomposable systems" in [12]. It is claimed there that those composition schemata suffice for the representation of the most complex phenomena human beings can handle at all. Consequently, they should be general enough for data base purposes as well.

In fact, one may show that the abstraction method suffices to represent those semantic concepts as:

- object-attribute-value relationships [24]
- compound objects [8]
- compound attributes [8]
- n:n, n:1 and 1:n relationships [25]
- unidirectional, bidirectional and neutral relationships [5,26]
- intrarelational dependencies [27]
- relations [3]
- interrelational dependencies [8,19]
- entities [6,8]

While some of these constructs are very well understood, some others are still rather vague. A more careful analysis shows that those concepts whose operational characteristics are properly described as well are semantically clear and comprehensive.

We do not want to argue here whether the list given above encompasses the proper semantic primitives (or primitives at all) for the conceptual schema of a data base. All we want to say is that there is a need for a proper specification of primitives and their proper composition. We do not even think there is a need to have one or a small number of primitives. We would rather like to provide the user a reliable instrument to define his own application oriented primitives whenever he feels like doing so. The abstraction concept provides the framework a user needs to perform this task.

Abstract objects impose through their type specification some restrictions with respect to their permissible compositions of components and consequently with respect to the operations permissible on them. The specification of permissible compositions and operations, however, is in fact a representation of meaning in terms of semantic invariants and manipulation characteristics compatible with these invariants. (We may also call it the specification of a state space for an object and of the operations whose execution will always lead to a legal state in the state space.)

4. D-GRAPHS

Although the notion of abstraction may be considered as a generic concept for the representation of knowledge, one may show that it is necessary to allow abstract objects to be composed repeatedly in a hierarchic fashion. The repeated application of the abstraction concept leads then to a hierarchically structured net. In order to refine and complete a symbolic representation, we provide only those extensions of the net which correspond to new abstractions. One can see very easily that the hierarchic abstraction concept may not be represented within a tree-like composition schema. One can imagine very many situations where components are the constituents of more than one abstract object (the concept of a domain in the relational model as a constituent of more than one relation is an example for such a composition). Thus we propose a graph representation which permits the representation of "logically shared" components. The representation graph for the knowledge embedded in a data base will therefore be a directed acyclic graph. We will call those representational graphs D-graphs later on in this paper. The notion of dependency we introduced above prevents us from building more complex structures than those D-graph structures in a straightforward way.

One may then define D-graphs as follows.

4.1. The definition of D-graphs

A D-graph (Dependency-graph) is composed of two kinds of nodes: terminal nodes which represent atomic (non-decomposable) objects and nonterminal nodes representing abstract objects. With the directed arcs of this graph we associate the relationship "contains". (As we have seen, the meaning of "contains" is not the same in all cases. In some cases it may represent a set inclusion relation - in others another coupling.) Common subcomponents of different abstract objects are represented as nodes to which a number of arcs point. The number of components of an abstract object is depicted by the number of emanating arcs from the node representing this abstract object.

We use the following graphical depiction of D-graphs (the arcs are supposed to point downwards).

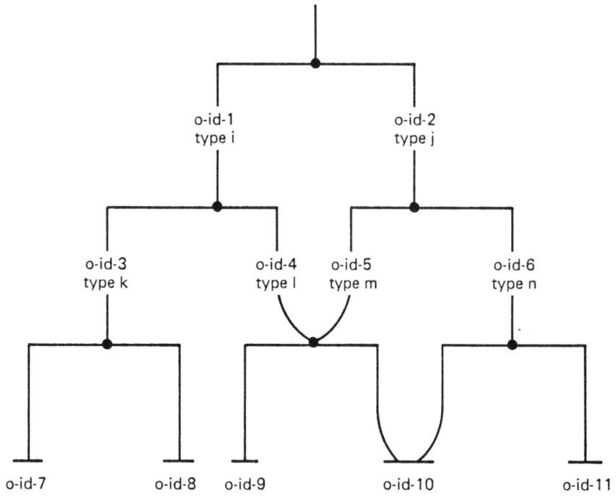

Definitions:

(1) Nodes in the D-graph represent data base objects
(2) Selector labels identify objects and denote their type
(3) Objects have an information content which may include other objects. If an object B is part of the information content of object A, an arc is drawn from A to B carrying the object identifier B as a selector in the D-graph to indicate this containment.
(4) Every data base object has a type associated with it, and every object is a member of exactly one type.
(5) With their type specification we define the information content of data base objects (their composition of more primitive objects) and their changing properties expressed in terms of the operations permissible on them.

This definition indicates that all objects have to be distinct in the data base and that objects may be created only if they are distinct from all existing objects. The definition also indicates that objects, once created, must exist at least as long in the data base as they are part of the information content of any other object. A more elaborate definition of D-graphs may be found in [23]. In order to avoid a misinterpretation of the concept it should however be noted again that the D-graph is by no means the representation of an access structure. In fact arbitrary complex access structures for the components of an abstract object may be described in the abstract object's type specification. The D-graph provides instead different abstract descriptions of collections of primitives.

4.2. The semantics of D-graphs

One may represent arbitrary deep decompositions of complex phenomena (or arbitrary complex abstractions composed of primitive facts) within a D-graph framework. The semantics of abstract objects is determined by their inherited properties (from higher level abstract objects) and by their dependents (their components). The semantic analysis of an abstract object encompasses therefore the scanning and semantic analysis of its ancestor and sibling objects (until one reaches terminal objects).

Data base objects may belong to the information content of a number of other - more abstract - data base objects. A component may then have a slightly different meaning in the different abstract objects encompassing it. The different semantics of a component in different abstract objects are due to different preconditions on manipulations of the component objects as specified in the abstract objects' type specification. We therefore say an abstract object specifies a context for the interpretation of the description of its component objects.

Example

The relationship OCCUPANCY which denotes the dependency among NUMBER OF PASSENGERS and AVAILABLE SEATS must be a (≤)-relationship within an airplane context but may be a ($\lesseqgtr$)-relationship in a train context.

The abstract object specifies one particular universe of discourse and the meaning of the components within the universe. It is obvious then that the meaning of an object may be narrowed by means of preconditions, and it may be broadened by referencing it in other contexts.

With the context specification the concept also offers means to define context specific operations. This, in turn, is a precondition for the representation of

- compositions of components and their meaning preserving manipulations for arbitrary complex objects;
- overlapping complex objects;
- relationships among relationships;
- views (i.e., different mental models);
- and of independent modules of the data base's information content (in order to support the distribution of the data base.

For an in depth explanation of these semantic constructs within the D-graph framework, we refer - due to the lack of space in this description - to [23].

5. CONCLUSION

The representation of knowledge in terms of both data models and semantic nets requires the definition and enforcement of integrity constraints. One may roughly distinguish two types of integrity assertions:

The first type of integrity constraints are those which are necessary, since the data model does not support the specification of all types of dependencies which one would like to enforce in order to model the reality in an adequate way.

The abstraction concept, however, has been developed to offer exactly this. One may even conclude that the necessity to define such an integrity constraint follows from the existence of a more abstract mental model which incorporates the dependent models as components.

The second kind of integrity constraints which have to be represented are supposed to compensate another disadvantage of other representations. They provide means for a more complete characterization of (1) the static characteristics of already defined abstract objects, e.g., the set of valid components of an abstract object, and (2) the behavioral characteristics of already defined abstract objects, e.g., how objects of a certain type may be manipulated.

These integrity constraints are in fact restrictions on the set of possible compositions of components in a certain context and restrictions on the permissible operations in the components. Thus, the abstraction concept as introduced above may be considered as the natural means to specify those constraints as well. This in fact indicates that choosing proper abstractions and specifying them in a detailed manner makes the rather unnatural distinction between meaning represented in terms of data models or semantic nets and in terms of integrity assertions superfluous.

With this result we are able to fulfill one of the requirements defined in the first section of the paper. How some of the other requirements - in particular how the concept supports views and manipulations of the data base through different views - may be met with the D-graph model may be found in [23], some others have still to be elaborated.

REFERENCES

[1] Simmons, R. F. "Semantic Networks: Their Computations and Use for Understanding English Sentences," in [2].

[2] Schank, R. C. and Colby, K. M. (1973) "Computer Models of Thought and Language," W. H. Freeman and Co., San Francisco.

[3] Codd, E. F. (1970) "A Relational Model of Data for Large Shared Data Banks," Comm. ACM 13, 6.

[4] CODASYL Systems Committee. (1974) "Report of the CODASYL Data Base Task Group," ACM.

[5] Abrial, J. R. (1974) "Data Semantics," in J. W. Klimbie and K. L. Koffeman (eds.) Data Base Management, North Holland.

[6] Chen, P. P. S. (1976) "The Entity-Relationship Model: Toward a Unified View of Data," ACM Transactions on Data Base Systems 1 (1), pp. 9-36.

[7] Roussopoulos, N. and Mylopoulus, J. (1975) "Using Semantic Networks for Data Base Management," in Proceedings of the International Conference on Very Large Data Bases, Sept. 22-24, 1975, Framingham, Mass. (ACM, New York).

[8] Schmid, H. A. and Swenson, J. R. (1975) "On the Semantics of the Relational Model," in ACM SIGMOD International Conference on Management of Data, May 14-16, 1975, San Jose, California, W. F. King (ed.).

[9] Senko, M. E. (1975) "Information Systems: Records, Relations, Sets, Entities, and Things," Information Systems 1 (1), pp. 1-13.

[10] Sowa, J. R. (1976) "Conceptual Graphs for a Data Base Interface," IBM J. Res. and Dev. 20 (4), pp. 336-357.

[11] Sundgren, B. (1974) "Conceptual Foundations of the Infological Approach to Data Bases," in J. W. Klimbie and K. L. Koffeman (eds.), Data Base Management, North Holland.

[12] Simon, H. A. (1962) "The Architecture of Complexity," Proc. of the American Philosophy Society, Vol. 106, No. 6.

[13] Koestler, A. (1967) The Ghost in the Engine, Henry Regency Co.

[14] Nijssen, G. M. "A Gross Architecture for the Next Generation Data Base Management Systems in [15].

[15] Nijssen, G. M. (ed.) (1976) Modelling in Data Base Management Systems, North Holland.

[16] Norman, D. A. and Rumdhart, D. E. (1975) Explorations in Cognition, Freeman, San Francisco.

[17] Codd, E. F. (1972) "Relational Completeness of Data Base Sublanguages," in Rustin, R. (ed.) Data Base Systems, Prentice Hall, Englewood Cliffs.

[18] Smith, J. M. and Smith D. C. P. (1976) "Data Base Abstraction," in Proceeding of the ACM Conference on Data: Abstraction, Definition, and Structure, March 1976, Salt Lake City.

[19] Weber, H. "A Semantic Model of Integrity Constrains on a Relational Data Base," in [15].

[20] Langefors, B. (1974) "Theoretical Aspects of Information Systems for Management," in Information Processing, North Holland.

[21] Hammer, M. M., Howe, W. G., and Wladawski, T. (1974), "An Interactive Business Definition Language," SIGPLAN Not. 9, 4.

[22] Woods, W. A. (1975) "What's a Link: Foundations for Semantic Networks," in Bobrow, D. G. and Collins, A., Representation and Understanding, Academic Press.

[23] Weber, H. (1976) "The D-graph Model of Large Shared Data Bases: A Representation of Integrity Constraints and Views as Abstract Data Types," IBM Research Report RJ1875.

[24] Raphael, B. (1964) "A Computer Program Which 'Understands'," AFIPS Conference Proceedings.

[25] Engels, R. W. (1972) "A Tutorial on Data Base Organization," Annual Review in Automatic Programming, Vol. 7, Part 1, Pergammon Press.

[26] Kent, W. (1976) "New Criteria for the Conceptual Model," in Lockemann, P. C. and Neuhold, E. J., Systems for Large Data Bases, North Holland.

[27] Codd, E. F. (1972) "Further Normalization of the Data Base Relational Model," in Rustin, R., Data Base Systems, Prentice Hall, Englewood Cliffs.

E. Morlet and D. Ribbens, (Eds.), International Computing Symposium 1977.

PRIVACY PROTECTION - IS IT JUST AN ENGINEERING ISSUE?

H. R. Schuchmann,
Siemens AG,
Munich, Western Germany

During the last years the problems related to the use of computers have expanded from merely technical concerns to include more and more issues of a sociological or even political nature. The discussion on protection of information privacy, which has been going on for about ten years now, is an obvious indication of this broader view. This paper reviews the problem of privacy, summarizes results from efforts to protect privacy, and outlines expected impacts of technical improvements in computer architecture on both the privacy problem and possible solutions for it.

1. INTRODUCTION

A technical tool like the computer has a certain impact on sociological and political aspects of society. This is emphasized by the term "computer revolution", coined in analogy to "industrial revolution". Hedberg /1/ points out that this effect runs through four distinguishable phases, which indicate the changing relationship between the triggering event and the effects on its environment. The first phase is one of "technical optimism: Here is the technology, let us built the machines". This is followed by a phase of "concern for safety", in which interest grows for "the latent physical conflict between men and machines". A third phase, the "ergonomic phase" acknowledges man as a "physio-anatomical system" which has to be considered already within the design phase of a technical tool. Finally, a "human-oriented design phase", in which the motivation for new technical design results predominantly from the intention to "build machines that will help human self-realization".

Regarding the state of the art of computer development from this point of view, we are currently in phase two. An obvious indication for this is the increased awareness of the impact of computers on their users and on those who are affected by computer applications. This awareness is especially pronounced in the discussion of information privacy which started about ten years ago and is reflected in a number of papers on this subject. Two quite early documents are most frequently referenced: A discussion by Petersen /2/ on various technical aspects of protection and its potential violation, and a study on sociological and political consequences of computer applications prepared by Westin /3/.

In the following presentation we are going to critically review this period of discussion on privacy. We start with the problem of privacy itself which, on closer inspection, is a twofold one. Various mechanisms have been considered in order to protect privacy, some of which have also been implemented. The results of these efforts will be summarized. Finally we want to point out technical improvements from which further impacts can be expected.

2. THE OBJECT OF PRIVACY

The notion of privacy is meaningful only with respect to an object. According to Webster's Dictionary there are two such relevant objects, namely property and person.

With respect to property, privacy denotes the quality of being private, i.e. of belonging to a particular person. This quality has the characteristic of a right. The right is violated if unauthorized access to private property occurs, independent of possible consequences to the property itself or to the proprietor.

With respect to a person, privacy denotes one's private life, i.e. one's personal affairs. It is an abstraction for a sphere within which personality can expand, a sphere consisting of thoughts, facts, actions etc. This privacy is not automatically violated by the very knowledge about it but only by a certain intention to make use of it.

Consequently, in regard to the application of computers there are two privacy problems to be distinguished. The first relates to multi-user systems where information has to be protected against unauthorized human access. The second relates to the application of information processing in human affairs, i.e. the decoding of knowledge from stored personal data and its evaluation. The point is, that protection of privacy in the first case is directed towards the user of the system - thus protecting the system which in turn is conceptually responsible for protecting users against each other - while in the second case it is directed towards the application of the system - thus protecting persons being in general not users of the system.

2.1 THE PRIVACY OF STORED INFORMATION

Multi-user systems have been introduced for two reasons, namely to achieve increased efficiency of a computer installation by keeping all of its parts permanently busy and to permit the sharing of data among several independent users. The first requires strict isolation, the second demands support of properly controlled cooperation. Stored information is the property of the user who created it and/or imported it into the system; hence he may distribute or deny the authorization to access his private information.

The attributes "private" or "public" thus indicate an access right.

Protection of information privacy therefore means protection of the ownership of information and the control mechanisms necessary to share private information. Both are primarily technical problems resulting from the transition from single to multi-user systems; they are therefore home-made problems and not application inherent.

The cause for a violation of the privacy may be unintentional, i.e. it may result from a temporary failure of the computer system or from a user error; the latter should be conceptually detectable by the system and can therefore be viewed as an error in designing the system. The motive for a deliberate attack may be an attempt to get some illegal benefits in using the system; other motives are destruction of information (sabotage) or illegal access to information (espionage).

Mechanisms internal to the computer system for protecting information privacy are based on sophisticated means of addressing indirection. They have been discussed systematically mainly by Dennis /5/ amd Lampson /6/. Their proposals have had major influence on the development of the MULTICS operating system /7/ which is the result of a long-term project studying the requirements for a secure operating system. A more general solution avoiding certain deficiencies of the MULTICS system is given by Jones /8/. Among several surveys on protection mechanisms, the paper by Saltzer /9/ seems to be the most accurate and comprehensive one.

Threats to information privacy from outside the computer system - e.g. by wiretapping or by masquerading - and potential safeguards against them, have so far only been discussed informally; there exists no closed model from which the various proposed mechanisms could be derived. Further there is no substantial progress in this area. Thus the early paper by Petersen /2/ is conceptuelly still up-to-date.

2.2 PERSONAL PRIVACY

The concept of personal privacy has no fixed meaning. Rather it depends on the political conviction of how the inherent conflict between the individual claim for autonomy and the public claim for surveillance and control can be solved. In a democracy the solution is based on a controlled balance between the diversity of individual interests and a kind of common interest represented by legitimate authorities.

It is difficult to define personal privacy precisely in this context. What is meant is a title to a private sphere, which is believed to be essential for each person. Westin /3/ points out, that privacy stands for personal autonomy, i.e. emotional release, self-evaluation, and the right to choose or not to choose partners for communication.

There exists a complex relationship between privacy and the knowledge of personal data. Certain personal data are available to everybody (e.g. name, address, profession), some of them can be gathered easily (e.g. data on personal behaviour) some of them are quite often not known to the person whom they characterize (e.g. certain medical data). Thus privacy is not necessarily violated by the very knowledge of such personal data but by gathering or using them against the interest of the person affected by it. Such violation may be caused unintentionally or deliberately.

The necessity of protecting personal privacy already existed before the use of the computer in public administration. The problem, however, has been substantially intensified with its introduction. Two aspects have to be considered, namely a political and a more conceptual one.

The political aspects refers to the balance between private and public influence. By means of centralized data bases, bureaucracies have a large amount of personal data at their disposal which can be evaluated within a a short amount of time. This fact increases the power of administrative institutions and encourages misuse. To compensate this effect several national proposals for privacy legislation have been discussed mainly in Great Britain, Sweden, the United States, and Germany; a few of them have become statute-law. They are conceptually based on four principles which, however, are not always intended to be realized in full strength: (1) The knowledge of a person about what personal data are recorded on him, (2) the requirement of the person's authorization to use and/or transfer his personal data, (3) the obligation to record all accesses to personal data, and finally (4) the commitment to keep all personal data permanently accurate and complete. These principles include the person's guarantee to be able to check - and potentially to claim - their observation.

A recently published comprehensive study on information processing in human affairs by Mowshowitz /10/ emphasizes the potential misuse of computerized data bases by bureaucracies. The author further argues that the often cited "increasing complexity of administrative tasks" which is used to justify the necessity for even more powerful computer support is in fact a "concomitant of the centralisation of power and not a 'natural' feature of social evolution". There seems to be a vicious circle between centralisation tendencies within the bureaucracies and the increased application of computer systems for administrative purposes.

This point is also stressed by Weizenbaum /4/ from a more conceptual point of view. The power of a new tool does not only enable its users to do things better and in some sense more efficiently. It also pushes away the insight that certain problems require a solution by structural reorganisation. This leads subsequently to a dependency on the tool without really a solving of the problem and finally makes the tool indispensable; the invention of the tool then appears to have happened just in time.

Another important point refers to the suitability of computerized models for human problems in general. Minsky /11/ has already discussed the fact, that a model does not only reflect more or less accurately that excerpt from reality which it intends to represent but it automatically includes the view of its originator. Thus a model is always subjective with respect to the selection of data and their subsequent interpretation. Personal data are a model of an individual, whether they are gathered and stored manually or by a computer. In the latter case, however, there is an obvious tendency to trust the output of a computer because the sheer amount of available data stored and the precision and speed with which they can be processed surpass human capabilities. Thereby it is quite often disregarded that the reliability of a computed result decisively depends on the accuracy of the stored input-data and on their adequate selection. This attitude is interpreted by Weizenbaum /4/ as a confusion of judgement and calculation resulting from the belief that conceptually all problems are those of technical computability. In his opinion "there are certain tasks which computers ought not be made to do, independent of whether computers can be made to do them".

3. EXPERIENCES WITH IMPLEMENTED PROTECTION MECHANISMS

In a figurative sense, protection is not a "boolean" quality which is either granted or not granted, but it is an "analog" quality. There exists a smooth transition from no protection at all to absolute protection. The latter never can be realized because it would require strict isolation which is contradictory to the claim for a certain degree of communication. The expense of protection increases exponentially with its efficiency which, however, cannot really be quantified on a general scale. For a certain implemented protection mechanism we can only state the conditions under which protection is granted; otherwise their effect is more or less undefined.

The environment of a computer application is quite often different from that which the system designers had in mind. We therefore want to find out how efficiently stored information is currently protected within a computer with existing protection mechanisms and what kind of threats to information privacy have occured in the past. Finally some economical aspects have to be considered.

3.1 THE EFFICIENCY OF PROTECTION MECHANISMS

There is much interest - especially in the academic area - in models for secure computer systems but most of them have never been tested for their efficiency under real conditions. This is due to the fact that the few implemented systems designed with security aspects in mind - e.g. MULTICS or ADEPT-50 - are not in wide use, while the majority of systems in use have not been designed to be secure. In a few cases security measures were added to a system after it had been already completed; the RSS approach of IBM for their OS/360 is an example of this strategy.

Studies on the vulnerability of concrete computer systems are likely to have been performed, however, their results are not published. There are mainly two exceptions: Attanasio /12/ checked the integrity of IBM's VM/370 and the Lawrence Livermore Laboratory published some results of an ongoing "Research in Secured Operating Systems" (RISOS), examining several powerful computer systems systematically.

Three general sources for the vulnerability of computer systems have been discovered which, however, are not very surprising. Current protection mechanisms are mainly built around the CPU and its primary storage, the secondary storage and the I/O mechanisms are therefore possible entry points for penetrators. The second weakness refers to system failures. Automatic reconfiguration and recovery, if systematically studied at all - as e.g. by Schell /13/ and Stern /14/ - usually do not take into account that in abnormal situations the protective power of a system should increase instead of decrease as it is currently the fact. Finally vulnerability increases quite often, if modifications, corrections, and functional enhancements are applied to the system.

From these results, it can be concluded that almost all current computer systems are not sufficiently secure. They are vulnerable because of their inconsistant level of protection mechanisms; thus the efficiency of their sophisticated mechanisms can be bypassed. Further, attempts for penetration which could be prevented by the system are in most cases not recorded; this makes it nearly impossible to get quantitative figures.

3.2 THREATS TO INFORMATION PRIVACY

From time to time newspapers present stories reporting on cases of sabotage and espionage in computer centers, e.g. penetrations into banking accounts, payroll systems, or booking systems. The question is whether this kind of attack represents a significant part of violations of information privacy.

At Stanford University Parker /15/ gathered 350 well-documented computer incidents in a "computer abuse case file" which was used to categorize the violations of system integrity. The results - as given by Nielson /16/ - indicate that in more than 30 % of the cases the integrity of data was violated manually outside the system storing the private data. This was done by alterations of data before their entry into the computer system and/or after their output from there, or by manipulating the application software in the design, implementation or maintenance stages. Violations by penetrating the system at runtime, i.e. through bypassing built-in protection mechanisms, occurred in 20 % of the registered cases. This result indicates that careful procedures around the computer system are probably more important to information privacy than technical means.

Human carelessness in handling personal data are another important source for violations of information privacy. The commissioner for data security in Hessen (GFR) reported quite recently on several incidents of this kinds: a police office submitted personal data to a private punching office, authentic data from an ordnance-survey office were used as test data and later found undestroyed on a waste area, material given to pollsters on request has been used to deduce private information.

Apparently, threats to privacy cannot be prevented with technical measures alone; in addition a certain awareness for the value of privacy and the acceptance of responsibility for its protection is necessary. Further, we should not expect a computer to solve human problems, which cannot be solved algorithmically at all.

3.3 ECONOMICAL ASPECTS

For a long time it was uphold that computerized data processing reduces costs. Meanwhile effective costs for using and maintaining computer installations - i.e. hardware and software - have been recorded and indicate, that the effect of the expected rationalization is often less impressive. The costs will further increase with additional hardware and software necessary to grant the privacy of personal data according to legislative regulations.

Up to now the cost of privacy has not effectively been measured on running systems. A comprehensive simulation under quite realistic circumstances, which has been carried out by Goldstein /17/, however, presents some quantitative results. The study is based on six personal data systems: a hospital computer network, two law-enforcement systems, a personnel system for employees and systems for a credit organisation and an insurance company. The results indicate initial privacy conversion costs as between 10 % and 600 % of the original development costs and an increase in the annual operating costs as between 10 % and 200 %. It will depend on how valuable the quality of personal privacy is estimated to be, whether either a redesign of the privacy legislation, or a reorientation in gathering more and more personal data will take place, if these figures are to be confirmed. As a third alternative, persons would have to pay more and more for services, even if they don't want them.

The violation of information privacy causes damages for which the holder of personal data is liable for compensation. These damages must, however, be seen in relation to other economical damages caused by the use of computers. For and on behalf of several European insurance companies, Diebold Europe /18/ recently presented a forecast until 1988 on economical losses caused by computer applications in three selected areas, namely management, process control and public administration. According to that study, total annual damages within Europe of about $ 2,700 Mill. are expected, which are to be doubled if all areas of computer application are included. They are spread for 42 % on user errors, 33 % on machine failures, 15 % on errors in programming and evaluation of results and the remaining 10 % on various effects including deliberate abuse of computers for fraud and espionage. These figures lead to the conjecture, that possible violations of information privacy are currently much more likely to be due to human errors without any malicious intention and that technical protection mechanism will have very little influence on them. The stimulation for deliberate attacks, however, might grow with the benefits an attacker can expect. The implementation of an "Electronic Funds Transfer System" (EFTS) which currently is discussed in the United States, could for example turn out to have a substantial impact into this direction.

4. SOURCES FOR TECHNICAL IMPROVEMENTS OF PRIVACY PROTECTION

Improvement of privacy protection does not necessarily require a "second generation" of protection mechanisms. A better understanding of what kind of data processing is suitable and how to adjust computer systems more effectively to their human users may reduce the privacy problem substantially. Three technical areas are expected to contribute to this development, namely improvements in data base technology, decentralisation of computer power, and the application of intelligent terminals at the man-machine interface level.

Accumulated data which are stored in a computer are a data base. Our current distinction between a file, a library, and a data base is as unconvincing as our distinction between primary storage, secondary storage for paging, and secondary storage for files. It reflects historical developments and aspects of technical implementation which need not be visible to the user of a computer system. Thus it is not surprising that the interest of well known researchers and research projects currently moves quite obviously from operating systems to data base systems. Dodd /19/, reporting from a workshop organized by the National Bureau of Standards (NBS) and the Association for Computing Machinery (ACM) in Florida in October 1975 outlines, that the current "state-of-the-art for data base design reminds one of that for building bridges a century ago". Concrete data is missing on the definition and current use of data base systems. Three major topics for further research are indicated, namely usability - including aspects of reliability - architecture, and improvements with respect to new models, relational interferences, natural languages and data base semantics. It can be expected that a more systematic and consistant way of storing and manipulating data within a computer, will also improve the protection of these data against unintentional errors, system failures, and deliberate attacks.

One of the basic principles in organizing a democratic society is the division of power. Currently this principle is partly overlayed by the conviction, that administrations using centralized computer installations perform more efficiently. This, however, results mainly from the high cost of hardware machinery. For the future, decreasing hardware costs will support a just beginning tendency for decentralization. This is triggered by three effects:

The obvious inflexibility of centralized computing power to handle "non-standard" cases, the high overhead to be paid for reliability, and the complexity of centralized systems which is reflected in the costs of their software. It seems to be more than a singular event that one of the most powerful banking houses in the United States - the New York City Bank - is currently investing great efforts in decentralizing various data processing activities. In conventional manual processing of personal data, decentralization has been the major protection against threats to personal privacy; computerized data processing is expected to move into this direction, too.

Experiences with current computer systems have demonstrated a high degree of human errors in using them; this is due to inadequate user interfaces. The situation is expected to change with the development of more intelligent terminals. "Intelligent" in this context means that the machinery will hide superfluous technical details, that it will be more adaptable to a specific user or task, and that it will be able to detect and prevent more user errors. Intelligent terminals could support for example the decentralisation of protection, and enable the surveillance of stored personal data by the person to whom they belong, for correctness and legality as provided by proposed privacy legislation. Currently we have the technical mechanisms to built intelligent terminals but on a broad scale we still do not have a clear concept of how to use them in a feasable manner. Putting a microprocessor into a conventional terminal does not automatically make it intelligent.

5. CONCLUSION

We have discussed the privacy problems raised by computer applications from two sides, namely as the problem of shielding private user data in a multi-user system against unauthorized access and as the problem to protect the privacy of an individual against computer aided violations through bureaucracies. Since several years there have been efforts in investigating both problems. The lack of commonly accepted goals and economical aspects of implementing proposed protection mechanisms have so far prevented a general breakthrough in this area. This is likely to change because the privacy problems become more urgent and the technological possibilities available now allow for practicable solutions.

Most technical tools developed in the past have had certain side effects which either emerge as consequences of the application of a tool which originally its designers were unaware of, or they result from changing the intention in using it. The difficulty to handle side-effects is due to their latency, to evaluate their harmlessness or the threshold of their harmful interference, and finally to invent countermeasures and to receive a feedback of their effect. Regarding for example the invention of X-rays, experiences show that - with a certain delay - a reasonable way could be found to prevent dangerous and irreversible side-effects without impeding their useful and economical application.

Current computer systems are already subject to several regulations for security: They must be constructed e.g. in a way, that no parts leading voltage can be touched, that video-terminals do not transmit X-rays and that the interference of radio frequency bands generated by the hardware is kept inside the computer cabinets. These regulations have their price but it seems quite natural to us that it be paid - in the case of a desk calculator as well as in the case of an installation for a large computer center.

There is no reason to doubt that the enormous power of information processing can be successfully applied to human affairs without overestimating its effect and without threatening personal privacy. The computer industry should recognize the challenge to use its technological improvements for avoiding the negative side effects of computers instead of searching mainly for new application areas. The political conclusion to be drawn is, that we are still in schedule with Orwell's /20/ famous vision for 1984 predicted nearly 30 years ago. If this fact will become more aware to the public opinion before reasonable means to prevent the possibility for total surveillance are in operation, a strong emotional resistance against computer applications in general is likely to grow. The opposition against nuclear power stations currently emerging in Germany is an example, that public concern about real or imaginary hazards for society have not been taken seriously.

With respect to privacy protection, we do not suggest a modern version of the country "Erewhon" invented more than hundred years ago by the English novelist Samuel Butler /21/, where it is forbidden to own machines. We only suggest to use our technical knowledge to built more reasonable machines, such that their undesirable side-effects are tolerable and can be kept under control.

Acknowledgement: The author wishes to thank Dr. Jan Witt for his helpful comments and Mrs. D. Ebert for stylistical improvements.

6. REFERENCES

/1/ Hedberg, B., Mumford, E., *"The design of computer systems"*, Proc. IFIP Conference on Human Choice and Computers, pp. 31-59, Vienna, April 1-5, 1974

/2/ Petersen, H.E., Turn, R., *"System implications of information privacy"*, AFIPS Spring Joint Computer Conference (1967), pp. 291-300

/3/ Westin, A.F., *"Privacy and Freedom"*, Atheneum, New York (1967)

/4/ Weizenbaum, J., *"Computer Power and Human Reason"*, Freeman, San Francisco (1976)

/5/ Dennis, J.B., van Horn, E.C., *"Programming Semantics for Multiprogrammed computations"*, CACM 9(1966)3, pp. 143-155

/6/ Lampson, B.W., *"Dynamic Protection Structures"*, AFIPS Fall Joint Computer Conference (1969), pp. 27-38

/7/ Organick, E.I., *"The MULTICS system: an examination of its structure"*, MIT Press (1972)

/8/ Jones, A.K., *"Protection in Programmed Systems"*, Ph.D. Thesis, Carnegie-Mellon University (1973), NTIS Doc No. AD-765 535

/9/ Saltzer, J.H., Schroeder, M.D., *"The Protection of Information in Computer Systems"*, Proc. IEEE 63 (1975)9, 1278-1308

/10/ Mowshowitz, A., *"The Conquest of Will: Information Processing in Human Affairs"*, Addison-Wesley (1976)

/11/ Minsky, M.L., *"Matter, Minds and Models"*, Reprinted in: Semantic information processing, edited by M. Minsky, MIT Press (1968)

/12/ Attanasio, C.R., Markstein, P.W., Phillips, R.J., *"Penetrating an Operating System: A Study of VM/370 Integrity"*, IBM Syst. J. 15 (1976)1, pp. 102-116

/13/ Schell, R.R., *"Dynamic Reconfiguration in a Modular Computer System"*, MIT Report MAC TR-86 (1971)

/14/ Stern, J.A., *"Back-Up and Recovery of On-Line Information in a Computer Utility"*, MIT Report MAC TR-116 (1974)

/15/ Parker, D.B., *"Computer Abuse Perpetrators and Vulnerabilities of Computer Systems"*, Proc. National Computer Conference (1976), pp. 65-73

/16/ Nielson, N.R., Ruder, B., Brandiss, D.H., *"Effective Safeguards for Computer System Integrity"*, Proc. National Computer Conference (1976), pp. 75-84

/17/ Goldstein, R.C., *"The Cost of Privacy"*, Ph. D. Thesis, Harvard University; a summary is given in: Datamation 21(1975)10, 65-69

/18/ Association Internationale pour l'Etude de l'Economie de l'Assurance, *"Studie über die Art und Bedeutung wirtschaftlicher Verluste bei Anwendung der Datenverarbeitungssysteme in Europa bis 1988"*, Informationsbrief Nr. 29, Genf (6. Juli 1976)

/19/ Dodd, G. (ed.), *"Data Base Technology - Present and Future"*, ACM SIGMOD Newsletter 8 (1976)1, pp. 81-106

/20/ Orwell, G., *"1984"*, Hartcourt, Brace and Company (1949)

/21/ Butler, S., *"Erewhon"*, (1872)

E. Morlet and D. Ribbens, (Eds.), International Computing Symposium 1977.
© North-Holland Publishing Company, 1977

PROGRAMMING LANGUAGES: LINGUISTICS & SEMANTICS

An Invited Tutorial.

Dines Bjørner,
Department of Computer Science, Bldg. 343,
Technical University of Denmark,
DK-2800 Lyngby, DENMARK.

Abstract: Basic aspects of the linguistics of various programming language construats are surveyed: their concrete grammatical and abstract syntactical specification; their possible translation into λ-algebra expressions and concrete, low-level machine-like simple statement sequences, as well as their more abstract denotational semantics description. The aim is to present varieties of analysis and synthesis tools used in understanding and designing meta- and source (programming) languages. The emphasis is on abstraction, and on enabling the student to follow the current literature on denotational semantics in particular and programming language design in general.

1. INTRODUCTION

Programming languages are our most important tool for getting useful work done on computers.It is therefore mandatory that we thoroughly understand this tool.The techniques used in this paper illustrate means by which careful analyses can be made of old programming languages,with the same techniques being equally well applicable to the design of new languages.This is the subject mainly of sect.5. Also: since all,or most,programs pass through processors for such languages,we must equally well be concerned about their correctness. This is the subject of [1] (of these proceedings). The view and techniques of sect.s 2-5 carry right into those of that reference. Sect.s 2-4 provide an encompassing survey of what could be considered the foundations of languages,programming and λ-algebra.The latter is used as the simple basis from which to explain linguistics and formulate semantics.

This tutorial does not survey differing 'schools of semantics',neither historically nor technically,but concentrates on excerpts of just one, the McCarthy/Irons/Landin/Reynolds/Strachey/Scott and Vienna line.Thus this survey, together with [1] represents the present author's current style of teaching parts of the subjects: programming linguistics, semantics and compiler specifications. We consider compiler engineering to be a therefrom quite distinct activity,having, as Naur [153] argues, more common parts with 'ordinary' programming, than it has distinguishing marks.

The presentational principle has been to serve you with more or less self-contained,'orthogonal' glimpses of a great variety of examples and techniques couched in a rigid frame and reflecting basically the linguistic structure of such languages as FORTRAN, ALGOL 60/68, PL/I, PASCAL and COBOL, not by specifically illustrating their particular constructs,but by illuminating common underlying notions.From such a basis,if we have properly succeeded,the reader should then be able to ask specific, meaningful and relevant questions about identified languages, and be able to answer most such questions using e.g. the techniques of this paper.

2. SYNTAX, SEMANTICS and PRAGMATICS

A language, L,consists of a set of sentences, P, a universe of discourse, D,about which the sentences speak,and a semantic meaning function, Ψ, which to any sentence, p,in P,ascribes its meaning d in D:

$$p \in P,\ \Psi(p)=d,\ d \in D.$$

d is said to be the denotation of p,p is said to be a syntactical (or: grammatical) domain object, d a semantical domain object,and Ψ the semantics of L.

$$L = \langle P,\Psi,D\rangle,$$
$$\Psi :\ P \rightarrow D.$$

Ψ is normally a function from the P domain into the D co-domain (or range).

2.1 Programming Languages

P is the set of syntactically represented programs (with or without their input data);D is, to a very gross approximation,the set of data type object classes;and Ψ is the elaboration function. For the case p is a program and its input data we take d to be the corresponding output data;then Ψ is the language interpreter,respectively the language compiler and target machine. For the case p is just the program we take d to be the function from input- to output data that p denotes.These two views will be re-iterated repeatedly below, and in [1],and corresponds (roughly speaking) to the computational,respectively the denotational view of semantics.

2.2 Concrete & Abstract Syntax

The study of the representational forms that P & D take belongs to syntax. By syntactical considerations we shall mean concerns and decisions of how programs and their (input) data are represented. We shall distinguish between two levels of syntactical problems: a concrete, and an abstract. Common to both is the specification of how programs (and data) are composable from lesser parts, e.g. such as are known as: blocks and procedures, and these again from declarations,statements and expressions;similarly for data: arrays and records being composable from other data,and eventually from scalar,or elementary objects.

In concrete syntax we are additionally concerned about actual uses of sequences of displayable symbols for purposes of communication between humans and man & machine. In abstract syntax we abstract from such,semantically irrelevant so-called syn=

tactic sugaring concerns [2-3].The most commonly accepted tool with which to syntactically specify programs concretely is that of the BNF (Backus-Normal/Naur-Form) Grammar [4-5]. We shall illus= trate its application. No one particular abstract syntax tool is in widespread use;we shall illus= trate one which seems to strike a balance between several contenders [6-8].Abstract syntax defini= tions do not specify symbol strings as do BNF grammars,but describe mathematically tractable ob= jects.Hence abstract syntax will also be used for the representational abstraction of semantic do= mains.In syntax we normally start with a-priori given (classes,categories or types of) simple ob= jects (sentences,data).From this basis the syntax then gives rules as to how composite (compound, structured or aggregate) objects (sentences,data) may/can be formed.

2.3 Denotational & Computational Semantics

The study of what the syntactical forms represent, i.e.what they stand for,label,name or denote,be= longs to semantics.

In denotational semantics we start from a basis which fixes the denotation of simple,syntactic ob= jects.Denotational semantics now specifies how the meaning of a composite (syntactic) object is to be gotten (derived) from those of the proper consti= tuent,syntactic objects.Obviously the form in which the semantic domains are defined may help or hinder the free,easy and transparent explication of the semantics.In denotaional semantics the objects de= noted are usually functional.We are almost lead to this property by the above insistance on deriving semantics of composite objects by composing seman= tics (i.e.denotations) of proper parts.We pursue denotational semantics since it affords a most suitable abstraction from which to develop inter= preters and compilers for varying user-profiles & target machines,as well as a mathematically clean reference with respect to which we either direct= ly prove/verify programs of the specified language correct,derive other program properties,or based on which we derive certain,so-called 'surface-pro= perties' [9-12] of the language.These amount to suitably constrained axiom (schema)s,and it appears that,so far,it is easier to prove program proper= ties based on axiom systems,than when appealing to the so-called 'elaboration functions' of denota= tional semantics.Other than this passing reference to axiomatic semantics we shall regrettably not touch upon this concept anymore in this tutorial [13-17].

In computational (mechanical,operational,...) se= mantics we start with an 'abstract machine'. This machine (vaguely) resembles our 'real' machine,i.e. it consists of various,"loosely coupled" 'state' components.The meaning of a program is now given with reference to its input data in terms of a stepwise computation on the abstract machine ac= cepting the input,undergoing a sequence of state transformations,and finally (it is hoped) yielding the output.This is more of the "stuff" we are norm= ally familiar with,and since 'real' programs are used for 'real' computations,i.e.since compilers must be able to generate code for 'real' machines effecting such computations,and since interpreters must directly 'simulate' such computations, -- sin= ce this be the reality,we shall in [1] be inter= ested in the design processes of deriving correct= ly functioning compilers and interpreters from de= notational semantics.

2.4 Pragmatics: Language Applications

The study of which syntactic forms to choose,and which semantic domains to favor or discard belongs to pragmatics.In pragmatics we are concerned with the selection of exactly such concrete representa= tions which are closest to the natural,technical, commercial or administrative 'jargon' of the user -- and of exactly such composite constructs which, in an affine way,expresses the basic,common and respective 'recipes' of the 'trade' for which the language is primarily geared ("numerical analysis", "business data processing","civil engineering de= sign automation",...); and of exactly such seman= tic domains which most relevantly reflects,and compares with,the data and processes of the primary application area.We shall totally omit any broader or deeper treatment of the various pragmatic rea= sons for in- or exclusion of data types and program (flow-of-control) constructs as they are manifested in actual commercial or experimental languages.

2.5 Programming Linguistics

Instead we shall,in sect.5,present an analysis of constructs common,as well as particular,to such languages.This amounts to a study of programming language constructs,syntactically and semantically, individually and comparatively.Such a study belongs to linguistics.

2.6 Summary

A language is a system of signs.Syntactics deals with combination of signs without regard to their specific significations,or their relation to the behavior in which they occur,and is the study of the formal relations of signs (symbols,...) to one another.Semantics deals with the significations of signs in all modes of signifying.Semantics is the study of the relations of signs to the objects to which the signs are applicable.Pragmatics deals with the origin,uses and effects of signs within the behavior in which they occur.Linguistics is the descriptive,empirical parts of syntax+semantics +pragmatics (=semiotics),hence it consists of prag= matics and the descriptive parts of syntax and se= mantics.By their descriptive parts we mean the de= scription and analysis of respectively syntactic & semantic features,of a given — or all — language(s) [18-27].

3. BASIC PROGRAMMING CONCEPTS

A program is a recipe for transforming,or proces= sing certain data,called input,into some other da= ta,called output. By data we shall understand "a representation of facts or ideas in a formalized manner capable of being communicated,transformed or manipulated by some process" [28].Data is usu= ally communicated between humans,and between hu= mans and machines according to,or in a certain no= tation. The signs used are not,but represent the data. A particular sign combination, when occurring in certain contexts, thus represents a particular data value. By value we shall understand "data viewed in a context where several or many different would be possible" [28]. The set of all data values of a particular programming language form the universe of discourse. It usually can be regarded as a collection of disjoint data value classes; each representing the objects of a distinct data type. A data type is here taken to be a class of objects and a family of operations applicable to these objects (possibly in combination with objects of other data types). With each operation, θ, of a data type we associate its logical type:

$$\underline{type}: \theta: D1\ D2\ \ldots\ Dn \rightarrow D$$

where $D1, D2, \ldots, Dn, D$ denote not necessarily distinct data type object classes. It expresses that the operation θ must only be applied to argument objects of respectively the types $D1, D2, \ldots, Dn$ and then that a result object of type D is yielded. n is said to be the arity of the operation:

$$\theta(d1, d2, \ldots, dn) = d$$

θ is said to specify a simple transformation (of $d1, d2, \ldots, dn$ into d). Composite transformations can be specified, e.g. by compositions of simple or composite transformations:

$$\underline{type}: \Theta 1: D11\ D12\ \ldots\ D1m \rightarrow D1$$
$$\underline{type}: \Theta 2: D21\ D22\ \ldots\ D2m \rightarrow D2$$
$$\ldots$$
$$\underline{type}: \Theta n: Dn1\ Dn2\ \ldots\ Dnm \rightarrow Dn$$

$$\theta(\Theta 1(d11, .., d1m), \Theta 2(d21, .., d2m), .., \Theta n(dn1, .., dnm))$$

Data can, in addition to transformations, be subject to processes. Computation is a term comprising both. A process is a set of transformations. A sequential process has all of its transformations proceed in a strict, a-priori given, linear order. The notion of data storage is implied by the concept of sequential process. The need for storing data arises from the need to keep results of one transformation waiting until a later stage, permitting intermediate stage transformations. The concept of a data store can be explained as a collection of locations, each location capable of holding, or containing a value. We generalize the data store notion into the concept of variable: "an identifiable ability to hold data with the possibility that these data enter into and are changed by the process described by a program". The value of a variable is "the data held by the variable at a given stage of a process" [28]. We talk also about the state of a (process or) computation as "the momentary association ($\vec{m}$) between variables and their *VAL*ues, i.e. between *LOC*ations and their contents", and we write $\Sigma = LOC \vec{m} VAL$ to denote the space (domain) of all such states, $\sigma \in \Sigma$. The fundamental programming language construct for syntactically specifying state-changing transformations is the statement; a statement is a request for state change; a statement, when executed, accepts an input state, σ, and (if it terminates) delivers an output state, σ'; and a statement, when viewed out of its context, denotes a state transformation function. Correspondingly: the fundamental programming language construct for syntactically specifying a *VAL*ue is the expression. The value represented by an expression is usually gotten by references to the current state, hence an expression denotes a function from states to values. Any programming language construct which changes, or potentially may change, the state, is said to (potentially) cause a side-effect. All statements cause side-effects. Expressions may be so composed (syntactically) that their evaluation may result in side-effects, hence the logical type of the denotation of statements and expressions are:

$$\underline{type}: Stmt: \quad \Sigma \rightarrow \Sigma$$
$$\underline{type}: Expr: \quad \Sigma \rightarrow \Sigma\ VAL$$

The 'process' by which the denotation, or the effect, of a statement, respectively expression, is gotten, is called interpretation, respectively evaluation. Elaboration is a term comprising both. The above distinctions will be folowed rather dogmatically in the rest of this tutorial. It is not an intrinsic one: in ALGOL 68 expressions and statements are grouped into a class of clauses with (syntactical) objects of either sub-class being permitted in contexts where we shall otherwise exemplify only a particular choice as determined by the above type definitions. The so-called 'orthogonality' of ALGOL 68 appears to stem partly from this 'consistency'. We group language constructs according to the criteria of applicative- & imperative-ness. To the imperative features of a language we count all such which explicitly change the state. The basic mechanism for 'enlarging' the state (domain-codomain) is that of declaration of variables. The update of variables, and hence of the state, is afforded by the so-called assignment (statement). All statements are imperatives. To the applicative features of a language we group the 'less dynamic, more static' constructs like expressions, the definition and application (as a concept) of functions (procedures, subroutines), and the notion of scope, i.e. the concepts of blocks and their local bindings. It is an important aspect of imperative features that their syntactical presentation includes the linear ordering of statements may be labelled (named) and so-called gotos used to effect "non-linear" computations over otherwise linearly composed statements. In order to achieve a close match between the composition of the program text and the computations effectable, structured statements are then introduced. A block is either an expression and specifies a value - aided by objects (values, functions) defined local to the block; or it is a statement and specifies a state change - aided by variables and subroutines defined local to the block. A procedure is either a function (type procedure) and then specifies a value computation; or it is a subroutine and then specifies a state change. A procedure is a special kind of "block" in a number of aspects. A (conventional) block is elaborated when encountered (in some 'containing' elaboration) - and in the *ENV*ironment (see below) at that 'time'. Any one procedure is a 'centralized' means of effecting the same elaboration from a variety of distinct places in the program text. The procedure concept thus involves definition & application. A procedure definition (when encountered in some elaboration) is not itself elaborated by being 'applied', but its position in the program text together with the em=

bracing elaboration determines the *ENV*vironment in which its body will be elaborated when activated. Thus a procedure is always basically elaborated in the defining,rather than the calling (invoking) environment.Activations of one and the same pro= cedure - from distinct places in the program text - can furthermore be handed distinct arguments provided so-called formal parameters have been de= fined for that procedure.In that case the proce= dure body is elaborated in an extended environment which in addition the bindings (see below) of the defining environment binds the formal parameters to their corresponding arguments.In summary: a pro= cedure has a name,a formal parameter list,and a block which we henceforth refer to as its body.

3.1 Meta Notions

A number of meta notions have already been used.

We have e.g.briefly touched upon such constructs as expressions and statements,blocks and procedu= res.In sect.5 we shall go into details concerning varieties of these and their proper semantic de= finition.Suffice it here to state a common proper= ty of such constructs: namely one we could term: containment.Expressions are composable from ex= pressions,hence the latter are said to be proper= ly contained within the former,which are then said to embrace the latter.Likewise for statements.Con= tainment,or as we shall call it,when it relates to syntactic structures,phrase-structure properties of statements usually determine rules for goto's, and containment properties of blocks and procedu= res,we say their nesting,determine rules for which identifiers of user-defined constructs (variables, labels,procedures,...) are accessible,known or de= fined.It is this (latter) property which,as we shall see,determine *ENV*ironments.

Thus we explain the denotational semantics of vari= ous constructs basically by means of two meta-no= tions:the abstract store,or state;and the environ= ment:

$$\Sigma = LOC \underset{m}{\rightarrow} VAL; \quad ENV = Id \underset{m}{\rightarrow} DEN$$

States are finite domain maps from *LOC*ations to *VAL*ues,and environments are likewise finite maps from program text *Id*entifiers to their *DEN*otations. The environment domain identifiers are (normally) exactly those of e.g.variables,procedures and la= bels defined in statically containing blocks and procedures,where by using the word:statically we intend to underline the property that containment is something that can be read from the text with= out recourse to a (dynamic) computation. Variable identifiers map to *LOC*ations,procedure identifiers to (partial,~) *FUN*ctions (→):

$$FUN = ARG^{*} \tilde{\rightarrow} (\Sigma \tilde{\rightarrow} \Sigma\ [VAL])$$

where *ARG* stands for argument values,and the pro= cedure is either a subroutine,and no (*nil*) value is yielded;or it is a type procedure,i.e. a func= tion yielding a *VAL*ue.Environments thus model the concept of scope of blocks and procedure bodies, whereas states model the notion of data storage. The state,σ,changes as rapidly as individual sta= tements are executed,and blocks and bodies enter= ed and left.An environment changes only as slowly as block and procedure activations are set-up and taken down,i.e.as blocks/bodies are entered and left.We say that the state is (more) dynamic,and the environment (more) static.Also:any block,re= gardless of its (potentially recursive) nesting (activation- or just program text) depth,can, through assignment change non-local variables,i.e. variables declared in any statically embracing,i.e. lexicographically enclosing,block or procedure -- or passed by reference from a dynamically embracing activation.But:no block or procedure activation can affect the environment of any embracing activation. We say that the state is global,and that the envi= ronments are local.

We shall,in contrast to our denotational viewpoint, explain the mechanical semantics of various con= structs in terms of a rather simple(-minded) ma= chine-like language (with liberal use of goto's), and in terms of activations.An activation is a con= cept related to blocks (and hence procedures too). Initiation of program execution signals the crea= tion of a bottom-most,the 'program' activation. Within the program,block or procedures may be in= voked.Their invocation means the pushing of an ac= tivation on top of the calling,invoking activation. Since blocks and procedures are normally entered and left in a truly bracketed,nested fashion,our activations behave like a stack.Normal termination of computation within a procedure or block thus means the popping of its,the top-most activation, with computation 'falling' back to the prior,the calling/invoking activation.Abnormal termination occurs when a goto or a goto-like exit occurs from within a block or procedure to a program point (e. g.label) in (normally) an embracing block or pro= cedure (activation).Such exits usually entail the popping of up to several activations.An activation finally enables an association between variable identifiers local to a block or procedure (includ= ing formal parameters),their location and value. Procedures may be recursively activated:either be= cause they are themselves (explicitly) recursive, by textually self-referential - or because they are invoked from other procedures which through chains of activations (backward) were invoked (im= plicitly) by the former.Hence a procedure is said to be recursive if two or more activations pertain= ing to the same text may be on the stack simulta= neously.If procedures,p,are permitted to yield procedure values,q,which themselves have their functionality depend on e.g.variables local to p - or if p may assign to variables global to p proce= dure values q local to p -, and if such procedure values may then be applied,then we are said to have what has become known as the FUNARG property.A feature quite desirable in especially the so-called artificial intelligence,AI,languages (FUNARG - FUNc tional ARGument,an unfortunate name).To understand its effect should be no problem,whereas to realize it in an efficient manner may be,since it calls for our abandoning the conventional stack of activations with its pushing/popping occurring in synchronism with block & body entry/exit.Instead we must retain all such activations whose variables (etc.) may be referred to by FUNARG functions.This in general calls for a tree-structured stack for its logical implementation.

3.2 Conclusion

The view enunciated in this section derives from those of Landin [30],in the area of distinguish= ing between applicative- & imperative features, Naur [28] when it comes to basic programming no= tions,and van Wijngaarden,Strachey and Scott when the subject is the relation between linguistics & semantic meta-notions [31-34].

4. THE λ-ALGEBRA & A META-LANGUAGE

In order that we may be able to base our subsequent linguistic & semantic descriptions on a minimum of 'machinery' we now give,as has become customary,a short introduction to relevant aspects of the λ-al= gebra [35-37]; whereupon we immediately,as is also usually done,sweeten [39,42] as well as extend this language to incorporate abstract data types.The re= sult is a meta-language (*META-IV*)[6,7],i.e. a lan= guage with which to describe other languages.

4.1 The λ-algebra

The λ-algebra consists of a set of objects,called λ-expressions,*λExpr*,and a number of reduction ope= rations (α,β,...).The latter map λ-expressions in= to λ-expressions.Thus $D \subset P = \lambda Expr$ (of sect.2) and $\Psi = \{\alpha,\beta,...\}$.Since $D \subset P$ we say that the λ-algebra of Church is a syntactic language,in that its seman= tics views certain λ-expressions as denoting them= selves - i.e.the syntactic forms.This is strictly speaking not the real intention with the λ-algebra: it was to have certain of these forms denote mathe= matical functions,not to 'simulate' them.Such an interpretation has been achieved by Scott [43],but other than this passing reference (but: [...44-45]) we shall not touch this area again.

4.1.1 λ-Expression Syntax

Since λ-expressions are basically self-denoting it is customary to use λ-expressions to 'mimic' con= ventional data type objects.This subject of defin= ability will,however,neither be considered in this tutorial.Hence the language needs only three forms:

BNF Grammar:

(1) <λExpr> ::= <Var>|<Appl>|<λFunct>
(2) <Var> ::= *id-1*|*id-2*|...|*id-n*|...
(3) <Appl> ::= (<λExpr> <λExpr>)
(4) <λFunct> ::= λ<Var>.<λExpr>

Program Schemas:

(5) *id*
(6) (*expr-f* *expr-a*)
(7) λ*id.expr-d*

Abstract Syntax:

(8) *E = V|A|F*
(9) *V = Id*
(10) *A :: E E*
(11) *F :: Id E*
(12) *Id* ⊂ *TOKEN*

The above summarizes three means of describing the syntactic (-expression 'program') domain. These are intuitively named as: variables, applications (of functions to arguments) and functions.Since no o= ther objects are required,we need,e.g.,not state constants,etc.

4.1.2 λ-Expression 'Semantics'

We shall here concentrate on only informal rules. The basic idea of the λ-algebra is to have:

(λ*id.expr-d* *expr-a*)

'denote' the functional application of the first part ('denoting' a function) to the second part. This is achieved ('mimiced') by calling for a re= placement,or: substitution,of all,so-called free occurrences of *id* in *expr-d* by *expr-a*! Example: (λx.3+x 7) shall 'reduce' to 10,where we have al= ready suggested the extension +,etc.λx.3+x is the function of x that 3+x is! Hence applying it to 7 should (with unexplained +) give 10. Informally:

(13) *x* is free in *x*.

(14) *x* is free in (*f a*) iff *x* is free in *f* or *a* or both.

(15) *x* is free in λ*y.e* iff *x*≠*y* and *x* is free in *e*.

x is bound otherwise.Thus λ*y.e* binds all free *y* in *e*!The above binding rules amount to an enunciation of a foundational scope concept and its rules. The form λ*id.expr* 'denotes' a function without naming it.

Reduction Rules

Since this is not to be a section on classical "λ-calculus",but only its application to explaining programming linguistics,we shall in the following assume that all identfiers of any λ-expression are distinct.The λ-algebra 'meaning' of a variable i= dentifier is itself.The λ-algebra 'meaning' of a λ-function: λ*id.expr* is λ*id.expr'* where *expr'* is the 'meaning' of *expr*.And finally:the meaning of application: (*expr-f* *expr-a*) is - in the CALL-BY-VALUE version - the meaning of (*expr-f'* *expr-a'*) which iff *expr-f'* = λ*x.expr-d* is the meaning of the expression resulting from the so-called β-re= duction rule whereby all free occurrences of *x* in *expr-d* are replaced by *expr-a'*;otherwise the mean= ing is: (*expr-f'* *expr-a'*).

4.2 A Meta-Language

We now (1) sugar the above syntactically,and (2) introduce data types (see sect.5.1).

(16) (*let id = expr;* *expr-d*) ~ (λ*id.expr-d expr*)

(17) *expr-f*(*expr-a*) ~ (*expr-f expr-a*)

(18) (*let f*(*x*) = *expr-d*; *expr-b*) ~ (λ*f.expr-b* λ*x.expr-d*)

and permitting recursive *f* definitions:

(19) (*letrec f*(*x*)=*e*; *e-b*) ~ (λ*f.e-b* Yλ*g*.λ*x.e*)

where Y is the so-called fixed-point-finding ope= rator which (can be given a λ-expression form,but otherwise) satifies the following reduction (>) schemata:

(20) YF > F(YF)

where F is any form.Using normal-order reduction where only left-most Y or λ are reduced,the above rules can now be used to 'find' the meaning of an extended (meta-language) expression.We generally mean,but always omit,rec.

Simple data types are the usual ones:rational numbers,integers,natural numbers and booleans together with their corresponding operations.An additional elementary data type is that of *TOKEN*s,the objects are otherwise un-analysed objects and the operations are just equality (=). Composite data types are: *SET*s ({...}) permitting union,intersection, complement,membership,powerset,proper subset,subset,equality and cardinality operations ($\cup,\cap,\setminus,\in$, $\mathcal{P},\subset,\subseteq,=$,*card*); *TUPLE*s (lists,sequences) ($\langle\ldots\rangle$) with *h*ead,*t*ail,*l*ength,*ind*exing ([.]),*elem*ents, equality (=) and pairwise- ($\frown$) & distributed concatenation (*conc*);*MAP*s (functions,normally finite, pre-computable *dom*ains (to *rng*es)) ([..→..]) with operations: merge two distinct *dom*ain maps ($\cup$), extend-override one map with/to another (+),application (*()*) and restriction ($\setminus$) of a map to the domain specified by the right-hand *SET* argument; *TREE*s (*mk*-θ(...)) with selector (*s*-θ) functions.

The above meta-language will slowly be unfolded in the subsequent sections.

4.3 Conclusion

The λ-algebra notions has had an enormous influence on the thinking of many language designers as witnessed by the representative entries in our reference list.With Scott's mathematical models we now have a firm mathematical foundation for our use of the λ-algebra ideas.Before they may have "made sense,without our looking closely or rigorously at the details -- inducing us to use it freely as an everyday algebra"(as will be done in the following)! [82].

We said above that the λ-algebra (as here described) was a 'syntactic' language.The mathematicians /logicians call it a formal system,thereby stressing that one is concerned only with form fiddling. Other formal systems of great lure and exciting interest to many programmers are so-called tree-substitution systems [46-53].They all basically share the so-called Church-Rosser problem/property,a characteristic related to the order in which reductions (may/can) occur and the related outcomes.In this respect one should finally not forget also to refer to the interesting formal system of the so-called Markov-Normal-Algorithms and W-grammars [54-55].

5. PROGRAMMING LANGUAGE LINGUISTICS

In the following 8 subsections we now give an abstract,terse survey of conventional programming language constructs.The treatment is 'abstract' in the sense of not exemplifying specific constructs of identified languages,but conceptualizations of these;it is also abstract in that we e.g.explain compound constructs by letting proper components remain 'un-interpreted',or by referring to explanations of other sections.Some of the coverage is suggestive of 'new' language design ideas.The survey is just that:only a few constructs within each area will be formalized using a variety of definition techniques:translations into either λ-algebra expressions incorporating the meta-language extensions or simple sequences of possibly labelled simple statements (including goto's;as well as formal semantics in terms of denotational models.Given the examples the reader should now be able to personally experiment with new features' formalization and to model existing features of old languages.By doing so the reader will now be able to ask meaningful, relevant questions and to succeed in more conclusive and complete answers.We should,of course have liked to provide special 'pointers' to existing commercial and experimental languages,and e.g.say:language X has such & such a feature with this variation relative to that of language Y's 'similar' feature.But time and space does not permit so.Neither shall we be able to the very important subject of how any one particular language 'offers' the mixture of concepts - their 'orthogonality',the relation to expected applications and the assumed underlying methodology whereby the language designers intended/hoped that users would be programming (viz.e.g.the rather distinct attitudes of APL and ALGOL-like programmers and corresponding modes of programming).Observe in the following the distinctness of presentational styles across the subsequent sections:sect's 5.1 and 5.3 presents rather complete,but somewhat informal surveys,sect.5.5 presents selected examples in differing styles,sect.5.7 presents a complete, 'orthogonalization',etc..In general see [56-79].

5.1 Data Types

Objects and Operations

A data type,*T* ,is an algebra,i.e.: a 'pair': $\langle D,\theta\rangle$; a collection,*D*,of objects;and a family,θ,of (primitive) operations.

Examples: The *integer* data type: $D=\{\ldots,-2,-1,0,1,\ldots\}$ and $\theta=\{+,-,/,*,\leq,\geq,=,<,>,=,\neq,\ldots\}$ where / denotes integer division.The *boolean* data type: $D=\{$*true*,*false*$\}$ and $\theta=\{\wedge,\vee,\equiv,\supset,\sim,\ldots\}$.The *character* data type: $D=\{$"*A*","*B*",...$\}$ and $\theta=\{=,\neq\}$.The *real* data type: $D=\{i/j \mid i,j\in D\mathit{integer} \wedge j\neq 0\}$ and $\theta=\{+,-,/,*,\uparrow$,*ln*,*log*,*ceil*,*floor*,..}.

Elementary and Composite Types

Elementary types are such whose objects are unstructured,i.e. such whose 'structure' is of no relevance to our use of them.Composite types then are such whose objects are decomposable into proper constituents of either elementary- &/or (other) composite objects.

Examples: All of the above exemplified types are elementary.Examples of composite objects are:the *array*-,the *record*- (or: *structure*-) and the *string* data type objects.

Generic Composite Object Functions

Three classes of generic operations are part of the algebraic,composite data type operations: constructors & destructors; access-,selector- &/or index-operations;and (type investigation) predicate functions.

Examples:Although uncommon in present languages, writing: $\langle o1,o2,\ldots,on\rangle$, $\langle\langle o11,o12,\ldots,o1n\rangle,\langle o21,o22,\ldots,o2n\rangle,\ldots,\langle om1,om2,\ldots,omn\rangle\rangle$ permits us to regard $\langle,,\ldots,\rangle$ as a constructor of/for arrays (*n* and *m*×*n* element vectors,respectively matrices of non-array objects,*oi*,and,*ojk*;etc.).A structure of type *T* (see below) whose immediate fields are of types *T1*,*T2*, ..,*Tn*,could e.g.give rise to the following make constructor: *mk-T(mk-T1(..),mk-T2(..),..,mk-Tn(..))*. String constructors are more common: in connection with proper component objects of elementary cha= racters: "*a*"⌢"*b*"⌢"*c*"⌢...⌢"*z*" the concatenation o= peration (⌢) constructs a string object.The *empty* vector (<>) or matrix (<<>,<>,..,<>>) are seldom= ly used notions,similar for structures.The *null* (or empty) string: "" is however an important de= vice.For the 'semantics' (i.e.properties of such empty objects),see later.

Examples: Access functions are: indexing for ar= rays: <...>[*i*], <<..>,<..>,..,<..>>[*i*,*j*] etc.;and selection for records: *s-Ti(mk-T(mk-T1(...),..., mk-Tn(...))* where *Ti* as a type name (e.g.:iden= tifier) is in the set of types names {*T1*,*T2*,.., *Tn*} .Substring extraction functions can likewise be defined: *substr(str,i,j)* extract from *str* the *j*-length substring starting with the *i*'th position. The depth of embedded arrays determines its rank or dimensionality.Indexing an array with an index= list specifying fewer indices than its rank,acces= ses a sub-array.Likewise,if *Ti* is a structure of structure types,etc.,then *s-Tjk(s-Ti(mk-T(mk-T1(...),...,mk-Tn(...))))* denotes a composite selec= tion with *s-Tjk(s-Ti(r))* usually being expressed as *s-Tjk·s-Ti(r)*,or if *t* is the name of the object *r* then in some languages: *t·s-Ti·s-Tjk* (as for in= dices).

Examples: Predicate functions are as rare in most languages as are the constructors: *is-array*<...> and *is-T(mk-T(...))* yields *true*,whereas *is-T*(<..>) and *is-array(mk-T(...))* and *is-Ti(mk-Tj(...))* with *i*≠*j* all should yield *false*.Given an object known to be an array one could test its rank &/or the bounds or just extents of certain,or all,dimen= sions: *rank*<<...>,...,<...>> is expected to yield 2 for a matrix,*bound*(<<*o11*,..,*o1n*>,..,<*om1*,..,*omn*>> [*1*]) should yield *n* and *bound*(<...>[*2*]) (to the same array type object) should yield *m*.

The above explications have already assumed some of the 'semantics' of the objects and operations of the data type;more complete accounts will be illustrated at the end of this sect.

Data Type Names & Definitions

Usually a programming language comes equipped with pre-defined elementary types.Based on these the language then usually permits the user to define new types,both elementary and composite.Pre-defi= ned data types are e.g. identified by given type names (*integer*,*real*,*boolean*,*character*,...).User- defined data types have names assigned to them by the user.The particular compositions permitted are then a distinguishing mark of the language.

Examples: Let *T*,*T'*,*T1*,*T2*,...,*Tn* be already defined (pre/user) data type names.Then *array T' of T*, *record(field T1 field T2... field Tn)* and *string of T* are then (potentially) typical of the logical type expressions for arrays,records (structures) and strings.Others are certainly possible: *stack T*, *list T*, *queue T*, *union of T1 or ... or Tn* etc.

Also: languages usually put (seemingly arbitrary)re= strictions on what object types may index arrays: *T'*is normally *integer*, *array integer of integer*, *array integerof* (*array integer of integer*),etc.,for respectively: vector,matrix & tensor (1-,2-,3-di= mension) array index elements,and usually with arbitrary conventions permitting extensive short- hand forms for expressing the above.New elementary ordered or unordered types may be defined by simple enumeration: (*e1*,*e2*,...,*en*) *ordered* or (*e1*,..,*en*) *unordered*,where *ei* are explicit constants (nume= rals,charcaters,truth signifiers) or are just iden= tifiers then standing for further un-analyzed *TO= KEN*s.Enumerations can be used for array index types.

Type Equations

Names can be given to (new) types,thus type equa= tions consists of definitional pairs: a left-hand definiendum,which is a user-ascribed new name (an identifier,e.g.;underlined or not);and a definiens right-hand side logical type expression of e.g.the above forms.A set of such definitions may be or= dered,not generally permitting the un-constrained recursive definition of types;or may be un-ordered - permitting such circular,or self-referential type definitions.

Examples: *types*: *A is (1,2,4,8); B is (red,blue, white); C is array B of A; D is record(field real, field C,field array C of union(D or nil))*, where *nil* is a void object (enabling in this case the recursion to 'terminate').

Field Names

The position of an index in an indexlist determines its 'function' (i.e. what it selects) uniquely.Two or more fields in a record data type may be of the same type,thus not permitting an un-ambiguous means of uniquely selecting proper structure components; or field types may be directly defined by some com= posite logical type expression rendering expressing a field selector ackward.For such cases languages introduce field names.

Example: *record(id1 field T1,id2 field T2, ..., idn field Tn)* where *idi*≠*idj* for *i*≠*j*.

Type Constructors and The Class/Module Concept

Some languages allow only pre-defined type con= structors (*array .. of ..*, *record(field .. field .. field ..)*, *string ..*).For these the language(s) then define generic functions as above.In addition to such pre-defined composite type schemata some languages permit the user to define so-called class or module types,for which the user has to define the generic functions - these normally then becomes rather applications-oriented.

Example: *T' is class (T initialized to I(...) with generic functions: f1(..)=(...) and f2(..)=(...) and ... and fn(..)=(...))* defines the class *T'* to be the objects denoted by the logical type expres= sion *T* whose initial values are determined by *I* and which can be manipulated (i.e.accessed,tested,upda= ted,...,re-structured (de-stroyed)) by the func= tions *fi*.Thus if *t* is such an object (or a name denoting it),then writing: *t.fi(...)* (with (...) denoting suitable arguments,see sect.5.7) may be an allowable construct of the language which ex=

presses that the function (denoted by) *fi* is to be applied to (this particular instance of) *t*, of an object of type *T'* possibly conditioned by the arguments (...).

Data Type Semantics

Except for informal explication of the generic functions on composite objects we have so-far begged the issue of what the operators 'mean': as we shall now illustrate: the 'meaning' of operators is 'something' which is intrinsically tied to the 'properties' of the objects. Several means of defining their relationships are possible. Two will be illustrated: one axiomatic, another 'constructive'.

Examples: Below is given a (tentative) definition of the algebra of (mathematical) sets, or, as we should term it: the abstract programming language data type whose objects are sets, and whose operations are: $\in, \cup, \cap, \subset, =, \setminus$, card, P.

(1) $\{\} \in SET$
(2) assume: $x, x1, x2 \in SET;\ y \in OBJECT$
(3) $\{y\} \cup x \in SET$
(4) $\sim(y \in \{\})$
(5) $y \in x \cup \{y\}$
(6) $y1 \neq y2 \supset (y1 \in x \cup \{y2\} \equiv y1 \in x)$
(7) $x1 \cup \{y\} \subset x2 \equiv x1 \subset x2 \wedge y \in x2$
(8) $x1 = x2 \equiv x1 \subset x2 \wedge x2 \subset x1$
(9) $x1 \subset x2 \equiv x1 \subset x2 \wedge \sim(x1 = x2)$
(10) $x \cup \{\} = x$
(11) $x1 \cup x2 = x2 \cup x1,\ c1 \cup (x2 \cup \{y\}) = (x1 \cup \{y\}) \cup x2$
(12) $x2 \cap \{\} = \{\}$
(13) $x \cap \{y\} = \underline{if}\ y \in x\ \underline{then}\ \{y\}\ \underline{else}\ \{\}$
(14) $x1 \cap x2 = x2 \cap x1,\ x1 \cap (x2 \cap \{y\}) = x1 \cap x2 \cup x1 \cap \{y\}$
(15) $\{\} \setminus x = \{\}$
(16) $\{y\} \setminus x = \underline{if}\ y \in x\ \underline{then}\ \{\}\ \underline{else}\ \{y\}$
(17) $(x1 \cup \{y\}) \setminus x2 = x1 \setminus x2 \cup \{y\} \setminus x2$
(18) $\underline{card}\{\} = 0,$
$\underline{card}(x \cup \{y\}) = \underline{if}\ y \in x\ \underline{then}\ \underline{card}x\ \underline{else}\ 1 + \underline{card}x$

This was a 'semantics' in the axiomatic style. Now a 'more' constructive specification of the same data type:

(1) $\{y1, y2, \ldots, yn\},\ n \geq 0$
(2) $y \in \{\ldots\} \equiv (\exists i)(yi = y)$
(3) $y \in S \cup T \equiv y \in S \vee y \in T$
(4) $y \in S \cap T \equiv y \in S \wedge y \in T$
(5) $y \in S \setminus T \equiv y \in S \wedge \sim(y \in T)$
(6) $S \subseteq T \equiv y \in S \supset y \in T$
(7) $S = T \equiv y \in S \equiv y \in T$
(8) $S \subset T \equiv S \in T \wedge \sim(S = T)$
(9) $\underline{card}\{\} = 0,\ \underline{card}((S \setminus \{y\}) \cup \{y\}) = 1 + \underline{card}S$

etcetera.

Conclusion

A taxonomy of the various issues/problems/techniques concerned with the programming language notion of data type has been reviewed. For scientific papers on the data type concept, spanning from the pragmatic issues with which the user is confronted to the theoretical ones based on which we e.g. may abstractly define higher-order, functional data types, are listed as references [80-93]. With the present material the reader should now be able to go to the everyday 'work-horse/favourite' language to investigate its 'arbitrary' limitations concerning data type objects and operations, as well as finding out how godd/bad their semantics has been specified. We refer to [89] for a survey of methods by which to define the semantics of data types. References [81,15] bring fine specifications.

5.2 Primitive Operator/Operand Expressions

Pre-supposing later material &/or relying on your previous knowledge: instead of writing out the constants denoting the objects one introduces short-hand names (identifiers) for them. And in order to specify/denote primitive data transformations one writes pre-, in-, and suffix expressions involving either such identifiers or the constants (or other 'expressions') and operators:

(1) *p-op e*
(2) *e1 i-op e2*
(3) *e s-op*

examples are:

(1') $-a$, *hlist*, *tlist*, *llist*, *card set*, *dom map*
(2') $a - b$, $a + b$, *set1* $\cup$ *set2*, *map1* + *map2*
(3') $n!$

(Selecting the *i*'th member of a list, or vector, must be considered an 'act' of functional application, and is hence treated in sect's 5.6-7.). The semantics of such expressions is simple: evaluate all (the, or both) operands, then apply the operation denoted by the operator to the resulting temporaries:

```
(4)  eval-expr(e)(env)=
       cases e:
        "op e"    → (let v:eval-expr("e")(env),
                         f:eval-func("op")(env);
                     f(v)),
        "e1 op e2" → (let v1:eval-expr("e1")(env),
                          v2:eval-expr("e2")(env),
                          f:eval-func("op")(env);
                     f(v1,v2)),
        "e op"    → (let v:eval-expr("e")(env),
                         f:eval-expr("op")(env);
                     f(v))

     type: eval-expr: Expr → ENV → (Σ → Σ VAL)
```

-- where further definition of 'missing' expression alternatives follows in sect.5.6. The *eval-func* is usually defined axiomatically, as above, in sect.5.1. The roles of *env*$\in$*ENV* and Σ was briefly covered in sect.3 and will be further unravelled in subsequent sections. The definition of the semantics is seen to structurally follow that of the syntax (1-2-3), and since it involved recursion, so does the evaluation function. The *v1*, *v2*, *v* objects are so-called temporaries. Finally observe that the depth of recursion is statically determinable from the form of the evaluated expression, and likewise are the correspondingly stacked number of temporaries. Let us finally state an abstract syntax for simple, operand/operator expressions:

(0") *E = P | I | S*
(1") *P :: POP E*
(2") *I :: E IOP E* ·
(3") *S :: E SOP*

where (.) it is not important whether *POP* is listed before or after *E* in the logical type expression (1"), and similarly for (2"-3"); and where (..) we presently leave *POP*, *IOP*, *SOP* unspecified.

5.3 Assignable Variables & The State

Variable Declarations

Variables are either explicitly- or implicitly declared. A variable is said to be explicitly declared iff a particular, syntactic ('kind of') imperative is textually distinguished whose purpose (semantics) it is to name the variable, to potentially associate attributes with it, and to effect, or make sure of the existence of an, allocation - with the proviso that no other mention of this variable can be made 'before' such a declaration clause has been elaborated:

$$(1)\quad (\underline{dcl}\ v;\ \overline{B(v)}) \quad\sim\quad \begin{aligned}&\lambda\sigma.(\underline{let}\ r\in REF\ \underline{be}\ \underline{s}.\underline{t}.\ r\sim\in\underline{dom}\sigma;\\ &\quad\underline{let}\ v=r;\\ &\quad\underline{let}\ \sigma'=B(v)(\sigma\cup[r\to\underline{undef}]);\\ &\quad\sigma'\setminus\{r\})\end{aligned}$$

Otherwise a variable is said to be implcitly declared by the first assignment dynamically attempted to a previously 'unknown' storage location. Elaboration of a declaration consists then in general of these actions: a storage location is set aside (allocated), an association between the variable's name and the location is established (e.g. in an *env*ironment), a set of attributes are also related to this variable name (and location) (usually an 'act' statically 'performed' by the compiler, see below), and the variable is initialized (e.g. to the *undefined*, some default defined value, or to the value of an initializing expression:

$$(\underline{dcl}\ v := e;\ B(v))$$

Variable Attributes

From any variable value one can deduce a type. The type of a variable (at some computation step) is the type to which its variable value (currently) belongs. The type is an attribute of the variable. The following are general attributes associatable with variables:

- type
- scope
- allocation class
- storage mapping
- initialization

These will now be dealt with in turn.

Free/Fixed/Union Type- and Type-less Languages

A language is said to be free type if the values of any variable are permitted to be ranging over any type:

$$(\underline{dcl}\ v := \underline{true};\ldots;v := 2;\ldots;v := \text{"ABC"};\ldots)$$

If, however, values of any one variable, are restricted to range only within objects of a specific type, but distinct variables may be so distinctly 'typed', then it said to be fixed type, provided no one object belongs to two or more types:

$$(\underline{dcl}\ v\ \ldots\ \underline{type}\ T;\ \ldots\ )$$

If a value belongs to two or more types, then we have a *union* type concept. A language all of whose variable values range within a single type which is not itself the (intricate) union of a(n interesting) variety of other, distinct (composite) types is said to be type-less.

Strong/Weak Typing - Coercion & Polymorphic Op's

(The natural *N*umbers form a subset of the *INT*e*G*er numbers, and these again of the rational *NUM*bers.) A language which forces any operation on any value to be typed "to within" a subset is said to be strongly typed. (Such a language would not permit:

$$(\underline{dcl}\ i := 1\ \underline{int};\ \underline{dcl}\ r := 1.7;\ \ldots\ r := r\times i;\ \ldots)$$

A language whose primitive operators accepts union type operands is said to be polymorphic. If the semantics of the operators convert all operands into a distinct (potentially non-union) type, then polymorphism is replaced by a so-called coercion scheme.

Example: the $\wedge$ in: $a\wedge b$ would be polymorphic if e.g. a and b could range over simple, elementary *booleans*, *arrays*s, *lists*, etc. of these, etc..

Scope & The Block Concept

The scope concept is usually introduced by tying it to the names of user-defined quantities such as variables, formal parameters (see sect.5.7), labels (see sect.5.8), procedures etc.. The scope rules of a language are the rules which establish relations between where names are defined and the (total) program text over which the name(s) can be used, and is then bound to the definition, i.e. its attributes. A language for which the scope of a name includes the entire program text is said to not explicitly possess a scope concept: no two definitions of the same name could hence occur, nor co-exist. One important aspect of the block concept is that it introduces a definite, textually limited scope for names. In particular: in a so-called block-structured language names defined in blocks have a scope which 'encompasses' all of this block, possibly save its local blocks, and all of their text, in which the names are redefined. Scope rules are normally statically determinable. In:

```
(dcl v ...
 ... v ...
    (dcl v ...
     ... v ...)
 ... v ...)
```

the 2nd and 5th occurrence of v are bound to the 1st definition, whereas the 4th occurrence is tied to the 2nd definition, i.e. 3rd occurrence. It would be instructive if the reader translated the above using (1) into proper (extended) λ-expressions, and 'verified/compared' the above scope rules with/to the bound/free rules for λ-expressions.

Allocation Classes

The act of 'ear-marking' specific storage for a variable is called allocation:

$$(2)\quad \begin{aligned}&\lambda\sigma.(\underline{let}\ r\in REF\ \underline{be}\ \underline{s}.\underline{t}.\ r\sim\in\underline{dom}\,\sigma;\\ &\quad\ldots\ \sigma\cup[r\to\underline{undefined}]\ldots\end{aligned}$$

the corresponding act of voiding this association is called freeing:

$$(3)\qquad \sigma'\setminus\{r\})$$

Variables may, irrespective of their scopes, have locations allocated (so-called) statically externally, statically internally or automatically. Extern=

ally allocated locations are such which exist in permanent storage before &/or after program com= putation.Statically internally allocated locations are such which are 'set aside' at the very start of program execution,and 'taken down' at the very end of same.When allocation 'matches' start-of-sco= pe and free 'follows' end-of-scope,then we have the automatic storage class.In that last case,a vari= able is said to be 'shielded' (or 'stacked') when scopes are temporarily suspended,e.g.by/in inner blocks.

```
(dcl v static ext ...
   (dcl v static int ...
      (dcl v automatic ...
         (dcl v static int ...
            (dcl v static ext ...
)...)...)...)...)
```

Nested redefinitions of automatic then refer to distinct allocations,whereas those of static norm= ally refer to 'pairwise' corresponding (internal, external) allocations.In a language not permitting recursion variable names can be uniquely renamed and each such name then refers to at most one lo= cation;with recursion,one & the same name may now refer to a set of (stacked) allocations.In a lan= guage with procedures permitting call by reference parameters two or more distinct names might get to stand for the same location,which is now said to be shared.With recursion &/or with sharing the current binding of names to locations is,in deno= tational expressions,modelled by *env*ironments;with= out either one need not interject *env*ironments be= tween program text variable names and their binding to storage (Σ) locations.

Storage Mapping

Higher level programming languages are 'higher-le= vel' only with respect to 'something'.Concerning data types,it is usually the case that an illusion is created of a 'virtual' machine possessing other types than those trivially provided by 'physical' machines.Distinctly declared variables (of espe= cially elementary types) are usually allocated in physical storage according to no semantic rules. For the case of e.g.arrays,if only non-array ele= ments,i.e.no subarrays,can be accessed,then arrays can likewise be arbitrarily 'laid-out' in storage. Of course:physical storage comes equipped with some ordering properties among locations.We say that a language has a storage mapping concept if its se= mantics either explicitly specifies,or the program= mer can control,how e.g.composite objects are laid out in (consecutive) storage - with the above defi= nition extending to groups of (not necessarily si= multaneously defined) variables.

Examples: Arrays may be spread out (so-called) row= wise,i.e. first co-ordinate elements first,then se= cond,etc..Groups of otherwise distinct variables may be 'overlaid/commoned' with one or several (de= fined) variables,forcing their allocation according to order of textual declaration/definition in the program text.

The pragmatics is clear:for arrays one may wish efficient access along specific axes,either for reason of subarray selection,iteration or both.Re= cord variables may be assigned to by reading data serially from unstructured (backing) store.

The State

The collection of all allocated variables form at any point in a computation the state:

$$\Sigma = REF \underset{m}{\to} VAL, \quad \sigma \in \Sigma \qquad\qquad LOC \sim REF$$

Allocations joins (∪) new locations to the *dom*ain of σ,freeing restricts (∖) the *dom*ain,and assign= ments update,by extend-override (+),for given lo= cations,the *rang*e values:

alloc:	$\sigma \cup [r \to \ldots]$	$r \notin dom\ \sigma$
free:	$\sigma \setminus \{r\}$	$r \in dom\ \sigma$
assign:	$\sigma + [r \to v]$	$r \in dom\ \sigma$

Assignment

The assignment statement specifies an update.Syn= tactically the form of an assignment usually has two parts:

$$var := expr$$

a target variable (list) and an expression (list). Semantically an evaluation of the two parts is re= quested:the denotation of the target variable (list) is to be that of a *LOC*action (list),and that of the expression (list),a *VAL*ue (list);then the storage is updated:

(1) $r := v \sim \lambda\sigma.(\sigma + [r \mapsto v])$

(2) $r := e \sim \lambda\sigma.(\underline{let}\ \langle\sigma', v\rangle = e(\sigma);\ \sigma' + [r \to v])$

Syntactic variations are:

(3) $v1, v2, \ldots, vn := expr$
(4) $v1 :=: v2$
(5) $(v1, v2, \ldots, vn) := (e1, e2, \ldots, en)$

corresponding semantically to:

(3') $(\underline{let}\ v : expr;\ //\{v1 := v, v2 := v, \ldots, vn := v\})$

(4') $(\underline{let}\ \ell1 : v1,\ \ell2 : v2;\ //\{v1 := \ell2, v2 := \ell1\})$

(5') $//\{v1 := e1, v2 := e2, \ldots, vn := en\}$

The above illuminates two aspects: arbitrary ('qua= si'-) parallel (//{..,. . . .,..}) order of evalua= tion of target variable references;and the distinc= tion between co-called left- and right-values.That is:that *var* in some 'context' stand for the *LOC*a= tion associated with the variable identified by and in other contexts stand for the *VAL*ue corre= sponding to such a *LOC*ation.

In a fixed type language the type of the values de= clared for *var* (*vi*) and those of the right-hand expressions (*expr*,*ei*) must 'match'.The pragmatic purpose of explicitly forcing the programmer to associate types textually with variable declara= tions is to enable,in a fixed type language,a sta= tic - i.e.compile-time - check on type correspon= dance.In particular it is (now) postulated that (compiler) functions,*extract-var-type* & *extract-expr-type*,can be written which applies to variable references,respectively expressions,and yields the type as given in the declaration.Thus the compile-plus-run-time (i.e.'static+dynamic') semantics of (simple) assignments can loosely be stated as follows:

```
int-asgn("var := expr")δρσ=
  (let v-tp = extract-var-type("var")δ,
       e-tp = extract-expr-type("expr")δ;
   if v-tp ≠ e-tp
     then DIAGNOSTICS
     else (let loc = eval-loc("var")δρσ,
               val = eval-val("expr")δρσ;
           result is(σ + [loc → val])))
```

type: *int-asgn*: $Asgn \to DICT \to ENV \to \Sigma \to \Sigma$

where δ is the compiler δictionary, based solely upon which types (of a fixed type language) can be uniquely determined. ρ is a run-time envi*ro*nment.

Target References, Super & Sub-Locations

The forms that expressions may take and their meaning was partly a subject of sect.5.2, and will also be the subject of e.g.sect.5.6. In this section we now take a rather superficial look at what syntactic forms target variable references may take, and on their meaning. For elementary data types, variable references are commonly simple *id*entifiers, and the environment maps these directly into locations. For compound data types, variable references to entire, compound objects are again usually simple identifiers. But since we may wish to access &/or selectively update proper components of these we may think of the location associated with the compound variable's simple identifier as being a 'super' location, consisting of a 'hierarchy' of sublocations, one for each proper (contained) value component. Some languages only permit array references to non-array elements, and hence one could instead model, in *ENV*, each proper array-element identification by its (sub)location. For arrays and array-elements we normally find these target variable references:

vid[*e*], *mid*[*e1*,*e2*], *mid*[*e1*,*], *mid*[*e*]

where *vid* & *mid* are simple identifiers and *e* (suitably decorated) is an (integer-valued) expression. Modelling array-locations hierarchically could, in one style, e.g. lead to:

$$\rho = \left[\, ..,\ vid \to \begin{bmatrix} i1 \to loc1 \\ .. \quad .... \\ il \to locl \end{bmatrix},\ mid \to \begin{bmatrix} \langle j1,k1\rangle \to loc11 \\ ..... \quad ..... \\ \langle jn,km\rangle \to locmn \end{bmatrix} .. \right]$$

where ρ thus maps vector-*id*entifiers into maps from vector indices (*i*) into corresponding locations, and matrix-*id*entifiers into maps from matrix index-lists (<*j*,*k*>) into corresponding element locations. The implied *eval-loc* function might in this case look like:

```
eval-loc("var")δρσ=
  cases "var":
   ("id"        → ρ(id),
    "vid(e)"    → (let i = eval-val("e")δρσ,
                       m = ρ(vid);
                   result is m(i)),
    "mid(e1,e2)"→ (let j = eval-val("e1")δρσ,
                       k = eval-val("e2")δρσ,
                       m = ρ(mid);
                   result is m(<j,k>)),
    ...            ...)
```

type: *eval-loc*: $Targ\text{-}Ref \to (DICT \to (ENV \to (\Sigma \to LOC)))$

i.e. the function specifies no state changes. For the case the index(list) expressions might additionally specify side-effect, the above function would have to be re-written, and its type changed:

type: *eval-loc*: $Targ\text{-}Ref \to (DICT \to (ENV \to (\Sigma \to \Sigma\ LOC)))$

We exemplify such formulae subsequently.

In summary: the purpose of the above illustrations have been (1) to bring into focus the semantics elaboration functions, their purpose, their structure and their potential recursive nature; (2) to illustrate the static, semi-static, and dynamic semantic domain objects (δ,ρ,σ); and finally (3) to exhibit certain modelling problems: viz.: that of modelling storage locations and storage values for compound data. This latter subject is considered at length and depth in [98-99]. We leave it to the reder to search there, and e.g. in [100], or personally set up, a model for e.g. record and field locations.

Binding: Free & Fixed Types vs. Interpreters & Compilers

Two data object type & value extremes can be identified: the statically based determination, i.e. solely from the program text, of what fixed type any program identifier in any context is bound to, versus the dynamically, i.e. run-time-only, based determination of this. This to be further compounded by the ability of certain object values to be dependent on scopes only dynamically determinable. We refer her in particular to functions as values - with this aspect otherwise being referred to the FUNARG subsection of sect.5.6. The problem is basically this: given any, say operator-operand, expression (of the source language), how is the operator to be understood for varying types of the operand(s)? In a fixed, strongly typed languagethis type is per definition (to be) statically checkable, and hence the meaning of the operator is unique - consequently a specific, definite length sequence of machine instructions can be set aside (compiled) for (from) this operator. In a free (or in cases, just weakly fixed) type language, one and the same physical such expression may be repeatedly evaluated in distinct (dynamic) contexts, giving distinct types to the operands, thus forcing each evaluation to apply different operator meanings depending on the 'incoming, actual' operand types - and thus, for each such expression, code must be set aside, or a common, run-time system routine must be available, for determining the appropriate type(s) and activating an appropriate operator instruction sequence from among a variety of such. Thus the two 'ends' of the above: "free to fixed binding" spectrum requires the intricate presence-, respectively permits the complete absence of run-time functions for determining types and selecting proper operator interpretations. This then corresponds to the interpreter versus the compiler situation. Behind the fixed versus free type notions stands a number of pragmatic issues. These span from applications determined factors to educational concerns. Applications, e.g. in the artificial intelligence (AI) area, appear to benefit, in their easy (re-)formulation from a type free language - especially one also possessing the FUNARG property. But some educators claim,what is called the 'advantages' of complete compile-time type-checking as opposed to the 'hard-to-understand' run-time messages any interpreter system could possibly generate upon in-explicable type mis-matches.The subject will not be discussed further here as we lack (the definition of) a proper,common,unanimously agreed-upon 'frame-of-reference' within which programming: conception,specification,realization,testing and usage occur!

Conclusion

References [38,94-95] discusses early attempts at λ-algebraisizing the store semantics;[98-99] offer more developed models;and [100] relates such store models to the lattice-theoretic mathematical semantics.

5.4 Simple/Basic Statements

Statement Compositions

It was argued,that when 'grand' overall input data transformations into output became "too complex" to specify by a simple,applicative expression (as is usually the case in mathematics) then we could 'chop' the transformation up into a sequence of simpler transformation steps.This necessitated assignable variables.We now return to the subject of sequences of transformations.A basic means of specifying these are by specifying simple or composite, structured compounds of statement sequences.In this section we treat only the inescapably necessary and sufficient linear (or 'simply-') compound-,the basic *if-then-* & *if-then-else-*,and the primitive *goto* statements.

Linear Compounds

Typical forms are: "*st1;st2;...;stn*",where,for the sake of subsequently needed generality,we let *sti* (for all *i*) be any statement - but,presently,in our semantic explication not containing *goto*s 'out' of any *sti*:

```
(1) int-cmp("st1;st2")ρσ=
       (let σ' = int-stmt("st1")ρσ;
        int-stmt("st2")ρσ')

    type: int-cmp: Stmt Stmt → (ENV → (Σ → Σ))
```

corresponds to:

(2) "*st1;st2*" ~ λσ.λρ.(*I*("*st2*")ρ(*I*("*st1*")ρσ))

which then explains linear compunds of 2 non-*goto* statements by functional application and functional composition.Sequences of more than 2 statements can then be explained,e.g.using the above:

(3) *st1;st2;...;stn* ≡ *st1*;(*st2*;(...(*stn-1*;*stn*)...))

whereby these are fragmented into nested compounds of 'pairs' of statements (properly adjusting for odd-even numbered sequences).The *I* used above represents an abbreviation of *int-stmt*.

Basic Conditionals

Typical forms are: "*if e then s*" and "*if e then s1 else s2*",etc..We shall not here dwell on the semantically un-interesting issue of 'dangling' *else* ambiguities such as: "*if e1 then if e2 then s1 else* ... " -- is this (unspecified) *else* clause that determined by the first or the second *then* clause?) -- nor on their syntactic resolution (*fis*).

```
(4) int-if("cond")ρ =
      cases "cond":
        ("if e            → (let b : eval-val("e")ρ;
          then s"            if b then int-stmt("s")ρ
                                  else I),
         "if e            → (let b : eval-val("e")ρ;
          then s1            if b then int-stmt("s1")ρ
          else s2 "               else int-stmt("s2")ρ)

    type: int-if: Cond → (ENV → (Σ → Σ))
```

maybe explains it somewhat circularly to you (in terms of meta-language *ifs*) - but,as in fact did previous elaboration function definitions,leave out the subsequently important issue of side-effect producing expression evaluations.We even left the state component out of the picture:

```
(5) int-if("cond")δρσ=
      cases "cond":
        "if e        → (let <σ',b> = eval-val("e")δρσ;
         then s1        if b
         else s2"          then int-stmt("s1")δρσ'
                           else int-stmt("s2")δρσ'),
      ...
```

catches more of the essence.Also we "forgot" to check the type of *e*:

```
(5')                 → (let typ = extract-type("e")δ;
                         if typ ≠ BOOLEAN
                            then DIAGNOSTICS
                            else (...)
```

ought be properly inserted.

Gotos

Linear compounds could only effect a single execution of any,and every,particular component statement.Basic conditionals woven into linear compounds could effect "even less" executions:namely one or none,by effectively steering a non-looping course. For certain kinds of data transformation,repetitive executions of textually the same statement(s) become desirable: either because it saves you writing more code,or because the computation iterates value-independently (i.e.identically) over array-elements,or because the computation resembles that of a value-dependent 'closure' operation on a compound structure ("graph"),or because all data elements cannot be in store at any one time - many distinct reasons,a single (presently undisputed) cure: the *goto*! There are two parts to the goto 'story' (as their is to a semantically interesting "parallel": the procedure): both syntactics and semantics: the *goto* statement itself,and the *labelling* of statements.In general:

(6) (*l1:s1;l2:s2;...;li:si;li':si';..;ln:sn*)

schematically depicts a list of labelled statements with *i'* stand for the *i* plus first list element.With

(7) *int-goto*("*goto lj*")δρσ = <σ,<JUMP,*lj*>>

being the model for *goto*s, and with *lsl* being an abbreviation for e.g. the above statement list,we might express the meaning of compound statements now (potentially) containing *goto*s as follows:

```
(8) int-lstl(lsl,"ℓi")ρσ=
      (let "(...;ℓi:sti;ℓi':sti';...)"= lsl;
       let <σ',flag> = int-stmt("sti")ρσ;
       if flag = CONTINUE
         then if i = l lsl
                then <σ',CONTINUE>
                else int-lstl(lsl,"ℓi'")ρσ'
         else (let <JUMP,"ℓj"> = flag;
               int-lstl(lsl,"ℓj")ρσ'))
```

where it is understood that all (previous & future) interpretation functions deliver a 'pair':

```
    type: Stmt* Label → (ENV→(Σ→(Σ (J | C))))
(9) J  =  (JUMP Label)
(10) C  =  CONTINUE
```

Instead of the repetitive & cumbersome 'flag' communication & testing we introduce meta-language features (*exit* & *trap exit*) which absorbs these into their semantics:

```
(11) int-lstl(lsl,j)ρ=
       (trap exit("ℓbℓ")
         with if (∃k∈ind lsl)(lsl[k]="ℓbℓ:...")
                then int-lstl(lsl,k)ρ
                else exit("ℓbℓ");
        for i = j to l lsl do int-stmt(lsl[i])ρ)
(12) int-stmt(stmt)ρ=
       cases stmt:
         ("goto ℓj" → exit("ℓj"),
          ...       → ...)
       type: int-lstl: Stmt*  N1 → (ENV → (Σ → Σ))
       type: int-stmt: Stmt      → (ENV → (Σ → Σ))
```

where the latter formulation depends on meta-formulae side-effect on a meta-program declared global storage which models the source-language state:

(13) *dcl stg* := [] *type LOC* $\underset{m}{\rightarrow}$ *VAL*

whereby:

(14) Σ = *REF* $\underset{m}{\rightarrow}$ *OBJ*, *stg*$\in$*REF*, *LOC*$\underset{m}{\rightarrow}$*VAL* $\in$ *OBJ*

Conclusion

The *exit* explication of *goto*s evolved from [101] via [102] to [6]. Its sufficiency has been demonstrated there by its application to ALGOL 60 and PL/I. Different approaches to expressing the semantics of 'jumps' was first given earlier by Landin [121,104-5] ;then developed by Lockwood-Morris [106] and Strachey & Wadsworth [107]. A study of the relations between this latter, so-called continuation-, and the *exit* semantics is given in [103], and of continuation semantics itself in [108]. Other, mostly axiomatic treatments of *goto*s can be found in e.g. [109-110].

5.5 Structured Statements

From the rather informal, seemingly in-systematic definitions of sect's 5.3-4 we now turn to increasingly more systematic & formal, abstract & concrete specifications. In the following subsections we give the syntax of programming constructs in basically three styles (see below) and their semantics in basically two styles: one resembling a compiling algorithm (but not being one, see [1]) - and thus explains the semantics in terms of expansions of ('sophisticated', structured) statements into statement sequences with *goto*s and labels; the other being an abstract, denotational model of the same. We do not, however, in this paper prove "equivalence".

Iteration

Syntax:

Program Schema:

```
(1) for cv := spec1, spec2, ..., specn do stmt-l
(2) spec-i  ~  expri by exprb to exprt
(3) spec-i  ~  expri          to exprt
(4) spec-i  ~  expri by exprb
(5) spec-i  ~  expri
```

BNF Grammar:

```
(6) <For>     ::=  for <Var> := <Spec-L> do <St-L>
(7) <Var>     ::=  <Id>
(8) <Spec-L>::=  <Spec> , <Spec-L> | <Spec>
(9) <Spec>    ::=  <Expr> by <Expr> to <Expr>   |
                   <Expr> to <Expr>              |
                   <Expr> by <Expr>              |
                   <Expr>
```

Abstract Syntax:

```
(10) For   ::  Id  Spec+  Stmt+
(11) Spec  =   Seq | One | Loop
(12) Seq   ::  Expr Expr Expr
(13) One   ::  Expr
(14) Loop  ::  Expr Expr
```

What we intend to illustrate here is the familiar iteration, DO-, or FOR-LOOP.

Semantics:

Translation:

We first 'translate' (e.g.) (1) into:

```
(15)  (for cv := spec1 do stmt-l;
       for cv := spec2 do stmt-l;
       ...
       for cv := specn do stmt-l)
```

and declare that the semantics of (1) (etc.) is identical (≡) to that of its rewritten forms (15). Then we define the semantics of the simpler forms as follows (4 cases): (16-18):

```
(16)   spec  ~  expri by exprb to exprt
(17') (dcl cv := expri;
       let by := exprb,
           to := exprt;
     L:if ~((by>0)∧(ccv<to) ∨ (by<0)∧(ccv>to))
         then goto OUT;
       stmt-l;
       cv := ccv + by;
       goto L;
   OUT: I)
```

assigns one kind of semantics by stipulating exactly one evaluation of each of: *expri*, *-b*, *-t*;

```
(17") (dcl cv := expri,
           by := exprb,
           to := exprt;
     L:if ~((cby>0)∧(ccv<cto) ∨ (cby<0)∧(ccv>cto))
         then goto OUT;
```

```
        stmt-l;
        by := exprb;
        to := exprt;
        cv := ccv + cby;
        goto L;
   OUT: I)
```

ascribes another semantics which prescribes repeated evaluations of *exprb* and *exprt*.

```
(18)  spec ~ expri to exprt
```

can be explained (away) in terms of the former by dynamically assigning *+1* or *-1* to *by* depending on *ccv ≤ to* (*cto*), respectively *ccv ≥ to* (*cto*).

```
(19)  spec ~ expri
(20)  (let cv := expri;
       stmt-l)
```

whereas:

```
(21)  spec  ~ expri by exprb
(22)  (dcl cv := expri;
       let by : exprb;
    L: stmt-l
       cv := ccv + by;
       goto L)
```

etc.,requires *stmt-l* to contain a *goto* out of the iterative,otherwise un-ending,loop.If however - as otherwise indicated by (15) - we wish to avoid the code-generation- and -space- wise redundant replication of (*n*) *stmt-l*'s,then the following expansion might serve:

```
(23) comment: spec ~ expri by exprb to exprt;
     L10:(dcl br := Lr1 type Label;
          dcl cv := expri1,
              by :='exprb1,
              to := exprt1;
          goto Ls;
     Lr1: cv := ccv + cby;
          if~((c by≤0)∧(ccv>cto)v(cby>0)∧(ccv<cto))
             then goto L20;
          goto Ls;
     comment: spec ~ expri;
     L20: br := L30;
          cv := expri2;
          goto Ls;
     ...
          ...
     comment: spec ~ expri by exprb;
     Ln0: br := Lrn;
          cv := exprin;
          by := exprbn;
          goto Ls;
     Lrn: cv := ccv + cby;
     Ls:  stmt-l;
          goto cbr;
     L(n+1)0:I)
```

Now the question is: which way would you specify it? The first way is less involved,requiring few ad-hoc,auxiliary variables,but might suggest a space-wise expensive (expansive) code to be generated;the last way (23) involves us in some tricky branch label administration,which for simple, (de-generate) but usually prevalent cases would have to be factored-out.And (if both solutions are sought for mixed cases) we would anyway have to show their equivalence.We therefore suggest the denotational semantics style:

```
(24) int-for(mk-For(id,spl,stl))=
  1  for i = 1 to lspl do
  2   cases spl[i]:
  3    mk-Seq(ei,eb,et)
  4    → (let vi : eval-expr(ei),
  5            vb : eval-expr(eb),
  6            vt : eval-expr(et);
  7        let for(j) = if ((vb≥0)∧(j>vt))v
  8                        ((vb≤0)∧(j<vt))
  9                        then I
 10                        else (stg := cstg+[id→j];
 11                              int-stmt-l(stl);
 12                              for((cstg)(id)+vb));
 13        for(vi)),
 14    mk-One(ei)
 15    → (let vi : eval-expr(ei);
 16        stg := cstg+[id→vi];
 17        int-stmt-l(stl)),
 18    mk-Loop(ei,eb)
 19    → (let vi : eval-expr(ei),
 20            vb : eval-expr(eb);
 21        let loop(j)=(stg := cstg+[id→j];
 22                     int-stmt-l(stl);
 23                     loop((cstg)(id)+vb));
 24        loop(vi))
```

To the above definition we usually attach the following:

Annotation: 0.The interpretation function takes as arguments a *For* statement,and operates,by side-effect,on a globally declared state (*stg*).From this definition we omit *environment*.1.The *stl* is executed zero,one or more times per each of the elements in *spl*.2.Settles the 'case' of either of the three specification forms.7 & 21.Looping is explained without *gotos* and *labels*.Instead recursively defined functions,*for* and *loop*,are established. 12 & 23.Since interpretation of *stl* may alter the controlled variable,*id*,we carry (*cstg*)(*id*)+*vb* rather than *j*+*vb* forward.

While-Do

Syntax:

Program Schema:

```
(25) while expr do stmt
```

BNF Grammar:

```
(26) <While> ::= while <Expr> do <Stmt>
```

Abstract Syntax:

```
(27) While :: Expr Stmt
```

We now intend to define the conditional loop construct by two extremes:

Semantics:

Translation:

```
(28) (dcl bool := expr;
   L: if ~cbool then goto OUT;
      stmt;
      bool := expr;
      goto L;
 OUT: I)
```

```
(29)int-while(mk-While(e,s))=
      (let wh()=if eval-expr(e)
                 then (int-stmt(s);
                       wh())
                 else I;
       wh())
    type: While → (Σ → Σ)
```

McCarthy Conditional Statement

Syntax:

Program Schema:

```
(1)  (e1  →  s1,
      e2  →  s2,
      ..     ..,
      en  →  sn)
```

BNF Grammar:

```
(2)  <McCarthy>  ::=  ( <ESList> )
(3)  <ESList>    ::=  <Ex-St> | <Ex-St> , <ESList>
(4)  <Ex-St>     ::=  <Expr> → <Stmt>
```

Abstract Syntax:

(5) *McCarthy* :: *(Expr Stmt)*$^+$

Some versions permit the last expression part (*en*) to be a reserved "catch all" expression, represented -- as it is in our own meta-language formulae -- e.g.by the symbol: *T*. If so, then *T* would be defined by <Expr>, respectively be (e.g.) the *QOUT*ation symbol *T* defined by *Expr*. Since neither the concrete, nor the abstract syntax presently expresses that any such *T* (*T*) be the last (*en*), we shall (either) repair the syntax (or make dynamic tests in our elaboration formulae for such constraints):

```
(1') (e1→s1,e2→s2,...,T→sn)

(2') <McCarthy>  ::= ( <ESList> ) |
                     ( <ESList> , T → <Stmt> )

(5') McCarthy :: (Expr Stmt)+ [Stmt]
```

Now: with *T* (*T*) not being in the syntactic category <Expr> (*Expr*), the evaluation function 'becomes' "simpler" or "cleaner" in that it does not have to test for, or consider, *T* as a special case -- only the *int-McC* interpretation function, the one that really ought be concerned, must make special tests:

Semantics:

Translation, Version 1

```
(6)  if e1 then s1          (6') if e1 then s1
           else                        else
     (if e2 then s2              (if e2 then s2
            else                         else
      (...                        (...
            else                         else sn ...))
      (if en then sn
             else error)...))

(7)  (dcl v := e1;          (7') ...
      if ~v then goto L2;        ...
      s1; goto OUT;              ...
  L2: v := e2;                   ...
      if ~v then goto L3;        ...
      s2; goto OUT;              ...
  L3:...                         ...
  Ln: v := en;               Ln: sn); OUT: I
      if v then error;
      sn); OUT:I
```

where we have used a bit of abbreviation in showing the two versions' two cases (with/without *T*).

Elaboration Functions:

As an exercise in varieties of displaying/expressing denotational semantics formulae we now give you four alternative formulations of the same semantics:

```
(8)  int-McC(mk-McCarthy(esl,t))=
       if esl= <>
         then (if t=nil
                 then error
                 else int-stmt(t))
         else (let <e,s> = h esl;
               let b : eval-expr(e);
               if b then int-stmt(s)
                    else
                     int-McC(mk-McCarthy(tesl,t)))

(9)  int-McC(mk-McCarthy(esl,t))(σ)=
       if esl=<>
         then (if t=nil then error
                        else int-stmt(t)(σ))
         else (let <e,s> = h esl;
               let <σ',b> = eval-expr(e)(σ);
               if b
                  then int-stmt(s)(σ')
                  else
                   int-McC(mk-McCarthy(tesl,t))(σ'))

(10)int-McC(mk-McCarthy(esl,t))=
      (trap exit() with I;
       for i=1 to l esl do
         (if eval-expr(s-Expr(esl[i]))
            then(int-stmt(s-Stmt(esl[i]));
                 exit)
            else I);
       if t=nil then error
                else int-stmt(t))

(11)int-McC(mk-McCarthy(esl,t))=
      (for i=1 to l esl do
         (let <e,s> = esl[i];
          let b : eval-expr(e);
          if b then (int-stmt(s);
                     goto OUT)
               else I);
       if t=nil then error
                else int-stmt(t);
     OUT:I)
```

with the logical type of all above variants:

type: *McCarthy* → (Σ → Σ)

being the same! In (8) the elaboration functions are thought of as applying to a globally declared state, whereas in (9) this state is explicitly 'dragged' around, and hence explicitly yielded. (11) is the goto transliteration of (10), both, as (8), applying to global state variables.

Conclusion

A number of structured statements have been formally specified using a variety of methods. It is left to the reader to similarly specify such constructs as e.g. the integer "casing", the Guarded

Commands of Dijkstra,or compounds of structured statements such as e.g. analyzed and suggested in [118].General references are [111-120].The sub= ject of 'translations' between recursive and non- recursive formulations,and of correctness of trans= lations belongs to the discipline of 'Program Sche= mata'.

5.6 Applicative Expressions

We have already,in sect.5.2 dealt with introducto= ry aspects of applicative expressions,and have fur= thermore presupposed familiarity with the *if-then-else* (applicative) expression,and its semantics. The McCarthy conditional expression is similar to that of the corresponding -statement,and the:

Cases Expression:

can be simply dealt with:

Syntax and Semantics:

```
(1) cases e0:          ~ (let v0 : e0;
      e11  →  e12,        (if v0 = e11 then e12
      e21  →  e22,                     else
      ...     ...         (if v0 = e21 then e22
      en1  →  en2                      else
                          (...
                                       else
                          (if v0 = en1 then en2
                                       else error)
                          ...))))
```

respectively:

```
(2)   T    →  en2      ~               else en2
                          ...))))
```

Block Expressions

Syntax and Semantics:

```
(3) (let v = expr-d;   ~ (λv.expr-b  expr-d)
     expr-b)
```

with the proviso that inner-most reductions of λ-expressions proceed first,i.e.call-by-value is the rule of the meta-language.Intuitively the idea is this: In the body,*expr-b*,the (constant) value of *expr-d* is used repeatedly.As a shorthand it is computed once,given the name *v* and all inten= ded occurrences of the subexpression *expr-d* in the body are instead just occurrences of the 'variable' *v*.The scope of *v* is *expr-b* — excluding any proper= ly contained parts of *expr-b* which are blocks in which *v* is *let* (*rec*) defined.*v* is a constant in all of *expr-b*.The implied notion of textual, or object,substitution,can be explained by the seman= tic domain object of environment(s) which binds free identifiers of *expr-b* to their meaning (val= ue).Now an evaluation function looks these free identifiers up in the argument environment:

```
(4) eval-expr("let v = exprd;exprb")env=
        (let env' = env + [v→eval-expr("exprd")env];
         eval-expr("exprb")env')
```

-- a rather circular definition of *let* by means of *let*,but given (1) all is clearer!

```
(5) eval-expr("id")env = env(id)
```

Recursive Definitions (Blocks cont'd)

For expresssions,which like:

```
(6)   (let f(n)=if n=0 then 1 else n*f(n-1);
       f(7))
```

requires the left- & righthand side *f*'s to denote the same object,in this case a function,and in par= ticular the factorial, some writers use:

```
(7)   (letrec f(n)=if n=0 then 1 else n*f(n-1));
       f(7))
```

to indicate that evaluation of the righthand side is to take place in the same environment as being created.In general:

```
(8)   (letrec f = λn.e1(f); e2)
```

where the righthandside denotes "the function of *n* that *e1(f)* is",is normally written:

```
(9)   (letrec f(n) = e1(f); e2)
```

and *e1(f)* is here written so,in order to indicate that *f* occurs (free) in *e1*! The semantics:

```
(10) eval-expr("(letrec f(n)=ed; eb)")env=
        (letrec env' = env +[f→eval-fun("λn.ed")env'];
         eval-expr("eb")env')
```

with:

```
(11) eval-fun("λn.e")env=
        (let f(a) = (let env' = env + [n→a];
                     eval-expr("e")env');
         result is f )
```

shall be understood as follows:the body, *eb* ,a *letrec* block,defining a function recursively,is evaluated in an environment,*env'*,which is that ex= tension (+) of the block embracing environment, *env*,which binds the name,*f*,of the defined function to the denoted function (*eval-fun("λn.ed")env'*) and otherwise binds names as in *env*.The function denoted by *f* is yielded by *eval-fun*.*eval-fun* when given a function definition,i.e.a syntactic object, *λn.expr-d* ,and an environment,*env*,called the de= fining environment (which in the *eval-expr* of the *letrec* block case was *env'*),yields a semantic do= main object,temporarily,but conveniently named *f*. It is a mathematical function.In particular: *f* is that function which when applied to an argument, say *a*,behaves like the righthandside of the *letrec* *env'* = ... definition.That is: the body, *ed* ,of the function definition is evaluated in an envi= ronment,*env'*,which is that extension of the defi= ning -- not applying -- environment,*env*,which binds the formal parameter (or: bound variable) name *n* to the object denoted by *a* and otherwise binds as *env*.

Two crucial things must be observed: the denotation of *f* is yielded by an evaluation of *λn.ed* in an en= vironment,*env'*,which binds *f* to that denotation. Thus recursion in *f* is explained by a recursive equation in *env'*.At this point you may wish to pause,wondering how this works.Mathematically it is (or has,at least after D.Scott's recent work, become) simple: *env'* is the smallest solution to the equation,i.e. is the *MAP* object which satis= fies the defining equation and whose *graph*,i.e. *SET* of domain-range pairs is contained in any o= ther solution to the equation.Now in this case it is simple.The *graph* must contain all of *env* and then just one more pair: <*f*,*f*> -- but here *f* is itself the smallest solution to the equation: *f(a)=...* !

Mechanically,i.e. implementation (compile- & exe=cution-)wise the situation is a bit more complica=ted.The discussion of solutions here leads us right into [1],and involves us in such commonly known subjects as: activation stacks, dynamic and static (calling and lexicographically preceding activa=tion) chains, display mechanisms,etc.,for the pro=per referencing of variables.The other notable thing is that the definiens in *eval-fun* is not e=valuated (in general: elaborated) when *eval-fun* is first invoked for the purpose of yielding *f*.This is just like in ordinary programming:all you ex=pect of a *Block* elaboration,when,in its prologue activities it encounters locally defined procedu=res,is that their bodies not be elaborated,but that their names be so bound such that when the proce=dure is called,say from any indefinitely nested, inner block,the body now be elaborated in the ex=tended defining-,rather than calling-,environment, which binds all formal parameter identifiers to their meaning -- etc..This then was the reason for bringing you a section on function definitions:to indoctrinate one proper way of viewing this seman=tically,disregarding implementational details & concerns (such a stack manipulations).In the next section we complete the treatment by looking in particular at parameter transfer mechanisms and also generalizing to procedures and macros, to subroutines and type functions.

The FUNARG Problem

Functions,like *f*,which are delivered out of their defining scope -- like *f* results from *eval-fun*'s body -- potentially lead to the so-called FUNARG situation.Mathematically everything is quite simple, by nothing so far said being changed.Implementation-wise matters are more serious.Referring more form=ally to [1] of these proceedings,it can be summa=rized:If no such function could be returned out of its defining scope then a simple linear stack could realize a block-structured & procedure-oriented language's concept of both static and dynamic (re=cursive) nesting.This means that when elaboration of a block or procedure body (which itself usually is a block) is terminated,then the corresponding activation (which is the realization of the envi=ronment (and storage for imperative languages)) can be popped off the stack -- deleted.With the so-called FUNctional ARGument (unfortunate name) pro=perty this deletion cannot occur for such blocks/ bodies which return(ed) functions depending on lo=cally defined objects.Deletion can,at the earliest, take place when the function can no longer be in=voked.This latter requires extensive (compile-time) control flow analysis of program texts as well as sophisticated (run-time) garbage-collection mecha=nisms [130].The stack itself would become strcutured as a tree.

5.7 Parameters, Procedures & Macros

Blocks are introduced into programming languages for basically two reasons: both pragmatic: (1) to enable the programmer to locally define types,con=stants,variables,procedures and labels with the explicit ability to (re-)use their identifying na=mes elsewhere for other purposes,thus bringing a=bout 'economy' of name varieties as well as text-ually tightly localizable (name,type)-pair corre=spondance checks; and (2) to enable efficient run-time allocation techniques for declared variables by permitting variables of disjoint blocks,i.e. blocks not satisfying a relative or mutual con=tainment property,to be mapped onto physically o=verlapping segments of actual storage.

A procedure definition is a centralized recipe for data dependently computing certain data &/or state transformations (repeatedly) required in a variety of contexts.The recipe usually calls for auxiliary variables to be used in the strictly local sense of not being elsewhere required.And thus,since elaboration of procedure definition local expres=sions anyway,invariable,at run-time,requires tem=poraries,i.e. local 'hidden' variables, -- proce=dure definition bodies are generalized to blocks, this permitting the same scope rules as for state=ment- and expression-blocks in general.

Typical (program schema) syntactic forms of blocks and procedures are:

```
(1)   begin
         Def-list ;
         Cmd-list
      end

(2')  pid: procedure(fid1,fid2,...,fidm)=
             parameters: fid1: type ftp1 by vrn1,
                         fid2: type ftp2 by vrn2,
                         ...
                         fidn: type ftpm by vrnm;
             Block
          end

(2")  Proc  returns t
```

where (1) is a *Block* and (2') a *Proc* ,and:

```
(3)   Def-list ~ Def1,Def2,...,Defn
(4)   Cmd-list ~ Cmd1;Cmd2;...;Cmdl
(5.1) Def      ~ dcl vi := vei type vti
(5.2) Def      ~ let cj = cej type ctj
(5.3) Def      ~ Proc
(6.1) Cmd      ~ lbl: Stmt
(6.2) Cmd      ~ Stmt
(7.1) Stmt     ~ call pid(e1,e2,...,em)
(7..)          ~ ...
```

with expressions: *ve*, *ce* and *ei* being of the forms previously covered in addition to:

```
(8..) Expr     ~ pid(e1,e2,...,em)
```

What we now have in mind to illustrate is the va=riety of calling features: CALL by *vrn*,where *vrn* is either VALUE, REFERENCE, NAME or formal PRO=CEDURE.ALGOL 60 features VALUE, NAME and PROCE=DURE.PL/I REFERENCE and PROCEDURE.In addition lan=guages restrict the kind of objects which may be VALUEs or REFERENCEs to such. Abstract syntacti=cally we summarize the above completely:

(9) *Block* :: $Id \underset{m}{\rightarrow} Def \quad Cmd^*$

(10) *Def* = *Dcl* | *Let* | *Proc*

(11) *Dcl* :: *Expr* *Type*

(12) *Let* :: *Expr* [*Type*]

(13) *Proc* :: $Parm^*$ *Block* [*Type*]

(14) *Parm* :: *Id* *Type* *By*

(15) *By* = V | R | N | P

```
(16) Cmd       =  Call | Return | ...
(17) Call      :: Id  Expr*
(18) Return    :: [Expr]
(19) Expr      =  Vref|Prefix|Infix|Fct-ref|Cst-ref
(20) Vref      =  Var-ref|Parm-ref|P-ref
(21) Var-ref   :: Id  Expr*
(22) Parm-ref  :: Id  Expr*  [N]
(23) Fct-ref   :: Id  Expr*
(24) Cst-ref   :: Id  Expr*
(25) P-ref     :: Id
(26) Prefix    :: Mop  Expr
(27) Infix     :: Expr  Dop  Expr
```

The *Def-list* (*Id* $\underset{m}{\rightarrow}$ *Def*) locally defines a number (*n*) of either declared variables, *vi*, initialized to the value of some expression, *vei*, and firmly fixed to be of some type, *vti*; or let constants, *cj*, which receive the value of expressions, *cej*, doubly checked to be of the type *ctj*; or procedures with name *pid*, a formal paramater list whose *q*'th element has type *vtq* and is to be called by *vrnq*, where *vrn* is the same as is *By* in the abstract. The procedure then has a body which is a block, and, if it is a type procedure (i.e. function) which explicitly returns a value, then a type, *t*, indicating the type of the returned value. Among executable possibly labelled -- statements we now include calls of procedures. Among expressions we similarly include references to functions, as well as to variables -- the latter potentially including an indexlist selecting elements of arrays. Expressions may also be references to constants or formal/bound variables.

Parameter Transfer Schemes

Values, or more precisely: denotations, can be communicated in either of four ways: (1) just plainly as the value of the argument expression (by VALUE), (2) as the reference to a storage cell containing that value (by REFERENCE or LOCATION), (3) as a reference returning function which is evaluated everytime the formal identifier, *fid*, is elaborated during a procedure invocation (by NAME), or (4) as a (formal) procedure (by PROCEDURE). Complications are these: in by VALUE a value is transferred, but, as in e.g. ALGOL 60, local, so-called 'dummy', variables are to be set up by the called procedure activation and initialized to this value, with the possibility that this dummy enter into update assignments in the body block of the procedure. In by REFERENCE the argument expression may e.g. be an operator/operand expression (*Fct-ref*, *Prefix* or *Infix*), in which case a similar dummy location must be set up, likewise only during invocation, and taken down upon normal, and abnormal termination. In by NAME the argument expression may similarly be e.g. an *Infix* expression with the requirement now that the reference yielding function being transferred always yield the same, dummy, location. This is in contrast to the interesting/trick-coding aspect of by NAME in which e.g. array element argument expressions result in functions (generally called thunks) which may yield distinct array element references for (repeated) distinct formal parameter elaborations.

Given the formal, denotational semantics viewpoint, we establish the following semantic domains:

```
(28) ENV    =  Id →m DEN
(29) DEN    =  LOC | VAL | FCT | THUNK
(30) LOC    ⊂  TOKEN
(31) VAL    =  ...
(32) FCT   :: [LOC](V|R|N|P)* DEN* →([LOC]→(Σ → Σ [VAL]))
(33) THUNK =   → (Σ→Σ LOC)
(34) STG    =  LOC →m VAL
(35) Σ      =  REF →m STG
```

Initializing our abstract machine to:

```
(36)  dcl Stg := []  type STG
```

we can now give a rather exhaustive/comprehensive mathematical semantics definition of all the major aspects of the block- and procedure concept, in particular one which models all the four parameter transfer/calling mechanisms hinted at above. The description now given would be far more complex were we to give a mechanical explication of the same problem.

```
(37)int-bl(mk-Block(d,cl))ρ=
      (let ρ'=ρ+[id→eval-def(id,d(id))ρ'|id∈domd];
       int-cmd-l(cl)ρ')

(38)eval-def(id,def)ρ=
      cases def:
       mk-Dcl(e,)→(let v : eval-expr(e)ρ,
                        l ∈ LOC be s.t. l ~∈ dom c Stg;
                   Stg := cStg ∪ [l → v];
                   return l),
       mk-Let(e,)→eval-expr(e)ρ,
       T          →eval-proc(id,def)ρ)

(39)eval-proc(pid,mk-Proc(pml,bl,t))ρ=
      (let byl = <s-By(pml[i])|i∈indpml>;
       let f(al)(loc)=
            (let ρ' =  ρ+[s-Id(pml[i])→al[i]|i∈indal];
                        +[pid →mk-FCT(loc,byl,f)];
             int-bl (bl)ρ');
             result is(mk-FCT(nil,byl,f)))

       note:(lal=lpml)∧(∀i∈indal)(extract-type(el[i])
                                   = s-Type(pml[i]))
            checks omitted,el is calling arg.expr's.

(40)int-cmd-l(cl)ρ=
     for i=1 to l cl  do int-stmt(s-Stmt(cl[i]))ρ

(41)int-stmt(st)ρ=
     cases st:
      mk-Asgn(r,e)→(let v : eval-expr(e)ρ,
                        l : eval-ref(r)ρ;
                    assign(l,v)),
      mk-Call(,)  →int-call(st)ρ,
      T           →...

(42)int-call(mk-Call(pid,el))ρ=
     (let mk-FCT(l,byl,f) = ρ(pid);
      let al : eval-arg-l(el,byl)ρ;
      f(al)(nil);
      free-dummy-locs(el,al,byl))

(43)free-dummy-locs(el,al,byl)=
     (let locs = {l|(((byl[i]=N)∧(~is-Vref(el[i]))∧
                    (l=(al[i])()))∨((bl[i]=V)∨
                    ((bl[i]=R)∧(~is-Var-ref(el[i]))))
                    ∧(l=al[i])) ∨ i∈ind el }
      Stg := cStg∖locs )

(44)eval-arg-l(el,byl)ρ=
     <eval-arg(el[i],byl[i])ρ | i ∈ ind el >
```

```
(45)eval-arg(e,by)ρ=
     cases by:
      N→eval-thunk(e)ρ,
      V→(let v : eval-expr(e)ρ,
             l ∈ LOC be s.t. l ~∈ dom c Stg;
         Stg := cStg ∪ [l → v];
         return l),
      R→(is-Var-ref(e)→eval-loc-ref(e)ρ,
         T → (let v : eval-expr(e)ρ,
                  l ∈ LOC be s.t. l ~∈ dom c Stg;
              Stg := cStg ∪ [l → v];
              return l)),
      P→ρ(e)
```

```
(46)eval-loc-ref(e)ρ=
     cases e:
      mk-Var-ref(id,el)
      → (let il : <eval-expr(el[i])ρ|i ∈ ind el >;
         sub-loc(ρ(id),il)),
      mk-P-ref(id)
      → (let mk-FCT(loc,,) = ρ(id);
         return(loc)),
      mk-Parm-ref(id,el,nm)
      → (let il : <eval-expr(el[i])ρ | i ∈ ind el >;
         cases nm:
           nil → sub-loc(ρ(id),il),
           N   → sub-loc((ρ(id))(),il))
```

note: *sub-loc* not defined. Its inclusion here presupposes a model of e.g. array-locations as cursorily sketched in sect. 5.3. Functions: *assign* and *content* are likewise not included, for the same reasons.

```
(47)eval-expr(e)ρ=
     cases e:
      mk-Prefix(o,e')
      → (let v : eval-expr(e')ρ;
         cases o: (MINUS → return(-v),...)),
      mk-Infix(e1,o,e2)
      → (let v1 : eval-expr(e1)ρ,
             v2 : eval-expr(e2)ρ;
         cases o: (ADD → return(v1+v2),...)),
      mk-Fct-ref(id,el)
      → (let mk-FCT(l,b,f)=ρ(id),
             l' ∈ LOC be s.t. l' ~∈ dom c Stg;
         Stg := cStg ∪ [l' → undefined];
         let al : eval-arg-l(el,al,b)ρ;
         f(al)(l');
         free-dummy-locs(el,al,b);
         let v' : (cStg)(l');
         Stg := cStg \ {l'};
         return(v')),
      mk-Cst-ref(id,el)
      → (let v = ρ(id);
         if el=<>
            then return v
            else
             (let il : <eval-expr(el[i])ρ|i∈ind el>;
              return v(il))),
      T (let loc : eval-loc-ref(e)ρ;
         content(loc))
```

```
(48)eval-thunk(e)ρ=
    (is-Vref(e)→(let th()=(let l : eval-loc-ref(e)ρ;
                                return l);
                 return th),
     T→(let l ∈ LOC be s.t. l ~∈ dom c Stg;
         Stg := cStg ∪ [l → undefined];
         let th() = (let v : eval-expr(e)ρ;
                         Stg := cStg + [l → v];
                         return l);
         return th)
```

with the elaboration function logical types being:

```
(37) type: int-bl:          Block                 ⇒
(38)       eval-def:        Id Def                ⇒
(39)       eval-proc:       Id Proc    → (ENV → FCT)
(40)       int-cmd-l:       Cmd                   ⇒
(41)       int-stmt:        Stmt                  ⇒
(42)       int-call:        Call                  ⇒
(43)       free-dummy-locs:Expr  DEN              ⇒
(44)       eval-arg-l:      Expr (V|N|R|P)*       ⇒ DEN*
(45)       eval-arg:        Expr (V|N|R|P)        ⇒ DEN
(46)       eval-loc-ref:    Expr                  ⇒ LOC
(47)       eval-expr:       Expr                  ⇒ VAL
(48)       eval-thunk:      Expr                  ⇒ THUNK
```

where ⇒ abbreviates: $\rightarrow$ *(ENV* $\rightarrow (\Sigma \rightarrow \Sigma))$ and ⇒ *OBJ* abbreviates: $\rightarrow$ *(ENV* $\rightarrow (\Sigma \rightarrow \Sigma$ *OBJ*$))$.

Macros

Whereas the logical type of a procedure denotation is essentially:

Proc: FCT ~ $DEN^* \rightarrow (\Sigma \rightarrow \Sigma\ [VAL]))$

that of a macro is essentially:

Macro: MAC ~ $DEN^* \rightarrow (ENV \rightarrow (\Sigma \rightarrow \Sigma\ [VAL]))$

That is: the defining environment of a procedure is encapsulated in the denotation *FCT*, but is absent from the macro denotation. The latter, when applied, takes the calling environment and arguments (DEN^*) to yield a function. In more familiar terms: a procedure is elaborated in the defining-, and a macro in the calling environments.

Conclusion:

No attempt was here made at illustrating the semantics of blocks and procedures (macros) mechanically. In [1] of these proceedings we systematically derive several, increasingly more concrete such descriptions from a denotational definition. The literature usually is very operational, and thus very detailed, when describing procedure semantics. But since several, fundamentally distinct means exist for implementing procedures [124-5,130-2] we decide to take the realization-independent route to understanding. Completely constrasting, diagrammatic, but still very operational, and not comprehensive, definition methods are those of [133-4]. Most operational definitions appear to suffer from the common decease of only explaining instances, special cases or examples, and not the general case. The axiomatic method [14-6,126] which we do not illustrate, instead suffers from presently not being able to cater generally for formal procedures as parameters, recursion and variable sharing -- the latter here being deemed a serious drawback.

5.8 Exceptions

By an 'exception' programming construct we shall vaguely understand an imperative language construct which denotes either a temporary or a permanent suspension of ordinary, phrase-structure based, iterative sequencing (flow-of-control) for the sake of temporarily,or permanently basing computations on phrase-structure-wise 'disjoint' program text parts.The above delineation is purposely left vague in order that we may include e.g. such constructs otherwise known as RETURNs, GOTOs, LEAVEs, EXITs, etc..The first and the latter two eventually being classifiable as 'label-free' GOTOs,i.e. EXITs to phrase-structure determined 'pro-' or 'epilogues' to the structured statements (procedures) which they eventually cause 'exits' from.We should also like to classify the PL/I-COBOL-like On-Condition notion as belonging the 'exception' programming.It will be given a rather complete,simplified model in [7] ,but see also [6] .In this tutorial we shall end our survey of linguistic issues and associated semantics modelling techniques and problems by now giving a model of a rather general GOTO scheme. Having understood this model the reader should then be able to construct definitions of e.g.the phrase-structured EXIT/LEAVE schemes as well as varieties of the present GOTO scheme.Among the latter we suggest that you try,yourself,simplifications such as:permitting only label constants, not permitting GOTOs out of procedures,or blocks, or both;respectively additional twists e.g.involving arbitrary GOTOs between alternate arms of IF-THEN-ELSE statements.

Informal Semantics Description: Our example language is block-structured and procedure-oriented. GOTOs are based on the *VAL*ues of *Expr*essions.These may then be either *Label* constants or *I*dentifiers denoting references (*LOC*ations) to *Label* variables (actual or formal),etc.A command list (Cmd^+) defines a level.A *Statement* of a command list,*cl*, which is itself a command list,*cl'*,defines a level one higher than that of the immediately containing *cl*.A GOTO can occur only to statements on the same or a lower level as that of the GOTO,and such that the target statement (that to which the GOTO occurs),if of a lower level,is that of a command list statically embracing the GOTO.In particular: GOTO out of a block shall also cause freeing of automatically allocated variables,and similarly for the pseudo-variables of BY-VALUE parameters of procedure *Call*s.A (further) twist has been introduced in order to illuminate modelling problems: the only *Command* of a *While* statement may be a statement which is a GOTO,or may contain a command list which contains a GOTO,to that *While* statement command!Such a GOTO should not (abnormally) terminate while-looping! No GOTOs into While's.

Modelling Notes: To model *Label* (actual or formal) variables we introduce two global state objects: *A*ctive- & *P*ast *A*ctivations -- being sets of *A*ctivation *ID*entifiers,allocated (to *aa*) when entering, and freed (from *aa*) when leaving a *Block*.Now *Labels* of distinct *Block*s may be identical,and lead to correspondingly distinguishable actions.The above also permits *Label* arguments to procedure *Calls*, and may be especially useful (or 'tricky',depending on your viewpoint/attitude) in recursion,allowing GOTOs to an arbitrary,programmer/dynamics controlled, 'earlier' (recursion) activation.The while problem (-twist) alluded to lead here to the use of twin functions,one *cue*ing (french: 'donner la replique',german: 'stichwort') the other.

Syntactic Domains

```
(1)  Prog  =  Block
(2)  Block :: (Id m→ (Dcl|Proc)) Cmd+
(3)  Cmd   :: s-Lbl:[Lbl]  Stmt
(4)  Dcl   :: Expr
(5)  Proc  :: Id+ Block
(6)  Stmt  =  Asgn|While|Block|Cmpd|Goto|Call|Ret
(7)  Asgn  :: Id Expr
(8)  While :: Expr Cmd
(9)  Cmpd  :: Cmd+
(10) Goto  :: Expr
(11) Call  :: Id Expr+
(12) Ret   :: ...
(13) Expr  =  Id|Lbl|...
(14) Id    ⊂  TOKEN
(15) Lbl   ⊂  TOKEN
```

Semantic Domains

```
(16) ρ,ρ' ∈ ENV = Id m→ (LOC|FCT|LAB)
(17) STG        = LOC m→ VAL
(18) VAL        = LAB|...
(19) LAB       :: Lbl AID
(20) AA,PA      ⊂ AID
(21) AID        ⊂ TOKEN
(22) Σ          = REF m→ (STG|AA|PA)
```

Global State Initialization

```
(23) dcl Stg := [] type STG,
(24)     aa  := {} type AA,
(25)     pa  := {} type PA;
```

Elaboration Functions

```
int-prog(p)=                                              (26)
 (trap exit(id) with error;
  int-bl(p)[])

int-bl(mk-Block(m,cl))ρ=                                  (27)
 (let aid : get-aid();
  (trap exit(id) with (epilogue(aid,m)ρ';
                       exit(id));
   let ρ' = ρ + [id→eval-def(m(id))ρ' | id ∈ dom m ]
           ∪ [l→ mk-LAB(l,aid) | l ∈ C-Lbls(cl)];
   int-cl(cl,1)ρ';
   epilogue(aid,m)ρ'))

eval-def(d)ρ=                                             (28)
 cases d:
  mk-Dcl(e)   → get-loc(e)ρ,
  mk-Proc(.)  → eval-proc(d)ρ

get-loc(e)ρ=                                              (29)
 (let l ∈ LOC be s.t. l ~∈ dom c Stg;
  Stg := cStg ∪ [l → eval-expr(e)ρ];
  return l )

get-aid()=                                                (30)
 (let aid ∈ AID be s.t. aid ~∈ caa ∪ cpa;
  aa := caa ∪ {aid};
  return aid)

C-Lbls(cl)=                                               (31)
 {s-Lbl(cl[i]) | i ∈ ind cl}∖{nil}              ∪
  union{S-Lbls(s-Stmt(cl[i])) | i ∈ ind cl }

S-Lbls(stmt)=                                             (32)
 cases stmt:
  mk-While(,c) → {s-Lbl(c)}∖{nil}∪S-Lbls(s-Stmt(c)),
  mk-Cmpd(cl)  → C-Lbls(cl),
  T            → {}
```

```
epilogue(aid,m)ρ=                                          (33)
  (//{aa := caa∖{aid},
      pa := cpa∪{aid}};
   let locs ={ρ(m(id)) | id ∈ dom m  ∧ is-Dcl(m(id))};
   Stg := cStg∖locs )

eval-proc(mk-Proc(idl,bl))ρ=                               (34)
 (let fct(al)=
        (let ρ' =ρ + [idl[i]→al[i] | i ∈ ind al];
         int-bl(bl)ρ');
  result is fct )

int-cl(cl,j)ρ=                                             (35)
 (trap exit(id) with
   cases id:
    mk-LAB(l,a)
     → if ρ(l)=id ∧ (∃!j ∈ ind cl)(s-Lbl(cl[i])=l)
         then (let j = (Δk)(s-Lbl(cl[k])=l);
                   int-cl(cl,j)ρ)
         else exit(id),
     T → exit(id);
   for i = j to l cl do
    int-st(s-Stmt(cl[i]))ρ)

int-st(s)ρ=                                                (36)
 cases s:
  mk-Asgn(id,e)
  → Stg := cStg + [ρ(id) → eval-expr(e)ρ],
  mk-While(e,c)
  → cue-int-wh(e,c,false)ρ,
  mk-Cmpd(cl)
  → int-cl(cl,1)ρ,
  mk-Goto(e)
  → exit(eval-expr(e)ρ),
  mk-Ret(...)
  → exit(RET),
  mk-Call(id,el)
  → (let ll : <get-loc(el[i])ρ | i ∈ ind el >;
      (trap exit(id') with
          (Stg := cStg ∖ rng ll;
           cases id': (RET → I, T → exit(id')));
       let fct =  ρ(id);
       fct(ll);
       Stg := cStg ∖ rng ll))

cue-int-wh(e,c,cue)ρ=                                      (37)
 (trap exit(id) with
   if id = ρ(s-Lbl(c))
    then cue-int-wh(e,c,true)ρ
    else exit(id);
  if cue
   then (int-st(s-Stmt(c))ρ;
           int-wh(e,c)ρ)
  else int-wh(e,c)ρ)

int-wh(e,c)ρ=                                              (38)
 if eval-expr(e)ρ
  then (int-st(s-Stmt(c))ρ;
          int-wh(e,c)ρ)
  else I

eval-expr(e)ρ=                                             (39)
  (is-Id(e)  → cStg(ρ(e)),
   is-Lbl(e) → ρ(e)'
   ...)
```

The *j* command list index passed to invocations of the *int-cl* elaboration function, like *cue*, serves as a cue to that (former) function, instructing it as where to begin! The technique of *cue-int*-functions was first reported by Jones in [6].

Conclusion:

With the techniques given above the reader should now be able to set up complete models for e.g. FORTRANs or COBOLs *GOTO* schemes, incl. the latters idea of *ALTER* - a construct which in essence restrictively introduces label variables into COBOL. We shall not here enter into any discussion of the appropriateness of *GOTO*, but only stress that once one has decided to include a variant of some exception (*GOTO*) mechanism, tools exist for its proper description. The one exemplified above is itself based on an exception construct of the meta-language - bu this *exit* construct can, however, be given a very simple, extended λ-expression definition [6,7] involving only applicative notions. For another, more powerful meta-notion: that of continuations, and examples of its use, we refer to [107,108,103]. For source language renditions of the *exit* idea we refer to [135, 136].

5.9 Concurrent/Parallel Program Constructs

This section is of necessity brief. Whereas, on one hand, many years of practice and study have shown the viability and demonstrated the foundational character of the constructs dealt with in all of the eight preceding subsections, and whereas there is some assurance that e.g. the above descriptional tools are proper and s fficiently powerful, that same, can, on the other hand, not be said for the concurrent/parallel programming constructs suggested in the 1960's. Also problems concerning their mathematical foundations exist which are yet to be understood. The 1970's have, however, seen the emergence of very promising ideas, and we shall therefore just take space out to refer to, and list references. [137-147] report on carefully motivated, mostly axiomatically modelled, and beautifully applied co-routine & concurrent programming constructs, and [148-152] represents attempts to provide a mathematical foundation for their proper characterization.

6. CONCLUSION

A number of programming language constructs have been isolated, and mechanical &/or denotational, abstract models have been given for their semantics. The treatm-nt has in parts been necessarily sporadic. A more complete, formal and thorough coverage is being planned for a monographic textbook on this and related subjects (sketched in [1,156-158]). It is the current authors' contention that university under-graduate courses in programming would benefit from an early introduction, into these courses, of denotational, rather than computational, descriptions. The latter is anyway 'experienced' by the programming student, the former would serve as an educational contrast, to broaden the mind, widen the outlook and deepen the understanding: setting the student free to more easily grasp, convert or adapt to, or even adopt new programming practices/languages. The idea in general is to be able to describe language constructs 'orthogonally', independently of one another, and then, dependent on their particular combination, in any one proposed, new language, to 'assemble' these subparts systematically into a complete language definition.

ACKNOWLEDGEMENTS

[154] must be credited for having stirred the authors' desire to formally & systematically 'orthogonalizing' the description of language constructs, and discussions with Jones [155] for having served as a first demonstration that it could be done are also,now greatly acknowledged.But more generally I should like to express my sincerest gratitude to my former colleagues at the IBM Vienna Lab.:H.Bekič,W.Henhapl,C.B.Jones,P.Lucas,K.Walk and,last but certainly not least:Prof.H.Zemanek,for having provided an inspiring and challenging milieu.

REFERENCES & BIBLIOGRAPHY -- a personal selection:

[1] D.Bjørner:"Programming Language:Formal Developement of Interpreters & Compilers",these proceedings.

Syntax:

[2] J.McCarthy:"Towards a Mathematical Science of Computations",in:'Information Processing',(ed. C.M.Popplewell) Proc.2nd IFIP Conf.,North-Holland Publ.,pp 21-28,1963.

[3] P.Lucas & K.Walk:"On the Formal Definition of PL/I",Ann.Rev.in:'Automatic Programming',vol. 6,pt.3,pp 105-152,1969.

[4] J.W.Backus:"The Syntax and Semantics of the Proposed Algebraic Language of the Zürich ACM-GAMM Conf.",Proc. IFIP,Unesco,Paris,Verlag Oldenburg,1959.

[5] J.W.Backus et.al.:"Report on the Algorithmic Language ALGOL 60",(ed.P.Naur) CACM,vol.3,no. 5,pp 299-314,1960.

[6] H.Bekič,D.Bjørner,W.Henhapl,C.B.Jones & P.Lucas:"A Formal Definition of a PL/I Subset", Pts.I-II,IBM Vienna Lab.Techn.Rept.TR25-139, Dec.1974.

[7] D.Bjørner:"META-IV: A Meta-Language for Abstract Software Specifications",Techn.Rept. (subm.for publ.) Techn.Univ.Denmark,Nov.1976.

[8] P.D.Mosses:"Compound Domain Descriptions", privately circulated,1976 (Comp.Sci.Dept., Århus Univ.,Denmark).

Axiomatic Semantics:

[9] J.E.Donahue:"The Mathematical Semantics of Axiomatically Defined Programming Language Constructs",IRIA Colloq.on:'Proving and Improving Programs',Arc et Senans,July 1-3,pp 353-367,1975.

[10] --:"Complementary Definitions of Programming Languages",Springer Lect.Notes in Comp.Sci., vol.42,1976.

[11] G.Ligler:"A Mathematical Approach to Language Design",Proc.2nd ACM SIGACT/SIGPLAN Symp.on 'Principles of Programming Languages',pp 41-53,ACM N.Y.,1975.

[12] --:"Surface Properties of Programming Language Constructs",ref 9,pp 299-323.

[13] C.A.R.Hoare:"An Axiomatic Basis for Computer Programming",CACM,vol.12,no.10,pp 576-583, 1969.

[14] --:"Procedures & Parameters:an Axiomatic Approach",in:'Semantics of Algorithmic Languages',(ed.E.Engeler) Springer Lecture Notes in Mathematics,vol.188,pp 102-116,1971.

[15] -- & N.Wirth:"An Axiomatic Definition of the Programming Language PASCAL",Acta Informatica, vol.2,no.2,pp 335-355,1973.

[16] W.P.de Roever:"Recursion and Parameter-Mechanisms,an Axiomatic Approach",Proc.2nd Colloq. on 'Automata,Languages and Programming',Springer Lect.Notes in Comp.Sci.,vol.14,pp 34-65, 1974.

[17] E.W.Dijkstra:"A Simple Axiomatic Basis for Programming Language Constructs",Indagationes Mathematicae,vol.36,pp 1-15,1974.

Semiotics:

[18] R.Carnap:"The Logical Syntax of Language",Harcourt,Brace & Co.,N.Y.,1937.

[19] --:"Introduction to Semantics",Harvard Univ. Press,Cambridge,Mass.1942.

[20] C.W.Morris:"Foundations of the Theory of Signs", in: Int'l Encyclopedia of Unified Sciences, vol.1,no.2,Univ.of Chicago Press,1938.

[21] --:"Signs,Language & Behavior",G.Brazilier, N.Y.,1955.

[22] G.Frege:"Über Sinn und Bedeutung",Zeitschrift für Philosophie und Philosophisches Kritik, vol.100,pp 25-50,1892.

[23] B.Russell:"On Denoting",Mind,vol.14,pp 479-493,1905.

[24] --:"The Principles of Mathematics",Allen and Unwin,London,1910.

[25] A.Church:"Introduction to Mathematical Logic", Princeton Univ.Press,N.J.,1956.

[26] W.V.Quine:"Word and Object",Technology Press, J.Wiley,MIT,Cambridge,Mass.,1960.

[27] H.Zemanek:"Semiotics and Programming Languages", CAM.,vol.9,no.3,pp 139-143,1966.

Basic Programming Ideas

[28] P.Naur:"A Concise Survey of Computer Methods", Studentförlag,Lund,Sweden,1974.

Foundational Semantics & Linguistics Modelling:

[29] J.McCarthy:"Recursive Functions of Symbolic Expressions and their Computation by Machines, pt.I",CACM,vol.3,no.4,pp 184-195,1960.

[30] P.J.Landin:"The Next 700 Programming Languages", CACM.,vol.9,no.3,pp 157-166,1966.

[31] C.Strachey:"Towards a Formal Semantics",in: 'Formal Language Description Languages for Computer Programming',(ed.T.B.Stell Jr.) Proc. IFIP Working Conf.,Vienna,North-Holland Publ., pp 198-220,1966.

[32] D.Scott & C.Strachey:"Towards a Mathematical Semantics for Computer Languages",in:'Computers & Automata',(ed.J.Fox) PIB MRI Symp.Ser. vol.XXI,Polytechnic Inst.of Brooklyn Press,71.

[33] A.van Wijngaarden'"Generalized ALGOL",Ann. Rev.in:'Automatic Programming',Pergamon Press, no.11,no.3,pp 17-26,1963.

[34] --:"Recursive Definition of Syntax and Seman= tics",ref 31,pp 13-24.

λ-Calculus/Algebra & Combinatory Logic:

[35] A.Church:"The Calculi of Lambda Conversion", Ann.of Math.Studies,vol.6,Princeton Univ.Press, N.J.,1941 (2nd ed.1951).

[36] H.B.Curry & R.Feys:"Combinatory Logic,vol.I", North-Holland Publ.,1958.

[37] H.B.Curry,J.R.Hindley & J.Seldin:"Combinatory Logic,vol.II",North-Holland Publ.,1972.

[38] P.J.Landin:"A Correspondance between ALGOL 60 and Church's Lambda Notation",CACM.,vol. 8,nos 2-3,pp 89-101,158-165,1965.

[39] --:"A Lambda Calculus Approach",in:'Advances in Programming and Non-Numeric Computations', (ed.L.Fox) Pergamon Press,pp 97-141,1966.

[40] --:"A Formal Description of ALGOL 60",ref 31, pp 266-294.

[41] J.H.Morris:"Lambda-Calculus Models of Program= ming Languages",Ph.D.Thesis,MIT,Proj.MAC Techn. Rept.,TR-57,Cambridge,Mass.,1968.

[42] A.Evans Jr.:"The Lambda-Calculus and its Re= lation to Programming Languages",Proc.ACM Nat'l.Conf.,pp 395-403,1968.

[43] D.Scott:"Lattic-Theoretic Models for Various Type-Free Calculi",Proc.4th Int'l.Cong.for 'Logic,Methodology and the Philosophy of Sci.', Bucharest,(ed.P.Suppes) North-Holland,pp 157-187,1973.

[...] 'λ-Calculus & Comp.Sci.Theory',(ed.C.Böhm) Symp.Proc.,Rome,Italy,Springer Lect.Notes in Comp.Sci.,vol.37,1975.

[44] C.P.Wadsworth:"Semantics and Pragmatics of the Lambda-Calculus",Ph.D.Thesis,Oxford Univ., Comp.Lab.,Prgr.Res.Grp.,1971.

[45] --:"The Relation between Computational and Denotational Properties for Scott's D_∞-Models of the Lambda-Calculus",SIAM J.Comput.,vol.5, no.3,pp 488-521,1976.

Substitution Languages:

[46] J.W.Backus:"Reduction Languages and Variable-Free Programming",IBM Res.Lab.,Rept.RJ-1010, San Jose,Ca.,1972.

[47] --:"Programming Language Semantics & Closed Applicative Languages",ibid RJ-1245,and in: 'Principles of Programming Languages',Proc. ACM SIGACT/SIGPLAN Conf.,Boston,pp 71-86,1973.

[48] W.C.Rounds:"Mappings and Grammars on Trees", Math.Sys.The.,vol.4,pp 257-287,1970.

[49] J.Engelfriet:"Bottom-Up & Top-Down Tree Trans= formations",Memo-19,Techn.Univ.Twente,Ensche= de,The Netherlands,1971.

[50] D.Bjørner:"Finite State Tree Transductions,pt. I",IBM Res.Lab.,Rept.RJ-1052,San Jose,Ca.,1972.

[51] J.W.Thatcher:"Tree Automata: An Informal Sur= vey",in:'Currents in Computing',(ed.A.Aho) Prentice-Hall,pp 147-172,1973.

[52] B.K.Rosen:"Tree Manipulating Systems & Church Rosser Theroems",JACM,vol.20,no.1,pp 160-187, 1973.

[53] J.Engelfriet & E.M.Schmidt:"IO & OI",Dept.of Comp.Sci.,DAIMI Rept.PB-47,Århus Univ.,1975.

[54] A.A.Markov:"Theory of Algorithms",trans.:Amer. Math.Soc.Trans.,vol.2,no.15,pp 1-14,1960 (1st. publ.in Russian,1951).

[55] J.E.L.Peck:"Two Level Grammars in Action",in Proc.IFIP Cong.74,North-Holland Publ.,pp 317-321,1974.

Languages:

ALGOL 60: [25,27]

[56] J.W.Backus,et.al.:"Revised Report on the Al= gorithmic Language ALGOL 60",(ed.P.Naur) CACM, vol.6,no.1,pp 1-17,1963.

[57] N.Wirth:"A Generalization of ALGOL",CACM.,vol. 6,pp 547-554,1963.

[58] -- & C.A.R.Hoare:"A Contribution to the Deve= lopment of ALGOL",CACM.,vol.9,no.6,pp 413-432,1966.

Euler:

[59] N.Wirth & H.Weber:"EULER - A Generalization of ALGOL and its Formal Definition,Pts.1 & 2", CACM,vol.9,nos.1-2,pp 13-23,89-99,1966.

PASCAL: [8]

[60] N.Wirth:"The Programming Language PASCAL", Acta Informatica,vol.1,no.1,pp 35-63,1971.

[61] A.N.Habermann:"Critical Comments on the Pro= gramming Language PASCAL",

CPL/BCPL: (otherwise 'un-related')

[62] D.W.Barron,J.N.Buxton,D.F.Hartley,E.Nixon & C.Strachey:"The Main Features of CPL",Comp. J.,vol.6,pp 134-143,1963.

[63] M.Richards:"BCPL Reference Manual",Techn.Memo. No.69/1,The Univ.Math.Lab.,Cambridge,UK,1969.

SIMULA 67:

[64] O.-J.Dahl & K.Nygaard:"SIMULA - An ALGOL-based Simulation Language",CACM.,vol.9,no.9,pp 671-678,1966.

[65] J.D.Ichbiah & S.P.Morse:"General Concepts of the SIMULA 67 Programming Language",Ann.Rev. in:'Automatic Progr.',Pergamon Press,pp 65-93,19

GEDANKEN:

[66] J.C.Reynolds:"GEDANKEN - A Simple,Type-Less Language based on the Principle of Complete= ness and the Reference Concept",CACM.,vol.13, no.5,pp 308-319,1970.

PAL: [42]

[67] A.Evans:"PAL - A Language Designed for Teaching

Programming Linguistics",Proc.ACM 23rd Nat'l Conf.,Brandin Sys.Press,Princeton,N.J.,pp 395-403,1968.

Lisp 1.5

[68] J.McCarthy et al.:"LISP 1.5 Programmar's Manual",MIT Press,Cambridge,Mass.,1962.

Bliss:

[69] W.A.Wulf et al.:"BLISS: A Language for Systems Programming",CACM.,vol.14,pp 780-790,1971.

SNOBOL:

[70] R.Griswold,J.Poage,I.Polonsky:"The SNOBOL-4 Programming Language",Prentice-Hall,1971.

[71] R.D.Tennent:"Mathematical Semantics of SNOBOL 4",ref 47,pp 95-107.

ALGOL 68: [55]

[72] A.van Wijngaarden et al.:"Report on the Algorithmic Language ALGOL 68",Acta Informatica, vol.5,pp 1-236,1975.

[73] P.Branquart,J.Lewi,M.Sintzoff & P.L.Wodon:"The Composition of Semantics in ALGOL 69",CACM., vol.14,no.11,pp 697-708,1971.

[74] H.Bekić:"An Introduction to ALGOL 68",in:'Ann. Rev.in Automatic Programming',Pergamon Press, vol.7,pt.3,1973.

[75] A.S.Tanenbaum:"A Tutorial on ALGOL 68",ACM Comp.Survey,vol.8,no.2,pp 155-190,1976.

[76] C.H.Lindsey & S.G.van der Meulen:"An Informal Introduction to ALGOL 68",North-Holland Publ.,1971.

[77] F.G.Pagan:"A Practical Guide to ALGOL 68", J.Wiley Inc.,N.Y.,1976.

COMIT:

[78] V.Yngve:"COMIT II Programming Manual",MIT Press,Cambridge,Mass.,1972.

APL:

[79] K.E.Iverson:"A Programming Language",J.Wiley & Sons,N.Y.,1962.

COBOL / FORTRAN / BASIC / PL/I [6](&: [48-50] in [1])

... -- consult your nearest bookshelf!

Data Types:

[80] D.Scott:"Data Types as Lattices",ref 45,pp 522-587.

[81] C.A.R.Hoare:"Notes on Data Structuring",in: 'Structured Programming',(eds.Dahl+Dijkstra+ Hoare) Academic Press,1972.

[82] --:"Recursive Data Structures",AIM-223,Stanford Univ.,Comp.Sci.Dept.,1973 (also publ.!).

[83] A.E. & M.J.Fischer:"Mode Modules as Representations of Domains",ref 47,pp 139-143.

[84] J.H.Morris:"Types are Not Sets",ref 47,pp 120-124.

[85] --:"Protection in Programming Languages",CACM vol.16,no.1,pp 15-21,1973.

[86] --:"Towards more Flexible Type Systems",Proc. 'Programming Symp.',Paris,April,1974,Springer Lect.Notes in Comp.Sci.,vol.19,pp 377-384,1974.

[87] J.C.Reynolds:"Towards a Theory of Type Structure",ref 86,pp 408-425.

[88] B.H.Liskov & S.N.Zilles:"Programming with Abstract Data Types",Proc.ACM SIGPLAN Conf.on 'Very High-Level Languages',SIGPLAN Notices, vol.9,no.4,pp 50-59,1974.

[89] --:"Specification Techniques for Data Abstractions",IEEE Trans.on Softw.Eng.,vol.SE-1,no.1, pp 7-19,1975.

[90] C.H.Lewis & B.K.Rosen:"Recursively Defined Data Types",pt.I:ref 47,pp 125-138;pt.II: IBM Ths.J.Watson Res.Ctr.,Rept.RC-4713,Yorktown Heights,N.Y.,1974.

[91] M.Newey:"Axioms and Theorems for Integer Lists and Finite Sets in LCF",AI-184,Stanford Univ., Comp.Sci.Dept.,1973.

[92] M.Wand:"On the Recursive Specifications of Data Types",in:'Category Theory applied to Computation & Control',(ed.E.Manes) Univ.of Mass.,Amherst,Springer Lect.Notes in Comp. Sci.,vol 25,pp 222-225,1975.

[93] D.Park:"On the Semantics of some Data Structures",in:'Machine Intelligence'(ed.D.Michie), Edinburg Univ.Press,vol.3,pp 351-371,1968.

Variables,Assignment & The Store:

[94] P.J.Landin:"An Analysis of Assignment in Programming Languages",Univac Sys.Prgr.Res.Grp., N.Y.,1965.

[95] C.Strachey:"Fundamental Concepts in Programming Languages",unpubl.lect.notes for the NATO Summer School,Copenhagen,1967.

[96] R.M.Burstall:"The Semantics of Assignment", ref 93,vol.2,pp 3-20,1968.

[97] J.W.de Bakker:"Axiomatics of Simple Assignment Statements",MR94,Math.Centrum,Amsterdam, pp 1-37,1968.

[98] H.Bekić & K-Walk:"Formalization of Storage Properties",ref 14,pp 28-61.

[99] K.Walk:"Modeling of Storage Properties of Higher-Level Languages",Int'l.J.Comp.& Inf. Sci.,vol.2,no.1,pp 1-24,1973.

[100] R.Milne & C.Strachey:"A Theory of Programming Language Semantics",Chapman and Hall,London, 1976.

Simple Goto Semantics:

[101] W.Henhapl & C.B.Jones:"On the Interpretation of GOTO Statements in the VDL",IBM Vienna Lab., Lab.Note LN25.3.065,1970.

[102] C.D.Allen,D.N.Chapman & C.B.Jones:"A Formal Definition of ALGOL 60",IBM British Labs,Techn. Rept.TR12.105,IBM UK,Hursley,1972.

[103] C.B.Jones:"Mathematical Semantics of GOTO: Exit Formulation and its Relation to Continuations",unpubl.,IBM Vienna Lab.,1976.

[104] P.J.Landin:"Getting Rid of Labels",Univac Sys.Prgr.Res.Grp.,N.Y.,1965.

[105] P.J.Landin:"A Generalization of Jumps and Labels",ibid,1965.

[106] F.Lockwood Morris:"The next 700 Formal Programming Descriptions",unpubl.notes,Univ.of Essex,1969.

[107] C.Strachey & C.P.Wadsworth:"Continuations - a Mathematical Semantics for Handling Full Jumps",PRG-11,Oxford Univ.Comp.Lab.,Prgr. Res.Grp.,1974.

[108] J.C.Reynolds:"On the Relation between Direct and Continuation Semantics",ref 16,pp 141-156.

[109] M.Clint & C.A.R.Hoare:"Program Proving:Jumps and Functions",Acta Informatica,vol.1,pp 214-224,1972.

[110] A.Wang:"An Axiomatic Basis for Proving Total Correctness of GOTO Programs",BIT,vol.16,no. 1,pp 88-102,1976.

Structured Control Structures:

[111] C.Böhm & G.Jacopini:"Flow Diagrams,Turing Machines and Languages with only two Formation Rules",CACM.,vol.9,no.5,pp 366-371,1966.

[112] D.C.Cooper:"Some Transformations and Standard Forms of Graphs with Applications to Computer Programs",ref 93,vol.2,pp 21-32,1968.

[113] E.Ashcroft & Z.Manna:"The Translations of 'GOTO' Programs to 'While' Programs",Stanford Univ.,Comp.Sci.Dept.,CS-188,1971.

[114] R.Kosaraju:"Analysis of Structured Programs", J.Comp.& Sys.Sci.,vol.9,no.3,pp 232-255,1974.

[115] H.D.Mills:"Matjematical Foundations for Structured Programming",IBM Corp.Rept.FSC72-6012, Fed.Sys.Div.,Gaithersburg,Md.,1972.

[116] W.W.Peterson,T.Kasami & N.Tokura:"On the Capabilities of while,repeat and exit statements", CACM.,vol.16,pp 503-512,1973.

[117] H.F.Ledgard & M-Marcotty:"A Genealogy of Control Structures",CACM.,vol.18,no.11,pp 629-639,1975.

[118] D.S.Wise,D.P.Friedmann,S.C.Shapiro & M.Wand: "Boolean-Valued Loops",BIT,vol.15,pp 431-451, 1975.

[119] E.W.Dijkstra:"Guarded Commands,Non-Determinacy and a Calculus for the Derivation of Programs",CACM.,vol.18,no.8,pp 453-457,1975.

[120] C.A.R.Hoare:"A Note of the 'FOR' Statement", BIT,vol.12,pp 334-341,1972.

Applicative Languages & Combinatory Programming:

[121]≡[30],see also: [46,47]

[122] W.H.Burge:"Combinatory Programming and Combinatorial Analysis",IBM J.of Res.& Dev., vol.16,no.5,1972,pp 450-461.

[123] --:"Recursive Programming Techniques",Addison-Wesley (IBM Systems Programming Ser.), 1975.

Blocks,Procedures & Macros: [7]

[124] E.W.Dijkstra:"Recursive Programming",Num. Mathematik,vol.2 ,no.5,pp 312-318,1960.

[125] --:"An ALGOL 60 Translator for the X1",Automatic Programming Bulletin,Ann.Rev.in: 'Automatic Progr',vol. 3,pp 329-356,1962.

[126] J.W.de Bakker:"Recursive Procedures",Math. Centre Tracts,vol.24,Amsterdam,1971.

[127] J.Moses:"The Function of FUNCTION in LISP", ACM SIGPLAN Bulletin,pp 13-27,1970;also: "... - or why the FUNARG Problem should be called the Environment Problem",Memo-248, AI-199,Proj.MAC,MIT,Cambridge,Mass.,1970.

[128] J.Weizenbaum:"The FUNARG Problem Explained", unpubl.note,Proj.MAC,MIT,1968.

[129] B.Wegbreit:"Procedure Closure in EL1",Comp. J.,vol.17,no.1,pp 38-43,197 .

[130] D.G.Bobrow & B.Wegbreit:"A Model and Stack Implementation of Multiple Environments", (1)Bolt-Beranek-Newman,Inc.,BBN-2334,1972; (2)CACM,vol.16,no.10,1973;(3)Proc.Int'l. Conf.on Art.Intell.,1973.

[131] W.Henhapl & C.B.Jones:"A Run-Time Mechanism for Referencing Variables",Inf-Proc.Letters, vol.1,no.1,pp 14-16,1971.

[132] P.Lucas:"Two Constructive Realizations of the Block Concept and their Equivalence", IBM Vienna Lab.,Techn.Rept.,TR25.085,1968.

[133] J.B.Johnston:"The Contour Model of Block-Structured Processes",Proc.Symp.on:'Data Structures in Programming Languages',ACM SIGPLAN Notices,vol.6,no.2,pp 55-82,1971.

[134] J.W.Thomas E E.I.Organick:"Visible Semantices for Programming Languages",ACM Nat'l Conf.,Proc.,pp 416-421,San Diego,Calif., (out of print!),1974.

Exceptions: [101-110]

[135] C.T.Zahn Jr.:"A Control Statement for Natural Top-Down Structured Programming",in: 'Programming',Symp.Paris,France,Springer Lect.Notes in Comp.Sci.,vol.19,pp 170-180, 1974.

[136] A.Halaas: Event Driven Control Statements", BIT,vol.15,pp 259-271,1975.

Co-Routines & Concurrent/Parallel Programming:

[137] O.-J.Dahl:"An Approach to Correctness Proofs of Semi-Coroutines",in:'Math.Found.of Comp. Sci.',Springer Lect.Notes in Comp.Sci.,vol. 28,pp 157-174,1975.

[138] A.Wang & O.-J.Dahl:"Coroutine Sequencing in a Block-Structured Environment",BIT,vol. 11,pp 425-449,1971.

[139] P.B.Hansen:"The Nucleus of a Multiprogramming System",CACM.,vol.13,no.4,pp 238-250, 1970.

[140] --:"Short-Term Scheduling in Multi-Programming Systems",Proc.ACM SIGOPS Symp.on:'Operating System Principles',pp 101-105,1971.

[141] --:"Structured Multiprogramming",ACM Comp. Survey,vol.15,pp 574-578,1972.

[142] --:"The Programming Language Concurrent PAS= CAL",IEEE Trans.on Softw.Eng.,vol.SE-1,no.2, pp 199-207,1975.

[143] A.N.Habermann:"Synchronization of Communica= ting Processes",CACM.,vol.15,no.3,pp 171-176, 1972.

[144] C.A.R.Hoare:"Towards a Theory of Parallel Programming",in:'Operating Systems Techni= ques'(eds.C.A.R.Hoare & R.H.Perrot) Academic Press,1972.

[145] --:"Parallel Programming: An Axiomatic Ap= proach",Stanford Univ.,Comp.Sci.Dept.,CS394, AI-219,1973 -- also in:Springer Lect.Notes in Comp.Sci.,vol.46,pp 11-39,1976.

[146] --:"Monitors: An Operating System Structuring Concept",CACM.,vol.17,no.10,pp 549-557,1974.

[147] --:"The Structure of an Operating System", (later)ref 145,pp 242-265.

[148] H.Bekić:"Towards a Mathematical Theory of Processes",IBM Vienna Lab.,Techn.Rept.,TR 25.125,1971.

[149] R.Milner:"An Approach to the Semantics of Parallel Programs",Proc.Convegno di Infor= matica Teorica,Univ.of Pisa,pp 285-..,1973.

[150] --:"Processes: A Mathematical Model for Com= puting Agents",Proc.Colloq.in Math.Logic, Univ.Bristol,England,1973.(North-Holland.)

[151] J.M.Cadiou & J.J.Levy:"Mechanizable Proofs about Parallel Processes",Proc.14th SWAT, IEEE,1973.

[152] B.K.Rosen:"Correctness of Parallel Programs - The Church-Rosser Approach",ref 9.

General:

[153] P.Naur:" Program Translation Viewed as a Ge= neral Data Processing Problem",CACM.,vol.9, no.3,pp 176-179,1966.

[154] H.F.Ledgard:"Ten Mini-Languages: A Study of Topical Issues in Programming Languages", ACM Comp.Survey.,vol.3,no.3,pp 115-146,1971.

[155] C.B.Jones:"Formal Specifications in Language Development",Proc.Symp.Wildbad,'Programming Methodology'(IBM Germany),Springer Lect.Notes in Comp.Sci.,vol.23,1974/75.

[156] D.Bjørner:"Abstract Software Specifications" &:"Software Abstraction Principles",Techn. Univ.Denmark,Techn.Monograph,resp.Rept.,Fall 1976.(112+46 pg)

[157] --:"Systematic Program Derivation" &:"... Techniques",Techn.Univ.Denmark,Techn.Mono= graph,resp.Rept.,Fall 1976.(72+46 pg)

[158] --:"Systematic Compiler Specifications",Techn. Univ.Denmark,Techn.Monograph (draft),Fall 1976.(155 pg)

[159] --:"A Short Introduction to the Engineering Art of Software Development",Techn.Monograph, Univ.Copenhagen,Feb.1976.(365 pg)

E. Morlet and D. Ribbens, (Eds.), International Computing Symposium 1977.

PROGRAM SPECIFICATIONS AND FORMAL DEVELOPMENT

C.B. JONES
IBM Arthur K. Watson International Education Centre
European Systems Research Institute - E.S.R.I.
Chaussée de Bruxelles 135
B - 1310 La Hulpe.
BELGIUM

This tutorial covers the subjects of precise program specification, program correctness proofs and stepwise refinement of programs. Particular emphasis is placed on the use and development of abstract data objects.

Introduction

This paper will attempt to survey some of the topics which are essential for a more rigorous approach to program development. The key idea which underlies this paper's view of the program development process is that it is possible to prove programs correct with respect to their specifications (see refs Floyd /1/, Naur /2/, Hoare /3/, Manna /4/). It is not the intent of this paper to argue that all programs should be formally proved correct : rather it is the extent to which the methods, which would be used in so doing, can be employed in making program development more rigorous, which this paper will try to convey. A specification must itself provide a precise statement of the desired effect of a program, and specifications are the subject of the first section below. A brief outline of the published concepts relating to proving programs correct is then given.

The likely extent and time scale of the impact of the methods is not the subject of this paper. It is, however, clear that whilst the ideas on program proofs are a cornerstone of the future work, their application to large programs will only be practicable in some stepwise development process (cf refs Naur /5/, Hoare /6/, Jones /7/, Dijkstra /8/, Wirth /9/). Furthermore, it is the opinion of the current author that application to a wider class of problems than those dealing with numerical calculations depends on the use of abstract data objects (refs Jones /7/, Hoare /10/ Wirth /11/). The section on specifications will introduce this concept and show its application to defining the task to be performed by a program. Rather than show the application of the proof techniques, which are described in the second section below, to a stepwise refinement of operations, the remaining section will show the part played by object refinement in a rigorous program development approach (cf ref Jones /12/).

Program specifications

If one wishes to cause a program to be developed it should be clear that, as in other walks of life, one must first create a precise statement of the task which is to be performed. The experience of the author would support going through this preliminary step even where requester and programmer are the same person. This paper will use the term "specification" to denote that description of a program which concentrates on what it should do without going into any details as to how the task might be accomplished.

The view of a specification as a contract between the eventual user of a program and its developer suggests a number of requirements. The technical requirements of :

- Precision
- Consistency
- Completeness

would argue for a formal language being used. Here "formal" is meant to distinguish those languages which have a precise semantics. It is well known that sentences can be constructed in "natural languages" (e.g. French, German, English) whose meaning can be, at best, a subject of debate. Programming languages are "formal" in the sense used here although, for a number of reasons which are indicated below, they are not suitable for specifications.

The technical requirements given above must not be allowed to obscure the fact that specifications must also be understood by human beings. This salutary observation brings the additional requirements of :

- Comprehensibility
- Organization

(Reasonable) length.

One of the aims of this paper will be to convince the reader that this latter group of requirements is also met by specifications which are written predominantly in formal notation.

The apparent qualification in the last sentence applies to large systems where a definition whose organization is made clear by a formal structure might be shortened by defining certain sub-functions in natural language. The structure of the definitions will have set the context. If the text is chosen so as to appeal to the knowledge common in one area then there should be little danger of imprecision. Most importantly, however, is the knowledge that the definition could be completed by formalising any areas which do become a subject of misunderstanding. This will, of course, only be possible to do in a non-disruptive way if the structure really has been properly thought out.

Before coming to specifying programs as such, it is convenient to consider how a function can be characterised implicitly. A function can be applied to values as arguments and will deliver values as results. If one wishes to describe the effect of a function one might use the notation of logic to specify the relationship required between the result delivered and the input value given. The advantage of such an implicit definition is that where the required operation goes beyond the simple expressions of the language in which one eventually has to write the function, it will frequently be easier to say what should be achieved. Suppose, for example, that the task of computing square roots to within some tolerance is to be specified. The statement that the required function, f say, is to yield a value when applied to x, say, such that its square is no more than a given tolerance, say t, away from x, can be written as :

$$\text{abs } (f(x,t)^2 - x) \leq t$$

This description of what f should do is certainly much shorter than the successive approximation algorithm which will be required to realise f. For many purposes it is also much more convenient: if f is to figure in some larger computations it will be its properties which are of importance not its eventual realisation.

The above specification is incomplete, however, in that no limitation as to what values f is capable of handling has been stated.

Whilst it could possibly be argued that the use of the arithmetic operators in the specification indicates that f should not be applied, for example, to character strings, there is as yet nothing to prevent application of f to negative numbers. In an example as simple as this it is, in fact, possible to specify the required constraint by stating a familiar set of values to which f can be applied.

A standard notation from mathematics to state the sets for the domain (permissable arguments) and range (results) is :

$$f : D \rightarrow R$$

where D and R are the names of known sets. In more complex cases there might be no convenient known set over which the function can be expected to operate (this is particularly the case when the input consists of a number of values and the function relies on a relationship holding between them) and it is again necessary to write a logical expression which characterizes the set.

To summarize then, a function can be implicitly characterized by stating its type, a "pre" condition limiting its domain and a "post" condition specifying the required relation between input and output values. For the square root example above, if Real is the set of real numbers the type might be written :

$$f : \text{Real} \quad \text{Real} \rightarrow \text{Real}$$

the limitation to the domain might be specified by the predicate :

$$\text{pre-}f\ (x,t) \equiv 0 \leq x$$

and the required function by the predicate :

$$\text{post-}f\ (x,t,r) \equiv \text{abs } (r^2 - x) \leq t$$

the implied specification being if :

$$\text{pre-}f\ (x,t)$$

holds, then :

$$\text{post-}f\ (x,t,f(x,t))$$

must be true.

Another example can be made of the well-known factorial function in which :

$$0\,! = 1$$

$$(n + 1)\,! = (n + 1).\ n\,!$$

If the set of natural numbers including zero (i.e. 0,1, 2 etc) is denoted by :

$$\text{Nat}^{\circ}$$

then the required function has the type :

$$\text{fact} : \text{Nat}^{\circ} \rightarrow \text{Nat}$$

No further constraint on the input values is required, the value computed should be such that:

$$\text{post-fact } (x,\ \text{fact}(x))$$

where :

$$\text{post-fact}(n,fn) \equiv fn = n\,!$$

It is worth noticing two things about this type description. The range elements have been specified as coming from the natural numbers excluding zero (i.e. 1,2,3 etc.) : since this can be deduced from the definition it is really redundant information but it will be found convenient when combining one function with others to have a note of its type. Secondly, it should be observed that the domain could have been shown as a wider set and the limitation (e.g. $0 \leq x$) stated as a pre-condition. There will be occasions where such choices are more difficult to resolve. The pre- and post-conditions given above are, in fact, predicates, that is functions from some given domain to the set of truth values (called Bool below); thus :

$$\text{pre-f} : \text{Real} \rightarrow \text{Bool}$$

$$\text{post-f} : \text{Real} \quad \text{Real} \quad \text{Real} \rightarrow \text{Bool}$$

One symbol ($\equiv$) for building up logical expressions has already been used : the full set used below is :

sign	read as
$\wedge$	and
$\vee$	or
$\supset$	implies
$\equiv$	equivalence
$\neg$	not
$\forall$	for all
$\exists$	there exists

It is not the aim of this paper to teach propositional and predicate calculus (for most purposes the above "readings" will be adequate) ref Kleene /14/ can be recommended for this purpose.

The ideas of characterizing a required function by giving its type and pre/post predicates will also be used in implicitly stating properties required of pieces of program. But it is important to be clear about the distinction between functions and programs. The essence of a digital computer is its store from which values can be retrieved, and into which new values may be stored.

This memory which can be overwritten at the machine level, has affected the design of nearly all programming languages via the notions of variable and assignment. In specifying a piece of program, then, it may be necessary to state a relation between input states and output states in addition to any other input and output values.

The importance of the notion of assignment can already be observed with the trivial example of factorial. Suppose it were to be realized, using an obvious notation, by the following recursive function :

$$\text{fact}(n) = \underline{\text{if}}\ n = 0\ \underline{\text{then}}\ 1\ \underline{\text{else}}\ n.\text{fact}(n-1)$$

then a particular evaluation might be :

$$\text{fact}(3) = 3.(2.(1.(1)))$$

mathematically there is no problem, but if it is actually computed this way by machine then the amount of storage required prior to computing the result is proportional to the value of n. Obviously, this is one objection to using recursion on this example and a more satisfactory program, which ends with the answer in variable fn, is :

```
c = 0;
fn = 1;
    DO WHILE (c ≠ n);
    c = c + 1;
    fn = fn.c;
    END;
```

In this solution, apart from the input and output variables (n,fn respectively) exactly one extra storage location is used regardless of the value of n. If, instead of factorial, an example involving arrays was under consideration, the role of variables which are overwritten within loops would be even more important.

To achieve, with parts of programs, the same implicit definition style which was used with functions it is first necessary to decide how to describe states. Essentially one has to record the variable names and their types. It is possible to do this completely formally but for the current purposes it is adequate to write, say :

$$\Sigma = \begin{array}{l} n : \text{Nat}^{\circ} \\ fn : \text{Nat}^{\circ} \\ c : \text{Nat}^{\circ} \end{array}$$

to indicate a class of states with three components (i.e. variables n,fn and c) with the given types.

It is now possible to regard a program as taking an input state and possibly some arguments and delivering an output state and possibly some result :

$$\text{PROG} : \Sigma \quad D \rightarrow \Sigma \quad R$$

It is however, a constraint on most languages that complete phrase structures (e.g. statements or blocks) cannot change the structure of the state. In ref Jones /15/ this fact was emphasized by showing the state as follows :

$$\text{PROG} :: \Sigma : \quad D \quad R$$

this can be read as "PROG runs on states of and can read and write the values of variables therein; in addition arguments in D are accepted and results in R created".

Characterizing a (part of a) program in a way analogous to that for characterizing functions can now be done by defining two predicates :

$$\text{pre-PROG} : \Sigma \ D \rightarrow \text{Bool}$$

$$\text{post-PROG} : \Sigma \ D \ \Sigma \ R \rightarrow \text{Bool}$$

For example, using Σ as above and the sequence of statements for computing factorial :

$$\text{pre-FACT}(\langle n,fn,c\rangle) \equiv 0 \leq n$$

$$\text{post-FACT}(\langle n,fn,c\rangle, \langle n',fn',c'\rangle) \equiv fn'=n!$$

Notice that in this example there are no auxiliary arguments and results : all data is in the state.

The use of post-conditions for functions and programs has provided an implicit means of characterizing the required object : it has been made possible to abstract from an algorithm the essential properties on which others rely viz. the result.

The subject of proving programs correct with respect to specifications of the sort given above will be returned to in the next section. For the time being the class of programs which can usefully be specified must be extended : so far it has only been indicated that one can provide descriptions of numerical problems.

In order to tackle problems of other types (e.g. string handling, commercial) it will be necessary to give more consideration to data objects. In particular the case will now be developed for using abstract data objects.

Suppose the need is for a system which records which students are in a given classroom. One can envisage sub-programs which record entry and exit and test function which can be used to determine whether a given student is in the classroom. Given a set of student names :

St-nm

how is one to specify the state on which the sub-programs work ? In the eventual program one might choose an array of character string variables and an index : modelling insertion is then adding a name in the "next" position of the array and moving the index; deletion is somewhat more tedious because the "empty position" in the array must be refilled; worst of all, if the test function is required very often the array search may be rather inefficient. In other words one might choose an entirely different representation ! The point is that in the specification one wants to describe what should happen and postpone the design of the data structures of the program until one's attention shifts to implementation. What then is to be done about describing the state in the specification ? The answer, in general, is "abstract". Use data structures which possess only those properties necessary to specify the required results. In this specific case the only fact of importance is whether a name is present or not and an appropriate abstraction would be a set of student names, writing :

$$\Sigma = \text{St-nm-set}$$

to define elements of Σ as containing some set of elements each of which are in the set St-nm, the types of the sub-programs can be given as :

$$\text{ENTER} :: \Sigma : \text{St-nm} \rightarrow$$

$$\text{EXIT} :: \Sigma : \text{St-nm} \rightarrow$$

$$\text{PRESENT} : \Sigma \ \text{St-nm} \rightarrow \text{Bool}$$

Furthermore, using an obvious set notation (see below) it is possible to specify :

$$\text{post-ENTER}(\sigma,s,\sigma') \equiv \sigma' = \sigma \cup \{s\}$$

$$\text{post-EXIT}(\sigma,s,\sigma') \equiv \sigma' = \sigma - \{s\}$$

$$\text{PRESENT}(\sigma,s) \equiv s \in \sigma$$

Having attempted to motivate the introduction of something as abstract as sets for the description of a very simple programming problem a brief review of the notation to be used will be given. Set values may be written by explicitly enumerating the values between braces :

$$\{x_1, x_2, \ldots, x_n\}$$

a special case being the empty set (which has zero elements) :

$$\{\ \}$$

Set values may also be given implicitly by enclosing in braces an expression in some bound variable and a range for that bound variable separated by a bar (which can be read as "such that") :

$$\{f(x) \mid p(x)\}$$

Thus, for example :

$$\{2^n \mid 0 \leq n \leq 3\} = \{1, 8, 2, 4\}$$

the odd order of the explicit value being shown only as a reminder that neither order nor multiple occurences play any part in set values. Certain special sets, some of which were used above, are :

$$\text{Bool} = \{\underline{\text{TRUE}}, \underline{\text{FALSE}}\}$$

$$\text{Nat} = \{1,2,\ldots\}$$

$$\text{Nat}^\circ = \{0,1,2,\ldots\}$$

$$\text{Int} = \{\ldots, -1, 0, 1, \ldots\}$$

Notice that only the first of these four sets has a finite number of elements. Three infix operators on sets which yield set values can be defined in terms of the test for presence:

$x \in S$: true if and only if x is a member of set S

Union :

$$S_1 \cup S_2 = \{x \mid x \in S_1 \vee x \in S_2\}$$

Intersection :

$$S_1 \cap S_2 = \{x \mid x \in S_1 \wedge x \in S_2\}$$

Difference :

$$S_1 - S_2 = \{x \mid x \in S_1 \wedge \neg(x \in S_2)\}$$

The two operators for testing subset and proper subset can also be defined :

$$S_1 \subseteq S_2 \equiv (x \in S_1 \supset x \in S_2)$$

$$S_1 \subset S_2 \equiv (S_1 \subseteq S_2 \wedge (\exists x \in S_2)(\neg(x \in S_1)))$$

(Notice that the "there exists" quantifier is used with a bound for the selection of elements).

The number of elements in a set is given by : card S.

What has been gained by taking this step back from the real world ? At the cost of learning a modest amount of notation a technique is now available for describing a class of problems more succinctly than they could be described by the normal data structures of programming languages (these, it should be realized, are themselves abstractions of the "real" machine). No constraints have been put on or implied about the implementation and the section on "Object refinement" will discuss how this freedom is used. Before introducing two further abstractions some more examples of the use of sets will be discussed.

Suppose a program is required which records which students are handing in answers to exercises. The state might be :

$$\Sigma = n : \text{St-nm-set}$$
$$y : \text{St-nm-set}$$

A new student who enrolls on the course will not have done any exercises, so :

$$\text{ENROLL} :: \Sigma : \text{St-nm} \rightarrow$$

$$\text{post-ENROLL}(\langle n,y\rangle, s, \langle n',y'\rangle) \equiv$$
$$n' = n \cup \{s\} \wedge y' = y$$

a successful exercise will be recorded by :

$$\text{SUCC} :: \Sigma : \text{St-nm} \rightarrow$$

$$\text{post-SUCC}(\langle n,y\rangle, s, \langle n',y'\rangle) \equiv$$
$$n' = n - \{s\} \wedge y' = y \cup \{s\}$$

The set of students who successfully completed the course may be determined by :

$$\text{COMPL} : \Sigma \rightarrow \text{St-nm-set}$$

$$\text{COMPL}(\langle n,y\rangle) = y$$

A less trivial example of an abstract specification is for a program which records equivalence relations. An equivalence relation is one which is :

transitive	: $x \equiv y \wedge y \equiv z \supset x \equiv z$
symmetric	: $x \equiv y \supset y \equiv x$
reflexive	: $x \equiv x$

Suppose a given finite set S is to be considered and the task is to construct a program which will accept a given list of pairs whose equivalence is to be assumed and then to respond to the question whether a given pair is equivalent considering all symmetric and transitive implications of the list of pairs given. (Such a system might be of use for recording the relationship of "sharing storage" in a compiler).

A way of modelling an equivalence relation over S is to view it as a partitioning of S into a number of non-empty, disjoint subsets of S. Two elements are then equivalent if and only if they are in the same subset. It is now a simple task to define the operations required in terms of a state which contains a set of objects each member of which is a subset of S :

$$R = (\text{S-set})\text{-set}$$

The extra constraints which require that all elements of S are contained in one of the elements of the state and that the sets are non-empty and pairwise disjoint provide the notion of validity :

$$v(r) = (\underline{\text{union}}\ r = S \wedge$$
$$s \in r \supset s \neq \{\} \wedge$$
$$s_1 \in r \wedge s_2 \in r \wedge s_1 \neq s_2 \supset s_1 \cap s_2 = \{\})$$

where "union" is an operator defined on sets of sets which yields a set of exactly the elements contained in each of the original sets. Thus if :

$$S = \{1, 2\}$$

the valid R's would be :

$$\{\{1\}, \{2\}\} \quad , \quad \{\{1,2\}\}$$

In the initial state the only equivalences are those given by reflexivity, thus :

$$\text{INIT} : \rightarrow R$$

$$\text{INIT}() = \{\{s\} \mid s \in S\}$$

Changes to an R can be recorded by the ENTER function which unites the sets containing the two elements which are now given as equivalent (notice that if the two elements are already equivalent the value is unchanged) :

$$\text{ENTER} : R \quad S \quad S \rightarrow R$$

$$ENTER(r,s,t) = \{e \mid e \in r \wedge \{s,t\} \cap e = \{\}\} \cup \{e_s \cup e_t \mid e_s \in r \wedge e_t \in r \wedge s \in e_s \wedge t \in e_t\}$$

As indicated above, the test for equivalence is now, simply :

$$EQUIV : R\ S\ S \rightarrow Bool$$

$$EQUIV\ (r,s,t) \equiv (\exists e \in r)(s \in e \wedge t \in e)$$

Notice that ENTER and EQUIV are total over states R as restricted by v, and that INIT creates valid states and ENTER preserves validity :

$$v\ (INIT\ ())$$

$$v\ (r) \supset v(ENTER(r,s,t))$$

This concludes the specification of the problem.

Sets are a useful abstraction but in developing specifications it will be worth having more tools at one's disposal. Consider an extension of the earlier "students in classroom" problem in which the aim is to know in which room a given student can be found. In an implementation we might have an array with one element for each student and store in these elements the room number currently occupied. The mere fact that this forces one to consider so early in the specification how the name will be transformed into an array index should alert one to the danger of getting involved in implementation details too early. Rather, consider defining the state of the system as a mapping from names to room numbers. This is written :

$$\Sigma = St\text{-}nm \rightarrow Room\text{-}no$$

The operations might be :

$$ARRIVE :: \Sigma : St\text{-}nm \rightarrow$$

$$MOVE :: \Sigma : St\text{-}nm \quad Room\text{-}no \rightarrow$$

$$LOCATE : \Sigma\ St\text{-}nm \rightarrow Room\text{-}no$$

In order to define these operations it will be necessary to introduce some notation for mappings. An explicit enumeration of a pairing of elements will be written :

$$[d_1 \mapsto r_1, d_2 \mapsto r_2, \ldots, d_n \mapsto r_n]$$

Notice that the d must all be different from each other. For the special case of the empty map :

$$[\,]$$

Maps may, like sets, be defined implicitly:

$$[x \mapsto f(x) \mid p\ (x)]$$

Thus :

$$[x \mapsto x^2 \mid x \in \{1:4\}] = [1 \mapsto 1, 2 \mapsto 4, 3 \mapsto 9, 4 \mapsto 16]$$

A mapping can be applied to a value and will yield the right hand element of the pair whose left hand element is the value to which the mapping was applied. Thus, calling the mapping to squares given above, M :

$$M\ (3) = 9$$

The sets of elements to which a mapping may be applied, its domain is given by :

$$\underline{d}M = \{1,2,3,4\}$$

The set of possible values resulting from applications, the range, is given by :

$$\underline{r}M = \{1,4,9,16\}$$

A map value obtained by overwriting the first map with the second where their domain elements match can be defined :

$$M_1 + M_2 = [d \mapsto r \mid (d \in \underline{d}\ M_2 \wedge r = M_2(d)) \vee (d \in \underline{d}\ M_1 \wedge \neg(d \in \underline{d}M_2) \wedge r = M_1(d))]$$

Providing that their domains are disjoint a union operator is available which is commutative (and thus easier to reason about) :

$$M_1 \cup M_2 = [d \mapsto r \mid (d \in \underline{d}\ M_1 \wedge r = M_1(d)) \vee (d \in \underline{d}\ M_2 \wedge r = M_2(d))]$$

Equiped with this notation the three student tracking operations can now be easily defined (in the first it is assumed that the entrance area has room number of zero) :

$$post\text{-}ARRIVE(\sigma,s,\sigma') \equiv \sigma' = \sigma \cup [s \mapsto 0]$$

$$post\text{-}MOVE\ (\sigma,s,n,\sigma') \equiv \sigma' = \sigma + [s \mapsto n]$$

$$LOCATE\ (\sigma,s) = \sigma(s)$$

In order to drive home the point about not choosing a representation for the implementation too early, consider that it is now necessary to add a further operation which checks (for safety reasons) whether any lecture room is overcrowded, if say there is a limit of 50 students per room, it is easy to write :

$$CHECK\text{-}SAFETY : \Sigma \rightarrow Bool$$

$$CHECK\text{-}SAFETY(\sigma) \equiv (\exists n)(\underline{card}\{s \mid \sigma(s)=n\} > 50)$$

Although easy to specify it would be potentially disastrous to implement if the array implementation mentioned above had been chosen. It is clear that no competent programmer would choose his final data representation until he had a clear idea of the total set of operations to be supported. The point being made here is that this should not prevent him recording something about parts of his specification. In order to do so he should not, however, guess a representation and see whether a different one is required for the actual realization. Rather, one should use an abstraction which contains the essential

relationships only. Thus one can be sure that these will be present in some form in the final implementation without prejudging what the representation should be.
Indeed the abstract model is ideal for couching questions like the relative frequencies of various primitive operations the answers to which must be determined in order to select the representation for good performance.

It is useful to note that where a model suggests itself as a disjoint partitioning of a set into a finite number of subsets, a mapping may prove to be a more convenient model. Thus the example given above of students who do exercises might have been defined :

$$\Sigma = St\text{-}nm \rightarrow \{\underline{Y}, \underline{N}\}$$

$$\text{post-ENROLL}(\sigma, s, \sigma') \equiv \sigma' = \sigma \cup [s \mapsto \underline{N}]$$

$$\text{post-SUCC}(\sigma, s, \sigma') \equiv \sigma' = \sigma + [s \mapsto \underline{Y}]$$

A slightly more interesting example which uses mappings can be built on a simplified version of a "bill of materials" problem. Suppose a manufacturer has a number of products each of which is either a base item (no sub-components) or a sub-unit which may be made-up from a number of components which are themselves either basic or sub-unit and so on. If the only need is to extract the set of basic units from any unit, the data required is :

$$Bom = P\text{-}no \rightarrow P\text{-}no\text{-}set$$

The complete set of sub-components can then be derived from an operation which would yield :

$$EXP : Bom \quad P\text{-}no \rightarrow P\text{-}no\text{-}set$$

$$EXP(bom,p) = \underline{if}\ bom(p) = \{\}\ \underline{then}\ \{p\}$$
$$\underline{else}\ \{p\} \cup \underline{union}\ \{ExP(bom,c) | c \in bom(p)\}$$

which can, in fact, be simplified to :

$$EXP(bom,p) = \{p\} \cup \underline{union}\ \{EXP(bom,c) | c \in bom(p)\}$$

The specification is simple and not just because the problem is a simplification of that actually faced by manufacturers.
What has been ignored is that the Bom itself may be huge, requiring the design of techniques for retrieval from secondary storage. Furthermore the EXP operation, or rather a more complicated version thereof, is likely to be required so often that the design of the representation must be governed by considerations of fast access to information on sub-assemblies. Here, however, these problems have been postponed until after the specification of other operations, such as those for updating Bom itself, have been considered.

One last abstraction will be introduced for the purposes of the current paper.

A useful abstraction of objects as simple as arrays and as complex as collections of data which are made to contain a pointer to the next linearly data element is the concept of "L i s t s".

As with sets and maps, the first items of notation to be introduced are those for explicitly displaying values :

$$\langle c_1, c_2, \ldots, c_n \rangle$$

$$\langle\rangle \qquad \text{empty list}$$

notice that here order is important.

It is sometimes convenient to have an implicit construction of list, but :

$$\langle f(x) \mid p(x) \rangle$$

cannot be permitted because it gives no guidance as to the order of the required list. With caution, constructions where the range of the predicate is over a clearly ordered set can be used, for example :

$$\langle x \mid 1 \leq x \leq 12 \wedge \text{is-prime}(x) \rangle =$$
$$\langle 1,2,3,5,7,11 \rangle$$

The first element of a list can be obtained by an operator which yields the head. Thus, denoting the list given above by P :

$$\underline{h}\ P = 1$$

The list which contains all of the elements except the first in the same order, is given by the tail, thus :

$$\underline{t}\ P = \langle 2,3,5,7,11 \rangle$$

Neither of these operations can be applied to empty lists whereas the length operator can :

$$\underline{l}\ P = 6 \quad , \underline{l}\langle\rangle = 0$$

notice that the length of a list is the number of items including duplicates in the list to which the operator is applied (counting any elements which are lists as one element), thus :

$$\underline{l}\langle 1, 1, \{1, 2\}, \langle 1, 2\rangle, \langle 1, 2\rangle\rangle = 5$$

A particular element of a list may be extracted by applying the list to an index (whose value must be between one and the length of the list), thus :

$$P(5) = 7$$

The use of the application suggests viewing a list as a mapping from a compact set of integers (the lowest being one) onto the elements. This further suggests :

$\underline{d}(P) = \{1:6\}$, $\underline{r}(P) = \{1,2,3,5,7,11\}$

of which the latter is of far greater utility.

The infix operator for creating a list value which contains the elements of one list followed by the elements of another is concatenation, thus :

$P\hat{}\langle c\rangle = \langle 1,2,3,5,7,11,c\rangle$

Lists only play a large part in specifications which contain many other abstract objects so that the simple examples given now may appear rather strained. Supppose the task is to define the operation of a stack. It would be possible to write :

Stack = El^*

which defines elements of Stack to be lists of which each element, if any, are members of El

TOP : Stack → El

TOP (st) = $\underline{h}$ st

POP : Stack → Stack

POP (st) = $\underline{t}$ st

PUSH : Stack El → Stack

PUSH (st,el) = $\langle el\rangle\hat{}$ st

Notice that TOP and POP work in the expected LIFO fashion but are undefined for empty stacks, also that since concatenation works only between lists the single element to be appended by PUSH has first to be made into a list.

Contrast this with FIFO queue :

Queue = El^*

DEQ : Queue → El

DEQ (q) = $\underline{h}$ q

TRN : Queue → Queue

TRN (q) = $\underline{t}$ q

ENQ : Queue El Queue

ENQ (q ,el) = $q\hat{}\langle el\rangle$

These three abstract objects (Sets, Maps and Lists) together with some obvious abstract syntax notation will suffice for the current paper. (For a more complete description see Bekic /20/). The choice is not meant to indicate that these are the only, nor even the most important ones.

In fact the catalogue should never be complete ! Not only should one consider what data concepts are appropriate when faced with a new problem area and develop notation, but also there is the possibility of characterizing objects axiomatically (cf. ref Guttag /16/. (It is interesting to compare in this context, the work on relational data bases where everything is represented via relations).

Before leaving the subject of abstractions it is, perhaps, worth anticipating the question of whether they should be added to our programming languages. Firstly, observe that current high level languages (e.g. FORTRAN, PL/I) are already offering data objects which abstract from details of the machine. But even with the simple example of an array, which permits the programmer to ignore the actual linear order of elements in storage, the implementation is not straightforward. A niave implementation is likely to be unacceptably inefficient; one which attempts to discern patterns in the programmers indexing through arrays, is faced with the problem of optimization across sequences of statements (this sort of optimization is referred to as "strength reduction"). All of the objects introduced above could, in their finite cases, be implemented in a programming language without undue difficulty. However, the scope for inefficiency and for complex optimization would be huge. It would seem, at least to this author, that although the use of abstraction is a proper tool for specifications, it is a fundamental part of the programmers task to find representations which fit the particular operations he requires.

Program Correctness Proofs

The subject of proving programs correct is introduced at this point in order to ensure that the reader has an awareness of the state of the art. The previous section has dealt with specifying what a program should do. Given a program text what link between it and its specification will be considered acceptable? The environment has for too long had to accept the claims of the programmer supported by the evidence of a few "test cases". Even assuming that these represented a sincere attempt on the part of the programmer (rather than an attempt to manufacture some evidence to persuade his user to accept a poor program) they were of little more use to the user than wishful thinking. The advances of the past years have now put programmers in the position where they have a more convincing way of supporting the claim that their program performs its required function : they can offer an argument for correctness. A program should produce a given result (non-determinism complicates the explanation somewhat but does not change the argument); the claim that a given program will always compute a result corresponding to its specification can be viewed as the statement of a putative theorem : if the theorem is true it can be proved correct. The techniques now avaialable for reasoning about programs should be understood by all programmers. As Harlan Mills has pointed out, knowing that one can do something without error is likely to have a large impact on one's tolerance to errors. Both for the original author of a program and anybody who has subsequently to understand the program, some record of the reasons why it is believed to be correct will be an immense aid to clear thinking.

An important warning must, however, be given in order to avoid misunderstanding. This section will present ways of writing the correctness proof for a given program.

This should not be interpreted as a suggestion that program construction should proceed in the sequence :

1) specify
2) program
3) prove

The only way one can expect to reach correct solutions to difficult problems is by decomposition. Thus the final program documentation envisaged will appear in a stepwise structure where each stage of development is supported by a correctness argument (cf. refs Hoare /6/, Jones /7/, Wirth /9/). The ideas underlying such a process are, however, more briefly represented in terms of program proofs and, since the next section will be involved with the stepwise development of data structures, this approach is adopted here.

For any programming language that one knows well, one can compute by hand what result a given program will yield for given input. Furthermore, with some thought, one should be able to derive statements about what a program does for any input. Essentially one is using knowledge about constructs of a language under consideration. Knowledge of this sort can be collected together to form a definition of a programming language. There are a number of distinct styles in which a language definition may be written. For the purposes of the current paper the style which has been called "axiomatic" (ref-3) will be used. (It is possible to prove that relationships exist between the various possible definitions of a language and it is possible, in fact, to regard the axioms as theorems of other definitions the question of how the "axioms" are obtained is not, however, of concern here).

A program can be considered to be correct, or otherwise, only in relation to some specification. As was indicated at the beginning of the preceding section it is normal to have one predicate which limits the class of input states to which the program is to be applied and another which specifies the relation required between input and output states.

For reasons which will shortly become apparent it is, in fact, more convenient to regard even the "post-condition" as a predicate of one state. The implications of this convenience will be discussed at the end of the current section.

Consider the sequence of assignments in, say PL/I :

```
y = 2 * x ;
z = 3 * y
```

regarding the state as containing three values in the order $\langle x, y, z \rangle$, one would expect the program (assuming no storage overlap) to transform :

$$\langle 1, 2, 3 \rangle \text{ into } \langle 1, 2, 6 \rangle$$

More generally any state with values :

$$\langle x_0, y_0, z_0 \rangle$$

will be transformed into one containing the values :

$$\langle x_0, (2 * x_0), (6 * x_0) \rangle$$

The above generalization is one from noting the effect of a particular test case to reasoning about sets of states. It is the aim of what follows to show how one can reason about the set of states which arise at various points in the program by means of predicates which characterize the sets. In other words the "axioms" which will be required to support reasoning about pieces of program will be such that they relate predicates over states. For a given operation OP the following style of writing assertions is adopted :

$$\{P\} \; OP \; \{Q\}$$

This can be interpreted as "if OP is applied to any state satisfying the predicate P it will create a state which will satisfy the predicate Q".

Consider then the example of a program which is to produce a quotient and remainder by integer division (in order to contrive an example which requires little explanation, it is assumed that no convenient operation is available in the given language and that an algorithm using successive substraction must be constructed). Given a dividend and divisor such that :

$$\text{pre-DIV}(\langle a, b, q, r\rangle) \equiv 0 \leqslant a \wedge 0 < b$$

then the required result is an output state for which :

$$\text{post-DIV}(\langle a,b,q,r\rangle) \equiv q * b + r = a \wedge 0 \leqslant r < b$$

Presenting the program which is to be proved correct in a PL/I-like syntax along with assertions, whose meaning will be discussed below, in braces :

```
DIV : PROC(a,b,q,r);
DCL(a,b,q,r)...;
{0≤a ∧ 0<b}
q = 0;
     {q*b+a=a ∧ 0≤a ∧ 0<b}
r = a;
     {q*b+r=a ∧ 0≤r ∧ 0<b}
DO WHILE (b≤r);
     {q*b+r=a ∧ b≤r ∧ 0<b}
r = r - b;
     {q*b+r+b = a ∧ 0≤r ∧ 0<b}
q = q + 1;
     {(q-1)*b+r+b=a ∧ 0≤r ∧ 0<b}
END;
     {q*b+r=a ∧ 0≤r<b}
END;
```

The first assertions (i.e. predicate on the values in the state) is written before any computation is performed. Since assertions are considered to apply to the states which can arise at the point in the flow where they are written, this is no more nor less than the pre-condition which was assumed to hold for all input states. The next two steps :

$$\{0 \leqslant a \wedge 0 < b\} \quad q = 0 \quad \{q*b+a=a \wedge 0 \leqslant a \wedge 0 < b\}$$

$$\{q*b+a=a \wedge 0 \leqslant a \wedge 0 < b\} \quad r = a \quad \{q*b+r=a \wedge 0 \leqslant r \wedge 0 < b\}$$

are, even if so far unmotivated, fairly obvious. The aim here, however, is to understand how a greater degree of certainty can be obtained about these intermediate assertions holding for all possible states. The statements which transform the state are in both cases assignments. The most convenient "axiomatic definition" of the assignment statement is the one which works backwards. Using, if P is some arbitrary predicate :

$$P_{x \rightsquigarrow e}$$

to denote the predicate which results from systematically substituting all (free) occurences of x within P by e, the axiom is :

$$\{P_{x \rightsquigarrow e}\} \quad x = e \quad \{P\}$$

This form may be made more intuitively obvious by the reading "if P is to be true of the values (including x) in the state after the assignment of the value of e to the variable x, then a predicate which differs from P only in that all mentions of x are replaced by the expression e must be true before the assignment". A few simple examples :

$$\{10 = 10\} \quad x = 10 \quad \{x = 10\}$$

$$\{0 \leqslant x\} \quad x = x + 1 \quad \{0 < x\}$$

$$\{0+a=a \wedge 0 \leqslant a \wedge 0 < b\} \, q=0 \, \{qb+a=a \wedge 0 \leqslant a \wedge 0 < b\}$$

$$\{q * b+a=a \wedge 0 \leqslant a \wedge 0 < b\} \quad r=a \quad \{qb+r=a \wedge 0 \leqslant r \wedge 0 < b\}$$

where, having dropped the identically true clause "0 + a = a", the last two are exactly the results required to establish the validity of the second and the third assertions of DIV.

(The above form of argument is, in fact, hiding the application of the rule for composing statements with ";" :

$$\text{if} : \{P\}OP1\{Q\} \, , \, \{Q\}OP2 \, \{R\}$$

$$\text{then} : \{P\}OP1 \; ; \; OP2 \; \{R\}$$

The remainder of this exposition also reasons in terms of assertions being true at points in the flow. This is not to be taken as an argument against the more elegant approach of ref Dijkstra /8/.

The next step is to verify the step from the third to the seventh (and last) assertion, since the "DO....END" can be regarded as a single statement. Notice that if the converse of the test in the while is conjoined (i.e. appended by " ") to the third assertion the result implies the final assertion :

$$q*b+r=a \wedge 0 \leqslant r \wedge 0 < b \wedge \neg(b \leqslant r) \supset q * b+r=a \wedge 0 \leqslant r < b$$

Now since all states which arise at the position of the third assertion have been shown to satisfy it and since "r < b" will be true of any of those states for which the loop gets executed zero times, the final assertion will be true for those states for which the flow control never enters the body of the loop.

The key to reasoning about those states which

are generated via one or more iterations of the body of the loop is to recognise what remains invariant in the loop. It has already been observed that if :

$P \equiv q * b + r = a \wedge 0 \leq r \wedge o < b$

$p \equiv b \leq r$

then :

P is the third assertion

$P \wedge \neg p$ implies the seventh assertion

Notice now :

$P \wedge p$ is the fourth assertion

P is equivalent to the sixth

Since the only states whose values will arise at the fourth assertion have come from the third or the sixth and have satisfied "p", then all states will indeed satisfy "P ∧ p" at the fourth providing only that the appropriate relationships hold between the fourth and sixth. This is easily verified by two applications of the assignment axiom :

$\{q*b+r=a \wedge b \leq r \wedge 0<b\}$ r = r - b $\{q*b + r + b = a \wedge 0 \leq r \wedge 0<b\}$

$\{q*b+r+b=a \wedge 0 \leq r \wedge 0<b\}$ q = q + 1 $\{(q - 1)*b + r + b = a \wedge 0 \leq r \wedge 0<b\}$

The correctness of the program with respect to its post-condition has thus been established for all states satisfying its pre-condition.

(The above argument on the loop has in fact used an "axiom" of the form :

if : $\{P \wedge p\}$ body $\{P\}$

then : $\{P\}$ DO WHILE p; body; END$\{P \wedge \neg p\}$

The axiom for the other standard way of building so called "structured code" is :

if : $\{P \wedge p\}$ S_1 $\{R\}$, $\{P \wedge \neg p\}$ S_2 $\{R\}$

then: $\{P\}$IF p THEN S_1 ; ELSE S_2 $\{R\}$)

The reader who has been patient enough to follow these deductions will have probably found them both tedious and have asked where the assertions actually came from. It is clear that the first and last assertions were required in that they represented the specification. The derivation of required pre-conditions across assignments was basically a mechanical process and four of the intermediate assertions could have been mechanically generated even if they had not been written. What is, however, required in addition to the pre- and post-conditions is one assertion within the loop. This "invariant" property P cannot, in general, be discovered mechanically (see ref Wegbreit /17/ for progress towards algorithms which work in some cases). It can be argued that the invariant captures the essence of the loop (it can in fact be used to generate the loop) and that if the programmer cannot provide it his loop is probably incorrect. It is certainly true that a well thought out invariant is the most useful comment one can be provided with when facing a loop written by another programmer.

One important qualification must be made to the above proof : it has in fact only shown that the final states will satisfy the post-conditions when they arise; it has not been proved that the program will terminate for all states satisfying its pre-condition. In this case, the necessary reasoning is straightforward and the key assertion ($0< b$) has been carried through the deduction. But in general, the step from the first result, called "partial correctness" to the termination proof can also require some inventiveness.

A further "loose end" can now be tied up. The post-condition here is, in fact, inadequate in that it only puts a requirement on the final state and would be satisfied by the program :

a=7; b=3; q=2; r=1

In other words the preservation of the initial values for the variables a and b has not been explicitly guaranted. In the literature this is frequently handled by using free variables to denote the initial values of the input variables. Some care is necessary in handling free variables within deductions. For this reason, and some stronger ones which relate to stepwise development, this author prefers to accept somewhat longer "axioms" (cf ref Jones /15/) and use post-conditions of state pairs. Before leaving the topic of proving results about sequences of operations it would be worth repeating that proofs of this sort are not envisaged for larger programs. Rather, the techniques occuring here would be used to indicate the main steps in a proof at each stage of a stepwise development.

Data Refinement

Programmers are normally familiar with the idea of presenting a development as a series of hierarchically arranged operations. The section on specifications began by showing how to document the requirements of an operation. If such an operation is available directly on the machine, or in the language, which is to be used for implementation, then the programmers task is trivial; if not available an operation must be decomposed into a number of simpler operations which could be used to fulfil the original objective. Each of the simpler operations would also be specified and, on the assumption that these specifications will be satisfactorily met, techniques like those of the last section can support an argument as to why a composition of such units will achieve the original task. The specifications of the assumed operations subsequently, of course, are subjected to the same treatment and one eventually has a comprehensible description to running a program.

The second part of the section on specifications proposed the use of abstract data types. Here again the specification can be thought of as a possible solution to the problem. If the language which is to be used possesses all of the required data types the development task may be at an end. On the other hand the data objects may be more abstract than those available and some further development therefore be required. Development steps from abstract to (more) concrete, termed "data refinement", are the subject of this section.

The advantages of developing a program in a style which separates the decisions made are primarily those derived from making the mental task more manageable. Thus the developer is more likely to produce a correct solution and a later reader will find the work far easier to comprehend. The separation of problems in the case of data is likely to bring an additional bonus in terms of efficiency of the final program.

The reason for this claim is the wide range of possible ways of implementing abstract data objects in terms of more familiar ones. The stepwise development process permits enough development to be performed to enable one to fully understand the operations (and their relative frequencies) to be performed on the abstract data objects, before one is forced to decide how to represent them.

There are indications of possible ways of representing of abstract objects in ref Wirth /11/ : here a condensed and somewhat different list is provided to indicate the range of choice. Only structured (i.e. composite) values will be discussed here. The simplest composite value is the Cartesian Product of a number of simpler values. Thus, in PL/I, given a number of simpler types, a type which allows one of each of the sub-types to occur can be achieved by declaring a structure. The range of choice in representing such a simple combination is naturally limited but even with PL/I one is presented with the options of packing into the smallest amount of storage possible or of alligning field on machine boundaries. The decision whether to try to conserve storage or to achieve faster access can thus be separated from the understanding of the required information content.

In the simplest case an array of values is dense (most values of interest) and of static size : the implementation in this case is simply concerned with linearizing the multidimensional collection of elements. If one dimension is to be allowed to increase, it is possible in, say PL/I, to avoid reserving storage for the largest possible overall size by having only a vector large enough to contain the maximum size of the expanding dimension and storing into this vector pointers to dynamically allocated (i.e. BASED) storage for arrays of the static dimensions. Rosenberg (e.g. ref /18/) has studied algorithms for mapping arrays which can expand in more than one of their dimensions. A sparse array (e.g. a large array where less than 5% of the values differ from zero) on the other hand is best considered as a general map (see below).

When introducing the abstraction of lists it was mentioned that the simplest concrete data type covered was a one dimensional array. This is an acceptable realization of the abstraction only if there is a known maximum length and there are only rare occasions when it is necessary to insert elements within the list. If either of these two limitations do not hold, then it may be necessary to organize the elements in a "linked list" type of structure where each data item is paired with a pointer to the next value.

The range of possiblities for implementing a set is far more interesting. If the set of values to be represented has a small maximum number of elements, although the range of possible elements is large, an array may be chosen to store the current elements. If, on the other hand, the class of potential elements is relatively small, it might be worth finding some relationship between the elements and the integers, so that set values can be represented as bit vectors where the interpretation of the bits denotes presence or absence of the corresponding element. The presence of suitable bit operations on the machine can lead to very efficient implementations of the set operations like union. Finally, if for example, the set which has been used to specify an operation has no maximum size, it may be necessary to employ a linked list type storage.

Finding a suitable representation for the abstraction of maps is again governed by the likely contents. It may be efficient to regard a map as a list of pairs (i.e. domain, range elements) and then consider how to handle the set. If application is to be frequent the pairs may have to be arranged into a list ordered on their first elements. An even faster access may be possible, at the expense of storage, if a hashing technique is used on the domain element to compute an address where the value may be located.

The above lists are not intended to be exhaustive. In fact, the real interest in finding realizations comes with those non-basic items which are built up in more complex ways. But it should be apparent that the amount of detail postponed by using abstractions is significant and, correspondingly, that development steps which involve choosing representations will require some thought.

It will be explained below how a step of Data Refinement can be proved correct. A necessary preliminary to being able to do this is to document the relationship between the abstract objects involved and their representations. In general the abstract object was chosen to contain a minimum of information (i.e. only that essential to the problem). A representation is likely to contain further information whose purpose is either finding a way around the data structure or making access more efficient.

Again in general, there will be a number of different values in the representation which correspond to the same abstract value. For example, suppose an operation were specified in terms of sets and an implementation is then sought in terms of lists, the set :

$$\{1, 2, 3\}$$

could be represented by :

$$\langle 1,2,3\rangle \text{ or } \langle 1,3,2\rangle \text{ or } \langle 2,1,3\rangle \text{ etc}$$

each of these representations has the same information from the abstract level, but has additional information about the order of the elements which was irrelevant before. There is then a "one : many" relationship between abstract values and their representations. The easiest way of documenting such a relationship is by a function which retrieves the essential information. Thus, for the example with lists and sets :

$$\text{retr-set} : X^* \rightarrow X\text{-set}$$

$$\text{retr-set}(xl) = \{xl(i) \mid 1 \leq i \leq \underline{l}xl\}$$

Examples below will indicate that this method of documenting the relationship extends to complex situations, even where a data object is restricted by a notion of validity.

Clearly, for a representation to be useful it must be capable of representing any value from the abstractions. The term "adequate" will be used for representations (R) of an abstraction (A) such that :

$$a \in A \supset (\exists r \in R)(a = \text{retr-r}(r))$$

Recall the example given of specifying a system for recording the students in a given classroom. The state was :

$$\Sigma = \text{St-nm-set}$$

and the operations defined by :

$$\text{post-ENTER}(\sigma, s, \sigma') \equiv \sigma' = \sigma \cup \{s\}$$

$$\text{post-EXIT}(\sigma, s, \sigma') \equiv \sigma' = \sigma - \{s\}$$

$$\text{PRESENT}(\sigma, s) \equiv s \in \sigma$$

The next step might be to choose a state which contains both an index, which maps names to numbers, and a status part, which records a boolean value(presence) for each student number :

$$\text{St-no} = \{1 : n\}$$

$$\Sigma 1 = \text{index} : \text{St-nm} \rightarrow \text{St-no}$$

$$\quad \text{status} : \text{Bool}^*$$

(The final data types might employ a BIT vector for status and an array of student names where the student number for a given name is its index in the array. This index could be found by retaining the names in order and using a binary search technique). The new state can be related to the original abstract Σ by :

$$\text{retr-}\Sigma : \Sigma 1 \rightarrow \Sigma$$

$$\text{retr-}\Sigma(\langle i,s\rangle) = \{sn \mid s(i(sn)) \wedge sn \in \underline{d}\ i\}$$

Thus retr-Σ generates a set of student names which is that subset of the domain of the index for which the "i(sn)" element of s has the value TRUE. Clearly $\Sigma 1$ is an adequate representation providing the domain of the index contains all of the student names and the length of the status bit list is such that all elements of "St-no" are valid indices.

It is now straightforward to give specifications for operations which use the revised state :

$$\text{ENTER1} :: \Sigma 1 : \text{St-nm} \rightarrow$$

$$\text{post-ENTER1}(\langle i_0, s_0\rangle, sn, \sigma 1_f) \equiv$$

$$\sigma 1_f = \langle i_0, (s_0 + [i_0(sn) \mapsto \underline{\text{TRUE}}])\rangle$$

$$\text{EXIT} :: \Sigma 1 : \text{St-nm} \rightarrow$$

$$\text{post-EXIT1}(\langle i_0, s_0\rangle, sn, \sigma 1_f) \equiv$$

$$\sigma 1_f = \langle i_0, (s_0 + [i_0(sn) \mapsto \underline{FALSE}]) \rangle$$

PRESENT1 :: $\Sigma 1$ St-name $\rightarrow$ Bool

PRESENT1$(\langle i_0, s_0 \rangle, sn) \equiv s_0(i_0(sn))$

Notice that the list has again been viewed as a mapping in order to provide a convenient notation for a change to a single element.

On such a simple example the correctness of this realization may appear obvious but it will serve as a useful vehicle for discussing the general method.

Given any starting state of $\Sigma 1$, say $\sigma 1$, there are two ways of arriving at an abstract state after an operation, say ENTER :

ENTER (retr-$\Sigma(\sigma 1)$, sn)

retr-Σ (ENTER1$(\sigma 1$, sn)) .

In other words one can either retrieve the abstract object and apply the original operation or one can apply the new operation and then retrieve the abstraction from the transformed representation. If, for all of the operations involved, it can be shown that the compositions are equal :

retr-Σ ° ENTER1 = ENTER ° retr-Σ

then the new state and set of operations will be said to "model" the abstraction (Milner has used the term simulation in ref /19/). The above constraint is only sufficient providing the set of states has also been shown to be adequate.

For the example of students in a given classroom it is easy to see :

retr-Σ(ENTER1 $(\langle i_0, s_0 \rangle, sn)$) =

ENTER (retr-$\Sigma(\langle i_0, d_0 \rangle)$, sn)

because, providing "sn" is a valid student name, both are :

$$= \{sn \mid sn \in \underline{d}\ i_0 \wedge s_0(i_0(sn))\} \cup \{sn\}$$

similarly :

retr-Σ(EXIT1 $(\langle i_0, s_0 \rangle, sn)$) =

EXIT(retr-$\Sigma(\langle i_0, d_0 \rangle)$, sn)

PRESENT1 $(\langle i_0, s_0 \rangle, sn)$ =

PRESENT(retr-$\Sigma(\langle i_0, s_0 \rangle)$, sn)

This completes the first example of Data Refinement step. To recap the steps. At some stage of development a "solution" exists which uses some class of abstract data objects and a set of operations thereon; a model is provided in terms of a representation for the objects and a new set of operations; the representation is related to the abstraction by means of a retrieve function; proving that the representation is adequate and that the new operations model the original ones concludes the development step. The specifications of the new operations may now be subjected to further refinement either of the data or of the operations. The discussion so far has assumed that the operations involved are all deterministic (functional rather relational specifications) : this problem and some relaxations relating to limitations of the domain of arguments by "pre-conditions" is not discussed in this paper. Just as with the proofs about program correctness shown in the preceding section, it is not likely that large programs would be proved correct in detail : there the assertions could be used to indicate the main lines of a correctness argument; here the documentation of a retrieve function will serve the same purpose.

In order to check his understanding the reader might like to consider a development of the example which records the room number in which any student can be found :

Σ = St-nm $\rightarrow$ Room-no

post-ARRIVE$(\sigma, s, \sigma') \equiv \sigma' = \sigma \cup [s \mapsto 0]$

post-MOVE$(\sigma, s, n, \sigma') \equiv \sigma' = \sigma + [s \mapsto n]$

LOCATE$(\sigma, s) = \sigma(s)$

Thus far, a model in terms of :

$\Sigma 1$ = index : St-nm $\rightarrow$ St-no

room : Room-no*

would appear appropriate. Write down the conditions for $\Sigma 1$ to be an adequate representation of Σ, the retrieve function, the operations which would be required on $\Sigma 1$, and an argument of correctness.

If the other operation is now considered :

CHECK-SAFETY$(\sigma) \equiv (\exists n)(\underline{card}\{s \mid \sigma(o) = n\} > 50)$

it might be decided to use a two dimensional array of bits for the room component

$\Sigma 1'$ = index : St-nm $\rightarrow$ St-no

room : St-no Room-no $\rightarrow$ Bool

Assuming slicing type operations (PL/I cross section R(*,m)) and operations for counting and locating bits in vectors, repeat the above tasks for $\Sigma 1'$.

As a final example consider again the problem of recording equivalence relations which was specified earlier. Implementation of this algorithm is complex in that the obvious approaches result in very bad performance in either data entry or response. The crudest data structure would simply record all of the pairs which are given to be equivalent : response to the question of

EQUIV for two elements can now be catastrophically slow. The fastest response to the question is achieved by storing a two dimensional array of bits which reflect not only the given equivalences but also all of those implied by the rules of symmetry transitivity and reflexivity : clearly accepting a newly ENTERed pair will be slow. The abstract data structure was a partitioning of the set of elements S into non-empty disjoint subsets. As was mentioned in connection with maps, such a partitioning can also be modelled by making a mapping from elements of S to some indicator set. The "Fisher-Galler" algorithm presents a good balance between the time used for update and response by providing a way of mapping all elements of the same partition onto a representative element for that set. Thus testing for equivalence is done by comparing representative elements. If this mapping were direct, the problem of finding all of the elements in the classes to be changed when a new ENTER is executed could also be rather time consuming. The Fisher-Galler algorithm in fact collects elements of the same sub-class into trees so that joining two trees requires only the grafting of the root of one on as a branch of the other. The trees are represented by having a mapping from each element of S to the element next up the tree ; a mapping to a <u>NIL</u> value is used to indicate the root of the tree and it is this root value which is used as the distinguishing mark of the sub-set.

Thus :

$$\Sigma = S \rightarrow [S]$$

Where the brackets indicate optional occurence and can be interpreted as adjoining an element <u>NIL</u> to the range of the mapping.

Defining functions :

ROOT(σ,i)=<u>if</u> σ(i) = <u>NIL</u> <u>then</u> i
<u>else</u> ROOT (σ,σ(i))

COLL(σ,r) = {e | ROOT(σ,e) = r}
<u>where</u> σ(r) = <u>NIL</u>

The relationship between R and Σ is :

retr-R(σ)={COLL(σ,r) | σ(r) = <u>NIL</u>}

The class of valid Σ is defined by the restriction that ROOT should always be defined :

$s \in S \supset (\exists r)(\text{ROOT}(\sigma,s) = r)$

The valid representations are easily seen to be adequate :

$v(r) \supset (\exists\sigma)(\ r = \text{retr-}\Sigma(\sigma))$

The developed operations which on the revised structures are :

INIT 1( ) =[s ↦ <u>NIL</u> | s ∈ S]

ENTER1(σ,s,t)=(<u>if</u> ROOT(σ,s)=ROOT(σ,t)
<u>then</u> σ
<u>else</u> σ + [ROOT(σ,t) ↦ ROOT(σ,s)])

EQUIV(σ,s,t) ≡ ROOT(σ,s) = ROOT(σ,t)

The results required, for example :

v1(σ)⊃retr-Σ(ENTER1(σ,s,t))=
ENTER(retr-Σ(σ) ,s,t)

are proved in ref. 12. From this stage it is straightforward to show that the following program is correct (notice that until this point nothing has been assumed about the nature of the set S. It is now assumed to be a subset of the integers).

```
BEGIN :
    DCL  A(1 : n) ... ;
INIT 2 :
    PROC;
    DCL ... ;
        DO i = 1 to UBD(A);
            A(i) = 0;
        { 1≤x≤i⊃A(i) = 0 }

        END;
        {retr-Σ(A) = INIT 1()}

    END;
ENTER 2 :
    PROC (s,t) ;
    DCL ... ;
        {σ= retr-Σ(A)}
    rs = ROOT 2 (s);
    rt = ROOT 2 (t);
        {rs = ROOT(σ,s)∧rt= ROOT(σ,t)}
    If rs ≠ rt
    THEN
        DO;
        A(rt) = rs;
        {retr-Σ(A)=σ+[ROOT(σ,t) ↦ ROOT(σ,s)]}

        END;
```

```
        {retr-Σ(A) = ENTER 1(σ,s,t)}

    END;

EQUIV 2 :
    PROC (s,t) RETURNS(BIT(1) ) ;
    DCL ... ;
        {σ = retr-Σ(A)}
    RETURN (ROOT 2(s) = ROOT 2 (t));
        { ≡(ROOT(σ,s) = ROOT(σ,t))}

    END;

ROOT 2 :
    PROC  (u) RETURNS (...) ;
    DCL ... ;
        { σ = retr- Σ (A) }
    i = u ;
    DO WHILE ( A (i) ≠ 0);
        i = A(i);

    END ;
        { i = ROOT(σ,u) }

    RETURN (i) ;
    END ;
...
END ;
```

With the conclusion of such a tutorial it would appear to be appropriate to recommend further reading. The two books Wirth /9/ and Wirth /11/ taken together provide a fairly complete and not too formal treatment of program development methods. For the student who is prepared to study a more formal approach Dijkstra /8/ will certainly repay the effort invested.

Acknowledgements.

Most of the current author's work in this area was done at the IBM Laboratory in Vienna. The author also gratefully acknowledges the stimulus of the discussions within IFIP Working Group 2.3.

References

/1/ R.W. Floyd, "Assigning Meaning to Programs", Proceedings of Symposia in applied Mathematics, Vol. 19, 1967.

/2/ P. Naur, "Proof of Algorithms by General Snapshots", BIT Vol. 6, 1966.

/3/ C.A.R. Hoare, "The Axiomatic Basis of Computer Programming", Comm. ACM, Vol. 12, pp 576 - 583, 1969.

/4/ Z. Manna, "Properties of Programs and the First Order Predicate Calculus", J. ACM, Vol. 16, pp 244-255, 1969.

/5/ P. Naur, "An Experiment on Program Development", BIT Vol. 12, pp 347 - 365, 1972.

/6/ C.A.R. Hoare, "Proof of a Program: FIND", Comm. ACM, Vol. 14, pp 39-45, 1971.

/7/ C.B. Jones, "Formal Development of Correct Algorithms : an Example Based on Earley's Recogniser", ACM SIGPLAN Notices, Vol. 7, N°1, 1972.

/8/ E.W. Dijkstra, " A Discipline of Programming", Prentice-Hall, 1976.

/9/ N. Wirth, "Program Development by Stepwise Refinement", Comm. ACM, Vol. 14, pp 221 - 227, 1971.

/10/ C.A.R. Hoare, "Proof of Correctness of Data Representations", Acta Informatica, Vol.1, pp 271 - 281, 1972.

/11/ N. Wirth, "Algorithms + Data Structures = Programs", Prentice-Hall, 1976.

/12/ C.B. Jones, "Data Abstraction in Program Development", (offered for publication).

/13/ C.B. Jones, "Formal Refinition in Program Development", (in) Springer Verlag Lecture Notes in Computer Science, N° 23, 1975.

/14/ S.C. Kleene, "Mathematical Logic", John Wiley & Sons, 1967.

/15/ C.B. Jones, "Formal Development of Programs", IBM Laboratory Hursley Report TR 12. 117, June 1973.

/16/ J.V. Guttag, "The Specification and Application to Programming of Abstract Data Types", Ph. D. Thesis, University of Toronto, 1975.

/17/ B. Wegbreit, " The Synthesis of Loop Predicates", Comm. ACM, Vol. 17, pp 102 - 112, 1974.

/18/ A.L. Rosenberg, "On Storing Arbitrarily Many Extendible Arrays of Arbitrary Dimensions", IBM Research Report RC 4800, 1974.

/19/ R. Milner, "An Algebraic Definition of Simulation Between Programs", Stanford University, AIM-142, Feb. 1971.

/20/ H. Bekic, D. Bjorner, W. Henhapl, C.B. Jones, P. Lucas, "A Formal Definition of a PL/I Subset", IBM Laboratory Vienna TR25.139, 1974.

E. Morlet and D. Ribbens, (Eds.), International Computing Symposium 1977.

PRINCIPLES OF DATA BASE SYSTEMS

M. VETTER

I B M European Systems Research Institute (E.S.R.I.)
La Hulpe (Belgium)

This paper (written as a tutorial) emphasizes the principles of data base systems (DBS) rather than describing current systems. The first part of the paper reviews the abstract representation of reality, purpose and functions of a DBS and ends by describing a possible DBS architecture. The second part covers what we would like to call 'data synthesis', i.e. the derivation of data structures (hierarchies, networks, relations) from an appropriate description of reality (i.e. from a conceptual view specification). The conclusion is that the intuitive approach used today to design data bases can be replaced by a much more scientific approach.

Although relations are covered only roughly throughout this paper it is fair to say that the author has been highly influenced by E.F. Codd's ideas on the relational approach. It would be misleading not to warn the reader that the text is somewhat biased and that there exist other valuable approaches not discussed in this paper.

PART I: DATA BASE SYSTEM ARCHITECTURE

1. REALITY AND ITS ABSTRACT REPRESENTATION

The real world consists of so called entities. Webster's Dictionary defines:

'An entity is a thing that has real or individual existence in reality or in mind'

and M.E. Senko [1] postulates:

'An entity is defined as anything that has reality and distinctness of being in fact or in thought'.

An entity may be therefore a real object (like a person (P1), a machine (M1), a student (S1), a building (B1) etc.), an association (like the relationships (man-wife), (student-course), (course-student) etc.) an abstract concept (like a particular colour (red), a particular skill (programmer), a particular course (C1) etc.) or an event. The entity conception allows representation of the real world in discrete units.

Every entity has distinct properties characterizing that entity. An entity property consists of a name (e.g. colour) and a value (e.g. red). If a particular building (B1) is considered as an entity then colour (grey) may be considered as an entity property. If colour (grey) is considered as an entity then density (low) may be considered as the entity property. Entities and entity properties may change their roles as follows from the next example: If a particular student (S1) is considered as entity then the courses (C1, C2, C3, ...) followed by student (S1) may be considered as entity property. If, on the other hand, a particular course (C1) is considered as entity then the students (S1, S2, S3, ...) following course (C1) may be considered as entity property. We state:

1. What we consider as an entity or an entity property depends completly on what we intend to achieve.

2. Entities and entity properties can reverse their roles.

3. Only relevant properties are used to characterize an entity. The relevance depends again completly on what we intend to achieve.

An entity set is a named collection of entities having similar properties. For example the expression

$$S = \{S1, S2, ...Sn\}$$

denotes the entity set S containing the students S1, S2, ...Sn.

An entity set identifier (or Key) is an entity property (or a combination of entity properties) allowing one to uniquely identify a given entity within an entity set.

Usually we refer to a particular entity by indicating (1st) the entity set name, (2nd) the name of an entity property (preferably the name of the entity set identifier) and (3rd) a value of the entity property (e.g. STUDENT/NAME/Brown). M.E. Senko [1] calls the triplet 'entity set name/entity property name/entity property value' the entry mechanism. This entry mechanism is unique if the entity set name is unique within the whole system and the property name is unique within an entity set.

M.E. Senko specifies in [1]: 'Information consists of facts (properties) about things (entities). These facts and things exist independently of any representation, but it is essentially impossible to deal with them conceptually except in terms of some representation'. We distinguish (1st) the format free and (2nd) the formatted representation of an entity set. Figure I.1 shows the format free representation of an entity set named S where particular entities (students) are mentioned with their properties. The entity set identifier is the student number S#.

With the formatted representation of an entity set all property values (e.g. red, green, blue) for a given property (e.g. colour) are collected and are presented as a group. Such a group is called an attribute. It consists of an attribute name and attribute values (also called: attribute occurrences or attribute instances) (see figure I.2).

A domain is the set of all attribute values for a given attribute. A domain is similar to an attribute but - having the characteristics of a set - it contains a particular attribute value only once. For example: (compare with figure I.2)

ENTITY	PROPERTIES
1st STUDENT	SEX/masculin, AGE/40, LOCATION/London, STATUS/married, SALARY/10'000, NAME/SA, NUMBER/S1
2nd STUDENT	NUMBER/S2, STATUS/single, SEX/feminin, SALARY/8'000, LOCATION/Brussels, NAME/SB, AGE/28

ENTITY IDENTIFIER: NUMBER

Figure I.1

ENTITY SET STUDENT (format free representation)

ENTITY	NUMBER	NAME	SEX	AGE	LOCATION	STATUS	SALARY
1st STUDENT	S1	SA	masc	40	London	married	10'000
2nd STUDENT	S2	SB	fem	28	Brussels	single	8'000
3rd STUDENT	S3	SA	fem	32	Geneva	single	9'500

ENTITY IDENTIFIER: NUMBER

Figure I.2

ENTITY SET STUDENT (formatted representation)

```
domain    STUDENT NUMBER = {S1, S2, S3}
attribute STUDENT NUMBER = (S1, S2, S3)

domain    STUDENT NAME   = {SA, SB}
attribute STUDENT NAME   = (SA, SB, SA)

domain    SEX            = {MASC, FEM}
attribute SEX            = (MASC, FEM,
                            FEM)
```

Note that a domain represents a set of values whereas an attribute represents a list of values. Note also that only attributes which are identical with their domains can be used as entity set identifier.

We are now in a position to specify the

2. PURPOSE OF A DATA BASE SYSTEM

The purpose of a Data Base System (DBS) is

1. To store and provide facts concerning entities (real objects and abstract concepts as described in chapter 1)

2. To provide the functions required to operate in an environment characterized by:

2.1. Multi usage: Multiple users are interrogating and updating the data base simultaneously.

2.2. User heterogeneity: Several user types with different information requirements and different skills have to be supported simultaneously. E.F. Codd distinguishes in [2] the following user types:

DP-profesionals (performing data manipulation at a rather low level) such as:

System and Data Control Staff: people responsible for the definition, creation and maintenance of DBS's.

Application Programmers: people responsible for the realization of sophisticated data base applications.

Non DP-profesionals (performing data manipulation at a fairly high level without requiring help from experts) such as:

On-line Job-trained Routine Users (or Parametric Users): persons whose interactions with the data base are an integral part of their job and who have quite predictable needs (e.g. for banking transactions, air flight reservations, etc.).

Analysts and Researchers: persons whose interactions with the data base are also an integral part of their job but who have quite unpredictable needs requiring access to any part of the data base.

Casual Users: persons who may occasionally interact with the data base and have again quite unpredictable needs.

Note that the user types mentioned above range from the most computer-sophisticated to the most computer-naive.

2.3. Instability: The environment of a DBS is quite unstable in so far as the information requirements of the different user types and the hardware technology are rapidly changing.

2.4. System-Surrounding-Integration: DBS's become more and more a prerequisite for daily work meaning that system failures may cause considerable work interruptions.

2.5. Economical considerations: DBS's tend to become rather expensive. The consequence is a high demand for DBS's allowing one to achieve with minimal costs as much as possible.

Having defined the purpose of a DBS we are now in a position to specify the

3. FUNCTIONS OF A DATA BASE SYSTEM

According to the two main DBS-purposes (compare with chapter 2) we distinguish the following DBS-functions:

1. Primary DBS-functions

These functions support:

1.1. Storage and maintenance of entity facts.

1.2. Presentation of entity facts from the stored representation on request.

The functions 1.1. and 1.2. are available through (1st) a Data Definition Language (DDL) which allows the system and data control staff to specify different data structures (views) and (2nd) preferably several Data Manipulation Languages (DML) supporting the application programmers and the different end users (parametric users, analysts/researchers and casual users).

We distinguish within a DBS (1st) physical structures (describing how data is technically stored on physical storage devices) and (2nd) logical structures (describing how data is presented to a user). Physical structures should allow storage of data without redundancy (or with system controlled redundancy only) since redundancy requires enhanced storage space as well as enhanced update activity and renders information consistency more difficult. On the other hand logical structures should simplify solving of practical problems. This is often achievable through structures containing redundant information. From this discussion it follows that the requirements for physical structures and those for logical structures differ considerably.

Another remark concerning logical structures is important: Since we distinguish data base users ranging from the most computer-sophisticated (system and data control staff, application programmer) to the most computer-naive (casual user) the DBS should provide the possibility to derive simultaneously complex logical structures as well as those of spartan simplicity from a given stored representation (physical structure). Actually the following structure types are discussed amongst experts:

Network structures
Hierarchical structures
Relations

(all these structure types will be explained in PART II of this paper).

Concerning the DML's the following versions are desirable within the same DBS:

For system/data control staff and application programmers: Sophisticated DML permitting specification of any operation.

For on-line job-trained routine users (parametric users): Preplaned stored procedures requiring specification of few parameters only.

For Analysts and Researchers: DML with high selection capabilities allowing specification of queries without resorting to programming loops or any other form of branched execution (compare with [4], [5] and [7]).

For casual users: Natural language providing these users (as E.F. Codd formulates in [2]) with at least the illusion of free use of their native language, so that they can express their requirements in an informal way (compare also with [16]).

If a DBS permits through its DDL to derive different types of data structures from a given stored representation then it provides structure type coexistence. If the DBS allows to operate different DML's simultaneously on the same data base then it provides language coexistence.

2. Secondary DBS-functions

These functions mainly allow one to overcome the problems caused by the environment in which a DBS has to operate. Included are functions allowing to overcome problems caused by:

2.1. Multi usage: Multi usage requires a DBS where it is possible to

2.1.1. Synchronize simultaneous user requests

Simultaneous user requests have to be synchronized to avoid possible loss of user modifications. The following example explains this statement:

Assume a data element DE1 having at time T1 a value of 10 (compare with the top of figure I.3). At time T1 user U1 requests DE1, modifies the value and updates the data base at time T3. Meanwhile (at time T2) user U2 is also requesting DE1 for update purpose (note that at time T2 DE1 has still the old value of 10). U2 modifies DE1 and updates the data base at time T4. This operation overwrites the modification from user U1 provided that the DBS contains no synchronization mechanism.

The solution to the problem consists (as can be seen from the bottom of figure I.3) in locking DE1 until U1 has terminated its modification. This locking mechanism which ensures data base consistency may cause however so called dead lock situations. The reason is the following:

Assume that at time T1 user U1 is requesting DE1 and user U2 DE2 both for update purpose requiring DE1 and DE2 to be locked. Assume further that at time T2 user U1 needs DE2 whereas user U2 requires DE1 (figure I.4).

The situation in figure I.4 represents a dead lock situation, meaning that neither request can be satisfied. The synchronization of simultaneous user requests requires therefore in addition to the locking mechanism that the DBS is able to detect and resolve (or to prevent) dead lock situations.

J.N. Gray points out in [3] that an important problem arising in the design of a DBS is choosing the lockable units, i.e. the data aggregates (e.g. data element values, interval of data element values, segment occurrences, segment types, files, data bases, etc.) which are locked as a unit. The finer the

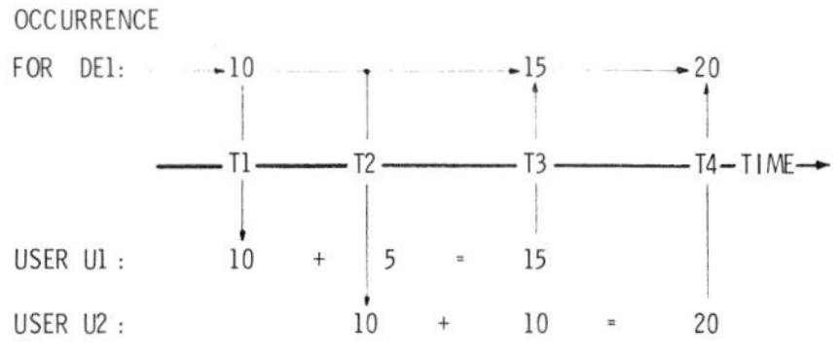

Figure I.3a
DATA BASE UPDATE WITHOUT SYNCHRONIZATION

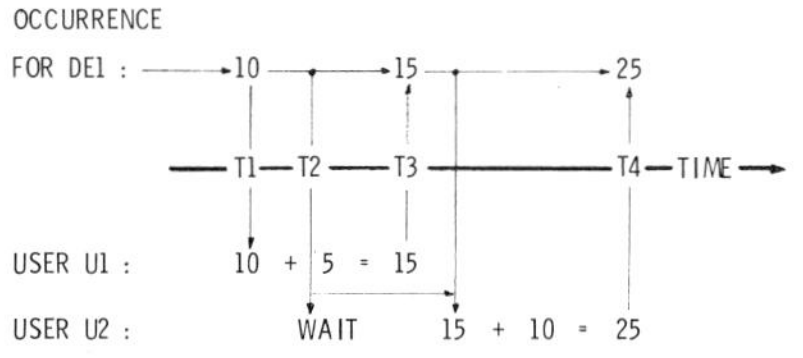

Figure I.3b
DATA BASE UPDATE WITH SYNCHRONIZATION

USER \ TIME	T 1	T 2
U 1	DE1	DE2
U 2	DE2	DE1

Figure 1.4
DEADLOCK SITUATION

lockable unit (e.g. a data element value or a segment occurrence) the more concurrent users can be supported simultaneously, because the propability that two users are requesting the same element at the same time becomes very low. On the other hand: the finer the unit of locking the higher the system overhead. This statement is particularly true for 'complex' transactions which access a large number of records invoking thereby the locking mechanism many times. From this discussion it follows that there exists an important trade-off between:

fine unit of locking (also called: fine granularity)

causing:
- high user concurrency
- high system overhead (for locking purpose)

coarse unit of locking (also called: coarse granularity)

causing:
- low user concurrency
- small system overhead (for locking purpose)

Depending on the number of concurrent users and the complexity of the transaction to be processed a DBS should therefore be able to dynamically choose the lockable unit such that the system overhead is minimized and a given response time can be guaranteed. This requires a DBS beeing able to handle coexisting lockable units of different sizes (granularities).

In addition, multi usage requires a DBS accepting specifications for:

2.1.2. Data base integrity constraints

Data base integrity constraints indicate the checks which must be applied by the DBS when a user attempts to change the content of a data base to ensure that the change is a valid one.

2.1.3. Security constraints

Security constraints indicate the checks which must be applied by the DBS to ensure that a user is authorized to perform the operation he is attempting.

2.1.4. User priorities

User priorities allow a DBS to decide in which order simultaneous user requests have to be satisfied.

2.2. User heterogeneity

User heterogeneity requires a DBS to allow:

2.2.1. Derive different views (data structures) from a given stored representation (structure type coexistence) and

2.2.2. Operate different data manipulation languages (DML's) simultaneously (language coexistence)

The primary DBS functions already discussed answer to these requirements.

2.3. Instability

Instability requires flexibility. In a DBS flexibility is achieved through data independence. We distinguish:

2.3.1. Storage structure (physical structure) independence

Storage structure independence is defined as the program immunity to changes in the storage structure (physical structure). Storage structure independence allows one in particular to change physical storage devices without affecting existing data base programs.

2.3.2. Growth independence

Growth independence is defined as the program immunity to growth in the conceptual view definition (describes how a section of the real world is represented within the data base). Growth independence allows one in particular to take additional entity facts into consideration without affecting existing data base programs.

2.4. System-surrounding integration

System-surrounding integration requires a DBS providing a high degree of reliability and availability through:

2.4.1. Restart features

allowing immediate and fast system restart after system failure without loosing data already introduced into the system.

2.4.2. Recovery features

allowing fast recreation of destroyed data bases without loosing data already introduced into the system.

2.5. Economical considerations

Require a DBS providing tuning and optimazation functions. The following functions are desirable:

2.5.1. Data base reorganization

Any data base requires usually from time to time a physical reorganization. The purpose of a reorganization is (1st) to reestablish the access time which may - as time goes on - decrease due to insertion operations and (2nd) to regain direct access storage space which (mainly for performance reasons) has not been freed after deletion operations. Depending on the ongoing data base update activity there exists an important trade-off between:

many reorganizations per time interval

causing: - lower access time
- higher system overhead (for reorganization purpose)

few reorganizations per time interval

causing: - higher access time
- lower system overhead (for reorganization purpose)

A DBS should therefore be able to:

- dynamically determine the optimum reorganization time interval depending on the ongoing data base update activity (compare with figure I.5)

- automatically initiate the reorganization of the data base

- reorganize the data base without interrupting the ongoing data base activity

2.5.2. Data base image copy

The data base recovery function (compare with the section 2.4.) requires that a data base image copy is taken periodically and that the ongoing data base activity is maintained on a so

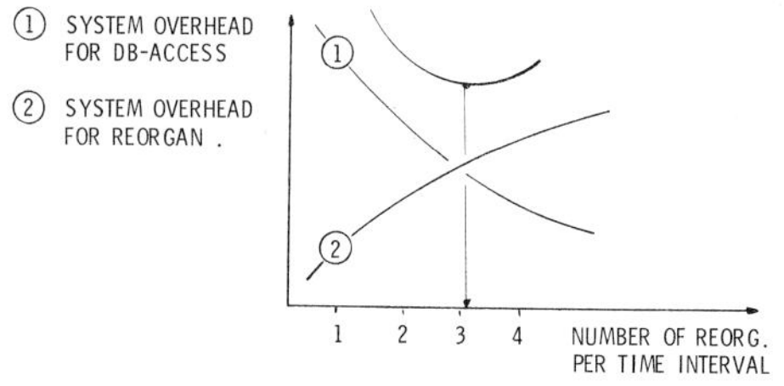

Figure I.5
OPTIMAZATION OF REORGANIZATION

called log tape. Given the trivial dependency: the smaller the log tape created since the last image copy the faster the recovery, there exists again an important trade-off between:

many image copies per time interval (resulting in small log tapes)

causing: - low recovery time
- high system overhead (for image copy purpose)

few image copies per time interval (resulting in voluminous log tapes)

causing: - higher recovery time
- lower system overhead (for image copy purpose)

A DBS should therefore be able to:

- dynamically determine the optimum image copy interval (or determine the image copy interval required to satisfy a given recovery time) depending on the ongoing data base update activity (compare with figure I.6)

- automatically initiate the execution of the image copy

- take the image copy without interrupting the ongoing data base activity

2.5.3. Store data without redundancy (or with system controlled redundancy)

The primary DBS functions already discussed answer to this requirement.

2.5.4. Accounting information

A DBS should be able to collect accounting information allowing one to charge individual users for their system usage.

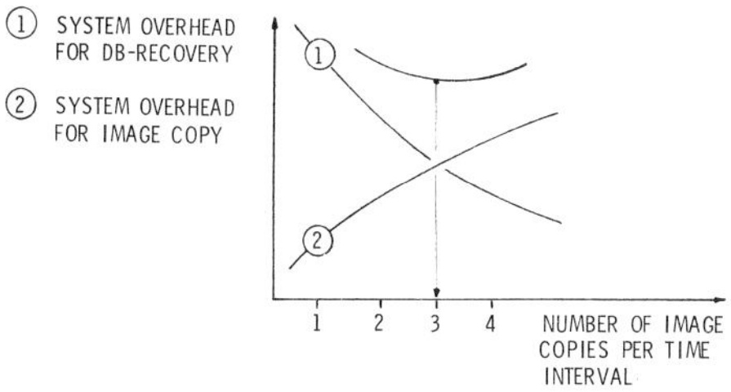

Figure I.6
IMAGE COPY OPTIMAZATION

2.5.5. Storage hierarchies

A DBS should be able to manage physical storage devices such that seldom used data is automatically located on slow but cheap devices and often used data on fast but expensive devices.

2.5.6. Distributed data bases

A DBS should be able to manage distributed data bases (i.e. a data base spread over several physical locations) such that data is automatically placed where it is most often used (allowing one to reduce data transmitting costs).

2.5.7. Statistical information

A DBS should provide any kind of statistical information allowing the system and data control staff to tune the system.

Having specified the purpose and the functions of a DBS we are now in a position to give a precise

4. DATA BASE SYSTEM DEFINITION

A DBS consists of a data base part and a system part.

The data base part (supported by the primary DBS functions) represents a nonredundant (or system controlled redundant) collection of interrelated data.

The system part (corresponding to the secondary DBS functions) guarantees a smooth and economic operation of the data base part such that several users with different information requirements and different skills may simultaneously interrogate and update the data base.

We are now able to understand how the different elements of a DBS are related to each other; in other words: we are now in a position to discuss the

5. ARCHITECTURE OF A DATA BASE SYSTEM

Figure I.7 shows a DBS architecture scheme derived (slightly simplified) from an ANSI/X3/SPARC group [8] proposition.

The scheme shows the different user types discussed in chapter 2, a box representing the primary DBS functions, another one - connected to the log tape - for the secondary DBS functions and finally the physical storage device. The box representing the primary DBS functions is subdivided into smaller boxes, showing the different views (data structures) and view interfaces supported by the primary DBS functions. We distinguish:

- the external views (also called: user subviews): describing how data is presented to a particular user

- the conceptual view (also called: global view, logical view): representing

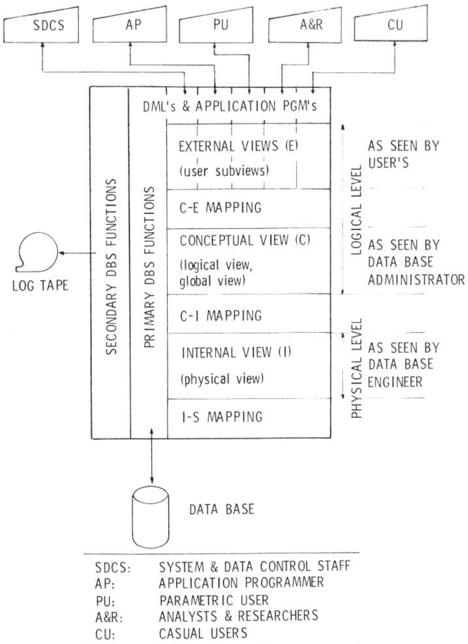

Figure I.7
DATA BASE ARCHITECTURE

the way information is seen by the data base administrator (i.e. the person or group of persons deciding which entity facts of an enterprise have to be considered in a DBS and being responsible for the stored information as an asset)

- the internal view (also called: physical view): describing how data is technically stored on physical storage devices.

Note that the notation: logical level refers to the external views and the conceptual view as a whole whereas the notation: physical level represents a synonym for internal view.

The conceptual view is the central reference point and serves to construct the external views as well as the internal view by means of mappings. We distinguish the following mappings:

- Conceptual view (C) - External view (E) mapping (C-E-mapping)

- Conceptual view (C) - Internal view (I) mapping (C-I-mapping)

- Internal view (I) - Physical Storage Device (S) mapping (I-S-mapping)

The mappings are specified by the data base administrator by means of a Data Definition Language (DDL). A DDL allows one therefore to describe the algorithm required to transform a given view (e.g. the conceptual view) into another view (e.g. the internal view or one of the external views).

With traditional DBS all the mappings have to be specified. More and more we begin to realize however that the C-I-mapping as well as the I-S-mapping can be mechanized. In other words: the way how to technically store data on physical storage devices can be derived from an appropriate conceptual view by means of data synthesis rules. PART II of this paper is mainly concerned with these aspects.

PART II: DATA SYNTHESIS

1. THE RELATIONSHIPS BETWEEN ENTITIES AND DATA BASE ELEMENTS

In PART I chapter 1 we pointed out, that entities belonging to an entity set are characterized by attributes. Realizing a DBS for an enterprise requires first of all that we determine which entity sets we want to have considered within the DBS and which attributes are of relevance for the enterprise. Relevant attributes are represented on the logical level of a DBS by Data Elements (DE) (to avoid misunderstandings we would like to mention that some authors are not distinguishing between attributes and DE's).

A DE consists (as an attribute) of a name and of values. A particular DE-value is called a DE-occurrence or a DE-instance.

Usually a DE has a corresponding element on the physical level of the DBS. This corresponding element is called a field. A field consists again of a name and of values. A particular field-value is called a field-occurrence or a field-instance. A field describes how and where a given DE is technically stored. It is important to note that not every DE has a corresponding field since there exist DE's whose values can be derived from field-values (e.g. average value, total value, maximum value, minimum value, etc.). To formulate it in a different way: the set of all the DE-values represents what may be presented to a given user whereas the collection of all the field-values represents what is technically stored on physical storage devices. The following statement follows immediately from the preceding discussion:

If {A} represents the set of all the attributes for a given entity set, {DE} the set of DE's corresponding to selected elements from {A} and {F} the set of fields corresponding to elements in {DE} then:

$$\{A\}\text{-cardinality} \geq \{DE\}\text{-cardinality} \geq \{F\}\text{-cardinality}.$$

The elements in {DE} are used to construct logical structures satisfying the needs of the different user types. The elements in {F} are used to construct physical structures taking physical storage device characteristics into consideration and allowing derivation of the logical structures mentioned before.

The following summary emphasizes the notation which will be used in the following chapters. (We would like to mention at this point that the field of data base systems possesses as yet no commonly agreed nomenclature. The following set of definitions therefore has to be considered as an attempt to reconsile different terminologies).

- Entities within an entity set are characterized by attributes.

- Some of these attributes have a corresponding element (called: data element DE) on the logical level of the DBS.

- Some of the DE's have a corresponding element (called: field) on the physical level of the DBS.

- A *data element group* (DE-group) is a collection of DE's presented to a user as a unit (e.g. <NAME, AGE, LOCATION>).

- A *DE-group occurrence* is a collection of DE-values from DE's of a DE-group (e.g. <NAME/Brown, AGE/38, LOCATION/Brussels>).

- A *logical structure* contains the DE's (arranged by DE-groups) required to *present* to a specific user facts concerning the entities of an entity set. A logical structure represents a general picture valid for all the entities of a set.

- A *logical structure occurrence* contains the DE-values (arranged by DE-group occurrences) from the DE's of a logical structure. A logical structure occurrence contains facts for a *specific* entity as seen by a particular user.

- A *logical data base* represents the collection of all the logical structure occurrences for the entities of a set.

- A *record* is a collection of fields. It indicates how these fields have to be arranged in order to be stored as a unit on a physical storage device.

- A *record occurrence* is a collection of field-values from fields of a record. It represents what is actually stored as a unit on a physical storage device.

- A *physical structure* contains the fields (arranged by records) which are *stored* for the entities of an entity set. A physical structure represents a general picture valid for all the entities of an entity set.

- A *physical structure occurrence* contains the field-values (arranged by record occurrences) from the fields of a physical structure. A physical structure occurrence contains for a *specific* entity those facts which are actually *stored*.

- A *physical data base* represents the collection of all the physical structure occurrences for the entities of an entity set.

Since (depending on different user requirements) the DE's used to present facts concerning the entities of a set may be structured in different ways, several logical structures as well as several logical data bases may reside in a DBS for a given entity set. However an entity set is always represented by only one physical structure and one physical data base.

2. DATA ELEMENTS

(The following notation is taken from [11])

A data element (DE) may be either

- a *key*: a DE is a key if each occurrence of this DE is able to uniquely identify an entity within a set (e.g. STUDENT-NO). Unique identification is often only achievable through several DE's. The concatenation of these DE's is called a *compound key*. The following notation is used: if the DE's DE1, DE2, DE3 are required for unique identification then the compound key is represented by DE1*DE2*DE3.

- an *attributive DE*: a DE is an attributive DE if it adds just further facts to the description of an entity without allowing to uniquely identify this entity within a set (e.g. AGE). An

Association

is a 'from-to'-relationship between two DE's. The 'from'-element is considered thereby as a key. Each key occurrence identifies (depending on the type of the association) 1 or several or no occurrence(s) of the 'to'-element. The notation (DE1,DE2) is used to represent an association from DE1 to DE2. We distinguish the following

Association types

1. Simple (or type 1) associations
2. Complex (or type M) associations
3. Conditional (or type C) associations.

The different association types have the following characteristics:

Simple (or type 1) associations

Each occurrence of the 'from'-DE identifies one and only one occurrence of the 'to'-DE. For example:

Association: (STUDENT-NO, ADVISOR-NO)

DE-occurrences:		
	S1	A1
	S2	A5
	S3	A2
	S4	A1
	S5	A1

(The type 1 association: (STUDENT-NO, ADVISOR-NO) indicates that a particular student has one and only one advisor.)

Complex (or type M) associations

Each occurrence of the 'from'-DE can identify any number (including 0) of occurrences of the 'to'-DE. For example:

Association: (STUDENT-NO, COURSE-NO)

DE-occurrences:		
	S1	C1
	S1	C2
	S1	C3
	S2	C1
	S2	C3
	S2	C6
	S2	C8

(The type M association (STUDENT-NO, COURSE-NO) indicates that a particular student may follow any number of courses.)

Conditional (or type C) associations

A conditional association is similar to a simple (type 1) association except that an occurrence of the 'from'-DE may or may not identify an occurrence of the 'to'-DE, depending on a given condition. For example:

Association: (EMPLOYEE, SPOUSE)

DE-occurrences:		
	E1	S1
	E2	S3
	E3	
	E4	S2

(The type C association (EMPLOYEE, SPOUSE) indicates that a particular employee may or may not have a (single) spouse.)

DE-Mapping

Between two related DE's one can distinguish two associations. Either of these associations can be called the forward association; the other association then is called the inverse association. Forward and inverse association together are called a DE-mapping. The following notation is used:

Given the DE's DE1 and DE2 then

((DE1, DE2)(DE2, DE1))

denotes the mapping between DE1 and DE2. The expression ((DE1, DE2)(DE2, DE1)) is usually abbreviated and becomes (X:Y) where X represents the type of the (forward) association (DE1, DE2) and Y the type of the (inverse) association (DE2, DE1). Figure II.1 summarizes all possible mapping types.

Note that the (C:C)-mapping represents a contradiction. It indicates: given a DE1-occurrence in (DE1, DE2) this occurrence may or may not (type C association) identify a DE2-occurrence and: given an identified DE2-occurrence this occurrence may or may not (type C association) identify a DE1-occurrence in (DE2, DE1) (an identified DE2-occurrence always identifies a DE1-occurrence).

We now show some DE-mapping examples.

(1:M)-example: ((S#, A#)(A#, S#))

(This (1:M)-mapping indicates that a particular student (represented by the student number S#) is advised by one advisor (represented by the advisor number A#) but a particular advisor may advise any number of students)

(M:M)-example: ((S#, C#)(C#, S#))

INVERSE ASSOC. / FORWARD ASSOC.	TYPE 1	TYPE M	TYPE C
TYPE 1	(1:1)	(1:M)	(1:C)
TYPE M	(M:1)	(M:M)	(M:C)
TYPE C	(C:1)	(C:M)	(C:C)

Figure II.1
MAPPING TYPES

(This (M:M)-mapping indicates that a particular student (represented by the student number S#) may follow any number of courses (represented by the course number C#) and a particular course may be followed by any number of students)

(C:1)-example: ((E#, SPN)(SPN, E#))

(This (C:1)-mapping indicates that a particular employee (represented by the employee number E#) may or may not have a (single) spouse (represented by the spouse name SPN) and that a spouse is married with one employee only).

In PART I chapter 2 we pointed out that one of the purposes of a DBS is to store and provide facts concerning entities (i.e. real objects, associations, abstract concepts). Using the mapping-types in figure II.1 for DE's corresponding to entity set identifiers allows us to represent how entities are related (associated) to each other. A DBS should therefore be able to handle all the mapping-types mentioned in figure II.1 (excluded is of course the contradictory (C:C)-mapping). In the following chapters we discuss which structure types are required to support the different mapping-types.

3. DE-GROUP/RECORD CONSIDERATIONS

(The following considerations are taken from [12])

In PART II chapter 1 we pointed out that a DE-group is a collection of DE's presented to a particular user as a unit. A DE-group has always a name and contains a distinguished DE (or a collection of distinguished DE's) whose occurrences allow to uniquely identify DE-group occurrences. This distinguished DE (respectively this collection of distinguished DE's) is called the DE-group key (respectively the DE-group compound key) and will be underlined throughout this paper. For example:

STUDENT (S#, SNAME, LOCATION)

denotes a DE-group called STUDENT with the DE's S# (student number), SNAME (student name) and LOCATION. S# (underlined) serves as the DE-group key.

To refer to a particular DE-group occurrence we use the notation 'DE-group-name(key/key-value)'. Thus, STUDENT(S#/S1) denotes a DE-group occurrence for the student with the student number S1.

Note that analogous remarks apply also to records, which - as already defined - indicate the fields to be stored as a unit. Thus, the above example could also denote a record called STUDENT with the fields S#, SNAME and LOCATION. S# (underlined) serves as the record key.

At first glance we are tempted to assume that any DE's can be combined in order to construct a DE-group provided that the result is 'semantically reasonable'. This statement however is true for retrieval operations only. For data base modifications (i.e. inserts, deletes and updates) DE's have to be combined according to precise rules in order to avoid so called anomalies in storage operations. The term 'anomalies in storage operations' is a collective notion for problems which may occur with data base insert, delete and update operations (we distinguish in fact anomalies in insert, delete and update operations).

Before discussing the rules mentioned above we would like to show that there exist a close correspondance between DE-groups and underlying records. Showing this correspondance will allow us to deduce that the following rules are applicable both to DE-groups and to records.

Suppose that the physical level of a DBS includes the following records:

Record: PROD(P#, PD, M#)

Record-occurrences:	P1	PA	M1
	P2	PB	M1

Record: EMP(E#, EN, M#)

Record-occurrences:	E1	EA	M1
	E2	EB	M1

with:
P#: part number
PD: part description
M#: machine number
E#: employee number
EN: employee name

Suppose now that a user requests (on the logical DBS level) the DE-group MANUF(P#, M#, E#) indicating the machines and the persons required to produce parts. The DE-group MANUF is created by mapping the records PROD and

EMP such that each record occurrence from PROD is concatenated with a record occurrence in EMP provided that both occurrences have a common M#-field value. The creation of MANUF requires in addition reduction of the concatenated record to the fields corresponding to the DE's in MANUF. This mapping procedure is described with the help of an appropriate DDL specification. The mapping yields:

DE-group:	MANUF(P#, M#, E#)
DE-group occurrences:	P1 M1 E1
	P1 M1 E2
	P2 M1 E1
	P2 M1 E2

(Note that for unique DE-group occurrence identification the compound key P#*E# is required).

Suppose now that a user desires to delete within MANUF just one DE-group occurrence (e.g. the 4th occurrence: <P#/P2, M#/M1, E#/E2>). Note that there is no way to reflect this deletion by means of corresponding deletions from PROD and EMP.

The phenomena discussed above (first described by E.F. Codd in [14]) does not occur if the set of DE's in a DE-group (used for storage operations) corresponds to a subset of fields from a single record. This subset must include at least the record key.

From this discussion it follows that designing DE-groups used for storage operations requires that the DE's of a particular DE-group correspond to the fields of a single record and that this record should not cause any problems in storage operations.

We are now in a position to discuss rules related both to the construction of DE-groups (used for storage operations) and records. The term segment will be used to stand for 'DE-group' (if the rules are used for the design of DE-groups) respectively 'record' (if the rules are used for the design of records).

Rule 1:

This rule specifies which associations are allowed between the key and attributive elements (AE). An attributive element is a DE which does not participate in a DE-group key (respectively a field which does not participate in a record key).

Given the mapping

((Key, AE) (AE, Key))

abbreviated by

(X:Y)

then X and Y may represent one of the following association types:

X: simple (type 1) association or conditional (type C) association

Y: simple (type 1) association or complex (type M) association

Thus, the segment concept supports the mapping-types: (1:1), (1:M), (C:1), (C:M)

We now show some examples:

(1:1)-example: ((S#, SS#) (SS#, S#))

The (1:1)-mapping indicates that S# (student number) and SS# (social security number) can be included in the same segment. Note that in this case both S# and SS# must be considered as key (E.F. Codd [13] would use the notation: primary key (for S#) and candidate key (for SS#)).

(1:M)-example: ((S#, AGE) (AGE, S#))

The (1:M)-mapping indicates that S# (student number) and AGE (student age) can be included in the same segment

(C:1)-example: ((S#, SPN) (SPN, S#))

The (C:1)-mapping indicates that S# (student number) and SPN (spouse name) can be included in the same segment.

Rule 2:

(This rule applies to segments having a compound key).

If the segment key is a compound key (e.g. DE1*DE2*DE3) then the association

(subset of compound key, AE)

must be a complex (type M) association.

We show the justification for this rule with help of an example:

Assume the following segment and segment occurrences:

Segment: STUDENT(S#, SN, C#, EV)

Segment-occ.:

S1	SA	C1	1
S1	SA	C2	2
S1	SA	C3	1
S2	SB	C1	6
S2	SB	C4	2
S3	SA	C2	5
S3	SA	C5	2

with:
- S#: student number
- SN: student name
- C#: course number
- EV: course evaluation
- S#*C#: segment key

We first apply rule 1 to the STUDENT segment:

In STUDENT we distinguish the following mappings between the segment key (S#*C#) and attributive elements (SN and EV):

((S#*C#, SN)(SN, S#*C#)): (1:M)-mapping
((S#*C#, EV)(EV, S#*C#)): (1:M)-mapping

Rule 1 is not violated since both mappings are of type (1:M).

We now apply rule 2 to the STUDENT segment:

In STUDENT we distinguish the following associations between key subsets (S# and C#) and attributive elements (SN and EV):

(S#, SN): simple (type 1) association
(C#, SN): complex (type M) association
(S#, EV): complex (type M) association
(C#, EV): complex (type M) association

Rule 2 is violated by the first association. The conclusion from this fact is that SN should not be included in the same segment as S#, C# and EV. Violating the rule causes anomalies in storage operations. For the actual example we recognize particularly: if a student changes his name, several segment occurrences have to be modified in order to avoid inconsistent results. The problem does not occur if the STUDENT segment is divided into two segments as follows:

Segment: S(S#, SN)

Segment-occ.:

S1	SA
S2	SB
S3	SA

Segment: SC(S#, C#, EV)

Segment-occ.:

S1	C1	1
S1	C2	2
.		
.		

(Note that the segments S and SC do not violate any rule discussed so far).

Rule 3:

No simple (type 1) associations are allowed between attributive elements of a segment.

We show the justification for this rule again with help of an example:

Assume the following segment and segment occurrences:

Segment: MANUF(P#, M#, E#)

Segment-occ.:

01	3	100
02	5	150
03	3	100
04	3	100
05	2	200
06	4	100

with:
- P#: product number (segment key)
- M#: machine number
- E#: employee number

We now test if the MANUF segment violates any rule discussed so far. We first apply rule 1 to the MANUF segment:

In MANUF we distinguish the following mappings between the segment key (P#) and attributive elements (M# and E#):

((P#, M#)(M#, P#)): (1:M)-mapping
((P#, E#)(E#, P#)): (1:M)-mapping

Rule 1 is not violated since both mappings are of type (1:M). The meaning of these mappings is that a given product is produced with one machine only but a given machine may produce different products. In addition: a given product is produced by the same person always but a given person may be responsible for several products.

Rule 2 does not have to be checked since the MANUF segment has no compound key.

We now apply rule 3 to the MANUF segment:

In MANUF we distinguish the following associations between attributive elements (M# and E#):

(M#, E#): simple (type 1) association
(E#, M#): complex (type M) association

Rule 3 is violated by the first association which indicates that a given machine is handled by one person only (the second association indicates that a given person is responsible for several machines). The conclusion from this fact is that M# should not be included in the same segment as P# and E# (respectively E# should not be included in the same segment as P# and M#). Violating the rule causes again <u>anomalies in storage operations</u>. For the actual example we recognize the following anomalies:

<u>Anomaly in update operations</u>: if a person responsible for a given machine changes, several segment occurrences have to be modified in order to avoid inconsistent results.

<u>Anomaly in insert operations</u>: it is not possible to store the relation between a person and a machine without knowing at least one product produced by this machine (note that a segment occurrence can only be inserted if at least the key value is known).

<u>Anomaly in delete operations</u>: if all the products produced by a given machine are deleted the relationship between the machine and the person responsible for this machine is also deleted.

To overcome these anomalies we have again to divide the MANUF segment into several segments. At first glance we may consider the following solutions:

Solution 1:	S1(<u>P#</u>, M#)	S2(<u>M#</u>, E#)
Solution 2:	S1(<u>P#</u>, M#)	S3(<u>P#</u>, E#)
Solution 3:	S3(<u>P#</u>, E#)	S2(<u>M#</u>, E#)

Although the above solutions are not violating any rule discussed so far, they are not equally good. To test the quality of the different solutions we check if they answer to the following requirements:

1. A given solution must represent the same information as the original segment; in other words: the original segment must be restorable.

2. The storage space required to store the information contained in the original segment has to be minimal.

We are now discussing which solution answers best to these requirements.

<u>Segment restorability</u>: The 3rd solution does not allow us to restore MANUF as it was because:

- In S3 the association (P#, E#) is simple (as in MANUF).

- In S2 the association (E#, M#) is complex (as in MANUF).

- Restoring MANUF from S2 and S3 using E# as link element yields a segment with a complex (P#, M#) association (note that this association is simple in the original MANUF segment). The consequence is that the 3rd solution does not allow us to determine which (single) machine is required to produce a given product. We have therefore to exclude solution 3.

<u>Minimizing storage space</u>: Assume that the original MANUF segment occurs n times. Solution 1 then requires:

for segment S1: n segment occurrences
for segment S2: m segment occurrences

therefore: (m+n) segment occ. required.

Note that m<n because the association (M#, P#) is complex (a given M#-value is identifying several P#-values which means that the <u>set</u> of M#-values is smaller than the <u>set</u> of P#-values).

Solution 2 requires:

for segment S1: n segment occurrences
for segment S3: n segment occurrences

therefore: 2n segment occ. required.

Since (m+n)<2n we eliminate solution 2.

The 4th rule indicates finally how to split a segment in order to get a solution answering to the preceding requirements.

<u>Rule 4</u>:

Attributive elements of a segment S being uniquely identified by other attributive elements of S have to be excluded from S. For each uniquely identifying attributive element an additional segment has to be created by combining the uniquely identifying element (which becomes the key of the new segment) with the excluded elements it identifies.

We now apply rule 4 to MANUF(P#, M#, E#).

In MANUF we distinguish the following mappings (the segment key P# is underlined):

((P#, M#)(M#, P#)): (1:M)-mapping
((P#, E#)(E#, P#)): (1:M)-mapping
((M#, E#)(E#, M#)): (1:M)-mapping

The attributive element E# is uniquely identified by the attributive element M#. E# is therefore excluded from MANUF. An additional segment is created by combining the uniquely identifying element M# (which becomes the key of the new segment) with the identified element E#. The solution obtained thereby corresponds to the optimum solution discussed before.

For the special case:

((M#, E#)(E#, M#)): (1:1)-mapping

either M# or E# have to be excluded from MANUF.

We summarize:

A segment consists of a key which identifies an entity type and attributive elements which describe this entity type in some way. These descriptive attributive elements are all independent of one another, in the sense that none is determined by any combination of the others.

The segment concept discussed so far supports the mapping types (1:1), (1:M), (C:1) and (C:M). The remaining mapping types discussed in PART II chapter 2 (i.e. (M:1), (M:M), (1:C) and (M:C)) are supported only by more complex structures which will be discussed in the remaining chapters.

Data structures are used both on the logical level of a DBS (to present entity facts) and on the physical level (to store entity facts). In fact we distinguish between logical structures (built on DE-groups) and physical structures (built on records). Since we would like first to discuss the general characteristics of data structures (regardless wether they are used on the logical or physical level) we are again using the segment notion to refer both to DE-groups and to records.

4. HIERARCHICAL STRUCTURES (TREE STRUCTURES)

A hierarchical structure (or tree structure) allows one to represent facts for a single entity type. Following rules apply to the construction of hierarchical structures:

Rule 1:

A hierarchical structure always starts with a root segment. The key of this segment corresponds to the identifier of the entity type to be described with the hierarchical structure.

Rule 2:

Additional segments (called dependants) may be added on a succeeding level. The segment on the preceding level becomes the parent of the new dependants. The addition of dependants is repeated horizontally (same level) and vertically (different level) as often as required (figure II.2).

As is well known every segment represents an entity type (PART II, chapter 3). The dependants in a hierarchical structure have however a special function in so far as they correspond to entity types serving as properties for the entity type identified by the root segment key (remember that any entity can become the property of other entities (PART I, chapter 1)).

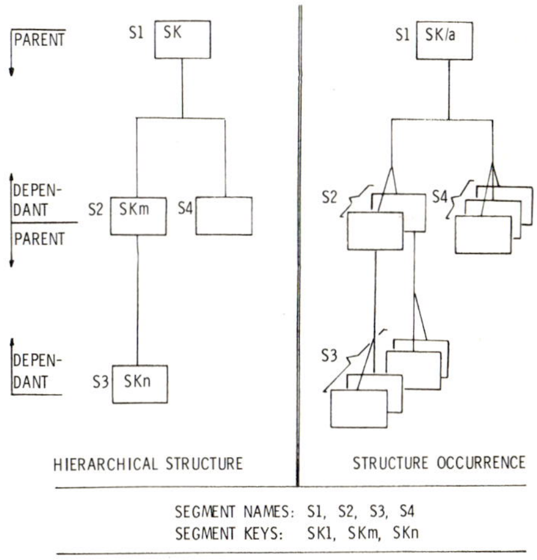

Figure II.2

Rule 3:

Given the mapping

((SKm, SKn)(SKn, SKm))

abbreviated by

(Xmn : Ynm)

where

SKm: general notation for a segment key on level m (parent segment key)

SKn: general notation for a segment key on level n where n=m+1 (dependant segment key)

then Xmn (type of the (parent, dependant)-association) and Ynm (type of the (dependant, parent)-association) may be:

Xmn: simple (type 1) association or complex (type M) association or conditional (type C) association

Ynm: always simple (type 1) association.

Rule 4:

Every segment (except the root) has only one entry point. This is due the fact that Ynm (type of the association (dependant,parent)) is simple and a given segment is accessable only via its parent. To indicate that an association can be used to access a segment the corresponding association type will be underlined throughout this paper. For hierarchical structures Xmn (type of the association (parent, dependant)) will therefore always appear underlined.

The following statement follows immediately from the preceding discussion:

If {(Xmn:Ynm)} represents the set of all the mappings between parent and dependant segments of a hierarchical structure then only (1:1)-, (M:1)- and (C:1)-mappings are contained within this set.

The consequence of rule 4 is that the access path to every segment within a hierarchical structure is unique (a segment is always only accessable via its parent). This means that a hierarchical structure represents a so called linear structure type.

We are now discussing the suitability of hierarchical structures with regard to their usage on the logical, respectively physical, level of a DBS.

1. Hierarchical structures as logical structures

We test the suitability by analyzing:

1.1. The ability to represent entity facts.

1.2. Ease of use for the realization of data base application programs.

1.1. Representability of entity facts: In PART I chapter 1 we pointed out that an entity is characterized by properties. We also stated that an entity may appear as a property of another entity.

On the logical level of a DBS an entity type is represented by a DE-group consisting of a key which identifies that entity type and attributive data elements which describe that entity type in some way. Remember that these descriptive data elements are all independent of one another, in the sense that none is determined by any combination of the others (PART II, chapter 3).

The fact that an entity type is used as property for another entity type means that the latter is associated (simple, complex or conditional) with the former. Applying this statement to the logical level of a DBS means that one has to be able to represent any association type between the DE-group containing the entity type identifier (i.e. the root) and DE-groups corresponding to entity types serving as entity properties (i.e. dependants). A hierarchical structure imposes no restrictions on doing so. Thus, hierarchical structures are quite suitable to represent facts for a particular entity type.

Representing entity facts by means of hierarchical structures may cause redundancy. The reason for this is two fold: first, redundancy within a single structure occurrence may occur because facts for a particular entity type are mentioned - although in a different context - several times within the same structure. Second, redundancy may occur through several structure occurrences because the underlying hierarchical structure only supports simple (dependant, parent)-associations. In reality however the association between the entity type corresponding to the dependant and the entity type corresponding to the parent may also be complex. Representing this situation by means of a hierarchical structure requires repetition of a given dependant occurrence whenever it has to appear underneath a parent occurrence.

It is important to recognize that redundancy on the <u>logical level</u> of a DBS is <u>not</u> a disadvantage but it simplifies the representation of entity facts quite drastically.

We now show an example.

Assume that by means of a hierarchical structure occurrence one would like to represent for a particular student (i.e. the entity) the courses he is following and the attendees of these courses. Figure II.3 shows on the left side a corresponding hierarchical structure (valid for all the students) and on the right side structure occurrences (valid for particular students only). Both, course entities and attendee entities are considered in this example as properties of a student entity. It is obvious that the entity type student corresponds to the entity type attendee. This means (according to the preceding explanations) that a particular structure occurrence necessarily contains redundancy since facts for an entity type (i.e. the entity type student, respectively the entity type attendee) are mentioned - although in a different context - several times within the same structure (e.g. facts for the student S#/S1 appear within the root occurrence as well as within an A (attendee) occurrence).

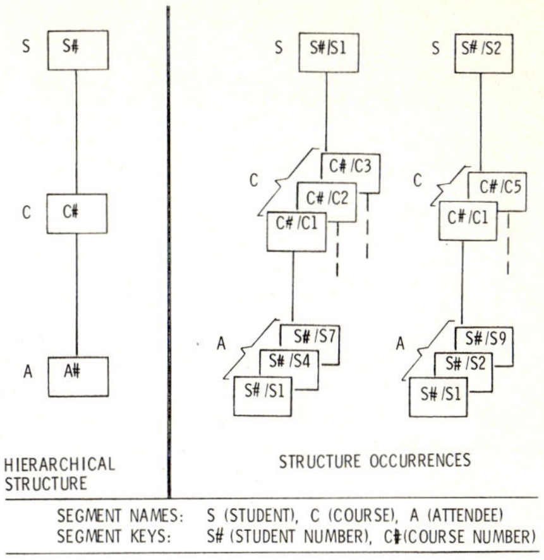

Figure II.3

It is obvious too that the mapping

((STUDENT, COURSE)(COURSE, STUDENT))

is of type (M:M) in reality. While it is possible to represent the complex (STUDENT, COURSE)-association by means of a complex (parent, dependant)-association the complex inverse (COURSE, STUDENT)-association may only - due to the restrictions for hierarchical structures - be represented by a simple (dependant, parent)-association. Representing the real situation by means of a hierarchical structure requires therefore to repeat the facts for a particular course whenever this course is followed by a student (e.g. facts for the course C#/C1 appear within different structure occurrences because this course is followed by several students.

1.2. <u>Ease of use</u>: The fact that a hierarchical structure is a <u>linear structure</u> (i.e. the access path to every segment is unique) has a positive impact on the effort required for the realization of data base application programs. It means that an application programmer has no choice on how to 'navigate' to a particular segment. This allows one to neglect - what we would like to call - the <u>navigation dimension</u> within an application program. The consequence is a drastic simplification in the design and realization of such programs. It is true that C.W. Bachman points out in [15] that '... the application programmer should accept the challenge of navigation within an n-dimensional data space' (a hierarchical structure represents only a 3-dimensional data space). Our opinion however is that every simplification (provided that it does not restrict the possibilities) contributes to an increase in the programmer's productivity and should therefore be taken into consideration.

We now try to illustrate the preceding assertions.

Assume that one would like to get an answer to the question: 'a particular student (e.g. S#/S1) is following which courses?'. Working with the hierarchical structure shown in figure II.3 one could formulate the answer to this question as follows:

{S(S#/S1)*C( )}

The above notation denotes the set of all the hierarchical paths created by individually concatenating the root occurrence S(S#/S1) with a C occurrence appearing underneath the root occurrence. There is only one interpretation for the above mentioned set since every path contained in the set is well defined.

2. Hierarchical structures as physical structures

From the preceding discussion it follows that hierarchical structures in many cases may cause redundancy. We pointed out in PART I chapter 3 that a physical structure should allow storage without redundancy (possibly with system controlled redundancy) since redundancy requires enhanced storage space as well as enhanced update activity and renders information consistency more difficult.

Hierarchical structures used on the physical level of a DBS may in addition cause anomalies in storage operations. We illustrate this assertion by means of an example:

Assume that the structure shown in figure II.3 is used on the physical level of a DBS. We immediately recognize the following anomalies:

Anomaly in update operations: if facts for a particular course change, several C (course) occurrences have to be modified in order to avoid inconsistent results.

Anomaly in insert operations: it is not possible to store facts concerning a course having no enrollments (to store a dependant requires storage of its parents up to the root level).

Anomaly in delete operations: if all the students following a particular course are deleted then the facts for this course will also disappear.

We summarize:

Hierarchical structures simplify representation and processing of entity facts. Since these advantages are particularly desirable when presenting data and working with data, hierarchical structures can by all means be used on the logical level of a DBS. However, hierarchical structures may cause redundancy and anomalies in storage operations. Since these disadvantages are particularly undesirable when storing data, hierarchical structures should not be used on the physical level of a DBS.

The following chapter discusses network structures - a structure type which does not show the disadvantages (redundancy, anomalies in storage operations) mentioned for hierarchical structures but, on the other hand does not have their advantages (simplified fact representation and processing) either.

5. NETWORK STRUCTURES (NETS)

A network structure (net) allows one to represent facts for several entity types. Following rules apply to the construction of network structures:

Rule 1:

A network structure represents (as a hierarchical structure) a collection of related segments. Each of these segments represents an entity type. No segment has a special function (like the root segment in a hierarchical structure). As a matter of fact any segment within a network structure can be used as starting point and obtains thereby a similar function to that of the root segment in a hierarchical structure (i.e. it identifies through its key the entity type to be described by means of the structure). A network structure allows one to describe as many entity types as there are segments within the structure. It goes without saying that whenever a segment is chosen to identify through its key an entity type then the remaining segments correspond to entity types serving as properties for the aforesaid entity type.

From the preceding discussion it follows that a single network structure allows one immediately to handle the reciprocal roles entities and entity properties may take (PART I, chapter 1). In contrast: the hierarchical approach requires a separate structure for each entity to be described.

Rule 2:

Given the mapping

((SKm, SKn)(SKn, SKm))

abbreviated by

(Xmn : Ynm)

where

SKm and SKn represent the segment keys of any two related segments m and n then

Xmn and Ynm may be of any type.

In a network structure any segment is accessable by any other related segment. This means that both, Xmn and Ynm have - according to the notation introduced in PART II, chapter 4 - to be underlined.

Rule 3:

We distinguish between simple and complex network structures. The difference is the following:

If {(Xmn : Ynm)} represents the set of all the mappings between related segments of a network structure then the structure is simple if the mapping set contains only (1:1)-, (1:M)-, (1:C)-, (M:1)-, (M:C)-, (C:1)- and (C:M)-mappings (in other words: if the mapping set contains no (M:M)-mapping). The structure is complex if the mapping set contains (besides others or exclusively) a (M:M)-mapping.

Rule 4:

Any complex network structure can be transformed into a simple network structure by replacing all (M:M)-mappings by two (M:1)-mappings using an additional segment (say LS) for linking purpose. The replacing (M:1)-mappings are defined as follows:

((SKm, LS)(LS, SKm)) and
((SKn, LS)(LS, SKn))

(Note that LS denotes the commonly used link segment).

The transformation mentioned above is in so far important as some data base software packages can handle simple network structures only. Transforming a complex structure into a simple one allows therefore to use such packages also for complex cases.

Rule 5:

A network structure can be transformed into a hierarchical structure by introducing redundancy. This transformation is in so far important as it allows the design of DBS which combines the advantages of network structures (discussed later in this chapter) with those of hierarchical structures.

We would like to illustrate the preceding explanations by means of an example.

Assume that one would like to represent by means of a network structure facts concerning the entities students (S), courses (C) and professors (P). We distinguish the following mappings between these entities:

1. ((S, C)(C, S)): (M:M)-mapping
2. ((S, P)(P, S)): (1:M)-mapping
3. ((P, C)(C, P)): (M:1)-mapping

The 1st mapping indicates that a student (S) is following any number of courses (C) and that a course may be followed by any number of students.

The 2nd mapping indicates that a student (S) is advised by one professor (P) only but a professor can advise any number of students.

The 3rd mapping indicates that a professor (P) may teach any number of courses (C) but a course is taught by one professor only.

The underlined association types indicate that one would like to access any segment from any other related segment.

Figure II.4 shows on the left side an appropriate network structure (valid for all students, courses and professors) and on the right side corresponding structure occurrences (valid for particular students, courses and professors only).

One recognizes immediately that the structure occurrences are free of

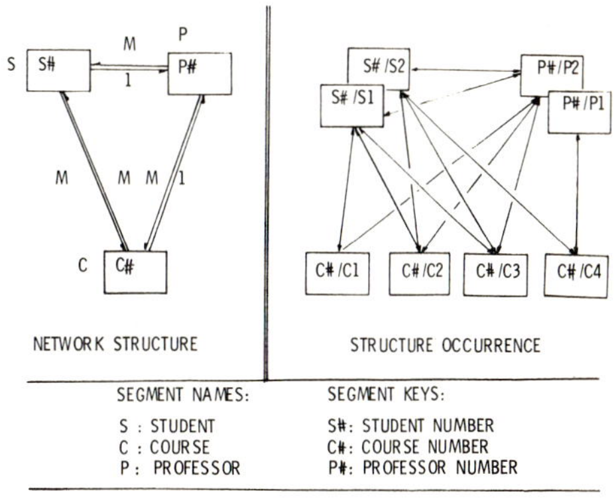

Figure II.4

redundancy. This is due to the fact that a given segment (respectively segment occurrence) has - in contrast to a hierarchical structure - several entry points. The consequence is that there exist usually several access paths to every segment (respectively segment occurrence). This means that a network structure represents a so called non linear structure type.

The network structure shown in figure II.4 is complex because it includes at least one (M:M)-mapping. The complex structure can be transformed into a simple one by converting the (M:M)-mapping

((S, C) (C, S))

into the following (M:1)-mappings (SC indicates the commonly used link segment):

((S, SC) (SC, S)) and
((C, SC) (SC, C))

The example presented in figure II.4 is used in figure II.5 again. The left side of figure II.5 shows occurrences for the (M:M)-mapping

((S#, C#) (C#, S#))

while the right side represents occurrences for the two (M:1)-mappings

((S#, S#*C#) (S#*C#, S#)) respectively
((C#, S#*C#) (S#*C#, C#)).

(Note that the commonly used link segment SC is only uniquely identifiable by the compound key S#*C#).

Figure II.6 finally shows three hierarchical structures (together with some structure occurrences) derived (according to rule 5) from the network structure presented in figure II.4. Note

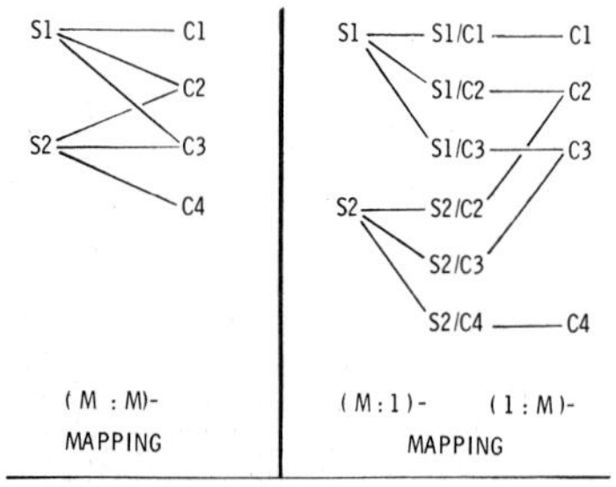

Figure II.5
MAPPING TRANSFORMATION

that at least 3 hierarchical structures had to be derived in order to describe the 3 entities S (students), C (courses) and P (professors).

We are now in a position to discuss the suitability of network structures with regard to their usage on the logical respectively physical level of a DBS.

1. Network structures as logical structures

We discuss the suitability by analyzing the same aspects as for hierarchical structures:

1.1. Representability of entity facts: Since all the mapping types (excluded of course the contradictory (C:C)-mapping) mentioned in figure II.1 are supported by network structures it goes without saying that this structure type causes no difficulties to represent any entity facts. Important is especially that this representation is possible without redundancy.

1.2. Ease of use: The fact that a network structure is a non linear structure type (i.e. there exist usually several access paths to a segment respectively to a segment occurrence)

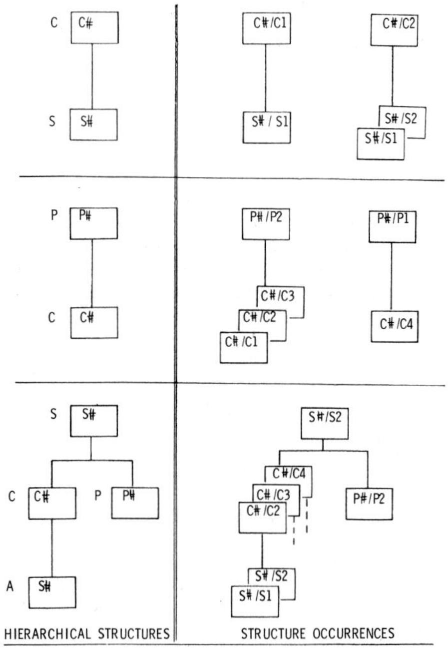

Figure II.6
HIERARCHICAL STRUCTURES DERIVED FROM NETWORK STRUCTURE (fig. II.4)

has a negative impact on the effort required for the realization of data base application programs. It means that an application programmer has to choose how to 'navigate' to a particular segment. Thus, the navigation dimension may not be neglected within an application program. The consequence is that more sophisticated programs are required to process network structures.

Since there exist usually alternative paths to navigate to a particular segment, one must be able to explicitly specify the path to be taken. The Data Base Task Group (DBTG) proposal from the CODASYL programming language committee [17] introduces for this (and other) purpose(s) the 'set' concept. To avoid confusion with a mathematical set, a DBTG-set will always appear within apostrophes throughout this paper. A 'set' is a named relationship between record types (segments in our notation). Alternative paths may then be specified by indicating the names of the 'sets' to be used.

Figure II.7 shows a possible DBTG implementation for the network structure mentioned in figure II.4. Since the DBTG proposal can handle simple networks but cannot handle complex networks without their being modified to a simple network form, the (M:M)-mapping

((STUDENT, COURSE)(COURSE, STUDENT))

appears in figure II.7 as the (M:1)-mappings

((S, SC)(SC, S)) and
((C, SC)(SC, C)).

The segment SC with the compound key S#*C# acts as link segment between the S (student) and C (course) segment. The arrows indicate complex (type M)

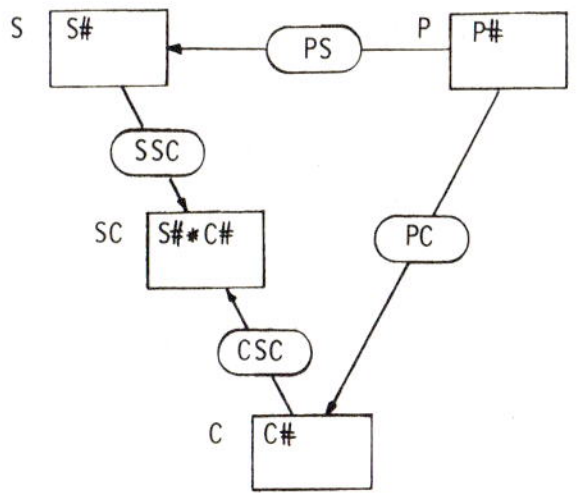

Figure II.7
DBTG-IMPLEMENTATION OF THE NETWORK SHOWN IN FIG. II.4

associations while a circle contains the name of a 'set'.

We are now in a position to illustrate the navigation dimension one has to consider when realizing application programs processing a network structure.

Assume that one would like to get an answer to the question: 'a particular student (e.g. S#/S1) is following which courses?'. Working with the network structure shown in figure II.7 one could formulate the answer to this question as follows:

{S(S#/S1)->[SSC]*SC( )->[CSC]*C( )}

Above notation denotes the set of all the paths created by individually concatenating the S(S#/S1)-occurrence with a SC-occurrence (obtained by using (indicated by: '->') the 'set' SSC) and with a C-occurrence (obtained by using the 'set' CSC).

More elaborate examples showing the impact of hierarchical, respectively network, structures with regard to the effort required for problem solving are mentioned in [12].

2. Network structures as physical structures

From the preceding discussion it follows that network structures are quite suitable with regard to their usage on the physical level of a DBS since they allow to store entity facts without redundancy. The fact that no segment has a special function means in addition that anomalies in storage operations will not occur.

We summarize:

Network structures allow one to avoid redundancy and do not cause anomalies in storage operations. Since these advantages are particularly desirable when storing data, network structures should by all means be used on the physical level of a DBS. However, the increased effort required to handle network structures makes their application on the logical level of a DBS debatable. A solution to the problem consists of using network structures for the storage of data and - since network structures can always be reduced to simpler forms - to use hierarchical structures for the presentation of data. The mapping between the physical level and the logical level (specified by the data base administrator once) would then include the algorithm required to transform the network into a hierarchy. Needless to say this approach (described in detail in [10]) lays a certain burden on the data base administrator and requires probably an increased initial effort. On the other side it decreases the effort required for the realization of application programs which - in the long term - possitively affects the productivity of the EDP department as a whole.

The structure types discussed so far are more or less reserved to the computer sophisticated users. For casual users whose importance will tremendously increase over the next future (compare e.g. with [14]) neither hierarchical nor network structures are ideal. The following chapter discusses relations which are - due to their simplicity - especially suited for casual users without excluding the more sophisticated users.

6. RELATIONS

A relation allows one to represent facts for a single entity type. E.F. Codd [18] gives the following definition:

Given the sets (domains) D1, D2, ..., Dn (not necessarily distinct) R is a relation on these n sets if it is a set of elements of the form:

(d1, d2, ..., dn) where

dj ∈ Dj for each j = 1, 2, ..., n.

Since a DBS has to store and provide facts for several entity types, several relations are required. A data base is therefore a finite collection of time varying relations defined over a finite set of domains.

Usually a relation is presented in the form of a table having the following properties:

1. Column homogeneity (the elements in a column are all of the same type, i.e. numeric or character string)

2. Each element is atomic (not decomposable)

3. Rows (called tuples) are distinct

4. The ordering of rows (tuples) is immaterial since the latter are identified by content and not by position

5. The ordering of columns is immaterial since the latter are identified by name and not by position.

We now show an example:

Given the domains (sets)

S# (student number) = {S1, S2, S3}
SN (student name) = {SA, SB}
SEX = {MASC, FEM}

then

STUDENT (S#, SN, SEX)

S#	SN	SEX
S1	SA	MASC
S2	SB	MASC
S3	SA	FEM

represents the relation STUDENT containing facts for the entity student. S#, SN, SEX are attributes (i.e. list of values). The attribute values are taken from equally named domains (set of values). Attributes (or attribute combinations allowing to uniquely identify a row (called tuple) are called candidate keys (in STUDENT only S# is a candidate key). One of the candidate keys (if there are several) is arbitrarily designed as the primary key (in STUDENT: S#) and appears usually underlined. Attributes participating in at least one candidate key are called prime attributes; the others are called non-prime attributes. The rules related to the construction of relations correspond to the normalization criterias introduced by E.F. Codd in [13]. We distinguish between 1st, 2nd and 3rd normal form relations. These normal forms are characterized as follows:

A relation is in 1st normal form if every value within the relation (i.e. each attribute value in each tuple) is an atomic (nondecomposable) data item (e.g., a number or a character string).

A relation is in 2nd normal form if it follows the rules 1 and 2 discussed in PART II, chapter 3 (E.F. Codd gives a different definition which yields however the same results as the rules 1 and 2).

A relation is in 3rd normal form if it follows rule 3 discussed in PART II, chapter 3 (again E.F. Codd gives a different definition).

From this discussion it follows that designing segments (i.e. DE-groups and records) according to the rules mentioned in PART II chapter 3 yield segments being (according to E.F. Codds definition) in 3rd normal form.

For the justification of the relational approach we refer to E.F. Codd's papers (especially [2]), to C.J. Date's book [19] and to [20] where the problem solving capabilities of the relational approach have been demonstrated for a complete range of complex manufacturing problems.

The following chapter discusses - starting from an appropriate description of the real world (i.e. from a conceptual view specification) - the synthesis of relations, respectively segments, which - as a matter of fact - follow the same construction rules as the former.

7. SYNTHESIS OF RELATIONS / SEGMENTS

We would like to discuss the steps required to synthesize relations (segments) starting from an appropriate real world description (i.e. a conceptual view specification) by means of an example:

Assume that one would like to represent within a DBS facts concerning the entities students (S), courses (C) and professors (P). Analyzing the real world we determine that following attributes are of relevance (for us):

S#: student number: identifier for the entity set S
SN: student name
SEX
C#: course number: identifier for the entity set C
CN: course name
EV: course evaluation
P#: prof. number: identifier for the entity set P
PN: professor name

In addition we determine the following mappings:

((S#, SN)(SN, S#)):	(1:M)
((S#, P#)(P#, S#)):	(1:M)
((S#, C#)(C#, S#)):	(M:M)
((S#, SEX)(SEX, S#)):	(1:M)
((C#, CN)(CN, C#)):	(1:1)
((C#, P#)(P#, C#)):	(1:M)
((P#, PN)(PN, P#)):	(1:M)

EV (evaluation) is a property of the relationship between the entity S (student) and C (course). This means that each EV-occurrence is related to a particular student (represented by a S#-occurrence) and a particular course (represented by a C#-occurrence). In other words: EV may be regarded to be related to the compound element S#*C#. Since a particular student provides one evaluation per course only the association from S#*C# to EV is simple (type 1). On the other hand, since a particular evaluation (e.g. 'good') might be given to several courses by several students the association from EV to S#*C# is complex (type M). We thus obtain the following mapping:

((S#*C#, EV)(EV, S#*C#)): (1:M)

The attributes and mappings specified so far reflect the section of the real world we would like to have considered within the DBS. As a matter of fact they represent the conceptual view specification introduced in PART I, chapter 5. In the following discussion we call the collection of mappings required to describe a section of the real world the conceptual mapping set.

We now start to synthesize relations, respectively segments, using above conceptual mapping set. It is necessary to emphasize at this point that this synthesis can and will be mechanized with future DBS's. Following steps are required:

1st step:

Take each entity identifier and determine (using the conceptual mapping set) the attributes to which the former is simply (type 1) or conditionally (type C) associated (PART II, chapter 3, rule 1). Each identifier is combined with the attributes it identifies as described, yielding thereby a first relation (respectively segment) version which obtains the name of the set whose identifier has been used.

For the actual example we thus obtain:

S(S#, SN, SEX, P#)
C(C#, CN, P#)
P(P#, PN)

2nd step:

Determine the mappings not yet considered within the conceptual mapping set.

For the actual example we obtain:

((S#, C#)(C#, S#)):	(M:M)
((S#*C#, EV)(EV, S#*C#)):	(1:M)

3rd step:

Transform each (M:M)-mapping into two (M:1)-mappings using an additional link element which becomes an additional relation (respectively segment) (PART II, chapter 5, rule 4). The key of the new relation (segment) is a compound key created by concatenating the attributes occurring in the (M:M)-mapping.

For the actual example we transform the (M:M)-mapping

((S#, C#)(C#, S#)).

and obtain thereby:

- An additional relation (segment), say SC, with the compound key S#*C#.
- The (M:1)-mappings:

  ((S#, S#*C#)(S#*C#, S#)) and
  ((C#, S#*C#)(S#*C#, C#))

4th step:

Repeat step 1 using however the compound keys obtained in step 3 and the mappings obtained in step 2 (excluding the (M:M)-mappings already considered in step 3).

For the actual example we obtain:

SC(S#, C#, EV)

Note that above relation does not violate rule 2 (PART II, chapter 3) since all possible subsets of the compound key S#*C# (i.e. S# and C#) are complex associated to EV. Thus, (S#, EV) is a complex (type M) association indicating that a student provides several evaluations and (C#, EV) is also a complex (type M) association indicating that a course obtains several evaluations.

5th step:

Apply rule 3 (PART II, chapter 3) to the relations (segments) obtained in the preceding steps. Relations (segments) violating rule 3 are split according to rule 4 (PART II, chapter 3).

For the actual example we recognize no simple (type 1) association between non-prime attributes (attributive elements). Thus rule 3 is not violated.

We show the final result:

S(S#, SN, SEX, P#)
C(C#, CN, P#)
P(P#, PN)
SC(S#, C#, EV)

We would like to comment the result as follows:

1. The result has been obtained by applying to an appropriate description of a real world section (i.e. the conceptual view specification) systematic rules. The conceptual view has been specified with the help of attributes and attribute associations.

2. The result obtained indicates which attributes can be combined and stored as a unit such that no anomalies in storage operations may occur.

3. If a particular attribute appears in two relations (segments) then it acts (in addition to its descriptive function) as a link element. Such attributes indicate how relations (segments) are linked to each other. We refer to such a link as a symbolic link.

For the actual example we distinguish the following symbolic links:

P.P# <-> S.P#: P# links P and S
P.P# <-> C.P#: P# links P and C
S.S# <-> SC.S#: S# links S and SC
C.C# <-> SC.C#: C# links C and SC

4. The keys K1 and K2 of two relations (segments) being involved in a symbolic link are always mapped as follows:

((K1, K2)(K2, K1)): (M:1) or (1:M) or (1:1)

These mappings are all supported by a simple network structure.

For the actual example we distinguish in particular:

For the symbolic link: P.P# <-> S.P#:
The (M:1)-mapping: ((P#,S#)(S#,P#))

For the symbolic link: P.P# <-> C.P#:
The (M:1)-mapping: ((P#,C#)(C#,P#))

For the symbolic link: S.S# <-> SC.S#:
The (M:1)-mapping: ((S#,S#*C#)(S#*C#,S#))

For the symbolic link: C.C# <-> SC.C#:
The (M:1)-mapping: ((C#,S#*C#)(S#*C#,C#))

5. From the preceding discussion it follows that the result obtained by going through the synthesis steps discussed above not only indicates which attributes can be combined and stored as a unit but also indicates how these units are related to each other. We recognize in particular that the

synthesis always yields a simple network structure. From this we conclude that relations may be stored on physical storage devices in a similar way as records in a simple network structure. In fact, some promising work [21] has already been done showing the feasibility of such an implementation.

6. The result obtained indicates also which attributes have to be processed as a unit when modifying the data base (remember that we pointed out in PART II chapter 3 that the attributes processed as a unit when modifying a data base have to correspond to a subset of attributes stored as a unit. We further pointed out that this subset must include at least the key of the stored unit).

7. The result obtained does not indicate which attributes have to be processed as a unit when retrieving from the data base. In fact, the unit used to retrieve from the data base can be designed as conveniently as necessary to solve a given problem. This means in particular that a relation (segment) used on the logical level to retrieve from a data base does not have to satisfy the 3rd normal form criteria (respectively the rules 1 to 4 discussed in PART II, chapter 3).

8. A real world section (described by an appropriate conceptual view) can be presented to a user in the form of (usually) several hierarchical structures and/or a single network structure and/or (usually) several relations. The mapping between the underlying physical structure (simple network structure) and the desired logical structure is specified by the data base administrator by means of a DDL (PART I, chapter 3).

For the actual example one can represent the facts concerning the entity sets S (students), C (courses) and P (professors) according to figure II.6 (note that at least 3 hierarchical structures are required) and/or according to figure II.7 (note that only one network structure is required) or by means of the following relations:

S(S#, SN, SEX, P#)

S1	SA	F	P2
S2	SB	M	P2

C(C#, CN, P#)

C1	CA	P2
C2	CB	P2
C3	CC	P2
C4	CD	P2

P(P#, PN)

P1	PA
P2	PB

SC(S#, C#, EV)

S1	C1	1
S1	C2	3
S1	C3	2
S2	C2	1
S2	C3	2
S2	C4	1

(The content of the relations reflects the same situation as figure II.4).

We would like to close this paper by the following

7. CONCLUSION

We have shown that the normalization criteria introduced by E.F. Codd [13] can be modified such that they allow one to synthesize (rather than to decompose) both relations and segments from an appropriate real world description (i.e. a conceptual view specification). We have also shown that facts concerning a real world section can be presented to a user in the form of (usually several) hierarchical structures and/or a single network structure and/or (usually several) relations. We strongly believe that all three approaches have their advantages and that future DBS will have to support the structure type coexistence discussed in PART I, chapter 3. It is obvious that a system providing structure type coexistence will not only allow us to benefit from all of the advantages inherent in the different structure types but will also simplify transition problems in so far as existing application programs could continue to use the structure type they have been designed for while new applications could be designed based on any structure type. Some interesting work [21] has already been done in this area, and there is good reason to be optimistic about the outcome. We are convinced that the answer to the data base problem is not an 'either or' but an 'as well as' approach.

Acknowledgement

The author would like to thank IBM for the assistance obtained in preparing this paper. It must be emphasized, however, that the author is entirely responsible for the contents of the paper. The oppinions expressed represent in no way an official statement on the part of IBM.

References

[1] Senko, M.E.; Altman, E.B.; Astrahan, M.M.; Fehder, P.L.: 'Data Structures and Accessing in Data Base Systems', IBM Systems Journal, Volume Twelve/Number One, 1973

[2] Codd, E.F.; Date, C.J.: 'Interactive Support for Non-programmers: the Relational and Network Approaches', IBM Research Report RJ 1400, June 6, 1974

[3] Gray, J.N.; Lorie, R.A.; Putzolu, G.R.; Traiger, I.L.: 'Granularity of Locks and Degrees of Consistency in a Shared Data Base', IBM Research Report RJ 1654, September 19, 1975

[4] Codd, E.F.: 'A Data Base Sublanguage Founded on the Relational Calculus', Proceedings of the 1971 ACM-Sigfidet Workshop on Data Description, Access and Control, San Diego, available from ACM, New York

[5] Codd, E.F.: 'Relational Completeness of Sublanguages', in 'Data Base Systems', Courant Computer Science Symposia 6, Prentice-Hall 1972

[6] Boyce, R.F.; Chamberlin, D.D.; King, W.F.; Hammer, M.M.: 'Specifying Queries as Relational Expressions: SQUARE', Proceedings ACM SIGPLAN-SIGIR Interface Meeting, Gaitherburg, Maryland, Nov. 4-6, 1973

[7] Astrahan, M.M.; Chamberlin, D.D.: 'Implementation of a Structured English Query Language', IBM Research Report RJ 1464, October 28, 1974

[8] ANSI/X3/SPARC: Interim Report: Study Committee on Data Base Management Systems. ACM SIGMOD Newsletter, 1975

[9] Blaser, A.; Schmutz, H.: 'Data Base Research: a Survey', IBM Germany, Heidelberg Scientific Center, Technical Report TR 75.10.009, November 1975

[10] Information Management System (IMS): System/Application Design Guide. IBM Form Number: SH20-9025

[11] Data Base Design Aid (DBDA): Designer's Guide. IBM Form Number: GH20-1627

[12] Vetter, M.: 'Hierarchische, netzwerkfoermige und relationalartige Datenbankstrukturen (mit ausgewaehlten Beispielen aus einem Fertigungsunternehmen), Dissertation, ETH Zurich (Swiss Institute of Technology), Mai, 1976

[13] Codd, E.F.: 'Further Normalization of the Relational Model', in 'Data Base Systems', Courant Computer Science Symposia 6, Prentice-Hall 1972

[14] Codd, E.F.: 'Recent Investigations in Relational Data Base Systems', Proceedings of the IFIP Congress on Information Processing, Stockholm 1974, available from North Holland, Amsterdam

[15] Bachman, C.W.: 'The Programmer as Navigator', Comm. ACM 16, No. 11, November 1973

[16] Codd, E.F.: 'Seven Steps to Rendezvous with the Casual User', IBM Research Report RJ 1333, January 17, 1974

[17] CODASYL Data Base Task Group: 'April 1971 Report', available from IFIP Administrative Data Processing Group, 40 Paulus Potterstraat, Amsterdam

[18] Codd, E.F.: 'A Relational Model of Data for Large Shared Data Banks', CACM 13, June 6, 1970

[19] Date, C.J.: 'An Introduction to Database Systems', Addison Wesley, 1975

[20] Vetter, M.: 'Problem Solving Capabilities of the Relational Algebra', Proceedings of the International Technical Conference on Relational Data Base Systems, IBM Scientific Center, Bari (Italy), June, 1976. Paper available from IBM-IEC library, Chaussee de Bruxelles 135, B-1310 La Hulpe (Belgium)

[21] Astrahan, M.M.; Blasgen, M.W.; Chamberlin, D.D.; Eswaran, K.P.; Gray, J.N.; Griffiths, P.P.; King, W.F.; Lorie, R.A.; McJones, P.R.; Mehl, J.W.; Putzolu, G.R.; Traiger, I.L.; Wade, B.W.; Watson, V.: 'System R: A Relational Approach to Data Base Management', IBM Research Report RJ 1738, February 27, 1976

E. Morlet and D. Ribbens, (Eds.), International Computing Symposium 1977.

THE ENTITY - ASSOCIATION MODEL : AN INFORMATION - ORIENTED DATA BASE MODEL

Alain PIROTTE
MBLE Research Laboratory
Avenue Van Becelaere 2
1170 Bruxelles.

For its users, a data base is not merely a collection of structured data. It is also a partial and biased representation of the real world, or rather the representation of a specialized knowledge about a part of the real world. Therefore, a complete definition of a user interface to a data base must take into account, in some way or another, the relationships between the subject matter in the real world and its model as it is viewed by the interface.

It has been frequently suggested that a portion of the real world can be viewed as a collection of entities which are qualified by their properties and whose interactions are expressed by relationships, also qualified by properties.

Structure is introduced in such a view of the subject matter by the process of abstraction. Only those properties are retained which are relevant to the information needs defined by specific applications.

This paper describes an implementation - independent formalism of data organization for data base interfaces. Design decisions for this formalism result from a combination of two sometimes conflicting requirements : (1) the requirement that data base schemas at the interface exhibit the natural structure of the information represented by the data; (2) the requirement that the data structures can be efficiently accessed and updated at the level of the interface.

The first requirement is approached by defining entities, associations among entities and properties of entities and associations as elementary objects in the data model, with interactions which approximate the behavior of their real world counterparts.

The second requirement could be fulfilled by defining a data manipulation language (DML) and by showing its effectiveness. This has not been done in this paper, and only indications are given concerning the semantics of convenient DML operations. The design of the data model presented here was constrained in order that its data base descriptions be translatable easily and in a reasonably faithful manner into data base descriptions in a form of the relational model. This aspect of the data model is discussed elsewhere [PIR76] : it contributes to keeping the model simple and it suggests that a retrieval language can be derived from a predicate calculus with "domain variables" [PIR76], with some similarity with well-established non-procedural relational languages. Nevertheless, even if the essential part of the data model of this paper can be defined without a more precise characterization of a DML, some aspects of the structure should be worked out in detail and evaluated in conjunction with their treatment by DML operations.

Section 2 of this paper presents the perception of information which has inspired the form of the data model. The basic structure of this model is defined in section 3. Examples in this paper relate to a simple example data base described in section 4 : it deals with computers, computer users and computer manufacturers. Sections 5 and 6 discuss the structural role of integrity constraints and show how they can be used to define an information-oriented normal form for associations.

2. Structure of the real-world information to be represented in a data base

When analyzing the structure of the information contained in a portion of the real world, it has often been found natural to distinguish the important individuals, usually called entities, and relationships among them [DEH74, KEN77, LIN74, MEA67, MOU76, SEN73] .

A *real-world entity* is a thing, abstract or concrete; it has an existence of its own and it forms a whole which can be distinguished from its environment, in particular from all other entities of interest.

For example, the following phrases might designate entities :
- *the MIX cpu model;*
- *the computer installed on the second floor of this building;*
- *John Smith;*
- *the company of which John Smith is an employee.*

Entities are the basic objects of the subject matter. *Relationships* describe various interactions among entities.
Examples of relationships :
- *the company of which John Smith is an employee* is a user of *the computer installed on the second floor of this building;*
- *the computer installed on the second floor of this building* has *a MIX cpu model.*

A *property* qualifies an entity or a relationship and it has no real significance without a qualified entity or relationship.

Example of properties of entities :
- *the color of John Smith's car;*
- *the price of the MIX cpu model.*

When attempting to describe a portion of the real world in terms of entities, relationships and properties of entities and of relationships, the analyst faces a number of difficult choices. Ideally, the correspondence between a portion of the real world and a faithful model of it should be one-to-one, in the sense that every "thing" in the real world should correspond to an "element" in the model and conversely. However, there are often many ways of perceiving and describing the same "reality". Actually, almost any particular decision made when describing a subject matter with entities, properties and relationships may be questionable as to the generality with which it models the real world (see e.g. [KEN77]).

Examples
- *the real-world concept of a "user" (i.e. a company which uses computer equipment) may be described either as an entity or as a relationship between e.g. a company entity and a computer entity or as a property of a company entity;*
- *the color of a person's hair or of a car is normally seen as a property in the context of data about persons or about registered vehicles : a color has no interest independently of an entity that it qualifies. On the contrary, hairdressers, car makers, physicists would probably view colors as entities, i.e. as things which by themselves are of considerable interest.*

Faithful models of the real world quickly become hopelessly complex if they want to be general. For reasons of efficiency, both of human activities and of machine processing, computer-oriented models must remain simple. Therefore, models of the real world to be used to build and document data bases correspond to the selection of one particular point of view in analyzing the real world. There is no absolute criterion for performing such a selection, and the only guidelines are the convenience and the relevance to the applications of the data base.

Thus, the analysis and design of a data base model is a process which involves abstraction and structuration. The applications of the data base dictate the choice of which part of the real world is the subject matter, of which entities and relationships are to be in the model and of which properties of entities and relationships are relevant. Structuration consists in grouping similar entities into sets and similar relationships into other sets according to the needs of the applications.

A faithful description of a portion of the real world could then be imagined as a kind of superposition of all the possible particular perceptions of that portion of the world.

3. Definition of the EPA model

The Entity-Property-Association (EPA) model describes the organization of data in the form of networks. The structure of EPA data bases is defined with the help of entities grouped in entity sets, values grouped in value sets, properties and associations.

3.1 Entity Sets

An entity is an elementary object in an EPA data base. Entities are grouped in entity sets, each of which has a unique name which distinguishes it from the other entity sets.

Entity sets and types

Whereas the number of entities in an entity set varies with time, an EPA entity set is meant to represent a set of real-world entities which share properties important for the purpose of the data base. The intentional (or time-independent) aspect of an entity set is formalized by associating a type with each entity set : each entity has the type of the entity set to which it belongs.

The existence of types in the data model enables the definition of type-checking rules which constrain DML operations. Thus, one such rule would prescribe that two entities may only be compared for equality if they have the same type. An alternative way to control the semantics of DML expressions consists in providing, for each type, a membership predicate in the DML : for any given entity, each such predicate tests whether the entity belongs to the entity set of the type associated with the predicate.

For EPA data bases, types realize a structuring tool : there is a common semantics, with respect to real world objects, for all objects of a type. There is no provision in the EPA model to represent formally this real world semantics, although it must be described informally, in some way or another. It consists of a description of which real world properties and relationships shared by real world entities are taken into account to group the corresponding EPA entities in an entity set. This analysis process is described precisely e.g. in [LIN74] .

At least three cases of overlapping entity sets can be imagined when analyzing real world situations. They can be modelled as EPA entity sets as follows :

(a) an entity set E is the union of two (or more) disjoint entity sets E1 and E2. Each entity in E has two types : the type associated with E and the type associated with either E1 or E2. A given entity may not change its types during its lifetime.

Example :

E represents models of computer peripherals, E1 representing models of tape drives and E2 models of disk drives.

(b) an entity set E is the union of two overlapping entity sets E1 and E2. Each entity in the intersection of E1 and E2 has three types associated respectively with E, E1 and E2, whereas an entity in E1 or E2 but not in their intersection only has two types. During its lifetime a given entity may move freely between E-E1, E-E2 and E1 E2 and change its types accordingly. A DML for the EPA model must provide the corresponding update operations.

Example :

E represents companies, E1 represents user companies and E2 manufacturer companies.

(c) an entity set E contains an entity set E1. A given entity has one type if it is in E-E1 and two types if it is in E1. As in case (b), a given entity may move from E-E1 to E1 and conversely.

Example :

E represents employees and E1 represent managers, with the hypotheses that all managers are employees, but that managers have in addition specific properties.

In cases (b) and (c), the types of an entity may change with time. This may be convenient for data modelling, but complicates the DML operations interacting with types and sub-types. For example, type-checking is a more complex operation when it is dynamic than when it is static.

3.2. Associations

EPA associations model relationships among entities in a perception of the subject matter. The definition of associations is similar to the definition of relations in a relational model.

An association has a name which distinguishes it from other associations. The extension of an association is a subset of an indexed Cartesian product of entity sets :

$$A \subseteq i1:E1 \times \dots \times in : Cn$$

for an association A with n domains noted ij : Ej, where ij is the role index and Ej the entity set of the j-th domain. Each index uniquely identifies a domain, and the domains of an association are unordered.

An element of the extension of an association is an instance of the association. Each instance of association models a relationship among entities in a perception of the subject matter.

A natural DML will probably not manipulate instances of associations as units without structure. The conclusions of [PIR76] about "tuple" and "domain" languages for the relational model are still more valid for the EPA model : a high-level and natural DML should treat entities as its elementary objects, like e.g. constants and ranges of variables, and associations as predicates among elementary objects; it should not have the analog of the "tuple" variables of some relational languages.

Defining types for associations would be easy, but this may not be very useful if the DML does not manipulate association instances as elementary objects.

A special form for associations, called primitive associations, is defined in section 6. It corresponds to an attempt to identify the elementary relationships of the subject matter, given all the structural information represented in an EPA data base.

The preceding definition of an association may be generalized to account for the fact that instances of an association may not be completely known. Therefore, the extension of an association is redefined as :

$$A \subseteq i1:(E1 \cup \{\omega\ e\}) \times \ldots \times in:(En \cup \{\omega\ e\})$$

where e is a maker which indicates that an entity is missing. Its use is further constrained by the following prescription : if an instance (a1,...,ak,...,an) belongs to an association A, then there cannot exist in A an instance (a1,...,ωe,...,...,an) which only differs in that ak has been replaced by ωe. More generally, there cannot exist an instance of an association all of whose "known" elements (i.e. entities) occur in corresponding roles in another instance.

Note that ωe is not an entity and therefore, in particular, that it does not belong to entity sets.

3.3 Properties

Besides entities and associations, the EPA model also defines properties of entities and of associations.

For example, cpu model entities have among their property values a dollar value and a word size. In a certain perception of the world, applications can be considered as property values of an association which describe the fact that computer configurations are used by companies.

Value Sets

Property values are grouped into *value sets* or *classes* of similar values. A value set has a *name* which distinguishes it from other value sets.

As for entity sets, a *type* is attached to each value set : it is the type of each value in the set. The definition of a type for a value set includes the definition of the legal operations for a DML. This definition includes the rule that values from different value sets are not comparable, whereas all values in a value set are comparable at least for equality and possibly for other operations.

Definition of properties

A *simple non-repeating property* of an entity set or of an association is defined, at every given moment, by a total function, which may change with time :

$$p : D \rightarrow V \cup \{\omega\ v\}$$

from the entity set or association D to a set composed of a value set V supplemented with a special value ωv.

Strictly speaking, there is one special value ωv per value set and it has the type of the value set. Its meaning is "existing but unknown value". Note the difference with the marker ωe which is not an entity.

An *instance of a property* p is a triplet (p,d,v), where d is an entity or an instance of an association and v is either v or a value in the value set of the property.

A property has a *name* which distinguishes it among other properties.

The definition of properties as total functions implies that all entities in an entity set share the same properties : the very existence of an entity at the EPA level implies the existence of values for all the properties defined for the entity set of the entity. However, some or even all the property values of an entity may be ωv, i.e. unknown.

Existence dependency of values

To exist in an EPA data base, a value must be the value of at least one property instance. This condition on values is called *existence dependency*. A similar notion has been defined in several other works [CHE76, DEH74, SCH75] .

For example, one can imagine a situation in which a dollar value is meaningless on its own : it acquires meaning only together with an entity (or an instance of an association) of which it is a property value, like the salary of somebody, the price of something.

On the contrary, unless an explicit constraint prevents it, an entity may have the value ωv for all its property instances : the existence of an EPA entity is not dependent on known values for its properties.

Semantics of properties

Like associations, properties are meant to represent well-defined real world relationships and their semantics can be derived by abstraction from the meaning of the real world relationships. A structural part of meaning is represented by defining a property as a function which is total on an entity set or an association, by defining the special values ωv and the existence dependency of values in a value set. But the particular meaning is not more represented for properties than for associations.

Attributes

An alternative definition of a property as a set of attribute-value pairs puts more emphasis on the dynamic character of a data base than a definition in terms of a total function which is rather a static definition.

An *attribute* is a pair entity-property name. The *value of an attribute* is a pair entity-property name. The value of an attribute is either ωv or a value in a value set associated with the property. For each entity, there is one attribute for each property defined for the entity set of the entity. An attribute is *permanently* associated with an entity : it is created when the entity enters the EPA data base and it is deleted together with the entity. An attribute has a value at all times, but this value may change with time. At any given moment, the extension of a property is the set of all attribute-value pairs associated with the property.

The definition of attributes may be seen as a step away from the definition of entities as indivisible wholes without structure. In effect, it may be argued that attributes are *parts of entities*. Actually for a given real world entity the two perceptions are possible. An EPA entity (which is a model of a particular perceptition of a real world entity) is viewed as a whole with permanent attributes, and it need not be required in the EPA model that the attribute values of an entity uniquely identify the entity. In other words, an entity *is not* the sum of some of its attribute values.

Example : the height of a human being is one of his permanent attributes, from his birth to his death. His existence implies the existence of his height although the exact value may change and is not necessarily known at all times.

The definition of attributes extends in an obvious way to properties of associations.

More about value sets

The choice to model a set of real world objects as an entity set or as a value set only reflects the biases of the intended applications of a data base. Therefore, the arguments for having overlapping entity sets in the EPA model could be transposed for value sets. However, entities are more central than values to the structural description of EPA data bases. Therefore defining overlapping EPA value sets may not be worth the extra complication of the model.

What may be relevant to some DML operations is the distinction between several kinds of value sets :

- some are not defined in extension but have a constructive semantics (e.g. *cardinal numbers*);
- others are defined in extension and are fixed during the lifetime of the data base (e.g. *continents*);
- still others are defined in extension and are essentially open-ended (e.g. *names of cpu models*).

It is a part of the definition of each particular data base to indicate of which kind are the value sets and to indicate rules for the external representation of values.

Simple repeating properties

So far, simple non-repeating properties have been defined. A *simple repeating property* is defined, at every given moment, by a total function, which may change with time :

$$p : D \rightarrow \{\omega v\} \cup 2^{V}$$

where $\mathcal{D}$ is an entity set or an association and $2^{\mathcal{V}}$ is the powerset of a value set $\mathcal{V}$.

The notion of attribute is defined as for non-repeating properties : the value of an attribute is either ωv or a subset of the value set of the property.

Examples :

- *the applications for which a particular company uses a particular configuration form a repeating property value of an instance of the association which states that companies use configurations;*
- *in a data base of employee data, the skills of employees could be described as a repeating property of employees represented as an entity set.*

A type could be associated in an obvious way to the values of a simple repeating property, and also to the values of all complex properties.

Complex properties

A *non-repeating complex property* is defined, at any instant, by a total function, which may change with time :

$$p : D \to (\{\omega v\} \cup \mathcal{V}1) \times \ldots \times (\{\omega v\} \cup \mathcal{V}n)$$

where $\mathcal{D}$ is an entity set or an association; $\mathcal{V}1,\ldots,\mathcal{V}n$ are value sets.

The attribute value of an entity (or of an instance of association) for a complex property is thus a tuple of n values.

Example : the address of a company entity can be represented as a complex property which comprises a street address, a city and a country.

When designing an EPA data base, the choice between a complex property with n components and n simple properties is arbitrary from the point of view of the EPA model : it depends on the particular semantics of the subject matter and on the manipulations required on the property values.

A *repeating complex property* is naturally defined as a total function from a particular entity set (or association) to the powerset of the Cartesian product of several value sets :

$$p : D \to 2^{(\{\omega v\} \cup \mathcal{V}1) \times \ldots \times (\{\omega v\} \cup \mathcal{V}n)}$$

Complex property values and entities

A complex property value, like an *address* in the example above, is very different from an entity. A complex property value, like a simple property value, does not exist by itself, i.e. if it is not the value of at least one attribute of an entity or an instance of an association. Furthermore, a complex property value is completely represented by its component values. As it is described above, an *address* is a *street address* plus a *city* plus a *country* and nothing more.

Further generalization of complex and repeating properties was not defined in order to keep a very clear distinction between a property value and an entity in the EPA model.

3.4 Identification of entities

Keys

Consider only the non-repeating properties of an entity set.

A *key* of the entity set is a property (resp. a list of properties) such that :

(1) each value from the range of the property (resp. each value from the Cartesian product of the ranges of the list of properties) is guaranteed *at all times* to be associated with zero or one entity in the entity set;

(2) a list of properties is a key only if none of its proper sublists satisfies point (1).

An entity set can have any number of keys, including zero. A key is denoted by the name or list of names of the properties it contains.

Remark that complex properties cannot be "split" in any way in a key.

As an extension, key values are sometimes called keys of entities.

Defining keys

A simple non-repeating property which is a key may be declared to be a *defining key*. The attribute values of a defining key may not be unknown and they may not change during the lifetime of the associated entities. Thus, in the case of a defining key property, the correspondence between entity set and value set is one-to-one and permanent.

At first, a value may appear as an entity reduced to its defining key, but there is more in the difference between entity and value. Entities can exist in an EPA data base without being involved in an instance of an association, whereas a value must always be the value of at least one attribute.

Identifiers

An identifier of an entity set is a generalization of a key : like key values, its instances uniquely identify entities in the entity set. An identifier consists of one or more non-repeating properties of the identified entity set and/or one or more non-repeating properties of the identified entity set and/ or one or more entity sets whose connection to the identified entity set is indicated by mentioning one or more associations.

Existence of defining keys

Since each real-world entity is unique, it can always be given a unique "name". Whether this name is natural, i.e. whether it exists in the real world modelled in the data base, is something else.

In business data processing, it is customary to associate a "reference code" with each entity : this code expresses the unicity of the entity in its entity set. If such subject matters are described as EPA data bases, then it must be required that each entity set possess a defining key.

In the human usage of ordinary language, the identification of entities is usually not so direct, and identifiers can be the only way to uniquely identify entities in the corresponding EPA data bases. This approach suppresses the need to invent artificial defining keys but it complicates the update operations.

In the example of section 4, defining keys have been chosen to reflect the fact that real world entities sometimes but not always have a unique and stable name.

Example : corporation entities have a defining key called "NAME". Then, for example, "the corporation named PHILIPS" is also "the PHILIPS corporation" or "PHILIPS", in the ordinary language of the subject matter. On the contrary, computer configurations are modelled as an entity set without a defining key.

3.5 Updates

This section sketches a possible semantics of update operations for the EPA model. Creation, deletion and modification take into account the specificity of entities, properties and associations. A detailed definition of updates should be done in conjunction with the design of a specific DML. Update operations are executed in sessions which, as a whole, verify the various consistency constraints (see section 5). However, the constraints may be violated at intermediate moments during a session.

Following the discussion of section 3.4, it is supposed that each entity set has at least one identifier, key or defining key and, at the instance level, that each entity is at all times identifiable; but, if an entity set has several means of identification, it is allowed that the particular means of identification of an entity change with time.

This is not the simplest scheme for the identification of entities.

Creation of an entity

A new entity enters the data base : the session involving the creation must result in establishing a unique identification for the entity. Property values can be given at the same time as the entity; all other attribute values of the entity are equal to ωv.

The creation of an entity can be associated with the creation of an instance of an association involving the entity being created, for example to establish an instance of an identifier for the new entity.

Creation of an instance of an association

This operation requires an identification of the entities involved, except those which are being created at the same time as the association instance and those which are missing and replaced by ωe.

Attribute values may be given for the instance; otherwise, they are equal to ωv.

Modification of an attribute value

This operation involves an access to an association instance, through identification of its entities, or to an entity. It is forbidden for a defining key value different from ωv. The value ωv is a legal new value, provided that, in the case of a property of an entity, the entity remain uniquely identifiable.

Deletion of an entity

The entity disappears with all its properties. It is replaced by ωe in the instances of associations in which it participated. If an instance of association then has the same known part as another instance of the same association, then the first instance is deleted.

If the deleted entity is part of an instance of an identifier of another entity and if the latter entity is not identified otherwise, then the deletion of the first entity must be part of a session which either ensures the identification of the second entity or deletes it as well.

Deletion of an association instance

The association instance is uniquely accessed by accessing its entities.

If the deleted instance is part of an instance of an identifier which is the unique identifier of an entity, then deletion of the association instance must be part of a session which restores the identification or which deletes the identified entity.

An association instance is deleted if it contains only ωe markers.

Modification of an association instance

The association instance is accessed by accessing its entities.

An ωe marker can be replaced by an entity.

An entity can be replaced by an ωe marker; if the modified instance has the same known part as another instance of the same association, then the modified instance is deleted. If the instance being modified is part of an essential identifier instance, then identification must be restored in the same session or the identified entity must be deleted.

This section shows that some sophistication may be introduced in update operations. A compromise must be worked out between the complexity of updates and the sophistication of the patterns of constraints, unknown elements and identifications which attempt to model corresponding the patterns in the real world.

4. An example of EPA data base

4.1 Network representation

An EPA data base can be given a pictorial representation in the form of a network, where nodes represent entity and value sets and arcs represent properties and associations. The unicity of entities is illustrated by representing each entity set only once. The different roles played by an entity set are represented by different property or association arcs leading to the same entity set node. On the contrary, as a consequence of both the unicity of entities and the strong link between an entity and its attributes, two equal property values, of the same or of two different properties, cannot be considered as identical : they belong to different attributes and, unless explicitly requested, a modification of one value does not affect the other. Therefore, a value set is represented as a node for each role that it plays in an EPA data base. Complex properties appear as trees.

This graphical representation of EPA data bases is inspired by that of [SCH75] .

4.2. Example

Figure 1 represents the entity sets, associations and properties of a simple example of EPA data base.

The following English sentences describe the example. They are followed by names of EPA associations and properties which correspond to them.

All computer configurations have exactly one model of cpu (A1). A configuration may possess a number of copies of a model of peripheral units, which are disk and tape drives (A2, P1). All configurations have a purchase value in dollars (P2). They support programming languages under operating systems (P3). They have a certain amount of core (P4). They were installed at a certain date (P5). A configuration may be used by user companies for one or more applications and under a certain usage category (A3,P6,P7).

All cpu models have one purchase value in dollars (P8). They are identified by a name (P10). They are characterized by the size in bits of their registers (P9). They are built by one manufacturer (A4).

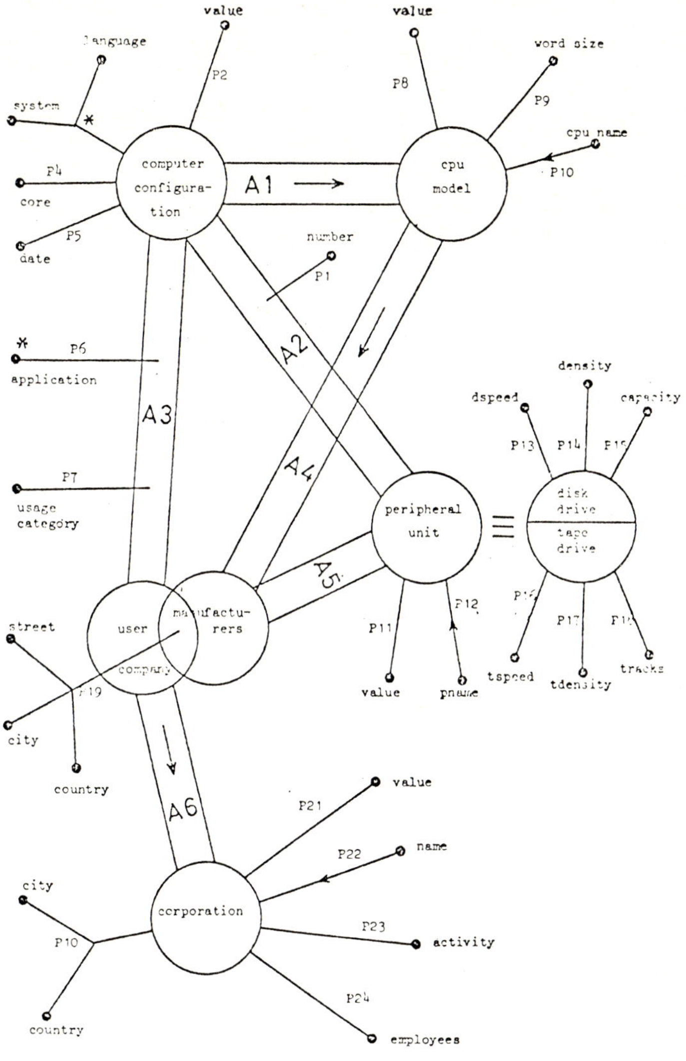

Figure 1.

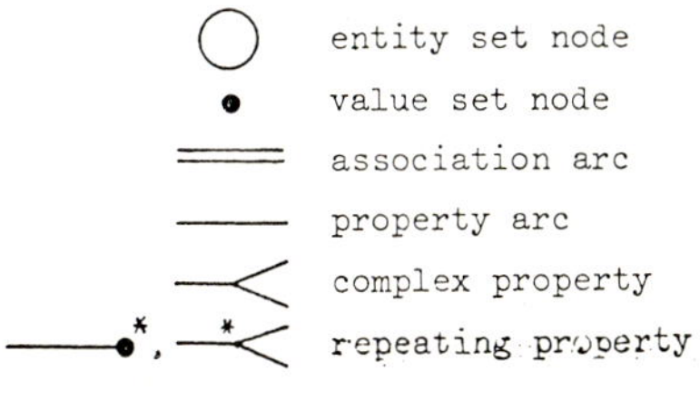

All models of peripherals have one purchase value in dollars (P11). They are identified by a name (P12). They are built by one or more manufacturers (A5).

All models of disk drive have a rotation speed in revolutions per minute (P13), a density in characters per track (P14), a capacity in characters (P15).

All models of tape unit have a speed in inches per second (P16), a number of tracks (P18) and one or more possible densities in characters per inch (P17).

All companies have one address, which comprises a street address, a city name and a country name (P19). They are controlled by one head office corporation (A6).

All corporations are characterized by a volume of sales in dollars (P21), a number of employees (P24), a certain number of domains of activity (P23) and a seat address which comprises a city name and a country name (P20). They are identified by a name (P22).

A gross view of the network of Fig. 1 shows associations which connect complex objects : these are entity set nodes surrounded by properties. The entity sets in the example have the following names, which have been abridged in Fig. 1 : *computer configuration, cpu model, disk drive model, tape drive model, peripheral unit, computer user, manufacturer, head office corporation.*

The entity set *company* is the union of the entity sets *computer user* and *manufacturer*. Fig. 1 shows that A6 concerns *companies*, A3 concerns *computer users* and A4 and A5 concern *manufacturers*. A particular *company* entity can be at the same time *user* and *manufacturer*.

The entity set *peripheral unit* is also the union of two entity sets : *disk drive* and *tape drive*. However the component sets are disjoint in this case.

The names of value sets which serve as lables, in an abridged version, in Fig. 1 are : *dollar value, programming language, operating system, amount of core memory, date, application, usage category, street, city, country, corporation name, activity, number of employees, peripheral model name, tape speed, tape density, number of tracks, disk speed, disk density, disk capacity, cpu name, word size.*

Units have been indicated in the English description for all the numerical value sets. The problems of unit conversions are not discussed here. They belong in the definition of a DML; conversion can be achieved by the simplest kind of function, i.e. a function C1 C2 from one value set C1 to another C2, which is similar to functions of the predicate calculus. Such conversions functions could be either explicitly invoked by the users or automatically inserted by the processor of the data manipulation language.

The external representation of values as strings of characters is not discussed either: it belongs in a user's manual of a DML. The internal representation of values is of course of no concern for an implementation-independent interface like the EPA model.

Arrows on property arcs indicate that a property is a defining key of an entity set. Arrows on association arcs indicate functional dependencies, which are defined in section 5. Role indices have not been indicated in associations, because, in the example, the same enity set does not occur twice in an association.

The names of associations and properties have been chose as simple labels in order to simplify Fig. 1, but also to insist on the fact that the particular real-world semantics of the subject matter is not represented in the EPA data base.

5. Integrity constraints

The simple EPA model, consisting of entity and value sets, associations and properties is not powerful enough to express all the structural information contained in a perception of the subject matter. There is a great variety of time-independent structural prescriptions which have to be expressed by other means. Several kinds of such prescriptions are particularly important.

Functional dependencies

Functional dependencies inside associations are defined as follows.

An entity set e1 from a domain of an association is functionally dependent on an entity set e2 from another domain of the association if, for every entity in e2, there is, at all times, zero or one entity in e1 associated with it in the instances of the association.

The dependency is noted e2→e1, with, in addition, an indication of the role indices if there are more than one domain of entity sets e1 and/or e2 in the association.

Note the difference with the existence dependency which links an entity set and each of its properties : for each entity there is exactly one attribute value for each property.

Functional dependencies in associations are easily generalized to groups of entity sets, by analogy with relations. Thus candidate keys and first, second and third normal forms (1NF, 2NF, 3NF) [COD72] can also be defined for associations.

Totalities

Totality of an association with respect to one of its domains is the prescription that every entity in the entity set of the domain participate in at least one instance of the association. In the example of section 4, A1 is total on the entity set *computer configuration:* the *cpu model* of every *configuration* must be known at all times to the data base. A3 is also total on the entity set *computer configuration* : every *configuration* is reported to be used by at least one *user company*.

The *absence of a totality* may sometimes be an important structural information. For example, if the entity sets *user* and *manufacturer* were not defined and if only their union *company* was present, then it would be important to state that neither A3 nor A4 nor A5 is total on *company*.

Totality in an association is similar to the existence dependency which holds for all properties.

Inclusion relationships

Inclusion relationships relate several subsets of the same entity set which participate in several associations.

For example, it can be prescribed that all *manufacturers of cpu models* also make *peripheral units*. This can also be expressed by requiring that the set of *manufacturers* which participate in A4 is at all times included in the set of *manufacturers* which participate in A5.

Totalities and inclusion relationships are defined in a similar manner for value sets, for their participation in properties of entity sets and associations.

Keys and identifiers

An identifier of an entity set has been defined in section 3.4 as a list of properties and associations whose instances uniquely identify the entities in the entity set.

Example : A computer configuration is identified by its cpu model (A1), its amount of core memory (P4) and one of its user companies (A3). The presence of this identifier implies that a company does not use more than one configuration with the same cpu model and the same amount of core. Another example of identifier is that of companies which are identified by their address (P19) and their head office corporation (A6).

A key is an identifier reduced to one or more non-repeating properties of the identified entity set.

Keys and identifiers generalize the definition of functional dependencies given above.

Other constraints

There remain constraints of various forms and generality. For example, the following prescriptions can be stated about the example of section 4 :

- *the value of a computer configuration is greater than the sum of the value of its cpu model and the value of its peripheral equipment;*
- *all corporations control at least one company whose address is in the country where they have their seat;*
- *all corporations with their seat in Holland use at least one computer whose cpu is manufactured by a company located in Holland;*
- *all manufacturers of any given peripheral unit are controlled by the same corporation.*

Definition of an EPA data base

From a logical point of view, the EPA network of entity sets, properties and associations is equivalent to the assertion that every instance of association and every instance of property is *true*, or equivalently, the assertion that the conjunction of instance is *true*.

Existence dependencies, functional dependencies, totalities and inclusion relationships express a limited form of quantification, whereas the possibility of defining unions of entity sets is equivalent to a limited form of disjunction. But the resulting "language" is not powerful enough to express all the prescriptions listed above.

The solution adopted in the relational model is to define a relational schema as a list of relations supplemented with constraints expressed in an assertion language.

Similarly, the structure of an EPA data base is defined as a list of entity sets, properties and associations supplemented with a list of constraints. These comprise constraints expressed in a special manner, i.e. keys, defining keys, identifiers, functional dependencies, totalities, inclusion relationships and also assertions written in an assertion language which could be derived from an EPA retrieval language.

The assertions are usually called "integrity" or "consistency" constraints because they are used to ensure the integrity of data bases by controlling the validity of updates. However, *these constraints also have a clear structural role, which is to make up for the weakness of the main formalism of data structure definition.* To take an image, constraints are as essential to the structure definition as unformalized syntax rules are essential to the syntactic definition of a language, which cannot be done only with e.g. context-free rules. Recent work on the structure of conceptual models seem to advocate a similar attitude towards constraints [SCH77] .

6. Primitive associations

An information-oriented data model like the EPA model must represent the fundamental relationships in a perception of the subject matter in such a way that they are visible and accessible in a striaghtforward manner.

Intra-and inter-association constraints

The structural description of an EPA data base is defined as a list of entity sets, a network of associations and of properties of entity sets and of associations and a list of constraints about the preceding elements.

Several special kinds of constraints have been presented in section 5. A frequent classifica- of constraints consists in distinguishing those which bear on a single association (intra-association) from those whose prescriptions extend over several associations (inter-association). However, considering the structure of information, there is no essential difference between implicit or explicit intra-association constraints and explicit inter-association constraints, since the former are changed into the latter when associations are split, and vice versa when they are joined.

Consider for example the splitting of an association R(X1, X2, X3) into two of its projections R1(X1, X2) and R2(X2,X3). Then, apart from intra-association constraints which may have been broken in the splitting, R1 and R2 represent the same structural information as R only if they are supplemented by a time-independent constraint R1(X2) = R2(X2) which states that the projections of R1 and R2 on their domain X2 are at all times equal. Thus, an implicit intra-association constraint has been transformed into an explicit inter-association constraint. Because of their simplicity, constraints of this kind are often overlooked in the literature, for example in the definition or relational normal forms.

Intra- and inter-association constraints can be sufficiently varied and complex that they can only be expressed in a powerful asserion language. Therefore, in general, they can alter in essential ways the structure as it is described by associations and properties alone.

An essential question then becomes the following : *What are the reasons, in a data model where considerations about implementation are absent, to group entity sets in associations in some cases and to separate them in several associations in other cases? In other words, what are the criteria to separate intra-association and inter-association structural semantics?*

Definition of primitive associations

The definition of primitive associations separates the constraints in two classes according to their generality. Then, the definition amounts to a test to be passed by associations and by the class of general constraints.

Schematically, the definition requires that entity sets be grouped in an association if and only if they are linked a sufficiently general piece of information.

Only an informal definition is given here. A more precise definition of the form of the most general constraints requires a more specific characterization of the assertion language for expressing constraints.

The *most general constraints* are defined as those which are expressible in terms of only entity sets or projections of entity sets in associations, and which can be verified only by examining all the elements in the concerned entity sets or projections of entity sets.

An *inclusion relationship* is defined as in the preceding section, as a test for equality or for inclusion of two projections concerning the same entity set.

An *association*, considered with all the intra-association constraints which concern it, *is primitive* if it cannot be split into other associations expressing the same structural semantics without introducing most general inter-associations constraints which are not inclusion relationships.

A *set of associations*, considered with all the intra and inter-association constraints concerning them, *is primitive* if (1) all the associations are primitive; (2) the most general inter-association constraints are only inclusion relationships.

The idea of requiring that a set of associations be primitive is that, since there is no essential difference between intra- and inter-associations constraints, the structure of information will appear more clearly when strongly connected entity sets are grouped together, instead of being separated in several associations and linked by a possibly hard to understand inter-association constraint.

On the other hand, another component of the definition prescribes that loosely related entity sets be separated in different associations as often as possible : an association should be split by projection if this does not give rise to most general constraints which are not inclusion relationships.

It must be emphasized that the definition of primitive associations only concerns the entity sets in the EPA associations. The reason is that associations of entity sets express the essential structural information, whereas properties are there to give details about this essential structure and to provide values to describe the entities and instances of associations. Properties do carry structural information, but differently : through their definition as total functions, through the repartition in simple, complex and repeating properties, through the definition of keys and identifiers and through introduction of integrity constraints.

All constraints which involve properties are excluded from most general constraints. For example the constraint that *all corporations with their seat in Holland use at least one computer whose cpu is manufactured by a company located in Holland* is not general enough to influence the groupings of entity sets in associations, in the example of section 4.

There can exist constraints which involve entity sets only and which are not most general. For example, the inter-association functional dependency which states that *all manufacturers of any given peripheral unit are controlled by the same corporation* is not most general, because it does not concern all *companies* in association A6 but only the *manufacturers*. Therefore A5 and A6 must not be joined into a ternary association.

Primitive, 3NF and irreducible associations

Primitive and 3NF associations are not really comparable, since the definition of 3NF associations (or relations) disregards the inter-assocation constraints generated during the normalization process. Therefore, not all primitive associations are 3NF and 3NF associations are not necessarily primitive either.

The simplest cases of transformations of 1NF and 2NF to 3NF have also been performed in primitive associations, namely the simplest removals of "non-full" and "transitive" functional dependencies on "candidate keys" [COD72] . However, as pointed out earlier, splitting associations always produces inter-association constraints and, in the EPA model, these must satisfy the definition of primitive associations. Therefore, there exist 1NF or 2NF primitive associations, in which intra-association dependencies (functional or not) prevent further splitting.

However these cases are normally not very frequent.

On the other hand, there are cases where primitive associations are smaller than 3NF ones. Primitive associations represent the essential groupings of entity sets in a particular perception of a part of the real world. Therefore, groupings irrelevant to structural considerations are eliminated by splitting associations. This idea is contrary to the concept of "optimal 3NF" [COD72] , which suggests to reduce the number of 3NF relations by grouping "non-prime" domains. It is often the case that an "optimal 3NF" relation represents several independent real-world relationships. If there is no intra-association constraint which prevents splitting, then there is at most one "non-prime" domain in a primitive association.

Another divergence between 3NF and primitive associations is that there are other cases in which a relation can be split than the presence of a functional dependency.

Suppose for example that a candidate ternary association A(CP,L,CF) expresses that *companies use languages on configurations*, where the entity sets are *companies, configurations* and *languages*, and where no functional dependency is present. Therefore the ternary association is 3NF. Suppose, in addition, that the semantics of the subject matter adds the intra-association constraint that *every company which uses a configuration uses all the languages available on the configuration.* This kind of constraint, recently called multi-valued dependency [FAG76, ZAN76] , permits the splitting of the ternary association into two associations which are primitive because the intra-association constraint has become an inclusion relationship. The two primitive associations express : A1(CP,CF) that *companies use configurations* and A2(CF,L) that *configurations have languages*, and the inclusion relationship expresses that their projections on *configurations* are equal. Remark that the particular semantics of A1(CP,CF) is really : *companies use all the languages of configurations*, but that *languages* are not explicitly mentioned.

An irreducible association [RIS73] is primitive. A set of irreducible associations is a primitive set of associations, if all the most general inter-association constraints are inclusion relationships. However there are primitive associations which are not irreducible. By definition, an association is irreducible if it cannot be split by projection into two other associations which can be joined together and produce the original association. Like the definition of 3NF, this definition disregards inter-association dependencies and the splitting of association can go too far for primitive associations.

Examples of primitive associations

The first example is that of a primitive, 3NF and irreducible ternary association. Its particular semantics is that *configurations have languages available on systems*, and the entity sets are *configurations, languages* and *systems*. An intra-association constraint (normally implicit) states that *not all languages of a configuration are available on all the systems of the configuration*. This constraint expresses that the association is irreducible, and therefore primitive and 3NF.

The second example has the same structure as an example in [DAT75] . It describes a ternary primitive association which is neither irreducible nor 3NF. It is about a situation in which *companies use configurations for applications*, and entity sets are *company, configuration* and *application*. In addition, there are two intra-association functional dependencies : *each configuration is used by only one company* and *each company works for each of its applications on only one configuration*. The ternary association is represented in Fig. 2

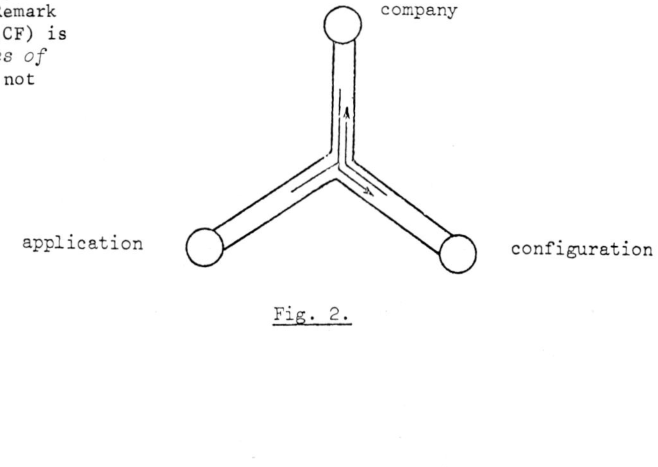

Fig. 2.

It is primitive, because its projection on *(company, configuration)* and *(company, application)* transforms one of the intra-association functional dependencies into an inter-association functional dependency, which is too complex to be acceptable for primitive associations but which does not concern the 3NF and irreducible associations.

The third example, represented in Fig. 3, is about a primitive quaternary association, which, as in the previous example, is neither irreducible nor 3NF. It expresses that *a company supplies to a client a peripheral model with a certain character code*, and entity sets are *company, client, peripheral* and *character code*. An intra-association functional dependency states that *each client has only one character code*, whereas a second intra-association dependency is that *each peripheral model is supplied with any character code;* the latter constraint is expressible for example by stating that a binary projection is equal to the Cartesian product of two unary projections.

The presence of the functional dependency entails that the association is 1NF and of course reducible : normalization to 3NF is obtained by projection into two associations involving *(client, character code)* and *(company, client, peripheral)*, but this process ignores the non-functional dependency which becomes a complex inter-association dependency.

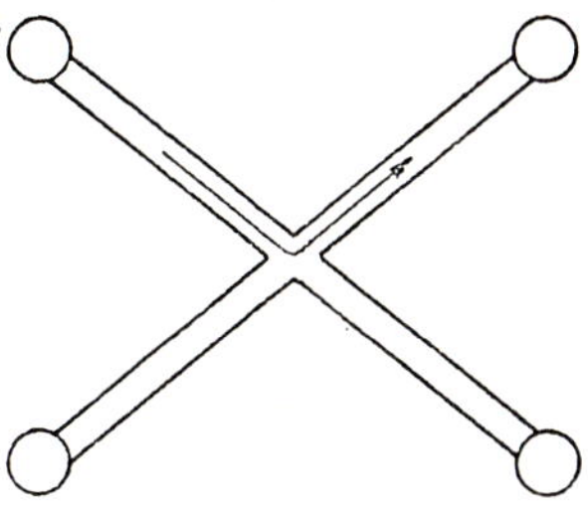

Fig. 3.

Complexity of primitive associations

At first, it may seem that refusing to split an association when an explicit intra-association relationship gets broken by the splitting could prohibitively increase the number of domains of primitive associations. There is indeed a correlation between the length of primitive associations and the complexity of situations described, but it does not seem much easier to build primitive associations with many domains than it is to build irreducible relations with many domains. This is particularly true when entity sets are chosen after natural language habits for the subject matter : natural language sentences are understandable only if they are reasonably short, and therefore the abstractions represented by natural language simple phrases have developed so that all the details of a situation can be described by short sentences.

7. Comparisons and conclusions

This paper takes the view that, for the purpose of designing a data base, a part of the real world can be naturally perceived as a network made of entities, property values and relationships among entities. The EPA network data model was defined as a formalism in which such perceptions of the real world can be expressed in a straightforward manner.

The important aspects of the EPA model are :

(1) the emphasis on entities, which are the essential objects in a particular perception of a subject matter; each entity has a single occurrence in an EPA data base and all pieces of information which concern it refer to this occurrence;

(2) the systematic consideration of the structural role of "integrity" or "consistency" constraints. Some of them, like the existence dependency of properties, are embodied in the definition of essential aspects of the network structure. Thus the definition of an EPA entity approximates the behavior of a real world entity : it is permanently associated with property values but its existence does not necessarily depend on its participation in associations;

(3) the definition of primitive associations, which is an approach to defining an information-oriented normal form for associations. By taking into account and classifying all the consistency constraints in a logical definition of a data base, this approach generalizes previous definitions of normal forms : the usual relational normal forms [COD72] , for which the only relevant constraints are functional dependencies, and also the relational normal forms which, in addition, take into account the multi-valued dependencies [FAG76, ZAN76]

The EPA model should be contrasted with the relational model, which is not adequate to express in a clear manner the structure of information. The relational model has fewer primitive constructions than the EPA model. Therefore, to maintain the difference of behavior between entities and values and between properties and associations, the relational model must introduce a large number of explicit consistency constraints. Entities and values may all be represented as values in the relational model, but relation tuples may also represent entities. Similarly, the distinction between properties and associations is not built-in.

The present definition of the EPA model was partly inspired by other works [SCH75, CHE76] which it generalizes in several respects. Schmid and Swenson [SCH75] have proposed a network model to express the semantics of a relational model. In their model, the distinction between "characteristic" and "independent" objects and also between "association" and "characteristic" relationships is based principally on the existence dependencies. However the distinction between characteristic and independent objects is not as sharp as the EPA distinction between entities and values, and, for example, the interpretation of functional dependencies among characteristic objects is not clear.

The EPA model may be used to express the semantics of a form of the relational model [PIR76] . This is done by building a model of information independently of relations, and by expressing the semantics of relational constructs by their correspondents in an EPA model. As the EPA structure is richer than the corresponding relational structure, this approach actually suggests a strategy for designing relational data bases.

The level 1 of the model proposed by Chen [CHE76] is similar to the EPA model, but it does not contain many details about the semantics of properties and none about the structure of relationships (i.e. associations).

This paper is a detailed proposal for an information-oriented data model, but this model can only be completely defined if it is supplemented with a data manipulation language and if its position in the architecture of a data base system is made precise. We believe that the EPA model can serve as a basis for a user-oriented interface, since it is implementation-independent and it is an adequate support to express the real-world semantics of data. The EPA model could also be used to build an information-oriented conceptual schema.

References

CHE76 CHEN, P.P., *The entity-relationship model. Toward a unified view of data,* ACM Transactions on Data Base Systems 1-1 (9-36), March 1976.

COD72 CODD, E.F., *Further normalization of the data base relational model,* In : Data Base Systems, Courant computer science symposium 6, Rustin editor, Prentice-Hall 1972, p. 33-64.

DAT75 DATE, C., *An introduction to data base systems,* Addison-Wesley, 1975.

DEH74 DEHENEFFE, C., HENNEBERT, H. PAULUS, W., *Relational model for a data base,* IFIP Congress 1974 (Stockholm), p. 1022-1025.

FAG76 FAGIN, R., *Multivalued dependencies and a new normal form for relational data bases,* IBM Report RJ 1812, July 1976.

KEN77 KENT, W., *Entities and relationships in information,* IFIP-TC2 working conference on modelling in data base management systems, Nice, January 1977. Proc. to appear (North Holland).

LIN74 LINDGREEN, P., *Basic operations on information as a basis for data base design,* IFIP Congress 1974 (Stockholm), p. 993-997.

MEA67 MEALY, G., *Another look at data*, AFIPS Fall Joint Computer Conference, 1967, p. 525-534.

MOU76 MOULIN, P., RANDON, J., SAVOYSKY, S., SPACCAPIETRA, S., TARDIEU, H., TEBOUL, M., *Conceptual model as a data base design tool*, Proc. IFIP-TC2 working conference on modelling in data base management systems, Freudenstadt, January 1976, Nijssen editor, North-Holland (1976), p. 221-238.

PIR76 PIROTTE, A., *Explicit description of entities and their manipulation in languages for the relational data base model*, Thèse de Doctorat, Université Libre de Bruxelles, Fac. Sc. Appl. Décembre 1976.

RIS73 RISSANEN, J., DELOBEL, C., *Decomposition of files, a basis for data storage and retrieval*, IBM Report RJ 1220, May 1973.

SCH75 SCHMID, H., SWENSON, J., *On the semantics of the relational data model*, Proc. ACM SIGMOD international conference on management of data, King editor, May 1975, p. 211-223.

SCH77 SCHMID, H., *An analysis of some constructs for conceptual models*, IFIP-TC2 working conference on modelling in data base management systems, Nice, January 1977. Proc. to appear (North-Holland).

SEN73 SENKO, M., ALTMAN, E., ASTRAHAN, M., FEHDER, P., *Data structures and accessing in data base systems*, IBM Systems Journal 12-1 (30-93), 1973.

ZAN76 ZANIOLO, C., *Analysis and design of relational schemata for data base systems*, Ph. D. Thesis, Univ. Calif. Los Angeles, July 1976.

E. Morlet and D. Ribbens, (Eds.), International Computing Symposium 1977.

Decisions in Operating Systems

Lutz H. Richter
Abteilung Informatik, Universität Dortmund,
D-4600 Dortmund 50, Germany

This paper explains the different decision marks to be observed in current operating systems. Fundamental principles are briefly reported. The main objective of the presentation is directed to the elaboration of functional primitives in operating systems and their influence over basic algorithmic decisions concerning the resource management. The principle of locality plays a central role, in the storage management and in the processor scheduling as well. With regard to the practical usage of the knowledge of modern operating system structures the problems of design and implementation and the security and protection of the system are of increasing importance.

Contents:

Introduction

With the introduction of comfortable input-output-control-systems and the techniques of multiprogramming and time shared access a new discipline has been created which was called operating system. Although a complete and unique definition of this term has not yet been agreed upon several names are used as synonyms, i.e. monitor, supervisor and executive system.

A very informal description of the term operating system includes all those programs of a digital computer system controlling and maintaining the performance of programs. Basic task of an operating system will be therefore the control of the computer system resources. System resources have to be understood in the most general possible way including central processing units (CPU's), various kinds of memories, input-output devices, data-sets, language compilers, utility programs etc. Managing all these physical and logical resources many decisions have to be made, most of them are not independent from the others. An expository contribution to this decision making task shall be the following paper.

Overview on the tasks and basic terms

The various programs making up an operating system have to take care of possible conflicts which may caused by the simultaneous demands on the components of the computing system. Besides the avoidance of resource conflicts a major task of an operating system is to facilitate the general usage of the system and to help to increase the overall efficiency of the different parts of the computing system.

Due to the distinct applications of computing systems diverse techniques are influencing the structure of the operating system. One possible classification is the following:

- real-time systems, i.e. process control, reservation systems, telephone switching systems
- data base systems, i.e. management information systems, inquiry systems

- universal operating systems, i.e. general batch processing systems, multiprogramming and multiprocessing systems, time sharing systems
- computer networks or general communication systems for message exchange

In order to get a view on the different tasks of an operating system a rough functional analysis will be used. The various resources of the computer have to be managed and depending upon the specific tasks we distinguish four components

- memory management
- processor management
- device management
- process management.

An explanation of these functions will be found in the following sections.

Decisions in operating systems and their objectives

All modern computing systems have a high degree of internal parallelism. There are many reasons for this simultaneous operation. Most of the applications do not fully utilize the simultaneously operable components and on the other hand an increase in speed of the entire system can be reached favourably by performing something in parallel.

But this parallelism involves serious problems for the operating system. Demands for resources are arriving simultaneously and the question which demand shall be serviced first requires several decisions concerning the priority of the originator of the demanded resource. The parallelism of the various components and its control in dependancy upon various objective functions is the platform for basic assumptions and the implied decisions within the operating system.

In this way the central processing unit and the different I/O-channels overlap in their operations that means they are performing instructions or transferring data resp. in parallel. This kind of multiprogramming results in several underlying principles of sequencing decisions which are necessary to realize the enqueue and dequeue operations.

Using parallelism in computing systems implies to distinguish two fundamentally different methods:

- the parallelism is used to perform different and independent tasks simultaneously
- one application is split up into several subtasks which can be performed in parallel.

Whereas the first kind of parallelism is identical with the already mentioned multiprogramming and allows arbitrary scheduling decisions the second form of concurrency is strongly dependent on the internal structure of the specific application. The scope of decisions in the latter kind of parallelism is much more restricted and far strictly embedded into the individual task. Regarding to the frequency of occurence the first case of parallelism is clearly more important than the second form described.

Objective functions guiding the decision mechanism in operating systems belong to the essential contributions of the pragmatic part of their construction.

1. Processes

The activities in a computing system are composed by the running programs. In order to describe these activities more precisely the term process is commonly used. Programs running at a computing system are characterized by

- given sequences of elementary operations are performed consecutively onto the basis of the underlying algorithm
- the sequence of these operations is fully determined by the current state of the program
- the actual used execution time is irrelevant with respect to sequence of executed statements.

But programs of the described form are not suitable to be used for the construction of operating systems. The reasons are

- operating systems have to control all components of the computing system and the parallel usage of these components must be managable
- the reactions of the operating system depend on the current state of all programs which shall be monitored by the operating system
- the influence of the behaviour of the operating system must be extremely time sensitive.

The mentioned difficulties led to the introduction of the new term process.

Definition of processes

Dennis/van Horn (1966) introduced as a process the center of activity within a sequence of primitive operations. A process is accordingly an abstract entity moving through the instructions of the program while this program is performed sequentially. Horning/Randell (1973) understand in their formal definition a process as a tupel of state variables, sets of state variables and state spaces. Computations are sequences of states within the state space beginning with an initial state and terminating with a terminal state. Activities characterize the assignments of values to the state variables. In this way an activity function is a transformation of states into activities. A process generates all sequences from the initial state by application of the activity function.

Processes may communicate with other processes. An explizit communication takes place by means of sending and receiving of messages. An implicit communication modifies the environment of the corresponding processes.

Justification of the necessity of communication and synchronization

For many reasons communications between processes for the purposes of their synchronisation is necessary. Let us consider cyclic sequential processes requesting write access to a shared data set. All business of the preparation of the access is uncritical and can be done in parallel by more than one process. However as soon as the data set is startet to get modified a careful synchronization between the different processes has to be installed in such a way that one process at a time only changes the contents of the data set. If the writing cannot be guaranteed to be done exclusively the resulting state of the data set is not uniquely determined. Therefore we have to take care that a process does the writing of shared data set in a so-called exclusive mode only. The same is true if two processes exchange a message. Usually the receiver is not prepared receiving the message and has to be initialized for the following communication procedure. Different principles of message communication can be applied and shall be described roughly later on.

Primitives of communication

Without knowledge of the explizit structure of the used hardware and software a set of communication primitives can be defined. Each of these primitives is appendet by various parameters for the identification of the participating processes and in order to localize the exchanged messages. The following operations are sufficient to implement a message exchange (without broadcasting):

The operation H(ALLO) initializes a communication and contains four parameters (the identifications of the involved processes both, the buffer for system messages and an event field for status information). A similar parameter set is used also for the other operations: S(END), R(ECEIVE), W(AIT) and A(NY RECEIVE).

The last mentioned operation signals a general readiness to receive from any sender.

These communication primitives are applicable for process communication of processes residing as well on the same as on different processors.

Various techniques for synchronization

Synchronizing two or more concurrently running processes means to take care that at certain instances one process is progressing only. Always a process reaches within its flow a section which requires that one process may execute instructions only, a so-called mutual exclusion must be performed.

One synchronization method uses explicit synchronization variables. Let us consider two cyclic processes consisting of an exclusive and of an uncritical section each. Before entering the critical or exclusive section each process has to check whether the other process ist not just in its critical section. The following solution has been proposed by the Dutch mathematician Dekker and uses three synchronization variables. Two of these variables s_1 and s_2 are dedicated to the processes 1 and 2 resp. and the third variable serves as a common synchronization variable. All three variables are initialized by 1 (see fig.1)

The implementation of synchronization procedures by means of explicit synchronization variables is awkward for many reasons. At the beginning of its critical section each process has to ask for the permission to enter. If this permission cannot be given immediately the corresponding process has to repeat this application continuously. This keeps the host process busy in a rather unproductive manner. Another problem with explicit synchronization variables is to guarantee that the checking section ist undivisable and cannot be interfered by the other process. All the necessary provisions need considerable effort.

```
                         integer s,s1,s2;

          PROCESS 1                              PROCESS 2

begin                                     begin
    p1: s1:= 0;                               p2: s2:= 0
    q1: if s2=1 then goto e1;                 q2: if s1=1 then goto e2;
        if s=1  then goto q1;                     if s=2  then goto q2;
        s1:= 1;                                   s2:= 1;
        r1: if s=2 then goto r1;                  r2: if s=1 then goto r2;
    e1: exclusive section 1;                  e2: exclusive section 2;
        s:= 2; s1:= 1;                            s:= 1; s2:= 1;
        ...;                                      ...;
        uncritical section;                       uncritical section;
        ...;                                      ...;
        goto p1;                                  goto p2;
end;                                      end;
```

Figure 1

A more simpler solution for the synchronization problem has been given by Dijkstra (1968), who introduced semaphores as state variables. Semaphores can be understood as data of the type non-negative integer which may be manipulated by two special operations only. Both operations the P- and the V-Operation are undivisable primitives and have to be applicated at the beginning and at the end of a critical section resp. If s indicates a semaphore the two mentioned operations can be defined as follows:

```
P(s):if s≥1 then s:= s-1
                 and the process execu-
                 ting P proceeds
            else the process executing
                 P has stopped and is
                 switched in a blocked
                 state. The semaphore
                 s is entered into the
                 waiting list of s.

V(s): s:= s+1
      if waiting list s not empty
         then one process is selected
              from the waiting list and
              is awakened from its
              blocked state this means it
              is eligable to proceed.
         The process issuing V proceeds.
```

The value used for the initialization of a semaphore determines the number of processes which may execute the critical section simultaneously.

As example we consider the well-known producer-consumer-problem. A producer process generates a certain kind of articles and puts them in a buffer as long as this buffer has its n positions not yet filled. A consumer process takes these articles from the buffer and consumes them. Any activity at the buffer must be synchronized and this is done by means of the semaphore 'buffer'. Two additional semaphores 'empty' and 'filled' regulate the contents of the buffer. The three used semaphores are initialized in the following manner

empty:= 0; filled:= n; buffer:= 1 .

A complete symmetric solution of the producer-consumer-problem will now be running in the form described in fig. 2 .

For many applications the synchronization with one semaphore per operation is not sufficient. Patil (1971) and Presser (1975) therefore propose an extension to apply the P- and V-Operations onto a list of semaphores. With this generalization several synchronization tasks can be solved far less restrictive.

producer process	consumer process
<u>begin</u>	<u>begin</u>
pp: produce article;	cp: P(filled);
P(empty);	P(buffer);
P(buffer);	get article from buffer;
put article into buffer;	V(buffer);
V(buffer);	V(empty);
V(filled);	consume article;
<u>goto</u> pp;	<u>goto</u> cp;
<u>end</u>;	<u>end</u>;

Figure 2

Deadlocks

As concurrently running processes demand the resources (processor, main memory, I/O units, data sets, programs etc.) independently but ordered timely, situations may occur that some or all of processes mutually block up due to simultaneous requests for certain resources. The roundabout traffic is a well-known example for this situation.

A deadlock can be described by the simultaneous occurence of the following four conditions:

(1) processes request and get granted exclusive control on the required resources

(2) resources are allocated in a non-preemptive way

(3) processes control exclusively some resources and request additional

(4) it exists a closed chain of processes in such a way that each process holds resources which are requested by the next process in the chain.

Analyzing deadlocked system states one distinguishes two basically different methods:

- detection and elemination of deadlocks
  Processes involved in a deadlock are removed from the system and the resources allocated to them are released.
- prevention of deadlocks
  Each request for an additional resource is checked for a potentially implied deadlock before it is granted. These deadlock avoidance procedures require certain a-priori knowledge about the distribution of further resource requests.

2. Memory Management

The management of primary memory plays a very important role within each operating system. Decisions concerning the allocation of memory have a far-reaching influence over all other resource management principles.

Two different allocation schemes can be applied. The static store management assumes that the actual memory requirements are known in advance and the corresponding allocation decisions of the available memory can be fixed for a certain amount of time. Contrary to the static store management the dynamic allocation abandons all a-priori knowledge. Obviously the dynamic store management corresponds far more the reality.

Store organization and virtual memory

Programs process data during their execution. In order to identify these data or objects uniquely they are given names. The set of all names constitute the name space. If an object resides in a memory it has an address. The set of all addresses or of all objects residing in any memory we call the address space. The subset of all those objects which are in the main or primary memory forms the so-called storage space.

It will be the task of the memory management to organize the association between name space, address space and storage space.

At the most existing systems with dynamic memory management as well the storage space as the address space are partitioned in equal sized blocks called page frames and pages resp. In this way a program may be loaded in a scattered form this means that blocks belonging to the same program do not need to be loaded into adjacent page frames. If the number of pages in the address space is greater than the number of page frames in the storage space we are speaking of virtual storage. The transformation from the address space into the storage space and vice versa is done by certain strategies implemented in the operating system.

Supposed the address space A consists of n pages and the storage space S contains m(≤n) page frames. Then we define the address-translation function f: A→S by

$$f(i) = \begin{cases} k & \text{if page frame k contains page i} \\ \text{undefined} & \text{otherwise} \end{cases}$$

If one page includes z words a valid virtual address v is determined as a pair (i,d) by means of the address-translation function so that

$$v=(i-1)\cdot z+d \quad \text{and} \quad 0 \le d < z \quad .$$

Correspondingly the real address r is

$$r=[f(i)-1]\cdot z+d \quad \text{and} \quad 0 \le d < z \quad ,$$

if f(i) ist defined. In case f(i) is undefined the referenced page must be loaded from the address space into the storage space and after completion f(i)=k indicates the page frame now housing the requested page i.

Rules and algorithms

Commonly the storage space S is completely occupied by pages from the address space A. If now a referenced page i must be loaded from A into S, and S does not contain unused page frames a replacement rule has to be applied to determine a page frame in S whose current page shall be replaced.

In opposition to the replacement rule the fetch rule defines the instant of time at which the referred page i will be loaded from A into S. If it is operated with completely filled storage space the loading of pages is done by demand only (demand paging).

If for certain reasons demand paging is not used the placement rule selects the page frame k in which a page i from A to S shall be loaded. In case of demand paging placement rule and replacement rule operate identically.

Paging systems are classified into two categories: static and dynamic partition systems. Correspondingly we have two classes of replacement algorithms. In a multiprogramming situation the storage space is shared by multiple programs. If the number of page frames in S dedicated to a certain program is fixed for the life time of that program we are speaking of fixed partition management. Replacement algorithms supporting fixed partition storage managment will be described in the following. Dynamic partition algorithms vary the number of page frames allocate to a specific program depending upon several parameters describing the behaviour of that program. Dynamic partition algorithms are explained in the next section.

Discussing fixed partition algorithms we denote by $M_m = \{W \mid W \subseteq N, |W| \le m\}$ the control states of the storage space S where $N= \{1,\ldots,n\}$ indicates the set of pages of A of a certain programm and $W \subseteq N$ the subsets on N. Let us a consider a multiprogramming system with l concurrently running programs then

$$M_m \ge Q_1 + Q_2 + \ldots + Q_l$$

describes the control states Q_j of l fixed storage space partitions with regard to the used replacement algorithm(s). The most well-known fixed partition algorithms are

- FIFO (first-in-first-out)

  if the referenced page belongs already to the control state, Q will not be changed; if a page has to be removed from S the page from the tail of the ordered control state Q will be chosen and the newly loaded page will be positioned at the head of Q.

- LRU (least-recently-used)

  the referenced page is always positioned at the head of Q regardingless whether it belongs already to Q or not; in case of a removal of a page the page from the end of Q is selected.

- MRU (most-recently-used)

  Contrary to the LRU-algorithm the MRU-algorithm replaces the most recently referred page.

- MFU (most-frequently-used)

  the control state is ordered decreasingly depending on the reference frequency of each page; removed is for a replacement the first page in Q and the newly loaded page is appended at the end of Q.

- LFU (least-frequently-used)

  the same like MFU but all ordering decisions are inverted.

- OPT (optimal replacement)

  In dependency on the further referenced pages in A always that page in Q is replaced which has the longest distance until it is referenced next. As this algorithm requires exact knowledge about future references it is of theoretical interest only.

Both algorithms LRU and OPT have a property which leads to the naming stack algorithms. This so-called inclusion property says that the subsets W_r and W_{r+1} (r and r+1 resp. denote the number of pages in S) fulfill $W_r \subseteq W_{r+1}$ or more precisely the first r elements in the related control states Q^r and Q^{r+1} are identical.

Principle of locality

All program behave more or less local during their life time that means during a time intervall certain pages are referenced more frequently than other pages. This set of pages will move through the pages in A with advancing time.

W define $W_p(t,\tau)$ as the working set of the program p at the time instant t consisting of all pages referenced during the last τ units of virtual time.

The term virtual time stands here for that time while the program under consideration is allowed to execute instructions. In a multiprogramming system this will be true obviously only during a part of the real time.

The size of the working set will depend upon the frequency of access to the same pages. We call the number of virtual time units between two consecutive references to the same page the interreference intervall x of that page.

Coming to the before mentioned dynamic partition algorithms we first mention the working set algorithm. At each time instant t those pages of A are mapped into S which belong to the working set $W(t,\tau)$. Obviously the size will vary with the time.

As the working set algorithm ist not quite simple to implement, Chu and Opderbeck (1972) proposed as an alternative the page fault frequency algorithm. Every time a page in A is referenced which does not already belong to S a page fault is generated. Now the page fault frequency algorithm uses the measured page fault frequency as the basic parameter for the storage allocation decision process. In general, a high page fault frequency indicates an inefficient program as too less page frames in S are assigned to that program. On the other hand, a low page fault frequency implies that a further increase in the number of the assigned page frames will not considerably improve the efficiency and might result in a waste of storage space. The policy of the page fault frequency algorithm is now the following: whenever the page fault frequencies exceed a certain limit L the number of allocated page frames will be increased until the page fault frequency does not longer rise above L. On the other hand, once the page fault frequency goes below L all those page frames which have not been referenced since the last page fault occurred are freed.

Using the principles of locality may result into a more flexible and above all more efficient storage management.

3. Processor Management

Amongst all resources in a computing system the processor(s) is(are) of the same importance than the memory. A program cannot proceed without being assigned to processor. In a system consisting of multiple concurrently running processes each user shall be suggested the impression that he is working with a virtual computer. It is the task of the operating system to perform the mapping of the virtual processors to the physically existing real processor(s).

Processor and processes

Let us consider all virtual processors and the processes served by them. Four different states of these processes can be distinguished.

(1) active : the virtual processor of this process is assigned to the real processor. The instructions of the corresponding program are executed.

(2) ready : the process has applied for the assignment of its virtual processor to the real processor. However at the time under consideration the allocation of the real processor is not yet

possible because another process still seizes the real processor.

(3) suspended: the process has been suspended from the state "active" because a missing page caused a page fault and a continuation of that process is not possible as long as the requested page has not yet been loaded.

(4) blocked: the corresponding process is waiting on the occurence of a certain event (i.e. the completion of a specific I/O, the ready state of another process etc.)

The transitions of these states are as follows:

After a process has acquired all necessary resources it is put into the state "ready" by the dispatcher of the operating system. The selection of a process from the set of ready processes is determined by discipline to be applied for the dequeuing. The process removed from the ready queue will be set into the state "active" as soon as the processor becomes available. There are several reasons for leaving the status "active". The occurence of an event may cause the switching of the process state. Whenever the allotted time slice has elapsed and the process again requests the processor then the process is returned to the queue of ready processes. The event of a missing page induces the state changing into "suspended". Any requested I/O may result the process to be switched into the state "blocked". After the required I/O has been done or the outstanding request has been fulfilled the process goes to the "ready" queue. The same happens after the page has been loaded for which a "suspended" process has been waiting. Consequently the following state transitions are allowed:

ready → active → ready

ready → active → suspended → ready

ready → active → blocked → ready

Ordering the ready queue always implies the application of a certain scheduling decision. Several different scheduling disciplines will be described in the following two sections.

Adaptive strategies for processor management

The most scheduling strategies suffer from the disadvantage that some process or task relevant scheduling variables are necessary, to come to a scheduling decision, which are not known or at least not known in advance.

The following two algorithms relax from this condition and apply again the principle of locality. But locality is understood here in a more general meaning. It is not restricted to the storage requirements only but extended to the processor behaviour, too.

Processes are monitoring their processor usage by themselves and apply these gathered data to predict the coming processor requirement. This forecast will be so much the better the higher the locality of the process behaviour is.

With a distance of Q time units the priority sequence G of processes is reconsidered and in dependancy on the foregoing behaviour of these processes permuted. For each of the N dispatchable processes and for each time slice Q a history value h_{ik} is calculated. If a process enters the system an initial value of $h_{io}=0$ will be assigned. At the end of each time slice Q the history values are recalculated by means of the following formula

$$h_{ik} = a_i + h_{i,k-1} - \frac{1}{N} \sum_{\nu=1}^{N} (a_\nu + h_{\nu,k-1}),$$

where a_i indicates the "active" time of process i during the last time slice Q. After this recalculation all tasks are sequenced in an increasing order. During the following time slice the process with the lowest history value has the highest priority to become active. If one determines the recursive development for the h_{ik} beginning with $h_{io}=0$ the weaknesses of the forementioned algorithms become apparent.

As each newly determined history value contains all processing ("active") times without consideration of their age the short-term behaviour will be unsufficiently modelled only. Furthermore small values of h_{ik} do not allow the conclusion that the corresponding processes are of small processor intensity. Therefore the high priority schedule of these processes might be wrong because these processes could have been at the end of the priority sequence and therefore never have had the chance to prove their real behaviour.

Both of the foregoing disadvantages are removed by the following algorithm

$$h_{ik} = \begin{cases} \frac{a_i}{b_i} + h_{i,k-1}(1-\frac{b_i}{Q}) & \text{if } b_i \neq 0 \\ h_{i,k-1} & \text{if } b_i = 0 \end{cases}$$

where

$$b_i = Q - \sum_{\nu=1}^{i-1} a_{[\nu]}$$

describes the maximum of the available processor time for process i during the foregoing time slice Q. The order of the processing times $a_{[\nu]}$ is identical with the priority sequence G at the last time slice. In this way each process i is normalized by the actual used active time a_i and is related to the available time b_i.

Those, on the basis of selfmonitoring, operating procedures of processor scheduling are applied in several commercially available operating systems (i.e. IBM/370-OS-VS, UNIVAC EXEC 8).

Various queuing disciplines

The user of a computing system gets its requested processor work by means of one or multiple time slices. The size of these time slices does not have to be fixed in advance. A user arrives at the system and is sequenced into the queue of the other users according to a certain strategy. If one time slice is sufficient to satisty the user requirements this user is leaving the system or the not yet completed order enters cyclically the queue again. This is repeated as long as the corresponding task has been finished.

With the frequency of the time slice length a task switching takes place in the processor which guaranties that each user is suggested having the entire system to his exclusive disposal. Distinguishing between short and long processor usage is important for the service order.

The distribution of the arrivals at the system is denoted by A(t) indicating the probability that the time between two successive arrivals is $\leq t$. Let B(t) the distribution of service times. With given A(t) and B(t) it is of interest to determine the time the user stays with the system. We indicate by T(t) the mean response time for users requiring t units processing time. Therefore the waiting time is $W(t) = T(t)-t$. Usually the distribution of the arrivals is modelled by a Poisson process with a mean arrival rate of λ users per time unit, i.e.

$$A(t) = 1 - e^{-\lambda t} \quad \text{with} \quad t \geq 0 \ .$$

In the following a few of the most important queuing disciplines are roughly sketched:

- First-Come-First-Served (FCFS)

  This is the most simple scheduling discipline and is primarily applied in batch systems. It turns out that the waiting time of a process is independent upon the service time. On the other hand the waiting times are considerably influenced by the processor intensity. A processor operating close to its saturation implies almost unlimited waiting times.

- Round Robin (RR)

  This cyclical scheduling procedure belongs to the most used algorithms in time sharing systems. Newly arriving requests are put in a FCFS manner at the end of the processor queue. After a task has been serviced for one time slice it is inserted again at the end of the queue (in contrary to FCFS where the not yet completed task is always put in front of the queue). In cyclical scheduling algorithms the response time is a linear function of the service time. The same is true for the waiting time. For an exponential service time distribution it may be shown that the mean response time for a task with an average service time is the same like for FCFS. Tasks with a less than average service time result under RR into a faster service than under FCFS.

- Foreground-Background-Strategy (FB)

  This scheduling procedure inserts the tasks in one of two processor queues. The first queue holds all requests arriving new at the system. After a first service quantum the not yet completed request is put at the end of the second processor queue. The second queue is serviced only after the first queue is emptied. Tasks from the second queue are serviced in a preemptive way which means that they can be interrupted as soon as a new task arrives. Short service time requests have a response time rate close to one. Long requests have to wait until all during the mean time arriving tasks have been serviced at last once.

However, there are many other scheduling systems in use which differ, from those described in some additional parameters only.

4. Problems of Design

Operating systems represent very large and complex software constructions. The methods of design and implementation have, therefore, to be organized and planned carefully in order to meet the goals of the realization. Design and implementation are often not strictly separable. If a system has been projected in a structured way then the implementation is the description of this structured design by means of a suitable programming language.

Of considerable interest are also problems of the correctness, of the reliability concerning the supported functions, and the qualitative and quantitative evaluation of the components of the system. In this concern many initial decisions must be made fixing important properties of the operating system to be implemented.

Different design techniques

There are different techniques known to design an operating system. In the most existing systems several of these techniques are applied.

Projecting a complex system one distinguishes several levels of specification. The concept of abstraction is used to take advantage of various levels in detail. In operating systems many different abstractions are possible. Starting with an abstraction a_1 one constructs a confined level a_2 which describes the same structures and properties than a_1 but with a higher degree of detail. In this way multiple levels of abstraction are defined called higher and lower levels of abstraction.

Another concept used in the description and development of operating systems is the principle of virtual machines. In this concern a virtual machine is a set of primitive operations describing the functional part of the system. As these primitives need not necessarily be provided by the hardware architecture this principle is named a virtual machine construction. It will be the task of the implementation to create a suitable mapping of the virtual machine onto the real hardware.

Most design methods use a common principle. By means of the definition of different layers the very complex construction of an operating system is stepwise separated into more simpler and better surveyable parts. Depending on orientation or the sequence resp. constructing these layers two distinct procedures are distinguished.

The bottom-up design starts with the real hardware as the lowest level and adds additional layers until the final system is reached. Various ratios of communicating between the different layers can be introduced.

An alternative method is the top-down construction. The complete functional specification of the projected operating system is used to refine stepwise the specification until the last refinement can be implemented at the real hardware.

Some other design methods have been used in the past but those vary only slightly from the mentioned principles.

Security and protection aspects

The computer and its surrounding operating system should be capable to protect the users or the processes resp. against illegal and erroneous influences implied by other users or processes resp. Such conflicts can result in

- the not permitted reading or copying of data of other users;
- the modification or erasing of strange data;
- the not explicitly allowed influence over resources kept by other users.

The last mentioned example may lead in a worst case to a breakdown of the whole system.

Generally spoken one denotes the problem of protecting an object against the unauthorized or unintentional influence by its surrounding as protection or security task. Mechanisms to solve this problem have to guaranty that no user is able to interfere other users. Basis of all protection systems is the closure of all surroundings and states within the system. Example for this is the well-known two-state-architecture provided in the hardware structure of several current computing systems.

If we distinguish subjects (processes) and objects (data, subjects) as elements in our system one may separate different access rights of subjects with respect to the objects. The term domain indicates an area of access rights. An abstract model uses an access matrix (Graham/ Denning) in which the rows represent the subjects and the columns the objects. A set of capabilities which describes the access rights of a subject over an object may be written as a list. A modification of an access right implies, therefore, a change of the capability list. Each element of the access matrix represents a list of capabilities running in a certain domain. In this way each subject consists of a pair (the process and its domain).

Concerning the implementation of those protection mechanisms one needs a certain hardware support. Most of the today commercially available systems do provide only very less features, necessary to implement advanced protection systems.

Fault-tolerant requirements

As the requirements for reliability of the computing systems are contineously increasing fault-tolerance provisions have become a widely accepted practice. Failures of the system have to be detected by the software. But as it is often rather difficult to locate uniquely the source of the failure, fault-tolerant behaviour of the software is very critical to be implemented. One way including software failure handling is redundancy. This redundancy requires programs which are sufficiently distinct from the original part which they are intended to back up.

In this connection the recovery block concept introduced by Randell (1975) must be mentioned. It consists of the provision of a primary and of an alternate module for each critical task. Furthermore a test facility is available which determines whether a module has executed correctly or not. Designing the system, an outstanding important decision is the answer to the question which features shall belong to the primary and which to the alternate module.

Wulf (1975) proposed four mechanisms, necessary to construct reliable operating systems:

- error confinement to limit the risk that errors may damage or destroy other parts of the system before they are detected;
- detection and categorization of potential failures by means of exposing inconsistencies in the processed data;
- reconfiguration facilities to remove failured units (hardware or software) from the system;
- restart features to recover from a failed system.

Again important decisions have to be made during the design phase of the operating system in order to incorporate fault-tolerance provisions in the developed system.

Summary

Decision making is an important tool during the design and implementation phase of an operating system. Selecting the right functional facilities, choosing amongst the various possible strategies for resource management, and prefering suitable construction techniques require careful decisions. But designing and implementing an operating system does not finish the line of decisions. Putting operating system in action again requires many decisions, concerning the adaption to the specific installation and its application. Although the user commonly simply gains from the services provided by the system he has still come to decisions induced by his individual usage of the operating system. Therefore the user's knowledge of the basic characteristics of the applied operating system is indispensable.

References

[1] Aho,A.V.;Denning,P.J.;Ullman,J.D.: Principles of Optimal Page Replacement, Journal of the ACM, 18 (1971), 80-93

[2] Chu,W.;Opderbeck,H.: The page fault frequency replacement algorithm, Proc. AFIPS FJCC, vol.41 (1972), 597-609

[3] Coffman,E.G.;Kleinrock,L.: Computer Scheduling Measures and their Countermeasures, Proc. AFIPS 32 (1968), 11-21

[4] Coffman,E.G.et al.: System Deadlocks, Computing Surveys, 3 (1971), 67-78

[5] Coffman,E.G.;Denning,P.J.: Operating Systems Theory, Prentice Hall, Englewood Cliffs (1973)

[6] Conway,R.W.;Maxwell,W.L.; Miller,L.W.: Theory of Scheduling, Addison-Wesley, Reading (1967)

[7] Denning,P.J.: The Working Set Model for Program Behaviour, Communications of the ACM, 11 (1968), 323-333

[8] Denning,P.J.: Virtual Memory, Computing Surveys, 2 (1970), 153-190

[9] Dennis,J.B.;van Horn,E.C.: Programming Semantics for Multiprogrammed Computations, Communications of the ACM, 9 (1966), 143-155

[10] Dijkstra,E.W.:
Cooperating Sequential Processes, in Multiprogramming Languages (Editor F.Genuys), Academic Press, New York (1968), 43-112

[11] Dijkstra,E.W.:
Hierarchical Ordering of Sequential Processes,
Acta Informatica, 1 (1971), 115-138

[12] Graham,R.M.:
Protection in an Information Processing Utility,
Communications of the ACM, 11 (1968), 365-369

[13] Habermann,A.N.:
Prevention of System Deadlocks,
Communications of the ACM, 12 (1969), 373-377,385

[14] Hansen,P.B.:
Operating System Principles,
Prentice Hall, Englewood Cliffs (1973)

[15] Hellerman,H.;Conroy,T.F.:
Computer System Performance,
McGraw-Hill, New York (1975)

[16] Horning,J.J.;Randell,B.:
Process Structuring,
Computing Surveys 5 (1973),5-30

[17] Kleinrock,L.:
A Continuum of Time Sharing Scheduling Algorithms,
Proc. AFIPS, 36 (1970), 453-458

[18] Madnick,S.E.;Donovan,J.J.:
Operating Systems,
McGraw-Hill, New York (1974)

[19] Mills,H.:
On the Development of Large Reliable Programs,
Record IEEE Symp.Comp.Software Reliability, New York (1973), 155-159

[20] Patil,S.S.:
Limitations and Capabilities of Dijkstra's Semaphore Primitives for Coordination among Processes,
MIT Project MAC Memo 57, Cambridge (1971)

[21] Presser,L.:
Multiprogramming Coordination,
Computing Surveys, 7 (1975), 21-44

[22] Randell,B.:
System structure for software fault-tolerance,
Proc.Interntl.Conf.on Reliable Software, ACM, New York (1975)

[23] Richter,L.:
Resource Allocation by means of HASP Conceptional Extensions,
Proc. of SHARE Europ.Ass., 15 (1970)

[24] Richter,L.:
Rechnernetzwerke - eine Aufgabe der praktischen Informatik,
Forschungsbericht der Universitat Dortmund, Bd.7 (1975)

[25] Richter,L.:
Betriebssysteme,
Teubner-Verlag, Stuttgart (1977)

[26] Wulf,W.:
Reliable hardware/software architecture,
IEEE TSE 2 (June 1975), 233-240

E R R A T A

INVITED PAPERS

R. Durchholz : TYPES AND RELATED CONCEPTS

p. 35, col. 1, line 2 should read:"subject. Although the report characterizes ......"

p. 35, col. 1, line 11 should read: "OF AREA). In any case there does exist a data ...."

p. 37, col. 1, line 10 should read: "and more complex ones than is indicated"

p. 37, col. 2, line 14 should read: "the set of all states or at least comprises all"

p. 33, col. 1, lines 10/11 should read: "less fuzzy. This is only to help the imagination and would of course require more elaboration if need be".

p. 33, col. 2, line 3 should read: "(12-34-56) be the (degererate) type with"

B. Meltzer : BRAINS AND PROGRAMS

p. 83, col. 1, structure should read :

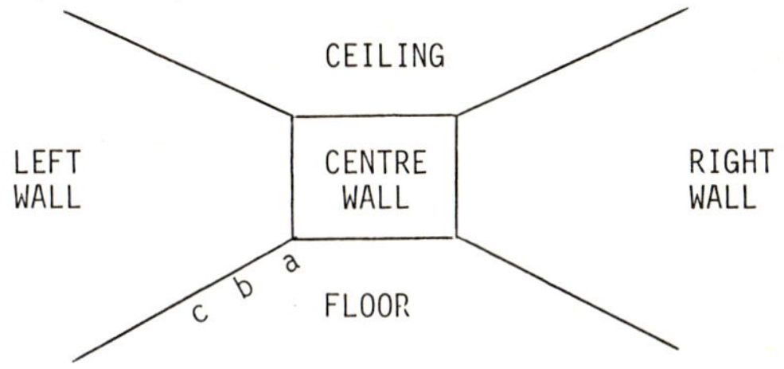

J.Y. Cotronis, P.E. Lauer : VERIFICATION OF CONCURRENT SYSTEMS OF PROCESSES

p. 198, col. 2, line 33 should read: $\forall[\tilde{M}]\varepsilon (M) : \forall p\varepsilon P : \tilde{M} (p) \leq 1$

p. 198, col. 2, line 50 should read : A variant V is a set of places such that the set of their input transitions is a subset of the set of their output transitions.

p. 200, col. 1, line 44 should read: is simpler than P but do the two nets possess.....

p. 201, col. 1, line 18 should read : Now we state Theorem 1 [12], which is true for a large class of nets.

p. 201, col. 1, line 20 should read : non-negative invariant is marked is not live-1 iff

p. 201, col. 2, line 12 should read : 0 0 1 1 0 0 1 1 1 1

p. 201, col. 2, line 14 should read : where $\gamma=C^{\cdot}V=(\qquad)$

p. 201, col. 2, line 18 should read : 1 0 0 1 1 0 0 1 0 0

p. 201, col. 2, line 19 should read : 0 0 1 1 0 0 1 1 1 1

p. 203, col. 2, line 26 should read : in Petri-net P. Then P deadlocks iff $P/t^1 \ldots t_n$

p. 204, col. 1, line 9 should read : 2) if $\beta_1 = tj$ $(1<j\leq n)$

p. 204, col. 1, line 13 should read : μ^1 and μ^2 are computations in P and no occur-

p. 204, col. 1, line 41 should read : Corollary: $P/t_1 \ldots t_n$ is not determinate iff P is

p. 205, col. 1, line 3 should read : For this net to deadlock inside the routine 1,2,3,4 place 1 must remain empty without being able to be marked again. So it must be a place in an emptyable variant. But there is not such variant since all of them contain an invariant which is marked. So this net does not deadlock inside the routine. We can argue similarly for routine 5,6,7,8.

p. 205, col. 2, line 11 should read : is for place 8 to be unmarked. This means that
p. 205, col. 2, line 21 should read : can prove it does not deadlock inside 3,4
p. 205, col. 2, line 22 should read : Also since 1,3 are right movers, 1,2 and 3,4
p. 205, col. 2, line 37 should read : 4,1

P. Ribeyre, P.Y. Saintoyant : A PREDICTIVE TOOL FOR THE IMPROVEMENT OF PROGRAM BEHAVIOR

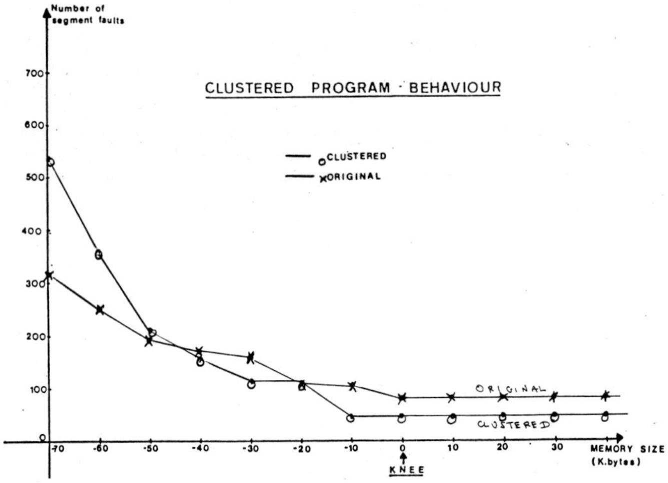

p. 286, col. 2. Figure 1 above replaces the one shown.

J. van den Bos : A DESIGN OF A COMMUNICATION SUPERVISOR FOR A LOCAL NETWORK EMPLOYING MONITORS

p. 323, col. 2, line 8 should read : ence 1977, no. 2, pp 173-177

G. Bucci, S. Golinelli : A DISTRIBUTED STRATEGY FOR RESOURCE ALLOCATION IN INFORMATION NETWORKS

1.	Page 5, line 6 from bottom: replace .. $_i = n_i$ (m,w)	with: .. $_i = \eta_i$ (m,w)
2.	Page 6, line after formula (7): replace ...=1-m.	with: ...=1-m_i.
3.	Page 6, line 16 right-hand: replace ...A_i (m,w) + $Z_i^o(m^i,w)$ m_i	with: ...$A_i(m^i,w)$ + $A_i^o(m^i,w)$ $\bar{m}_i$
4.	Page 6, formula (9) 2nd line: replace ....β_i (m,w))	with: ....η_i (m,w))
5.	Page 7, Proposition 3.1: replace $\rho(\hat{m},m) \geqslant 1$	with: $\rho(\hat{m},\tilde{m}) \geqslant 1$
6.	Page 8, line 3 left-hand: replace ....) > 1	with: ....) $\geqslant$ 1
7.	Page 9 formula (14) : replace $\underset{k\ I}{\text{and}}$ $\underset{k\ I}{\min}$	with: $\underset{k\varepsilon I}{\text{and}}$ $\underset{k\varepsilon I}{\min}$
8.	Page 10, Fig. 3 : replace $\rho(\hat{m},\tilde{m}) > 1$	with: $(\hat{m},\tilde{m}) \geqslant 1$
9.	Page 8, line 6 from the bottom : replace i/m_i...	with: i|m_i...